American Casebook Series
Hornbook Series and Basic Legal Texts
Black Letter Series and Nutshell Series

of

WEST PUBLISHING COMPANY
P.O. Box 64526
St. Paul, Minnesota 55164–0526

Accounting

FARIS' ACCOUNTING AND LAW IN A NUT-SHELL, 377 pages, 1984. Softcover. (Text)

FIFLIS, KRIPKE AND FOSTER'S TEACHING MATERIALS ON ACCOUNTING FOR BUSINESS LAWYERS, Third Edition, 838 pages, 1984. (Casebook)

SIEGEL AND SIEGEL'S ACCOUNTING AND FINANCIAL DISCLOSURE: A GUIDE TO BASIC CONCEPTS, 259 pages, 1983. Softcover. (Text)

Administrative Law

BONFIELD AND ASIMOW'S STATE AND FEDERAL ADMINISTRATIVE LAW, 826 pages, 1989. Teacher's Manual available. (Casebook)

GELLHORN AND LEVIN'S ADMINISTRATIVE LAW AND PROCESS IN A NUTSHELL, Third Edition, approximately 420 pages, 1990. Softcover. (Text)

MASHAW AND MERRILL'S CASES AND MATERIALS ON ADMINISTRATIVE LAW—THE AMERICAN PUBLIC LAW SYSTEM, Second Edition, 976 pages, 1985. (Casebook) 1989 Supplement.

ROBINSON, GELLHORN AND BRUFF'S THE ADMINISTRATIVE PROCESS, Third Edition, 978 pages, 1986. (Casebook)

Admiralty

HEALY AND SHARPE'S CASES AND MATERIALS ON ADMIRALTY, Second Edition, 876 pages, 1986. (Casebook)

MARAIST'S ADMIRALTY IN A NUTSHELL, Second Edition, 379 pages, 1988. Softcover.

(Text)

SCHOENBAUM'S HORNBOOK ON ADMIRALTY AND MARITIME LAW, Student Edition, 692 pages, 1987 with 1989 pocket part. (Text)

Agency—Partnership

FESSLER'S ALTERNATIVES TO INCORPORATION FOR PERSONS IN QUEST OF PROFIT, Second Edition, 326 pages, 1986. Softcover. Teacher's Manual available. (Casebook)

HENN'S CASES AND MATERIALS ON AGENCY, PARTNERSHIP AND OTHER UNINCORPORATED BUSINESS ENTERPRISES, Second Edition, 733 pages, 1985. Teacher's Manual available. (Casebook)

REUSCHLEIN AND GREGORY'S HORNBOOK ON THE LAW OF AGENCY AND PARTNERSHIP, Second Edition, 683 pages, 1990. (Text)

SELECTED CORPORATION AND PARTNERSHIP STATUTES, RULES AND FORMS. Softcover. 727 pages, 1989.

STEFFEN AND KERR'S CASES ON AGENCY-PARTNERSHIP, Fourth Edition, 859 pages, 1980. (Casebook)

STEFFEN'S AGENCY-PARTNERSHIP IN A NUT-SHELL, 364 pages, 1977. Softcover. (Text)

Agricultural Law

MEYER, PEDERSEN, THORSON AND DAVIDSON'S AGRICULTURAL LAW: CASES AND MATERIALS, 931 pages, 1985. Teacher's Manual available. (Casebook)

Alternative Dispute Resolution

KANOWITZ' CASES AND MATERIALS ON ALTERNATIVE DISPUTE RESOLUTION, 1024 pages,

Alternative Dispute Resolution—Cont'd

1986. Teacher's Manual available. (Casebook) 1990 Supplement.

RISKIN AND WESTBROOK'S DISPUTE RESOLUTION AND LAWYERS, 468 pages, 1987. Teacher's Manual available. (Casebook)

RISKIN AND WESTBROOK'S DISPUTE RESOLUTION AND LAWYERS, Abridged Edition, 223 pages, 1987. Softcover. Teacher's Manual available. (Casebook)

American Indian Law

CANBY'S AMERICAN INDIAN LAW IN A NUTSHELL, Second Edition, 336 pages, 1988. Softcover. (Text)

GETCHES AND WILKINSON'S CASES AND MATERIALS ON FEDERAL INDIAN LAW, Second Edition, 880 pages, 1986. (Casebook)

Antitrust—see also Regulated Industries, Trade Regulation

FOX AND SULLIVAN'S CASES AND MATERIALS ON ANTITRUST, 935 pages, 1989. Teacher's Manual available. (Casebook)

GELLHORN'S ANTITRUST LAW AND ECONOMICS IN A NUTSHELL, Third Edition, 472 pages, 1986. Softcover. (Text)

HOVENKAMP'S BLACK LETTER ON ANTITRUST, 323 pages, 1986. Softcover. (Review)

HOVENKAMP'S HORNBOOK ON ECONOMICS AND FEDERAL ANTITRUST LAW, Student Edition, 414 pages, 1985. (Text)

OPPENHEIM, WESTON AND MCCARTHY'S CASES AND COMMENTS ON FEDERAL ANTITRUST LAWS, Fourth Edition, 1168 pages, 1981. (Casebook) 1985 Supplement.

POSNER AND EASTERBROOK'S CASES AND ECONOMIC NOTES ON ANTITRUST, Second Edition, 1077 pages, 1981. (Casebook) 1984–85 Supplement.

SULLIVAN'S HORNBOOK OF THE LAW OF ANTITRUST, 886 pages, 1977. (Text)

Appellate Advocacy—see Trial and Appellate Advocacy

Architecture and Engineering Law

SWEET'S LEGAL ASPECTS OF ARCHITECTURE, ENGINEERING AND THE CONSTRUCTION PROCESS, Fourth Edition, 889 pages, 1989. Teacher's Manual available. (Casebook)

Art Law

DUBOFF'S ART LAW IN A NUTSHELL, 335 pages, 1984. Softcover. (Text)

Banking Law

LOVETT'S BANKING AND FINANCIAL INSTITUTIONS LAW IN A NUTSHELL, Second Edition, 464 pages, 1988. Softcover. (Text)

SYMONS AND WHITE'S TEACHING MATERIALS ON BANKING LAW, Second Edition, 993 pages, 1984. Teacher's Manual available. (Casebook) 1987 Supplement.

Business Planning—see also Corporate Finance

PAINTER'S PROBLEMS AND MATERIALS IN BUSINESS PLANNING, Second Edition, 1008 pages, 1984. (Casebook) 1990 Supplement.

Statutory Supplement. *See Selected Corporation and Partnership*

SELECTED CORPORATION AND PARTNERSHIP STATUTES, RULES AND FORMS. 727 pages, 1989. Softcover.

Civil Procedure—see also Federal Jurisdiction and Procedure

AMERICAN BAR ASSOCIATION SECTION OF LITIGATION—READINGS ON ADVERSARIAL JUSTICE: THE AMERICAN APPROACH TO ADJUDICATION, 217 pages, 1988. Softcover. (Coursebook)

CLERMONT'S BLACK LETTER ON CIVIL PROCEDURE, Second Edition, 332 pages, 1988. Softcover. (Review)

COUND, FRIEDENTHAL, MILLER AND SEXTON'S CASES AND MATERIALS ON CIVIL PROCEDURE, Fifth Edition, 1284 pages, 1989. Teacher's Manual available. (Casebook)

COUND, FRIEDENTHAL, MILLER AND SEXTON'S CIVIL PROCEDURE SUPPLEMENT. Approximately 450 pages, 1990. Softcover. (Casebook Supplement)

FEDERAL RULES OF CIVIL PROCEDURE—EDUCATIONAL EDITION. Softcover. Approximately 635 pages, 1990.

FRIEDENTHAL, KANE AND MILLER'S HORNBOOK ON CIVIL PROCEDURE, 876 pages, 1985. (Text)

KANE AND LEVINE'S CIVIL PROCEDURE IN CALIFORNIA: STATE AND FEDERAL 498 pages, 1989. Softcover. (Casebook Supplement)

Civil Procedure—Cont'd

KANE'S CIVIL PROCEDURE IN A NUTSHELL, Second Edition, 306 pages, 1986. Softcover. (Text)

KOFFLER AND REPPY'S HORNBOOK ON COMMON LAW PLEADING, 663 pages, 1969. (Text)

MARCUS, REDISH AND SHERMAN'S CIVIL PROCEDURE: A MODERN APPROACH, 1027 pages, 1989. Teacher's Manual available. (Casebook)

MARCUS AND SHERMAN'S COMPLEX LITIGATION–CASES AND MATERIALS ON ADVANCED CIVIL PROCEDURE, 846 pages, 1985. Teacher's Manual available. (Casebook) 1989 Supplement.

PARK'S COMPUTER-AIDED EXERCISES ON CIVIL PROCEDURE, Second Edition, 167 pages, 1983. Softcover. (Coursebook)

SIEGEL'S HORNBOOK ON NEW YORK PRACTICE, 1011 pages, 1978, with 1987 pocket part. (Text)

Commercial Law

BAILEY AND HAGEDORN'S SECURED TRANSACTIONS IN A NUTSHELL, Third Edition, 390 pages, 1988. Softcover. (Text)

EPSTEIN, MARTIN, HENNING AND NICKLES' BASIC UNIFORM COMMERCIAL CODE TEACHING MATERIALS, Third Edition, 704 pages, 1988. Teacher's Manual available. (Casebook)

HENSON'S HORNBOOK ON SECURED TRANSACTIONS UNDER THE U.C.C., Second Edition, 504 pages, 1979, with 1979 pocket part. (Text)

MURRAY'S COMMERCIAL LAW, PROBLEMS AND MATERIALS, 366 pages, 1975. Teacher's Manual available. Softcover. (Coursebook)

NICKLES' BLACK LETTER ON COMMERCIAL PAPER, 450 pages, 1988. Softcover. (Review)

NICKLES, MATHESON AND DOLAN'S MATERIALS FOR UNDERSTANDING CREDIT AND PAYMENT SYSTEMS, 923 pages, 1987. Teacher's Manual available. (Casebook)

NORDSTROM, MURRAY AND CLOVIS' PROBLEMS AND MATERIALS ON SALES, 515 pages, 1982. (Casebook)

NORDSTROM, MURRAY AND CLOVIS' PROBLEMS AND MATERIALS ON SECURED TRANSACTIONS, 594 pages, 1987. (Casebook)

RUBIN AND COOTER'S THE PAYMENT SYSTEM: CASES, MATERIALS AND ISSUES, 885 pages, 1989. (Casebook)

SELECTED COMMERCIAL STATUTES. Softcover. Approximately 1650 pages, 1990.

SPEIDEL'S BLACK LETTER ON SALES AND SALES FINANCING, 363 pages, 1984. Softcover. (Review)

SPEIDEL, SUMMERS AND WHITE'S COMMERCIAL LAW: TEACHING MATERIALS, Fourth Edition, 1448 pages, 1987. Teacher's Manual available. (Casebook)

SPEIDEL, SUMMERS AND WHITE'S COMMERCIAL PAPER: TEACHING MATERIALS, Fourth Edition, 578 pages, 1987. Reprint from Speidel et al., Commercial Law, Fourth Edition. Teacher's Manual available. (Casebook)

SPEIDEL, SUMMERS AND WHITE'S SALES: TEACHING MATERIALS, Fourth Edition, 804 pages, 1987. Reprint from Speidel et al., Commercial Law, Fourth Edition. Teacher's Manual available. (Casebook)

SPEIDEL, SUMMERS AND WHITE'S SECURED TRANSACTIONS: TEACHING MATERIALS, Fourth Edition, 485 pages, 1987. Reprint from Speidel et al., Commercial Law, Fourth Edition. Teacher's Manual available. (Casebook)

STOCKTON'S SALES IN A NUTSHELL, Second Edition, 370 pages, 1981. Softcover. (Text)

STONE'S UNIFORM COMMERCIAL CODE IN A NUTSHELL, Third Edition, 580 pages, 1989. Softcover. (Text)

WEBER AND SPEIDEL'S COMMERCIAL PAPER IN A NUTSHELL, Third Edition, 404 pages, 1982. Softcover. (Text)

WHITE AND SUMMERS' HORNBOOK ON THE UNIFORM COMMERCIAL CODE, Third Edition, Student Edition, 1386 pages, 1988. (Text)

Community Property

MENNELL AND BOYKOFF'S COMMUNITY PROPERTY IN A NUTSHELL, Second Edition, 432 pages, 1988. Softcover. (Text)

VERRALL AND BIRD'S CASES AND MATERIALS

Community Property—Cont'd

ON CALIFORNIA COMMUNITY PROPERTY, Fifth Edition, 604 pages, 1988. (Casebook)

Comparative Law

BARTON, GIBBS, LI AND MERRYMAN'S LAW IN RADICALLY DIFFERENT CULTURES, 960 pages, 1983. (Casebook)

GLENDON, GORDON AND OSAKWE'S COMPARATIVE LEGAL TRADITIONS: TEXT, MATERIALS AND CASES ON THE CIVIL LAW, COMMON LAW AND SOCIALIST LAW TRADITIONS, 1091 pages, 1985. (Casebook)

GLENDON, GORDON AND OSAKWE'S COMPARATIVE LEGAL TRADITIONS IN A NUTSHELL. 402 pages, 1982. Softcover. (Text)

LANGBEIN'S COMPARATIVE CRIMINAL PROCEDURE: GERMANY, 172 pages, 1977. Softcover. (Casebook)

Computers and Law

MAGGS AND SPROWL'S COMPUTER APPLICATIONS IN THE LAW, 316 pages, 1987. (Coursebook)

MASON'S USING COMPUTERS IN THE LAW: AN INTRODUCTION AND PRACTICAL GUIDE, Second Edition, 288 pages, 1988. Softcover. (Coursebook)

Conflict of Laws

CRAMTON, CURRIE AND KAY'S CASES–COMMENTS–QUESTIONS ON CONFLICT OF LAWS, Fourth Edition, 876 pages, 1987. (Casebook)

HAY'S BLACK LETTER ON CONFLICT OF LAWS, 330 pages, 1989. Softcover. (Review)

SCOLES AND HAY'S HORNBOOK ON CONFLICT OF LAWS, Student Edition, 1085 pages, 1982, with 1988–89 pocket part. (Text)

SEIGEL'S CONFLICTS IN A NUTSHELL, 470 pages, 1982. Softcover. (Text)

Constitutional Law—Civil Rights—see also Foreign Relations and National Security Law

ABERNATHY'S CASES AND MATERIALS ON CIVIL RIGHTS, 660 pages, 1980. (Casebook)

BARRON AND DIENES' BLACK LETTER ON CONSTITUTIONAL LAW, Second Edition, 310 pages, 1987. Softcover. (Review)

BARRON AND DIENES' CONSTITUTIONAL LAW IN A NUTSHELL, 389 pages, 1986. Softcover. (Text)

ENGDAHL'S CONSTITUTIONAL FEDERALISM IN A NUTSHELL, Second Edition, 411 pages, 1987. Softcover. (Text)

FARBER AND SHERRY'S HISTORY OF THE AMERICAN CONSTITUTION, 458 pages, 1990. Softcover. Teacher's Manual available. (Text)

GARVEY AND ALEINIKOFF'S MODERN CONSTITUTIONAL THEORY: A READER, 494 pages, 1989. Softcover. (Reader)

LOCKHART, KAMISAR, CHOPER AND SHIFFRIN'S CONSTITUTIONAL LAW: CASES–COMMENTS–QUESTIONS, Sixth Edition, 1601 pages, 1986. (Casebook) 1990 Supplement.

LOCKHART, KAMISAR, CHOPER AND SHIFFRIN'S THE AMERICAN CONSTITUTION: CASES AND MATERIALS, Sixth Edition, 1260 pages, 1986. Abridged version of Lockhart, et al., Constitutional Law: Cases–Comments–Questions, Sixth Edition. (Casebook) 1990 Supplement.

LOCKHART, KAMISAR, CHOPER AND SHIFFRIN'S CONSTITUTIONAL RIGHTS AND LIBERTIES: CASES AND MATERIALS, Sixth Edition, 1266 pages, 1986. Reprint from Lockhart, et al., Constitutional Law: Cases–Comments–Questions, Sixth Edition. (Casebook) 1990 Supplement.

MARKS AND COOPER'S STATE CONSTITUTIONAL LAW IN A NUTSHELL, 329 pages, 1988. Softcover. (Text)

NOWAK, ROTUNDA AND YOUNG'S HORNBOOK ON CONSTITUTIONAL LAW, Third Edition, 1191 pages, 1986 with 1988 pocket part. (Text)

ROTUNDA'S MODERN CONSTITUTIONAL LAW: CASES AND NOTES, Third Edition, 1085 pages, 1989. (Casebook) 1990 Supplement.

VIEIRA'S CONSTITUTIONAL CIVIL RIGHTS IN A NUTSHELL, Second Edition, 322 pages, 1990. Softcover. (Text)

WILLIAMS' CONSTITUTIONAL ANALYSIS IN A NUTSHELL, 388 pages, 1979. Softcover. (Text)

Consumer Law—see also Commercial Law

EPSTEIN AND NICKLES' CONSUMER LAW IN A NUTSHELL, Second Edition, 418 pages,

Consumer Law—Cont'd

1981. Softcover. (Text)

SELECTED COMMERCIAL STATUTES. Softcover. Approximately 1650 pages, 1990.

SPANOGLE AND ROHNER'S CASES AND MATERIALS ON CONSUMER LAW, 693 pages, 1979. Teacher's Manual available. (Casebook) 1982 Supplement.

Contracts

CALAMARI AND PERILLO'S BLACK LETTER ON CONTRACTS, Second Edition, approximately 450 pages, 1990. Softcover. (Review)

CALAMARI AND PERILLO'S HORNBOOK ON CONTRACTS, Third Edition, 1049 pages, 1987. (Text)

CALAMARI, PERILLO AND BENDER'S CASES AND PROBLEMS ON CONTRACTS, Second Edition, 905 pages, 1989. Teacher's Manual Available. (Casebook)

CORBIN'S TEXT ON CONTRACTS, One Volume Student Edition, 1224 pages, 1952. (Text)

FESSLER AND LOISEAUX'S CASES AND MATERIALS ON CONTRACTS—MORALITY, ECONOMICS AND THE MARKET PLACE, 837 pages, 1982. Teacher's Manual available. (Casebook)

FRIEDMAN'S CONTRACT REMEDIES IN A NUTSHELL, 323 pages, 1981. Softcover. (Text)

FULLER AND EISENBERG'S CASES ON BASIC CONTRACT LAW, Fifth Edition, approximately 1100 pages, 1990. (Casebook)

HAMILTON, RAU AND WEINTRAUB'S CASES AND MATERIALS ON CONTRACTS, 830 pages, 1984. (Casebook)

JACKSON AND BOLLINGER'S CASES ON CONTRACT LAW IN MODERN SOCIETY, Second Edition, 1329 pages, 1980. Teacher's Manual available. (Casebook)

KEYES' GOVERNMENT CONTRACTS IN A NUTSHELL, Second Edition, approximately 530 pages, 1990. Softcover. (Text)

SCHABER AND ROHWER'S CONTRACTS IN A NUTSHELL, Third Edition, approximately 438 pages, 1990. Softcover. (Text)

SUMMERS AND HILLMAN'S CONTRACT AND RELATED OBLIGATION: THEORY, DOCTRINE AND PRACTICE, 1074 pages, 1987. Teacher's Manual available. (Casebook)

Copyright—see Patent and Copyright Law

Corporate Finance

HAMILTON'S CASES AND MATERIALS ON CORPORATION FINANCE, Second Edition, 1221 pages, 1989. (Casebook)

Corporations

HAMILTON'S BLACK LETTER ON CORPORATIONS, Second Edition, 513 pages, 1986. Softcover. (Review)

HAMILTON'S CASES AND MATERIALS ON CORPORATIONS—INCLUDING PARTNERSHIPS AND LIMITED PARTNERSHIPS, Fourth Edition, approximately 1250 pages, 1990. (Casebook) 1990 Statutory Supplement.

HAMILTON'S THE LAW OF CORPORATIONS IN A NUTSHELL, Second Edition, 515 pages, 1987. Softcover. (Text)

HENN'S TEACHING MATERIALS ON THE LAW OF CORPORATIONS, Second Edition, 1204 pages, 1986. Teacher's Manual available. (Casebook)

Statutory Supplement. *See Selected Corporation and Partnership*

HENN AND ALEXANDER'S HORNBOOK ON LAWS OF CORPORATIONS, Third Edition, Student Edition, 1371 pages, 1983, with 1986 pocket part. (Text)

SELECTED CORPORATION AND PARTNERSHIP STATUTES, RULES AND FORMS. Softcover. 727 pages, 1989.

SOLOMON, SCHWARTZ AND BAUMAN'S MATERIALS AND PROBLEMS ON CORPORATIONS: LAW AND POLICY, Second Edition, 1391 pages, 1988. Teacher's Manual available. (Casebook) 1990 Supplement.

Statutory Supplement. *See Selected Corporation and Partnership*

Corrections

KRANTZ' CASES AND MATERIALS ON THE LAW OF CORRECTIONS AND PRISONERS' RIGHTS, Third Edition, 855 pages, 1986. (Casebook) 1988 Supplement.

KRANTZ' THE LAW OF CORRECTIONS AND PRISONERS' RIGHTS IN A NUTSHELL, Third Edition, 407 pages, 1988. Softcover. (Text)

ROBBINS' CASES AND MATERIALS ON POST-CONVICTION REMEDIES, 506 pages, 1982. (Casebook)

Creditors' Rights

BANKRUPTCY CODE, RULES AND OFFICIAL FORMS, LAW SCHOOL EDITION. Approximately 875 pages, 1990. Softcover.

EPSTEIN'S DEBTOR-CREDITOR RELATIONS IN A NUTSHELL, Third Edition, 383 pages, 1986. Softcover. (Text)

EPSTEIN, LANDERS AND NICKLES' CASES AND MATERIALS ON DEBTORS AND CREDITORS, Third Edition, 1059 pages, 1987. Teacher's Manual available. (Casebook)

LOPUCKI'S PLAYER'S MANUAL FOR THE DEBTOR-CREDITOR GAME, 123 pages, 1985. Softcover. (Coursebook)

NICKLES AND EPSTEIN'S BLACK LETTER ON CREDITORS' RIGHTS AND BANKRUPTCY, 576 pages, 1989. (Review)

RIESENFELD'S CASES AND MATERIALS ON CREDITORS' REMEDIES AND DEBTORS' PROTECTION, Fourth Edition, 914 pages, 1987. (Casebook) 1990 Supplement.

WHITE'S CASES AND MATERIALS ON BANKRUPTCY AND CREDITORS' RIGHTS, 812 pages, 1985. Teacher's Manual available. (Casebook) 1987 Supplement.

Criminal Law and Criminal Procedure—see also Corrections, Juvenile Justice

ABRAMS' FEDERAL CRIMINAL LAW AND ITS ENFORCEMENT, 866 pages, 1986. (Casebook) 1988 Supplement.

AMERICAN CRIMINAL JUSTICE PROCESS: SELECTED RULES, STATUTES AND GUIDELINES. 723 pages, 1989. Softcover.

CARLSON'S ADJUDICATION OF CRIMINAL JUSTICE: PROBLEMS AND REFERENCES, 130 pages, 1986. Softcover. (Casebook)

DIX AND SHARLOT'S CASES AND MATERIALS ON CRIMINAL LAW, Third Edition, 846 pages, 1987. (Casebook)

GRANO'S PROBLEMS IN CRIMINAL PROCEDURE, Second Edition, 176 pages, 1981. Teacher's Manual available. Softcover. (Coursebook)

HEYMANN AND KENETY'S THE MURDER TRIAL OF WILBUR JACKSON: A HOMICIDE IN THE FAMILY, Second Edition, 347 pages, 1985. (Coursebook)

ISRAEL, KAMISAR AND LaFAVE'S CRIMINAL PROCEDURE AND THE CONSTITUTION: LEADING SUPREME COURT CASES AND INTRODUCTORY TEXT. Approximately 725 pages, 1990 Edition. Softcover. (Casebook)

ISRAEL AND LaFAVE'S CRIMINAL PROCEDURE—CONSTITUTIONAL LIMITATIONS IN A NUTSHELL, Fourth Edition, 461 pages, 1988. Softcover. (Text)

JOHNSON'S CASES, MATERIALS AND TEXT ON CRIMINAL LAW, Fourth Edition, approximately 790 pages, 1990. Teacher's Manual available. (Casebook)

JOHNSON'S CASES AND MATERIALS ON CRIMINAL PROCEDURE, 859 pages, 1988. (Casebook) 1990 Supplement.

KAMISAR, LaFAVE AND ISRAEL'S MODERN CRIMINAL PROCEDURE: CASES, COMMENTS AND QUESTIONS, Seventh Edition, 1593 pages, 1990. (Casebook) 1990 Supplement.

KAMISAR, LaFAVE AND ISRAEL'S BASIC CRIMINAL PROCEDURE: CASES, COMMENTS AND QUESTIONS, Seventh Edition, 792 pages, 1990. Softcover reprint from Kamisar, et al., Modern Criminal Procedure: Cases, Comments and Questions, Seventh Edition. (Casebook) 1990 Supplement.

LaFAVE'S MODERN CRIMINAL LAW: CASES, COMMENTS AND QUESTIONS, Second Edition, 903 pages, 1988. (Casebook)

LaFAVE AND ISRAEL'S HORNBOOK ON CRIMINAL PROCEDURE, Student Edition, 1142 pages, 1985, with 1989 pocket part. (Text)

LaFAVE AND SCOTT'S HORNBOOK ON CRIMINAL LAW, Second Edition, 918 pages, 1986. (Text)

LANGBEIN'S COMPARATIVE CRIMINAL PROCEDURE: GERMANY, 172 pages, 1977. Softcover. (Casebook)

LOEWY'S CRIMINAL LAW IN A NUTSHELL, Second Edition, 321 pages, 1987. Softcover. (Text)

LOW'S BLACK LETTER ON CRIMINAL LAW, Revised First Edition, approximately 430 pages, 1990. Softcover. (Review)

SALTZBURG'S CASES AND COMMENTARY ON AMERICAN CRIMINAL PROCEDURE, Third Edition, 1302 pages, 1988. Teacher's Manual available. (Casebook) 1990 Supplement.

Criminal Law and Criminal Procedure— Cont'd

UVILLER'S THE PROCESSES OF CRIMINAL JUSTICE: INVESTIGATION AND ADJUDICATION, Second Edition, 1384 pages, 1979. (Casebook) 1979 Statutory Supplement. 1986 Update.

VORENBERG'S CASES ON CRIMINAL LAW AND PROCEDURE, Second Edition, 1088 pages, 1981. Teacher's Manual available. (Casebook) 1990 Supplement.

Decedents' Estates—see Trusts and Estates

Domestic Relations

CLARK'S HORNBOOK ON DOMESTIC RELATIONS, Second Edition, Student Edition, 1050 pages, 1988. (Text)

CLARK AND GLOWINSKY'S CASES AND PROBLEMS ON DOMESTIC RELATIONS, Fourth Edition. Approximately 1125 pages, 1990. Teacher's Manual available. (Casebook)

KRAUSE'S BLACK LETTER ON FAMILY LAW, 314 pages, 1988. Softcover. (Review)

KRAUSE'S CASES, COMMENTS AND QUESTIONS ON FAMILY LAW, Third Edition, 1433 pages, 1990. (Casebook)

KRAUSE'S FAMILY LAW IN A NUTSHELL, Second Edition, 444 pages, 1986. Softcover. (Text)

KRAUSKOPF'S CASES ON PROPERTY DIVISION AT MARRIAGE DISSOLUTION, 250 pages, 1984. Softcover. (Casebook)

Economics, Law and—see also Antitrust, Regulated Industries

GOETZ' CASES AND MATERIALS ON LAW AND ECONOMICS, 547 pages, 1984. (Casebook)

MALLOY'S LAW AND ECONOMICS: A COMPARATIVE APPROACH TO THEORY AND PRACTICE, Approximately 152 pages, 1990. Softcover. (Text)

Education Law

ALEXANDER AND ALEXANDER'S THE LAW OF SCHOOLS, STUDENTS AND TEACHERS IN A NUTSHELL, 409 pages, 1984. Softcover. (Text)

Employment Discrimination—see also Women and the Law

ESTREICHER AND HARPER'S CASES AND

MATERIALS ON THE LAW GOVERNING THE EMPLOYMENT RELATIONSHIP, 962 pages, 1990. Teacher's Manual available. (Casebook) Statutory Supplement.

JONES, MURPHY AND BELTON'S CASES AND MATERIALS ON DISCRIMINATION IN EMPLOYMENT, (The Labor Law Group). Fifth Edition, 1116 pages, 1987. (Casebook) 1990 Supplement.

PLAYER'S FEDERAL LAW OF EMPLOYMENT DISCRIMINATION IN A NUTSHELL, Second Edition, 402 pages, 1981. Softcover. (Text)

PLAYER'S HORNBOOK ON EMPLOYMENT DISCRIMINATION LAW, Student Edition, 708 pages, 1988. (Text)

PLAYER, SHOBEN AND LIEBERWITZ' CASES AND MATERIALS ON EMPLOYMENT DISCRIMINATION LAW, Approximately 810 pages, 1990. (Casebook)

Energy and Natural Resources Law—see also Oil and Gas

LAITOS' CASES AND MATERIALS ON NATURAL RESOURCES LAW, 938 pages, 1985. Teacher's Manual available. (Casebook)

SELECTED ENVIRONMENTAL LAW STATUTES— EDUCATIONAL EDITION. Softcover. Approximately 1040 pages, 1990.

Environmental Law—see also Energy and Natural Resources Law; Sea, Law of

BONINE AND MCGARITY'S THE LAW OF ENVIRONMENTAL PROTECTION: CASES—LEGISLATION—POLICIES, 1076 pages, 1984. Teacher's Manual available. (Casebook)

FINDLEY AND FARBER'S CASES AND MATERIALS ON ENVIRONMENTAL LAW, Second Edition, 813 pages, 1985. (Casebook) 1988 Supplement.

FINDLEY AND FARBER'S ENVIRONMENTAL LAW IN A NUTSHELL, Second Edition, 367 pages, 1988. Softcover. (Text)

RODGERS' HORNBOOK ON ENVIRONMENTAL LAW, 956 pages, 1977, with 1984 pocket part. (Text)

SELECTED ENVIRONMENTAL LAW STATUTES— EDUCATIONAL EDITION. Softcover. Approximately 1040 pages, 1990.

Equity—see Remedies

Estate Planning—see also Trusts and Estates; Taxation—Estate and Gift

LYNN'S AN INTRODUCTION TO ESTATE PLANNING IN A NUTSHELL, Third Edition, 370 pages, 1983. Softcover. (Text)

Evidence

BROUN AND BLAKEY'S BLACK LETTER ON EVIDENCE, 269 pages, 1984. Softcover. (Review)

BROUN, MEISENHOLDER, STRONG AND MOSTELLER'S PROBLEMS IN EVIDENCE, Third Edition, 238 pages, 1988. Teacher's Manual available. Softcover. (Coursebook)

CLEARY, STRONG, BROUN AND MOSTELLER'S CASES AND MATERIALS ON EVIDENCE, Fourth Edition, 1060 pages, 1988. (Casebook)

FEDERAL RULES OF EVIDENCE FOR UNITED STATES COURTS AND MAGISTRATES. Softcover. Approximately 380 pages, 1990.

GRAHAM'S FEDERAL RULES OF EVIDENCE IN A NUTSHELL, Second Edition, 473 pages, 1987. Softcover. (Text)

LEMPERT AND SALTZBURG'S A MODERN APPROACH TO EVIDENCE: TEXT, PROBLEMS, TRANSCRIPTS AND CASES, Second Edition, 1232 pages, 1983. Teacher's Manual available. (Casebook)

LILLY'S AN INTRODUCTION TO THE LAW OF EVIDENCE, Second Edition, 585 pages, 1987. (Text)

MCCORMICK, SUTTON AND WELLBORN'S CASES AND MATERIALS ON EVIDENCE, Sixth Edition, 1067 pages, 1987. (Casebook)

MCCORMICK'S HORNBOOK ON EVIDENCE, Third Edition, Student Edition, 1156 pages, 1984, with 1987 pocket part. (Text)

ROTHSTEIN'S EVIDENCE IN A NUTSHELL: STATE AND FEDERAL RULES, Second Edition, 514 pages, 1981. Softcover. (Text)

Federal Jurisdiction and Procedure

CURRIE'S CASES AND MATERIALS ON FEDERAL COURTS, Fourth Edition, approximately 1125 pages, 1990. (Casebook)

CURRIE'S FEDERAL JURISDICTION IN A NUTSHELL, Third Edition, approximately 260 pages, 1990. Softcover. (Text)

FEDERAL RULES OF CIVIL PROCEDURE—EDUCATIONAL EDITION. Softcover. Approximately 635 pages, 1990.

REDISH'S BLACK LETTER ON FEDERAL JURISDICTION, 219 pages, 1985. Softcover. (Review)

REDISH'S CASES, COMMENTS AND QUESTIONS ON FEDERAL COURTS, Second Edition, 1122 pages, 1989. (Casebook) 1990 Supplement.

VETRI AND MERRILL'S FEDERAL COURTS PROBLEMS AND MATERIALS, Second Edition, 232 pages, 1984. Softcover. (Coursebook)

WRIGHT'S HORNBOOK ON FEDERAL COURTS, Fourth Edition, Student Edition, 870 pages, 1983. (Text)

Foreign Relations and National Security Law

FRANCK AND GLENNON'S FOREIGN RELATIONS AND NATIONAL SECURITY LAW, 941 pages, 1987. (Casebook)

Future Interests—see Trusts and Estates

Health Law—see Medicine, Law and

Human Rights—see International Law

Immigration Law

ALEINIKOFF AND MARTIN'S IMMIGRATION PROCESS AND POLICY, Second Edition, approximately 1100 pages, October, 1990 (Casebook)

    Statutory Supplement. *See Immigration and Nationality Laws*

IMMIGRATION AND NATIONALITY LAWS OF THE UNITED STATES: SELECTED STATUTES, REGULATIONS AND FORMS. Softcover. Approximately 400 pages, 1990.

WEISSBRODT'S IMMIGRATION LAW AND PROCEDURE IN A NUTSHELL, Second Edition, 438 pages, 1989, Softcover. (Text)

Indian Law—see American Indian Law

Insurance Law

DEVINE AND TERRY'S PROBLEMS IN INSURANCE LAW, 240 pages, 1989. Softcover. Teacher's Manual available. (Course book)

DOBBYN'S INSURANCE LAW IN A NUTSHELL, Second Edition, 316 pages, 1989. Softcover. (Text)

KEETON'S CASES ON BASIC INSURANCE LAW,

Insurance Law—Cont'd

Second Edition, 1086 pages, 1977. Teacher's Manual available. (Casebook)

KEETON'S COMPUTER-AIDED AND WORKBOOK EXERCISES ON INSURANCE LAW, 255 pages, 1990. Softcover. (Coursebook)

KEETON AND WIDISS' INSURANCE LAW, Student Edition, 1359 pages, 1988. (Text)

WIDISS AND KEETON'S COURSE SUPPLEMENT TO KEETON AND WIDISS' INSURANCE LAW, 502 pages, 1988. Softcover. (Casebook)

WIDISS' INSURANCE: MATERIALS ON FUNDAMENTAL PRINCIPLES, LEGAL DOCTRINES AND REGULATORY ACTS, 1186 pages, 1989. (Casebook)

YORK AND WHELAN'S CASES, MATERIALS AND PROBLEMS ON GENERAL PRACTICE INSURANCE LAW, Second Edition, 787 pages, 1988. Teacher's Manual available. (Casebook)

International Law—see also Sea, Law of

BUERGENTHAL'S INTERNATIONAL HUMAN RIGHTS IN A NUTSHELL, 283 pages, 1988. Softcover. (Text)

BUERGENTHAL AND MAIER'S PUBLIC INTERNATIONAL LAW IN A NUTSHELL, Second Edition, 275 pages, 1990. Softcover. (Text)

FOLSOM, GORDON AND SPANOGLE'S INTERNATIONAL BUSINESS TRANSACTIONS—A PROBLEM-ORIENTED COURSEBOOK, 1160 pages, 1986. Teacher's Manual available. (Casebook) 1989 Documents Supplement.

FOLSOM, GORDON AND SPANOGLE'S INTERNATIONAL BUSINESS TRANSACTIONS IN A NUTSHELL, Third Edition, 509 pages, 1988. Softcover. (Text)

HENKIN, PUGH, SCHACHTER AND SMIT'S CASES AND MATERIALS ON INTERNATIONAL LAW, Second Edition, 1517 pages, 1987. (Casebook) Documents Supplement.

JACKSON AND DAVEY'S CASES, MATERIALS AND TEXT ON LEGAL PROBLEMS OF INTERNATIONAL ECONOMIC RELATIONS, Second Edition, 1269 pages, 1986. (Casebook) 1989 Documents Supplement.

KIRGIS' INTERNATIONAL ORGANIZATIONS IN THEIR LEGAL SETTING, 1016 pages, 1977. Teacher's Manual available. (Casebook) 1981 Supplement.

WESTON, FALK AND D'AMATO'S INTERNATIONAL LAW AND WORLD ORDER—A PROBLEM-ORIENTED COURSEBOOK, Second Edition, approximately 1305 pages, 1990. Teacher's Manual available. (Casebook) Documents Supplement.

Interviewing and Counseling

BINDER AND PRICE'S LEGAL INTERVIEWING AND COUNSELING, 232 pages, 1977. Teacher's Manual available. Softcover. (Coursebook)

BINDER, BERGMAN AND PRICE'S LAWYERS AS COUNSELORS: A CLIENT CENTERED APPROACH, Approximately 400 pages, October, 1990 Pub. Softcover. (Coursebook)

SHAFFER AND ELKINS' LEGAL INTERVIEWING AND COUNSELING IN A NUTSHELL, Second Edition, 487 pages, 1987. Softcover. (Text)

Introduction to Law—see Legal Method and Legal System

Introduction to Law Study

HEGLAND'S INTRODUCTION TO THE STUDY AND PRACTICE OF LAW IN A NUTSHELL, 418 pages, 1983. Softcover. (Text)

KINYON'S INTRODUCTION TO LAW STUDY AND LAW EXAMINATIONS IN A NUTSHELL, 389 pages, 1971. Softcover. (Text)

Judicial Process—see Legal Method and Legal System

Jurisprudence

CHRISTIE'S JURISPRUDENCE—TEXT AND READINGS ON THE PHILOSOPHY OF LAW, 1056 pages, 1973. (Casebook)

Juvenile Justice

FOX'S CASES AND MATERIALS ON MODERN JUVENILE JUSTICE, Second Edition, 960 pages, 1981. (Casebook)

FOX'S JUVENILE COURTS IN A NUTSHELL, Third Edition, 291 pages, 1984. Softcover. (Text)

Labor and Employment Law—see also Employment Discrimination, Social Legislation

FINKIN, GOLDMAN AND SUMMERS' LEGAL PROTECTION OF INDIVIDUAL EMPLOYEES, (The La-

Labor and Employment Law—Cont'd

bor Law Group). 1164 pages, 1989. (Casebook)

GORMAN'S BASIC TEXT ON LABOR LAW—UNIONIZATION AND COLLECTIVE BARGAINING, 914 pages, 1976. (Text)

LESLIE'S LABOR LAW IN A NUTSHELL, Second Edition, 397 pages, 1986. Softcover. (Text)

NOLAN'S LABOR ARBITRATION LAW AND PRACTICE IN A NUTSHELL, 358 pages, 1979. Softcover. (Text)

OBERER, HANSLOWE, ANDERSEN AND HEINSZ' CASES AND MATERIALS ON LABOR LAW—COLLECTIVE BARGAINING IN A FREE SOCIETY, Third Edition, 1163 pages, 1986. (Casebook) Statutory Supplement.

RABIN, SILVERSTEIN AND SCHATZKI'S LABOR AND EMPLOYMENT LAW: PROBLEMS, CASES AND MATERIALS IN THE LAW OF WORK, (The Labor Law Group). 1014 pages, 1988. Teacher's Manual available. (Casebook) 1988 Statutory Supplement.

Land Finance—Property Security—see Real Estate Transactions

Land Use

CALLIES AND FREILICH'S CASES AND MATERIALS ON LAND USE, 1233 pages, 1986. (Casebook) 1988 Supplement.

HAGMAN AND JUERGENSMEYER'S HORNBOOK ON URBAN PLANNING AND LAND DEVELOPMENT CONTROL LAW, Second Edition, Student Edition, 680 pages, 1986. (Text)

WRIGHT AND GITELMAN'S CASES AND MATERIALS ON LAND USE, Third Edition, 1300 pages, 1982. Teacher's Manual available. (Casebook) 1987 Supplement.

WRIGHT AND WRIGHT'S LAND USE IN A NUTSHELL, Second Edition, 356 pages, 1985. Softcover. (Text)

Legal History—see also Legal Method and Legal System

PRESSER AND ZAINALDIN'S CASES AND MATERIALS ON LAW AND JURISPRUDENCE IN AMERICAN HISTORY, Second Edition, 1092 pages, 1989. Teacher's Manual available. (Casebook)

Legal Method and Legal System—see also Legal Research, Legal Writing

ALDISERT'S READINGS, MATERIALS AND CASES IN THE JUDICIAL PROCESS, 948 pages, 1976. (Casebook)

BERCH AND BERCH'S INTRODUCTION TO LEGAL METHOD AND PROCESS, 550 pages, 1985. Teacher's Manual available. (Casebook)

BODENHEIMER, OAKLEY AND LOVE'S READINGS AND CASES ON AN INTRODUCTION TO THE ANGLO-AMERICAN LEGAL SYSTEM, Second Edition, 166 pages, 1988. Softcover. (Casebook)

DAVIES AND LAWRY'S INSTITUTIONS AND METHODS OF THE LAW—INTRODUCTORY TEACHING MATERIALS, 547 pages, 1982. Teacher's Manual available. (Casebook)

DVORKIN, HIMMELSTEIN AND LESNICK'S BECOMING A LAWYER: A HUMANISTIC PERSPECTIVE ON LEGAL EDUCATION AND PROFESSIONALISM, 211 pages, 1981. Softcover. (Text)

KEETON'S JUDGING, 842 pages, 1990. Softcover. (Coursebook)

KELSO AND KELSO'S STUDYING LAW: AN INTRODUCTION, 587 pages, 1984. (Coursebook)

KEMPIN'S HISTORICAL INTRODUCTION TO ANGLO-AMERICAN LAW IN A NUTSHELL, Third Edition, approximately 302 pages, 1990. Softcover. (Text)

REYNOLDS' JUDICIAL PROCESS IN A NUTSHELL, 292 pages, 1980. Softcover. (Text)

Legal Research

COHEN'S LEGAL RESEARCH IN A NUTSHELL, Fourth Edition, 452 pages, 1985. Softcover. (Text)

COHEN, BERRING AND OLSON'S HOW TO FIND THE LAW, Ninth Edition, 716 pages, 1989. (Text)

COHEN, BERRING AND OLSON'S FINDING THE LAW, 570 pages, 1989. Softcover reprint from Cohen, Berring and Olson's How to Find the Law, Ninth Edition. (Coursebook)

Legal Research Exercises, 3rd Ed., for use with Cohen, Berring and Olson, 229 pages, 1989. Teacher's Manual available.

ROMBAUER'S LEGAL PROBLEM SOLVING—

Legal Research—Cont'd

ANALYSIS, RESEARCH AND WRITING, Fourth Edition, 424 pages, 1983. Teacher's Manual with problems available. (Coursebook)

STATSKY'S LEGAL RESEARCH AND WRITING, Third Edition, 257 pages, 1986. Softcover. (Coursebook)

TEPLY'S LEGAL RESEARCH AND CITATION, Third Edition, 472 pages, 1989. Softcover. (Coursebook)

    Student Library Exercises, 3rd ed., 391 pages, 1989. Answer Key available.

Legal Writing

CHILD'S DRAFTING LEGAL DOCUMENTS: MATERIALS AND PROBLEMS, 286 pages, 1988. Softcover. Teacher's Manual available. (Coursebook)

DICKERSON'S MATERIALS ON LEGAL DRAFTING, 425 pages, 1981. Teacher's Manual available. (Coursebook)

FELSENFELD AND SIEGEL'S WRITING CONTRACTS IN PLAIN ENGLISH, 290 pages, 1981. Softcover. (Text)

GOPEN'S WRITING FROM A LEGAL PERSPECTIVE, 225 pages, 1981. (Text)

MELLINKOFF'S LEGAL WRITING—SENSE AND NONSENSE, 242 pages, 1982. Softcover. Teacher's Manual available. (Text)

PRATT'S LEGAL WRITING: A SYSTEMATIC APPROACH, 422 pages, 1989. Teacher's Manual available. (Coursebook)

RAY AND RAMSFIELD'S LEGAL WRITING: GETTING IT RIGHT AND GETTING IT WRITTEN, 250 pages, 1987. Softcover. (Text)

SQUIRES AND ROMBAUER'S LEGAL WRITING IN A NUTSHELL, 294 pages, 1982. Softcover. (Text)

STATSKY AND WERNET'S CASE ANALYSIS AND FUNDAMENTALS OF LEGAL WRITING, Third Edition, 424 pages, 1989. Teacher's Manual available. (Text)

TEPLY'S LEGAL WRITING, ANALYSIS AND ORAL ARGUMENT, 576 pages, 1990. Softcover. Teacher's Manual available. (Coursebook)

WEIHOFEN'S LEGAL WRITING STYLE, Second Edition, 332 pages, 1980. (Text)

Legislation

DAVIES' LEGISLATIVE LAW AND PROCESS IN A NUTSHELL, Second Edition, 346 pages, 1986. Softcover. (Text)

ESKRIDGE AND FRICKEY'S CASES AND MATERIALS ON LEGISLATION: STATUTES AND THE CREATION OF PUBLIC POLICY, 937 pages, 1988. Teacher's Manual available. (Casebook) 1990 Supplement.

NUTTING AND DICKERSON'S CASES AND MATERIALS ON LEGISLATION, Fifth Edition, 744 pages, 1978. (Casebook)

STATSKY'S LEGISLATIVE ANALYSIS AND DRAFTING, Second Edition, 217 pages, 1984. Teacher's Manual available. (Text)

Local Government

FRUG'S CASES AND MATERIALS ON LOCAL GOVERNMENT LAW, 1005 pages, 1988. (Casebook)

MCCARTHY'S LOCAL GOVERNMENT LAW IN A NUTSHELL, Third Edition, approximately 400 pages, 1990. Softcover. (Text)

REYNOLDS' HORNBOOK ON LOCAL GOVERNMENT LAW, 860 pages, 1982, with 1990 pocket part. (Text)

VALENTE'S CASES AND MATERIALS ON LOCAL GOVERNMENT LAW, Third Edition, 1010 pages, 1987. Teacher's Manual available. (Casebook) 1989 Supplement.

Mass Communication Law

GILLMOR, BARRON, SIMON AND TERRY'S CASES AND COMMENT ON MASS COMMUNICATION LAW, Fifth Edition, 947 pages, 1990. (Casebook)

GINSBURG'S REGULATION OF BROADCASTING: LAW AND POLICY TOWARDS RADIO, TELEVISION AND CABLE COMMUNICATIONS, 741 pages, 1979 (Casebook) 1983 Supplement.

ZUCKMAN, GAYNES, CARTER AND DEE'S MASS COMMUNICATIONS LAW IN A NUTSHELL, Third Edition, 538 pages, 1988. Softcover. (Text)

Medicine, Law and

FURROW, JOHNSON, JOST AND SCHWARTZ' HEALTH LAW: CASES, MATERIALS AND PROBLEMS, 1005 pages, 1987. Teacher's Manual available. (Casebook) 1989 Supplement.

HALL AND ELLMAN'S HEALTH CARE LAW AND

Medicine, Law and—Cont'd

ETHICS IN A NUTSHELL, 401 pages, 1990. Softcover (Text)

KING'S THE LAW OF MEDICAL MALPRACTICE IN A NUTSHELL, Second Edition, 342 pages, 1986. Softcover. (Text)

SHAPIRO AND SPECE'S CASES, MATERIALS AND PROBLEMS ON BIOETHICS AND LAW, 892 pages, 1981. (Casebook)

SHARPE, BOUMIL, FISCINA AND HEAD'S CASES AND MATERIALS ON MEDICAL LIABILITY, Approximately 500 pages, September, 1990 Pub. (Casebook)

Military Law

SHANOR AND TERRELL'S MILITARY LAW IN A NUTSHELL, 378 pages, 1980. Softcover. (Text)

Mortgages—see Real Estate Transactions

Natural Resources Law—see Energy and Natural Resources Law, Environmental Law

Negotiation

GIFFORD'S LEGAL NEGOTIATION: THEORY AND APPLICATIONS, 225 pages, 1989. Softcover. (Text)

WILLIAMS' LEGAL NEGOTIATION AND SETTLEMENT, 207 pages, 1983. Softcover. Teacher's Manual available. (Coursebook)

Office Practice—see also Computers and Law, Interviewing and Counseling, Negotiation

HEGLAND'S TRIAL AND PRACTICE SKILLS IN A NUTSHELL, 346 pages, 1978. Softcover (Text)

STRONG AND CLARK'S LAW OFFICE MANAGEMENT, 424 pages, 1974. (Casebook)

Oil and Gas—see also Energy and Natural Resources Law

HEMINGWAY'S HORNBOOK ON OIL AND GAS, Second Edition, Student Edition, 543 pages, 1983, with 1989 pocket part. (Text)

KUNTZ, LOWE, ANDERSON AND SMITH'S CASES AND MATERIALS ON OIL AND GAS LAW, 857 pages, 1986. Teacher's Manual available. (Casebook) Forms Manual. Revised.

LOWE'S OIL AND GAS LAW IN A NUTSHELL,

Second Edition, 465 pages, 1988. Softcover. (Text)

Partnership—see Agency—Partnership

Patent and Copyright Law

CHOATE, FRANCIS AND COLLINS' CASES AND MATERIALS ON PATENT LAW, INCLUDING TRADE SECRETS, COPYRIGHTS, TRADEMARKS, Third Edition, 1009 pages, 1987. (Casebook)

MILLER AND DAVIS' INTELLECTUAL PROPERTY—PATENTS, TRADEMARKS AND COPYRIGHT IN A NUTSHELL, Second Edition, approximately 440 pages, 1990. Softcover. (Text)

NIMMER'S CASES AND MATERIALS ON COPYRIGHT AND OTHER ASPECTS OF ENTERTAINMENT LITIGATION ILLUSTRATED—INCLUDING UNFAIR COMPETITION, DEFAMATION AND PRIVACY, Third Edition, 1025 pages, 1985. (Casebook) 1989 Supplement.

Products Liability

FISCHER AND POWERS' CASES AND MATERIALS ON PRODUCTS LIABILITY, 685 pages, 1988. Teacher's Manual available. (Casebook)

NOEL AND PHILLIPS' CASES ON PRODUCTS LIABILITY, Second Edition, 821 pages, 1982. (Casebook)

PHILLIPS' PRODUCTS LIABILITY IN A NUTSHELL, Third Edition, 307 pages, 1988. Softcover. (Text)

Professional Responsibility

ARONSON, DEVINE AND FISCH'S PROBLEMS, CASES AND MATERIALS IN PROFESSIONAL RESPONSIBILITY, 745 pages, 1985. Teacher's Manual available. (Casebook)

ARONSON AND WECKSTEIN'S PROFESSIONAL RESPONSIBILITY IN A NUTSHELL, 399 pages, 1980. Softcover. (Text)

MELLINKOFF'S THE CONSCIENCE OF A LAWYER, 304 pages, 1973. (Text)

PIRSIG AND KIRWIN'S CASES AND MATERIALS ON PROFESSIONAL RESPONSIBILITY, Fourth Edition, 603 pages, 1984. Teacher's Manual available. (Casebook)

ROTUNDA'S BLACK LETTER ON PROFESSIONAL RESPONSIBILITY, Second Edition, 414 pages, 1988. Softcover. (Review)

SCHWARTZ AND WYDICK'S PROBLEMS IN LE-

Professional Responsibility—Cont'd

GAL ETHICS, Second Edition, 341 pages, 1988. (Coursebook)

SELECTED STATUTES, RULES AND STANDARDS ON THE LEGAL PROFESSION. Softcover. Approximately 600 pages, 1990.

SMITH AND MALLEN'S PREVENTING LEGAL MALPRACTICE, 264 pages, 1989. Reprint from Mallen and Smith's Legal Malpractice, Third Edition. (Text)

SUTTON AND DZIENKOWSKI'S CASES AND MATERIALS ON THE PROFESSIONAL RESPONSIBILITY FOR LAWYERS, 839 pages, 1989. Teacher's Manual available. (Casebook)

WOLFRAM'S HORNBOOK ON MODERN LEGAL ETHICS, Student Edition, 1120 pages, 1986. (Text)

Property—see also Real Estate Transactions, Land Use, Trusts and Estates

BERNHARDT'S BLACK LETTER ON PROPERTY, 318 pages, 1983. Softcover. (Review)

BERNHARDT'S REAL PROPERTY IN A NUTSHELL, Second Edition, 448 pages, 1981. Softcover. (Text)

BOYER'S SURVEY OF THE LAW OF PROPERTY, Third Edition, 766 pages, 1981. (Text)

BROWDER, CUNNINGHAM, NELSON, STOEBUCK AND WHITMAN'S CASES ON BASIC PROPERTY LAW, Fifth Edition, 1386 pages, 1989. Teacher's Manual available. (Casebook)

BRUCE, ELY AND BOSTICK'S CASES AND MATERIALS ON MODERN PROPERTY LAW, Second Edition, 953 pages, 1989. Teacher's Manual available. (Casebook)

BURKE'S PERSONAL PROPERTY IN A NUTSHELL, 322 pages, 1983. Softcover. (Text)

CUNNINGHAM, STOEBUCK AND WHITMAN'S HORNBOOK ON THE LAW OF PROPERTY, Student Edition, 916 pages, 1984, with 1987 pocket part. (Text)

DONAHUE, KAUPER AND MARTIN'S CASES ON PROPERTY, Second Edition, 1362 pages, 1983. Teacher's Manual available. (Casebook)

HILL'S LANDLORD AND TENANT LAW IN A NUTSHELL, Second Edition, 311 pages, 1986. Softcover. (Text)

KURTZ AND HOVENKAMP'S CASES AND

MATERIALS ON AMERICAN PROPERTY LAW, 1296 pages, 1987. Teacher's Manual available. (Casebook) 1988 Supplement.

MOYNIHAN'S INTRODUCTION TO REAL PROPERTY, Second Edition, 239 pages, 1988. (Text)

Psychiatry, Law and

REISNER AND SLOBOGIN'S LAW AND THE MENTAL HEALTH SYSTEM, CIVIL AND CRIMINAL ASPECTS, Second Edition, approximately 1127 pages, 1990. (Casebook)

Real Estate Transactions

BRUCE'S REAL ESTATE FINANCE IN A NUTSHELL, Second Edition, 262 pages, 1985. Softcover. (Text)

MAXWELL, RIESENFELD, HETLAND AND WARREN'S CASES ON CALIFORNIA SECURITY TRANSACTIONS IN LAND, Third Edition, 728 pages, 1984. (Casebook)

NELSON AND WHITMAN'S BLACK LETTER ON LAND TRANSACTIONS AND FINANCE, Second Edition, 466 pages, 1988. Softcover. (Review)

NELSON AND WHITMAN'S CASES ON REAL ESTATE TRANSFER, FINANCE AND DEVELOPMENT, Third Edition, 1184 pages, 1987. (Casebook)

NELSON AND WHITMAN'S HORNBOOK ON REAL ESTATE FINANCE LAW, Second Edition, 941 pages, 1985 with 1989 pocket part. (Text)

Regulated Industries—see also Mass Communication Law, Banking Law

GELLHORN AND PIERCE'S REGULATED INDUSTRIES IN A NUTSHELL, Second Edition, 389 pages, 1987. Softcover. (Text)

MORGAN, HARRISON AND VERKUIL'S CASES AND MATERIALS ON ECONOMIC REGULATION OF BUSINESS, Second Edition, 666 pages, 1985. (Casebook)

Remedies

DOBBS' HORNBOOK ON REMEDIES, 1067 pages, 1973. (Text)

DOBBS' PROBLEMS IN REMEDIES. 137 pages, 1974. Teacher's Manual available. Softcover. (Coursebook)

DOBBYN'S INJUNCTIONS IN A NUTSHELL, 264 pages, 1974. Softcover. (Text)

Remedies—Cont'd

FRIEDMAN'S CONTRACT REMEDIES IN A NUTSHELL, 323 pages, 1981. Softcover. (Text)

LEAVELL, LOVE AND NELSON'S CASES AND MATERIALS ON EQUITABLE REMEDIES, RESTITUTION AND DAMAGES, Fourth Edition, 1111 pages, 1986. Teacher's Manual available. (Casebook)

MCCORMICK'S HORNBOOK ON DAMAGES, 811 pages, 1935. (Text)

O'CONNELL'S REMEDIES IN A NUTSHELL, Second Edition, 320 pages, 1985. Softcover. (Text)

SCHOENBROD, MACBETH, LEVINE AND JUNG'S CASES AND MATERIALS ON REMEDIES: PUBLIC AND PRIVATE, Approximately 807 pages, 1990. Teacher's Manual available. (Casebook)

YORK, BAUMAN AND RENDLEMAN'S CASES AND MATERIALS ON REMEDIES, Fourth Edition, 1029 pages, 1985. Teacher's Manual available. (Casebook)

Sea, Law of

SOHN AND GUSTAFSON'S THE LAW OF THE SEA IN A NUTSHELL, 264 pages, 1984. Softcover. (Text)

Securities Regulation

HAZEN'S HORNBOOK ON THE LAW OF SECURITIES REGULATION, Second Edition, Student Edition, approximately 1000 pages, 1990. (Text)

RATNER'S MATERIALS ON SECURITIES REGULATION, Third Edition, 1000 pages, 1986. Teacher's Manual available. (Casebook) 1989 Supplement.

    Statutory Supplement. *See Selected Securities Regulation*

RATNER'S SECURITIES REGULATION IN A NUTSHELL, Third Edition, 316 pages, 1988. Softcover. (Text)

SELECTED STATUTES, REGULATIONS, RULES, DOCUMENTS AND FORMS ON SECURITIES REGULATION. Softcover. 1272 pages, 1990.

Social Legislation

HOOD, HARDY AND LEWIS' WORKERS' COMPENSATION AND EMPLOYEE PROTECTION LAWS IN A NUTSHELL, Second Edition, 361 pages, 1990. Softcover. (Text)

LAFRANCE'S WELFARE LAW: STRUCTURE AND ENTITLEMENT IN A NUTSHELL, 455 pages, 1979. Softcover. (Text)

MALONE, PLANT AND LITTLE'S CASES ON WORKERS' COMPENSATION AND EMPLOYMENT RIGHTS, Second Edition, 951 pages, 1980. Teacher's Manual available. (Casebook)

Sports Law

SCHUBERT, SMITH AND TRENTADUE'S SPORTS LAW, 395 pages, 1986. (Text)

Tax Practice and Procedure

GARBIS, STRUNTZ AND RUBIN'S CASES AND MATERIALS ON TAX PROCEDURE AND TAX FRAUD, Second Edition, 687 pages, 1987. (Casebook)

MORGAN'S TAX PROCEDURE AND TAX FRAUD IN A NUTSHELL, Approximately 382 pages, 1990. Softcover. (Text)

Taxation—Corporate

KAHN AND GANN'S CORPORATE TAXATION, Third Edition, 980 pages, 1989. Teacher's Manual available. (Casebook)

WEIDENBRUCH AND BURKE'S FEDERAL INCOME TAXATION OF CORPORATIONS AND STOCKHOLDERS IN A NUTSHELL, Third Edition, 309 pages, 1989. Softcover. (Text)

Taxation—Estate & Gift—see also Estate Planning, Trusts and Estates

MCNULTY'S FEDERAL ESTATE AND GIFT TAXATION IN A NUTSHELL, Fourth Edition, 496 pages, 1989. Softcover. (Text)

PENNELL'S CASES AND MATERIALS ON INCOME TAXATION OF TRUSTS, ESTATES, GRANTORS AND BENEFICIARIES, 460 pages, 1987. Teacher's Manual available. (Casebook)

Taxation—Individual

DODGE'S THE LOGIC OF TAX, 343 pages, 1989. Softcover. (Text)

GUNN AND WARD'S CASES, TEXT AND PROBLEMS ON FEDERAL INCOME TAXATION, Second Edition, 835 pages, 1988. Teacher's Manual available. (Casebook) 1990 Supplement.

HUDSON AND LIND'S BLACK LETTER ON FEDERAL INCOME TAXATION, Third Edition, approximately 390 pages, 1990. Softcover. (Review)

Taxation—Individual—Cont'd

KRAGEN AND MCNULTY'S CASES AND MATERIALS ON FEDERAL INCOME TAXATION—INDIVIDUALS, CORPORATIONS, PARTNERSHIPS, Fourth Edition, 1287 pages, 1985. (Casebook)

MCNULTY'S FEDERAL INCOME TAXATION OF INDIVIDUALS IN A NUTSHELL, Fourth Edition, 503 pages, 1988. Softcover. (Text)

POSIN'S HORNBOOK ON FEDERAL INCOME TAXATION, Student Edition, 491 pages, 1983, with 1989 pocket part. (Text)

ROSE AND CHOMMIE'S HORNBOOK ON FEDERAL INCOME TAXATION, Third Edition, 923 pages, 1988, with 1989 pocket part. (Text)

SELECTED FEDERAL TAXATION STATUTES AND REGULATIONS. Softcover. Approximately 1650 pages, 1991.

SOLOMON AND HESCH'S PROBLEMS, CASES AND MATERIALS ON FEDERAL INCOME TAXATION OF INDIVIDUALS, 1068 pages, 1987. Teacher's Manual available. (Casebook)

Taxation—International

DOERNBERG'S INTERNATIONAL TAXATION IN A NUTSHELL, 325 pages, 1989. Softcover. (Text)

KAPLAN'S FEDERAL TAXATION OF INTERNATIONAL TRANSACTIONS: PRINCIPLES, PLANNING AND POLICY, 635 pages, 1988. (Casebook)

Taxation—Partnership

BERGER AND WIEDENBECK'S CASES AND MATERIALS ON PARTNERSHIP TAXATION, 788 pages, 1989. Teacher's Manual available. (Casebook)

Taxation—State & Local

GELFAND AND SALSICH'S STATE AND LOCAL TAXATION AND FINANCE IN A NUTSHELL, 309 pages, 1986. Softcover. (Text)

HELLERSTEIN AND HELLERSTEIN'S CASES AND MATERIALS ON STATE AND LOCAL TAXATION, Fifth Edition, 1071 pages, 1988. (Casebook)

Torts—see also Products Liability

CHRISTIE AND MEEKS' CASES AND MATERIALS ON THE LAW OF TORTS, Second Edition, 1264 pages, 1990. (Casebook)

DOBBS' TORTS AND COMPENSATION—PERSONAL ACCOUNTABILITY AND SOCIAL RESPONSIBILITY FOR INJURY, 955 pages, 1985. Teacher's Manual available. (Casebook) 1990 Supplement.

KEETON, KEETON, SARGENTICH AND STEINER'S CASES AND MATERIALS ON TORT AND ACCIDENT LAW, Second Edition, 1318 pages, 1989. (Casebook)

KIONKA'S BLACK LETTER ON TORTS, 339 pages, 1988. Softcover. (Review)

KIONKA'S TORTS IN A NUTSHELL: INJURIES TO PERSONS AND PROPERTY, 434 pages, 1977. Softcover. (Text)

MALONE'S TORTS IN A NUTSHELL: INJURIES TO FAMILY, SOCIAL AND TRADE RELATIONS, 358 pages, 1979. Softcover. (Text)

PROSSER AND KEETON'S HORNBOOK ON TORTS, Fifth Edition, Student Edition, 1286 pages, 1984 with 1988 pocket part. (Text)

ROBERTSON, POWERS AND ANDERSON'S CASES AND MATERIALS ON TORTS, 932 pages, 1989. Teacher's Manual available. (Casebook)

Trade Regulation—see also Antitrust, Regulated Industries

MCMANIS' UNFAIR TRADE PRACTICES IN A NUTSHELL, Second Edition, 464 pages, 1988. Softcover. (Text)

OPPENHEIM, WESTON, MAGGS AND SCHECHTER'S CASES AND MATERIALS ON UNFAIR TRADE PRACTICES AND CONSUMER PROTECTION, Fourth Edition, 1038 pages, 1983. Teacher's Manual available. (Casebook) 1986 Supplement.

SCHECHTER'S BLACK LETTER ON UNFAIR TRADE PRACTICES, 272 pages, 1986. Softcover. (Review)

Trial and Appellate Advocacy—see also Civil Procedure

APPELLATE ADVOCACY, HANDBOOK OF, Second Edition, 182 pages, 1986. Softcover. (Text)

BERGMAN'S TRIAL ADVOCACY IN A NUTSHELL, Second Edition, 354 pages, 1989. Softcover. (Text)

BINDER AND BERGMAN'S FACT INVESTIGATION: FROM HYPOTHESIS TO PROOF, 354 pages, 1984. Teacher's Manual available. (Coursebook)

Trial and Appellate Advocacy—Cont'd

CARLSON AND IMWINKELRIED'S DYNAMICS OF TRIAL PRACTICE: PROBLEMS AND MATERIALS, 414 pages, 1989. Teacher's Manual available. (Coursebook)

GOLDBERG'S THE FIRST TRIAL (WHERE DO I SIT? WHAT DO I SAY?) IN A NUTSHELL, 396 pages, 1982. Softcover. (Text)

HAYDOCK, HERR, AND STEMPEL'S FUNDAMENTALS OF PRE-TRIAL LITIGATION, 768 pages, 1985. Softcover. Teacher's Manual available. (Coursebook)

HEGLAND'S TRIAL AND PRACTICE SKILLS IN A NUTSHELL, 346 pages, 1978. Softcover. (Text)

HORNSTEIN'S APPELLATE ADVOCACY IN A NUTSHELL, 325 pages, 1984. Softcover. (Text)

JEANS' HANDBOOK ON TRIAL ADVOCACY, Student Edition, 473 pages, 1975. Softcover. (Text)

LISNEK AND KAUFMAN'S DEPOSITIONS: PROCEDURE, STRATEGY AND TECHNIQUE, Law School and CLE Edition. 250 pages, 1990. Softcover. (Text)

MARTINEAU'S CASES AND MATERIALS ON APPELLATE PRACTICE AND PROCEDURE, 565 pages, 1987. (Casebook)

NOLAN'S CASES AND MATERIALS ON TRIAL PRACTICE, 518 pages, 1981. (Casebook)

SONSTENG AND HAYDOCK'S TRIAL: THEORIES, TACTICS, TECHNIQUE, Approximately 650 pages, 1990. Softcover. (Text)

SONSTENG, HAYDOCK AND BOYD'S THE TRIALBOOK: A TOTAL SYSTEM FOR PREPARATION AND PRESENTATION OF A CASE, 404 pages, 1984. Softcover. (Coursebook)

WHARTON, HAYDOCK AND SONSTENG'S CALIFORNIA CIVIL TRIALBOOK, Law School and CLE Edition. Approximately 300 pages, 1990. Softcover. (Text)

Trusts and Estates

ATKINSON'S HORNBOOK ON WILLS, Second Edition, 975 pages, 1953. (Text)

AVERILL'S UNIFORM PROBATE CODE IN A NUTSHELL, Second Edition, 454 pages, 1987. Softcover. (Text)

BOGERT'S HORNBOOK ON TRUSTS, Sixth Edition, Student Edition, 794 pages, 1987. (Text)

CLARK, LUSKY AND MURPHY'S CASES AND MATERIALS ON GRATUITOUS TRANSFERS, Third Edition, 970 pages, 1985. (Casebook)

DODGE'S WILLS, TRUSTS AND ESTATE PLANNING–LAW AND TAXATION, CASES AND MATERIALS, 665 pages, 1988. (Casebook)

KURTZ' PROBLEMS, CASES AND OTHER MATERIALS ON FAMILY ESTATE PLANNING, 853 pages, 1983. Teacher's Manual available. (Casebook)

McGOVERN'S CASES AND MATERIALS ON WILLS, TRUSTS AND FUTURE INTERESTS: AN INTRODUCTION TO ESTATE PLANNING, 750 pages, 1983. (Casebook)

McGOVERN, KURTZ AND REIN'S HORNBOOK ON WILLS, TRUSTS AND ESTATES–INCLUDING TAXATION AND FUTURE INTERESTS, 996 pages, 1988. (Text)

MENNELL'S WILLS AND TRUSTS IN A NUTSHELL, 392 pages, 1979. Softcover. (Text)

SIMES' HORNBOOK ON FUTURE INTERESTS, Second Edition, 355 pages, 1966. (Text)

TURANO AND RADIGAN'S HORNBOOK ON NEW YORK ESTATE ADMINISTRATION, 676 pages, 1986. (Text)

UNIFORM PROBATE CODE, OFFICIAL TEXT WITH COMMENTS. 615 pages, 1989. Softcover.

WAGGONER'S FUTURE INTERESTS IN A NUTSHELL, 361 pages, 1981. Softcover. (Text)

WATERBURY'S MATERIALS ON TRUSTS AND ESTATES, 1039 pages, 1986. Teacher's Manual available. (Casebook)

Water Law—see also Energy and Natural Resources Law, Environmental Law

GETCHES' WATER LAW IN A NUTSHELL, Second Edition, approximately 441 pages, 1990. Softcover. (Text)

SAX AND ABRAMS' LEGAL CONTROL OF WATER RESOURCES: CASES AND MATERIALS, 941 pages, 1986. (Casebook)

TRELEASE AND GOULD'S CASES AND MATERIALS ON WATER LAW, Fourth Edition, 816 pages, 1986. (Casebook)

WEST'S LAW SCHOOL
ADVISORY BOARD

JOHN A. BAUMAN
Professor of Law, University of California, Los Angeles

CURTIS J. BERGER
Professor of Law, Columbia University

JESSE H. CHOPER
Dean and Professor of Law,
University of California, Berkeley

DAVID P. CURRIE
Professor of Law, University of Chicago

YALE KAMISAR
Professor of Law, University of Michigan

MARY KAY KANE
Professor of Law, University of California,
Hastings College of the Law

WAYNE R. LaFAVE
Professor of Law, University of Illinois

RICHARD C. MAXWELL
Professor of Law, Duke University

ARTHUR R. MILLER
Professor of Law, Harvard University

ROBERT A. STEIN
Dean and Professor of Law, University of Minnesota

JAMES J. WHITE
Professor of Law, University of Michigan

CHARLES ALAN WRIGHT
Professor of Law, University of Texas

CONSUMER LAW
CASES AND MATERIALS
Second Edition

By

John A. Spanogle
Professor of Law
The George Washington University

Ralph J. Rohner
Dean and Professor of Law
The Catholic University of America

Dee Pridgen
Professor of Law
University of Wyoming

Paul B. Rasor
Professor of Law
Washburn University

AMERICAN CASEBOOK SERIES®

WEST PUBLISHING CO.
ST. PAUL, MINN., 1991

American Casebook Series, the key number appearing on the front
cover and the WP symbol are registered trademarks of West Publishing
Co. Registered in U.S. Patent and Trademark Office.

COPYRIGHT © 1979, 1982 WEST PUBLISHING CO.
COPYRIGHT © 1991 By WEST PUBLISHING CO.
                     50 West Kellogg Boulevard
                     P.O. Box 64526
                     St. Paul, MN 55164–0526

Library of Congress Cataloging-in-Publication Data

Spanogle, John A., 1934–
    Cases and materials on consumer law. — 2nd ed. / John A.
  Spanogle, Mary Dee Pridgen, Paul B. Rasor.
        p.   cm. — (American casebook series)
    Rev. ed. of: Consumer law / by John A. Spanogle and Ralph J.
  Rohner.
    Includes index.
    ISBN 0–314–78651–1
    1. Consumer protection—Law and legislation—United States—Cases.
  2. Consumer credit—Law and legislation—United States—Cases.
  I. Pridgen, Mary Dee, 1949–   . II. Rasor, Paul B. III. Spanogle,
  John A., 1934–   Consumer law. IV. Title. V. Series.
  KF1608.S66 1991
  343.73'071—dc20
  [347.30371]   90–45540
                                                          CIP

ISBN 0–314–78651–1

            (S., R., P. & R.) Consumer Law 2d Ed. ACB   ∞

To
Pam, Kathy and Sharon,
Monica,
Ken and Keiko
and
Carol, Lisa and Noel

*

Preface to the Second Edition

*The answers may have changed,
but the questions remain the same.*

In the eleven years since the first edition of this casebook was published, almost every aspect of consumer law has been rewritten. The FTC has taken itself out of the "cutting edge" problems of deceit regulation. A litigation-prone Truth in Lending Act has been replaced by a nearly case-less Truth in Lending Simplification Act. Several approaches to consumer problems which seemed to be promising in 1979 have seemingly not had any great impact. Examples include class actions and the FTC Credit Practices Rule, and other Trade Regulation Rules. "Unconscionability," with only one prominent exception, is used more by corporations than by consumers. Even the federal-state tension and balance which permeated the first edition has shifted— both ways. State usury laws have been "deregulated" and preempted. On the other hand, the use of state "Baby FTC Acts" has grown to fill the gaps left by federal FTC inaction.

—AND YET—

The basic fact patterns analyzed in the Problems of the first edition still exist, with their tension between protecting consumers and allowing creditors and sellers to do business. Thus, a surprising number of the Problems used in the first edition are still useful teaching tools, and have been kept in this second edition. Some of the old scams have disappeared, and some new ones have appeared, and related Problems have been added, amended or deleted as necessary.

It's a different story with the cases and notes. Except for a few classics, or where historical development was needed, most of the cases have been replaced and notes rewritten.

The overall organization of the first edition has been maintained, with its four-Part division into: I. Regulation of Information, II. Regulation of Conduct, III. Regulation of Prices, and IV. Enforcement of all the above. Within those four Parts, there has been some rearrangement. The chapters in Part II relate to three different stages of the consumer transaction: pre-contractual relations (Chapters 3 and 4), obligations during performance (Chapters 5 and 6), and debt collection (Chapters 7, 8 and 9). Part III is broken into chapters on regulation of prices of goods and services (10), state regulation of interest rates (11), federal regulation of interest rates (12), an evaluation of these regulations (13), and the upside-down world of credit insurance (14).

Evaluations of the utility of regulation are attempted at the end of Chapters 2 (information), 4 (credit availability), 6 (cut-off of defenses), 9 (coercive collection) and in all of Chapter 13 (interest rate regulation). We believe that such evaluations are an integral part of any Consumer Law course.

Two new coauthors, Dee Pridgen and Paul Rasor, have joined the team for this second edition. One of the strengths of the first edition was its presentation of the tension between federal and state law in the consumer law area. Since the two original authors are now based in Washington, it seemed appropriate to bring in coauthors who were "outside the Beltway."

Each of the authors thanks all the other coauthors for their feedback, direction and support. Even though we are scattered around the country, overnight mail, the fax machine, the computer and the airplane allowed each of us to participate in the drafting (and redrafting) of all parts of the book. This book may be an example of Tofler's "Third Wave," where geographical boundaries no longer limit what we can do, as long as we can communicate.

We also wish to thank multiple classes of students who read through mimeo versions of earlier drafts of this book, and who helped to improve it by their reactions and constructive comments. It is appropriate that their comments are reflected throughout the book, and their enthusiasm helped us complete it, for they are the ultimate consumers of our effort.

We could not have written this manuscript without the help from each of our schools of our secretarial staffs, librarians, colleagues and deans. To all of them, we give a heartfelt "Thank you." Dee Pridgen especially wishes to acknowledge the financial support she received from the George Hopper Faculty Research Fund.

November, 1990

JOHN A. SPANOGLE
RALPH J. ROHNER
DEE PRIDGEN
PAUL B. RASOR

Preface to the First Edition

Too often, the materials for a consumer protection course start and end with theoretical problems, and have no substance in between. They seem to be based on an assumption that consumer protection laws are either only theoretically possible or some aberrant fluke of legislative madness which will not be repeated.

These materials proceed from a different set of assumptions: (1) Consumer protection statutes and caselaw doctrines are pervasive within the legal structure. (2) They are growing. (3) They are not likely to disappear, but are more likely to increase. (4) Even though they concern widely disparate subject-matter, there are likely to be common doctrinal and practical threads running through them, and it is our job to try to discover these threads.

Another problem with some consumer protection materials is that they rely on long quotations from law review articles, reports and other textual material to present information. There is now sufficient caselaw to provide a core of teaching materials. There are statutes also, in abundance. In many areas, the cases amply set forth both the present practices and the present legal doctrines. However, these cases should be read in the same manner as those for any other course—to evaluate and critique not only the holding of the case, but also its underlying assumptions, statute, and policies.

One pattern running throughout these materials is to compare judge-made law and legislation dealing with the same problem. Thus, where cases are presented, there will usually be discussions of statutory provisions dealing with the same problem.

The authors hope that these materials will enable students to do several things. One is to grasp a reasonable portion of the array of substantive law applicable in consumer transactions, with an appreciation both of its complexity and of its recurrent themes. Another is to appreciate the "hidden" workings of the consumer marketplace—the economic motives and consequences of transaction patterns. An equally important goal is to persuade students—most of whom instinctively applaud anything labeled "consumer protection"—that current statutory and caselaw approaches, and the policy choices underlying them, are not beyond criticism. If iconoclasm is perceived in these materials, it is intended.

For the purposes of this book, "consumer transactions" include those in which individuals enter into consensual arrangements for the purchase of property or services, or for the borrowing of money. These materials treat of the various legal rules designed to protect the consumer's *economic* expectations in those transactions. We therefore do not address such matters as products liability, or the regulation of product safety, or the rights of consumers in landlord-tenant or employment relationships, or other kinds of "transactions" in which consumers engage. Considerable attention is given to credit transactions since those present more, and more complex, legal issues than do cash transactions, and have generated more sweeping statutory controls.

These materials obviously build on concepts and rules treated in basic contracts courses, and in courses on sales, negotiable instruments and secured financing. This book is designed, however, to include ample prefatory and review material so that students need not have taken commercial law courses before taking Consumer Law. Neither of the authors treats those commercial courses as prerequisites, although one of us "recommends" that students take them first. In any event, students may profitably consult a basic commercial law hornbook, such as J. White & R. Summers, Uniform Commercial Code (1972), or R. Braucher & R. Riegert, Introduction to Commercial Transactions (1977).

Each of the authors first acknowledges that the other has contributed more than half the book. It is for this reason that the order of our names on the cover was chosen by coin flip.

To our students, past, present and future, we owe a debt beyond calculation. It is their interest and enthusiasm, their challenges, their critiques and their perceptions, that make this effort worthwhile.

We also acknowledge, with gratitude and affection, the support, encouragement and inspiration provided by two esteemed teachers of the law, Professors Homer Kripke and Fairfax Leary, Jr. In many ways, large and small, they are a part of this book and of the law it portrays.

There are many other people to whom we owe thanks for their help: Professor Jack Ayer, who was kind enough to share his unpublished materials with us, and whose materials furnished a springboard for many of our ideas. Our colleagues, who critiqued parts of the materials, especially Dick Bell, Grace Blumberg, Marjorie Girth, Nils Olsen, George Priest, Jack Schlegal, Paul Spiegelman, and Urban Lester. The mistakes and heresies in the final product, however, are ours, not theirs. And last but not least, our families, who did not tell us too often how absent we were.

April, 1979

JOHN A. SPANOGLE
RALPH J. ROHNER

Summary of Contents

PART IV. WEAPONS FOR ENFORCEMENT

*

Table of Contents

PART III. REGULATION OF PRICES AND ALLOCATION OF RESOURCES

Table of Cases

The principal cases are in bold type. Cases cited or discussed in the text are roman type. References are to pages. Cases cited in principal cases and within other quoted materials are not included.

*

Table of Statutes

*

CONSUMER LAW

CASES AND MATERIALS

Second Edition

*

CONSUMER LAW
Cases and Materials

You shall not deprive the
poor man of justice
in his suit.

* * *

Nor shall you favour the poor
man in his suit.

Exodus 23, Verses 6, 3

INTRODUCTION

Consumer Law has its own analytical format and organization—one which attempts to synthesize the seemingly random bits and pieces of "reform" legislation into a coherent pattern. This book is designed around such a format, and approaches the law of consumer transactions in four Parts which correspond to what we believe are four distinct philosophies of consumer protection. Or, since these several theories tend to intersect and criss-cross in their application, one might approach the book in terms of four separate levels of consciousness through which anyone dealing with consumer problems must pass—whether the person be a consumer advocate, industry representative, legislator or regulator.

These four philosophies, or levels of consciousness, each have a separate Part in these materials, and are: (1) regulation of information disclosure, (2) regulation of conduct, (3) regulation of prices, including resource allocation and credit availability, and (4) enforcement of the regulatory provisions.

The book lets the student see that all four "philosophies" may need to be brought to bear—that a sound legal response to a given problem may require some aspects of disclosure, some direct regulation, efficient and effective enforcement, and due consideration of the availability of the market to adjust or be adjusted.

Thus, the book does not follow more "obvious" organization patterns, because we believe that consumer law does have a set of concepts which are uniquely its own, and we hope the book will help to analyze

(S., R., P. & R.) Consumer Law 2d Ed. ACB—3

1

them. For this reason, the organization does not depend upon the law of torts or general commercial law; it does not develop material in a strictly chronological pattern, either in terms of historical evolution or transactional stages; nor does it separate the material into federal laws and state laws, or into private consumer rights and public agency enforcement powers. Indeed, usury laws and rate regulation—which might have the longest ancestry in the law—are deferred until relatively late in the book while the basic consumer protection mandate of the Federal Trade Commission appears much earlier, as does the Truth in Lending Act, a legal infant barely twenty years old.

A primary level of attack on any perceived pattern of consumer abuse, dealt with in *Part I,* is to regulate the disclosure of information to consumers, both as to accuracy and completeness. Regulation of informational conduct has deep roots and wide acceptance in our society: Truth in Lending is a contemporary example, but proscriptions against deceptive advertising have been with us for years, and the common law action of deceit is an even more ancient concept. The traditional negative constraints on disclosure (through liability for misrepresentation or breach of express warranty) are compared to the affirmative disclosure requirements embodied in many current laws. This Part also allows some comparison of alternative legal devices: a common law *stare decisis* approach, a generalized statutory standard, such as the Federal Trade Commission's "unfair or deceptive acts or practice," or a detailed and technical statute such as Truth in Lending.

The problem-solver soon learns that disclosure does not eliminate all problems, and that more direct regulation of abuses is necessary. Thus statutes are passed, or judicial decisions are rendered, prohibiting certain described conduct, or prohibiting "unfair" conduct generally, or requiring sellers and creditors to take certain measures for their customers' protection. This is the meat of *Part II.* Many different regulatory tools are considered, and again the emphasis is on a comparison of different consumer protection techniques: one using caselaw doctrines ("unconscionability", e.g.) or very general statutes, as a flexible tool; the other using very precisely drawn statutes or regulations as a more directed tool. But, alas, the problem-solver now realizes that, even after many of these statutes are enacted, the problems still do not go away—or worse, they multiply because of regulatory complexity or lax enforcement, or because merchant and creditor ingenuity devises new practices.

Part III then brings us to what might be called "resource allocation" questions. What do we do to the presumably open and competitive marketplace when we attack consumer abuses symptomatically, in band-aid fashion? Is it possible to curtail the truly abusive practices without unduly increasing the cost of goods or services to all consumers and without placing those goods or services beyond the reach of poor or less-creditworthy consumers? What are the consequences of controlling the price of money (through usury laws and the like) but not the price of goods? How do we assure participation in the consumer transaction market for both consumers and their suppliers? Although these questions could be explored in many areas, we concentrate on price and interest ceilings, in the belief that the effects are exposed more dramatically there, and more data is available.

Finally, the problem-solver comes to realize that all the substantive decision making in the world does not solve all the problems because no one is enforcing the laws already in place. Thus *Part IV* examines the different methods of seeking effective enforcement of consumer protection laws. To what extent should consumers be given (or left with) private rights to be vindicated informally or through private lawsuits? To what extent should public agencies serve as policemen of the consumer market place, and with what powers?

These materials attempt to take the student through this process of thinking. Hopefully all of this will engender the type of analysis which creates cross-currents of thought to design non-traditional solutions to traditional problems.

A Note to Our Colleagues in the Chair—Students Should Not Read

We thought that a note on teaching methodology might be helpful. We have tried to present these materials through both cases and formal problems. One of the co-authors uses cases more extensively in class, another focuses more on problems in class with the cases usually considered as background information. We have tried to design these materials so that they can be used by teachers of either persuasion, and by those in the middle. The formal problems do not cover exactly the same issues as the cases, and so each can be used to build on the other.

In all chapters, we try to present examples and illustrations of attempts to regulate conduct, and the problems created by such attempts, rather than to present a comprehensive summary of all consumer protection law. The materials also show that some regulatory concepts appear both in consumer credit and in other statutes or caselaw. Thus, the basic idea is to lead the student through consumer protection processes, using cases and statutes in one area of abuse to illustrate each protection process. Then, notes or problems have been added to show how the same process can be used to protect consumers in another area or from a different abuse. This may not be the only organizational principle, but we think it is one which is natural, and will make the concepts learned become obsolete more slowly. Since the substance of consumer protection changes so fast, we do not think we can use present substantive law as an organizational principle. But what we can do, through this process-oriented organization, is to enable the student to fit more recent substance into the organizational pattern, as illustrations of further and different uses of already-developed processes (or as new processes, if they are such).

A second common principle is the continuous comparison of (1) caselaw (2) general concept statutes (such as the FTC Act) and (3) more specific statutes (such as the Truth in Lending Act and the Uniform Consumer Credit Code (U3C)). The contrast of general-language statutes with specifically-worded statutes is deliberate, and we hope will lead throughout the course to an increasing debate about the comparative effectiveness of each as a protective device in different circumstances. This debate should continue into Part IV on enforcement. Thus, we seek to promote a continuous analysis of these two basically different approaches to regulation of industry conduct.

A third principle is to use primary authorities wherever possible, in preference to secondary authority materials. Where we had a choice between presenting a transactional pattern through a law review article or a case, we have tried to use the case, on the ground that the student is more likely to read a case more carefully. Secondary materials generally have been limited to those which present commercial and social science background, usually through field work investigation.

By the way, if you are a student and have read this section, you have just been part of a demonstration project. Many consumer protection statutes require a legend to appear on consumer contracts which reads as follows:

"Notice to Consumer: Read this paper before you sign it."

Many consumer and industry representatives believe this is a waste of effort and print. Instead, most of them believe that it would be more effective to require a legend which states:

"Notice to Consumer: You may NOT read this paper before you sign it."

What do you think?

The Statutory Cast of Characters

—or, where do we find the "rules of the game"?

Consumer law is not exclusively statute law, but it is predominantly so. Many of the statutes fall into categories whose names are bandied about by insiders in a manner that is likely to bewilder a stranger. Here is a sort of scorecard calculated to give you brief identifications of the major statutory players.

A. State Legislation:

The Uniform Commercial Code (UCC) ought to be the fountainhead of consumer law, since it covers sales, negotiable instruments, and security arrangements in financing. But it is not. With only a few exceptions, the UCC does no more than set some outer limits of consumer protection. This was done deliberately by the drafters of the UCC for at least two reasons. First, they made a more or less conscious decision to leave the tough consumer questions for another day. This, unfortunately, does not necessarily mean that the UCC is neutral on consumer issues. Instead, by refusing to deal with them, the UCC often treated consumer issues as though they did not exist, and left consumer transactions under the same regulations as merchant-to-merchant transactions. Second, the UCC sales warranty provisions have been outmoded almost since the start. What is more broadly termed "products liability" law has swept on by, and left sales warranties in the eddy behind.

Retail Installment Sales Acts (RISA's) are specialized consumer statutes adopted in nearly all states to regulate the content of credit sale transactions. RISA's may regulate disclosure terms, finance charges, credit insurance and remedies on default, among other things. Some cover only autos; some, other goods. The first RISA's were enacted in the 1930's well before the UCC, and they co-exist in more or less uneasy alliance with the UCC today.

Small Loan Acts are laws that regulate the conduct of lenders who specialize in making loans to consumers, normally at rates well above what is allowed by general usury laws. Most of these acts owe their genesis to a Uniform Small Loan Act promulgated by the Russell Sage Foundation in 1916. The limited scope of these laws generally includes licensing provisions and restrictions on the rates and terms of small loans.

The U3C and the MCCA are two proposed "reform" statutes in the field of consumer credit that would embrace many of the topics previously dealt with by other legislation. The U3C is the Uniform Consumer Credit Code. An original version was approved by the National Conference of Commissioners of Uniform State Laws in 1968, and the revised version (U3C) was published in 1974. The 1974 revisions were both organizational and substantive. Thus, references will be given in these materials primarily to the 1974 U3C, and only secondarily to its obsolete predecessor, the 1968 version.

The 1968 U3C was so poorly received by consumer groups that they created their own competing proposed legislation—the National Consumer Act (NCA). It was produced in 1969 by the National Consumer Law Center with funds provided by the U.S. Office of Economic Opportunity. In 1973, a revised version of it was proposed as the Model Consumer Credit Act (MCCA). Again, references in these materials will be given primarily to the MCCA, and only secondarily to the NCA.

It is probably not a burlesque to say that the U3C is the industry and the MCCA the consumer reform proposal—but the characterization does not suggest the full flavor of the debate. At this point the U3C has been adopted by half a dozen states (Colorado, Idaho, Indiana, Kansas, Oklahoma, Utah and Wyoming), but each state has included a number of non-uniform variations. The NCA provided much of the substance of the new Wisconsin Consumer Act and piecemeal amendments to other consumer laws. Perhaps more important, Iowa, Maine, South Carolina and West Virginia have each enacted hybrid versions containing some U3C, some MCCA, and some local variants—and these were the last four states to take any comprehensive action in the credit area.

Little FTC Acts have been enacted by many states, and are of increasing importance in state protection of consumers. They are analogous to the Federal Trade Commission Act, discussed below, and are applicable to unfair or deceptive acts or practices in either credit or cash transactions. In this area, there is model state legislation, such as the Uniform Consumer Sales Practices Act.

One arguably unfortunate result of the tension between the U3C and the MCCA was that there is no uniformity among the states in their consumer legislation. In addition, there have been piecemeal, *ad hoc* amendments to all state consumer credit legislation. In fact the crazy-quilt pattern of state statutes in this area has been the occasion for an ever-increasing *federal* intervention.

B.   Federal Legislation:

The Consumer Credit Protection Act (CCPA) 15 U.S.C.A. § 1601 et seq., passed by Congress in 1968, is the first major foray by the federal government into the field of consumer credit control. As Chapter 2 indicates, it was substantially amended in 1982, and all discussion in this text concerns the current version. Title I of the CCPA is the Truth in Lending Act (TIL) which requires certain disclosures in consumer credit sales and loans, regulates credit advertising, and allows "cooling off" periods in certain mortgage transactions. The Truth in Lending title has been amended several times to add new chapters on credit billing practices (the Fair Credit Billing Act) and consumer leases (the Consumer Leasing Act).

Titles II and III of the original CCPA place limits on wage garnishment, and provide criminal penalties for extortionate loans. The CCPA has also been amended to add new titles dealing with credit reporting agencies (Title VI, The Fair Credit Reporting Act), discrimination in credit transactions (Title VII, The Equal Credit Opportunity Act), collection agency practices (Title VIII, The Fair Debt Collection Practices Act), and electronic funds transfers (Title IX, The Electronic Funds Transfer Act).

The Federal Trade Commission Act, 15 U.S.C.A. § 41 *et seq.,* establishes broad authority for that Commission to regulate "unfair and deceptive acts or practices in or affecting commerce," principally under Section 5 of that Act. However, due to recent interpretations by the Commission, the Act is not now used extensively, even though the analogous state "little FTC" Acts have become more prominent in state enforcement.

The FTC Act now authorizes the Commission to issue Trade Regulation Rules which have the full force of law and which in effect add another whole layer of governmental regulation. Existing TRRs include those on "Cooling Off Period for Door-to-Door Sales", "Preservation of Consumers' Claims and Defenses", and "Credit Practices".

The *Magnuson–Moss Warranty Act,* 15 U.S.C.A. § 2301 *et seq.,* establishes certain minimum requirements for written warranties offered by suppliers of consumer products.

C. Caveat!

This is only a partial scorecard. There are probably countless bits and pieces of state law which impact on consumer transactions; some of these may have broader application, others may be narrow *ad hoc* consumer protection measures. Together—and because widespread adoption of the U3C has stalled—the body of state statutory law constitutes a hodgepodge at least equal to that existing in the commercial area before adoption of the Uniform Commercial Code.

In addition, of course, some areas of the "law" of consumer transactions are only sketchily dealt with in statutes specifically drawn for consumer protection. One such area is the basic law of creditor remedies. Parts of the UCC and the U3C touch on this area, and the Federal Trade Commission promulgated a fairly limited Trade Regulation Rule on the subject in 1984, but the existing statutory benchmarks provide little more than general guidance.

Finally, despite the relatively narrow coverage areas of the current federal laws and rules, their impact is substantial because of their nationwide applicability and the accompanying preemption of inconsistent state laws. Your authors disagree, frankly, on where the significant consumer protection activity will occur in the years ahead. We all agree that in areas of new transactions or concern, federal law is likely to take precedence because the process of enactment is quicker. In areas of already known conflict, however, one of us believes that the nitty-gritty work of identifying and responding to consumer needs, and providing meaningful enforcement, will be at the state and local level— with or without a "uniform" state code. Another is of the view that the federal takeover of the consumer protection area will continue by statute and rule.

D. A note on editorial style and supplementary materials:

In order to conserve space, we have regularly dropped citations from judicial opinions without marking the deletions. We have also frequently omitted footnotes of the court; those footnotes that remain bear the court's numbering.

A copy of West's Selected Commercial Statutes is a necessary adjunct to this text. Teachers may also wish to supply students with copies of new or revised federal regulations; these are generally available without cost from Federal Reserve Banks or Federal Trade Commission Regional Offices.

Especially in the case of federal statutes, section numbering often differs between the original act and its U.S.C.A. version. We use the section numbers of the original acts, since this is the way they appear in the Selected Commercial Statutes supplement.

The most frequently cited specialized reporting services are the Commerce Clearing House Consumer Credit Guide, hereafter CCH–CCG, and the Commerce Clearing House Trade Regulation Reporter, hereafter CCH–TRR.

Part I

REGULATION OF INFORMATION

Introduction

Regulation of marketplace information is a traditional governmental activity. At Common Law use of the writ of deceit dates back to the thirteenth century. Part I raises two basic questions in regard to regulation of information: First, how truthful must the information be? Second, must seller give any information at all, and, if so, how complete must it be?

Chapter 1 considers the first of these questions. A seller of goods has traditionally been permitted some leeway in describing the goods ("puffing his wares") in order to persuade a potential buyer to buy them. Where does "puffing" end, and deception begin? The Common Law resolution of this tension has changed over time, and continues to change. In addition, the states have moved forward at very different rates, so that conduct considered deceptive in one state may be permissible in another state at the same time. The difficulties in remedying misleading conduct led to statutory reform, first at the federal level with the FTC Act and later at the state level with "Little FTC Acts" or "UDAPs". However, regulation of information may at some point infringe on the seller's First Amendment right to free speech, which creates another set of analytical problems.

Chapter 2 deals with a different problem: Can the government compel the seller or creditor to disclose information when the seller or creditor would prefer to remain silent? Thus, the problem for the consumer is not that the information given is not reliable, but that insufficient information is given. The federal government's efforts at this type of regulation date from the 1938 enactment of the Food, Drug and Cosmetic Act (21 U.S.C.A. § 301 et seq.). Another such federal regulation is the Truth in Lending Act (15 U.S.C.A. § 1601 et seq.) and regulation Z (12 C.F.R. Part 226), both of which can be found in West's Selected Commercial Statutes. We will focus on the Truth in Lending Act as an illustration of compulsory disclosure legislation, and examine the underlying information problems, the statutory approach and its difficulties, and the perceived effect of the regulation.

Chapter 1

REGULATION OF VOLUNTARY DISCLOSURE

SECTION A. THE COMMON LAW APPROACH—DECEIT AND OTHER TORT DEVICES

The consumer's need for reliable information in order to make intelligent purchasing decisions is self-evident. The law has therefore long afforded redress for purchasers who rely to their detriment on seller representations which prove to be false. The formulations of these legal rules have differed, however, depending on the nature of the transaction, the blameworthiness or innocence of the speaker, and the form of remedy sought by the injured buyer. In transactions involving the sale of goods (chattels), sellers are held to any express "warranties" they make as part of the sale, regardless of any intent to deceive or mislead the buyer. Rescission based on mistaken understandings of one or both parties is a traditional equitable remedy. The tort action for deceit, on the other hand, is premised more on seller's fault and buyer's justifiable reliance. The following excerpt from the watershed case of Derry v. Peek, 14 App.Cas. 337, 359, 374–75 (House of Lords, 1889), distinguishes the tort from the equitable remedy:

"This action is one which is commonly called an action of deceit, a mere common-law action." This is the description of it given by Cotton, L.J., in delivering judgment. I think it important that it should be borne in mind that such an action differs essentially from one brought to obtain rescission of a contract on the ground of misrepresentation of a material fact. The principles which govern the two actions differ widely. Where rescission is claimed it is only necessary to prove that there was misrepresentation; then, however honestly it may have been made, however free from blame the person who made it, the contract, having been obtained by misrepresentation, cannot stand. In an action of deceit, on the contrary, it is not enough to establish misrepresentation alone; it is conceded on all hands that something more must be proved to cast liability upon the defendant, though it has been a matter of controversy what additional elements are requisite. I lay stress upon this because observations made by learned judges in actions for rescission have been cited and much relied upon at the bar by counsel for the respondent. Care must obviously be observed in applying the language used in relation to such actions to an action of deceit. * * *

I think the authorities establish the following propositions: First, in order to sustain an action of deceit, there must be proof of fraud, and nothing short of that will suffice. Secondly, fraud is proved when it is shewn that a false representation has been made (1) knowingly, or (2) without belief in its truth, or (3) recklessly, careless whether it be true or false. Although I have treated the second and third as distinct cases, I think the third is but an instance of the second, for one who makes a statement under such circumstances can have no real belief in the truth of what he states. To prevent a false statement being fraudulent, there must, I think, always be an honest belief in its truth. And this probably covers the whole ground, for one who knowingly alleges that which is false, has obviously no such honest belief. Thirdly, if fraud be proved, the motive of the person guilty of it is immaterial. It matters not that there was no intention to cheat or injure the person to whom the statement was made. * * *

In my opinion making a false statement through want of care falls far short of, and is a very different thing from, fraud, and the same may be said of a false representation honestly believed though on insufficient grounds. * * *

The following cases and problems are a summary review of the evolution of doctrine—particularly in the law of deceit. The student should be on the lookout for those aspects of deceit which distinguish it from equitable rescission or breach of warranty, and for changing standards of seller responsibility for misstatements.

In other words, the law of deceit has been a known and used consumer protection device for decades, starting long before any perceived "consumer" movement. It has not, however, been a static doctrine. Many of the "elements" of such a cause of action actually measure society's expectations of the consumer, and the amount of protection he should be afforded—the opinion v. fact dichotomy, reliance, inducement, lack of knowledge of falsity, intention of the deceiver—i.e., was the victim's reliance justifiable? As the following materials show, these standards have changed, and have offered less protection in the past. The policy question which overrides the technicalities is: What criteria should be used under present societal conditions?

1. WHERE HAVE WE COME FROM?—THE TRADITIONAL DOCTRINE

PROSSER AND KEETON, TORTS

(5th Ed., 1984).

The tort action for damages, commonly referred to as the action for deceit, is of very ancient origin. There was an old writ of deceit known as early as 1201, which lay only against a person who had misused legal procedure for the purpose of swindling someone. At a later period this writ was superseded by an action on the case in the nature of deceit, which became the general common law remedy for fraudulent or even nonfraudulent misrepresentation resulting in actual damage. In particular, it was extended to afford a remedy for many wrongs which we should now regard as breaches of contract, such as false warranties in the sale of goods. Its use was limited almost entirely to cases of direct transactions between the parties, and it came to be regarded as inseparable from some contractual relation. It was not until 1789, in Pasley v. Freeman, which is the parent of the modern law of deceit, that the action was held to lie where the plaintiff had had no dealings with the defendant, but had been induced by his misrepresentation to deal with a third person. After that date deceit was recognized as purely a tort action, and not necessarily founded upon a contract. At about the same time, the remedy for a breach of warranty was taken over into the action of assumpsit, and it was thus established that it had a contract character. Thereafter the two lines of recovery slowly diverged, although some vestiges of confusion between the two still remain in many courts, particularly as to the measure of damages. The distinction was made clear in the English courts by decisions holding that the tort action of deceit requires something in the way of knowledge of the falsity of the statement and an intention to mislead, while the contract action on a warranty does not.

The elements of the tort cause of action in deceit which at last emerged from this process of development frequently have been stated as follows:

1. A false representation made by the defendant. In the ordinary case, this representation must be one of fact.

2. Knowledge or belief on the part of the defendant that the representation is false—or, what is regarded as equivalent, that he has not a sufficient basis of information to make it. This element often is given the technical name of "scienter."

3. An intention to induce the plaintiff to act or to refrain from action in reliance upon the misrepresentation.

4. Justifiable reliance upon the representation on the part of the plaintiff, in taking action or refraining from it.

5. Damage to the plaintiff, resulting from such reliance.

As will be seen, some of these elements have undergone modification or qualification in some jurisdictions. In addition, it must be repeated that such an action of deceit is only one of several possible remedies for various forms of misrepresentation * * *.

* * *

[M]isrepresentation may be found in statements which are literally true, but which create a false impression in the mind of the hearer, as is sometimes the case where a complicated financial statement is issued by a seller of securities.

In addition to such representations by word or conduct, which might be called definite or positive, deceit, as well as other remedies, may be based upon an active concealment of the truth.

A much more difficult problem arises as to whether mere silence, or a passive failure to disclose facts of which the defendant has knowledge, can serve as the foundation of a deceit action. It has commonly been stated as a general rule, particularly in the older cases, that the action will not lie for such tacit nondisclosure. This rule of course reflected the dubious business ethics of the bargaining transactions with which deceit was at first concerned, together with a touch of the old tort notion that there can be no liability for nonfeasance, or merely doing nothing.

* * *

To this general rule, if such it be, the courts have developed a number of exceptions, some of which are as yet very ill defined, and have no very definite boundaries. The most obvious one is that if the defendant does speak, he must disclose enough to prevent his words from being misleading.

Another exception is found where the parties stand in some confidential or fiduciary relation to one another, such as that of principal and agent, executor and beneficiary of an estate, bank and investing depositor, majority and minority stockholders, old friends, or numerous others where special trust and confidence is reposed.

* * *

A statement of opinion is one which either indicates some doubt as to the speaker's belief in the existence of a state of facts, as where he says, "I think this is true, but I am not sure," or merely expresses his judgment on some matter of judgment connected with the facts, such as quality, value, authenticity and the like, as where he says, "This is a very fine picture." It is not, however, the form of the statement which is important or controlling, but the sense in which it is reasonably understood. The parties are expected to deal at arm's length and to beware of one another, and each is supposed to be competent to look after his own interests, and to draw his own conclusions. So long as he has not been misled by positive statements of fact, he has no right to rely upon the judgment of his opponent.

The intent which underlies an intentional misrepresentation is a more complex matter than the relatively simple intention in the case of assault and battery. It involves the intent that a representation shall be made, that it shall be directed to a particular person or class of persons, that it shall convey a certain meaning, that it shall be believed, and that it shall be acted upon in a certain way. * * * The intent which becomes important is the intent to deceive, to mislead, to convey a false impression. Obviously this intent, which has been given the name of "scienter" by the courts, must be a matter of belief, or of absence of belief, that the representation is true; * * *.

There is of course no difficulty in finding the required intent to mislead where it appears that the speaker believes his statement to be false. Likewise there is general agreement that it is present when the representation is made without any belief as to its truth, or with reckless disregard whether it be true or false. Further than this, it appears that all courts have extended it to include representations made by one who is conscious that he has no sufficient basis of information to justify them. A defendant who asserts a fact as of his own knowledge, or so positively as to imply that he has knowledge, under circumstances where he is aware that he will be so understood when he knows that he does not in fact know whether what he says is true, is found to have the intent to deceive, not so much as to the fact itself, but rather as to the extent of his information.

When the plaintiff seeks relief of an equitable character, as by rescission of the transaction and recovery of what he has parted with, a more liberal rule usually is applied. * * * It was not until as late as 1889 that the House of Lords, in the leading case of Derry v. Peek, clearly identified the deceit action with intentional misrepresentation, and left negligence and strict responsibility to be dealt with by other remedies.

Misrepresentation and mistake were recognized very early as a basis for jurisdiction of courts of equity because of the inadequacies of the legal remedy of damages to deal with the injuries resulting therefrom. The most common equitable remedies for misrepresentation were rescission or reformation of the contract, deed, lease, or other written transaction or requiring the defendant who had been unjustly enriched as a consequence of performance from the mistaken party to hold the money or property he had received subject to a constructive trust, or an equitable lien. Thus, so far as misrepresentation is concerned, most courts have held that it is unnecessary to establish for restitution the mental element of knowledge commonly required in the tort action of deceit, and it is sufficient to show an honest misrepresentation, or even, in some cases, a mere mistake. Likewise, unless he is excused by special circumstances, the plaintiff must restore what he has himself received.

Not only must there be reliance but the reliance must be justifiable under the circumstances.

It is a sufficient indication that the person deceived is not held to the standard of precaution, or of minimum knowledge, or of intelligent judgment, of the hypothetical reasonable man, that people who are exceptionally gullible, superstitious, ignorant, stupid, dim-witted, or illiterate, have been allowed to recover when the defendant knew it, and deliberately took advantage of it. * * * The other side of the shield is that one who has special knowledge, experience and competence may not be permitted to rely on statements for which the ordinary man might recover, and that one who has acquired expert knowledge concerning the matter dealt with may be required to form his own judgment, rather than take the word of the defendant. * * * Earlier decisions, under the influence of the prevalent doctrine of "caveat emptor," laid great stress upon the plaintiff's "duty" to protect himself and distrust his antagonist, and held that he was not entitled to rely even upon positive assertions of fact made by one with whom he was dealing at arm's length.

––––––––

The following case will help you appreciate the way courts used to respond to problems of alleged deceit. This judicial approach reflected the societal values, including consumer expectations, of the time.

SWINTON v. WHITINSVILLE SAVINGS BANK

Supreme Judicial Court of Massachusetts, 1942.
311 Mass. 677, 42 N.E.2d 808.

QUA, JUSTICE.

The declaration alleges that on or about September 12, 1938, the defendant sold the plaintiff a house in Newton to be occupied by the plaintiff and his family as a dwelling; that at the time of the sale the house "was infested with termites, an insect that is most dangerous and destructive to buildings"; that the defendant knew the house was so infested; that the plaintiff could not readily observe this condition upon inspection; that "knowing the internal destruction that these insects were creating in said house", the defendant falsely and fraudulently concealed from the plaintiff its true condition; that the plaintiff at the time of his purchase had no knowledge of the termites, exercised due care thereafter, and learned of them about August 30, 1940; and that, because of the destruction that was being done and the dangerous condition that was being created by the termites, the plaintiff was put to great expense for repairs and for the installation of termite control in order to prevent the loss and destruction of said house.

There is no allegation of any false statement or representation, or of the uttering of a half truth which may be tantamount to a falsehood. There is no intimation that the defendant by any means prevented the plaintiff from acquiring information as to the condition of the house. There is nothing to show any fiduciary relation between the parties, or that the plaintiff stood in a position of confidence toward or dependence upon the defendant. So far as appears the parties made a business deal at arm's length. The charge is concealment and nothing more; and it is concealment in the simple sense of mere failure to reveal, with nothing to show any peculiar duty to speak. The characterization of the concealment as false and fraudulent of course adds nothing in the absence of further allegations of fact.

If this defendant is liable on this declaration every seller is liable who fails to disclose any nonapparent defect known to him in the subject of the sale which materially reduces its value and which the buyer fails to discover. Similarly it would seem that every buyer would be liable who fails to disclose any nonapparent virtue known to him in the subject of the purchase which materially enhances its value and of which the seller is ignorant. The law has not yet, we believe, reached the point of imposing upon the frailties of human nature a standard so idealistic as this. That the particular case here stated by the plaintiff possesses a certain appeal to the moral sense is scarcely to be denied. Probably the reason is to be found in the facts that the infestation of buildings by termites has not been common in Massachusetts and constitutes a concealed risk against which buyers are off their guard. But the law cannot provide special rules for termites and can hardly attempt to determine liability according to the varying probabilities of the existence and discovery of different possible defects in the subjects of trade. The rule of nonliability for bare nondisclosure has been stated and followed by this court. It is adopted in the American Law Institute's Restatement of Torts, § 551. See Williston on Contracts, Rev.Ed., §§ 1497, 1498, 1499.

The order sustaining the demurrer is affirmed, and judgment is to be entered for the defendant.

* * *

Notes

1. In Babb v. Bolyard, 194 Md. 603, 72 A.2d 13 (1950), buyer-plaintiff alleged that used car seller-defendant had misrepresented that the "dealer's price" of a 1946 Buick was $3000, when in fact it was only $1986. The court directed a verdict for seller on the ground that "a representation as to value is only an expression of opinion, not a statement of fact." Buyer did not have the right "as a person of ordinary prudence to rely upon the alleged misrepresentation."

2. Of poignant interest to students may be the case of Trustees of Columbia University v. Jacobsen, 53 N.J.Super. 574, 148 A.2d 63 (App.Div. 1959). The University sued a former student on promissory notes given for his tuition, only to be met by a counterclaim for fraud. The gravamen of the student's claim was that the University had falsely represented that it would teach "wisdom." These allegedly false and deceitful representations were to be found in catalogs, brochures, inscriptions on University buildings. Key among them was the University's motto: "In lumine tuo videbimus lumen."

Problem 1

Southern Land Co. sold a 400 acre farm to Saxby, representing it to contain 150 acres of timber, of which about 20 acres had been "burned over," and representing that cordwood would sell for $4 per cord. Saxby bought the farm and found that it did contain 400 acres; there were 140 acres of timber, of which 75 acres had been burned over; and cordwood has and does sell for only $2 per cord. Has Saxby a successful cause of action for either of the misrepresentations? Cf., Saxby v. Southern Land Co., 109 Va. 196, 63 S.E. 423 (1909) ("merely expressing his opinion"); but see, Richard v. A. Waldman & Sons, Inc., 155 Conn. 343, 232 A.2d 307 (1967) (innocent misrepresentation actionable if declarant has the means of knowing, ought to know, or has a duty to know.)

2. WHERE ARE WE NOW?—THE PRESENT DOCTRINE OF DECEIT

The common law doctrine has changed as the marketplace has evolved. In older cases, courts were much more likely to find that statements made by sellers were merely expressions of opinion rather than actionable misstatements of fact. This attitude has changed over the years. For example, in Ragsdale v. Kennedy, 286 N.C. 130, 209 S.E.2d 494 (1974), defendant bought corporate stock from plaintiff. Plaintiff failed to disclose increases in the corporation's debt, a reduction in its cash on hand, and a general deterioration in its financial condition. Instead, plaintiff had described the corporation as a "gold mine" and a "going concern." Defendant's counterclaim for fraud was held to state a claim on the ground that, since plaintiff chose to speak about the corporation's finances, he must make "a full and fair disclosure as to the matters he discusses." In addition, the court stated that "suppression" of defects known to the seller, but not to the buyer, also constituted fraud. Note the two different approaches to the concept: one concerned with misleading half-truths, the other concerned with requiring affirmative disclosure, even if the seller prefers to remain totally silent.

PROSSER AND KEETON, TORTS
(5th Ed., 1984).

It is now held that assertions of fact as to the quantity or quality of land or goods sold, the financial status of corporations, and similar matters inducing commercial transactions, may justifiably be relied on without investigation, not only where such investigation would be burdensome or difficult, as where land which is sold lies at a distance, but likewise where the falsity of the representation might be discovered with little effort by means easily at hand.

The requirement of justifiability according to the Second Restatement of Torts refers to whether or not the representation relates to a matter about which a reasonable person would attach importance in determining a choice of action. It relates therefore to (a) immaterial misrepresentation, (b) opinions and statements of intention that are commonly regarded as dealer's talk or puffing, and (c) statements about the law.

The courts have developed numerous exceptions to the rule that misrepresentations of opinion are not a basis for relief. Apparently all of these may be summed up by saying that they involve situations where special circumstances make it very reasonable or probable that the plaintiff should accept the defendant's opinion and act upon it, and so justify a relaxation of the distrust which is considered admirable between bargaining opponents. Thus where the parties stand in a relation of trust and confidence, as in the case of members of the same family, partners, attorney and client, executor and beneficiary of an estate, principal and agent, insurer and insured, close friendship, and the like, it is held that reliance upon an opinion, whether it be as to a fact or a matter of law, is justifiable, and relief is granted.

Further than this, it has been recognized very often that the expression of an opinion may carry with it an implied assertion, not only that the speaker knows no facts which would preclude such an opinion, but that he does know facts which justify it. There is quite general agreement that such an assertion is to be implied where the defendant holds himself out or is understood as having special knowledge of the matter which is not available to the plaintiff, so that his opinion becomes in effect an assertion summarizing his knowledge. Thus the ordinary man is free to deal in reliance upon the opinion of an expert jeweler as to the value of a diamond, of an attorney upon a point of law, of a physician upon a matter of health, of a banker upon the validity of a signature, or the owner of land at a distance as to its worth, even though the opinion is that of his antagonist in a bargaining transaction.

* * *

* * * For the most part, the courts have limited deceit to those cases where there is an intent to mislead, and have left negligence and strict liability to be dealt with in some other type of action.

PIETRAZAK v. McDERMOTT

Supreme Judicial Court of Massachusetts, 1960.
341 Mass. 107, 167 N.E.2d 166.

WILLIAMS, JUSTICE.

This is an action of contract or tort in which the first count of the declaration alleges deceit and the second count breach of warranty in connection with the sale by the defendants of a house and land to the plaintiffs. The case came before a judge of the Superior Court upon the plaintiffs' motion for judgment on the report of an auditor whose findings of fact were not final. The judge found generally for the plaintiffs. The defendants "treating the finding as an allowance" of the plaintiffs' motion excepted to the "order for judgment."

The auditor found that in the spring of 1955 the defendants, who we assume were husband and wife, were building a single one story frame dwelling house in Lowell. When it was substantially completed, Angie Pietrazak, one of the plaintiffs and wife of the other plaintiff, looked at it with a view to a possible purchase. She went back on a number of occasions to examine it and "discussed" the house and its purchase price with the builder, the defendant McDermott. As a result of seeing a puddle of water in the middle of the cellar floor on one of her visits, Mrs. Pietrazak asked McDermott about water in the cellar and discussed with him whether the cellar would be dry. McDermott stated "that he built a good house and that there would be no water in the cellar." He later repeated the statement "prior to passing papers."

No purchase and sale agreement was executed. Papers were passed and title transferred by the defendants to the plaintiffs on June 23, 1955, at a price of $12,000. The latter moved in on July 1 and in the following months panelled a portion of the cellar and laid a tile floor. They built and furnished a so called "rumpus" room. In September during a heavy rainstorm water entered the cellar to such an extent that the fire department was called to pump it out. "Thereafter on many occasions of heavy rainstorms, prolonged rainy periods, or snow thaws, water entered the cellar." It came in "at various points between the foundation and the cellar floor, and, until the holes were filled with cement, at places in the foundation walls where steel tie rods were imbedded." The water caused damage to the cellar and to personal property. The cost of "corrective" work to prevent water entering the cellar will be $850. The damage to personal property and the cost of refinishing the cellar is $100.

The auditor found that "the defendants did not know that water would enter the cellar at the points described, nor that it would enter in any substantial quantities when * * * [McDermott] made the statement" that "there would be no water in the cellar." He made the statement "in good faith and had no intention of deceiving or defrauding the plaintiffs." It "was made of his own knowledge and was a false though innocent misrepresentation of a material fact, * * * the plaintiffs relied upon the truth of this statement * * * and * * * it was an essential factor in their being induced to buy this house."

In conclusion the auditor reported, "I find for the plaintiffs on count 2 of the declaration in the amount of $950. I, therefore, find for the plaintiffs and assess damages in the amount of $950." See Mahoney v. C. & R. Const. Co., 311 Mass. 558, 559, 42 N.E.2d 255. The first sentence appears to be a ruling of law that the plaintiffs could recover on count 2 for breach of warranty. As such it is not strictly a part of the report which is to be considered only on the facts found. It was the duty of the trial judge and is now our duty to enter a correct judgment on the facts reported. We are in the same position as the trial judge in respect to both fact and law. The question whether as matter of law the plaintiffs could recover for breach of warranty in relation to a transaction which did not involve the sale of tangible chattels has not been argued and need not be decided. See Prosser on Torts (2d ed.) p. 546. The findings of fact by the auditor are sufficient to warrant the entry of judgment for the plaintiffs on count 1 for deceit. He found that the statement "there would be no water in the cellar" was made by McDermott as of his own knowledge and was a false representation of a material fact. It was not a mere expression of opinion as to the dryness of the cellar. McDermott appears to have been the builder of the house and his assertion could reasonably have been understood by Mrs. Pietrazak to mean that the construction of the house was such as to preclude the entrance of water. If a statement of fact which is susceptible of actual knowledge is made as of one's own knowledge and is false, it may be the basis for an action of deceit without proof of an actual intent to deceive.

Exceptions overruled.

Notes

1. Can *Pietrazak* be reconciled with the older common law deceit cases? Has the requirement of intent to deceive been eliminated, or did the builder implicitly make a deliberately false statement? See Litchfield v. Hutchinson, 117 Mass. 195, 198 (1875) ("[t]he falsity and fraud consist in representing that he knows the facts to be true, of his own knowledge, when he has not such knowledge").

2. In Fogarty v. Van Loan, 344 Mass. 530, 183 N.E.2d 111 (1962), the buyer bought a house from the builder, who was employed as a printer. Before the sale, seller had said the cellar had "a good concrete floor, good foundation walls" and that it was a "nice well-built house." There had been no water in the cellar before the sale. A month after the sale, the buyers found water in the cellar. Seller told them "not to be concerned, any new house will have water in the cellar, [and] that it will disappear when the earth around the foundation becomes firm." When asked if he would stand behind the house if anything went wrong, he replied: "Oh yes, I will stand behind it, there is nothing wrong with the house." When the cellar continued to leak, Buyer sued Seller in deceit. The court held that Buyer had not proved a case of deceit. "The Pietrazak case goes to the verge and we are not disposed to extend it. * * * [F]alse statements of opinion, of conditions to exist in the future, or of matters promissory in nature are not actionable. * * * [W]ords of hope or expectation are converted by an interested memory into statements of quality and value when the expectation has been disappointed. The line between what is actionable and what is not in cases of this sort is often difficult to draw. * * * But the line exists, and we think that the trial judge drew it correctly. * * *"

Can you distinguish *Pietrazak* and *Fogarty?* Did the court distinguish them? What is left of the concept articulated in *Pietrazak?*

3. In both *Pietrazak* and *Fogarty* the seller-builder was speaking with first hand knowledge of the home's construction. What result would you expect if the statements about water damage were made instead by a real

estate broker employed by the owner to market the home? To what extent is such a broker chargeable with knowledge of the actual physical condition of the home? Would a consumer buyer place more (or less) reliance on the statements of such a broker than on the statements of the actual owner-builder?

In Berryman v. Riegert, 286 Minn. 270, 175 N.W.2d 438 (1970), broker had viewed the premises and knew that each lot-owner would have to rely on his own separate water and sewer systems. There was evidence that water had seeped into the basement and pooled in the yard during the preceding five years, but it was unclear whether the broker actually knew this. The broker said to the buyers: "You can see for yourself that it is a high and dry lot * * *. After the rains we have had here, if there is no water here now, there never should be any." The basement later flooded. In buyers' action against the broker for deceit, the court observed that the test was whether the broker falsely represented an "existing material fact, susceptible of knowledge, knowing it to be false or without knowing whether it was true or false, * * * under such circumstances that such person [buyer] was justified in so acting [in reliance on the statement]." The court held:

> It may be true that Miller [the broker] did not actually know that there had been a water problem in the neighborhood either from surface flow or seepage. Those facts were nevertheless susceptible of knowledge by Miller. It would seem that such information should be available to an experienced real estate broker, who should know his merchandise. * * * The parties were not on an equal footing. Defendants had superior knowledge of the problems that might be encountered in the purchase of the Riegert home. Because of plaintiffs' inexperience in this field, they had a right to rely upon the representations of defendants. * * *

We conclude that the evidence, viewed as a whole, supports the verdict for plaintiffs.

4. Is it possible to generalize from these cases involving the sale of homes to sales of other kinds of property? Should a used car dealer [and the individual salesman as well] be charged with a duty to investigate and disclose defects in the cars they sell? Cf., the Federal Trade Commission's "Used Car Rule," 16 C.F.R. Part 455. How about a department store selling appliances packaged at the factory?

5. For a comprehensive and innovative analysis of the modern approach to misrepresentation issues, see Shapo, "A Representational Theory of Consumer Protection: Doctrine, Function and Legal Liability for Product Disappointment," 60 Va.L.Rev. 1109 (1974).

LINDBERG CADILLAC CO. v. ARON

Court of Appeals, Missouri, 1963.
371 S.W.2d 651.

WOLFE, JUDGE.

This is an action in fraud in which the defendant is charged by the plaintiff with concealing defects in an automobile which he traded to plaintiff in part payment of the purchase price of a new car which the plaintiff sold to him. The trial was to the court, which found for the plaintiff in the sum of $759.00 and costs. After an unavailing motion for a new trial, the defendant appealed.

[Defendant traded in a used Cadillac to plaintiff automobile dealer, failing to mention that the car had cracks on each side of the engine block. Defendant was aware of the cracks, and had had a service station fill them with a sealer and cover them with a compound. The plaintiff dealer looked the car over and drove it a bit but did not discover the cracked block, and allowed defendant $2,290 on the trade-in. Plaintiff learned of the cracks when a subsequent buyer returned the Cadillac, complaining of an overheating problem. Plaintiff refunded the buyer's money and subsequently resold the car for half of the defendant's trade-in credit.]

The first point he raises is that the appellant failed to make a prima facie showing of fraud, and that the court should have found for the defendant. The appellant asserts in support of this that he made no misrepresentation, and that his mere silence cannot be held to have been fraudulent where the matter was open to investigation by the party alleged to have been defrauded. This constitutes a complete disregard of the facts. Silence can be an act of fraud. In one of our earliest cases, McAdams v. Cates, 24 Mo. 223, l.c. 225, our Supreme Court stated:

"If, in a contract of sale, the vendor knowingly allow the vendee to be deceived as to the thing sold in a material matter, his silence is grossly fraudulent in a moral point of view, and may be safely treated accordingly in the law tribunals of the country. Although he is not required to give the purchaser all the information he possesses himself, he can not be permitted to be silent when his silence operates virtually as a fraud. If he fails to disclose an intrinsic circumstance that is vital to the contract, knowing that the other party is acting upon the presumption that no such fact exists, it would seem to be quite as much a fraud as if he had expressly denied it, or asserted the reverse, or used any artifice to conceal it, or to call off the buyer's attention from it."

The reason for the rule is that since matters are not what they appear to be and the true state of affairs is not discoverable by ordinary diligence, deceit is accomplished by suppression of the truth.

We have in the facts before us more than a failure to speak. There is also a positive fraudulent concealment. In the case of Jones v. West Side Buick Auto Co., 231 Mo.App. 187, 93 S.W.2d 1083, decided by this court, we have before us facts quite similar in effect to those here under consideration. There a fraudulent seller turned back the speedometer in the car sold to 22,400 miles, when the car had in fact been driven 48,800 miles. There was no verbal or written representation by the seller, but the buyer, relying upon the mileage registered on the speedometer, purchased the car. We held that the buyer had been defrauded by the deception, stating: " * * * a representation is not confined to words or positive assertions; it may consist as well of deeds, acts, or artifices of a nature calculated to mislead another and thereby to allow the fraud-feasor to obtain an undue advantage over him." The acts of the defendant as stated above were designed to, and did, defraud the plaintiff, and there is no merit to the contention that a case in fraud was not made.

* * *

We find no error present, and the judgment is affirmed.

Notes

1. Would the holding in this case apply where the seller replaced a broken odometer with one showing fewer miles than the car had actually been driven, and said nothing to the prospective buyer? See Osborn v. Gene Teague Chevrolet Co., 254 Or. 486, 459 P.2d 988 (1969).

2. Continued problems with turned-back odometers produced the Federal Motor Vehicle Information and Cost Savings Act, 15 U.S.C.A. §§ 1981–1991, effective in 1973, which makes it unlawful to alter odometer readings. The Act provides a private cause of action to aggrieved buyers. See Alley v. Chrysler Credit Corp., 767 F.2d 138 (5th Cir.1985); Duval v. Midwest Auto City, Inc., 425 F.Supp. 1381 (D.Neb.1977), aff'd, 578 F.2d 721 (8th Cir. 1978). There are also criminal sanctions for violators. See United States v. Schmuck, 776 F.2d 1368 (7th Cir.1985), aff'd, ___ U.S. ___, 109 S.Ct. 1443, 103 L.Ed.2d 734 (1989), discussed infra pages 896–897.

Problem 2

Carol DePrey received a letter from the Oakwood Shores Resort which stated: "You are called upon to visit our resort, learn about the valuable opportunities available to you in purchasing a time share in our resort property, and then claim one of the Grand Prizes available for good listeners: one 1990 BMW automobile, or one certificate entitling you to $10,000 worth of gold bullion. No purchase is required; and Mrs. DePrey, you are guaranteed to be awarded a prize." Carol immediately took the week off from work, jumped into her car, drove 250 miles to Oakwood Shores, listened patiently to its salesman pitch the time share, and then asked for her prize. She was somewhat surprised when the prize proffered was a book about the 1984 Olympics. She refused to accept that book, and asked for "her BMW." Oakwood responded that she did not win a Grand Prize, which was available only to time share purchasers. Instead, as a non-purchaser, she had won only "a prize"—the book.

Carol consults you. Has she a cause of action against Oakwood? What representations were made by Oakwood? Which ones were false? Did Carol justifiably rely on them?

Is it proper to look at the letter as a whole, and ask the court to look at the total effect of all the language rather than specific words or phrases? Do the cases permit this latter approach?

How has Carol been hurt? How would her damages be measured? Would you take this case on a contingent fee basis?

Problem 3

Buck N. Ham bought an unmounted diamond from Fleur D. Lee for $1,000 cash, to be made into an engagement ring. The diamond was to be sent away to be mounted, and then returned to Fleur; Buck was to pick it up from Fleur. Under the contract, Buck was to insure the diamond from the date of sale.

Fleur had two shops, one on Tower Road and one on Paris Avenue. Buck asked where the diamond was, because he needed to tell his insurer; and Fleur mistakenly replied that it was at the Tower Road shop, when it was really at Paris Avenue. Buck called his insurance agent Rich E. Loo, had a rider put on his insurance policy to cover the diamond at the Tower Road location, and left town for a one-week trip. During that week, the diamond was stolen. The insurer refuses to pay because Tower Road is a safer location than Paris Avenue. Has Buck a successful cause of action against Fleur for the misrepresentation? Cf., International Products Co. v. Erie R. Co., 244 N.Y. 331, 155 N.E. 662 (1927). Did Fleur "intend to deceive" Buck? Or was this a negligent mistake? Under what circumstances should liability attach for mistakes?

Notes

1. In real estate transactions, the traditional doctrine is that, upon closing, the buyer's acceptance of deed "merges" all the obligations under the sales contract into the deed. Consequently, a real estate buyer could not thereafter claim a contractual breach of promise or warranty by seller. This is why so many deceit cases involve land sales, and courts have been imaginative in interpreting the common law requirements of the tort of deceit. The merger doctrine is now under attack in many states, especially in the warranty context. See pp. 406–409, infra.

3. WHERE ARE WE GOING?—THE DEVELOPING DOCTRINES OF DECEIT

JOHNSON v. DAVIS
Supreme Court of Florida, 1985.
480 So.2d 625.

ADKINS, JUSTICE.

* * *

In May of 1982, the Davises entered into a contract to buy for $310,000 the Johnsons' home, which at the time was three years old. The contract required a $5,000 deposit payment, an additional $26,000 deposit payment within five days and a closing by June 21, 1982. The crucial provision of the contract, for the purposes of the case at bar, is Paragraph F which provided:

F. *Roof Inspection:* Prior to closing at Buyer's expense, Buyer shall have the right to obtain a written report from a licensed roofer stating that the roof is in a watertight condition. In the event repairs are required either to correct leaks or to replace damage to facia or soffit, seller shall pay for said repairs which shall be performed by a licensed roofing contractor.

The contract further provided for payment to the "prevailing party" of all costs and reasonable fees in any contract litigation.

Before the Davises made the additional $26,000 deposit payment, Mrs. Davis noticed some buckling and peeling plaster around the corner of a window frame in the family room and stains on the ceilings in the family room and kitchen of the home. Upon inquiring, Mrs. Davis was told by Mr. Johnson that the window had had a minor problem that had long since been corrected and that the stains were wallpaper glue and the result of ceiling beams being moved. There is disagreement among the parties as to whether Mr. Johnson also told Mrs. Davis at this time that there had never been any problems with the roof or ceilings. The Davises thereafter paid the remainder of their deposit and the Johnsons vacated the home. Several days later, following a heavy rain, Mrs. Davis entered the home and discovered water "gushing" in from around the window frame, the ceiling of the family room, the light fixtures, the glass doors, and the stove in the kitchen.

Two roofers hired by the Johnsons' broker concluded that for under $1,000 they could "fix" certain leaks in the roof and by doing so make the roof "watertight." Three roofers hired by the Davises found that the roof was inherently defective, that any repairs would be temporary because the roof was "slipping," and that only a new $15,000 roof could be "watertight."

The Davises filed a complaint alleging breach of contract, fraud and misrepresentation, and sought recission of the contract and return of their deposit. The Johnsons counterclaimed seeking the deposit as liquidated damages.

* * *

We find that the Johnsons' statements to the Davises regarding the condition of the roof constituted a fraudulent misrepresentation entitling respondents to the return of their $26,000 deposit payment. In the state of Florida, relief for a fraudulent misrepresentation may be granted only when the following elements are present: (1) a false statement concerning a material fact; (2) the representor's knowledge that the representation is false; (3) an intention that the representation induce another to act on it; and, (4) consequent injury by the party acting in reliance on the representation.

The evidence adduced at trial shows that after the buyer and the seller signed the purchase and sales agreement and after receiving the $5,000 initial deposit payment the Johnsons affirmatively repeated to the Davises that there were no problems with the roof. The Johnsons subsequently received the additional $26,000 deposit payment from the Davises. The record reflects that the statement made by the Johnsons was a false representation of material fact, made with knowledge of its falsity, upon which the Davises relied to their detriment as evidenced by the $26,000 paid to the Johnsons.

The doctrine of caveat emptor does not exempt a seller from responsibility for the statements and representations which he makes to induce the buyer to act, when under the circumstances these amount to fraud in the legal sense. To be grounds for relief, the false representations need not have been made at the time of the signing of the purchase and sales agreement in order for the element of reliance to be present. The fact that the false statements as to the quality of the roof were made after the signing of the purchase and sales agreement does not excuse the seller from liability when the misrepresentations were made prior to the execution of the contract by conveyance of the property. It would be contrary to all notions of fairness and justice for this Court to place its stamp of approval on an affirmative misrepresentation by a wrongdoer just because it was made after the signing of the executory contract when all of the necessary elements for actionable fraud are present. Furthermore, the Davises' reliance on the truth of the Johnsons' representation was justified and is supported by this Court's decision in *Besett v. Basnett,* where we held "that a recipient may rely on the truth of a representation, even though its falsity could have been ascertained had he made an investigation, unless he knows the representation to be false or its falsity is obvious to him."

In determining whether a seller of a home has a duty to disclose latent material defects to a buyer, the established tort law distinction between misfeasance and nonfeasance, action and inaction must carefully be analyzed. The highly individualistic philosophy of the earlier common law consistently imposed liability upon the commission of affirmative acts of harm, but shrank from converting the courts into an institution for forcing men to help one another. This distinction is deeply rooted in our case law. Liability for nonfeasance has therefore been slow to receive recognition in the evolution of tort law.

In theory, the difference between misfeasance and nonfeasance, action and inaction is quite simple and obvious; however, in practice it is not always easy to draw the line and determine whether conduct is active or passive. That is, where failure to disclose a material fact is calculated to induce a false belief, the distinction between concealment and affirmative representations is tenuous. Both proceed from the same motives and are attended with the same consequences; both are violative of the principles of fair dealing and good faith; both are calculated to produce the same result; and, in fact, both essentially have the same effect.

Still there exists in much of our case law the old tort notion that there can be no liability for nonfeasance. The courts in some jurisdictions, including Florida, hold that where the parties are dealing at arms's length and the facts lie equally open to both parties, with equal opportunity of examination, mere nondisclosure does not constitute a fraudulent concealment. The Fourth District affirmed that rule of law in *Banks v. Salina,* and found that although the sellers had sold a home without disclosing the presence of a defective roof and swimming pool of which the sellers had knowledge, "[i]n Florida, there is no duty to disclose when parties are dealing at arms length."

These unappetizing cases are not in tune with the times and do not conform with current notions of justice, equity and fair dealing. One should not be able to stand behind the impervious shield of caveat emptor and take advantage of another's ignorance. Our courts have taken great strides since the days when the judicial emphasis was on rigid rules and ancient precedents. Modern concepts of justice and fair dealing have given our courts the opportunity and latitude to change legal precepts in order to conform to society's needs. Thus, the tendency of the more recent cases has been to restrict rather than extend the doctrine of caveat emptor. The law appears to be working toward the ultimate conclusion that full disclosure of all material facts must be made whenever elementary fair conduct demands it.

* * *

We are of the opinion that the same philosophy regarding the sale of homes should also be the law in the state of Florida. Accordingly, we hold that where the seller of a home knows of facts materially affecting the value of the property which are not readily observable and are not known to the buyer, the seller is under a duty to disclose them to the buyer. This duty is equally applicable to all forms of real property, new and used.

In the case at bar, the evidence shows that the Johnsons knew of and failed to disclose that there had been problems with the roof of the house. Mr. Johnson admitted during his testimony that the Johnsons were aware of roof problems prior to entering into the contract of sale and receiving the $5,000 deposit payment. Thus, we agree with the district court and find that the Johnsons' fraudulent concealment also entitles the Davises to the return of the $5,000 deposit payment plus interest. We further find that the Davises should be awarded costs and fees.

BOYD, CHIEF JUSTICE, dissenting.

I respectfully but strongly dissent to the Court's expansion of the duties of sellers of real property. This ruling will give rise to a flood of litigation and will facilitate unjust outcomes in many cases. If, as a matter of public policy, the well settled law of this state on this question should be changed, the change should come from the legislature. Moreover, I do not find sufficient evidence in the record to justify rescission or a finding of fraud even under present law. I would quash the decision of the district court of appeal.

* * *

I do not agree with the Court's belief that the distinction between nondisclosure and affirmative statement is weak or nonexistent. It is a distinction that we should take special care to emphasize and preserve. Imposition of liability for seller's nondisclosure of the condition of improvements to real property is the first step toward making the seller a guarantor of the good condition of the property. Ultimately this trend will significantly burden the alienability of property because sellers will have to worry about the possibility of catastrophic post-sale judgments for damages sought to pay for repairs. The trend will proceed somewhat as follows. At first, the cause of action will require proof of actual knowledge of the undisclosed defect on the part of the seller. But in many cases the courts will allow it to be shown by circumstantial evidence. Then a rule of constructive knowledge will develop based on the reasoning that if the seller did not know of the defect, he should have known about it before attempting to sell the property. Thus the burden of inspection will shift from the buyer to the seller. Ultimately the courts will be in the position of imposing implied warranties and guaranties on all sellers of real property.

* * *

LAYMAN v. BINNS

Supreme Court of Ohio, 1988.
35 Ohio St.3d 176, 519 N.E.2d 642.

The dispute between the parties arises from the sale of a home in January 1978 by the vendors-appellants (Mr. and Mrs. Bradley O. Binns) to the purchasers-appellees (Mr. and Mrs. F. Garry Layman). Purchasers claim that vendors fraudulently concealed a structural defect in the house.

In 1970 or 1971, vendors hired a builder to construct the home. When it was nearly completed, backfilling around the cinder block foundation caused the foundation to give way resulting in a bow in the south basement wall. Steel I-beams were installed to support the bowed wall.

In 1977, vendors listed the home for sale and told their realtor about the basement wall problem and the corrective measures which were taken. The realtor told his sales staff about the defective wall but such information was omitted from the property listings.

The Laymans, with their agent, viewed the Binnses' house in December 1977. Mr. Binns did not accompany purchasers to the basement and he did not mention the bowed wall to the Laymans or their agent. Mr. Layman saw the I-beams but did not question their purpose because he thought they were part of the structure. Mr. Layman did inquire about utility bills and moisture at the east end of the basement. Mr. Binns explained that moisture usually entered the basement during excessive rain in the spring.

The purchase contract, signed by the parties, specified that it was the entire agreement between the parties, that no representations had been made other than those in the contract, and that the purchasers were relying upon their own inspection as to the condition and character of the dwelling. Purchasers paid $75,000 in cash to vendors, and moved into the house in February 1978.

In 1981, a foreclosure action was filed against the purchasers. Later, it was voluntarily dismissed. The purchasers then made an unsuccessful effort to sell the property at private sale. During that time, the defective basement wall was called to their attention by a realtor. Faced with estimates ranging from $32,000 to $49,612 to remedy the defect, they elected to lower their asking price from $125,000 to $75,000. The house still did not sell.

* * *

The trial court (following a bench trial) determined that the structural defect in the wall was known to vendors and "was not apparent upon inspection to inexperienced persons" such as the purchasers. The court found that the vendors had an affirmative duty to call the defect to the purchasers' attention and held that such failure amounted to fraud. The court awarded $40,000 in damages, but declined to assess punitive damages since there was no active concealment of the defect. The court of appeals affirmed.

The cause is before this court pursuant to the allowance of a motion to certify the record.

HERBERT R. BROWN, JUSTICE.

The determinative issue raised on appeal is whether recovery is barred by application of the doctrine of *caveat emptor* (let the buyer beware). We find that it is for the reasons set forth below.

The doctrine of *caveat emptor,* although virtually abolished in the area of personal property, remains a viable rule of law in real estate sales.

* * *

The doctrine of *caveat emptor* is one of long standing. Since problems of varying degree are to be found in most dwellings and buildings, the doctrine performs a function in the real estate marketplace. Without the doctrine nearly every sale would invite litigation instituted by a disappointed buyer. Accordingly, we are not disposed to abolish the doctrine of *caveat emptor.* A seller of realty is not obligated to reveal all that he or she knows. A duty falls upon the purchaser to make inquiry and examination.

To make the doctrine operate fairly, courts have established certain conditions upon the rule's application. We summarize and adopt these conditions as follows: (1) the defect must be open to observation or discoverable on reasonable inspection, (2) the purchaser must have an unimpeded opportunity to examine the property and (3) the vendor may not engage in fraud. We measure the case before us against these requirements.

I

The defect here was open to observation. Mr. Layman (one of the purchasers) saw the steel bracing that supported the defective wall. The Laymans contend that Mr. Layman was not an expert and should not be held to have knowledge of the defect simply because he saw a symptom of it. If the issue were the cause of the defect or the remedial effectiveness of the beams, we might agree. However, the test is whether the defect was open to observation. Here, witnesses who viewed the basement detected the bow and steel beams with little effort. The defect was described as obvious and highly visible. The basement wall was bulging.

II

The purchasers had an unhindered opportunity to examine the basement. Mr. Layman saw the steel beams, yet failed to inspect the wall in detail or to ask about the purpose of the beams. The purchasers had a duty to inspect and inquire about the premises in a prudent, diligent manner.

III

This brings us to the final, and pivotal, question. On the facts in this case, did the vendors engage in fraud?

The purchasers admit that no active misrepresentation or misstatement of material fact was made. However, they argue that failure to disclose the bow in the wall constituted fraudulent concealment.

An action for fraud may be grounded upon failure to fully disclose facts of a material nature where there exists a duty to speak. This court has held that a vendor has a duty to disclose material facts which are latent, not readily observable or discoverable through a purchaser's reasonable inspection.

The non-disclosure in this case does not rise to the level of fraud for the reason that the defect here was not latent. It could have been detected by inspection. Thus, the purchasers must show an affirmative misrepresentation or a misstatement of a material fact in order to demonstrate fraud and thereby preclude application of the doctrine of *caveat emptor*. This, they failed to do.

IV

We hold that the doctrine of *caveat emptor* precludes recovery in an action by the purchaser for a structural defect in real estate where (1) the condition complained of is open to observation or discoverable upon reasonable inspection, (2) the purchaser had the full and unimpeded opportunity to examine the premises, and (3) there is no evidence of fraud on the part of the vendor. The judgment of the court of appeals is reversed and final judgment is hereby entered in favor of appellants.

Judgment reversed.

LOCHER, JUSTICE, concurring in part and dissenting in part.

Although I have no quarrel with the law expressed in the syllabus, I cannot concur in its application by the majority to the facts of this case.

In my view, the trial court properly found that the structural defect in the basement wall was not readily apparent upon reasonable inspection by persons inexperienced in such matters, like the Laymans.

* * *

Furthermore, the majority's analysis applies an unreasonably high standard for the purpose of determining whether the Laymans should have observed or discovered the defective wall. In concluding that the defect was open to observation, the majority states that "witnesses who viewed the basement detected the bow and steel beams with little effort." These witnesses were persons with experience in the construction, appraisal and sales of homes. However, the standard by which purchasers of real property should be measured in order to determine whether they should have observed or discovered a structural defect is that of "ordinarily prudent persons of their station and experience confronted with the same or similar circumstances." *Traverse v. Long* (1956), 165 Ohio St. 249, 252, 59 O.O. 325, 326, 135 N.E.2d 256, 259. Because the Laymans have little or no experience in the construction or buying of homes, it is simply unreasonable to compare them to persons with specialized knowledge in the fields of construction and real estate, as opposed to ordinarily prudent persons of like experience. Accordingly, I would affirm the trial court's judgment that persons of the Laymans' experience would not have discovered the defect upon reasonable inspection.

For these reasons, I respectfully dissent.

Notes

1. After *Johnson*, is there any longer a meaningful distinction between misfeasance (deceit by affirmative misrepresentation) and nonfeasance (deceit by silence)? Should there be? Is the dissenting Justice right that this trend will ultimately lead to imposing implied warranties of quality on all sellers of real estate? If it did, would that be a good rule? Would it be in line with current consumer expectations and societal values? Note that the majority stated that its ruling applied to *all* forms of real property, both new and used. This means that the duty to disclose applies to Mr. & Mrs. Average Homeowner as well as to developers. Is this a good rule? Note also that this rule goes considerably beyond the UCC for personal property, where only professional sellers are held to the implied warranty of merchantability. See UCC § 2–314. Has the court in Johnson created an implied warranty of merchantability in real estate sales? The dissenting Justice seems to think so, doesn't he? See infra pages 406–409, for a discussion of the implied warranty of habitability as applied to the sale of residential real estate.

2. Could the sellers in *Johnson* have made a "merger" argument? If they had, do you think it would have worked?

3. The history of consumer law, especially in seller-buyer transactions, has in general seen the slow demise of the doctrine of caveat emptor. Presumably, *Johnson* is some proof that this trend continues. Lest you think that the view is unanimous, however, compare the *Layman* case. Which case do you think represents the future of the law of deceit and misrepresentation, *Johnson* or *Layman*? Why?

4. WHERE ARE WE GOING?—A DIFFERENT CAUSE OF ACTION?

WARD DEVELOPMENT CO. v. INGRAO

Court of Appeals, Maryland, 1985.
63 Md.App. 645, 493 A.2d 421.

GETTY, JUDGE.

This action arose when thirteen plaintiffs, all homeowners in the Foxhall North Subdivision in Montgomery County, sued three defendants—Ward Development Co., Inc., the developer of the subdivision; Long and Foster Real Estate, Inc., Ward's real estate broker; and William Conrad Behrens, a selling agent with Long & Foster—for fraudulent and negligent misrepresentation. ⁕ ⁕ ⁕ After a three week trial in the Circuit Court for Montgomery County, a jury returned a verdict for the homeowners on the negligent misrepresentation count and assessed damages against the defendants totaling $55,048.00. Appellant Ward now appeals from the judgments entered on the jury verdicts. ⁕ ⁕ ⁕

NEGLIGENT MISREPRESENTATION

The Foxhall North Subdivision is a residential real estate development constructed by Ward Development Co., Inc. On March 2, 1978, Ward employed Long & Foster Real Estate, Inc., to sell thirty-eight homes located in the subdivision. On April 3, 1978, Long & Foster employed William Conrad Behrens to be the selling agent for the homes. The homes involved in the present suit were sold by Behrens for Long & Foster and Ward between May 27, 1978 and March 6, 1979. As the issue presented here is in the context of a motion for directed verdict (former Rule 552), the evidentiary background will be stated in a light most favorable to the homeowners.

During the bargaining period for the purchase of the homes Behrens told the homeowners that the neighborhood would consist of only 38 or 39 homes and that the road going through the subdivision, Rippling Brook Drive, would dead-end and terminate permanently at the edge of the subdivision. Shortly after the homeowners purchased their homes, however, Rippling Brook Drive was extended and construction was begun on additional homes in the area. In addition, the homeowners' contracts of sale contained the following clause:

"The estimated cost of deferred water and/or sewer connection charge for which the purchaser is liable is $_____ payable over a period of 35 years."

Each homeowner's contract was filled in with an estimated cost of the sewer and water connection charge; the amounts varied between $250 and $900, "payable over a period of 35 years." When the homeowners received their Montgomery County tax bills for 1979, however, they discovered that their annual sewer and water connection charges were much greater than their contracts had indicated. For example, the contract of one homeowner, Arnold Kaplan, contains an estimate that his deferred water and sewer connection charge would be "$400.00 payable over a period of 35 years" (roughly, an $11.42 annual charge). Kaplan's actual deferred water and sewer connection charge for 1979 was $71.59. The other homeowners testified to similar discrepancies between the sewer and water connection charge as stated in their contracts and the charge which was actually assessed.

In order to explain the reason for the discrepancies, some background information on water and sewer benefit charges in Montgomery County is necessary. Each property owner in Montgomery County is subject to two water and sewer benefit charges. The first charge is termed a "front foot benefit assessment" and is levied to repay bonds sold by the Washington Suburban Sanitary Commission to finance the costs of main water and sewer lines constructed during a given year. The second charge, termed a "house connection charge," is levied to recover the construction costs for connecting water and sewer lines to individual homes. The front foot benefit assessment is an annual charge for 33 years but may also be paid off at any time in one lump sum. The house connection charge is in the nature of a lump sum, but may be deferred and paid off in installments over a 33–year period.

In the instant case the amount Behrens stated in each property owner's contract to be the "sewer and/or water connection charge * * * payable over 35 years" was actually Ward's estimate of a combined total of the property owner's house connection charge plus his front foot benefit assessment for one year (1979).

At the conclusion of the trial, the jury returned verdicts in favor of the homeowners as follows:

(a) No finding of fraud as to any defendant;

(b) $6,006 against all defendants (jointly and severally) for damages incurred as a result of negligent misrepresentation as to the extension of Rippling Brook Drive;

(c) $13,494 against all defendants (jointly and severally) incurred as a result of negligent misrepresentation as to the sewer and water annual assessments;

(d) $41,554 against defendant Ward solely, incurred as a result of negligent misrepresentation as to the sewer and water annual assessments.

Ward now asserts that the trial court erred in denying Ward's motion for directed verdict as to the homeowners' claim for negligent misrepresentation of their sewer and water connection charges.[1] Ward argues that the homeowners' evidence of a negligent misrepresentation was legally deficient in two respects, to-wit:

A. The homeowners failed to show a misrepresentation of a material fact.

B. The homeowners failed to show a misrepresentation as to a past or existing fact.

For the following reasons, we find that the trial court did not err in denying Ward's motion for a directed verdict.

The tort of negligent misrepresentation is one of recent origin in Maryland. The Court of Appeals initially recognized the cause of action in 1938 * * *.

* * * In *Martens Chevrolet v. Seney,* 292 Md. 328, 439 A.2d 534 (1982), the Court * * * outlined the principal elements of negligent misrepresentation as follows:

(1) the defendant, owing a duty of care to the plaintiff, negligently asserts a false statement;

(2) the defendant intends that his statement will be acted upon by the plaintiff;

(3) the defendant has knowledge that the plaintiff will probably rely on the statement, which, if erroneous, will cause loss or injury;

(4) the plaintiff, justifiably, takes action in reliance on the statement; and

(5) the plaintiff suffers damage proximately caused by the defendant's negligence.

The *Martens* Court went on to hold that the buyer of an automobile dealership could bring an action for negligent misrepresentation against the seller for allegedly misinforming the buyer regarding the dealership's financial status.

Turning now to the present case, Ward argues that the trial court erred in denying Ward's motion for a directed verdict because the homeowners failed to prove that the misrepresentation regarding the sewer and water connection charge was a material one. We note first that nowhere in the *Martens* opinion does the Court of Appeals specify that the misrepresentation of a "material fact" is an element of the tort of negligent misrepresentation. An element which is specified, however, is that the plaintiff must justifiably take action in reliance on the misrepresentation. The requirement of justifiable reliance is, by implication, inextricably bound up with the requirement of materiality. An immaterial representation could not, by definition, influence the reasonable man. We conclude, therefore, that for a plaintiff justifiably to take action in reliance on a statement, that statement must be a representation of a material fact.

In defining what is meant by a material fact, Ward quotes the following language from *Babb v. Bolyard,* "[t]he fraud must be material, by which is meant, without it, that the transaction would not have been made." We find a better definition of what constitutes a material fact in Restatement (Second) of Torts, § 538 (1977):

"The matter is material if (a) a reasonable man would attach importance to its existence or non-existence in determining his choice of action in the transaction in question; or (b) the maker of the representation knows or has reason to know that its recipient regards or is likely to regard the matter as important in determining his choice of action, although a reasonable man would not so regard it."

In the instant case, at least one of the homeowners testified that had she known that the actual sewer and water connection charge was as great as it was, she would have contemplated the contract further or at least have done additional comparative shopping. This testimony and the evidence as a whole compels us to conclude that the question of whether the misrepresentation regarding the sewer and water connection charge was one of a material fact was one properly submitted to the jury.

Ward next asserts that the homeowners failed to show that the misrepresentation of the sewer and water connection charge was a representation of a past or existing fact. Ward argues that the statement regarding the charge was merely an estimate and cannot therefore be the basis for a suit for negligent misrepresentation. We disagree. The Court of Appeals has stated that an action for fraudulent misrepresentation will not lie for the unfulfillment of promises or the failure of future events to materialize as predicated.

We recognize the difference between a promise of future events and an estimate by one knowledgeable in a particular field. In the latter situation, redress may be had for representations as to future facts and not merely as to past or existing facts. As stated by the commentators Fleming and Gray, "[i]t is not surprising * * * that courts have been increasingly willing to hold predictive statements material where the circumstances indicate to the addressee that the speaker has a factual basis for his predictions so that the existence of facts is implied by the representations." In the instant case, the homeowners relied on Ward and its agents as knowledgeable in the field of real estate. Ward, as the developer of the subdivision, and Behrens, as the real estate selling agent, held themselves out as knowledgeable in matters such as the charge for a sewer and water connection. The homeowners were entitled to rely on that estimate to a reasonable extent. But the charge stated in the contract was so far removed from the actual charge it cannot properly be termed a reasonable estimate and can only be explained as a misrepresentation. Therefore, we hold that the estimate of the sewer and water connection charge was actionable under a theory of negligent misrepresentation.

* * *

JUDGMENT AFFIRMED AS TO LIABILITY FOR MISREPRESENTATION AS TO WATER AND SEWER CONNECTION CHARGES. REMANDED FOR NEW TRIAL ON THE ISSUE OF DAMAGES RESULTING THEREFROM.

Problem 4

Bill Bones bought a used car from dealer Sam Silver for $3000 cash. Sam made no written or oral representations about the car, and in the contract of sale Sam effectively disclaimed all warranties. One week later Bones discovered that the car had cracks on each side of the engine block, rendering the engine unusable. Silver did not know of the cracked block, as he does not regularly do any mechanical work on the used cars he sells.

Calvin Consumer had sold the car to Sam for $2000 cash some weeks earlier. During the preceding winter the car's engine coolant had frozen, causing the block to crack, and before selling the car to Sam Calvin had filled the cracks with a "sealer" and covered the filled cracks with a compound which hid them. Calvin had said nothing to Sam.

Does Bill have an action against Sam for deceit? For negligent misrepresentation? Does Sam have an action against Calvin for deceit? Cf., Lindberg Cadillac v. Aron, supra. The "representations" (silence about the condition of the engine) are the same in each case. Is the difference in Sam's and Calvin's knowledge critical to the actionability of their conduct?

Should Sam's ability to recover against Calvin depend upon whether Bones recovered against Silver? Should Bones' ability to recover against Sam depend on whether Sam can in turn recover from Calvin? Does Bill Bones have a cause of action directly against Calvin? Cf., Hanberry v. Hearst Corp., 276 Cal.App.2d 680, 81 Cal.Rptr. 519 (1969).

Notes

1. In Easton v. Strassburger, 152 Cal.App.3d 90, 199 Cal.Rptr. 383 (1984), the court used a negligence theory to impose on the real estate broker "a duty to conduct a reasonably competent and diligent inspection of property he has listed for sale in order to discover defects for the benefit of the buyer."

In the *Easton* case, the real estate agent overlooked certain "red flags" that should have alerted him to the fact that the house suffered from soil erosion problems. Despite this, the agent did not request any testing and did not inform the buyer that there were potential soil problems. There had been some mudslides during the tenure of the sellers, necessitating corrective action, but the sellers did not tell the real estate agent about these events.

The buyer sued when a mudslide occurred shortly after the purchase and reduced the value of the house from $170,000 to $20,000.

The appellate court upheld the judgment against the listing agent. Emphasizing that this was a case of "simple negligence," the court noted that to establish liability:

> * * * respondent was not required to show that appellant had actual knowledge of the soils problems (as would have been required to prove intentional misrepresentation or fraudulent concealment) or that a misrepresentation had been made as to the soils condition of the property (as is required to establish negligent misrepresentation). We are concerned here only with the elements of a simple negligence action; that is, whether appellant owed a legal duty to respondent to

use due care, whether this legal duty was breached, and finally whether the breach was a proximate cause of appellant's injury.

The *Easton* court rejected an argument that the duty to disclose defects should be limited to those actually known by the agent:

> * * * If a broker were required to disclose only known defects, but not also those that are reasonably discoverable, he would be shielded by his ignorance of that which he holds himself out to know. * * * Such a construction would not only reward the unskilled broker for his own incompetence, but might provide the unscrupulous broker the unilateral ability to protect himself at the expense of the inexperienced and unwary who rely upon him.

What if the defect was obvious to the buyer? Would that eliminate the real estate agent's duty to inspect and disclose?

2. The *Easton* decision has been followed in Gouveia v. Citicorp Person-to-Person Financial Center, 101 N.M. 572, 686 P.2d 262 (1984); and cited with approval in some other states. See, e.g., Secor v. Knight, 716 P.2d 790, 795 n. 1 (Utah 1986). A Fourth Circuit case applying Maryland law declined to adopt the Easton approach, however, noting it would be a "sweeping change" in Maryland law, and that:

> Moreover, we hesitate to impose a duty on realtors to investigate property and report defects to prospective buyers because such an obligation could conflict with the fiduciary duties that realtors normally owe to property sellers under Maryland law.

Herbert v. Saffell, 877 F.2d 267, 274–275 (4th Cir.1989).

3. After the *Easton* decision the California Legislature enacted Cal. Civil Code §§ 2079–79.5, which places duties on real estate brokers, and § 2373, which places duties on real estate sellers. The former was interpreted in Smith v. Rickard, 205 Cal.App.3d 1354, 254 Cal.Rptr. 633 (1988) as "no more than a codification of that case (*Easton*)."

4. Eighteen jurisdictions have adopted the rule articulated in the Restatement (Second) of Torts, § 552C:

> (1) One who, in a sale, rental or exchange transaction with another, makes a misrepresentation of a material fact for the purpose of inducing the other to act or to refrain from acting in reliance upon it, is subject to liability to the other for pecuniary loss caused to him by his justifiable reliance upon the misrepresentation, even though it is not made fraudulently or negligently.

> (2) Damages recoverable under the rule stated in this section are limited to the difference between the value of what the other has parted with and the value of what he has received in the transaction.

What does this formulation do to the common law of deceit? What is the likely rationale for this approach to misrepresentation?

Problem 5

Harry and Harriet Hopeful were anxiously seeking a moderately-priced mobile home in which to spend their retirement years just outside of Buffalo, New York. They visited the sales lot of Comfy Mobile Homes, Inc., and were attracted to a used Victoria two-bedroom model. Concerned about the severe winters in the area, the Hopefuls asked the salesman whether the unit was well-built and heated. The salesman innocently responded that this was a "good solid home, as good as any others on the lot," that it "had a good electric heater," and that they "sold many similar units without complaints" about their heatability. The sales manager of Comfy, who was standing nearby, overheard the discussion but said nothing, even though she was aware that this particular mobile home had been kept in Florida by its prior owners, and was uninsulated. In fact, the lack of insulation explained the very low price being asked for it.

The Hopefuls examined the unit to their heart's content, and agreed to buy it. The contract of sale, which they browsed through while the salesman was doing other paperwork, contained the following clause in 10–point boldface type:

> The purchaser has examined the mobile home agreed to be sold and is familiar with the physical condition thereof. The seller has not made and does not make any representations of any kind as to the physical condition, suitability, or operating costs of said unit, and purchaser acknowledges that no such representations have been made.

> It is understood and agreed that all prior understandings and agreements between the parties are merged in this contract, and that neither party is relying upon any statement or representation not embodied in this contract.

Please assume that the contract also contained an effective disclaimer of all warranties, so that the Hopefuls cannot recover on any cause of action based on a warranty claim.

The following December they became frigidly aware of the lack of insulation, and aware also that they were running up astronomical heating bills trying to keep the place even tolerably warm.

Evaluate Harry and Harriet's chances of recovering from Comfy on a deceit or a negligence cause of action. Compare City Dodge, Inc. v. Gardner, 232 Ga. 766, 208 S.E.2d 794 (1974) and Bill Spreen Toyota, Inc. v. Jenquin, 163 Ga.App. 855, 294 S.E.2d 533 (1982), with Danann Realty Corp. v. Harris, 5 N.Y.2d 317, 184 N.Y.S.2d 599, 157 N.E.2d 597 (1959).

Note on Warranties

Apart from the tort law of deceit or negligence, buyers may be able to recover from sellers on the basis of "warranties" as to the quality of the goods. Historically, the seller's liability for "express" warranties originated as a part of the common law action of assumpsit—i.e., the seller bore responsibility for the represented quality of the goods as a part of his contractual undertaking. For many and varied reasons of policy, later courts and legislatures also found warranty obligations "implied" in the contract. The Uniform Commercial Code states these warranty concepts in sections 2–313, 2–314, and 2–315. See also J. White & R. Summers, Uniform Commercial Code, chs. 9–12 (3d Ed., 1988).

For our purposes, the important points to grasp are the reasons for and consequences of characterizing one form of seller misrepresentation as the *tort* of deceit, and another form of misstatement as a *contractual* breach of warranty. The former rests on the breach of a duty to speak truthfully to those who justifiably rely on the statements, while the latter derives from the notion of a freely assumed (dickered) contractual undertaking. As the contracting process in consumer sales became more formalized, through standardized contract forms and "take it or leave it" attitudes by sellers, open negotiations between sellers and buyers over the quality of goods disappeared. Where contracts shifted the risk of serious injury to consumer buyers, courts responded by imposing quality responsibilities on sellers regardless of their contracts, through the doctrine of strict liability in tort. And in much the same way, the traditional doctrine of deceit has always served as a check on the seller's ability to avoid responsibility for express representations by clever contract gimmicks (such as a "merger" clause triggering the parol evidence rule).

We look more closely at limitations on the seller's freedom to avoid warranty liability in Chapter 6, infra. For now students should note that warranty and deceit may sometimes be parallel routes to seller liability, but that each theory has its unique ingredients and limitations. In many cases one theory or the other may be invocable, but not both; at times they may overlap.

SECTION B. THE STATUTORY APPROACH—FEDERAL AND STATE

1. FEDERAL REGULATION—THE FTC ACT

The prior section dealt with the common law standards of informational accuracy available to private parties in private disputes. But the community's distaste for deception is often reflected in broad statutory mandates to public agencies to prohibit marketplace misrepresentation. For example, the Securities & Exchange Commission performs this function for the protection of securities investors.

The dominant agency in the consumer area is the Federal Trade Commission. Section 5(a)(1) of the Federal Trade Commission Act, 15 U.S.C.A. § 45, declares in majestic simplicity:

Unfair methods of competition in or affecting commerce, and unfair or deceptive acts or practices in or affecting commerce, are hereby declared unlawful.

One particular "unfair or deceptive act or practice" is defined in FTC Act § 12, 15 U.S.C.A. § 52, as the dissemination of "any false advertisement" likely to induce the purchase of food, drugs, devices, or cosmetics. The Act expressly defines "false advertising" in section 15(a)(1) as an advertisement which is "misleading in a material respect." The remainder of the Act is concerned with procedures for implementing these broad prohibitions. The remedies available to the FTC are discussed infra Chapter 17, Section C.

Not surprisingly, a distinct body of jurisprudence has grown up around the Commission's mandate, much of it dealing with the standards for accuracy of advertising and promotional material. In reading what follows, compare the substantive rules developed by the Commission and the courts to those applied in common law actions in the preceding section.

The following excerpt, from the court's opinion in Federal Trade Com'n v. Sterling Drug, Inc., 317 F.2d 669 (2d Cir.1963), summarizes the legal principles traditionally applied by the Commission in advertising cases:

> The legal principles to be applied here are quite clear. The central purpose of the provisions of the Federal Trade Commission Act under discussion is in effect to abolish the rule of *caveat emptor* which traditionally defined rights and responsibilities in the world of commerce. That rule can no longer be relied upon as a means of rewarding fraud and deception, and has been replaced by a rule which gives to the consumer the right to rely upon representations of facts as the truth. In order best to implement the prophylactic purpose of the statute, it has been consistently held that advertising falls within its proscription not only when there is proof of actual deception but also when the representations made have a capacity or tendency to deceive, i.e., when there is a likelihood or fair probability that the reader will be misled. For the same reason, proof of intention to deceive is not requisite to a finding of violation of the statute; since the purpose of the statute is not to punish the wrongdoer but to protect the public, the cardinal factor is the probable effect which the advertiser's handiwork will have upon the eye and mind of the reader. It is therefore necessary in these cases to consider the advertisement in its entirety and not to engage in disputatious dissection. The entire mosaic should be viewed rather than each tile separately. * * *

> Unlike that abiding faith which the law has in the "reasonable man," it has very little faith indeed in the intellectual acuity of the "ordinary purchaser" who is the object of the advertising campaign.

>> "The general public has been defined as 'that vast multitude which includes the ignorant, and unthinking and the credulous, who, in making purchases, do not stop to analyze but too often are governed by appearances and general impressions.' The average purchaser has been variously characterized as not 'straight thinking,' subject to 'impressions,' uneducated, and grossly misinformed; he is influenced by prejudice and superstition; and he wishfully believes in miracles, allegedly the result of progress in science * * *. The language of the ordinary purchaser is casual and unaffected. He is not an 'expert in grammatical construction' or an 'educated analytical reader' and, therefore, he does not normally subject every word in the advertisement to careful study."

> 1 Callman, Unfair Competition and Trademarks § 19.2(a)(1), at 341–44 (1950), and the cases there cited.

It is well established that advertising need not be literally false in order to fall within the proscription of the act. Gone for the most part, fortunately, are the days when the advertiser was so lacking in subtlety as to represent his nostrum as superlative for "arthritis, rheumatism, neuralgia, sciatica, lumbago, gout, coronary thrombosis, brittle bones, bad teeth, malfunctioning glands, infected tonsils, infected appendix, gall stones, neuritis, underweight, constipation, indigestion, lack of energy, lack of vitality, lack of ambition and inability to sleep * * *." See Federal Trade Commission v. National Health Aids, Inc., 108 F.Supp. 340, 342 (D.Md.1952). The courts are no longer content to insist simply upon the "most literal truthfulness," Moretrench Corp. v. Federal Trade Commission, 127 F.2d 792 at 795, for we have increasingly come to recognize that "Advertisements as a whole may be completely misleading although every sentence separately considered is literally true. This may be because things are omitted that should be said, or because advertisements are composed or purposefully printed in such way as to mislead." Donaldson v. Read Magazine, 333 U.S. 178, 188, 68 S.Ct. 591, 597, 92 L.Ed. 628 (1948). There are two obvious methods of employing a true statement so as to convey a false impression: one is the half-truth, where the statement is removed from its context and the nondisclosure of its context renders the statement misleading; a second is the ambiguity, where the statement in context has two or more commonly understood meanings, one of which is deceptive.

Problem 6

The FTC staff seeks a cease and desist order against advertising claims made by Andreotti Co., the maker of "Engine Shield." Engine Shield is an oil additive which consists of oil containing extremely small particles of colloidal graphite. When added to the oil in an automobile engine, the particles become suspended in the engine oil. The Engine Shield ads claim that "Engine Shield actually becomes part of the metal of cylinder walls, permeating the pores, and reducing friction by 50%."

The staff has presented experts who testified that "the viscosity and other properties and qualities of engine oil are not affected by the presence or absence of colloidal graphite." This is true for the oil either in bulk or as a thin film, and it is also true whether a motor is operated under "full-film" or "boundary" (negligible or no film of oil) conditions. The effect of oil containing Engine Shield upon the metal surfaces of an engine are the same as the same oil without Engine Shield, and no more.

"In tests made on bearings with plain oil and also with graphite oil, it has been determined that in the presence of an ample supply of oil, Engine Shield had no measurable effect on the friction, power, or economy of a gasoline engine. No reduction of friction is accomplished by conditioning a motor with Engine Shield."

The Commission staff also has reports of tests made by the United States Bureau of Standards on Engine Shield, which conclude:

"1. In the presence of an ample supply of oil, Engine Shield has no measurable effect on the friction, power, or economy of a gasoline engine.

"2. No reduction of friction whatever was found after the engine had operated the equivalent of more than 1,000 miles as directed."

On the other hand, Andreotti Co. presented experts who made their own tests and who testified:

"＊ ＊ ＊ The graphite deposited from the Engine Shield probably lubricated the bearing and enabled it to run longer and with less friction after the supply of oil had been cut off than would the small amount of oil which remained in the bearing alone. Bearings can undoubtedly be designed to run with graphitic lubrication alone. However, such a bearing would be incapable of sustaining loads comparable to those which can safely be put on an equal bearing lubricated with oil. The bearing in which the test was made at the North Dakota State College would probably have done as well with any form of graphite lubricant. ＊ ＊ ＊ The possible benefit of the graphite would occur if for any reason the oil supply should so diminish that metallic contact would occur in the absence of the graphite.

＊ ＊ ＊

"Well, the fact that we did get this improved economy and the decrease in friction, of my value of 36%, I think would not invalidate the claims of 50%, for, after all, our condition was at the one speed. Perhaps if we had selected another speed it would have been a little more than 36%, so it met these claims of 50%. I think that is merely relative. I do know it would improve the frictional properties to a substantial amount."

(a) Are the advertising claims for Engine Shield deceptive, misleading, or unfair? Should Andreotti Co. be prohibited from making these claims?

(b) What if Andreotti proved their 50% reduction claim, but only *after* the FTC complaint was filed. Have they misrepresented anything?

(c) If a cease and desist order is issued, how should it be worded? Should Andreotti Co. be prohibited from advertising Engine Shield in any way, or is some lesser prohibition proper? What claims should Andreotti be prohibited from making?

Problem 7

Charles of the Ritz manufactures a cosmetic preparation named "Rejuvenescence Cream." The advertising makes no claims of any kind for this cosmetic, it only repeats the name, and shows the faces of lovely women (with very healthy looking facial skin) in the background. The ads do describe the cream as containing "a vital organic ingredient" and certain "essences and compounds" which bring to the user's skin "the quality and texture of youth." The ads also ask the question: "Don't you want to keep looking young?"

The Commission staff seeks a cease and desist order against this advertising, on the ground that it falsely represented that Rejuvenescence Cream will rejuvenate and restore youth or the appearance of youth to the skin, regardless of the condition of the skin or the age of the user. This claim was deemed false because external applications of cosmetics cannot overcome skin conditions which result from systemic causes or from physiological changes occurring with the passage of time. There is no treatment known to medical science by which changes in the condition of the skin of an individual can be prevented or by which an aged skin can be rejuvenated or restored to a youthful condition.

Two medical experts, one a leading dermatologist, testified for the Commission; and both affirmatively stated that there was nothing known to medical science which could act as a rejuvenating agent and preserve or restore the youthful appearance of the skin. There was no testimony to the contrary; but Charles of the Ritz asserts that, since neither expert had ever used Rejuvenescence Cream or knew what it contained—Charles of the Ritz being unwilling to reveal its secret formula—their testimony was not substantial evidence to support the position of the Commission staff.

Charles of the Ritz also asserts that the use of the name "Rejuvenescence Cream" does not make a representation that the product rejuvenates and restores a youthful appearance to the skin. However, the Commission staff supplies an unabridged Webster's Dictionary which treats "rejuvenescense" as a common word meaning "a renewing of youth", and having "rejuvenation" as a synonym. The Commission's two medical experts both testified that the word meant "restoration of youth" to them.

(a) Is this label a misrepresentation? Is it misleading? What are the criteria for each?

(b) Is anyone being harmed by this label? Consider whether consumers are being harmed, and also whether competitors are being harmed. If there is harm to either, is it material or significant?

(c) What level of persons should the Commission try to protect? The choices include "the reasonably intelligent consumer," "the average consumer," and "the most naive hypothetical consumer," as well as other points on the spectrum of sophistication. Can the Commission insist upon the most literal truthfulness, such that the ad cannot possibly be misconstrued? Or advertising so clear that, in the words of the prophet Isaiah, "wayfaring men, though fools, shall not err therein"? See the *Standard Oil* case, infra.

(d) Must the Commission staff prove actual deception of the public—or at least some members of the public? The traditional rule is that representations having "a tendency or capacity to deceive" are unlawful. Does that entitle the Commission to speculate about the effect of words and claims on the consuming public? What evidence of misleading should the FTC staff gather to obtain the cease and desist order? Should they commission the taking of a public poll? Suppose Charles of the Ritz' attorney offers to stipulate that, if thirty members of the consuming public were called to testify, sixteen of them would testify they understand "Rejuvenescence" means "restoration of youth", while fourteen would testify that they didn't have any idea what the word means. Should the FTC accept the offer? If they do, should they pursue other evidence that the label is misleading, or is the stipulation sufficient?

(e) In determining whether the content of a message is misleading, how relevant are the meanings of individual words obtained from dictionaries? How relevant are "trade meanings"?

Cf. Charles of the Ritz Distributors Corp. v. Federal Trade Commission, 143 F.2d 676 (2d Cir.1944).

Notes

Traditionally, the FTC felt obliged to protect the ignorant and the unwary, a la *Charles of the Ritz,* supra.

In an apparently conflicting strand of FTC doctrine, other cases of this era held that exaggerations would be discounted by consumers as mere "puffing." See Carlay Co. v. FTC, 153 F.2d 493 (7th Cir.1946).

If consumers are so gullible as to believe that a cream can rejuvenate skin, will these same consumers scoff at claims that a diet is "easy" or an engine oil is the "perfect lubricant"? Is the FTC's puffery doctrine really just a resurrection of the old fact/opinion dichotomy from common law deceit? See I. Preston, The Great American Blow-up, Puffery in Advertising and Selling (1975).

Under the FTC's Deception Policy adopted in 1983, a deceptive trade practice would include only that which would be "likely to mislead" the "consumer acting reasonably under the circumstances." The new policy and its implications will be discussed in more detail, infra pages 54–64.

STANDARD OIL CO. OF CAL. v. FEDERAL TRADE COM'N

United States Court of Appeals, Ninth Circuit, 1978.
577 F.2d 653.

KENNEDY, CIRCUIT JUDGE:

* * *

The case concerns three television commercials that promoted a gasoline additive known as F–310. [Standard Oil was the manufacturer of F–310 and Batten, Barton, Durstine & Osborn (BBD & O) was the advertising agency that developed the advertisements in question.] The commercials were broadcast on television from January 9 to June 9, 1970. Two commercials were based on demonstrations which were designed to afford viewers a visual comparison of automobile exhaust before and after using F–310. See Appendix I. In one, a large clear balloon was attached to the exhaust pipe of an idling automobile. The balloon was shown inflating with black, opaque vapor, while the announcer described it as "filling with dirty exhaust emissions that go into the air and waste mileage." The announcer then stated that "Standard Oil of California has accomplished the development of a remarkable gasoline additive, Formula F–310, that reduces exhaust emissions from dirty engines." He informed the viewer that the same car was run on six tankfuls of Chevron F–310 and the result was "no dirty smoke, cleaner air." To prove the point, a clear balloon was again shown being attached to the car. This time the balloon inflated with transparent vapor. In conclusion the television viewer was told: "Chevron with F–310 turns dirty smoke into good, clean mileage. There isn't a car on the road that shouldn't be using it."

The second commercial, known as the bag demonstration, was similar to the commercial just described except that the automobile was completely enclosed in a transparent bag. In the before segment of the demonstration, the automobile was hidden from view by black exhaust smoke. In the after segment the automobile was plainly visible, thus illustrating the effects of using the F–310 additive.

The third commercial considered by the Commission focused on a meter dial labeled "exhaust emissions." The dial showed a scale from 0 to 100. The word "clean" labeled the 0 extremity, and the word "dirty" was printed under 100. Once again a before-and-after format was used, with the meter pointing to 100 before use of F–310 and to 20 afterwards. The announcer's accompanying message was: "[A]fter just six tankfuls of Chevron F–310—exhaust emissions reduced." The commercial again closed with the message that: "There isn't a car on the road that shouldn't be using it."

On May 19, 1970 the FTC advised Standard that it objected to the advertisements because it was not clear that the car depicted in the before segment of each commercial had been driven previously with a gasoline that was deliberately formulated to accelerate carbon deposits, resulting in an especially dirty engine. The FTC expressed concern that the commercials did not indicate either that the degree of improvement in gasoline mileage and pollution reduction would vary according to the condition of the engine, or that the gasoline used to prepare the test cars for the before part of the sequence caused much dirtier engines than would have been caused by normal gasoline.

Standard submitted an assurance of voluntary compliance to the Commission on May 25, 1970. Beginning June 10 the commercials were altered by superimposing on the film phrases such as, "Very Dirty Engine Purposely Used to Provide Severe Test," and "Degree of Improvement in Your Car Depends on Condition of Engine."

On December 29, 1970 the Commission filed a complaint against Standard and BBD & O based on the commercials as they were presented prior to June 10, 1970, specifying eleven charges of false advertising. The charges were sweeping. The FTC alleged not only that the ads were misleading in the respects indicated above, but also that F–310 did not reduce pollution to any significant degree. * * *

* * * Specifically, the Commission found that the commercials falsely represented (1) that use of F–310 would result in a complete reduction of air pollutants; (2) that all cars would show the same degree of improvement as was illustrated by the reduction of pollution in the exceptionally dirty engine; (3) that the use of F–310 would affect all types of exhaust emissions; and (4) that the meter used in the third commercial portrayed an eighty percent reduction of pollution with F–310. Based on these findings the Commission held that Standard and BBD & O had violated section 5 and issued broad cease and desist orders against them.

* * *

The Commission's Findings

Although the law is intended to protect "that vast multitude which includes the ignorant, the unthinking and the credulous," *Aronberg v. FTC,* 132 F.2d 165, 167 (7th Cir.1942), neither the courts nor the Commission should freely speculate that the viewing public will place a patently absurd interpretation on an advertisement. On the facts before it, the Commission could not properly have found that these ads claimed that F–310 removed all harmful chemical emissions from automobile exhaust. We do not think that any television viewer would have a level of credulity so primitive that he could expect to breathe fresh air if he stuck his head into a bag inflated by exhaust, no matter how clean it looked. If that were the whole case, we would agree with the petitioners and overturn the Commission's order in its entirety. But the Commission's opinion made a different point. The Commission was concerned with the ads' implicit statements about the degree of reduction in auto emissions and the effect of that reduction on the pollution problem.

Exhaust emissions are of two types: visible and transparent. The visible elements (black smoke and particulate matter) contribute less to pollution than the transparent elements. The Commission determined that the public is not aware of this fact. In support of this finding, it cited a study made by BBD & O with respect to the very commercials in question here. BBD & O, in reporting on this study to Standard, concluded from a survey it had made that only fourteen percent of motorists are aware that most polluting elements in automobile exhaust are invisible.

Hydrocarbons and carbon monoxide, two common exhaust pollutants which generally are transparent, were reduced by fifty percent and thirty-three percent, respectively, after use of F–310 in tests run on cars with very dirty engines. The additive had no effect at all on lead compound auto emissions which are also prime contributors to air pollution. The ads gave the public no indication whatsoever of the degree of reduction of invisible pollutants with use of F–310. Moreover, since the public, at least before it analyzes the question fully, is unaware that the visible pollutants eliminated by F–310 are not the most troublesome part of exhaust pollution, the complete disappearance of black smoke may indicate a greater pollution reduction than is actually achieved by the product. References in the ads to "no dirty smoke, cleaner air" and "turns dirty smoke into good, clean mileage" reinforced that erroneous impression.

* * *

The Commission found that a substantial portion of the viewing audience would believe that the automobiles in all three advertisements were representative of most automobiles, and petitioners do not cite evidence in the record to contradict that conclusion. That representation, clear and implicit in the ads, simply was not true. Heavy engine deposits were built up in the test vehicles by use of a special, extra-dirty fuel to show a more dramatic difference between the before-and-after sequences. It is conceded that only a small percentage of cars on the road would have similar engine conditions before using F–310. Thus most cars, although they would be cleaned by the detergent effects of F–310, would not show as large an improvement as was demonstrated by the ad. The statement made in each advertisement that "[t]here isn't a car on the road that shouldn't be using it" seemed to promise similar results for all cars, thus reinforcing the misleading impression that the condition of the demonstration vehicle was representative of the condition of most automobiles. * * *

The issue before us as to each of the ads is whether the record supports the Commission's interpretation of the meaning the commercial would have to the average viewer, and the Commission's determination of the accuracy of that message.

The Commission found that the public is acutely aware of the air pollution problem and that it is a matter of public importance for advertisements which play upon this concern to be accurate and precise. Implicit in the Commission's opinion is a finding that commercial messages might lead the average viewer, in his anxiety to help solve the pollution problem, to overreact even though upon careful reflection he might see for himself the limitations inherent in the advertiser's claim.

* * *

Here the Commission found that the predominant visual message was misleading, and that it was not corrected or contradicted by the accompanying verbal message in the advertisements. "[T]he Commission may determine for itself [the deceptive nature of the representations] through visual inspection and analysis." *United States Retail Credit Ass'n v. FTC,* 300 F.2d 212, 217 (4th Cir.1962); *Carter Products, Inc. v. FTC,* 268 F.2d 461, 495 (9th Cir.), *cert. denied,* 361 U.S. 884, 80 S.Ct. 155, 4 L.Ed.2d 120 (1959). In making this determination the Commission is entitled to "draw upon its own experience in order to determine (even) in the absence of consumer testimony, the natural and probable result of the use of advertising expressions." *Carter Products, Inc.,* 268 F.2d at 495 (parenthetical in original). Based on those principles and our review of the record, we find substantial evidence to support the Commission's finding that the three advertisements were misleading.

* * *

Problem 8

The Colgate–Palmolive Company advertises that its shaving cream "Rapid Shave" outshaves them all. Its commercials on television are designed to show that Rapid Shave softens even the toughness of sandpaper—a claim which the company has verified in laboratory tests. If real sandpaper were used for the TV demonstration, however, the inadequacies of television transmission make it appear to viewers to be nothing but plain paper—that is, its texture is not visible. The commercials therefore use a simulated prop, or "mock up," made of plexiglass to which sand is applied. As an announcer intones the qualities of Rapid Shave and particularly its ability to shave sandpaper, a razor neatly "shaves" clean the plexiglass mock-up which has been soaked with Rapid Shave.

(a) Is the undisclosed use of a plexiglass substitute a deceptive act subject to FTC prosecution? See FTC v. Colgate–Palmolive Co., 380 U.S. 374 (1965).

(b) What claim or claims are being made in this ad? Which, if any, are deceptive?

(c) Would the answer be the same in the case of—

— the use of mashed potatoes to depict ice cream being enjoyed by children, because real ice cream would melt under the TV lights?

— the use of blue sheets to produce an image of "white" sheets in a detergent commercial, where an actually white sheet would appear a dingy grey?

— putting marbles in a bowl of soup so that the solid ingredients would be forced to the top and be more visible? See Campbell Soup Co., 77 F.T.C. 664 (1970).

In each case, what has the manufacturer misrepresented, if anything? Who stands to lose thereby, and what do they stand to lose? Is this sort of policing worth the expenditure of government time, effort and money? Why? What social interest is served thereby?

Notes

1. The *Colgate–Palmolive* case cited in Problem 8, supra, was one of several to reach the Supreme Court in the 1960s in which the Commission seemed to press for a broader notion of deceptiveness. See also FTC v. Mary Carter Paint Co., 382 U.S. 46, 86 S.Ct. 219, 15 L.Ed.2d 128 (1965) ("free" can of paint of two-for-the-price-of-one sales). Nonetheless there was surprising agreement on the unfocused misuse of resources by the FTC in the period before 1970. See both the Nader Report (Cox, Fellmeth &

Schultz, The Consumer and the FTC (1969)) and the American Bar Association Report (Report of the ABA Commission to Study the FTC (1969)).

Problem 9

The Wonder Bread Company sponsors a series of TV ads that tout the superior nutritional value of its product. The text of the ad includes

> These are the "Wonder Years," the formative years one through twelve when your child develops in many ways, actually grows to 90% of her adult height * * *

> To help make the most of these "Wonder Years," serve nutritious Wonder Enriched Bread. Wonder helps build strong bodies in 12 ways. Carefully enriched with foods for body and mind. Wonder Bread tastes so good, and it is so good for growing child, for active adult.

While the announcer is talking, the TV screen shows a child eating Wonder Bread and then actually growing rapidly from a very young child to a twelve-year old. The commercial ends with the announcer urging parents

> * * * to help make the most of her "Wonder Years," her growth years, serve Wonder Bread. Wonder helps build strong bodies twelve ways.

In its complaint, the FTC alleges that these ads falsely represent that Wonder Bread is "an extraordinary food for producing dramatic growth in children." Does the ad in fact make this representation, and if so, how? Assuming that all "enriched" breads are of equal nutritional value, is the Wonder Bread claim true or false? See ITT Continental Baking Co., Inc. v. FTC, 532 F.2d 207 (2d Cir.1976), affirming with modifications the opinion of the Commission, 83 F.T.C. 865 (1973).

Notes

1. Do you agree with the FTC's interpretation of what this ad is representing to the consumer? How should the Commission go about interpreting the meaning of advertisements? The traditional judicial view, deferring to the FTC's expertise on the matter, was expressed in *Standard Oil,* supra, pages 48–49:

2. Advertisers usually perform elaborate consumer studies, or "copy tests" to determine whether they are conveying the message they want to convey. Why should five FTC Commissioners in Washington, D.C. feel they have the expertise to determine what consumers are taking from a particular television commercial if even the advertisers themselves don't feel qualified to do this? See Pitofsky, Beyond Nader: Consumer Protection and the Regulation of Advertising, 90 Harv.L.Rev. 661, 678 (1977). Many commentators have suggested that the FTC be required to use survey evidence in interpreting the meaning of advertisements. See Gellhorn, Proof of Consumer Deception Before the Federal Trade Commission, 17 U.Kan.L.Rev. 559 (1969); Preston, Data–Free at the FTC? How the Federal Trade Commission Decides Whether Extrinsic Evidence of Deceptiveness Is Required, 24 Am.Bus.L.J. 359 (1986); Comment, The Use and Reliability

of Survey Evidence in Deceptive Advertising Cases, 62 Or.L.Rev. 561 (1983); Comment, FTC Deceptive Advertising Regulation: A Proposal for the Use of Consumer Behavior Research, 76 N.W.U.L.Rev. (1982).

The Commission itself in a 1984 case declared that if the purported implied claim in an advertisement was not clearly made, it would require complaint counsel to offer extrinsic evidence in the form of consumer surveys, evidence of marketing principles applicable to similar situations, or adequately supported expert opinions. See In re Thompson Medical Co., 104 F.T.C. 648, 789–90 (1984), aff'd 791 F.2d 189 (D.C.Cir.1986), cert. denied, 479 U.S. 1086, 107 S.Ct. 1289, 94 L.Ed.2d 146 (1987).

One author has suggested that the Commission should abandon the impossible task of trying to determine "the" meaning of advertisements, and instead should balance the costs of eliminating any misleading interpretations against the benefits to consumers. See Craswell, Interpreting Deceptive Advertising, 65 B.U.L.Rev. 657 (1985). See also Preston & Richards, Consumer Miscomprehension and Deceptive Advertising: A Response to Professor Craswell, 68 B.U.L.Rev. 431 (1988).

STERLING DRUG, INC. v. FEDERAL TRADE COMMISSION

United States Court of Appeals, Ninth Circuit, 1984.
741 F.2d 1146.

Hug, Circuit Judge:

In this appeal from a decision of the Federal Trade Commission, Sterling Drug, Inc. seeks review of a determination that it disseminated false advertising for its nonprescription analgesic products. Sterling contests findings by the Commission that its advertising was deceptive. It contends that the provisions of the cease and desist order are not warranted by the record and that the order applies to more of Sterling's products than is warranted by the record. We uphold the findings and enforce the order.

I

Facts and Procedural History

Sterling Drug, Inc. ("Sterling") manufactures nonprescription internal analgesic products, including Bayer Aspirin, Bayer Children's Aspirin, Vanquish, Cope, and Midol. In February 1983, the Federal Trade Commission issued an administrative complaint against Sterling in which it was alleged that certain Sterling advertisements violated sections 5 and 12 of the Federal Trade Commission Act, 15 U.S.C. §§ 45 and 52. On the same day, the Commission also charged that two of Sterling's competitors had engaged in deceptive advertising practices. Those complaints named Bristol–Myers Company, which manufactures Bufferin and Excedrin, and American Home Products Corporation, which produces Anacin and Arthritis Pain Formula.

The cases were partially consolidated before an administrative law judge, who held joint hearings on issues common to the three cases.

After extensive pretrial discovery, the ALJ held a separate hearing in this case in 1979–80. He heard testimony from forty witnesses, including experts in the fields of medicine, pharmacology, and advertising. He also reviewed hundreds of exhibits and a large volume of scientific publications submitted in conjunction with the testimony of the expert witnesses.

The ALJ found each of the companies liable for violations of the Act and issued broad cease and desist orders barring future violations. Each of the companies appealed to the Commission. In each case, the Commission affirmed the ALJ's decision as modified.

* * *

B. Discussion

In its examination of the complaint, the Commission distinguished three distinct types of advertising claims. The first type, establishment claims, suggests that a product's superiority has been scientifically established. An advertiser may make this type of representation through the use of specific language, such as "medically proven," or through the use of visual representations.

The second type of claim is a representation that suggests the product is superior without claiming that superiority has been scientifically established. The claimed superiority may refer to therapeutic efficacy or may describe the product's pharmaceutical attributes, such as freshness, purity, color, and shelf life. The Commission requires that the advertiser have a reasonable basis to support a claim of product superiority.

The third type of claim is puffing. These claims are either vague or highly subjective, *e.g.,* "Bayer works wonders," and therefore no substantiation of the claim is required.

* * *

b. Establishment of Therapeutic Superiority

The Commission determined that several advertisements for Bayer Aspirin represented the product to be therapeutically superior and claimed that superiority had been scientifically established. Sterling first contends that those advertisements, read as a whole, merely claimed Bayer's pharmaceutical superiority, not its therapeutic superiority. Its second contention is that there was no establishment claim.

* * *

The Commission held it did not need to consider whether Sterling had a reasonable basis to claim Bayer was therapeutically superior, since in every case Sterling had also claimed that Bayer's therapeutic superiority was scientifically established. It concluded that Sterling lacked the substantiation to make these establishment claims. The Commission held that establishment claims could be substantiated only if Sterling relied upon two well-controlled clinical studies that indicated Bayer was superior.

Sterling refutes the conclusion that it made establishment claims, arguing that the text of its advertisements made no explicit assertion that Bayer's therapeutic superiority was established. However, the Commission's conclusions were based upon visual aspects of the advertisements, rather than only on the text. These visual representations included pictures of medical and scientific reports from which consumers could infer that Bayer's effectiveness had been objectively evaluated. The Commission noted that the advertisements conveyed a "serious tone" or a "scientific aura" that also implied scientific approval of the product.

A determination of false advertising can be based upon deceptive visual representations. It is within the Commission's expertise to determine what inferences consumers may draw from such representations. We defer to that expertise and affirm the conclusion that Bayer was advertised to have scientifically established therapeutic superiority.

* * *

b. *Establishment of Therapeutic Claims*

Sterling does not contest the Commission's conclusion that it made therapeutic efficacy claims as to Cope. However, it claims these representations did not include the assertion that Cope's superiority was established.

The Commission based its conclusion on the visual aspects of advertisements for Cope. It cited as an example a television advertisement in which an announcer discussed Cope's efficacy in conjunction with his description of "important studies" on pain relief. The announcer held a copy of the "important studies." In the background were shelves lined with "ponderous books." We agree with the Commission that the combination of the visual and oral representations was apt to convey to consumers a message of proven efficacy.

The Commission found Sterling could not substantiate its claim that Cope's therapeutic efficacy was established. Sterling does not challenge that finding on appeal.

3. *Findings Concerning Midol*

The complaint charged Sterling with failing to disclose Midol's aspirin content. The Commission held that a mere failure to disclose the presence of aspirin in advertising for aspirin-based analgesics was not misleading. It concluded, however, that it was a deceptive practice to disseminate advertising that implied aspirin-based products did not contain aspirin. It found that certain Midol advertisements did create that impression, and it illustrated its finding with this radio advertisement:

> Midol starts to work fast with an exclusive formula that helps stop periodic pain * * * and its medically approved ingredients give effective relief from headache and low backache. All in all, Midol's unique formula gets you through those days in comfort.

The Commission concluded that the term "exclusive formula" conveyed the message that Midol's analgesic ingredient was not aspirin. It also criticized an advertisement that claimed Midol was made from an "exclusive formula with medication ordinary pain relievers don't give you."

The failure to disclose material information may cause an advertisement to be deceptive, even if it does not state false facts. We must reject Sterling's contention that these advertisements were not intended to suggest that Midol's analgesic ingredient was unique. The illustrative advertisements specifically state that the unique ingredient relieves pain. We agree with the Commission that consumers could easily infer the unique pain reliever was something other than ordinary aspirin.

* * *

Notes

1. Why the emphasis in modern FTC advertising cases on advertising substantiation rather than deception? Does this unfairly shift the burden of proof from the Commission to the advertiser?

2. What is the legal basis for the FTC's requirement of prior substantiation for claims made in advertising?

Originally the FTC held that it would be "unfair" for an advertiser to make a product claim without a "reasonable basis." In a 1972 case, the Commission based the requirement on marketplace fairness, pointing to the "imbalance of knowledge and resources between a business enterprise and each of its customers," concluding that "economically it is more rational, and imposes far less cost on society, to require a manufacturer to confirm his affirmative product claims rather than impose a burden upon each individual consumer to test, investigate, or experiment for himself." In re Pfizer, Inc., 81 F.T.C. 23, 62 (1972).

Subsequent cases have based the substantiation requirement on a more limited deception theory. For instance, when Firestone said its tires stop "25% quicker," the FTC said the advertiser was impliedly representing to consumers that the claim was backed by scientific proof. In re Firestone Tire & Rubber Co., 81 F.T.C. 398, 450–51 (1972), aff'd 481 F.2d 246, 250–51 (6th Cir.), cert. denied, 414 U.S. 1112, 94 S.Ct. 841, 38 L.Ed.2d 739 (1973).

3. What level of substantiation is required by the FTC? The Commission's Policy Statement Regarding Advertising Substantiation, 49 Fed.Reg. 30999 (1984), says that an advertiser must have at least the amount and type of substantiation it claims to have in the ad. Otherwise, the advertiser must have a "reasonable basis." What level of substantiation was claimed for the superiority claims for Bayer and Cope in the Sterling Drug case? Was the requirement of two well-controlled clinical studies justified?

Problem 10

An aspirin commercial claims that an academic study published in the New England Journal of Medicine concluded that taking one aspirin tablet every other day could significantly reduce the risk of heart attack in men over 35. Would two well-controlled clinical studies be required or could the advertiser simply rely on the article itself for its substantiation?

Notes

1. Most consumers have heard the slogan: "Hospitals trust Tylenol." What they have not heard is that hospitals recommend—or at least pass along—Tylenol *because* its manufacturer consistently sets Tylenol's price to hospitals lower than that of competing products. Is Tylenol's slogan misleading?

2. Most consumers have also heard the slogan: "Hospitals recommend acetaminophen, the aspirin free pain reliever in Anacin–3, more than any other pain reliever." How can this and Tylenol's slogan both be true? Well, hospitals use Tylenol (because of the favorable price) and Tylenol does contain acetaminophen—as does Anacin–3. Is Anacin's slogan misleading? Would you consider either slogan to be only a half-truth? Does the FTC Act require more?

Query: Whither Now the FTC and "Deception"?

In October of 1983, a divided Commission issued a "Policy Statement on Deception," in the form of a letter to Congress. The new policy has been characterized as either a succinct restatement of existing FTC standards for proving a deceptive practice, or a throwback to common law deceit. The new policy was used for the first time in the 1984 case of *Cliffdale Associates.*

CLIFFDALE ASSOCIATES

Federal Trade Comm., 1984.
103 F.T.C. 110.

OPINION OF THE COMMISSION

By MILLER, CHAIRMAN: Cliffdale Associates, Jean–Claude Koven, and Arthur N. Sussman were charged with unfair methods of competition and unfair or deceptive acts or practices in violation of Section 5 of the Federal Trade Commission Act. Specifically, the complaint charged that respondents misrepresented the value and performance of an automobile engine attachment known as the Ball–Matic Gas Save Valve ("Ball–Matic"). The complaint also charged that respondents lacked a reasonable basis for their performance claims for the Ball–Matic.

Administrative Law Judge Miles J. Brown held that respondents had engaged in false and deceptive advertising and had lacked a reasonable basis for the claims made in their advertisements and promotional materials, in violation of Section 5 of the FTC Act. Both sides appeal from the ALJ's initial decision. We generally agree with the ALJ's findings and conclusions and, except as noted in this opinion, we adopt them as our own.

I. Background

A. The Respondents

1. Cliffdale Associates

Cliffdale is a Connecticut corporation headquartered in Westport, Connecticut. The company is engaged in mail order marketing of different products, including the Ball–Matic. Company sales for the year ending December 31, 1979, were $692,998.

* * *

B. The Product

The Ball–Matic was marketed as a gasoline conservation automobile retrofit device. The Ball–Matic is one of a number of "air bleed" devices designed to allow additional air to enter a car's engine in order to improve gasoline mileage.

* * *

II. Legal Standard for Deception

The complaint pleads both an unfairness and a deception theory for each alleged violation of Section 5. (Complaint ¶ 6, 7, 8, 11.) However, deception was the standard under which the claims were actually tried, and it is the Commission's view that this was the appropriate approach.

In finding the representations in respondents' advertisements to be deceptive the ALJ accepted complaint counsel's articulation of the standard for deception. He concluded that "any advertising representation that has the tendency and capacity to mislead or deceive a prospective purchaser is an unfair and deceptive practice which violates the Federal Trade Commission Act." We find this approach to deception and violations of Section 5 to be circular and therefore inadequate to provide guidance on how a deception claim should be analyzed. Accordingly, we believe it appropriate for the Commission to articulate a clear and understandable standard for deception.

Consistent with its Policy Statement on Deception, issued on October 14, 1983, the Commission will find an act or practice deceptive if, first, there is a representation, omission, or practice that, second, is likely to mislead consumers acting reasonably under the circumstances, and third, the representation, omission, or practice is material. These elements articulate the factors actually used in most earlier Commission cases identifying whether or not an act or practice was deceptive, even though the language used in those cases was often couched in such terms as "a tendency and capacity to deceive".

The requirement that an act or practice be "likely to mislead", for example, reflects the long established principle that the Commission need not find *actual* deception to hold that a violation of Section 5 has occurred. This concept was explained as early as 1964, when the Commission stated:

> In the application of [the deception] standard to the many different factual patterns that have arisen in cases before the Commission,

certain principles have been well established. One is that under Section 5 actual deception of particular consumers need not be shown.

Similarly, the requirement that an act or practice be considered from the perspective of a "consumer acting reasonably in the circumstances" is not new. Virtually all representations, even those that are true, can be misunderstood by some consumers. The Commission has long recognized that the law should not be applied in such a way as to find that honest representations are deceptive simply because they are misunderstood by a few. Thus, the Commission has noted that an advertisement would not be considered deceptive merely because it could be "unreasonably misunderstood by an insignificant and unrepresentative segment of the class of persons to whom the representation is addressed. In recent cases, this concept has been increasingly emphasized by the Commission.

The third element is materiality. As noted in the Commission's policy statement, a material representation, omission, act or practice involves information that is important to consumers and, hence, likely to affect their choice of, or conduct regarding, a product. Consumers thus are likely to suffer injury from a material misrepresentation. A review of past Commission deception cases shows that one of the factors usually considered, either directly or indirectly, is whether or not a claim is material.

Although the ALJ in this case used the phrase "tendency and capacity to deceive" in his initial decision, we find after reviewing the record that his underlying analysis shows that the three elements necessary for a finding of deception are present in this case.

* * *

III. The Question of Liability

The obvious first step in analyzing whether a claim is deceptive is for the Commission to determine what claim has been made. When the advertisement contains an express claim, the representation itself establishes its meaning. When the claim is implied, the Commission will often be able to determine the meaning through an examination of the representation, including an evaluation of such factors as the entire document, the juxtaposition of various phrases in the document, the nature of the claim, and the nature of the transaction.

In other situations, the Commission will require extrinsic evidence that reasonable consumers interpret the implied claims in a certain way. The evidence can consist of expert opinion, consumer testimony, contests, surveys, or any other reliable evidence of consumer interpretation. In all instances, the Commission will carefully consider any extrinsic evidence that is introduced.

A. Descriptive Claims

a. Were the Claims Made?

[The Commission found that the Ball–Matic device was represented to be an "important new invention," "needed in every car," and would provide "enhanced fuel economy."]

2. Were the Claims Deceptive?

Having determined that respondents made the claims as charged, we must next determine whether the claims were false in a material respect, and thus likely to injure consumers.

a. Ball–Matic as an Important New Invention

The evidence presented at trial amply documented that the Ball–Matic is a simple air-bleed device similar to many other such devices that have been marketed over the years. Clearly the Ball–Matic is not new. In fact, the Commission has already issued cease and desist orders against various marketers of two such devices, the Albano Air Jet and the G.R. Valve, both of which are virtually identical in design to the Ball–Matic. Air-bleed devices have been around a long time and, as the ALJ found, are considered to be of little value by the automobile industry.

The claim that the Ball–Matic was a new invention was expressly made. Having found such a claim to have been made, and that the claim is false, the Commission may infer, within the bounds of reason, that it is material. We therefore conclude that the ALJ was correct in holding that this claim was deceptive.

b. Ball–Matic Needed in Every Vehicle

The ALJ correctly concluded from the evidence presented at trial that most automobiles manufactured after 1974 have carburetors set to perform at such a lean air/fuel mixture that little, if any, fuel economy could be expected by using an air-bleed valve such as the Ball–Matic. There are, therefore, a significant number of consumers as to whom the claim of increased fuel economy is untrue. Accordingly, we agree with the ALJ that the claim that every car and truck needs the Ball–Matic is an express statement contrary to fact.

As with the "new invention" claim, this misrepresentation concerned a material aspect of the product. In the first place the claim was expressly made, and the Commission may infer materiality. In any event, the claim that the Ball–Matic is needed on every car would tend to induce all consumers (including those owning cars for which it has no utility) to buy the device. Those consumers who cannot in fact profit from the Ball–Matic will have relied on the representation to their detriment. Thus, the ALJ was correct in concluding that this claim was deceptive.

c. *Efficiency Claims*

The ALJ found the representation that the Ball–Matic would significantly improve fuel economy when installed in a typical car and used under normal driving conditions to be false. We agree. The record discloses that even under conditions most likely to produce benefits from the Ball–Matic, the fuel savings do not approach those claimed by respondents. Respondent's consumer tests and testimonials also fail to support these claims and, as the ALJ found, are not a recognized way of testing fuel economy.

Claims about enhanced fuel efficiency resulting from use of the Ball–Matic are clearly material to consumers. While consumers will not necessarily expect to achieve the specific fuel economy level represented in a particular advertisement, the performance claimed in the ads should be representative of consumers' expected savings from the Ball–Matic. It was not, and the advertisements were therefore deceptive.

* * *

COMMISSIONER PATRICIA P. BAILEY CONCURRING IN THE RESULT IN PART AND DISSENTING IN PART

The issues pertaining to liability in this case are not complicated. Indeed, the application of established law to the facts in *Cliffdale* can lead to only one conclusion: these respondents have violated Section 5 of the Federal Trade Commission Act in a number of ways, as set forth in this opinion, in their marketing of the Ball–Matic Gas Save Valve. Thus, I concur fully in the findings of liability. However, I must disassociate myself from the confusing and wholly unorthodox reformulation of the traditional test for finding deception, which has been announced in this opinion as the relevant legal standard. * * *

Legal Standard for Deception

This is an uncomplicated case involving a number of advertising claims, which are clearly false and deceptive, that could have been addressed with swift and sure justice under existing law. Unfortunately, a majority of the Commission has chosen to use the case as a vehicle to set forth a new legal standard which has little to do with the case and much to do with an ill-advised undertaking to rewrite the law of deception.

Applying a shorthand variant of the oft-repeated standard for deception, Administrative Law Judge Miles J. Brown concluded in the Initial Decision that "any representation that has a tendency or capacity to mislead or deceive a prospective purchaser is an unfair or deceptive practice which violates the Federal Trade Commission Act." The Commission's opinion dismisses this articulation as being "circular and therefore inadequate to provide guidance on how a deceptive claim should be analyzed." In its place is substituted a new formulation, promoted as "a clear and understandable standard", which states that the Commission will find deception where "first, there is a representation, omission, or practice that is likely to mislead, second, consumers acting reasonably under the circumstances, and third, the representation, omission or practice is material."

Notwithstanding assertions to the contrary, none of these three elements, as defined in the opinion, (or for that matter in the appended Policy Statement) correctly states the factors expressly relied upon in prior Commission cases and by reviewing courts to determine whether a deceptive representation or practice has occurred. Rather, a complete and accurate statement of the elements of deception has typically and traditionally included the three-part formula that an act or practice have the tendency or capacity to mislead a substantial number of consumers in a material way. While the two statements may at first glance seem semantically similar, the fact is that this reformulation departs from current law in several significant respects, all of which have the potential to heighten the Commission's evidentiary burden considerably and thereby limit the time-honored reach of its deception authority. For this reason, I dissent from the legal standard employed in the opinion and believe it is important to examine each of these new elements separately.

The majority's first criterion for deception is that there be a claim, omission or practice that is "likely to mislead" consumers. It is true that the courts have occasionally used this or similar phrasing, such as "the likelihood or propensity" of deception, interchangeably with tendency or capacity. I certainly do not object to and indeed am sympathetic with such usage where the primary goal appears to be to avoid the repetitious use of standard phraseology in the discussion of well-grounded legal principles. Here, however, the majority makes unmistakable its intent to *exchange* the phrase tendency or capacity for the term likely, with only the brief explanation that it is meant to convey an understanding that "actual" deception need not be shown. As that was never in doubt, it does not explain the use of the term likely generally, and it certainly does not make clear how its use will be more instructive in assessing deception.

Unfortunately, neither the opinion nor the appended Policy Statement offers additional explanation for this stated preference, leaving us all to guess as to any real or intended distinction from the "tendency or capacity" analysis. A standard Webster's definition of likely, "having a high probability of occurring or being true", suggests, however, that the purposeful substitution of this term for tendency or capacity may well be intended to raise, or may be construed so as to raise, the burden of proof the Commission must meet in demonstrating that deception has occurred. A careful reading of the opinion and the Policy Statement lends support to this inference; recurring references are made to the need for extrinsic evidence of consumer interpretations in many instances where it is not presently required, suggesting a need for the Commission to establish a higher level of probability that deception may have occurred in any particular instance.

Although the Commission has often admitted and relied in the past upon evidence about the effect of an act or practice on consumers, such a showing has not been required by reviewing courts, which have regularly affirmed that such matters are committed to the discretion of the FTC. Thus, use of the term "likely" here may be fairly perceived to be at least a partial retreat from the Commission's traditional position that it may on the basis of its own expertise determine what representations a seller has made to the public.

The second requirement is that an act or practice be likely to mislead consumers "acting reasonably under the circumstances." Of the three newly introduced elements, I believe this is on its face the most divorced from prior precedent and also the most likely to produce troubling results.

While the precise wording has varied a bit from decision to decision, the concept underlying the existing analytical construct has remained constant: a claim or practice must deceive a "substantial number" of consumers in order to trigger a finding of deception. Importantly, this standard affords protection to consumers and business merchants alike. Thus, it is well recognized that, if a claim is directed at a particular audience, the test is whether it could deceive a significant portion of that group. At the same time, while it is clear that a practice need not mislead all or even a majority of consumers, the Commission will not base findings of law violations on the idiosyncratic interpretations or the unreasonable misunderstandings of an insignificant and unrepresentative segment of a seller's audience.

The substantial numbers test is not intended to lead to the strict quantification of the number of consumers who have been misled by a claim or practice and has, therefore, never required the introduction of external evidence concerning such numbers. Rather the concept provides the Commission with a flexible sliding scale upon which it can typically infer whether or not a significant number of consumers could be deceived from its own examination of the conduct at hand and surrounding circumstances, often based on general information concerning the size and composition of a specific target audience. Even when extrinsic evidence is available, the Commission does not rely exclusively on such documentation in reaching its decision.

Despite the forty-odd year application by the Commission and the courts of a substantial numbers formula, the opinion injects this alternative precept and unknown quantity, the "reasonable consumer," into the law of deception. Again, there is little helpful explanation as to why.

* * *

The consequences of this hastily constructed house of cards, devoid as it is of any support in Commission precedent, accompanying explanation, or meaningful application in this particular case, may be far reaching. Practically speaking, one obvious result may be to complicate and delay Commission trial proceedings. If the reasonableness of consumer interpretations becomes a litigable issue—and there is every reason to believe that future respondents' counsel will assure that it will be under the new standard—survey evidence or expert testimony regarding consumer attitudes and actions may be mandated in even the simplest Commission cases. The introduction of such evidence will, in turn, raise difficult questions about related evidentiary issues, such as whether new discovery and cross-examination rights concerning survey methodology and results have been created. It does not take a seer to predict that the real beneficiaries of these procedural complications and the ensuing delay will be FTC respondents and their counsel, and not the Commission or the public.

Another unfortunate but foreseeable consequence of the introduction of a reasonable consumer standard is to cast the courts adrift in their efforts to understand and apply to Commission cases what is clearly a departure from prior law. What, for example, are the elements of a reasonable consumer test? Without more, the courts may logically turn for guidance to certain common law principles, such as the standard of "ordinary prudence or care" attributable to the hypothetical "reasonable man" in tort law. Although principles such as these are useful tools to establish objective standards for judging individual conduct which may result in physical or emotional harm to others, comparable concepts have no place in the examination of *consumer* behavior in the marketplace, as the Commission has made clear in the past. Thus, while the Commission has indicated that it will not subject sellers to every interpretation made by an "insubstantial and unrepresentative segment" of the seller's audience, it has at the same time faithfully adhered to the enduring proposition that consumers are entitled to take commercial representations at face value and need not mistrust them. I believe the imposition of a "reasonable consumer" test as an element of the legal standard for deception may seriously jeopardize this guiding principle of deception law, which has permitted and encouraged the Commission to spread its protective mantle over the uninformed and credulous, those with understandable but often unreasonable hopes, those with limited reasoning abilities, such as children, and even "average" consumers whose guard may be down or who may behave somewhat carelessly in the face of deceptive conduct.

Although the Policy Statement promises to continue the traditional protections afforded such groups, a reasonable consumer standard, like the rejected doctrine of caveat emptor, is analytically unsuited for such purposes. By definition the term reasonable means "possessing sound judgment." Thus, while the Commission may logically continue to consider "reasonable consumer interpretations" in instances where it may be one acceptable approach, such as in cases involving major national advertising campaigns aimed at mass audiences, traditional Commission fraud cases, focusing as they generally do on seller exploitation of *unreasonable* consumer judgments and actions, will never lend themselves in an appropriate way to such an analysis. Unlike the "substantial numbers" test, which by design encompasses both types of cases by focusing on the likely reactions of a seller's intended audience—whatever human frailties the group may exhibit—to a marketing message, the majority's approach will, I believe, require much analytical sleight of hand if the protections long promised and provided by the FTC to vulnerable consumers is to continue.

The third and last element of the new deception triumvirate is a requirement that the representation, practice, or omission be "material". Of the new requirements, this has the potential to be the wolf in sheep's clothing. The Commission has long held that a challenged act or practice must be misleading in a material respect in order to be found deceptive. Additionally, the opinion accurately states that materiality has been generally defined to include any sort of consumer preference which is likely to affect the purchasing decision or post-purchase use of the product. And, perhaps most significantly, the opinion carefully and correctly disavows any requirement of a specific finding that actual injury has occurred.

Just when all appears to be going well, however, the opinion (and at greater length the Policy Statement) introduces a series of new concepts which appear to qualify standard principles of materiality in a restrictive fashion. At one point the opinion seems to equate materiality with the actual effects of claims or practices on consumer conduct, and the Policy Statement expressly states that "injury and materiality are different names for the same concept" and that deception will be found where an act or practice "misleads * * * to the consumer's detriment." (Detriment is, of course, legally defined as injury.) The Policy Statement also notes that injury exists if consumers would have chosen differently "but for" the misleading act or practice, suggesting that reliance and causation are elements of materiality.

While I don't pretend to understand the full import of these statements, they certainly imply the possible imposition in at least some cases of new evidentiary requirements that are contrary to current law. Because Section 5 protects consumer preferences generally, including subjective preferences, materiality can be found without reference to objective injury or "detriment." Moreover, because purchasers may be influenced by a combination or variety of factors, it may be virtually impossible to establish that a particular misrepresentation caused consumers to choose differently, much less that they were "injured" in some respect by the selection made. Hence, under the law, (t)he fact that consumers were not harmed because they would have purchased the product anyway * * * is not relevant."

Opinion and Policy Statement conclusions that injury and materiality are synonymous, that causation and reliance must be shown, or even that the likelihood of consumer detriment must be demonstrated in every case do not square with these accepted understandings of materiality. Like the other elements of the new deception standard, the effects of such requirements may well be to raise the burden of proof regarding materiality generally in FTC cases, while at the same time seriously jeopardizing more complicated cases in which specific consumer harm is not easily demonstrated. I am particularly concerned that a restrictive materiality test may serve to undermine the Commission's ad substantiation doctrine. If actual injury or even the likelihood of harm must be shown in all events, the Commission may, in addition to demonstrating a lack of substantiation, be forced to prove falsity in many advertising cases where it is not presently required, in order to establish the necessary link to concrete consumer detriment.

[Commissioner Pertschuk filed a similar "dissent".]

Notes

1. Would the claims in the *Cliffdale* case have been held deceptive under the traditional standard? Did the application of the new deception policy make any difference to the outcome of this case?

2. Do you agree with Commissioner Bailey that the FTC has scaled back the standards of deceptiveness under sections 5 and 12 of the FTC Act? If so, in exactly what respects has the standard changed?

3. The FTC's 1983 "Policy Statement on Deception," published in 5 CCH–TRR ¶ 50,455 (1983), created something of a brouhaha. It was issued in response to a request from a congressional committee for an FTC statement of the current law against deception. Upon receipt of the "Policy Statement," the chairman of that committee described it as inaccurate and unresponsive, and suggested that the Commission was attempting to "rewrite a 45–year history of law enforcement." At subsequent hearings there were vitriolic exchanges between Committee Chairman John Dingell (D.Mich.) and then-FTC Chairman James C. Miller, III as to the propriety of the Commission's 3–2 vote in support of the deception "restatement." See 46 Antitrust & Trade Reg.Rep. (BNA) 641–42 (1984). Is this anything more than a political tempest in a teapot? With the fairly rapid changes in the membership of the FTC (Chairman Miller left the Commission in 1985), or changes in the party in power (the president appoints FTC Commissioners), is it likely that the "Policy Statement" and decisions like that in *Cliffdale Associates* signal a dramatic change in the FTC's long-term deception enforcement policy? What legal effect does a "policy statement" have on future Commissions? Should Congress amend the FTC Act to reflect the new policy?

4. There is already some judicial recognition that the FTC is applying a more stringent theory of deception. Southwest Sunsites, Inc. v. Federal Trade Com'n, 785 F.2d 1431 (9th Cir.1986): new standard "imposes a greater burden of proof on the FTC to show a violation of Section 5," and the new formulation is "more narrow than, but completely subsumed in, the prior theory."

5. For more in-depth discussions of the 1983 deception policy statement and its possible effects see Bailey & Pertschuk, The Law of Deception: The Past as Prologue, 33 Am.U.L.Rev. 849 (1984); Ford & Calfee, Recent Developments in FTC Policy on Deception, 50 J. of Marketing 82 (July 1986); Sullivan, The FTC's Deceptive Advertising Policy: a Legal and

Economic Analysis, 64 Or.L.Rev. 593 (1986); Note, The FTC and Deceptive Trade Practices: A Reasonable Standard?, 35 Emory L.J. 683 (1986).

Problem 11

A travel agency advertised a meeting as being of special interest to cancer patients. At the meeting, the speaker promoted a trip to the Phillipines that would include an opportunity for travelers to witness and take advantage of "psychic surgery," whereby cancerous tumors are removed without cutting the skin. A film was shown demonstrating psychic surgery. Many terminally ill patients purchased the trip, only to find out that the "surgery" shown on the film was done through sleight of hand techniques, and was a complete fraud.

You are a staff attorney at the FTC. Will you be able to persuade the Commission to issue a complaint in this case under the 1983 Deception Policy? Cf. In re Travel King, 86 F.T.C. 715 (1975).

Notes

1. Implicit assertions in ads can still be misleading under the new *Cliffdale* standard, as long as reasonable consumers would consider the information important. See Thompson Medical Co., Inc., 104 F.T.C. 648 (1984). The emphasis on reasonable consumer reaction is not always helpful to the advertiser. In F.T.C. v. Atlantex Associates, 1987–2 Trade Cases 67,788 (S.D.Fla.1987) (unpublished case), a seller of oil and gas drilling program partnerships showed that it did disclose the risks in its investments in some instances. The court stated, however, that the net impression given consumers was deceptive and enjoined the practices. Does this analytical approach indicate a possible return to the traditional standard?

2. What about advertisers who were prohibited from particular representations under the traditional standard? Can they now seek to reopen prior orders on the basis that their representations would not violate the new, *Cliffdale* standard? Should they be allowed to do so?

Note: "Unfairness"

The operative language of Section 5 of the FTC Act proscribes "*unfair* or deceptive" conduct. Virtually all of the FTC's advertising activity draws on the deceptiveness term, as well as the specific prohibition of "false" advertising in Section 12. But the disjunctive phrase "unfair *or* deceptive" clearly suggests that the Commission can act independently on unfairness grounds, and it has done so on occasion, for instance, in the Credit Practices Rule. See infra Chapter 3, pages 214–217.

The traditional criteria for determining whether a practice was unfair, consisted of three prongs:

> (1) whether the practice, without necessarily having been previously considered unlawful, offends public policy as it has been established by statutes, the common law, or otherwise—whether, in other words, it is within at least the penumbra of some common-law, statutory, or other established concept of unfairness;

(2) whether it is immoral, unethical, oppressive, or unscrupulous;

(3) whether it causes substantial injury to consumers.

This language was originally used by the Commission in a proposed regulation that would have required a health warning in cigarette advertising, 29 Fed.Reg. 8324, 8355 (1964) (the rule was later superseded by legislation requiring a warning label in ads and on packages for cigarettes, Cigarette Labeling and Advertising Act of 1965, codified at 15 U.S.C.A. §§ 1331–40).

The Commission has occasionally challenged advertising or marketing practices as being "unfair" without also being "deceptive." The best example is Philip Morris, Inc., 82 F.T.C. 16 (1973), where the Commission took a consent order from a company that distributed free razor blade samples in newspapers, with obvious risk of injury to consumers, especially children. Also noteworthy was the FTC's 1978 proposal to regulate advertising on TV programs aimed primarily at children. The proposed Rule would have banned or severely limited the kinds of food and toy commercials that dominate the Saturday morning cartoon shows. While these ads were rarely "deceptive" in the conventional sense, the Commission argued that they *unfairly* took advantage of the susceptibilities of the young viewing audience. By congressional dictate, however, this rulemaking was aborted in 1980. See FTC Act § 18(i), 15 U.S.C.A. § 57a(i): "The Commission shall not have any authority to promulgate any rule in the children's advertising proceeding ＊ ＊ ＊ on the basis ＊ ＊ ＊ that such advertising constitutes an unfair act or practice."

In the wake of criticism of the Children's Advertising Rule proposed in 1978, the Commission issued a policy statement on unfairness in 1980 that was intended to fend off legislative restrictions. The 1980 policy places primary emphasis on consumer injury (which must be substantial, not outweighed by countervailing benefits, and must be an injury that consumers could not reasonably avoid). Public policy has become a secondary confirming factor, and public morality has been dropped completely. Thus, the unfairness doctrine has lost its original intuitive meaning based on moral considerations, and has become more of a cost-benefit analysis, with a slant toward consumer sovereignty. See generally Averitt, The Meaning of "Unfair Acts or Practices" in Section 5 of the Federal Trade Commission Act, 70 Geo.L.J. 225 (1981).

The Commission has also held that failure to disclose certain information can be "unfair" although not necessarily deceptive. In In re International Harvester Co., 104 F.T.C. 949 (1984), the complaint charged that Harvester's gasoline-powered tractors were subject to a phenomenon known as fuel geysering, or the forceful ejection of hot fuel through a loosened gas cap. The complaint charged also that fuel geysering could result in serious fires, sometimes involving the tractor operator; that Harvester had been aware of this for many years; that it did not adequately notify its customers of the danger; and that the operators therefore took inadequate measures to protect themselves. The ALJ found all this to be both deceptive and an unfair practice under § 5. The Commission reversed the finding of deception, but upheld the finding that this constituted an unfair practice. It also ruled that no corrective order was necessary, since Harvester had already begun issuing adequate warnings.

In its opinion, the Commission analyzed the unfairness issue in the following way:

> The Commission's unfairness jurisdiction provides a more general basis for action against acts or practices which cause significant consumer injury. This part of our jurisdiction is broader than that involving deception, and the standards for its exercise are correspondingly more stringent. It requires the complete analysis of a practice which may be harmful to consumers. To put the point another way, unfairness is the set of general principles of which deception is a particularly well-established and streamlined subset.

> Over the past four years the Commission has devoted considerable attention to clarifying these general principles. In 1980 we prepared a formal policy statement describing our jurisdiction over unfair practices. The statement took as its point of departure the familiar language of the *Sperry & Hutchinson* case. It declared that most unfairness cases would be brought under the consumer injury theory identified in that decision. It also systematized the essential elements of that theory. An actionable consumer injury must be: (1) substantial; (2) not outweighed by any offsetting consumer or competitive benefits that the practice produces; and (3) one which consumers could not reasonably have avoided.

> The first element to this analysis is that the injury must be substantial. Unlike deception, which focuses on "likely" injury, unfairness cases usually involve actual and completed harms. While in most cases the harm involved is monetary, the policy statement expressly noted the "unwarranted health and safety risks may also support a finding of unfairness."

> The second element is that the conduct must be harmful in its net effects. This is simply a recognition of the fact that most conduct creates a mixture of both beneficial and adverse consequences. In analyzing an omission this part of the unfairness analysis requires us to balance against the risks of injury the costs of notification and the costs of determining what the prevailing consumer misconceptions actually are. This inquiry must be made in a level of detail that deception analysis does not contemplate.

> Finally, the third element is that the injury be one that consumers could not reasonably have avoided through the exercise of consumer choice. This restriction is necessary in order to keep the FTC Act focused on the economic issues that are its proper concern. The Commission does not ordinarily seek to mandate specific conduct or specific social outcomes, but rather seeks to ensure simply that markets operate freely, so that consumers can make their own decisions.

> To accomplish these goals the Commission may require that consumers be given the information that is critical to an informed choice. There is also a need for principled limits on this concept, of course, since virtually any piece of information may be useful to some consum-

ers. While this balance must ultimately be struck in the context of the individual case, the Commission has decided on certain general principles. In most cases it is appropriate to limit mandatory disclosure to those core aspects of a transaction that virtually all consumers would consider essential to an informed decision. These are the same basic characteristics discussed above in connection with common-law merchantability: (1) information bearing on fitness for intended use, and (2) information bearing on significant hidden safety hazards.

* * * In an assessment of unfairness, on the other hand, we conduct a full cost-benefit analysis, in which we weigh the consumer benefits of disclosure against their likely costs, and so there is less risk of an overbroad result. We can therefore take a more inclusive view of the information that must be disclosed under this approach.

In short, an omission may be found unfair even though it is not deceptive. * * *

* * * The unfairness theory, it will be recalled, is the Commission's general law of consumer protection, for which deception is one specific but particularly important application. Unfairness calls for a somewhat more detailed analysis of a challenged practice. This focuses on three criteria: (1) whether the practice creates a serious consumer injury; (2) whether this injury exceeds any offsetting consumer benefits; and (3) whether the injury was one that consumers could not reasonably have avoided. We find that all three criteria are satisfied in the present case.

There clearly has been serious consumer injury. At least one person has been killed and eleven others burned. * * *

The second criterion states the consumer injury must not be outweighed by any countervailing benefits to consumers or to competition that the practice also brings about. This inquiry is particularly important in the case of pure omissions. Since the range of such omissions is potentially infinite, the range of cost-benefit ratios from actions to force disclosure is infinite as well, raising the possibility that a particular action may be ill-advised. We believe that this criterion is also satisfied in the present case, however. The consuming public has realized no benefit from Harvester's non-disclosure that is at all sufficient to offset the human injuries involved.

The principal tradeoff to be considered in this analysis is that involving compliance costs. More information may generally be helpful to consumers, but all such information can be produced only by incurring costs that are ultimately born as higher prices by those same consumers. * * *

Here, however, we have no doubt that such a calculation favors disclosure. Harvester's expenses were not large in relation to the injuries that could have been avoided. Nor do we mean to rule out the possibility that some other, less expensive form of notification—such as a clearly worded warning in the operating manual—would also have been sufficient. We therefore conclude that the costs and benefits in this case satisfy the second unfairness criterion.

Finally, the third unfairness criterion states that the injury must be one that consumers could not reasonably have avoided. Here tractor operators could in fact have avoided their injuries by following a few relatively simple safety rules. If they had refrained from removing the cap from a hot or running tractor—something that both the owner's manuals and common knowledge suggested was a dangerous practice—fuel geysering would have been completely precluded. Harvester therefore argues that one necessary element of unfairness is not present.

Upon full consideration, however, we believe that this element is satisfied as well. The issue here is whether the safety rules for these tractors were adequately disclosed. Whether some consequence is "reasonably avoidable" depends, not just on whether people know the physical steps to take in order to prevent it, but also on whether they understand the necessity of actually taking those steps. We do not believe that this need was fully appreciated here. Farmers may have known that loosening the fuel cap was generally a poor practice, but they did not know from the limited disclosures made, nor could they be expected to know from prior experience, the full consequences that might follow from it. This is therefore not a situation in which the farmers themselves are primarily responsible for their own accidents.

* * *

Since fuel geysering was a risk that they were not aware of, they could not reasonably have avoided it. This is so even though they had been informed of measures to prevent it. Such information was not the same thing as an effective warning:

> [I]mplicit in the duty to warn is the duty to warn with a degree of intensity that would cause a reasonable man to exercise for his own safety the caution commensurate with the potential danger.

Such a warning was not provided in this case. We therefore find that the three elements of unfair conduct are present, and that Harvester's non-disclosures violated Section 5 of the FTC Act.

* * *

Conclusion

This case is in most respects a routine dispute over the proper contours of consumer information disclosure. We have resolved that dispute by holding that disclosure was necessary here.

En route to that holding we also had to identify the proper legal framework to use when assessing pure omissions. We have decided that such omissions should be judged as cases of possible unfairness rather than of possible deception. Since pure omissions do not most probably reflect deliberate acts on the part of the sellers, we cannot be confident, without a cost-benefit analysis, that a Commission action would do more good than harm. Yet a cost-benefit analysis is required only under an unfairness and not under a deception approach. We will therefore treat these matters in unfairness terms in order to ensure that such an analysis is made. In so deciding we hope to have added something further to the clarity and rigor of our statute, so that decisions on the merits may henceforth be made and predicted with greater precision.

Notes

1. Why did the majority of the Commission in *International Harvester* consider it preferable to deal with the omission of adequate safety information as an unfairness matter, rather than as a deceptive trade practice?

2. Do advertisers have any more concrete guidance from the new policy statement as to what information they must disclose in order to avoid a charge of unfairness than they did under the old standard? See Craswell, The Identification of Unfair Acts and Practices by the Federal Trade Commission, 1981 Wis.L.Rev. 107 (1981); Rice, Consumer Unfairness at the FTC: Misadventures in Law and Economics, 52 Geo.Wash.L.Rev. 1 (1983).

Problem 12

You are one of the five Federal Trade Commissioners. The staff has asked the Commission to issue a complaint against the manufacturer of Ole Chew smokeless tobacco for unfair or deceptive trade practices. The complaint would be based on an advertising campaign featuring a well known Country & Western singer who urges viewers to "get a lift without the smoke." None of the Ole Chew advertisements or any other smokeless tobacco ads make any mention of a health risk associated with use of the product.

Research sponsored by the U.S. Department of Health and Human Services shows that smokeless tobacco increases the risk of oral cancer in regular users by about 10%. An FTC survey of smokeless tobacco users also shows that 95% of them are aware in a general way that smokeless tobacco can be harmful to the health of the user.

Assume for the purposes of this problem that the federal legislation requiring health warnings in cigarette advertising does not apply to smokeless tobacco, and that no other federal or state legislation requires health warnings for smokeless tobacco.

Would you vote in favor of issuing a complaint? Based on deception, unfairness or both?

2. STATE REGULATION—"UDAPS" AND "LITTLE FTC ACTS"

The burden of policing advertising practices does not rest exclusively with the Federal Trade Commission. Today, in every state, there are statutes which parallel and supplement the F.T.C. Act and under which state authorities are often empowered to regulate deceptive advertising and other information practices. Many of these state laws use the language of § 5 of the F.T.C. Act to describe the conduct subject to regulation. For this reason, they are often known as "little FTC Acts." They are also often referred to as "UDAP" statutes, for "unfair or deceptive acts or practices." For a general discussion see Leafer and Lipson, Consumer Actions Against Unfair or Deceptive Acts or Practices: The Private Uses of Federal Trade Commission Jurisprudence, 48 Geo.Wash.L.Rev. 521 (1980).

These state laws are not uniform; indeed, they vary widely among the states. The National Conference of Commissioners on Uniform State Laws (the same wonderful people who brought you the UCC, U3C, and others) attempted to unify the differing pieces of state legislation by offering the Uniform Consumer Sales Practices Act for enactment by the states. The UCSPA is set forth in full in your statutory supplement. To date, however, the uniform act has been enacted only in Utah. In addition, the Kansas statute is modelled basically on the uniform act.

Despite the lack of uniformity, however, there are many common elements among the various state statutes. For example, all of them address in some way the overall problem of deception and other unfair practices in consumer transactions. All (or nearly all) of them provide for administrative enforcement by some agency of the state, often the attorney general. Most of them also provide for private actions by consumers, something not available under the federal law. Finally, they all contain penalty provisions of some kind, although these range from injunctive remedies to treble damages or other monetary penalties. There are greater differences among these laws in coverage, that is, in types of transactions regulated or classes of suppliers or consumers covered. Finally, there are differences in types of behavior regulated. Some statutes state prohibitions in only general terms ("deceptive practices," for example); others prohibit long lists of specific conduct. An insightful compilation and analysis of the various state laws can be found in the National Consumer Law Center publication "Unfair and Deceptive Acts and Practices" (1988, 2d Ed., with cumulative supplements): these volumes are part of NCLC's Consumer Credit and Sales Legal Practice Series. See also D. Pridgen, *Consumer Protection and the Law*, chapters 3–7 (1986 with annual updates).

To what extent should state courts, interpreting their own statutes, borrow from the vast experience and jurisprudence built up over the years under the federal F.T.C. Act? Consider the following.

MARSHALL v. MILLER

Supreme Court of North Carolina, 1981.
302 N.C. 539, 276 S.E.2d 397.

MEYER, JUSTICE.

Plaintiffs, residents of a mobile home park in Greensboro, North Carolina, bring this action seeking damages from defendants, owners and managers of the park. Each of the plaintiffs seeks damages for certain misrepresentations allegedly made by defendants concerning services which defendants would provide to plaintiffs, lessees of lots in the mobile home park. Plaintiffs offered evidence, and the jury found as fact, that defendants had led plaintiffs to believe that they would be furnished the following services or amenities by the mobile home park:

two playgrounds, one basketball court, one swimming pool, adequate garbage facilities and pickup, complete yard care, paved and lighted streets and common facilities. The jury further found that, during the period between 7 October 1974 and the filing of this action on 7 October 1977, defendants had failed to provide any of those facilities or services. Based on these findings of fact by the jury, Judge Alexander determined as a matter of law that certain of defendants' misrepresentations constituted unfair or deceptive acts or practices in or affecting commerce within the meaning of G.S. 75–1.1. * * *

The Court of Appeals found error in several of the issues submitted to the jury. Our review is limited to Issue No. 4, which was as follows:

Did the defendant, after October 7, 1974, without the intent and/or the ability to perform lead the plaintiffs or any of them to believe that he would provide the following equipped facilities for their use, reasonable wear and tear accepted (sic)?

(a) Two playgrounds

ANSWER: Yes

(b) One basketball court

ANSWER: Yes

(c) One swimming pool

ANSWER: Yes

(d) Household water

ANSWER: No

(e) Adequate garbage facilities and pickup

ANSWER: Yes

(f) Complete yard care, that is, mowing and trimming

ANSWER: Yes

(g) Paved streets

ANSWER: Yes

(h) Lighted streets

ANSWER: Yes

(i) Common facilities

ANSWER: Yes

The Court of Appeals deemed that statement of the issue erroneous because defendants could be adjudged to have committed unfair or deceptive acts without a showing that they acted in bad faith.

In determining that bad faith was an essential element of plaintiffs' claim, the Court of Appeals recognized that G.S. 75–1.1(a) closely follows the portion of Section 5 of the Federal Trade Commission Act codified at 15 U.S.C. § 45(a)(1) (hereinafter FTC Act). In fact, the language of our statute is identical to that section of the FTC Act. Both acts further provide for government enforcement, our state Act through actions brought by the Attorney General to obtain mandatory orders. (G.S. 75–14). The court may impose civil penalties in suits instituted by the Attorney General in which the defendant is found to have violated G.S. 75–1.1 and the "acts or practices which constituted the violation were, when committed, specifically prohibited by a court order or knowingly violative of a statute." G.S. 75–15.2. Unlike our own statutory scheme, however, the FTC Act confers no private right of action upon an injured party.

Rather, the provisions for private enforcement found in our statute are more closely analogous to Section 4 of the Clayton Act, which provides for private suits with treble damage recovery for violation of federal antitrust laws. 15 U.S.C. § 15 (1976).

It is established by earlier decisions of this Court that federal decisions interpreting the FTC Act may be used as guidance in determining the scope and meaning of G.S. 75–1.1. Federal courts have uniformly held that the FTC may issue a cease and desist order to enforce Section 5 where an act or practice has a capacity to deceive, regardless of the presence or absence of good faith on the part of the offending party. Although recognizing the precedential value of FTC decisions, the Court of Appeals held that, because our state Act provides for a private action, federal decisions to the effect that bad faith was not necessary to show a violation of the FTC Act were not dispositive. Good faith, said the Court of Appeals, may be irrelevant where the Attorney General seeks injunctive relief under G.S. 75–14, a remedy analogous to an FTC cease and desist order, but it should be relevant where a party is potentially liable in a private action for treble damages under G.S. 75–16. Our task is to determine whether the intent of the Legislature will be more fully served if the addition of a private action under our statute brings with it a concomitant requirement that a private party must show bad faith in order to recover treble damages. In resolving that question, we are guided by two other questions: (1) what was this State's unfair and deceptive trade practice act intended to accomplish, and (2) how can the purpose for which the law was passed be most fully realized.

Between the 1960's and the present, North Carolina was one of forty-nine states to adopt consumer protection legislation designed to parallel and supplement the FTC Act. * * *

Such legislation was needed because common law remedies had proved often ineffective. Tort actions for deceit in cases of misrepresentation involved proof of scienter as an essential element and were subject to the defense of "puffing." Proof of actionable fraud involved a heavy burden of proof, including a showing of intent to deceive. *Ragsdale v. Kennedy*, 286 N.C. 130, 209 S.E.2d 494 (1974). Actions alleging breach of express and implied warranties in contract also entailed burdensome elements of proof. A contract action for recision or restitution might be impeded by the parol evidence rule where a form contract disclaimed oral misrepresentations made in the course of a sale. Use of a product after discovery of a defect or misrepresentation might constitute an affirmance of the contract. Any delay in notifying a seller of an intention to rescind might foreclose an action for recision. Against this background, and with the federal act as guidance, North Carolina and all but one of her sister states have adopted unfair and deceptive trade practices statutes.

* * *

As mentioned above, the Court of Appeals felt that, as this was a private action rather than one instituted by the Attorney General, good faith was a proper defense. There is some authority in other jurisdictions for such a distinction. *See, e.g., Bartner v. Carter*, 405 A.2d 194 (Me.1979) (where "loss of money or property" is an essential element of the claim, private action showing mere proof of capacity to deceive is insufficient).

We reach the contrary result for several reasons. First, nothing in our earlier decisions in *Hardy* and *Johnson* limits the precedential value of FTC jurisprudence to cases or actions brought by the Attorney General. Indeed, both cases actually involved private litigants. Second, unlike statutes enacted by some of our sister states, there is no explicit statutory requirement of a showing of bad faith in G.S. 75–1.1. Finally, as discussed above, under the standards for determining what is unfair and deceptive according to *Johnson*, the intent or good faith belief of the actor is irrelevant.

In an area of law such as this, we would be remiss if we failed to consider also the overall purpose for which this statute was enacted. The commentators agree that state statutes such as ours were enacted to supplement federal legislation, so that local business interests could not proceed with impunity, secure in the knowledge that the dimensions of their transgression would not merit federal action. Given the small dollar amounts often involved in such suits, statutory provision for treble damages found in G.S. 75–16 serves two purposes. First, it makes more economically feasible the bringing of an action where the possible money damages are limited, and thus encourages private enforcement. Second, it increases the incentive for reaching a settlement. Further provision for attorney fees, found in G.S. 75–16.1, also encourages private enforcement in the marketplace. The dissimilarity in language used by our Legislature in G.S. 75–1.1 and G.S. 75–16.1, in that willfulness is specifically mentioned in the latter, was apparently not accidental. The fact that attorney fees may only be awarded upon a specific finding that defendant acted "willfully" indicates, rather clearly we think, that the omission of willfulness, intentional wrongdoing or bad faith as an essential element under G.S. 75–1.1 was deliberate, and supports the result in this case. We further note that G.S. 75–16.1 also provides that an unsuccessful plaintiff may be charged with defendant's attorney fees should the court find that "[t]he party instituting the action knew, or should have known, the action was frivolous and malicious." This is an important counterweight designed to inhibit the bringing of spurious lawsuits which the liberal damages provisions of G.S. 75–16 might otherwise encourage.

Were we to agree with the Court of Appeals, we think we would seriously weaken the effectiveness of G.S. 75–1.1 and circumvent the intent of the Legislature. Except as modified herein, we adopt the opinion of the Court of Appeals.

MODIFIED AND AFFIRMED.

Problem 13

Sergeant and Mrs. Bilko went to their local mobile home dealer in Fayetteville, North Carolina to look at a mobile home. They were concerned about the cost of moving the home, since they could be subject to a transfer at any time. They asked the salesman if the army would pay for the moving costs of the home if they had to move, and the salesman assured them (in good faith) that the military would pay. The Bilkos did not check this out with the Base Transportation Office, but went ahead and bought the mobile home on the word of the salesman. Bilko was transferred to California a few months later, and he was informed that the army would pay only $5,000 of the $8,000 cost of moving. The Bilkos could not afford the $3,000 so they left their mobile home in North Carolina and sued the dealer under the North Carolina Unfair and Deceptive Trade Practices Act. Have they stated a cause of action under the UDAP? What criteria will the court use to determine whether the salesman's acts were deceptive? Would they have prevailed in a common law action for deceit? See Strickland v. A & C Mobile Homes, 70 N.C.App. 768, 321 S.E.2d 16 (1984).

Query: In any state with a UDAP statute like North Carolina's and caselaw like Marshall v. Miller—no good faith defense, liability measured only by a "tendency to deceive" standard, and treble damages plus attorney's fees—will consumers ever again have to grapple with the components of common law deceit (scienter, materiality, reliance)? Have the state UDAPs relegated common law deceit to the history books for consumer transactions?

[Your authors disagree on this. One of us believes there will always be a need to invoke deceit theory in cases not covered by a UDAP statute (such as sales of real estate, or insurance, or in credit or banking transactions), and that a deceit claim is always a useful backup count even in actions under a UDAP law, especially if the conduct is so egregious that a fraud count may justify punitive damages. Another of us is convinced that the relaxed deception and unfairness theories evidenced in FTC jurisprudence and in the state UDAPs are the wave of the present and future for consumer law. Those state laws will continue to be interpreted or amended in an expansive way, for all forms of consumer transactions, until the common law strictures of deceit will become altogether irrelevant.]

Further Query: During the 1980s, state attorneys general, dissatisfied with the apparent lack of vigor at the FTC in regulating national advertising, started to challenge television commercials touting such nationwide favorites as McDonalds' Chicken McNuggets, Kraft's Cheez Whiz and

Arby's "lean meal" using their authority under state UDAPs. Is this an appropriate use of state UDAPs? Will suits under different state laws impose undue burdens on national advertisers? Is this an area that should be preempted by federal law?

HESLIN, COM'R OF CONSUMER PROTECTION v. CONNECTICUT LAW CLINIC OF TRANTOLO AND TRANTOLO

Supreme Court of Connecticut, 1983.
190 Conn. 510, 461 A.2d 938.

PETERS, ASSOCIATE JUSTICE.

The principal issue in this appeal is whether an investigative demand of Mary M. Heslin, the Connecticut Commissioner of Consumer Protection (commissioner), issued to attorneys suspected of engaging in deceptive trade practices, exceeds the commissioner's statutory authority and unlawfully exercises a power vested by the constitution of Connecticut exclusively with the state judiciary. The case arose when the defendant, Connecticut Law Clinic of Trantolo & Trantolo, refused to comply with an investigative demand issued to it by the plaintiff commissioner pursuant to the Connecticut Unfair Trade Practices Act. General Statutes §§ 42–110a through 42–110q (CUTPA, the act). Upon the defendant's refusal to comply, the commissioner sought an order requiring compliance from the Superior Court. The trial court, holding the regulation of attorney conduct to be a matter exclusively within the control of the judicial branch of the state government, dismissed the commissioner's application. From this judgment of dismissal, the commissioner has appealed. We find error and remand for further proceedings.

The investigative demand in controversy, in accordance with General Statutes § 42–110d(c), provided the defendant with a description of the alleged practices under investigation. These alleged practices included unfair or deceptive use of the terms "clinic" and "law clinic" in the defendant's advertising, misrepresentations by the defendant as to its fees and as to the fees of other attorneys performing the same services, and referrals by the defendant to the law firm of Trantolo & Trantolo, which caused those referred to pay higher legal fees than the fees advertised by the defendant. * * *

CUTPA was designed by the legislature to "put Connecticut in the forefront of state consumer protection." It endows the commissioner with broad powers: to investigate suspected violations of the act; to define, through the promulgation of regulations, what may constitute unfair or deceptive acts or practices; and to subpoena witnesses, conduct hearings, and issue cease-and-desist orders to persons determined to have violated the act. The commissioner may also seek enforcement of the act in the Superior Court; which is authorized to enjoin violations of the act and to "make such additional orders or judgments as may be necessary to restore to any person in interest any moneys or property, real or personal, which may have been acquired by means of any practices prohibited by this chapter * * *." General Statutes § 42–110d(e).

CUTPA contains no language expressly including or excluding attorneys from its purview. Since the defendant does not claim that it falls within one of the act's general exceptions, the question on appeal is whether the provision of legal services constitutes "the conduct of any trade or commerce." The act defines trade or commerce as "the advertising, the sale or rent or lease, the offering for sale or rent or lease, or the distribution of any services and any property, tangible or intangible, real, personal or mixed, and any other article, commodity, or thing of value in this state." General Statutes § 42–110a(4).

It is not surprising that CUTPA is textually inconclusive on the question of whether the practice of law is included within the conduct of trade or commerce. In 1973, before lawyers engaged in advertising and when few lawyers were incorporated, existing precedents tended to exclude the work of the legal profession from the category of trade or commerce. * * *

We need not speculate about the intent of CUTPA's drafters, because the act contains its own guide to statutory construction. It provides, in § 42–110b(b): "It is the intent of the legislature that in construing subsection (a) of this section, the commissioner [of consumer protection] and the courts of this state shall be guided by interpretations given by the Federal Trade Commission and the federal courts to Section 5(a)(1) of the Federal Trade Commission Act (15 U.S.C. 45(a)(1)), as from time to time amended."

Although the federal courts have not directly addressed the issue of whether the Federal Trade Commission Act (FTC Act) applies to attorneys, the existing decisions provide considerable guidance. The United States Supreme Court has recently affirmed application of the FTC Act to other professionals. That court, furthermore, has, since the passage of CUTPA, decided that the practice of law may constitute the conduct of a trade or commerce under the Sherman Anti–Trust Act, 15 U.S.C. § 1. * * * In light of the above, it is reasonable to conclude that the federal courts would construe the FTC Act as applying to attorneys.

If we look to interpretations of the FTC Act given by the federal trade commission itself, we need exercise fewer cautions. As early as 1964, an attorney who had prepared a dunning letter and had participated in a collection scheme violative of 15 U.S.C. § 45(a)(1) was held to have himself violated the FTC Act and was enjoined from using threats of legal action in connection with the unlawful scheme. More recently, the federal trade commission has unequivocally stated its official position that state-regulated professions, including the practice of law, are not and should not be exempted from coverage of the FTC Act.

* * *

We need not in this case decide whether every provision of CUTPA permits regulation of every aspect of the practice of law by every member of the bar of this state. For now, we need conclude only that CUTPA's regulation of "the conduct of any trade or commerce" does not totally exclude all conduct of the profession of law. For the purpose of sustaining an investigatory demand, we conclude that CUTPA applies to the conduct of attorneys.

* * *

Notes

1. Can you argue with a straight face that the provision of legal services is *not* a part of "trade or commerce?"

2. On the other hand, aren't consumers already well protected by the availability of malpractice suits against lawyers or doctors who handle their cases in a negligent manner and by the oversight of state professional conduct committees? Is placing the professions under the jurisdiction of state UDAPs a matter of regulatory overkill?

3. The state of Washington has held that the state's Consumer Protection Act applies to the "entrepreneurial" aspects of legal and medical practice (e.g., billing and advertising), but not to the quality of legal advice and services. See Short v. Demopolis, 103 Wash.2d 52, 691 P.2d 163 (1984). Is this the proper compromise?

4. Should other regulated industries, such as insurance and securities transactions, be exempt from state UDAPs? If you were a state legislator, what would you want to know about the regulatory system before determining whether an exemption from the little FTC Act would be appropriate? What are the dangers of UDAP coverage of a regulated industry?

A few courts have found that the practice of law is itself exempt as a regulated industry, since admission to the practice of law is regulated by the legislative and judicial branches of state government. See Rousseau v. Eshleman, 128 N.H. 564, 519 A.2d 243 (1986).

5. Although buying a house is typically one of the largest purchases most consumers make in a lifetime, and one where arguably the consumer is most in need of legal protection, the states are divided on whether or not real estate transactions are included within their state UDAPs. Often the statutes are limited to acts or practices involving the sale of "goods or services," a phrase which is usually interpreted to exclude real property. A similar issue has arisen with regard to the coverage of deceptive or unfair practices in connection with rental housing. On the other hand, many state UDAPs specifically include real estate and rental of residential housing within the definition of consumer transactions.

Problem 14

Open your statutory supplement to the Uniform Consumer Sales Practices Act. Considering it as a model, or as representative of other state UDAPs, answer the following:

(a) What are the standards of conduct the UCSPA imposes on suppliers? See §§ 3 and 4. What is the difference between those sections? Are the specific, enumerated instances of deceptive and unconscionable acts exhaustive, or merely examples?

(b) Does the UCSPA consciously adopt prevailing Federal Trade Commission standards on unfair or deceptive acts or practices? See §§ 1(4) and 14. Query: If the Cliffdale Associates case, supra p. 54, reflects a change in FTC deception theory, does that mean an automatic change in state UDAP doctrines as well? See Karns, Redefining "Deceptive" Advertising Under the Illinois Consumer Fraud and Deceptive Business Practices Act After Cliffdale Associates, 1985 S.Ill.U.L.J. 1.

(c) Are the powers given to the "Enforcing Authority" (typically a state attorney general or Consumer Protection Office) equivalent to, or stronger or weaker than, those of the Federal Trade Commission? See §§ 5–10, particularly § 9. For example, could the Enforcing Authority sue and ask the court to void an entire class of customer contracts procured through deception, and to refund any customer deposits? What are the pre-conditions for any such remedy?

There are numerous examples of state officials successfully suing under state UDAPs for either injunctive or monetary relief, or both. Some recent examples include: State ex rel. McLeod v. VIP Enterprises, Inc., 286 S.C. 501, 335 S.E.2d 243 (App.1985) (injunction and civil penalties for illegal "pyramid" scheme); State by Abrams v. Stevens, 130 Misc.2d 790, 497 N.Y.S.2d 812 (1985) (injunctive relief and restitution for misleading ads for "free" merchandise); Barry v. Arrow Pontiac, In., 100 N.J. 57, 494 A.2d 804 (1985) (cease and desist order for ads misrepresenting "dealer's invoice price"). See also infra Chapter 17, Sec. B, pages 812–824.

(d) What private remedies are available to aggrieved consumers? See § 11. Are they adequate? Is there any particular incentive for consumers to incur the expenses and worry of litigating over what will typically be modest amounts of money? See § 11(e). Are attorneys' fees recoverable if a consumer's action is settled in his favor prior to trial? Could an individual consumer sue to enjoin a deceptive advertising campaign without having first bought the product? Cf. § 11(a). See also infra Chapter 16, Sec. D.

(e) On the other hand, how certain are you of success under the UCSPA? Consider, for example, the position of the Hopefuls in Problem 15 below.

Problem 15

Re-read Problem 5 on p. 37, supra. [Harry and Harriet Hopeful bought an uninsulated trailer from Comfy Mobile Homes after Comfy's salesman had innocently made multiple oral statements concerning its quality ("good solid home, as good as any others"), while the informed sales manager stood silently by.] You represent the Hopefuls. Assume you are in a jurisdiction that has enacted the UCSPA.

(a) First, even if you can prove all the above facts, has Comfy violated either § 3 or § 4 of the UCSPA? Is Comfy's alleged conduct within any of the specific enumerated instances of deception and unconscionable acts, or will you have to fit it into the broad, general language? If the latter, what are the requirements and criteria for finding conduct to be "unconscionable" or "deceptive"? Can FTC decisions be used? Can common law deceit cases be used?

(b) Second, if the Hopefuls prove a violation of the Act, what remedies are they entitled to? In particular, can they have the contract cancelled and get their money back? Can they recover the costs of insulating the mobile home? Can they recover "pain and suffering" damages for shivering through a Buffalo winter?

(c) Third, after your initial interview with the Hopefuls, how much of the facts will you be aware of? (e.g., the presence of the sales manager? her knowledge?) How solid is your evidence concerning any statements (precise wording?) of the salesman? or, the relative quality of the actual trailer? Note that it is after that interview that you will probably decide how seriously you will pursue this case. Does the award of attorneys' fees to the successful consumer make this case look like a sure winner to you now?

Notes

1. Many states provide for double or treble damages for violation of the state UDAP, although in some states damages are multiplied only if the plaintiff shows that the violation was knowing or deliberate. Also, in most states only the prevailing plaintiff may obtain attorneys' fees, not the prevailing defendant.

2. Has the private right of action under state little FTC Acts made the issue of individual suits for violation of the FTC Act a moot question? Does the proliferation of private suits under state UDAPs pose the same danger of inconsistent standards for "unfair and deceptive trade practices" that seemed to worry the judges considering implying a private right of action under the FTC Act? See infra Chapter 17, Sec. B. pages 855–858, for a discussion of the merits of an implied private right of action under the FTC Act.

3. In State of Maine v. Sears, Roebuck and Co., unreported, Maine Superior Ct. Kennebec Co., 1985, the state's Attorney General charged Sears with violating the state Unfair Trade Practices Act. Sears advertised sales of its appliances stating, "Each of these advertised items is readily available for sale as advertised." However, the advertised appliances were "not actually kept in stock at Sears stores, but are stored at central warehouses and then delivered to stores or customers generally seven to fourteen days after order." The court found that the "reasonable import of the statement is that the goods are indeed available at the store," which they were not; but also found that both the advertising statement and the appliance distribution system arose out of a 1977 consent agreement between Sears and the FTC. The consent agreement approved the distribution system and mandated the specific language in Sears ads. The court then stated:

> This advertising statement was imposed by the Federal Trade Commission with recognition that the central warehousing plan for storage

and sale of white goods was in operation. If Maine law is to be interpreted consistently with the mandates of the Federal Trade Commission, therefore, the Sears central warehousing plan for white goods, and the advertising statement having Federal Trade Commission approval, must gain approval under 5 M.R.S.A. § 207, absent an outrageous or strained interpretation of law or a "sweetheart" deal by the F.T.C. which is not suggested in this case. In drafting section 207, the Legislature went to unusual lengths to assure that Maine courts would follow F.T.C. guidance in interpreting the law. Thus, § 207–1 specifies:

> "It is the intent of the Legislature that in construing this section the courts will be guided by the interpretations given by the Federal Trade Commission and the Federal Courts to section 5(a)(1) of the Federal Trade Commission Act (15 U.S.C.A. 45(a)(1)), as from time to time amended."

But for the strong legislative mandate to follow Federal Trade Commission direction, the Court's view of the "each items available" statement might be different in light of the substantial evidence of Sears availability problems.

4. Is this a judicial pronouncement that Maine law must follow FTC concepts, even if they change (as in Cliffdale), or even if Maine precedent must be overturned? Or, is the pronouncement merely that Maine law cannot conflict with prior FTC orders, so that Sears need not attempt to satisfy conflicting directions from federal and state agencies?

5. If the Maine statute directs the state courts to follow FTC Act concepts, should the court be guided by current FTC doctrine, the FTC doctrines recognized at the time of the enactment of the Maine statute, the court's analysis of most likely FTC doctrine in the future—or, should the court follow its own analysis, using FTC doctrine as one component of a multi-faceted balancing equation? Compare UCSPA §§ 1(4) and 14(1) to § 207–01 of the Maine statute. Do they state the same concepts?

6. The court states that the FTC–Sears consent order was not a "sweetheart" deal. According to the consent order, "once the customer indicates desire to buy the [advertised] item, the Sears employee must offer to write up *an order* for the item" (Emphasis added.) However, according to the consent order, even while offering to write up the order, the Sears employee "may also attempt to get the customer to 'trade up' by suggesting that the customer look at a higher priced item with more features * * *." Do you think that the 7–14 day delay in the availability of the advertised item will have any impact on the employee's "attempt to get the customer to 'trade up' "? Note that delayed availability is built into Sears' system, and the FTC-mandated legend gives the public a false sense of security. For more on bait and switch tactics, see Chapter 3, below.

PENNINGTON v. SINGLETON
Supreme Court of Texas, 1980.
606 S.W.2d 682.

[Singleton, who was not in the business of selling boats and had never sold a boat before, sold his used boat, motor and trailer to

Pennington. Singleton represented that $500 worth of work had been done on the goods, and that they were in "excellent condition" and "just like new." In fact, the goods were defective, with a cracked gear housing which was inadequately repaired, but Singleton did not know this. Pennington relied on the statements. When the defects were discovered, Pennington sued Singleton both in common law fraud and under the Texas Deceptive Trade Practices—Consumer Protection Act (DTPA). The trial court concluded that Pennington had not proved the elements of a common law fraud, but could recover under DTPA. On appeal, Singleton argued that DTPA was inapplicable to a seller who is not in the business of selling those goods (a nonmerchant). The Texas court of civil appeals initially affirmed the trial court, but on rehearing "reversed the judgment of the trial court and rendered the judgment that Pennington take nothing."]

To provide individual consumers with a method and incentive to discourage deceptive trade practices, the legislature included § 17.50, thereby creating a private cause of action for mandatory treble damages. Section 17.50(a) has four subdivisions, which list categories of prohibited conduct. A finding that the defendant's acts fall within one of these subdivisions may entitle the plaintiff to the remedies allowed by § 17.50(b).

* * *

Section 17.50(a)(1) provides that a consumer may maintain an action for violations of § 17.46. Section 17.46(a) declares unlawful any "[f]alse, misleading, or deceptive acts or practices in the conduct of any trade or commerce."

* * *

APPLICABILITY OF THE DTPA TO NONMERCHANTS

By cross-point Singleton urges that the DTPA does not apply to an isolated sale of a good by one who is not engaged in the business of selling that good. We agree with the court of civil appeals' first opinion, which held that the Act cannot reasonably be construed as so restricted. Section 17.46 prohibits false, misleading, or deceptive acts in "trade or commerce." "Trade" and "commerce" are broadly defined in § 17.45(6) as "the advertising, offering for sale, sale, lease, or distribution of any good or service, of any property, tangible or intangible, real, personal, or mixed, and any other article, commodity, or thing of value, wherever situated, and shall include any trade or commerce directly or indirectly affecting the people of this state." Section 17.50(a)(1) allows a private cause of action for "any person's" unlawful trade practice. "Person" is defined in § 17.45(3) as "an individual, partnership, corporation, association, or other group, however organized." No exception is provided for persons engaged in trade or commerce who are not in the business of selling; other exemptions are allowed in § 17.49.

The legislature explicitly defined the type of transactions included within the DTPA and the persons against whom a private action may be brought. No indication is made that persons not in the business of selling are to be excluded. Furthermore, it is reasonable to assume that the private action was included in the DTPA to provide a remedy for one-time abuses that could not be adequately handled by state enforcement. For these reasons, we hold that a private cause of action is available against nonmerchants as well as merchants.

LANTNER v. CARSON

Supreme Court of Massachusetts, 1978.
374 Mass. 606, 373 N.E.2d 973.

[Plaintiffs bought a used home from defendants, "subject to the following: Water turned on, well functional, and water tests acceptable." Prior to the written agreement, seller represented that evident damage to ceilings was a result of a defective roof which had been repaired; and that the second floor fireplace was stuffed with paper "to avoid drafts", but was otherwise in good working order. Subsequently, the water pump failed, the well ran sufficiently dry to suck sand into the pipes, the roof leaked because original roof damage had not been repaired, and the fireplace was found to be reconstructed of "newspaper bricks" (newspaper coated with plaster and painted black) and unusable. Buyers repaired the defects and then sued seller under the state Consumer Protection Act.]

[The court first noted that the act provided a private right of action to "any person who purchases ∗ ∗ ∗ property ∗ ∗ ∗ [for] household purposes and thereby suffers loss ∗ ∗ ∗ as a result of the use ∗ ∗ ∗ by another person of an unfair or deceptive act ∗ ∗ ∗ declared unlawful by section two." Section 2 proscribed "unfair or deceptive acts ∗ ∗ ∗ in the conduct of any trade or commerce." "Trade" and "commerce" were defined to include advertising or selling any real or personal property.]

The plaintiffs argue that the terms of §§ 1 and 2 are broad enough to reach *any* type of commercial exchange, regardless of the nature of the transaction or the character of the parties involved. According to the plaintiffs, the Legislature made no distinction in the statute between the professional salesperson or business person, and the amateur, the individual who may sell a consumer item only on an isolated basis. Therefore, they argue, the remedial provisions of § 9 should be available to the consumer who purchases from an individual homeowner, regardless of the fact the transaction is not in pursuit of the seller's ordinary course of business. We do not agree with this expansive reading.

First, the statute does not specifically define the phrase "in the conduct of any trade or commerce." Nevertheless, we may infer its meaning from reading the statute as a whole. In so doing, we observe that, contrary to the plaintiffs' assertions, G.L. c. 93A creates a sharp distinction between a business person and an individual who participates in commercial transactions on a private, nonprofessional basis.

For example, where § 9 affords a private remedy to the individual consumer who suffers a loss as a result of the use of an unfair or deceptive act or practice, an entirely different section, § 11, extends the same remedy to "[a]ny person who engages in the conduct of any trade or commerce." In *Slaney v. Westwood Auto, Inc.*, we concluded that by these terms, § 11 extends the consumer protection remedies of G.L. c. 93A to the "businessman." Indeed, this construction is a necessary one. Were we to interpret the phrase "in the conduct of any trade or commerce" as the plaintiffs suggest, to apply to any commercial transaction whatsoever, the "persons" covered by §§ 9 and 11 would be identical. Section 11 would thus be superfluous—merely a repetition of § 9. We have stated that "[a]n intention to enact a barren and ineffective provision is not lightly to be imputed to the Legislature." Therefore, we conclude that with respect to G.L. c. 93A, where the Legislature employed the terms "persons engaged in the conduct of any trade or commerce," it intended to refer specifically to individuals acting in a business context.

* * *

Finally, we note that our conclusions with respect to the scope of G.L. c. 93A are not inconsistent with the statute's broadly protective legislative purpose. In *Dodd v. Commercial Union Ins. Co.*, we stated that the basic policy of G.L. c. 93A was "to regulate business activities with the view to providing * * * a more equitable balance in the relationship of consumers to persons conducting business activities." An individual homeowner who decides to sell his residence stands in no better bargaining position than the individual consumer. Both parties have rights and liabilities established under common law principles of contract, tort, and property law. Thus, arming the "consumer" in this circumstance does not serve to equalize the positions of buyer and seller. Rather, it serves to give superior rights to only one of the parties, even though as nonprofessionals both stand on an equal footing.

Judgment affirmed.

Notes

1. Note that both the Texas and Massachusetts statutes are limited to acts occuring "in trade or commerce," yet they reach diametrically opposed results regarding the coverage of nonmerchant sellers. Which case has the better approach to determining whether a consumer who purchases an item from another private individual should be able to use the pro-plaintiff provisions of state little FTC Acts or be relegated to his or her common law remedies?

2. Zeeman v. Black, 156 Ga.App. 82, 273 S.E.2d 910 (1980) took a slightly different approach to reach the conclusion that Georgia's Fair Business Practices Act was not applicable to the private sale of a home. The Georgia appellate court noted that the objective of the statute was to eliminate deceptive practices in the "consumer marketplace," meaning the underlying transaction had to involve a business person as well as a consumer. Furthermore, the Georgia law was patterned on the FTC Act,

which contains a "public interest" standard, meaning only suits affecting the "public interest" can be brought under that Act. Hence, a dispute between two individuals, when the seller does not sell to the general public, was not a matter affecting the public interest.

SECTION C. CONSTITUTIONAL LIMITATIONS ON ADVERTISING REGULATION

Before 1973 it had been axiomatic that "commercial" speech enjoyed no special first amendment protections, and legislatures and agencies were free to regulate advertising and similar marketplace communications at will. The basis for this assumption was an almost offhand opinion of the Supreme Court in the case of Valentine v. Chrestensen, 316 U.S. 52, 62 S.Ct. 920, 86 L.Ed. 1262 (1942), where the Court rejected a free speech challenge to a handbilling ordinance. Under that law Chrestensen was restrained from distributing a double-faced handbill: one side advertised tours of a former Navy submarine he owned; the other side contained a protest against New York City's refusal to allow him the use of a city pier. In sustaining the ordinance, the Court acknowledged that laws could not "unduly burden" free speech in public places, but continued:

> We are equally clear that the Constitution imposes no such restraint on government as respects purely commercial advertising. Whether, and to what extent, one may promote or pursue a gainful occupation in the streets, to what extent such activity shall be adjudged a derogation of the public right of user, are matters for legislative judgment ∗ ∗ ∗. If the respondent was attempting to use the streets of New York by distributing commercial advertising, the prohibition of the code provision was lawfully invoked against his conduct. 316 U.S. at 54–55, 62 S.Ct. at 921, 86 L.Ed. at 1265.

In 1973 there began a series of Supreme Court decisions which together clearly expand the degree of First Amendment protection for commercial advertising. Many students will have encountered this line of cases in constitutional law courses, but a summary of them is useful. Note that virtually all these cases involve statutory or regulatory prohibitions of advertising based on its informational *content,* not on its deceptiveness.

In Pittsburgh Press Co. v. Pittsburgh Com'n on Human Relations, 413 U.S. 376, 93 S.Ct. 2553, 37 L.Ed.2d 669 (1973), a divided court upheld an ordinance that forbade newspapers from running help-wanted ads in sex-designated columns. Conceding that these ads, though "classic examples of commercial speech," were not *entirely* without First Amendment protection, the Court stressed that regulation is justified where the advertised activity (discriminatory hiring practices) was itself illegal:

> "Any First Amendment interest which might be served by advertising an ordinary commercial proposal and which might arguably outweigh the governmental interests supporting the regulation is alto-

gether absent when the commercial activity itself is illegal and the restriction on advertising is incidental to a valid limitation on economic activity."

Two years later, in Bigelow v. Virginia, 421 U.S. 809, 95 S.Ct. 2222, 44 L.Ed.2d 600 (1975) the Court invalidated a state statute which prohibited the advertising of abortion services and made such advertising a misdemeanor. The ads in question, published in the Virginia Weekly, promoted a low cost abortion clinic in New York, where abortions were lawful. The Court applied a "balancing" test, concluding that Virginia "may not, under the guise of exercising internal police powers, bar a citizen of another State from disseminating information about an activity that is legal in that State." 421 U.S. at 824–25, 95 S.Ct. at 2234–35, 44 L.Ed.2d at 613.

In the 1976 landmark decision in Virginia State Board of Pharmacy v. Virginia Citizens Consumer Council, Inc., 425 U.S. 748, 96 S.Ct. 1817, 48 L.Ed.2d 346 (1976), the Court rejected as unconstitutional a state statute barring the advertising of prescription drug prices. The opinion acknowledged the purely economic interest of the pharmacist who wants to advertise prices, but stressed the concomitant interests of society as a whole, and of individual consumers, to a free flow of market information. Against these considerations, the purported justification for the law—to assure professional standards for pharmacists—carried little weight. The Court also distinguished situations where commercial speech was false or misleading:

> Nor is there any claim that prescription drug price advertisements are forbidden [under the Virginia statute] because they are false or misleading in any way. Untruthful speech, commercial or otherwise, has never been protected for its own sake. Obviously, much commercial speech is not provably false, or even wholly false, but only deceptive or misleading. We foresee no obstacle to a State's dealing effectively with this problem. The First Amendment, as we construe it today, does not prohibit the State from insuring that the stream of commercial information flow cleanly as well as freely.

In Central Hudson Gas & Electric Corp. v. Public Service Commission of New York, 447 U.S. 557, 100 S.Ct. 2343, 65 L.Ed.2d 341 (1980), the Court reviewed a state regulation, emanating from the days of the OPEC oil embargo in 1973, that prohibited electric utilities from advertising that promoted the use of electricity. The regulation was sustained in the state courts, but the Supreme Court found that it violated the First Amendment because the complete suppression of speech was more extensive than necessary to further the State's interest in energy conservation. After reviewing its prior holdings, the Court summarized the test to be applied:

> In commercial speech cases, then, a four-part analysis has developed. At the outset, we must determine whether the expression is protected by the First Amendment. For commercial speech to come within that provision, it at least must concern lawful activity and not

be misleading. Next we ask whether the asserted governmental interest is substantial. If both inquiries yield positive answers, we must
determine whether the regulation directly advances the governmental
interest asserted, and whether it is not more extensive than is necessary to serve that interest.

The *"Central Hudson* formula"* now guides any evaluation of restrictions on advertising content. But is it being applied in the same
spirit in which it was first articulated? Consider the following case.

POSADAS DE PUERTO RICO ASSOCIATES v. TOURISM COMPANY OF PUERTO RICO

Supreme Court of the United States, 1986.
478 U.S. 328, 106 S.Ct. 2968, 92 L.Ed.2d 266.

JUSTICE REHNQUIST delivered the opinion of the Court.

In this case we address the facial constitutionality of a Puerto Rico
statute and regulations restricting advertising of casino gambling
aimed at the residents of Puerto Rico. Appellant Posadas de Puerto
Rico Associates, doing business in Puerto Rico as Condado Holiday Inn
Hotel and Sands Casino, filed suit against appellee Tourism Company
of Puerto Rico in the Superior Court of Puerto Rico, San Juan Section.
Appellant sought a declaratory judgment that the statute and regulations, both facially and as applied by the Tourism Company, impermissibly suppressed commercial speech in violation of the First Amendment and the equal protection and due process guarantees of the
United States Constitution. The Superior Court held that the advertising restrictions had been unconstitutionally applied to appellant's past
conduct. But the court adopted a narrowing construction of the statute
and regulations and held that, based on such a construction, both were
facially constitutional. * * * We now hold that we have jurisdiction
to hear the appeal, and we affirm the decision of the Supreme Court of
Puerto Rico with respect to the facial constitutionality of the advertising restrictions.

In 1948, the Puerto Rico Legislature legalized certain forms of
casino gambling. * * *

The Act also provided that "(n)o gambling room shall be permitted
to advertise or otherwise offer their facilities to the public of Puerto
Rico."

* * *

Because this case involves the restriction of pure commercial
speech which does "no more than propose a commercial transaction,"
Virginia Pharmacy Board v. Virginia Citizens Consumer Council, Inc.,
425 U.S. 748, 762, 96 S.Ct. 1817, 1825, 48 L.Ed.2d 346 (1976), our First
Amendment analysis is guided by the general principles identified in
Central Hudson Gas & Electric Corp. v. Public Service Comm'n, 447
U.S. 557, 100 S.Ct. 2343, 65 L.Ed. 341 (1980). Under Central Hudson,
commercial speech receives a limited form of First Amendment protection so long as it concerns a lawful activity and is not misleading or

fraudulent. Once it is determined that the First Amendment applies to the particular kind of commercial speech at issue, then the speech may be restricted only if the government's interest in doing so is substantial, the restrictions directly advance the government's asserted interest, and the restrictions are no more extensive than necessary to serve that interest. 447 U.S., at 566, 100 S.Ct., at 2351.

The particular kind of commercial speech at issue here, namely, advertising of casino gambling aimed at the residents of Puerto Rico, concerns a lawful activity and is not misleading or fraudulent, at least in the abstract. * * * The interest at stake in this case, as determined by the Superior Court, is the reduction of demand for casino gambling by the residents of Puerto Rico. * * * These are some of the very same concerns, of course, that have motivated the vast majority of the 50 States to prohibit casino gambling. We have no difficulty in concluding that the Puerto Rico Legislature's interest in the health, safety, and welfare of its citizens constitutes a "substantial" governmental interest.

The last two steps of the Central Hudson analysis basically involve a consideration of the "fit" between the legislature's ends and the means chosen to accomplish those ends. Step three asks the question whether the challenged restrictions on commercial speech "directly advance" the government's asserted interest. In the instant case, the answer to this question is clearly "yes." The Puerto Rico Legislature obviously believed, when it enacted the advertising restrictions at issue here, that advertising of casino gambling aimed at the residents of Puerto Rico would serve to increase the demand for the product advertised. We think the legislature's belief is a reasonable one, * * *.

Appellant argues, however, that the challenged advertising restrictions are underinclusive because other kinds of gambling such as horse racing, cockfighting, and the lottery may be advertised to the residents of Puerto Rico. Appellant's argument is misplaced for two reasons. First, whether other kinds of gambling are advertised in Puerto Rico or not, the restrictions on advertising of casino gambling "directly advance" the legislature's interest in reducing demand for games of chance. Second, the legislature's interest, as previously identified, is not necessarily to reduce demand for all games of chance, but to reduce demand for casino gambling. * * * In other words, the legislature felt that for Puerto Ricans the risks associated with casino gambling were significantly greater than those associated with the more traditional kinds of gambling in Puerto Rico. In our view, the legislature's separate classification of casino gambling, for purposes of the advertising ban, satisfies the third step of the Central Hudson analysis.

We also think it clear beyond peradventure that the challenged statute and regulations satisfy the fourth and last step of the Central Hudson analysis, namely, whether the restrictions on commercial speech are no more extensive than necessary to serve the government's interest. The narrowing constructions of the advertising restrictions announced by the Superior Court ensure that the restrictions will not affect advertising of casino gambling aimed at tourists, but will apply only to such advertising when aimed at the residents of Puerto Rico. Appellant contends, however, that the First Amendment requires the Puerto Rico Legislature to reduce demand for casino gambling among the residents of Puerto Rico not by suppressing commercial speech that might encourage such gambling, but by promulgating additional speech designed to discourage it. We reject this contention. We think it is up to the legislature to decide whether or not such a "counterspeech" policy would be as effective in reducing the demand for casino gambling as a restriction on advertising. The legislature could conclude, as it apparently did here, that residents of Puerto Rico are already aware of the risks of casino gambling, yet would nevertheless be induced by widespread advertising to engage in such potentially harmful conduct.

In short, we conclude that the statute and regulations at issue in this case, as construed by the Superior Court, pass muster under each prong of the Central Hudson test. We therefore hold that the Supreme Court of Puerto Rico properly rejected appellant's First Amendment claim.

Appellant argues, however, that the challenged advertising restrictions are constitutionally defective under our decisions in Carey v. Population Services Int'l, 431 U.S. 678, 97 S.Ct. 2010, 52 L.Ed.2d 675 (1977), and Bigelow v. Virginia, 421 U.S. 809, 95 S.Ct. 2222, 44 L.Ed.2d 600 (1975). In *Carey*, this Court struck down a ban on any "advertisement or display" of contraceptives, and in *Bigelow*, we reversed a criminal conviction based on the advertisement of an abortion clinic. We think appellant's argument ignores a crucial distinction between the *Carey* and *Bigelow* decisions and the instant case. In *Carey* and *Bigelow*, the underlying conduct that was the subject of the advertising restrictions was constitutionally protected and could not have been prohibited by the State. Here, on the other hand, the Puerto Rico Legislature surely could have prohibited casino gambling by the residents of Puerto Rico altogether. In our view, the greater power to completely ban casino gambling necessarily includes the lesser power to ban advertising of casino gambling, and *Carey* and *Bigelow* are hence inapposite.

Appellant also makes the related argument that, having chosen to legalize casino gambling for residents of Puerto Rico, the First Amendment prohibits the legislature from using restrictions on advertising to accomplish its goal of reducing demand for such gambling. We disagree. In our view, appellant has the argument backwards. As we noted in the preceding paragraph, it is precisely because the government could have enacted a wholesale prohibition of the underlying conduct that it is permissible for the government to take the less intrusive step of allowing the conduct, but reducing the demand through restrictions on advertising. It would surely be a Pyrrhic victory for casino owners such as appellant to gain recognition of a First Amendment right to advertise their casinos to the residents of Puerto Rico, only to thereby force the legislature into banning casino gambling by residents altogether. It would just as surely be a strange constitutional doctrine which would concede to the legislature the authority to totally ban a product or activity, but deny to the legislature the authority to forbid the stimulation of demand for the product or activity through advertising on behalf of those who would profit from such increased demand. Legislative regulation of products or activities deemed harmful, such as cigarettes, alcoholic beverages, and prostitution, has varied from outright prohibition on the one hand, * * * to legalization of the product or activity with restrictions on stimulation of its demand on the other hand * * *. To rule out the latter, intermediate kind of response would require more than we find in the First Amendment.

* * *

For the foregoing reasons, the decision of the Supreme Court of Puerto Rico that, as construed by the Superior Court, section 8 of the Games of Chance Act of 1948 and the implementing regulations do not facially violate the First Amendment or the due process or equal protection guarantees of the Constitution, is affirmed.

It is so ordered.

JUSTICE BRENNAN, with whom JUSTICE MARSHALL and JUSTICE BLACKMUN join, dissenting.

* * * I do not believe that Puerto Rico constitutionally may suppress truthful commercial speech in order to discourage its residents from engaging in lawful activity.

* * *

I see no reason why commercial speech should be afforded less protection than other types of speech where, as here, the government seeks to suppress commercial speech in order to deprive consumers of accurate information concerning lawful activity. * * * [N]o differences between commercial and other kinds of speech justify protecting commercial speech less extensively where, as here, the government seeks to manipulate private behavior by depriving citizens of truthful information concerning lawful activities.

"Even though 'commercial' speech is involved, (this kind of restriction) strikes at the heart of the First Amendment. This is because it is a covert attempt by the State to manipulate the choices of its citizens, not by persuasion or direct regulation, but by depriving the public of the information needed to make a free choice. . . . (T)he State's policy choices are insulated from the visibility and scrutiny that direct regulation would entail and the conduct of citizens is molded by the information that government chooses to give them * * *" Central Hudson, supra, 447 U.S., at 574–575, 100 S.Ct., at 2355–2356 (Blackmun, J., concurring in judgment).

* * * Accordingly, I believe that where the government seeks to suppress the dissemination of nonmisleading commercial speech relating to legal activities, for fear that recipients will act on the information provided, such regulation should be subject to strict judicial scrutiny.

* * *

* * * Where the government seeks to restrict speech in order to advance an important interest, it is not, contrary to what the Court has stated, "up to the legislature" to decide whether or not the government's interest might be protected adequately by less intrusive measures. Rather, it is incumbent upon the government to prove that more limited means are not sufficient to protect its interests, and for a court to decide whether or not the government has sustained this burden. In this case, nothing suggests that the Puerto Rico Legislature ever considered the efficacy of measures other than suppressing protected expression. More importantly, there has been no showing that alternative measures would inadequately safeguard the Commonwealth's interest in controlling the harmful effects allegedly associated with casino gambling. Under these circumstances, Puerto Rico's ban on advertising clearly violates the First Amendment.

[The additional dissent of Mr. Justice Stevens is omitted].

Notes

1. Does the *Posadas* holding undermine, or add qualifications to, any of the earlier Supreme Court decisions on advertising regulation?

2. Could Congress, or a state legislature, now ban *all* advertising for tobacco products, alcoholic beverages, handguns, massage parlors, or abortion clinics?

Problem 16

A Virginia pharmacist, now that he may advertise prices of drugs, decides to promote their sale. He runs the following ad in the local newspaper:

"Pain getting you down? Insist that your physician prescribe demerol. You pay a little more than for aspirin, but you get a lot more relief."

"Can't shake the flu? Get a prescription for tetracycline from your doctor today."

"Don't spend another sleepless night. Ask your doctor to prescribe Seconal without delay."

(a) Assuming these ads are not technically untruthful, can the Federal Trade Commission, or a state legislature or agency, ban them? Are they "deceptive" under the FTC Act? Could the government justify the ban on the ground that there are dangers in the overuse of prescription drugs and that these dangers are increased when advertising generates patient pressure on physicians to prescribe them?

(b) Prescription drug advertising might take various forms, and your reaction to the advertising might be influenced by the amount and format of the information disclosed. For example, a drug ad might dryly recite all the specific details, including recommended dosage, limitations on use, and possible side effects, that the Food & Drug Administration requires in the "PPIs" (Patient Package Inserts) that accompany the product when it is sold. Or the ad may be a lyrical tribute to "Valium time" (approximating recent commercials for "Miller time"). Or the ads might emphasize only the price and not any medical properties of the prescription drug. Under the guidelines of the Supreme Court, can the advertisement's informational content (or lack of it) be considered in applying the First Amendment test from *Central Hudson?*

(c) Even if certain advertising messages cannot be banned altogether, the Court's decisions acknowledge that governments may impose "time, place, and manner" restrictions on advertising. For example, the pharmacist in *Virginia Board* might not be allowed to advertise his drug prices from a sound truck in the middle of the night in residential neighborhoods. Could the ads described at the top of this problem be prohibited in publications aimed at senior citizens, or at children? In publications kept in doctors' waiting rooms? On prime time TV? In connection with part (b) of this problem, could the ads be prohibited *unless* they include all the detail from the PPI?

BOLGER v. YOUNGS DRUG PRODUCTS CORP.

Supreme Court of the United States, 1983.
463 U.S. 60, 103 S.Ct. 2875, 77 L.Ed.2d 469.

[Youngs engaged in the manufacture, sale and distribution of contraceptives. Youngs publicized its products in part through unsolicited mailings, including information pamphlets discussing the desirability and availability of prophylactics in general or Youngs' products in particular. When informed in 1979 by the Postal Service that its mailings violated a federal law against the mailing of contraceptive advertisements (39 U.S.C. 3001(e)(2), Youngs brought an action for declaratory and injunctive relief. Since the Postal Service had conceded that the prohibition would not extend to noncommercial speech, it became necessary for the Court to determine whether the informational pamphlets were or were not commercial speech.]

* * *

Most of appellee's mailings fall within the core notion of commercial speech—"speech which does 'no more than propose a commercial transaction.'" *Virginia State Board of Pharmacy v. Virginia Citizens Consumer Council, Inc.,* 425 U.S., at 762, 96 S.Ct., at 1825, quoting *Pittsburgh Press Co. v. Human Relations Comm'n,* 413 U.S. 376, 385, 93 S.Ct. 2553, 2558, 37 L.Ed.2d 669 (1973). Youngs' informational pamphlets, however, cannot be characterized merely as proposals to engage in commercial transactions. Their proper classification as commercial or non-commercial speech thus presents a closer question. The mere fact that these pamphlets are conceded to be advertisements clearly does not compel the conclusion that they are commercial speech. See *New York Times v. Sullivan,* 376 U.S. 254, 265–266, 84 S.Ct. 710, 718–719, 11 L.Ed.2d 686 (1964). Similarly, the reference to a specific product does not by itself render the pamphlets commercial speech.[13] See *Associated Students v. Attorney General,* 368 F.Supp. 11, 24 (CD Cal. 1973). Finally, the fact that Youngs has an economic motivation for mailing the pamphlets would clearly be insufficient by itself to turn the materials into commercial speech. See *Bigelow v. Virginia,* 421 U.S. 809, 818, 95 S.Ct. 2222, 2230, 44 L.Ed.2d 600 (1975); *Ginzburg v. United States,* 383 U.S. 463, 474, 86 S.Ct. 942, 949, 16 L.Ed.2d 31 (1966); *Thornhill v. Alabama,* 310 U.S. 88, 60 S.Ct. 736, 84 L.Ed. 1093 (1940).

The combination of *all* these characteristics, however, provides strong support for the District Court's conclusion that the informational pamphlets are properly characterized as commercial speech. The mailings constitute commercial speech notwithstanding the fact that they contain discussions of important public issues such as venereal disease and family planning. We have made clear that advertising which "links a product to a current public debate" is not thereby entitled to the constitutional protection afforded noncommercial speech. *Central Hudson Gas & Electric Corp. v. Public Service Comm'n,* 447 U.S., at 563, n. 5, 100 S.Ct., at 2350, n. 5. A company has the full panoply of protections available to its direct comments on public issues, so there is no reason for providing similar constitutional protection when such statements are made in the context of commercial transactions. See *ibid.* Advertisers should not be permitted to immunize false or misleading product information from government regulation simply by including references to public issues. Cf. *Metromedia, Inc. v. City of San Diego,* 453 U.S. 490, 540, 101 S.Ct. 2882, 2909, 69 L.Ed.2d 800 (1981) (Brennan, J., concurring).

We conclude, therefore, that all of the mailings in this case are entitled to the qualified but nonetheless substantial protection accorded to commercial speech.

* * *

13. One of the informational pamphlets, "Condoms and Human Sexuality," specifically refers to a number of Trojan-brand condoms manufactured by appellee and describes the advantages of each type.

The other informational pamphlet, "Plain Talk about Venereal Disease," repeatedly discusses condoms without any specific reference to those manufactured by appellee. The only reference to appellee's products is contained at the very bottom of the last page, where appellee is identified as the distributor of Trojan-brand prophylactics. That a product is referred to generically does not, however, remove it from the realm of commercial speech. For example, a company with sufficient control of the market for a product may be able to promote the product without reference to its own brand names. Or, a trade association may make statements about a product without reference to specific brand names. See, *e.g., National Commission on Egg Nutrition v. FTC,* 570 F.2d 157 (CA7 1977) (enforcing in part an FTC order prohibiting false and misleading advertising by an egg industry trade association concerning the relationship between cholesterol, eggs, and heart disease). In this case, Youngs describes itself as "the leader in the manufacture and sale" of contraceptives. Brief for the Appellee at 3.

[Applying the *Central Hudson* formula, the Court then concluded that the challenged statutory provisions were more extensive than necessary to protect the government's interests.]

Problem 17

Jerry Leadhaber is a Professor of Communication at New York County College. He has recently organized a group called the Young Educated Supporters for Egg Generated Greatness (YES–EGG). YES–EGG has mounted a significant nation-wide educational campaign to convey the message that eggs are "good for you" and are needed by all persons as a major part of their diet. The three major themes in YES–EGG's campaign, as they appeared in the media are:

"There is no significant scientific evidence that eating eggs increases the risk of heart or circulatory disease."

"There is scientific evidence that eggs, and dietary cholesterol, decrease the risk of heart and circulatory disease; and that avoiding eggs increases those risks."

"Eating eggs does not increase the blood cholesterol level in a normal person, because the human body increases its manufacture of cholesterol in an amount equal to any decrease in intake of dietary cholesterol."

Professor Leadhaber states that his opinions are based on his own studies of nutrition, and those of his friend Professor Pshaw, a Professor of Engineering. Neither of their studies have been published, as they are both being "fine-tuned," but Professor Leadhaber and other members of YES–EGG state their complete and sincere belief in the veracity of their statements. They also dismiss all studies leading to a contrary conclusion (which include all published studies on the subject) as "quackery" and "unscientific".

The FTC staff wants to seek a cease and desist order requiring YES–EGG to include in any of its "educational" statements an express acknowledgement that "many medical experts believe that increased consumption of eggs, and other dietary cholesterol, may increase the risk of heart disease." However, the staff is concerned about First Amendment freedom of speech issues, because YES–EGG asserts that any such inclusion will make its whole educational campaign counter-productive. It further asserts that on a subject of intense national debate, such an order would preclude one side from making its case to the public, which in turn would clearly subvert the First Amendment.

(a) The staff seeks your analysis of the First Amendment issues. Is this "commercial speech", or non-commercial speech? Does it matter? To what extent is this speech protected by the First Amendment? If *every* published study finds a link between eggs, cholesterol and heart disease—does this take away YES–EGG's (or Leadhaber's) right to dissent and disagree? (If the Nobel Peace Prize Committee and all the American media agree that Bishop Tutu is a hero, does that take away Jerry Falwell's right to dissent and disagree?)

(b) Would it make any difference if the FTC staff could prove that all of YES–EGG's financial support came from a trade association of egg producers and marketers? Why? Suppose the FTC staff could prove that the egg producers trade association had hired Professor Leadhaber to create YES–EGG and to conduct a promotional and advertising campaign which would counteract the anti-egg, anti-cholesterol information? Any difference?

(c) Does the FTC staff's proposed disclosure go too far? I.e., is it more extensive than necessary to cure the potential deception?

(d) What if YES–EGG had used the name "National Commission on Egg Nutrition?" Would that be misleading? What would be an appropriate remedy compatible with the first amendment? Cf. FTC v. National Commission on Egg Nutrition, 517 F.2d 485 (7th Cir.1975), cert. denied, 426 U.S. 919, 96 S.Ct. 2623, 49 L.Ed.2d 372 (1976).

Notes

1. A leading cigarette manufacturer published a series of "editorial advertisements" in various magazines. A typical advertisement was headlined "Of Cigarettes and Science" and summarized a scientific study that had concluded there is no link between cigarette smoking and heart disease. The ad did not mention any particular brand of cigarette, but was signed and paid for by "R.J. Reynolds Corporation." The Federal Trade Commission issued a complaint alleging that the ad was false and misleading. R.J. Reynolds contended it was just making its contribution to the public debate on the health consequences of smoking cigarettes, that its editorial ad was not commercial speech, and thus the FTC had no jurisdiction to regulate it. The Administrative Law Judge dismissed the complaint, but a divided Commission remanded the case for further proceedings. The majority noted that the advertisements referred to a specific product, cigarettes, and discussed an attribute (i.e., the link between smoking and heart disease) which was a concern of purchasers. See In re R.J. Reynolds Tobacco Co., 54 Antitrust & Trade Reg.Rep. (BNA) 681 (April 14, 1988). This case was settled the following year.

Do all the Supreme Court holdings discussed in this section apply equally to *print* media (newspapers, magazines) and to *electronic* media (radio and television)? Before you leap to the apparently obvious conclusion that of course they do, consider the following:

In *Bigelow* the Supreme Court inserted this qualifying footnote, 421 U.S. at 825 n. 10, 95 S.Ct. at 2234 n. 10, 44 L.Ed.2d at 613 n. 10:

"Nor need we comment here on the First Amendment ramifications of legislative prohibitions of certain kinds of advertising in the electronic media, where the "unique characteristics" of this form of communication "make it especially subject to regulation in the public interest * * *.""

The Court cited, inter alia, Capital Broadcasting Co. v. Mitchell, 333 F.Supp. 582 (D.D.C.1971), aff'd, 405 U.S. 1000, 92 S.Ct. 1289, 31 L.Ed.2d 472 (1972). That case had sustained the constitutionality of the Cigarette

Smoking Act of 1969 which flatly prohibited cigarette advertising on any medium of electronic communication.

Similarly, in *Virginia State Board of Pharmacy,* the Court stressed that "the special problems of the electronic broadcast media are ＊ ＊ ＊ not in this case," again citing the *Capital Broadcasting* case, 425 U.S. at 773, 96 S.Ct. at 1831, 48 L.Ed.2d at 365.

The Court again affirmed the special status of the broadcast media in Federal Communications Comm. v. Pacifica Foundation, 438 U.S. 726, 98 S.Ct. 3026, 57 L.Ed.2d 1073 (1978), the Court approved FCC censure for a radio station which had broadcast, in mid afternoon, comedian George Carlin's "seven dirty words" monologue. Noting that "it is broadcasting that has received the most limited First Amendment protection," the Court offered several reasons for permitting tighter regulation of the airwaves: (1) "the individual's right to be let alone plainly outweighs the First Amendment rights of the intruder"; (2) "broadcasting is uniquely accessible to children, even those too young to read."

The Court has not expressly retreated from, or modified, these holdings since *Central Hudson.* Has the Court effectively carved out radio and TV advertising from the First Amendment protection available in other media, leaving broadcast advertising subject—like cigarette ads—to unfettered regulation by Congress, the FTC or the states?

Sidebar on Charitable Solicitations

Soliciting for charitable causes has become big business, or at least it is an ever present occurrence, as anyone who has a telephone or receives mail can testify. These campaigns are now increasingly directed by professional fundraisers, and the expenses involved may leave very little for the actual work of the charitable organization to whom people believe they are contributing. Is this activity a potential fraud on the public that can be regulated in the same manner as other commercial speech?

In a series of cases starting in 1980, the Supreme Court has concluded that charitable solicitations are not commercial speech, even when conducted by professional fundraisers. Furthermore, percentage limits on the amount that must go to actual charitable activities, excluding administrative costs and the costs of the solicitation itself, are unconstitutional because such restrictions could limit protected information dissemination and advocacy activities that are tied up in the solicitation itself. See Schaumburg v. Citizens for a Better Environment, 444 U.S. 620, 100 S.Ct. 826, 63 L.Ed.2d 73 (1980); Secretary of State of Maryland v. Joseph H. Munson Co., 467 U.S. 947, 104 S.Ct. 2839, 81 L.Ed.2d 786 (1984).

While the Court has looked rather favorably on required disclosures in the commercial speech area, it struck down a North Carolina statute that would have required professional fundraisers to disclose the percentage of contributions collected during the previous 12 months that were actually turned over to charity. Riley v. National Federation of the Blind of North Carolina, 487 U.S. 781, 108 S.Ct. 2667, 101 L.Ed.2d 669 (1988). The majority concluded that this disclosure would hamper fundraising efforts, particularly for the small or unpopular charities who rely on professionals and receive a relatively small return due to the difficulty of finding donors. The state could deal with fraud by purported charities through more direct measures. Id. Chief Justice Rehnquist, joined by Justice O'Connor, dissented, asserting that the statute was an economic regulation with an incidental effect on speech, and thus the court should not have applied any type of heightened scrutiny. The required disclosure was deemed equivalent to mandatory disclosure requirements for securities transactions.

Chapter 2

COMPULSORY DISCLOSURE OF INFORMATION

SECTION A. INTRODUCTION

1. DISCLOSURE LAWS IN GENERAL

Chapter 1 concerned the regulation of information which may be voluntarily disclosed to a consumer. Beyond this form of regulation, many laws also *require* that suppliers of some consumer products provide certain information about those products. Some of these laws are of quite recent origin; others have been on the books for years. They cover a wide array of transactions and they affect all of our day to day lives.

Perhaps the oldest and best known of these compulsory disclosure requirements are those created by the Federal Food, Drug & Cosmetic Act, 21 U.S.C.A. § 301 et seq., first enacted in 1938. The regulations under this Act contain specifications as to the labelling of contents and ingredients for food, drugs, and cosmetics. See 21 C.F.R. Parts 101 (food), 201 (drugs), and 701 (cosmetics). The original Act was supplemented in 1966 by the Fair Packaging and Labelling Act, 15 U.S.C.A. § 1451 et seq.

In this chapter, we will focus on the Truth in Lending Act (TILA), perhaps the most intricate and controversial mandatory disclosure law ever enacted.

2. THE FUNDAMENTAL PROBLEM: OBSTACLES TO CREDIT SHOPPING

Credit costs on a product such as a car or major appliance can be as varied as the price of the product itself. Let's say you are in the market for a new stereo system. You probably expect prices to vary widely among stores. If you shop around, you might save as much as two hundred dollars or more.

But what about credit costs? You probably have several sources of credit available to you to purchase the stereo. For example, you might use a credit card. Or, you might obtain an installment sales contract from the seller or a loan from a third party such as a credit union or small loan company. Many consumers assume that all creditors charge roughly the same rates, but this is not true. For example, if your stereo cost $800 and you were financing the entire amount, finance charges might range from $96 for a two year credit union loan, to $288 on a typical credit card (over two years), to $320 for a loan from a consumer finance company. The difference in credit costs might be as much or more than your price savings. Yet the evidence suggests that you are much less likely to shop around for credit. Why?

Actually, there are several major obstacles in your path. One is the difficulty of direct comparison. How do you compare, for example, the relative costs of (1) a credit union installment loan of $800 for three years at a cost ("finance charge") of $144, with (2) a credit card charge of 1½% per month on an average daily unpaid balance (which changes constantly), with (3) the seller's two-year installment plan which costs $240, with (4) a small loan company's offer to pay for your new stereo and consolidate $1500 of your other bills for only $55 a month for five years?

A second major obstacle is that creditors often charge different rates to different customers. You may not know what rate you will get until after your loan has been approved. Moreover, many creditors do not advertise their terms. Automobile finance companies often advertise rates for new car transactions, but how often do you see bank or small loan company rates advertised specifically? Instead, you are more likely to see statements like "low bank rates" or "you're good for more." As a result, price comparison for credit costs cannot be done casually, by looking at price tags, but instead requires asking questions of the potential creditor.

A third major obstacle is that you may not know whether a given creditor will consider you to be creditworthy. (Neither, for that matter, may the creditor, at least not without some investigation.) Further, you are unlikely to know the minimum criteria the creditor uses to determine creditworthiness, and you may have heard of examples of creditor rejections which seemed arbitrary to you. Thus, like many consumers, you might end up approaching creditors "hat in hand," without knowing whether they will even do business with you. In contrast, you normally expect a seller of goods to do business with *any* buyer who offers cash.

One question to keep in mind as you study the material in this chapter is whether these obstacles have been overcome, or at least reduced, by TIL.

3. ALTERNATIVES TO COMPULSORY DISCLOSURE

Mandatory disclosure laws have been used in an enormous variety of situations. There are warnings not only on consumer contracts, see U3C § 3.203, but also on cigarette packages and x-ray machines and toasters and children's toys. These warnings and other disclosures have larger purposes such as increasing competition or consumer safety. But if these things are the real goals, why not regulate them directly instead of relying on disclosure laws? I.e., why not simply require low prices or safe toys, rather than simply warn consumers to watch out for high prices and unsafe toys?

As we will see later in this book, disclosure laws are not the whole story, and there is much direct regulation of consumer transactions. Laws regulating the cost of credit have been around for thousands of years, for example. In Chapters 11 and 12, we will examine their modern counterparts in detail. There are also many substantive regulations of other aspects of most consumer contracts. This type of regulation has increased dramatically during the past two decades. Does this mean that disclosure laws are not as important? As you study the material in this chapter, you should ask yourself (occasionally) whether legislative responses other than disclosure laws might better achieve the goals they seek to accomplish.

4. ANTECEDENTS OF TRUTH IN LENDING

There were some early efforts by the Federal Trade Commission to deal with the problem of credit disclosure, especially the potential for deception caused by the various non-uniform ways of stating interest rates.

FORD MOTOR COMPANY v. FEDERAL TRADE COMMISSION

United States Court of Appeals, Sixth Circuit, 1941.
120 F.2d 175.

HAMILTON, CIRCUIT JUDGE.

This is a petition by the Ford Motor Company to review an order of the Federal Trade Commission requiring it to cease and desist from the use of the word "six percent" or the figure and symbol "6%" in certain forms of advertising in connection with the cost of, or the additional charge for, the use of a deferred or installment payment plan of purchasing automobiles manufactured by it.

The so-called "six percent plan" of financing the retail sale of automobiles was first used in 1935 by the General Motors Corporation, through its wholly-owned subsidiary, the General Motors Acceptance Corporation and was as follows:

"General Motors Acceptance
Corporation

"Reduces Time Payment Costs
"On New Cars
"With a new 6% Plan
"Simple as A, B, C

"A—Take Your Unpaid Balance

"B—Add Cost of Insurance

"C—Multiply by 6%—12 Months' plan

"(One-half of one percent per month for periods more or less than 12 months)

"That's your whole financing cost. No extras. No service fees. No other charges.*

" * In some states a small legal documentary fee is required.

"GMAC announces today a new, economical way to buy any new General Motors car from General Motors dealers all over the United States.

"It's the plan you've been waiting for—a plan you can understand at a glance. It is far simpler and more economical than any other automobile time payment arrangement you've ever tried.

"Actually as simple as A, B, C—this new plan provides for convenient time payments of the unpaid balance on your car—including cost of insurance and a financing cost of 6%. This represents a considerable reduction in the cost of financing car purchases. It is not 6% interest, but simply a convenient multiplier anyone can use and understand. Nothing is added in the way of so-called service or carrying charges. There are no extras. Simply a straightforward, easy-to-understand transaction.

"This single step brings the world's finest cars within reach of thousands who have long needed new cars. When you buy a new Cadillac or Buick, Chevrolet or Pontiac, Oldsmobile or LaSalle, on this new plan, you actually save money!

* * *

"(Block here asking owners to make comparison with other finance plan.)

"Offered Only by Dealers in
Chevrolet Cars & Trucks—Pontiac
Oldsmobile—Buick—LaSalle
Cadillac"

General Motors, through its subsidiaries, published many thousands of advertisements featuring this so-called "6% plan," some with the above explanation, others merely referring to a "6%" plan without explanation.

Other leading automobile manufacturing concerns promptly announced similar plans, all featuring the "6%" plan, determined approximately in the same manner as the General Motors, the first to do so being Chrysler, followed by Nash Motors, Reo, Hudson, Graham–Paige, Packard and the petitioner, all appearing in advertisements in newspapers of general and wide circulation and all featuring in a conspicuous manner, the symbol "6%" or the words "six percent," and all determined in the same manner as the plan of petitioner.

* * *

In January 1936, petitioner announced it had adopted the "6%" plan and issued throughout the country the advertisement found in the margin.

Petitioner published many similar advertisements, some with the explanatory data in the advertisement quoted in the margin, others merely referring to the plan as follows:

"Ask your Ford dealers about the new $25–a–month new U.C.C. 6% finance plan."

"6% Plan of Financing. Total cost of credit is only ½% monthly on original unpaid balance and insurance.

"(6% for 12 months)"

* * *

The "6%" plan was computed in actual practice as follows:

On a new car, the purchase price of which is $643 and on which the purchaser makes a down payment of $243, there is an unpaid balance of $400 due and if the dealer furnishes the insurance, its cost on the above transaction would be $15, the total balance to be paid by the purchaser would be $415 and where this amount is paid according to the 6% plan (or ½ of 1% a month) in eighteen consecutive monthly payments of substantially $25 each, the charge of ½ of 1% a month for 18 months, or 9% on $415 would be $37.35, which, added to the original balance of $415, makes a total sum of $452.35.

This same transaction with an unpaid balance of $415 paid in a like manner at $25 a month over a period of eighteen months on a straight 6% simple interest per annum basis, computed on the declining balances as reduced by monthly installments, would amount to $19.34 interest charge or $18.01 less than the charge made pursuant to petitioner's plan. Comparative tables prepared by an expert accountant in evidence in the case indicated that the credit charge under petitioner's "6%" plan amounted to approximately 11½% simple annual interest.

The 6% plans of all of petitioner's competitors were also computed in the above described manner and the average member of the public was under the impression the "6%" plan as advertised by petitioner and the other manufacturers meant 6% simple interest annually on the remaining balance after deducting each successive monthly payment.

The cars manufactured by petitioner at Dearborn, Michigan, and sold through retail dealers to the retail purchasers thereof throughout the United States and in the District of Columbia are in the regular flow of interstate commerce. The Commission found that the statements contained in petitioner's advertising matter with reference to its "6%" plan had the tendency to mislead and deceive, and did mislead and deceive, a substantial part of the purchasing public into the erroneous belief that petitioner's finance plan or method as outlined contemplates a simple 6% interest charge upon the deferred and unpaid balance of the purchase price of cars and tended to cause, and has caused, the public to purchase automobiles from the petitioner through its dealers and agents because of this mistaken belief, when the actual credit charge, computed in accordance with the "6%" plan, amounts to approximately 11½% simple annual interest on the unpaid balance of the installments due on cars sold. It also found that these acts and practices of petitioner tended to unfairly divert trade to the petitioner and its dealers from competitors who correctly represented the cost of the credit charges for purchasing cars on the installment or deferred payment plan and a substantial injury had been done by petitioner to competitors in commerce among and between the various states of the United States and the District of Columbia.

The order to cease and desist of the Commission is found in the margin.

* * *

The relevant portion of Section 5 of the Federal Trade Commission Act as it read at the time the present complaint was issued, Act of September 26, 1914, c. 311, 38 Stat. 717, 719, 720, 15 U.S.C.A. § 45, is as follows: "That unfair methods of competition in [interstate and foreign] commerce are hereby declared unlawful."

* * *

Unfair methods of competition as used in the Act may consist generally of false advertising of a product, process or method which misleads, or has the capacity or tendency to mislead, the purchasing public into buying such product, process or method in the belief it is acquiring one essentially different. The question does not depend upon the purpose of the advertisement nor upon the good or bad faith of the advertiser. The point for consideration here is whether, under the facts and circumstances in connection with the publication of the advertisement, the language in and of itself, without regard to good or bad faith, is calculated to deceive the buying public into believing it is purchasing petitioner's cars at one price when in fact it is purchasing them at another. A prerequisite to the application of the statute in any case is the unfair interference with interstate trade and such deception of the public as to cause it to buy and pay for something which it is in fact not getting.

Petitioner contends that the method of competition here complained of is not unfair within the meaning of the Act nor of the foregoing general rule, as it long has been the established practice of automobile manufacturers and vendors of merchandise on the deferred payment plan to charge an advance over what would be charged in a cash sale and that it also has been the common practice of banks and small loan companies to advertise loans with a percentage added to the principal payable over fixed periods without calculating interest upon a declining balance. It also charges that the Federal Housing Administration and the Federal Electric Home and Farm Authority, two governmental agencies, use the same plan. It thus argues that the present advertisements were subject to the interpretation only that petitioner was adding a charge to the cash price of its cars because of the extension of credit to the purchaser.

The practices in the automobile industry or those in similar related enterprises are immaterial, if petitioner's advertisements misled the members of the public into purchasing its cars at a higher cost than they otherwise would have paid.

A method inherently unfair does not cease to be so because the falsity of the public representation has become so well known to those engaged in identical or similar enterprises as to no longer deceive them.

The average individual does not make, and often is incapable of making, minute calculations to determine the cost of property purchased on the deferred payment plan. Mechanization, industrialization, and urbanization have transformed the structure of our society and raised to the proportions of a major social problem, the protection of the installment purchaser against his own ignorance and the pressure of his need.

The present advertisement must be considered from the view of the prospective purchasers of petitioner's cars and, in determining its capacity or tendency to mislead, must be judged from its general fabric, not its single threads.

* * *

The primary consideration in carrying out the purpose of the present Act is the promotion and continuance of free enterprise and competition in interstate commerce. Installment credit in varying forms is widely used in this country in the purchase of many types of property and especially affects the manufacturers of automobiles. No one can deny it is in the public interest in the sale on credit of such devices to prevent the use of methods which have a tendency and capacity to mislead the purchasing public and to unfairly damage the manufacturer's present or potential competitors and that such practices may be restrained. * * * When misleading advertisements attract customers by means of deception perpetrated by the advertiser, it is presumed that business is thereby unfairly diverted from a competitor, who truthfully advertises his process, method or goods.

* * *

Advertising goes hand in hand with volume of production and retail distribution. It operates to increase the demand for and availability of goods and to develop quickly consumers' acceptance of the manufactured products. Expressed another way, it breaks down consumers' resistance, creates consumers' acceptance and develops consumers' demand.

* * *

Cease and desist orders of the Commission should go no further than reasonably necessary to correct the evil complained of and preserve the rights of competitors and the public and we are of the opinion that the order here did not violate this rule, but was necessary to protect the public against the species of deception alleged in the complaint. The Commission's findings are supported by substantial evidence. Petition denied and order of Commission affirmed.

Notes

1. Since the FTC's order was affirmed, shouldn't that have established a sufficient law of deceptive advertising of credit terms? Why didn't it? Do you think it would have been better to have continued the case law approach (as in *Ford*) to these problems, rather than the "affirmative action" approach in TILA? See also Tashof v. Federal Trade Commission, 437 F.2d 707 (D.C.Cir.1970).

2. Ford used the "add-on" formulation in its advertising, and the FTC found it deceptive when compared with "simple annual" interest. Did the FTC find that consumers understood the "6%" ads to state simple interest? If "add-on" computations were commonplace even in the 1930s, how could Ford's use of this formula constitute an unfair method of competition?

3. As the *Ford* case reflects, before the Truth in Lending Act, perhaps the largest problem in the disclosure of credit costs was lack of uniformity. The National Commission on Consumer Finance (NCCF) described the situation as follows in its 1972 report:

> Prior to enactment of TIL, information given consumers about their credit arrangements ranged from very little to what TIL now requires. Most consumers were told the amount of their monthly payments and the due dates. Provisions for additional information varied widely among credit grantors, types of credit, and states.
>
> The greatest lack of uniformity was in the quotation of the amount and rate of the finance charge. Some credit grantors provided neither figure, showing only the number and amount of monthly payments and the dollar sum. While many creditors disclosed the dollar amount of the finance charge or provided enough data so that it could be ascertained, they stated the *rate* of charge in a variety of ways.
>
> (1) In some cases no rate of finance charge was quoted.
>
> (2) Retailers, finance companies and some banks often quoted the rate as a dollar add-on—an expression of the dollar amount of the finance charge per annum in relation to the *initial* unpaid balance. For instance, the finance charge on a new car loan might have been stated as $7 per $100 per year, indicating that on a 3–year loan of $2,000 the dollar amount of the finance charge was $420 ($140 × 3 years). The APR on such a contract is 12.83 percent. Prior to the effective date of TIL, add-on rates were heavily advertised.
>
> (3) Commercial and industrial banks often quoted rates on a discount basis—a statement of dollars per $100 of initial unpaid bal-

ance on the assumption that the finance charge was deducted from the face amount of the note at the time credit was extended. A charge of $7 per $100 of initial unpaid balance *discounted* for 3 years is equivalent to an APR of 16.01 percent.

(4) Many consumer finance companies, almost all credit unions, and most commercial banks and retailers offering revolving credit accounts stated a monthly rate applied to a defined balance. Banks and retailers often quoted a rate of 1½ percent applied monthly. If applied to daily unpaid balances from the date of credit extension, as in the case of credit unions, the APR was equivalent to 12 times the monthly rate.

(5) A final procedure was to fragment the finance charge so that part appeared as an add-on or discount rate and part as a flat fee or extra charge. For example, industrial loan companies in Georgia charged 8 percent a year discount (to 18 months) plus a flat fee of 8 percent on the first $600 of initial unpaid balance. Thus a 6–month loan of $500 carried a finance charge of $68.14 or an annual rate of 45.33 percent.

National Commission on Consumer Finance, *Consumer Credit in the United States* 169–70 (1972). Obviously, comparative shopping was difficult or impossible under these conditions.

4. Did you understand the underlying transaction in the Ford case? Understanding how the financing arrangements work in a typical automobile purchase can be useful. In many ways it is a prototype of several consumer transactions you will encounter throughout this book.

There are three players in the auto purchase game: the consumer, the dealer, and the finance company. (Actually there are others as well, including the manufacturer, one or more insurance companies, etc.; but for our purposes we can ignore them.) Let's say you have just agreed to buy a new Fuddmobile from Elmer's Auto for $8,500. After making a down payment of $1,000, you will finance the $7500 balance over three years at, say, 10% APR (more on what "APR" means shortly). Your payments will be $242 a month for 36 months. You will pay a total, over the three year period, of $8712. The extra $1212 is the "finance charge," or the price you must pay for the privilege of buying on credit. (More on this shortly, too.)

In Elmer's office, you will sign a Retail Installment Sales Contract (or something similar). This contract will contain not only the credit and payment terms, but also such things as warranty terms and much more. The contract will also grant to Elmer a security interest in your car to secure payment of your credit obligation. Among other things, this security interest will give Elmer the right to repossess your car if you default on the loan.

Now Elmer, like most dealers, probably does not have the financial resources to handle customers' credit transactions. He needs cash to buy more inventory, pay his employees, and so on. So, to get some cash, Elmer will assign his rights in (or "sell") your contract to a finance company, Fudd Motor Acceptance Corp. (FMAC). You will learn about this assignment because you will soon get a little coupon booklet in the mail from

FMAC. The booklet will instruct you to make all your monthly payments to FMAC, not to Elmer, and it is FMAC who will come looking for your car if you default.

SECTION B. DISCLOSURE IN CREDIT TRANSACTIONS: THE TRUTH IN LENDING ACT

1. BACKGROUND

Disclosure of the costs of credit in consumer credit transactions has been through several phases of development, and its history generally illustrates the possibilities and problems of consumer protection legislation. The *Ford Motor* case, for example, illustrates one approach—use of a statute with very generalized provisions ("misleading and deceptive") to regulate voluntary disclosures by creditors. Of course, this worked only if creditors chose to advertise, and only as long as they were subject to the then limited jurisdiction of the FTC. The Truth in Lending Act, in contrast, represents the other extreme—compulsory disclosure and regulation through a detailed statute.

The first draft of truth in lending legislation, introduced in the late 1950s, followed the generalized approach of the FTC analysis and would have required creditor simply (a) to disclose the interest rate to be charged, and (b) to disclose that interest rate as a simple annual rate on a declining balance. The reaction of the consumer credit industry was to ask for clarification, rather than to debate whether compulsory disclosure was warranted or not. The debate then focused upon what charges should be considered as within "interest", and how to calculate the appropriate rate. The proponents of the statute tried to respond to the ever-more-detailed requests for clarification by adding details through many redrafts over approximately a decade, but there were always more potential uncertainties.

By 1968, it was apparent that the statute could never be drafted to the degree of certainty that the creditors wanted. Instead, the statute could be made relatively clear for most typical transactions, and the Federal Reserve Board would be given the power to issue regulations to clear up any remaining problems or uncertainties. This decision made, the Truth in Lending Act was enacted in 1968, to become effective in 1969, 15 U.S.C.A. § 1601 et seq. The Board issued Regulation Z to fill in the statutory gaps, and it continues to amend Regulation Z whenever further (potential) ambiguities and uncertainties are discovered.

All of this was fine in theory, but the actual experience was something else. Together, the statute and regulations were technically complex, and difficult to understand. After a few years, a huge body of case law and administrative interpretations had been built up. All this led to "disclosure statements" which kept increasing in length and complexity. Creditors found it nearly impossible to comply, and it became great sport among consumer lawyers to nit-pick disclosure statements for violations. Moreover, there was growing evidence that consumers couldn't understand them anyway.

These problems led to the Truth in Lending Simplification and Reform Act of 1980 (effective 1982), the present law. The simplification was intended primarily to reduce the amount of information creditors had to disclose to consumers, and to reduce creditor liability for violations of the Act. There is some disagreement as to whether the Reform Act has accomplished all of its goals. But there is no doubt that it is now much easier for creditors to comply and much harder for consumers to sue for violations. The case law has diminished from a flood to a trickle. See Rohner, Truth in Lending "Simplified": Simplified?, 56 N.Y.U.L.Rev. 999 (1981).

The Federal Consumer Credit Protection Act (CCPA) has been expanded and further amended several times. For example, in 1970, §§ 132 through 134 were added to deal with unauthorized credit card transactions. These amendments were followed by the addition of The Fair Credit Reporting Act (FCRA), §§ 601–22, in 1971; the Fair Credit Billing Act (FCBA), §§ 161–171, in 1973; the Equal Credit Opportunity Act (ECOA), §§ 701–09, in 1974 and 1976; the Consumer Leasing Act (CLA), §§ 181–187, in 1976; the Fair Debt Collection Practices Act (FDCPA), §§ 801–18, in 1977; and the Electronic Funds Transfer Act (EFTA), §§ 901–20, in 1979. The CCPA "tree" then stopped growing branches, although none of the acts has been repealed, and only the basic disclosure provisions of TILA have been modified significantly.

To work at all in the truth in lending area, you must know more than the TILA; you must also become familiar with the Federal Reserve Board's implementing regulation, known as Regulation Z. Reg. Z is found officially in 12 C.F.R. Part 226; it is also found in West's Selected Commercial Statutes booklet. Regulation Z contains the gory details of the disclosures and other rules creditors must follow. Like the statute Reg. Z was completely rewritten in 1980. While it is still quite complex, most students find the regulation much easier to read than the statute, although there are times when this will not work. The Board has also issued (and continually updates) a lengthy Official Staff Commentary on Reg. Z. This commentary is essential for practitioners, since it often gives examples and answers questions raised by ambiguities in the regulation.

Note on the Effect of Regulation Z

What weight should the courts give Reg. Z or the Board's official or unofficial comments? Courts have always treated administrative interpretations with a certain degree of deference. After all, an agency which specializes in a particular subject matter is likely to have a good deal of useful insight. After the decision of the United States Supreme Court in Ford Motor Credit Co. v. Milhollin, 444 U.S. 555, 100 S.Ct. 790, 63 L.Ed.2d

22 (1980), however, the Federal Reserve Board's positions have taken on even greater significance in TIL matters.

In *Milhollin,* the issue was whether acceleration clauses had to be disclosed in closed-end credit transactions. Neither the statute nor the regulation addressed this issue (then or now), and the Courts of Appeal had disagreed. The Board, however, had taken the position that this disclosure was not required. The Supreme Court ruled that in all truth in lending cases, the Board's opinions and interpretations should be followed unless they are "demonstrably irrational." 444 U.S. at 565, 100 S.Ct. at 796. As a practical matter, this ruling means that the Board's regulations and comments are law.

Note on Rate Calculations

Truth in Lending uses the term "annual percentage rate," or "APR." It is based on "actuarial" or simple interest calculations. For students (and teachers) who have difficulty mastering the arithmetic of the various methods of computing rates, we supply the following. It is one of the clearer explanations your authors have seen. (It is worth reading carefully both here and also later in connection with the material on rate regulation in Chapter 11.)

OEO LEGAL SERVICES TRAINING PROGRAM, MEMORANDUM

(April 1972).*

I. INTRODUCTION

[T]he Federal Truth in Lending Act * * * provides a standardized method of computing and disclosing finance charges * * * and an annual percentage rate (APR) * * *. The federal standard [for computing an APR] is computed on an annual basis by the actuarial method while state statutes concerned with imposing maximum rates are inevitably phrased in terms of the add-on or discount method. * * *

The distinction between the different methods is significant. For example, an extension of $100 in credit for one year, payable in 12 monthly regular installments at 8 percent, involves the following Finance Charges and APR's depending upon the method of computing the 8 percent:

Computation Method	Finance Charge	APR
Actuarial	$4.39	8%
Add–On	8.00	14.45%
Discount	8.70	15.68%

* * *

II. COMMON METHODS OF COMPUTING FINANCE CHARGES

A. *Why Simple Math Doesn't Help*

When confronted with the task of computing the unknown of any one of the four key variables in a credit transaction—finance charge (C), amount of credit extended (A), rate (R) or period of time extended in years (T)—the almost instinctive response is to solve for the unknown through the use of the formula: $C = A \times R \times T$. Thus, $8.00 is the finance charge on the $100.00 credit extended at 8% for one year. Right? Yes, if the total debt (A + C) is paid in a single installment at the end of the period. But the formula does not work if any part of the total debt is paid prior to the expiration of the full period. The reason is that the debtor has not had the total use of the amount of the credit for the full period.

When portions of the credit are paid back regularly, at even intervals throughout the full period (as is typical for consumer credit), the departure from the formula is even more extreme. In the case of monthly payments, that portion of the credit which is repaid in the first installment has been enjoyed by the debtor for only one month and has not been properly entered into a formula which contemplates the use of the credit for an entire year. The standard simple formula cannot work, therefore, to solve for any of the variables of consumer credit. For example, in the case of a charge of $8.00 for $100.00 payable in 12 monthly installments, the rate is 14.45 percent when expressed as an APR.

B. *The Actuarial, or Interest on Declining Balances, Method*

This is also referred to as the method to obtain "true" or "simple" interest. And, since it is the method required by Truth in Lending, it is rapidly becoming known as the APR method. This is the classical method, interest having been calculated by this method for at least a couple of thousand years, with the sole exception of consumer credit. By custom, and now by Federal law, the rate is expressed *per year.* For periods less than a year the ratio is constant; at 12% per year the rate per month is 1%, or per quarter, 3%, etc.

The actuarial method is simple and readily adaptable to an open ledger bookkeeping approach of calculation. That is, if you know the APR and the amount of credit, you can compute, by use of the simple formula discussed above ($C = A \times R \times T$), the amount of each installment allocable to finance charges, the balance going to reduce the amount of credit outstanding. Thus, on $100.00 at an APR of 14.45% payable in monthly installments of $9.00 each:

Installment	Finance Charge	Repayment per Installment	Balance
1	$1.21	$ 7.79	$92.21
2	1.11	7.89	84.32
3	1.02	7.98	76.34
etc.	etc.	etc.	etc.
12	$8.00	$100.00	

Using this approach you can, in a very backhanded way, analyze a transaction installment-by-installment and check the accuracy of a creditor's disclosures. On a 36 installment transaction this process can become a bit tedious. It only works, however, when approached one installment at a time. There is, unfortunately, no simple algebraic formula for the actuarial method whereby the rate can be conveniently solved for as an unknown (unless you enjoy solving equations which involve unknowns raised to a power equivalent to the number of installments).

The solution is to use the conversion tables prepared by the Federal Reserve for Truth in Lending (available for $1.00 from your nearest FED; reprinted in the Truth in Lending Handbook of the National Consumer Law Center. * * *

C. The Add–On Method

This method, generally contemplated by the statutes which regulate installment financing of goods and services, is probably the simplest to calculate. Statutes using the add-on method are typically phrased in terms of dollars per hundred per year. The simple formula can be used to check compliance with a statutory maximum. Merely apply simple multiplication of the add-on rate times the amount of credit extended times the years extended.

As indicated in II A, above, this formula disregards the fact that installments will be paid in monthly. That's the deceptive quality of add-ons. As a result the APR is, roughly usually just a bit less than double the add-on rate. For example, an 8 percent add-on for $100.00 for one year, payable in monthly installments, is the equivalent of 14.45% APR. To solve for the APR when the add-on rate or the finance charge is known to be accurate, you must use a conversion table.

D. The Discount Method

Traditionally, bankers have used this method of expressing rates, particularly for short term loans. Discount means that something has been subtracted, not added as in the add-on method. That means the finance charge (interest) is taken from the amount of credit extended at the outset, from the top so to speak. Thus, in the case of $100.00 at the 8% discount, for one year, the consumer actually gets only $92.00, not $100.00. Expressing the same transaction in add-on terms, since the debtor is getting only $92.00 and paying $8.00 finance charge, it is an add-on of 8.7%. The APR is 15.7%. The effect of discount rates then is not unlike add-on, except even more exaggerated. For short terms the discount rate will be about one-half of the true APR. At about one year it will start to become less than half and as the time for repayment extends, it will become a smaller and smaller percentage of the true APR. For example, an 8% discount rate is equivalent to 15.7% APR at one year, 17.3% at two years, 18.8% at three years and 22.3% at five. At 10 years of monthly installments, an 8% discount is the equivalent of 49.6% APR!

2. FORMAT—CLOSED–END AND OPEN–END TRANSACTIONS

The mandatory disclosure rules of the Truth in Lending Act are applicable to both "open-end" (revolving) credit and "closed-end" (fixed term) credit. The distinction between open- and closed-end credit is important, because both the form and the content of the required disclosures are different for each type. As a result, you should become familiar with them right away. A good place to start would be the definitions contained in Reg. Z § 226.2(a).

Most types of consumer transactions are easy to classify. A closed-end transaction usually involves a single loan or advance of funds, often in a purchase money transaction such as a new car loan or a home mortgage. An open-end transaction, on the other hand, is a revolving account. Here, the parties agree in advance that the borrower may engage in repeated transactions, and may also replenish or increase the amount of credit available by repayment. The prototype open-end arrangement is the credit card. Today, there are also more sophisticated types of open-end transactions such as home equity loans.

Problem 1

The form on the following page is the model form suggested by the Federal Reserve Board for closed-end credit sales. See Reg. Z, Appendix H–10. It is commonly referred to as the "federal box." From this disclosure statement, can you follow this transaction and the calculations represented in the form?

(a) What is the total cost of the car and its financing? What are the component parts of that cost?

(b) What amount does Ms. Green have to pay in installments? How was the difference paid? How much is each installment? How often? How long?

(c) Did she get a good deal on the *credit* part of the transaction? What rate is she paying for credit?

(d) Did you have any difficulty following the figures and calculations, or are there problems in comprehending it at a glance? Can you improve its comprehensibility? How? Are all the figures presented of equal importance? If not, which ones are crucial? Are they "conspicuous"? Is it helpful to have the APR disclosed to two decimal places?

(e) Compare this form to the one in Problem 2A, infra. Which is more comprehensible? Is the primary difference the format, or the underlying transaction?

(f) Identify each of the items which is a required TIL disclosure under Reg. Z § 226.18.

(g) Is it important to know that there was a $25 application fee charged in this transaction? Where does it show up in the disclosures?

Big Wheel Auto   Alice Green

ANNUAL PERCENTAGE RATE The cost of your credit as a yearly rate.	FINANCE CHARGE The dollar amount the credit will cost you.	Amount Financed The amount of credit provided to you or on your behalf.	Total of Payments The amount you will have paid after you have made all payments as scheduled.	Total Sale Price The total cost of your purchase on credit, including your downpayment of $ _1500 –_
14.84 %	$1496.80	$6107.50	$7604.30	$9129.30

You have the right to receive at this time an itemization of the Amount Financed.
☐ I want an itemization.   ☒ I do not want an itemization.

Your payment schedule will be:

Number of Payments	Amount of Payments	When Payments Are Due
36	$211.23	Monthly beginning 6-1-81

Insurance
Credit life insurance and credit disability insurance are not required to obtain credit, and will not be provided unless you sign and agree to pay the additional cost.

Type	Premium	Signature	
Credit Life	$120 –	I want credit life insurance.	_alice Green_ Signature
Credit Disability		I want credit disability insurance. Signature	
Credit Life and Disability		I want credit life and disability insurance. Signature	

Security: You are giving a security interest in:
☒ the goods being purchased.
☐ _____.

Filing fees $ _12.50_   Non-filing insurance $ _____

Late Charge: If a payment is late, you will be charged $10.

Prepayment: If you pay off early, you
☒ may   ☐ will not   have to pay a penalty.
☒ may   ☐ will not   be entitled to a refund of part of the finance charge.

See your contract documents for any additional information about nonpayment, default, any required repayment in full before the scheduled date, and prepayment refunds and penalties.

I have received a copy of this statement.
alice Green   _5-1-81_
Signature   Date

_____
e means an estimate

Problem 2A

The form on the following page is from Meyers v. Clearview Dodge Sales, 539 F.2d 511 (5th Cir.1976), a classic TILA case from the pre-simplification era. It involves a closed-end transaction. Review this form and consider whether the information it discloses is helpful to the consumer.

(a) Answer the same questions for this form that you answered for the form in Problem 1.

(b) Review items numbered 1 through 14 in the Meyers form in light of the disclosure rules now required in Reg. Z § 226.18. What information is retained from the existing form? Which items are dropped or modified? Are important items deleted? Why?

84-291-5163 (12/71) Louisiana

SALE AND CHATTEL MORTGAGE

No.

Buyer's (Mortgagor's) and Co-Buyer's Name and Address	Seller's (Mortgagee's) Name and Address
Cheryl Meyers 316 33nd st. N. O. La.	Clearview Dodge Sales, Inc. 4848 Veterans Blvd. Metairie, La.

The undersigned Seller (mortgagee) hereby sells, and the undersigned Buyer (which means Buyer [mortgagor] or Buyers [mortgagors], jointly and severally), having been quoted both a time price and a lower cash price, hereby purchases from Seller on a time price basis, subject to the terms and conditions set forth herein, including the reverse hereof (which are incorporated herein by reference), the below described motor vehicle(s) (hereinafter called "property"), delivery and acceptance of which in good order hereby are acknowledged by Buyer. In order to secure payment of said Total of Payments and the promissory note executed herewith and any other indebtedness which now exists or may hereafter accrue from Buyer to Seller and assigns pursuant hereto, not to exceed a maximum amount of 50% of the original principal of the said note (without this mortgage being a waiver by Seller of the vendor's lien and privilege which are hereby expressly reserved), Buyer does hereby specially mortgage, affect and hypothecate the property to the Seller and assigns forever, the property to remain so mortgaged and hypothecated until all amounts due hereunder, and under said note, are fully paid in cash. Seller may cause the property to be seized and sold under executory or other legal process should such action be required pursuant to the conditions under this mortgage, in the manner provided by applicable law. Buyer binds himself not to alienate the property to the prejudice of this mortgage and hereby confesses judgement in favor of Seller or any subsequent holder of said note for the principal, delinquency and collection charges, interest if any, attorney's fees, taxes, assessments, license fees and all other expenses, charges and costs to the extent permitted by applicable law. Buyer hereby expressly waives the benefit of appraisement and all laws conferring the same, and expressly waives the issuance of the notice and demand for payment provided by Article 2639 and the delays prescribed by Article 2331 of the Louisiana Code of Civil Procedure or any other laws pertaining thereto, Buyer hereby expressly agreeing to the immediate seizure of said property in the event of suit herein. The property will be located in the Parish of _____ , State of Louisiana.

	Year	Make	Cyl	Model	Body Style	Vehicle No.
☐ NEW ☒ USED	1972	Dodge	8	Swinger	2 Dr.	LH23G2R138710

CHECK ALL SPEC EQUIP: ☐ RADIO ☐ HEATER ☐ AUTO TRANS. ☐ POWER STEERING ☐ POWER BRAKES ☐ POWER WINDOWS ☐ POWER SEATS ☐ AIR CONDITION ☐ DESCRIBE OTHER

DESCRIPTION OF TRADE-IN	YEAR	MODEL	MAKE

DISCLOSURE STATEMENT

1. Cash Price (including accessories, delivery, installation charges and sales taxes, if any)	$ 3534.20	***4.** PHYSICAL DAMAGE INSURANCE against accidental damage to the property for a term of **12** months as checked: ☒ Comprehensive Coverage; ☒ Fire-Theft and Additional Coverage; ☒ $100.00 Deductible Collision; ☐ Towing and Labor (if included, cost of $_____ is included in premium). Insurance settlement will be based upon actual cash value of property at time of loss, not exceeding limits of liability set forth in policy, and payable to Buyer, Seller or assignee of Seller, as interests may appear. **BUYER MAY CHOOSE THE PERSON THROUGH WHICH THE INSURANCE IS TO BE OBTAINED.**
2. Downpayment: Consisting of –		
a. Cash Downpayment	$ 400.20	
b. Trade-in	n.a.	
c. Total Downpayment (2a & b)	400.20	****4.** CREDIT LIFE AND/OR ACCIDENT AND HEALTH INSURANCE according to terms and conditions set forth in policy or certificate of insurance issued by (check)
3. Unpaid Balance of Cash Price (1 – 2c)	3134.00	☐ The John Hancock Mutual Life Insurance Company, Boston, Mass., under its Group Policy No. 17680-GCI.
4. Other Charges: Consisting of –		IF OTHER POLICY, ☐ NAME INSURER HOME OFFICE ADDRESS
* a. Physical Damage Insurance	163.00	See Notice to Buyer on reverse side of Buyer's Copy if Credit Life Insurance is Authorized
** b. Credit Life Insurance	n.a.	**BUYER IS NOT REQUIRED TO OBTAIN CREDIT LIFE AND/OR ACCIDENT AND HEALTH INSURANCE COVERAGE.**
** c. Accident & Health Insurance	n.a.	The undersigned hereby affirms that (i) if a charge for credit life insurance is set forth in item 4b of this Disclosure Statement or (ii) if a charge for credit accident
d. Taxes (not included in Cash Price)	n.a.	and health insurance is set forth in item 4c of this Disclosure Statement, each such
e. Official Fees	n.a.	charge was disclosed in writing to the undersigned prior to the execution by the
f.	n.a.	undersigned of this statement and after such disclosure the undersigned specifically
g.	n.a.	affirms that the undersigned desires to obtain the insurance for which such charge,
h. Total Other Charges (4a, b, c, d, e, f & g)	163.00	if any, is set forth in item 4b or item 4c. The undersigned agrees that no insurance
5. Unpaid Balance (Amount Financed) (3 + 4h)	3297.00	coverage is included in this contract unless a charge for such coverage is included in
6. FINANCE CHARGE	791.16	item 4b or 4c.
7. Deferred Payment Price (1 + 4h + 6)	4488.36	
8. Total of Payments (5 + 6)	4088.16	BUYER'S SIGNATURE X DATE
9. ANNUAL PERCENTAGE RATE	14.5%	CO-BUYER'S SIGNATURE X xxxxxxxxxxxxxxxxxxxxxxxxxxxxxxxxxx DATE

10. Repayment Schedule: The Total of Payments is payable by Buyer at Seller's office designated herein, or at such office of any holder of this mortgage, in **36** instalments of $ **113.56** each, and one final instalment of $ **0**, commencing on the **10** day of **August**, 19 **72**, and on the same day of each successive month thereafter, in accordance with the terms of a certain promissory note of even date herewith, which note, having been paraphed 'Ne Varietur' by the undersigned Notary Public for identification with this Act, has been delivered to the Seller who acknowledges receipt thereof.

11. Balloon Payment: $ _____ due, _____ , 19 ___ Insert amount of any payment which is more than twice the amount of an otherwise regularly scheduled equal payment. Balloon Payment shall be paid when due and may not be refinanced.

12. Delinquency Charges: Seller may collect, and Buyer hereby agrees to pay, a delinquency and collection charge on any instalment which shall not have been paid within 10 days after the date on which it becomes due and payable, in an amount not exceeding 5% of each such unpaid instalment, or $5, whichever is less. In addition to such delinquency charge, Buyer shall reimburse Seller for actual out-of-pocket collection expenses not exceeding $150 and attorneys fees of 25% of the total amount due and payable hereunder, with a minimum of $15 if this Sale and Chattel mortgage is referred to an attorney for collection.

13. Security Interest: Seller shall have a mortgage, lien and privilege, in the property until all amounts due under this Sale and Chattel Mortgage are paid in full.

14. Prepayment Rebate: Buyer may prepay his obligations under this contract in full at any time prior to maturity and receive a refund credit computed in accordance with the Rule of 78s. Such rebate will be computed after first deducting from the finance charge an acquisition charge in the amount of $25.00; provided, however, that no acquisition charge will be made if more than one half of the term of this mortgage shall have elapsed. No rebate will be made in an amount of less than $1.00.

DECLARATION OF GOOD HEALTH—Applicable Where A Charge Has Been Authorized in 4b Above and Insurance Under John Hancock Group Policy No. 17680-GCI is Proposed: I, the Buyer proposed for life insurance, in order to induce John Hancock to effect such insurance, do hereby declare that to the best of my knowledge and belief I am now in good health. I hereby authorize any physician or hospital to disclose to John Hancock in the event of my death all information concerning my medical history prior to the date of this contract.

LIABILITY INSURANCE COVERAGE FOR BODILY INJURY AND PROPERTY DAMAGE CAUSED TO OTHERS IS NOT INCLUDED.
Notice to the Buyer: Do not sign this contract before you read it (BOTH SIDES) or if it contains any blank spaces. You are entitled to an exact copy of the contract you sign.

Executed this **26** day of **June**, 19 **72**, and a completely filled-in copy delivered to Buyer who acknowledges receipt thereof. Accepted by the Seller and assigned to Chrysler Credit Corporation in accordance with the terms of the Assignment set forth on the reverse hereof.

Buyer Signs X S/Cheryl Meyers	Co-Buyer Signs X		
Seller: Clearview Dodge Sales, Inc.	By S/A. J. Keller		Title Sect Treas
Witness X S/N. Revon	Witness X S/L. Marino		

State of Louisiana, Parish of _____ Orleans _____ SS: 　　**AFFIDAVIT OF WITNESS**

On this ___26___ day of ___June_____, 19 _72_, before me, a Notary Public personally appeared ___L. Marino_____, a subscribing witness to the foregoing document, well known to me, who, being first duly sworn, did depose and say that said instrument was executed by the parties thereto in the presence of the affiant and of the other attesting witness as their free act and deed and that their genuine signatures appear thereto.

Subscribed and sworn to before me the day and year aforesaid.

Notary Public	Witness
S/D. Casey	S/L Marino
	X

PROMISSORY NOTE

$ _____4088.16_____　　Metairie _____, Louisiana, _____June 26_____, 19 _72_.
　(Total of Payments)

FOR VALUE RECEIVED, I (we jointly, severally and in solido) promise to pay to BEARER the sum of

___Four Thousand Eighty Eight and 16/100_____ dollars ($ _4088.16_) in
　　　　　　　　　　　(Total of Payments)

instalments of $ ___113.56_____ each, and one final instalment of $ _____, commencing on the ___10___ day of __August_____, 19 _72_, and on the same day of each successive month thereafter until paid, together with a delinquent and collection charge on each instalment in default for 10 days or more in an amount not in excess of 5% of each such instalment, or $5, whichever is less, plus actual out-of-pocket expenses of collection not to exceed $150 and attorney's fees of 25% of the total amount due and payable hereunder, with a minimum of $15, if this promissory note is referred to an attorney for collection. If any instalment of this note be not paid when due or if the undersigned fails to comply with any of the terms and conditions of the Sale and Chattel Mortgage securing payment of this note, then all unpaid instalments shall, at holder's option immediately become due and payable without notice or demand. All parties hereto, including endorsers and guarantors, hereby severally waive presentment, demand for payment, protest and notice of non-payment and protest and diligence in bringing suit against any part hereto, and all endorsers and guarantors consent that the time of payment may be extended from time to time after maturity without notice. All exemptions are hereby waived.

(vertical text: RETURN Mortgage 19__ As per Sale and of this)

(vertical text: PAYMENT)

Buyer Signs	Co-Buyer Signs
X　　S/ Cheryl Meyers	X

　　　　　　　　　　　　　　　　　　　　　　　　　　　　　[B9853]

BUYER

Problem 2B

Redesign the document used by Clearview Dodge in the Meyers transaction so that it complies with present law, using the "federal box" form from Problem 1. Remember that the creditor will probably want to retain somewhere in the new contract *all* of the terms of the earlier contract. Remember, too, that everything found in the underlying contract will not appear in the TILA box. To get you started, here are some specific questions (refer to Reg. Z §§ 226.17 and 226.18 for additional help):

　　1. Where on the contract should the "federal box" be located? Must the TILA disclosures literally be placed in a black-bordered box, or are there other ways to group and segregate them?

　　2. Can the TILA disclosures include explanatory information about the security interest, the insurance coverage, the prepayment rebate, or the expected assignment of the contract to Chrysler Credit Corp.?

　　3. Can the box be rearranged so that the information is placed in a different order?

　　4. If the creditor decides to give the TILA disclosures on a separate piece of paper from the credit contract, may it include in the "box" information that identifies the transaction, such as the date, a contract number, and the consumer's name and signature?

GOLDBERG v. DELAWARE OLDS, INC.

United States District Court, District of Delaware, 1987.
670 F.Supp. 125

FARNAN, DISTRICT JUDGE.

This case arises under the Truth in Lending Act ("TILA"), 15 U.S.C. §§ 1601–1693r (1982). The Court has federal question jurisdiction * * *. The issue presented is whether, in a Conditional Sales Contract, an assignee-bank's right of set-off against deposits may be disclosed in the "Federal Box". For the reasons discussed below, I conclude that such information may be placed in the Federal Box. Summary judgment shall therefore be entered in favor of codefendants Delaware Olds, Inc. ("Delaware Olds") and Bank of Delaware ("the Bank").

I. FACTUAL BACKGROUND.

The material facts are not in dispute. Plaintiff Samuel E. Goldberg initiated this action after purchasing a car from Delaware Olds. * * * Delaware Olds immediately assigned the Contract to the Bank.

The Contract which memorialized the transaction was written on a standard form provided by the Bank. At issue in this lawsuit is the special, boxed-in section of the Contract entitled "DISCLOSURES REQUIRED BY FEDERAL LAW AND MADE BY SELLER" ("the Federal Box"). Under TILA, the Federal Box is a conspicuously segregated portion of the Contract containing federally-mandated disclosures. In the Contract between the Goldbergs and Delaware Olds, the Federal Box included the federally-required disclosures, as well as a disclosure that states: "If this CONTRACT is assigned to Bank of Delaware, it will have the right of set-off against deposits owed by it to BUYER."

The Goldbergs paid the entire amount due under the Contract within one year and shortly thereafter plaintiff Samuel Goldberg initiated this action against Delaware Olds, claiming that the disclosure in the Federal Box of the Bank's right of set-off violated the TILA and entitled plaintiff to an award of statutory damages. Pursuant to Fed.R. Civ.P. 14, Delaware Olds sought relief against the Bank as a third-party defendant, requesting indemnification from the Bank should Delaware Olds be held liable to the plaintiff. Because the Contract at issue was drafted entirely by the Bank and supplied to Delaware Olds as a form for use in originating automobile financing on behalf of the Bank, the Bank sought to intervene as a party defendant. The Court granted the Bank's Motion to Realign and the Bank now appears in this action as a party defendant.

II. CROSS–MOTIONS FOR SUMMARY JUDGMENT.

* * *

The TILA sets forth specific mandatory requirements relating to the form in which disclosures are to be made in closed-end credit transactions such as the one involved in this action. Certain information is to be "conspicuously segregated from all other terms, data or information provided in connection with a transaction. * * * " In the Official Staff Commentary the Board expressed a preference for segregating this information by outlining it in a box, by use of bold print dividing lines, or by some other method calculated to set off the mandatory disclosures from the rest of the Contract. The information which must be segregated from the rest of the Contract language is set forth in 12 C.F.R. § 226.18. The regulations mandate that the Federal Box "shall not contain any information not directly related to the disclosures required under § 226.18." The Bank contends that the disclosure of its right of set-off was required under TILA and Regulation Z as a security interest and, alternatively, that the information is directly related to the mandatory disclosure of a creditor's security interest and therefore permissible under 12 C.F.R. § 226.17(a). The plaintiff, on the other hand, argues that a right of set-off is not a security interest, nor is it information directly related to a security interest. In the alternative, plaintiff maintains that even if the Court is of the opinion that the Bank's right of set-off was a security interest, it was not a security interest of the non-bank creditor, Delaware Olds. I will discuss each of these contentions separately.

First, is the bank's right of set-off against a borrower's deposit accounts within the scope of the term "security interest"?

A review of the limited case law available and other authorities indicate that a bank's right of set-off against a depositor's account is not, within the ordinary understanding of the term, a security interest that would require disclosure under the TILA.

* * *

Revised Regulation Z defines the term "security interest" as follows:

> An interest in property that secures performance of a consumer credit obligation and that is recognized by state or federal law. It does not include incidental interest such as interest in proceeds, accessions, additions, fixtures, insurance proceeds * * * premium rebates, or interests in after acquired property. For purposes of disclosure under Section * * * 226.18 [closed-end disclosures], the term does not include an interest that arises solely by operation of law * * *.

Regulation Z, § 226.2(a)(25).

This definition of security interest is narrower than the definition set forth in the earlier Regulation Z, § 226.2(gg). The commentators acknowledge that a fair amount of post-revision confusion continues to surround the status of a right of set-off vis-a-vis security interest disclosures. *See, e.g.,* R. Rohner & F. Miller, *The Law of Truth In Lending,* 5-74 (1984). These commentators note that an early version of the proposed Commentary stated that set-offs were security interests and should be disclosed accordingly. However, the Board ultimately declined to include the "right of set-off" in subsequent proposed Commentaries or in the final text. Consequently, the disclosure of a right of set-off is not specifically treated in the Commentary. At least one commentator has stated that by not including set-off in the commentary to Regulation Z, it was intended that creditors rely on state law to determine whether it is disclosable in the Federal Box. I have examined Delaware law and have found nothing to indicate that the right of set-off is to be treated as either a statutory or non-statutory security interest. At best Delaware law is unclear.

Since I have concluded that the right of set-off is not a security interest and, therefore, the bank may not disclose set-off as a security interest in the Federal Box, it is necessary to discuss the issue of whether the bank's right of set-off is "directly related" to any of those items that must be placed in the Federal Box. I conclude that it is.

The regulations delineate the terms that must be segregated on the agreement and set forth separately in the Federal Box. Included in the list of information to be segregated is "the fact that the creditor has a or will acquire a security interest in the property purchased as part of the transaction, or in other property identified by item or type." 12 C.F.R. § 226.18(m). 12 C.F.R. § 226.17(a)(1) states that the Federal Box "shall not contain any information not *directly related* to the disclosures required under § 226.18" (emphasis added, footnotes omitted). The purpose of this change was to avoid "information overload." Since the bank's right to set-off is not a security interest, the issue becomes whether the right to set-off is "directly related" to the security interest assigned by Delaware Olds to the Bank.

The regulations do not define the term "directly related." The official commentary, however, offers several examples of what might be considered "directly related." This list is meant to provide examples only and is not intended to be exclusive. Among the items of information considered "directly related" are a description of a grace period after which a late payment charge will be imposed, and the conditions under which a demand feature may be exercised. Both of these examples involve notice to the debtor of extra charges or method of payment.

Although a bank's right to set-off is not included in the examples given, set-off certainly seems analogous to and possibly subsumed in the broad concept of method of payment. For example, when a security interest is assigned by Delaware Olds to the Bank, the set-off provision becomes a method of payment that may be used if the debtor defaults on his or her obligation to the Bank. It seems to me that this is information that is helpful and important to consumers and assists them in understanding more fully the remedies that may be available to their creditor.

I have no doubt, given the Congress' intent, that it is preferable to include set-off information in the Federal Box rather than hide it in the cavernous small print so common in the notorious debtor-creditor financing agreements of days past. In the present case, there is not even a hint that the Bank's inclusion of the right to set-off statement was intended to obscure the information required in the box, but it is plain its inclusion was designed to straightforwardly inform consumers of a significant remedy that the Bank might exercise on the occurrence of a default.

III. CONCLUSION.

For these reasons, I hold that the security interest Delaware Olds obtained in the Goldberg vehicle and later assigned to the Bank must be disclosed in the Federal Box and that the information concerning the Bank's right of set-off is directly related to the security interest of Delaware Olds and, therefore, the right of set-off may be disclosed in the box.

Finally, having reached the conclusion that the Bank's right of set-off is disclosable because it is directly related to mandatory information, there is no need to address plaintiff's remaining contention. Accordingly, I will enter an Order granting defendants' Motion for Summary Judgment and denying plaintiff's.

Notes

1. Why does the TILA require disclosure of a security interest? Is this a useful piece of information in a law designed to disclose credit *costs?* Is a consumer likely to find a creditor who will make a car loan on an *unsecured* basis? If not, of what shopping value is the disclosure? Does this disclosure tell the consumer anything she doesn't already know? Remember that under the Uniform Commercial Code, there must be a written security agreement describing the collateral. UCC § 9–203(1)(a).

2. Does the argument in Goldberg begin to remind you of the classic "how many angels can dance on the head of a pin?" Even if the court had found a violation, wouldn't it have been just another "technical" violation that increases credit costs? On the question of "technical" violations compare Mars v. Spartanburg Chrysler Plymouth, Inc., 713 F.2d 65 (4th Cir.1983), with Streit v. Fireside Chrysler–Plymouth, Inc., 697 F.2d 193 (7th Cir.1983).

3. Is there anything harmful in the form used by the Bank of Delaware. Look again at the form in Problem 1. How many clauses (each one being 24 words in length) could you squeeze into the "federal box."? Alternatively, how many such clauses would you need to squeeze in before all the information "conspicuously segregated" (presumably because of its importance) becomes just another undifferentiated jumble of important *and* not-so-important terms?

Prefatory Note

Problems 1 and 2 and *Goldberg* each concerned a closed-end transaction. The following Problems and materials concern open-end transactions. One major difference is that there is periodic, recurring contact between the parties to the open-end transaction, in addition to the initial contact which created their contractual relationship. Thus, for the open-end transaction TIL requires the creditor to furnish the consumer with both an "initial disclosure statement", Reg. Z § 226.6, and "periodic statements," Reg. Z § 226.7. What must the creditor disclose in such "periodic statements"?

Problem 3

The form on the following two pages is a "periodic statement" from a current open-end credit card account. Refer to Reg. Z § 226.7, and answer the following questions:

1. Is there a "free ride" or grace period? If so, how long is it? Why would a creditor let customers have a free ride? Is it really free?

2. Is any credit shopping purpose served by the periodic statement? When does it come?

3. Note that individual transactions must be identified in the periodic statement. See Reg. Z § 226.8. Different methods of creditor billing practices are contemplated. The billing procedure described in § 226.8(a)(1) is known as "country club" billing, while the procedures described in (a)(2) and (a)(3) are often called "descriptive billing." Which of these procedures is used in this form? How can you tell?

4. Do you understand the method used to compute the unpaid balance on the account? How does it work?

5. How is the finance charge calculated? Does the creditor simply multiply the outstanding balance by the periodic rate? Do you think that an APR of 18% will always produce the same amount of finance charge?

6. Does this form comply with Reg. Z §§ 226.5 and 226.7?

PLEASE RETAIN BOTTOM PORTION OF YOUR STATEMENT. IT IS YOUR PERMANENT RECORD.
PLEASE REPORT ANY BILLING DISCREPANCIES ON THIS BILL TO US IMMEDIATELY.

NBD DELAWARE BANK
P.O. BOX 15438
WILMINGTON, DE   19850

CLOSING DATE OF BILLING PERIOD	PAST DUE	MINIMUM PAYMENT	NEW BALANCE	DUE DATE	VISA ACCOUNT NUMBER	MASTERCARD ACCOUNT NUMBER
11/15/88		25.00	513.30	12/10/88		

$

☐ INDICATE ADDRESS CHANGE ON REVERSE SIDE AND CHECK HERE

INSERT AMOUNT OF YOUR PAYMENT
ALLOW SUFFICIENT TIME FOR MAILING

MAIL PAYMENT TO   075201   000051330 000002500 0

NBD DELAWARE BANK
P.O. BOX 15111
WILMINGTON, DE   19850

● PLEASE DETACH AND ENCLOSE TOP PORTION WITH REMITTANCE TO INSURE PROPER CREDIT ●

TO REPORT LOST OR STOLEN CARD TELEPHONE   **1 313 680 0288**

NBD SERVICE CORP.
AUDITOR
900 TOWER DRIVE
TROY, MI   48098

SEND BILLING INQUIRIES TO THIS ADDRESS

FINANCE CHARGE RATES

	PERIODIC RATE		ANNUAL PERCENTAGE RATE	
	UP TO ■	OVER ■	UP TO ■	OVER ■
PLAN TYPE	OPTION B		OPTION B	
PURCHASES	1.5000%	■	18.0000%	■
CASH ADVANCES	1.2450%	■	14.9400%	■

TRANS DATE MO DY	REFERENCE NUMBER	CARD USED	POSTING DATE MO DY	DESCRIPTION	AMOUNT
	**=FOR CUSTOMER SERVICE			PLEASE CALL 1=800=428=8462==	
	THANK YOU FOR YOUR NBD BANCARD RELATIONSHIP.				
1108	74127008313254009210296	V	1109	TIME LIFE MUSIC RICHMOND VA	20.45
1028	74412008308902379031665	V	1104	LE PICARDY TOPEKA KS	51.83
1101	7520100110188	V	1101	ANNUAL FEE WILMINGTON DE	18.00
1016	74399008299160363247015	V	1026	BIG BOY RESTAU00999268 WASHINGTON NC	16.02
1015	74692118295224501084899	V	1024	JOHN F KENNEDY CENTER WASHINGTON DC	79.00
1014	74399008294160761968241	V	1021	BIG BOY RESTAU00999268 WASHINGTON NC	13.76
1015	74399008294160761966203	V	1021	BIG BOY RESTAU00999268 WASHINGTON NC	14.89
1013	74387138292001155953863	V	1019	MARROCCO II WASHINGTON DC	41.05
1014	74399008292013290026688	V	1019	AMTRAK 00005986 WASHINGTON DC	55.75
1014	74692118292224486069462	V	1019	LLL INCORPORATED GAITHERSBURG MD	29.60
1014	00034270900	V	1017	PAYMENT THANK YOU	32.81CR
1015	99999901	V	1017	INTEREST REVERSAL = 10/14/88 PAYMENT	.98CR

PREVIOUS BALANCE OF	– PAYMENTS	– CREDITS	+ PURCHASES	+ CASH ADVANCES	FINANCE CHARGE		PLEASE PAY AT LEAST MINIMUM PAYMENT BY DUE DATE	= NEW BALANCE OF
					ON PURCHASES	ON CASH ADVANCES		
202.04	32.81	.98	340.35		4.70			513.30

VISA ACCOUNT NUMBER	YOUR CREDIT LIMIT	YOU HAVE UNUSED CREDIT OF	TOTAL FINANCE CHARGE	AVERAGE DAILY BALANCE		CLOSING DATE OF BILLING PERIOD	MINIMUM PAYMENT
				PURCHASES	CASH ADVANCES		
	1500.00	986.70	4.70	313.93		11/15/88	25.00

DUE DATE   12/10/88

MASTERCARD ACCOUNT NUMBER

See other side for important information.
CARD USED: M means MasterCard, V means Visa. "CR" means Credit.

Information About Your Account

Finance Charges and Computing Your Balance. Below are the calculations for each Option. Please be sure to read the portion about your Option. The Option you selected is shown on the other side of this statement.

(1) Options A and B.

There is no finance charge on purchases if the New Balance shown on your periodic statement is paid in full by the due date of the statement in which the purchases first appear. If not paid, finance charges on purchases will be figured from the date of each purchase. Finance charges on cash advances will be figured from the date of each advance. To determine the finance charge, we multiply the periodic rate for purchases by the average daily balance of purchases and we multiply the periodic rate for cash advances by the average daily balance of cash advances. We add these two figures together to get the finance charge. We separately calculate the average daily balances of cash advances and purchases so that you may save finance charges on purchases by paying your New Balance in full by the due date. We use the following method to figure your average daily balances:

(a) **Purchases.**

(i) Current Period: The daily balance is the beginning balance each day in the current billing period less any payments or adjustments credited that day. The daily balance does not include finance charges or current purchases. These daily balances are added and then divided by the number of days in the period. This is the average balance for the current period.

(ii) Previous Period New Purchases: The daily balance is the beginning balance of new purchases of each day of the previous billing period, plus any purchases made that day less any payments and adjustments credited that day. It does not include finance charges or purchases from other billing periods. These daily balances are added and then divided by the number of days in the previous period. This is the average daily balance for new purchases for the previous period.

(iii) If the New Balance on the previous statement was not paid in full by the statement Due Date, the average daily balance for the current period is added to the average daily balance for new purchases for the previous period. The total is the average daily balance of purchases.

(b) **Advances.**

(i) The daily balance is the beginning balance on each day in the current period, plus any advances made that day, and less any payments or adjustments credited that day. Finance charges are not included in the daily balance.

(ii) The daily balances are added up and divided by the total number of days in the period. This result is the average daily balance of cash advances.

(2) Option C.

Finance charges will be figured from the date of each purchase or advance. To determine finance charge, we multiply the periodic rate by the average daily balance for purchases and by the average daily balance for cash advances. We add these two figures together to get the finance charge. We use the following method to figure your average daily balances:

(a) **Purchases.**

(i) The daily balance is the beginning balance on each day in the current period, plus any purchases made that day, and less any payments or adjustments credited that day. Finance charges are not included in the daily balance.

(ii) The daily balances for the current period are added up and divided by the total number of days in the period. This is the average daily balance for purchases.

(b) **Advances.**

(i) The daily balance is the beginning balance on each day in the current period, plus any advances made that day and less any payments or adjustments credited that day. Finance charges are not included in the daily balance.

(ii) The daily balances for the current period are added up and divided by the total number of days in the period. This is the average daily balance for cash advances.

Liability for Unauthorized Use. You must notify us at once if your card or checks are lost or stolen. You may be liable for the unauthorized use of your card or checks. You will not be liable for unauthorized use of your card that occurs after you notify us of the loss, theft or possible unauthorized use in writing at the address on the front of the statement or orally at the telephone number on your statement. In any case, your liability for unauthorized use of your card will not exceed $50 dollars.

Crediting Payments. Payments received by mail before noon on a banking day at the address for payments shown on the front of this statement will be credited as of that day. In all other cases, payments will be credited within 5 days after receipt. The crediting date is the transaction date shown on the face of the statement.

Foreign Transactions. Foreign currency transactions are converted to U.S. Dollars under the then current rules of MasterCard and/or Visa, as the case may be.

Billing Rights Summary _____

In Case of Errors or Questions About Your Bill

If you think your bill is wrong, or if you need more information about a transaction on your bill, write us on a separate sheet at the address on the front of this statement as soon as possible. We must hear from you no later than 60 days after we sent you the first bill on which the error or problem appeared. You can telephone us, but doing so will not preserve your rights.

In your letter, give us the following information:

● Your name and account number.

● The dollar amount of the suspected error.

● Describe the error and explain, if you can, why you believe there is an error. If you need more information, describe the item you are unsure about.

You do not have to pay any amount in question while we are investigating, but you are still obligated to pay the parts of your bill that are not in question. While we investigate your question, we cannot report you as delinquent or take any action to collect the amount you question.

Special Rule for Credit Card Purchases

If you have a problem with the quality of goods or services that you purchased with a credit card, and you have tried in good faith to correct the problem with the merchant, you may not have to pay the remaining amount due on the goods or services. You have this protection only when the purchase price was more than $50 and the purchase was made in your home state or within 100 miles of your mailing address. (If we own or operate the merchant, or if we mailed you the advertisement for the property or services, all purchases are covered regardless of amount or location of purchase.)

Note on Calculating the Unpaid Balance

Disclosures in open-end accounts must include a description of the method used to determine the unpaid balance on which the finance charge will be computed. As most creditors know (but most consumers do not), the method a creditor uses can have a significant impact on an individual account. The following material explains the most common methods.

McALISTER AND DESPAIN, CREDIT CARD YIELDS UNDER ALTERNATIVE ASSESSMENT METHODS

2 J. Retail Banking 56, 57–59, 68 (1980).*

Previous Balance. Also known as the "beginning balance." Finance charges are calculated on any beginning unpaid balance shown on the current month's statement before deducting payments or credits received during the billing period and before adding purchases made during the billing period. Thus, the period's credits and debits are treated symmetrically in that both are excluded from the balance upon which the finance charge is assessed. Payments are applied first to any unpaid finance charges and then to principal. If the previous balance is paid in full, no finance charge is assessed. If no payment is made, the unpaid finance charge may become part of the principal balance owed, although the practice varies among creditors.

Adjusted Balance. Finance charges are calculated on the basis of any beginning unpaid balance shown on the current month's billing statement less payments and credits received during the current billing period, but before adding the current month's purchases. The date of payment on an account is irrelevant to the calculation. On the closing date of the account, payments are first applied to any unpaid finance charges and then to principal. If no payment is made, the unpaid finance charge may become part of the new balance owed.

Ending Balance. Finance charges are based on the balance owed at the end of each billing period, including purchases, payments, and credits occurring during the current month. Thus, the period's credits and debits are treated alike in that both are included in the balance on which the finance charge is assessed. Payments are applied first to any unpaid finance charges before application to principal. If no payment is made, the unpaid finance charge may become part of the principal balance owed. Note that no "free ride" is given the customer who pays the account in full unless there is, indeed, no outstanding balance at the end of the month.

Average Daily Balance Including Debits (ADBW). Finance charges are based on the "average" unpaid balance owed during the billing period. This includes all purchases, payments, and credits transacted during the billing period. It is calculated by dividing the sum of the daily unpaid balances, excluding unpaid finance charges, by the number of days in the billing period. Payments are applied first to any unpaid finance charges then to principal. In the event no payment is made on the account, the finance charge is carried forward as a memo balance (i.e., a balance upon which no finance charges are assessed) until a payment sufficient to cover the unpaid finance charge is made. Under this method no finance charge is imposed if the account has a zero balance at the beginning of the billing cycle or if at any time in the billing period the total of payments and other credits equals or exceeds the opening balance.

Average Daily Balance Excluding Debits (ADBX). Sometimes referred to as the "modified" average daily balance, this method calculates finance charges on the basis of an "average" monthly balance, which is computed by dividing the sum of the daily unpaid balances (excluding the sum of the daily debit balances and unpaid finance charges) by the number of days in the billing cycle. Thus, unlike the

Adjusted Balance method, the timing of the payment affects the size of the finance charge. Payments usually are applied first to any unpaid finance charge, then to principal. If no payment is made, the unpaid finance charge is carried forward separately, not as part of the principal balance, until payment in sufficient amount to cover the unpaid finance charge is made. No finance charge is imposed if the account has a zero balance at the beginning of the billing period or if the total of payments and credits during the period equals or exceeds the opening balance.

"True" (Actuarial) Average Daily Balance (TADB). Finance charges are based on the "average" unpaid balance during the billing period, including all purchases, payments, and credits on the account during the period. It is calculated in exactly the same way as ADBW except that finance charges are assessed on the average daily balance whether or not the account was paid off during the month (where the sum of credits and payments is equal to or greater than the previous month's balance). Thus, there is no "free ride" under this billing method as there is with ADBW.

* * *

Average Daily Balance Methods. The three ADB methods are also closely related. The ADBX method disregards increases in the average daily balance resulting from the current month's purchases, but gives the consumer credit for decreases in the average daily balance due to the current month's payments and credits. TADB and ADBW take both debits and credits into account in figuring finance charges. The two latter methods differ only in that TADB assesses a finance charge whenever there is any balance active within the month, while ADBW makes no assessment when the account is paid off.

These factors produce certain relationships between the three average daily balance methods. First, ADBX finance charges can never exceed ADBW charges. However, they can equal one another, as, for instance, when there are no purchases during a billing period. Second, ADBW finance charges can never exceed TADB charges. The charges can be equal, in fact, whenever the account is not paid off, regardless of any other activity.

The main argument against TADB, as compared to ADBW, is its acceptability to customers and its administrative complexity. When a TADB account is paid in full and no new purchases are made, a finance charge assessed on the average daily balance during the month would be billed alone in the subsequent month. This amount would typically be small relative to usual monthly payments and would often be disregarded by consumers. In addition, the collection costs of these amounts would usually be large relative to the possible revenues.

* * *

Recent Developments. In recent years a new type of average daily balance system has been initiated by a few firms. While this method was not considered in the samples, it is worth mentioning. For purposes of discussion, this newer method will be referred to as ADBR, or simply "retro."

ADBR operates much as an ADBX system insofar as finance charges are not assessed on purchase balances accrued during the current billing cycle of an account. However, if the total of credits and payments in a cycle are less than the previous statement balance (i.e., if the account is not paid off in full), finance charges are assessed *retroactively* in the succeeding month from original date of purchase on the current purchase balance. In other words, no finance charge is assessed during a month on current purchases; but if the account is not paid in full during the following cycle, those same purchases will accrue finance charges from their original date of purchase or date of posting to the account.

SCHMIDT v. CITIBANK (SOUTH DAKOTA) N.A.

United States District Court, District of Connecticut, 1987.
677 F.Supp. 687.

DORSEY, DISTRICT JUDGE.

Plaintiff seeks declaratory and injunctive relief and damages for defendant's alleged violation of the Truth-in-Lending Act ("TILA" or "Act"), 15 U.S.C. § 1601, *et seq.* and Conn.Gen.Stat. § 36–393, *et seq.* Plaintiff and defendant entered into an open-end credit agreement for a VISA credit card. Plaintiff claims that, during the one year ending at the filing of the complaint, defendant failed to disclose as required by both state and federal law.

Cross-motions for summary judgment on the issue of defendant's liability will be considered together.

* * *

ALLEGED TILA VIOLATIONS

1. *Annual Percentage Rate and Finance Charge*

Plaintiff first claims that defendant has violated 15 U.S.C. § 1632(a) and 12 C.F.R. § 226.5(a) by failing to disclose on its monthly periodic billing statement the terms "Annual Percentage Rate" and "Finance Charge" in a conspicuous manner. * * *

(a) Finance Charge

Plaintiff argues that in assessing the conspicuousness of the term "Finance Charge" (located in the Account Summary Section), the court should consider the completed form and the language located under the heading "Activity Since Last Statement:"

LATE CHARGE

ADVANCES*FINANCE CHARGE*PERIODIC RATE

ATTENTION! YOUR ACCOUNT IS DELINQUENT TO AVOID AN ADDITIONAL LATE CHARGE, PLEASE PAY THE MINIMUM AMOUNT DUE IMMEDIATELY. IF PAID, THANK YOU.

YOUR ACCOUNT HAS BEEN REVIEWED AND YOUR CASH AD-
VANCE LIMIT WAS DECREASED TO $300. IF YOU HAVE ANY
QUESTIONS, PLEASE CALL US.

Section 1632(a) requires that the term "Finance Charge" be more
conspicuous "than other terms, data, or information provided in connection with a transaction." Thus, the statute requires that the completed
periodic form, not the *un* completed periodic form, be considered in
determining the conspicuousness of the specified terms. But § 1632(a)
also notes that what is clear and conspicuous should be determined "in
accordance with the regulations of the Board." Section 226.5(a)(2) of
the regulations provides that conspicuousness should be determined in
relation to the other required disclosure terms—not in relation to other
language which may appear on the statement. Thus, even though the
computer typed language on the November 19, 1984 form, is of a print
type and a pitch which is substantially larger than the "Finance
Charge" print type and pitch and typed in capital letters versus the
"Finance Charge" which is printed in upper and lower case letters,
such does not provide support for plaintiff's argument. Indeed, the
rationale for not extending the requirements of the statute to additional language is evident in this situation. It seems a plausible conclusion
that the most important aspect of the November 19, 1984 statement is
defendant's personal message or warning to plaintiff about the status of
his account. It would seem somewhat illogical that a statute, which
has as its core the requirement that a creditor deal fairly, honestly and
openly with its debtor, would require that a message such as that
reproduced above take a back seat to the notation of the "Finance
Charge." The reason that the Act requires that "finance charge" and
"annual percentage rate" be printed conspicuously is because it helps
the consumer become "aware of the costs of credit and enabl[es] him to
undertake comparative shopping for credit." The purpose of the Act is
not served if, after the consumer has contracted for credit, the creditor
is penalized for warning him about the status of his account.

* * *

(b) Annual Percentage Rate

As to plaintiff's claims regarding the term "Annual Percentage
Rate," it is necessary to consider § 226.7(d) and (g). Section 226.5(a)(2)
provides that where the terms "Finance Charge" and "Annual Percentage Rate" are used under § 226.7(d) they need not be more conspicuous.
See § 226.5(a)(2), n. 9; Federal Reserve Board Comments, Part 226,
Supp. 1, at 684. Section 226.7(d) provides for disclosure of periodic
rates. A periodic rate is defined as "a rate of finance charge that is or
may be imposed by a creditor on a balance for a day, week, month, or
other subdivision of a year." 12 C.F.R. § 226.2(a)(21). Under
§ 226.7(d), a creditor must furnish the consumer with "[e]ach periodic
rate that may be used to compute the finance charge, the range of
balances to which it is applicable, and the corresponding annual percentage rate." (Footnotes omitted). Section 226.7(g) requires that the

annual percentage rate, as determined by § 226.14, be provided "[w]hen a finance charge is imposed during the billing cycle."

Defendant argues that in this case the "Annual Percentage Rate" need not be more conspicuous as it falls within the exception of note 9. Although the rationale of note 9 is not explained in the regulations, it seems clear that it was not meant to supplant the requirement of § 226.5(a)(2). Section 226.7(d) refers to the *corresponding* annual percentage rate, *viz*, the rate which, when coupled with the periodic rate pursuant to some set mathematical formula, becomes the applicable finance charge. The Federal Reserve Board's comments are instructive:

> In disclosing the annual percentage rate that corresponds to each periodic rate, the creditor may use "corresponding annual percentage rate," "nominal annual percentage rate," "corresponding nominal annual percentage rate," or similar phrases. [However,] [w]hen the corresponding rate is the same as the actual percentage rate * * * required to be disclosed (§ 226.7(g)), the creditor need disclose only one annual percentage rate, but *must use the phrase "annual percentage rate."*

Federal Reserve Board Comment, Part 226, Supp. 1, at 691. Note 9 excepts the corresponding annual percentage rate simply because it is not of primary concern to the consumer. It is the finance charge and the annual percentage rate which are the terms which best enable the consumer to understand the cost of the credit he is undertaking and to undertake comparison shopping. The individual figures which go into that calculation hardly provide a consumer with any meaningful basis to fulfill either of these two objectives.

The term "Annual Percentage Rate" is of the exact same type size, degree of boldness, and pitch as the terms "Periodic Rate" and "Nominal Annual Percentage Rate." It is not, therefore, more conspicuous and, as such, defendant has not complied with the Act.

Accordingly, plaintiff's motion as to the conspicuousness of the term "Annual Percentage Rate" is granted; plaintiff's motion as to the conspicuousness of the term "Finance Charge" is denied.

2. *Failure to Disclose Method of Calculation*

Plaintiff also alleges that defendant failed to disclose its method for determining the balance to which it applied the periodic rate. The credit statement contains the following:

The Balance Subject to Finance Charge For Purchases:

The Balance Subject to Finance Charge is the average of the daily balances outstanding at the close of business each day during the billing period, consisting of the Previous Balance, less Payments and Credits credited on or before that day, plus Purchases, Fees and Adjustments charged on or before that day. * * * There is no

Finance Charge if we receive payment of your Previous Balance in full on or before the Payment Due Date shown on your previous statement.

(footnote omitted).

Plaintiff complains that this statement is defective in that it does not: (1) indicate that defendant calculates the finance charge, at least in part, by applying the periodic rate to the balance; (2) explain how the average daily balance is determined; (3) distinguish between average daily balance and daily balance; and (4) indicate how current transactions are treated. Section 1637(b)(7) requires a periodic billing statement setting forth "[t]he balance on which the finance charge was computed and a statement of how that balance was determined." To help ensure that this requirement is complied with, the Federal Reserve Board has proposed model forms which, if followed, immunize the creditor from a claim that it has not complied with the Act. Use of the forms is not required, however. *Id.* The Model Form in this instance, provides:

> We figure [a portion of] the finance charge on your account by applying the periodic rate to the "average daily balance" of your account (including current transactions). To get the "average daily balance" we take the beginning balance of your account each day, add any new [purchases/advances/loans], and subtract any payments or credits, [and unpaid finance charges]. This gives us the daily balance. Then, we add up all the daily balances for the billing cycle and divide the total by the number of days in the billing cycle. This gives us the "average daily balance."

Appendix G–1(d) (brackets in original).

(a) Insufficient Notation That Finance Charge is Calculated by Applying Periodic Rate to Average Daily Balance

Plaintiff's claim that the billing statement is deficient because it fails to note that the finance charge is calculated by applying the periodic rate to the average daily balance is without merit. Section 227.7(e) requires disclosure of the "amount of the balance to which a periodic rate was applied and an explanation of how that balance was determined." It does not require disclosure of how the finance rate is calculated because that information has already been provided in the initial disclosure statement. Since it is the borrower's balance which changes from one periodic statement to the next, it is this calculation with which he should be provided in order to verify the creditor's information. Thus, although full compliance with Appendix G–1 might simplify reading a periodic statement, compliance with § 227.7(e) does not require the first sentence of the Model Form on periodic statements.

(b) Insufficient Description of "Average Daily Balance" Method

Defendant argues that it has adequately defined the "average daily balance." This is not so. Although the model form may seem somewhat simplistic, TILA recognized that not all borrowers are mathematicians. By combining the latter four sentences of Appendix G–1(d) into one sentence, defendant has complicated an otherwise straightforward explanation. An average borrower could read the clause beginning with "consisting" as modifying "the average of the daily balances" or just one daily balance. It is unclear as to whether the adjustments are to be made to the previous balance or to a daily balance. So also is it unclear whether the adjustments are made to each day's balance. Indeed, defendant's memorandum explanation of its formula is clearer than is the actual formula. Defendant's Opposition Memorandum and Memorandum in Support of Motion for Summary Judgment at 18 ("This is the 'average daily balance' method. In order to determine the balance subject to finance charge the defendant on a daily basis adds or subtracts all debits and credits to or from the balance existing on the previous day, takes the closing balance at the end of the day and then averages the closing balances for the billing period."). Defendant's articulation does not explain, with adequate clarity, the method of calculating the balance to which the periodic rate is applied.

(c) Failure to Define "Daily Balance" and
"Average Daily Balance"

As noted above, defendant's paraphrase of the Model Form has confused the explanation of the "average daily balance." Separate descriptions of "daily balance" and "average daily balance" would have clarified the formula.

* * *

3. Failure to Adequately Disclose Address for Billing Inquiries

Plaintiff lastly argues that defendant has violated 15 U.S.C. § 1637(b)(10) which requires a creditor to disclose the "address to be used by the creditor for the purpose of receiving billing inquiries from the obligor." * * *

Plaintiff claims that defendant's report is deficient in that it (1) lists two different addresses thus making it unclear as to which address is intended for billing inquiries; and (2) fails to provide a precautionary instruction about telephone conversations. * * * Quite clearly, as to plaintiff's first alleged error,—that defendant's inclusion of two addresses is confusing—there is no basis for liability. Defendant adequately explains the difference between the two addresses; one for payment, the other for customer service. The form is not unclear in this regard.

As to plaintiff's second alleged error, that defendant has not provided a precautionary instruction about telephone calls, defendant has not complied. Both the regulation and the Model Forms, *see* 12 C.F.R. Part 226, App. G–3 and G–4, contain the precautionary instruction that inquiries made by telephone will not preserve the consumer's rights. * * *

CONCLUSION

Accordingly, plaintiff's motion for summary judgment on the issue of liability is:

(1) granted as to the conspicuousness of the term "Annual Percentage Rate;" denied as to the term "Finance Charge;"

(2) denied as to the claim of failure to note that the finance charge is calculated by applying the periodic rate to the average daily balance; granted as to defendant's insufficient description of the average daily balance method; granted as to the failure to define "daily balance" and average daily balance; and denied on defendant's alleged failure to emphasize; and

(3) denied as to the claimed confusion relating to two addresses; granted as to the failure to provide a precautionary instruction and/or failure to make the billing address clear and conspicuous.

* * *

SO ORDERED.

Notes

1. Which average daily balance method does Citibank use? Did you understand the description of that method as used in Citibank's form? Do you think the average consumer would understand the description? Is the description used in the Federal Reserve Board's model clause any better?

2. Even if you do understand the method of computing the unpaid balance, what do you know that is helpful? For example, would you know (or would you have known before reading this chapter) that there were several methods of computing the "average daily balance"? Would you know how the method used by any particular creditor compares to other available methods?

3. Compare the method of computing the unpaid balance used by Citibank with the method used in the form on page 121. Assuming both banks applied the same APR, which account gives the consumer the better deal?

Home Equity Loans

In recent years, so-called "home equity loans" have become widespread. The home equity loan, as it is currently used in most parts of the country, is sort of a cross between the traditional closed-end second mortgage and the typical credit card open-end account. Like a credit card account, the consumer is allowed to draw on a pre-established line of credit at varying times and in varying amounts. Like a second mortgage, the lender will take a security interest in the consumer's home to secure the outstanding balance.

When home equity loans first appeared, it seemed clear enough that they were open-end transactions, but the TIL disclosures for open-end transactions were written primarily for credit card accounts. Most credit card accounts are unsecured, but home equity loans are potentially more risky for consumers, because upon default the consumer could lose his or her house. The existing disclosures did not adequately address this problem.

As a result of all this, in 1988 Congress passed the Home Equity Loan Consumer Protection Act of 1988. This act added several new provisions to the Truth in Lending Act. See TILA §§ 127A, 137, and 147. In addition, in 1989 the Board added corresponding amendments to Reg. Z to implement the new act. For each home equity loan transaction, lenders now must make three sets of disclosures. The first must be made at the time the application is given to the consumer. See Reg. Z § 226.5b(b). The second corresponds to the initial disclosure statement on credit card accounts. Normally, this set of disclosures will be given at closing, along with the other contract documents. See Reg. Z § 226.6(e). Finally, as in all open-end accounts, a periodic disclosure statement containing the details of the current activity in the account must be provided each month (or other period). Reg. Z § 226.7. Refer to these statutory and regulatory provisions as you work through the following problems.

Problem 4A

The form on the following pages is the model suggested by the Board as the disclosure to be given at the time of application. Review it in light of Reg. Z § 226.5b(d).

(a) Can you follow the disclosures so that you have a basic understanding of the transaction? If you were about to take out a home equity loan, would this information help you understand what you were getting into? Would it help the average consumer?

(b) Are all of the disclosures useful? If not, which ones would you eliminate? Can you think of any other information which should be disclosed?

(c) Are the disclosures too complex? Will the average consumer (who hasn't taken a law school course on consumer law) be able to understand them? Can you suggest ways in which the disclosures could be simplified?

IMPORTANT TERMS
of our
HOME EQUITY LINE OF CREDIT

This disclosure contains important information about our Home Equity Line of Credit. You should read it carefully and keep a copy for your records.

Availability of Terms: To obtain the terms described below, you must submit your application before April 1, 1989.

If these terms change (other than the annual percentage rate) and you decide, as a result, to not enter into an agreement with us, you are entitled to a refund of any fees that you paid to us or anyone else in connection with your application.

Security Interest: We will take a mortgage in your home. You could lose your home if you do not meet the obligations in your agreement with us.

Possible Actions: Under certain circumstances, we can (1) terminate your line, require you to pay us the entire outstanding balance in one payment, and charge you certain fees, (2) refuse to make additional extensions of credit, and (3) reduce your credit limit.

If you ask, we will give you more specific information concerning when we can take these actions.

Minimum Payment Requirements: You can obtain advances of credit for 10 years (the "draw period"). During the draw period, payments will be due monthly. Your minimum monthly payment will equal the greater of $100 or $\frac{1}{360}$th of the outstanding balance plus the finance charges that have accrued on the outstanding balance.

After the draw period ends, you will no longer be able to obtain credit advances and must pay the outstanding balance over 5 years (the "repayment period"). During the repayment period, payments will be due monthly. Your minimum monthly payment will equal $\frac{1}{60}$th of the balance that was outstanding at the end of the draw period plus the finance charges that have accrued on the remaining balance.

Minimum Payment Example: If you made only the minimum monthly payments and took no other credit advances, it would take 15 years to pay off a credit advance of $10,000 at an ANNUAL PERCENTAGE RATE of 12.00%. During that period, you would make 120 monthly payments varying between $127.78 and $100.00 followed by 60 monthly payments varying between $187.06 and $118.08.

Fees and Charges: To open and maintain a line of credit, you must pay the following fees to us:

Application fee: $150 (due at application)

Points: 1% of credit limit (due when account opened)

Annual maintenance fee: $75 (due each year)

You also must pay certain fees to third parties. These fees generally total between $500 and $900. If you ask, we will provide you with an itemization of the fees you will have to pay to third parties.

Minimum Draw and Balance Requirements: The minimum credit advance that you can receive is $500. You must maintain an account balance of at least $100.

Tax Deductibility: You should consult a tax advisor regarding the deductibility of interest and charges under the plan.

Variable–Rate Information: The plan has a variable-rate feature, and the annual percentage rate (corresponding to the periodic rate) and the minimum payment can change as a result.

The annual percentage rate includes only interest and not other costs.

The annual percentage rate is based on the value of an index. The index is the monthly average prime rate charged by banks and is published in the *Federal Reserve Bulletin*. To determine the annual percentage rate that will apply to your account, we add a margin to the value of the index.

Ask us for the current index value, margin and annual percentage rate. After you open a line, rate information will be provided on periodic statements that we will send you.

Rate Changes: The annual percentage rate can change each month. The maximum ANNUAL PERCENTAGE RATE that can apply during the plan is 18%. Except for the 18% "cap," there is no limit on the amount by which the rate can change during any one-year period.

Maximum Rate and Payment Examples: If you had an outstanding balance of $10,000 at the beginning of the draw period, the minimum monthly payment at the maximum ANNUAL PERCENTAGE RATE of 18% would be $177.78. This annual percentage rate could be reached during the first month of the draw period.

If you had an outstanding balance of $10,000 at the beginning of the repayment period, the minimum monthly payment at the maximum ANNUAL PERCENTAGE RATE of 18% would be $316.67. This annual percentage rate could be reached during the first month of the repayment period.

Historical Example: The following table shows how the annual percentage rate and the minimum monthly payments for a single $10,000 credit advance would have changed based on changes in the index over the past 15 years. The index values are from September of each year. While only one payment amount per year is shown, payments would have varied during each year.

The table assumes that no additional credit advances were taken and that only the minimum payment was made each month. It does not necessarily indicate how the index or your payments will change in the future.

Year	Index	Margin*	ANNUAL PERCENTAGE RATE	Minimum Monthly Payment
	(%)	(%)	(%)	
1974	12.00	2	14.00	$144.44
1975	7.88	2	9.88	$106.50
1976	7.00	2	9.00	$100.00
1977	7.13	2	9.13	$100.00
1978	9.41	2	11.41	$105.47
1979	12.90	2	14.90	$126.16
1980	12.23	2	14.23	$117.53
1981	20.08	2	18.00 **	$138.07
1982	13.50	2	15.50	$117.89
1983	11.00	2	13.00	$100.00
1984	12.97	2	14.97	$203.81
1985	9.50	2	11.50	$170.18
1986	7.50	2	9.50	$149.78
1987	8.70	2	10.70	$141.50
1988	10.00	2	12.00	$130.55

* This is a margin we have used recently.

** This rate reflects the 18% maximum rate limitation.

Problem 4B

The document on the following pages is part of a home equity loan contract used by a real-life lender at the time the TIL home equity amendments went into effect. Assume you are counsel for the lender. The chief loan officer has asked for your opinion as to whether this contract may continue to be used under these amendments. If not, she has asked that you prepare a draft of a form which does comply, incorporating any changes or improvements you feel are necessary or desirable. In addition, the loan officer has asked the following questions:

(a) Since this is an open-end account, do we have to make the usual initial disclosures under Reg. Z § 226.6? If so, does our form comply? I am especially concerned about the Finance Charge and APR disclosures.

(b) Reg. Z § 226.6(e) suggests that we will have to repeat many of the disclosures given at the time of application. Do any of these rules apply to our form? I'm especially unsure about which variable rate disclosures must be repeated.

(c) In the model application disclosures (Problem 4A), the Board seems to assume that the underlying contract will have separate "draw" and "repayment" phases. But our contract does not do this; instead, we have a true revolving account. Is this something we should worry about? Could we use the model form at the time of application? If we did, would we have to change our contract?

(d) Must we make the variable rate disclosures required by Reg. Z § 226.19(b)? Or does that rule apply only to closed-end contracts?

EXECUTIVE OPEN END CREDIT AGREEMENT AND INITIAL DISCLOSURE STATEMENT

Borrower(s)   Loan No.

Address of Property   Date

INITIAL ANNUAL PERCENTAGE RATE (APR)
CREDIT LIMIT

This is your EXECUTIVE OPEN END CREDIT AGREEMENT with First Federal Savings and Loan Association (hereinafter "Agreement"). It contains important information concerning your rights and obligations, and includes certain disclosures required under federal law. You should read the Agreement carefully before signing.

Throughout this Agreement, the words "you," "your" and "yours" refer to the borrower(s) named above, and the words "we," "us," and "Association" refer to First Federal Savings and Loan Association, and any other person or entity to whom its rights may be assigned, as the content may require.

2. Open End Credit: Your loan is set up as an Open End Line of Credit. This enables you to borrow all or any part of your Credit Limit, repay amounts borrowed, and re-borrow to the Credit Limit. The maximum Line of Credit for this loan is set forth at the top of this Agreement with the heading "CREDIT LIMIT." Nevertheless, we reserve the right to cancel the Line of Credit as described in the Loan Documents, and to convert the Loan to a Closed End Credit Loan.

* * *

3. Loan Secured By Mortgage: As security for the repayment of your loans and other obligations chargeable to your Executive account, you are giving us a mortgage on the dwelling ("Property") which you occupy as your principal residence, all as more fully described in the mortgage document. The mortgage will remain in effect as long as you have your Executive account, even during periods when your account balance may be zero. The mortgage will be released only after your Executive account has been closed, and all loans and other obligations chargeable to it have been repaid. Regardless of whether this is an individual account or a joint account, anyone who has an ownership interest in the dwelling must sign the mortgage. If you are married, then your spouse must sign the mortgage, even if he or she is not on the deed.

4. Executive Open End Credit Access: Following the expiration of your three (3) day right to cancel, as provided elsewhere in this Agreement, your Executive Open End Line of Credit will become available for your use. Your Line of Credit shall be accessible (a) in person at any office of First Federal or (b) by presentment of special Executive drafts bearing your Executive account number. Your use of an Executive draft shall be treated by us as a request for a Cash Advance to be paid directly to the named payee under the terms of this Agreement and the other Loan Documents. Advances shall be deemed to have been made at the time of presentment of such drafts, and payment by us shall constitute a Cash Advance to you of such amount pursuant to this Agreement. You will owe us all amounts borrowed by use of your Executive account plus any finance charges and any other charges or fees provided for in this Agreement or in any of the other Loan Documents:

* * *

6. Finance Charge: If you have a balance in your account, we will send you a monthly statement. It will show separately your new cash advances, the previous balance, the FINANCE CHARGE, any other charges, the minimum payment due and the date the payment is due.

A FINANCE CHARGE will be imposed on each Cash Advance from the date the Cash Advance is made to the date paid in full.

We will compute the amount of FINANCE CHARGE by adding together any FINANCE CHARGE due to the imposition of the daily interest rate for each billing cycle. These charges are computed in the following manner:

(a) Periodic Finance Charge:

(i) To compute the Periodic Finance Charge, we start with the previous balance, excluding any unpaid FINANCE CHARGE or other charges from previous billing cycles.

(ii) Each day of the billing cycle, we subtract payments and credits and add new advances and charges posted to your account. This gives us the actual daily balance ("Balance Subject to Finance Charge").

(iii) Then, we multiply the Balance Subject to Finance Charge by the Daily Interest Rate to obtain the Daily Finance Charge.

(iv) Finally, at the end of the billing cycle, we add together each of the Daily Finance Charges incurred during the billing cycle, and the sum of these charges is the "Periodic Finance Charge."

(b) Daily Interest Rate:

(i) The Daily Interest Rate applied to the Balance Subject to Finance Charge will be a figure which is two percentage points above the "Prime Rate" (or its substitute) in effect, divided by 365. The "Prime Rate" for purposes of this Agreement and the Loan Documents means the Prime Rate for commercial banks in the United States published on the first business day of each month in the Wall Street Journal, Midwest Edition (see the "Money Rates" column). If the Prime Rate is published as a range of rates, the weighted average of the rates will be used. If the Wall Street Journal discontinues publishing the Prime Rate described above, the association may substitute any national or regional index chosen by the Association which measures interest rates or the rate of inflation, applying a conversion factor which will convert the index value to a value most similar to the Prime Rate used initially.

(ii) The Daily Interest Rate will be subject to change on the first business day of each month, and all changes to the Daily Interest Rate shall become effective on the next day.

(iii) IN NO EVENT WILL THE INTEREST RATE OF THIS LOAN BE INCREASED TO MORE THAN 18.0% A.P.R.

7. Payment on the Account: You must pay at least a minimum monthly payment on your account equal to two percent (2%) of the outstanding balance disclosed on your current monthly billing statement, or $50.00, whichever is greater, plus current monthly insurance premiums or charges for dishonored payments, if any. Your minimum payment (plus any past due payments) is due on or before the due date specified on the billing statement.

If the outstanding balance is less than $50.00, the entire balance must be paid in full. You may at any time pay more than the minimum amount due, or even the full amount without a penalty. There is no "free period" within which payments may be made in order to completely avoid FINANCE CHARGES. FINANCE CHARGES will be assessed beginning with the day that loan advances or other charges are posted to your account. The sooner you pay your total balance, the less you will have to pay in FINANCE CHARGES.

* * *

25. Notice of Your Right to Cancel: Because you are giving us a mortgage on your principal dwelling as security for your Executive open end loan account, you will have three (3) business days after you sign this Agreement and the mortgage to cancel or rescind your Executive account. This right to cancel also applies to anyone who has an ownership interest in the dwelling and lives there with you, whether they have signed this Agreement or not. Along with your copies of this Agreement, we are giving you notices of right to cancel which contain more information about your right to cancel. If anyone having the right to cancel does so exercise his or her right, the cancellation will terminate the Executive account. Because of the three business day cancellation period, we must wait until that period has expired before making loans available to you under your Executive account.

NOTICE TO CONSUMER: 1. DO NOT SIGN THIS AGREEMENT BEFORE YOU READ IT, OR IF IT CONTAINS ANY BLANK SPACES; 2. YOU ARE ENTITLED TO A COPY OF THIS AGREEMENT; 3. YOU MAY REPAY THE UNPAID BALANCE AT ANY TIME WITHOUT PENALTY.

BORROWER: CO–BORROWER:

_____   _____

FIRST FEDERAL SAVINGS &
LOAN ASS'N.

By ——————————   Date ——————————————

3. TIMING—WHEN MUST DISCLOSURES BE MADE?

The Truth in Lending Act's preamble emphasizes that its purpose is "to assure a meaningful disclosure of credit terms so that the consumer will be able to compare more readily the various credit terms available to him and avoid the uninformed use of credit." To accomplish this, it would seem necessary to put the disclosures into the consumer's hands at a time when there is a realistic opportunity to use them for comparative shopping.

In evaluating the materials that follow, consider: (1) when in fact does the TILA require the disclosures to be made; and (2) as of that time, how useful are they to the consumer?

The general rules on timing of TILA disclosures are found in Reg. Z §§ 226.5(b) (for open-end credit) and 226.17(b) (for closed-end credit).

————

The timing rules of the TILA have been severely criticized. The following excerpt is typical:

LANDERS AND ROHNER, A FUNCTIONAL ANALYSIS OF TRUTH IN LENDING
26 U.C.L.A.L.Rev. 711, 715–16 (1979).*

There is a fundamental fallacy in the present approach to TIL disclosures. From the beginning, the disclosure requirements were premised on the notion that the TIL statement should include the particulars of the transaction that the consumer is considering. But the disclosures cannot be made until the consumer and the creditor have negotiated a basic agreement whose particulars can be ascertained. Thus, there must always be a fixing of prices and terms before the consumer receives the disclosure statement.

The Act resolves this dilemma by permitting creditors to make the disclosures as part of the contracting process, or in other words, after some sort of preliminary agreement has been reached that permits the preparation of the disclosure forms. Thus, the disclosures come at, or very shortly before, the consummation of a transaction to which the consumer is already verbally and psychologically committed. At this point, comparative shopping by the consumer is unlikely. Moreover, it is equally unlikely that at this point the consumer will opt to pay with cash. Thus, the present Act does not put usable credit information into the consumer's hands at a time when it will affect transactional behavior.

Note

The preceding comment is directed toward disclosure in the closed end transaction under TILA. How accurate are the authors' observations? Consider as illustrative, the two basic transactions in Problems 5 and 6, below. When does TILA require disclosures to be made? (And, are the TILA rules on this point free from ambiguity?) How useful are the disclosures to the consumer when made?

Problem 5

Wanda has been shopping for a new car. She finally decided that a new Honda Civic was the "perfect" car for her. At the dealership, she picked out the model and decided on the various options she wanted included. She bargained with the dealer, and they reached an agreement on the price. At that time, she put down $100 and signed a purchase order, but it had no provisions concerning financing or credit. A few weeks later, Honda delivered the car to the dealership, which in turn called Wanda. When Wanda arrived to pick up her car, the dealer asked her how she wanted to pay for it. Wanda responded that she needed to finance the car, so she filled out a credit application which was approved, signed a purchase money security agreement with the dealer and drove away.

At what point in the transaction must the dealer make the TILA disclosures to Wanda? At that point is Wanda likely to use them for comparison shopping? Are they likely to influence her decision or cause her to change her mind about the car? Are they likely to influence her decision or cause her to change her mind about the financing of the car?

Read Reg. Z § 226.17(b). When does "consummation" of this transaction occur? Does TILA determine when "consummation" occurs? Or, is this concept dependent upon state contract law? If the latter, will the timing of federally-mandated disclosure vary from state to state?

The Official Commentary to the Truth in Lending Simplification and Reform Act, 46 Fed.Reg. 50 292 (1981), states:

2(a)(13) "Consummation:

1. State law governs. When a contractual obligation on the consumer's part is created is a matter to be determined under applicable law; Regulation Z does not make this determination. Consummation does not occur merely because the consumer has made some financial investment in the transaction (for example, by paying a nonrefundable fee) unless, of course, applicable law holds otherwise.

2. Credit v. sale. Consummation does not occur when the consumer becomes contractually committed to a sale transaction, unless the consumer also becomes legally obligated to accept a particular credit arrangement. For example, when a consumer

pays a nonrefundable deposit to purchase an automobile, a purchase contract may be created, but consummation for purposes of the regulation does not occur unless the consumer also contracts for financing at that time.

Problem 6

Lucy and Schroeder have been house hunting. After several weeks, they finally discovered the perfect little bungalow. They submitted a bid to the seller's agent, a real estate broker, which was contingent upon their obtaining financing. The sellers accepted their bid, and it was then their duty to apply for financing in a timely fashion. On the advice of the real estate broker, they went to Ace Mortgage Co. for a mortgage loan. There they filled out and signed an application form, giving their entire economic history, and paid an application fee of $200. Three weeks later, Ace called and said that their credit had been approved, and Ace then mailed to them a letter committing itself to make the loan. One month later, the parties "closed" on the house. At closing, Ace advanced funds to the seller, and Lucy and Schroeder signed a note and mortgage.

When must Ace make the TILA disclosures? At that time, are Lucy and Schroeder likely to be influenced in their decision about buying the home? Are they likely to be influenced to change their minds about the financing of the house?

When is "consummation" of this transaction? Should disclosure depend upon local real estate law? Note that there are special disclosure requirements for "residential mortgage transaction" under Reg. Z § 226.19(a), and that "good faith estimates" of the figures must be given "before consummation." At what time should Ace send these estimates to Lucy and Schroeder?

Prefatory Note

Open end transactions also have disclosure timing problems. There is the same great temptation for creditors to leave some items out of credit application forms and to send initial disclosure forms only after the application has been approved. Under such a system of disclosure, shopping for credit card credit can be accomplished only by filling out an application, and few consumers are willing to fill out multiple applications. A separate problem has arisen concerning the "annual membership fee" levied by many credit card issuers, and the timing of the disclosure of its existence and amount.

Problem 7A

Last Bank has been issuing VISA cards for years. Potential cardholders who come into the bank see a bank officer who takes information from them and fills out an application form. At the end of the interview, the potential cardholder signs the application form, which the bank keeps. The consumer gets nothing from the bank in writing at that time.

When the consumer's credit is approved, Last Bank mails them a letter of congratulations, the initial disclosure statement with the disclosures required by Reg. Z § 226.6, and the credit card itself. This initial disclosure statement says quite clearly that "the annual membership fee for a Last Bank VISA card is $15, which is due and payable upon acceptance of the card." Is this procedure in conformity with TILA? See Reg. Z §§ 226.5(b) and 226.6.

Credit Card Solicitations

Increased competition in the credit card market in recent years has led to the widespread use of mass solicitations. Banks and other card issuers mail solicitation brochures to potential customers from pre-screened mailing lists. These brochures often tell consumers that they have been "specially selected" and "already approved to enjoy the convenience of a VISA card," and that all they have to do is call the bank at a designated number. When a customer calls, the card and the initial TIL disclosures are typically mailed within a few days.

In the past, these solicitation brochures normally did not contain any of the TIL disclosures, although at times (for example, when the soliciting bank's rates were below those of other banks in the area) they did mention the APR then being charged. Congress thought that consumers should have more information than was typically given to them, so in 1988 it enacted the Fair Credit and Charge Card Disclosure Act of 1988. This act added subsections (c) through (g) to TILA § 127, and the law now requires a series of specific disclosures to be made in credit card solicitations. To implement the new law, the Board added a whole new section to Reg. Z, § 226.5a, as well as a couple of new subsections, (e) and (f), to § 226.9. Consult those sections as you work through the following problems.

Problem 7B

The form on the following page is a solicitation received by one of your co-authors at about the time the new rules went into effect. Does it comply?

Problem 7C

You represent Last Bank. Last's credit card officer has also told you that Last is considering initiating an aggressive new advertising campaign for its credit cards. Among other things, it plans to use telemarketing solicitations and to distribute application forms in "take one" displays in local merchant outlets. Under the new law, what information must be disclosed in these forms of advertising?

Please detach and return in the enclosed postage-paid envelope.

Acceptance Certificate

NAME AND ADDRESS	PLEASE TELL US ABOUT YOURSELF

NOTE: YOUR NAME AND ADDRESS WILL APPEAR ON YOUR ACCOUNT AS SHOWN BELOW. PLEASE PRINT CORRECTIONS.

Social Security No.   Date of Birth (Mo./Day/Yr.)

☐ Own Home ☐ Other
☐ Rent

Home Phone And Area Code   Name On Phone Bill

PAUL B. RASOR
2847 SW MULVANE ST
TOPEKA, KS 66611-1665

Previous Home Address   Years There

City, Town, Or Post Office   State   Zip

PLEASE TELL US ABOUT YOUR WORK

Business Name Or Employer | Position | Check Here if ☐ Retired ☐ Self-Employed | Years At Job

Business Phone And Area Code | If Retired Or Self-Employed, Bank Name And Account Number

Business Bank Address, Number And Street | City, Town, Or Post Office | State

PLEASE GIVE US SOME FINANCIAL INFORMATION

☐ Money Market Funds/NOW Acct. (Joint Or Individual) Institution | ☐ Checking Account (Joint Or Individual) Institution | ☐ Savings Account CD Treasury Bills (Joint Or Individual) Institution

☐ MasterCard/Visa ☐ Diners Club | ☐ American Express ☐ Department Store | ☐ Gasoline ☐ Sears | ☐ Other

Your Total Personal ANNUAL Income $ | Other Household Income $ | Source(s) Of Other Income

You do not have to include alimony, child support, spouse's annual income, separate maintenance or other income unless you want us to consider it in connection with this application.

* * *

DISCLOSURES

Annual Percentage Rate	Variable Rate Index and Spread	Annualized Membership Fee
19.8% for Purchases and Cash Advances.	Does Not Apply.	$20.

Grace Period/Free Ride Period
On purchases you will have a grace period or "free ride" period (up to 25 days) calculated from the statement closing date to the payment due date. If you do not pay your new balance in full by the payment due date, you will be assessed a finance charge on the then outstanding balance and on future purchases from the date such purchases are posted to your account. On cash advances, finance charges are assessed from the day you take the cash advance until the day we receive payment in full.

Cash Advance Fees and Transaction Fees
If taken at a financial institution, 2% of amount of advance but not less than $2 or more than $10. If taken at Automated Teller Machine, $1.75 per transaction.

Late Payment Fees
The fee is $10 for each billing period in which your minimum payment is not received within 25 days after payment due date.

Over the Limit Fees and Other Charges
Over the Limit Fee—None. *Bad Check Fee*—$10. *Minimum Finance Charge*—50¢ for each billing period in which a finance charge, based on a periodic rate, is payable. *Collection Fees*—lawyers' fees plus court costs and any other fees as allowed by law.

[F10478]

Notes

1. Do you think that the new credit card disclosure rules for solicitations will solve the timing problems? How will they help consumers who take the initiative themselves (rather than responding to a solicitation) when applying for a credit card?

2. Will the new rules do anything for consumers who apply for closed-end credit? Would it be possible to design similar rules for closed-end transactions?

3. Another way to get credit information to consumers in time for it to be meaningful is to require certain disclosures in credit advertising. Should creditors be required to advertise? For those creditors who do advertise, should there be minimum requirements as to the kinds of information that is disclosed? We will consider the problem of credit advertising immediately below.

4. CREDIT ADVERTISING

STATE v. TERRY BUICK, INC.

New York Supreme Court, Duchess County, 1987.
137 Misc.2d 290, 520 N.Y.S.2d 497.

JAMES D. BENSON, JUSTICE.

This action for an injunction under 15 U.S.C. § 1664 (Truth in Lending Act) General Business Law Article 22–A and CPLR § 6301 enjoining Terry Buick, Inc. from continuing to advertise the terms for credit on vehicles it is selling in an illegal, false and deceptive manner is determined as follows:

In this action, the State of New York sues a retail automobile dealer for a judgment enjoining it from continuing several advertising practices which it claims violate General Business Law §§ 350 and 350–a as well as 15 U.S.C. § 1664(d) and Regulation Z, 12 C.F.R. § 226.24 (Truth in Lending Act). The thrust of the claim is that the defendant did not disclose its payment and financing terms in the sale of automobiles "clearly and conspicuously". At the heart of the controversy are two advertising practices in which the defendant (1) displayed large signs in its showroom window which read "NO MONEY DOWN" "$99 MO" and, (2) the announcement of the actual terms of each sale on $2\frac{1}{4}'' \times 3\frac{3}{8}''$ stickers, legible only upon close inspection, attached to the windshields of vehicles offered for sale.

The proof was clear that the defendant operated an automobile dealership business on Route 9, a very busy public highway in Poughkeepsie. At the time of the events of which the plaintiff complains, the defendant displayed large yellow signs across the street-side face of its building in block letters which read "NO MONEY DOWN INSTANT CREDIT" and in the showroom window beneath it, "$99/MO." The windshields of many of the used cars offered for sale in the yard also bore a large painted sign which read "$99/MO or $199/MO". The record also shows that the defendant attached small stickers to the windshields of each car offered for sale, not legible from the highway, which stated the terms of sale. These announcements showed the stock number of the car, the price, the down payment, the term in months and the average interest rate applied to installment payments. It was not clear whether these stickers were attached before or after the litigation was commenced.

On June 29, 1987, Terry Buick stipulated that it would remove, forthwith, the signs on the building which read "NO MONEY DOWN" and "$99/MO".

The Court viewed the defendant's place of business with the attorneys and examined a number of the windshield stickers. They were legible only upon inspection from a distance of a few feet and set forth the financial details of each offer. Examination of the stickers showed that almost every offering required a down payment to obtain $99 per month financing. Other used cars had only "$99/MO" painted on their windshields. According to the testimony of one witness, the salesman did not know the price of several of such cars. He testified that no cars were offered for sale for $2,000 down and $99 per month.

[TILA] § 1664(d) reads as follows:

* * *

General Business Law § 350 reads:

"False advertising in the conduct of any business, trade or commerce or in the furnishing of any service in this state is hereby declared unlawful."

Section 350–a of that law reads:

"The term "false advertising" means advertising, including labeling, which is misleading in a material respect; and in determining whether any advertising is misleading, there shall be taken into account (among other things) not only representations made by statement, word, design, device, sound or any combination thereof, but also the extent to which the advertising fails to reveal facts material in the light of such representations with respect to the commodity to which the advertising relates under the conditions prescribed in said advertisement, or under such conditions as are customary or usual."

The Court's inspection of the defendant's place of business and its advertising material showed beyond question that the announcement signs were a "come on" designed to lure the eager seeker of a good deal. It also showed that "what you see is not what you get". We have not given the testimony of the undercover agent much weight. It was a contrived tactic practiced upon a relatively guileless salesman by a young woman who pretended to be a purchaser. Her testimony is not necessary, however, to convince the Court that defendant's public announcement of its deals fell far short of the candid display which the law requires. The law requires full disclosure described in the plain language of the statute. A look at the defendant's advertising scheme leads directly to the conclusion that it was designed to attract customers by half truths or falsity. No customer could buy a car on the terms boldly announced on the face of the building. The defendant's intentions did not have to be explained by testimony. No undercover agent was needed to obtain admissions. The message spoke for itself and could not be misread. It was "misleading in a material respect".

Truth in lending laws were not adopted for the canny shopper. They were made for the gullible and those easily led. The Court of Appeals decided in *Guggenheimer v. Ginzburg,* 43 N.Y.2d 268, 273, 401 N.Y.S.2d 182, 372 N.E.2d 17 that, "In weighing a statement's capacity, tendency or effect in deceiving or misleading customers, we do not look to the average customer but to the vast multitude which the statutes were enacted to safeguard, including the ignorant, the unthinking and the credulous who, in making purchases, do not stop to analyze but are governed by appearances and general impressions." The plaintiff was not required to show that anyone had been deceived or that the advertising had injured anyone. It met its burden by showing its misleading effect.

The defendant's violation of Federal and New York State truth in lending laws has been demonstrated.

* * *

The motion for an order granting a preliminary injunction enjoining the defendant Terry Buick, Inc. from continuing to advertise the terms for credit on vehicles it is selling in an illegal, false and deceptive manner is granted.

Notes

1. Under the TILA, what is the precise basis for the court's ruling? Is it that the advertisement was not "clear and conspicuous"? Do the general format requirements of Reg. Z found in §§ 226.5(a) and 226.17(a) apply to credit advertising? If so, how should they be applied in radio and television advertising?

2. Why is the New York attorney general the plaintiff in the lawsuit? Could a consumer who had shopped for or purchased a car at Terry Buick have brought a suit? See also Smeyres v. General Motors Corp., 820 F.2d 782 (6th Cir.1987).

3. Did Terry Buick's advertising comply with Reg. Z § 226.24(c)? Note that this section uses the "trigger" concept. That is, certain terms must be disclosed as a complete package if any one of the listed "trigger" terms are advertised. What is the rationale for requiring a package disclosure? Should other terms have been included in the "trigger" list?

4. Reconsider the Ford Motor Co. case, supra at page 99. There, the F.T.C. attacked credit advertising in general deceptive practice terms, rather than as being in violation of a detailed disclosure statute. At the time, of course, there was no TILA; indeed, federal law looked much like the New York statute involved in Terry Buick. Which approach do you feel provides a better tool for dealing with deceptive advertising?

Problem 8

Examine closely the advertisement from a local auto dealership reprinted on the following page. Does it comply with the requirements for credit advertising contained in the TILA? See Reg. Z. § 226.24.

Problem 9

What do you think of the rebate offer in the ad on the previous page? Assume that you have purchased a new car in response to this ad. Assume also that after your down payment, a balance of $10,000 is left on the price of the car and that the rebate on this car is $1,000. You are now confronted with a choice: Do you take the low APR or do you take the rebate? If you elect the low rate, you would finance this $10,000 balance at 2.9% for, say, 36 months. If you take the rebate, you would have to take an APR at a higher market rate, say 10%. Of course, you could also reduce the amount financed (unpaid balance) by applying the rebate to the price.

   1. Which is the better deal? Are you better off financing $10,000 at 2.9% over 36 months, or $9,000 at 10% over 36 months? How can you tell? (About two-thirds of car buyers confronted with this choice elect the low rate.)

   2. If it should turn out that the overall economic effect of the two deals is about the same, is it deceptive to advertise and offer a choice between large cash rebates and too-good-to-be-true APRs?

   3. Assume you elect the 2.9% APR. What APR should be stated in the TIL disclosures? 2.9%? But might the rebate be a hidden finance charge? If so, wouldn't that increase the APR? And wouldn't a creditor who fails to disclose the rebate as a finance charge, or who discloses the APR as 2.9%, be making a grievously incorrect disclosure? You will be better able to evaluate this question after you have read the material in the following section. See Problem 12, infra.

5. THE EDGES OF A CONCEPT—WHAT IS A FINANCE CHARGE?

As noted above, these materials do not pretend to cover all Truth in Lending issues. We turn now, however, to the item that is central to the credit cost disclosure function of TIL—the finance charge. The concept of "finance charge" is probably the most important concept in the TILA, so it is worth some effort to understand it. First, if a creditor imposes a finance charge in a consumer transaction, that fact alone brings him within the scope of the TILA. See the definition of "creditor" in TILA § 103. Secondly, the finance charge is the figure which translates into the "annual percentage rate" (APR), especially in closed-end transactions. While "finance charge" is expressed in dollars, "APR" is expressed in percentages. Thus, the finance charge tells the consumer the real cost of credit, while the APR tells the comparative cost. It works in the same way as other comparative cost expressions such as cents per pound or dollars per gallon. At this point, you should examine Reg. Z § 226.4 in some detail. You might also take a look at § 226.22(a)(1).

Caveat: TIL "Finance Charges" and State Law Interest Rates

Truth in Lending regulates only the *disclosure* of credit costs; it does *not* set usury limits or otherwise regulate the permissible amounts of interest charges. This function remains that of the states. As we will see in a later chapter, state rate-ceiling legislation is a hodgepodge of rules which set different rates for different kinds of transactions, often stating permissible rates as "add-ons," "discounts," monthly carrying charges, and so on and on. State laws also often specifically permit certain additional charges to be imposed beyond the basic "interest" ceiling. There is absolutely no uniformity from state to state with respect to maximum rates or the method of calculating those charges. Thus the uniform disclosure rules of Truth in Lending will often produce disclosed "finance charges" and "annual percentage rates" quite different from the numerical rate limits set by state law. Students should not be mystified at seeing TIL disclosures that appear high: TIL begins with a half-heartedly inclusive definition of finance charge, and then requires that the APR be stated as a simple-interest percentage. These factors in combination lead to *disclosed* TIL rates which in many cases are numerically higher than (but not violative of) those state rate ceilings which are expressed in non-simple interest terms.

FIRST ACADIANA BANK v. FEDERAL DEPOSIT INSURANCE CORP.

United States Court of Appeals, Fifth Circuit, 1987.
833 F.2d 548.

PATRICK E. HIGGINBOTHAM, CIRCUIT JUDGE:

First Acadiana Bank seeks review of a final administrative order by the Federal Deposit Insurance Corporation. The FDIC found the Bank in violation of the Truth-in-Lending Act and FDIC regulations and ordered the Bank to reimburse certain customers. We affirm.

In 1984, the FDIC notified First Acadiana Bank of Eunice, Louisiana, that it was in violation of the Truth-in-Lending Act and FDIC regulations. Since October 1, 1982, the Bank's policy has been to require each car-loan borrower to employ a bank-approved attorney to prepare a valid chattel mortgage on the car. For two-thirds of such customers, these legal fees were included in the amount financed by the Bank. The amount of the fee was always determined by the attorney and ranged from $55 to $151 per loan.

When the Bank financed such a fee, it did not add it to the "finance charge" listed on the disclosure form presented to the borrower. Nor was the fee included in the computation of the annual percentage rate (APR) listed on the same form. Had these fees been included in the finance charge, the APR in any given loan would have been from half a point to ten points higher than that quoted by the Bank. However, the fees were included in the category "amount financed" and separately disclosed to the borrower.

After the Bank refused to alter its policy pursuant to the compliance examiner's report, the FDIC Board of Review issued a Notice of Charges and of Hearing. An administrative law judge entered an initial decision against the Bank that the FDIC's Board of Directors adopted in whole.

The FDIC order commands the Bank to cease and desist from failing to include the attorneys' fees as part of the finance charge on its disclosure form. The Board also ordered the Bank to identify all consumer automobile loans it made since October 1, 1982, in which the finance charge and annual percentage rate were understated. The Bank must then reimburse each borrower to the extent of the understatement.

* * *

Under the Act's definition, the attorneys' fees obviously constitute part of the finance charge. Payment of the fees was "incident to the extension of credit," because the Bank would not extend credit otherwise. Likewise, the attorneys' fee to perfect a mortgage is not "of a type payable in a comparable cash transaction," because a cash sale would involve no security interest.

In addition, the fees were "imposed directly or indirectly by the creditor," and thus within the Act's definition. The Bank contends that the fee was imposed not by the Bank but by the attorney perfecting the mortgage insofar as the attorney set the amount of the fee and kept the proceeds. According to the Bank, its policy was simply the practical consequence of Louisiana's strict requirements for a valid chattel mortgage.

We reject the Bank's approach. The Bank has required its borrowers, as a condition to the extension of credit, to pay an avoidable economic cost. Louisiana law does not require the Bank to take a mortgage on a car loan, or to have an attorney complete the mortgage documents. The fact that the precise amount of the fee was set by a third party makes no difference.

We also do not agree that the disputed fees could be finance charges only if the Bank had retained them. *Cf. Abbey v. Columbus Dodge, Inc.*, 607 F.2d 85, 86 (5th Cir.1979) (finance charge includes filing fee only partly retained by lender). Although the Bank retained no fee, it retained a substantial benefit from the attorneys' services: a perfected security interest.

It would be difficult to reconcile any other interpretation with the Act's explicit examples of finance charges, several of which involve payments to third parties. "Finders fees," a "fee for an investigation or credit report," or an insurance premium against the borrower's default all may be set and retained by a party other than the lender.

* * *

Affirmed.

JERRE S. WILLIAMS, CIRCUIT JUDGE, specially concurring:

The opinion for the Court omits a highly significant fact in this case, and as a result reaches a conclusion which extends the definition of "finance charges" under the law beyond reasonable statutory limits.

The critical fact is that the Bank recommended two attorneys regularly who were closely associated with the Bank to draft the chattel mortgages which the Bank required. The inclusion of those fees in the "amounts financed" portion of the disclosure form was automatic, and the bank collected the fees and paid the attorneys. Under these circumstances I agree that these fees were finance charges.

At least some of the chattel mortgages were drafted by other attorneys in the community who were not recommended by and had no connection with the Bank. The FDIC takes the position that the fees charged by those attorneys also are finance charges of the Bank but then specifically eschews any attempt to take action against the Bank for failure to include those fees on the ground of pragmatic difficulty.

Since the opinion for the Court does not properly distinguish between a wholly independent action by a lawyer which is necessary and properly required by the Bank before it will issue a loan from the "in house" actions of the Bank in this case, I find it important to dispute this broad interpretation of the statute by the FDIC and by the panel opinion.

I start with the proposition that it is reasonable and sound for a Bank to require that before it gives an automobile loan it will demand a chattel mortgage. It is also reasonable for the Bank to require that the chattel mortgage be drafted by a lawyer. These are simply qualifications which a Bank has a right to make before it will engage in the voluntary act of granting a loan on an automobile. We are not here testing the right of the Bank to demand professional qualifications. Under the reasoning of the panel opinion, if the chattel mortgage had been drafted by the applicant on a standard form sold in the stores or anyone else, the cost of purchasing the form would, under the reasoning of the majority, constitute a "finance charge". If the Bank required that such loan applications be typed, the cost of typing the applications would be a finance charge. If the automobile in question had been purchased at a foreclosure sale, the cost of obtaining the requisite documents to establish clear title from the court clerk would also be a finance charge. I suppose even the ink or pencil used by an individual applicant to fill out an application would be a finance charge.

* * *

Notes

1. Do you agree with the "parade of horribles" raised by the concurring opinion? Under the majority ruling, could the cost of ink really be a finance charge? Are Louisiana creditors hindered in their attempts to take security in car loans?

2. Could a lawyer ethically prepare a security agreement under the circumstances described in the opinion? Who is the client? Who pays the fees? Whose interest would the lawyer understand she is to protect?

3. Examine the list of items in Reg. Z § 226.4(b) and (c) more closely. Notice, for example, that "points" paid by the buyer are included, (b)(3), while "points" paid by the seller are not, (c)(5). Why? ("Points" are front-end charges imposed by a lender on a seller or buyer, typically in real estate sales.) No matter which party gets charged initially with the points, who eventually pays them?

4. What is the rationale for the exclusions in Reg. Z § 226.4(c)(7)? Wouldn't those items be included in the finance charge but for the special exclusion? Do these exclusions distort the APR disclosed in real estate transactions? Do they reflect the power of the real estate lobby?

5. Students should now appreciate the double significance of determining that a particular charge is within or without the finance charge. If it is in, it increases the numerator of the fraction that becomes the APR. If it is excluded, it not only decreases the numerator by the amount of the charge, it also increases the denominator. Thus, the mathematical effect is compounded, and the APR decreases dramatically. This is so because items excluded from the finance charge are usually (unless prepaid in cash) included in the "amount financed."

Problem 10

Reconsider the Home Equity Loan plan reproduced on page 133. This plan will carry several charges which any given consumer might or might not incur. Assume that the following charges may be imposed under the plan. Which of them are "finance charges" under Reg Z § 226.4?

A. Charges when the account is opened:

1. $50 application fee.

2. $25 "commission" to the employee who personally solicits the consumer's application.

3. $250 settlement charges (appraisal, credit report, title search, deed preparation and recording, and title insurance premium).

B. Regular recurring charges:

1. Interest at a daily periodic rate of .049315 on outstanding balances.

2. Service charge of $1 for the handling of each draft used to draw on the credit line.

3. Monthly premium for credit life insurance.

4. Semi-annual premium for property insurance on the consumer's home.

C. Extraordinary charges:

1. $5 fee for stopping payment on a draft.

2. $15 fee for sending a monthly payment check which bounces.

3. Fees for late payment or for exceeding the credit limit.

4. Attorney's fees and foreclosure costs in the event of default.

HEFFERMAN v. BITTON

United States Court of Appeals, Ninth Circuit, 1989.
882 F.2d 379.

SNEED, CIRCUIT JUDGE:

The district court below ordered lender Bernard Brill to pay consumer Diane K. Hefferman a $1000 civil penalty plus costs and attorney's fees for failing to comply with the Truth in Lending Act (TILA). Hefferman, dissatisfied with the civil penalty, appeals from the court's refusal to order Brill to refund the interest and loan costs that she has paid him. Brill cross-appeals from the judgment against him and the denial of attorney's fees. Lenders Edward F. Reid, Bernadette Y. Bitton, and Nathan Bitton, whom the court dismissed as defendants, also cross-appeal from the denial of attorney's fees. We affirm the district court's refusal to award additional relief to Hefferman, reverse its judgment against Brill, and affirm its denials of attorney's fees.

I.

FACTS AND PROCEEDINGS BELOW

On September 24, 1984, Brill, Reid, and the Bittons loaned Hefferman $22,000 in exchange for three notes secured by a single deed of trust on Hefferman's condominium in Walnut Creek, California. Hefferman promised in the notes to repay $3080 to Brill, $7920 to Reid, and $11,000 to the Bittons at sixteen percent interest in twenty-three installments due each month from November 1, 1984, to October 1, 1986, with a single balloon payment afterwards. Before giving her the money, the lenders withheld $2,200 for a broker's fee (finance charge) and $297 for title insurance, escrow fees, and recording fees. Hefferman, and the third parties to whom she assigned the money, thus received a total of $19,503. She used $389.77 of this amount for her first installment payment.

The lenders provided Hefferman with a one-page "Federal Truth-in-Lending Disclosure Statement" patterned closely on model forms published by the Federal Reserve Board. The disclosure statement contained two apparent inconsistencies that the parties did not notice immediately. First, the lenders listed the "Amount Financed" as $19,800 at the top of the form but as $22,000 at the bottom of the form. Second, they stated the "Total of Payments" as $29,040.01, * * *.

* * *

We begin by determining whether Brill violated TILA's elaborate disclosure requirements. We conclude that he did not.

* * *

The $19,800 figure at the top of the lenders' disclosure statement complies with the requirements of [§ 128(a)(2)(A)]. The principal amount ($22,000), plus the charges financed by Hefferman which are not part of the finance charge or principal ($0), minus the finance charge withheld from the proceeds of the credit ($2,200), equals $19,800.

Section 1638(a)(2)(B) enables creditors to clarify the calculation of the amount financed through an itemization. * * * The lenders provided an itemization on the one-page disclosure statement pursuant to this provision. The itemization satisfies (i) by showing that the lenders paid Hefferman $10,941.28 directly. It satisfies (ii) by stating a credit of $389.77 for the first payment on the loan. It satisfies (iii) by listing individual charges of $297 for title insurance, escrow fees and recorder fees, $4279.77 for taxes, $1,699.18 for "Central Bank," and $2,193.00 for "PMBIc." Finally, it satisfies (iv) by listing $2,200 as a finance charge.

The lenders, therefore, correctly stated the amount financed and they correctly itemized it. A problem arose only when they decided to use the official sample format for the itemization that the Federal Reserve Board has provided in 12 C.F.R. pt. 226, app. H, at H–3 (1988). This sample format includes a line, immediately above the itemization figures, reading "Itemization of the Amount Financed of $_____." The lenders copied this line onto his disclosure statement but had difficulty filling in the blank space. Although the amount financed technically was $19,800, the itemization added up to $22,000. The difference in the figures stems from a distinction made by the statute; section 1638(a)(2)(B)(iv) requires the lenders to include the $2,200 finance charge in the itemization but § 1638(a)(2)(A)(iii) instructed them to omit it in calculating the amount financed.

The lenders, admittedly, created some confusion by placing $22,000 in the sample format's blank space because they made the disclosure statement inconsistent. But some confusion was unavoidable. Stating $19,800 in the space also would have created confusion because it would not comport with the itemization. In the past, we always have required lenders to comply strictly and completely with all of TILA's requirements. Yet, it makes no sense to convert TILA from a shield protecting consumers into a sword allowing them to strike lenders who have followed the statute and its regulations as closely as logic permits. We thus decline to find an error in the lenders' disclosure of the amount financed.[1]

* * *

We conclude that, despite the peculiarities in the disclosure statement, Hefferman has failed to convince us to hold Brill liable for violating any of TILA's disclosure requirements. * * *. We conclude that Hefferman had no right to rescission and we reverse the district court's award to Hefferman of the civil penalty, attorney's fees, and costs.

* * *

1. To hold otherwise would mean that only by filing two statements, one using the $22,000 figure as the amount financed and the other the $19,800 figure, together with a note of explanation, could the lender hope to deflect the borrower's sword. Even this might fail because it could be argued that complexity obscured truth.

Notes

1. If Hefferman received $19,503 and was to make a "Total of Payments" of $29,040, isn't the "Finance Charge" equal to ($29,040 − 19,503) $9537? Under Reg. Z § 226.4(a) that would seem to be the "cost of consumer credit as a dollar amount" in this transaction, including all charges "payable directly or indirectly by the consumer." See TILA § 106(a). Can you explain why this general, but basic, regulatory definition should not be followed to its logical conclusion?

2. Should a "broker's fee" be included in "finance charge"? In this case it is a fee, not to a real estate broker, but to a loan broker," as a fee for finding a willing lender. See TILA § 106(a)(3). If such a fee should be included in the finance charge, can it *also* be part "Amount Financed"? The definition of that term in TILA § 128(a)(2)(A) and in Reg. Z § 226.18(b) seems to indicate that the designations are mutually exclusive.

3. If the $2200 broker's fee *is* part of the "Finance Charge," why should it be one of the parts of an itemized amount financed? Your response to that question may be determined by your concept of what is the purpose of the optional itemization established by TILA § 128(a)(2)(B). Note the difficulties in fixing a firm label on "costs of credit" which are paid to third parties.

4. One effect of increasing the amount of the "Amount Financed" is that it proportionally reduces the A.P.R., even if the Finance Charge is not affected. Has the *Hefferman* court given creditors a new way to play games in rate reduction? See the following materials on "hidden finance charges."

Hidden Finance Charges

YAZZIE v. REYNOLDS

United States Court of Appeals, Tenth Circuit, 1980.
623 F.2d 638.

WILLIAM E. DOYLE, CIRCUIT JUDGE.

In this federal Truth-in-Lending Act case, the plaintiffs-appellants seek reversal of an order of the United States District Court of the District of New Mexico. The cause was disposed of on summary judgment. * * * The claim is that Reynolds violated the Truth-in-Lending Act and Federal Reserve Regulation Z, 12 C.F.R. § 226.1 *et seq*. The crux of the claim is that Reynolds failed to disclose a finance charge and to express it as an annual percentage rate when, in fact, the allegation is, a finance charge was imposed on credit customers.
* * *

There is no dispute about the facts:

Reynolds, who does business in Gallup, New Mexico, as Ben's Auto Sales, was engaged in retail sale of used cars. 98% of his sales were pursuant to installment contracts which provided for four or more payments payable on a prearranged schedule. * * * The practice was that the price was the same regardless of whether the buyer agreed to pay cash or to pay for the car in installments. Furthermore, Reynolds, according to the stipulated facts, did not sell the contracts at a discount to any other individual or financing institution. There were, nevertheless, expenses in collecting delinquent payments and repossessing automobiles. According to the evidence, this service was performed by Reynolds' salesmen. They were given notice at the outset of their employment that they would be, from time to time, required to make collections or repossessions and they did so. Reynolds would sometimes furnish an automobile for the purpose of performing this service. The salesmen would make the collections and sometimes would repossess the vehicle by connecting it to the salesman's car through the use of a towing bar.

The trial court ruled that there had been a failure to prove that Reynolds' automobiles were artificially priced so as to hide finance charges, or that there were any real differences between the cash price and the deferred payment price. The court found also that the evidence failed to establish the existence of hidden finance charges and that the contract language was not confusing. Each of the transactions was negotiated face-to-face by the plaintiffs with the salesmen, and the agreed price was in accordance with an oral agreement. The trial court determined that costs incurred by Reynolds for extension of credit were part of his regular business expenses; that these are not in any way reflected in the price which he charged installment customers.

The important issue in the case is whether this single-price sales approach was intended to and did conceal the cost of credit so as to circumvent the Truth-in-Lending Act, 15 U.S.C. § 1601, *et seq.* and 12 C.F.R. § 226.4. * * * [T]he contract provided under the heading of "Finance Charge" and "Annual Percentage Rate" a zero. Also, each contract contained a space labeled "cash price" and another space stating "Deferred Payment Price." On each contract the appellee disclosed the "Deferred Payment Price" as an amount equal to the "Cash Price." * * *

Plaintiffs contend:

1. That a finance charge under the statute is imposed on credit buyers where the creditor has an insignificant percentage of cash sales and incurs substantial costs in connection with the extension of credit. * * * Finance charges within the meaning of the Act are, as we have noted above, all charges payable by the person to whom the credit is extended, and charges "imposed directly or indirectly by the creditor as an incident to the extension of credit * * *" 15 U.S.C. § 1605. The obvious object is to prevent hidden, undisclosed costs whereby the credit buyer is unable to know the identity of the credit items. If any such finance items were added to the cost of the automobile and charged the buyer, it is essential that they be disclosed to the buyer in order that he or she can make informed decisions. In other words, the defendant was required to disclose any sums of money which stemmed from the credit transaction. The automobiles which were sold were not expensive, but

the number of payments were in excess of four. The same pattern was present in every instance. Also, the evidence established that 98% of the sales made by the defendant provided for payment in more than four installments, and that there were necessarily costs which grew out of this way of doing business. Books had to be kept on the status of each sale, receipts had to be given when payments were made, and fees were paid for collection of delinquent payments in nearly all of the instances in which there was a time contract. Defendant had a vehicle used for collections and repossessions with a tow bar. Furthermore, he suffered losses on account of unpaid and uncollected bills. The cash customers were charged the same amount as the credit customers, but credit customers necessarily required added expenditure, particularly those customers that required trips to relatively distant towns for the purpose of making the collection or repossessing the vehicle. It is not difficult to infer from the record before us that the purchase price to the credit customer, at least some part of it, was used to defray the costs of collection or repossession, or both. * * * In the light of the Act, a single price for both cash and credit transactions, notwithstanding that the vast portion of the business of the defendant-appellee involved installment payments which are costly, tends to show that the defendant is seeking to avoid the requirements of the Truth-in-Lending Act. In other words, the evidence in the case raises at least a factual issue as to whether these transactions are a ploy which has been designed to avoid the Truth-in-Lending Act.

* * *

The judgment of the district court must, then, be reversed and the cause must be remanded for further proceedings consistent with the expressions contained herein.

Notes

1. For a more recent case reaching the same result and citing *Yazzie* with approval, see In re Stewart, infra, at page 649.

2. Two important questions are presented by the Yazzie case: (a) if a credit seller buries credit costs in his general overhead, must he make any TIL disclosures at all; and (b) if so, must the creditor somehow allocate a specific portion of those costs to a given transaction, identify it as a "finance charge," and compute it into an APR?

The answer to the first question is easy: Yes. See the definition of "creditor" in Reg. Z § 226.2(a)(17). Reynolds, in the case, complied with this rule; he did give his customers a disclosure statement. The answer to the second question is more difficult. Note that Reynolds disclosed a "$0.00" finance charge and a "0%" APR. Is this correct? As the court notes, it is indisputable that there were at least some credit costs. These include at least the collection and handling costs, to say nothing of the lost opportunity costs. But are those costs measurable? Should a creditor be forced to divide a "unitary" price, for example (the same for all customers, cash or credit), into amount financed and finance charge per transaction?

If we do not require the creditor to do this, how can the comparative shopping purpose of truth in lending be fulfilled?

3. If you were counsel for the consumers in Yazzie, what factual information would you want to introduce on a new motion for summary judgment or at trial? I.e., how would you go about proving that there is in fact an identifiable finance charge in these transactions?

4. At least one of your authors thinks that the law should require creditors who bury finance charges to make the following disclosure:

WARNING: THE PRICE OF THIS CAR HAS BEEN ARTIFICIALLY INFLATED BY THE LARGE COSTS OF OUR CREDIT OPERATIONS. IF YOU ARE PAYING CASH, YOU ARE SUBSIDIZING OTHER CUSTOMERS WHO ARE PAYING ON CREDIT.

Problem 11A

Jane Consumer buys a new compact disc player from Cal's Discount Audio Shop, and pays the $200 price using her VISA card. While Jane will have to repay her bank the $200, Cal got only $192 out of the transaction. This is because the bank charges a 4% "merchant discount" to merchants who honor the cards. The discount covers costs such as handling paperwork, advancing credit to the merchant, and collecting from Jane and other cardholders. Jane's monthly statement, however, makes no mention of the 4% merchant discount, nor is that amount computed into the finance charge or APR disclosed to Jane. Has the issuing bank violated the TILA? If so, why is it that no card issuer includes information about merchant discounts on its monthly statements? If not, can you distinguish Yazzie?

Problem 11B

Suppose Cal decided to encourage customers to pay cash for stereo equipment by offering cash customers a 4% discount, while continuing to charge credit-card customers the full price. The 4% discount is clearly a finance charge, is it not? See Reg. Z § 226.4(b)(9). But must Cal, or the card issuing bank, compute and disclose it as such? See Reg. Z § 226.4(c)(8) and TILA § 167(b). Would the analysis change if, instead of reducing the price for cash customers, Cal imposed a "surcharge" of 4% on customers who paid by credit card? See TILA § 103(p) and (q). Should it make a difference?

Problem 12

Reconsider the credit advertising problem on page 144. Is 2.9% the true cost of credit to the consumer? If the rebate is really a finance charge because the consumer can get it only by electing a higher rate (and your authors agree, for once, that it is), shouldn't it be disclosed as such and calculated into the APR? But if the rebate comes from the manufacturer, is the *dealer* obligated to make this disclosure? Would it make any difference in the analysis if the dealer was required to "buy down" the APR by making a cash payment to the finance company? Should the amount of the "buy down" be included in the finance charge?

HENDLEY v. CAMERON–BROWN CO.

United States Court of Appeals, Eleventh Circuit, 1988.
840 F.2d 831.

VANCE, CIRCUIT JUDGE:

The question in this appeal is whether appellee, a mortgage company, properly disclosed the terms of appellants' discounted variable rate loans as required by the Truth In Lending Act, 15 U.S.C. §§ 1601–1693r. Appellants argue that the mortgage company failed to disclose fully the circumstances which would increase the initial interest rate. Finding that appellee was technically in compliance with the regulations and that appellee's good faith effort protected any disclosure inadequacies, the district court for the Middle District of Georgia granted appellee's motion for summary judgment. We reverse.

I.

In the spring of 1984, appellants, the Hendleys and the Blacks, obtained discounted variable rate mortgage loans from appellee to finance the purchase of their homes. One feature of the variable rate loans was the annual adjustment of the interest rate. The annual interest rate was based on an "index plus margin" formula which was determined by adding to the margin, preset at 2.79%, the current index. Appellants claim that they were informed that the interest rate on the loans would adjust annually in the same direction as the index. The Hendleys closed their $69,250 loan on April 30, 1984. On the next day, May 1, 1984, the Blacks closed their $80,025.46 loan. At closing, appellants received a Truth In Lending Disclosure Statement. This disclosure statement identified the mortgage as a variable rate loan and provided that "[t]he interest rate may increase during the term of this transaction if the index increases."

Approximately forty-five days before the end of the loan's first year, appellee informed appellants that the interest rate for the second year would increase from 9.875% to 11.875%. Appellee claims that this increase was based on the "index plus margin" formula provided in the loan agreement checked by the 2% annual cap.[2] Objecting to this increase, appellants filed suit claiming that appellee failed to comply with the disclosure requirements of the Truth In Lending Act. Because the index actually declined in the second year from 10.53% to 9.61%, appellants maintain that the increase is inconsistent with the disclosure statement's language that the interest rate would be adjusted annually in the same direction as the index. Appellants argue that appellee failed to disclose the initial index and that the initial interest rate was discounted or lower than the rate would be if it were calculated by using the "index plus margin" formula. According to appellants these undisclosed facts created other circumstances for an increased

---

2. The annual adjustment was subject to a 2% cap, up or down, each year and an overall cap of 5.75% for the lifetime of the loan.

interest rate and the failure to disclose this information violated statutory and regulatory disclosure requirements.

The district court ruled that the mortgage company technically complied with the requirements of the Truth In Lending Act and its regulations. The district court found that the initial index information "was not explicitly disclosed" and that the disclosure statement failed to disclose that the initial interest rate was discounted. The court nevertheless held that appellee technically complied with the disclosure requirements due to the lack of specific guidance for discounted variable rate loans. Since the discounted variable rate loan was a new product in early 1984 and the application of Regulation Z, 12 C.F.R. § 226, to these loans was not clear, the court ruled that "any inadequacies are protected by [appellee's] good faith effort at compliance."

II.

Congress enacted the Truth In Lending Act to ensure meaningful disclosures in consumer credit transactions. *See* 15 U.S.C. § 1601(a). The Federal Reserve Board ("Board") promulgated Regulation Z to execute the purposes of the Truth In Lending Act. The Board established the disclosure requirements for variable rate loans in 12 C.F.R. § 226.18(f). This provision provides:

> If the annual percentage rate may increase after consummation, the following disclosures [are required]:

> (1) The circumstances under which the rate may increase.

* * *

We hold that appellee did not comply with the first requirement by fully disclosing the "circumstances under which the rate may increase." The disclosure statement provided that "the interest rate may increase during the term of this transaction if the index increases." This, however, was not the only circumstance which could cause an increase in the interest rate. As the district court stated, "[t]he problem is that the statement fails to note that the initial interest rate is discounted, creating the possibility of an increase even when the index does not rise." Due to the initial discounted interest rate, the annual interest rate could increase if the index remained constant, or even if the index declined. Absent this information, the disclosure failed to meet regulatory standards.

* * *

Appellee also argues that even if the disclosure were improper, it is insulated from liability under 15 U.S.C. § 1640(f) because it acted in good faith in accordance with the Board's official interpretation of regulation § 226.18(f). * * * Section 1640(f) "does not protect a creditor who *fails* to conform with a regulation or interpretation through an honest, good faith mistake." So a creditor's honest and reasonable but mistaken interpretation is not protected. Appellee's belief that the regulation did not require further disclosure based on its mistaken interpretation of the regulation and reliance on an inapplicable interpretation does not protect it from liability. As a matter of law, the section 1640(f) good faith defense is not available.

III.

Accordingly, we reverse the district court's decision granting summary judgment in favor of appellees and remand for further proceedings consistent with this opinion.

REVERSED and REMANDED.

Notes

1. Variable rates present some formidable problems under the Truth in Lending disclosure scheme, because not only the APR but also the number and amount of payments may change. Do you think that this is an area where consumers are particularly vulnerable and therefore need some additional protection? Why? Read Reg. Z §§ 226.18(f) and 226.19(b). Do these provisions require disclosure of all the important features of variable rate loans? Is there information you would like to see disclosed that is not included? Do they provide consumers with enough information so they can properly analyze and compare the various new types of alternative mortgages such as graduated payment (not variable rate) mortgages, growth equity mortgages, reverse annuity mortgages, etc.?

2. Consumer spokespersons have argued vigorously for the need for a "worst case" hypothetical example to show the borrower the largest possible increase under the particular variable rate plan. Do current regulations require such a disclosure? What would be the worst case example for a mortgage with no rate or payment caps?

3. Read Reg. Z § 226.30. This provision was added in 1987 after Congress enacted the Competitive Equality Banking Act of 1987. This provision goes beyond the normal scope of truth in lending and actually imposes a substantive requirement, a "lifetime cap" on the rate which may be imposed. Does it say what the "cap" should be? Are creditors really limited by this rule?

4. For more discussion of variable rate mortgages, see chapter 12, infra at page 694.

SECTION C. DISCLOSURE IN OTHER TRANSACTIONS

1. CONSUMER LEASES

During the early 1970's, leasing of automobiles and other durable consumer goods became a popular alternative to buying these items. Because the original TILA did not expressly cover leases, Congress added the Consumer Leasing Act (CLA) to it in 1976. See TILA §§ 181–187. The CLA requires certain disclosures to be made in lease transactions which exceed four months. Federal Reserve Board Regulation M, like its TIL counterpart, Reg. Z, spells out the details.

Of particular concern to Congress was the so-called open-end or "net" lease. This arrangement typically guaranteed the lessor a specified return on the lease, and also made the lessee responsible for a deficiency at the end of the lease term if the value of the car dropped below a certain pre-arranged level. As a result, the consumer ran the risk of depreciation. Continuing the approach of the TILA, the CLA does not regulate the substance of consumer lease transactions; instead, it is merely a disclosure law. The CLA is not difficult to apply or understand in the average case. See, e.g., Blum v. General Motors Acceptance Corporation, 185 Ga.App. 714, 365 S.E.2d 474 (1988).

A more troublesome type of consumer lease is the so-called "rent-to-own" contract. These transactions have dramatically increased their share of the consumer goods market during the past decade or so. Unlike auto leases, which are typically for terms of years, the typical rent-to-own contract obligates the consumer on a week to week basis. This keeps these contracts out of the reach of the CLA. But are they subject to the TILA? Consider the following.

REMCO ENTERPRISES, INC. v. HOUSTON
Kansas Court of Appeals, 1984.
9 Kan.App.2d 296, 677 P.2d 567.

HARRY G. MILLER, JUDGE:

The defendant Alice Houston appeals from the trial court's denial of her two counterclaims against plaintiff Remco Enterprises, Inc. The plaintiff cross-appeals from the trial court's denial of its petition seeking past-due rental payments and possession of a television set which plaintiff had rented to defendant.

The plaintiff is in the business of renting television sets and other appliances. At the time of the trial, the defendant was a 20–year–old single mother of three who had completed only the ninth grade in school and was dependent upon aid to dependent children welfare payments of $320 per month.

On September 11, 1980, plaintiff and defendant entered into a rental agreement with an option to purchase a stereo component set. This agreement provided that if the defendant made 69 weekly payments of $12 each, she would become the owner of the stereo set.

On September 13, 1980, plaintiff and defendant entered into a rental agreement with an option to purchase a console color TV set. This agreement provided that if the defendant made 104 weekly payments of $17 each, she would become the owner of the TV set.

Both agreements were identical but for the number and the amount of payments, and provided that defendant could cancel the agreement at any time by returning the rented property. The agreements also obligated the plaintiff to maintain the equipment.

Defendant complied with the agreement for the stereo set and made the final payment to plaintiff on January 4, 1982. Plaintiff accordingly transferred the ownership of the stereo set to the defendant. On January 23, 1982, with 36 weekly payments remaining on the TV set, defendant made her last payment. On February 1, 1982, plaintiff sued defendant to recover the TV set and past-due rental payments. The defendant counterclaimed alleging that plaintiff had violated the Truth in Lending Act (TILA), 15 U.S.C. § 1601 *et seq.* (1976) and amendments thereto, and the unconscionability provisions of the Kansas Consumer Protection Act, K.S.A. 50–623 *et seq.* and amendments thereto. * * *

In Count I of defendant's counterclaim, the defendant alleged that the "Rental Agreement with Option to Purchase" covering the TV set was in fact a disguised credit sale, and that plaintiff violated the TILA and Regulation Z, 12 C.F.R. § 226 (1980), by failing to disclose the amount of the finance charge and by failing to express the amount of the finance charge in an annual percentage rate. Plaintiff argues that the above disclosures were not required since the agreement was not a "credit sale" within the meaning of the TILA.

* * *

Plaintiff does not contest that defendant had the option to become the owner of the TV set for no additional consideration upon her compliance with her contractual obligations. Nor does plaintiff contest defendant's assertion that the total payments required over the 104 week period, $1,768, was in excess of the aggregate value of the TV set. Rather, plaintiff argues that because the defendant had the right to terminate the agreement at any time after making the first week's payment of $17, she was not contractually obligated to pay any sum substantially equivalent to or in excess of the aggregate value of the TV set which had a retail value of $850.

The rental agreement makes it clear that the defendant had the right to terminate the agreement at the end of any week without penalty in this provision:

> "TERMINATION BY RENTER: Renter may terminate this agreement at the end of any rental period by return of the property to owner. Renter is *required* to rent the property for only one rental period."

The agreement also makes it clear that the "rental period" is for one week, and that plaintiff agrees to maintain the TV set in good working order and repair it during defendant's use and possession of it.

* * *

Modified Regulation Z, promulgated by the FRB subsequent to the passage of the Truth in Lending Simplification & Reform Act of 1980, in defining the term "credit sale" specifically excludes a bailment or lease that is terminable without penalty at any time by the consumer. 12 C.F.R. § 226.2(a)(16) (1983). This revised definition reveals the current intent of the FRB that rental agreements such as the one involved herein are not "credit sales" and are not subject to the disclosure requirements of the TILA or Regulation Z.

We therefore conclude that the trial court's ruling that the rental agreement between the plaintiff and the defendant was not a "credit sale" within the meaning of the TILA was not erroneous.

Defendant next contends that the trial court erred in not finding that the excessive price charged by plaintiff and the unfair advantage gained by the plaintiff due to the defendant's poverty and limited education violated the unconscionability provisions of the Kansas Consumer Protection Act, K.S.A. 50–623 *et seq.* and amendments thereto.

* * *

In the present case, the contract called for defendant to pay $1,768 for the set that had a retail value of $850. This allowed plaintiff a profit of $918, or an increase of 108% over the retail price, a near 2:1 ratio. No cases have been cited in which a comparable retail price discrepancy formed the basis for a finding of unconscionability.

The 108% markup in the present case does not shock the conscience of this court when the circumstances surrounding the execution of the contract, including its commercial setting and its purpose and actual effect, are considered.

Although defendant would have had to pay 108% more than a cash customer, defendant received the benefit of not being responsible for service or repairs to the TV set, of not having to undergo a credit check or make a down payment, and of having the option to return the set and cancel the agreement at any time after one week. Most importantly, she received the benefit and use of a TV set which she might not have otherwise had. Although in retrospect it may seem to have been a bad bargain, the price disparity does not rise to the level of unconscionability.

Defendant further argues that the agreement was procedurally unconscionable because of defendant's financial and educational background. The trial court found that defendant knew that she could return the set at any time she desired to terminate the agreement, that she knew how to multiply 104 (weeks) times 17 (dollars), that she was of average intelligence and was not taken advantage of by the seller. Defendant testified that she read the agreement and knew how to multiply. She fully complied with the stereo agreement, and exercised her option to purchase the stereo. The record is devoid of any evidence of any deceptive or oppressive practices, overreaching, intentional misstatements, or concealment of facts by plaintiff.

* * *

The trial court's denial of defendant's counterclaims is affirmed.

Notes

1. The court is correct, is it not, that the current TILA does not cover rent-to-own contracts. Since the CLA does not cover them either, it appears that suppliers of consumer goods under these contracts have carefully structured the transactions so that they fall in the statutory

cracks. Does any disclosure law apply to them? Should there be a disclosure law for these transactions? For example, in the Remco contract, the total amount of the rental payments is not disclosed. Is the court's comment that the consumer "knew how to multiply 104 times 17" a sufficient answer?

2. Wasn't it obvious to all parties that Ms. Houston intended to buy the TV set? She had already paid off the stereo, and there was evidence (not discussed by the court) that both parties understood this from the beginning. There was also evidence that Remco's business is directed mainly at low income consumers who cannot get loans but who want to buy TV sets and other items, and that a substantial percentage of "lessees" do in fact pay off and buy the items. If all this is so, isn't the transaction really a secured credit sale? Isn't the distinction between a "lease" and a "sale" completely phony on these facts? See, e.g., Clark v. Rent–It Corp., 685 F.2d 245 (8th Cir.1982), cert. denied, 459 U.S. 1225, 103 S.Ct. 1232, 75 L.Ed.2d 466 (1983). See also Ayer, On the Vacuity of the Sale/Lease Distinction, 68 Iowa L.Rev. 667 (1983).

3. Consider the figures. Ms. Houston was to pay $17 a week for 104 weeks for a TV set worth $850. If this was a credit sale, the entire $918 mark-up would have to be disclosed as a finance charge, not so? What APR would this have produced? Would you believe approximately 93.50%?! Of course, this was not disclosed. It is unlikely that a court would tolerate this level of return in a credit transaction (indeed, it would be criminal in many states), yet the court said that this did not shock its conscience. Does it shock yours? Does it surprise you? Does it make you reluctant to buy a TV on a rent-to-own basis?

4. At least since 1984, bills have been regularly introduced in Congress to amend the CCPA by adding a new title which would require certain disclosures in consumer lease-purchase agreements not covered by the either the TILA or the CLA. None of these bills has ever passed. In an attempt to fill this statutory gap, several states have enacted disclosure laws for rent-to-own and similar contracts. These laws typically require disclosure of the total amount of all payments, the initial payment, other charges, penalties, and the like. See, e.g., Mich.Comp.Laws Ann. §§ 445.951 et seq. They do not, however, require the supplier to calculate and disclose the credit sale equivalent of finance charge and APR. Without this, can the consumer truly evaluate the relative merits of the deal?

5. The extremely high rate of return in the Remco lease is typical of rent-to-own agreements; in fact, many produce even higher returns. Usury laws in most states protect consumers against having to pay such exorbitant rates in loan and credit sale transactions, but usury laws normally do not apply to lease transactions. A few states, however, have recently begun to address the problem of exorbitant rates of return in lease transactions. We will look at a few examples in Chapter 11.

2. OTHER DISCLOSURE LAWS

Compulsory disclosure is not limited to credit transactions. Although there is no general "Truth in Selling" Act, there are other consumer protection statutes which have mandatory disclosure features. There are also disclosure regulations covering other subjects and products from cars to beer. Disclosure in food and drug labelling goes back several decades. The labelling requirements for alcoholic beverages can be found at 27 C.F.R. Parts 4 (wine), 5 (distilled spirits), and 7 (malt beverages). Most early disclosure rules, like the food and drug laws, were concerned primarily with public health and safety. Only relatively recently have disclosure laws been used to address purely economic concerns. This, of course, is the primary emphasis of the TILA.

There are also several product disclosure laws relating to automobiles. For example, the Motor Vehicle Information and Cost Savings Act, 15 U.S.C.A. § 1981 et seq., enacted in 1972, requires anyone who sells (or even gives away) a motor vehicle to make a written disclosure of the odometer reading and its accuracy. Used car dealers must put a FTC disclosure form on the window of used cars for sale. See 16 C.F.R. Part 455. The Environmental Protection Agency requires that new vehicles carry stickers which indicate projected fuel economy. See 40 C.F.R. Part 600. There are also labelling rules for tires. See 16 C.F.R. Part 228.

Another important disclosure law is the Interstate Land Sales Full Disclosure Act, 15 U.S.C.A. §§ 1701–20. The ILSFDA was enacted in 1968, the same year as the TILA. It requires that subdivision developers and others who sell or lease 100 or more lots of unimproved land as part of a common promotion file a complex "statement of record" in the Office of Interstate Land Sales Registration. This office is a division of the Department of Housing and Urban Development. The statement is supposed to contain details about both the land and the developer. In addition, when individual lots are sold, the developer must furnish a very detailed property report to the prospective purchaser before any contract is signed. Finally, the purchaser is given a cooling-off period, during which he may rescind the entire transaction. While this rescission right is similar to the right of rescission under the TILA, see pages 196–205, infra, the overall scheme of the ILSFDA more resembles the securities laws than the truth in lending laws.

Another disclosure law, which we will encounter elsewhere in these materials, is the Magnuson–Moss Warranty Act, 15 U.S.C.A. §§ 2301–12, enacted in 1975, which sets federal standards for written product warranties. We will study this law in more detail in chapter 6.

State law can also provide its share of mandatory disclosure laws. The most visible results of a state mandatory disclosure law are the "unit prices," which many state statutes require grocers to post in their stores, representing the price of a given item by pound, quart, or other standard measure. See, e.g., Mass.Gen.Laws Ann. ch. 94 § 183, N.J.

Stat.Ann. 56:8–21, N.Y.Agric. & Mkts.Law § 193–h (McKinney). The purpose of such statutes is to promote comparative food shopping, and they resulted from the perceived failure of different types of disclosures required by the Fair Packaging and Labeling Act (15 U.S.C.A. § 1451, et seq.). See, Schrag, Local Government and Consumer Protection, Consumer Protection Compliance, No. 4, at 8 (1971).

Generally, the number of shoppers using unit pricing is difficult to obtain since the percentage varies according to who is sponsoring the study. One study, conducted in 1972 by Compusamp for Super-marketing Magazine, revealed that 80% of consumers surveyed found unit pricing "very helpful and that those who were the oldest, poorest and best educated seemed to like it the most." New York Times, Feb. 29, 1972, at 45, col. 4. On the other hand, only a month earlier, the Consumer Research Institute, which provides research data to the food industry, concluded that most consumers are unaware of and disinterested in unit pricing. Shabecoff, United Pricing Called Something of A Dud, N.Y. Times, Jan. 31, 1972, at 22, col. 1. Out of 2400 shoppers interviewed, 65% said they noticed the labels and from this group only 74% said they understood them, with 23.5% saying they saved money by using them. There is an equally great division concerning the costs of unit price disclosure.

The most ambitious disclosure statute is New York's "Plain Language" Act. The text of this statute is reproduced below.

N.Y.GEN.OBL.LAW (McKINNEY)

§ 5–702. Requirements for Use of Plain Language in Consumer Transactions

a. Every written agreement entered into after November first, nineteen hundred seventy-eight, for the lease of space to be occupied for residential purposes, or to which a consumer is a party and the money, property or service which is the subject of the transaction is primarily for personal, family or household purposes must be:

    1. Written in a clear and coherent manner using words with common and every day meanings;

    2. Appropriately divided and captioned by its various sections.

Any creditor, seller or lessor who fails to comply with this subdivision shall be liable to a consumer who is a party to a written agreement governed by this subdivision in an amount equal to any actual damages sustained plus a penalty of fifty dollars. The total class action penalty against any such creditor, seller or lessor shall not exceed ten thousand dollars in any class action or series of class actions arising out of the use by a creditor, seller or lessor of an agreement which fails to comply with this subdivision. No action under this subdivision may be brought after both parties to the agreement have fully performed their obligation under such agreement, nor shall any creditor, seller or lessor who attempts in good faith to comply with this subdivision be liable for such penalties. This subdivision shall not apply to agreements involving amounts in excess of fifty thousand dollars nor prohibit the use of words or phrases or forms of agreement required by state or federal law, rule or regulation or by a governmental instrumentality.

b. A violation of the provisions of subdivision a. of this section shall not render any such agreement void or voidable nor shall it constitute

    1. A defense to any action or proceeding to enforce such agreement; or

    2. A defense to any action or proceeding for breach of such agreement.

All this is but a small sampling of a very long list of federal and state statutes and regulations that impose affirmative disclosure duties on suppliers of consumer products.

The questions to be asked in each case are: What is being disclosed to the consumer? How is it being disclosed? Is he likely to find it? Will he understand it if he does find it? Is the information given him limited? If so, will he recognize the limitation? Can he be misled by the limitations in the information disclosed? What is the cost to the merchant of disclosing the information? Is the benefit to the consumer worth this cost?

Problem 13

Sauce for the Gander.

If you believe that compulsory disclosure of interest rates is a good idea, then you should also decide whether that general concept should be applied to lawyers and their fees.

Under the District of Columbia Rules of Professional Conduct, Rule 1.5 (effective in 1991), lawyers must give to each new client a written statement indicating the "basis or rate" of the lawyer's fee. This statement must be given to the new client "before, or within a reasonable time after, commencing the representation." In the past, many lawyers have advised other lawyers to do so, because it is both a good business practice (avoiding ambiguities and disputes) and good public relations (clients' expectations can then be firm). In D.C. and elsewhere, it was an "ethical recommendation" before it became a "rule".

Would you support making such disclosure mandatory as a "consumer protection" measure? If not, can you articulate why creditors should disclose rates, but lawyers should not? If you cannot articulate such a reason, should we repeal TILA?

SECTION D. AN EVALUATION—WHAT IS THE EFFECTIVENESS OF MANDATORY DISCLOSURE?

What results has Truth in Lending produced? There is general disagreement on the answer to this question. The following material represents some of the divergent views. After you have read it, you should consider your own position on mandatory disclosure laws. For example, do you think they have accomplished any of their stated goals (discussed below)? Have they made consumer credit contracts more understandable to the average consumer? Are they worth all the trouble and expense? Before you can fairly evaluate these issues, you need to have some idea of just what it was these laws were designed to accomplish in the first place.

Purposes of Disclosure Laws

Disclosure laws like the Truth in Lending Act are obviously intended to inform consumers, but to what ends? And do these laws have purposes other than informational? Consider the following possibilities:

a. *A market function.* Many observers believe that well-informed consumers have a positive effect on the overall consumer market. The theory is that if there are enough well-informed consumers, suppliers of goods and services will compete for their business. The increased competition, in turn, will reduce prices. This may sound like a tall order, but this market function was emphasized by advocates of truth in lending in the very earliest Congressional hearings on the subject. For a more detailed discussion of this idea, see Schwartz and Wilde, Intervening in Markets on the Basis of Imperfect Information: A Legal and Economic Analysis, 127 U.Pa.L.Rev. 630 (1979).

b. *A prescriptive or "best buy" function.* The idea here is that well-informed consumers make better decisions. For example, a consumer who knows that the price of a TV set is lower at store A than store B will probably buy the TV from store A, all other things being equal. If all other things are not equal, however, for example if store A is too far away or store B has a better warranty, the consumer might buy at store B. The point is that the decision should be made intelligently and with full awareness of the options. See TILA § 102, which reflects this philosophy. The term "best buy" comes from Whitford, The Functions of Disclosure Regulation in Consumer Transactions, 1973 Wis.L.Rev. 400.

c. *A descriptive or "alert" function.* Rather than providing refined shopping information, the basic TIL disclosures might serve merely as warning signals for credit offerings that are far out of line. For example, a consumer might not respond to the difference between APRs of 11.00% and 11.35%, but should react to an APR of 42.00% or even 2.00%. For an elaborate analysis of this "alert" function, see Landers and Rohner, *A Functional Analysis of Truth in Lending,* 26 U.C.L.A.L.Rev. 711 (1979).

d. *A "contract synopsis."* Whether used for shopping purposes or not, the TIL disclosures provide an understandable summary of the contract, and may be useful later on when the consumer wants to verify contract terms.

e. *A law reform device.* The need to disclose contract terms clearly and conspicuously may prompt creditors to rethink contract boilerplate that is archaic or unnecessary. It also might stimulate law reform by flushing out harsh terms formerly hidden in the fine print shadows. See 26 U.C.L.A.L.Rev. at 740–45.

f. *A "rough justice" mechanism.* The civil penalty provisions of the TILA permit consumers to use claims of TIL violations for leverage where the real underlying grievance (abusive or deceptive practices) would be hard to prove. See Landers, *Some Reflections on Truth in Lending,* 1977 U.Ill.L.F. 699.

g. *Long-term consumer education.* Repeated encounters with TIL disclosures, with their standardized terminology, should produce better informed consumers over time. See 26 U.C.L.A.L.Rev. at 737–50.

h. *A "political" function.* This is a cynical view which holds that disclosure laws are not really expected to have any impact. Instead, they are nothing more than political responses to demands for pro-consumer legislation. This works because the laws appear to be pro-consumer, and because the average consumer is not sophisticated enough to realize that the laws really don't help. See Whitford, supra, 1973 Wis.L.Rev. at 435–39.

Notes

1. Can you think of any other purposes mandatory disclosure laws might serve? Do you think any disclosure law can be expected to accomplish all of this? Might there be harmful side effects?

2. How does the purpose of a disclosure law relate to the actual disclosures which should be required? For example, if the purpose is to increase competition, should the disclosures be limited to cost elements (APR and finance charge)? If the goal is general awareness, should the disclosures be simple rather than detailed? And how is this goal served by making disclosures on a transaction-by-transaction basis? Should information about interest rates be collected and distributed to the public? See TILA § 136.

The following chart is taken from the Washington Post, May 28, 1978, at E4 *. It compares the levels of consumer awareness found in studies conducted before and soon after the TILA took effect (1969, 1970), and in the Federal Reserve Board's 1977 Consumer Credit Survey. If a similar study were conducted today what do you think it would show?

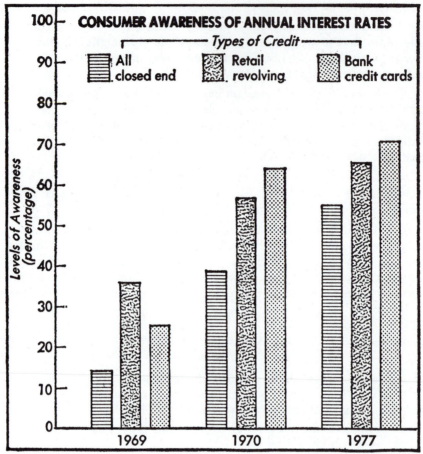

By Bill Perkins—The Washinbgton Post

WHITFORD, THE FUNCTIONS OF DISCLOSURE REGULATION IN CONSUMER TRANSACTIONS

1973 Wisc.L.Rev. 400, 420–23, 431–32.*

The continued reliance on disclosure as an important technique for regulating consumer transactions is contrary to the advice of many commentators, who have argued that although not positively harmful, such regulation is typically almost useless. The concern of these critics has not been principally with the difficulty in obtaining seller compliance with disclosure regulation, but rather with the alleged lack of effect either on consumer behavior or on the substance of transactions. They correctly point out that the proponents of disclosure regulation typically presume that conspicuous and comprehensible disclosure will cause many consumers to change their buying behavior so as either to refrain from buying particular products or services that they otherwise would have bought, or to shop more carefully among competing products or services. Once this effect takes hold, many proponents of disclosure regulation seem to presume, sellers will be forced to compete with regard to the disclosed aspects of the transactions they offer, with the result that all or nearly all consumer transactions will become "fairer," or more "proconsumer." Critics argue this scenario rarely if ever takes place because the disclosed information either is not learned by consumers, or if it is, it is not used by them in reaching purchase decisions. The critics uniformly contend that this description of the effects of disclosure applies particularly to the response of low income consumers to disclosure regulation. But many critics also argue or assume that middle and upper class consumers react in a substantially similar way.

* * *

A variety of possible explanations have been offered for the limited impact of truth-in-lending on consumer buying behavior. Some of the explanations relate directly to the lack of impact on the lower economic classes. It has been suggested, for example, that many poor have few outlets for credit available to them. Even if these poor comparatively shopped for credit, in many instances the only choice that would be available to them would be either to obtain credit from whoever offered it or to do without the often necessary goods or services the credit would purchase. Unless the latter is perceived as a realistic alternative, there is little incentive for these persons even to become aware of interest rates or total finance charges.

Another suggested explanation for the limited impact of truth-in-lending, and one that is most interesting for purposes of evaluating disclosure regulation generally, is that most consumers are not motivated to shop comparatively for the lowest interest rate, at least with regard to all but their largest credit transactions. A variety of possible reasons have been advanced for this lack of motivation. If the amount borrowed is not large, often the amount to be saved by obtaining the lowest available interest rate is not sufficient to justify the inconvenience and costs of comparative shopping. Many consumers apparently prefer to use an established or other source of credit known to be available, perhaps in order to avoid the anxieties of asking for credit from an unfamiliar institution—for example, a bank, which frequently will offer the lowest available interest rate. Even when some comparative shopping for credit occurs, consumers—particularly low income consumers—are apparently more concerned with the size of the required downpayment and monthly payments than with interest rates. No doubt there are also many other reasons for a lack of motivation to shop comparatively for low interest rates.

* * *

Nevertheless, on the available evidence, the criticisms of disclosure regulation discussed in the introduction appear sound, both empirically and theoretically.

It does not follow from this conclusion, however, that traditional precontract disclosure should be abandoned as a regulatory technique, if the alternative is no disclosure regulation at all. My previous analysis has suggested such regulation may sometimes have very useful impact in highly oligopolistic markets. Even in relatively competitive markets, the benefits to society of compulsory disclosure can exceed its costs even though there is no voluntary disclosure because the private benefits of such disclosure to an individual seller are less than his costs. The societal benefits of compulsory disclosure may not always be limited to savings realized by consumers who use the information. Changing the shopping behavior of only a very small number of consumers can sometimes have impact on the substantive content of a much larger number of transactions. If one assumes a competitive market and a product or contractual term that is highly standardized and not susceptible to differentiation to meet the desires of different sets of consumers, then changing the behavior of only a marginal group of consumers may set off a competition for that group and in the process produce changes in the content of the transactions of a very large number of consumers. Thus, because "interest rate" is a term which is difficult for a seller to differentiate according to the buying motivations of his customers, some expected this "marginal buyer" effect to take hold under truth-in-lending and lead to a competitive reduction in interest rates. However, no such effect is yet observable.

Not only may the benefits of compulsory disclosure exceed those of voluntary disclosure, but it is at least possible for the costs of compulsory disclosure to be less than the costs of voluntary disclosure. If only one or a few sellers are trying to disclose previously unavailable information, they may be forced to use relatively expensive communication techniques, such as media advertising, in order to reach consumers with whom they do not ordinarily come into contact. Traditional disclosure regulation, however, by providing for disclosure only in the contract, rarely requires sellers to expend more than is necessary to hire a lawyer to draft a few additional forms. And since all sellers must disclose, inclusion in the contract will make the information available to most consumers who might use it.

LANDERS AND ROHNER, A FUNCTIONAL ANALYSIS OF TRUTH IN LENDING

26 U.C.L.A.L.Rev. 711, 722–26 (1979).*

B. INFIRMITIES IN TRUTH IN LENDING

1. *Cognitive Overload*

The consumer's behavior in the transaction will not be affected if the credit disclosures are so numerous and, in conjunction with other contract provisions, so formidable as to create a "cognitive overload." That is, the consumer becomes overwhelmed by the aggregate mass of words and figures and reacts by ignoring the disclosures entirely.

A typical retail installment sale contract may be printed on both sides of a legal-sized sheet of paper containing the pertinent credit information, descriptions of the item purchased, warranty and servicing information, credit and property insurance provisions, and much more. The credit disclosures may be interspersed among the other items on the face of the form and some disclosures may refer to other disclosures in other portions of the form. The completed document is given to the consumer at a time and under circumstances that are not conducive to careful reading and study. Many consumers are simply unable to sort out, process, and evaluate all of the information presented. The unconscious response may be to ignore everything—except, perhaps, a quick confirmation that this is in fact the "right" contract.

There is, admittedly, no "hard" evidence that this is occurring in the case of Truth in Lending Statements. But, in a recent and provocative study, Professor Jeffrey Davis has shown that consumer understanding may be increased by dropping some disclosures and simplifying others, thus suggesting that some type of information excesses may inhere in the present requirements. This phenomenon of cognitive overload also has been postulated in other disclosure contexts, and there is no reason to doubt that something of the sort occurs with respect to credit disclosures as well. Available studies suggest that typical consumers can manage six, seven, or maybe eight "bits" of information, but that more than eight likely will produce overload results. Obviously, the present Act requires disclosure of substantially more than this quantum level. Indeed, the nature of the information involved in a credit context, and the relative stressfulness of the situation, suggest that cognitive overload is more likely to occur in the case of credit disclosures than in those cases where it has been identified already. Clearly, a consumer will not use disclosed information for shopping purposes if he has not focused on it.

Of course, some consumers can process more complex information. There is no "correct" way to make this sort of policy judgment. However, if the purpose of the Act is to influence a substantial portion of the credit-consuming public, attention must be paid to the phenomenon of cognitive overload for the mass of consumers.

There are several theoretical ways to reduce information overload, but each presents its own difficulties and may frustrate other desired functions of the disclosure scheme. The most obvious response is to reduce the number of items disclosed to within the manageable range of six or eight that is suggested by the empirical data. To do this, however, means deciding that some of the information now disclosed is expendable. Which items should go?

* * *

2. Dysfunction in the Delivery of Information

Common sense suggests that an individual's ability to comprehend information is related to the conditions under which the information is imparted and must be learned. Most TIL disclosures are given under circumstances that are extremely stressful and not suited to careful deliberation and analysis. Usually, at least in closed end transactions, the information is given by a person sitting or standing in close proximity to the consumer. The physical conditions are likely to be at least mildly intimidating—a "sterile" bank, a small room, other persons milling around. The consumer may be distracted by children, noise, interruptions, or unrelated conversation; and there may be subtle references to the need for speed. The person with whom the consumer "negotiates" the credit arrangement may be an authority figure (the "credit man") who is separated from the sales activities and is somewhat forbidding. The consumer may lack a desk and paper and pencil to make any calculations. This is not to say that consumers will not do their best, but it does suggest that whatever optimum value can be obtained from TIL transactional disclosures is not likely to be attained, indeed, even approached, under such conditions.

Many consumer credit transactions arise in connection with the purchase of a product. The consumer may suffer from what might be called a "decisional overload." That is, the credit terms are likely to have much less significance in the consumer's eye than the color, model, brand name, accessories, and cash price of the item purchased. The consumer is likely to give much more thought to, and be much more excited about, the overall purchase than its credit aspect which, after all, will be only a fraction of the total investment. Fully aware of the credit cost implications, the consumer may give them no more significance than the cost of the air conditioning in the car he is purchasing; "credit" is something he must tolerate to get behind the wheel. Indeed, from the consumer's point of view, the decision to get air conditioning has greater economic significance than the credit terms since the cost of air conditioning almost always exceeds any saving which might be obtained by shopping for credit.

Consumer surveys demonstrate that consumers making a purchase on credit consider product-related decisions to be more important than credit-related decisions. Moreover, it may be that the typical consumer is simply unable to evaluate multiple components of the transaction and weigh them as part of an overall package. Instead, the consumer may just shop for price and significant options and defer to the credit-seller on other matters.

SCHWARTZ & WILDE, "INTERVENING IN MARKETS ON THE BASIS OF IMPERFECT INFORMATION: A LEGAL AND ECONOMIC ANALYSIS"

127 U.Pa.L.Rev. 630, 675–77 (1979).*

The objection that consumers would not absorb data from comparative price lists stems from the concept of "information overload" currently in vogue. This concept asserts that when consumers are provided with too much information they make dysfunctional decisions; the circuits become "overloaded." Recent experiments, however, fail to support the existence of this phenomenon. The evidence to date shows that more information enables consumers to make better purchase decisions than they would make were they uninformed, with a "better" purchase decision defined as one that yields an outcome that more closely approximates a consumer's actual preferences. This is not to say that the information overload phenomenon never occurs, but instead that it has not been verified under experimental conditions. Moreover, no one can predict when consumers will experience "overload" in real world situations. Thus, that information overload may occur if "too much" information is provided is an observation of little relevance to decisionmakers. To be sure, consumers could decide that the potential gains from absorbing new information would exceed the costs. Given the potential savings that the provision of comparative price and term information could yield, however, assertions that such information would not be used are premature.

The administrative costs of a comparative price information program could, however, exceed the welfare gains. It would be expensive to create and maintain price-gathering and promulgating agencies, to identify the firms and products that should be included on each list—for example, Los Angeles consumers may care little about Anaheim prices—and to police firms to ensure that transaction prices are not significantly higher than the prices firms provide to the listing agency. Nevertheless, because providing consumers with inexpensive comparative price data would be so useful in moving markets toward competitive equilibria, it is a reform that decisionmakers should seriously consider.

See also Grether, Schwartz, & Wilde, The Irrelevance of Information Overload: An Analysis of Search and Disclosure, 59 S.Cal.L.Rev. 277 (1986).

Argumentative Observations

At least one of your authors believes that greatest single gain produced by Truth in Lending is the standardization of credit terminology and mathematics, especially the concepts of "finance charge" and "APR." In addition, this author thinks that disclosure forces to the surface many contract provisions which otherwise would be buried in the fine print, and that this is a good thing. As for consumer awareness, however, this author suspects that truth in lending has had a smaller impact than events such as the economic crisis of the late 1970's and early 1980's which put interest rates in the world's headlines, or the widespread advertising during the 1980's of ridiculously (and deceptively) low rates for car loans.

This author also questions the usefulness of any law that assumes consumers will actually read something. If it is true, as many scholars suggest, that our society is about one-third functionally illiterate, then disclosure laws must be justified on some other basis. Besides, laws designed to influence shopping behavior presuppose the ability to shop around and chose among offers of credit. For a large (and growing) portion of the population, this is not the case. This author would not, however, like to see TILA repealed. He believes that the standardizing effect alone makes it worth the effort.

Another author believes that assistance to the two thirds of the population which *is* functionally literate is justified. To that author, although TILA is not a panacea for everyone, it is assistance which is available and helpful for those who choose to use it. Further, that author believes that there are many more credit options, and much more credit shopping, today than there were in the 1960s, before TILA.

Part II

REGULATION OF CONDUCT

Even if all relevant information is perfectly obtainable at no cost, there will still be situations in which the consumer needs further protection. Thus, regulation of merchant and creditor conduct (in addition to regulation of information flow) is often deemed necessary. Thus, in the chapters which follow, the questions to be asked are whether the problems in each transaction can be solved by disclosure alone, or whether some additional form of protection should be provided. If further protection is needed, what form should it take: A right of action after the abuse is discovered? A restructuring of the transaction to make the abuse more difficult to realize? Other?

Regulation of conduct can occur at many different points of the transaction. The following chapters organize the regulation according to the time at which the problem arises. Chapters 3 and 4 deal with abuses which arise at the formation of the contract, or which prevent its formation due to discrimination. Chapters 5 and 6 deal with abuses which arise during the performance of the contract, including the question: "Do I have to pay for goods that don't work right?" Chapters 7, 8 and 9 deal with various aspects of the debt collection process—informal, self-help repossession and court-based enforcement devices.

Chapters 4, 6 and 9 contain sections which explore the issues related to evaluating the costs and benefits of the current regulations of conduct.

Chapter 3

ABUSES AT THE FORMATION OF THE CONTRACT

SECTION A. THE DEAL THAT IS "TOO GOOD TO BE TRUE"—BAIT AND SWITCH

STATE v. AMERICAN TV & APPLIANCE OF MADISON, INC.

Supreme Court of Wisconsin, 1988.
146 Wis.2d 292, 430 N.W.2d 709.

CALLOW, JUSTICE.

This is a review of a published decision of the court of appeals, *State v. American TV*, 140 Wis.2d 353, 410 N.W.2d 596 (Ct.App.1987). That decision reversed an order of the circuit court for Dane county, Judge P. Charles Jones, granting a motion to dismiss the state's complaint for failure to state a claim in this forfeiture action. We reverse the decision of the court of appeals because the state cannot prevail, even if the facts alleged in the complaint are true.

The state filed a complaint against American TV & Appliance of Madison, Inc., (American) alleging that in January, 1985, American ran the following radio advertisement one hundred sixty-four times on twenty-two radio stations:

There are lots of good quality washers and dryers on the market. But when you ask which ones [sic] the best automatic washers and dryers, well it's simple. There's Speed Queen, Maytag and all the rest. Sears makes good washers and dryers there are lots of other good brands. But the best washers and dryers are made by Maytag and Speed Queen. And at American we have both of them and they're on sale for our January white sale. A clearance sale on the finest washers and dryers you can buy. This week a Speed Queen washer and dryer set is reduced to 499. This week you can buy the finest for less than $500. Both the Speed Queen washer and dryer set for 499. Speed Queen, the choice of more commercial laundra-mats than any other washer because they last. Because Speed Queen uses the same transmission in

176

home washes [sic] as they use in commercial washers. When it comes to washers and dryers, there's Maytag, Speed Queen and all the rest. And during American's closeout January white sale you can buy the best like a Speed Queen washer and dryer pair for 499 at American. Why pay more at Sears.

The state contends that this advertisement violated secs. 100.18(1) and (9)(a), Stats. The complaint alleges that American ordered twenty of these $499 Speed Queen sets at a cost of $520 per set. In addition, the complaint alleges that American ordered one hundred thirty-three more expensive washer and dryer sets. Sixty-five of these sets contained more features and were "visually more sophisticated" than the $499 sets. American purchased these for $518. The other sixty-eight sets cost American up to $604 and were of an even higher quality. The complaint states that, although American sold only four of the $499 sets during the sale, the state "believes that a much larger number" of the more expensive sets were sold. In addition, American sold a large number of non-Speed Queen washers and dryers at higher prices.

The complaint also alleges that American employs a commission system under which a salesperson receives commission only on the sale of items at a price greater than the wholesale cost. Since American sold these sets at $21 below cost, the salespersons received no commission on their sale.

The state's complaint alleges that the advertisement is not a bona fide offer to sell the $499 set and that American used the advertisement to induce potential buyers to come to the store where it discouraged the purchase of the $499 set and tried to sell the more expensive unadvertised sets. The state alleges that the following eight indicia reveal American's deceptive intent: (1) the loss of money on sales of the $499 set; (2) the disproportionate number of unadvertised sets purchased for sale; (3) the disproportionate number of unadvertised sets sold; (4) the large expense of advertising a set upon which American would lose money; (5) the plain appearance of the $499 set and the lack of certain features found in more expensive sets, even though the $499 set was advertised as the "best" and "finest"; (6) the commission structure discouraging sales of the $499 set; (7) the training received by sales persons encouraging them to direct customers to the more expensive models; and (8) the fact that American did not permit credit card purchases of the $499 set.

Based upon these allegations, the state, in its complaint, makes two claims for relief. First, it claims that the advertisement is untrue, deceptive or misleading in violation of sec. 100.18(1), Stats. Second, it claims that the advertisement is a part of a plan or scheme, the purpose or effect of which is not to sell the merchandise as advertised, in violation of sec. 100.18(9)(a).[2]

* * *

2. Section 100.18(9)(a), Stats., provides: "It is deemed deceptive advertising, within the meaning of this section, for any person or any agent or employe thereof to make, publish, disseminate, circulate or place before the public in this state in a newspaper

II. *Bait and Switch.*

The state's second claim for relief is based upon sec. 100.18(9)(a), Stats. There are three elements which must be alleged to state a claim under this provision. First, there must be an advertisement. Second, there must be a plan or scheme of which the advertisement is a part. Third, the purpose or effect of this plan must be to not sell the product as advertised.

The state insists that American violated this provision because its advertisement induced customers to visit the stores and then it switched them from the $499 set to more expensive models. The state bases its claim on the eight indicia of intent which, it claims, reveal a purpose not to sell the $499 set as advertised.

Missing from the complaint are allegations tending to prove that, apart from any purpose not to sell the merchandise as advertised, there was a plan or scheme to carry out such a purpose. The state's complaint is more conspicuous by what it does not allege than by what it does allege. It does not allege that the $499 sets were not available to customers. It does not allege that the $499 sets were not sold to customers. To the contrary, it acknowledges four sets *were* sold. It does not allege that the sets displayed were defective. It does not allege that salespersons discouraged any actual customers from buying the $499 model and then switched them to more expensive models. The complaint does not allege any improper overt act.

The complaint does not allege anything except that there were incentives for American to try to sell the more expensive models and that, in fact, it stocked and sold more of those models. All profit motivated retailers recognize these incentives and hope to sell their more profitable items, if possible. Section 100.18(9)(a), Stats., cannot be interpreted to make unlawful such an incentive. The statute requires a plan or scheme which is not demonstrated in this complaint.

Notwithstanding this deficiency in its complaint, the state attempts to rely upon FTC cases and guides for support of its position. It does so to no avail. The cases upon which the state relies do not find the existence of bait and switch merely from the kind of indicia of intent listed by the state. Indeed, the state recognizes that the federal cases often focus on disparagement of the advertised product, and it argues that disparagement occurred in this case. It contends that the $499 set was "plain" and lacked many features found in the more expensive models, and thus disparaged itself.

or other publication or in the form of book, notice, handbill, poster, bill, circular, pamphlet, letter, sign, placard, card, label or over any radio or television station or in any other way similar or dissimilar to the foregoing, an advertisement, announcement, statement or representation of any kind to the public relating to the purchase, sale, hire, use or lease of real estate, merchandise, securities, service or employment or to the terms or conditions thereof which advertisement, announcement, statement or representation is part of a plan or scheme the purpose or effect of which is not to sell, purchase, hire, use or lease the real estate, merchandise, securities, service or employment as advertised."

This contention is without merit. The federal cases relied upon by the state, in which the merchandise was found to be self-disparaging, involve defective or poor quality merchandise. In *Household Sewing Machine Co.,* 52 F.T.C. 250, 263–64 (1955), the advertised sewing machine would not perform certain advertised functions and was exceptionally noisy. Similarly, in *Carpets "R" Us, Inc. et al.,* 87 F.T.C. 303, 320–21 (1976), the carpet was of a "poor" quality and appearance. In both cases there was also verbal disparagement by salespersons. By contrast, the state alleges neither verbal disparagement nor defective merchandise. "Plainness" does not constitute defectiveness. The federal cases simply do not support the state's claim.

The state further contends that American disparaged the set by displaying it next to the more sophisticated models. This argument, too, must be rejected. The state points to *Southern States Distributing Co., et al.,* 83 F.T.C. 1126, 1166 (1973), in which swimming pool salespersons induced customers to switch from an economy pool to a deluxe pool by exhibiting two models side by side. However, the FTC's opinion makes it clear that the side-by-side exhibition itself was not the deceptive act. It was that Southern States had constructed the two models in such a way as to misleadingly embellish the expensive model.

The state also relies upon *Carpets "R" Us,* 87 F.T.C. at 320, 321, and *Wilbanks Carpet Specialists, Inc., et al.,* 84 F.T.C. 510, 520 (1974), claiming that side-by-side exhibitions of products disparaged the lower priced items. However, unlike the perfectly functional, albeit plain, washer and dryer set in this case, the lower priced carpets in those cases were of poor quality and disparaged themselves.

Section 100.18(9)(a), Stats., does not require a retailer to display different items in a product line in separate areas of the store out of fear that the less expensive models will compare unfavorably. Side-by-side exhibition, far from being evidence of a bait and switch plan, is helpful to consumers. It enables them to balance price differences with feature differences in order to arrive at the most efficient decision for them, given their tastes and resources.

Failing in its attempt to show disparagement, the state also argues that a showing of disparagement is not needed. Instead, it insists that a finding of bait and switch may be inferred from the advertisement itself and minimal sales resulting from it. It relies upon cases such as *Central Carpet Corp., Inc.,* 85 F.T.C. 1022 (1975), and *Tashof v. Federal Trade Commission,* 437 F.2d 707 (D.C.Cir.1970). What these cases conclude, however, is that, in addition to minimal sales of the product, the court must find bait advertising.

The cases demonstrate that a bait advertisement is one which is false or misleading. In *Tashof,* 437 F.2d at 709, an advertisement offering glasses "complete" for $7.50 was misleading bait advertising because this price applied only to customers who had their own prescriptions. The supposedly "complete" package did not include a free eye examination as some signs and flyers indicated. Similarly, in

Central Carpet, 85 F.T.C. at 1031, the advertisement itself was deceptive as "the carpeting was not suitable for the uses for which advertised."

The FTC and federal courts have not made a finding of bait and switch simply on the basis of a low number of sales resulting from a *true* advertisement. As we stated above, American's advertisement is not false or misleading and, hence, is not bait advertising. These cases are not applicable to this case.

The FTC Guides in 16 C.F.R. sec. 238.3 (1988) likewise do not support the state's position. As this court noted in *State v. Amoco Oil Co.,* 97 Wis.2d 226, 243, 293 N.W.2d 487 (1980), the Guides are interpretive rules which "do not carry the force and effect of law." Section 238.3 of the Guides reads as follows:

Discouragement of purchase of advertised merchandise.

No act or practice should be engaged in by an advertiser to discourage the purchase of the advertised merchandise as part of a bait scheme to sell other merchandise. Among acts or practices which will be considered in determining if an advertisement is a bona fide offer are:

(a) The refusal to show, demonstrate, or sell the product offered in accordance with the terms of the offer,

(b) The disparagement by acts or words of the advertised product or the disparagement of the guarantee, credit terms, availability of service, repairs or parts, or in any other respect, in connection with it,

(c) The failure to have available at all outlets listed in the advertisement a sufficient quantity of the advertised product to meet reasonably anticipated demands, unless the advertisement clearly and adequately discloses that supply is limited and/or the merchandise is available only at designated outlets,

(d) The refusal to take orders for the advertised merchandise to be delivered within a reasonable period of time,

(e) The showing or demonstrating of a product which is defective, unusable or impractical for the purpose represented or implied in the advertisement,

(f) Use of a sales plan or method of compensation for salesmen or penalizing salesmen, designed to prevent or discourage them from selling the advertised product.

The circuit court correctly determined that the first five acts listed in sec. 238.3 are the very type of overt acts which the state, in its complaint, has not alleged. Only subparagraph (f), referring to the use of a commission system, applies to this case.

The existence of a commission system is not determinative evidence of a bait and switch plan or scheme. Commission systems merely reflect the general profit motivation which governs all retail operations. Consequently, the federal cases which discuss a commission plan as evidence of bait and switch also rely upon many other evidences of a plan or scheme which are not present in this case. For example, in *Southern States,* 83 F.T.C. at 1166, in addition to the commission system, there was actual product disparagement. *See also Carpets "R" Us,* 87 F.T.C. at 320–21 (finding both verbal disparagement and self-disparagement of the product). Neither the federal cases nor Guides support the state's position.

* * *

For the reasons set forth, we conclude that the state's complaint fails to state a claim upon which relief can be granted.

The decision of the court of appeals is reversed.

STEINMETZ, JUSTICE (dissenting).

* * *

A cause of action based on sec. 100.18(9)(a), Stats., does not require facts to show the defendant's improper overt act. In light of Wisconsin's rules of notice pleading, sec. 100.18(9)(a) only requires that a plaintiff allege facts from which it can be reasonably inferred that such a plan or scheme exists. It is inconceivable that such a plan or scheme cannot be reasonably inferred from the complaint which alleged: (1) American's purchase of only 20 washers while running the advertisement 164 times; (2) American's cost was $21 over the selling price; (3) American's purchase of 133 more expensive washer-dryer sets; (4) American sold only four of the sets in its four stores; and (5) the salesperson's commission structure which provided no commissions on these sets. The majority incorrectly concludes that no plan or scheme could even reasonably be inferred from the complaint.

The majority also mentions that the FTC Guides, 16 C.F.R. sec. 238.3 (1988), aid in determining whether a certain practice is violative of sec. 100.18(9)(a), Stats. The majority concedes that sec. 238.3(f) of the Guides was alleged by the state. However, 238.3(c) provides:

> (c) The failure to have available at all outlets listed in the advertisement a sufficient quantity of the advertised product to meet reasonably anticipated demands, unless the advertisement clearly and adequately discloses that supply is limited and/or the merchandise is available only at designated outlets.

American's advertisement contained no limitation. American ran 164 advertisements on 22 radio stations, yet American ordered only 20 of the advertised sets. The question of whether American ordered a sufficient quantity of the washer-dryer sets to meet reasonably anticipated demands is a matter of proof.

Because the allegations in the complaint do provide sufficient facts from which it could be reasonably inferred that secs. 100.18(1) and 100.18(9)(a), Stats., were violated, I would affirm the court of appeals which reinstated the complaint.

I am authorized to state that CHIEF JUSTICE NATHAN S. HEFFERNAN and JUSTICE SHIRLEY S. ABRAHAMSON join this dissenting opinion.

Query: Would compulsory disclosure of contract terms, as in TIL, have been helpful here? Would a "plain English" statute have any impact? What is it that needs to be disclosed?

Problem 1

Elder & Johnson Co., a department store, advertised a new, full-size, electric sewing machine for sale at a price of $26, as a "Thursday Only Special." Connie Craft saw the ad and immediately hurried downtown to Elder & Johnson's only store in order to buy the advertised sewing machine. She was the third person in the door, but the salesman informed her that the store had only two of the $26 machines, and she was too late. The salesman also informed her, however, that the store had stocked "hundreds" of a "better-quality" sewing machine, at a "bargain" price of $175.

Could the Wisconsin Attorney General obtain an injunction against such conduct? Could the FTC obtain a cease and desist order under § 5 of the FTC Act?

Notes

1. The Federal Trade Commission has also prosecuted "bait and switch" practices in the aluminum siding industry. See, e.g., All–State Industries v. Federal Trade Com'n, 423 F.2d 423 (4th Cir.1970). "The FTC receives more consumer complaints about practices in the home improvements industry than in any other single industry, according to unofficial estimates," reports Susan Wagner in the Federal Trade Commission 161 (1971). You may want to ask yourself why siding is so peculiarly susceptible to fraudulent selling techniques—a question you may be better able to answer after reading subsequent portions of this material. Meanwhile, you may care to ponder the remarks of a former door-to-door salesman. He said he never sold siding himself, but "whenever I went into a new neighborhood I'd look for the house with the siding on it because I knew they would buy anything!"

2. What are the critical elements of proof of illegal bait-and-switch? In Household Sewing Machine Co., Inc., 76 F.T.C. 207, 239 (1969) the Commission observed:

> The examiner seemed to be saying that since no one "took" the "bait," no one was "switched."
>
> To define bait and switch in terms of offers or refusals of offers misconceives the essential nature of the practice. Our decisions relating to bait and switch are grounded on a factual determination that the advertised product is not an offer which the seller seriously intends the buyer to accept, but a "come on" which will lead to the sale of a higher priced product. Whether the bait is actually taken or not is of no moment. On the contrary and as the record of this case plainly shows, the assumption of the bait and switch perpetrator is that the bait will probably *not* be "taken" (or at least not swallowed) but will serve as an opening gambit to get the salesman over the doorstep. Insofar as the examiner required proof of actual offers to buy the used

machines, and subsequent refusals by respondents to sell, he erred—
these factors are not material in establishing an illegal "bait and
switch" scheme.

3. Related to bait and switch is the tactic apparently employed by
some retail grocers of advertising a special to lure "traffic" into the store
without stocking adequate supplies to meet expected demand. A 1967–68
FTC study of grocery stores in the District of Columbia and San Francisco
showed an 11% unavailability rate and considerable consumer dissatisfaction with the situation. Thus, in 1971, the FTC promulgated a trade
regulation rule requiring grocers to stock an adequate supply to meet the
expected demand for advertised specials. 16 C.F.R. Part 424. Defenses
were nonexistent unless the grocer maintained records showing the lack of
inventory was beyond his control.

In a controversial 1986 report, the FTC staff said that the paperwork
and other costs of complying with the advertised specials rule exceeded the
benefits by millions of dollars every year. They recommended that the
rule be repealed or significantly amended.

In 1989, the Commission published amendments to the rule. 54 Fed.
Reg. 35,456 (Aug. 28, 1989). In the accompanying Statement of Basis and
Purpose, the Commission noted that although overall unavailability rates
have been reduced by about 50 percent since the original rule's promulgation, surveys indicated that consumers were not much inconvenienced by
unavailability and would be willing to tolerate much greater unavailability
rates to avoid higher grocery prices. The record also indicated significant
costs borne by grocers from overstocking, monitoring, and recordkeeping.
The amended rule seeks to reduce these costs while retaining the consumers' benefits by

— allowing broader use of limited availability disclosures in advertis-
    ing,

— eliminating recordkeeping requirements, and

— allowing food retailers to offer rainchecks or comparable value
    substitutes if they cannot supply the advertised item.

The Commission majority expressed their faith that the competitive system
would provide grocers with ample incentive to avoid disappointing their
customers. In the event that some grocers were to take advantage of the
new more lenient standards to engage in deliberate understocking without
adequate disclosure, however, the Commission asserted that its Bait Advertising Guides (discussed in the *American Television* case, supra) would still
be applicable.

As amended, the rule now reads as follows:

§ 424.1 Unfair or deceptive acts or practices

In connection with the sale or offering for sale by retail food stores
of food, grocery products or other merchandise to consumers in or
affecting commerce as "commerce" is defined in Section 4 of the
Federal Trade Commission Act, 15 U.S.C. 44, it is an unfair or deceptive act or practice in violation of Section 5(a)(1) of the Federal Trade
Commission Act, 15 U.S.C. 45(a)(1), to offer any such products for sale

at a stated price, by means of an advertisement disseminated in an area served by any stores which are covered by the advertisement if those stores do not have the advertised products in stock and readily available to customers during the effective period of the advertisement, unless the advertisement clearly and adequately discloses that supplies of the advertised products are limited and/or the advertised products are available only at some outlets.

§ 424.2   Defense

No violation of § 424.1 shall be found if: (a) The advertised products were ordered in adequate time for delivery in quantities sufficient to meet reasonably anticipated demand; (b) the retailer offers a 'raincheck' for the advertised products; (c) the retailer offers at the advertised price or at a comparable price reduction the same type of product at least comparable in value to the advertised product; or (d) the retailer offers other compensation at least equal to the advertised value.

4. The Uniform Consumer Sales Practices Act (UCSPA), § 3(b), lists a number of seller representations that are deceptive. One of them is the representation "that the subject of a consumer transaction will be supplied in greater quantity than the supplier intends." Does this adequately deal with bait and switch practices? What should a seller do who has only a limited quantity of the advertised item but is perfectly willing to sell them? See UCSPA § 3(b)(6) and the Comment thereto (in West's Selected Commercial Statutes).

5. Would such rules prohibit sellers from engaging in "loss leader" selling—where goods are offered at a loss in order to attract customers who will (hopefully) purchase other goods at a profit?

In Electrolux Corp. v. Val–Worth, Inc., 6 N.Y.2d 556, 190 N.Y.S.2d 977, 161 N.E.2d 197 (1959) a seller advertised "rebuilt" vacuum cleaners at a very attractive price in order to gain admittance to people's homes, where efforts were made to switch the buyers to more expensive new machines. A competitor of the seller sought an injunction, which the trial court denied. The appellate court reversed:

> The majority of the [lower court] took the view that an injunction here would impinge upon "loss leader" selling where a merchant offers goods at a loss in order to attract customers to whom he can make other more profitable sales. But this is not a situation where a person comes into a store attracted by a bargain and buys other items as well. Here, the customer, who is, as indicated by the dissenting Justice below, trapped in his own home, is faced with a choice between the rebuilt machine as to which only he made inquiry and the new machine, with the salesman using all of his talents to effectuate the "switch". Furthermore, it is not common for the average consumer to purchase two vacuum cleaners at one time, which demonstrates how this scheme uses plaintiff's good name as a weapon against itself in a highly competitive market. Finally, one cannot say that it is normal business ethics for a merchant to discourage sales of items which he has advertised in glowing terms in order to sell different *unadvertised*

goods. Thus, it is difficult to see how an injunction on these facts would impinge upon ordinary "cut-rate" or "loss-leader" selling practices.

6. Another cousin to bait and switch practices is the gimmick of underestimating repair costs, or of making more expensive repairs than the customer had authorized. A number of states and localities have legislated directly on this matter. See e.g., Cal.Bus. & Prof.Code § 9884.9, and Bennett v. Hayes, 53 Cal.App.3d 700, 125 Cal.Rptr. 825 (1975).

7. In *American TV*, the suit was brought by the state attorney general. Can an individual consumer challenge a bait and switch practice under state law? See Williams v. Bruno Appliance & Furniture Mart, 62 Ill.App.3d 219, 19 Ill.Dec. 537, 379 N.E.2d 52 (1978). Can an individual consumer challenge a bait and switch practice under federal law?

Problem 2

Ace Mortgage Co. makes home mortgage loans. Its practice is to quote an interest rate to prospective borrowers, and offer to "lock in" the quoted rate for a period of 60 days from the date of the loan application. If the loan is not closed within the 60 day period, the quoted rate no longer applies, and Ace then applies the going market rate (usually higher). After receiving a series of complaints from consumers around the state, the attorney general's office began investigating Ace's lending practices. It found that during the previous six months, only 30% of the loans Ace actually made were closed within the 60 day "lock-in" period. All others were closed from a week to three weeks later, and always at higher rates. When asked about this, Ace's loan officer told the attorney general's investigator, "sometimes it just takes a little longer to handle all the paperwork and get the deal closed." You are the assistant attorney general in charge of the case, and the "UDAP" in your state contains language similar to that found in § 3 of the Uniform Consumer Sales Practices Act. Do you think Ace's practice amounts to an illegal bait and switch? Would you recommend prosecution?

SECTION B. THE DEAL THAT CONTEMPLATES FINDING OTHER SUCKERS—REFERRAL SALES AND PYRAMID SCHEMES

No inducement has quite the surface attraction as the prospect of getting something for nothing, or making lots of money from minimal effort. Both lures seem to persist in the consumer marketplace. One of the most common varieties is the "referral sale" where customers are induced to buy by promises of commissions, rebates or other credits for supplying the names of other potential customers. In most of these cases the basic purchase price the consumer agrees to pay is highly inflated, and the promises of referral commissions prove illusory.

In one such referral sales plan the court described the operation as follows:

> Mancen, agent of defendant World Wide Distributors, Inc., called upon the plaintiffs about January 23, 1961, and outlined to them "a program for direct advertising." He represented to them that if they purchased a breakfront, he would pay them $5 for each letter they wrote to a friend requesting an appointment for World Wide's agent to explain the details of a sound advertising program and $20 for each sale made to any such person. Their friends whose names they furnished were to be given the same opportunity to profit from supplying names of their friends. He said the plaintiffs would realize sufficient money to pay for the breakfront and to enable them to send their daughter to college. He persuaded the plaintiffs to sign, without reading, a purchase agreement, an attached judgment note in blank and an "Owner's Participation Certificate." The plaintiffs were given forms by World Wide of letters to be sent to their friends and they prepared 60 of them for mailing, but received only $80. When asked for the balance due them under the contract they were told that the bookkeeper was ill, that the matter would be taken up, that the check was on the desk awaiting the treasurer's signature, and similar excuses. Under the terms of the purchase agreement, the plaintiffs agreed to "sign the attached note providing for 30 monthly installments of $35.98 or a total of $1,079.40." (It was alleged that the fair retail price of the breakfront was less than one-fifth this amount.) The first payment was to be made in 45 days.
>
> * * * The note for $1,079.40, with interest, was purchased by Peoples National Fund, Inc. on January 25, 1961, for $831 and judgment was entered thereon February 7, 1961. It is hardly necessary to add that World Wide is now nowhere to be found. Within approximately a year its principals, unnamed in the record, had operated first under the name of Carpet Industries, then under State Wide, and finally under World Wide Distributors.

Norman v. World Wide Distributors, Inc., 202 Pa.Super. 53, 195 A.2d 115 (1963). The court concluded that the referral plan "was a fraudulent scheme based on an operation similar to the recurrent chain letter racket," and noted that in twenty months of operation "it would require *17 trillion* salesmen to carry on" the plan as it was described to the consumers.

In *Norman*, the basis for the customer's suit was common law fraud. In many cases of this type, however, state authorities and aggrieved consumers challenged referral sales as illegal lotteries. This approach had varying degrees of success. See, e.g., Braddock v. Family Finance Corp., 95 Idaho 256, 506 P.2d 824 (1973). The following excerpt from the dissenting opinion in the *Braddock* case shows how these schemes work:

> The element of chance which permeated Sease's scheme in the instant case is heightened by its so-called chain-letter effect. Coinci-

dentally, the factual discussion in *Sherwood & Roberts* applies precisely to Sease's "allotment privilege" and its chain-letter effect:

"＊ ＊ ＊ For ease of demonstration, respondents must earn 12 commissions of $100 each in order to get, as promised, something for nothing. This means that 12 of respondents' referrals must purchase as respondents did; they, in turn, to get something for nothing, must find 12 more people to purchase, and so forth, as follows:

	Number of Purchasers
	1
1st round	12
2d round	144
3d round	1,728
4th round	20,736
5th round	248,832

"Soon the scheme will run itself out; the market will become saturated." Sherwood & Roberts–Yakima, Inc. v. Leach, supra, 409 P.2d at 163.

I would take judicial notice that in 1968 the population of Coeur d'Alene, Idaho was less than 20,000 people. If every man, woman, and child in Coeur d'Alene bought a stereo set, the allotment privilege had to play itself out and the market become completely saturated between the third and fourth round. The inherent fallacies and dangers of such sales referral schemes are aptly stated:

"[t]he inherent fallacy of all referral contracts [is] the 'chain letter effect.' Any given single buyer may get the benefit of his agreement, if none of the foregoing defects arise. And if the referral payment could be earned simply by providing a name at random, regardless of the potential customer's financial condition or his ownership of the item or need for the service in question, all buyers could satisfy their obligation; the telephone directory would assure that. But the seller could ill afford such an arrangement. The seller will therefore restrict the buyers in providing names: to earn a payment the buyer must provide the name of a person who actually buys the product or service, or at least one who could afford it, who is presently without it, and who has not been referred. The seller must thus insure himself a chance to convert names into sales to stay in business.

"*This restriction means that no matter how large the financial resources or how pure the methods of the seller, the success of the buyers as a group depends on an inexhaustible supply of bona fide potential customers. Whatever the number of referrals required of each buyer to avail himself of the full benefits, there cannot be enough remaining potential customers to prolong the chain indefinitely.* The early and rapid success of the plan (should such occur) only hastens its end, as far as the buyers are concerned. The last buyers in any given market, whether because of the seller's failure or the exhaustion of potential customers, must pay for whatever benefit their predecessors received, without themselves benefiting at all. This feature is built into most of the plans—thus if the seller can hold on long enough to exhaust the market, he will ultimately make enormous profits from the last round of buyers. And the buyer who is unaware of the history, in his area, of the particular plan offered him is at a considerable disadvantage." (Emphasis supplied) Comment, Referral Sales Contracts: To Alter or Abolish, 15 Buffalo L.Rev. 669, 684–685 (1966).

506 P.2d at 828–29. In *Braddock*, the court found, over a strong dissent, that the challenged scheme was not an illegal lottery. Today, many states have laws which address the problem of referral sales directly. See, e.g., U3C § 3.309; UCSPA § 3(b)(11). Which approach do you think works best?

Query: Would compulsory disclosure of contract terms, as in TIL, be helpful in these cases? Would the New York Plain English law have any impact? What is it that needs to be disclosed?

Problem 3

Crafty Siders, Inc., a purveyor of home siding, makes the following statements to selected potential customers: "We are using a new method of advertising. We are not going to pay newspapers, TV, or radio anymore, for they already make enough money. Instead we are going to pay our customers to advertise for us, and let you use those payments from us to practically pay for your new siding. If you buy from us, we will offer you $25 per month to let us erect a sign in your front yard saying that your home has our siding." Of course, the sign remains in customer's front yard only so long as it is effective—i.e., only so long as it or the customer produces new sales, but the customer does not know that, yet. Is this actionable as a referral sale, or under any other principle, under the case-law, the U3C or the UCSPA? The applicable section of the U3C would be § 3.309.

Would it make a difference if the customer knew from the beginning that the term of the sign placement depended upon continuously generating new sales?

Note on Pyramid Sales

Akin to referral sales is pyramid marketing. As its name suggests, the technique involves the selling of the right to sell, indefinitely, in an inverted pyramid fashion. The "genius" at pyramid selling was Glenn Turner whose Koscot (cosmetics) and Dare-to-be-Great (self-improvement course) pyramids earned him (1) a great deal of money; (2) prosecutions by countless federal, state and local officials; (3) eventual bankruptcy and dismemberment of his corporate empire.

Turner's selling scheme utilized high pressure group sessions (Golden Opportunity, or GO meetings) replete with flashing $100 bills, exuberant salesmen, and promises of vast annual incomes. In the Koscot plan, consumers could purchase the right to sell cosmetics; but, more important-ly, they could purchase the right to sell distributorships (or sub-franchises) to others who in turn could sell cosmetics or new distributorships. Each such sale would earn an override commission for the original enrollee, larger of course, for sales of distributorships than for actual sales of cosmetics products. Dare-to-be-Great was similar, the actual product consisting of nothing more than a cassette tape extolling Turner's own philosophy of success. The pyramid scheme obviously suffers from the same mathematical impossibility as referral sales—several rounds of distributorship sales would exhaust the population of the world.

Turner, and other pyramid marketers, have been successfully prosecuted on numerous grounds: fraudulent sales practices, postal fraud, sales of unregistered securities, antitrust violations, and others. See, e.g., Kugler v. Koscot Interplanetary, Inc., 120 N.J.Super. 216, 293 A.2d 682 (1972). See generally Note, 61 Geo.L.J. 1257 (1973). The story of the Turner enterprises is told with flair by the newspaper reporter who first publicized his operations. See R. Maxa, "Dare to be Great" (Wm. Morrow & Co., 1977).

PEOPLE ex rel. FAHNER v. WALSH

Appellate Court of Illinois, 1984.
122 Ill.App.3d 481, 77 Ill.Dec. 691, 461 N.E.2d 78.

HOPF, JUSTICE:

On July 30, 1979, the Attorney General filed a complaint which alleged that defendants had violated the Act (Ill.Rev.Stat.1977, ch. 121½, pars. 261, *et seq.*) by selling interests in a plan known as the "Circle of Platinum." Under this plan, a person would purchase a list of six names, paying $500 to the seller and $500 to the person whose name was first on the list. The purchaser then made two copies of a new list, on which his or her own name was added as sixth, the name which had been first was eliminated, and each other name was moved up one position. The purchaser then attempted to sell these two lists to two new people who were told to repeat the process. The plan thus represented that, for an investment of $1,000, a person could make profits of up to $32,000 from an endless chain of recruiting additional purchasers.

* * *

The first issue we consider on appeal is the question of whether Woolbright's activities violated the Consumer Fraud and Deceptive Practices Act (Ill.Rev.Stat.1981, ch. 121½, pars. 261 *et seq.*). The Act prohibits "unfair or deceptive acts or practices * * * in the conduct of any trade or commerce" (Ill.Rev.Stat.1981, ch. 121½, par. 262). These terms are incapable of precise definition, so whether a given practice is unfair or deceptive must be determined on a case-by-case basis.

* * * Although Woolbright indicated that there was a possibility of losing the initial $1,000 he also stated that this "investment" could be recouped when the participant sold his or her two lists. Woolbright represented that although there was no guarantee there was also a great potential for gain, with receipts beginning when the participant's name reached the number one position on circulating lists. While

Woolbright claimed that the people he dealt with did not expect exorbitant gains, Woolbright told people that the plan worked and repeated, without investigating their veracity, various stories of great success with the plan. As the plan contemplated that the number of circulating lists would double at each step, it was held out to be possible to make up to $32,000 just by the sale of two lists. Woolbright testified that the DeKalb, LaSalle and Rockford newspapers covered the story of people who had bought the lists. One such article stated that a State's Attorney had stated that as long as the lists were not carried through the mail it was not mail fraud. Copies of the article were passed out at some of the parties. Woolbright encouraged and assisted people in his chain to sell their lists and kept track of the identity of people in the chain.

There are some facts which suggest that Woolbright was attempting to comply with the law, in that he declared his gains for income tax purposes, ceased his activities after being served with summons in this case, and had opinions from several sources, including a State's Attorney, that the plan was legal. However, Woolbright did not know whether the pyramid scheme was legal. Demand for lists admittedly dropped when the Attorney General became involved.

* * *

While there are no cases that have directly applied the issue presented in the case at bar, we believe the statute in question was violated. Pyramid programs, such as the "Circle of Platinum", which induce a person to participate on the representation that he or she cannot only regain the purchase price, but also reap profits by selling the plan to others, are inherently deceptive and contrary to public policy. The deception arises because the market eventually becomes saturated and the seemingly endless chain must end; consequently, many participants cannot even recoup their investments, let alone make a profit.

Additionally, such schemes involve aspects of a lottery, in that the controlling inducement to participate is the lure of an uncertain gain. This also renders these programs deceptive, unfair, and violative of consumer protection laws, regardless of whether criminal prohibitions against lotteries also are violated. Due to these considerations, marketing programs based on a pyramid principle have been found to violate other consumer protection statutes. Consequently, we believe the "Circle of Platinum" should be found to be a violation of the Illinois Act. Contrary to defendants' suggestion this conclusion is bolstered by the Act's prohibition of chain referral sales practices which evidences a general policy against techniques of this type, a distinguishable but analogous situation. See Ill.Rev.Stat.1981, ch. 121½, par. 262A.

Notes

1. The *Walsh* case relies on the state "little FTC Act's" general prohibition against "unfair and deceptive trade practices." The FTC itself

has used this approach in combatting pyramid schemes, and could use it to even better effect, as suggested in Stone & Steiner, The Federal Trade Commission and Pyramid Sales Schemes, 15 Pac.L.J. 879 (1984).

2.   Many states have enacted specific legislation banning pyramid or "multi-level" sales plans.   Illinois defines a prohibited pyramid sales scheme as follows:

> [A]ny plan or operation whereby a person in exchange for money or other thing of value acquires the opportunity to receive a benefit or thing of value, which is primarily based upon the inducement of additional persons, by himself or others, regardless of number, to participate in the same plan or operation and is not primarily contingent on the volume or quantity of goods, services, or other property sold or distributed or to be sold or distributed to persons for purposes of resale to consumers.

Ill.Rev.Stat. Ch. 121½, par. 261(g).

State attorneys general relying on such statutes have had mixed results.   Compare People ex rel. Hartigan v. Dynasty System Corp., 128 Ill. App.3d 874, 83 Ill.Dec. 937, 471 N.E.2d 236 (1984);   State ex rel. Edmisten v. Challenge, 54 N.C.App. 513, 284 S.E.2d 333 (1981) (defendants' conduct fell within statutory definition of pyramid sales);   with State ex rel. Miller v. American Professional Marketing, 382 N.W.2d 117 (Iowa 1986) (defendant's sales plan was a legitimate multilevel distributing plan, and did not fall within the prohibited category defined in the statute).

3.   Illegal pyramids sometimes lead to criminal prosecution.   See, e.g., Schrader v. State, 69 Md.App. 377, 517 A.2d 1139 (1986), cert. denied, 309 Md. 326, 523 A.2d 1014 (1987).

4.   Another kind of pyramiding is often used in consumer loan transactions to increase the yield on finance charges.   We will look at this technique in detail in chapter 5.

5.   Can you articulate what it is that distinguishes a deceptive or unfair pyramid scheme from the Avon lady?

Problem 4

The State of Illinois has brought a case against a company called Ultramax, which operates the Ultramax Buyers' Service and the Ultramax Matrix, a multi-level marketing plan.   For a payment of $36 a month, subscribers to the Buyer's Service may purchase products and services at a discount from various suppliers who have agreements with Ultramax.   Subscribers are also entitled for no extra fee to become Matrix "marketers" by signing an agreement with the company and undergoing some modest training.   All 10,874 subscribers to the Buyers' Service have also signed marketer agreements, although only 10% of these are "active," i.e., up to date on their fee payments.

A marketer earns commissions on the $36 monthly subscription fees paid by new subscribers he sponsors, and also earns commissions on the fees paid by new subscribers sponsored by the original subscribers, and so on up to the ninth level.   Each marketer must recruit at least three new subscribers.   A marketer's monthly commission check increases according to a schedule on each of the nine levels. At Level 1, he earns a commission of 1% of the $36 fee paid by each of his subscribers at that level ($1.08 a month, assuming three subscribers). However, at Level 9, the marketer would have 19,683 subscribers in his down-line organization, and his commission at this level is 6% of each $36 fee, or $42,515.28 per month.

The FTC's definition of an illegal pyramid includes as an essential element the right to receive rewards in return for recruiting other participants where the rewards are unrelated to the sale of the product to ultimate users. The FTC has also identified other characteristics typical of pyramid schemes, such as requiring a recruit to pay a large sum as an entry fee or to pay for a large non-refundable inventory, pressuring of members to recruit more participants, and "endless chains" or downlines with no limits.

The State's complaint alleged that the Ultramax marketing plan violates the Illinois Consumer Fraud and Deceptive Business Practices Act, Ill.Rev.Stat. ch. 121½, ¶ 261(g) (quoted in the preceding notes). On these facts, Ultramax has filed a motion to dismiss. What arguments would you make on behalf of Ultramax? The State Attorney General? How should the trial court rule on the motion? See People ex rel. Hartigan v. Unimax Inc., 168 Ill.App.3d 718, 119 Ill.Dec. 558, 523 N.E.2d 26 (1988).

SECTION C. LOCUS PENITENTIAE—HOME SOLICITATION AND OTHER COOLING–OFF PERIODS

Problem 5

A state attorney general has brought an action for injunctive and restitutionary relief, under a statute authorizing such actions against any "unfair, deceptive, fraudulent or unconscionable sales practices." You are the trial court judge in the case, and the following evidence has been presented before you. Without proof of overt misrepresentations by the seller, is there a basis for your court to enjoin these sales practices? Does the fact that the sales pitch was made in the consumer's home make any difference? See Kugler v. Romain, 58 N.J. 522, 279 A.2d 640 (1971), from which the following facts are drawn.

Defendant was engaged in the installment sale of so-called educational books and related materials in New York and New Jersey. He operated under the trade name Educational Services Company from an office in New York City.

Sales solicitations were made exclusively through house-to-house canvass by defendant's employees. No advance appointments were made. The solicitors simply descended upon a selected section of a municipality and undertook by house-to-house calls to sell a package of books which was described in large type on the contract presented to the prospective customers as "A Complete Ten Year Educational Program." It was also indicated thereon that the package was the product of the "Junior Institute," and nearby was the plea "Give your child its chance." In engaging his sales personnel, defendant sought persons who were "sales oriented" and extroverted. They were trained by defendant and his sales manager. The sales force fluctuated in number depending upon the season; the number was greater in the summer, reaching 30–35 persons. Defendant's "crew leader" transported them by car to the New Jersey area to be covered.

The geographical areas to be the subject of sales solicitation were primarily the urban centers of Newark, Paterson, Elizabeth and Rahway. They were chosen by defendant who was familiar with them and the class of people to be sought out by his sales force. Within these target areas, the sales solicitations were consciously directed toward minority group consumers and consumers of limited education and economic means. Persons with incomes of less than $5000 a year were favored; some buyers were welfare recipients. Sales among these people were thought to be "easier." Although the canvassing was door-to-door, ordinances in the municipalities involved in this case which required licensing or registration were ignored.

Defendant's educational package consisted of the following books and materials:

1. Questions Children Ask (1 Vol.)
2. Child Horizons (4 Vols.)
3. New Achievement Library (5 Vols.)
4. High School Subjects Self-Taught (4 Vols.)
5. Science Library (1 Vol.)
6. Play-Way French and Spanish Records (2 45 r.p.m. Records)
7. Tell Time Flash Card Set.

Additionally a "bonus" volume—a Negro History, a World Atlas or a Bible—was offered either along with the original package or after completion of payment.

The printed contract form marked "Retail Installment Obligation," which was presented to the customer for signature, consisted of a single sheet covered with printed matter on both sides. The cash and time sale prices were printed on the face of the contract, the former at $249.50, and the latter at $279.95, less a $9 down payment which was obtained whenever possible. Apparently no one paid the cash price. Also printed on the face in small print was the statement: "This order is not subject to cancellation and set is not returnable."

The wholesale price for the basic package, including the bonus items, was $35 to $40. Thus the cash sale price was six or seven times the wholesale price. Defendant's sales personnel were paid on a commission basis, ranging from $16.50 to $33 per sale; the amount paid depended upon whether (1) he secured the $9 down payment; (2) he obtained the customer's home telephone number; (3) the customer was not self-employed; and (4) the customer had been employed for at least 1½ years. In most cases the commission averaged $16.50. The crew leader also worked on a commission basis and additionally received an over-ride commission of $5 on every approved order of a member of his crew.

The Attorney General offered uncontradicted expert evidence that in view of industry-wide practices the maximum retail price which should have been charged for the entire package was approximately $108–$110. He offered persuasive evidence that the books had little or no educational value for the children in the age group and socio-economic position the defendant represented would be benefitted by them.

The testimony showed that as to the New Achievement Library, three of the five volumes dealing with Nature, Science and Civilization, represented "very poor, watered-down articles which cover the * * * areas very superficially." They were of "extremely little use" or value as a means of raising the educational level of the children they were supposed to help. Another volume entitled "Getting Acquainted with Your Opportunities in Education" was extremely poor both in quality and content. Although the volume required a tenth grade reading level, it contained articles which the witness characterized as obsolete at the time it was being sold and irrelevant to 98% of its intended readers. "Child Horizons," consisting of four volumes and designed for children 6 to 10 years of age, was said to have no relevance to children whose unfortunate socio-economic conditions did not make them susceptible to the concepts and ideas reflected therein. It was, according to the expert, like giving calculus to a person who had never studied simple algebra. As to "High School Self Taught," the four volumes were useless not merely for members of a minority group but for basic education for any individual. They might have some value for refreshment purposes for a person who has been through high school, "but for one to self teach, it is just impossible." Similar comments were made about other books in the package. Taken as a whole, the witness said that, in his judgment, the books

> * * * "will serve no purpose in improving the intellectual level of these children, arousing their intellectual curiosity and compensating for the deficient intellectual climate in which they are being raised."

Defendant offered no contradictory proof on this subject.

The Attorney General produced 24 consumers who testified concerning their own experiences with defendant's sales personnel which led to the execution of the printed form purchase contracts. In no case was there any real explanation of the obligation being assumed upon signing the contract. Many buyers, relying on the representations of defendant's agents, did not read the form being signed.

Query: Would compulsory disclosure of contract terms, as in TIL, have been helpful here? Would the New York Clear Language Act have any impact? What is it that needs to be disclosed?

A Radical Departure—Restructuring the Transaction

Although Attorney General Kugler was successful in his efforts to enjoin the particular door-to-door selling scheme depicted in the problem above, it was with great difficulty, for he had not only to litigate both at the trial and appellate levels, but also to litigate very difficult fact issues at the trial. This enormous investment of attorney resources was required because his only weapon was a general-language consumer fraud statute; it will not happen very often. The problem therefore raises the question whether there might be a better legal response to this kind of imposition, one which does not make the outcome depend on post-contract litigation over the existence of fraud in the transaction?

Note that controls on disclosure, through fraud doctrines or legislation like TIL have an obvious limitation. They still permit the seller or creditor to construct the transaction and its terms however he chooses, and to hold the consumer to his signed obligation, so long as pertinent information is disclosed accurately before the magic moment of contract consummation. The consumer has little or no real chance to reflect on the sales pitch, the disclosures or the contract document before becoming legally obligated.

One way of breaking this Gordian knot is to restructure the transaction pattern in such a way that consumers *do* have an opportunity for reflection, for second-thoughts, and for careful reading of disclosures and other documents—an opportunity, in other words, to "cool off." Because of situations like those in Problem 5, supra, this cooling-off notion has gotten particular acceptance in legislation dealing with door-to-door sales. The usual format of these statutes is to provide that consumers will have a specified period after signing a contract within which they may disavow, or cancel, it without penalty by notifying the seller of their election to do so. The seller or creditor is required to inform the consumer of this right, and to provide the consumer with written cancellation forms to be returned if the consumer elects to cancel. Often the seller is prohibited from delivering goods or otherwise performing the contract until the period has expired.

The rationale for such substantive interference with the parties' freedom of contract is succinctly stated in an opinion of the Arizona Supreme Court sustaining the constitutionality of a home-solicitation "cooling off" statute. Arizona v. Direct Sellers Ass'n, 108 Ariz. 165, 494 P.2d 361 (1972). Quoting from a legislative committee report, the court stated:

> Although, without doubt, unethical sales techniques are employed in all methods of retailing, * * * this bill [is limited] to direct selling. This is partially because * * * a disproportionate number of door-to-

door sales involve misleading or high pressure sales tactics, and partially because of certain of the unique characteristics of direct selling which seem to leave the consumer particularly vulnerable: The buyer has not made a conscious decision, as by entering a store, to expose himself to a sales pitch. * * * The buyer has no way of screening the type of salesman who comes to his door, as he does in choosing the stores in which he shops. The buyer may feel intimidated into making a purchase from a salesman within the home, for there is no place to which he or she can readily escape. The buyer * * * has no opportunity for comparing value. And finally, the selling company does not have the same opportunity to police the conduct of its salesmen and their representations in the buyer's home, as it does when they operate within a store.

In addition, door-to-door sellers commonly work on commission, and are often well-trained. And, as Problem 5 above suggests, door-to-door sellers can pick their neighborhoods on the basis of income, ethnic makeup, or other demographic factors, to maximize their chances of success.

Notes

1. Recurrent abuses in door-to-door selling have prompted legislative responses other than cooling-off period requirements. One is the prohibition of "referral" sales, discussed in the preceding section. Another is the imposition of licensing or registration requirements on door-to-door sellers. Do you think these techniques work better than cooling-off periods?

2. The idea of cooling-off legislation first gained currency not in this country, but in England, where it was embodied in the Hire–Purchase Act of 1964. Individual states in the United States began adopting cooling-off statutes in the middle 1960's. See Sher, The Cooling–Off Period in Door-to-Door Sales, 15 U.C.L.A.L.Rev. 717 (1968). The U3C provides for a cooling-off period in home solicitation sales. See U3C §§ 3.501–3.505. The various state laws on the subject are varied, and they do not all operate under the same conditions or in the same types of transactions. Yet all of them are similar in that they address the basic issue of high pressure sales in the consumer's home. In 1972, the FTC promulgated a trade regulation rule requiring a cooling-off period in all door-to-door sales, whether for cash or on credit. The regulation can be found at 16 C.F.R. § 429.1, and it can also be found in West's Selected Commercial Statutes. Again, while the FTC rule is similar to most of the state statutes in its basic ideas, many of the state statutes differ in some of the details of specific coverage.

The federal Truth in Lending Act also provides a cooling-off period in certain transactions in which a security interest is retained in the consumer's home. See TIL § 125; Reg. §§ 226.15 (open-end transactions) and 226.23 (closed-end transactions). Unlike the FTC rule and the state statutes, there is no requirement of a door-to-door sale. However, home improvement contractors, the primary target of the TIL provision, often use door-to-door sales methods, and then take a second mortgage in the consumer's home to secure the debt. As a result, the criteria which trigger both provisions may be met in many transactions. See, for example, the Cole case immediately below.

One important policy issue raised by these different provisions is to decide which transactions need a cooling-off period and which do not. For example, is it possible to identify the characteristics of those transactions for which cooling-off periods have been provided? Are there others which should be included?

COLE v. LOVETT

United States District Court, Southern District of Mississippi, 1987.
672 F.Supp. 947, aff'd, 833 F.2d 1008 (5th Cir.).

TOM S. LEE, DISTRICT JUDGE.

* * *

On Tuesday, November 9, 1982, at approximately six o'clock p.m., plaintiffs Norman and Judy Cole were visited by two representatives of Capitol Roofing, Tony Stepp and Ken Smith. After describing the siding proposed to be sold to the Coles and installed on their home, Stepp estimated the cost of covering the Cole home at $4900. This sales call resulted in plaintiffs', on the same evening, signing a contract for the installation of vinyl siding on their home. During this transaction, Stepp presented a number of documents to the Coles for their signatures, including a work order contract, home improvement retail installment contract security agreement and disclosure statement (disclosure statement), loan application, notice of right to cancel, and deed of trust. Although all of the documents were signed by plaintiffs, they both testified that the only document they actually saw was the work order contract. Stepp had represented to them that the papers they were signing included a work order, credit application and insurance papers. According to the Coles, the papers were arranged one on top of the other, with the contract being the top paper. As Stepp presented the papers for their signature, he lifted only so much of a document as was necessary to obtain their signatures at the bottom of each page. When the transaction was completed, the Coles were given a single carbon copy of the work order contract and a copy of the disclosure statement. According to the Coles' testimony, which the court credits, they received no copies of the remaining documents.

Shortly after Stepp and Smith left the home, plaintiffs discussed the matter and decided to hold off on the transaction with Capitol Roofing. They wished to obtain more estimates and have time to decide if they really wanted the siding. Early the next morning, Judy Cole called Capitol Roofing and informed Stepp that she and her husband had decided to wait, to which Stepp replied that the papers had been processed, the workers would be out at the end of the week, and there was nothing he could do.[2]

---

2. Stepp, at trial, admitted having received a phone call from Judy Cole early on the morning following the consummation of the transaction, but claimed that she had called him to discuss the color of the siding to be applied. Stepp's explanation of the call was inconsistent with an earlier version related by J.L. Lovett on

Frustrated and not knowing what else to do, Mrs. Cole accepted Stepp's explanation. Upon returning home from work that day, she discovered the Capitol Roofing installation crew putting siding on the home. She did not tell them to leave because she believed that she and her husband were bound since they had signed the contract. Subsequently, on November 27, after the job was completed, plaintiffs signed a completion certificate acknowledging their satisfaction with the work which had been done. Immediately upon completion of the paperwork, including the completion certificate, Capitol Roofing assigned the contract to defendant UCM.[3] At trial, there was testimony from two UCM employees, John Nowell and Marvin Murray, regarding UCM's normal procedure for handling the purchase of a retail installment contract from Capitol Roofing. According to their testimony, once an application for a potential customer was approved, Capitol Roofing would furnish UCM with the disclosure statement and notice of right to rescind. The UCM employees would communicate with the customer to verify that the customer had received the required forms, and that they understood the terms and knew with whom they were dealing. Although it was established at trial that this was UCM's normal procedure, the Coles firmly denied having been contacted by anyone from UCM and the court so finds.

Despite continuing problems with the siding and repeated unsuccessful calls by Judy Cole to Capitol Roofing requesting that the problems be remedied, plaintiffs made monthly payments to UCM. However, after having made eleven payments, the Coles became totally frustrated and discontinued further payment. They subsequently retained counsel who, by letter dated December 19, 1984, informed both J.L. Lovett and UCM that the Coles desired to exercise their right of rescission under the Truth–In–Lending Act (TILA), 15 U.S.C. §§ 1601–1693 (1982), and their right of cancellation pursuant to the Mississippi Home Sales Solicitation Act (MHSSA), Miss.Code Ann. §§ 75–66–1—11 (Supp.1986). Upon receiving no response from defendants, plaintiffs instituted this action on November 7, 1985, seeking to enforce their right of rescission and alleging breach of express and implied warranties by defendants. UCM counterclaimed alleging the Coles' default under the contract.

the telephone to Charles Ramberg, attorney for plaintiffs. Lovett told Ramberg that Mrs. Cole had called on November 10 to demand that the work begin immediately. This discrepancy leads the court to credit the testimony of Judy Cole regarding her conversation with Stepp on November 10.

3. United Companies Mortgage, as Capitol Roofing's assignee, became subject to all of the Coles' claims and defenses against Capitol Roofing by virtue of a provision in the contract that, "[a]ny holder of this consumer credit contract is subject to all claims and defenses which the debtor could assert against the seller of goods or services obtained pursuant hereto or with the proceeds hereof. Recovery hereunder by the debtor shall not exceed amounts paid by the debtor hereunder." This provision was contained in the contract pursuant to the Federal Trade Commission Holder in Due Course Rule, 16 C.F.R. § 433.2 (1986).

Truth–in–Lending Act

The TILA and its implementing Regulation Z require that prior to the consummation of a consumer credit sale, the creditor make certain disclosures to the obligor and give the obligor notice of his right to rescind the transaction. The consumer has until midnight of the third business day following consummation of the transaction or delivery of notice of the right to rescind, or delivery of all material disclosures, whichever occurs last, to rescind the transaction. If the required notice or material disclosures are not delivered, the right to rescission extends for three years following consummation of the transaction.

The first violation which plaintiffs contend entitles them to rescind the transaction under TILA is the failure of Capitol Roofing to disclose the security interest that was being acquired in their home. Under TILA, the right to rescind is available in any "credit transaction in which a security interest is or will be retained or acquired in the consumer's principal dwelling." 12 C.F.R. § 226.23(a)(1). * * * Plaintiffs, on the other hand, testified that neither Smith nor Stepp informed them that their home would be security for the siding contract. Neither of them recalled having signed a deed of trust. The disclosure statement signed by the Coles did not mention a deed of trust but contained the following language:

Security: Buyers are giving a security interest in:

—the goods or property being purchased.

X land located at *P.O. Box D'Lo, MS.*

* * * The court credits the testimony of the Coles and is of the opinion that Capitol Roofing did not disclose to them the fact that a security interest was being acquired in their home. Therefore, under the rationale of *Williamson*, this constituted a material violation of TILA and Regulation Z, 15 U.S.C. § 1635(a), 12 C.F.R. §§ 226.18(m), 226.23(a)(1) and (3), and plaintiffs are entitled to rescind.

The plaintiffs next charge that Capitol Roofing failed to furnish them with notice of their right to rescind as required by TILA. TILA and Regulation Z expressly require the creditor in a consumer credit transaction, in which a security interest is being conveyed in the property used by the consumers as their principal dwelling, to provide each consumer who own[s] an interest in the property two copies of a notice of the right to rescind. At trial, Stepp testified that he verbally informed the Coles of their right to rescind the transaction and gave them each two copies of a notice of right to cancel form which contained the required information. Capitol Roofing introduced a document entitled "notice of right to cancel" with an acknowledgement of receipt of form signed by both plaintiffs and dated November 9, 1982. However, the Coles claimed that they had never seen the notice of right to cancel and that, despite their having signed the acknowledgement portion of the document, neither of them ever received copies of the notice form. Moreover, both testified that Stepp never explained the right of rescission and, in fact, after her discussion with Stepp on November 10, Judy Cole was under the impression that she and her husband were bound by having signed the contract. The effect of the Coles' signatures on the acknowledgement is governed by 15 U.S.C. § 1635(c) which provides that a written acknowledgement of receipt of disclosures by a TILA creditor "does no more than create a rebuttable presumption of delivery thereof." As it appears from the testimony that the Coles were unaware of any right of recission and did not learn of their right until much later upon consulting with an attorney, the court is of the opinion that the Coles have effectively rebutted the presumption of delivery. The court finds that plaintiffs were not informed of their right to rescind and that, notwithstanding their signing an acknowledgement of receipt of forms, they never received copies of the notice. The failure by Capitol Roofing to provide each of the plaintiffs with the required notice constituted a violation of TILA and entitled them to rescind the transaction. As they were never given proper notice of their right to rescind, they timely exercised this right, having notified defendants of their rescission within three years following consummation of the transaction. *See* 15 U.S.C. § 1635(f).[5]

* * *

As a result of Capitol Roofing's violations of TILA, plaintiffs were entitled to rescind the transaction. After the Coles served notice on defendants of their election to cancel the transaction, defendants were required to "return to the [Coles] any money or property given as earnest money, down payment, or otherwise, and [were required to] take any action necessary or appropriate to reflect the termination of any security interest created under the transaction." 15 U.S.C. § 1635(b); 12 C.F.R. § 226.23(d)(2). Plaintiffs' attempt at cancellation was met with total inaction by defendants. Consequently, the Coles are entitled to the cancellation of the finance charges in their transaction, and to have the security interest in their home voided.

MISSISSIPPI HOME SOLICITATION SALES ACT

In addition to their TILA claims, plaintiffs have alleged violations of the MHSSA. Like TILA, the MHSSA imposes notice and disclosure requirements upon a seller in a transaction which is a "home solicitation sale." A home solicitation sale is defined as "a consumer credit sale of goods or services in which the seller * * * engages in a personal solicitation of the sale at a residence of the buyer and the buyer's agreement or offer to purchase is there given to the seller. . . ." Miss.Code Ann. § 75–66–1. This section excludes from coverage sales which are initiated by the buyer.

In the present case, there was substantial disagreement between the parties as to the manner in which the initial contact between Capitol Roofing and the Coles occurred. Stepp testified that in November 1982 Capitol Roofing had installed siding on the home of Wanda

---

5. While TILA provides for the assessment of civil penalty damages against creditors for noncompliance with the Act, an action to recover such damages must be brought within one year from the date of the violation. 15 U.S.C. § 1640(a) and (c). Because the Coles did not file their lawsuit until more than one year following consummation of their transaction, no penalty damages lie under the Act.

Collins, a neighbor of the Coles. He claimed that while the crew was working at the Collins home, Judy Cole approached a member of the installation crew and, as a result of a conversation between them, the applicator told Ken Smith to see if the Coles wanted siding. According to Stepp's version, the sales call was at the instance of Judy Cole. The Coles' testimony that their first contact with anyone from Capitol Roofing occurred when Smith and Stepp came to their home on November 9 was corroborated by Wanda Collins, who explained that she had suggested to Stepp that Judy Cole might be interested in purchasing siding. Mrs. Cole had commented on the improved appearance of the Collins home after the siding was applied, and Stepp promised Wanda Collins a $100 commission on any referrals by her which resulted in sales. The court finds that the sales call by Stepp and Smith was the result of a referral by Wanda Collins and was not at the Coles' request. Consequently, this transaction constituted a "home solicitation sale" within the meaning of MHSSA.

Section 75–66–3 of MHSSA provides the buyer a right to cancel a home solicitation sale until midnight of the third business day following the day on which the buyer signs an agreement or offer to purchase. With limited exceptions, none of which are applicable here, the seller is required to obtain the buyer's signature on a statement, executed simultaneously with the agreement to purchase, which must conspicuously inform the buyer of his rights under the Act. Until the seller has complied with the notice provisions of the Act, the buyer may cancel the home solicitation sale by notifying the seller "in any manner and by any means of his intention to cancel." Miss.Code Ann. § 75–66–5(4). Defendants did not suggest that they provided the Coles with the notice required by MHSSA. Rather, their sole defense to plaintiffs' MHSSA claim was that the transaction was not a home solicitation sale and compliance was therefore unnecessary.[10] As the court has concluded that the transaction constituted a home solicitation sale, and as Capitol Roofing never informed the Coles of their right to cancel under the Mississippi Act, the Coles properly and timely exercised their right to cancel by letter from their attorney to defendants dated December 19, 1984.

The obligations of the parties to a home solicitation sale upon cancellation are set forth in part at Miss.Code Ann. § 75–66–7(1) which requires the seller, within ten days of cancellation of a home solicita-

10. At trial, defendants also took the position that they were not required to comply with the disclosure requirements of MHSSA since the state statute conflicts with TILA and Regulation Z. This assertion is predicated upon 15 U.S.C. § 1632(b) and 1638(b)(1), implemented at 12 C.F.R. § 226.28(a)(1), which provides that state law disclosure requirements that are inconsistent with the requirements under TILA are preempted to the extent of the inconsistency. "A state law is inconsistent if it requires a creditor to make disclosures or take actions that contradict the requirements of the federal law." Id. Defendants did not explain or identify which requirements of MHSSA that they contend are inconsistent with the disclosure requirements of TILA. The court has compared the requirements of these statutes and concludes that, while MHSSA requires additional disclosures, it does not require inconsistent disclosures. Thus, defendants' argument is without merit.

tion sale, to tender to the buyer "any payments made by the buyer and any note or other evidence of indebtedness." If the seller complies with this obligation, he is allowed to retain a cancellation fee of five percent of the cash price, not to exceed any cash down payment. Miss.Code Ann. § 75–66–7(3). Until the seller complies, "the buyer may retain possession of the goods delivered to him by the seller or has a lien on the goods in his possession or control for any recovery to which he is entitled." Miss.Code Ann. § 75–66–7(4). Section 75–66–9 provides in pertinent part that

> (1) Except as provided in section 75–66–7, within a reasonable time after a home solicitation sale has been cancelled or an offer to purchase revoked, the buyer upon demand must tender to the seller any goods delivered by the seller pursuant to the sale. * * * *If the seller fails to demand possession of goods within a reasonable time after cancellation or revocation, the goods become the property of the buyer without obligation to pay for them.* For the purpose of this section, forty (40) days is presumed to be a reasonable time. (emphasis supplied)

> *   *   *   *   *   *   *   *   *

> (3) If the seller has performed any services pursuant to a home solicitation sale prior to its cancellation, the seller is entitled to no compensation except the cancellation fee provided in this chapter.

Although MHSSA was enacted in 1974, there has been no construction of the provisions relating to the various rights and obligations of the buyer and seller upon cancellation. Under TILA, as construed by the Fifth Circuit, a creditor forfeits any interest in the property delivered an obligor if the obligor tenders the property or its reasonable value and the seller fails to take possession of the property within twenty days of tender. In order for the forfeiture provision to apply, the obligor must make tender, irrespective of any actions on the part of the creditor. *See Gerasta v. Hibernia,* 575 F.2d 580 (5th Cir.1978). Under the clear wording of MHSSA, however, if within a reasonable time of cancellation, the seller fails to demand a return of the property from the buyer, the property becomes that of the buyer, and the buyer is no longer obligated to pay for it. In addition, the buyer is entitled to a return of all sums paid and cancellation of any security interest granted to the seller. In the present case, neither Capitol Roofing nor UCM demanded a return of the property from plaintiffs within a reasonable time or at any time. Hence, as a result of defendants' noncompliance with the requirements of MHSSA, they are required to cancel the deed of trust and to return to plaintiffs payments made in the amount of $1703.57. The Coles are also entitled to cancellation of the underlying contract. Finally, as a result of Capitol Roofing's failure to demand possession of the siding within a reasonable time after cancellation, the siding became the property of the Coles and they are relieved of any further obligation to pay for it.

While the transaction that included installation of the siding on the home of the Coles was a sale of services, as well as a sale of goods, a seller who has performed services pursuant to a home solicitation sale prior to its cancellation is entitled to no compensation except the five percent cancellation fee provided by Miss.Code Ann. § 75–66–7(3). The cancellation fee is not available if the seller fails to comply with his duties upon cancellation, or if the buyer voids the sale on any ground independent of his right to cancel. Miss.Code Ann. § 75–66–7(3). In this case, Capitol Roofing failed to comply with the requirement in section 75–66–7(1) to tender to the buyer payments made and the evidence of indebtedness within ten days after cancellation of the sale. Thus, Capitol Roofing is not entitled to any cancellation fee.

Defendants have urged that the court condition rescission or cancellation upon the Coles' payment to defendants of the reasonable value of the siding. The defendants could have avoided what may seem like a harsh result in the first instance, if they had complied with the clear requirements of MHSSA. At the time of the transaction with the Coles, the defendants wholly failed to inform the Coles of their rights, thus leaving them vulnerable to subsequent actions by Capitol Roofing. Then, Capitol Roofing, despite Judy Coles' request to hold off on the siding, began work immediately, before the expiration of the three-day cancellation period, thus placing the Coles in a position of accepting goods and services they were not certain they wanted. Capitol Roofing attempted to deprive plaintiffs of their right to rescind, first, by failing to inform them of the right and, secondly, by subtly forcing them to accept the siding. For those reasons, the court concludes that, although rescission is an equitable remedy and conditions may be placed on the exercise of that right, the equity in this case does not lie with the defendants. As one court has observed,

> If this result appears to deal harshly with merchants who have fully performed under their contracts, it seems clear to this court that the message which the legislature has attempted to convey by the enactment of [The California Solicitation Sale Act] is "Caveat Vendor". Merchants, put on notice by the statute, can easily and inexpensively protect themselves, * * *, by including a right to cancel provision and an accompanying notice of cancellation as a matter of course in all contracts signed outside their trade premises.

Weatherall Aluminum Products Company v. Scott, 71 Cal.App.3d 245, 249, 139 Cal.Rptr. 329, 331 (1977); *see also Louis Luskin and Sons, Inc. v. Samovitz*, 166 Cal.App.3d 533, 539, 212 Cal.Rptr. 612, 615 (1985) (attempt to pressure buyers by part performance within three-day cancellation period was precisely conduct home solicitation sales act was intended to prevent).

As the court has concluded that plaintiffs have established violations of both TILA and MHSSA, and that under MHSSA the Coles have no obligation to pay for the siding on their home, this court need not consider the breach of warranty claims alleged by plaintiffs. Further, plaintiffs are entitled to cancellation of the transaction under both MHSSA and TILA, and UCM is entitled to no relief on its counterclaim for damages as a result of plaintiffs' default on the underlying contract. Defendants are also required, pursuant to Miss.Code Ann. § 75–66–7(3), to return to the Coles the sum of $1703.57, representing the total of payments made by the Coles.

The court directs counsel to meet and confer for the purpose of exploring the possibilities of reaching agreement on a reasonable attorney's fee. If counsel cannot within fifteen days of the date of entry of this memorandum reach agreement on the attorney's fee, counsel for the plaintiffs is directed to submit a statement of costs and time spent preparing this case and the court, after giving defendant an opportunity to be heard, will award costs and a reasonable attorney's fee in such amounts as it deems proper.

A separate judgment shall be submitted by the parties in accordance with this opinion.

Notes

1. Truth in Lending extends the right to rescind for up to three years if the initial (material) disclosures or disclosure of the right to rescind are not given properly. 12 C.F.R. §§ 226.15(a)(3) & .23(a)(3). Cases in which the consumer successfully exercises the right to cancel within the initial three days virtually never get to court. Thus, the vast majority of reported TIL rescission cases will involve the stickier issues that come up when the right to cancel is invoked long after the transaction was concluded. See generally R. Rohner, The Law of Truth in Lending ¶ 8.02[2] (1984). See also Pridgen, Truth in Lending's Right of Rescission: The Well Has Not Run Dry, 43 Cons.Fin.L.Q. 49 (1989).

2. In the principal case, why did the three day cooling-off period fail to work for the Coles?

3. Why were the Coles able to claim a remedy under both the federal TILA and the Mississippi Home Solicitation Sales Act? Why didn't they allege a violation of the FTC Door-to-Door Sales Rule?

4. In the *Cole* case, Capitol Roofing left a paper trail attempting to show compliance with Truth in Lending, which was contradicted by the testimony of the consumers. Would their tactics have worked in a court less inclined to believe the testimony of the consumer plaintiffs? Were the consumers negligent in not reading the papers they signed? Was the remedy too harsh on the creditor?

5. The furor over establishing a legal right to rescind may obscure the fact that many sellers customarily allow a customer to return goods purchased and be free of obligation, not because of any legal requirement, but simply as matter of business goodwill. If this policy is so well established, why not make the cooling-off period a matter of general contract law, rather than restricting it to situations involving second home mortgages and home solicitations?

6. In 1988 the FTC affirmed the continuing need for its door-to-door sales rule, but it granted an exemption for sales at public car auctions and at arts and crafts fairs. See 53 Fed.Reg. 45,455, effective December 12, 1988. Is there a relevant distinction between these types of situations and the scenario involving the Coles?

Problem 6

Ima Victim, a homeowner, called repairman Sam Slick, reported that her air conditioner was not operating properly and asked Sam to come to her home and repair it. Sam arrived, inspected the unit and reported that Ima needed a new condenser, which Sam would obtain and install for her. Sam also reported that the house seemed to be very dry—a condition which could be cured by installing a humidifier—and that he could obtain and install one of those also. Ima agreed to both the new condenser and the humidifier. Sam wrote up an installment contract for both, but did not give any notices relating to a three-day cooling-off period.

(a) Are rescission notices required by the FTC Door-to-Door Sales Rule in this case? See 16 C.F.R. § 429.1, Note 1, reproduced in West's Selected Commercial Statutes. Is this a door-to-door sale? Did the buyer initiate the contact in such a manner as to preclude application of the rule? Note that it may be possible to treat the air conditioner and the humidifier separately from a policy standpoint, but would it make any sense to have different legal requirements for each?

(b) Are rescission notices required under TIL § 125? Note that Sam will undoubtedly acquire a "mechanic's lien" on Ima's real estate for his service and labor. See Reg. Z § 226.2(a)(25).

(c) If both TIL and the FTC Rule require such notices, with which must Sam comply? See FTC Rule, Note 1(a)(2).

(d) Would it make any difference if Ima's house was not her residence, but instead was a rental house she owned? See Louis Luskin and Sons, Inc. v. Samovitz, 166 Cal.App.2d 533, 212 Cal.Rptr. 612 (1985).

The Seller's Case

It is easy to sympathize with the repentant consumer in the door-to-door high-pressure sales transaction. But is that the only way to look at the issue? Consider the following remarks of William P. Youngclaus, managing director of The National Remodelers Association, at a public hearing on an earlier draft of the Uniform Consumer Credit Code: National Conference of Commissioners on Uniform State Laws, Special Committee on Retail Installment Sales, Consumer Credit, Small Loans and Usury, Proceedings, Public Hearing on Second Tentative Draft of the Uniform Consumer Credit Code 257–59 (June 16–17, 1967):

> * * * I'd like to also point out that there are a lot of unethical consumers, if I may. They probably outnumber by many, many times the unethical contractors, or anybody else, [laughter] and I would like

to see some way of protecting the small businessman, who will be at the mercy of some of these people. [Laughter]

Let me give you an example. This happens quite frequently. You will get a call that you want a fast job done. Your sister-in-law is getting married Saturday, the party is at your house, and we'd like to get new storm windows. So this guy comes over and signs a contract for ten or fifteen storm windows at about $40 apiece.

So he signs a contract for ten storm windows, a couple of storm doors, a total bill of $680, an installment sale. There are a couple of conditions on doing this: (1) that you take down my old storm windows, and I want a trade-in value; so you give him fifty bucks, when they are really junk. They don't fit anything else. And the other condition was that you would get the storm windows down, and get the windows and sashes painted for me, because this party is coming up.

Okay, he signs it. The guy comes over the next morning. They take the storm windows off. He gets his sashes painted, windows painted. The following morning he gets a notice of a cancellation * * *.

Does Youngclaus have a legitimate complaint? Measure it against any existing "cooling-off" statute. Does the statute protect against this sort of abuse? How would you protect against it?

Note on "Emergency Repairs"

The FTC Rule, the U3C and Reg. Z each provide (in slightly different language) that their three day cooling-off provisions do not apply in emergencies if the consumer requests the goods or services be furnished without delay. FTC Rule 16 C.F.R. § 429.1, Note 1(a)(3); U3C § 3.502(5); Reg. Z; 12 C.F.R. § 226.23(e). Why are emergency waivers included in these laws? What is the scope of the problem perceived? Does this exception provide a device for evading the statute? Consider the following problem.

Problem 7

The Flaky Furnace Co. establishes the following sales technique: "Heating engineers" are sent to homes, where they gain the permission of the owner to dismantle the furnace for a free inspection. The result of many inspections is an assertion that the furnace needs repairs and is so dangerous that it cannot be reassembled and operated safely, or at least that Flaky's employees would not want to guarantee its safety if the owner insisted upon reassembly without repair. When the owner agrees to repair the furnace, both he and Flaky's employee go to a notary public, where the owner makes an affidavit that he requests the repairs without delay because of an emergency. Has the owner a cause of action against Flaky under the U3C "home solicitation sales" provisions? Has he a cause of action under any other provisions of either proposed statute?

Could the FTC obtain a cease and desist order against this conduct? Before promulgating its door-to-door sales Rule the FTC had repeatedly attempted to regulate similar conduct, apparently without lasting effect. See Holland Furnace Co. v. Federal Trade Com'n, 295 F.2d 302 (7th Cir.1961). Why did it then *design* a Trade Regulation Rule with a potential loophole built in?

Note on Telephone Sales

Can the hard sell work just as well over the telephone as in person? Or are consumers better able to resist a telephoned solicitation? The FTC door-to-door sales rule specifically exempts telephone sales, 16 C.F.R. § 429.1, Note 1(a)(4), as does the U3C § 3.501. However, a growing minority of states specifically include telephone sales in their cooling-off statutes. See Pridgen, Consumer Credit and the Law, Appendix 15A (1990). In other states that do not address the issue directly, courts have interpreted the statute to include telephone solicitations. See, e.g., People v. Toomey, 157 Cal.App.3d 1, 203 Cal.Rptr. 642 (1984); Brown v. Martinelli, 66 Ohio St.2d 45, 419 N.E.2d 1081 (1981). Consider the following.

Problem 8

Vic Video, a 21 year old aging adolescent, recently got a telephone call from a representative of Software Unlimited, who wanted to sell him a subscription to a monthly video game service for his home computer. The salesperson asserted the games were the top of the line, were compatible with all makes of computers, and would cost "only pennies a day." Vic verbally agreed to subscribe. Three days later he received his first set of games and a bill in the mail for $32 for the first month. The video games were also of poor quality and would not work properly on his brand of computer.

Vic's state has a law that requires a three day cooling-off period for "home solicitation sales" which are defined in pertinent part as:

> (a) * * * a sale of consumer goods or services in which the seller or a person acting for him engages in a personal solicitation of the sale at a residence of the buyer, including solicitations in response to or following an invitation by the buyer, and the buyer's agreement or offer to purchase is there given to the seller or a person acting for him, or in which the buyer's agreement or offer to purchase is made at a place other than the seller's place of business. It does not include a transaction or transactions in which:

> * * *

> (2) the transaction was conducted and consummated entirely by mail or by telephone if initiated by the buyer, and without any other contact between the seller or his representative prior to the delivery of goods or performance of the service.

Can Vic claim that he should have been given a three day cooling-off period under his state law? Would it do him any good if he could?

SECTION D.   THE DEAL THAT MAKES YOU "GOOD FOR MORE"—TAKING LOTS OF SECURITY

One of the most common credit problems is the over commitment of the consumer—their debt is so high that it can never be paid off. For many creditors who lend to low income consumers, as long as the consumer can continue to pay interest regularly, such a loan is still profitable. Most such loans involve "security" to the creditor in one form or another, and this section explores what can and cannot be taken as security for the loan—and why.

Why should the law limit what a consumer can offer as security? After all, it *is* the consumer's property; can't he do anything he wants to with his own assets? Some limitations seem to be easily accepted— e.g., prohibiting the taking of "a pound of flesh" or the proverbial "first-born child"—without a great deal of analysis. But other types of security demand more analysis. Consumers may be asked to put up as security for loans their automobiles, shares of stock, furniture, works of art, the family jewels, or any other property they own. They may also be asked to put up property they do not yet own, through after acquired property clauses, or their future wages, through wage assignments, or even the assets of third parties, through surety or "co-signer" arrangements.

The law contains many restrictions on a creditor's ability to take security in consumer loans, ranging from a mild limitation on the effect of after-acquired property clauses in UCC Article 9 (which applies to both commercial and consumer loans), to broader restrictions in the FTC Trade Regulation Rule on Credit Practices, to multiple prohibitions on several types of security in many state Retail Installment Sales Acts. We will examine four types of restrictions as illustrations of the concepts, trends and sources of law: cross-collateral clauses, household goods, wage assignments and co-signers. For further discussion of these issues, see Rasor, Limitations on Taking and Enforcing Security Interests in Consumer Credit Transactions, in 1B P. Coogan, et al., eds., Secured Transactions under the Uniform Commercial Code, ch. 20AA (1984).

When security is restricted, a mixture of problems can usually be identified, so there is no predominant rationale. Problems include: the lack of notice or understanding by the consumer or third party concerning what is at stake, the lack of economic value in the assets given as security, the necessity of the assets (wages, tools of the trade) to keep the consumer functioning as an economic entity, and a significant disproportion between the monetary return to the creditor from the assets and the harm to the consumer from their loss. In all such cases, it is believed likely that the creditor seeks extra security because of significant doubts about the consumer's ability to pay. However, none of the regulatory devices available under current law approaches that problem directly by attempting to deter the creditor from making "improvident loans."

1. CROSS–COLLATERAL CLAUSES

If I borrow to buy a TV, is there any problem in putting up the TV as collateral? If I later purchase a stereo, is there any problem in putting up the stereo? In putting up both items? When do I own the TV, "free and clear"? Does it matter whether I understand all these details about circumstances I hope will never happen? What is the market value of a cheap, used "Daveno," three tables, and two lamps?

WILLIAMS v. WALKER–THOMAS FURNITURE CO.

United States Court of Appeals, District of Columbia Circuit, 1965.
350 F.2d 445.

J. SKELLY WRIGHT, CIRCUIT JUDGE:

Appellee, Walker–Thomas Furniture Company, operates a retail furniture store in the District of Columbia. During the period from 1957 to 1962 each appellant in these cases purchased a number of household items from Walker–Thomas, for which payment was to be made in installments. The terms of each purchase were contained in a printed form contract which set forth the value of the purchased item and purported to lease the item to appellant for a stipulated monthly rent payment. The contract then provided, in substance, that title would remain in Walker–Thomas until the total of all the monthly payments made equaled the stated value of the item, at which time appellants could take title. In the event of a default in the payment of any monthly installment, Walker–Thomas could repossess the item.

The contract further provided that "the amount of each periodical installment payment to be made by [purchaser] to the Company under this present lease shall be inclusive of and not in addition to the amount of each installment payment to be made by [purchaser] under such prior leases, bills or accounts; *and all payments now and hereafter made by [purchaser] shall be credited pro rata on all outstanding leases, bills and accounts* due the Company by [purchaser] at the time each such payment is made." (Emphasis added.) The effect of this rather obscure provision was to keep a balance due on every item purchased until the balance due on all items, whenever purchased, was liquidated. As a result, the debt incurred at the time of purchase of each item was secured by the right to repossess all the items previously purchased by the same purchaser, and each new item purchased automatically became subject to a security interest arising out of the previous dealings.

On May 12, 1962, appellant Thorne purchased an item described as a Daveno, three tables, and two lamps, having total stated value of $391.10. Shortly thereafter, he defaulted on his monthly payments and appellee sought to replevy all the items purchased since the first transaction in 1958. Similarly, on April 17, 1962, appellant Williams bought a stereo set of stated value of $514.95.[1] She too defaulted shortly thereafter, and appellee sought to replevy all the items purchased since December, 1957. * * *

Appellants' principal contention, rejected by both the trial and the appellate courts below, is that these contracts, or at least some of them, are unconscionable and, hence, not enforceable. In its opinion in Williams v. Walker–Thomas Furniture Company, 198 A.2d 914, 916 (1964), the District of Columbia Court of Appeals explained its rejection of this contention as follows:

"Appellant's second argument presents a more serious question. The record reveals that prior to the last purchase appellant had reduced the balance in her account to $164. The last purchase, a stereo set, raised the balance due to $678. Significantly, at the time of this and the preceding purchases, appellee was aware of appellant's financial position. The reverse side of the stereo contract listed the name of appellant's social worker and her $218 monthly stipend from the government. Nevertheless, with full knowledge that appellant had to feed, clothe and support both herself and seven children on this amount, appellee sold her a $514 stereo set.

"We cannot condemn too strongly appellee's conduct. It raises serious questions of sharp practice and irresponsible business dealings. A review of the legislation in the District of Columbia affecting retail sales and the pertinent decisions of the highest court in this jurisdiction disclose, however, no ground upon which this court can declare the contracts in question contrary to public policy. We note that were the Maryland Retail Installment Sales Act, Art. 83 §§ 128–153, or its equivalent, in force in the District of Columbia, we could grant appellant appropriate relief. We think Congress should consider corrective legislation to protect the public from such exploitive contracts as were utilized in the case at bar."

We do not agree that the court lacked the power to refuse enforcement to contracts found to be unconscionable. In other jurisdictions, it has been held as a matter of common law that unconscionable contracts are not enforceable. While no decision of this court so holding has been found, the notion that an unconscionable bargain should not be given full enforcement is by no means novel. * * * Since we have never adopted or rejected such a rule, the question here presented is actually one of first impression.

Congress has recently enacted the Uniform Commercial Code, which specifically provides that the court may refuse to enforce a contract which it finds to be unconscionable at the time it was made. 28 D.C.Code § 2–302 (Supp. IV 1965). The enactment of this section, which occurred subsequent to the contracts here in suit, does not mean that the common law of the District of Columbia was otherwise at the time of enactment, nor does it preclude the court from adopting a

1. At the time of this purchase her account showed a balance of $164 still owing from her prior purchases. The total of all the purchases made over the years in question came to $1,800. The total payments amounted to $1,400.

similar rule in the exercise of its powers to develop the common law for the District of Columbia. In fact, in view of the absence of prior authority on the point, we consider the congressional adoption of § 2–302 persuasive authority for following the rationale of the cases from which the section is explicitly derived. Accordingly, we hold that where the element of unconscionability is present at the time a contract is made, the contract should not be enforced.

Unconscionability has generally been recognized to include an absence of meaningful choice on the part of one of the parties together with contract terms which are unreasonably favorable to the other party. Whether a meaningful choice is present in a particular case can only be determined by consideration of all the circumstances surrounding the transaction. In many cases the meaningfulness of the choice is negated by a gross inequality of bargaining power. The manner in which the contract was entered is also relevant to this consideration. Did each party to the contract, considering his obvious education or lack of it, have a reasonable opportunity to understand the terms of the contract, or were the important terms hidden in a maze of fine print and minimized by deceptive sales practices? Ordinarily, one who signs an agreement without full knowledge of its terms might be held to assume the risk that he has entered a one-sided bargain.[8] But when a party of little bargaining power, and hence little real choice, signs a commercially unreasonable contract with little or no knowledge of its terms, it is hardly likely that his consent, or even an objective manifestation of his consent, was ever given to all the terms. In such a case the usual rule that the terms of the agreement are not to be questioned should be abandoned and the court should consider whether the terms of the contract are so unfair that enforcement should be withheld.

In determining reasonableness or fairness, the primary concern must be with the terms of the contract considered in light of the circumstances existing when the contract was made. The test is not simple, nor can it be mechanically applied. The terms are to be considered "in the light of the general commercial background and the commercial needs of the particular trade or case." Corbin suggests the test as being whether the terms are "so extreme as to appear unconscionable according to the mores and business practices of the time and place." 1 Corbin, op. cit. supra Note 2. We think this formulation correctly states the test to be applied in those cases where no meaningful choice was exercised upon entering the contract.

---

8. See Restatement, Contracts, § 70 (1932); Note, 63 Harv.L.Rev. 494 (1950). See also Daley v. People's Building, Loan & Savings Ass'n, 178 Mass. 13, 59 N.E. 452, 453 (1901), in which Mr. Justice Holmes, while sitting on the Supreme Judicial Court of Massachusetts, made this observation:

"* * * Courts are less and less disposed to interfere with parties making such contracts as they choose, so long as they interfere with no one's welfare but their own. * * * It will be understood that we are speaking of parties standing in an equal position where neither has any oppressive advantage or power * * *."

Because the trial court and the appellate court did not feel that enforcement could be refused, no findings were made on the possible unconscionability of the contracts in these cases. Since the record is not sufficient for our deciding the issue as a matter of law, the cases must be remanded to the trial court for further proceedings.

So ordered.

* * *

Notes

1. Would compulsory disclosure of contract terms, as in TIL, avoid this problem? See Reg. Z § 226.18(m) and (p). Would the New York plain English law help? What is it that needs to be disclosed? Could you write a cross-collateral clause in plain English?

2. You should be aware that the court did *not* find the Walker–Thomas contract unconscionable in fact. Rather it remanded the case for findings on possible unconscionability. The case was settled at that point, and so constitutes uncertain precedent on the legality of the contract involved.

3. Some commentators have argued that the unconscionability doctrine is too vague and undefined; and that, especially in evaluating clauses in a contract, it can be used only in a subjective manner. Thus, the argument is that any decision based upon the unconscionability doctrine must reflect only the judge's intuitive reaction to the fact pattern, and cannot create useful precedent. The most famous presentation of this line of reasoning is in Leff, "Unconscionability and the Code—The Emperor's New Clause," 115 U.Pa.L.Rev. 485, 544–45 (1967) *:

> Or instead let us consider the case of a poor, ignorant lady, with seven children, who signed a contract (pursuant to which she bought a stereo set she couldn't afford) making all goods bought from a certain seller, whenever bought, security for any outstanding balance owed the seller, such that on default he could take anything back, even things really already paid for. That hearing might sound as follows:

> Buyer's Counsel: Mr. Walker–Thomas, what is the purpose of this so-called "add-on clause"?

> Seller: It gives us an extra hook over the buyers. Sometimes you can squeeze a little more out by repossessing some of the items bought earlier and reselling them. It makes it easier to convince the buyers that if they don't pay up they're going to get hurt bad.

> Counsel: What is the effect of this provision?

> Seller: It's hard to tell, but we think it helps a little.

> Counsel: Helps do what?

> Seller: Helps make more money.

Counsel:	What about commercial setting? Does everybody use this clause?
Seller:	How would I know? What am I, some kind of conspiracy? I guess whoever can use it uses it.
Counsel:	What would happen if you didn't use such a provision in your contract?
Seller:	I'd make less money.
Counsel:	What if you sold only to people who could afford it?
Seller:	I'd make much less money.
Counsel:	Doesn't your conscience bother you?
Seller:	Wha?

4. Others argue that there can be analytical content to such decisions, including the *Williams* case. In such cases, the court is required to balance interests, just as it is in many contexts. How would one use a balancing test in a case like Williams? To begin, it could be argued that there is no public policy against cross-collateral clauses in any jurisdiction where there is no explicit statutory provision in a retail installment sales act. But against this might be set up the fact that prohibitions against such clauses are widespread in other jurisdictions and can be read as establishing general business standards. Still further, the seller might argue that he needs the additional collateral in cases where repayment is especially insecure. If that seller only uses the cross-collateral clause for very risky transactions, its use is based on a clearly-perceived, and arguably legitimate, interest of the seller. On the other hand, if the clause appears routinely on all the seller's credit forms, that legitimate interest is open to question.

Perhaps more important, however, is the concept of deriving public policy from the widespread enactment of reform legislation, even if it had not been enacted in the relevant jurisdiction. Consider Spanogle, "Analyzing Unconscionability Problems," 117 U.Pa.L.Rev. 931, 961–62 n. 151 *:

It has been suggested that the security arrangement permitting all of Mrs. Williams' prior purchases to be repossessed upon default at any time, even though the payment period for the prior purchases has been extended, was not patently unconscionable because provisions allowing cross-collateral clauses appear in the various state retail installment sales acts. This assertion fails to recognize that there are three basic kinds of cross-collateral clauses. (1) The payments may be pro-rated to keep a balance owing on all prior purchases until the final payment is made on the last purchase. Such an arrangement extends the duration of the payments on the first purchase. (2) The first consolidated payments may be applied first to complete the payment on prior purchases. Such an arrangement accelerates payments on the first purchases. (3) The payments may be pro-rated to pay off all the purchases in the order they were made. Under such an arrangement, subsequent purchases do not affect the payment schedule of prior contracts. Walker–Thomas involved the first type of arrangement. The retail installment sales acts, however, invariably adopt either the second or the third alternatives, or a combination of them. The acts do not permit the perpetual extension of prior purchase payment periods by subsequent purchase contracts.

5. What good would it do the consumers of the United States, or even the District of Columbia, if the court in *Williams* had found the clause to be unconscionable? Would Walker–Thomas be prohibited from using the clause in the future? Who is bound by the court's ruling? Would a statutory approach be better? Well over 30 states have statutes on the subject of cross-collateral clauses; most are similar to the model proposed by the U3C. See §§ 3.302 and 3.303. Do these provisions prohibit the type of clause used by Walker–Thomas? How?

6. The principal argument against decisions like *Williams* is that, without such clauses, lenders may be unwilling to lend to poorer consumers, restricting credit to them unduly. Who is better able to resolve this kind of an issue, a court or a legislature?

2. HOUSEHOLD GOODS

It was once standard practice for small loan companies to take so-called "blanket" security interests in a consumer's household goods as collateral for a consumer loan. Under these arrangements, a consumer's furniture was at risk even for transactions in which the collateral was completely unrelated to the purpose of the loan. Since March 1, 1985, however, blanket security interests have been essentially abolished by the Federal Trade Commission's Trade Regulation Rule on Credit Practices, 16 C.F.R. Part 444. Section 444.2(a)(4) of that rule makes it an unfair act or practice under the F.T.C. Act for a lender or retail installment seller to take or receive from a consumer any obligation that "constitutes or contains a non-possessory security interest in household goods other than a purchase money security interest." The full text of the rule can be found in West's Selected Commercial Statutes.

The Credit Practices Rule was first proposed in 1975, and it was the subject of intense debate for a decade. In 1980, the staff of the FTC's Bureau of Consumer Protection issued a lengthy report on the then proposed rule. Over 50 pages of this report were devoted to the problem of blanket security interests. The following excerpt should help you understand the reason for the rule.

CREDIT PRACTICES, STAFF REPORT AND RECOMMENDATION ON PROPOSED TRADE REGULATION RULE
192–228 (1980).

In return for the credit they receive consumers are often required to give their creditors a security interest in the property they own at the time credit is extended or may obtain after the credit transaction is consummated. ∗ ∗ ∗ Loans secured by non-possessory liens on debtor's household goods and personal effects [have become] increasingly common. Between 1900 and the present, the use of security interests has become standard business practice in the consumer credit market.

Specifically at issue in this proceeding are two kinds of security interests affecting consumers' property. The first is a broadly cast lien on all of a consumer's household goods taken in connection with a loan. The second is the reservation of a security interest in specific property which is not the subject of a credit sale as additional security for the sale. Both forms of security interest give rise to a right to seize property from a consumer, inflicting a substantial forfeiture on the consumer. They also equip a creditor with a capacity to threaten the consumer with extreme deprivation to induce the consumer to acquiesce to the creditor's demands, whether or not the demands are reasonable.

∗ ∗ ∗

The practice of securing consumer loans with a blanket security interest in household goods (HHG) appears to be almost universal, based on this record. Finance companies are the preeminent users, and HHG security interests are found in a majority of finance company loan contracts. However, banks also avail themselves of such security as do credit unions and even, occasionally, savings and loan associations. While retail installment sales acts tend to restrict retailers to a purchase money lien on the goods sold, the record also reveals that certain retailers rely on HHG security interests as additional collateral in credit sale transactions.

An HHG security interest may be created by the mere expedient of checking a box appearing in the text of a standard form agreement. In such cases, the description of covered property is cast only in the most general terms, giving consumers little notice of the nature and extent of the collateral they are pledging to secure the loan. Consumers may thus be completely unaware, in a given instance, of what is subject to a security interest. Under current interpretations of Article Nine of the U.C.C., the simple inclusion of the term "household goods" is sufficient to encumber all of the personal property owned by the consumer.

The majority of HHG security interests are taken in connection with extensions of credit made under small loan acts where the amount financed is limited, generally between 1200 and 1500 dollars. Moreover, a substantial number of these loans are refinancings or consolidations of pre-existing indebtedness where the consumer receives little or no cash disbursement. In many cases debtors consummate a series of refinancings with one company over many years.

∗ ∗ ∗

While the median amount financed in consumer loans tends to be between 1200 and 1500 dollars, HHG security interests are frequently taken to secure substantially smaller extensions of credit. In this connection, HHG security is employed by finance companies which are licensed to lend no more than 300 dollars. Moreover, the record reflects instances where co-signors as well as the primary debtor are impelled to pledge all of their household goods when they guarantee the loan of another. In such cases, the co-signor receives no consideration for a pledge of all of his or her personal property.

* * *

The vast majority of industry witnesses conceded that household goods have little, if any, economic value to creditors. Their value is psychological. * * * When consumers run into difficulty, the blanket security interest in household goods enables a creditor to threaten the consumer with the loss of all personal property located in the home.

* * *

[T]he National Consumer Law Center found that non-purchase money security interests were the single most common basis for threats and harassment of consumers of all of the creditors' remedies surveyed.

The abuse occurred in 77% of the cases studied, and injury resulted just as frequently. Anxiety was the most common, followed by disruption of household finances and other delinquency. Costly financings were reported in 40% of the instances, and distinct out-of-pocket expenses were reported 30% of the time and payment of the [sic] disputed debt as often (31%). Unreasonable settlements, and abandonment of bona fide defenses all occurred 25%, if not more frequently. Loss of job time and marital instability each occurred 20% of the time.

In summary, three out of every four cases involving a delinquent account secured by non-purchase money collateral lead to harassment; and in two of every four situations, injury results.

The findings of the National Consumer Law Center Survey are borne out by the testimony received in this proceeding.

* * *

While seizure of household goods is rare, when it occurs it may have devastating consequences. It may occur in the context of divorce, where a wife finds herself financially devastated and deprived of her personal belongings, or without baby furniture, or a refrigerator. Repossessed furniture may be taken to the dump or auctioned for a tiny fraction of its replacement value. For the debtor, the replacement value is a true measure of the cost of the repossession. This fact was acknowledged by the industry as well as by consumer witnesses. Thus, seizure often means the infliction of a cost which is grossly disproportionate to the benefit obtained. This is particularly true of cross-collateral clauses where a debtor faces the loss of many purchases for the failure to pay for one.

In the context of seizure, the disproportionate impact of blanket security interests thus becomes all the more apparent. Debtors lose property which is of great value to them and little value to the creditor. While creditors are entitled to payment, such security interests offer little economic return to creditors at great economic and social cost.

FTC CREDIT PRACTICES RULE STATEMENT OF BASIS AND PURPOSE AND REGULATORY ANALYSIS

49 Fed.Reg. 7740, 7744 (March 1, 1984).

* * *

In consumer credit transactions, the rights and duties of the parties are defined by standard-form contracts, over most of which there is no bargaining. The economic exigencies of extending credit to large numbers of consumers each day make standardization a necessity. The issue, however, is whether the contents of these standard form contracts are a product of market forces.

Although market forces undoubtedly influence the remedies included in standard form contracts, several factors indicate that competition will not necessarily produce optimal contracts. Consumers have limited incentives to search out better remedial provisions in credit contracts. The substantive similarities of contracts from different creditors mean that search is less likely to reveal a different alternative. Because remedies are relevant only in the event of default, and default is relatively infrequent, consumers reasonably concentrate their search on such factors as interest rates and payment terms. Searching for credit contracts is also difficult, because contracts are written in obscure technical language, do not use standardized terminology, and may not be provided before the transaction is consummated. Individual creditors have little incentive to provide better terms and explain their benefits to consumers, because a costly education effort would be required with all creditors sharing the benefits. Moreover, such a campaign might differentially attract relatively high risk borrowers.

For these reasons, the Commission concludes that consumers cannot reasonably avoid the remedial provisions themselves. Nor can consumers, having signed a contract, avoid the harsh consequences of remedies by avoiding default. When default occurs, it is most often a response to events such as unemployment or illness that are not within the borrower's control. Thus, consumers cannot reasonably avoid the substantial injury these creditor remedies may inflict.

* * *

Problem 9

On February 1, Ms. Williams purchased a refrigerator on credit from Walker–Thomas, the contract to be paid over a three year period. On June 1, Ms. Williams sought to buy a stereo on credit from Walker–Thomas. The credit manager said he would approve the stereo contract if he had additional collateral. Ms. Williams offered to put up, as collateral, all her presently owned furniture and appliances, including her equity in the refrigerator.

(a) What collateral can Walker–Thomas safely take under the decision in the principal case?

(b) What can it safely take under the U3C? See §§ 3.301–3.303.

(c) What can it safely take under the FTC Credit Practices Rule? Are cross-collateral clauses prohibited by the rule?

(d) Does the FTC Rule help solve Ms. Williams' problems with Walker–Thomas? Does it help her establish that the furniture store's conduct was unconscionable or otherwise violated state law?

(e) Assume Walker–Thomas took the refrigerator and the stereo under a cross-collateral arrangement. Assume also that Ms. Williams filed bankruptcy. What portion, if any, of the security interest may she set aside under Bankruptcy Code § 522(f)? Are both items purchase money transactions? See Pristas v. Landaus of Plymouth, Inc., 742 F.2d 797 (3d Cir.1984).

Notes

1. The rule does not directly prohibit blanket security interests in household goods, yet that is its effect. Why? Does the FTC have the authority to amend state law by abolishing certain types of security interests? If not, does it have the authority to accomplish the same thing through the back door of unfair trade practices? The validity of the Credit Practices rule was upheld in American Financial Services Ass'n v. F.T.C., 767 F.2d 957 (D.C.Cir.1985). Note also that the FTC's rule technically applies only to those lending institutions within the regulatory jurisdiction of the FTC, such as small loan companies and retail sellers. Before the rule went into effect, small loan companies were the principal users of blanket security interests. However, the Federal Reserve Board has also adopted a credit practices rule which is nearly identical to the FTC rule and which applies to banks, institutions beyond the reach of the FTC. See 12 C.F.R. Part 227.

2. Why should purchase money security interests in household goods continue to be allowed? If furniture loses its value almost the minute the consumer gets it home, wouldn't any attempt to repossesses it have to be for reasons other than economic ones? Is a creditor who repossess furniture ever likely to recoup the entire debt? If a consumer buys but doesn't pay for a new sofa, is she likely to be surprised when the creditor comes to take it back? Is she likely to be surprised when the same creditor wants to take the refrigerator as well? Does this help explain the rule?

3. Notice that the FTC rule does not prevent nonpossessory security interests in things like stereo systems, jewelry, and works of art. Why? Is it because these items may be considered to be luxuries? If so, is it proper for the FTC to decide which property is "luxury" property? Is it because these items are more likely to maintain their value than ordinary household furniture? May a creditor still use a "blanket" type form or a check-box method of taking these items as collateral?

4. Several states also restrict or prohibit non-purchase money security interests in household goods. Some retail installment sales acts, for example, restrict sellers to security in either the goods sold or closely related goods. U3C § 3.301 is of this type. At least three states, Connecticut, Iowa, and Wisconsin, apply the same restrictions to lenders as well. In

addition to statutory approaches, at least one state court, in a well-known case, has held that blanket household goods security interests were unconscionable. State v. Avco Financial Services of New York, 70 A.D.2d 859, 418 N.Y.S.2d 52 (1979). This ruling was reversed on appeal, however, on procedural grounds. State v. Avco Financial Services of New York, 50 N.Y.2d 383, 429 N.Y.S.2d 181, 406 N.E.2d 1075 (1980). With the FTC rule in effect, will these state law restrictions continue to have any viability?

5. The federal Bankruptcy Code, in § 522(f), permits a consumer debtor to set aside certain pre-bankruptcy transfers which created a security interest or other lien on certain categories of exempt property. This includes non-possessory, non-purchase money security interests in household goods. Like the FTC rule, this provision was designed to alleviate the harshness of blanket security interests. This provision was added to the law by the bankruptcy reform act of 1978. It caused an enormous stir in bankruptcy circles, first over its validity, see United States v. Security Industrial Bank, 459 U.S. 70, 103 S.Ct. 407, 74 L.Ed.2d 235 (1982), and later over its application to refinancing and the like, see e.g., In re Matthews, 724 F.2d 798 (9th Cir.1984). Now that the FTC rule has wiped out these sorts of secured transactions, does Bankruptcy Code § 522(f) matter anymore?

6. Are rules restricting security unduly paternalistic? Don't they amount to a restriction on the alienability of the consumer's property? A provision in a private contract such as a security agreement, for example, which purported to restrict the debtor's ability to sell or grant a security interest in particular property would almost certainly be unenforceable. See UCC § 9–311. Why should the FTC or a state legislature be able to tell consumers what they may or may not do with their own property?

3. OTHER FORMS OF "SECURITY"

a. *Wage assignments*

A wage assignment, as the name suggests, is a device under which consumers assign their future earnings to their creditors. Traditionally, wage assignments were taken at the time credit was extended, but most often the creditor treated them as fall-back security and did not exercise his rights under the assignment until after a default. At that time, the creditor would simply notify the consumer's employer to begin paying all or a portion of the consumer's wages directly to the creditor. Nearly all wage assignments were irrevocable.

As you can imagine, wage assignments are a particularly harsh form of security. By the mid–1980s, over half the states had severely restricted their use or outlawed them altogether. U3C § 3.305 is typical. In addition, the FTC Credit Practices Rule outlaws certain forms of irrevocable wage assignments. See § 444.2(a)(3). In its original draft, this rule matched most state laws on the subject and outlawed all forms of wage assignments. As finally adopted, however, the rule incorporates several exceptions. It now permits irrevocable "payroll deduction plans." What is the difference between irrevocable wage assignments and a "payroll deduction plan"?

b. Co-signers

A creditor can add a substantial measure of contractual security to a consumer transaction by requiring a co-signer—a spouse, parent, friend or relative whose creditworthiness compensates for any weaknesses in the debtor's own. Over the years, many observers of the consumer credit industry felt that unpaid co-signers such as parents and rich uncles did not really understand the nature of their obligation. For example, many believed that the creditor must sue the principal debtor before suing the co-signer. In most cases, this is not true. The co-signer is liable in his capacity as maker of the note, and the creditor may ordinarily come after the parent without bothering about the broke kid. See UCC § 3–415.

Because of concern about widespread misunderstanding of co-signer obligations, the FTC included in its Credit Practices Rule a provision which requires a special disclosure to consumer co-signers. See § 444.3. The U3C contains a similar provision. See § 3.208. Do you think this disclosure will cause many potential co-signers to refuse to sign? Do you think it will help them better understand their obligations?

Note

What accounts for the different treatment of these two types of non-property security? That is, why are wage assignments regulated substantively by being outlawed or severely restricted, while co-signer obligations are regulated solely through disclosure? Does this make sense? Do you think co-signers should be outlawed? (Would you have made it to law school without one?)

4. OVERLOADING THE CONSUMER—IS IT A PROBLEM OF MECHANISMS OR RESULT?

The preceding materials focus on particular contract, sales, or security mechanisms as the oppressive feature of the transaction analyzed. One link between them is their ability to induce the consumer to incur unreasonably high amounts of debt. Would it be possible to conclude, without referring to any particular contract gimmick, that creditors have a recognizable responsibility not to extend credit where doing so is likely to get the consumer in over his head? Professor Countryman in "Improvident Credit Extension: A New Legal Concept Aborning?," 27 Maine L.Rev. 1, 15–17 (1975) * , argues for the concept of "improvident credit extension," and offers an example of what he means:

> I invoke the consolidated Chapter XIII (bankruptcy) cases of Richard and Nancy Lowell, which came before Judge Poulos in late 1972, and in which the Industrial Bank of Maine filed three claims. Judge Poulos's opinion gives the essential facts:

* Copyright © 1975 by the Maine Law Review, Reprinted by permission of the publisher.

* * *

Industrial acquired the Lowells as customers by purchasing their account from Dial Finance in August of 1969. The Lowells previously had borrowed $296.20 from that company in May of that year. In connection with that loan, Dial reported on the back of its ledger card that the Lowells were "Overloaded—can't manage money. Always in fin. trouble—keep low." Yet, in a span of less than thirteen months, beginning September 30, 1969, Industrial made six additional loans to the Lowells ranging from $84 to $3420. By October 14, 1970, they were eventually obligated, through renewals, on three loans simultaneously, totaling the face amount of $6282. * * * The Lowells were heavily indebted by the fall of 1970 [before the last loan from Industrial]. They owed $10,063.65 on a house which they purchased in 1966 for $12,600. They also owed $4,986 to Industrial and had other debts amounting to $7,103.63 for a grand total of $22,153.28. * * *

> The Lowells were then obligated to pay monthly installments totaling approximately $600 from their combined net monthly wages of $780, leaving them as a family of five with only about $45 weekly. * * *

Judge Poulos disallowed all three of Industrial's claims as usurious. More importantly, he also retained jurisdiction to permit the Chapter XIII trustee and the Lowells to determine whether they would file a counterclaim for (1) damages for the usury and costs under Maine statutes applicable to Industrial or (2) "compensable and exemplary damages" for injury sustained by the Lowells because Industrial "granted a series of improvident loans, deliberately charged excessive interest, and engaged in other unconscionable activities." Since Maine had no statutes dealing with unconscionable or improvident loans, a counterclaim based on an improvident loan apparently would have had to be founded on common law tort doctrine.

It should be noted, however, that this 1975 suggestion does not seem to have borne any fruit. Why not? See also, Hersbergen, "The Improvident Extension of Credit As An Unconscionable Contract," 23 Drake L.Rev. 225 (1974).

Queries:

1. Why would a creditor extend credit to anyone knowing there was a substantial likelihood of default? Cf., U3C § 5.108(4)(a).

2. How should "improvident credit extension" be defined? (Countryman's suggestion is in 27 Maine L.Rev. at 23).

3. Should it be unlawful to sell fancy stereos to welfare recipients?

Chapter 4

ASSURING ACCESS TO THE MARKET

Consumers may never experience the benefits (or frustrations) of certain consumer transactions if they are arbitrarily denied the opportunity to engage in them at all—the door is shut to them from the start. A merchant's or creditor's refusal to deal with otherwise eligible consumers may be due to many things. The materials in this chapter examine two causes: (1) misinformation about the consumer's qualifications, and (2) discrimination.

SECTION A. CREDIT REPORTING

1. CREDIT GRANTING AND THE CREDIT REPORTING INDUSTRY

In the United States today, there are over 1600 credit reporting agencies. A reporting agency, or "credit bureau," as they are known, can be found in nearly every community of any size. It used to be that these credit bureaus maintained their own records and kept files on individual consumers, often in manila folders stuffed with pieces of paper and tucked away in filing cabinets. No longer. Not only have nearly all credit bureaus become fully automated, but most of them no longer rely on their own records. Instead, they get most of their information from one of the three large national institutions which now dominate the credit reporting industry: Credit Bureau Incorporated (CBI), located in Atlanta; TRW Inc., Information Services Division, of Cleveland; and Trans Union Credit Information Company, of Chicago. Each of these organizations maintains data bases on consumers all over the country, and they make this information available to the local bureaus through affiliation or other similar arrangements. An affiliate of TRW, for example, will have a computer terminal in its office, and when someone requests a credit report on a particular consumer, the local bureau will simply dial up TRW's computer and receive a printout of the data on that consumer. In addition, the industry trade organization, Associated Credit Bureaus, through its subsidiary ACB

222

Services, routinely obtains the records of credit grantors around the country and makes them available to local credit bureaus. The local bureaus normally supplement the information they get from the large national institutions with local information such as records from local merchants and court records such as divorce filings.

The following material contains a more detailed discussion of the operations of credit reporting agencies.

RASOR, FINANCIAL INFORMATION, IN 1 G. TRUBOW, ED., PRIVACY LAW AND PRACTICE
¶ 3.01[4]–[5] (1987).*

Credit reporting agencies, or credit bureaus, are clearinghouses for information about individuals. They gather and supply to credit grantors and others vast amounts of data about the financial status and other personal attributes of those individuals. They are considered "one of the most important sources of information about the paying habits of consumers." Their information gathering and reporting practices raise a host of financial privacy issues.

There are two distinct types of credit reporting agencies in the consumer reporting industry. The first is the familiar local credit bureau; the second is the less familiar, but equally ubiquitous, investigative reporting agency. They are distinguished by the nature of information they gather, the types of reports they prepare, and the types of subscribers who use their reports. Each will be described and discussed in turn. * * *

Credit bureaus are used primarily by credit grantors, and the information they gather and report to their subscribers is normally confined to credit and financial information. Individual files always include appropriate identifying information such as the consumer's full name and aliases, address, and social security number. Also, they normally include employment information such as position, income, spouse's income, place and length of employment (present and former), and other sources of income. A full credit history commonly appears, showing all existing lines of credit, payment habits, amounts, due dates, and more. Finally, the file will include significant (and much insignificant) public record information, including arrest and conviction records, bankruptcies, tax and other liens, and lawsuits. Even newspaper clippings commonly appear.

Next to public records, the main sources of all this information are credit grantors themselves. Most large credit grantors with computer-based record-keeping systems disclose customer account information to credit bureaus every month. They simply supply their computer tapes (or copies) either to a central source, to which automated credit bureaus have access, or to local credit bureaus directly. This shared information will normally include customer name, account number, account type, date and type of last activity, scheduled payment dates, date account was opened, highest credit accumulated, amounts currently owing or past due, any indication of billing disputes, and the grantor's rating. The rating typically discloses the customer's usual manner of payment, and is coded so users can discern payment habits ("pays within 30 days"; "pays between 60 and 90 days after due"; "repossession"; "placed for collection"; "skip"; etc.).

* * *

The investigative reporting industry is dominated by Equifax Services, Inc., based in Atlanta. Equifax alone maintains files on over fifty million Americans and issues more than twenty million reports a year. The principal consumers of these reports are prospective employers and insurance companies; creditors rarely use them.

Investigative reports are distinguished by both the character and the sources of the information they contain. Under the federal Fair Credit Reporting Act, an "investigative consumer report" is one in which any or all of the information is obtained through personal interviews with the subject's neighbors, friends, associates, co-workers, and the like. While public records and other traditional sources of information are used, the personal interview is the mainstay.

Investigators are trained in interviewing techniques and are encouraged to "not be afraid to ask personal questions." Open-ended questions such as "How much does X drink?" or "What's your opinion of X's home life; how do you think of him as a family man?" are encouraged because they provide leads for further investigation. There is evidence that this digging is not entirely objective. Investigators for Equifax, for example, are apparently asked specifically to identify "anything adverse about reputation, life style, or home environment." In other instances, investigators are subject to "adverse information quotas" under which they are expected to produce a certain quantity of derogatory information on the individuals in whose lives they are meddling.

These questionable interrogation practices seem "designed to provoke gossip," and the reports produced often read like scandal sheets. Along with routine information on employment and finances, they typically include discussions of the subject's use of alcohol and drugs (legal and illegal), domestic problems, sexual practices, and general reputation. One of the most astonishing features of this business is that insurance companies and other subscribers base important decisions about people's lives on this sort of information, despite the fact that it "may have no bearing at all on risk [and] be of no importance in underwriting."

* * *

Notes

1. There is a continuing trend toward centralization in the credit reporting industry. In 1989, there were five large national institutions.

Two of those have now merged into two of the remaining three. This centralization does have significance for the consumer. Many items of information about individual consumers which were traditionally thought of as local are now becoming national. Many creditors with essentially local, rather than regional or national, customer bases are sending their monthly account tapes to credit bureaus around the country or to the large national data bases. Thus, a credit bureau in Laramie, Wyoming, will likely have in its files (or be able to obtain from its computer terminals) records of a loan you have with a bank in Topeka, Kansas.

2. While local credit bureaus may have a primary relationship with one of the large national institutions, they normally have access to all three data bases. All it takes is a membership or user fee. One of your co-authors visited a local bureau to see what was in his files, and within minutes a report was obtained from four of the (then) five large agencies. (This bureau did not maintain relations with the fifth.) All contained most of the same data, although some were more current and more complete than others. (This is because not all credit grantors maintain relationships with all large agencies, so some accounts may appear in a TRW file, for example, while others show up in a CBI file. Many, of course, will appear in both.) Together, these reports contained information which was remarkable both in its detail and its currency. They included, for example, the current balance and monthly payment of his home mortgage, the exact amount of his last American Express statement, and whether he had been late (or more precisely, whether any creditor had reported him late) in any payments to any creditor during the past 24 months. (He hadn't; or at least they hadn't.) There was even information on long-since paid off or unused accounts. The reports were in moderately different formats, but most looked more or less like the form reprinted on p. 231. Have a look. Can you decipher the information contained in this report? Is Joe's credit record good or bad? How can you tell? You may even want to visit your local credit bureau and look at your own file. It may surprise you.

3. What types of problems arise in this process in the absence of regulation? Consider the following:

Hearings before the Subcommittee on Consumer Affairs of the Committee on Banking and Currency, House of Representatives, 91st Cong., 2nd Sess., on H.R. 16340, March 23, 1970 (pp. 241–242):

Prepared Statement of M. Eugene Williamson, Washington D.C.

My tale begins with a form letter I received in August 1967 from the Frost–Arnett Company, a credit or collection outfit in Nashville, Tennessee. It was the first of a series of threatening letters that I was to get from the same company over the next four to six months. All of these letters were dunning me for an alleged claim of $132.87. That is the amount I was supposed to have owed to the Shell Oil Company.

One would assume on reading that first letter that I had already been contacted a number of times and that I had made no effort either to acknowledge or dispute the claim. In truth, it was the first I had heard of the claim, either from Frost–Arnett or from Shell. Actually, the total amount due on my statement from Shell in July 1967 was $11.20, an amount which I had paid by the time I received my next statement (dated August 24, 1967). The August statement showed a total amount due of $5.88.

At no time did I get an overdue statement or a threatening letter from the Shell Oil Company. All of the threats to date have been addressed to me by credit companies. No, it is incorrect to say that these threats have been addressed to me. Rather they have been addressed to a Mrs. M.E. Williamson. I am clearly a Mister.

I wrote to Frost–Arnett immediately and tried to make it clear that I was not the guilty Williamson, and that I would appreciate it if Frost–Arnett would get together with Shell's computer and get the facts straight.

I told them that I had no record of any claim from Shell amounting to $132.87. I also told them that the credit card number for the Mrs. M.E. Williamson being sought was 466–107–091. My credit card number was 248–870–222.

My letter was ignored, and Frost–Arnett continued to flex its muscles with absurd letters that threatened to file papers, issue summonses, dispatch officers, bring on trials, lien on my estate, and do all manner of other nonsense.

I stated my case again to Frost–Arnett in at least one more letter. No relief. The threats continued. So next I wrote the Shell Oil Company and asked that someone please clear up the matter. Shell ignored the fact that the guilty credit card number (466–107–091) did not belong to me. Shell sent to me Xerox copies of the credit slips that were supposed to have been signed by me or by my wife. Most of the credit slips (which total $132.87) were written on a service station in Point Pleasant, Maryland. I had never heard of either the station or Point Pleasant, Maryland. Also, the signatures on the credit slips were neither mine nor my wife's. My full name is Marion Eugene Williamson. My usual signature is M. Eugene Williamson. Although my wife would sometimes write "Mrs. M.E. Williamson," she would often write simply "Mrs. Gene Williamson." She dislikes the name Marion as much as I do. The name on the credit slips written in an unfamiliar hand, was either "Mrs. M.E. Williamson" or "Mrs. Melvin E. Williamson."

I don't know of a Melvin E. Williamson any more than I know of a Point Pleasant, Maryland, or of a time when I could have run up an unpaid bill of $132.87 to the Shell Oil Company. In fact, most of my gas and oil purchases were made on the credit card of another oil company (who has never found the need to track me down with a collection agency).

I pointed all of this out in my next letter to Shell, at which time I also returned my credit card (in two pieces). To repeat, the account number on that card was 248–870–222. The guilty number was and is and ever shall be 466–107–091.

For some reason, I heard no more of the matter until about six months ago, when I received another threatening letter for the same $132.87. But this letter came to me from The Credit Bureau, Inc., located here in Washington, D.C., at 222 6th Street, N.W. It also has another address, which is P.O. Box 1617. This letter was signed by a Mr. Harry Baker, to whom I tried to explain the situation by telephone. He agreed to look into the matter if I would forward to him all of the earlier correspondence from Frost–Arnett and Shell, including the Xerox copies of the credit slips. I did so, and a few days later, Mr. Baker called me to say that he had finally caught up with the illusive Mrs. Williamson, and that I was off the hook. He did not return to me my correspondence from Frost–Arnett and Shell; nor did he return the credit slips.

A few weeks ago I received another threat (dated May 1, 1969) from the same collection firm, The Credit Bureau, Inc. This one was signed by C. Baylor of the Collection Department. This form said: "Regarding account of Shell Oil Company $132.87. The statement you requested is enclosed. Your remittance of the balance due is expected by return mail." I had requested no such statement. I thought the matter was closed. A notation at the top of this form reads as follows: "Important Notice. This seriously delinquent account becomes part of your permanent credit record in our files."

This could be a matter of bitter regret when requests for future credit or employment are denied. Prompt payment helps build a good record. I called Mr. Baylor and tried (although rather heatedly) to give him a history of the matter and also to tell him of my discussions with Mr. Harry Baker some months ago. Mr. Baylor's reply was pay the $132.87, or my credit rating would be in trouble. My attorney told me we would sue if the credit company continued to hound me. Mr. Baylor told me to sue, then, because he was not giving up. I said a few other words not to be readily misunderstood.

I'm waiting to see what happens next.

Note on Common Law Liability

Absent any statute, what might Mr. Williamson be able to do about the problems he described? At common law, consumers who discovered that a credit reporting agency had issued a report which contained false information had to sue in defamation. This avenue normally led nowhere. The reason was that nearly all jurisdictions applied the doctrine of qualified privilege to reporting agencies. This meant that the plaintiff was not entitled to the usual presumption of damages in defamation cases. It also meant that before plaintiffs could recover, they had to show malice. This is nearly impossible to do. Credit reporting agencies simply gather and report information in what, for them, are routine business transactions. They almost never know personally any of the people they report on, and they are not likely to act with malice toward a particular consumer. As a result, the qualified privilege operated almost as a grant of absolute immunity. See, e.g., Dun & Bradstreet, Inc. v. Robinson, 233 Ark. 168, 345 S.W.2d 34 (1961). The same was true in cases against the creditor who may have caused the confusion by reporting the erroneous information in the first place. Defamation was the only theory, and the qualified privilege applied. See, e.g., Ford Motor Credit Co. v. Holland, 367 A.2d 1311 (D.C. App.1977).

2. REGULATION OF AGENCY FILES—CLEANING UP INAC-CURATE INFORMATION

The Fair Credit Reporting Act

The federal Fair Credit Reporting Act (FCRA) was enacted in 1970 to deal with privacy and other issues raised by the flow of information into and out of credit reporting agencies. The FCRA regulates many aspects of credit bureau practices and provides remedies to individuals when these statutory mandates are not followed. Several states have enacted similar statutes, but most of the state laws are carbon copies of the federal statute. This chapter will focus on the FCRA. The FCRA is codified at 15 U.S.C.A. § 1681 et seq., and is Title VI of the omnibus Consumer Credit Protection Act (CCPA). It is also found in West's Selected Commercial Statutes.

Unlike the Truth in Lending Act, the FCRA does not carry with it a set of regulations which credit bureaus and others must follow. However, the Federal Trade Commission, the agency charged with enforcement of the FCRA, has, over the years, written several interpretations and advisory letters on many aspects of the FCRA. In addition, in 1990, the F.T.C. issued an official commentary to the FCRA which consolidates and updates the various policy statements and interpretations the F.T.C. had given over the years. See 16 C.F.R. Part 600, effective May 4, 1990. It is sure to be a useful source of guidance in the future application of the FCRA. The FCRA relates to different aspects of the credit-granting procedure—the formation of a file on a consumer, the information in the file, and use of that information.

Follow carefully the scenario called for under the Act. If a consumer is denied credit, insurance or employment on the basis of a consumer report, the user must so notify the consumer and identify the consumer reporting agency from which the report was obtained. FCRA (CCPA) § 615(a). The consumer may then get from that agency the "nature and substance" of the information in the file. § 609. This disclosure need only be made if the consumer appears at the agency during normal business hours or prearranges for telephone disclosure. § 610. If the consumer challenges information in the file, the consumer reporting agency must reinvestigate and delete inaccurate or unverified information, or accept a "brief statement" of the consumer's dispute. § 611. On the consumer's request, a corrected report must be furnished to any person who had recently received the inaccurate report. § 611(d). Reporting agencies must maintain "reasonable procedures" to assure accuracy, exclude obsolete information, and limit reports to permissible purposes. § 607. Liability attaches to negligent or willful non-compliance. §§ 616 and 617.

Do these requirements strike you as clear? Adequate? Fair? Before answering, consider:

— Is the rejected consumer told what information led to the rejection? Told by whom?

— Is the consumer told of his or her right to learn the contents of the file? Read § 615(a) carefully.

— Is the consumer permitted to *see* his or her file? Handle it? Copy it?

— Will the credit reporting agency personnel be able to tell the consumer *why* she was denied credit, insurance or employment?

— Except when rejected in a specific transaction, how is a consumer even to know that information is being kept on file about him? In which credit reporting agencies?

Problem 1

Fleur D. Lee applies to Commercial Credit Corp. (CCC) for a $5500 loan to buy a car. CCC asks Credit Bureau to send it a report on Fleur. The Credit Bureau report shows that Fleur defaulted on a prior car loan, and CCC denies Fleur's application. What, if anything, must CCC tell Fleur? See FCRA (CCPA) § 615.

If Fleur then goes to Credit Bureau "to straighten things out", what must it tell her? Must it tell her the name of the prior creditor? Must it tell her exactly what it told CCC? See §§ 609, 610. Does this part of the statute furnish clear guidance as to what must be disclosed and what may be withheld? If there is some other negative information in Fleur's file, is she likely to learn it?

If Fleur admits that she defaulted on the prior loan, but asserts that it was because the car became inoperable and was not fixed under a valid warranty, what should Credit Bureau do? See § 611. Reinvestigate? Believe the lender? Believe Fleur? Become judge and jury?

If Fleur's side of the story is incorporated into Credit Bureau's report, is that likely to induce CCC to make the loan? Is it likely to make Fleur feel better? Of what practical effect is the statutory procedure?

Note

The FCRA did not abolish common law defamation actions for false information in consumer reports, but it did codify the qualified privilege. See FCRA § 610(e). In addition, in Thornton v. Equifax, Inc., 619 F.2d 700 (8th Cir.), cert. denied, 449 U.S. 835, 101 S.Ct. 108, 66 L.Ed.2d 41 (1980), the court held that a federal standard, not a state standard, was to be used under this section to determine whether sufficient malice had been established to get past the privilege. The appropriate federal standard was held to be that used in the famous case of New York Times Co. v. Sullivan, 376

U.S. 254, 84 S.Ct. 710, 11 L.Ed.2d 686 (1964): knowledge that the report was false or reckless disregard of whether it was false. As a result, it seems unlikely that a common law action against a credit reporting agency can be successful in a consumer case. On the other hand, since common law actions were invariably unsuccessful even before the FCRA, perhaps consumers haven't lost much by this provision. For further discussion of these issues, see Maurer, Common Law Defamation and the Fair Credit Reporting Act, 72 Georgetown L.J. 95 (1983).

a. Consumer Access to Files

While most of the duties imposed by the FCRA fall on the reporting agencies, users of credit reports such as creditors and insurance companies also have some obligations. Perhaps the most important is that found in FCRA § 615, which requires users who act adversely to notify consumers that they considered a credit report in their decision. This, in turn, makes consumers aware of the report so they can, if they want, go to the credit reporting agency and check their file for accuracy. It is likely that learning of adverse action by a creditor is the primary means through which most consumers become aware of credit bureau files. This rule complements a similar rule in the Equal Credit Opportunity Act (ECOA), which we will consider more fully in Part B of this chapter. See Fischl v. General Motors Acceptance Corp., infra at page 275. Question: Why is there no notification requirement if the creditor acts favorably towards the consumer? Doesn't the good consumer, as much as the bad consumer, have an interest in knowing who has been snooping in his files?

Note, too, that users of investigative reports have a further obligation, under most circumstances, to notify consumers in advance that a report will be made. See FCRA § 606. Why this additional notification requirement for investigative reports? What is it that makes a report "investigative"? See FCRA § 603(e), and see Millstone v. O'Hanlon Reports, Inc., infra at page 250.

Problem 2

One Sunday evening, Sam Tudent was munching popcorn and sipping on a cool one while watching "60 Minutes." One of the segments contained an interview with a person who was complaining about the problems he had been having with his credit records. Sam began to be concerned about the information that might be kept in a file somewhere about him. He does not want to apply for credit, but he is curious to know what information about his life is being gathered, and by whom.

(a) How and where should he begin to look?

(b) Suppose Sam discovers that Local Credit Bureau has a file on him. If he goes over to the Credit Bureau, will he be entitled to see or touch his file? Would it help him if he could? What if the "file" consists entirely of electronic blips or other coded items that only trained personnel could understand?

(c) Suppose Local had issued a report on Sam to a finance company within the past two months. Must Local tell Sam about this? Does Sam have a right to see the report given to the finance company? Is a "consumer report" the same as a "file"? Which will have the most information? See FCRA § 603(d) and (g).

(d) If Sam was allowed to see the report issued on him, it might look like the form below. Do you think Sam would be able to understand it? Do you understand it? Based on this report, do you think Jonathan Customer is a good credit risk? How can you tell?

Credit Profile

```
TCA1                              Inquiry Information
RTS 3122250X1J CONSUMER JONATHON QS.,10655 B 91502,
P-1314 S 92708,235 E 14202,S-548603388,Y-1951,T-18010005,
3-AJAX HARDWARE/2035 BROADWAY/LOS ANGELES CA 90019,L-BIRCH
```

PAGE 1	DATE 2-28-90	TIME 11:23:14	PHP26	V177	TCA1

```
JONATHON QUINCY CONSUMER        SSN: 548-60-3388      EMPL: AJAX HARDWARE
10655 BIRCH STREET              YOB: 1951             2035 BROADWAY
BURBANK CA 91502                SPOUSE: S             LOS ANGELES CA 90019
RPTD: 12-88                                           RPTD: 4-87

FACS+ SUMMARY:
SSN NOT ISSUED AS OF 12-89                    TELEPHONE ANSWERING SVC:
                                              ABC ANSWER-ALL
FROM 11-01-89 # OF INQS WITH THIS SSN=8       10655 BIRCH ST
FROM 11-01-89 # OF INQS WITH THIS ADDR=15     BURBANK CA 91502
                                              213.555.1212

PROFILE SUMMARY:
PUBLIC RECORDS-------1   PAST DUE AMT------$956    INQUIRIES----3   SATIS ACCTS---2
INSTALL BAL----$24,078   SCH/EST PAY-----$1,000*   INQS/6 MON---0   NOW DEL/DRG---1
R ESTATE BAL-------N/A   R ESTATE PAY-------N/A     TRADELINES---5   WAS DEL/DRG---2
REVOLVNG BAL------$437   REVOLVNG AVAIL-----83%     PAID ACCTS---1   OLD TRADE--5-80

NATIONAL DERIVED RISK SCORE = 259         SCORE FACTORS: F,A,J,D

PUBLIC RECORDS:
 CO SPR CT SANTA ANA          10-19-86    3019999        $1,200      JUDGMT SAT
 CASE: 7505853              PLAINTIFF: ALLIED COMPANY
```

SUBSCRIBER ACCOUNT # SUBSCR #	TYPE	TERMS	ECOA	DATE OPN BAL DATE LAST PAY	AMT/TYPE BALANCE MONTH PAY	STATUS DATE $PASTDUE	ACCT STATUS PYMT HISTORY IN PRIOR MOS
MOUNTAIN BK 3562A0197325346R5 1139999	SEC	60	2	1-87 1-26-90 12-89	$43,000 O $19,330 $956	1-90 $956	30 3 TIMES CCCCCC1C1CCC CCCCCCCCCCCC
HILLSIDE BK 291445C8119 3149999	AUT	48	5	3-89 1-15-90 12-89	$6,300 O $4,748	1-90	CURR ACCT CCCCCCCCCC

```
** ACCOUNT WAS IN DISPUTE-NOW RESOLVED-REPORTED BY SUBSCRIBER **
```

| HEMLOCKS 98E543184026 3309999 | CHG | REV | 2 | 10-89 2-05-90 | $1,000 L $437 $44 E | 2-90 | CURR ACCT NCCC |

```
INQUIRIES:
 CAL AUTO                       3-22-89      $8,700       1926599
 1016597317
            AUT      48
 HILLSIDE BK                    2-18-89                   3149999

+++++ MORE
```

Credit Profile

Inquiry Information

TCA1 RTS 3122250X1J CONSUMER JONATHON QS.,10655 B 91502

PAGE 2	DATE 2-28-90	TIME 11:23:14	PHP26	V177	TCA1

```
>>>> CHECKPOINT >>>>> SS# IS 548063388/OTHER FILE IDENT: ZIP IS 91503
JONATHON QUINCY CONSUMER          SSN: 548-06-3388     EMPL: ACE HARDWARE
10655 BIRCH STREET                YOB: 1951            RPTD: 10-82
BURBANK CA 91503                  SPOUSE: S
RPTD: 5-84

  CENTRAL BANK                    2-85      $16,000 O             PD WAS 30
  4590345859403                1-31-90                   1-90    CCCC1CCCCCCC
  1234567      SEC    60    2  12-89                             CCCCCCCCCCCC

  BAY COMPANY                     5-80      $1,600 L             CUR WAS 60
  4681123R101                  1-21-90          $0       7-89    CCCCCC1CCCCC
  3339999      CHG    REV   1   8-89                             CCCCCCCC21CC

INQUIRIES:
  SMITH BROS FINANCE CO          10-24-88                6586868

CONSUMER RELATIONS CONTACT: CREDIT BUREAU OF SOUTHERN CALIFORNIA
100 OCEAN BLVD, SANTA MONICA CA 92000  818.233.0000

END
```

Problem 3

Klinger has just moved out of an apartment he rented from Potter. Potter claims Klinger owes him $150 for repairs and cleaning, but Klinger disputes that he owes any money to Potter.

Potter is a member of RentCheck, an association of local landlords which maintains files on all local tenants. All of the information in RentCheck's files comes from those landlords. Potter reports to RentCheck that Klinger is a "messy tenant who did not properly clean the premises at the end of the rental term when he left."

Klinger now goes to several other landlords seeking to rent an apartment. Each landlord calls RentCheck to determine whether there is a file on Klinger and what it says. After hearing what was in the file, each landlord turned Klinger down, but said nothing about RentCheck or its files to Klinger.

Has anyone violated the FCRA? Note that the information on Klinger had nothing to do with his *creditworthiness*. Does that matter?

PINNER v. SCHMIDT

United States Court of Appeals, Fifth Circuit, 1986.
805 F.2d 1258.

HUNTER, DISTRICT JUDGE

[Pinner worked as an outside salesman for a Sherwin–Williams store that was managed by Schmidt. There was tension between Pinner and Schmidt, and Pinner left in late 1980. Pinner had a personal charge account with Sherwin–Williams which reflected a balance of $171.11 when he left, although "the evidence at trial tended to show that the correct balance was $121.71." Pinner believed that Schmidt had entered several fictitious charges on his account. Sherwin–Williams is a subscriber of Chilton, a credit reporting agency.]

Sherwin–Williams executive Robert Stewart classified Pinner's account as delinquent in June, 1980, and again in January, 1981. This information was relayed to Chilton at these times and was included in Pinner's credit file. Sherwin–Williams made no mention of Pinner's objections to the amounts allegedly due. Stewart also reported the account as delinquent to a collection agency. On October 8, 1981, Pinner attempted to purchase tires on credit but was refused after the tire company routinely consulted Chilton for Pinner's credit history. It was at this point that Pinner learned of the delinquent account report. Pinner then requested and received a copy of his credit report from Chilton showing his account as delinquent. He also received materials which explained the procedure to follow if he disputed any part of the report. On January 11, 1982, Pinner's attorney sent a letter to Chilton notifying them that Pinner disputed the accuracy of the Sherwin–Williams charges. The letter clearly set forth the dispute between Pinner and Schmidt over the charge account and requested an investigation of the accuracy of the balance. Chilton employees contacted Sherwin–Williams and received verification from Schmidt that Pinner's account remained delinquent.

In February, 1982, Pinner was denied charge accounts by D.H. Holmes Company, Ltd., and Danny's Clothing Store. Both stores advised him in writing that the denials of credit were based on information they received from Chilton. Pinner again requested a copy of his credit report. The report he received, issued two months after his attorney's letter notifying Chilton that the account was disputed, still indicated that he had an undisputed delinquent account with Sherwin–Williams. In fact Chilton never amended Pinner's credit file to show the account balance was disputed. After suit was filed, however,

Chilton noted in the file "Litigation Pending." The notation did not specify whether Pinner was plaintiff or defendant in the litigation.

Pinner sought recovery against Schmidt and Sherwin–Williams under La.Civ.Code Ann. art. 2315 (West Supp.1986) on several theories including damage to his creditworthiness and reputation and damages for humiliation and mental distress. Pinner also made claims against Sherwin–Williams for non-compliance with the Fair Credit Billing Act, 15 U.S.C.A. §§ 1666–1666j (West Supp.1986), and against Chilton for both negligent and willful violations of the Fair Credit Reporting Act (FCRA), 15 U.S.C.A. §§ 1681n and 1681o (West Supp.1986).

* * *

* * * The trial judge entered a judgment holding Schmidt, Sherwin–Williams and Chilton liable in solido for the $100,000 compensatory damages. Chilton alone was cast for $100,000 punitive damages. Each defendant filed a motion for judgment notwithstanding the verdict or alternatively for a new trial or a remittitur, 617 F.Supp. 342. The motions were denied. This appeal followed.

II. CHILTON'S LIABILITY UNDER THE FCRA

Congress, in enacting the FCRA, sought to require consumer reporting agencies to adopt reasonable procedures for meeting the needs of commerce for consumer credit in a manner both fair and equitable to the consumer. 15 U.S.C.A. § 1681(b). The legislative history of the FCRA indicates that its purpose is to protect an individual from inaccurate or arbitrary information about himself in a consumer report that is being used as a factor in determining the individual's eligibility for credit, insurance, or employment.

The facts of this case present two possible bases of liability under the FCRA. First, the FCRA provides that in preparing a consumer report a credit reporting agency must "follow reasonable procedures to assure maximum possible accuracy of the information concerning the individual about whom the report relates." 15 U.S.C.A. § 1681e(b). This section imposes a duty of reasonable care in the preparation of a consumer report. *Thompson v. San Antonio Retail Merchants Association,* 682 F.2d 509, 513 (5th Cir.1982). Second, the FCRA imposes a duty upon reporting agencies to reinvestigate and to delete information found to be inaccurate or no longer verifiable once the consumer has protested the inclusion of the material. 15 U.S.C.A. § 1681i. A negligent violation of either of these sections subjects the credit reporting agency to liability for any actual damages sustained as a result of the violation, together with the costs of the action and a reasonable attorney's fee. 15 U.S.C.A. § 1681o. A willful violation of either section subjects the agency to punitive damages as well. 15 U.S.C.A. § 1681n.

* * *

The record reveals evidence from which a jury could find a negligent violation of § 1681i. Once Chilton received notice of the dispute over the Sherwin–Williams account from Pinner's attorney it was obligated to re-verify the accuracy of the delinquent entry. The letter informed Chilton of the Pinner–Schmidt dispute. It was unreasonable for Chilton to contact only Schmidt in its reinvestigation.

The Sixth Circuit has held that where a credit agency knew of a dispute between the consumer and creditors and where the consumer had complained about his consumer report, merely making two telephone calls to the creditors was insufficient to re-verify the information contained in the report. *Bryant v. TRW, Inc.,* 689 F.2d 72, 79 (6th Cir. 1982). Here, Chilton not only called the creditor to re-verify the report but consulted the man they knew to have had disagreements with Pinner in the past. Because of Schmidt's involvement, contacting only him was insufficient to reverify the entry as Chilton was required to do under § 1681i(a). If, as Chilton argues, there was no other authority to turn to to verify Pinner's account, Chilton should have deleted the information altogether, as is required by § 1681i(a).

* * *

We have carefully considered each argument presented by Chilton with the premise that our assigned role is neither to re-try the case de novo nor to supplant the jury verdict so long as it is supported by substantial evidence. We find that the district court was eminently correct in denying Chilton's motions for directed verdict, judgment notwithstanding the verdict, or a new trial in regard to negligent violations of the FCRA.

We can see nothing in this fact situation, however, to justify a finding that Chilton willfully violated the Act. Punitive damage awards are permitted even without malice or evil motive, but the violation must have been willful under 15 U.S.C.A. § 1681n. *Fischl v. General Motors Acceptance Corporation,* 708 F.2d 143 (5th Cir.1983). In each case where punitive damages have been allowed the defendant's conduct involved willful misrepresentations or concealments. In *Millstone v. O'Hanlon Reports, Inc.,* 528 F.2d 829 (8th Cir.1976) punitive damages were found to be proper when the agency sought at every step to block the consumer in his attempts to exercise his rights under the FCRA. There, the agency mislead the consumer about the contents of his credit file on three separate occasions. The reports it issued were "rife with innuendo, misstatement, and slander," and the agency did not reveal the contents of the credit file until the commencement of litigation. 528 F.2d at 834. In *Collins v. Retail Credit Co.,* 410 F.Supp. 924 (E.D.Mich.1976) the agency's report contained statements about the plaintiff regarding her excessive drinking and "alleged instances of low moral character." 410 F.Supp. at 927. The agency also refused to disclose the contents of her file on at least one occasion. *Id.*

Chilton's conduct in this case in no way resembles the actions of the defendants in *Millstone* and *Collins.* Chilton promptly furnished Pinner with a copy of his credit report when he requested one. No effort was made to conceal anything and the information contained in the credit file was limited to the report on the delinquent Sherwin–Williams account. There was unrefuted testimony from Chilton employees establishing that they attempted to contact Pinner's attorney to relay that Chilton had reaffirmed the accuracy of his credit history. The telephone calls were not returned. Under the plain language and legislative history of § 1681n, punitive damages are appropriate only where the violation has been willful. "Willful" is a word of many meanings—its construction often influenced by its context. But here there is simply nothing to even suggest that Chilton willfully set out to do Pinner harm. There is no evidence that they knowingly and intentionally committed an act in conscious disregard for the rights of others. The jury's award of punitive damages lacked any evidentiary support whatsoever. The facts and controlling case law mandate that the punitive damage award be vacated. It is.

* * *

In summary: As to Chilton, we reverse and render as to the punitive damage award; we affirm the judgment appealed from as to compensatory damages, except as to the amount of those damages. We find $25,000 to be the maximum possible recovery for those damages and order a conditional remittitur. We reverse as to Schmidt and Sherwin–Williams.

AFFIRMED IN PART, REVERSED IN PART AS TO CHILTON with conditional REMITTITUR. REVERSED AS TO SCHMIDT AND WILLIAMS.

Note

Each section of the FCRA is highly qualified by various conditions. It is fair to say that the FCRA is one of the most condition- and qualification-ridden statutes enacted by Congress in recent decades. Can you recognize the conditions on the regulations illustrated by the problems above? For each condition recognized, can you predict whether it will prevent disclosure in the usual case, or only in a limited number of cases? Can you recognize the interest of the consumer reporting agency which is being protected? Has the FCRA succeeded in balancing fairly the conflicting interests of the consumer and the agency?

Problem 4

There are two guys from Syracuse named James Andrew O'Brian and James Andre O'Brian. James Andrew is a lawyer who continuously over estimates his future income. He bought a BMW, but could not keep up the payments, and it was repossessed. He bought a ritzy town-house—same story. He now has $9,000 in unpaid entertainment bills on his American Express card.

James Andre, on the other hand, has no blemishes on his credit record at all. He just graduated from plumbers school, and wants to take a well-earned motoring vacation out West. He applied to Amoco, Exxon and Mobil for credit cards. All three companies ask for credit reports from the Credit Bureau Co. of New York (CBC) on "James A. O'Brian", because this is how James Andre filled in their application forms. Exxon and Mobil receive reports from CBC on James Andre's credit record, and promptly issue credit cards to him. Amoco, however, receives from CBC a report on James Andr*ew*'s credit record, and promptly denied the credit card application, giving a proper FCRA § 615 notice.

If James Andre visits CBC, will he learn about the information Amoco received, or only what is in *his* file? See FCRA § 609(a). Since all the information in his file is correct, there seems to be no perceptible problem. However, one piece of information will be *missing* from James Andre's file: there is no record in it of CBC furnishing a report to Amoco. How likely is he to notice that? Note that his attorney should note the discrepancy and pursue it. Does that give you a better appreciation of the reasons for FCRA § 609(a)(3)? If CBC's mistake is discovered, can James Andre force it to send a new report to Amoco?

b. Credit Repair Organizations—The Newest Scam?

Have you seen ads like this? In recent years, so-called credit repair organizations have been springing up all over the country. What do these organizations really do? Do they bring salvation for the consumer in need, or do they merely increase that need? Consider the following materials.

HEARING BEFORE THE SUBCOMMITTEE ON CONSUMER AFFAIRS AND COINAGE OF THE COMMITTEE ON BANKING, FINANCE AND URBAN AFFAIRS, HOUSE OF REPRESENTATIVES

100th Cong., 2d Sess., on H.R. 458, September 15, 1988 (pages 3–4):

Statement of Kenneth P. Walton, Deputy Assistant Director, Criminal Investigation Division, Federal Bureau of Investigation:

In this case, information was received by our Newark division in late 1986, that Credit–Rite, Inc., doing business in Palmyra, NJ, was defrauding consumers through a scheme wherein they promised to repair the credit of people with poor credit profiles.

Credit–Rite, Inc. was operated principally by president, James T. Gray, its acting president, franchise director, Jeffrey Roberts, and its credit repair manager, Donald Gray. It was in operation from approximately mid–1985 to February 1987.

Credit–Rite, Inc. sold franchises to investors throughout the United States for a fee of between $5000 to $30,000. The franchisers solicited consumers with poor credit profiles and signed them to contracts which guaranteed 100 percent credit repair within 18 months. The contract was usually sold to the consumer for $650 with initial deposits of between $50 and $250. Once a franchiser sold a contract, the contract would be forwarded to the main office of Credit–Rite in Palmyra, NJ, where an account would be established under the client's name. Credit–Rite, Inc. would then send billings to the consumers on the remaining balance due on the contract. When Credit–Rite, Inc. received the monthly payment from the client, a percentage of that fee was to be sent to the originating franchise.

The FBI received numerous inquiries from consumer affairs offices of several States each claiming to have received complaints from consumers advising they had paid Credit–Rite, Inc. for credit repair when, in fact, no credit repair had taken place.

Credit–Rite, Inc. guaranteed, for a fee, to repair the negative credit histories of clients to the point where the clients could apply for any credit that they desired and would not be denied credit based solely on their credit history. Investigation determined that "credit repair", as marketed by Credit–Rite, Inc., could not be performed since credit reporting is governed by the Fair Credit Reporting Act. As you are aware, this act provides that certain accurately reported negative credit entries, including late payments, collection accounts, and charge-offs may remain on the credit reports for up to 7 years, while bankruptcy may remain for 10 years. Other entries, such as liens and judgments, remain on a credit report until paid. Therefore, one cannot guarantee a claim to be able to "repair" an accurate credit report. The Fair Credit Reporting Act provides that only inaccurate information on a credit report may be removed.

The principal method used by Credit–Rite, Inc. in attempting to remove negative credit entries from an accurate credit report was by disputing the accuracy of the entry. Credit reporting agencies are required, under the Fair Credit Reporting Act to investigate and respond to consumer disputes within a reasonable time, which has been interpreted by the Federal Trade Commission as 30 days from receipt of the dispute. Credit–Rite, Inc. operated under the premise that by inundating the credit bureaus with disputes, the credit bureaus would become mired and unable to respond to the disputes within the period of time proscribed by law. This would result in the disputed item being removed from the credit history report.

Credit–Rite, Inc. also attempted to remove or upgrade existing negative items on a credit report by "negotiating" with a creditor to delete or upgrade the entry in return for the client making partial or full payments to the creditor. By and large, creditors realize that by succumbing to this type of negotiation; they undermine the integrity of the credit reporting system they depend upon for granting credit. Therefore, negotiations were generally not successful.

Credit–Rite, Inc. attempted to utilize a combination of disputes and negotiations, whereby, they arranged with clients to repay a portion of existing bad debt. Once a partial payment was made, a dispute was sent to the credit bureau stating the account was paid and should be so reflected on the current credit report.

The FBI investigation revealed Credit–Rite, Inc. sold over 9,000 "repair" contracts through 33 franchise locations throughout the United States. Credit–Rite, Inc. totaled over $6 million in business volume and available records reveal approximately $2.3 million in revenues were actually received.

The three principals of Credit–Rite, Inc. were indicted in November 1987, for devising a scheme to defraud the public through the guaranteed "repaired credit" contracts sold through Credit–Rite, Inc. franchises.

Notes

1. The three principals involved in the Credit–Rite operation were all convicted of federal crimes, including mail fraud and conspiracy. James Gray was sentenced in July, 1988, to 7 years in prison. Donald Gray received a sentence of 3 years, and Jeffrey Roberts got 15 months. Restitution orders were also entered. At the criminal trial, the three defendants changed their pleas to guilty during the testimony of one witness.

2. H.R. 458, the bill that was the subject of the Congressional hearing excerpted above, is entitled The Credit Repair Organizations Act. It is described as "a bill to prevent consumer abuses by credit repair organizations." A similar bill has been introduced in the Senate. Neither bill has yet become law, but about half the states have enacted laws which regulate the activities of credit repair organizations. Most of these laws require repair organizations to advise consumers of their rights under the FCRA and to fully disclose the services they will provide. They also prohibit repair organizations from taking money from consumers in advance unless they post a bond, and they commonly give consumers a three-day cooling-off period. Do you think a bonding requirement and notice rules are enough to protect consumers from the possible dangers posed by these organizations? Jeffrey Roberts, one of the principals of Credit–Rite, didn't think so. He told Congress flat out that these organizations should be banned entirely. Why? At least one state, Georgia, has chosen this path and has prohibited these organizations entirely.

3. The credit reporting industry has come out four-square against credit repair organizations, calling them "rip-offs" and other similar names. Why?

4. Supporters of credit repair organizations claim that consumers need representatives to help deal with stubborn credit reporting agencies. They claim that many credit reporting agencies do not cooperate when consumers want to see their files, and the presence of a repair organization representative helps. Would you advise a friend who had credit problems to use one of these organizations? Can it do anything that your friend could not do for herself? Is your friend likely to understand all of her rights under the FCRA? Is she likely to feel comfortable sitting alone in the credit bureau office while going over her file?

5. Are the practices of credit repair organizations deceptive or misleading under the F.T.C. Act or state "UDAP" statutes? The FTC did file complaints against Credit–Rite and its principals, charging that they falsely and deceptively claimed that the company could substantially improve consumers' credit records and failed to honor the company's money-back guarantee. Consent decrees were reached. See F.T.C. v. Credit–Rite, Inc., No. 88–1206 (GEB), District Court of New Jersey (1988).

6. People who have credit problems sometimes do things even more desperate than go to repair organizations. Sometimes they go to so-called "credit doctors." Credit doctors are thieves who use computers to raid credit bureau files, steal good credit histories, and then sell them to desperate people with bad credit records. Their method of operation is remarkably simple. They might buy a credit bureau access code from an underpaid clerk in a local retail establishment, for example. Using their own computers, they then tap into the credit bureau's records, search until they find a file with a good credit record and the same name as their "patient's," and copy the good file into the patient's file. Naturally, this procedure often ruins the record of the innocent person whose file was raided. Doesn't all this make you wish your name was Spanogle or Pridgen or Rasor instead of Smith or Thompson? See especially Thompson v. San Antonio Retail Merchants Ass'n, infra at page 246.

3. REGULATION OF MISINFORMATION IN REPORTING: HOW ACCURATE DOES AN AGENCY HAVE TO BE?

Read FCRA § 607(b). Notice that credit reporting agencies are under no obligation to make accurate reports. Rather, they must use "reasonable procedures to assure maximum possible accuracy." This means that when an agency issues a report with false information, that fact alone is not enough to establish liability for violating the FCRA. Instead, the consumer must show that the agency's procedures didn't measure up to the statutory standard. Of course, the fact that false information got into a report might be some indication that procedures were faulty somewhere along the line, but normally this by itself is insufficient to prove a case.

Note that FCRA does not distinguish between ordinary credit bureaus and investigative reporting agencies. Yet, as discussed earlier, the operations differ in each type of institution. For this reason, the procedures each might follow to comply with the statutory standard might differ as well. Accordingly, we will look at each type independently. *Koropoulos* and *Thompson,* the first two of the following cases, involve ordinary credit bureaus. The third case, *Millstone,* involves an investigative reporting agency. Keep the differences in mind as you read the cases.

KOROPOULOS v. CREDIT BUREAU, INC.

United States Court of Appeals, District of Columbia Circuit, 1984.
734 F.2d 37.

WALD, CIRCUIT JUDGE:

Plaintiffs, George and Katelina Koropoulos, appeal the district court's dismissal of their suit alleging that the Credit Bureau Incorporated of Georgia (CBI), violated the Fair Credit Reporting Act (FCRA or Act), 15 U.S.C. §§ 1681–1681t, by failing "to follow reasonable procedures to assure maximum accuracy" of credit reports it issued in response to inquiries on Mr. and Mrs. Koropoulos. The district court granted CBI's motion for summary judgment on the basis of facts it found uncontested: that the report CBI issued on Mr. Koropoulos was accurate and that CBI had issued no report on Mrs. Koropoulos. We find, however, that there are genuine issues of material fact as to whether the report on Mr. Koropoulos was accurate within the meaning of the FCRA. * * * We therefore vacate the grant of summary judgment and remand the case for appropriate action by the trial court.

I. BACKGROUND

On June 7, 1976, Mr. Koropoulos borrowed $2,034.92 from Virginia National Bank (VNB), to be paid off in twelve monthly installments beginning in July, 1976. Mr. Koropoulos subsequently defaulted on the loan; VNB charged the loan off as a bad debt and referred it to Nationwide Credit Corporation (NCC) for collection. Mr. Koropoulos paid the loan in full to NCC, the final payment occurring in November, 1977. NCC kept a 40% collection fee on the payments by Mr. Koropoulos, and sent the remaining 60% of his payments to VNB.

In 1981, the Bank of Virginia denied Mr. Koropoulos' application for a credit card, allegedly on the basis of a credit report from CBI. At about the same time, Lord & Taylor turned down Mrs. Koropoulos' application for a credit card, also allegedly because of a credit report from CBI. Over the next few months Mr. Koropoulos was denied credit on a number of occasions; each time he claims that the lending institution mentioned a CBI credit report as the reason for denial.

In January, 1982, after plaintiffs' attorney contacted CBI, it disclosed Mr. Koropoulos' file to the plaintiffs. The file reported the VNB loan as having a current status of "I9" with a "0" balance. According to CBI's own definition, the "I9" status indicates that VNB either wrote the loan off as a bad debt, placed it for collection, instituted a civil suit against the debtor to collect it, or determined that the debtor "skipped" (*i.e.,* could not be located). The "0" balance indicates that the balance, as it appears on VNB's books, is zero.

On June 1, 1982, plaintiffs filed suit alleging that this characterization of the VNB loan was misleading because it indicated to potential creditors that VNB wrote the loan off as a total loss, and that Mr. Koropoulos never paid the debt. In fact, CBI knew in November 1977 that Mr. Koropoulos had paid off the loan in full. Less than a month later, CBI moved for summary judgment on the grounds that the information it reported on Mr. Koropoulos was entirely accurate and that it never issued a credit report on Mrs. Koropoulos.

* * *

II. THE VNB LOAN

A. *The Accuracy Defense*

* * *

Many cases construing section 1681e(b) have limited liability of credit reporting agencies to technically inaccurate reports—reports which include false information—and have dismissed actions where reports were factually correct but nonetheless misleading or materially incomplete. For example, one district court held that a report that the plaintiff had declared bankruptcy was accurate, within the meaning of section 1681e(b), despite its failure to mention that the consumer had withdrawn his bankruptcy petition and fully repaid his debts. The district court here followed this line of cases in dismissing plaintiffs' claims. It noted that CBI clearly states, in explanations provided to its customers, that a classification of "9" applies to any debt charged off as a loss, referred for collection, requiring a civil action, or uncollectible because the debtor "skipped." Mr. Koropoulos' loan was charged off as a bad debt by VNB, and therefore, the district court reasoned, came within CBI's classification of "9". The district court also found that CBI "adjusted Mr. Koropoulos' credit report to reflect a '0' balance for the VNB loan," upon notification by VNB that the loan had been paid. It considered the affidavit of plaintiffs' expert, attesting that the "9–0" designation would be read as indicating a total default on the loan, to be irrelevant because it found the report itself "totally accurate."

First of all, we do not agree with the district court that section 1681e(b) makes a credit reporting agency liable for damages only if the report contains statements that are technically untrue. Congress did not limit the Act's mandate to reasonable procedures to assure only technical accuracy; to the contrary, the Act requires reasonable procedures to assure "maximum accuracy." The Act's self-stated purpose is "to require that consumer reporting agencies adopt reasonable procedures for meeting the needs of commerce for consumer credit * * * in a manner which is fair and equitable to the consumer, with regard to the confidentiality, accuracy, relevancy, and proper utilization of such information." 15 U.S.C. 1681e(b). Certainly reports containing factually correct information that nonetheless mislead their readers are neither maximally accurate nor fair to the consumer who is the subject of the reports.

* * *

* * * [W]e find more in line with congressional intent and purpose the position taken in [*Alexander v. Moore & Associates, Inc.,* 553 F.Supp. 948 (D.Haw.1982)]:

> [S]ection 1681e(b) of the Act, fairly read, would apply to consumer reports even though they may be technically accurate, if it is shown that such reports are not accurate to the maximum possible extent. The inquiry however would not end there. The statute does not flatly require maximum possible accuracy, only that the consumer reporting agency must follow *reasonable procedures* to assure such accuracy. Thus, the determination of this issue would seem to involve a balancing test.
>
> Under this approach, the court, in determining whether a violation of 1681e(b) has occurred, would weigh the potential that the information will create a misleading impression against the availability of more accurate [or complete] information and the burden of providing such information. Clearly the more misleading the information [*i.e.,* the greater the harm it can cause the consumer] and the more easily available the clarifying information, the greater the burden upon the consumer reporting agency to provide this clarification. Conversely, if the misleading information is of relatively insignificant value, a consumer reporting agency should not be required to take on a burdensome task in order to discover or provide additional or clarifying data, and it should not be penalized under this section if the procedures used are otherwise reasonable.

553 F.Supp. at 952 (emphasis in original).

Applying that interpretation in this case, we find that the district court's dismissal of the Koropoulos' claims by summary judgment on the grounds that the information in the report was technically accurate, regardless of any confusion generated in the recipients' minds as to what it meant, was improper. We find there is a genuine issue of fact as to whether the report was sufficiently misleading so as to raise the issue of whether CBI's procedures for assuring "maximum possible accuracy" were reasonable. The affidavit of plaintiffs' expert stated that "the only reasonable interpretation of the Code [CBI's classification of the VNB loan] is that * * * the creditor took a loss of $2182 on the account after the account was placed for collection." It also impugned the affidavit of Janice Cummings, a CBI manager, as "not accurate in that it states that the Code signifies that plaintiff [Mr. Koropoulos] had fully paid off his account." Were the plaintiffs' expert to be credited, the report could be found to be misleading, since in fact VNB did not take a total loss, and Mr. Koropoulos did repay the debt.

* * *

* * * Summary judgment on the issue of whether the report was misleading is thus not appropriate at this juncture in the case. Indeed,

it was granted by the district court on an altogether different theory which we reject—that the report was technically accurate.

B. Incomplete Credit Reports

Plaintiffs also argue that even if the report on the VNB loan is not misleading, CBI's classification system is so imprecise that, as a matter of law, it fails to constitute a reasonable procedure to assure maximum possible accuracy. Specifically, they object to "CBI * * * classif[ying] all adverse information into a single '9' category." *Id.* at 21. CBI relies on the explanation it gives its customers, which clearly states that a "9" rating means the "debtor failed to pay back a loan in a timely fashion and the creditor had to take extraordinary measures to collect the debt." The issue we must decide is whether using the classification "9" for all bad debts, whether ultimately paid or not, renders the report of the VNB loan sufficiently incomplete that plaintiffs may invoke the protection of section 1681e(b).

* * *

In introducing the bill which ultimately became the FCRA, Senator Proxmire reviewed the types of inaccuracy that can harm credit consumers. He explicitly addressed "[i]ncomplete information" as a type of inaccuracy distinct from misleading information, stating that "[b]ecause of the increased computerization and standardization of credit bureau files, all of the relevant information is not always reflected in a person's files." 115 Cong.Rec. 2411 (1969). The conference report's explanation of section 1681e(b) is also a significant indicator that that section covers incomplete, as well as false and misleading reports. * * *

* * *

Having thus concluded that the FRCA imposes some duty on credit reporting agencies to assure their reports are not overly imprecise, we do not suggest that the Act requires all relevant credit information be included in agencies' reports: The Act only requires that agencies adopt reasonable procedures to ensure complete and precise reporting. *Cf. Moore,* 553 F.Supp. at 952 (discussing reasonable procedures to assure reports are not misleading). Imprecise or incomplete reports that are not misleading, although undesirable, are not as noxious as erroneous and misleading ones. * * *

The reasonableness requirement thus severely limits an agency's duty to maximally assure precise and complete reporting. Nevertheless, Congress apparently felt that, at some point, certain distinctions, such as those between bankruptcy and wage earner plans, may be so fundamental to the message credit report conveys that it is reasonable to place a burden on the credit reporting agency to report them.

Plaintiffs argue that lumping together all bad debts, ranging from loans totally paid off after referral for collection to flagrant defaults where the debtor has "skipped" town, is unreasonable, and that it is fundamental to the accuracy of a credit report under section 1681e(b) that such disparate circumstances be distinguished. CBI's explanation of its Code, which it gives to its customers, itself states that the "9" classification even includes debts that were not repaid because the debtor declared bankruptcy, *see* Affidavit of Eugenia A. Murray, Exhibit C, App. at 93; that would seem very much at odds with the section's purpose. In this case, the record is too sparse for us to conclude at this early stage in the proceeding either that CBI's "9" classification is so broad that it unreasonably fails to distinguish between fundamentally different credit histories, or that it is sufficiently narrow to be reasonable. The parties did not address the reasonableness of the "9" classification in the district court, and the record is therefore devoid of such evidence as: (1) the likelihood that a potential creditor would deny credit to an individual who has failed to pay back a loan, but would grant it to one who repayed [sic] the loan after the loan was referred for collection; and (2) the burden imposed on agencies by requiring a distinction between "skips," loans never repaid, loans repaid after referral for collection, and loans repaid only after civil suit is instituted. We therefore leave to the district court the determination whether the "9" classification is unreasonable *per se.*

* * *

IV. Conclusion

We find that genuine issues of material fact exist with respect to whether (1) CBI negligently issued a misleading or incomplete report, in violation of 15 U.S.C. § 1681e(b), and (2) CBI negligently or willfully issued a report for an impermissible purpose, a violation of 15 U.S.C. § 1681b(3)(A). For the foregoing reasons we vacate the district court's grant of summary judgment for CBI, and remand for further proceedings consistent with this opinion.

It is so ordered.

Notes

1. On remand, what result do you think will be reached on the plaintiff's claim that the report was inaccurate and misleading? Were Bank of Virginia and Lord & Taylor in fact misled? Does this matter?

2. Do you agree with the claim that CBI's classification scheme was inherently misleading? The reporting form used by CBI in Koropoulos was once the standard of the consumer reporting industry. Today, however, this form has been discontinued in favor of a form like the one reproduced on page 231. Note that this form does not contain any classification codes. The industry still recognizes these codes, but they are seldom used. Instead, the report merely shows the payment record of the consumer and leaves it to the interested creditor to make classifications or other judgments. Which style of credit report do you think creditors would prefer? Which would be less likely to be misinterpreted?

3. In early cases under the FCRA, the courts commonly held that truth (or at least accuracy) was a complete defense. See, e.g., Todd v. Associated Credit Bureau Services, Inc., 451 F.Supp. 447 (E.D.Pa.1977), aff'd, 578 F.2d 1376 (3d Cir.1978), cert. denied, 439 U.S. 1068, 99 S.Ct. 834,

59 L.Ed.2d 33 (1979). This, presumably, grew out of the Act's defamation background. After *Koropoulos,* is this defense still available to credit bureaus who issue misleading or partially false reports?

4. While it may seem like credit bureaus know everything there is to know about most of us, presumably there is always some information about a particular consumer that never finds its way into a credit bureau file. Where might creditors look for other information?

5. Suppose a credit bureau receives inaccurate information from a creditor. Suppose further that in future credit reports the credit bureau reports accurately the information it received. Does it have any liability under the FCRA? Reconsider Pinner v. Schmidt, at page 233, supra; and see Bryant v. TRW, Inc., 689 F.2d 72 (6th Cir.1982) (cited and discussed in *Pinner*).

Problem 5

You are counsel to Credit Bureau Co. of New York (CBC). Another attorney has posed a hypothetical to CBC which was just like the facts in Problem 4 (two guys from Syracuse named James Andrew O'Brian and James Andre O'Brian, and one was denied credit because CBC sent Amoco the other's credit record). CBC wants you to give it three types of advice:

(a) How can it change its procedures so as to prevent such a problem from arising?

(b) Does FCRA § 607 *require* that it change its procedures in the ways you recommended above?

(c) If the facts in Problem 4 had occurred, would James Andre have had a cause of action against either CBC or Amoco? If so, what would have been his damages? See Thompson v. San Antonio Retail Merchants Ass'n. below.

THOMPSON v. SAN ANTONIO RETAIL MERCHANTS ASS'N

United States Court of Appeals, Fifth Circuit, 1982.
682 F.2d 509.

PER CURIAM:

This case involves the liability of the San Antonio Retail Merchants Association (SARMA) for an inaccurate credit report. Gulf Oil Corporation (Gulf) and Montgomery Ward (Ward's) denied credit to William Douglas Thompson, III, on the basis of erroneous credit information furnished by SARMA. The district court, after a nonjury trial, entered judgment for Thompson in the sum of $10,000 actual damages and $4,485 attorneys' fees. SARMA appeals.

I. BACKGROUND

SARMA provides a computerized credit reporting service to local business subscribers. This service depends heavily upon credit history information fed into SARMA's files by subscribers. A key mechanism used by SARMA to update its files is a computerized "automatic capturing" feature. A subscriber must feed certain identifying information from its own computer terminal into SARMA's central computer in order to gain access to the credit history of a particular consumer. When presented with this identifying information, SARMA's computer searches its records and displays on the subscriber's terminal the credit history file that most nearly matches the consumer. The decision whether to accept a given file as being that of a particular consumer is left completely to the terminal operator. When a subscriber does accept a given file as pertaining to a particular consumer, however, the computer automatically captures into the file any information input from the subscriber's terminal that the central file did not already have.

The disadvantage of an automatic capturing feature is that it may accept erroneous information fed in by subscribers, unless special auditing procedures are built into the system. In the instant case, SARMA failed to check the accuracy of a social security number obtained by its automatic capturing feature. The social security number is the single most important identifying factor for credit-reference purposes. As a result, the computer erroneously began to report the bad credit history of "William Daniel Thompson, Jr.," to subscribers inquiring about "William Douglas Thompson, III."

In November 1974, William Daniel Thompson, Jr., opened a credit account with Gordon's Jewelers (Gordon's) in San Antonio, listing his social security number as 457–68–5778, his address as 132 Baxter, his occupation as truck loader, and his marital status as single. He subsequently ran up a delinquent account of $77.25 at Gordon's that was ultimately charged off as a bad debt. When Gordon's voluntarily reported the bad debt, SARMA placed the information and a derogatory credit rating into file number 5867114, without any identifying social security number.

In early 1978, the plaintiff, William Douglas Thompson, III, applied for credit with Gulf and with Ward's in San Antonio. He listed his social security as 407–86–4065, his address as 6929 Timbercreek, his occupation as grounds keeper, and his wife as Deborah C. On February 9, 1978, Gulf's terminal operator mistakenly accepted file number 5867114 as that of the plaintiff. SARMA's computer thereupon automatically captured various information about William Douglas Thompson, III, including his social security number, into file number 5867114. At that point, the original file, which was on William Daniel Thompson, Jr., became a potpourri of information on both the plaintiff and the original William Daniel Thompson, Jr. The name on the file remained that of William Daniel Thompson, Jr. The social security number became that of the plaintiff, the current address and employer became that of the plaintiff, a former address and employer became that of William Daniel Thompson, Jr., and the wife's name became that of the plaintiff's wife.

Shortly thereafter, Ward's terminal operator ran a credit check on the plaintiff, was given the garbled data, and accepted file number 5867114 as that of the plaintiff. As a result of the adverse information regarding the Gordon's account, Ward's denied the plaintiff credit. The plaintiff applied for credit at Ward's in May 1979 and was again rejected.

On February 21, 1978, Gulf requested a "revision" of file number 5867114, a procedure which entails a rechecking of information in a file with respect to a particular creditor or creditors. Following its usual procedures, SARMA would call Gordon's to verify in detail the information in the file. Although this was probably done, whoever contacted Gordon's apparently failed to check the social security number of Gordon's delinquent customer and take corrective action when it was received. Instead, the adverse information remained in the file under the plaintiff's social security number after Gulf's revision request, and Gulf denied the plaintiff credit.

The adverse information remained in the plaintiff's file during 1978 and the first five and a half months of 1979. During all of this time the plaintiff thought he had been denied credit from Ward's and Gulf because of a 1976 Texas felony conviction for burglary. He had received a five-year probationary sentence, but subsequently gained fulltime employment and straightened out his life. In June of 1979, plaintiff's wife learned from her credit union in processing an application for a loan that her husband's adverse credit rating resulted from a bad debt at Gordon's. The plaintiff knew he had never had an account at Gordon's so he and his wife went directly to their place of business. After waiting some two hours he was informed that there had indeed been a mistake, their credit record was for William Daniel Thompson, Jr.

The plaintiff and his wife went to SARMA with this information in an attempt to purge the erroneous credit information. They spoke with an individual and showed birth registration and drivers license information revealing his name to be William Douglas Thompson III. The entire process required some three hours. Nevertheless SARMA thereafter mailed appellee a letter addressed to William Daniel Thompson III. Appellee's wife again returned to SARMA. Following this SARMA once again addressed appellee in another letter as William Daniel Thompson III. Appellee again returned to SARMA—yet again SARMA wrote still another letter with the same incorrect name. Further, though SARMA's policy was to send corrections made on a file to any subscribers who had made inquiry about it within the last six months, SARMA failed to notify Ward's of the corrections. The plaintiff filed an action in state court on October 4, 1979. It was not until October 16, 1979, that SARMA informed Ward's of the erroneous credit information. On November 5, 1979, the action was removed to the federal district court. After a bench trial, the district court found that denials of credit to the appellee by Gulf and Ward's were caused by SARMA's failure to follow reasonable procedures to assure the maximum possible accuracy of its files. The district court awarded plaintiff actual damages in the sum of $10,000 plus attorneys' fees in the sum of $4485.

II. THE LIABILITY ISSUE

Under 15 U.S.C. § 1681o of the Fair Credit Reporting Act (Act), a "consumer reporting agency" is liable to "any consumer" for negligent failure to comply with "any requirement imposed" by the Act. In the instant case, the district court determined that SARMA was liable under section 1681o for negligent failure to comply with section 1681e(b) of the Act.

Section 1681e(b) does not impose strict liability for any inaccurate credit report, but only a duty of reasonable care in preparation of the report. That duty extends to updating procedures, because "preparation" of a consumer report should be viewed as a continuing process and the obligation to insure accuracy arises with every addition of information.

Applying the reasonable-person standard, the district court found two acts of negligence in SARMA's updating procedures. First, SARMA failed to exercise reasonable care in programming its computer to automatically capture information into a file without requiring any minimum number of "points of correspondence" between the consumer and the file or having an adequate auditing procedure to foster accuracy. Second, SARMA failed to employ reasonable procedures designed to learn the disparity in social security numbers for the two Thompsons when it revised file number 5867114 at Gulf's request. * * *

With respect to the first act of negligence, George Zepeda, SARMA's manager, testified that SARMA's computer had no minimum number of points of correspondence to be satisfied before an inquiring subscriber could accept credit information. Moreover, SARMA had no way of knowing if the information supplied by the subscriber was correct. Although SARMA did conduct spot audits to verify social security numbers, it did not audit all subscribers. With respect to the second act of negligence, SARMA's verification process failed to uncover the erroneous social security number even though Gulf made a specific request for a "revision" to check the adverse credit history ascribed to the plaintiff. SARMA's manager, Mr. Zepeda, testified that what should have been done upon the request for a revision, was to pick up the phone and check with Gordon's and learn, among other things, the social security number for William Daniel Thompson, Jr. It was the manager's further testimony that the social security number is the single most important information in a consumer's credit file. In light of this evidence, this Court cannot conclude that the district court was clearly erroneous in finding negligent violation of section 1681e(b).

III. AWARD OF DAMAGES

The district court's award of $10,000 in actual damages was based on humiliation and mental distress to the plaintiff. Even when there are no out-of-pocket expenses, humiliation and mental distress do constitute recoverable elements of damage under the Act. * * *

SARMA asserts that Thompson failed to prove any actual damages, or at best proved only minimal damages for humiliation and mental distress. There was evidence, however, that Thompson suffered humiliation and embarrassment from being denied credit on three occasions. Thompson testified that the denial of credit hurt him deeply because of his mistaken belief that it resulted from his felony conviction:

> I was trying to build myself back up, trying to set myself up, get back on my feet again. I was working sixty hours a week and sometimes seventy. I went back to school. I was going to school at night three nights a week, four nights a week, three hours a night, and [denial of credit] really hurt. It made me disgusted with myself.

> * * *. [I needed credit to] be able to obtain things that everybody else is able to obtain, to be able to buy clothes or set myself up where I can show my ability to be trusted.

> We didn't even have a bed. It was pretty bad. We were hurting. Everything we had to do, we had to save up and pay cash for strictly. It was just impossible to do it any other way.

Further, the inaccurate information remained in SARMA's files for almost one and one-half years after the inaccurate information was inserted. Even after the error was discovered, Thompson spent months pressing SARMA to correct its mistakes and fully succeeded only after bringing a lawsuit against SARMA. This Court is of the opinion that the trial judge was entitled to conclude that the humiliation and mental distress were not minimal but substantial.

* * *

The judgment of the district court is

Affirmed.

Notes

1. In *Thompson*, how did the creditors get the reports? Did any of SARMA's employees touch the file? If not, who caused the problem? If it wasn't SARMA, why is SARMA liable? Should someone else be held liable?

2. Does William Daniel Thompson, Jr., have a claim against anyone? Who? On what grounds?

MILLSTONE v. O'HANLON REPORTS, INC.

United States District Court, Eastern District of Missouri, 1974.
383 F.Supp. 269.

WANGELIN, DISTRICT JUDGE.

This action is before the Court for decision on the merits following the trial to the Court sitting without a jury.

Plaintiff, James C. Millstone (herein Millstone) brought this action alleging violation of 15 U.S.C.A. § 1681 et seq., commonly known as the

"Fair Credit Reporting Act", against the defendant, O'Hanlon Reports, Inc. (herein O'Hanlon). The Court being fully apprised of the premises hereby makes the following findings of fact and conclusions of law.

FINDINGS OF FACT

1. This Court has jurisdiction over the subject matter of this suit and the parties hereto pursuant to 15 U.S.C.A. § 1681p.

2. The plaintiff, James C. Millstone, is an Assistant Managing Editor of the St. Louis Post–Dispatch, a local daily newspaper. He has worked for the Post–Dispatch in various positions since 1958. Prior to his return to the St. Louis area in 1971, he worked in Washington, D.C. as a correspondent for approximately seven years covering various federal agencies, including the White House, and had an FBI clearance to travel with Presidents Johnson and Nixon.

3. The defendant, O'Hanlon Reports, Inc., is a corporation, formerly known as the National Inspection Bureau, Inc., d/b/a O'Hanlon Reports, Inc., operating under the laws of the State of New York and licensed to do business in the State of Missouri as well as most of the States of the Union. It has as its purpose the investigation and collection of information concerning consumers of predominantly real property insurance and automobile insurance.

4. In August of 1971, Millstone and his family moved to St. Louis, Missouri, so that he might take up his duties as news editor for the St. Louis Post–Dispatch. He thereafter contacted his insurance agent, Norman Kastner, and asked Kastner to place auto insurance for him. Kastner placed the policy with Firemen's Fund Insurance Company. The policy took effect on November 15, 1971, and several days later Millstone, in accordance with 15 U.S.C.A. § 1681d received a notice that a personal investigation would be made in connection with the new policy.

5. On December 20, 1971, Walter McPherson from the Firemen's Fund Insurance Company informed Kastner (and Kastner informed Millstone) that the policy would be cancelled. After assurances from Kastner of Millstone's character and reputation, the insurance company reversed its decision the following day. Millstone voluntarily cancelled the policy.

6. Millstone discovered from McPherson that the cancellation had been brought about because of a consumer credit report which had been made by the defendant, O'Hanlon Reports, Inc.

7. On December 22, 1971, Millstone went to the office of O'Hanlon Reports where he spoke to William O'Connell, the Office Manager. Millstone was told that he was entitled to know what was in his report but that O'Hanlon was entitled to reasonable notice of ten (10) days before giving the information. When Millstone protested, O'Connell called the New York Home Office of O'Hanlon and allowed Millstone to speak to a Kenneth Mitchell. Mitchell told Millstone that the information would be available as soon as possible but that he could not give

disclosure immediately because the Millstone file was en route from St. Louis to New York through the mails. After Millstone left the office, O'Connell then mailed the file to New York.

8. On December 28, 1971, Millstone received the disclosure of the information in its file from O'Connell at the O'Hanlon offices. O'Connell read the disclosure from a single sheet of paper which had been prepared by David Slayback, the Vice President of O'Hanlon. The disclosure sheet stated in part that:

> "The file shows that you are very much disliked by your neighbors at that location [Millstone's Washington residence], and were considered to be a 'hippy type'. The file indicates that you participated in many demonstrations in Washington, D.C., and that you also housed out-of-town demonstrators during demonstrations. The file indicates that these demonstrators slept on floors, in the basement and wherever else there was room on your property. The file shows that you were strongly suspected of being a drug user by neighbors but they could not positively substantiate these suspicions. You are shown to have had shoulder length hair and a beard on one occasion while living in Washington, D.C. The file indicates that there were rumors in the neighborhood that you had been evicted by neighbors from three previous residences in Washington, D.C. prior to living at the 48th Street, N.W. location."

This disclosure sheet which Millstone was not allowed to examine was the only item that Millstone was informed of by O'Connell.

9. After protesting virtually all the information contained in the disclosure, Millstone asked O'Connell to explain certain facts contained therein. O'Connell told Millstone that he had no further information and could not answer the questions. He told Millstone that his instructions from the Home Office were only to read the disclosure sheet prepared in New York and to take careful note of any dispute from the customer. At no time was Millstone allowed to look at the actual consumer report file maintained by O'Hanlon upon him, nor were any actual portions of that file read to Millstone at any time by Mr. O'Connell.

10. O'Connell once again called New York and allowed Millstone to speak. David Slayback defended the method and propriety of disclosure to Millstone and neither would nor could explain such matters as the basis and meaning of the statement that Millstone was strongly suspected of being a "drug user".

11. Slayback ordered the Manager of his Silver Springs office, the office which had conducted the original investigation of Millstone, to re-investigate the information. Raymond T. Jonas, the Branch Manager, took approximately three days to complete the re-investigation and then sent his report to the New York office. This re-investigation report contained statements that the Millstone children had "torn up" part of a neighbor's garden and that Mrs. Millstone had used terms such as "pig", and "old hag" to a neighbor and his wife and that she

was considered by the neighbors to be a "paranoid", and that Mr. Millstone was considered to be a "hippy type" because he allowed peace demonstrators to stay in his house. Mrs. Millstone was also alleged to have stated that she would allow her children to use drugs.

12. On or about January 12, 1972, O'Connell notified Millstone that the re-investigation was completed and at a meeting between the two read to Millstone both the first and second disclosure sheets along with a cover letter written by Mr. Slayback to the Firemen's Fund Insurance Company. The thrust of these documents was to correct the previous allegations that Millstone was a: "drug user", "hippy type" and the statements about the "peace demonstrators staying at the Millstone residence".

*   *   *

18. O'Hanlon's procedures for making disclosure to Millstone were in conformity with previously planned procedural processes explained to managers of the defendant's branch offices several months prior to the effective date of the Fair Credit Reporting Act. These procedures were contained in a handbook which each manager received and which was introduced into evidence at the trial as plaintiff's exhibit 13 (herein referred to as Manual). The procedures called for in the Manual state in pertinent part:

> The important thing is to NEVER check the files in the presence of the consumer *   *   * (Manual, § 609–610–611, p. 1.).
>
> Prior to the time of your appointment with the consumer, you will have received the Statement of Disclosure from the Home Office. At the time of your appointment, ANY and ALL information you may have relating to the consumer, such as copies of files, copy of your statement, index cards, etc. are to be in your desk drawer, OUT OF SIGHT, of the consumer. You are not to show anything, or acknowledge that you have anything, other than the Statement of Disclosure.
>
> Actual disclosure will be accomplished by reading the Statement of Disclosure to the consumer. The statement is to be read word for word, at your normal reading speed. It is not to be read slowly enough for anyone to copy down word for word, nor is it to be read so fast that the Consumer will not understand what you are saying. Part or all of the Statement of Disclosure may be re-read if the Consumer indicates that he did not understand what you are telling him. The Consumer and/or the person with him may not have a copy of the Statement, nor may they be allowed to read the Statement, or touch it. (emphasis added by capitalization is that contained in the Manual) (Manual, p. 1–2).

19. The original report on Millstone was prepared by Alexander Mayes, an employee of defendant in defendant's Silver Springs office. Mayes contacted four neighbors of the Millstones on the block where they last lived while residing in Washington, D.C.

20. Of the four persons contacted, one refused to speak to Mayes, two others told him that they knew of trouble in the neighborhood but

knew nothing first hand and wished not to become involved. All the data recovered in Mayes' report was gleaned from a discussion with one neighbor identified as one McMillan, now deceased. Mayes gathered the data in a period of less than one-half hour. Mayes worked on a commission basis and received approximately one-third of the fee charged by the defendant, which amounted approximately to $1.85 in the Millstone investigation.

21. The time spent by defendant's agents on gathering information for automobile insurance reports is anywhere from ten minutes to one-half hour. The data gathered for real estate insurance transactions may take slightly longer.

22. An investigator for O'Hanlon such as Mayes would average 140 to 160 reports every two weeks.

* * *

27. Concerning the disclosure procedures followed in the instant case, Slayback testified that the first disclosure was incomplete, and the reason therefor was his rush to satisfy Millstone's demand for disclosure; in his letter of January 20, 1972, he informed Millstone that the reason for the exclusion was that he had not received the information from his Silver Springs office at the time that he prepared the first disclosure. He stated that Millstone's "utter lack of reasoning and judgment" could be implied from the contents of the first consumer report.

* * *

CONCLUSIONS OF LAW

* * *

The remainder of this action revolves around the questions of whether or not defendant O'Hanlon is liable under Section 1681n and Section 1681o of this aforecited title. Section 1681n allows the recovery of actual damages, costs and reasonable attorneys fees along with punitive damages for willful non-compliance with the Act in question, and Section 1681o allows actual damages along with costs and attorneys fees for negligent non-compliance with this Act. The standard of care imposed by the aforecited statutory sections is that:

> Whenever a consumer reporting agency prepares a consumer report it shall follow reasonable procedures to assure maximum possible accuracy of the information concerning the individual about whom the report relates. 15 U.S.C.A. § 1681e(b).

It is clear to this Court as the trier of fact that the defendant was in violation of § 1681e(b), in that its procedures of gathering personal information about consumers, such as Millstone, was only from neighbors from the consumer's residence and that these items were not verified. The evidence also shows that defendant's agent Mayes knowingly included false information in the report which defendant compiled concerning Millstone. In his report agent Mayes refers to a poll of four neighbors, with full knowledge that he spoke only to three neighbors. Also, the report repeatedly asserts that all of the sources were in agreement when Mayes in fact received information from only one source, Mr. McMillan. Considering the prior unblemished record of Millstone and the fact that defendant's own operations Manual concerning such derogatory information states: "When adverse information is developed, it should be verified by at least one other source to avoid the reporting of any prejudicial or inaccurate information", the actions of O'Hanlon's agent Mayes are so wanton as to be certainly a willful non-compliance with the standard of care imposed by the Act. These actions by defendant's agent Mayes are so heinous and reprehensible as to justify the harsh damages imposed by Section 1681n. Defendant's methods of reporting on consumer's credit backgrounds as shown at trial were so slipshod and slovenly as to not even approach the realm of reasonable standards of care as imposed by the statute. * * *

Independent of the previously discussed willful violation of the statute is the defendant's violation of § 1681g(a)(1) in that it failed to disclose, and continued until pre-trial discovery forced such disclosure, the nature and substance of all the information contained in its files concerning Millstone. To say that O'Hanlon was parsimonious in its disclosures in this case would be an exercise in understatement. Defendant has stated to the Court that its policy remains not to disclose certain information to consumers which O'Hanlon itself deems appropriate. The previously quoted sections of defendant's operation Manual are ample evidence of plaintiff's attitudes and actions concerning this matter. Millstone was forced to return to defendants' offices on several occasions and each time was able to elicit a little more information from the defendant which concerned him. At no time until this lawsuit was joined and discovery was undertaken did O'Hanlon inform Millstone of the entire amount of information concerning him in O'Hanlon's files. * * *

* * *

In regards to damages, the Court further finds that although plaintiff suffered no lost wages nor incurred medical expenses on the account of the injuries therein, he suffered by reason of his mental anguish and had symptoms of sleeplessness and nervousness which were amply testified to, and because of the repeated and numerous times in which plaintiff had to contact O'Hanlon, in many cases having to leave his employment for meetings on account of the defendant's actions as stated above, the plaintiff is entitled to actual damages in the amount of $2,500.00.

Considering the willful non-compliance of O'Hanlon with the requirements of the statute, this Court will assess the sum of $25,000 against defendant O'Hanlon as punitive damages in this action. This Court also finds that the sum of $12,500 will be awarded to plaintiff from defendant for attorneys fees, and the Court will further order that defendant pay costs in this matter. In consequence, judgment for the plaintiff as stated above will be entered.

Notes

1. Millstone was affirmed on appeal, in an opinion by Mr. Justice Clark, sitting by designation, which concluded:

> There can be no doubt that O'Hanlon willfully violated both the spirit and the letter of the Fair Credit Reporting Act, 15 U.S.C. § 1681 et seq., by trampling recklessly upon Millstone's rights thereunder. We therefore find no abuse of discretion or other error in the award.

Millstone v. O'Hanlon Reports, Inc., 528 F.2d 829, 835 (8th Cir.1976).

2. What is the difference between a "consumer report" and an "investigative consumer report"? See FCRA § 603(d)–(e). Do different standards or procedures apply for investigative reports? Should they? Why? See FCRA §§ 606 and 614.

3. O'Hanlon's manual said that adverse information should be verified by at least one other source. How could Mayes, the investigative agent, have done that in this case? Would it have been sufficient simply to ask another neighbor? Wouldn't this just reinforce the neighborhood gossip?

4. The information contained in the credit report was obviously false, wasn't it? How else could Millstone have won his case? Yet, the insurance company obviously believed that it was true, and it based an insurance decision on that information. But even if it was true, what do Millstone's personal living habits have to do with his eligibility for insurance? Does the FCRA contain a requirement that the information in a credit report be relevant? Should it? If your answer is yes, who do you think should decide which information is relevant?

5. When Millstone visited the O'Hanlon offices, could he have insisted on knowing which neighbor supplied the damaging information? See FCRA § 609(a)(2). Could Millstone have joined the neighbor, McMillan, as a defendant in the FCRA suit? See FCRA § 610(e). How about a common law action for defamation against McMillan?

6. With the growing concern for personal privacy, should consumers be given greater control over the collection and dissemination of personal information about them? How? Review FCRA § 606. Suppose this section were amended to require the consumer's explicit *permission* before an investigative consumer report was prepared. Would this be good or bad? What would it achieve as a practical matter?

The Final Report of the Privacy Protection Study Commission, created by Congress in 1974, contains a number of recommendations for amendments to the Fair Credit Reporting Act. Key among them is the suggestion that the responsibility for accuracy and content of the report be shared between the reporting bureau and the users of the report:

Redistribution of Responsibility

The Fair Credit Reporting Act establishes liability for the accuracy, timeliness, and completeness of investigative reports, but currently places it exclusively on the inspection bureaus and investigative agencies that prepare them. The user of a report bears no responsibility for the conduct of the investigative support organization that put the report together, nor is it under any obligation to inform the support organization when it discovers an error. Indeed, the likelihood that it will discover an error is low, since the FCRA only allows an individual to check and, if necessary, correct the copy of an investigative report that the support organization retains. The Act gives him no parallel right with respect to the same report in the hands of the insurer or employer user. The user's responsibility is limited to notifying the individual that a report may be requested, describing, upon request, the scope of the investigation, and, if an adverse decision results, notifying the individual of the name and address of the inspection bureau or private investigative agency that prepared the report.

The Commission's solution to this problem is to place the insurer and employer in a position of joint responsibility with the investigative support organization. While accountability for the contents of a report would remain with the organization that prepares it, the user would be liable if it repeatedly did business with any support organization that consistently engaged in objectionable practices. Moreover, by requiring the user, as well as the preparer of a report, to disclose its contents to the individual whom it concerns and to cope with certain types of deficiencies in it that the individual may allege, the user is given a strong incentive to deal only with support organizations that produce reports of high quality.

Some investigative support organizations currently have contracts with their users that make the user who discloses the contents of a report to its subject the liable party in any law suit that may result. The effect, of course, is to keep the user from disclosing anything to the individual, and the Commission's recommendation would therefore make such contracts null and void. Finally, the Commission's "expectation of confidentiality" recommendations and proposed authorization requirements are worded in such a way as to compel support organizations to live by the same ground rules on third-party access to reports as the insurers and employers who use them. In practical terms, this means that a report prepared on an individual for one purpose will no longer be useable for another purpose without his authorization, thereby giving him some control over the circulation of information about him which has been generated in service of markedly different record-keeping relationships he maintains or seeks to establish.

Privacy Protection Study Commission, Personal Privacy in an Information Society 342–43 (1977).

Try your hand at drafting statutory language to amend the FCRA to accomplish the above objectives!

Problem 6

Dart N. Yan works for Wholesale Fact Investigations Co. (which is a competitor of O'Hanlon). He is basically a nice guy, but he has his problems. Not only does he have to produce information as fast as his O'Hanlon counterparts (see Findings of Fact 20–22 in *Millstone*), but each month he is also expected to produce "negative information" about the subjects of his reports in a certain percentage of those reports. This quota on negative information varies from 6% to 16%. On June 25, Dart made an employment investigation report on Fleur D. Lee who was unemployed and seeking a job as a waitress. As part of the 30 minute investigation, Dart interviewed Fleur at her apartment. It was the end of June, and Dart had filed almost no reports having any negative information that month. When Dart filed his report, there was no negative information on Fleur, except the following notation: "This interviewer is unable to say that his attentions would not have been welcome after the end of the interview." When Rich E. Loo, the prospective employer, read that, he decided not to hire Fleur. Further, this information is now contained in Wholesale Fact's basic file on Fleur, and other employers have also decided not to hire her.

Fleur now consults you. All she knows is that she has been unable to find work for about 90 days and that she has received a form letter from each prospective employer naming some company she has never heard of—and has thrown the letters away. What information can you obtain? How? Would obtaining that information require going to court? Fleur cannot afford to pay for litigation.

Once you discover the information in the report, can you require Wholesale Fact to retract it? Dart may stand by his story. Must you go to court? Against whom? Fleur still can't afford that. What alternatives are provided by the statute?

What is the principal defect in Wholesale Fact's system? Is there any statutory regulation of such aspects of the system? Who could take action against such aspects? What action? See In re Equifax, 96 F.T.C. 844 (1980), set aside in part, Equifax, Inc. v. F.T.C., 678 F.2d 1047 (11th Cir.1982).

4. MISUSE OF REPORTS: INVASIONS OF PRIVACY—WHO CAN SEE YOUR FILE?

Read FCRA §§ 603(d), 604, 608, and 619, and then read the following case.

YOHAY v. CITY OF ALEXANDRIA EMPLOYEES CREDIT UNION

United States Court of Appeals, Fourth Circuit, 1987.
827 F.2d 967.

FRANK A. KAUFMAN, SENIOR DISTRICT JUDGE:

On July 26, 1983, Patricia Ryan (Ryan), an attorney on retainer with the City of Alexandria Employees Credit Union (Credit Union) in connection with the collection of delinquent accounts and other matters, either used, or caused an employee of the Credit Union to use, the Credit Union's computer to obtain information from the Credit Bureau of Georgia, Inc. (CBI), with whom the Credit Union had a contract and a computer tie, concerning Ryan's ex-husband, Stephen Yohay (Yohay). At the time of the incident in question, Ryan and Yohay were engaged in a state court custody trial concerning their son. Prior to the incident in question, Yohay's second wife had brought an assault charge against Ryan of which Ryan had been acquitted. Furthermore, according to Ryan, Yohay had accused Ryan of charging gasoline to one of Yohay's credit cards. Ryan had remarried Arlen Justice (Justice), Secretary–Treasurer of the Credit Union and Deputy Chief of Police for the City of Alexandria, who had introduced Ryan to the Credit Union's Board of Directors before Ryan was placed on a retainer by the Credit Union.

At the trial of the within cases, Ryan testified that she had sought information from CBI regarding Yohay's credit in order to compare the numbers of Yohay's credit card accounts with their earlier established joint credit card accounts to ensure that Yohay was no longer using those previously established joint credit arrangements. Also during the trial, Andrea Martin, the Credit Union's assistant manager, testified that Donna Hatton, an employee of the Credit Union, had told her (Martin) that she (Hatton) had obtained the credit report on Yohay from CBI at the request of George Filopovich, the Credit Union's manager and a friend of Justice.

The Credit Union had a contract with CBI permitting the Credit Union to obtain credit information from CBI for appropriate purposes. The trial testimony revealed that the Credit Union had posted no rules or guidelines concerning the running of credit checks and that seemingly anyone, who could obtain physical access to the computer on the Credit Union's premises, could access CBI's files for any reason.

Yohay first became aware that CBI had furnished credit information to the Credit Union when Yohay obtained from CBI a copy of his credit records in March, 1984. Those records revealed that a credit check of Yohay had been run by the Credit Union on July 26, 1983. Since Yohay had had no relationship with the Credit Union, Yohay wrote a letter to the Credit Union inquiring as to the reason for the credit check. The president of the Credit Union, in responding to such inquiry, informed Yohay that the Credit Union had run the check at the request of Ryan.

Yohay filed the within action against the Credit Union pursuant to the Fair Credit Reporting Act (FCRA), 15 U.S.C. § 1681 *et seq.*, seeking punitive damages, costs, and attorneys' fees, but not seeking compensatory damages. The Credit Union filed a third-party complaint against Ryan for indemnification.

Prior to or during the jury trial, the district court ruled as a matter of law or as a matter of undisputed fact, as follows: (1) that "on or about July 26, 1983, Patricia Ryan, using the facilities of the defendant, City of Alexandria Employees Credit Union, obtained a consumer report regarding Stephen Yohay from CBI, a consumer reporting agency, for a purpose not permitted by the Fair Credit Reporting Act"; (2) that Ryan had acted as an employee and an agent for the Credit Union within the scope of her employment and agency in obtaining the information about Yohay from CBI; (3) that punitive damages could be awarded to Yohay by the jury against the Credit Union if the jury found that the Credit Union's failure to comply with the Act had been "willful," that is, if the Act had been violated "voluntarily and intentionally, and not because of negligence, mistake, accident or other innocent reason"; (4) that to award punitive damages under the Act, the jury "need not find that the Credit Union acted with malice or bad intention"; and (5) that the Credit Union was entitled as a matter of law to indemnification from Ryan for any damages awarded in these cases by the jury to Yohay against the Credit Union.

In effect, the only factual questions presented to the jury by the district court were (1) whether the Credit Union had acted willfully and, if so, (2) the amount of punitive damages to be awarded to Yohay against the Credit Union. The jury awarded Yohay $10,000 for punitive damages. The trial court subsequently granted, in part, Yohay's petition for attorney's fees and costs against the Credit Union. The trial court also ordered that Ryan indemnify the Credit Union for (1) the award of punitive damages to Yohay; (2) the award of attorney's fees and costs to Yohay; and (3) the attorney's fees incurred by the Credit Union in defending itself against Yohay's claim.

In the within appeals, the Credit Union and Ryan assert numerous errors by the court below. For reasons which will be discussed herein, we conclude that each of those challenges is without merit.

* * *

CIVIL LIABILITY

The Credit Union and Ryan were "user[s] of information" obtained from CBI, "a consumer reporting agency." *See* 15 U.S.C. § 1681a(f) and § 1681n. *See* discussion *infra* at 973–974. As such, if either the Credit Union or Ryan "willfully fail[ed] to comply with any requirement imposed" by the FCRA, each is liable to the "consumer"—in these cases Yohay—for actual and punitive damages as well as costs and attorney's fees. *See* 15 U.S.C. § 1681n.

Pursuant to section 1681b, in the absence of a court order, *see* 15 U.S.C. § 1681b(1), or written instructions from the consumer, Yohay, *see* 15 U.S.C. § 1681b(2), or any of the grounds set forth in section 1681b(3)(A–E), inclusive, CBI could not lawfully provide either the Credit Union or Ryan with the information regarding Yohay.

In *Heath v. Credit Bureau of Sheridan, Inc.,* 618 F.2d 693, 697 (10th Cir.1980), the Tenth Circuit has taken the position that a person such as Ryan—who, as the district court concluded herein before trial in the context of undisputed facts, obtained from CBI the consumer report in question for purposes not permitted by section 1681b—could not be held civilly liable under section 1681b. Herein, we need not reach that issue because of the view we take with respect to section 1681q.

In *Hansen v. Morgan,* 582 F.2d 1214, 1216 (9th Cir.1978), the Ninth Circuit incorporated the criminal provisions of section 1681q into sections 1681n and 1681o and held that a user who obtains a consumer report under false pretenses, as those words are used in section 1681q, can be civilly liable under either section 1681n or section 1681o. In *Hansen,* Judge Carter wrote that "[t]he standard for determining when a consumer report has been obtained under false pretenses will usually be defined in relation to the permissible purposes of consumer reports which are enumerated in 15 U.S.C. § 1681b," *id.* at 1219 (footnote omitted), "that obtaining a consumer report * * * without disclosing the impermissible purpose for which the report is desired can constitute obtaining consumer information under false pretenses, and that the facts in this case demonstrate that the consumer report was so obtained." *Id.* at 1219–20 (footnote omitted). We agree with and accordingly adopt the reasoning of the Ninth Circuit in *Hansen,* and also conclude that the facts in these cases before us disclose that the report was obtained under false pretenses.

Accordingly, each of the two users—the Credit Union and Ryan—is subject to civil liability under section 1681n if each user's individual non-compliance with section 1681b was willful. In the within cases the record shows that Ryan obtained the report from CBI, as the district court found before trial, for "a purpose not permitted by" the FCRA and also without in any way disclosing to CBI the impermissible purpose for which she sought the report. The trial record discloses more than sufficient evidence to support the jury's implicit conclusion that the Credit Union acted willfully. For example, the evidence of the friendly relationship between the manager of the Credit Union, Filopovich, and Ryan and her second husband, Justice, indicated that Filopovich was cognizant of Ryan's improper purpose.

PUNITIVE DAMAGES

The FCRA specifically provides that punitive damages may be awarded "as the court may allow," 15 U.S.C. § 1681n(2), if the defendant's noncompliance with the provisions of the Act is willful. Actual damages are not a statutory prerequisite to an award of punitive damages under the Act. The award of punitive damages in the absence of any actual damages, in an appropriate case, comports with the underlying deterrent purpose of the FCRA.

Furthermore, "[p]unitive damages awarded under section 1681n are within the discretion of the court and malice or evil motive need not be found for such an award, but the violation must be willful."

The district court correctly instructed the jury that punitive damages may be awarded if the jury found "that the defendant acted under circumstances amounting to willful or wanton disregard of the plaintiff's rights." *See Pinner,* 805 F.2d at 1263. As discussed *supra,* there is considerable evidence in the record to support the jury's implicit finding that the Credit Union consciously ignored the rights of Yohay.

AGENCY OF RYAN

The record supports the district court's determination that there was no genuine factual dispute that Ryan was an agent of the Credit

Union and had apparent authority to obtain the credit report, even if Ryan lacked actual authority so to do. Accordingly, the Credit Union is liable to Yohay for Ryan's wrongful actions as its agent pursuant to the doctrine of respondeat superior. * * *

Seemingly, anyone who used the Credit Union's computer to access CBI's files appeared—from CBI's perspective—to have authority to gain such access. In that regard it is to be noted that the Credit Union had not posted any guidelines to users of the computer informing them of the circumstances under which such credit information could be obtained. Indeed, the Credit Union had posted the code which provided access to the computer system, enabling anyone with the physical opportunity to use the system to access CBI's files. The record also indicates that the credit check was run by Donna Hatton, an employee of the Credit Union, at the direction of George Filopovich, the manager of the Credit Union. There is little or no question about the apparent, if not the actual, authority of Filopovich to have ordered a credit check from CBI. Accordingly, the Credit Union would be liable to Yohay for Ryan's actions, regardless of whether Ryan had actual or apparent authority to obtain the information about Yohay from CBI.

* * *

Affirmed and Remanded.

Problem 7

Smith and Wesson were running against each other in a hotly contested election for Congress. The campaign was becoming increasingly negative, and a campaign worker for Smith thought it would be interesting to see whether a credit report on Wesson would turn up anything they could use against him. The Smith people asked Morgan, a Smith supporter, to get the report. Morgan owned a retail store in the community and was a member of the credit bureau. Morgan called Local Credit Bureau and asked for a report on Wesson. Morgan did not state what the report was to be used for, and Local did not ask. Local issued the report.

In Wesson's lawsuit against Local and Morgan for violating the FCRA, Local defends by arguing that the FCRA simply does not apply to this report. Under the definition in FCRA § 603(d), Local argues, a report is a "consumer report" only if it is issued for credit, insurance, employment, or "other purposes authorized under section 604." Since this report was not issued for any of the listed purposes, it is outside the scope of the FCRA, and Wesson has no remedy. As Wesson's counsel, how do you respond?

Problem 8

Ready Bank wants to expand the cardholder base for its VISA cards. Instead of doing a blind mass mailing of application forms, however, Ready wants to target the people it believes are the best prospects. It wants Local Credit Bureau to help identify these prospects. To do this, Ready provides Local with its credit criteria and a list of potential customers. It asks Local to run the list through its computerized credit files, delete the names that don't meet Ready's criteria or otherwise have an adverse credit record, and then submit a final "approved" list to Ready. Ready will then send its usual advertising to everyone on the final list, inviting them to become VISA cardholders. This time, you are Local's attorney, and it wants to know whether it can do this without violating the FCRA. After reading FCRA § 604, what is your advice?

Problem 9

The Department of Social Services in your state has announced an aggressive new program to track down and collect unpaid child support payments from delinquent parents. The Department wants to use credit bureau information in its program. Specifically, it has asked Local Credit Bureau to furnish it with a computer terminal that will allow it direct access to Local's files. The terminal would be similar to those supplied to merchants, lenders and other regular users of credit information. The Department wants to use the information from the files to help locate delinquent parents and determine whether their financial circumstances warrant legal action. Local wants to cooperate, but it is concerned that the proposal might run afoul of the FCRA. If you are Local's counsel, after reading FCRA §§ 604 and 608, what will you advise it to do?

Note on Constitutional Implications of Credit Reporting

In Chapter 1, we considered the impact of the First Amendment's limited protection of commercial speech on the ability of the FTC and other government agencies to regulate advertising practices. While it may seem less immediately obvious, these same First Amendment issues are raised in the credit reporting context. After all, what is a credit report if not commercial speech? This raises the possibility that regulation of credit reporting practices, through the FCRA or otherwise, might be unconstitutional. In fact, in Equifax Services, Inc. v. Cohen, 420 A.2d 189 (Me.1980), the Supreme Judicial Court of Maine held portions of the Maine FCRA unconstitutional on these very grounds. To date, no court has applied this ruling to the federal FCRA, but it seems only a matter of time until these arguments are raised.

Constitutional issues may arise in other ways. In Dun & Bradstreet, Inc. v. Greenmoss Builders, Inc., 472 U.S. 749, 105 S.Ct. 2939, 86 L.Ed.2d 593 (1985), the Supreme Court held that the qualified privilege, traditionally given to credit reporting agencies under common law doctrines (see page 227, supra), has no constitutional basis. Thus, the Constitution does not require states to continue giving this protection to agencies who issue false credit reports. Nevertheless, it seem unlikely that any state court or legislature would overturn this doctrine. And, as we have seen, in the consumer context at least, this may be a moot issue since the FCRA codified the privilege in § 610(e).

For a more detailed discussion of these constitutional issues, see Rasor, Financial Information, in 1 G. Trubow, ed., Privacy Law and Practice ¶ 3.03[5] (1987).

SECTION B. CREDIT DISCRIMINATION

1. THE PRE–ECOA PROBLEM—DISCRIMINATION BY CREDITORS AND ITS EFFECTS ON THE AVAILABILITY OF CREDIT

Cash sellers are not likely to "discriminate" against any particular class of buyer, at least in the sense of refusing to accept the stated price in legal tender, because there is little motivation to do so. But it is the very nature of a credit transaction for the creditor to be "discriminating" in his choice of customers: the creditor will want some reasonable assurance that the borrower will be able to (and disposed to) repay the credit as scheduled. The desire for this assurance will prompt creditors to obtain credit reports and otherwise to evaluate the creditworthiness of the prospective borrower, in order to make the best possible prediction about the likelihood of repayment.

The process of determining creditworthiness has, in the past, been a very private and proprietary matter for most creditors. That is, they rarely advertise or publicize the details of their credit granting criteria, with the result that consumers often must apply for credit as supplicants, hopeful of the creditor's beneficence, and disappointed that their qualifications should be found wanting in some unknown aspect. From the creditor's point of view, since he takes the risk of non-payment, he is entitled to set the qualifying standards.

This state of affairs might not give rise to concern were it not for two considerations. For one, the judgments of loan officers or creditor actuaries are not infallible; for another, credit is no longer either a luxury to be dispensed by whim nor an opiate for the groveling poor—it has become a virtual necessity for most consumers, to purchase homes, automobiles, and the quality of lifestyle our society promises. In this setting it becomes understandable that lawmakers should take an interest in assuring the fairest policies in credit granting.

Before the ECOA was enacted in 1974, there was much evidence of widespread discriminatory lending practices. The following material summarizes some of the evidence.

NATIONAL COMMISSION ON CONSUMER FINANCE, CONSUMER CREDIT IN THE UNITED STATES
152–54 (1972)

With respect to sex discrimination in the field of consumer credit, testimony presented at the hearings can be summarized as follows:

1. Single women have more trouble obtaining credit than single men. (This appeared to be more characteristic of mortgage credit than of consumer credit.)

2. Creditors generally require a woman upon marriage to reapply for credit, usually in her husband's name. Similar reapplication is not asked of men when they marry. * * *

3. Creditors are often unwilling to extend credit to a married woman in her own name. * * *

4. Creditors are often unwilling to count the wife's income when a married couple applies for credit. * * *

5. Women who are divorced or widowed have trouble re-establishing credit. Women who are separated have a particularly difficult time, since the accounts may still be in the husband's name.

The anecdotal evidence was supplemented by a survey of 23 commercial banks conducted by the St. Paul Department of Human Rights. A man and a woman with virtually identical qualifications applied for a $600 loan to finance a used car without the signature of the other spouse. Each applicant was the wage earner, and the spouse was in school. Eleven of the banks visited by the woman "either strictly required the husband's signature or stated it was their preference although they would accept an application and possibly make an exception to the general policy." When the same banks, plus two additional banks that would make no commitment to the female applicant, were visited by the male interviewer, six said that they would prefer both signatures but would make an exception for him; one insisted on both signatures; and six "told the male interviewer that he, as a married man, could obtain the loan without his wife's signature."

Many practices to which witnesses objected have been inherited from past decades, if not centuries. They fail to reflect the times. The extensive publicity that accompanied the Commission's hearings has caused many credit grantors to reexamine their policies with respect to the existence of sex discrimination. In a competitive market, creditors responsive to these complaints will capture business from their more archaic competitors.

* * *

Racial Discrimination

Historically, minority groups have faced discrimination in the nation's economic and social structures.

* * *

Frederick D. Sturdivant, alone and in collaboration with Walter T. Wilhelm, narrowed exploration of a nationwide problem to the Los Angeles area. In "Poverty, Minorities and Consumer Exploitation," Sturdivant and Wilhelm found that credit charges were frequently used by merchants in ghetto areas of Los Angeles as a vehicle to practice economic, racial and ethnic discrimination against installment buyers. Their study indicated that economic discrimination was a feature of any type of ghetto marketplace, and that within those marketplaces price or credit discrimination might be practiced against other minorities who went outside their own area to shop in another ghetto business district.

* * *

2. REGULATION OF OVERT DISCRIMINATION—THE BASIC ECOA SCHEME

In 1974, Congress responded to the findings of the National Commission on Consumer Finance and to other evidence of lending discrimination by enacting the Equal Credit Opportunity Act (ECOA), CCPA § 701 et seq., 15 U.S.C.A. § 1601 et seq. In its original form, the ECOA prohibited discrimination only on the basis of sex and marital status. In 1976, however, it was broadened considerably, and the ECOA now also prohibits discrimination on the basis of race, color, religion, national origin, age, receipt of public assistance benefits, and the good faith exercise of rights under the CCPA.

As with the Truth in Lending Act, the Federal Reserve Board has issued a set of implementing regulations and an official staff commentary interpreting the ECOA. The regulations are known as Regulation B and are found at 12 C.F.R. part 202. Both the regulation and the ECOA itself can also be found in West's Selected Commercial Statutes supplement.

Problem 10

Dan Jones, recently divorced, and Dorie Smith, a single 24 year old assistant librarian, cohabit and apply jointly to First Federal Savings & Loan Association for a purchase money mortgage loan. Their application describes the $66,000 home they intend to purchase and notes Dan's salary of $18,500 and Dorie's of $12,800. Their respective credit histories, verified by First Federal, are flawless. Nonetheless, Dan and Dorie are turned down for their mortgage. Together they visit First Federal where the loan officer explains that its action is based on a corporate policy that it will not deal with people who are "living in sin," because it wishes to discourage such conduct.

Under any of the statutory or caselaw material we have seen thus far, do Dan and Dorie have any rights against First Federal? Would they have any rights under the Equal Credit Opportunity Act, discussed below? See ECOA § 701(a).

Problem 11

Dan and Dorie then apply to Second Federal Savings and Loan Association for a purchase money mortgage. Again, they are turned down. When they visit Second Federal, the accommodating loan officer explains that the association's action is based on an analysis of all of its mortgages over the past ten years. According to that analysis, single and recently divorced men are more likely to default than married men; and women in Dorie's age bracket tend to leave the work force after a few years to become mothers and housewives. In addition, the loan officer says, married couples are statistically much more stable obligors than unmarried co-applicants. All in all, he concludes, there is too much risk for the association in their application. Read Markham v. Colonial Mortgage Service Co., below.

The association's required income for the $62,000 mortgage Dan and Dorie seek is $31,000, which makes them a border-line case in any event. The association's 10–year analysis of its mortgages shows that, in over 10% of the instances involving employed women in Dorie's age bracket where the woman's income was necessary to meet the association's required income level, it soon ceased and the borrowers defaulted on their loans. Second Association discounted Dorie's income by 10%, as an experience factor, and therefore Dan and Dorie do not meet the income requirements.

If Dan and Dorie ask you to represent them, would you take their case? Is there unlawful "discrimination" in this case? Is it unlawful in the constitutional sense of a deprivation of civil liberties under color of law, or only in an economic sense of an unfair application of criteria? If the latter, in what sense is it unfair?

Problem 12

Suppose, in Problem 10, that the two people who applied jointly to First Federal Savings & Loan Association were Dan Jones and Don Smith, living together in an openly homosexual relationship. Their house costs the same as in Problem 10, their income figures are the same as for Dan and Dorie in Problem 10, and they are turned down for the same reason, and First refused to pool their incomes, so they did not meet First's income guidelines. Do Dan and Don have a claim under ECOA?

MARKHAM v. COLONIAL MORTGAGE SERVICE CO., ASSOCIATES

United States Court of Appeals, District of Columbia Circuit, 1979.
605 F.2d 566.

SWYGERT, CIRCUIT JUDGE.

The Equal Credit Opportunity Act, prohibits creditors from discriminating against applicants on the basis of sex or marital status. We are asked to decide whether this prohibition prevents creditors from refusing to aggregate the incomes of two unmarried joint mortgage applicants when determining their creditworthiness in a situation where the incomes of two similarly situated married joint applicants would have been aggregated. The plaintiffs in this action, Jerry and Marcia Markham [formerly Marcia Harris], appeal the judgment of the district court granting defendant Illinois Federal Service Savings and Loan Association's motion for summary judgment. We reverse.

* * *

[Harris and Markham submitted a joint mortgage application to Colonial Mortgage Service Co., which passed the application on to Illinois Federal Service Savings and Loan Association.]

* * * On February 1, the loan committee of Illinois Federal rejected the plaintiffs' application. On February 3, the eve of the settlement date, plaintiffs were informed through a B.W. Real Estate agent that their loan application had been denied because they were not married. They were advised that their application would be resubmitted to the "investor"—who was not identified—on February 8, but that approval would be contingent upon the submission of a marriage certificate.

On February 8, the Illinois Federal loan committee reconsidered the plaintiffs' application, but again denied it. A letter was sent that date from Illinois Federal to Colonial–Philadelphia, which letter stated that the application had been rejected with the statement: "Separate income not sufficient for loan and job tenure."

On February 9, 1977 plaintiffs filed this suit, alleging violation of the Equal Credit Opportunity Act. After the district court separately granted the motions of Illinois Federal and the other defendants for summary judgment on May 25, 1978, plaintiffs brought this appeal.

* * *

We turn to a consideration of whether the Equal Credit Opportunity Act's prohibition of discrimination on the basis of sex or marital status makes illegal Illinois Federal's refusal to aggregate plaintiffs' income when determining their creditworthiness. Illinois Federal contends that neither the purpose nor the language of the Act requires it to combine the incomes of unmarried joint applicants when making that determination.

We start, as we must, with the language of the statute itself.
* * *

It shall be unlawful for any creditor to discriminate against any applicant, with respect to any aspect of a credit transaction—

(1) on the basis of * * * sex or marital status
* * *

This language is simple, and its meaning is not difficult to comprehend. Illinois Federal itself has correctly phrased the standard in its brief: The Act forbids discrimination "on the basis of a person's marital status, that is, to treat persons differently, all other facts being the same, because of their marital status. * * *" Illinois Federal does not contend that they would not have aggregated plaintiffs' income had they been married at the time. Indeed, Illinois Federal concedes that the law would have required it to do so. Thus, it is plain that Illinois Federal treated plaintiffs differently—that is, refused to aggregate their incomes—solely because of their marital status, which is precisely the sort of discrimination prohibited by section 1691(a)(1) on its face.

Despite the section's clarity of language, Illinois Federal seeks to avoid a finding of prohibited discrimination by arguing that it was not the Congressional purpose to require such an aggregation of the incomes of non-married applicants. It can be assumed, *arguendo,* that one, perhaps even the main, purpose of the act was to eradicate credit discrimination waged against women, especially married women whom creditors traditionally refused to consider apart from their husbands as individually worthy of credit. But granting such an assumption does not negate the clear language of the Act itself that discrimination against *any* applicant, with respect to *any* aspect of a credit transaction, which is based on marital status is outlawed. . . .

Illinois Federal expresses the fear that a holding such as we reach today will require it to aggregate the incomes of all persons who apply for credit as a group. Lest it be misinterpreted, we note that our holding is not itself that far-reaching. It does no more than require Illinois Federal to treat plaintiffs—a couple jointly applying for credit— the same as they would be treated if married. We have not been asked to decide what the effect of the Act would have been had plaintiffs not applied for credit jointly. Nor do we have before us a question of whether the Act's marital status provision in any way applies to a situation where more than two people jointly request credit. We hold only that, under the Act Illinois Federal should have treated plaintiffs—an unmarried couple applying for credit jointly—the same as it would have treated them had they been married at the time.

* * *

Notes

1. The violation seems obvious, doesn't it? Yet can you point to any specific rule in the ECOA or Reg. B which was broken?

2. How would you answer the creditor's argument that it was simply concerned about the continuity of the plaintiffs' income? After all, isn't that something a creditor ought to be worried about? And see Reg. B § 202.6(b).

MILLER v. AMERICAN EXPRESS CO.

United States Court of Appeals, Ninth Circuit, 1982.
688 F.2d 1235.

BOOCHEVER, CIRCUIT JUDGE:

Virginia Miller brought an action in district court alleging a violation of the Equal Credit Opportunity Act (ECOA), 15 U.S.C. §§ 1691 *et seq.,* after her American Express card was cancelled following the death of her husband. * * *

Maurice Miller, plaintiff's late husband, applied for and received an American Express credit card in 1966. His account was denominated a Basic Card Account. Later in 1966, plaintiff Virginia Miller applied for and was granted a supplementary card. Her application was signed by her husband as the basic cardholder and by her. Mrs.

Miller agreed to be personally liable for all charges made on her supplementary card. Her card bore a different account number from her husband's card, was issued in her own name, required a separate annual fee, and bore a different expiration date from Mr. Miller's card. The Millers used their American Express cards until Mr. Miller passed away in May, 1979. Two months after her husband's death, Mrs. Miller attempted to use her card during a shopping trip and was informed by the store clerk that her account had been cancelled. This was the first notice she received of the cancellation. Subsequently, Amex informed her that her account had been cancelled pursuant to a policy of automatically terminating the account of a supplementary cardholder upon the death of a basic cardholder. Amex invited her to apply for a basic account. Her application for a new account consisted merely of filling out a short form, entitled "Request to Change Membership status from Supplementary to Basic Card member," which did not require any financial or credit history data. Amex issued Mrs. Miller a new card, apparently on the basis of her thirteen year credit history in the use of the card it had just cancelled. Mrs. Miller brought suit against Amex for violation of the ECOA.

* * * The court awarded summary judgment to Amex without specifying its reasons.

ANALYSIS

The issues on this appeal are whether Amex's policy of cancelling a spouse's supplementary account upon the death of the basic cardholder violates the ECOA and whether a plaintiff must always show discriminatory intent or effect to establish an ECOA violation. The facts are undisputed, therefore, we must decide whether the substantive law was correctly applied. We hold that there has been credit discrimination within the meaning of the ECOA and that partial summary judgment on the issue of liability should have been granted to Mrs. Miller, rather than to Amex.

The ECOA makes it unlawful for any creditor to discriminate with respect to any credit transaction on the basis of marital status. 15 U.S.C. § 1691(a)(1). It also authorizes the Board of Governors of the Federal Reserve System (Board) to prescribe regulations, and creates a private right of action for declaratory and equitable relief and for actual and punitive damages.

In order to carry out the purposes of the ECOA, the Board promulgated the regulations codified at 12 C.F.R. §§ 201.1 *et seq.* Section 202.7(c)(1) provides that a creditor shall not terminate the account of a person who is contractually liable on an existing open end account on the basis of a change in marital status in the absence of evidence of inability or unwillingness to repay. Under certain circumstances, a creditor may require a reapplication after a change in the applicant's marital status. 12 C.F.R. § 202.7(c)(2).

Mrs. Miller's Amex card was cancelled after her marital status changed from married to widowed. Under § 202.7(c)(2), Amex could have asked her to reapply for credit, but instead it first terminated her card and then invited reapplication. There was no contention or evidence that her widowhood rendered Mrs. Miller unable or unwilling to pay, indeed, Amex's prompt issuance of a new card to her indicates that she was considered creditworthy.

Amex has argued that there was no violation of the ECOA for three reasons: that Section 202.7(c) was beyond the scope of the Board's authority, that Mrs. Miller was not "contractually liable on an existing open end account" within the meaning of § 202.7(c), and that the termination did not constitute discrimination on the basis of marital status because it occurred pursuant to a policy of automatic cancellation of all supplementary cardholders whether they were widow, widower, sibling, or child of the basic cardholder. We hold that § 202.7(c) was within the scope of the Board's authority under the ECOA, and that Mrs. Miller was within the protection of the regulation.

I

AUTHORITY FOR SECTION 202.7(c)

* * * Section 2.207(c) is directly addressed to one of the evils that the ECOA was designed to prevent: loss of credit because of widowhood. It was therefore within the discretion allowed the Board to define termination of credit as a result of the death of a spouse as credit discrimination.

II

APPLICATION OF SECTION 202.7(c)

A. Coverage of the Regulation: Contractual Liability on an Open End Account

By its terms, § 202.7(c) reaches only terminations of existing open end accounts on which the creditholder is contractually liable. * * * "Contractually liable" means "expressly obligated to repay all debts arising on an account by reason of an agreement to that effect." 12 C.F.R. § 202.2(i). Amex has argued that the reference to persons "contractually liable" was meant to exclude spouses who are only "users" of accounts. The Federal Reserve Board's comments, made when the "contractually liable" phrase was added in 1975, indicate that the phrase was designed to exclude a "user" who might be liable for a specific debt charged to a spouse's account, *"but [who] is not liable on the contract creating the account."* 40 Fed.Reg. 49,298 (1975) (emphasis added).

Mrs. Miller was not, however, merely a user of her husband's basic account. She was personally liable under the contract creating her supplementary account for all debts charged on her card by any person. For example, Mrs. Miller would have been personally liable for even charges made on her supplementary card by her husband, the basic cardholder.

* * *

Amex's cardholder agreement provides that "by either signing, using or accepting the Card, you will be agreeing with us to everything written here" and that "[i]f you are a Supplementary Cardmember, you are liable to us for all Charges made in connection with the Card issued to you * * *." This language made Mrs. Miller "contractually liable" for all debts on her supplementary account.

* * * [In] *Anderson v. United Finance Co.*, 666 F.2d 1274, 1277 (9th Cir.1982), * * * we held that there was credit "discrimination" within the meaning of the ECOA when a regulation promulgated under the ECOA was violated. No showing of any specific intent to discriminate was required. As another court has noted, not requiring proof of discriminatory intent is especially appropriate in analysis of ECOA violations because "discrimination in credit transactions is more likely to be of the unintentional, rather than the intentional, variety." *Cherry v. Amoco Oil Co.*, 490 F.Supp. 1026, 1030 (N.D.Ga.1980).

If specific intent is not proved, we nevertheless do not think that a statistical showing of an adverse impact on women is always necessary to the plaintiff's case. The ECOA's history refers by analogy to the disparate treatment and adverse impact tests for discrimination which are used in employment discrimination cases under Title VII. * * * Read in full, the Senate Report allows but does not limit proof of credit discrimination to the two traditional Title VII tests for employment discrimination. It also expressly recognizes that a creditor's conduct in an individual transaction may be considered to determine the existence of credit discrimination, quite apart from intent or from a statistical showing of adverse impact.

The conduct here was squarely within that prohibited by § 202.7(c). Mrs. Miller's account was terminated in response to her husband's death and without reference to or even inquiry regarding her creditworthiness. It is undisputed that the death of her husband was the sole reason for Amex's termination of Mrs. Miller's credit. Amex contends that its automatic cancellation policy was necessary to protect it from noncreditworthy supplementary cardholders. The regulations, however, prohibit termination based on a spouse's death in the absence of evidence of inability or unwillingness to repay. Amex has never contended in this action that the death of her husband rendered Mrs. Miller unable or unwilling to pay charges made on her card. The fact that the cancellation policy could also result in the termination of a supplemental cardholder who was not protected by the ECOA, such as a sibling or friend of the basic cardholder, does not change the essential fact that Mrs. Miller's account was terminated solely because of her husband's death. The interruption of Mrs. Miller's credit on the basis of the change in her marital status is precisely the type of occurrence that the ECOA and regulations thereunder are designed to prevent.

We hold that the undisputed facts show, as a matter of law, that Amex violated the ECOA and regulations thereunder in its termination of Mrs. Miller's supplementary card. For this reason, we reverse the district court's grant of summary judgment for Amex and instruct that partial summary judgment should be awarded to Mrs. Miller on the issue of liability. The case is remanded for further proceedings consistent with this opinion.

POOLE, CIRCUIT JUDGE, dissenting.

The majority today holds in effect that a credit practice need not be discriminatory to violate the Equal Credit Opportunity Act (the Act). Because this holding is contrary to the clear language and purpose of the Act, I respectfully dissent.

Applicability of § 202.7(c)

* * *

The majority correctly finds that the liabilities imposed upon supplementary cardholders are inconsistent with mere "authorized user" status.

Violation of § 202.7(c)

It is a fact that American Express cancelled appellant's supplementary card after the death of her husband. Section 202.7(c), however, does not prohibit the termination of an account after a change in an applicant's marital status; it prohibits only the termination of an account "on the basis of" such a change. Since the change in appellant's marital status was not the basis for American Express's decision to cancel her supplementary card, there has been no violation of § 202.7(c).

Notes

1. What damages did Virginia Miller suffer as a result of American Express' action?

2. The court refers to the "disparate treatment" and "disparate impact" test for proving employment discrimination under Title VII. Here, the court merely holds that the discrimination in this case is so open that no such fact development is needed. Note that ECOA § 701(a) is stated in terms of a direct prohibition which does not require such indirect proof.

However, it should also be understandable that not all discrimination will be so open. Where the discrimination is more disguised the "disparate treatment" and "disparate impact" tests are still available under ECOA. Cases and problems raising these issues will be treated later in this section.

Problem 13

Jane applied for an individual loan from Ace Finance. All credit checks and other verifications were done solely in Jane's name. Ace agreed to make the loan if she would put up her sailboat as security. The sailboat was jointly owned by Jane and her husband, Dick. As a result, Ace has asked you to advise it whether it can require the signature of both Jane and Dick on the security agreement without violating ECOA. If Ace also wanted Dick to sign the underlying promissory note, would your answer be the same? Secured credit issues are governed by Reg. B § 202.7(d)(4). Does that provision decide issues concerning both the security agreement and the note?

Problem 14

Dagwood and Blondie are separated, and divorce proceedings are pending. Blondie wants to buy her own home, and applied to Ace Savings and Loan for a home mortgage loan. Ace believes that Blondie's income is sufficient to support the amount of the mortgage, but it would also rely on the security of the mortgage interest in the house. It does not fully understand the impact of Dagwood's current relationship on that mortgage interest. Thus, it wants Dagwood to co-sign the mortgage and wants you to advise it whether a demand for Dagwood's signature would violate ECOA. Read Reg. B § 202.7.

Note

Most lenders base their loan decisions primarily on their estimates of future earnings. The existing assets of the borrower normally impact these decisions only if the loan is secured. In unsecured loans, co-signers will be required where the borrower's future earnings seem too small. The co-signer may be any person with sufficient earnings to make the combined earnings qualify for the loan.

Should these policies be different in community property states? In those states, a lender prefers to consider only the future earnings of a married applicant, and not the future earnings of the married applicant's spouse, unless the spouse will co-sign. If the lender actually restricts its valuation of future earnings this way, is it violating ECOA? See United States v. ITT Consumer Financial Corp., 816 F.2d 487 (9th Cir.1987). See also Taylor, The Equal Credit Opportunity Act's Spousal Co-signature Rules and Community Property States: Regulatory Haywire, 37 Sw.L.J. 1039 (1984); Taylor, The Equal Credit Opportunity Act's Spousal Co-signature Rules: Suretyship Contracts in Separate Property States, 48 Alb. L.Rev. 382 (1984).

Notification of Adverse Action

Like the FCRA, the ECOA requires a creditor who has taken "adverse action" to send a notice to the credit applicant. See ECOA § 701(d) and Reg. B §§ 202.2 and 202.9. For an elaborate discussion of exactly what constitutes "adverse action," see Jochum v. Pico Credit Corp. of Westbank, Inc., 730 F.2d 1041 (5th Cir.1984). Just what sort of notice must the creditor give?

FISCHL v. GENERAL MOTORS ACCEPTANCE CORP.

United States Court of Appeals, Fifth Circuit, 1983.
708 F.2d 143.

POLITZ, CIRCUIT JUDGE:

Terry Fischl sued General Motors Acceptance Corporation (GMAC), alleging that its failure to furnish specific reasons for denying him credit, and to disclose that this denial was predicated in whole or part on information derived from a credit reporting agency, violated the Equal Credit Opportunity Act (ECOA), 15 U.S.C. § 1691 *et seq.*, Regulation B promulgated thereunder, 12 C.F.R. § 202, and the Fair Credit Reporting Act (FCRA), 15 U.S.C. § 1681 *et seq.* Following a bench trial, the district court entered judgment for GMAC. We reverse and remand.

Factual and Procedural Background

On September 27, 1980, Fischl applied in writing to O.E. Harring, Inc., a New Orleans automobile dealership, for credit covering $12,000 of the $15,000 purchase price of a 1980 BMW automobile. A Harring salesman referred Fischl's credit application to GMAC, communicating the information by telephone. After transcribing this information on an application form, GMAC employees contacted Credit Bureau Services, a local credit reporting service, and obtained a consumer report on Fischl.

Both the application and the consumer report reflected that Fischl, a 27 year-old single homeowner, made mortgage payments of $564.80 per month. Although he held two sales jobs and earned a total monthly income of approximately $4,000, the credit report erroneously referred to one position as past employment. Credit references listed on the application were VISA, MasterCharge, Diner's Club and General Electric Credit Corporation. The credit report disclosed that Fischl had achieved an A–1 credit rating on current accounts with two area retailers, the New Orleans Public Service, First Homestead, and VISA or MasterCharge. An account in good standing with Sears, Roebuck and Company was mistakenly described in the report as a credit inquiry.

After reviewing the application and report, Robert Bell, GMAC's credit supervisor, determined that Fischl's credit background was deficient in terms of duration and extent; specifically, there were no sustained monthly payments of an amount comparable to that required to finance the purchase of the BMW. Based on these factors, Bell decided that credit at the level requested should not be extended, a decision approved by Lester Robinson, Bell's immediate superior.

On October 3, 1980, Fischl received a form letter from GMAC advising that his application had been rejected and noting, as the reason therefor, that "credit references are insufficient." The portion of the form letter designed to disclose the creditor's use of information from outside sources was marked "disclosure inapplicable." That same day, Fischl secured a copy of his credit report from Credit Bureau Services which reflected GMAC's inquiry. In subsequent telephone conversations with Bell and Robinson, both of which he initiated, Fischl learned that GMAC had received a consumer report from a credit reporting service. During these conversations, more specific reasons for the denial of credit were advanced and the name and address of the credit bureau were given. Shortly thereafter, Fischl secured a $12,000 loan from an area bank at a lower rate of interest than that offered by GMAC.

Equal Credit Opportunity Act

The district court found that GMAC's adverse determination letter adequately informed Fischl of the basis for rejection of his credit application and, because the reason assigned therein was similar to one proposed in the Federal Reserve Board's (Board) model checklist, 12 C.F.R. § 202.9(b)(2), that the creditor was insulated from liability under 15 U.S.C. § 1691e(e). Fischl contends that the district court erred in holding that GMAC provided him with the specific reasons for credit denial mandated by 15 U.S.C. §§ 1691(b)(2) and (3) and Regulation B, 12 C.F.R. § 202.9. He argues that the reason cited in GMAC's adverse determination letter, "credit references are insufficient," does not afford notice of the actual grounds for the denial, to-wit, the brevity of his credit history and the excessiveness of the amount he wished to finance when measured against the size of his current credit obligations.

* * *

* * * [A] creditor electing to provide a statement of reasons for denial or termination of credit in accordance with § 1691(d)(2)(A) must apprise the applicant in writing of the specific reasons for its adverse action. Section 202.9(b)(2) reiterates the specificity requirement set forth in § 1691(d)(3), dictates the inclusion of the "principal" reasons for adverse action, and advises creditors that completion of the model form contained therein assures compliance with § 202.9(a)(2)(i). * * * With respect to the proper use of the sample form outlined in § 202.9(b)(2), the Board emphasized:

> The sample form is illustrative and may not be appropriate for all creditors. It was designed to disclose those factors which creditors most commonly consider. Some of the reasons listed on the form could be misleading when compared to the factors actually scored. In such cases, it is improper to complete the form by simply checking the closest identifiable factor listed. For example, a creditor that considers only bank references (and disregards finance company references altogether) should disclose "insufficient bank references" (not "insufficient credit references"). Similarly, a creditor that considers bank references and other credit references as separate factors should treat the two factors separately in disclosing reasons. The creditor should either add those other factors to the form or check "other" and include the

> appropriate explanation. In providing reasons for adverse action, creditors need not describe how or why a factor adversely affected an applicant. For example, the notice may say "length of residence" rather than "too short a period of residence."

12 C.F.R. § 202.901(f).

After considering the notice transmitted in light of the congressional language and purpose of § 1691(d), we find that GMAC's perfunctory reliance on the Board's sample checklist was manifestly inappropriate. While it resembles the category of "insufficient credit references" deemed acceptable by the Board, § 202.9(b)(2), the reason for refusal of credit noted by GMAC, "credit references are insufficient," arguably communicates a different meaning. The Board's statement connotes quantitative inadequacy; that of GMAC implies some qualitative deficiency in Fischl's credit status. GMAC's statement does not signal the nature of that deficiency and, since the name and address of the credit bureau was not supplied, did not provide the mandated opportunity for the applicant to correct erroneous information.

Assuming, *arguendo,* that GMAC's phrase "credit references are insufficient" conveys substantially the same message as its regulatory counterpart, the notice provided in this case fails to satisfy the informative purposes of the ECOA. Upon receipt of GMAC's adverse determination letter, Fischl found himself in the dilemma described by one commentator:

> The "insufficient credit references" reason has been severely criticized by rejected applicants because it fails to tell them how they can meet the creditor's requirements. The statement only raises the question of what "sufficient" is, and without further explanation, an applicant is left to speculate as to what will meet the creditor's standards.

Given that a combination of factors contributed to GMAC's adverse credit determination, the reason articulated was misleading, or at best excessively vague. *See Carroll v. Exxon Co., U.S.A.,* 434 F.Supp. 557 (E.D.La.1977). A GMAC employee acknowledged at trial that "many things can come under the definition of 'credit references are insufficient'." Being unaware of the creditor's minimum standards of creditworthiness, Fischl was unable to translate this reason into concrete criteria. He could neither improve his credit application, correct any misinformation in his credit record, or guard against discrimination, thus thwarting both the educational and protective objectives of the ECOA. GMAC's subsequent oral clarification of the factors which actually motivated its adverse decision did not remedy this omission. Consistent with the Board's recent admonition that the protection of § 1691e(e) may not be invoked where factors delineated in the sample checklist are misleading by comparison to those actually weighed, or do not coincide with those in fact relied upon, *see* 12 C.F.R. § 202.901(f), we conclude that GMAC's conduct fell squarely within that proscribed by § 1691(d) and Regulation B.

Fair Credit Reporting Act

Fischl next argues that the district court erred in finding, first, that credit was not denied in whole or part on the basis of information contained in the consumer report issued by Credit Bureau Services, within the meaning of 15 U.S.C. § 1681m(a) and, second, that GMAC's oral disclosure of the name and address of the agency in response to Fischl's inquiry complied with the statute. Credit was not refused, in the district court's estimation, "because of information *in* the report; nothing adverse was there * * * [rather, Fischl] was denied credit, in a sense, for what was *not* in the report: there was not sufficient evidence * * * of his ability to sustain high monthly payments." (emphasis by the trial court.)

Section 1681m(a)'s disclosure requirement is triggered "[w]henever credit * * * for personal * * * purposes * * * is denied * * * either wholly or partly because of information contained in the consumer report from a consumer reporting agency * * *." * * * The purpose of the notification provision is to enable the subject of a consumer report to request disclosure from the reporting agency of the nature and scope of the information in his file.

Disclosure is not conditioned upon the creditor's consideration of derogatory or negative information in a consumer report in arriving at an adverse decision, so long as that decision is attributable wholly or in part to information in the report.

* * * Thus a creditor could, upon obtaining a consumer report, discover that a prospective borrower had established an excellent credit record over a period of years, yet determine that qualifications revealed in the report did not meet its own standards of creditworthiness. Under these circumstances, disclosure would be mandated.

Such is the case herein. Fischl's application for credit was denied in part because of information in a report prepared by a credit reporting service. This information was incomplete and misleading. The details of his credit history set forth in the report, when evaluated under GMAC's judgmental criteria, did not furnish a sufficient guarantee of financial responsibility to support an extension of credit in the amount sought. GMAC concluded that the record of Fischl's current obligations did not justify a prediction that he could successfully undertake the monthly payments contemplated.

Despite its reliance on data contained in the credit report, when reporting to Fischl via the form letter of October 3, 1980, GMAC did not disclose this information, advising instead that disclosure was inapplicable. This action did not comport with § 1681m(a). Similarly, GMAC's subsequent oral response to Fischl's inquiry, noting the name and address of the credit bureau, did not suffice under the statute. We need not and do not decide whether the notice required by § 1681m(a) must be written, nor do we decide the mandated timing for the notice. Those questions remain for another day.

* * *

REVERSED and REMANDED for further proceedings consistent herewith.

Note

Did Terry Fischl suffer any damages? Was he required to show any discrimination? Is the notice requirement just another of those "technical" rules that increases costs in credit transactions?

Problem 15. Branch managers at Ace Finance Co. decide whether to grant credit according to their own "gut feeling" about the applicant. They all have many years' experience at making such judgments, and their "uncollectables" are low. In addition, these branch managers also take the usual data on applicants (income, length of time on the job, etc.), but this is not what they rely upon in "close cases."

Fleur D. Lee, a recent graduate with a promised $80,000/year job at Dewey, Cheatham, and Howe, applied to Ace for a $25,000 loan to buy a new BMW. Ace's local branch manager, Buck N. Ham, took her application and talked with her for about 10 minutes. During that time, he called her "girl" about a dozen times. The last time he did that, Fleur interrupted him and told him that that was an inappropriate and demeaning form of reference. The interview ended soon thereafter. Fleur has a spotless credit record, and her salary would meet Ace's requirements for a $25,000 loan.

Buck has a negative "gut feeling" about Fleur's application, and wants to decline it. He knows that, under ECOA, he will have to send her an "adverse action letter." He asks your advice as to what to say in the letter is the reason for denying the application.

(a) Would you advise Buck to state that Fleur's credit application was denied due to "short length of employment history" and "currently unemployed"? See Reg. B § 202.9, Reg. B Appendix C, and *Fischl.*

(b) Would you advise Buck to state that he has a "negative gut feeling" about the likelihood of repayment of this loan? See ECOA § 701(a).

(c) Would you advise Buck not to state a specific reason for denial, but instead under Reg. B § 202.9(a)(2)(ii) to notify Fleur of her right to request a statement of specific reasons? Is this likely to solve Buck's problem, or only delay its resolution?

(d) Would you advise Buck to ignore his "gut feeling" and approve the credit application?

(e) Would you give none of the above as advice, and advance an alternative?

(f) Having made whatever advice you chose under (a)–(e), did it assist the policies underlying ECOA?

3. THE NEW INDUSTRY—MODERN (POST–ECOA) CREDIT GRANTING SYSTEMS

Traditionally, creditors used their own subjective judgment as the "system" to evaluate the creditworthiness of their applicants. Credit officers in lending institutions relied on their past experience and perhaps on institutional guidelines in making their decisions. Many creditors continue to use this approach.

Such "judgmental systems" have been criticized, however. For example, critics charge that credit officials often have a poor or a distorted recollection of past experiences. Another potential problem is that institutional guidelines may be outdated and may not reflect large-scale changes in the applicant pool over time. Often these problems lead to inadvertent discrimination. See generally, Hsia, Credit Scoring and the Equal Opportunity Act, 30 Hastings L.J. 371 (1978).

More recently, a system of evaluating credit applicants known as "credit scoring" has been developed as an alternative to the traditional judgmental systems. The following material will give you a good idea of how these systems are created and how they are used by creditors.

CAPON, CREDIT SCORING SYSTEMS: A CRITICAL ANALYSIS
46 J. Marketing 82, 83–86 (1982).*

The basic procedure for developing credit scoring systems involves the selection of samples of goods and bads from the creditor's files. Upwards of 50, and as many as 300 * * * potential predictor characteristics are obtained from the application blank. A multivariate statistical technique such as regression or discriminant analysis * * * is employed, frequently in a stepwise manner, to identify those predictor characteristics, typically from eight to twelve, which contribute most to separation of the two groups. These selected characteristics, determined in part by the initial set of characteristics available from the application blank and in part by the data, and their point values are unique to an individual system. An example of a regionally based system of a major national retailer is shown in Table 1.

An applicant for credit is evaluated in a credit scoring system by simply summing the points received on the various application characteristics to arrive at a total score. This score may be treated in a number of ways depending on the system design. In the single cut-off method, the applicant's total score is compared to a single cut-off point score. If this score exceeds the cut-off, credit is granted; otherwise the applicant is rejected. More complex systems are based on a two-stage process. For example, the applicant's total score may be compared to two cut-off figures. If the score exceeds the higher cut-off, credit is awarded automatically, while if it falls below the lower cut-off, credit is automatically denied. If the score is between the two cut-offs, credit history information is obtained, scored, and the points added to the total score obtained from the application blank. If this new score is above a new higher cut-off, credit is awarded; if not, credit is denied.

TABLE 1
Major National Retailer's Final Scoring Table for Application Characteristics

Zip Code		Time at Present Address	
Zip Codes A	60	Less than 6 months	39
Zip Codes B	48	6 months–1 year 5 months	30
Zip Codes C	41	1 year 6 months–3 years 5	
Zip Codes D	37	months	27
Not answered	53	3 years 6 months–7 years 5	
		months	30
Bank Reference		7 years 6 months–12 years 5	
Checking only	0	months	39
Savings only	0	12 years 6 months or longer	50
Checking & Savings	15	Not answered	36
Bank name or loan only	0		
No bank reference	7	Time with Employer	
Not answered	7	Less than 6 months	31
		6 months–5 years 5 months	24
Type of Housing		5 years 6 months–8 years 5	
Owns/buying	44	months	26
Rents	35	8 years 6 months–15 years 5	
All other	41	months	31
Not answered	39	15 years 6 months or longer	39
		Homemakers	39
Occupation		Retired	31
Clergy	46	Unemployed	29
Creative	41	Not answered	29
Driver	33		
Executive	62	Finance Company Reference	
Guard	46	Yes	0
Homemaker	50	Other references only	25
Labor	33	No	25
Manager	46	Not answered	15
Military enlisted	46	Other Department Store/Oil	
Military officer	62	Card/Major Credit Card	
Office staff	46	Department store only	12
Outside	33	Oil Card only	12
Production	41	Major credit card only	17
Professional	62	Department store and oil	
Retired	62	card	17
Sales	46	Department store and credit	
Semi-professional	50	card	31
Service	41	Major credit card and oil	
Student	46	card	31
Teacher	41	All three	31
Unemployed	33	Other references only	0
All other	46	No credit	0
Not answered	47	Not answered	12

*   *   *

The creditor sets his/her cut-off values on the basis of the probabilities of repayment and nonpayment associated with the various point scores and the tradeoffs between type I and type II errors. The higher an acceptance cut-off is set, the lower the type I error (accepting applicants who fail to repay), while the lower a rejection cut-off value, the lower the type II error (failing to accept applicants who would have repaid).

The critical distinction between extant credit scoring systems and other methods of credit evaluation is the absence, in credit scoring, of an explanatory model. While judgmental systems are based, however imperfectly, upon a credit evaluator's explanatory model of credit performance, credit scoring systems are concerned solely with statistical predictability. Since prediction is the sole criterion for acceptability, any individual characteristic that can be scored, other than obviously illegal characteristics, has potential for inclusion in a credit scoring system. A partial list of characteristics used by creditors in the development of their systems is presented in Table 2.

TABLE 2
Partial List of Factors Used to Develop Credit Scoring Systems

Telephone at home	First letter of last name
Own/rent living accommodations	Bank savings account
Age	Bank checking account
Time at home address	Zip code of residence
Industry in which employed	Age of automobile
Time with employer	Make and model of automobile
Time with previous employer	Geographic area of U.S.
Type of employment	Finance company reference
Number of dependents	Debt to income ratio
Types of credit reference	Monthly rent/mortgage payment
Income	Family size
Savings and loan references	Telephone area code
Trade union membership	Location of relatives
Age difference between man and wife	Number of children
	Number of other dependents
Telephone at work	Ownership of life insurance
Length of product being purchased	Width of product being purchased

Few of these variables bear an explanatory relationship to credit performance. At best they might be statistical predictors whose relationship to payment performance can exist only through a complex chain of intervening variables. The overwhelming concern of creditors for prediction and a total unconcern for other issues was perhaps most tellingly demonstrated in the exchange between Senator Carl Levin (D., Michigan) and William Fair, chairman of Fair, Isaac and Company, the leading developer of credit scoring systems, at the Senate hearings on S15. Senator Levin asked Mr. Fair whether he *should be allowed* to use certain characteristics in the development of credit scoring systems (*Credit Card Redlining* 1979, p. 221):

> **Senator Levin:** "You feel that you should be allowed to consider *race?*" (emphasis added)
>
> **Mr. Fair:** "That is correct."
>
> **Senator Levin:** "Would the same thing be true with *religion?*"
>
> **Mr. Fair:** "Yes."
>
> **Senator Levin:** "Would the same thing be true with *sex?*"
>
> **Mr. Fair:** "Yes."
>
> **Senator Levin:** "Would the same thing be true with *age?*"
>
> **Mr. Fair:** "Yes."
>
> **Senator Levin:** "The same thing be true with *marital status?*"
>
> **Mr. Fair:** "Yes."
>
> **Senator Levin:** "*Ethnic origin?*"
>
> **Mr. Fair:** "Yes."

This exchange demonstrates very clearly that in the development of credit scoring systems, for Fair, Isaac and Company at least, no issue other than statistical predictability is of any consequence.[3] Although professing a commitment to obey the law, Fair, Isaac and Company, if statistical predictability were found and it were so able, would provide its customers with credit scoring systems that discriminated on the basis of *race, religion, sex, age, marital status* and *ethnic origin*.

Notes

1. In a footnote, the author of the above article noted:

A logical extension of Mr. Fair's position would allow the inclusion of such characteristics as color of hair (if any), left or right-handedness, wear eyeglasses, height, weight, early morning drink preference (tea, coffee, milk, other), first digit of social security number, last digit of social security number, sexual preference (none, same, different, both), educational level, sports preference (football, baseball, tennis, soccer, golf, other), and favorite movie star (select from list), if it could be shown that they were statistically related to payment performance.

Is he correct? Assuming a creditor did use some of these factors in its evaluation system, would that violate the ECOA or Reg. B? Is there a requirement that factors used in a scoring table be intuitively related to creditworthiness? See Reg. § 202.6(a).

2. Does Table 1 make sense to you? Answer the following questions:

    a. In the "occupation" category, how would you score a law professor? A Congressman?

    b. Which factor carries the greatest weight? Why? How are relative weights determined?

c. How many points do you get for a good credit history or a high income?

d. How much does long-term stability in your job or your residence count?

e. Is whether the table makes sense to you even relevant under the ECOA?

3. Notice that the ECOA imposes certain limitations on the types of information a creditor can gather. See Reg. B § 202.5(c) and (d). Why restrict a creditor's access to information? Are any of the characteristics listed in these provisions relevant to a credit decision? Which ones? Under what circumstances?

4. Could a credit scoring system have a built-in bias? Evaluate the following argument: "The computer scoring system is discriminatory * * * because major values in the system are assigned to characteristics (industry employing and type of employment) which have a significant correlation with sex." Shuman v. Standard Oil of California, 453 F.Supp. 1150, 1156 (N.D.Cal.1978). Does this argument seem to hold with the scoring system described above?

5. Can scoring systems be justified on a cost-benefit analysis? One prominent economist has suggested that "[d]iscrimination is largely a matter of basing decisions on incomplete information: generalizing from a person's race or sex to his or her character or ability." R. Posner, The Economics of Justice, 345 (1981). Do you agree? Professor (now Judge) Posner also suggests that the cost of information is a major factor in processes such as hiring or credit granting. It is easier and cheaper to follow a flat rule against hiring former criminals, for example, than it is to investigate the individual circumstances in each case. Do you agree? Does this sort of analysis help explain the use of scoring systems?

6. When a creditor uses a scoring system, how should it state the reasons for adverse action? Can it simply disclose the fact that the applicant did not receive a high enough score? How will the lender even know the actual reason for the action if the computer merely manipulates a bunch of numbers? The Federal Reserve Board has issued the following Official Staff Commentary, ¶ 202.9(b)(2)–4, 5, which addresses this problem. Does it help?

4. *Credit scoring system.* If a creditor bases the denial or other adverse action on a credit scoring system, the reasons disclosed must relate only to those factors actually scored in the system. Moreover, no factor that was a principal reason for adverse action may be excluded from disclosure. The creditor must disclose the actual reasons for denial (for example, "age of automobile") even if the relationship of that factor to predicting creditworthiness may not be clear to the applicant.

5. *Credit scoring—method for selecting reasons.* The regulation does not require that any one method be used for selecting reasons for a credit denial or other adverse action that is based on a credit scoring system. Various methods will meet the requirements of the regulation. One method is to identify the factors for

which the applicant's score fell furthest below the average score for each of those factors achieved by applicants whose total score was at or slightly above the minimum passing score. Another method is to identify the factors for which the applicant's score fell furthest below the average score for each of those factors achieved by all applicants. These average scores could be calculated during the development or use of the system. Any other method that produces results substantially similar to either of these methods is also acceptable under the regulation.

Problem 16

Nationwide Retailers Co. has just adopted a credit scoring system. In fact, it adopted the exact scoring system described in Table 1 of Capon article, above. It requires a score of at least 225 to grant any loan. [For example, a secretary, with a new rental address in Zip Code C and a new employer, and with only an oil company credit card and both a checking and a savings account at her bank, and no finance company reference, will score 244.]

Constance Baker is a teacher who took a new job, and also rented a furnished apartment in Zip Code C, one year ago. She has a checking account at her bank; but has an account with a mutual money market fund, rather than a bank savings account. She has credit cards from oil companies and from other department stores. She once got a loan from a finance company and pre-paid it.

At the end of her first year in her new job, Constance decided to move to a better apartment, which was not furnished. She did, however, find the perfect furniture for the new apartment at Nationwide.

She then applied to Nationwide for credit. However, as Table 1 demonstrates, she scored only 188 on its scoring system (Zip Code: 41; Bank Ref.: 0; Housing: 35; Occupation: 41; Time at Address: 30; Time with Employer: 24; Fin. Co.: 0; Credit Card: 17). Nationwide asks you what it should say as a "statement of specific reasons" for its denial of credit. What is your advice? Is the Official Staff commentary, above, helpful?

Note that the factors for which her score fell furthest below the averages may be the Bank and Finance Co. References. Should Nationwide tell Constance to 1) open a savings account (even though that is financially counterproductive) and 2) don't tell us about your finance company loan? Or, should it tell her that her score is below average (the secretary new to town) in seven different categories?

If you were Constance, what would *you* want to be told, and why? Is that likely to be disclosed under ECOA?

4. MODERN, DISGUISED DISCRIMINATION

Proving discrimination is not easy, nor are the legal theories easy to articulate and understand. The most highly developed body of case law under any federal discrimination statute is no doubt that applying the Equal Employment Opportunity Act (EEOA, not to be confused with the ECOA), Title VII of the Civil Rights Act of 1964, 42 U.S.C.A. § 2000e et seq. Under Title VII, the courts have applied two separate legal theories or tests to determine whether discrimination exists in individual cases. These are (1) the disparate impact, or "effects," test, and (2) the disparate treatment test. You may think of these tests basically as devices to help focus the court's inquiry and evaluate the difficult issues of evidence and proof which are inevitable in discrimination cases. These same tests are often applied in credit discrimination cases under the ECOA, so you should have some understanding of how they work.

Perhaps it is easier if we begin with the disparate treatment test. Here, the plaintiff normally alleges that an employer or creditor treated her less favorably than other people in her position, and that the difference in treatment was due to her race or sex or some other improper characteristic, rather than her qualifications. To win a case under this test, the plaintiff must prove that the discrimination, or disparate treatment, was intentional. Proving subjective intent is always difficult; the defendant is not likely to testify that "our policy is simple; we don't hire blacks." Recognizing this, the courts have articulated a series of burden-shifting mechanisms which make the proof issues somewhat more objective. These mechanisms have been articulated in various forms, but, in general, the plaintiff can establish a prima facie case by showing that the employer continued to seek applicants with similar qualifications after having rejected the plaintiff. The burden of going forward then shifts to the defendant-employer. He may rebut the plaintiff's case by showing that there was a legitimate, non-discriminatory reason for his decision. If the defendant can do this, the plaintiff gets one final shot. She may still prevail if she can show that the so-called legitimate reason offered by the defendant was merely a pretext for discrimination. As you might imagine, it is sometimes hard to keep track of all these shifting burdens.

The disparate impact test, or "effects" test as it is often called, is quite different. To start, the plaintiff does not have to prove that the discrimination was intentional. Instead, the operative idea is that employment or credit practices which appear to be neutral might nevertheless create disparities among groups, especially to the disadvantage of groups the law wishes to protect such as minorities or women. Further, this might happen quite irrespective of the employer's or creditor's intent. Thus, a plaintiff who relies on this theory must prove the existence and extent of these disparities, and must also prove that the disparities were caused by the specific practice being challenged.

In disparate impact cases, it is important to remember that the court is looking for evidence of disparities among entire groups, and not simply individual instances of discrimination. As a result, the evidence is likely to be highly statistical and quite complex. It will probably include elaborate information about applicant pools, percentages of employees (or credit recipients) from various groups, and other statistical data. If the evidence shows that the effect of the challenged practice is to create a "statistically significant" disparity in treatment among the various groups (an issue over which the experts are sure to disagree), the plaintiff has established a prima facie case. As in the disparate treatment cases, the burden then shifts to the defendant. He may escape liability if he can demonstrate that the challenged practice is nevertheless legitimate, despite its adverse impact on the protected group. Normally this involves a showing that the practice has a manifest relationship to job performance (or creditworthiness), or was otherwise justified by business necessity.

Traditionally, the disparate impact (effects) test has been applied in cases in which the employer has used some objective criteria such as standardized aptitude tests or height and weight requirements. In the credit context, this test would seem to work best in cases in which the creditor used a credit scoring system. The disparate treatment test, on the other hand, has traditionally been applied in cases in which the employer's decision was based on some form of personal judgment or other subjective factors. In the credit context, this test would thus seem most appropriate in cases in which the creditor used a traditional judgmental evaluation system.

This does not mean, however, that the tests are limited to these types of cases. For example, the Supreme Court ruled recently that the disparate impact test could be used in cases in which the employment decision was subjective. Watson v. Fort Worth Bank and Trust, 487 U.S. 977, 108 S.Ct. 2777, 101 L.Ed.2d 827 (1988). So, in these cases, as well as in cases in which the decision was based on a combination of objective and subjective factors (a standardized test plus a personal interview, for example), the plaintiff can still use the "effects" test to make out a prima facie case, at least if the data is there. Presumably, *Watson* would also apply to credit cases, so that plaintiffs could challenge a judgmental credit evaluation system by showing that it had a disparate impact on a protected group.

This material can be quite difficult to understand, at least in the abstract. Worse, just when you think you have it figured out, the Supreme Court is sure to issue a new opinion which changes the rules. For example, the most recent effects test case in the employment area seems to have changed the longheld understanding of the various proof burdens. See Wards Cove Packing Co., Inc. v. Atonio, ___ U.S. ___, 109 S.Ct. 2115, 104 L.Ed.2d 733 (1989). No doubt there will be other changes (or "clarifications") in the future. And, as this book goes to press, Congress is considering changes to EEOA.

Meanwhile, the following material will give you some exercise in applying these concepts to cases involving alleged credit discrimination.

CHERRY v. AMOCO OIL CO.

United States District Court, Northern District of Georgia, 1980.
490 F.Supp. 1026.

ORINDA DALE EVANS, DISTRICT JUDGE.

The above-captioned case was tried to the Court sitting without a jury on April 29–30, 1980. Having considered the evidence adduced at the trial, together with the briefs and arguments of counsel, the Court finds in favor of Defendant Amoco Oil Company. Specifically, the Court finds and concludes as follows:

I. SUMMARY OF CASE

Plaintiff is a white woman who resides in a predominantly non-white residential area in Atlanta, Georgia. She applied for but was denied a gasoline credit card by Defendant Amoco Oil Company. She seeks damages under the Equal Credit Opportunity Act, which provides in part that it is unlawful for a creditor to discriminate against a credit applicant on the basis of race. She contends the reason for rejection of her application was race-related and that as such, said denial is proscribed by the Act.

Defendant Amoco Oil utilizes a complex computerized system to evaluate credit card applications. The system takes into account 38 objective factors in scoring each application, including level of income, occupation, and Amoco's prior credit experience in the U.S. Postal Service zip code area where the applicant resides. The information provided with respect to each of the 38 factors is scored by the computer. Credit is granted to those who receive a passing aggregate score; it is automatically denied to others.

Amoco's testimony indicated that its scoring system assigns a low rating to those zip code areas in which it has had unfavorable delinquency experience. Of those Atlanta zip code areas bearing the prefix 303–, low ratings were assigned to all predominantly non-white zip code areas as well as to many predominantly white areas. Plaintiff's zip code area, 30310, was assigned a rating of 1, the least desirable rating on a scale of 1 to 5. The evidence showed without dispute that if Plaintiff lived in a zip code area rated 3 or above, and all other information including level of income shown on her application had remained constant, she would have been granted a credit card by Amoco.

Plaintiff asserts that Amoco's utilization of zip code ratings is racially discriminatory. She contends she has standing to complain of such discrimination because she was adversely affected by it; to wit, she lives in a predominantly non-white zip code area which has been low-rated by Amoco's system.

Plaintiff produced two witnesses, herself and a sociologist. Plaintiff's testimony established that she received a letter from Amoco indicating her application had been turned down; the letter specified that one of the reasons was "our previous credit experience in your immediate geographical area." Plaintiff testified she was humiliated and embarrassed by rejection of her credit card application. She further testified she subsequently has had to reveal this denial on other credit applications, but there was no testimony that she has been denied other credit. In short, Plaintiff presented no testimony of actual damages, unless the statutory term "actual damages" is to be interpreted by the Court as permitting an award of damages for mental anguish.

Plaintiff's other witness testified he had received from Plaintiff's counsel a list of those Atlanta zip code areas bearing a 303 prefix which were rated 1 or 2 by Amoco, along with information as to credit application acceptance rate in each area. He then compiled, based on estimates derived from 1970 census data, percentage estimates of non-white population in each of these areas. These two sets of percentages were then correlated on a scattergram he prepared. * * * As may be seen from an examination of the scattergram, it shows a significant correlation between acceptance rate/percentage of white population or conversely, rejection rate/percentage of non-white population.

Defendant Amoco produced witnesses who opined that the methodology used by Plaintiff was faulty for various reasons. Amoco claimed the scattergram was based on incorrect demographic data and that even assuming the correctness of the data reflected in the scattergram, it did not prove anything about relationship between use of zip code ratings and rejection of black credit applicants, because (1) it made the unsupported assumption that the reason for rejection was the applicant's residence in his particular zip code area and (2) it made the unsupported assumption that Amoco's applicant pool for each zip code area reflected the racial composition of the population as a whole.

II. LAW APPLICABLE

* * *

Dealing with the damages question first, the Court holds that it is not necessary for plaintiff to prove actual damages to be entitled to relief. In this case, Plaintiff did state she was humiliated by Amoco's failure to grant her credit and that she felt she had been damaged by having to reveal the refusal of credit on future credit applications. This does not constitute proof of actual damage. However, it is clear to the Court that the Act did not envision the necessity of proof of actual damages as a prerequisite to entitlement to punitive damages, equitable or declaratory relief, or attorney's fees. * * * Therefore, the Court determines that should a violation be found, it has the power to award Mrs. Cherry punitive damages, even where no actual damages have been shown.

The question of what a plaintiff must show under the Equal Credit Opportunity Act to make out a prima facie case is a more subtle one. The Court notes that the drafters of the regulations accompanying the Act, *see* 12 C.F.R. § 202.6, footnote 7 as well as the legislative history of the Act, assume that the "effects test" will be utilized in cases under the Equal Credit Opportunity Act.

The so-called "effects test" is derived from a decision of the U.S. Supreme Court, *Griggs v. Duke Power Company*, 401 U.S. 424, 91 S.Ct. 849, 28 L.Ed.2d 158 (1971), a Title VII case under 42 U.S.C. § 2000e, et seq. There, the employer required persons hired in the labor department of its power generating facility to have a high school diploma. The effect of this requirement was to exclude a significantly higher percentage of black applicants from qualifying for employment than white applicants. In reversing the Fourth Circuit Court of Appeals' determination that Title VII required proof of intent to discriminate, and that such intent could not be inferred from mere disparate impact of the diploma requirement on black persons, the Supreme Court held that Title VII not only proscribes intentionally discriminatory conduct but also looks to the consequences of conduct, whether intent to discriminate is present or not. It held that plaintiff's evidence of disparate impact on a protected class was sufficient to make out a prima facie case. At that point, it became the employer's burden to show that the job requirement was related to job performance.

Although there are significant differences between the scope and purpose of Title VII and the Equal Credit Opportunity Act, and between the employment and credit settings, the court nonetheless concludes that use of an effects test concept is an available method for a plaintiff to make out a prima facie case. This conclusion is based upon the Court's assumption that otherwise, the Act will provide a remedy only in those rare cases where a company deciding on credit expressly states it is denied for a prohibited reason. Also, the Court is cognizant of the fact that discrimination in credit transactions is more likely to be of the unintentional, rather than the intentional, variety. The employment setting necessarily involves day-to-day dealings and contact between employer and employees; the relationship between a creditor and its customers tends to be more attenuated. Presumably, the creditor will act in whatever manner it deems best calculated to assure the creditworthiness of its customers and the maximum sales of its products. More personal considerations are not likely to be a factor. However, a given creditor could operate under the notion that a particular class of persons protected under the Act, are, for whatever reason, less reliable or creditworthy than others and may consciously or subconsciously select criteria which will have a tendency to "screen out" applicants in that class. If so, such criteria should be subjected to scrutiny to see if they are really necessary to meet legitimate business objectives, namely, accurately predicting creditworthiness.

The Court notes, however, that utilization of the effects test based on statistical methodology is apt to be quite difficult for a plaintiff. In the first place, the Act specifically proscribes inquiry by the creditor into the race, sex or marital status of a credit applicant, except in loans secured by residential real estate. Therefore, a creditor will not have direct information indicating the racial or other profile of its applicants or of the class of persons whose credit applications were granted. The conventional statistical methodology for showing disparate effect of a facially neutral test or practice is to compare representation of the protected class in the applicant pool with representation in the group actually accepted from the pool. If the statistical disparity is significant, then plaintiff is deemed to have made out a prima facie case.

III. FINDINGS AND CONCLUSIONS

Here, Plaintiff did not seek to make a statistical comparison based on the actual applicant pool. Presumably this was not done because it could not be, based on the specific proscription in the Act. Instead, she attempted to show that the zip code criterion has a disparate impact on black people by showing that the percentage of applicants rejected in various low-rated zip code areas correlated to the percentage of black population in each of said zip code areas. This evidence does not make out a prima facie case.

The Court agrees with Amoco's contention that Plaintiff's proof fails to show that the zip code ratings tend to adversely affect black applicants disproportionately. Rather, it shows only that the computerized grading system taken as a whole tends to reject a disproportionate number of persons living in predominantly black areas. In other words, it is deficient for two reasons: (1) It does not test the effect of zip code as a criterion involved but rather tests the effect of the overall 38–criteria grading scheme and (2) it does not deal with either an actual applicant pool or with one which could reasonably be assumed to possess the approximate characteristics of the applicant pool.

Having rejected the only theory advanced by Plaintiff herein, the Court nonetheless looks to see if other theories exist by which Plaintiff might prevail, based on the evidence introduced at the trial.

The Court does not think that proof of disparate impact need be shown by statistics in every case nor need it be shown by proof of actual disproportionate exclusion from the applicant pool. Because of the particular nature of the criterion complained of here, it may be possible to gain some enlightenment as to its effect from examination of the zip code map and the demographic data before the Court.

If the housing pattern in Atlanta is such that virtually all white persons live in neutrally-rated or high-rated zip code areas, but virtually all black persons live in low-rated areas, then the zip code criterion becomes suspect. Indeed, if the zip code/race correlation is high enough, the criterion itself takes on racial aspects so that it may be considered as a mere substitute for consideration of the applicant's race. The Court's examination of the evidence here indicates that no distinct racial pattern is evident, however. The low-rated zip code areas bearing prefix 303—on which Plaintiff's proof is based are not all predominantly black. In fact, the majority of them are predominantly white. Further, looking at the aggregate population of all such low-rated areas, one finds that 60% of such population is white and 40% is black.

A possible problem with zip code ratings in an area with a segregated housing pattern, such as Atlanta, is that as a result of actual or perceived lack of housing opportunities, black persons of all economic strata may tend to be grouped in certain zip code areas. If so, and if the economic housing pattern for white persons differs, it could mean there is a greater likelihood that an otherwise qualified black applicant would live in a low-rated zip code area than a similarly qualified white credit applicant. In order to test this hypothesis, it would be necessary to construct a hypothetical applicant pool on some basis reasonably gauged to approximate the actual applicant pool—for example, an income qualified group. By looking at both the economic and racial composition of various areas of the city, one might determine whether the zip code ratings adversely affect income-qualified black persons more than income-qualified whites. Thus, if the segregated housing pattern in Atlanta means that the zip code ratings penalize a high percentage of income-qualified black persons but only a low percentage of income-qualified white persons, then Plaintiff will have made out a prima facie case. At that point, it becomes Defendant's burden to show that the zip code ratings make Amoco's credit evaluation system more predictive than it would be otherwise.

The problem here, however, is that the Court does not have before it the data necessary to make such an analysis. Although the Court has some personal familiarity with the racial and economic makeup of various areas of the city, this general knowledge is an insufficient basis for such an analysis. Further, the Court notes that certain facts run counter to a theory that zip code ratings penalize income-qualified blacks but not income-qualified whites in Atlanta. For example, zip code areas 30305 (Buckhead) and 30309 (Ansley Park, Brookwood Hills) both of which are rated 2 by Amoco, are well-known as predominantly moderate to high income white areas. Therefore, even if the Court were to take liberal judicial notice of facts not presented to it by counsel, there would nonetheless be insufficient evidence from which to draw a conclusion as to whether Amoco's use of zip code ratings treats otherwise qualified white applicants and otherwise qualified black applicants in a significantly different manner.

For the foregoing reasons, the Clerk is DIRECTED to enter judgment in favor of Defendant Amoco Oil Company, with costs cast upon Plaintiff.

So ordered.

Notes

1. Do you agree with the opinion? If your credit application was turned down because you live in a black neighborhood (whether you are black, white, or green), haven't you been discriminated against? Compare O'Dowd v. South Central Bell, 729 F.2d 347 (5th Cir.1984).

2. Did the plaintiff's attorneys collect the correct statistical data? If you had represented the plaintiff, what additional evidence could you have used to strengthen your case? In Wards Cove Packing Co., Inc. v. Atonio, ___ U.S. ___, 109 S.Ct. 2115, 104 L.Ed.2d 733 (1989), the court had this to say about the data needed to establish a case:

> It is [this] comparison—between the racial composition of the qualified persons in the labor market and the persons holding at-issue jobs—that generally forms the proper basis for the initial inquiry in a disparate impact case. Alternatively, in cases where such labor market statistics will be difficult if not impossible to ascertain, we have recognized that certain other statistics—such as measures indicating the racial composition of "otherwise qualified applicants" for at-issue jobs—are equally probative for this purpose.

___ U.S. at ___, 109 S.Ct. at ___, 57 U.S.L.W. at 4586. Does this help? How should this language be applied in Cherry? Does the fact that the creditor used a scoring system make the problem more difficult? How?

3. The federal government was involved in the Cherry case. The U.S. Attorney General filed an amicus brief supporting the plaintiff's position that Amoco's use of ZIP codes amounted to racial discrimination. Independently, the F.T.C. had been after Amoco to stop using ZIP codes. On the very day Cherry went to trial, Amoco settled with the F.T.C. and agreed to stop using ZIP codes in its scoring system and to pay a civil penalty of $200,000.

4. Are anti-discrimination laws doomed to fail? Evaluate the following argument:

> [Assume that] blacks are discriminated against in credit and employment because (for whatever reason) their performance in these areas is on average poorer than whites'. Some states and the federal government pass laws to prevent discrimination against blacks. Barred from using race as proxy for employment suitability and credit-worthiness, employers and lenders cast about for other proxies and settle on arrest records, conviction records, bankruptcies, judgments, and the like. They do this not because they are trying to discriminate against blacks but because they want to screen out (or into lower wage or higher interest-rate categories) people who do not meet their qualification at normal prices. If, however, race is a reasonably close proxy for the underlying characteristics in which the employer and creditor are interested, and if the substitute proxies are also reasonably accurate, then the substitute proxies will have almost the same effect on the racial composition of employees and borrowers as explicit use of the racial proxy had. The ban on discrimination will have little impact.

R. Posner, The Economics of Justice, 302 (1981). Do you think ZIP code is a proxy for race? For creditworthiness? Is the use of proxies illegal under the ECOA?

Problem 17

A small loan company in New York has studied the ECOA and Regulation B carefully, and wants to avoid any consideration of prohibited bases under that law. It therefore analyzes all its credit files for the past twenty years, and finds that type of employment and place of residence both are good predictors of creditworthiness. Based on that analysis, the company determines it will make no further loans to persons who work as domestics, bartenders, busboys or cab drivers, nor to persons who live in certain neighborhoods in Harlem, the Bowery, or Fire Island. Is the company safe from an ECOA challenge? Is it important that demographic studies would place large numbers of blacks, Jews, Puerto Ricans and women in those jobs and those neighborhoods?

GROSS v. U.S. SMALL BUSINESS ADMIN.

United States District Court, Northern District of New York, 1987.
669 F.Supp. 50.

McCurn, District Judge.

I. Background

On June 12, 1980, plaintiff, Sally Gross, filed suit against the United States Small Business Administration (SBA) and its District Director, J. Wilson Harrison. Suit was brought pursuant to the ECOA alleging that the SBA and Harrison discriminated against the plaintiff on the basis of sex or marital status in their denial of her loan applications. In particular, plaintiff complained that credit applications she had made in 1975, 1976 and 1977 were improperly denied. In addition, she alleged that [the] February 9, 1978 reconsideration regarding the 1977 loan application was denied on the basis of her sex or marital status.

* * *

II. Relevant Law

* * * The plaintiff may ground her case on either a disproportionate impact theory under *Griggs v. Duke Power Co.*, 401 U.S. 424, 91 S.Ct. 849, 28 L.Ed.2d 158 (1971), or a disparate treatment analysis under the widely held test articulated in *McDonnel Douglas Corp. v. Green*, 411 U.S. 792, 93 S.Ct. 1817, 36 L.Ed.2d 668 (1973). * * *

There was little or no evidence produced at trial which would support a disparate impact claim, and plaintiff admitted in her closing argument that the proof was best analyzed under the disparate treatment test of *McDonnel Douglas*. Consequently, the plaintiff must present facts from which one can infer that the actions taken by the defendants, if unexplained, more likely than not were the result of unlawful discrimination. To meet this *prima facie* burden, she must offer proof that:

(1) she belongs to a minority or protected class,

(2) she applied for and was qualified for a loan,

(3) despite her qualifications she was rejected, and

(4) males or married females of similar credit stature were given loans, or were treated more favorably than plaintiff in the application process.

If she is successful, the burden shifts to the defendants to articulate a legitimate, non-discriminatory reason for the denial of credit. If the defendants produce such evidence, the plaintiff may still prevail if she can prove by a preponderance of the evidence that a discriminatory reason more likely motivated the defendants, or that the defendants' proffered explanation is unworthy of credence or is a pretext for discrimination.

III. APPLICATION OF THE RELEVANT LAW TO THE PRESENT CONTROVERSY

Plaintiff, a licensed real estate broker, established her real estate business in 1968. She operated out of her home from 1968 through some time in 1974 when she purchased an office located at 6888 E. Genesee Street, Fayetteville, New York. In 1975, with an eye toward expanding her business, the plaintiff sought bank financing guaranteed by the SBA. When the bank refused to grant her request, she turned to the SBA for direct financial assistance. She made an application to the SBA for an $100,000 loan on September 3, 1976, which was denied. She then made an application for a $95,000 loan on June 15, 1977, which was also denied. After the latter denial she sought reconsideration of her 1977 application by letter dated February 9, 1978. This reconsideration request was in the amount of $153,583.56, revised from the 1977 request for $95,000. Her application was again rejected.

As noted previously, the only claim before this court is whether the plaintiff's 1978 reconsideration request was denied because of her sex or marital status. Consequently, facts concerning that request and denial are most probative. Facts concerning the earlier applications provide background information, however, and will be noted where necessary.

A. *Prima Facie Case*

The court finds that the plaintiff has failed to establish a *prima facie* case of improper discrimination under the ECOA. While the plaintiff has clearly proved that she is a member of a protected class and that she unsuccessfully applied for credit from the defendants, there is considerable question about whether she has demonstrated that she was qualified for a loan, and that males or married females of similar credit stature were given loans, or were treated more favorably than plaintiff in the application process.

For the purpose of evaluating her prima facie case only, the court resolves the question of the plaintiff's loan qualifications in her favor.

* * *

The court cannot resolve the question about plaintiff's proof of the fourth element of the *prima facie* case in her favor, however. Ms. Gross offered scant evidence to demonstrate that males or married females of similar credit stature were given loans, or were treated more favorably than her in the application process. Plaintiff's proof in regard to this element of her case was primarily concerned with the SBA's approval of a 1978 loan application made by a male, Pat Bombard, in the name of Pat Bombard Buick, Inc. Plaintiff asserts that this "male" application was similar to hers in amount and in that Bombard, like plaintiff, had had some credit problems. (The SBA loan officer's report on the Bombard application and on plaintiff's 1976 application indicated that the SBA was concerned with the "payment slowness" of both individuals.) Unfortunately for the plaintiff, the similarity ends here. First, Bombard's business was considerably different than that of the plaintiff. Bombard operated a retail automobile dealership. The SBA, or any other lender, would be concerned with Bombard's cost of carrying inventory, inventory turnover, inventory financing, etc. The plaintiff's business was, on the other hand, service oriented. Lenders would be concerned with a different set of data with respect to such a business. Second, and most important, the loan officer's report on Bombard's 1978 loan indicates that Bombard had overcome an earlier debt problem by selling financed property. There is no indication that plaintiff had overcome debt problems in a similar or other manner.

The plaintiff has failed to demonstrate that she and Bombard were of similar credit stature. Consequently, the court refuses to attach any significance to the fact that Bombard was granted a loan and the plaintiff was not. * * *

B. Legitimate Reasons for Plaintiff's Denial

Even if the court were to determine that plaintiff had established her *prima facie* case, the defendants have clearly met their burden of articulating legitimate, nondiscriminatory reasons for the denial of credit. The defendants offered an abundance of evidence to support their position that all of plaintiff's applications, including the 1978 reconsideration in issue here, were denied because the defendants rightfully considered the plaintiff to be a credit risk, not because of her sex or marital status.

When plaintiff applied for direct loans from the SBA in 1976, 1977, and 1978, she was delinquent on a SBA loan of $10,000 granted in 1968. Because plaintiff demonstrated an inability to timely make the relatively small debt service payments of $109 per month on this loan, the defendants were understandably concerned about her ability to make payments roughly tenfold that amount.

Moreover, a comparison of plaintiff's financial statements and accounting ratios derived therefrom with standard ratios for comparable real estate businesses demonstrates that the defendants' concern about plaintiff's repayment ability was understandable. Compared to other comparable businesses analyzed by Robert Morris Associates, plaintiff's business was highly leveraged in that debt to net worth ratios for the plaintiff's business were at least five times that of the reported average. It is easy to see that any lender, including the SBA, would be concerned with a loan applicant who was so heavily burdened.

* * *

In addition, the defendants were concerned about the plaintiff's management ability. They believed she overestimated her business' growth potential in the competitive real estate field. This overconfidence resulted in too rapid an expansion, which in turn resulted in debt that could not be serviced from income. A related concern was that plaintiff intended to use a large portion of SBA loan proceeds to service existing debt, an apparently ineligible use under SBA guidelines.

Finally, the defendants questioned the reliability of information supplied to the SBA by the plaintiff. For example, the income shown on the plaintiff's financial statements differed substantially from the income shown on her corresponding tax returns. Although the plaintiff offered some explanation for the discrepancies at trial, the court concludes that the defendants were reasonably concerned about the reliability of information supplied by Ms. Gross. Given the above, and the testimony of defendant Harrison that plaintiff's sex or marital status never entered into the SBA's consideration of her applications, the court determines that the defendants have proved that they had legitimate, non-discriminatory reasons for denying plaintiff's 1978 reconsideration request.

* * *

IV. CONCLUSION

The plaintiff has failed to establish a *prima facie* case of improper discrimination under the ECOA. Even if she had met that burden, the defendants have articulated legitimate, non-discriminatory reasons for her denial, which the plaintiff has failed to rebut. Judgment shall be entered on behalf of the defendants.

IT IS SO ORDERED.

Notes

1. Ms. Gross was applying for a business loan. Are business loans within the scope of the ECOA?

2. One court has noted that "creditor-lender transactions do not conveniently fit the scenario adopted in *McDonnell* to evaluate employment discrimination cases." Williams v. First Federal Savings & Loan Association, 554 F.Supp. 447, 450, (N.D.N.Y.1981), aff'd, 697 F.2d 302 (2d Cir.1982). Do you agree? Did the court in *Gross* properly articulate the test?

3. What additional evidence could Ms. Gross have presented to the court? Where would this information come from? Is she likely to be able to find any "males or married females of similar credit stature [who] were treated more favorably" than she was by this creditor? Would it help if she could show that after she was turned down by the SBA, she was granted credit from another creditor based on exactly the same information?

4. Assume that Ms. Gross had applied for a loan to open a pool hall. Assume also that she had presented evidence that the loan officer had said "women shouldn't be running pool halls." Would this be sufficient to establish a prima facie case under the disparate treatment test? What if all of the legitimate reasons (cited by the court) for denying her loan were still present? How should the test be applied if the lender's motives in denying the loan were mixed, that is, based partly on proper criteria (past performance on other loans) and partly on improper criteria (sexual stereotypes)? See Price Waterhouse v. Hopkins, 490 U.S. 228, 109 S.Ct. 1775, 104 L.Ed.2d 268 (1989).

5. REDLINING—DISCRIMINATION IN HOME MORTGAGE LENDING

NOTE, ATTACKING THE URBAN REDLINING PROBLEM

56 B.U.L.Rev. 989, 989–90, 996–97 (1976).*

The term "redlining" describes the process used by banks and other lending institutions in systematically refusing to grant mortgages and make home improvement loans in specific urban neighborhoods. When lenders redline, mortgage loans with reasonable terms often are not available for any house in a neighborhood, regardless of the creditworthiness of the borrower or the condition of the building. The logic behind this practice is that investment in neighborhoods that are undergoing the initial stages of deterioration involves an unjustifiable risk with depositors' money.

Redlining appears in a variety of forms. The most common of these is the outright denial of loans within a particular locale. More subtle, although frequently as effective, is the granting of a mortgage with substantially less favorable terms than might be available in a more desirable location. Thus, the lender might demand shorter repayment periods or higher interest rates, thereby requiring inflated monthly debt service payments. In other instances, the institution might offer a loan at a low loan to value ratio and thereby force the urban purchaser either to shoulder a greater downpayment or to negotiate a costly second mortgage elsewhere. Similarly, a lender might underappraise the value of the property, thus forcing the buyer to make up the difference between the deflated appraised value and the true selling price. Finally, the institution might actually relocate itself outside of the urban neighborhood, generally by establishing a branch office in a more desirable area and subsequently phasing out the original facility. Whatever form redlining takes, its effect is always the same—to dissuade buyers from investing in disfavored neighborhoods and to encourage them to look elsewhere.

Redlining can have a considerable impact upon an urban community. Neighborhood vitality bears a direct relationship to the adequate availability of mortgage credit. Because of the enormous costs involved, very few individuals can afford to buy or even repair a home with their savings alone. Thus, to a large extent, institutional lenders determine the futures of individual urban neighborhoods. Those neighborhoods that receive adequate funding will remain viable while those that do not are likely to decay. As a result, redlining can often be a self-fulfilling prophecy; frequently, a lender's fear that an area is on the decline ultimately causes that decline to occur.

* * *

The major effect of institutional redlining practices is to severely limit the availability of adequate mortgage credit in a community. In most instances, the neighborhoods being starved for credit are the very same neighborhoods from which the financial institutions that utilize the practice draw their deposits. Thus, local residents cannot draw upon their collective funds. Instead, these funds frequently provide the financing necessary for the development of distant suburban communities, areas that pose little risk and thereby provide desirable lending forums to the institutional lenders. This removal of capital from areas of collection to different areas for investment is technically known as "disinvestment."

* * *

Note

In addition to the ECOA, there are two other federal laws which prohibit redlining practices in certain housing loans. The first came with other post-civil war legislation as part of the Civil Rights Act of 1866, 42 U.S.C.A. § 1982:

Property rights of citizens. All citizens of the United States shall have the same right, in every State and Territory, as is enjoyed by white citizens thereof to inherit, purchase, lease, sell, hold and convey real and personal property.

The second, of more recent vintage, appeared with the wave of civil rights legislation in the 1960's. This is the Fair Housing Act, Title VIII of the Civil Rights Act of 1968, 42 U.S.C.A. § 3601 et seq. Section 3605 of this Act states:

Discrimination in financing of housing. After December 31, 1968, it shall be unlawful for any bank, building and loan association, insurance company or other corporation, association, firm or enterprise whose business consists in whole or in part in the making of commercial real estate loans, to deny a loan or other financial assistance to a person applying therefor for the purpose of purchasing, constructing, improving, repairing, or maintaining a dwelling, or to discriminate against him in the fixing of the amount, interest rate, duration, or other terms or conditions of such loan or other financial assistance, because of the race, color, religion, sex, or national origin of such person or any person associated with him in connection with such loan or other financial assistance or the purposes of such loan or financial assistance, or of the present or prospective owners, lessees, tenants, or occupants of the dwelling or dwellings in relation to which such loan or other financial assistance is to be made or given.

Consider the application of these statutes as you read the following materials.

Problem 18

Willie Acton grew up in the black ghetto of a large city. His athletic ability made him a basketball star in high school, but not quite good enough for college scholarship offers. There was also the matter of several juvenile arrests and convictions, one for assault and one for running numbers slips. After high school Willie joined the army and spent several years at various bases in the southwest. He got an honorable discharge and, as he put it, "I got my head on straight." Since his parents had separated he went to work as an apprentice electrician (hoping to develop skills learned in the service) for a company in Tucson, Arizona. Six months later he transferred to the company's Memphis, Tennessee, offices. A year after that he moved back to the city where he grew up, partly to be close to his sister, but also to take what he thought would be a better job. The job did not work out well—Willie's lack of seniority precluded promotion to jobs for which he thought he was qualified—so he moved to another minority-run company in the same city.

About this same time he married, and the couple rented a larger apartment closer to Willie's job in the inner city area. Willie's sense of frugality led him to maintain a modest savings account in a nearby savings and loan association.

About a year and a half later Willie and his wife thought it was about time they bought a house. Both of them agreed they wanted to stay in the downtown area, and they located a home for sale in Willie's old neighborhood. The house was about forty years old; it needed paint and a new roof, but it was spacious and the Actons could see all kinds of possibilities for renovating and redecorating it themselves.

But when the Actons applied to their savings and loan association for mortgage credit, they were turned down, politely but firmly. The loan officer told Willie that he didn't qualify on several grounds: (1) his prior criminal record; (2) his frequent job changes; (3) the unsuitability of the home as mortgage collateral, it being in a borderline area with generally deteriorating property values, and almost exclusively blue collar workers living there.

The Actons have hired your firm to represent them. What theories might you develop on their behalf? Be prepared to suggest what additional information would be needed to support your theories, and how you could obtain that information.

THOMAS v. FIRST FEDERAL SAV. BANK OF INDIANA

United States District Court, Northern District of Indiana, 1987.
653 F.Supp. 1330.

MOODY, DISTRICT JUDGE.

On Tuesday, January 20, 1987, a bench trial commenced in this action brought by plaintiffs James and Rosie Thomas and the Northwest Indiana Open Housing Center, Inc. (the "Center") against defendant First Federal Savings Bank of Indiana ("First Federal") and Joseph Kurpis a/k/a Rudy Kurpis, a vice president and loan officer for First Federal. Both plaintiffs and defendants were represented by counsel throughout the trial in this case. On Wednesday, January 21, 1987, plaintiffs rested their case and defendants, immediately thereafter, moved for an involuntary dismissal pursuant to Fed.R.Civ.P. 41(b); the court took defendants' dismissal motion under advisement. On Thursday, January 23, 1987, after considering all the evidence and having determined the credibility of witnesses based on their respective demeanor and interests, the Court GRANTED defendants' 41(b) dismissal motion. The court now renders the following Findings of Fact and Conclusions of Law pursuant to Fed.R.Civ.P. 52(a).

I.

Findings of Fact

Plaintiffs alleged that defendants discriminated against the Thomases based on their race and "red-lined" the neighborhood where the Thomases lived in violation of the Fair Housing Act, 42 U.S.C. §§ 3604 and 3605, the Civil Rights Act of 1866, 42 U.S.C. §§ 1981 and 1982, and the Equal Credit Opportunity Act, 15 U.S.C. §§ 1691, et seq.

Plaintiffs James and Rosie Thomas are black citizens of the United States residing in Gary, Indiana. The plaintiff Center is a not-for-profit corporation organized under the laws of Indiana and supported by private contributions, foundation grants and contracts with certain cities. The purpose of the organization is to further the goals of the Fair Housing Act and to promote equal opportunity in housing in northwest Indiana. The Center's activities include referral services, housing and financial counseling to minority homeseekers, investigation of complaints of housing discrimination and legal representation in actions involving discrimination.

Defendant First Federal is a mutual thrift institution chartered under section 5 of the Homeowners Loan Act of 1933, 12 U.S.C. §§ 1461 et seq. As such, First Federal is subject to the constitution and laws of the United States and to all rules, regulations and orders issued by the Federal Home Loan Bank Board ("Bank Board"). Defendant Rudy Kurpis is, and was at the time of the incidents herein, a vice president and loan officer for First Federal.

On March 29, 1984, James Thomas went to the main office of First Federal located at 545 Broadway, Gary, Indiana to apply for a loan with the intention of using the money to pay off a $6,000.00 balance owing on a conditional sales contract for the purchase of real estate property located at 742 Johnson Street, Gary, Indiana and to make some necessary repairs on that property. The 742 property is located next door to the Thomases' residence which is located at 756 Johnson Street, Gary, Indiana. Mr. Thomas met with Mr. Kurpis and, after one discussion, Thomas decided to apply for a second mortgage on his residence at 756 Johnson in the amount of $7,100.00.

A loan application was filled out by Kurpis with information provided by Thomas. Both James and Rosie Thomas were applicants for the loan and were to be liable under the mortgage note. Because the Thomases planned to use their home at 756 Johnson as collateral for the loan, Kurpis explained that First Federal required an appraisal of the property.

After the Thomases paid an application fee of $200.00, Kurpis informed them that a real estate appraiser would be sent to their home on a particular date. There was some confusion about the exact location and time of the scheduled appraisal and it was not until the third scheduling that the appraiser showed up.

At that third appointment, Mr. Thomas met Mr. Beckham who was employed by First Federal for 25 years as its in-house and chief appraiser. Beckham was deceased at the time of trial. Thomas testified that he showed Beckham the entire house and pointed out to him the many renovations and improvements that the Thomases had made to their home. * * * After completing the tour of the house, Mr. Thomas testified that Beckham told him that if the house were located anywhere else it would be worth $100,000.00 and that the Thomases should have no problem getting the $7,100.00 loan.

Approximately two to three weeks after Beckham had visited their residence, the Thomases had not heard from First Federal on the status of their loan application. Rosie Thomas called Kurpis and was informed that their loan application had been denied because their loan-to-value ratio had exceeded First Federal's guidelines. Kurpis further explained that there was no reason for the loan application to go before First Federal's loan committee for additional review because it would be denied on the basis of the loan-to-value ratio.

The Thomases had a first mortgage on their home at 756 Johnson of approximately $17,000.00 and they were requesting a second mortgage of $7,100.00. The total mortgage debt, had the loan been approved, would have been $24,100.00. Beckham appraised the 756 Johnson property at $22,000.00. When comparing the total mortgage debt, $24,100.00, to the appraised value of the property, $22,000.00, the loan-to-value ratio ($24,100.00 divided by $22,000.00) was over 105%. First Federal's guidelines for loan approval required that the loan-to-value ratio be 80% or less.

The Thomases received an "adverse action" letter from First Federal, dated June 26, 1984, signed by Rudolph Kurpis, which stated that the reason their application had been denied was that the "value of Property ratio to Mtg., 1st & 2nd. exceeded 105% Policy is 80%."

*   *   *

At trial, plaintiffs offered the testimony of another real estate appraiser, George Wilkes, who appraised the value of their home at 756 Johnson. Wilkes testified that he had been in the real estate appraisal business, in northwest Indiana, for over 13 years. However, he admitted that he was not a registered member of any recognized society of appraisers. Wilkes appraised the Thomases' home on January 10, 1987, at $40,000.00; *   *   *.

Wilkes testified that there are essentially three "accepted" methods used by appraisers: (1) cost approach; (2) market sales approach; and (3) income approach. *   *   * The market sales approach, perhaps the most commonly employed method, involves a comparison between the subject property and "comparable" pieces of property, usually three in number. *   *   *

Wilkes was critical of Beckham's appraisal and took exception with many of Beckham's adjustments in his comparable sales analysis.

*   *   *

Wilkes provided no testimony whatsoever on the intent of Beckham, Kurpis, or First Federal when making appraisals and processing loan applications. Wilkes' testimony, at best, established that he did not approve of many of Beckham's subjective determinations, however, Wilkes admitted that Beckham was consistent in making his evaluations; that is, there was no evidence that Beckham appraised an individual's home or a home in a particular neighborhood any differently than others similarly situated.

Additionally, Wilkes testified that it was quite possible that the Thomases' home was "overimproved" for the neighborhood it was in.

*   *   *

*   *   *

II.

Conclusions of Law

*   *   *

Plaintiffs alleged violations of the Federal Housing Act, 42 U.S.C. § 3604 and 3605; the Equal Credit Opportunity Act, 15 U.S.C. §§ 1691 *et seq.;* and the Civil Rights Act of 1866, 42 U.S.C. §§ 1981 and 1982. In making its conclusions of law, the court will address the statutory violations in turn.

A.

Fair Housing Act

* * *

Initially, the court finds that a fair and liberal reading of plaintiffs' complaint in this action reveals two separate theories of recovery under the Fair Housing Act. First, plaintiffs allege that defendants discriminated individually against the Thomases' by denying their loan application on the basis of their race. Second, plaintiffs' complaint alleges that defendants denied the Thomases' loan application because of First Federal's practice of "red-lining" the Thomases' neighborhood. Red-lining is defined as "mortgage credit discrimination based on the characteristics of the neighborhood surrounding the would-be borrower's dwelling."

* * *

[T]he court holds that in order for plaintiffs to establish a prima facie case of racial discrimination under section 3605, they must prove (1) that they were members of a protected class; (2) that they applied and were qualified for a loan from defendants; (3) that the loan was rejected despite their qualifications; and (4) that defendants continued to approve loans for applicants with qualifications similar to plaintiffs.

Applying this standard to the facts as presented by plaintiffs at trial, the court finds that plaintiffs failed to establish a case under section 3605. Plaintiffs satisfied elements (1) and (3) in that they demonstrated that the Thomases, as black citizens, were members of a protected class and that they were denied a loan. However, plaintiffs failed to present any credible evidence on whether the Thomases were qualified for the loan or that First Federal made loans to other applicants who had similar qualifications.

One of First Federal's requirements for loan applicants is that their loan-to-value ratio, based on the appraised value of the collateral for the loan, be 80% or less. The Thomases did not meet First Federal's standard as their ratio was computed to be in excess of 105%. Plaintiffs do not dispute or challenge the legitimacy of First Federal's guideline of 80%; instead, they argue that First Federal undervalued the Thomases' home in violation of the Fair Housing Act. Plaintiffs maintain that First Federal undervalued the Thomas home because of their race or, alternatively, because First Federal red-lined their neighborhood.

In theory, the court agrees that a defendant cannot escape liability under the Fair Housing Act by artificially lowering the appraised value of a home for a prohibited reason like race. Plaintiffs need not prove actual intent to discriminate on the part of defendants in order to make out a violation of the Fair Housing Act. However, plaintiffs must show that "race was a motivating consideration in the [defendants'] decision" not to make the loan.

* * *

Here, after plaintiffs presented all their evidence, they still had not shown that defendants' knowledge of the Thomases' race contributed in any degree to either defendants' decision not to make the loan or in appraising the Thomas home.

* * *

In support of their red-lining theory, plaintiffs rely heavily upon the alleged statement by Beckham to James Thomas that if the Thomas home were anywhere else it would be worth $100,000.00. * * * Wilkes testified that it was quite possible that the Thomas home was "overimproved" for the neighborhood. Thus, even assuming that Beckham made such a statement, the court finds that the most logical inference to draw is that Beckham was referring to the overimproved condition of the Thomas home when compared with other houses in the area.

Finally, plaintiffs attempted to present statistical evidence, presumably in support of their red-lining theory. This evidence consisted entirely of the mortgage loan disclosure statements prepared by First Federal for the years 1983 and 1984 pursuant to the Home Mortgage Disclosure Act, 12 U.S.C. §§ 2801 *et seq.* and 12 C.F.R. §§ 203.1 *et seq.* These reports show the number and the amounts of the loans issued by First Federal in 1983 and 1984. The reports break the information down by the types of loans (*e.g.*, FHA, FmHA and VA; conventional; home improvement; multi-family dwellings; and non-occupant loans) and the community (*e.g.*, Gary, East Chicago, Hammond, and the remainder of Lake County). Reading these reports allows the court to compare both the number and the dollar amounts of loans made by First Federal in Gary, based on the type of loans, with loans made in East Chicago, Hammond and the remainder of Lake County.

It appears from this presentation that plaintiffs attempted to prove their claim under a "disparate impact" analysis. That such an avenue of recovery is available in the context of the Fair Housing Act was made clear by the Seventh Circuit * * *.

The court holds that plaintiffs' statistical evidence is not sufficient as a matter of law to establish a violation of section 3605. Plaintiffs' attorneys offered no explanation of the meaning of these figures, they made no attempt to present evidence which would allow the court to draw any inferences from them. This evidence, standing alone, does not establish that race played any part in First Federal's decisions to make loans to people in Gary; no reasonable inferences can be drawn in that direction. Although section 3605's red-lining prohibition makes it illegal to discriminate on the basis of certain characteristics of the plaintiff's neighborhood (*e.g.*, race, color, religion, sex or national origin), there are numerous legitimate business factors that go into a decision to make a loan which do not form the basis of a violation under section 3605. * * * The loan-to-value ratio was the dispositive factor in First Federal's decision to deny the loan. Such a factor is a legitimate business criterion and its use is not a violation of section 3605.

After considering all of plaintiffs' evidence, the court finds that the strength of their statistical evidence was nonexistent; that defendants had a legitimate business interest and basis for denying the loan; and that there was no evidence, apart from the conclusory statements by the Thomases, demonstrating a discriminatory intent on the part of defendants.

The incomplete and disjointed nature of the statistical evidence here fairly characterizes plaintiffs' presentation of their case in general. Throughout the two days of testimony plaintiffs' counsel never articulated a complete and coherent theory of recovery. The erratic nature of their presentation was exacerbated by plaintiffs' counsels' apparent lack of preparation and unfamiliarity with the Federal Rules of Evidence. The court recognizes that the substantive issues in redlining cases can be complex and are often difficult to prove, especially when a plaintiff relies on statistical evidence.

But the complaint in this case was originally filed over two years ago, in October of 1984, which means plaintiffs had ample time to adequately prepare for trial. This is especially true because plaintiffs did not spend any time or energy trying to negotiate or otherwise resolve their dispute with First Federal before filing suit. Given the plaintiff Center's stated goal of enhancing the cooperation between the Center and local landlords and financial lending institutions, *Davis v. Mansards,* 597 F.Supp. 334, 348 (N.D.Ind.1984), it would make more sense for the Center to contact a potential defendant at least once in an effort to resolve their dispute before rushing to trial.

* * * [T]he court GRANTS defendants judgment on plaintiffs' Fair Housing Act claims.

B.

Equal Credit Opportunity Act

Plaintiffs also alleged violations of the Equal Credit Opportunity Act ("ECOA").

* * *

As discussed earlier, there was no evidence at trial that the Thomases were treated any differently than other loan applicants by First Federal. The overwhelming evidence at trial established that First Federal neither intentionally discriminated against the Thomases nor that the effect of First Federal's loan practices had an impermissible adverse impact on black applicants. *See Cherry v. Amoco Oil Co.* (applying disparate impact analysis to the ECOA). Accordingly, the court GRANTS defendants judgment on plaintiffs' ECOA claims.

C.

Section 1981 and 1982

Finally, Thomases alleged that First Federal discriminated against them because of their race violating 42 U.S.C. §§ 1981 and 1982 regarding equal rights under the law.

* * *

To prevail on a claim under either section 1981 or 1982, plaintiffs must prove intentional discrimination on the part of defendants. Again, as discussed previously, the evidence at trial made no showing of intentional discrimination on the part of defendants. Because plaintiffs adduced no direct proof of discriminatory intent they seem to rely, once again, on indirect proof.

The court holds that the overwhelming evidence at trial established that First Federal's loan practices did not have an impermissible adverse impact on black applicants. Therefore, the court GRANTS defendants judgment on plaintiffs' section 1981 and 1982 claims.

CONCLUSION

Based on the foregoing, the court finds that defendants should prevail on all of plaintiffs' claims and it is hereby ADJUDGED that plaintiffs take nothing by their complaint. The Clerk of the Court is directed to ENTER JUDGMENT in favor of defendants.

Notes

1. What are the differences in proof required in cases brought under § 1982, the ECOA, and the FHA? Why would a plaintiff bother to allege violations of all three statutes when the basic issue, discrimination, is the same?

2. In a companion case, Evans v. First Federal Savings Bank of Indiana, 669 F.Supp. 915 (N.D.Ind.1987), the court noted that to state a case under § 1982, the plaintiff must show that the defendant' conduct impaired a property interest. The court held that procurement of financing is a protected property interest sufficient for the purpose, and the plaintiffs survived a motion to dismiss as to this portion of the complaint. But having a property interest in one thing; proving discrimination is quite another. Based on the result in *Thomas,* how do you think this claim will come out in the end?

3. As in the cases we studied earlier in this chapter under the ECOA, the plaintiffs in *Thomas* tried to prove their case using both the disparate treatment and the disparate impact (effects) tests. They failed in both. Why? What were the weaknesses in their case? What evidence would you suggest to overcome these weaknesses? Where and how would you go about gathering this evidence?

4. A practice often complained of by neighborhood groups is that of housing insurance redlining. Obviously the inability to obtain insurance can be just as great an impediment to housing availability as can the inability to obtain financing. Is insurance redlining prohibited by any of

the federal laws we have studied in this chapter? See Mackey v. Nationwide Insurance Companies, 724 F.2d 419 (4th Cir.1984).

5. In *Thomas*, the court referred to data gathered by the plaintiffs through the Home Mortgage Disclosure Act of 1975, 12 U.S.C.A. § 2801 et seq. This Act requires all depository lending institutions to compile and make available to the public the number and total dollar amount of all mortgage loans for each fiscal year, grouped according to census tract or zip code area. The theory is that individuals and groups, by analyzing the data, will be able to discover redlining practices and use public pressure, deposit withdrawals, or other means to attack offensive practices. A related statute is the Community Reinvestment Act of 1977, 12 U.S.C.A. § 2901 et seq. This Act requires financial supervisory agencies to consider, in their periodic and other reviews of financial institutions, whether these institutions are meeting the credit needs of the entire community, including low- and moderate-income neighborhoods. This can be done when new institutions apply for charters, when existing institutions merge with others or open branches, or during the course of ordinary examinations.

Do you think either of these statutes is likely to have much impact? From time to time, community groups are able to gather data under the HMDA and use it through the CRA to intervene in regulatory proceedings involving mergers or other activities of lending institutions in their areas. Often the process is essentially political; a group might simply present the information and then threaten to bog down the regulatory process until the institution makes a commitment to lend in poor neighborhoods. Enforcement by regulatory agencies themselves, however, is another matter. The Associated Press reported in February, 1989, that the Federal Reserve Board had rejected a request by a large Chicago bank to purchase a small Arizona bank because it had not met its responsibilities under the CRA. The story also noted that this was the first time the Board had ever penalized a bank for failure to comply with the CRA.

6. In addition to the various statutes, there are many federal regulations which prohibit redlining practices. These regulations apply not only to lending, but also to advertising, appraisal, and other services. See 12 C.F.R. parts 27, 338, and 528. As to appraisals, the regulations state that a lender may not rely on an appraisal which it knows or should know "is discriminatory on the basis of the age or location of the dwelling." 12 C.F.R. § 528.2a(a). Would this help in a case like *Thomas*?

7. For more on redlining in general, see R. Schafer and H. Ladd, Discrimination in Mortgage Lending (1981). See also Wisniewski, Mortgage Redlining (Disinvestment): The Parameters of Federal, State and Municipal Regulation, 54 U.Det.J.Urb.L. 367 (1977).

Effectiveness of Anti–Redlining Laws

How effective are anti-redlining laws? Do you think they actually reduce discrimination in housing loans? On January 22, 1989, the Atlanta Journal–Constitution sent shock waves through the nation's mortgage industry by reporting that black applicants are rejected by savings and loan institutions more than twice as often as white applicants. The newspaper analyzed records involving 10 million loan applications (for $1 trillion in loans) at 3100 institutions, all across the country, between 1983 and 1988. The records showed that racially discriminatory redlining practices have not only persisted, but seem to have grown worse during the 1980s. Some of the findings were:

— High-income blacks are rejected at the same rate as low-income whites.

— Rejection rates in integrated neighborhoods (at least 25% minority) penalize both white and black applicants; applicants (of all races) in high-income integrated areas are rejected at the same rate as applicants in poor white neighborhoods.

— The disparities exist throughout the country, although they were highest in the midwest and plains states (where blacks were rejected 2½ times more often than whites), and lowest in northeast (1½ times).

— The disparities did not reflect any pattern which could be correlated to city size, percent of minority population, or income gap between whites and blacks.

— Race is a much better predictor of the success of a loan application than sex or marital status (i.e., apparent racial discrimination is much higher than apparent discrimination based on sex or marital status).

Of course, data involving rejected applications do not, by themselves, prove systematic discrimination. (Do you see why?) Nevertheless, these findings are very disturbing; they suggest an enormous problem in the lending practices of institutions throughout the United States.

The findings of the Atlanta Journal–Constitution have been confirmed by other studies. On the specific issue of redlining, the Federal Reserve Bank of Boston reported on August 31, 1989, the results of a study it had done on mortgage lending practices in Boston between 1982 and 1987. This report noted that the percentage of loans made in predominately black neighborhoods was "significantly lower" (only half the rate) than that in white neighborhoods.

In July of 1989, a report was released on a major study of racial inequality and trends in the overall society during the past four decades. This report, "A Common Destiny: Blacks and American Society," noted that blacks are more likely than whites to be excluded from buying or renting housing in certain residential areas, to be quoted higher prices, and to be "steered" toward segregated areas.

Federal enforcement policies have also contributed to the problem. For example, during the 1980s the Reagan administration significantly decreased enforcement of the ECOA, FHA, and other anti-discrimination laws. Regulatory agencies have the authority to refer cases of credit discrimination to the Justice Department for prosecution, but none has done so for more than a decade. The information obtained by the Atlanta Journal–Constitution has been available in agency files and computers for years, but apparently no one ever bothered to analyze it before.

Question

As a result of the Atlanta Journal–Constitution story, many expressions of outrage and calls for investigation have been voiced by civil rights advocates and politicians. What do you think should be done about all this? If you were counsel for a Congressional committee looking into the problem, what would you recommend? Should the law be amended? How? (Is the problem one of law?) If you were counsel for a bank or other mortgage lender, what would you recommend, if anything, as a response to the reports cited above?

SECTION C. AN EVALUATION OF THE COSTS AND BENEFITS OF REGULATION OF ACCESS TO THE MARKET

Before the amendment of ECOA to require disclosure of reasons for adverse action, Congress was treated to the following before-the-fact estimate of the cost of actually giving reasons for adverse action:

> Sears Roebuck and Company stated that its annual estimated cost for such compliance would be approximately $5 per letter.   *   *   * Even if all creditors could operate as efficiently as Sears, the aggregate annual cost of this requirement could easily amount to hundreds of millions of dollars. The requirement is staggeringly inflationary.

Testimony of National Retail Merchants Association, Hearings on S. 483, S. 1900, S. 1927, S. 1961, and H.R. 6516, Subcommittee on Consumer Affairs, U.S. Senate Committee on Banking, Housing and Urban Affairs 399 (1975).

After enactment, the Federal Reserve Board surveyed actual costs of furnishing rejected applicants with statements of reasons for adverse action under Reg. B § 202.9. In addition, it also surveyed the actual costs of married persons' rights to have separate credit histories for joint accounts under Reg. B § 202.10; and the costs of handling disputes with credit card holders under FCBA and Reg. Z § 226.14.

BOARD OF GOVERNORS OF THE FEDERAL RESERVE SYSTEM, "EXERCISE OF CONSUMER RIGHTS UNDER THE EQUAL CREDIT OP-PORTUNITY AND FAIR CREDIT BILLING ACTS"

64 Fed.Res.Bull. 363 (1978).

In November 1977 the Board of Governors initiated a survey of selected large creditors to determine to what extent consumers were exercising their rights under the Equal Credit Opportunity Act and the Fair Credit Billing Act. The survey was also designed to determine the cost to creditors of complying with these laws.   *   *   *

In order to obtain information from a national cross-section of consumers with a minimum burden on the consumer credit industry, the Board selected nine large creditors that were believed to have readily available records. ＊ ＊ ＊

SEPARATE CREDIT HISTORY

Under Regulation B married persons have the right to a separate credit history. All creditors with open-end credit contracts were required to send a notice advising their married customers of this right by June 1, 1977, unless the company already had arranged to maintain access to the account records for each person entitled to use the account. ＊ ＊ ＊

The total initial mailing of somewhat less than 48.5 million notices by the seven companies yielded more than 5 million returns (about 11 per cent) from customers who requested the maintenance of separate credit histories. ＊ ＊ ＊

1. Separate credit history

Creditor	Notices				
	Number sent	Number of return requests	Percentage resulting in requests	Total cost (dollars)	Average cost per notice sent (dollars)
Federated Department Stores	5,600,536	471,875	8.4	64,880	.012
J.C. Penney	10,252,692	818,659	8.0	64,556	.006
Sears	23,000,000	3,000,000	13.0	68,095	.003
Bank of America	3,130,529	326,783	10.4	88,697	.028
First National Bank of Chicago	861,453	82,561	9.6	5,000	.006
Maryland National Bank	1,056,365	77,501	7.3	23,940	.023
Shell Oil	4,500,000	430,000	9.6	45,000	.010
American Express [1]	. . .	. . .	. . .	. . .	. . .

	Cost of dual reporting of credit records, in dollars					
	Processing initial requests	Reporting new information	Total for initial returns	Average initial cost per account	Cost of reporting new accounts per account	Annual maintenance cost of dual reporting per account
Federated Department Stores	31,575	[2]62,466	94,041	.20	.00 to 1.50	[3]39,825
J.C. Penney	12,061	31,614	43,675	.05	Negligible	Negligible
Sears	[1]94,134	55,555	149,689	.05	.01	88,667
Bank of America	55,543	36,744	92,287	.28	.10	3,600
First National Bank of Chicago	6,571	13,571	20,142	.24	.14	23,880
Maryland National Bank	22,392	5,470	27,862	.36	.12	13,600
Shell Oil	19,700	9,900	29,600	.07	Negligible	3,000
American Express [4]	. . .	. . .	. . .	. . .	. . .	

1. American Express provides separate access to its credit records for each credit-card holder and, therefore, was not required to send a special notice.

2. Excludes two divisions that maintain manual operations and report to credit-reporting agencies only on demand.

3. Represents estimates from only five divisions.

4. Reported as additional cost, estimated at $900,000, of annotating history record cards to reflect the requested changes.

Direct cost estimates for the nearly 50 million notices sent totaled $360,168; however, since some companies were unable to identify and include all administrative costs, this figure accounted for only a portion of the total cost. Furthermore, Penney's noted that the inclusion of the required notice with the billing statement displaced advertising inserts, which resulted in a loss of sales estimated at $665,000. * * * Although all of the reporting companies enclosed the required notice with the monthly billing statement, Bank of America noted that it had spent $68,000 to mail the notice separately to inactive BankAmericard accounts.

The identifiable costs of printing, processing, and mailing each notice averaged slightly less than 1 cent. There was considerable variation among the companies, however, with the average identifiable cost per notice ranging from a low of 0.3 cent to a high of 2.8 cents.

Processing the more than 5 million returns and initially reporting the new information to the credit-reporting agencies cost a little more than $450,000 for the seven companies, or an average of about 9 cents per request. * * *

Once the reporting of credit records on a dual basis for existing accounts had been completed, the cost of reporting new accounts on that basis ranged from "negligible" or "nominal" to about 14 cents per account. Federated Department Stores reported a range from "negligible" to $1.50 for its divisions. The cost of maintaining dual reporting varied widely, from "negligible" to nearly $89,000 a year. * * * [M]aintaining any dual reporting system may involve a significant element of fixed cost or that the wide variation in reporting maintenance costs may be the result of the different approaches used in estimating costs.

ADVERSE ACTION NOTICES

The revisions in Regulation B that became effective June 1, 1977, required creditors to inform rejected credit applicants of the reasons for the denial either initially or upon request. Sears, First National Bank of Chicago, Bank of America, and 1 of the 13 divisional respondents of Federated Department Stores furnished all rejected credit applicants with the reasons for the adverse action at the time of the denial. The other companies provided reasons for denial only upon request. Maryland National Bank received such requests from 12 per cent of rejected applicants; Federated Department Stores, from 20 per cent; and American Express, from 23 percent. Shell stated that each month about 4,600 rejected applicants requested the specific reasons for the denial.

Many of the rejected credit applicants who were initially given reasons for credit denial supplied additional information, and a high proportion of these were then granted credit. * * *

2. Adverse action on applications for credit

Creditor	Applicants rejected for credit who			Average cost per account of providing reasons for credit denial (dollars)	
	Requested reasons for denial (per cent)	Were given reason, then provided more information (per cent of col. 1)	Provided more information and were given credit (per cent of col. 2)	Initially	Upon request
	(1)	(2)	(3)	(4)	(5)
Federated Department Stores	20	34	26	[1].43	22 to 5.25
J.C. Penney	([2])	n.a.	n.a.	. . .	.56
Sears	[3]100	4	59	.59	. . .
Bank of America	[3]100	8	75	1.07	2.20
First National Bank of Chicago	[3]100	([4])	33	.60	. . .
Maryland National Bank	12	45	35	. . .	4.14
Shell Oil	([5])	70	72	.55	.38
American Express	23	30	60	1.75	3.00 to 5.25

1. Represents an estimate by one division only.

2. Approximately 13.3 per cent wrote to J.C. Penney regarding their rejection, but it is not known how many asked for specific reasons.

3. All rejected credit applicants were given the reasons initially.

4. Approximately 3,000 of the 8,600 rejected applicants per month requested reconsideration, and some provided additional information.

5. Approximately 4,600 rejected applicants per month requested specific reasons for denial.

n.a.—Not available.

3. Experience with fair credit billing

Creditor	Average number of active accounts billed monthly	Average number of billing statement inquiries	Billing statement inquiries (per cent)	Number of formal inquiries asserted monthly	Annual cost of billing error statements (dollars)
Federated Department Stores	3,366,000	86,000	2.55	4,400	[1]47,447
J.C. Penney	12,082,395	113,575	.94	n.a.	[2]7,308
Sears	18,600,000	n.a.	n.a.	9,167	([3])
Bank of America	2,464,469	119,164	4.84	3,047	([3])
First National Bank of Chicago	901,000	57,000	6.33	5,000	([3])
Maryland National Bank	301,000	2,606	.87	134	([3])
Shell Oil	3,500,000	37,000	1.06	1,150	[4]67,300
American Express	3,800,000	86,000	2.26	n.a.	[5]25,760

1. Represents estimate of printing costs only for monthly mailing.

2. The billing error statement is printed on the back of the billing statement and the costs reported are those for printing the full billing statement provided to those persons who raise billing inquiries.

3. The billing error statement is printed on the back of the billing statement and no specific costs were reported.

4. Mails the statement semiannually but estimates that mailing the shorter monthly statement would cost $347,000 per year.

5. Represents estimate of printing costs only for mailing semiannual statements.

n.a.—Not available.

Federated Department Stores estimated that about one-third of those requesting reasons for credit denial during the first 7 months after the revised Regulation B went into effect provided additional information, and in one-fourth of these cases credit was granted. The highest proportions were shown by Shell; almost 70 per cent of those requesting specific reasons supplied additional information, and in three-fourths of those cases credit was granted (Table 2).

The cost of providing reasons for the denial of credit to the rejected applicants varied widely. For the three companies that provided reasons initially, the average cost per rejected account ranged from 59 cents to $1.07. For the other companies the average cost of responding to specific requests for reasons for credit denial varied from 22 cents to $5.25.

Billing Inquiries

A considerable number of credit customers raised questions concerning their billing statements each month (Table 3). The extent of the increase in the number of customer inquiries since the billing-error sections were incorporated into Regulation Z is not known, but the figures reported by the eight creditors for recent months showed that the proportion of monthly billing statements questioned ranged from about 1 per cent for Penney's, Maryland National Bank, and Shell to about 5 per cent for Bank of America and 6 per cent for the First National Bank of Chicago. Only a small proportion of these questions were submitted according to the formal procedures provided by Regulation Z, but most of the companies indicated that they had treated all questions alike, whether presented in a formal or informal manner.

Notes

1. What would account for the wide difference between the $5.00 estimate and the 59¢ actual cost to Sears of an adverse action letter? Before you assume that there was any intentional misrepresentation, consider the difference in the quality of thinking about cost minimization by a Sears attorney before enactment of the legislation and the thinking about cost minimization by professional managers after enactment.

2. Whatever the reason for the differences between cost estimates and actual costs, what is the likely effect upon Sears, credibility before future legislative or agency hearings?

Attempting a Cost-benefit Analysis

The previous materials have analyzed only the costs related to the applicable regulations, and that is but one-half of the equation involved in a cost-benefit analysis.

Problem 19

Can you compare the costs and benefits of adverse action notices from the data in the Federal Reserve Bulletin, supra, at least as to the stores surveyed? Could you do so with further data? The data in the article include the average cost per account of the notices, and the proportion of rejected applicants who requested reasons for denial. However, in only two instances, in the footnotes, are actual numbers of requests given. Would such actual numbers be necessary for your analysis?

On the benefit side, the data provide percentage figures which allow computation of the proportion of consumers receiving notices who were given credit after being rejected. Are the percentages of consumers who exercise their rights high or low? Does this level of consumer activity justify the costs involved? Do you have enough data to make cost-benefit calculations? How do you value, in dollar terms, the ability to obtain credit—especially after a denial? It may be a blessing to most, but a disaster to some. What is the worth, in dollar terms, to a rejected person of being given reasons for denial of their credit application? In purely economic terms, that may depend upon whether the reasons can be overcome or not, but surely that analysis does not measure psychological factors.

In other words, is any attempt to compare costs and benefits of regulation likely to depend ultimately upon some evaluation of subjective, non-economic factors?

Chapter 5

ABUSES DURING PERFORMANCE

SECTION A. PAYMENT SCHEDULES AND CHARGES

1. PENALTIES AND REBATES FOR PREPAYMENT OR AC-CELERATION

Consumer debts often get prepaid. Prepayment may come voluntarily, as when the consumer simply pays off early, or involuntarily, as when the creditor accelerates the debt after default. Or, it may happen as the result of a refinancing or the like.

Today, we think of the debtor's right to prepay and the creditor's right to accelerate as routine incidents of the consumer credit relationship. Yet, neither of these options existed at common law. The debtor had no right to prepay a debt unless there was a contract provision or a statute which permitted it. See, e.g., Davis v. Hinton, 519 S.W.2d 776 (Tenn.1975). (Why would a creditor refuse to take full payment from a debtor who wanted to give it?) Today, most states have statutory provisions which expressly give the debtor the right to prepay most consumer debts. The U3C provision is typical; see U3C § 2.509. Even when no statute applies to a given transaction, a clause permitting prepayment (usually for a fee) is routinely included.

Acceleration is similar. Unless there is a clause in the contract giving him the right to do so, a creditor normally may not accelerate a debt simply because the debtor defaults on a single payment. Today, of course, acceleration clauses are commonplace. (See chapter 8, infra, for consideration of some problems surrounding the exercise of acceleration clauses.)

Prepayment by any means, whether through voluntary prepayment, acceleration, or refinancing, means that the transaction stops short of its original time schedule. This, in turn, has an effect on finance charges. The most important effect is that not all of the finance charges will have been earned as of the point of prepayment. This naturally raises the question whether the creditor must give the debtor some sort of rebate to account for these unearned charges. The answer means real dollars to the consumer, either as a deduction from the balance owing or as a credit on the refinanced obligation. Today, most states require that the creditor rebate unearned finance charges. Again, the U3C is typical; see § 2.510. But what proportion of a precomputed finance charge is "earned" by the creditor at any given point along the payment schedule? At first glance it might seem logical that if a consumer prepays a loan midway through its term, the consumer should get a rebate or credit of half the finance charge. But a creditor earns the finance charge not in proportion to the amount of time that has expired, but in proportion to the amount of money outstanding during a given period of time.

For an example, assume an obligation whose face amount is $1296, consisting of $1200 principal and $96 interest at 8% add-on (14.45% APR), payable in twelve equal monthly installments of $108. During the first month the consumer has the use of the full $1200 of principal. During the second month (assuming debtor repays $100 of principal), the consumer has the use of $1100; during the third month, $1,000, and so on. During these first few months, therefore, the creditor bears the greatest risk. Conversely, in the last three months, the consumer has the use of only $300, $200, and $100, respectively, of the creditor's funds. As a result, the creditor calculates that at the end of six months much more than half the agreed-upon finance charge has been "earned." If the consumer prepays at this point, the finance charge "rebate" will be a relatively small sum.

One method of calculating earned interest is the so-called "Rule of 78s," which takes its name from the sum of the digits 1 through 12. When the Rule of 78s is applied to the example above, consisting of $1200 principal and $96 finance charge, in the first month the creditor earns 12/78ths of the agreed on interest, or $14.77. After two months the creditor has earned 23/78th, the first 12/78ths plus 11/78ths. In the third month the creditor earns an additional 10/78ths. After six months, the creditor calculates earnings of $70.15, or 57/78ths of $96. Prepayment after six months will therefore produce a rebate of only $25.85.

The Rule of 78s is overly simplistic, because it assumes repayment of an equal amount of principal each month. A true actuarial computation, by contrast, would apply each monthly payment first to accrued interest, and then to principal reduction. Actuarially, in the above example, of the consumer's first payment of $108, $14.45 would be treated as earned interest, and $93.55 credited toward principal. Of the second payment, $12.20 would be interest and $95.80 would be principal reduction. This more precise method would produce a rebate after six months of $26.47—slightly higher than that calculated by the Rule of 78s.

Although these methods involve some fairly intricate mathematical calculations, students ought to be able to appreciate the principles involved without retaking mathematics courses. An exquisite exposition of the various computational methods, and of their dollars and cents consequences, may be found in Hunt, "The Rule of 78: Hidden Penalty for Prepayment in Consumer Credit Transactions," 55 B.U.L. Rev. 331 (1975). Mr. Hunt's point is that, while the Rule of 78s is relatively easy to use, it produces somewhat smaller rebates than a true actuarial computation. Further, although it is relatively close to actuarial computations for one, two or three year loans, it is much more inaccurate (and favorable to the creditor) for loans of longer than four years.

All of this raises a number of legal questions:

(a) Should the law permit creditors to use an easier though less generous method of calculating rebates on prepayment? Would it make sense to require use of the actuarial method in longer-term transactions where the distortions may be greater? See U3C § 2.510(1), (4) and (5). In recent years, a few states have amended their consumer credit laws to require creditors to use the actuarial method in some or all transactions. See, e.g., Kan.Stat.Ann. § 16a–2–510(3) (actuarial method must be used in all consumer transactions after July 1, 1988); Idaho Code § 28–42–307(3) (actuarial method must be used for loans over 61 installments).

(b) When a creditor accelerates a defaulted debt, the consumer will almost certainly not "prepay" the whole accelerated balance immediately. It may be necessary for the creditor to sue, which may take months or longer before any judgment is entered or collected. Does it make sense to talk of rebates in connection with acceleration? See U3C § 2.510(7).

(c) Should the law recognize that a creditor may incur certain expenses in merely writing a particular loan, and permit the creditor to retain some minimum portion of the finance charge no matter when the obligation is prepaid? See U3C § 2.510(2). Does a provision like this encourage "flipping"? (See Section A2, below.)

(d) How should Truth in Lending handle disclosures about rebates? Before simplification in 1980, Reg. Z required that creditors identify the method used in computing unearned finance charges. The Board had said that simple reference to the name of the method, e.g., "rule of 78s," was good enough. Do you think consumers were helped by such a disclosure? What do creditors today need to disclose about rebates? See Reg. Z § 226.18(k). Is this disclosure meaningful? Does the required reference to the contract documents help? See Reg. Z § 226.18(p). Hasn't the issue of whether and how to disclose the use of the rule of 78s simply been sidestepped under present TIL law?

(e) Since the rule of 78s always results in a smaller refund than the actuarial method, might it be deceptive to use the rule of 78s without explaining the difference? Consider the following.

LANIER v. ASSOCIATES FINANCE, INC.

Supreme Court of Illinois, 1986.
114 Ill.2d 1, 101 Ill.Dec. 852, 499 N.E.2d 440.

JUSTICE MILLER delivered the opinion of the court:

After paying the balance of an installment loan in September 1983, eight years prior to its due date in 1991, plaintiff Alma Lanier instituted a class action against defendants, Associates Finance, Inc., and its alleged parent corporation, Associates Corporation of North America. Plaintiff's class was comprised of persons who had prepaid, or were currently parties to, credit obligations entered into with the defendant Associates Finance, in which the credit agreements computed interest payments according to the Rule of 78's. The plaintiff contended that use of the Rule of 78's to compute interest in loans made to unsophisticated borrowers, absent explanation to the borrower about the effects of the rule upon early repayment, was fraudulent and violated unspecified provisions of the Consumer Fraud and Deceptive Business Practices Act (Ill.Rev.Stat.1981, ch. 121½, pars. 261 through 271).

The circuit court of Cook County granted defendants' motion to dismiss plaintiff's lawsuit, * * *.

On August 24, 1981, plaintiff obtained a loan in the amount of $24,961.68 from defendant Associates Finance, Inc., at a stated annual percentage rate of 21.59%. In addition, plaintiff was required to pay a service fee of $748.85. The loan was secured by a first mortgage on plaintiff's home and was to be repaid in monthly installments over a 10–year period. The loan agreement provided for prepayment of the outstanding balance of the loan, with a refund of the unearned finance charge computed according to the Rule of 78's, in the following language:

> "This Loan Agreement may at the option of the Borrower(s) be paid in whole or in part prior to the last payment date. If Borrower(s) prepays the loan in full, the Lender will allow a refund credit of the interest charge for the months prepaid using the 'Rule of 78's' method. No portion of the service fee will be refunded. No refund less than $1.00 will be made."

After making 23 monthly installment payments totaling $11,854.57, plaintiff inquired of Associates Finance as to the amount required to pay off her loan at that time. Associates informed plaintiff that the payoff figure was $27,706. Plaintiff paid that amount and initiated the present lawsuit.

Plaintiff states that, because defendants used the Rule of 78's to compute the interest on her loan, the amount required for plaintiff to pay off the balance of her loan was $4,654.42 more than it would have been had the defendant Associates Finance computed the interest on the loan according to the actuarial method. Plaintiff claims that, because of the Rule of 78's, plaintiff was charged an effective annual interest rate of 31.31% for the 23–month period ending when she paid off her loan, rather than the 21.59% APR stated in the agreement. Plaintiff argues that, since the effect of the rule on interest refunds following early repayment is understood by few borrowers, the defendants had an obligation to explain the Rule of 78's at the time of the loan.

* * *

The parties agree that the loan-agreement form provided by defendant Associates Finance and signed by plaintiff did not explain how the Rule of 78's operates; the agreement also did not inform borrowers that the Rule of 78's would yield a lower finance-charge rebate upon prepayment than would the actuarial method of computing these rebates.

* * *

In count II, the plaintiff alleges that the defendants fraudulently misrepresented the interest rate in the loan agreement. Plaintiff claims that although the loan contract recited an annual percentage rate of interest of 21.59%, the actual interest rate charged was much higher because the plaintiff prepaid her loan and the defendant computed the resulting interest rebate under the Rule of 78's. Plaintiff notes that, because the Rule of 78's attributes a higher proportion of the total interest charge to the early months of the loan term than to the final months of the term, use of the Rule of 78's to determine the interest rebate upon prepayment results in an actual interest rate for the period in which the loan was outstanding higher than the rate stated in the loan agreement. Plaintiff contends that the defendants knew that it was likely, from a statistical standpoint, that the loan would be repaid before its scheduled due date and that the result would be a higher effective interest rate than that listed in the loan agreement.

* * *

In the present case, the plaintiff and the defendant Associates Finance agreed upon a loan term of 10 years. The plaintiff, however, paid her obligation in full after approximately 23 months. That the effective interest rate for the 23–month period is different than the APR stated in the loan agreement does not mean that the APR stated in the agreement was misrepresented. The APR is calculated according to the full agreed-upon period of the loan, and is not meant to reflect the various interest rates which might result if a borrower pays his credit obligation in full prior to its due date. Under the Truth in Lending Act, all creditors covered by the Act must compute and disclose the APR and the loan finance charge in the same way. There is no requirement under the Truth in Lending Act that the APR figure equal the interest percentage at each interim period in the loan if the borrower chooses to pay his credit obligation prior to its due date. In the case of the plaintiff's loan, the effective interim rates of interest would vary daily. Listing the changing interim rates on the loan agreement would be both difficult and confusing.

The plaintiff in the present case cannot successfully claim that the defendant committed common law misrepresentation by properly stating the APR on the loan agreement. Under the plaintiff's argument, a creditor would find himself in the anomalous position, whenever the APR and the rate for any period less than the full loan term differed, of being guilty of common law misrepresentation by specifically complying with the mandates of the Federal Truth in Lending Act. We find, contrary to the plaintiff's assertion, that by listing an APR of 21.59% as defined by the Truth in Lending Act, the defendant did not misrepresent the interest rate per annum in the event of prepayment by the plaintiff.

In addition to her claims under common law, plaintiff also alleges that the failure of defendant Associates Finance to explain the operation of the Rule of 78's violates the Consumer Fraud and Deceptive Business Practices Act. The plaintiff has not specified in her complaint, however, which provisions of the Consumer Fraud Act were violated. In response to the plaintiff's claim, the defendant maintains that it complied with the disclosure requirements of the Federal Truth in Lending Act, and that compliance with the Federal act is a defense to liability under the Illinois statute.

* * *

Section 10b(1) of the Consumer Fraud Act provides that the Consumer Fraud Act does not apply to "[a]ctions or transactions specifically authorized by laws administered by any regulatory body or officer acting under statutory authority of this State or the United States." (Ill.Rev.Stat.1981, ch. 121½, par. 270b(1).) Under this provision, conduct which is authorized by Federal statutes and regulations, such as those administered by the Federal Reserve Board, is exempt from liability under the Consumer Fraud Act. The disclosure in the loan transaction between the plaintiff and the defendant complies with Federal Regulation Z, and thereby comports with the Truth in Lending Act. Because the Act is a law administered by the Federal Reserve Board, we find that, under section 10b(1) of the Consumer Fraud Act, the defendant's compliance with the disclosure requirements of the Truth in Lending Act is a defense to liability under the Illinois Consumer Fraud Act in the present case.

Although not raised in her complaint, plaintiff maintains here that, due to the harsh effects of the Rule of 78's on persons such as herself who prepay their credit obligations, the Rule of 78's is subject to judicial control as violative of the public policy of Illinois. Plaintiff cites a report of the Senate Committee on Banking, Housing, and Urban Affairs which called the use of the Rule of 78's on long-term credit transactions "indefensible," and encouraged State legislatures to prohibit use of the rule in long-term consumer credit obligations. However, the decision to prohibit the use of the Rule of 78's in consumer credit transactions is not a matter for the courts, but rather involves policy decisions more properly addressed by the legislature. We decline, therefore, to restrict or prohibit use of the Rule of 78's on public policy grounds, but we urge the legislature to promptly consider this matter which reflects an apparent injustice under the law as it currently exists.

Finding neither misrepresentation nor a violation of the Consumer Fraud and Deceptive Business Practices Act, we affirm the judgment of the appellate court.

Judgment affirmed.

Notes

1. The "hidden penalty" effect of the rule of 78s leaves the rule open to all kinds of challenges. In *Lanier,* its use was challenged as deceptive. See also Drennan v. Security Pacific National Bank, 28 Cal.3d 764, 170 Cal. Rptr. 904, 621 P.2d 1318 (1981). Other challenges have been mounted under the TILA and under state usury laws. Under the pre-simplification version of the TILA, the creditor had to describe any penalty charge imposed on prepayment, and explain how the penalty would be computed. When creditors used the rule of 78s to determine rebates, consumers often charged that this produced a hidden penalty and that this penalty had to be disclosed. However, consumers rarely got very far with this argument. Both the Board and the courts routinely ruled that the lesser rebate produced by the rule of 78s was not a penalty within the meaning of the TILA. (See Reg. Z § 226.18(k)(1) for current disclosure requirements.)

The usury challenge was based on the effect of the front-end bunching of interest charges as described in the Lanier case. Assume, for example, that a usury statute set a ceiling of 24% APR for the Lanier loan. The court noted that the effective rate at the point of prepayment was 31.31%. Does this mean that the loan was usurious? Remember that all methods even out in the end; if Ms. Lanier had paid according to the original schedule, the total rate for the entire contract would have been 21.59% no matter which method of accounting or rebating the creditor used. Remember, too, that the existence of usury must be determined according to the terms of the original obligation. At the time the loan was signed, could anyone have known that Ms. Lanier would not pay off according to the original schedule? In Winkle v. Grand National Bank, 267 Ark. 123, 601 S.W.2d 559 (1980) the court held that a note which was not usurious on its face or if paid according to it terms could not be made usurious through application of the rule of 78s on acceleration. But see Garrett v. G.A.C. Finance Corp., 129 Ga.App. 96, 198 S.E.2d 717 (1973), where the court held a loan to be usurious under the Georgia Industrial Loan Act when it was accelerated at the half-way point but less than half the total interest was refunded. (Does this make sense?)

2. Another method of computing unearned interest is known as the "pro rata" method. This method ignores normal amortization principles and is based instead purely on time. For example, if a loan is paid off halfway through its term, the consumer would be entitled to a rebate of half the finance charges. This method is almost never used anymore (except in Georgia; see note 3). Why? Does it make sense? If you were a lender and had a choice of methods to use, which would you choose?

3. Most state statutes which address the problem of rebates speak specifically only to prepayment; they normally do not mention acceleration. This has led to some confusion when creditors have applied the method stated for prepayment to other contexts. In Georgia, litigation over this problem apparently became something of a cottage industry during the early and middle 1980s. For example, in Bozeman v. Tifton Federal Savings & Loan Ass'n, 164 Ga.App. 260, 297 S.E.2d 49 (1982), reversed on other grounds, 324 S.E.2d 199, the court held that the Motor Vehicle Sales Finance Act, which expressly permitted use of the rule of 78s in cases of voluntary prepayment, did not allow it to be used in cases of acceleration. And in Carter v. First Federal Savings & Loan Ass'n, 179 Ga. App. 532, 347 S.E.2d 264 (1986), the court said in effect that the pro rata method must be used in these cases. To the same effect is Fitch v. G.M. A.C., 181 Ga.App. 7, 351 S.E.2d 215 (1986). See also Palace Industries, Inc. v. Craig, 177 Ga.App. 338, 339 S.E.2d 313 (1985) (rule of 78s improper on acceleration under Retail Installment Homes Solicitation Act). These cases echo the *Garrett* case (cited in note 1) a decade earlier, ruling on the same issue under the Georgia Industrial Loan Act. However, in Varner v. Century Finance Corp., Inc., 253 Ga. 27, 317 S.E.2d 178 (1984), the court ruled that the Industrial Loan Act, which also expressly mentions the rule of 78s only in the context of prepayment, nevertheless authorizes the rule of 78s in connection with a refinancing. See also Harlow v. Walton Loan Corp., 174 Ga.App. 311, 329 S.E.2d 616 (1985) (rule of 78s allowed on refinancing). Are these approaches consistent? Why have a different rebate rule for voluntary prepayment (or refinancing) than for acceleration? Isn't the earned portion of the finance charge always the same at any specified point in the transaction regardless of the reason the transaction was cut short?

4. If you represented Georgia lenders, would you recommend adding a clause to their contracts which said that on default and acceleration the consumer would get a pro rata rebate of interest? See Brown v. Associates Financial Services Corp., 179 Ga.App. 398, 346 S.E.2d 873 (1986).

----

2. RENEWING THE PREVIOUS DEAL—REFINANCING AND "FLIPPING"

The previous material introduced you to the important concepts of earned and unearned finance charges, and revealed some of the dangers hidden in the notion of rebates. But what happens in cases in which the debt is renewed, or rolled over, before it has been completed? Might there be a danger that a rebate method which favors the creditor (or a failure to rebate at all) could compound the problem? And what of multiple renewals? These are important real life issues: well over half, and perhaps as many as two-thirds, of consumer finance company loans are refinanced at least once. Consider the following.

IN THE MATTER OF WILLIAM SYLVESTER BRANCH, DEBTOR

Referee, United States District Court, Eastern District of Tennessee, 1966.

Printed in Hearings before the Subcommittee on Consumer Affairs of the
Committee on Banking and Currency, House of Representatives,
90th Congress, 1st Session on H.R. 11601, Consumer Credit
Protection Act, Part 2 (1967) p. 962.

MEMORANDUM OPINION

*   *   *

William Sylvester Branch, the above debtor, filed an original petition under Chapter XIII on February 21, 1966. The debtor is 46 years old, married, and employed as a porter at the East Tennessee Tuberculosis Hospital, earning $200.00 per month. With his petition, he submitted his wage earner plan providing for payment out of his future earnings and wages the sum of $20.00 each week. The plan further provided that Merit Finance Company (Merit), a secured creditor, received fixed monthly payments of $60.00. Merit, on March 9, 1966, filed its proof of claim in the amount of $2,870.00, accepting the debtor's plan.

Merit is an industrial loan and thrift company operating under the provisions of Tennessee Code Annotated. Secs. 45–2001–45–2017. Merit asserts that it holds a note secured by a second mortgage on the debtor's home, and a security interest in the debtor's household goods and an automobile, all executed November 19, 1965, at Knoxville, Tennessee. Merit's claim is based upon the following transactions.

(1) On December 22, 1964, the debtor negotiated a loan with Merit. He executed a note in the sum of $72.00 payable in 12 monthly installments of $6.00 each. Merit's ledger card (Account No. 63–235) indicates the $72.00 note was made up of the following items and charges:

Cash received by debtor	$59.04
Interest	4.32
Investigation charge	2.88
Life insurance premium	1.44
Accident and health premium	4.32
Total of note	72.00

(2) On January 23, 1965, the first loan was renewed or "flipped." [1] The debtor executed a new note in the amount of $378.00 payable in 18 monthly payments of $21.00 each. Merit's ledger card (Account No. 63–337) indicates the following items and charges:

---

1. "Industrial loan and thrift companies * * * freely engage in the practice of 'flipping,' whereby a borrower who has repaid a portion of a loan is allowed to make or is enticed to make another loan whereupon the new loan is set up combining the new amount with the old balance on which all allowable charges have already been made, and the full amount of allowable charges is again imposed on the new balance." *Final Report of the Legislative Council of the 80th General Assembly, State of Tennessee (1968).*

Payment to Merit on unpaid balance old loan (credit given for insurance premium rebate, $4.94) .... $ 68.06
Paid Franklin Finance Company for borrower 108.00
Cash to borrower 95.11
Property insurance 15.00
Interest 34.02
Investigation charge 15.12
Life insurance premium 11.34
Accident and health premium 28.35
Recording fee (security agreement, household furniture) 3.00
     Total of note 378.00

Repayments by debtor: $21.00—February 22, 1965; $84.00—March 6, 1965.

(3) On March 6, 1965, the second loan was renewed or "flipped." Merit's ledger card (Account No. 63–483) indicates a new note in the amount of $552.00 was executed, payable in 24 monthly installments of $23.00 each. The ledger card indicates the following items and charges:

Payment to Merit on unpaid balance old loan (rebate insurance premium, $45.58) $227.42
Cash to borrower 149.70
Interest 66.24
Investigation charge 22.08
Life insurance premium 22.08
Accident and health premium 41.40
Property insurance premium 22.08
Recording fee 1.00
     Total of note 552.00

Repayment by debtor: $21.85—April 24, 1965 (late fee charged $1.15); $23.00—July 1, 1965.

(4) On August 10, 1965, the third loan was renewed or "flipped" and a new note executed in the amount of $672.00, repayable in 24 monthly installments of $28.00 each. Merit's ledger card (Account No. 63–1074) indicates the following items and charges:

Payment to Merit on unpaid balance old loan (rebate insurance premium, $56.72) $450.43
Cash to debtor 9.89
Interest 80.64
Investigation fee 26.88
Life insurance premium 26.88
Accident and health premium 50.40
Property insurance premium 26.88
     Total of note 672.00

Repayments on the above loan appears as follows: $28.00—September 9, 1965; $28.00—October 9, 1965.

(5) On November 19, 1965, the fourth loan was renewed or "flipped" and this time a note executed in the sum of $2952.00, payable

in 36 monthly payments of $82.00 each. Merit's ledger (Account No. 63–1396) indicates the following items and charges:

Payment to Merit on unpaid balance old loan (rebate insurance premium, $79.90)	$536.10
Paid City Finance Company	1,044.00
Paid Consolidated Credit Company	72.00
Cash received by debtor	10.28
Interest	531.36
Investigation charge	118.08
Life insurance premium	177.12
Accident and health premium	280.44
Property insurance premium	177.12
Recording fee	5.50
Total of note	2,952.00

Repayment by debtor on this loan: $82.00— ...., 1966.

A résumé of the debtor's five loans with Merit, from December 22, 1964 to November 19, 1965, indicates the following:

Received by debtor or paid to others for his benefit	$1,548.02
Interest charges	716.58
Investigation charges	185.04
Insurance premiums (net after rebate)	678.41
Recording charges	9.50

Repayments by the debtor total $287.85. As indicated heretofore Merit says the debtor owes it $2870.00 at this time.

The question before the court is whether Merit's claim is free from usury. In Chapter XIII proceedings, where a loan of money is involved, General Order 55(4) places the burden of proof upon the claimant to show that its claim is free from usury. In my opinion Merit's claim is not free from usury and such usurious charges must be disallowed.

To creditors and leaders in the business community who are constantly asking why there is such a large number of bankruptcy petitions filed in Tennessee each year, an analysis of the financing charges in the loans under consideration in this opinion furnishes one of the principal answers.

Usury

* * *

By their nature, devices to conceal usury have the appearance of legality: the disguised transaction is usurious for the very reason that the true intent of the parties to the transaction, differs from the apparent or professed intent. It is, therefore, necessary to discover every fact that shows the true character of the transaction and to apply the fundamental principles of interest and usury, regardless of the disarming form in which the transaction may have been cast.

INTEREST

* * * The legal rate of interest in this state is fixed by Tennessee Code Annotated 47–14–104 at the rate of six dollars ($6.00) for the use of one hundred dollars ($100) for one (1) year. "* * * and every excess over that rate is usury."

Tennessee Code Annotated 45–2007(f) authorizes industrial loan and thrift companies "* * * to deduct interest in advance on the face amount of the loan for the full term thereof."

* * *

As pointed out heretofore the first loan was "flipped" four times within a period of eleven months; total benefits received by the debtor amounted to some $1548.02; interest totaling $716.58 was charged. In no instance was interest rebated when the loan was "flipped."

It will also be observed from the notes filed in this proceeding that in every instance interest has been charged on interest, e.g., consider the fifth loan made by the debtor. The debtor executed a note in the amount of $2952.00 which includes interest amounting to $531.36. The interest figure was arrived at by charging interest on the face amount of the note, to which the interest had already been added, thus interest is charged on interest.

Did the "flipping" of the loans by Merit in the transactions under consideration enable it to obtain an excess over the legal rate of interest? T.C.A. 47–14–103, 104.

When the first loan was made, the debtor executed a note in the amount of $72.00. This amount includes $4.32 interest for twelve months. One month later the loan was "flipped." The face amount of the new note includes $68.06 payment to Merit on the first loan (rebate given for insurance premiums). Although the debtor had already been charged with interest on $72.00 for twelve months, the $68.06 balance is added into the face amount of the second note ($378.00) and interest is again charged—this time for eighteen months. In the third loan interest is again charged on $227.42 remaining unpaid on the second loan, again for eighteen months. In the fourth loan interest is again charged on $450.43 balance on the third loan, this time for a thirty-six month period. In the fifth loan interest is again charged on $536.10 balance on the fourth loan, again for a thirty-six month period. These transactions indicate interest on interest on interest on interest on interest. Yet the statute says the legal rate of interest in this State is $6.00 for the use of $100.00 for one year "and every excess over that rate is usury." T.C.A. 47–14–103, 104.

When the first loan was made the debtor was entitled to the use of $72.00 for one year. He was charged $4.32 interest. When the loan was "flipped" at the end of one month, however, he was again charged interest on $68.06 of the original $72.00. Six per cent interest on $72.00 for one month (deducted in advance) is $0.36. Yet the debtor was given no rebate for interest when the loan was "flipped."

* * *

Had new loans been made instead of "flipping" the prior loans Merit could not have charged interest on the old loan, e.g., the second loan would have been for $203.11 plus legal charges, which total considerably less than the $378.00 note executed by the debtor. The same is true of the other loans. When the third loan was "flipped" the debtor received only $9.89; the face amount of the note was increased however from $552.00 to $672.00 even though the debtor had repaid $44.85 on the third loan. The reason for "flipping" the loans is obvious.

It is my conclusion that Merit "flipped" the loans so that it could again collect interest (and investigation charges) on the old balances even though interest (and investigation charges) had already been imposed. Does such practice constitute usury under the Tennessee statute and decisions?

If the transaction is intended as a device to evade the statute, it constitutes usury. * * *

It is my conclusion that the "flipping" of loans in the transactions under consideration was a plan or scheme to enable Merit to obtain an excess over the legal rate of interest. The consent or cooperation of the debtor is immaterial. The transaction is a continued one; although new advances were made and new instruments were executed, each note refers to the previous one.

INVESTIGATION CHARGES

Tennessee Code Annotated 45–2007(i) authorizes industrial loan and thrift companies—

"To charge for services rendered and expenses incurred in connection with investigating the moral and financial standing of the applicant, security for the loan, investigation of titles and other expenses incurred in connection with the closing of any loan an amount not to exceed four dollars ($4.00) per each one hundred dollars ($100) of the principal amount loaned, and a proportionate amount for any greater or lesser amount loaned, provided no charge shall be collected unless a loan shall have been made."

It will be noted that Merit in each instance deducted a flat 4% investigation charge. Is Merit entitled to these charges?

* * *

At the hearing on Merit's claim in this proceeding the loan company introduced no proof in support of its charges for investigation. Under the statute it would be entitled to reimbursement for actual expenses incurred in connection with its investigation, assuming, of course, that some expense was incurred. In my opinion the statute does not authorize a flat 4% fee to be deducted from every loan made, regardless of whether any investigation expense is incurred. The purpose of the statute is to reimburse the lender for actual expenses incurred, not to authorize collection of additional interest.

It will also be noted from an examination of Merit's note that the 4% investigation fee has been charged on the face amount of the note which includes the amount of the loan, insurance premiums, interest and the investigation fee itself. The statute authorizes a charge "not to exceed four dollars ($4.00) per each one hundred dollars ($100) of the *principal amount loaned.*" (Italics added.) This raises the question of whether Merit's instrument is usurious on its face and therefore unenforceable. White v. Kaminsky, 196 Tenn. 180, 185. It does not appear necessary at this time to determine this question, however. Merit's claim will be allowed in an amount equitable to the parties involved.

Although Merit failed to show that it incurred any expense in investigating the debtor's moral and financial standing, security for the loan, etc., when given an opportunity to do so, its first investigation charge will be allowed in accordance with Cobb v. Puckett, supra. All other investigation charges will be disallowed.

INSURANCE PREMIUMS

Tennessee Code Annotated 45–2007(k) authorizes industrial loan and thrift companies to require at the expense of the borrower, insurance against the hazards to which the collateral used to secure the loan is subject, *and upon failure of the borrower to supply such insurance,* to procure the same. It further authorizes them to accept, *but not require,* as collateral, insurance against the hazards of death or disability of a borrower.

* * *

Mr. John N. Culvahouse issued the life and accident and health and property insurance policies as agent for American Bankers Insurance Company of Florida. Mr. Culvahouse is manager of Merit Finance Company. Apparently the debtor was given one or more certificates along with various other documents when the loans were negotiated. The certificates refer to a "master policy" but the debtor was not given a copy of the master policy nor was one filed with the court. When questioned by the court concerning the insurance, the debtor testified:

"To tell you the truth I didn't know anything about it."

The debtor signed a so-called "Insurance Authorization" in which he purportedly made application to the insurance company, declaring that "the purchase (of insurance) is entirely voluntary and has not been made compulsory by the creditor." It is my conclusion however that the debtor signed the insurance applications without knowledge of their contents, just as he signed all documents placed in front of him. His testimony that the signing "was right fast and right quick" aptly describes the transactions in which the debtor signed financing statements, security agreements, deeds of trust, insurance applications, and possibly other forms, many in triplicate.

This conclusion is fully supported by an examination of one of the documents signed by the debtor. I refer to the so-called deed of trust on his home. This incredible instrument (Ex. 1) provides that a vendor (not otherwise identified in the instrument) for the consideration of $200.00 contracts and agrees to sell to a purchaser (also not identified) certain real estate which in fact is the debtor's home. This instrument further recites a sale price of $7750.00 payable in monthly installments of $90.22 each. Mr. Culvahouse testified that certain language was copied inadvertently from another instrument when this so-called trust deed was prepared. This instrument as well as all other instruments was prepared in the loan company office. The trust deed further provides that the debtor is indebted to Merit in the sum of $2952.00 payable in 36 monthly installments of $82.00 each, "*with interest thereon from date at 6 per cent per annum.*" As heretofore stated, interest amounting to $531.36 had already been added into the $2952.00 note. Again, Mr. Culvahouse testified that the inclusion of interest in the trust deed was a mistake. Yet this is one of the instruments the loan company would have the court believe was signed by the debtor with full knowledge of its contents. These may have been mistakes but clearly it shows that the debtor was signing all instruments placed in front of him by the loan company officials, including an instrument with provisions that even the loan company officials now say are erroneous, without having the slightest knowledge of what he was signing.

Merit's officials testified that the loan in this instance was handled exactly in the same manner as all other loans. I am sure this is true. A review of some nine claims filed by Merit in Chapter XIII proceedings now pending in this court indicates that in every instance life and accident and health insurance premiums have been included, as well as a flat 4 per cent investigation charge, plus interest thereon.

In my opinion, the "tie-in" sale of credit insurance in connection with small loan transactions is being used to evade the statutory limitations on the costs of the loan. The practice followed by Merit is the same practice followed by most, if not all, loan companies in this area. In most instances, if not all, the lenders are profiting by the transactions in that there are "adjustments" between the lender and the insurance company of the premiums charged, if not an actual retention by the company of a part of the premium.

In the case before the court, Mr. Culvahouse, manager of Merit, testified that at the end of the year "so much per cent" of the insurance premiums was returned to Merit's home office by the insurance company. Thus it is clear that Merit is profiting from the insurance transactions.

It is my conclusion that all insurance charges must be stricken from Merit's claim, as well as all interest and investigation fees charged thereon.

* * *

Although all insurance charges deducted by Merit will be stricken, the debtor will be required to furnish Merit, within ten days, insurance against the hazards to which its collateral is subject. This coverage will be obtained from an insurance carrier of the debtor's own choosing.

* * *

CONCLUSIONS

* * * Merit's claim is allowed in an amount deemed equitable to the parties involved; the money advanced by Merit will be repaid in full with interest.

Merit's claim will be allowed as follows:

Loan No.	Principal allowed	Investigation fee	Interest	Total
63–235	$59.04	$2.88	....	$65.46
		....	$3.54 (12 months)	
63–337	206.11	....	$18.54 (18 months) ...	224.65
63–483	150.70	....	$18.08 (24 months) ...	168.78
63–1074	9.89	....	1.18 (24 months) ...	11.07
63–1396	1,126.28	....	202.68 (36 months) ...	1,328.96

Total 1,798.92

Less payments made by debtor 287.85

Claim allowed 1,511.07

ORDER

At Knoxville, Tennessee, in said district, on the 8 day of June, 1966.

In accordance with the foregoing findings of fact and conclusions of law, it is

ORDERED, that claim No. 5, filed by Merit Finance Company on the 9 day of March, 1966, be, and the same hereby is, allowed as a secured claim in the amount of $1,511.07.

CLIVE W. BARE,
Referee in Bankruptcy.

Notes

1. What exactly happened to Mr. Branch? How did he, within a space of 14 months, escalate from a cash loan of $59.04 to an obligation for $2,952.00?

2. The bankruptcy referee addresses three "evils" presented in the case: (a) collecting double interest each time the loan was flipped; (b) charging fees for investigations not actually conducted; and (c) imposing insurance charges without Branch's agreement. How does, or should, the law deal with these "evils"?

(a) In each of Branch's transactions, the full amount of the interest for the expected term of the loan was precomputed and discounted. Recall that the discount method of computing interest produces a very high rate of return when converted to the "APR" actuarial method. (See the discussion of interest rate calculation methods in chapter two, page 108.) In Branch, when each loan was refinanced, the prior loan balance (including the precomputed interest) was incorporated into the new loan amount, on which new interest charges were computed and discounted. This produced the interest-on-interest result. The double interest windfall is dealt with in the U3C in § 2.504. Without trying to do the math, can you articulate how this rule would have benefited Mr. Branch?

(b) Separate charges for credit investigations are not permitted under the U3C. That is, such charges, if they exist, must be included within the finance charge. See U3C § 1.301(20)(a)(iv). Under the TILA, these charges would also be included in the finance charge, and they would therefore be reflected in the disclosed APR. See Reg. Z § 226.4(b)(4). But to the extent that a creditor can fit such charges into the finance charge without exceeding the rate ceiling, does anything in the U3C or the TILA prevent a creditor from charging for investigations never actually conducted? Would a "little F.T.C. Act" or "UDAP" statute help?

(c) The voluntariness of insurance is covered in Article 4 of the U3C; see particularly §§ 4.104 and 4.106. Are these rules significantly different from the Tennessee law applied in Branch? Cf. Reg. Z § 226.4(d). (We will consider credit insurance in more detail in Chapter 14.)

3. Consumer loans often contain "balloon" payment provisions. A balloon payment is a payment, usually scheduled at the end of a loan obligation, which is abnormally large when compared to the other payments. Balloons have the effect of making the early payments smaller than they would otherwise be, and this enables many consumers to manage loans they could not otherwise manage. It also causes many consumers to be unprepared to make the final balloon payment, and refinancing is a typical result. Refinancing of balloon payments, of course, raises all the dangers inherent in any refinancing. Are balloon payments an evil the law should address in some way? If so, how? The U3C represents one statutory approach to this problem. See §§ 2.308 and 3.308.

4. An issue related to flipping is that of financing a loan over an exceptionally long term. Sometimes this is done when a loan is refinanced. Is this a problem? Doesn't a longer term mean smaller payments for the consumer? Consider the *Besta* case, immediately following.

Problem 1

Assume the facts of *Branch* in a jurisdiction which has enacted the U3C. What relief could Mr. Branch seek in a private action? See U3C §§ 2.401, 2.501–2.510, and 5.201(2) and (3).

BESTA v. BENEFICIAL LOAN CO. OF IOWA

United States Court of Appeals, Eighth Circuit, 1988.
855 F.2d 532.

BEAM, CIRCUIT JUDGE.

Betty L. Besta appeals from an order of the district court dismissing her claim that her loan agreement with Beneficial Finance Company of Iowa (BFC) is unconscionable. We reverse.

BACKGROUND

The loan at issue (Loan II) was written on May 2, 1983, and in part refinanced an earlier loan made in 1981 (Loan I).

* * *

Besta made 18 of the 36 payments due on Loan I. At that time, she needed $500.00 to finish her basement.

* * *

Besta was laid off from her job soon after Loan II was made. She fell in arrears. To prevent BFC from foreclosing on her assets, she filed this rescissionary action. BFC counterclaimed for the amount then owing—$2986.86. The district court found in BFC's favor on both claims.

* * *

THE STATE LAW QUESTION

Katherine Keest, an expert witness, presented undisputed testimony that the Besta loan if paid over 36 months instead of 72 months would have cost Besta a total of $2541.88 instead of $5400.00—and her installment payments would have been $5.00 per month *less*. The question before us, then, is whether Iowa law was correctly applied when the district court concluded that it was not unconscionable for BFC to arrange to finance Loan II over a six-year period without informing Besta of a more advantageous three-year option.

The district court concluded that all of the insurance charges under Loan II were lawful. For a six-year loan, the court was correct. However, the thrust of Keest's testimony—she was a consumer lending specialist—was that lending $1442.23 over six years, with the insurance premiums necessary for a six-year loan, was an arrangement no fair person would propose.

Her testimony was that the longer the loan period, the higher the insurance premiums. By adding the increased premiums to the cash advanced, BFC propelled the loan principal to an ever higher amount, and in this case, made the principal amount exceed $2000.00.

With the loan principal greater than $2000.00, the lender could then take a valid mortgage on the borrower's home. (Iowa Code Annot. § 537.2307 corroborates Keest's testimony on this point.) The real estate mortgage allegedly necessitated the charging of additional recording and other fees with regard to the security taken. These fees were, in turn, added to the principal amount which then required the payment of still higher insurance premiums. Interest, of course, runs for six years on this entire amount.

The following chart illustrates the effect of Loan II being stretched to six years when compared to the terms calculated by Keest under a three-year agreement (Exh. 69). The terms for Loan I, a BFC loan that was for three years, substantiates the accuracy of Keest's figures.

	Loan I	Loan II	Exh. 69
Amount Requested	$1000.00	$ 500.00	$ 500.00
Cash Advanced	$1249.33	$1442.23 [1]	$1444.46
Disability Insurance	$ 79.34	$ 275.40	$ 96.59
Life Insurance	$ 40.72	$ 210.60	$ 49.57
Household Contents			
Insurance	$ 93.96	$ 486.00	$ 114.38
Recording Fees	$ 15.00	$ 184.00	$ _____
Amount Financed	$1478.35	$2598.23	$1705.00
Annual Percentage Rate	24%	28.09%	28.09%
Number of Payments	36	72	36
Amount Per Payment	$ 58/mo.	$ 75/mo.	$70.61/mo.
Amount of Interest to Pay	$ 609.65	$2801.77	$ 836.88
Total Amount to Repay	$2088.00	$5400.00	$2541.88

UNCONSCIONABILITY

*   *   *

Iowa courts have considered as factors unfair surprise, lack of notice, disparity of bargaining power and substantive unfairness. Courts find that a bargain is unconscionable "if it is such as no man in his senses and not under delusion would make on the one hand, and as no honest and fair man would accept on the other." *Smith v. Harrison*, 325 N.W.2d 92, 94 (Iowa 1982). While we think Loan II was substantively unfair because there was no reasonable basis for writing the loan for a six-year period, we need not base our decision on such a finding. Instead, we hold that not telling Besta that she could have repaid the same loan with lower monthly payments in one-half the time deprived her of fair notice and amounted to unfair surprise—clearly no person in her senses would have accepted the more expensive term. This constituted, at least, procedural unconscionability.

Similarly, we see no reasonable social or economic reason for structuring Loan II for six years with its attendant higher costs without first explaining and comparing the costs of a three-year loan.

*   *   *

Moreover, finding Loan II unconscionable will not *   *   * adversely affect the supply of lendable funds by limiting a lender's ability to protect his loan portfolio. No evidence was offered or claim made that BFC would not have made Besta a loan under a three-year agreement with only her personal property and motor vehicle as collateral. Indeed, the evidence is contrary. While we have been unable to locate testimony or a document showing the amount at which BFC estimated the value of the personal property, Besta's valuation of personal proper-

---

    1. $877.76 of this amount was the unpaid balance from Loan I. It is unclear from the record whether this amount reflects any credit given for refund of any part of the $214.02 in insurance premiums charged in conjunction with Loan I even though only one half of the payments under Loan I had come due at the time of the refinancing.

ty form lists her household contents at a worth of $2775.00 for insurance purposes. The value of her motor vehicle is unknown. Therefore, the inescapable conclusion is that a real estate mortgage was not necessary to persuade BFC to make Besta the loan.

Additional evidence of this is the fact that the amount financed under Loan I was $1478.35 and BFC had only the household goods and automobile as security for the transaction. This suggests that BFC would have considered itself secure had it extended Besta the loan calculated by Keest—$1705.00 for three years.

* * *

Considering the Code policies and the circumstances surrounding Loan II, executing this loan for six years without disclosure of the three year option was an unconscionable practice—both under Iowa common law and the Iowa Consumer Credit Code. We reverse the district court and remand for rescissionary relief—but direct that BFC may collect on its judgment as if a three-year loan had been written, and find that BFC should have recourse to only those assets which would have been available as security under a three-year loan. As further relief, the district court should award Besta her reasonable attorney fees pursuant to section 537.5108(6) of the Iowa Consumer Credit Code.

Notes

1. In *Branch* the court addressed the abuses of flipping as a usury problem, and in *Besta* the court resorted to the unconscionability doctrine to address an abusive loan practice. But aren't these approaches rather clumsy? Wouldn't a direct approach to the problem be better? For example, as we have seen, the U3C addresses the flipping problem not through interest rate ceilings, but through mandated rebates of unearned interest. But what about the long-term loan problem? Iowa has the U3C, yet none of its specific rules seemed to help. Many state small loan acts set maximum time limits for small loans; the U3C has adopted this approach in § 2.308. Why didn't this rule help in *Besta?* Do these sorts of rules prevent a consumer from continually refinancing (and escalating) his indebtedness? Should they?

2. Another approach to the twin problems of flipping and long terms is represented in the Maine Consumer Credit Code, Maine Rev.Stat.Ann. Tit. 9A. Maine has adopted the U3C, but in a non-uniform amendment to § 2.308 it requires loans whose original APR is above 18% to be dropped to 8% after 37 months. This rule applies regardless of any deferral, renewal, refinancing, consolidation, or extension of the original loan. See Maine Rev.Stat.Ann.Tit. 9A, § 2–308(3). Does this provision have the same goal as the uniform provision? Which approach is more likely to be an effective counter to the abuses presented by *Branch* and *Besta?*

3. CHARGES ON DEFAULT AND ACCELERATION

This section further develops the problems confronting the overextended consumer borrower.

HAYES v. FIRST NAT. BANK OF MEMPHIS

Supreme Court of Arkansas, 1974.
256 Ark. 328, 507 S.W.2d 701.

FOGLEMAN, JUSTICE.

The question presented by this appeal is whether "late charges" made on an installment purchase contract and a charge made for an extension agreement voided the entire debt for usury. We conclude that they did not.

Billy R. and Betty J. Hayes, husband and wife, purchased a mobile home from C. & G. Mobile Homes at Camden. After making a down payment, the balance of the purchase price to be financed amounted to $4,399 to which were added charges for insurance which brought the total to $5,010.40 to be paid in 84 equal installments. When the maximum time price differential allowable was added, the total to be paid under the contract amounted to $6,985.40, which was to be paid in installments of $83.16. Incorporated into the agreement was a clause by which the buyers agreed to pay a default charge equal to 5% of any payment in arrears for more than five days or $5, whichever was the lesser, but in no event to exceed the maximum default or delinquency charge permitted by law.

The contract was assigned to the First National Bank of Memphis, which furnished the forms on which it was made out. There were delinquencies in 24 payments which resulted in the making of "late charges" totaling $99.56. Appellants attempted to justify their tardiness by their alleged inability to obtain delivery of insurance policies covered by the contract or to have defects repaired by the seller or manufacturer of the mobile home. On January 2, 1970, when two installments were past due, appellee granted Mr. and Mrs. Hayes an extension for which it charged $41, which was one-half of 1% of the balance then due. It appears that "late charges" were debited to the Hayes account to be collected, without interest, after all other payments had been made. The extension agreement charge was paid prior to February 25, 1970. In effect, the extension agreement postponed the entire schedule of payments for 60 days, i.e., the maturity date of each subsequent payment was 60 days later than it otherwise would have been.

After a considerable period of delinquency, the bank instituted this suit to replevy the mobile home. Appellants answered, alleging that the conditional sales contract was void and unenforceable for usury, and filed a bond to retain the mobile home. * * *

Judgment was rendered for $3,089.69 with interest from the date of the judgment (February 6, 1973) and attorney's fees and cost. The amount of the judgment was the balance of the account after unearned premiums from insurance were credited. This amount did not include the unpaid "late charges."

Appellants state one point for reversal. It is:

The court erred in failing to dismiss the plaintiff's case on the ground of usury.

Appellants argue that, since payments of $83.16 were delinquent for a total of only 1,079 days, the maximum legal charges would have been interest at 10% per annum on $83.16 for that period, which they calculate as $24.57. In considering this matter, we should say, at the outset, that the burden of showing that the contract was usurious rested upon appellants. * * * Actually, usury will not be presumed, imputed or inferred where an opposite result can be reached. In determining whether a contract is usurious, it must be viewed as of the time it is entered into and it must be presumed that it will be performed according to its terms.

We have held that a "late charge" is in the nature of a penalty for delinquency and does not render the transaction usurious, even when provided for in the instrument evidencing it. The rationale of these cases and others like them is that agreements for penalties to induce prompt payment are free from usury, because the buyer has it in his power to avoid the penalty by discharging the debt when it is due. This is not to say that an agreement of this sort will not be declared usurious if it is shown to be mere contrivance to avoid usury and the real intention is a loan or forbearance of money and the taking of more than legal interest. But such an intention must first be made manifest from the agreement itself or from extraneous proof. There is nothing here to give the slightest indication that the charges were provided for in this contract with any such intention and the limitation placed on their amount would imply a contrary intention. If the penalty was too severe, appellants were relieved of it by the court, and appellee did not appeal.

The payment for the extension is a different matter. There can be no doubt that it is a charge for the forbearance of money, which simply means that the person to whom it is due foregoes payment in cash and waits for all or part of his money until a later date. We have not attempted to apply the test mathematically, however, because, even if the extension agreement was usurious, the original contract is not tainted by it, because the facts and circumstances existing at the time that contract was entered into, rather than the subsequent actions of the parties, determine whether it is usurious.

This being the case, there could be no justification for dismissing appellee's suit on the original contract, and the judgment must be affirmed.

BYRD, J., dissents.

Notes

1. Can you articulate the rationale for allowing late charges and deferral ("extension") charges?

2. As in the *Branch* approach to flipping, the court resorts to the usury laws to address the problem of late charges. (While most courts follow *Hayes,* the cases are not uniform.) But are usury laws really designed to deal with this problem? Would some other approach be better? Could late charges be characterized as liquidated damages, for example? If so, how should a court decide whether a particular charge was permissible? See Garrett v. Coast and Southern Fed. Savings and Loan Ass'n, 9 Cal.3d 731, 108 Cal.Rptr. 845, 511 P.2d 1197 (1973). Or, would a straight-forward statutory approach which set maximum charges be better? For the U3C approach, see §§ 2.502 and 2.503. If Arkansas had the U3C, would the charge imposed by the creditor have been permissible?

3. Another type of problem often associated with late charges is that of "pyramiding." Consider the following:

Problem 2A

Buck N. Hamm borrowed $4000 from Fleur D. Lee, and was obligated to pay it back at a rate of $100 per month, on the first day of each month. The contract also provided that Fleur could assess a late charge of $5 for any payment more than 15 days late. The January, February, and March payments were on time. The April payment was 20 days late. (It was tax time.) The May, June and July payments were all paid on time. Fleur's computer assessed Buck a $5 late charge in April, applied $5 of the May payment to pay it, then found the May payment short, assessed another $5 for May, applied $5 of the June payment to pay it, and will continue doing this forever. Is this permissible? See U3C § 2.502(3); F.T.C. Credit Practices Rule, 16 C.F.R., at § 444.4.

Problem 2B

Assume Buck missed the April payment altogether, but made the May, June, and July payments on time. Fleur's computer applied the May payment to April, and assessed a $5 late charge. It then applied the June payment to May, and assessed another $5 late charge. It will apply the July payment to June, and so on, and continue to assess late charges forever. Is this permissible? See also Steed v. First Union National Bank, 58 N.C.App. 189, 293 S.E.2d 217, review denied, 306 N.C. 751, 295 S.E.2d 763 (1982).

SECTION B. PLASTIC EXPLOSIVES—CREDIT AND DEBIT CARDS

A phenomenon of recent decades is the widespread consumer use of plastic cards to pay for goods and services. These cards may be used to draw on a line of credit (credit cards), or to gain access to deposit accounts for cash withdrawals and the like (debit cards). An important feature of both types of plastic is that they contemplate ongoing account relationships with the institutions which issue the cards.

Traditionally, credit cards were issued by three types of institutions: (1) retail stores, such as Sears or Penney's (or their equivalent, gasoline companies); (2) banks or other depository institutions, for bank cards such as VISA or MasterCard; and (3) "travel and entertainment" companies such as American Express or Diner's Club. Debit cards, on the other hand, were issued exclusively by banks and other depository institutions. Today, however, these traditional lines are blurring, and many cards have both credit and debit features. Many bank credit cards, for example, now permit direct access to deposit accounts; and debit cards often may be converted into credit devices by allowing consumers to overdraw their accounts.

Many different kinds of problems can arise in the course of these account relationships, problems that often defy solution under conventional contract principles. The materials that follow address some of these recurring problems, both for credit cards and debit cards. The legal system traditionally drew a sharp distinction between debit and credit, and the rules you will study in this section reflect this. As you work your way through the materials, you should consider whether the legal system has responded adequately to the growing tendency in the consumer finance industry to blur this traditional distinction.

Note on Source Materials

Most of the rules regulating the consumer credit card relationship are found in the Truth in Lending Act, especially in chapter 4 of the TILA (enacted separately in 1974 as the "Fair Credit Billing Act), §§ 161–171. The Reg. Z counterparts can be found generally in §§ 226.12 and 226.13.

For debit cards, another federal statute applies. This is the Electronic Fund Transfer Act of 1978, 15 U.S.C.A. §§ 1693–1693r. The EFTA was codified as Title IX of the federal Consumer Credit Protection Act. It, too, carries with it a Federal Reserve Board regulation, Reg. E, 12 C.F.R. Part 205. Both the EFTA and Reg. E appear in West's Selected Commercial Statutes, right along with the TILA and Reg. Z.

1. BILLING DISPUTES—THE UNRESPONSIVE COMPUTER AND OTHER GREMLINS

Problem 3

Joachim McGillicuddy receives his monthly MasterCard billing statement from Big Bank, the bank which issued Joachim's card. The statement contains a charge for $43 for "lingerie" purchased from a store in Reno, Nevada. Joachim thinks to himself, "I'm no transvestite, and besides, I've never even been to Reno. There must be some mistake." He writes a careful letter to Big Bank, explaining that there must be another Joachim McGillicuddy somewhere whose charge was erroneously put on his statement. Joachim gets no reply, but next month gets another statement. He writes again. No answer. He calls. And calls. Finally he sends a collect telegram. Six months after Joachim received the first erroneous statement, Big writes to Joachim, saying it has checked the sales slip and believes it is in fact his signature. Big therefore "regrets" it could not respond more promptly, but flatly refuses to credit Joachim with either the $43 or the $4.02 in finance charges that accrued over the six months.

(a) Do any of the disclosure or regulatory rules we have encountered thus far provide Joachim with any usable rights against Big Bank? Is there any way Joachim could force Big to adjust his account promptly? (Couldn't he just cancel his card?)

(b) It was largely in response to stories like this one that Congress enacted the Fair Credit Billing Act (cited above in Note on Source Materials). What are the rights and duties of Joachim and Big Bank under the FCBA? See Reg. Z § 226.13.

Notes

1. What is a "billing error" which triggers the FCBA error-resolution provisions? In Problem 3, for example, could Joachim invoke these provisions if his monthly statement reflected a charge for carpeting which he in fact had purchased, but which was never delivered by the store? Suppose the carpet was delivered and installed, but Joachim later discovered defects in it? See Reg. Z § 226.13(a). We will consider the question of the card issuer's potential liability for defective goods in chapter 6.

2. Once a billing error procedure is initiated by the consumer, the card issuer must conduct a "reasonable investigation" of the claim. Reg. Z § 226.13(f). What does this require the issuer to do? For example, Joachim may claim that he does not remember making any purchase from a boutique in Reno. Big Bank may have received only an electronic transmission of transaction data through the MasterCard network; i.e., it may not have an actual copy of the sales slip submitted by the store. Must it contact the store to verify the transaction, such as by getting a copy of the sales slip (if one still exists)? (Neither Reg. Z nor the Board's commentary speak to this point.) Could Big satisfy its duty by simply reviewing its own internal records?

3. Suppose Big Bank investigates promptly and reports to Joachim that it remains convinced of the genuineness of his signature on the Reno sales slip. What can Joachim do now? See Reg. Z § 226.13(h). Can Big cancel Joachim's card, or sue to recover the disputed $43? If it does, can it also report its actions to the local credit bureau?

4. How is a card holder supposed to know what to do in order to exercise his rights under the FCBA? For that matter, how is he supposed to know that he even has any rights? See Reg. Z §§ 226.6(d) and 226.7(k). Suppose that on the day after Joachim received the statement showing the disputed lingerie charge, he called Big Bank and told it of the alleged error, and then sent a photocopy of the statement with a circle around the disputed item. Would this be sufficient to trigger the FCBA procedures?

5. A related problem is that of the "shrinking billing period." Most credit card plans contain a "free ride" period, that is, they permit the cardholder to avoid finance charges by paying the entire balance within a certain period. Sometimes this period is stated in actual time, such as "within 25 days"; other times it is measured by reference to a stated due date. But what happens if the card issuer takes its time about getting the statement to the consumer? If the end of the free ride period is, say, October 10, but the consumer doesn't get the statement until October 5, the benefit of the grace period is all but lost. Consumers complained about this problem, too, and Congress responded to it by adding TILA § 163 to the Fair Credit Billing law. This section is clearly a compromise, is it not? Is it fair to consumers? To card issuers?

6. During the 1980s there was a shift from "country club" billing to "descriptive" billing systems. Creditors now give the consumer a monthly statement with brief, computer-generated descriptions of transactions during the billing period. Under "country club" billing, they had sent actual copies of the sales slips signed at the point of sale. In descriptive billing systems, the merchant's bank captures the payment and other information about the transaction, and then "truncates," or destroys, the sales slips. The information is then routed electronically to the card issuing bank. Naturally, this system is cheaper and more efficient to operate than the old paper-based "country club" systems. And, the less information required to be sent, the quicker and cheaper it is. But at some point, doesn't the terseness of the description make it difficult or impossible for the consumer to verify the statement?

What should be the limits of brevity in descriptive billing? Review the detailed provisions of Reg. Z § 226.8. If you use your VISA card to purchase half a dozen different items of cosmetics at a drugstore, what will your monthly statement "identify"? Would it be sufficient merely to say, for example, "Rexall # 78, Ashtabula"? Would the description be any different if you used the drug store's own credit card? Should it be?

7. Are there any error resolution procedures for closed-end credit accounts? Should there be? Are consumers as likely to get into disputes with their closed-end creditors as with their credit card issuers? If they do get into a dispute, should they have fewer rights? See Bailey v. Capitol Motors, Inc., 307 Md. 343, 513 A.2d 912 (1986); Jacobs v. Marine Midland Bank, N.A., 124 Misc.2d 162, 475 N.Y.S.2d 1003 (Sup.Ct.1984).

Problem 4

Paul Porter sought to withdraw $100 from his checking account at First Bank via the automated teller machine. When no money was dispensed, he reported the problem to a bank official (whose name he can no longer remember) and was told the matter would be investigated. A few weeks later, he tried to withdraw $200 through the ATM, and again no money appeared although he had pushed all the necessary buttons. He repeated the process a second time, to no avail. He again reported the problem to the bank management. To his dismay, his next bank statement showed one withdrawal of $100 and two of $200 which he never actually received. The next day, Porter comes to your office seeking legal advice on whether he can recover the $500. What will you tell him? See EFTA § 908 and Reg. E § 205.11. See also Porter v. Citibank, N.A., 123 Misc.2d 28, 472 N.Y.S.2d 582 (N.Y.City Civ.Ct.1984).

Notes

1. Are the error resolution procedures under the EFTA for debit cards comparable to those under the FCBA for credit cards? If not, where do they differ? Are there important transactional differences which justify different procedures? Don't forget that if a consumer disputes an item on a credit card bill, he can always refuse to pay until the dispute gets resolved. But if the bank charged the consumer's deposit account for an erroneous item, the consumer will lose the use of those funds while the dispute is pending unless the account is recredited during the interim. (People who live from paycheck to paycheck will understand the importance of this issue.) Is the bank required to recredit the consumer's account? See EFTA § 908(a) and (c); Reg. E § 205.11(c).

2. In disputes like the one illustrated in Problem 4, isn't the allocation of the burden of proof decisive? Who should have the burden of proof? Which party has access to the records which are most likely to reveal the truth? (Are any records likely to reveal the truth?) If the burden of proof is on the bank, isn't there a danger that consumers will make false claims? If so, is the danger any greater in consumer banking transactions than in other areas?

3. Why should error resolution procedures be limited to credit card and EFT accounts? Why shouldn't they apply as well to ordinary checking accounts? (They don't, do they? See the definition of "electronic fund transfer" in EFTA § 903(6).) Many checking accounts have EFT features as well; that is, consumers may write checks or use their debit cards against the same account. Normally, the consumer receives a single monthly statement showing all activity, both electronic and paper-based. If the statement contained some mistakes, would the error resolution procedures apply only to the EFT items, but not to the check items? Does this make sense?

Prefatory Note. What if the dispute escalates to the point that the card issuer cancels the card? Or, what if the card is simply "wrongfully dishonored," even without a pre-existing dispute? There certainly is a dispute after the dishonor.

Problem 5

Following the advice he heard on TV, Fred Consumer never leaves home without his American Express card. He has embarked on a two-week vacation to Hawaii, and when he arrives at the hotel, he proffers his card to pay for his room. The clerk consults by phone with the American Express authorization service, and then tells Fred: "American Express says you are delinquent on your account. Your card is cancelled as of now, and I am instructed to keep it." Fred does not have enough cash or other credit cards to cover his hotel bill, and so has to cancel his vacation. Does he have a cause of action against American Express? Does the answer depend on whether American Express is correct or mistaken about Fred's delinquency?

GRAY v. AMERICAN EXPRESS CO.

U.S. Court of Appeals, District of Columbia Circuit, 1984.
743 F.2d 10.

MIKVA, CIRCUIT JUDGE.

We are called upon to determine what rights, if any, appellant Oscar Gray has against American Express arising from the circumstances under which it cancelled his American Express credit card. The District Court granted summary judgment to American Express; we vacate that judgment and remand for further proceedings.

I. BACKGROUND

Gray had been a cardholder since 1964. In 1981, following some complicated billings arising out of deferred travel charges incurred by Gray, disputes arose about the amount due American Express. After considerable correspondence, the pertinence and timeliness of which we will detail below, American Express decided to cancel Gray's card. No notification of this cancellation was communicated to Gray until the night of April 8, 1982, when he offered his American Express card to pay for a wedding anniversary dinner he and his wife already had consumed in a Washington restaurant. The restaurant informed Gray that American Express had refused to accept the charges for the meal and had instructed the restaurant to confiscate and destroy his card. Gray spoke to the American Express employee on the telephone at the restaurant who informed him, "Your account is cancelled as of now."

The cancellation prompted Gray to file a lengthy complaint in District Court, stating claims under both diversity and federal question jurisdiction. He alleged that the actions of American Express violated the contract between them, known as the "Cardmember Agreement," as well as the Fair Credit Billing Act (the "Act"), 15 U.S.C. §§ 1666–1666j, Pub.L. 93–495, Tit. III, 88 Stat. 1511 (1974). The District Court granted summary judgment for American Express and dismissed the complaint.

The surge in the use of credit cards, the "plastic money" of our society, has been so quick that the law has had difficulty keeping pace. It was not until 1974 that Congress passed the Act, first making a serious effort to regulate the relationship between a credit cardholder and the issuing company. We hold that the District Court was too swift to conclude that the Act offers no protection to Gray and further hold that longstanding principles of contract law afford Gray substantial rights. We thus vacate the District Court's judgment and remand.

II. DISCUSSION

A. *The Statutory Claim*

Fair Credit Billing Act seeks to prescribe an orderly procedure for identifying and resolving disputes between a cardholder and a card issuer as to the amount due at any given time.

* * *

1. *The Billing Error*

The billing dispute in issue arose after Gray used his credit card to purchase airline tickets costing $9312. American Express agreed that Gray could pay for the tickets in 12 equal installments over 12 months. In January and February of 1981, Gray made substantial prepayments of $3500 and $1156 respectively. He so advised American Express by letter of February 8, 1981. There is no dispute about these payments, nor about Gray's handling of them. At this point the numbers become confusing because American Express, apparently in error, converted the deferred payment plan to a current charge on the March bill. American Express thereafter began to show Gray as delinquent, due at least in part to the dispute as to how and why the deferred billing had been converted to a current charge.

The District Court held that Gray failed to trigger the protection of the Act because he neglected to notify American Express in writing within 60 days after he first received an erroneous billing. Gray insists that his first letter to American Express on April 22, 1981, well within the 60 day period set forth in the statute, identified the dispute as it first appeared in the March, 1981 billing. According to Gray's complaint, the dispute continued to simmer for over a year because American Express never fulfilled its investigative and other obligations under the Act.

The District Court made no mention of the April 22, 1981 letter, deeming instead a September, 1981 letter as the first notification from Gray as to the existence of a dispute. We conclude that the District Court erred in overlooking the April letter.

Gray's April 22, 1981 letter complained specifically about the March bill and the miscrediting of the prepayments. Whatever the import and impact of other correspondence and actions of the parties, we hold that, through this earlier letter, Gray triggered the procedural protections of the Act. The letter enabled the card issuer to identify the name and account number, indicated that the cardholder believed that an error existed in a particular amount and set forth the cardholder's reasons why he believed an error had been made. The later correspondence and activities may be treated as evidentiary in nature—sufficient perhaps to show that American Express fulfilled all of its obligations under the Act, but not pertinent to the question of whether the Act was triggered in the first place.

2. *Reporting and Collection Efforts*

Gray alleged in count III that, notwithstanding his having given notice of dispute under § 1666 through his letters, American Express nevertheless turned over his account for collection to a bill collection agency. The District Judge dismissed this count (misdesignating it as count IV) by concluding that it failed to state a claim for relief. The District Court erred. *See* 15 U.S.C. §§ 1640(a), 1666a. We think that count III states an independent cause of action under § 1666a because Gray's April 22, 1981 correspondence brought the dispute within the Act's coverage. The question of American Express' compliance with the reporting and collection requirements of the Act also warrants consideration on remand.

3. *The Act and the Cardmember Agreement*

As we have indicated above, the District Court summarily resolved Gray's statutory claims by wrongly concluding that the Act did not apply. On appeal, American Express also urges that, even if the Act is otherwise pertinent, Gray was bound by the terms of the Cardmember Agreement which empowered American Express to cancel the credit card without notice and without cause. The contract between Gray and American Express provides:

> [W]e can revoke your right to use [the card] at any time. We can do this with or without cause and without giving you notice.

American Express concludes from this language that the cancellation was not of the kind prohibited by the Act, even though the Act regulates other aspects of the relationship between the cardholder and the card issuer.

Section 1666(d) of the Act states that, during the pendency of a disputed billing, the card issuer, until it fulfills its other obligations under § 1666(a)(B)(ii), shall not cause the cardholder's account to be restricted or closed because of the failure of the obligor to pay the amount in dispute. *See also* 12 C.F.R. § 226.14(d). American Express seems to argue that, despite that provision, it can exercise its right to cancellation for cause unrelated to the disputed amount, or for *no* cause, thus bringing itself out from under the statute. At the very least, the argument is audacious. American Express would restrict the efficacy of the statute to those situations where the parties had not agreed to a "without cause, without notice" cancellation clause, or to those cases where the cardholder can prove that the sole reason for cancellation was the amount in dispute. We doubt that Congress painted with such a faint brush.

The effect of American Express's argument is to allow the equivalent of a "waiver" of coverage of the Act simply by allowing the parties to contract it away. Congress usually is not so tepid in its approach to consumer problems. *See* 118 Cong.Rec. 14,835 (1972) (remarks by Sen. Proxmire, principal proponent of the Act, concerning a technical amendment to a predecessor bill later carried over into the Act; its purpose was to prevent "possible evasion" by precluding the creditor from including a pre-dispute waiver provision in the card agreement); 119 Cong.Rec. 25,400 (1973) (remarks by Sen. Proxmire on S. 2101, another predecessor: "The legislation seeks to establish a system for *insuring* that billing disputes or inquiries are resolved in a fair and timely manner.") (emphasis added).

Moreover, the consumer-oriented statutes that Congress has enacted in recent years belie the unrestrained reading that American Express gives to the Act in light of its contract. Waiver of statutory rights, particularly by a contract of adhesion, is hardly consistent with the legislature's purpose. The rationale of consumer protection legislation is to even out the inequalities that consumers normally bring to the bargain. To allow such protection to be waived by boiler plate language of the contract puts the legislative process to a foolish and unproductive task. A court ought not impute such nonsense to a Congress intent on correcting abuses in the market place.

* * *

Thus we hold that the Act's notice provision was met by Gray's April 22, 1981 letter and remand the case to the District Court for trial of Gray's statutory cause of action. American Express will be obliged to justify its conduct in this case as fully satisfying its obligations under the Act.

* * *

C. *Discovery*

Because the case is to be remanded for further proceedings, we think it appropriate to comment on the appellee's extraordinary use of interrogatories below. It appears to be of some significance to this case that Gray is a lawyer, because only a lawyer, tenacious even beyond the professional custom, would have been able to withstand the expenses and excesses of this litigation. Perhaps the presence of a lawyer-plaintiff caused American Express particular concern that occasioned their plethora of interrogatories; perhaps it was the shorter, but nonetheless substantial, set of interrogatories that plaintiff served on defendant. Whoever was the instigator and whatever the reason, the various sets of interrogatories and their answers are in the hundreds of pages. They run as far afield as inquiring the name of every law firm that plaintiff had been affiliated with since 1951 to asking all of the "professional credentials" that he had acquired in his lifetime; from psychiatrists consulted since 1978 to meals eaten at the fated restaurant since the suit was filed. The length, scope and detail of the interrogatories propounded by American Express suggest a strategy of attrition rather than a legitimate discovery of the facts needed to resolve a dispute over the account.

* * *

On remand, we think the trial court should take the quantity and relevance of the discovery into account in setting the case for trial and in determining what, if any, further discovery should be allowed, and in deciding whether sanctions for abusive litigation practices are appropriate.

The size of the record and the vigor with which the defenses have been pursued make it apparent that only a stubborn professional could seek to avail himself of the protection guaranteed by statute and the common law. The courts must exercise control so that access to justice is not foreclosed by such tactics at the preliminary stages of suit. Deep pockets and stubbornness ought not be prerequisites to bringing a case like this one to issue.

CONCLUSION

The District Court's order of summary judgment and dismissal is hereby vacated. The case is remanded for further proceedings consistent with this opinion.

So Ordered.

2. UNAUTHORIZED USE

The three most likely forms of consumer payment (other than cash) are personal check, credit card, and debit card. The most familiar to most of us is probably the check. There is a well-developed body of law concerning liability for forged or unauthorized checks. The bank may not charge its customer's account for any check which is not "properly payable." See Uniform Commercial Code (UCC) § 4–401. Further, any forged or unauthorized signature is "wholly inoperative" to bind a customer. UCC § 3–404. As a result, a consumer whose check book is stolen and whose signature is forged is not responsible for payment of the forged checks. If the bank has charged its customer's account for these checks, it must reimburse the customer, unless the bank can demonstrate that the customer has ratified the payment or that the customer's negligence contributed to the forgery. See UCC §§ 3–404, 3–406, 4–406.

Does this approach make sense in the credit card or debit card context? Whether it does or not, Congress took a different approach. In fact, Congress took a different approach for credit cards than for debit cards, and neither approach matches that for checks. As you read the following materials, you should consider whether it makes any sense to have different rules for allocating losses due to forgeries and other frauds for each type of payment. After all, why should a consumer's risk vary according to which piece of plastic he pulls out of his pocket? Or, to be more precise, why should the risk vary according to which piece of plastic the thief pulls out of the consumer's stolen wallet?

Problem 6A

Robin Hood steals Sam Tudent's wallet with his MasterCard in it. Sam never notifies the issuing bank of the theft. During the next 30 days, Hood charges $1500 worth of goods and services on Sam's Master-Card, each charge being less than $50. What must the issuing bank plead and prove before it can recover anything from Sam? If it does plead and prove all those things, how much is it entitled to recover? How many "unauthorized uses" occurred?

Problem 6B

Sam Tudent has used his VISA credit card for a year now, and it is about to expire. VISA sends him a replacement credit card, but Sam is so irritated at VISA because of the way it has handled his account that he throws both the new and the old credit cards in the trash. Someone retrieved the new VISA card and purchased goods worth $100 with it.

Was this an "unauthorized use" of the VISA credit card? See TILA § 133. Was the card an "accepted" credit card? (Was it "accepted" by Sam?) See TILA § 103(l) and Reg. Z § 226.12(a) and footnote 21. If the credit card is an "accepted credit card" under the TILA, what effect does that have on whether the purchaser is an "authorized user" of the credit card or not?

Problem 6C

Sally Tudent has used her VISA debit card to access funds in her deposit account for a year now, and it is about to expire. VISA sends her a replacement VISA debit card. However, Sally doesn't like either the ATMs or the debit cards, so she throws both the new and the old debit cards in the trash. From then on, she plans to access the funds in her account only through the use of negotiable instruments. Someone retrieves the new debit card and immediately takes it to First Bank's nearest ATM and uses it to withdraw $100 in cash.

Is this an "unauthorized transfer" under the EFTA? See EFTA § 903(1). Is there any reason to treat this situation differently from the situation in Problem 6B? Please consider not only the language of the statutes and regulations, but also the various risks to the parties involved in each situation.

Courts have applied common law agency principles to interpret questions involving unauthorized signatures on negotiable instruments. See UCC §§ 3–403 and 3–404. Can this approach be used successfully in other payment systems? What about in credit card transactions? See TILA § 103(o), and Walker Bank & Trust Co. v. Jones, infra. How about in debit card transactions? See EFTA § 903(11). Are the terms "actual, implied or apparent authority" any more clearly defined than they are in the UCC? Is the definition found in EFTA § 903(11) a step towards more clear boundaries for liability, or is it more confusing than the application of common law principles? Do we need the definitions to be clearer?

WALKER BANK & TRUST CO. v. JONES

Supreme Court of Utah, 1983.
672 P.2d 73, cert. denied 466 U.S. 937, 104 S.Ct. 1911, 80 L.Ed.2d 460 (1984).

HALL, CHIEF JUSTICE:

At issue in these consolidated cases is the liability of defendants to plaintiff Walker Bank for expenses allegedly incurred by defendants' separated spouses upon credit card accounts established by the plaintiff bank in the names of the defendants. Defendants appeal from adverse summary judgment orders on the grounds that their rights under the Federal Truth in Lending Act were violated.

A. DEFENDANT BETTY JONES

In 1977, Defendant Jones established VISA and Master Charge accounts with plaintiff Walker Bank (hereinafter "Bank"). Upon her request, credit cards were issued on those accounts to herself and her husband in each of their names.

On or about November 11, 1977, defendant Jones informed the Bank, by two separate letters, that she would no longer honor charges made by her husband on the two accounts, whereupon the Bank immediately revoked both accounts and requested the return of the credit cards. Despite numerous notices of revocation and requests for surrender of the cards, both defendant Jones and her husband retained their cards and continued to make charges against the accounts.

It was not until March 9, 1978, that defendant Jones finally relinquished her credit cards to the Bank, and then only after a persuasive visit to her place of employment by a Bank employee. At the time she surrendered her cards, the balance owing on the combined accounts (VISA and Master Charge) was $2,685.70. Her refusal to pay this balance prompted the Bank's institution of this suit to recover the same.

B. DEFENDANT GLORIA HARLAN

In July, 1979, defendant Harlan, who was prior to that time a VISA cardholder at plaintiff Bank, requested that her husband, John Harlan, be added to the account as an authorized user. The Bank honored this request and issued a card to Mr. Harlan. Shortly thereafter, at some point between July and the end of 1979, the Harlans separated and defendant (Mrs.) Harlan informed the Bank by letter that she either wanted the account closed or wanted the Bank to deny further extensions of credit to her husband.

Notwithstanding the explicit requirement in the account agreement that all outstanding credit cards be returned to the Bank in order to close the account, defendant Harlan did not tender either her card or her husband's at the time she made the aforementioned request. As to her card, she informed the Bank that she could not return it because it had been destroyed in the Bank's automated teller. Notwithstanding, however, she returned the card to the Bank some three months later (March, 1980).

In the interim period, i.e., after defendant's correspondence with the Bank regarding the exclusion of her husband from her account and prior to the relinquishment of her card, several charges were made (purportedly by Mr. Harlan) on the account for which the Bank now seeks recovery. The Bank has sued only Mrs. Harlan, as owner of the account.

Defendants' sole contention on appeal is that the Federal Truth in Lending Act (hereinafter "TILA") limits their liability, for the unauthorized use of the credit cards by their husbands, to a maximum of $50. The specific section of the Act upon which this contention rests is 15 U.S.C. § 1643.

* * *

The Bank's rejoinder is that § 1643 does not apply, inasmuch as defendants' husbands' use of the credit cards was at no time "unauthorized use" within the meaning of the statute. Whether such use was "unauthorized," as that term is contemplated by the statute, is the pivotal question in this case.

* * *

Defendants' [sic] aver that the effect of their notification to the Bank stating that they would no longer be responsible for charges made against their accounts by their husbands was to render any subsequent use (by their husbands) of the cards unauthorized. This notification, defendants maintain, was all that was necessary to revoke the authority they had once created in their husbands and thereby invoke the § 1643 limitations on cardholder liability.

The Bank's position is that unauthorized use within the meaning of § 1643 is precisely what the statutory definition (§ 1602(*o*) *supra*) says it is, to wit: "[U]se * * * by a person * * * who does not have actual, implied, or apparent authority * * *," and that notification to the card issuer has no bearing whatsoever on whether the use is unauthorized, so as to entitle a cardholder to the statutory limitation of liability. We agree with this position.

* * *

The Bank maintains that defendants' husbands clearly had "apparent" authority to use the cards, inasmuch as their signatures were the same as the signatures on the cards, and their names, the same as those imprinted upon the cards. Accordingly, it contends that no unauthorized use was made of the cards, and that defendants therefore cannot invoke the limitations on liability provided by the TILA.

Again, we find the Bank's position to be meritorious. Apparent authority exists:

> [W]here a person has created such an appearance of things that it causes a third party reasonably and prudently to believe that a second party has the power to act on behalf of the first person * * *.[5]

As previously pointed out, at defendants' request their husbands were issued cards bearing the husbands' own names and signatures. These cards were, therefore, a representation to the merchants (third parties) to whom they were presented that defendants' husbands (second parties—cardbearers) were authorized to make charges upon the defendants' (first parties—cardholders) accounts. This apparent authority

5. *Wynn v. McMahon Ford Co.,* Mo. App., 414 S.W.2d 330, 336 (1967).

conferred upon defendants' husbands by reason of the credit cards thus precluded the application of the TILA.

In view of our determination that the TILA has no application to the present case, we hold that liability for defendants' husbands' use of the cards is governed by their contracts with the Bank. The contractual agreements between defendants and the Bank provided clearly and unequivocally that *all* cards issued upon the accounts be returned to the Bank in order to terminate defendants' liability. Accordingly, defendants' refusal to relinquish either their cards or their husbands', at the time they notified the Bank that they no longer accepted liability for their husbands' charges, justified the Bank's disregard of that notification and refusal to terminate defendants' liability at that time.

The dissent expresses concern that the decision of the Court imposes an unreasonable burden on the cardholder. We disagree because in our opinion justice is better served by placing the responsibility for the credit escapades of an errant spouse (or son, daughter, mother, father, etc.) on the cardholder rather than the Bank. The cardholder is not left powerless to protect against misuse of the card. He or she need only surrender the cards and close the account, just as the defendants in the instant case were requested by the Bank to do.

Affirmed.   No costs awarded.

DURHAM, JUSTICE (dissenting):

I dissent from the majority opinion because I believe that the federal statute and the specific cardholder agreements in question relieve the defendants of liability for the unauthorized use of their credit cards by their spouses.

* * *

First, the result of the majority opinion runs counter to the purpose of § 1643 of the TILA, which has been described as follows:

> The federal credit card statute reflects a policy decision that it is preferable for the issuer to bear fraud losses arising from credit card use.
>
> * * * [I]ssuers are in a better position to control the occurrence of these losses. They not only select the merchants who may accept the card and the holders who may use it, but also design the security systems for card distribution, user identification, and loss notification. Hence, *the statutory choice of issuer liability assures that the problem of credit card loss is the responsibility of the party most likely to take efficient steps in its resolution.*

Weistart, *Consumer Protection in the Credit Card Industry: Federal Legislative Controls,* 70 Mich.L.Rev. 1475, 1509–10 (1972) (citations omitted) (emphasis added).

Under the present circumstances, I acknowledge that the burden or risk of liability should initially fall on the cardholder because use of the credit card by a spouse is, and remains, authorized until notice is given to the card issuer that the authority to use the credit card is revoked.

However, once the cardholder notifies the card issuer of the revocation of that authority, it is clear that the card issuer is in the best position to protect itself, the cardholder and third parties. The card issuer can protect both itself and the cardholder by refusing to pay any charges on the account, and it can protect third parties by listing the credit card in the regional warning bulletins. The issuer need only terminate the existing account, transfer all existing charges to a new number, and issue a new card to the cardholder. * * * Thus, in conformance with the purpose of § 1643 of the TILA, the better holding in this case, as a policy matter, is that, after notification to the card issuer, the cardholder should be relieved of all liability for the unauthorized use of the credit card by an estranged spouse.

Second, the language of § 1643 and the law of agency require that the defendants be relieved of liability. As the majority opinion recognizes, state law determines the question of whether the defendants' husbands are clothed with "apparent authority." * * * Under Utah law, a husband or wife may terminate an agency created in the spouse in the same manner as any other agency. The majority opinion holds that the defendants' husbands' use was authorized because the husbands had "apparent authority." This is apparently a reference to the relationship between the husband and third-party merchants who rely on the husband's possession of a credit card with his name and matching signature on it. It cannot refer to the existence of apparent authority vis-a-vis the Bank, because the Bank has been *expressly notified* of the revocation of all authority. I fail to see why the existence of "apparent authority" as to third-party merchants should govern the liability of a cardholder whose spouse "steals" a card in the context of marital difficulties, any more than it would govern in the case of a cardholder whose card is stolen before delivery and bears a "matching signature" forged thereon by a thief.

It is well recognized that apparent authority exists only to the extent that the *principal* represents to a third person that another is one's agent. In the present case, with respect to the Bank, the husbands' authority, actual, implied and apparent, was specifically terminated by the defendants (the principals) when the Bank was notified that the husbands' authority to use the defendants' credit cards was revoked. Thus, after notification, the husbands' use was unauthorized and both § 1643 and the provisions of the cardholder agreements relieved the defendants of all liability for charges incurred by their husbands subsequent to that notification.

* * *

Finally, the majority opinion ignores the impracticality of imposing the burden on a cardholder of obtaining a credit card from an estranged spouse in order to return it to the Bank. It is unrealistic to think that estranged spouses will be cooperative. Moreover, it is extremely unwise to arm one spouse with a weapon which permits virtually unlimited spending at the expense of the other. As is illustrated by the facts of these cases, where the whereabouts of the unauthorized spouse are unknown, the cardholder may be powerless to acquire possession of his or her card and return it to the Bank, which, according to the majority opinion, is the only way to limit liability. One result of the majority opinion will surely be to encourage the "theft" by divorcing spouses of credit cards they were authorized to use during the marriage and the liberal use of those cards at the other spouse's expense.

* * *

YOUNG v. BANK OF AMERICA NATIONAL TRUST & SAVINGS ASSOCIATION

California Court of Appeal, 1983.
141 Cal.App.3d 108, 190 Cal.Rptr. 122.

LOW, PRESIDING JUSTICE.

Defendant Bank of America appeals from a judgment awarding plaintiff Young $150,000 in compensatory and treble damages based upon a finding that the Bank violated provisions of the Song–Beverly Credit Card Act of 1971. Plaintiff reported to the Bank that her credit card had been stolen, but the Bank tenaciously sought collection of charges she did not make. In awarding damages, the jury considered her claim for emotional distress. We affirm.

Under the Credit Card Act (Civ.Code, § 1747 *et seq.*) a credit card issuer is required to correct billing errors within 60 days of notification by the cardholder. The Credit Card Act also prohibits the card issuer from communicating unfavorable credit information to a third party while a billing dispute is under investigation. A cardholder who is injured as a result of the wilful violations of either of these provisions may collect damages, which can be trebled in the court's discretion. (Civ.Code, §§ 1747.50, 1747.70.)

In her complaint for declaratory relief and damages, plaintiff alleged that she notified the Bank that her credit card had been stolen; that the charges thereafter incurred were unauthorized; that despite being so informed the Bank refused to remove these charges from her account; and that the Bank knowingly communicated this erroneous credit information to a credit reporting service, all in violation of Civil Code sections 1747.50 and 1747.70.

Following a bifurcated trial on the issues of liability and damages, the trial court found and concluded that Young was not liable for the charges to her account, and limited her liability to the Bank in the amount of $50 pursuant to former Civil Code section 1747.20. That section limited the cardholder's liability for the unauthorized use of a credit card to $50, on condition that the cardholder inform the card issuer that the card was lost or stolen within a reasonable time after the event. A jury tried the issue of damages and returned a general verdict in favor of respondent for $50,000. The trial court concluded that the Bank's conduct was wilful and callous and trebled the damage award as permitted under Civil Code sections 1747.50, subdivision (c) and 1747.70, subdivision (d).

The facts, as stated in an agreed statement submitted to the trial court are as follows: On May 24, 1979, plaintiff permitted her friend Jerry Wooden to use her BankAmericard Visa credit card issued by the Bank for the sole purpose of purchasing a one-way airplane ticket to Hawaii, in the approximate sum of $150, on condition that Wooden telephone plaintiff every day from Hawaii and return the credit card to her when he returned to California. Wooden disappeared after May 24th; he never telephoned Young and did not return her credit card to her. On May 26, 1979, Young telephoned the Bank and informed them that her credit card had been stolen and to cancel it effective immediately. On September 3, 1979, the Bank recovered the credit card, but not before Wooden or some other person incurred $2,198.32 in charges. The Bank refused to adjust Young's balance and billed her for the charges.

The evidence at the damages phase of trial established that on June 13, 1979, Young visited the Monterey branch of the Bank and confirmed her earlier telephone call. She later wrote a letter to the Bank repeating her earlier report that her credit card was stolen. During the investigation of the disputed charges, the Bank informed TRW credit reporting service that Young had exceeded her credit limit and that her account was thirty days past due. The Bank did not notify TRW that a dispute existed. Neither did the Bank advise Young of the unfavorable credit report. For several weeks following the reported loss, Bank employees made numerous telephone calls to Young's parents' home and her place of work regarding the outstanding balance on her account and continued to send her statements demanding payment of the disputed amount.

In January 1980, Young applied for and was refused a credit card from the Monterey branch of the Valley National Bank. The decision to reject the application was based on the unfavorable TRW credit report. Young's credit report reflected a "negative" credit profile indicating that her account was 120 days delinquent with a balance due of $2,198. Young testified that she suffered emotional stress.

In support of its first contention, the Bank argues that since Wooden had apparent authority to use the credit card, the credit card could not be considered lost or stolen within the meaning of Civil Code section 1747.20. We disagree.

The former statute provided: "If an accepted credit card is lost or stolen after the credit card has reached the cardholder, and the cardholder notifies the card issuer within a reasonable time by telephone, telegraph, letter, or any other reasonable means after discovery of loss or theft or after the time in which a reasonable man in the exercise of ordinary care would have discovered the loss or theft, the cardholder is not liable for any unauthorized use of the credit card. In no event shall the liability of a cardholder for the unauthorized use of a credit card exceed fifty dollars ($50)." (Repealed by Stats.1982, ch. 545, § 6; and replaced by § 1747.10, Stats.1982, ch. 545, § 5 [limits liability for unauthorized use to $50].)

"Unauthorized use" as defined in former Civil Code section 1747.02, subdivision (f) means:

> [T]he use of a credit card by a person, other than a cardholder, (i) who does not have actual, implied, or apparent authority for such use and (ii) from which the cardholder receives no benefit. "Unauthorized use" does not include the use of a credit card by a person who has been given authority by the cardholder to use the credit card. Any attempted termination by the cardholder of such person's authority is ineffective as against the card issuer until such time as the cardholder complies with such procedures as may be required by the card issuer to terminate such authority. Furthermore, following the card issuer's receipt of oral or written notice from a cardholder indicating that it wishes to terminate the authority of a previously authorized user of a credit card, the card issuer shall follow its usual procedures for precluding any further use of a credit card by an unauthorized person.

(Amended by Stats.1982, ch. 545, § 2.)

The facts support the trial court's finding that the credit card was stolen and Wooden's use of it was unauthorized. After receiving the credit card, Wooden failed to perform as promised; i.e., to telephone daily, to limit the use of the card to one plane ticket and to return the card shortly. It may be reasonably concluded that he took it under false pretenses, never intending to return it to Young. (See *People v. Fujita* (1974) 43 Cal.App.3d 454, 467–468, 117 Cal.Rptr. 757.) Wooden retained possession of the credit card beyond any permission given, with intent to deprive Young permanently of the benefits of ownership. Therefore, the credit card was stolen within the meaning of the statute.

It is not significant that Young had voluntarily loaned the credit card to Wooden in the first instance or that the name on the card could denote that the cardholder was male or female. On May 26, 1979, two days after Wooden disappeared, Young informed the Bank that the card was stolen and that any subsequent use was unauthorized. Young had fulfilled her duties under the statute and the trial court properly limited her liability to $50.

* * *

The judgment is affirmed.

Notes

1. Are *Walker Bank* and *Young* reconcilable in their treatment of the "apparent authority" issue? Why did Jones' estranged husband have apparent authority to use the credit card while Young's friend did not? Several courts have struggled with this issue. See also Oclander v. First Nat. Bank of Louisville, 700 S.W.2d 804 (Ky.App.1985); Fifth Third Bank/ Visa v. Gilbert, 17 Ohio Misc.2d 14, 478 N.E.2d 1324 (Mun.Ct.1984).

In Mastercard v. Town of Newport, 133 Wis.2d 328, 396 N.W.2d 345 (App.1986), the city had established a corporate MasterCard account for use by the city clerk for certain official purposes. When the clerk exceeded her authority and made several personal charges, the court held the city liable for all of them. The court said that the $50 limit was intended to apply only if the card was lost or stolen. But, "when, as here, a credit cardholder authorizes another to use the card for a specific purpose, and the other person uses it for another purpose, such a use is not an 'unauthorized use' within the meaning of [the TILA]." 396 N.W.2d at 348. Do you think this is correct? Does it make sense to base liability for credit card fraud losses on a legal doctrine as slippery as state agency law? Compare the treatment of debit card losses, below.

2. As the dissent in *Walker Bank* points out, a cardholder who wants to terminate the authority of a former spouse to use the account has something of a dilemma. What action would you recommend be taken? Is there an equivalent dilemma for the bank? If the *Young* view is correct, what can the bank do to protect itself and its participating merchants from unauthorized card charges? How do you think the holdings in *Walker Bank* or *Young* will affect bank policies?

3. The authorized user practice raises other issues. As described in the *Walker Bank* case, an account is often opened in the name of one person, and other named persons (often spouses or children) are authorized to use the account. Separate cards, embossed in the names of the other persons, may be issued. These users are not contractually liable to the card issuer for charges they incur on the account; instead, the issuer normally relies on the credit standing of the primary account holder. But if the authorized user incurs charges for himself (or his children whom he has an obligation to support), might the issuer be able to recover directly from the user under a theory of quasi- or implied contract or family "necessaries"? See Sears Roebuck & Co. v. Ragucci, 203 N.J.Super. 82, 495 A.2d 923 (1985).

4. Several states have set ceilings on cardholder liability for unauthorized use; most of these are similar to that in California and follow the federal $50 pattern. Some set other limits. See, e.g., North Dakota Cent. Code § 51–14.1–02 ($100). Do these statutes have any effect? Or, does the TILA preempt them?

5. While consumers may think of credit card fraud in relatively small terms ($50 at a time, for example), banks and law enforcement agencies have a different perspective. Credit card fraud is big business. In 1983 alone, the total losses from credit card fraud in the United States were estimated at $560 million, with another $100 million in losses due to EFT fraud. In 1984, Congress sought to combat this by enacting the Credit Card Fraud Act of 1984, 18 U.S.C.A. § 1029. This Act makes it a federal crime to use fraudulently either a credit card or a debit card, or to manufacture or distribute phony cards.

Problem 7

Father entrusts his son Prodigal with his debit card and personal identification number (PIN) so that Prodigal can get $50 from a nearby automated teller machine for his Saturday night date. Instead, Prodigal drops out of sight and begins withdrawing $100 a week from Father's account. Father, hoping that Prodigal will return and beg forgiveness, does not notify the bank. When total withdrawals reach $2,000 and it becomes apparent that Prodigal has no plans to return, Father demands that the bank reimburse his account.

(a) Must the bank do so? See EFTA §§ 903(11) and 909; Reg. E § 205.6.

(b) Would the result be different if Prodigal had taken the card and PIN from Father's wallet without permission?

OGNIBENE v. CITIBANK, N.A.

Civil Court of the City of New York, New York County,
Small Claims Part, 1981.
112 Misc.2d 219, 446 N.Y.S.2d 845.

MARA T. THORPE, JUDGE:

Plaintiff seeks to recover $400.00 withdrawn from his account at the defendant bank by an unauthorized person using an automated teller machine. The court has concluded that plaintiff was the victim of a scam which defendant has been aware of for some time.

Defendant's witness, an assistant manager of one of its branches, described how the scam works: A customer enters the automated teller machine (ATM) area for the purpose of using a machine for the transaction of business with the bank. At the time that he enters, a person is using the customer service telephone located between the two automated teller machines and appears to be telling customer service that one of the machines is malfunctioning. This person is the perpetrator of the scam and his conversation with customer service is only simulated. He observes the customer press his personal identification code into one of the two machines. Having learned the code, the perpetrator then tells the customer that customer service has advised him to ask the customer to insert his Citicard into the allegedly malfunctioning machine to check whether it will work with a card other than the perpetrator's. When a good samaritan customer accedes to the request, the other machine is activated. The perpetrator then presses a code into the machine, which the customer does not realize is his own code which the perpetrator has just observed. After continuing the simulated conversation on the telephone, the perpetrator advises the customer that customer services has asked if he would try his Citicard in the allegedly malfunctioning machine once more. A second insertion of the cards permits cash to be released by the machine, and if the customer does as requested, the thief has effectuated a cash withdrawal from the unwary customer's account.

Plaintiff testified that on August 16, 1981, he went to the ATM area at one of defendant's branches and activated one of the machines with his Citibank card, pressed in his personal identification code and withdrew $20.00. While he did this a person who was using the telephone between plaintiff's machine and the adjoining machine said into the telephone, "I'll see if his card works in my machine." Thereupon he asked plaintiff if he could use his card to see if the other machine was working. Plaintiff handed it to him and saw him insert it into the adjoining machine at least two times while stating into the telephone, "Yes, it seems to be working."

Defendant's computer records in evidence show that two withdrawals of $200.00 each from plaintiff's account were made on August 16, 1981, on the machine adjoining the one plaintiff used for his $20.00 withdrawal. The two $200.00 withdrawals were made at 5:42 p.m. and 5:43 p.m. respectively; plaintiff's own $20.00 withdrawal was made at 5:41 p.m. At the time, plaintiff was unaware that any withdrawals from his account were being made on the adjoining machine.

The only fair and reasonable inferences to be drawn from all of the evidence are that the person who appeared to be conversing on the telephone observed the plaintiff enter his personal identification code into the machine from which he withdrew $20.00 and that he entered it into the adjoining machine while simulating a conversation with customer service about that machine's malfunctioning. It is conceded in the testimony of defendant's assistant branch manager that it would have been possible for a person who was positioned so as to appear to be speaking on the telephone physically to observe the code being entered into the machine by plaintiff. Although plaintiff is not certain that his card was inserted in the adjoining machine more than twice, the circumstances indicate that it was inserted four times. No issue of fraud by plaintiff or anyone acting in concert with him has been raised by defendant. Having observed plaintiff's demeanor, the court found him to be a credible witness and is of the opinion that no such issues exist in this case.

The basic rights, liabilities and responsibilities of the banks which offer electronic money transfer services and the consumers who use them have been established by the federal legislation contained in 15 U.S.C.A. 1693 et seq., commonly called the Electronic Fund Transfers Act (EFT). Although the EFT Act preempts state law only to the extent of any inconsistency (15 U.S.C.A. 1693q), to date New York State has not enacted legislation which governs the resolution of the issues herein. Therefore, the EFT Act is applicable.

The EFT Act places various limits on a consumer's liability for electronic fund transfers from his account if they are "unauthorized." Insofar as is relevant here, a transfer is "unauthorized" if 1) it is initiated by a person other than the consumer and without actual authority to initiate such transfer, 2) the consumer receives no benefit from it, and 3) the consumer did not furnish such person "with the card, code or other means of access" to his account. 15 U.S.C.A. 1693a(11).

In an action involving a consumer's liability for an electronic fund transfer, such as the one at bar, the burden of going forward to show an "unauthorized" transfer from his account is on the consumer. The EFT Act places upon the bank, however, the burden of proof of any consumer liability for the transfer. 15 U.S.C.A. 1693g(b). To establish full liability on the part of the consumer, the bank must prove that the transfer was authorized. To be entitled to even the limited liability imposed by the statute on the consumer, the bank must prove that certain conditions of consumer liability, set forth in 15 U.S.C.A. 1693g(a) have been met and that certain disclosures mandated by 15 U.S.C.A. 1693c(a)(1) and (2) have been made.

Plaintiff herein met his burden of going forward. He did not initiate the withdrawals in question, did not authorize the person in the ATM area to make them, and did not benefit from them.

However, defendant's position is, in essence, that although plaintiff was duped, the bank's burden of proof on the issue of authorization has been met by plaintiff's testimony that he permitted his card to be used in the adjoining machine by the other person. The court does not agree.

The EFT Act requires that the consumer have furnished to a person initiating the transfer the "card, code, or other means of access" to his account to be ineligible for the limitations on liability afforded by the Act when transfers are "unauthorized." The evidence establishes that in order to obtain access to an account via an automated teller machine, both the card and the personal identification code must be used. Thus, by merely giving his card to the person initiating the transfer, a consumer does not furnish the "means of access" to his account. To do so, he would have to furnish the personal identification code as well. See 12 C.F.R. 205.2(a)(1), the regulation promulgated under the EFT Act which defines "access device" as "a card, code or other means of access to [an] * * * account *or any combination thereof*" (emphasis added).

The court finds that plaintiff did not furnish his personal identification code to the person initiating the $400.00 transfer within the meaning of the EFT Act. There is no evidence that he deliberately or even negligently did so. On the contrary, the unauthorized person was able to obtain the code because of defendant's own negligence. Since the bank had knowledge of the scam and its operational details (including the central role of the customer service telephone), it was negligent in failing to provide plaintiff-customer with information sufficient to alert him to the danger when he found himself in the position of a potential victim. Although in June, 1981, after the scam came to defendant's attention, it posted signs in its ATM areas containing a red circle approximately 2½ inches in diameter in which is written "Do Not Let Your Citicard Be Used For Any Transaction But Your Own", the court finds that this printed admonition is not a sufficient security measure since it fails to state the reason why one should not do so. Since a customer of defendant's electronic fund transfer service must employ both the card and the personal identification code in order to withdraw money from his account, the danger of loaning his card briefly for the purpose of checking the functioning of an adjoining automated teller machine would not be immediately apparent to one who has not divulged his personal identification number and who is unaware that it has been revealed merely by virtue of his own transaction with the machine.

Since the bank established the electronic fund transfer service and has the ability to tighten its security characteristics, the responsibility for the fact that plaintiff's code, one of the two necessary components of the "access device" or "means of access" to his account, was observed and utilized as it was must rest with the bank.

For the foregoing reasons and in view of the fact that the primary purpose of the EFT Act and the regulation promulgated thereunder is the protection of individual consumers (12 C.F.R. 205.1(b)), the court concludes that plaintiff did not furnish his code to anyone within the meaning of the Act. Accordingly, since the person who obtained it did not have actual authority to initiate the transfer, the transfer qualifies as an "unauthorized" one under 15 U.S.C.A. 1693a(11) and the bank cannot hold plaintiff fully liable for the $400.00 withdrawal.

To avail itself of the limited liability imposed by the Act upon a consumer in the event of an "unauthorized" transfer, the bank must demonstrate 1) that the means of access utilized for the transfer was "accepted" and 2) that the bank has provided a way which the user of the means of access can be identified as the person authorized to use it. 15 U.S.C.A. 1693g(a) and (b). One definition of "accepted" under the Act is that the consumer has used the means of access. 15 U.S.C.A. 1693a(1). Both of the foregoing conditions of liability have been met here since plaintiff used the means of access to his account to withdraw the $20.00 and had been given a personal identification code.

Additionally, the bank must prove that it disclosed to the consumer his liability for unauthorized electronic fund transfers and certain information pertaining to notification of the bank in the event the consumer believes that an unauthorized transfer has been or may be effected. 15 U.S.C.A. 1693c(a)(1) and (2) and 1693g(b). Defendant did not establish that it made such disclosures to plaintiff. Accordingly, it is not entitled to avail itself of the benefit of the limited liability for unauthorized transfers imposed upon consumers by the Act.

For the foregoing reasons, judgment shall be for plaintiff in the sum of $400.00.

Notes

1. The New York Attorney General also brought a case against Citibank based on the ATM problems and won injunctive relief, damages, and restitution. Citibank agreed to pay nearly $500,000 to customers who had been victims of the scam discussed in the preceding case. Afterwards, Citibank changed its software.

2. In *Ognibene*, why wasn't the customer responsible for $50 of the $400 loss? Did the bank's lawyer make a mistake somewhere?

3. When an unauthorized transfer is alleged, EFTA § 909(b) places the burden of proof squarely upon "the financial institution" to show authorization. Can the burden be met simply by presenting the record of the payment order, and alleging that a PIN is necessary to access the computer? Consider the following excerpt from Judd v. Citibank, 107 Misc. 2d 526, 435 N.Y.S.2d 210 (N.Y.City Ct.1980), decided under pre-EFTA concepts:

> From the testimony adduced at trial it appears that the funds in question were withdrawn from plaintiff's account on February 26, 1980 between 2:13 and 2:14 P.M., and on March 28, 1980 between 2:30 and 2:32 P.M. Plaintiff testified and produced a letter from her employer to the effect that she was at work on both occasions and could not have made the said withdrawals. Citibank produced computer printouts documenting the withdrawals in issue, which printouts were explained (translated) by the bank's witness, the branch manager. Defendant asserts that the funds in question were and could have been withdrawn from the Judd account by use of a validated Citicard at a Citibank electronic teller, coupled with entry of the correct [PIN]. Citibank has submitted a statement in support of its contention that it has effected stringent security measures to prevent the unauthorized use of Citicards. Plaintiff testified that not only did she not let anyone else use her Citicard but that she never told anyone her [PIN] and never wrote it down.

> The question presented is a basic one, of evidence, burdens and credibility: Has plaintiff proven her case by a fair preponderance of the credible evidence? In this case we are met with a credible witness on the one hand and a computer printout on the other. It is evident that there was no opportunity to cross examine the computer or the printout it produced. * * *

> * * * [T]his court is not prepared to go so far as to rule that where a credible witness is faced with the adverse "testimony" of a machine, he is as a matter of law faced also with an unmeetable burden of proof. It is too commonplace in our society that when faced with the choice of man or machine we readily accept the "word" of the machine everytime. This, despite the tales of computer malfunctions that we hear daily. Defendant's own witness testified to physical malfunctions of the very system in issue.

> This court, as trier of the fact, finds that plaintiff has proven her case by a fair preponderance of the credible evidence. * * *

4. Congress established the National Commission on Electronic Fund Transfers in 1974. This commission issued a final report three years later, and the report formed much of the basis for the EFTA. The commission had recommended that losses should fall on the customer if the customer was negligent. This rule would have followed the UCC's treatment of fraud losses for forged checks. As finally enacted, however, the EFTA contains no reference to negligence. Does that mean that the customer loss limits apply even if the customer wrote his PIN on his card?

5.   What happens if a state law is different?   Michigan followed the UCC model in its EFT law, and imposes liability on the customer if the bank can prove "that the customer's negligence substantially contributed to the unauthorized use."   Mich.Comp.Laws Ann. § 488.14.   Does this mean debit cardholders in Michigan must be more careful than cardholders in Kansas?   Is EFTA § 919 relevant?

Problem 8

Late at night you are confronted on the street by a robber who demands "your money or your life."   You have no cash, but the robber spots your plastic Firstbank debit card.   At gunpoint, you are marched to the bank's 24–hour teller machine and instructed to withdraw $1000.   After deliberating (a la Jack Benny), you do so, and give the money to the robber, who disappears.   Can you insist that Firstbank recredit your account?

Problem 9

An employee in the computer department at Firstbank has devised a way to steal money from customer accounts without using any card or personal identification number.   His scheme involves manipulating the computer program in such a way that electronic transfers are made from customer accounts to an account in the employee's name.   When the thefts are discovered, you realize that he has "hit" your account to the tune of $500.   Must the bank reimburse you?   Was this an "unauthorized" transfer within the meaning of the EFTA?   If not, does that make them "authorized" and binding on you?

Chapter 6

CUTTING OFF CONSUMER
CLAIMS AND DEFENSES

SECTION A. INDUSTRY CONDUCT BEFORE
REGULATION—THE LAW MERCHANT AND
THE UCC

Introductory Note

Traditional legal doctrines impose substantial responsibilities on sellers for the honesty, quality and safety of their performance. A dissatisfied customer may recover damages upon proof of seller's negligence, or breach of implied or express warranties. A buyer may recover damages or rescind if there was fraud in the transaction, or misrepresentation by the seller.

Also, by traditional rules, a third party who purchased the seller's contractual right to payment took those rights subject to the consumer's defenses against the seller. Thus the fact that a consumer's obligation was assigned to a bank or other financer did not, alone, diminish the consumer's rights.

But for all these conventional principles there were equally well-established bypasses which sellers and creditors could use to reduce or eliminate their exposure to liability. In the setting of contractual warranties, which were perceived to arise from the contractual agreement of the parties, the parties—at least the *dominant* party—were free to contract away those responsibilities. And for third party financers the law supplied the doctrine of "negotiability" of commercial paper with its resultant protection for bona fide purchasers of such paper ("holders in due course").

The Uniform Commercial Code retained most of the conventional wisdom. As between seller and buyer, any affirmation of fact, promise, description or sample creates an express warranty that the goods will conform, if such representation is a part of the "basis of the bargain." UCC § 2–313. In addition, merchant sellers warrant the "merchantability" of their wares, i.e., their fitness for ordinary use. UCC § 2–314. Sellers may also impliedly warrant that their goods are suitable for particular purposes. UCC § 2–315. Against these warranties, however, stand the "disclaimer" rules of UCC § 2–316 through which warranties may be avoided by specific and conspicuous language, by buyer's failure to see patent defects, or even by use of shorthand phrases like "as is." Thus, with only the UCC as a benchmark, a seller can reduce his duty to merely delivering something that meets the basic contract description ("one RCA portable TV"). And under the parol evidence rule inclusion of a "merger" clause would avoid liability for seller's oral statements (or mis-statements), UCC § 2–202. Finally, even if seller gave a warranty, he could scale down buyer's remedy. UCC § 2–719.

As for the protection of third party assignees, the UCC is equally solicitous. If a bank or finance company purchased from a dealer a "negotiable instrument" (UCC § 3–104) under circumstances where it qualified as a "holder in due course" (UCC § 3–302), the creditor could enforce the instrument free from all consumer defenses except a small number of "real" defenses (UCC § 3–305). Alternatively, the third party may acquire virtually identical protection by having the dealer insert a "waiver of defense" clause in the underlying consumer obligation. Furthermore, such a clause is implied into any secured sale involving a negotiable note. See UCC § 9–206(1).

For 20th century consumer transactions, the implications of these rules and sub-rules are easy to see. Sellers and creditors, who could be expected to be in a position to dictate the form and content of their mass-produced consumer contracts, did just that. Warranty "disclaimers" became boiler-plate. Negotiable promissory notes (or their functional twins, "waiver of defense" clauses) became standard formalities in credit transactions. Consumers were left with little more than ownership rights in cars that would not run, furniture that fell apart, and appliances that defied repair.

The materials that follow trace the law's response to this state of consumer disability. First through the courts, and then through the legislatures, the law with respect to consumer claims and defenses has been turned virtually upside down. Sweeping "reforms" have been instituted within recent years. These materials look first at a sampling of traditional practices, and then explore two of the developing streams:

(1) the attack on warranty disclaimers and remedy limitations; and

(2) the elimination of holder in due course protections.

The questions to be asked are: What were the abuses? Are the responses sufficient? Excessive? What new problems do they create?

FIRST NAT. BANK OF ELGIN v. HUSTED

Illinois Court of Appeals, 1965.
57 Ill.App.2d 227, 205 N.E.2d 780.

DAVIS, JUSTICE.

This is an appeal from an Order entered by the Circuit Court denying defendants' motion to open a judgment in the sum of $672.18, confessed against them on January 27, 1964, by plaintiff, First National Bank of Elgin.

The judgment was based on a Retail Installment Contract entered into by defendants, as buyers, and Reed Motors Inc., as seller, in connection with the sale of a 1958 Ford. The customary warrant of attorney and confession clause were on the reverse side of the contract, under the heading "Covenants and Conditions", along with the "Dealer's Assignment", whereby said contract was assigned to plaintiff, without recourse.

Defendants signed the contract on the face thereof, but did not sign on the reverse side. The face of the contract recited: "Buyer and Seller agree that the 'Covenants and Conditions' printed on the reverse side hereof are incorporated herein by reference and constitute a part of this contract."

* * *

The Retail Sales Contract was dated August 29, 1963, and was assigned to plaintiff August 30, 1963. Defendants, by said contract, acknowledged notice of intended assignment of the contract, and agreed to make all payments to assignee, and their answer admitted said assignment. The contract, on its face, provided that payments were to be made at the First National Bank of Elgin.

The motion to open the judgment, and to file answer, and the affidavit in support thereof, alleged that defendants purchased the Ford in question on August 29, 1963, from Reed Motors Inc., upon warranty that it was in good operating condition; that on September 1, 1963, defendants observed that the car did not operate properly, and that it became inoperative, and was damaged by fire; that thereafter, on September 2, 1963, Reed Motors Inc., promised to repair the car upon delivery thereof to it; that said car was delivered to Reed Motors Inc., but was never repaired, and was later sold by Reed Motors Inc., or plaintiff; and that neither Reed Motors Inc., nor plaintiff, its assignee, sold said car until December 2, 1963, which sale was not within a reasonable time after the re-taking, and hence there was an election of remedies under section 23 of the Retail Installment Sales Act, (Ill.Rev. Stat.1963, Chap. 121½, section 247) and thereby defendants have been released from any obligations to Reed Motors Inc., or plaintiff. Defendants' affidavit also charged lack of notice of the assignment and failure of consideration.

* * *

Defendants further charge that plaintiff was not a holder in due course of the Retail Installment Contract, and, therefore, the defenses which they have asserted are available against the plaintiff. However, the contract provided: "Buyer agrees to settle all claims against Seller directly with Seller and will not set up any such claims against Seller as defense, counterclaim, set-off, cross complaint or otherwise in any action for the purchase price or possession brought by any assignee of this contract."

The Uniform Commercial Code, provides:

"(1) Subject to any statute or decision which establishes a different rule for buyers of consumer goods, an agreement by a buyer that he will not assert against an assignee any claim or defense which he may have against the seller is enforceable by an assignee who takes his assignment for value, in good faith and without notice of a claim or defense, except as to defenses of a type which may be asserted against a holder in due course of a negotiable instrument under the Article on Commercial Paper. (Article 3). A buyer who as part of one transaction signs both a negotiable instrument and a security agreement makes such an agreement.

"(2) When a seller retains a purchase money security interest in goods the Article on Sales (Article 2) governs the sale and any disclaimer, limitation or modification of the seller's warranties."

(Ill.Rev.Stat.1963, Chap. 26, Sec. 9–206).

The first sentence of this subsection permits a contractual waiver of certain defenses by the buyer, and it is in accord with prior Illinois case law. Commercial Credit Corp. v. Biagi, 11 Ill.App.2d 80, 82, 136 N.E.2d 580 (1st Dist.1956). While this section provides that either the legislature or the courts may establish a different rule, we view this as a legislative function, the exercise of will rather than judgment, and we are reluctant to change the prior decisional law.

* * *

Thus, a buyer may contractually waive, as against an assignee, any defenses except those enumerated in Articles 3–305(2) and 9–206(2). The defenses which defendants, as buyers, seek to assert against plaintiff are: failure of consideration; lack of notice of assignment; breach of express and implied warranties; subsequent promises and failure to repair the car, and an election to retain the car arising by failure to resell it within a reasonable time after the re-taking. In absence of allegation in defendants' affidavit that plaintiff did not take the assignment for value, in good faith, and without notice of claim or defense, and in view of the date of the contract and assignment, we believe that plaintiff is an assignee for value, in good faith, and without notice of claim or defense.

The buyers' defenses of failure of consideration, and subsequent promise and failure to repair the car were waived, as against the plaintiff, assignee, under Article 9–206 of the Uniform Commercial Code.

* * *

The Retail Installment Sales Act contains no provisions relative to warranties. The exclusion and modification of warranties is governed by article 2–316 of the Uniform Commercial Code. Its purpose is to protect the buyer from unbargained language of disclaimer by denying effect to such language when inconsistent with the contract language of express warranty, and it permits the exclusion of implied warranties by conspicuous language in the contract. It provides that "all implied warranties are excluded by expressions like 'as is', 'with all faults' or other language which in common understanding calls the buyer's attention to the exclusion of warranties and makes plain that there is no implied warranty." It also provides that there is no implied warranty where "the buyer before entering into the contract has examined the goods or the sample or model as fully as he desired or has refused to examine the goods * * *."

The contract in question, immediately beneath the names of the parties, in language printed in the size type of all of the words of the paragraphs of the contract, provided: "Buyer acknowledges delivery, examination and acceptance of said car in its present condition." The "Covenants and Conditions" of the contract contained the following language, printed in the same size type: "This agreement constitutes the entire contract and no waivers or modification shall be valid unless written upon or attached to this contract, and said car is accepted without any express or implied warranties, agreements, representations, promises or statements unless expressly set forth in this contract at the time of purchase." The contract contained no express warranties pertaining to the car.

We believe that the words "in its present condition" are similar to the words "as is" or "with all faults", and have the effect of excluding implied warranties. Further, the buyer acknowledged examination of the car and this precludes an implied warranty. Consequently, the defenses of express and implied warranties were not available to the defendants.

* * *

Consequently, we hold that the trial Court properly denied defendants' motion to open the judgment in question. A motion to open up a judgment by confession is addressed to the sound discretion of the court and the order thereon will be reversed only for an abuse of such discretion. We find no such abuse of discretion in the case at bar; therefore judgment of the trial Court is affirmed.

Judgment affirmed.

Note

Consider the extensive variety of devices available to this creditor to cut off consumer defenses: disclaimer of warranty, merger clause, waiver of defense clause, negotiable note, confession of judgment clause, acknowledgment of receipt in good condition, default judgment. Each of these can operate independently, which means that the prohibition of only one or some of them does not completely obviate the consumer's problems.

Problem 1

Robbin Hood bought a used car on credit from Alan Dale, doing business as Dale Dodge Dealers. The contract of sale conspicuously stated that the car was sold "as is" and "with all faults". Hood drove the car off the lot and used it for 30 days. Then the car became inoperable, and Dale refused to repair, replace or refund. Does Hood have a successful cause of action against Dale under the UCC? See UCC § 2–316(2), (3); Chamberlain v. Bob Matick Chevrolet, Inc., 4 Conn.Cir. 685, 239 A.2d 42 (1967).

Problem 2

Hood bought a new car from Dale on credit. The contract of sale contained an express warranty with a one-year duration. After 30 days the car became inoperable. Can Hood safely stop making payments on the car? See UCC §§ 2–607(1), 2–717.

This may seem like an academic question in this simple transaction; presumably if seller sues buyer for the price buyer will defend and seek a set-off under UCC § 2–714 for breach of warranty. The issue becomes less academic, however, when we include the very real possibility of default judgments, and the effects of security interests and garnishments, all discussed later in this Part.

At the least, remember that there is a major distinction between buyer's ability to go to court and sue for breach of warranty, and buyer's ability to use self-help in the form of withholding payments. The right to exercise self-help seems deeply imbedded in our folklore; many dissatisfied consumers instinctively react by withholding payments, often with sad results. In reality self-help under the UCC is very limited, for UCC § 2–717 requires some moderately intricate "dance steps" as conditions to its use. The buyer must *notify* the seller of his intention to deduct damages from the payments, and may deduct only the damages caused by the breach of warranty—not the entire price. How likely is it that an unadvised consumer will adhere to these restrictions?

Problem 3

(a) Hood bought a new car from Dale on credit. The contract of sale had no disclaimers of warranty, limitations on remedy, or waiver of defense clause. The contract was assigned to Tuck Trust Co. for value. Hood refuses to pay because the car soon became inoperable. Has Tuck a successful cause of action against Hood? See Restatement, Second, Contracts §§ 152, 167; Sponge Divers' Ass'n v. Smith, Kline & French Co., 263 Fed 70 (3d Cir.1920); UCC §§ 9–318(1)(a), 2–714.

Note that the issues raised after Problem 2 (consumer self-help and rescission) are somewhat more complex when a third party is involved. Everything can still be worked out in contested litigation, but repossession, default judgments and the like are still problems. At the least, you should understand that retaining defenses against an assignee does not get the consumer buyer home free, even where there is a warranty.

(b) Same facts as in (a), except that this time the car is sold "as is." Dale assigns the credit contract to Tuck Trust Co. for value. If Hood refuses to pay because the car is inoperable, does Tuck have a successful cause of action against Hood? See Problem 1, supra.

Note that a disclaimer of warranties may be used to "cut off defenses" against a third party, and will be effective in doing that if the disclaimer is effective in protecting the seller itself.

Problem 4

(a) Hood bought a new car from Dale on credit. The contract of sale contained an express warranty with a one-year duration. It also contained a clause:

> "I (We) will settle all claims of any kind against SELLER directly with SELLER and if SELLER assigns this note I (we) will not use any such claim as a defense, setoff or counterclaim against any effort by the holder to enforce this instrument."

Dale assigned the credit contract to Tuck. After 30 days the car became inoperable, and Dale refuses to repair, replace or refund. If Hood refuses to pay because the car is inoperable, does Tuck have a successful cause of action against Hood? See UCC § 9–206; Root v. John Deere Co., 413 S.W.2d 901 (Ky.1967).

(b) Same facts as (a), except that this time Hood signs a negotiable promissory note which is then purchased by Tuck. When the car becomes inoperable, Hood refuses to pay. Does Tuck have a successful cause of action against Hood? See UCC §§ 9–206, 3–305.

SECTION B. CUTTING OFF THE CONSUMER BUYER'S RIGHTS AGAINST THE SELLER— DISCLAIMERS OF WARRANTY AND LIMITS ON REMEDIES

1. REVOCATION OF ACCEPTANCE UNDER THE UCC: CONSUMER SALVATION OR CONSUMER NIGHTMARE?

The Uniform Commercial Code is the foundation of all modern warranty law. It applies to both consumer and business transactions. The UCC is premised on the notion that the parties to a transaction are equals who can agree or not agree to anything they please.

The consumer who has purchased a defective product usually wants to return it and get his money back. Obviously, an effective warranty disclaimer may preclude this remedy. UCC § 2–316. Even if the warranty has not been disclaimed, however, there may be another obstacle facing the consumer, namely, a limitation of remedy clause. UCC § 2–719. A new car buyer whose remedy for breach of warranty is limited to repair or replacement of defective parts may soon get frustrated when he finds he must take the car back to the garage again and again. Also, the consumer will likely want a remedy against the "deep pocket" manufacturer, but lack of privity may also be a problem under the UCC.

The consumer does have some rights under the UCC itself, including the right to revoke acceptance of defective goods. UCC 2–608.

Courts have become more lenient in upholding these rights in consumer cases. This is not to say there is a yellow brick road that will inevitably lead the consumer to the desired goal, however.

Note the various land mines awaiting the unwary consumer-buyer. To revoke acceptance under § 2–608 the consumer must:

— show substantial impairment of value,

— show that non-discovery of the defect was "induced either by difficulty of discovery before acceptance or by the seller's assurances,"

— revoke acceptance within a "reasonable time after the buyer * * * should have discovered [the defects]" and "before any substantial change,"

— properly notify the seller of the alleged breach, and

— refrain from further use of the goods.

Despite these difficulties, revocation of acceptance has been called "the consumer buyer's most important remedy under Article 2." B. Clark & C. Smith, The Law of Product Warranties 7–15 (1984).

McCULLOUGH v. BILL SWAD CHRYSLER–PLYMOUTH

Ohio Supreme Court, 1983.
5 Ohio St.3d 181, 449 N.E.2d 1289.

On May 23, 1978, appellee, Deborah A. McCullough (then Deborah Miller), purchased a 1978 Chrysler LeBaron from appellant, Bill Swad Chrysler–Plymouth, Inc. (now Bill Swad Datsun, Inc.). The automobile was protected by both a limited warranty and a Vehicle Service Contract (extended warranty). Following delivery of the vehicle, appellee and her (then) fiance informed appellant's sales agent of problems they had noted with the car's brakes, lack of rustproofing, paint job and seat panels. Other problems were noted by appellee as to the car's transmission and air conditioning. The next day, the brakes failed, and appellee returned the car to appellant for the necessary repairs.

When again in possession of the car, appellee discovered that the brakes had not been fixed properly and that none of the cosmetic work was done. Problems were also noted with respect to the car's steering mechanism. Again, the car was returned for repair and again new problems appeared, this time as to the windshield post, the vinyl top and the paint job. Only two weeks later, appellant was unable to eliminate a noise appellee complained of that had developed in the car's rear end.

On June 26, 1978, appellee returned the car to appellant for correction both of the still unremedied defects and of other flaws that had surfaced since the last failed repair effort. Appellant retained possession of the vehicle for over three weeks in order to service it, but even then many of the former problems persisted. Moreover, appellant's workmanship had apparently caused new defects to arise affecting the car's stereo system, landau top and exterior. Appellee also experienced difficulties with vibrations, the horn, and the brakes.

The following month, while appellee was on a short trip away from her home, the automobile's engine abruptly shut off. The car eventually had to be towed to appellant's service shop for repair. A few days later, when appellee and her husband were embarked on an extensive honeymoon vacation, the brakes again failed. Upon returning from their excursion, the newlyweds, who had prepared a list of thirty-two of the automobile's defects, submitted the list to appellant and again requested their correction. By the end of October 1978, few of the enumerated problems had been remedied.

In early November 1978, appellee contacted appellant's successor, Chrysler–Plymouth East ("East"), regarding further servicing of the vehicle. East was not able to undertake the requested repairs until January 1979. Despite the additional work which East performed, the vehicle continued to malfunction. After May 1979, East refused to perform any additional work on the automobile, claiming that the vehicle was in satisfactory condition, appellee's assertions to the contrary notwithstanding.

On January 8, 1979, appellee, by letter addressed to appellant, called for the rescission of the purchase agreement, demanded a refund of the entire purchase price and expenses incurred, and offered to return the automobile to appellant upon receipt of shipping instructions. Appellant did not respond to appellee's letter, and appellee continued to operate the car.

On January 12, 1979, appellee filed suit against appellant, East, Chrysler Corporation, and City National Bank & Trust Co., seeking rescission of the sales agreement and incidental and consequential damages. By the time of trial, June 25, 1980, the subject vehicle had been driven nearly 35,000 miles, approximately 23,000 of which were logged after appellee mailed her notice of revocation. The trial court dismissed the action as to East, the bank and Chrysler Corporation, but entered judgment for appellee against appellant in the amount of $9,376.82, and ordered the return of the automobile to appellant. The court of appeals subsequently affirmed, determining that appellee had properly revoked her acceptance of the automobile despite her continued use of the vehicle, which use the appellate court found reasonable.

The cause is now before this court pursuant to the allowance of a motion to certify the record.

LOCHER, JUSTICE.

The case at bar essentially poses but a single question: Whether appellee, by continuing to operate the vehicle she had purchased from appellant after notifying the latter of her intent to rescind the purchase agreement, waived her right to revoke her initial acceptance. After having thoroughly reviewed both the relevant facts in the present cause and the applicable law, we find that appellee, despite her extensive use of the car following her revocation, in no way forfeited such right.

* * *

Although the legal question presented in appellant's first objection is a novel one for this bench, other state courts which have addressed the issue have held that whether continued use of goods after notification of revocation of their acceptance vitiates such revocation is solely dependent upon whether such use was reasonable. Moreover, whether such use was reasonable is a question to be determined by the trier of fact.

The genesis of the "reasonable use" test lies in the recognition that frequently a buyer, after revoking his earlier acceptance of a good, is constrained by exogenous circumstances—many of which the seller controls—to continue using the good until a suitable replacement may realistically be secured. Clearly, to penalize the buyer for a predicament not of his own creation would be patently unjust. As the court stated in *Richardson v. Messina* (1960), 361 Mich. 364, 369, 105 N.W.2d 153, 156:

> * * * It does not lie in the seller's mouth to demand the utmost in nicety between permissible and impermissible use, for the perilous situation in which the purchaser finds himself arises from the imperfections of that furnished, for a consideration, by the seller himself.

* * *

In ascertaining whether a buyer's continued use of an item after revocation of its acceptance was reasonable, the trier of fact should pose and divine the answers to the following queries: (1) Upon being apprised of the buyer's revocation of his acceptance, what instructions, if any, did the seller tender the buyer concerning return of the now rejected goods? (2) Did the buyer's business needs or personal circumstances compel the continued use? (3) During the period of such use, did the seller persist in assuring the buyer that all nonconformities would be cured or that provisions would otherwise be made to recompense the latter for the dissatisfaction and inconvenience which the defects caused him? (4) Did the seller act in good faith? (5) Was the seller unduly prejudiced by the buyer's continued use?

It is manifest that, upon consideration of the aforementioned criteria, appellee acted reasonably in continuing to operate her motor vehicle even after revocation of acceptance. First, the failure of the seller to advise the buyer, after the latter has revoked his acceptance of the goods, how the goods were to be returned entitles the buyer to retain possession of them. Appellant, in the case at bar, did not respond to appellee's request for instructions regarding the disposition of the vehicle. Failing to have done so, appellant can hardly be heard now to complain of appellee's continued use of the automobile.

Secondly, appellee, a young clerical secretary of limited financial resources, was scarcely in position to return the defective automobile and obtain a second in order to meet her business and personal needs.

A most unreasonable obligation would be imposed upon appellee were she to be required, in effect, to secure a loan to purchase a second car while remaining liable for repayment of the first car loan.

Additionally, appellant's successor (East), by attempting to repair the appellee's vehicle even after she tendered her notice of revocation, provided both express and tacit assurances that the automobile's defects were remediable, thereby, inducing her to retain possession. Moreover, whether appellant acted in good faith throughout this episode is highly problematic, especially given the fact that whenever repair of the car was undertaken, new defects often miraculously arose while previous ones frequently went uncorrected. Both appellant's and East's refusal to honor the warranties before their expiration also evidences less than fair dealing.

* * *

Appellant maintains, however, that even if appellee's continued operation of the automobile after revocation was reasonable, such use is "*prima facie* evidence" that the vehicle's nonconformities did not substantially impair its value to appellee, thus precluding availability of the remedy of revocation. Such an inference, though, may not be drawn. As stated earlier, external conditions beyond the buyer's immediate control often mandate continued use of an item even after revocation of its acceptance. Thus, it cannot seriously be contended that appellee, by continuing to operate the defective vehicle, intimated that its nonconformities did not substantially diminish its worth in her eyes.

* * *

Whether a complained of nonconformity substantially impairs an item's worth to the buyer is a determination exclusively within the purview of the factfinder and must be based on objective evidence of the buyer's idiosyncratic tastes and needs. Any defect that shakes the buyer's faith or undermines his confidence in the reliability and integrity of the purchased item is deemed to work a substantial impairment of the item's value and to provide a basis for revocation of the underlying sales agreement. Clearly, no error was committed in finding that the fears occasioned by the recurrent brake failings, steering malfunctions and other mechanical difficulties, as well as the utter frustration caused by the seemingly endless array of cosmetic flaws, constituted nonconformities giving rise to the remedy of revocation.

* * *

On the basis of the foregoing analysis, we affirm the judgment of the court of appeals.

Judgment affirmed.

HOLMES, JUSTICE, dissenting in part and concurring in part.

I concur in the syllabus law as set forth in this case, but would remand to the trial court for a determination of the amount due the dealer from the buyer as a setoff due to the buyer's use of the goods after revocation. Both the court of appeals and this court state that

Swad should be entitled to such an offset against the judgment for the reasonable value of the use of the automobile after the revocation. However, both courts summarily dispense with such an offset by stating that Swad introduced no evidence to establish the reasonable value of the automobile's use.

The need for any such evidence when the appellant was asserting that the buyer had waived any right to revoke acceptance would, from the standpoint of trial procedure, have been highly questionable. The seller should be given an opportunity to present evidence of the reasonable value of such use, or the trial court should take judicial notice of the fair market value of the use of such an automobile.

GASQUE v. MOOERS MOTOR CAR CO., INC.

Supreme Court of Virginia, 1984.
227 Va. 154, 313 S.E.2d 384.

RUSSELL, JUSTICE. * * *

In accordance with established standards of appellate review, we must view the evidence in the light most favorable to the parties prevailing below. The buyers took delivery of a new Fiat from Mooers on February 21, 1979. At various subsequent times, they reported to Mooers that they had experienced a water leak, a loose gearshift lever, difficulty shifting into second and third gear, heater malfunction, an inoperative clock and interior light, a loose wire under the dash, blown fuses, a piece missing from a front door, automatic choke problems, difficulty starting, fast idling, difficulty closing the rear door on the driver's side, difficulty opening the rear door on the passenger's side, excessive oil consumption, loud vibrations, and various other noises and rattles. In addition, they claimed that the reclining front seat broke, and that they experienced repeated difficulty with the foot-long plastic extension to the gearshift lever, which pulled loose.

The buyers returned the car to Mooers on March 13, March 23, an unspecified date in May, June 22, June 27, July 20, and August 6, 1979, for service. On each occasion, Mooers repaired the items complained of, without charge, although Mooers could find no evidence of some of the problems described by the buyers. Mooers conceded that the car experienced a recurring problem with the gearshift extension and testified that this defect affected three out of seventy cars of this model which it had recently sold. Mooers' service manager testified that the gearshift extension would come off only if used improperly by pulling it upward and that the car was still operable without the extension. The car was in fact driven for thousands of miles while subject to this defect. Although Mooers thought a permanent repair of this problem could be accomplished, the difficulty continued up to the time of trial.

The buyers consulted counsel, who, on September 19, 1979, wrote to Mooers and to Fiat demanding "a full refund including interests and expenses for the times that the vehicle was in the shop or, in the alternative, the replacement of said automobile."

The buyers continued to drive the Fiat, except when it was left with Mooers for service. When the car was last in Mooers' shop for repairs on August 6, it had 4,543 miles on the odometer. When buyers' counsel wrote to Mooers on September 19, he stated that the car had been driven 5,400 miles. At the time of trial on May 21, 1980, the car had been driven over 8,000 miles. The buyers testified that they purchased a used Volkswagen in November 1979, and permanently parked the Fiat, which by then had been driven 8,000 miles, in their driveway.

* * *

A buyer's right to revoke acceptance does not arise from every breach of warranty, notwithstanding the availability of damages for the breach; it arises only where the value of the goods to the buyer is substantially impaired. The test of such impairment is not, however, a diminution in value of the goods on the open market, or to the average buyer, but rather a substantial impairment of value to the particular buyer involved.

* * *

How may this be shown? Undoubtedly, there may be a purchaser of an automobile who wants it for an unusual and special purpose, such as display in a collection of antique vehicles. But the burden would be on the buyer to show such a special need. In the absence of such a showing, the fact-finder is entitled to infer that the goods are needed by the buyer for their customary and ordinary purpose—simple transportation in the case of an automobile. In the instant case, there was persuasive evidence that the Fiat in question substantially fulfilled that purpose. It had been driven 5,400 miles by the time the buyers sought to revoke acceptance and an additional 2,600 miles thereafter. The trial court applied a standard of "driveability" as the test of whether the car's value to the buyers was substantially impaired. While such a standard would not be of universal application, we cannot say that it was erroneous where the buyers failed to prove any need for the car beyond ordinary transportation. Accordingly, the trial court's finding in this respect was supported by evidence and will not be disturbed on appeal.

* * * Revocation of acceptance must be made promptly, or within a reasonable time after acceptance, and the buyer may not use the goods to a material degree and then attempt to revoke. * * * But after giving notice of revocation, the buyer holds the goods as bailee for the seller. The buyer cannot continue to use them as his own and still have the benefit of rescission; his continued use becomes wrongful against the seller, unless induced by the seller's instructions or promises.

Exceptions have been made to the rule in mobile home cases, where departure from the home before resolving the litigation would cause undue hardship to the buyer and where the buyer's continued occupancy might be the best means of safeguarding the property for a seller who refuses to take it back. But this reasoning has no application to the continuing use of an automobile, which ordinarily depreciates in value with every mile it is driven.

Applying these principles to the case at bar, the buyers' delay, at least until after August 6, was reasonable in light of the seller's continuing efforts to effect repairs, which were only partially successful. But it is equally clear that the buyers' continued use of the car after giving notice of revocation of acceptance on September 19, during which time they drove it 2,600 miles, was entirely inconsistent with their position as a bailee, maintaining custody only to safeguard the car for the seller. Such personal use of what they contended to be the seller's property does not meet the standard of commercial reasonableness, and the trial court correctly so held.

The trial court correctly struck the evidence against Fiat. The remedy of revocation of acceptance was the sole relief available to the buyers under their bill of complaint, as noted above. This remedy lies only against a seller of goods, not against a remote manufacturer. This is so because the remedy, where successful, cancels a contract of sale, restores both title to and possession of the goods to the seller, restores the purchase price to the buyer, and as fairly as possible, returns the contracting parties to the *status quo ante*. The remote manufacturer, having no part in the sale transaction, has no role to play in such a restoration of former positions.

The buyers argue that this limitation on revocation revivifies the "archaic doctrine of privity." We disagree. A remote manufacturer is liable to a buyer for damages arising from negligence or from breach of warranty, and the defense of lack of privity has been abolished as to such cases. Code § 8.2–318. But the remedy of revocation of acceptance under Code § 8.2–608 is conceptually inapplicable to any persons other than the parties to the contract of sale sought to be rescinded.

For these reasons, the decree will be

Affirmed.

Notes

1. Why was the value of the car substantially impaired in the *McCullough* case but not in *Gasque*? Is the test for substantial impairment of value objective or subjective? Does the Code language itself provide a clue? See Jorgensen v. Pressnall, 274 Or. 285, 545 P.2d 1382 (1976).

2. In *McCullough*, the court held that the consumer could continue to use the car after revocation of acceptance. Do you agree? Should it make any difference whether the product is a car or a mobile home? What if the consumer did not use the disputed product but instead rented a replacement to be used while repairs were being made. Should the consumer be allowed to recover the rental costs of the replacement?

3. If you had represented either of the consumers in these cases, would you have advised them to continue making payments after notice of revocation had been sent? Why or why not?

4. In *Gasque*, the court ruled that the consumer could have no remedy against Fiat. Do you agree? What happens if the dealer is in bankruptcy or goes out of business? Does the ruling in *Gasque* mean that revocation is no longer available as a consumer remedy?

2. THE ASSAULT ON WARRANTY DISCLAIMERS AND LIMITATIONS ON REMEDIES

This section presumes that students have at least passing familiarity with the UCC provisions on warranties, disclaimers, and remedy limitations. UCC §§ 2–313 to 2–316, and 2–719. See generally J. White and R. Summers, Uniform Commercial Code Chs. 9–12 (3d Ed. 1988). Our focus here is primarily on the consumer's claim for *economic loss,* rather than on the broader questions of product liability involving the doctrine of strict liability in tort under Restatement (Second) Torts, § 402A.

The judicial assault on warranty disclaimers began with the landmark case of Henningsen v. Bloomfield Motors, Inc., 32 N.J. 358, 161 A.2d 69 (1960). Ten days after her husband had purchased a new Plymouth, Helen Henningsen was injured when the car's steering mechanism failed. The sale contract had included a limited warranty against defective parts, and a remedy limited to replacement of such parts. In a long and rambling decision, Judge Francis denied effect to the disclaimer and limitation of remedy provisions, both as against Bloomfield Motors and against the Chrysler Corporation, citing the "gross inequality of bargaining position occupied by the consumer" and the "public policy" of protecting "the ordinary man against the loss of important rights."

Even in the context of purely economic loss, courts have often found ways within the parameters of the UCC to help the consumer get around warranty disclaimers and remedy limitations. Consider the following.

STREAM v. SPORTSCAR SALON, LTD.

New York City Civil Court, Queens County, 1977.
91 Misc.2d 99, 397 N.Y.S.2d 677.

CHARLES H. COHEN, JUDGE.

In this action the buyer of a used car seeks to recover the purchase price from the seller based upon a claim of breach of warranty.

* * *

Following a contract dated February 28, 1976 for the sale and purchase of this used car, plaintiff on March 5, 1976 paid to defendant the balance of the purchase price which totalled $2,688 (although the bill of sale dated March 5, 1976 set forth a price of $2,750.50). On or about March 10, 1976 the car was delivered to plaintiff who accepted it.

On or about April 12, 1976 the car broke down after having been driven about 300 miles. Prior to the breakdown, the engine had been losing oil and plaintiff's son had been adding oil. Defendant's employee, who examined the car after it had been towed to defendant's premises on April 12, 1976, stated that the engine had "seized" and was out of oil. After some discussion, defendant agreed to put another engine in the car. On April 20, 1976 plaintiff, after making reference to the defective engine as well as to other defects such as a defective odometer, notified defendant that plaintiff elected to "rescind" the sale and demanded the return of the purchase price. This notice further stated that plaintiff would consider "re-accepting" the car "if and when all the conditions described above are corrected, all without prejudice" to the rescission. Defendant performed work on the car and on May 1, 1976 plaintiff's son picked it up. A few days later, with the engine continuing to leak oil, the car again broke down. After the car was examined by plaintiff's mechanic, it was again towed and delivered to defendant's premises. At about the same time, on May 6, 1976, the car's certificate of title was delivered to defendant and plaintiff notified defendant that plaintiff "elected * * * to stand upon" the previous notice of rescission and again demanded the return of the purchase price and stated that upon defendant notifying plaintiff "that the funds are available, we shall arrange to have the check and license plates picked up." The car remains at defendant's premises with plaintiff's license plates apparently still on it.

* * *

1. THE CONDITION OF THE CAR

* * *

Based upon the testimony concerning the breakdowns of the car and the attendant oil leaks, and buttressed by the testimony of plaintiff's mechanic, the court finds that the engine was defective when the car was sold by defendant to plaintiff, that the engine subsequently installed by defendant was defective and that the car was inoperable each time it was towed to defendant's premises.

* * *

2. THE WARRANTIES MADE AND THEIR BREACH

The contract of sale on defendant's form dated February 28, 1976 states in paragraph 7: "It is expressly agreed that there are no warranties, express or implied, made by either the dealer or the manufacturer on the motor vehicle, chassis or parts furnished hereunder. * * *" The bill of sale on defendant's form dated March 5, 1977 has stamped on it the statement "Limited Used Car Warranty" without further explanation. In another one of defendant's forms entitled "One Year Mechanical Guarantee" dated March 9, 1976 (referred to as a warranty in testimony given by defendant's service manager) and signed by both parties, defendant "agrees that it will protect the purchaser from any cost of repairs other than normal maintenance and wear on the vehicle * * * during the term of this guarantee for one repair or replacement on each of the specified parts, subject to the terms and conditions hereinafter set forth: A. Engine * * * This guarantee is only valid for a mechanical failure. This does not cover normal wear." While this paper further states that "You have the finest guarantee on your car that is offered anywhere in the world" and also states that this is defendant's "famous one-year mechanical guarantee on parts and labor. This guarantee guards you against unforseen (sic) costly repairs on your car for one full year," it contains many exclusions and conditions including one stating that the limit of liability for loss shall not exceed "either (1) the actual cash value of the vehicle at the time of loss or (2) the reasonable value of the repair or replacement including labor thereon" and another stating that defendant "assumes no liability whatsoever except for the terms of the guaranteed (sic) as expressly stated herein. Representatives or agents of Sportscar Salon, Ltd., are not authorized to amend or change either verbally or in writing the terms and conditions of this guarantee."

Defendant does not rely on the express denial of warranties as set forth in the contract of sale. It could hardly do so since the subsequent bill of sale it issued declares that there is a "Limited Used Car Warranty" and the "Guarantee" makes what defendant itself regards as certain warranties. Indeed, as already noted, defendant's service manager in his testimony referred to warranties made with respect to the car. Considering the fact that these papers were forms prepared by defendant, any ambiguity concerning their interpretation must be construed against defendant and in favor of plaintiff.

Moreover, the impact of UCC Art. 2 must be considered. Although the car was not purchased for any particular purpose (UCC 2–315) so that the implied warranty of fitness for a particular purpose does not come into play, * * * the more general implied warranty of merchantability * * * [is implied] unless excluded or modified in accordance with UCC 2–316 * * *

There is no mention of the word "merchantability" in any of the papers involved in this case. Therefore, the implied warranty of merchantability remained in effect by virtue of subsection (2) unless subsection (3) came into effect. The phrases quoted in subsection (3) were not used in the various papers involved, and while the contract of sale had an inconspicuous disclaimer of all warranties in paragraph 7, under the circumstances of this case, where the contract of sale was followed by the bill of sale and guarantee indicating that there were in fact some warranties, this disclaimer was ineffective. Accordingly, the implied warranty of merchantability is applicable to the sale of this car.

The court finds that by virtue of the defective engine in the car, defendant breached the express warranty relating to the engine as set forth in the "Guarantee" and also breached the implied warranty of merchantability in that the car, with that defective engine, was not fit for driving—the ordinary purpose for which it was to be used.

3. THE RECOVERY OF THE PURCHASE PRICE AS A REMEDY UPON A
BREACH OF WARRANTY

Defendant contends that under no circumstances can plaintiff recover the purchase price. It contends that its obligation was limited to the repair and replacement of defective parts and that it satisfied this obligation by replacing the car's engine.

The buyer's remedies in general are set forth in UCC 2–711 which includes the following language which may be applicable to the situation presented in this case: "Where * * * the buyer * * * justifiably revokes acceptance then with respect to any goods involved * * * the buyer may cancel and whether or not he has done so may in addition to recovering so much of the price as had been paid * * *." Thus, if plaintiff justifiably revoked acceptance, she may be in a position to recover the purchase price under UCC 2–711. However, in determining whether plaintiff is entitled to this relief—assuming a justifiable revocation of acceptance—consideration must be given to any attempt to limit or modify remedies in accordance with UCC 2–316(4) which states: "Remedies for breach of warranty can be limited in accordance with the provisions of this Article on liquidation or limitation of damages and on contractual modification of remedy (Sections 2–718 and 2–719)." * * *

An examination of the language used in the express warranty reveals that while reference is made to "repairs" and "replacement", it is not "expressly agreed" that plaintiff's remedy was limited to repair and replacement. Indeed, the language used is in terms of limitation of "liability" rather than in terms of limitation of "remedies". As pointed out in Official Comment 2 to UCC 2–719:

"Subsection (1)(b) creates a presumption that clauses prescribing remedies are cumulative rather than exclusive. If the parties intend the term to describe the sole remedy under the contract, this must be clearly expressed."

Accordingly, the court concludes that the remedy of "repair and replacement" is not exclusive and that the remedy permitting the recovery of the purchase price is available to plaintiff.

Moreover, the court notes that in the beginning of the "Guarantee" there is a provision for "one repair or replacement" of the engine. In this case, there was a repair and replacement which still left the car with a defective engine. Even if the "Guarantee" were effective in limiting plaintiff's remedy to repair and replacement, under these circumstances such an exclusive or limited remedy failed "of its essential purpose", and under UCC 2–719(2) any "remedy may be had as provided in this Act." Indeed, under the circumstances of this case, if plaintiff's remedy were to be limited to "one repair or replacement" of the engine, such a limitation might very well be unconscionable. Further, even if the language in the "Guarantee" as well as in the contract of sale and bill of sale are regarded as ambiguous, this language appears in forms prepared by defendant and any such ambiguity is to be resolved against defendant.

Also, as observed in Part 2, hereof, there is, in addition to the express warranty, the implied warranty of merchantability. Since there has been no mention of merchantability in the papers prepared by defendant, there may be no limit on the remedy available to plaintiff—who seeks to recover the purchase price—by reason of the breach of the implied warranty of merchantability.

4. THE RECOVERY OF THE PURCHASE PRICE BY PLAINTIFF

Having determined that the recovery of the purchase price is a remedy open to the plaintiff, it must be determined whether plaintiff is entitled to recover the purchase price. As noted in Part 3 hereof, in order for plaintiff to enforce the available remedy of the recovery of the purchase price, it was necessary that she be in a position where she "justifiably revokes acceptance". In view of the defective condition of the car as found in Part 1 hereof, any revocation of acceptance would be justifiable. It must then be determined whether plaintiff did in fact revoke her acceptance of the car.

This involves the consideration of UCC 2–608 ∗ ∗ ∗

The car, with its defective engine which rendered it inoperable, was a "commercial unit" (see UCC 2–105(6)) "whose non-conformity substantially impairs its value". Plaintiff accepted it within the meaning of UCC 2–608(1)(b). Plaintiff, an ordinary purchaser of a car, did not know of the defective engine when she accepted the car and this defect could not be readily discovered by her at the time of purchase—aside from the fact that defendant assured her concerning the good condition of the car. The car broke down the first time on April 12, 1976 and revocation of acceptance was made eight days later on April 20, 1976. This revocation was made within a reasonable time, particularly in light of the discussions had during that period. Also, paragraph 3 of the conditions of the "Guarantee" required that no action shall lie against defendant unless it "shall have been given up to seven days from the date of first notice to effect inspection and arrange for appointment to repair vehicle." After the car had been redelivered to plaintiff and again broke down, plaintiff within a few days informed defendant that she "elected ∗ ∗ ∗ to stand upon the notice of rescission. ∗ ∗ ∗" (While UCC 2–608 uses the words "revocation of acceptance" rather than rescission, the use of the word "rescission" in the notices sent to defendant was sufficient. See Official Comment. The car and the certificate of title, which were delivered to defendant, together constituted a complete tender of ownership. ∗ ∗ ∗

∗ ∗ ∗

CONCLUSION

Judgment is directed in favor of plaintiff against defendant for the sum of $2,688 with interest from May 6, 1976.

Notes

1. Other courts have held that attempted disclaimers of the implied warranty of merchantability are invalid because not written in the proper language, or not sufficiently conspicuous. See Christopher v. Larson Ford Sales, 557 P.2d 1009 (Utah 1976); Blankenship v. Northtown Ford, Inc., 95 Ill.App.3d 303, 50 Ill.Dec. 850, 420 N.E.2d 167 (1981).

2. Consumers have also been relatively successful under the Code in arguing that an exclusive remedy—free repair—has "failed of its essential purpose." UCC § 2–719(1)(b). In most cases, if the vehicle or other product still does not operate as it should after the seller has been given a reasonable chance to repair, the limited remedy has failed of its essential purpose, and the buyer can invoke other remedies. Numerous cases follow this pattern. See, e.g., Volkswagen of America, Inc. v. Harrell, 431 So.2d 156 (Ala.1983); Ford Motor Co. v. Mayes, 575 S.W.2d 480 (Ky.App.1978); McCullough v. Bill Swad Chrysler–Plymouth, Inc., supra p. 370, Osburn v. Bendix Home Systems, Inc., 613 P.2d 445 (Okl.1980), Jacobs v. Rosemount Dodge–Winnebago South, 310 N.W.2d 71 (Minn.1981).

3. As is illustrated by the previous case, once the consumer overcomes the warranty disclaimer and remedy limitation, he may still have to satisfy UCC § 2–608 to revoke acceptance and obtain a refund. State lemon laws, discussed infra pages 400–406, streamline this procedure by permitting consumers to obtain revocation and refund (or a replacement vehicle), without having to prove failure of essential purpose or substantial impairment of value.

Problem 5

Robbin Hood bought a new car from Dale on credit. The contract of sale contained the following "Warranty" clause:

> Seller warrants this car to be free from defects in material and workmanship for 12 months or 12,000 miles, whichever comes first. Seller makes no other EXPRESS WARRANTY, and NO IMPLIED WARRANTIES of MERCHANTABILITY OR FITNESS. Seller's obligation under this warranty is limited to repair or replacement of defective parts without charge to Buyer.

Thirty days after the sale, as Hood was driving on the expressway, a cotter pin in the steering mechanism broke. Hood could not control the car, and it crashed into a bridge abutment. Hood was injured and the car was totally destroyed. Dale is willing to stipulate that the cotter pin was defective, and is willing to give Hood a replacement cotter pin, but is not willing to offer more. If Hood sues Dale under the UCC, how would this case be decided? See not only UCC § 2–316, but also § 2–719. Which would be more applicable to the last quoted clause in the contract? Section 2–719(3) may determine the effect of the clause on the part of the suit concerning physical injury, but Hood is also concerned with economic loss—i.e. the cost of repairing or replacing the car. How much does the UCC help Hood in obtaining redress for the loss of the car? See *Stream,* supra. Could Hood also recover the cost of renting a substitute car? See UCC § 2–715.

Note that strict product liability (in tort) would provide a separate avenue for Hood to seek redress for his physical injuries. But Hood has also incurred repair costs and other expenses. For these, recovery under strict product liability is more problematical. See Morrow v. New Moon Homes, below.

Note

Though victorious, the plaintiff in *Stream* had to find her rights within the confines of the Uniform Commercial Code. The questions remain whether the risk of defective products should be removed altogether from the contracting power of the parties and whether the policy reflected in *Henningsen* applies with equal force to economic loss as well as to personal injuries.

These questions flirt with a wholesale examination of the developing law of products liability, whose full scope is beyond this book. We will go only so far as to offer the following case, which is ultimately not a strict products liability case, but which touches on several main themes:

— Should a seller's responsibility for the quality of goods be characterized as "strict liability in tort"? What are the consequences of such a characterization?

— Should warranty or strict liability claims lie against remote suppliers—i.e., should privity of contract barriers fall—where defective goods cause economic loss but not personal injury?

— To what extent should sellers, remote or immediate, be free to reduce their liabilities by contractual provisions?

MORROW v. NEW MOON HOMES, INC.

Supreme Court of Alaska, 1976.
548 P.2d 279.

RABINOWITZ, CHIEF JUSTICE.

This appeal raises questions concerning personal jurisdiction over, and the liability of, a nonresident manufacturer of a defective mobile home that was purchased in Alaska from a resident seller.

In October of 1969, Joseph R. and Nikki Morrow bought a mobile home from Golden Heart Mobile Homes, a Fairbanks retailer of mobile homes. A plaque on the side of the mobile home disclosed that the home had been manufactured in Oregon by New Moon Homes, Inc. The Morrows made a down payment of $1,800, taking out a loan for the balance of the purchase price from the First National Bank of Fairbanks. The loan amount of $10,546.49, plus interest of 9 percent per year, was to be repaid by the Morrows in 72 monthly installments of $190.13 each.

At the time of the purchase, the Morrows inspected the mobile home and noticed that the carpeting had not been laid and that several windows were broken. Roy Miller, Golden Heart's salesman, assured them that these problems would be corrected and later made good his assurances. Miller also told the Morrows that the mobile home was a "good trailer", " * * * as warm as * * * any other trailer." After the sale, Miller moved the Morrows' mobile home to Lakeview Terrace, set it up on the space the Morrows had rented, and made sure that the utilities were connected. Then the troubles started.

On the first night that the mobile home's furnace was in use, the motor went out and had to be replaced. The electric furnace installed by the manufacturer had been removed by someone who had replaced the original with an oil furnace. The furnace vent did not fit, and consequently the "stove pipe" vibrated when the furnace was running. Subsequent events showed the furnace malfunction was not the primary problem with the mobile home.

About four days after the mobile home had been set up, the Morrows noticed that the doors did not close all the way and that the windows were cracked. The bathtub leaked water into the middle bedroom. In March of 1970 when the snow on the roof began to melt, the roof leaked. Water came in through gaps between the ceiling and the wall panels, as well as along the bottom of the wallboard. A short circuit developed in the electrical system; the lights flickered at various times. When it rained, water came out of the light fixture in the hallway. Other problems with the mobile home included the following: the interior walls did not fit together at the corners; the paneling came off the walls; the windows and doors were out of square; the door frames on the bedroom doors fell off and the closet doors would not slide properly; the curtains had glue on them; and the finish came off the kitchen cabinet doors.

Despite all these problems, the Morrows continued to live in the mobile home and make the loan payments. Golden Heart Mobile Homes was notified many times of the difficulties the Morrows were having with their mobile home. Roy Miller, the Golden Heart salesman with whom the Morrows had dealt, did put some caulking around the bathtub, but otherwise he was of little assistance. Finally, sometime before April 1, 1970, Nikki Morrow informed Miller that if Golden Heart did not fix the mobile home the Morrows wanted to return it. Miller said the Morrows would "[h]ave to take it up with the bank." Subsequently, Golden Heart went out of business.

The First National Bank of Fairbanks was more sensitive to the Morrows' plight. Upon being informed by the Morrows that they intended to make no further payments on the mobile home, bank personnel went out and inspected the home several times. In addition, on May 27, 1970, the bank wrote to New Moon Homes, Inc. in Silverton, Oregon. Its letter informed New Moon of the problems the Morrows were having with their New Moon mobile home and asked whether New Moon expected to send a representative to Fairbanks since Golden

Heart, the dealer, was no longer in business. Apparently, New Moon did not respond to the bank's letter.

A short time later the Morrows' counsel wrote a letter to New Moon Homes notifying New Moon that the Morrows intended to hold the company liable for damages for breach of implied warranties. About a month later the Morrows separated, with Nikki Morrow continuing to live in the mobile home. She continued to make payments to First National because she "couldn't afford Alaskan rents." Nikki Morrow eventually moved out of the mobile home but made no effort to sell or rent it because she considered it "not fit to live in." In October of 1971 the Morrows filed this action against both New Moon Homes and Golden Heart Mobile Homes, alleging that defendants had breached implied warranties of merchantability and fitness for particular purpose in manufacturing and selling an improperly constructed mobile home. * * *

* * *

* * * The critical question in this case is whether the Morrows, as remote purchasers, can invoke the warranties attributable to the manufacturer which arose when New Moon passed title of the mobile home to the next party in the chain of distribution. In other words, do the implied warranties of merchantability and fitness run from a manufacturer only to those with whom the manufacturer is in privity of contract?

* * *

The more difficult question before this court is whether we should extend this abolition of privity to embrace not only warranty actions for personal injuries and property damage but also those for economic loss. Contemporary courts have been more reticent to discard the privity requirement and to permit recovery in warranty by a remote consumer for purely economic losses. In considering this issue we note that economic loss may be categorized into direct economic loss and consequential economic loss, a distinction maintained in the Code's structure of damage remedies. * * *

The claim of the Morrows in this case is one for direct economic loss.

A number of courts recently confronting this issue have declined to overturn the privity requirement in warranty actions for economic loss. One principal factor seems to be that these courts simply do not find the social and economic reasons which justify extending enterprise liability to the victims of personal injury or property damage equally compelling in the case of a disappointed buyer suffering "only" economic loss. There is an apparent fear that economic losses may be of a far greater magnitude in value than personal injuries, and being somehow less foreseeable these losses would be less insurable, undermining the risk spreading theory of enterprise liability.

Several of the courts which have recently considered this aspect of the privity issue have found those arguments unpersuasive. We are in agreement and hold that there is no satisfactory justification for a remedial scheme which extends the warranty action to a consumer suffering personal injury or property damage but denies similar relief to the consumer "fortunate" enough to suffer only direct economic loss.

* * *

* * *

The fear that if the implied warranty action is extended to direct economic loss, manufacturers will be subjected to liability for damages of unknown and unlimited scope would seem unfounded. The manufacturer may possibly delimit the scope of his potential liability by use of a disclaimer in compliance with AS 45.05.100[2–316] or by resort to the limitations authorized in AS 45.05.230[2–719]. These statutory rights not only preclude extending the theory of strict liability in tort, supra, but also make highly appropriate this extension of the theory of implied warranties. Further, by expanding warranty rights to redress this form of harm, we preserve " * * * the well developed notion that the law of contract should control actions for purely economic losses and that the law of tort should control actions for personal injuries." We therefore hold that a manufacturer can be held liable for direct economic loss attributable to a breach of his implied warranties, without regard to privity of contract between the manufacturer and the ultimate purchaser. It was therefore error for the trial court to dismiss the Morrows' action against New Moon for want of privity.

Our decision today preserves the statutory rights of the manufacturer to define his potential liability to the ultimate consumer, by means of express disclaimers and limitations, while protecting the legitimate expectation of the consumer that goods distributed on a wide scale by the use of conduit retailers are fit for their intended use. The manufacturer's rights are not, of course, unfettered. Disclaimers and limitations must comport with the relevant statutory prerequisites and cannot be so oppressive as to be unconscionable within the meaning of AS 45.05.072[2–302]. On the other hand, under the Code the consumer has a number of responsibilities if he is to enjoy the right of action we recognize today, not the least of which is that he must give notice of the breach of warranty to the manufacturer pursuant to AS 45.05.174(c) (1)[2–607(3)(a)]. The warranty action brought under the Code must be brought within the statute of limitations period prescribed in AS 45.05.242[2–725]. * * *

Reversed and remanded for a new trial in accordance with this opinion.*

Problem 6

If, in Problem 5, Dale goes out of business and is judgment proof, which of these losses can Hood pass back to the manufacturer, Chrysler Corp.? What obstacles must Hood overcome to reach the "deep pocket"

---

* The omitted footnotes from the court's opinion contain a wealth of reference material on the issues discussed.

of the manufacturer? Will he be able to revoke acceptance and obtain a refund?

D. PRIDGEN, CONSUMER PROTECTION AND THE LAW
§ 13.07[2] (1986).*

PRIVITY

The doctrine of privity has been criticized as a relic of the past. In today's marketplace large corporations manufacture and advertise consumer products sold through mere conduits, such as the local supermarket or car dealer. They are in a much better position than the immediate seller to prevent the introduction of defective products into the stream of commerce, and to spread the loss among all consumers. The mere fact that the manufacturer has not contracted directly with the actual buyers upon whom it relies for its profits should not relieve it of responsibility. As a leading treatise on the UCC stated:

> It is possible that lack of privity as a defense to a cause of action will be only a historic relic in the year 2,000. It is a doctrine in hasty retreat; its current vitality is largely in cases in which plaintiffs seek recompense for economic loss.[4]

* * *

Lack of vertical privity, *i.e.*, when the consumer has not purchased directly from the defendant-manufacturer, but rather from a retail dealer, poses the more important obstacle to consumer warranty suits. The issue commonly arises when the dealer has successfully disclaimed all warranties, or when the dealer is financially insolvent or otherwise incapable of satisfying the consumer's claim. The UCC does not address vertical privity.[7] Some states have eliminated this barrier through legislation,[8] but mostly the matter has been left to the courts.

Most courts permit the consumer to sue the manufacturer directly for breach of an express warranty.[9] As the New York Court of Appeals concluded, the warranty "which effectively induces the purchase, is frequently that given by the manufacturer through mass advertising and labeling to ultimate business users or to consumers with whom he has no direct contractual relationship." [10] By "beaming" its warranty to the ultimate consumer, the manufacturer voluntarily takes on the responsibility to abide by its provisions. In a variation on this typical

---

* Reprinted with permission from "Consumer Protection and the Law." Copyright Clark, Boardman Co., Ltd., New York, N.Y.

4. J. White & R. Summers, Handbook of the Law Under the Uniform Commercial Code 411 (2d ed. 1980).

7. *See* UCC § 2–318, comment 3.

8. These states include Kansas, Maine, Massachusetts, Mississippi, New Hampshire, South Carolina and Virginia. *See* B.

Clark & C. Smith, *The Law of Product Warranties* 10–9 to 10–10 (1984).

9. *See, e.g.,* Randy Knitwear, Inc. v. American Cyanamid Co., 11 N.Y.2d 5, 226 N.Y.S.2d 363, 181 N.E.2d 399 (1962) (while this is a commercial case, the principle of manufacturer liability without privity for express warranties is equally applicable in consumer cases).

10. *Id.,* 181 N.E.2d at 402.

case, a Washington appellate court held that a subsequent buyer of a mobile home still under warranty could sue the manufacturer directly because the express warranty was not limited to the "original purchaser." [11] There are some exceptions to the trend toward eliminating the vertical privity requirement for breach of express warranty, however, with some states clinging to the old rule.[12]

Courts have been more reluctant to jettison the vertical privity rule in cases alleging purely economic loss due to breach of the implied warranty of merchantability.[13] A growing minority of influential opinions has concluded, however, that the citadel of privity should come down here too.[14] For instance, in the leading case of *Morrow v. New Moon Homes,* a couple purchased a mobile home from a dealer who later went out of business. The home was so defective it was virtually uninhabitable. The Alaska Supreme Court concluded "there is no satisfactory justification for a remedial scheme which extends the warranty action to a consumer suffering personal injury or property damage but denies similar relief to the consumer 'fortunate' enough to suffer only direct economic loss." [15] Any fear of potentially unlimited liability for manufacturers should be allayed by the UCC provisions permitting warranty disclaimers and limited remedies.[16]

One last vestige of the vertical privity rule arises when the buyer attempts to revoke acceptance and obtain a refund from the manufacturer. Some courts hold that revocation is only available against the immediate seller, and that an action against the manufacturer, although not completely barred by lack of privity, is limited to damages.[17] The Oregon courts permit revocation against the manufacturer only if the dealer acted as the manufacturer's agent, and was not itself the seller.[18] Other cases have held squarely that once the barrier of vertical privity is knocked down, the buyer should have the full array of UCC remedies to which he or she is otherwise entitled, including revocation and refund.[19]

11. Lidstrand v. Silvercrest Industries, 28 Wash.App. 359, 623 P.2d 710 (1981).

12. *See, e.g.,* Stewart v. Gainesville Glass Co., Inc., 233 Ga. 578, 212 S.E.2d 377 (1975).

13. *See, e.g.,* Rocky Mountain Fire & Casualty Co. v. Biddulph Oldsmobile, 131 Ariz. 289, 640 P.2d 851, 856 (1982); Koellmer v. Chrysler Motors Corp., 6 Conn. Cir. 478, 276 A.2d 807 (1970), *cert. denied,* 160 Conn. 590, 274 A.2d 884 (1971).

14. *See, e.g.,* Gherna v. Ford Motor Co., 246 Cal.App.2d 639, 55 Cal.Rptr. 94, 102 (1966); Manheim v. Ford Motor Co., 201 So.2d 440 (Fla.1967); Santor v. Karagheusian, Inc., 44 N.J. 52, 207 A.2d 305 (1965); Nobility Homes of Texas, Inc. v. Shivers, 557 S.W.2d 77 (Tex.1977).

15. Morrow v. New Moon Homes, Inc., 548 P.2d 279, 291 (Alaska 1976).

16. *Id.* at 291–92.

17. *See* Gasque v. Mooers Motor Car Co., 227 Va. 154, 313 S.E.2d 384, 390 (1984).

18. *See* Clark v. Ford Motor Co., 46 Or. App. 521, 612 P.2d 316 (1980); Gaha v. Taylor–Johnson Dodge, Inc., 53 Or.App. 471, 632 P.2d 483 (1981).

19. *See* Durfee v. Rod Baxter Imports, Inc., 262 N.W.2d 349 (Minn.1977) (distributer liable for revocation and refund when dealer became insolvent); Volkswagen of America, Inc. v. Novak, 418 So.2d 801 (Miss.1982) (an amendment to the Mississippi Commercial Code had abolished privity of contract for breach of warranty claims); Ventura v. Ford Motor Corp., 180 N.J.Super. 45, 433 A.2d 801, 811–12 (1981).

In sum, the privity doctrine is still an issue in consumer warranty cases against a distant manufacturer, but its dominance is fading. The trend is to permit warranty actions up the chain of distribution without regard to privity of contract. Yet the old rule still prevails in some jurisdictions, particularly with regard to purely economic injury caused by a breach of the implied warranty.

Note on Non–Uniform Amendment to the UCC

The provision set out below represents a direct legislative attack on warranty disclaimers and remedy limitations. Which is preferable, this statutory approach, or continued caselaw development? Does this statute affect both personal injury and economic loss cases? Does it moot the other issues raised in *Morrow?* Would enactment of this statute induce manufacturers to discontinue using language in their contracts similar to that in Problem 5, supra?

MARYLAND COMMERCIAL CODE

Section 2–316.1: Limitation of Exclusion or Modification of Warranties.

(1) The provisions of § 2–316 shall not apply to sales of consumer goods, as defined by § 9–109, services or both.

(2) Any oral or written language used by a seller of consumer goods and services, which attempts to exclude or modify any implied warranties of merchantability and fitness for a particular purpose or to exclude or modify the consumer's remedies for breach of those warranties, is unenforceable. However, the seller may recover from the manufacturer any damages resulting from breach of the [above-described] warranty. * * *

(3) Any oral or written language used by a manufacturer of consumer goods, which attempts to limit or modify a consumer's remedies for breach of the manufacturer's express warranties, is unenforceable, unless the manufacturer provides reasonable and expeditious means of performing the warranty obligations.

This is a non-uniform amendment to the UCC, as enacted in Maryland. Connecticut, the District of Columbia, Maine, Massachusetts, and Vermont have enacted similar provisions. See also Kan.Stat.Ann. 50–639 and W.Va. Code, 46A–6–107.

Some, but not all, of these statutes eliminate the requirement of vertical privity as well. Mississippi prohibits the limitation of remedies for breach of the implied warranty, Miss.Code § 75–2–719(4), and by virtue of having repealed UCC § 2–316, prohibited the exclusion or modification of the implied warranty of merchantability as well. See Beck Enterprises, Inc. v. Hester, 512 So.2d 672 (Miss.1987).

For an excellent analysis of these state laws, see B. Clark & C. Smith, The Law of Product Warranties ¶ 8.05[2] (1984).

Problem 7

(a) Sam Tudent bought a car from Muck Motors in Maryland. After the sale, and after he had paid cash for the car, Sam realized that he had received a "standard warranty" exactly like that in Problem 5, supra p. 382. Before any defect in the car has appeared, he consults you. What, if anything, can he do?

(b) Same transaction as in (a) except that a month after the sale the car becomes inoperable. What can Sam do?

(c) Would you have any additional suggestions for Sam if his state has enacted a "little FTC Act?" Are there any advantages to pleading the case as an unfair or deceptive trade practice, rather than a simple breach of warranty? Any disadvantages?

3. THE MAGNUSON–MOSS WARRANTY ACT

Notes

1. The Magnuson–Moss Warranty Act (MMWA), 15 U.S.C.A. §§ 2301–11, was enacted in 1975 and can be found in West's Selected Commercial Statutes. In this legislation, Congress attempted to address some common consumer problems with warranties, namely:

(1) complex language that rendered warranty terms incomprehensible to most people,

(2) warranties which appeared to give meaningful warranty protection but turned out to be much less than expected, and

(3) lack of meaningful access to the courts to enforce consumers' rights under their warranties.

The MMWA was hailed as a major piece of consumer protection legislation, but it also has many limitations.

The Magnuson–Moss Act is primarily a detailed disclosure law. The MMWA does not require the issuance of a warranty, nor does it regulate the substance of most warranty terms. Just as Truth in Lending is based on the theory that informed comparison shopping for credit would improve competition in the consumer credit market, so too the MMWA assumes that better informed consumers would select products with better warranties. This in turn would induce manufacturers to compete on warranty terms. Competition on warranties could ultimately lead to better quality products, since strong warranties normally will not accompany weak products. See generally C. Reitz, Consumer Protection Under the Magnuson–Moss Warranty Act (2d ed. 1987).

2. Following are the basic features of the MMWA.

The Act requires disclosures of the terms of warranties in *simple and readily understood language.* This has proven to be difficult to achieve in practice. MMWA § 102. 16 C.F.R. Part 700 (Hereafter Rule 700, 701, etc.)

The Act requires *pre-sale availability,* i.e., the exact text of the written warranty must be available to consumers before they buy. MMWA § 102(b)(1)(A) and Rule 702. This permits consumers to comparison shop for the best warranty, if they so desire. In 1987, the FTC amended the presale availability rule to give the retailer considerably more flexibility on the manner in which the text of the warranty is to be made available. Under the new rule, a retailer may simply make warranties available on request, provided he posts a sign to that effect. 52 Fed.Reg. 7574 (Mar. 12, 1987).

The Act requires *standard terminology* for warranties. Written warranties on consumer goods must be called either "full" or "limited." "Full" warranties must meet certain standards. MMWA §§ 103, 104 and 105, and Rule 700. All other written warranties must be called "limited."

The Act imposes *limits on disclaimers of implied warranties*. Sellers who offer written warranties on consumer products *may not* disclaim entirely any implied warranty that arises under state law, although they may limit the duration of the implied warranty. MMWA § 108. This very important provision gives consumers a way around warranty disclaimers in their contracts.

The Act provides a *private right of action* for aggrieved consumers. The Act gives consumers the right to enforce the warranty provisions of *their own individual contracts* or to sue for damages for violations of the Act. MMWA § 110(d). Unlike the Truth in Lending Act, however, the MMWA Act does not provide for minimum statutory penalties. The consumer is limited to proven damages, and may be awarded costs and attorney's fees.

The Act permits suit in either federal or state court. A consumer can sue in state court for ordinary breach of warranty under MMWA and thereby be awarded attorney's fees. Federal actions are more limited. The jurisdictional amount for a federal action is $50,000, and there must be at least 100 individuals for a class action. Cf. Seybold v. Francis P. Dean, Inc., 628 F.Supp. 912 (W.D.Pa.1986).

Finally, the Act attempts to facilitate the establishment of *informal dispute resolution* procedures for resolving warranty disputes. MMWA § 110(a)(2) and Rule 703. This aspect of the law did not have much impact at first. As states passed lemon laws in the 1980s that incorporate by reference the FTC/MMWA rule on informal dispute resolution, however, many automobile manufacturers established such procedures.

3. As is the case for most consumer protection legislation, the MMWA is limited in scope to warranties on "consumer" products. Unlike some other statutes, however, the MMWA uses an "objective" test, i.e., whether the product is "normally used for personal, family or household purposes," rather than the particular buyer's purpose. MMWA § 101(1). Thus, a business that purchased a car for deliveries may be able to argue its warranty is within the coverage of the Act because cars are normally used for family or personal purposes. On the other hand, a flat bed truck used for personal reasons would not come within the scope of MMWA because it is normally a commercial vehicle. See Crume v. Ford Motor Co., 60 Or. App. 224, 653 P.2d 564 (1982).

4. The operative portions of the MMWA are also limited to "written warranties," as defined in the Act. How does this term differ from express

or implied warranties in the UCC or warranties enforceable under the common law of contracts?

On the question whether the MMWA has real utility for the lemon-buying consumer, consider the following case.

VENTURA v. FORD MOTOR CORP.
Superior Court of New Jersey, Appellate Division, 1981.
180 N.J.Super. 45, 433 A.2d 801.

[When his new car proved seriously defective, and unrepairable, Ventura sued Marino Auto Sales (the dealer) and Ford (the manufacturer) for breach of warranty. Marino cross-claimed against Ford for indemnification. The trial court awarded Ventura rescission and damages against Marino Auto Sales, and allowed Marino to recover over against Ford. The lower court also awarded Ventura $5,165 in attorney's fees against Ford, but denied Ventura's claim for punitive and treble damages. Ford appeals.]

[W]e affirm plaintiff's recovery. We conclude that, despite Marino Auto's attempted disclaimer of all warranties, plaintiff can recover from Marino Auto for the breach of implied warranty of merchantability. We also uphold the award of counsel fees against Ford pursuant to the Magnuson–Moss Warranty Act.

The contract of sale between Marino Auto and plaintiff conspicuously contained the following legend on its face:

> The seller, MARINO AUTO SALES, Inc., hereby expressly disclaims all warranties, either expressed or implied, including any implied warranty of merchantability or fitness for a particular purpose, and MARINO AUTO SALES, Inc., neither assumes nor authorizes another person to assume for it any liability in connection with the sale of the vehicle.

On the back of this sales order-contract were the following terms which were made part of the contract:

> 7. It is expressly agreed that there are no warranties, express or implied, made by either the selling dealer or the manufacturer on the motor vehicle, chassis or parts furnished hereunder except, in the case of a new motor vehicle the warranty expressly given to the purchaser upon the delivery of such motor vehicle or chassis.
>
> The selling dealer also agrees to promptly perform and fulfill all terms and conditions of the owner service policy.

For the purpose of this opinion we will assume that the disclaimer of implied warranties of merchantability and fitness was effective under the Uniform Commercial Code, N.J.S.A. 12A:2–316. Since the dealer passed on to the purchaser a warranty from the manufacturer, we will not consider whether the attempted disclaimer by Marino Auto should be voided as unconscionable and contrary to public policy under N.J.S.A. 12A:2–302, even though such disclaimer could foreclose rescission or other remedies against the dealer and, without privity between buyer and manufacturer, rescission has been held ordinarily unavailable, under the Code against the manufacturer. * * * It may be argued that the dealer's conduct in transmitting Ford's warranty to plaintiff, the reference to such warranty in paragraph 7 on the back of the purchaser order-contract, and the undertaking "to promptly perform and fulfill all terms and conditions of the owner service policy," are inconsistent with a disclaimer of all warranties and that such a disclaimer is an unreasonable construction. The contract in the *Henningsen* case contained the identical obligation to perform all terms and conditions of the owner service policy. The combination of the dealer's undertaking and the automobile manufacturer's warranty was interpreted in *Henningsen* to rebut the disclaimer of implied warranty of merchantability by the dealer. The court held that the attempt to limit liability to the replacement of defective parts was contrary to public policy and void with respect to a claim for personal injuries resulting from an accident caused by defects in an automobile. However, we need not explore these issues further because the Magnuson–Moss Warranty Act has solved many of the problems posed by the intricacies confronting consumers under the preexisting law of sales.

The Magnuson–Moss Warranty–Federal Trade Commission Improvement Act, supra, was adopted on January 4, 1975, 88 Stat. 2183. Its purpose was to make "warranties on consumer products more readily understandable and enforceable." Note, 7 Rutgers–Camden L.J. 379 (1976). The act enhances the consumer's position by allowing recovery under a warranty without regard to privity of contract between the consumer and warrantor, by prohibiting the disclaimer of implied warranties in a written warranty, and by enlarging the remedies available to a consumer for breach of warranty, including the award of attorneys' fees. * * *

* * *

We will first consider the application of this act to the dealer, Marino Auto. As quoted above, paragraph 7 of the purchase order-contract provides that there are no warranties, express or implied, made by the selling dealer or manufacturer except, in the case of a new motor vehicle, "the warranty expressly given to the purchaser upon delivery of such motor vehicle * * *." This section also provides: "The selling dealer also agrees to promptly perform and fulfill all terms and conditions of the owner service policy." Ford contended in the trial court that Marino Auto had "a duty" to properly diagnose and make repairs, that such duty was "fixed both by the express warranty * * * which they passed on * * * and by the terms of [paragraph 7 of the contract with plaintiff]" by which Marino Auto expressly undertook "to perform its obligations under the owner service policy." See 15 U.S.C.A. § 2310(f); 16 C.F.R. § 700.4 (1980). The provision in paragraph 7 in these circumstances is a "written warranty" within the meaning of § 2301(6)(B) since it constitutes an undertaking in connection with the sale to take "remedial action with respect to such product in the event that such product fails to meet the specifications set forth in the undertaking * * *." In our view the specifications of the undertaking include, at the least, the provisions of the limited warranty furnished by Ford, namely:

LIMITED WARRANTY (12 MONTHS OR 12,000 MILES/19,312 KILOMETRES) 1978 NEW CAR AND LIGHT TRUCK

Ford warrants for its 1978 model cars and light trucks that the Selling Dealer will repair or replace free any parts, except tires, found under normal use in the U.S. or Canada to be defective in factory materials or workmanship within the earlier of 12 months or 12,000 miles/19,312 km from either first use or retail delivery. All we require is that you properly operate and maintain your vehicle and that you return for warranty service to your Selling Dealer or any Ford or Lincoln–Mercury Dealer if you are traveling, have moved a long distance or need emergency repairs. Warranty repairs will be made with Ford Authorized Service or Remanufactured Parts.

THERE IS NO OTHER EXPRESS WARRANTY ON THIS VEHICLE.[4]

The record does not contain a written description of the "owner service policy" which the dealer agreed to perform. Nevertheless, since Ford is the appellant here, we take its contentions at trial and documents in the record to establish the dealer's obligation to Ford and to plaintiff to make the warranty repairs on behalf of Ford (subject to the right of reimbursement or other terms that may be contained in their agreement). For the purpose of this appeal we are satisfied that the dealer's undertaking in paragraph 7 constitutes a written warranty within the meaning of 15 U.S.C.A. § 2301(6)(B). Accordingly, having furnished a written warranty to the consumer, the dealer as a supplier may not "disclaim or modify [except to limit in duration] any implied warranty to a consumer * * *." The result of this analysis is to invalidate the attempted disclaimer by the dealer of the implied warranties of merchantability and fitness.[5] Being bound by those implied warranties arising under state law, N.J.S.A. 12A:2–314 and 315, Marino Auto was liable to plaintiff for the breach thereof as found by the trial judge, and plaintiff could timely revoke his acceptance of the automobile and claim a refund of his purchase price. N.J.S.A. 12A:2–608 and N.J.S.A. 12A:2–711. Zabriskie Chevrolet, Inc. v. Smith, 99 N.J.Super. 441, 240 A.2d 195 (Law Div.1968). In this connection we note that the

---

4. The warranty also provided:

TO THE EXTENT ALLOWED BY LAW:

1. ANY IMPLIED WARRANTY OF MERCHANTABILITY OR FITNESS IS LIMITED TO THE 12 MONTH OR 12,000–MILE/19,312–KM DURATION OF THIS WRITTEN WARRANTY.

2. NEITHER FORD NOR THE SELLING DEALER SHALL HAVE ANY RESPONSIBILITY FOR LOSS OF USE OF THE VEHICLE, LOSS OF TIME, INCONVENIENCE, COMMERCIAL LOSS OR CONSEQUENTIAL DAMAGES.

Some states do not allow limitations on how long an implied warranty lasts or the exclusion or limitation of incidental or consequential damages, so the above limitations may not apply to you.

This warranty gives you specific legal rights, and you also may have other rights which vary from state to state.

5. The same holding would apply if the undertaking by Marino Auto to perform the "owner service policy" is construed as a "service contract." 15 U.S.C.A. § 2308(a), supra.

trial judge found that plaintiff's attempted revocation of acceptance was made in timely fashion, and that finding has adequate support in the evidence.

As the trial judge noted, 15 U.S.C.A. § 2310(d)(1) provides that a consumer who is damaged by the failure of a warrantor to comply with any obligation under the act, or under a written warranty or implied warranty or service contract, may bring suit "for damages and other legal and equitable relief * * *." Although the remedy of refund of the purchase price is expressly provided by the Magnuson–Moss Warranty Act for breach of a full warranty, granting this remedy under state law for breach of a limited warranty is not barred by or inconsistent with the act. 15 U.S.C.A. § 2311(b)(1) provides that nothing in the act restricts "any right or remedy of any consumer under State law or other Federal law." See also 15 U.S.C.A. § 2311(c)(2). Thus, for breach of the implied warranty of merchantability, plaintiff was entitled to revoke acceptance against Marino Auto, and a judgment for the purchase price less an allowance for the use of the vehicle was properly entered against Marino Auto. N.J.S.A. 12A:2–608 and 711. Cf. 15 U.S.C.A. § 2301(12) which defines "refund" as the return of the purchase price "less reasonable depreciation based on actual use where permitted" by regulations.

[The court also held that Ventura also could have recovered against Ford for Ford's breach of its limited warranty.]

Notes

1. Would you have taken this case before the MMWA was passed? See also GMAC v. Jankowitz, 216 N.J.Super. 313, 523 A.2d 695 (1987).

2. In *Ventura*, the buyer gave the dealer ample opportunity to attempt a cure, as required by MMWA § 110(e). A North Dakota buyer was no doubt chagrined to learn that he was not entitled to any damages under MMWA when the defects raised in the suit had not been reported to the seller. Byron v. Gerring Industries, Inc., 328 N.W.2d 819 (N.D.1982). In *Byron*, the court required the plaintiff buyer who had brought an unsuccessful MMWA action to pay defendant seller's expert witness fees under a North Dakota state law.

Problem 8

Under the facts of problem 5, supra, page 382, will Hood be able to get damages for breach of the implied warranty against the manufacturer if he brings suit under the MMWA? Would the answer depend on state law? See MMWA §§ 101(3), (4) & (7), and 110(d)(1), and consider the following case.

SZAJNA v. GENERAL MOTORS CORP.

Supreme Court of Illinois, 1986.
115 Ill.2d 294, 104 Ill.Dec. 898, 503 N.E.2d 760.

[Plaintiff Szajna brought a class action against GM for substituting Chevette transmissions in 1976 Pontiac Venturas. He alleged that the use of the inferior transmission breached the implied warranty of merchantability. GM alleged that although it had given a limited warranty on the car, Szajna could not sue GM for breach of implied warranty because of lack of vertical privity. The Illinois Supreme Court construed the MMWA to assist the buyer in this instance, as follows.]

Section 2308 provides:

> "No supplier may disclaim or modify (except as provided in subsection (b) of this section [limiting the duration of an implied warranty to the duration of a 'limited' written warranty]) any implied warranty to a consumer * * * if (1) such supplier makes any written warranty to the consumer * * * or (2) at the time of sale, or within 90 days thereafter, such supplier enters into a service contract with the consumer which applies to such consumer product." (15 U.S.C. sec. 2308(a) (1976).)

This section raises the question as to whether it modifies implied-warranty State-law provisions to the extent that any written warranty given by a manufacturer to a remote purchaser creates an implied warranty by virtue of Magnuson–Moss. At the very least we must acknowledge that the provisions of section 2308 clearly demonstrate the policy of Magnuson–Moss to sustain the protection afforded to consumers by implied warranties.

The Act broadly defines "consumer" in section 2301(3) as "a buyer (other than for purposes of resale) of any consumer product, any person to whom such product is transferred during the duration of an implied or written warranty * * * and any other person who is entitled by the terms of such warranty * * * or under applicable State law to enforce against the warrantor * * * the obligations of the warranty." (15 U.S.C. sec. 2301(3) (1976).) It has been suggested that this broad definition of "consumer" and the provisions of section 2310(d)(1) (15 U.S.C. sec. 2310(d)(1) (1976)), which section authorizes a "consumer" to maintain a civil action for damages for failure of a "supplier" or "warrantor" to comply with any obligation of a written or implied warranty, effectively abolish vertical privity. We do not think we can focus on any one section of Magnuson–Moss but should read the sections referred to together to accomplish the purpose of Magnuson–Moss of furnishing broad protection to the consumer.

In resolving this murky situation we find helpful, and accept, Professor Schroeder's analysis and suggestion as a reasonable solution. In cases where no Magnuson–Moss written warranty has been given, Magnuson–Moss has no effect upon State-law privity requirements because, by virtue of section 2301(7), which defines implied warranty, implied warranty arises only if it does so under State law. However, if a Magnuson–Moss written warranty (either "full" or "limited") is given by reason of the policy against disclaimers of implied warranty expressed in Magnuson–Moss and the provisions authorizing a consumer to sue a warrantor, the nonprivity "consumer" should be permitted to maintain an action on an implied warranty against the "warrantor." (Schroeder, *Privity Actions Under the Magnuson–Moss Warranty Act,* 66 Calif.L.Rev. 1, 16 (1978).) The rationale of this conclusion, though not specifically articulated by Professor Schroeder in the article, would hold that under Magnuson–Moss a warrantor, by extending a written warranty to the consumer, establishes privity between the warrantor and the consumer which, though limited in nature, is sufficient to support an implied warranty under sections 2–314 and 2–315 of the UCC. The implied warranty thus recognized, by virtue of the definition in section 2301(7) of Magnuson–Moss, must be one arising under the law of this State.

The appellate court in this case held that while the parties were in privity for purposes of the provisions of the express written limited warranty which General Motors had extended, they were not in privity for the purposes of implied warranty. This holding is in conflict with our holding herein and will therefore be reversed. The appellate court, in the same sentence, stated that implied warranties were "specifically disclaimed by the expressed warranty." The written warranty in this case limited any implied warranties to the duration of the written warranty. Thus, the part of the warranty referred to by the appellate court as disclaiming implied warranties may properly be referred to as a limitation on the duration of an implied warranty. * * * Szajna here contends that the issue of disclaimer was not raised, briefed or argued by GM in either the circuit or appellate courts and should not have been considered by the appellate court. These issues, it is argued, are affirmative defenses which, because of other provisions of the UCC and Magnuson–Moss, may or may not be applicable to this transaction. GM also has stated that it does not believe the disclaimer-limitation issue can be resolved fully on the basis of the allegations of Szajna's complaint and therefore did not address these questions in its briefs. In light of this, we find that the trial court erred in dismissing count I, and this cause will be remanded to the circuit court of Cook County.

* * *

Notes

1. Compare the approach in *Szajna* to that in Feinstein v. Firestone Tire & Rubber Co., 535 F.Supp. 595 (S.D.N.Y.1982) in which Plaintiffs brought a class action suit under MMWA against the manufacturer, Firestone, for breaching the implied warranty of merchantability regarding defective tires. The question arose whether buyers who did not purchase their tires directly from Firestone could assert a claim of breach of implied warranty against the manufacturer with whom they were not in privity of contract, and the court stated:

As to questions of law, we have noted that the Magnuson–Moss Act, in respect of claims for breaches of implied warranty, looks to state law for the definition of what an "implied warranty" is. Plaintiffs say this causes no difficulty, since U.C.C. §§ 2–314 and 2–714 "are identical in 49 states and provide a uniform legal basis for its resolution." That is an over-simplification; even within the U.C.C. implied warranty umbrella, state law may differ in such significant areas as vertical privity and the availability of punitive damages.

2. Footnote 13 in the Feinstein opinion provided this further analysis:

13. The question of vertical privity arises because the *Feinstein* plaintiffs (as well as the other plaintiffs) seek to represent classes of owners or purchasers of Firestone tires, whether or not they purchased the tires from Firestone. If a contractual relationship is necessary between plaintiff and defendant to sustain a claim for breach of an implied warranty, those putative class members who did not purchase directly from Firestone have no claim. The laws of the states are not uniform on this issue. See cases cited in Firestone's main brief at 38 n. 42. I do not accept plaintiffs' argument that, at least in respect of claims for breach of implied warranty, the Magnuson–Moss Act definitions of "supplier" and "consumer," 15 U.S.C. § 2301(4) and (3), render state law concepts of privity irrelevant; it is the definition section itself which, at § 2301(7), defines "implied warranty" as "arising under State law . . . ." If state law requires vertical privity to enforce an implied warranty and there is none, then, like the yeastless souffle, the warranty does not "arise." This conclusion is reached in Miller & Kanter, *Litigation Under Magnuson–Moss,* 13 U.C.C.L.J. 10, 21 (1980):

> "The UCC position on the need for privity in implied warranty cases is apparently not affected by the federal Act. The expansive definition of 'consumer' includes anyone to whom a product is transferred during the implied warranty period. However, the creation and extent of the implied warranty are left up to state law; if the state law holds that privity is essential to the implied warranty right, then probably the implied warranty simply does not survive transfer, and thus there is no one to whom the product is transferred within the implied warranty period. This interpretation is supported by legislative history which uses a privity requirement for implied warranties as an example of a state law on the creation of implied warranties not intended to be altered by the federal Act. In some states, a distant supplier will be held to give an implied warranty to consumers, while in others vertical privity remains a requirement for implied warranty suits."

I do not read *Ventura v. Ford Motor Co.,* 180 N.J.Super. 45, 433 A.2d 801 (N.J.Super.App.Div.1981) or *Hyde v. General Motors Corp.,* No. 21306/80 (Sup.Ct.N.Y.Cty. October, 1981), cited by plaintiffs, as requiring a different result.

Problem 9

The Avis Skewer Company has always sold its barbecue skewers on a "satisfaction guaranteed" basis, giving dissatisfied customers either a refund or a replacement. This guarantee is good for ten days, and Avis specifically limits its liability to refund or replacement by excluding responsibility for consequential damages.

The Hertz Skewer Company has always given a lifetime guarantee that "Our skewer will withstand trampling by herds of elephants forever. If it doesn't, we will repair or replace it for free." Hertz also excludes responsibility for consequential damages.

The National Skewer Company offers a ten year warranty against all defects, with guaranteed repair or replacement upon payment of a $5 handling charge. It also limits all implied warranties of merchantability or fitness to the same ten year period.

The Budget Skewer Company has always sold its skewers "as is".

Under the Magnuson–Moss Warranty Act, how must each company describe its guarantees in the future? Which description is likely to sound better in an advertising campaign? Which, in fact, is the best warranty? Is the average consumer likely to understand correctly what each type of guarantee really means? See Magnuson–Moss Warranty Act, §§ 103, 104.

Problem 10

Sam Silver thinks he has figured a way to beat the MMWA. In selling food freezers, he makes no express warranties of any kind, and his bill of sale explicitly disclaims any implied warranties. Within the week or two following each sale, Silver's employees call each customer and offer to sell (separately) a maintenance agreement under which Silver's repairmen will replace any defective freezer parts without charge. These maintenance agreements cost $50 per year, and (according to their small print) are automatically renewed unless the customer cancels in writing. Has Silver sidestepped the Act? See MMWA § 106.

Suppose a consumer buys the maintenance agreement the first year, but cancels it at the end of the year. Three months later the freezer stops working, in the process spoiling several hundred dollars worth of food. Does the consumer have any rights? See MMWA § 108(a) and (c).

Problem 11

Before MMWA, Dale Dodge Dealers used a form contract which contained both of the clauses recited in Problem 5, supra p. 382. Now that MMWA is effective, Dale wishes to know whether it must change the *substance* of its form contract. Does MMWA § 108 create any problem for Dale? It also wishes to know whether it will need to change the wording of its form contract. How must the contract be designated? See MMWA §§ 103–104.

Problem 12

Muck Motors, located in Maryland and subject to its UCC § 2–316.1 variation (as in Problem 8) dropped all warranty disclaimers and limitations on remedies from its form contracts after the enactment of UCC § 2–316.1. Now it wants to redraft its form contracts again, at least to limit the remedies available to its buyers, on the ground that MMWA pre-empts state legislation on the subject. Is Muck correct? See MMWA § 111(b) and (c). Which of these two subsections is applicable?

Note that the MMWA Regulations have a "plain language" requirement of their own. See MMWA § 102(a), 16 CFR 701.3(a) (reproduced in West's Selected Commercial Statutes). But also note the FTC's approach to disclosure of warranty provisions in such states as Maryland. See § 701.3(a)(7), (8). Can MMWA–authorized forms mislead consumers as to the effectiveness of limitations on remedies? Is this language as informative to the Maryland consumer as the pre–MMWA forms which often stated after a disclaimer: "Not applicable in Massachusetts or Maryland"?

4. LEMON LAWS

HONIGMAN, "THE NEW 'LEMON LAWS': EXPANDING UCC REMEDIES"

17 UCC L.Jour. 116 (1984).*

* * *

Lemon laws typically allow the purchaser of a new motor vehicle to rescind his or her purchase if the new vehicle requires service for the same warranty problem four or more times during the manufacturer's warranty period or first year of service, whichever occurs first, or if the vehicle is out of service for more than thirty days during this period.

* * *

The new lemon laws are a distinctly different remedy than Section 2–608 of the UCC, which allows revocation of acceptance. Under lemon laws it is the manufacturer, not the dealer, who is responsible for refunding the consumer's purchase price, while under Section 2–608, the dealer, as seller, is normally the only party who may be sued. Lemon laws allow consumers recovery of the purchaser price and collateral charges, or a replacement vehicle at the manufacturer's option, while Section 2–608 allows consumers consequential damages for loss of use in addition to the purchase price but affords the seller no replacement option. Lemon laws, with the exception of New Hampshire's, allow rescission only for breach of express warranty, while Section 2–608 allows revocation of acceptance for any breach of warranty, whether express or implied. * * *

All of the lemon law states, with the exception of Florida, require that the warranty breach be substantial as a condition of invoking the remedy. Section 2–608 also requires that the warranty breach be substantial. In contrast, the rescission provisions mandated for "full warranties" under the Magnuson–Moss Act only require that the warrantor has failed to remedy any warranty defect after a reasonable number of attempts. However, since most new car warranties are "limited warranties" under the definition of the Act, the Magnuson–Moss Act has had little effect on the lemon car problem. * * *

* Reprinted by permission of the publisher from the UCC Law Journal. © Warren, Gorham & Lamont 1984.

There is little doubt that the new lemon laws reflect a widespread public demand that new cars, trucks, and other motor vehicles be of high quality, without hidden defects, and that service under manufacturers' warranties be promptly and effectively performed. The new lemon laws are part of a continuing trend to replace the individual contract bargained for between the consumer and merchant in the marketplace, with a legislative contract bargained for between industry representatives and consumer interest groups under the mediation of legislative committees.

Yet lemon laws do not really change the underlying spirit or purpose of Section 2–608 of the UCC, which is to allow consumers to revoke their acceptance of a product if the manufacturer or seller fails to cure a substantial warranty defect within a reasonable time. Lemon laws by providing objective guidelines for determining reasonable time, and by encouraging the use of informal settlement procedures, should contribute to the Code's purpose of encouraging parties to minimize their losses by working out their differences together.

CHMILL v. FRIENDLY FORD–MERCURY OF JANESVILLE, INC.

Court of Appeals of Wisconsin, 1988.
144 Wis.2d 796, 424 N.W.2d 747.

SUNDBY, JUDGE.

This case requires an interpretation of sec. 218.015, Stats. (1983–84), Wisconsin's Lemon Law. Friendly Ford–Mercury of Janesville, Inc., and Ford Motor Company appeal a judgment under the law requiring them to replace the Chmills' Ford Tempo with a comparable new motor vehicle. We affirm.

I.

BACKGROUND OF THE CASE

On November 26, 1983, the Chmills purchased a demonstrator 1984 Ford Tempo, from Friendly Ford–Mercury of Janesville, Inc. Friendly Ford gave the Chmills a new-car warranty which expired May 4, 1984 when the Chmills had driven the vehicle 12,000 miles.

The trial court found that between the date of purchase and April 2, 1984, the Chmills on at least five occasions had reported a "pulling" problem to Friendly Ford and had left the vehicle with it to be repaired. In December 1984, the Chmills received a recall notice from Ford concerning a rear wheel alignment problem. On December 10, 1984 the Chmills presented the vehicle to Friendly Ford for repair pursuant to the recall notice. The rear wheels were realigned to attempt to correct the alignment and tire wear problems.

On December 8, 1984 the Chmills sought relief from the Ford Consumer Appeals Board. Friendly Ford's service manager responded that recent road tests had shown that the allegation of a "pulling" problem was unfounded. However, he agreed that a tie rod was defective and it was replaced. According to the Chmills the pulling problem continued. They commenced this action July 15, 1985. The defendants established that as of the final day of trial, June 27, 1986, the Chmills had driven the vehicle 78,000 miles.

* * *

The trial court made a finding of fact and a conclusion of law that the pulling problem constituted a nonconformity which substantially impaired the use, value and safety of the vehicle. [Under the Wisconsin statute, if such a nonconformity remains unrepaired after a reasonable attempt, the manufacturer must, at the consumer's option, either replace the vehicle with a comparable new one, or refund the purchase price.]

"Nonconformity" is defined in sec. 218.015(1)(f), Stats., which provides:

> "Nonconformity" means a condition or defect which substantially impairs the use, value or safety of a motor vehicle, and is covered by an express warranty applicable to the motor vehicle, but does not include a condition or defect which is the result of abuse, neglect or unauthorized modification or alteration of the motor vehicle by a consumer.

* * *

IV.

SUBSTANTIAL IMPAIRMENT

The defendants argue that because the Chmills drove the vehicle 78,000 miles, it does not have a substantial impairment as a matter of law. They rely on cases decided under the Uniform Commercial Code: *Gasque v. Mooers Motor Car Co., Inc.,* 227 Va. 154, 313 S.E.2d 384 (1984).

Cases decided under the U.C.C. are inapposite because nonconformity thereunder is determined solely under a value standard. Uniform Commercial Code sec. 2–608(1) (sec. 402.608(1), Stats.) permits a buyer to revoke his acceptance of a commercial unit whose "nonconformity substantially impairs its value to him." This is a far different standard from the sec. 218.015(1)(f), Stats., standard which defines a nonconformity in terms of use and safety as well as value.

In *Gasque,* 313 S.E.2d at 389, the fact that the vehicle had substantially fulfilled its primary purpose—simple transportation—was held to satisfy the requirements of the code. However, that a vehicle has served its primary purpose of providing "simple transportation" does not satisfy the use, value and safety standard of sec. 218.015(1)(f), Stats. We therefore reject the defendant's argument that because the Chmills drove the defective vehicle for 78,000 miles, there was, as a matter of law, no substantial impairment within the meaning of sec. 218.015(1)(f). Each case must be examined on its facts under the standard of sec. 218.015(1)(f).

The trial court found that, on her way home from the dealership, Mrs. Chmill discovered that the vehicle pulled to the left. The pulling problem continued and the vehicle was returned to Friendly Ford in December, 1983 for repair. Thereafter, through April of 1984 and no less than once each month, Mrs. Chmill returned the vehicle to Friendly Ford for repair of the pulling problem. The Chmills testified that Friendly Ford's service manager told them the vehicle should be replaced or repurchased since it was defective and could not be repaired. This testimony was unchallenged. An experienced car salesman and buyer for a Buick–Pontiac dealership testified that because of the pulling defect, the value of the vehicle was substantially less than the price paid by the Chmills. From these facts and testimony the trial court found that the pulling problem substantially impaired the use, value and safety of the vehicle. That finding is not clearly erroneous. We affirm the trial court's determination that the facts in this case fulfill the legal standard of "substantial impairment."

V.

ATTEMPTS TO REPAIR

We consider next the defendants' claim that there were not four attempts to repair the vehicle as required by sec. 218.015(1)(h)1, Stats.

To be entitled to recovery under sec. 218.015(2)(b), Stats., a consumer must establish that "after a reasonable attempt to repair the nonconformity [it] cannot be repaired." Section 218.015(1)(h) provides in part:

"Reasonable attempt to repair" means any of the following occurring within the term of an express warranty applicable to a new motor vehicle or within one year after first delivery of the motor vehicle to a consumer, whichever is sooner:

1. The same nonconformity with the warranty is subject to repair by the manufacturer or any of its authorized motor vehicle dealers at least 4 times and the nonconformity continues.

The defendants "vigorously dispute" the trial court's finding of fact that between the date of purchase of the vehicle and April 2, 1984, Mrs. Chmill had on at least five occasions left the vehicle with Friendly Ford to correct the pulling defect. However, they accept that finding for decision-making purposes. They suggest that a vehicle is not "subject to repair" unless the dealer has attempted to repair it. The defendants argue that the record shows that Friendly Ford did not attempt to repair the vehicle four times within the warranty period because the defective condition could not be verified by it.

The construction of the statute urged by the defendants would lead to an unreasonable result. If an acknowledged defect cannot be diagnosed by the service agency no matter how many times the consumer presents the vehicle for repair, the consumer is without recourse. Remedial statutes should be construed to suppress the mischief and advance the remedy which the statute intended to afford. We reject the defendant's hypertechnical construction of the statute as unreasonable. We conclude that the Chmills complied with the statute when on at least four occasions within the warranty period they presented the vehicle to Friendly Ford to be repaired.

* * *

Judgment affirmed, and cause remanded for further proceedings consistent with this opinion.

Note

Connecticut was one of the first states to pass a lemon law and it has been a leader among the states in continuing to fine tune and improve the law. Following is the 1987 version of the Connecticut lemon law:

CHAPTER 743b

AUTOMOBILE WARRANTIES

§ 42–179. **New motor vehicle warranties**
* * *

(b) If a new motor vehicle does not conform to all applicable express warranties, and the consumer reports the nonconformity to the manufacturer, its agent or its authorized dealer during the period of two years following the date of original delivery of the motor vehicle to a consumer or during the period of the first eighteen thousand miles of operation, whichever period ends first, the manufacturer, its agent or its authorized dealer shall make such repairs as are necessary to conform the vehicle to such express warranties, notwithstanding the fact that such repairs are made after the expiration of the applicable period.

* * *

(d) If the manufacturer, or its agents or authorized dealers are unable to conform the motor vehicle to any applicable express warranty by repairing or correcting any defect or condition which substantially impairs the use, safety or value of the motor vehicle to the consumer after a reasonable number of attempts, the manufacturer shall replace the motor vehicle with a new motor vehicle acceptable to the consumer, or accept return of the vehicle from the consumer and refund to the consumer, lessor and lienholder, if any, as their interests may appear, the following: (1) The full contract price including, but not limited to charges for undercoating, dealer preparation and transportation and installed options, (2) all collateral charges, including, but not limited to, sales tax, license and registration fees, and similar government charges, (3) all finance charges incurred by the consumer after he first reports the nonconformity to the manufacturer, agent or dealer and during any subsequent period when the vehicle is out of service by reason of repair, and (4) all incidental damages as defined in section 42a–2–715, less a reasonable allowance for the consumer's use of the vehicle.

* * *

It shall be an affirmative defense to any claim under this section (1) that an alleged nonconformity does not substantially impair such use, safety or value or (2) that a nonconformity is the result of abuse, neglect or unauthorized modifications or alterations of a motor vehicle by a consumer.

(e) It shall be presumed that a reasonable number of attempts have been undertaken to conform a motor vehicle to the applicable express warranties, if (1) the same nonconformity has been subject to repair four or more times by the manufacturer or its agents or authorized dealers during the period of two years following the date of original delivery of the motor vehicle to a consumer or during the period of the first eighteen thousand miles of operation, whichever period ends first, but such nonconformity continues to exist or (2) the vehicle is out of service by reason of repair for a cumulative total of thirty or more calendar days during the applicable period, determined pursuant to subdivision (1) of this subsection. ＊ ＊ ＊

(f) If a motor vehicle has a nonconformity which results in a condition which is likely to cause death or serious bodily injury if the vehicle is driven, it shall be presumed that a reasonable number of attempts have been undertaken to conform such vehicle to the applicable express warranties if the nonconformity has been subject to repair at least twice by the manufacturer or its agents or authorized dealers within the express warranty term or during the period of one year following the date of the original delivery of the motor vehicle to a consumer, whichever period ends first, but such nonconformity continues to exist. ＊ ＊ ＊

(g) No motor vehicle which is returned to the manufacturer and which requires replacement or refund shall be resold or leased in the state without clear and conspicuous written disclosure of the fact that such motor vehicle was so returned prior to resale or lease.

＊ ＊ ＊

(i) Nothing in this section shall in any way limit the rights or remedies which are otherwise available to a consumer under any other law.

(j) If a manufacturer has established an informal dispute settlement procedure which is certified by the attorney general as complying in all respects with the provisions of Title 16 Code of Federal Regulations Part 703, as in effect on October 1, 1982, and with the provisions of subsection (b) of section 42–182, the provisions of subsection (d) of this section concerning refunds or replacement shall not apply to any consumer who has not first resorted to such procedure.

§ 42–180. Costs and attorney's fees in breach of warranty actions

In any action by a consumer against the manufacturer of a motor vehicle, or the manufacturer's agent or authorized dealer, based upon the alleged breach of an express or implied warranty made in connection with the sale or lease of such motor vehicle, the court, in its discretion, may award to the plaintiff his costs and reasonable attorney's fees or, if the court determines that the action was brought without any substantial justification, may award costs and reasonable attorney's fees to the defendant.

Problem 13

Robbin Hood bought a new Dodge station wagon for $12,000 from Dale Dodge in Bridgeport, Connecticut. The car came with an express warranty which states in full:

LIMITED WARRANTY

The manufacturer warrants this car to be free from defects in material and workmanship for 12 months or 12,000 miles, whichever comes first. Manufacturer makes no other express warranty, and any implied warranty of merchantability or fitness is limited to the 12 month or 12,000 mile duration of this written warranty. The buyer's exclusive remedy under this warranty is repair or replacement of defective parts, which will be done without charge to the buyer.

Dale Dodge furnished a separate document to Hood, which stated in pertinent part:

The selling dealer agrees to perform all repairs required under this warranty as an agent of the manufacturer but makes absolutely NO EXPRESS OR IMPLIED WARRANTY OF MERCHANTABILITY OR FITNESS.

The automatic transmission has broken down four times since Hood purchased the car and each time the repair failed to correct the problem. Dale now says he will replace the transmission.

It is now 9 months since Hood bought the car, and the odometer reads 10,220 miles. Hood comes to you for legal advice. He confides that the car is really too expensive for him so he would prefer to get his money back and rescind the whole transaction.

(a) Is Hood in a better position under the Connecticut lemon law than he would be with only the UCC? (b) With the UCC and MMWA? (c) What if the manufacturer has instituted an informal dispute resolution system? See infra pages 753–760 for a discussion of possible preemption of state lemon laws regulating informal dispute resolution procedures that are also governed by FTC Rule 703.

5. REAL ESTATE

Thus, far, we have said nothing about warranties in the sale of real estate. The law of warranties in realty sales may be just about one hundred years behind that of personal property warranties. Neither the UCC nor the MMWA are applicable.

TAVARES v. HORSTMAN

Supreme Court of Wyoming, 1975.
542 P.2d 1275.

RAPER, JUSTICE

* * *

The defendant, a land developer and builder, sold the plaintiffs a tract of land; the defendant built a home for plaintiffs on the property under an oral agreement with no express warranty. A warranty deed with only the usual covenants of title was delivered. Within a little over a year, the septic tank system backed sewage to a depth of about three inches into the plaintiffs' basement before it was discovered. A plumber was called; after pumping out the tanks a couple of times, he advised that something would have to be done about the system. Defendant was called and informed of this nasty predicament. He dug down to the discharge pipe, perforated the line and let the raw sewage flow into an open trench. Nothing further was done. Plaintiffs called him to do something further but he said he could not work on it because he had to go on a vacation. The stinking situation was so deplorable that plaintiffs called in an experienced septic tank contractor. The system had to be rebuilt because of its inadequacy. The soil in the area of the drainage field was of tight gumbo so a particular design and manner of installation was necessary. The contractor who rebuilt the system testified that the problems with the one he replaced were several. The defendant had installed foundation drainage pipe all around the house and constructed it to discharge into the septic tank system, causing an overload of the sewage disposal scheme. There was not enough capacity for the size home it was to serve. The excess water caused the drainage field to waterlog, backed effluent into the tanks, killed the bacterial actions supposed to be taking place there and, in turn, blocked the flow of sewage from the house. Having no place else to go, the noxious waste covered the basement floor. Plaintiffs expended $2,083.00 to correct the condition.

* * *

Since World War II homes have been built in tremendous numbers. There have come into being developer-builders operating on a large scale. Many firms and persons, large and small operators, hold themselves out as skilled in home construction and are in the business of building and selling to individual owners. Developers contract with builders to construct for resale. Building construction by modern methods is complex and intertwined with governmental codes and regulations. The ordinary home buyer is not in a position, by skill or training, to discover defects lurking in the plumbing, the electrical wiring, the structure itself, all of which is usually covered up and not open for inspection.

A home buyer should be able to place reliance on the builder or developer who sells him a new house. The improved real estate the average family buys gives it thoughtful pause not only because of the base price but the interest involved over a long period of time. This is usually the largest single purchase a family makes for a lifetime. Some may be able to pay cash but we cannot single out that buyer in the formulation of a rule.

It ought to be an implicit understanding of the parties that when an agreed price is paid that the home is reasonably fit for the purpose for which it is to be used—that it is reasonably fit for habitation. Illusory value is a poor substitute for quality. There is no need for the buyer to be subjected to the harassment caused by defects and he deserves the focus of the law and its concern. The significant purchase of a new home leads logically to the buyer's expectation that he be judicially protected. Any other result would be intolerable and unjust, as the cases which follow demonstrate.

[The court then discusses a number of cases that held there is an implied warranty of habitability attached to the sale of a new home.]

We now reach defendant's claim that it is not necessary that the work be done perfectly and any implied warranty that may have existed has expired. Some question exists as to what should be the period of implied warranty. We appreciate that different parts of construction may have a different expected life, such as a foundation compared to a roof. We have no problem in the present case because the septic tank system failed before a minimum life expectancy had been reached; its breakdown is traced to the negligent design and is considered a major component of a residence not served by a county or municipal sewer system. * * * We likewise hold that the duration of liability is determined by the standard of reasonableness. The premature failure of a sewer system is no trifling matter, so we cannot accept defendant's contention that it was of minor consequence; the house was rendered uninhabitable.

In summary then, we hold that under the circumstances of this case, the rule of caveat emptor no longer protects the builder-vendor because it is unrealistic in the light of the change that has emerged in the morals of the marketplace. That doctrine was based upon an arms-length transaction between seller and buyer and contemplated comparable skill and experience, which does not now exist; they are not in an equal bargaining position and the buyer is forced to rely on the skill and knowledge of the builder.

We further hold along with a vast majority of courts that where a vendor builds new houses for the purpose of sale, the sale carries with it an implied warranty that it is constructed in a reasonably workmanlike manner and is fit for habitation.

* * *

Problem 14

Hovel Homes constructed a new home for Jack and Jill Hill. Two years later, Hill was transferred to another state and the Hills sold their home to Humpty Dumpty. Several months after he moved in, Dumpty gradually became aware that the electrical wiring was defective and dangerous. He determined that it would cost $4,000 to have the wiring brought up to standard. He wants to sue Hovel for breach of the implied warranty of habitability. Thus far his state has only recognized an implied warranty for the benefit of the original purchaser. Should the implied warranty extend to Humpty Dumpty? What are the arguments on each side? Compare Moxley v. Laramie Builders, Inc., 600 P.2d 733 (Wyo.1979) with Crowder v. Vandendeale, 564 S.W.2d 879 (Mo.1978).

Notes

1.   Some 44 states recognize through judicial decisions an implied warranty of habitability running from the builder/seller to the original buyer.

2.   By 1989 only 16 states had extended liability for defects from the builder to subsequent purchasers, and some of these are based on a negligence theory, not warranty.   See D. Pridgen, *Consumer Protection and the Law,* Appendix 18B (1986, with 1990 update).   Other states have held firm on the idea that the warranty does not go farther than the first buyer. See Ellis v. Robert C. Morris, Inc., 128 N.H. 358, 513 A.2d 951 (1986).

3.   No state implies a warranty of habitability from the seller of a used home who was not the original builder.   A disappointed buyer in the latter type of transaction would be relegated to common law fraud remedies, or a state "little FTC act," if applicable.

4.   The National Conference of Commissioners on Uniform State Laws (which brought you the UCC and the U3C) has proposed legislation to govern real estate transactions.   In 1975 the Conference promulgated, and in 1977 amended, the Uniform Land Transactions Act, which was intended to be to real estate what the UCC and U3C are to transactions in goods.   It codified an implied warranty of habitability for real estate sales.   For better or worse, the ULTA was never adopted in any state, although a few states have legislated an implied warranty of habitability for new homes. See, e.g., Md. Real Prop. Code Ann. 10–201(b)–(c);   Conn.Gen.Stat.Ann. § 47–118(a);   Minn.Stat. 327A.02, subd. 1;   N.J.Stat.Ann. 46:3B–3(b);   Va. Code 55–70.1.

5.   Unlike the situation for new homes, it is much more common for states to have enacted legislation mandating express and implied warranties to be given by developers of condominiums or other types of common-ownership residential or recreational property.   Almost one-third of the states have passed such laws, many of them derived from either the 1977 or 1980 Uniform Condominium Act or the 1982 Uniform Common Interest Ownership Act.   See Diamond & Raines, Consumer Warranty Issues in the Sale of Residential Condominiums, 20 Real Prop. Probate & Trust J. 933 (1985).   The following provisions on implied warranties and disclaimers are identical in both acts.

UNIFORM CONDOMINIUM ACT

§ 4–114.   [Implied Warranties of Quality]

(a) A declarant and any person in the business of selling real estate for his own account warrants that a unit will be in at least as good condition at the earlier of the time of the conveyance or delivery of possession as it was at the time of contracting, reasonable wear and tear excepted.

(b) A declarant and any person in the business of selling real estate for his own account impliedly warrants that a unit and the common elements in the condominium are suitable for the ordinary uses of real estate of its type and that any improvements made or contracted for by him, or made by any person before the creation of the condominium, will be:

(1) free from defective materials; and

(2) constructed in accordance with applicable law, according to sound engineering and construction standards, and in a workmanlike manner.

(c) In addition, a declarant and any person in the business of selling real estate for his own account warrants to a purchaser of a unit that may be used for residential use that an existing use, continuation of which is contemplated by the parties, does not violate applicable law at the earlier of the time of conveyance or delivery of possession.

(d) Warranties imposed by this section may be excluded or modified as specified in Section 4–115.

(e) For purposes of this section, improvements made or contracted for by an affiliate of a declarant (Section 1–103(1)) are made or contracted for by the declarant.

(f) Any conveyance of a unit transfers to the purchaser all of the declarant's implied warranties of quality.

§ 4–115. [Exclusion or Modification of Implied Warranties of Quality]

(a) Except as limited by subsection (b) with respect to a purchaser of a unit that may be used for residential use, implied warranties of quality:

(1) may be excluded or modified by agreement of the parties; and

(2) are excluded by expression of disclaimer, such as "as is," "with all faults," or other language which in common understanding calls the buyer's attention to the exclusion of warranties.

(b) With respect to a purchaser of a unit that may be occupied for residential use, no general disclaimer of implied warranties of quality is effective, but a declarant and any person in the business of selling real estate for his own account may disclaim liability in an instrument signed by the purchaser for a specified defect or specified failure to comply with applicable law, if the defect or failure entered into and became a part of the basis of the bargain.

Problem 15

Harry Hovel, President of Hovel Homes, would like to get into the business of building quickie condominium developments for retired persons. His jurisdiction has enacted the Uniform Condominium Act, which Hovel has heard will impose special warranty standards on residential condominium sales. He wants to disclaim all such warranties. He asks you whether an "as is" clause will accomplish his goal. Will it? If not, what can you put in his contract which will be effective? See U.S.C.A. 4–115(b).

Notes

1. How clear are the standards of the warranty stated in § 4–114? Would it be better or worse to rely on common law development of warranties for condominiums?

2. Should warranty legislation be developed for mobile home purchasers? Are mobile homes covered by the UCC? Seventeen states have enacted laws mandating some type of warranty on new mobile homes, usually a one year warranty against defects. See D. Pridgen, Consumer Protection and the Law, Appendix 17A (1986). A proposed FTC regulation that would have addressed problems of poor warranty performance in the mobile home industry was withdrawn in 1986.

3. Should similar warranty notions be applied with respect to apartments and other rental property? Some of the landmarks in this important area of landlord-tenant law are: Javins v. First National Realty Corp., 428 F.2d 1071 (D.C.Cir.1970); Boston Housing Authority v. Hemingway, 363 Mass. 184, 293 N.E.2d 831 (1973).

SECTION C. THE DEMISE OF SPECIAL PROTECTION TO THIRD–PARTY LENDERS (HOLDERS IN DUE COURSE)

1. THE JUDICIAL ASSAULT

Problem 16

Mr. and Mrs. Lundstrom agreed to buy a TV set from Electronics, for $995; simultaneously they executed to Electronics a separate agreement to participate in a "Referral Sales Plan" under which they would get $50 for each purchaser they referred to Electronics. The Lundstroms signed both a conditional sale contract and a negotiable promissory note for the TV. Continental Thrift purchased the conditional sale contract and the negotiable promissory note for the TV from Electronics, but it did not purchase the Referral Sales Plan agreement.

In order to keep the two transactions separate, Continental had the Lundstroms tape-record their understanding that the TV sale contract was separate from the Referral Sales Plan agreement. Continental also insisted that the Lundstroms give it a signed receipt for the TV; and Continental phoned the Lundstroms to confirm delivery, and their understanding of the two separate agreements. This was Continental's regular practice in financing Electronics' sales.

Electronics never paid the Lundstroms for any referrals, and is now insolvent. With only the UCC in effect in the jurisdiction, can the Lundstroms successfully defend a collection action brought by Continental? Compare Lundstrom v. Radio Corp. of America, 17 Utah 2d 114, 405 P.2d 339 (1965), with Unico v. Owen, 50 N.J. 101, 232 A.2d 405 (1967).

Notes

1.   The protections traditionally available to financers through various "cut-off" devices have now been largely eliminated by the FTC Trade Regulation Rule treated infra at pp. 413–423.   But the years preceding the Rule's promulgation saw a concentrated attack on holder in due course, in caselaw and in state statutes.   These developments are important background for the FTC Rule itself.

2.   Many courts reacted negatively to attempts to separate the consumer's duty to pay from the seller's duty to perform.   A variety of theories were used, but most commonly courts would either hold that the waiver of defense clause was void as against public policy under the circumstances, or the lender would be so closely connected to the sales transaction as to lose all claim to being a "good faith" holder in due course without notice of defenses.

The case of Fairfield Credit Corporation v. Donnelly, 158 Conn. 543, 264 A.2d 547 (1969) is typical of the public policy approach.   The Donnellys were lured into purchasing a color television on credit with the offer of being able to earn $50 for each potential new customer they referred to the seller.   The consumers bought it on credit, but did not sign a negotiable promissory note.   Instead, they executed an installment sale contract which included a waiver of defense clause, in fine print on the back: "The Buyer will settle all claims against the Seller directly with such Seller and will not assert or use any such claim as a defense against the assignee." Such clauses are authorized by UCC § 9–206.   Soon after delivery of the set, it became apparent that it was not working properly and that the seller was not going to make good on its service contract.   The Donnellys stopped making payments on the set, and were sued by the assignee of the credit contract.   Meanwhile, the seller went out of business and disappeared from the jurisdiction.   The assignee's attempt to hide behind the standard waiver of defense clause was in vain.   The Connecticut Supreme Court condemned the use of such clauses in consumer credit contracts, noting how often they appeared "in fine print and couched in technical language the significance of which is difficult for the ordinary consumer to appreciate."   The court also pointed to the recent passage of several consumer protection measures by the state legislature as evidence that "there exists in Connecticut a very strong public policy in favor of protecting purchasers of consumer goods" and concluded that "for a court to enforce a waiver of defense clause in a consumer-goods transaction would be contrary to that policy."   Thus, the assignee was not entitled to collect the balance due since the seller had more or less defaulted on its obligations.   However, the decision had an impact only on recoveries via a contract with a waiver of defense clause, and not necessarily on recoveries via a negotiable instrument.

3.   Unico v. Owen, 50 N.J. 101, 232 A.2d 405 (1967) typified a parallel approach which denied protection to the holders of negotiable notes on the basis of a close working relationship ("close-connectedness") between the seller and financer.   While these lines of caselaw provided ample precedent for challenging holder in due course status in particular cases, they did not

destroy the doctrine itself, which continued in the UCC. Nor were these lines of caselaw ever unanimous. See Block v. Ford Motor Credit Co., 286 A.2d 228 (D.C.App.1972); Randolph Nat. Bank v. Vail, 131 Vt. 390, 308 A.2d 588 (1973).

4. Holder in due course devices are dealt with in the U3C. See §§ 3.307, 3.404 for provisions barring the conventional techniques for generating defense-free consumer paper.

In fact, so widespread was the consensus against holder in due course in consumer transactions that, even prior to promulgation of the FTC Rule in 1975, more than forty state legislatures had acted to abolish it in at least some situations—some prohibited it generally, some limited the prohibition to narrow classes of transactions. In many states, consumers were given a limited period of time after receiving notice of an assignment, ranging from five to ninety days, to raise their claims against the assignee. See generally, Rohner, "Holder in Due Course in Consumer Transactions: Requiem, Revival, or Reformation?", 60 Cornell L.Rev. 503 (1975).

5. As long as the seller is available to provide redress to the aggrieved consumer, why shouldn't the consumer be expected to pursue the real malefactor? Shouldn't holder in due course protection continue to be available for the financer unless the seller has gone bankrupt or moved away? Note that the U3C does not limit its prohibitions to such situations.

6. What is the argument for total prohibition of holder in due course protection? Is it predicated on the theory that consumers should be able to recover damages in lawsuits against financers, or on hopes that financers would assist in resolving or preventing disputes over the quality of merchandise? If the latter, why and how are financers expected to perform such services?

In terms of risk allocation, the old rules allocated the risk of sellers' misconduct to consumers. By abolishing holder in due course, this risk is now borne by financers. Through what analysis does it make more sense to allocate risks to financers than to consumers?

7. Suppose the consumers in *Donnelly* had proved they had grounds to rescind the underlying contracts for fraud. Could they have gotten an affirmative recovery—damages or a refund of money already paid—from the financer? Or, suppose a consumer suffers $1 million in personal injuries from a defective car; can the consumer recover this sum from the bank holding the credit contract? Under the case law? Under the U3C?

2. THE FTC ASSAULT

Note on Disclosure

In the late 1960s the Federal Trade Commission began an attack on holder in due course protections for creditors, using a disclosure technique. On the now-familiar theory that disclosure would go a long way toward solving consumer problems, the Commission reasoned that it was unfair and deceptive for retailers to take negotiable instruments or waiver-of-defense clauses without clearly explaining to consumers the resulting loss of rights.

In one leading case, involving a seller of aluminum siding, the FTC concluded that the appropriate remedy for such deception was to require the seller to disclose affirmatively to the purchaser that:

> any conditional sales contract, promissory note or other instrument of indebtedness executed by a purchaser * * *, at the seller's option and without notice to the purchaser, may be assigned to a finance company or other third party to whom the purchaser will thereafter be indebted and against whom the purchaser's claims or defenses [on the contract] may not be available.

All–State Industries of North Carolina, Inc. v. Federal Trade Com'n, 423 F.2d 423, 425 (4th Cir.1970), cert. denied, 400 U.S. 828, 91 S.Ct. 57, 27 L.Ed. 2d 58 (1970).

Query: Assume a seller complies with the FTC order by incorporating into its contract the exact language used by the Commission, above. How enlightening is this disclosure for the typical consumer? How do you think the aluminum siding purchaser would react to this information?

This FTC attempt to deal with the problem on a case-by-case basis was no more successful than the earlier attempt to deal with misleading disclosure of interest rates. See Ford Motor Co. v. FTC, supra p. 99. However, when the FTC finally did move, in 1976, it used the device of a Trade Regulation Rule and moved effectively.

FTC Trade Regulation Rule on "Preservation of Consumer Claims and Defenses"—A Federal Broadside Attack on Holder in Due Course

In 1975, the Federal Trade Commission determined that "[I]t constitutes an unfair and deceptive practice to use contractual boilerplate to separate a buyer's duty to pay from a seller's duty to perform". Preservation of Consumer's Claims and Defenses, Statement of Basis and Purpose, 40 Fed.Reg. 53,506, at 53,524 (1975). The Holder in Due Course Rule abrogated the use of the holder in due course doctrine in consumer credit transactions by requiring sellers to include a notice in all consumer credit sales instruments stating that any subsequent holder is subject to all claims and defenses that could be asserted against the seller. See 16 C.F.R. Part 433 (set forth in West's Selected Commercial Statutes).

The Commission adopted an economically oriented rationale focusing on the effect of the seller's post-purchase conduct on the consumer's economic welfare when it adopted the Holder in Due Course Rule. See Preservation of Consumers' Claims and Defenses, Statement of Basis and Purpose, 40 Fed.Reg. at 53,522–24.

> The Commission believes that relief under Section Five of the FTC Act is appropriate where sellers or creditors impose adhesive contracts upon consumers, where such contracts contain terms which injure consumers, and where consumer injury is not off-set by a reasonable measure of value received in return. In this connection, the Commission's authority to examine and prohibit unfair practices in or affecting commerce in the manner of a commercial equity court is appropriately

applied to this problem. Where one party to a transaction enjoys substantial advantages with respect to the consumers with whom he deals, it is appropriate for the Commission to conduct an inquiry to determine whether the dominant party is using an overabundance of market power, or commercial advantage in an inequitable manner.

TINKER v. DE MARIA PORSCHE AUDI, INC.

Court of Appeal of Florida, 1984.
459 So.2d 487.

[Plaintiff Tinker purchased a used Jaguar from De Maria Porsche Audi, based in part on representations by the sales agent that the automobile was in good operating condition, was powered by its original engine and had never been involved in a major accident. As it turned out, the car soon developed problems, and Tinker discovered that the Jag had been involved in a major collision, and that it was not powered by the original engine. Tinker won his fraud claim against De Maria. However, the bank that purchased Tinker's credit contract and promissory note from De Maria was awarded $4,500 on its counterclaim against Tinker for the balance due on the Jaguar. The preprinted installment sales contract contained the required FTC notice in bold letters.]

Whether the jury's finding of fraud by De Maria is, as contended by Tinker, an absolute defense to the Bank's counterclaim for the balance owed on the contract, depends on the legal efficacy of the "Notice" provision which was included. Appellant expressed some uncertainty at trial as to how the provision operates.

The Notice is required by federal law in all consumer credit contracts made in connection with purchase money loans, such as installment sales contracts where the consumer executes the sales agreement together with a promissory note, both of which are, through a preprinted assignment clause, assigned to a bank which is closely affiliated with the seller. The effect of the federal rule is to defeat the holder in due course status of the assignee institutional lender, thus removing the lender's insulation from claims and defenses which could be asserted against the seller by the consumer.

Prior to the passage of the rule, consumers were caught in a "no-win" situation when the seller failed to remedy the defect either because of its unwillingness or its disappearance from the market. The institutional lenders then took advantage of protections under the holder in due course doctrine when the consumer sought to assert seller misconduct as a defense to the creditor's suit for payment on the note. The rule is expressly designed to compel creditors to either absorb seller misconduct costs or seek reimbursement of those costs from sellers.

Although we have found no cases directly on the point, it is clear that not only does the Notice clause entitle the buyer to withhold the balance of the purchase price owed to the creditor when the seller's contractual duties are not fulfilled, but it gives the buyer a complete defense should the creditor sue for payment. * * *

* * * We hold that the fraud found to have been perpetrated by De Maria constituted a complete defense to the Bank's counterclaim for the balance owed on the installment sales contract,[7] which disposes of appellant's contention that the verdicts were inconsistent.

EACHEN v. SCOTT HOUSING SYSTEMS, INC.

United States District Court, Middle District of Alabama, 1986.
630 F.Supp. 162.

THOMPSON, DISTRICT JUDGE.

The material facts of this case are undisputed. Charles and Mary Eachen purchased a Scott Showcase Mobile Home from Lawler Mobile Homes, Inc. of Phenix City, Alabama on June 10, 1983. The home was purchased on credit. In addition to a bill of sale, the Eachens and Lawler Mobile Homes signed an Alabama Mobile Home Retail Installment Contract and Security Agreement. That agreement contained the [FTC required language]. On the day of sale, Lawler Mobile Homes assigned the agreement to Citicorp.

The Eachens became dissatisfied with the mobile home because it allegedly contained serious defects in material and workmanship. Both Lawler Mobile Homes and Scott Housing, the manufacturer of the home, attempted to remedy the alleged defects, but the Eachens remained dissatisfied. Sometime before September 1985, Lawler filed for bankruptcy, thereby automatically barring any legal proceeding against it.

* * *

[The Eachens brought suit against Citicorp and Scott Housing for breach of warranty.]

Citicorp's first theory is that it is entitled to full summary judgment because, as assignee of the seller, it can be liable under Alabama law for the Eachens' claim only as a matter of *defense to* or *set-off against* a claim by the assignee. Since Citicorp has instituted no legal proceedings against the Eachens to collect unpaid funds, it continues, the Eachens are barred from maintaining this lawsuit. Citicorp rests this argument on the final phrase in a provision of the Alabama Consumer Finance Law:

> With respect to a consumer credit sale or consumer lease, an assignee of the rights of the seller or lessor is subject to all claims and defenses of the buyer or lessee against the seller or lessor arising out of the sale or lease, notwithstanding an agreement to the contrary, but the assignee's liability under this section may not exceed the amount owing to the assignee at the time the claim or defense is asserted against the assignee. *Rights of the buyer or lessee under this section can only be*

---

7. Under 16 C.F.R. § 433.2, Tinker could have sued the Bank for restitution to recover payments already made, in addition to defending against the Bank's counterclaim for payment. 40 Fed.Reg. at 53524.

asserted as a matter of defense to or set-off against a claim by the assignee.

1975 Alabama Code § 5–19–8 (emphasis added).

Citicorp's first theory lacks merit because the Eachens premise their lawsuit not on Alabama law but rather on the 1975 FTC regulation reported at 16 C.F.R. § 433.2 (1984) ("Preservation of Consumer's Claims and Defenses"). This federal regulation makes it "an unfair or deceptive act or practice" under the Federal Trade Commission Act, 15 U.S.C.A. § 41, *et seq.,* for a seller, directly or indirectly, to take or receive a consumer credit contract which fails to contain the provision regarding claims and defenses set forth in the consumer contract issued to the Eachens.

This regulation was specifically intended, according to the FTC, to provide that "a consumer can * * * maintain an *affirmative action* against a creditor who has received payments for a return of monies paid on account." 40 Fed.Reg. 53524 (1975) (emphasis added). The FTC expressly rejected amendments to the regulation that would limit the consumer to a "defense" or "setoff." The FTC stated,

> Many industry representatives suggested that the rule be amended so that the consumer may assert his rights only as a matter of defense or setoff against a claim by the assignee or holder. Industry representatives argued that such a limitation would prevent the financer from becoming a guarantor and that any limitation in the extent of a third party's liability was desirable.
>
> The practical and policy considerations which militate against such a limitation on affirmative actions by consumers are far more persuasive.

40 Fed.Reg. 53526 (1975) (footnotes omitted). The FTC observed, among other things, that if the consumer is limited to a purely defensive position the assignee-creditor may elect not to sue for the balance due when the consumer's defenses seem to have merit and the seller is judgment proof. The FTC observed that

> The most persuasive reason for not limiting a consumer to a wholly defensive position is the situation referred to in Professor Guttman's testimony. A consumer may stop payment after unsuccessfully attempting resolution of a complaint with the seller, or he may have finally discovered that the seller has moved, gone out of business or reincorporated as a different entity. During this period the consumer may have been making payments to the financer in good faith, notwithstanding the prior existence of defenses against the seller.
>
> If the consumer stops payment, he may be sued for the balance due by the third party financer. The financer may, however, elect not to bring suit, especially if he knows that he would be unable to implead the seller and he knows the consumer's defenses may be meritorious. Under such circumstances the financer may elect to not sue in the hopes that the threat of an unfavorable credit report may move the consumer to pay.

40 Fed.Reg. 53527 (1975). Indeed, assuming that the Eachens can prevail on their warranty claim—an assumption which this court must make on Citicorp's motion for summary judgment—it appears that the objectionable scenario described by the FTC could very well be applicable here unless the regulation is enforced.

Citicorp argues, nonetheless, that the limitation in Alabama's section 5–19–8 should be engrafted onto the FTC regulation. It supports this argument by citing the following isolated language from an introductory paragraph to certain FTC Enforcement Guidelines issued in 1976:

> The manner and procedure by which a buyer may assert claims and defenses is governed by the terms of the contract and by applicable state law.

41 Fed.Reg. 34594 (1976). Citicorp's argument is meritless.

First, Citicorp has lifted this language out of 1976 Enforcement Guidelines addressing the regulation's definition of a "purchase money loan." Allowing affirmative actions by consumers against assignee-creditors was not addressed in these Guidelines. Therefore, it is apparent that the Guidelines and the language in them were not intended as an authoritative statement on the extent to which consumers could bring actions against assignee-creditors under the regulation.

But more importantly, it is apparent that when the quoted language from the Guidelines is read in conjunction with the history and purposes of the FTC regulation, the language is intended to mean that one must look to state law and the terms of the contract to determine the "manner and procedure" by which a consumer may affirmatively maintain an action against a creditor. For example, as noted by the FTC, an affirmative action against a creditor "will only be available where a seller's breach is so substantial that a court is persuaded that rescission and restitution are justified. The most typical example of such a case would involve non-delivery, where delivery was scheduled after the date payments to a creditor commenced." 40 Fed.Reg. 53524 (1975). The FTC staff has also observed that

> Where a local jurisdiction has a two-year statute of limitations on contract claims, such claims and defenses would be extinguished after two years. Where a local jurisdiction imposes a rule analogous to laches or equitable estoppel, consumer claims and defenses would continue to be subject to such a limitation, and the consumer would have a duty to notify the potential defendant of his contention within a reasonable time.

41 Fed.Reg. 20024 (1976).

Moreover, to adopt Citicorp's understanding of the quoted language would mean that the FTC had authorized individual states to rescind the 1975 regulation to the extent the regulation specifically authorized consumers to bring affirmative actions against assignee-creditors. This drastic result is not supported by the regulation either on its face or by its history. The regulation neither expressly nor impliedly provides that states are authorized to rescind the 1975 regulation, in whole or in part; nor does a searching review of the history of the regulation uncover anything that would indicate such authorization, either expressly or impliedly.

* * *

The Eachens may therefore assert their warranty claim against Citicorp under the FTC regulation, irrespective of whether Citicorp has filed a lawsuit against the Eachens.

Citicorp's second theory is that it is entitled to partial summary judgment prohibiting the Eachens from recovering on their warranty claim more than they have paid under the contract to Citicorp. The Eachens concede this theory. The contract expressly provides that recovery by the debtor against an assignee-creditor is limited to amounts paid by the debtor.

The court will therefore grant partial summary judgment to Citicorp prohibiting the Eachens from recovering from Citicorp more than they have paid to Citicorp under the contract.

An appropriate order will be entered.

Problem 17

Robbin Hood bought a new car from Dale Dodge Dealer on Credit. The cash price was $7,000. Hood was allowed $1,000 for his trade-in. Hood financed the $6,000 balance by executing a 48 month installment contract, which included the unpaid principal balance and $1,680 in finance charges; monthly payments are $160. Chrysler gives a one-year limited warranty on the car under the Magnuson–Moss Warranty Act. Dale makes no express warranties, nor does he adopt the manufacturer's written warranty. Dale simply acts as a conduit for the manufacturer's warranty and serves as designated representative to do work under that warranty. Hood signed a contract (security agreement) containing the FTC notice.

The contract is then negotiated to Tuck Trust Co. "with recourse" for $6,500, in good faith and without notice. After three months, the clutch burns out. Dale claims that clutches are not covered by the warranty (the Chrysler Motors Service Manual agrees), and refuses to fix it for free. In fact, Dale is on the verge of bankruptcy.

Hood consults you. You are aware that a successful action in court will require at least $1,000 worth of your time and $100 incidental expenses for a recovery of less than $500.

With the FTC required language clearly present, what can you safely advise Hood to do? Is there anything you can now accomplish as Hood's attorney which you could not have done under the UCC?

Notes on the Effect of the FTC Rule

1. Are American consumers better off now that the holder in due course concept has generally been eliminated? Why or why not? See Geva, Optimality and Preservation of Consumer Defenses—A Model for Reform, 31 Case Wes.L.Rev. 51 (1980); Rohner, Holder in Due Course in Consumer Transactions: Requiem, Revival, or Reformation?, 60 Cornell L.Rev. 503 (1975); Schwartz, Optimality and the Cutoff of Defenses Against Financers of Consumer Sales, 15 B.C. Ind. & Com.L.Rev. 499 (1974).

2. Would it be safe for the attorney representing consumers in credit transactions simply to forget about the holder in due course issue as a relic of the past, and to view the legislative and judicial reforms preceding the FTC Rule as merely an interesting chapter in legal history? The FTC Rule, by requiring a clause to be inserted into all consumer credit contracts, allows the consumer to assert claims against the third party financer by relying on her own contract, not upon a claimed violation of federal law. But in the event the consumer is confronted with a credit contract not containing the FTC notice, what avenues are left for the consumer? Could the consumer assert that the seller was guilty of an unfair or deceptive trade practice under the state "little FTC act"? See Iron & Glass Bank v. Franz, 9 Pa. D. & C.3d 419 (Pa.Ct. Common Pleas 1978). Or could the debtor rely on the pre-existing state laws that limited the doctrine of holder in due course? Or even the old cases holding waiver of defense clauses void as against public policy, or cases holding that closely connected holders of consumer credit paper do not qualify as holders "in due course"? See *Unico* and *Donnelly,* supra pages 412–413. See generally D. Pridgen, Consumer Credit and the Law § 14.06 (1990).

Problem 18

Same facts as Problem 17. There is a contract that contains a standard waiver of defense clause, but there is *no* FTC notice—after the effective date of the FTC Rule.

(a) Can Tuck enforce this contract free of Hood's claims and defenses? Would you take Hood's case under these circumstances? See UCC §§ 3–302, 1–201(19), (25).

In other words, if the creditors do not put in the "Notice" required by the FTC, what can the aggrieved consumer do about it? Can he take direct action, or can only the FTC do that? See infra Chapter 17, pages 855–858.

(b) Could Tuck enforce this contract free of Hood's defenses in a state which has enacted the U3C? Are U3C §§ 3.307, 3.404 more effective than the FTC Rule? See U3C § 5.201.

(c) Can Hood fall back on case law such as the *Donnelly* and *Unico* cases, supra?

Notes

1. Only a few courts have specifically addressed the issue of what a consumer can do in the face of a contract that does not contain the FTC

notice. In a case where the consumer plaintiffs were attempting to assert TIL claims against holders of their credit contracts that did not contain the FTC provision, the court said:

> The "Holder in Due Course" Rule, by its own terms, does not create any claims or defenses for consumers in consumer credit contracts. Rather, the Rule provides only that failure to include the required provision in any consumer credit contract shall be an unfair or deceptive act or practice, within the meaning of Section 5 of the Federal Trade Commission Act, * * * Any rights of the consumer under the terms of the required provision itself come into existence only when the provision is in fact included in the consumer credit contract. Therefore, any rights that this provision creates or preserves against holders are contractual rights only, and can be enforced by plaintiffs only if their contracts contained this provision.

Vietnam Veterans of America, Inc. v. Guerdon Industries, Inc., 644 F.Supp. 951, 964–65 (D.Del.1986).

2. The *Vietnam Veterans* case and others have raised the issue whether the Holder Rule was meant to allow consumers to raise TIL disclosure claims against assignees even in the presence of the FTC provision. The Truth in Lending Act provides that assignees are liable only for violations which are "apparent on the face" of the document. 15 U.S.C.A. § 1614. Does the insertion of the FTC provision into a credit contract make assignees liable for nonapparent violations? Or would this be invalid as an attempt by regulation to amend a congressional statute? See Vietnam Veterans, supra, 644 F.Supp. at 965, n. 10; Cox v. First National Bank, 633 F.Supp. 236 (S.D. Ohio 1986).

3. Only the *seller* is liable for accepting a consumer credit contract that fails to contain the required FTC notice. An amendment which would have extended the FTC Rule to third party creditors was proposed soon after the Holder Rule was promulgated but it languished in a state of limbo at the Federal Trade Commission for over 10 years. The proposal has now been dropped. 53 Fed.Reg. 44,456 (Nov. 3, 1988). The Commission noted that there is "little evidence to suggest that creditor participation in cutting off consumer's claims is prevalent." Id. at 44,457.

Problem 19

Same facts as Problem 17, i.e., Dale puts the FTC notice in the contract which is assigned to Tuck. This time, however, Tuck asserts that the clause is inoperative since Hood had planned to use the car in his business, and thus, this is not a "consumer credit contract," as specified in the FTC Rule. Is Tuck correct that the clause would have no effect if Hood was purchasing the car for his business?

If Tuck wants to print one credit contract that could be used for both consumer and nonconsumer credit, without taking on more liability than is required by law, can he make the FTC notice conditional on the consumer's purpose?

See Jefferson Bank & Trust Co. v. Stamatiou, 384 So.2d 388 (La. 1980); In re Gray, 49 B.R. 540 (E.D.Va.1985); First New England Financial Corp. v. Woffard, 421 So.2d 590 (Fla.App.1982).

Note on Financer's Recourse

Financer liability under the FTC Rule is vicarious; the real party responsible for malperformance is the seller whose conduct gave rise to the consumer's claim or defense. How would one counsel a bank or other financer to shift liability under the FTC Rule back to the seller? Ordinarily, one would provide in the dealer-financer contract for a means of passing the loss back to the dealer automatically. The following excerpt on dealer participation plans, reserve accounts and recourse arrangements illustrates the normal bank-dealer relationships available to provide protection from any loss through dealer default. Thus, it is possible, with planning, for a bank to arrange for contractual recourse against the dealer if the consumer refuses to pay due to alleged defaults by the dealer, and to create a reserve account under the control of the bank which allows the bank to charge back such defaults automatically. Under such conditions, the bank's costs are not likely to rise, although the seller's costs will do so to the extent of current unredressed defaults.

The FTC clearly assumed, and intended, that its Rule would naturally lead financers to insist on stronger recourse agreements or larger dealer reserves. But, financers may not always be in a competitive position to obtain these protections. What can such a financer do, in the face of increased exposure to liability? Is it "subrogated" to the consumer's rights if it accedes to the asserted defense?

On the other hand, what are the probable repercussions for a thinly-capitalized retailer who needs to liquidate his consumer paper quickly, when his regular source of financing demands a stronger recourse agreement or larger reserves?

WARREN, REGULATION OF FINANCE CHARGES IN RETAIL INSTALMENT SALES *
68 Yale L.J. 839, 857–59 (1959).

To the General Motors Acceptance Corporation (GMAC) is attributed the origination, in 1925, of dealer participation, the practice by which finance companies rebate to retailers a portion of the finance charges paid by consumers. This innovation—which in the sales-finance world proved to be the rough equivalent of the invention of the wheel—was employed to offset the competitive advantage of independent finance companies. In 1924, these companies had begun to turn dealers' heads with the inelectable attractions of nonrecourse financing. Until that year, automobile financing was a rudimentary process in which a sales-finance company's principal accommodation to its dealers was converting their paper into cash. No dealer profit was anticipated from this transaction, and no risk was assumed by the finance companies, for all paper was purchased with full recourse against the dealer in case of consumer default. After GMAC's spectacular success with its dealer-participation plan, similar schemes quickly spread throughout the automobile financing business.

Dealer-participation plans today take differing forms. If a financing institution is purchasing a dealer's paper on a nonrecourse basis, a part of the finance charge may be immediately rebated to the dealer. The rebate is, in effect, the price the financer is willing to pay for the privilege of purchasing the consumer paper to gain the lucrative finance fees. The bulk of automobile and appliance financing, however, is done under some form of recourse plan, usually involving a repurchase agreement. In automobile financing under a repurchase arrangement, the financing agency ordinarily pays into a reserve account a portion of the finance charge on paper purchased from a particular dealer. Such payments continue until the account reaches either a minimum dollar amount or, more commonly, a percentage of the dealer's outstanding paper (usually three per cent). Upon default by a buyer and repossession by the financer, the dealer is obligated to repurchase the vehicle, and the unpaid balance of the note is charged to the reserve account. The dealer's liability may be limited to the amount of the fund in reserve. Once the stipulated reserve-account balance is attained, subsequent sums payable under the dealer-participation agreement are periodically distributed to the dealer. Since the dealer's share of the finance charges typically ranges from one-fifth to one-third, dealer participation constitutes a major element of his income. * * *

Problem 20

Same facts as Problem 17, Hood and Tuck mutually agree that Dale has breached a warranty and that Hood is entitled to deduct $50 from the amount financed. There is no agreement between Tuck and Dale for recourse due to losses caused by breaches of warranty. On what theory might Tuck recover the $50 from Dale? See UCC § 3–417(2)(d) and (3). Is Dale bound by the agreement between Hood and Tuck? How *should* Tuck handle such assertions by consumers?

3. THE ASSAULT ON DIRECT FINANCING—PURCHASE MONEY LOANS

We have thus far looked only at the typical pattern in which the consumer executes a credit obligation to a retail dealer, who in turn "discounts" that obligation to a third-party financer. Consumers, however, may lose their right to assert claims and defenses in other financing arrangements—arrangements of which the FTC was quite aware, and which it collectively refers to as "purchase money loans." Note, for example, that the FTC Rule, 16 C.F.R. 433.2(b), contains a distinct and separate Notice requirement for such loans.

A Review Problem and a "Loophole"

Problem 21

Robbin Hood bought a new car from Dale for $6000 cash plus his trade-in. Before contracting with Dale, Hood had borrowed $6000 from Tuck Trust Co., agreeing to repay the $6000 plus $1680 interest in 48 monthly payments of $160. Chrysler gives a one-year limited warranty on the car. Dale makes no express warranties, nor does he adopt the manufacturer's written warranty. He simply acts as conduit for the manufacturer's warranty.

After three months, the clutch burns out. Dale will not repair it for free. In fact, Dale is on the verge of bankruptcy. What rights does Hood have against Tuck, either under the FTC Rule, or otherwise?

Problem 22

Robbin Hood bought a used car from William Scarlet, doing business as "Scarlet's Auto Sales, the Home of Guaranteed Credit," under the following circumstances: Hood visited Scarlet's lot seeking a used car for $500. Scarlet showed him several $500 cars, but also told him of their known and suspected defects, and said he could not give a warranty with any of them. Hood decided he did not want any of them. Then Hood saw just the car—for $1500. Scarlet said it was "a beautiful car" and that he could give a 30–day limited warranty on it.

Unfortunately Hood didn't have $1500. Scarlet offered to help. Scarlet said he had a friend, John Little, who ran the Little Finance Co., which might make a loan to Hood as a "special favor" to Scarlet. Actually, Scarlet had an agreement with Little that Little would lend to all of Scarlet's customers if Scarlet would bring *all* of his credit customers to Little. The agreement was crucial to Scarlet who operated on a shoestring and could not have guaranteed financing through any bank—and all of his customers needed financing. The deal was profitable to Little because many of Scarlet's customers were low credit risks, and he got them all, not just the high risk ones.

So, Scarlet drove Hood to see Little. Little went through all the motions of running a credit check, just enough to make Hood nervous, and then approved the loan. Hood borrowed $1500 from Little, and executed a promissory note promising to repay the principal and $300 interest in 24 monthly payments of $75 each. None of the contract documents contained the FTC notice. Little then gave Hood a check for $1500 payable to "Robbin Hood and William Scarlet." Hood endorsed the check and gave it to Scarlet. Scarlet delivered the car keys to Hood, who drove it away. Three days later, the clutch burned out. Scarlet claims the clutches are not covered by the warranty, and refuses to fix it for free. In fact, Scarlet is on the verge of bankruptcy.

(a) What are Scarlet's obligations under the FTC Rule? What are Little's obligations? What rights does Hood have against Little under the FTC Rule? See 16 C.F.R. §§ 433.1(d) and 433.2(b).

(b) What rights does Hood have against Little under the U3C? See § 3.405.

Notes

1. The preceding two problems reflect the patterns in which direct loans to the consumer create, ostensibly, two separate contracts, a cash sale, and an independent loan. To the extent the independence of these two transactions is feigned—by the form of the contracts, as in Problem 22—the creditors have fashioned a new type of holder in due course status.

Analysis of this pattern under the UCC was dreary. Courts appeared unable to shed conventional jargon, or to perceive substance over form in even the most blatant situations. See, e.g., Waterbury Sav. Bank v. Jaroszewski, 4 Conn.Cir. 620, 238 A.2d 446, 4 UCC Rep.Ser. 1049 (1967); Slaughter v. Jefferson Federal Sav. & Loan Ass'n, 538 F.2d 397 (D.C.Cir. 1976).

2. The need for direct legislation to handle this problem was generally recognized, but there was little agreement on its exact content. See Littlefield, Preserving Consumer Defenses: Plugging the Loophole in the New UCCC, 44 N.Y.U.L.Rev. 272 (1969); Comment, "Dragging the Body"— Deceptive Automobile Financing in Pennsylvania: With Proposed Legislative Remedies, 34 U.Pitt.L.Rev. 429 (1973). The U3C treats "interlocking loans" in § 3.405. However, very few states enacted legislation dealing with direct or interlocking loans.

3. A forced consensus emerges from the FTC Rule's complex notion of "purchase money loan." The Commission has elaborated on the purchase money loan concept in an official "Statement of Enforcement Policy," 41 Fed.Reg. 34594 (1976). The following excerpts are from the Commission's Staff Guidelines on the Trade Regulation Rule concerning Preservation of Consumers' Claims and Defenses:

Purchase Money Loans

(1) *General Considerations*

The Rule states that a seller may not accept money which a consumer obtained via a "purchase money loan", as that term is defined in the Rule, unless the consumer credit contract made in connection with the loan contains the required provision preserving the consumer's claims and defenses. Where a "purchase money loan" is used to finance a sale, the seller is obligated to insure that the consumer's loan contract contains the required Notice before he consummates the Sale.

* * *

Failure to include purchase money loans would make avoidance of the Rule both easy and inevitable. In the course of the rulemaking proceedings the Commission learned that where the use of promissory notes and waivers of defenses in "indirect" consumer contracts has been prohibited by state law a marked increase in the use of direct loans to achieve the same ends has occurred. Whether direct or indirect financing is used, the basic problem of the separation of duties remains the same.

The Commission also concluded that when a creditor and a seller are working together to finance sales by means of consumer loans, the creditor has, or should have, access to information, resources, and business procedures which place him in a position to assess the likelihood of seller misconduct and make appropriate provisions for dealing with it. The creditor has access to sources of commercial information not easily available to the average consumer buyer, and if he transacts business with the seller repeatedly over a period of time he knows from his own experience whether the seller is basically fair or not. A creditor who deals regularly with a seller is in a position to establish economic ways of shifting the risk back to the seller, through recourse or reserve arrangements.

Where there is no such established relationship between the seller and the lender these reasons for the Rule do not apply. The Commission concluded that the Rule should not cover the situation where a buyer obtains financing from a lender who neither receives referrals from the seller nor is affiliated with the seller by common control, contract, or business arrangement.

Problem 23

In a small town in Iowa there are three banks and three auto dealers. The banks do not buy dealer paper, but do routinely make auto loans to customers who buy from one of the local dealers. Loan proceeds are always disbursed in the form of joint-payee checks (payable to the consumer and the dealer), and the dealers' employees routinely execute financing statements and certificate of title applications on the banks' behalf and mail them to the appropriate state offices. The bank loan officers pretty much know the dealers' credit managers on a first-name basis. Each of the auto dealers is on the board of directors of one of the banks. When customers inquire about credit terms, the dealers' employees will often suggest they seek bank loans.

(a) Are these "purchase money loans" within the Rule?

Note how the FTC Staff Guidelines, supra, construe "common control" as a test for the existence of a purchase money loan: " * * * if the two companies are owned by a holding company or by substantially the same individuals, if one is a subsidiary of the other, or if they are under common control in any other way."

Those Guidelines further suggest that there is no "referral" relationship where seller merely "provides his buyers with a list of local credit outlets and takes no other action."

The FTC's Statement of Enforcement Policy, supra, also says that neither the issuance of joint-payee checks, nor the fact that seller and lender must confer over the security interest, "in itself" creates an affiliation relationship. But what happens when several of these factors are present together?

(b) If they are purchase money loans, who must do what to comply with the Rule?

(c) Iowa has enacted a consumer credit code which contains a provision identical to U3C § 3.405. Would these bank loans also be interlocking loans under that section?

Problem 24

(a) Tuck Trust Co. provides Dale with inventory financing and regularly purchases consumer paper from Dale. Hood, unaware of this relationship and altogether on his own, approaches Tuck for a loan of $6000 to pay the balance of the price of the car. Must the FTC Notice appear in the loan agreement? If it does, what are Hood's rights against the bank?

(b) If Tuck Trust Co. refuses to put the Notice in the loan agreement, has it violated the Rule? See 16 C.F.R. 433.1(j), and 433.2(b).

(c) Assume Hood's transaction with Tuck is a purchase money loan within the FTC Rule. Tuck, however, does not inquire how Hood plans to spend the money. Dale does not inquire where Hood got his $6000. The loan agreement does not contain the Notice. Is this a violation? See FTC Statement of Enforcement Policy, 41 Fed.Reg. 34594.

The "Interlocking Loan" Not Covered by the FTC Rule—Real Estate Transactions

Can holder in due course problems arise in areas not covered by the FTC Rule, such as real estate transactions? If so, what protection does the consumer have in that transaction?

1. The FTC Rule applies only to credit sales of goods or services, and thus does not apply to real estate. Also, the U3C excludes real estate sales where the finance charge does not exceed 12 per cent per year. U3C § 1.301(12). This would eliminate most first mortgage residential real estate transactions.

2. In the typical home purchase and mortgage transaction, the buyer approaches the lender directly, rather than obtaining credit from a seller who negotiates the paper to the lender. Thus, lender liability issues in real estate transactions usually involve direct loans, rather than assignments or negotiable instruments.

3. Home improvement loans using second mortgages as security can also create problems for the consumer. In such cases, the courts generally refuse to find the lender liable for the contractor's fraud or breach of warranty, unless the lender was aware of or should have been aware of the underlying defenses or is somehow connected with the contractor. See Slaughter v. Jefferson Federal Sav. & Loan Ass'n, 538 F.2d 397 (D.C.Cir.1976).

4. There may well be interlocking relationships between the real estate seller and the lender. For instance, in a landmark California case, Connor v. Great Western Sav. & Loan Ass'n, 69 Cal.2d 850, 73 Cal. Rptr. 369, 447 P.2d 609 (1968), the financing institution was heavily

involved in a disastrous development project in which residences were severely damaged due to poor construction decisions. Here, the savings and loan, Great Western, "became much more than a lender content to lend money at interest on the security of real property. It became an active participant in a home construction enterprise. * * *" 447 P.2d at 616. Great Western purchased land ahead of construction and "warehoused" it for the developer's later purchase at a substantial profit to the lender. It actively reviewed plans and specifications, suggested selling prices, held a right of first refusal to supply mortgage loans to purchasers, and received fees from the developer for every purchaser obtaining financing. *Id.* A divided California Supreme Court, in a majority opinion by Chief Justice Traynor, held that under these circumstances the lender would be liable to the purchasers of the defective homes for negligence in failing to correct the obvious structural problems. *Id.*

Other courts have reached similar conclusions. A Michigan case held a direct lender liable for the fraud of the seller where it had reason to know that the seller had likely engaged in fraud. Jeminson v. Montgomery Real Estate & Co., 396 Mich. 106, 240 N.W.2d 205 (1976), facts contained in 47 Mich.App. 731, 210 N.W.2d 10 (1973). The Alabama Supreme Court found a mortgage lender could be liable for the failings of a home improvement contractor, but only if the borrowers could show that they had asked for and were relying on the promised inspections by the bank to protect them from problems of nonperformance by the contractor. Rudolph v. First Southern Fed. Sav. & Loan Ass'n, 414 So.2d 64 (Ala.1982).

5. Does the nature of the liability imposed in *Connor* and the other cases cited in note 4 differ from that imposed in *Donnelly,* supra page 412, or through the FTC Holder Rule? Do the different transactional contexts warrant different rules?

6. Despite the authority of a Traynor opinion, the decision in *Connor* has not been well received. The California legislature and the legislatures in many other states have enacted statutes protecting lenders from liability where they act solely as financing agencies. Also, later cases in California and elsewhere have limited *Connor* to its somewhat unusual facts. See Wierzbicki v. Alaska Mutual Sav. Bank, 630 P.2d 998 (Alaska 1981); Bradler v. Craig, 274 Cal.App.2d 466, 79 Cal.Rptr. 401 (1969); Callaizakis v. Astor Development Co., 4 Ill.App.3d 163, 280 N.E.2d 512 (1972); Clark v. Grover, 132 Mich.App. 476, 347 N.W.2d 748 (1984); Allison v. Home Sav. Ass'n of Kansas City, 643 S.W.2d 847 (Mo.App.1982); Schenectady Sav. Bank v. Bartosik, 77 Misc. 2d 837, 353 N.Y.S.2d 706 (1974).

One authority has warned that "[t]he potential for lender liability under a *Connor* theory is real. Even though the case has been frequently distinguished, its theory has been occasionally applied to impose liability on financial institutions who operate outside the scope of normal lending activity."   G. Nelson & D. Whitman, Real Estate Finance Law 12.11, at 930 (2d ed. 1985).

7. Should the issue of lender liability in residential real estate be dealt with by legislation or administrative rule, rather than on a case by case basis? Why or why not?

Problem 25

Hovel Homes, a California builder, decided to develop a parcel of land. It borrowed the purchase price and all development costs from First Bank. In return Hovel promised to place all construction and long-term mortgages on homes in the parcel with First Bank. For any mortgages not so placed, Hovel was to pay First Bank a penalty amount of 5% of the mortgage placed elsewhere. First Bank did not examine the plans of the houses to be built, nor did it conduct any on-site inspections.

After the houses were built, the foundations cracked because they were poorly designed, resulting in substantial damage to many houses. Hovel is nearly judgment proof, so the disgruntled home buyers sue both Hovel and First Bank. What result under *Connor*? Would the FTC Holder Rule or the U3C have any impact?

Suppose that halfway through the project, the developer's financial position became so precarious that First Bank put its own employee in charge of the completion of the houses. Would this change the outcome? Cf. Dunson v. Stockton, Whatley, Davin & Co., 346 So.2d 603 (Fla.App.1977).

4. CARD ISSUER LIABILITY FOR DEFECTIVE GOODS

Bank credit cards like Visa, and "travel and entertainment" cards like American Express, involve at least three parties: the bank (or other company) as card issuer, the consumer as cardholder, and the merchant who honors the card. In the early 1970s it was a very controversial question whether a consumer could justifiably refuse to pay the card issuer if the merchant supplied defective goods or services in a credit card transaction. The legal question is a variation of the "holder in due course" issue, and may well be the predominant context in which this issue arises in the future. That is, was the card issuer so closely involved in the merchant's sales practices as to incur a vicarious liability for the merchant's defective performance.

Card issuers obviously preferred not to be liable for defective merchandise sold by the retailers who honored their cards, and waiver of defense clauses were common in credit card agreements. But in 1974 the Fair Credit Billing Act (Chapter 4 of the TIL Act) sharply curtailed the card issuers' ability to shield themselves from cardholder claims or defenses relating to transactions with participating merchants. See TIL Act § 170; Reg. Z § 226.12(c).

Note the relationship between this statute and the FTC Rule on Preservation of Consumers' Claims and Defenses. By its own terms, the FTC Rule does not apply to a person acting "in the capacity of a credit card issuer." Does this reflect the FTC's conclusion that there are no problems in the credit card area, or the Commission's reluctance to confront Congress over credit cards? Should a department store which offers its own revolving charge account plan, involving the use of credit cards, have to include the FTC Rule "Notice" in its cardholder agreements?

Problem 26

Similar facts to those in Problem 17, supra, p. 419, Robbin Hood bought a new car from Dale Dodge Dealers, located in Hood's hometown, but this time Hood finances the $6,000 balance of the price on his Mastercard—a credit card issued to him by Nottingham Bank. Chrysler gives a one-year limited warranty on the car, and Dale makes no express warranties. After three months, the clutch burns out. It will cost about $500 to fix. Hood went to Dale and asked that the clutch be repaired under the warranty, but Dale refused. Hood made the same request a second time, but was again refused. Dale is on the verge of Bankruptcy.

When Dale refuses to fix the car, what can you safely advise Hood to do, under FCBA § 161, 15 U.S.C.A. § 1666, and § 170, 15 U.S.C.A. § 1666i? See also, Reg. Z §§ 226.12(c), 226.13(a).

Notes

1. What is the rationale for the $50 and 100 mile limitations in FCBA § 170? See Brandel & Leonard, Bank Charge Cards: New Cash or New Credit, 69 Mich.L.Rev. 1033 (1971).

2. The exceptions built into FCBA § 170 by Congress have caused few practical problems. But for those who like theoretical puzzles, consider whether a consumer can withhold payment of his credit card bill in any of the following situations:

(a) He buys a defective set of cutlery from a company out-of-state (and more than 100 miles away) by responding to a flier included with his MasterCard monthly billing statement. See Reg. Z § 226.12(c) (3)(i), Note 26, at 6.

(b) He uses his VISA card to purchase a 10–speed bike at a local store, for $120. The bike's brakes lock, throwing him to the ground and breaking his arm. The bike is undamaged and can be adjusted at no cost. Is a breach of warranty cause of action one which arises out of contract *and not* out of tort?

(c) He buys a ladder ($25) and three gallons of paint ($10 each) in order to paint his garage. The ladder breaks and the paint peels. See Reg. Z § 226.12(c).

Problem 27

Saul Brenner took his car to Kramer Auto Service for repairs. The repairs to be made were agreed upon and estimated to cost $25. When Brenner returned for the car, the bill read $51.02. Kramer had performed additional services, and, of course, demanded to be paid for them. Brenner objected that the extra services were not needed, but Kramer became obdurate and gave Brenner an option: either Brenner paid, or Kramer would keep possession of the car. Brenner paid by using his VISA card. What can Brenner do now to resolve this dispute? Complaining directly to the merchant is not likely to be effective; and if he has already paid, the burden of initiating litigation is on him. But, has he already paid? See Fair Credit Billing Act (CCPA) §§ 161, 170, 15 U.S.C.A. §§ 1666, 1666i; Reg. Z § 226.12(c). If Brenner is a person who always pays within 30 days, how much of his VISA card account would you advise him to pay to avoid finance charges?

Can Brenner use § 161, 15 U.S.C.A. § 1666—that is, is this a "billing error" under FCBA? See Reg. Z § 226.13(a)(3). If not, should Brenner withhold the amount allowed under § 161 and Reg. Z § 226.13(d)? Note that analysis of this issue requires comparison of the availability and overlap of Sections 161 and 170, and of Reg. Z §§ 226.12 and 226.13. In particular, compare and contrast Reg. Z §§ 226.12(c)(1) and 226.13(d)(3). Does Hood get positive rights from the regulations? Even if not supported by statutory language? See TIL § 105, 15 U.S.C.A. § 1604.

IZRAELEWITZ v. MANUFACTURERS HANOVER TRUST CO.

Civil Court of the City of New York, Kings County, Small Claims Part, 1983.
120 Misc.2d 125, 465 N.Y.S.2d 486.

DECISION

IRA B. HARKAVY, JUDGE.

As the texture of the American economy evolves from paper to plastic, the disgruntled customer is spewing its wrath upon the purveyor of the plastic rather than upon the merchant.

Plaintiff George Izraelewitz commenced this action to compel the Defendant bank Manufacturers Hanover Trust Company to credit his Mastercharge account in the amount of $290.00 plus finance charges. The disputed charge, posted to Plaintiff's account on July 16, 1981, is for electronic diagrams purchased by Plaintiff via telephone from Don Britton Enterprises, a Hawaii-based mail order business.

On September 9, 1981 Plaintiff advised Defendant bank, Manufacturers Hanover Trust Company (Trust Company), that the diagrams had been unsuitable for his needs and provided Defendant with a UPS receipt indicating that the purchased merchandise had been returned to Don Britton. Defendant's Customer Service Department credited Plaintiff's account and waived finance charges on the item. Trust Company subsequently proceeded to charge back the item to the merchant. The merchant refused the charge back through The 1st Hawaii Bank, and advised Defendant bank of their strict "No Refund" policy. Don Britton also indicated that Plaintiff, during the course of conversation, had admitted that he was aware of this policy. On April 1, 1982 Defendant advised Plaintiff that his account would be redebited for the full amount. At two later dates, Plaintiff advised Trust Company of said dispute, denied knowledge of the "No Refund" policy and stated that the goods had been returned. The Trust Company once again credited Plaintiff's account and attempted to collect from Don Britton. The charge back was again refused and Plaintiff's account was subsequently redebited.

Bank credit agreements generally provide that a cardholder is obligated to pay the bank regardless of any dispute which may exist respecting the merchandise. An exception to this rule arises under a provision in the Truth in Lending Law which allows claimants whose transactions exceed $50.00 and who have made a good faith attempt to obtain satisfactory resolution of the problem, to assert claims and defenses arising out of the credit card transaction, if the place of the initial transaction is in the same state or within 100 miles of the cardholder. Consumer Credit Protection Act, 15 U.S.C.A. § 1666i.

It would appear that Plaintiff is precluded from asserting any claims or defenses since Britton's location exceeds the geographical limitation. This assumption is deceiving. Under Truth in Lending the question of where the transaction occurred (e.g. as in mail order cases) is to be determined under state or other applicable law. Truth in Lending, 12 CFR, § 226.12(c). Furthermore, any state law permitting customers to assert claims and defenses against the card issuer would not be preempted, regardless of whether the place of the transaction was at issue. In effect, these federal laws are viewed as bare minimal standards.

In *Lincoln First Bank, N.A. v. Carlson,* 103 Misc.2d 467, 426 N.Y.S.2d 433 (1980), the court found that:

> "(T)he statement that a card issuer is subject to all defenses if a transaction occurred less than 100 miles from the cardholder's address, does not automatically presume a cardholder to give up all his defenses should the transaction take place at a distance of greater than 100 miles from the mailing address." *Id.* at 436.

The facts at bar do not warrant a similar finding. Whereas in *Lincoln, supra,* the cardholder's defense arose due to an alleged failure of the card issuer itself to comply with statutory rules, the Defendant herein is blameless. The geographical limitation serves to protect banks from consumers who may expose them to unlimited liability through dealings with merchants in faraway states where it is difficult to monitor a merchant's behavior. These circumstances do not lend the persuasion needed to cast-off this benefit.

Considering, arguendo, that under the Truth in Lending Act, Plaintiff was able to assert claims and defenses from the original transaction, any claims or defenses he chose to assert would only be as good as and no better than his claim against the merchant. Accordingly, Plaintiff's claim against the merchant must be scrutinized to ascertain whether it is of good faith and substantial merit. A consumer cannot assert every miniscule dispute he may have with a merchant as an excuse not to pay an issuer who has already paid the merchant.

The crux of Plaintiff's claim, apparently, is that he returned the diagrams purportedly unaware of merchant's "No Refund" policy. The merchant contends that Plaintiff admitted that he knew of the policy and nonetheless used deceptive means to return the plans; in that they were sent without a name so they would be accepted; were not delivered to an employee of the company; were not in the original box; and showed evidence of having been xeroxed.

"No Refund" policies, per se, are not unconscionable or offensive to public policy in any manner. Truth in Lending Law "(n)either requires refunds for returns nor does it prohibit refunds in kind." Truth in Lending Regulations, 12 CFR, § 226.12(e). Bank-merchant agreements, however, usually do contain a requirement that the merchant establish a fair policy for exchange and return of merchandise.

To establish the fairness in Don Britton's policy, the strength of the reasons behind the policy and the measures taken to inform the consumer of it must necessarily be considered. Don Britton's rationale for its policy is compelling. It contends that printing is a very small part of its business, which is selling original designs, and "once a customer has seen the designs he possesses what we have to sell." Britton's policy is clearly written in its catalog directly on the page which explains how to order merchandise. To compensate for not having a refund policy, which would be impractical considering the nature of the product, Britton offers well-advertised backup plans with free engineering assistance and an exchange procedure, as well, if original plans are beyond the customer's capabilities. The Plaintiff could have availed himself of any of these alternatives which are all presumably still open to him.

On the instant facts, as between Plaintiff and the Defendant bank, Plaintiff remains liable for the disputed debt, as he has not shown adequate cause to hold otherwise.

Judgment for Defendant dismissing the complaint.

Query: Exactly what does *Izraelewitz* hold as to the meaning of Reg. Z § 226.12(c)(3)(ii)? Did the disputed transaction "occur" in New York or Hawaii? What is the purpose of the limitations in that paragraph of Reg. Z?

Problem 28

In *Izraelewitz*, supra, assume the court had allowed the consumer to assert the claim against the bank. Must the bank swallow the loss, or can it recover the funds previously paid to Don Britton, the seller? Cf. Schorr v. Bank of New York, 91 A.D.2d 125, 458 N.Y.S.2d 244 (1983).

Note on EFTs

Until the 1978 enactment of the Electronic Funds Transfer Act (CCPA Title XI) resolved some of them, there were many open questions about customer rights in electronic funds transfer systems (EFTs). The question arose because many EFTs use a plastic card, called a "debit card" in their operations. The debit card looks like a credit card, but it is used to transfer the customer's funds, not to draw upon a line of credit—which is what the credit card does. However, this distinction blurs easily, especially when the "debit card" allows "overdraft privileges," which essentially creates a line of credit. The issue of whether to have separate rules for debit cards, different from the rules for credit cards, was hotly debated.

Is it conceivable that holder in due course questions will arise in the EFT environment? That is, might the financial institution which offers a debit card plan to consumers be held accountable for defective goods purchased with those cards, on analogy to the "purchase money loan" concept, or to the holding in Connor v. Great Western Savings & Loan Association, 73 Cal.Rptr. 369, 447 P.2d 609 (1968)?

SECTION D. THE COSTS OF REGULATING DEVICES CUTTING OFF CONSUMERS' CLAIMS AND DEFENSES

The FTC's Trade Regulation Rule on Preservation of Consumers' Claims and Defenses was bitterly attacked by the credit industry, in part on grounds that the increased exposure to consumer claims and defenses would make financers reluctant to extend consumer credit, thus drying up credit sources for auto, mobile home, furniture and similar purchases. Then–Federal Reserve Board Chairman Arthur Burns went so far as to write the FTC shortly before the Rule took effect in May 1976, asserting:

> [W]e believe that the consumer credit business may be seriously disrupted if the Rule goes into effect on May 14, 1976, as scheduled. Such disruption, if it occurs, could have harmful consequences for the economy.

Letter from FRB Chairman Burns to FTC Chairman Collier, May 5, 1976.

A year later, an independent newsletter surveyed the reactions of the major industry groups, and of the regulatory agencies.

CAPITOL REPORTS, INC., WASHINGTON CREDIT LETTER

May 16, 1977, p. 3.*

[T]here is little in the way of hard evidence from industry critics which suggests the rule has had a deleterious effect. For example, a spokesperson for *Independent Bankers,* which had predicted that "people will never lend money again," now says the association "hasn't heard a thing" from its members since shortly after the rule went into effect. "If there has been an adverse effect, we haven't heard about it here in Washington."

At the *American Bankers Association* a spokesperson says that at the beginning "we received sacks full of letters from members saying they were getting out of indirect lending altogether, but lately, there seems to be a lack of interest in the rule." And, says a spokesperson for the *National Consumer Finance Association,* there are "no statistics, no indication at all that creditors have made good their threat to get out of consumer lending because of the rule." A few have, he conceded, but adds, "nobody's wept over them; they should have gotten out anyway."

Consumer Bankers Association, the only financial trade association which did not predict a virtual end to consumer lending as a result of the rule, has had "zero flak" from its members, according to a spokesperson, who adds that CBA members have experienced "no losses and very few law suits."

Things also appear to have quieted down at the regulatory agencies. The *National Credit Union Administration* reports nothing on the rule from members and very little except "verbal comments to our Administrator" from credit union officials. In fact, the rule has had a therapeutic effect, says a spokesperson, because "everybody has had to review their practices and that's good."

At the *Federal Reserve Board,* an official reports some "retrenchment" particularly in the areas of mobile homes, used cars and home improvements—all expected—but he was unable to say how *much.* And, a Board economist further explained, his office has little in the way of economic impact figures on the effects of the rule "simply because there hasn't been any." * * *

Notes and Questions

1. On what basis would the chairman of the Federal Reserve Board predict a "serious disruption" of business with "harmful consequences for the economy"? Would such a prediction be based on data from past experience, econometric models, basic economic theory, or political biases?

* Copyright © 1977 by Capitol Reports, Inc. Reprinted by permission of the publisher.

The excerpt from Capitol Reports indicates that the estimated harm was exaggerated. Will the FRB prediction concerning the "Holder" Rule influence subsequent predictions? Their credibility?

2. On the other hand, is there any data concerning the benefits to consumers? There is a great deal of anecdotal evidence, but none of it has been systematically gathered. In the words of one observer, is consumer protection "gesture" or "reality"? See Kripke, "Gesture and Reality in Consumer Credit Reform," 44 N.Y.U.L.Rev. 1 (1969).

3. What are the costs of industry compliance? To date, the Federal Reserve Board has not done a study on the economic effects of the "Holder" Rule which would be comparable to their study of ECOA, reviewed supra in Chapter 4, Section D. Could their failure to do such a study be argued to indicate a greater likelihood of any particular result?

4. There may be further developments in this area, however. The FTC is now reviewing the "Holder" Rule, and is seeking comments:

The Regulatory Flexibility Act requires the Federal Trade Commission to conduct a periodic review of rules issued by the Commission that have or will have a significant economic impact upon a substantial number of small entities.

The Holder Rule was promulgated by the Commission on November 18, 1975 and became effective on May 14, 1976. This periodic review is conducted in accordance with the Commission's plan for periodic review of rules * * *.

At the same time the Commission promulgated the Holder Rule, it commenced a proceeding ("Holder II") to amend the Rule to extend it to third-party creditors. In 1979, the Commission approved the Holder II amendment in principle. Before final action on the amendment, however, the Commission articulated more specific criteria for exercising its unfairness authority and for issuing trade regulation rules. The record for the Holder II amendment, therefore, was developed under a different legal standard from the one the Commission now applies. The Commission has reevaluated the Holder II record in light of its current legal standards for determinations of unfairness and for the evaluation of proposed trade regulation rules, and has determined that the evidence is inadequate to support issuance of the proposed amendment. In particular, the record contains little evidence of consumer injury occurring after the Holder Rule became effective and little evidence to suggest that creditor participation in cutting off consumers' claims is prevalent. Accordingly, the Commission has decided to terminate the Holder II proceeding without issuing an amended rule.

The objective of the review initiated by this notice is to determine whether any part of the Holder Rule has had a significant impact on a substantial number of small entities and, if so, whether any such impact can be reduced consistent with the objectives of the Rule. In addition, the Commission requests comments on a number of other issues relating to the operation of the Rule.

For purposes of this review, the Commission poses the following questions for public comment: * * *

1. Has the Rule had a significant economic impact (costs and/or benefits) on a substantial number of small entities? What kinds of costs has the rule imposed on small entities? Have small but established entities found it more difficult to obtain credit since the Rule became effective in May 1976? Have new small entities found it more difficult to arrange sources of closed-end credit (purchasers for sales finance contracts or third parties to make purchase money loans) for their customers since May 1976? * * *

53 Fed.Reg. 44456 (1988)

Postscript

The doctrine of negotiability, and the cutting off of issuers' defenses, originated at a time when promissory notes and drafts were expected to circulate widely through many unknown hands before payment. By 1975, when the FTC issued the Holder Rule, this circulation pattern had changed radically. At that time, promissory notes were issued by a consumer-maker to a retailer-payee, and then the paper was sold once to a financer-endorsee, who held it until it was fully paid off. For paper with such limited circulation, the FTC Rule made sense; the FTC Statement of Basis and Purpose clearly indicates that this typical limited circulation pattern is an underlying assumption of the Holder Rule.

However, in the 1980s the banks developed a "secondary market" in consumer notes, whereby a bundle of 1000 or more notes would be sold by one financer to another. (A similar secondary market had been developed in the 1970s for bundles of home mortgages and promissory notes.) Thus, the notes signed by consumers now may have a new and different circulation pattern—from consumer-maker to retailer-payee to financer # 1–endorsee to financer # 2 to financer # 3 and so on * * *. And, perhaps most important, this entire secondary market developed *after* the FTC Holder Rule, and originated using non-negotiable consumer paper.

How could this happen? Chairman Burns' statement, supra, indicates that the then-typical limited circulation pattern "may be seriously disrupted" by the Holder Rule. Instead, circulation of consumer notes became more widespread. Does that indicate that negotiability and cutting-off of defenses is in fact less important than it was thought to be? In the secondary market, how can financer # 3 protect itself from consumer defaults?

Chapter 7

ABUSIVE COLLECTION PRACTICES

SECTION A. INTRODUCTION

In this and the next two chapters, we will consider the practices creditors use to collect consumer debts. We will also examine in detail the legal framework within which creditors are supposed to operate, and what happens when they don't. Each of these chapters deals with a different aspect of the collection process. This chapter focuses on what might be called "informal" collection processes. These are primarily processes a creditor might use before going to court or attempting to seize any of the debtor's property. Here, too, we introduce the larger social and economic arena in which debtor defaults occur.

In the next chapter, our focus is on secured consumer transactions and on the remedies a secured creditor has that distinguish him from an unsecured creditor. Finally, in Chapter 9, we address coercive collection tactics which involve going to court or seizing the debtor's property apart from any contract right to do so. The student will soon appreciate that the concerns of the legal system and the role of lawyers are quite different in each of these contexts.

1. COLLECTION TACTICS

How does a debt collector go about his business? The following material addresses various issues involved in the informal collection process. As you read it, think about the different concerns of the collector and the debtor. For example, as the Caplovitz material (infra, page 448) demonstrates, most consumers who do not pay have understandable reasons (loss of job, sudden medical emergency, etc.). Do you think a debt collector is likely to be sympathetic to these problems? Also consider the various collection tactics described below. Do you think a consumer would be likely to consider them as harassment? Would a creditor have a different view?

GRANT, "RESORT TO THE LEGAL PROCESS IN COLLECTING DEBTS FROM HIGH RISK CREDIT BUYERS IN LOS ANGELES—ALTERNATIVE METHODS FOR ALLOCATING PRESENT COSTS"

14 UCLA L.Rev. 879, 885–92 (1967).*

III. COLLECTION PRACTICES

The vast majority of consumer debts are paid promptly or after minimal collection efforts have been made.[22] However, the magnitude of the collection effort is disguised when couched in terms of percentages. Sellers who extend credit to high risk buyers, expecting a high proportion to default, rely heavily on efficient and streamlined collection operations which reduce the costs of proceeding against delinquent accounts.

The exhaustiveness of the creditor's initial collection effort is a function of his size and the extensiveness of his collection facilities. The large department store, retail merchant, or finance company, with credit departments that service a number of branches, can afford the large-scale, specialized operation required to collect efficiently all but the most difficult accounts. The smaller creditor can only make minimal collection efforts himself before he turns the account over to a collection specialist—an attorney who specializes in collection work or a collection agency. The more successful his own initial collection efforts, the less costly it is to the creditor.[24]

The large creditor may employ special personnel to follow up accounts and to initiate the collection process for delinquent accounts. Typically, one to three routine notice letters are sent to the delinquent customer, the first around ten days after payment becomes due. Nothing more is done until the account is considered a collection problem, a point which varies with the particular creditor.[25]

When the account is considered a collection problem, it is normally turned over to an employee who specializes in collection, for more personal handling if the size of the operation warrants this degree of specialization. The collector will contact the debtor personally, by letter or telephone, and will attempt to make arrangements for the

22. Consensus of Interviews. On the national average, the delinquency rate on installment credit is between 1% and 2% of the amount of credit extended, and the net loss rate is below that by an undetermined amount. California Assembly Interim Committee on the Judiciary, Proceedings on Attachments, app. B (June 23, 1964).

24. Collection agencies normally keep 50% of the amount collected as their fees.

The collection attorney may be on retainer or may keep a percentage of the total amount collected by him; usually, however, this amounts to less than half. Interviews with creditors' attorneys.

25. For example, a large consumer credit card issuer turns an account over to a "collector" if no payment has been received after 15 days from the date of the first notice letter; on the other hand, one large retail seller does not consider the account a collection problem until it has been delinquent for two months.

settlement of the account if possible.[26] For example, if the customer has been out of work because of some temporary illness, arrangements might be made to reschedule payments, deferring the date of the next payment due. The largest creditors may employ field representatives who attempt to contact the buyer personally at his home if he has not responded to the collector's previous efforts.

How closely the account is followed, how soon personal contact is made, and how much time is devoted to solving the customer's individual problems varies with the size and specialization of the credit department. This phase is, however, the most important one in debt collection. All of the creditors interviewed found it less costly and more satisfactory in terms of future business with the customer to work out an alternative payment plan with the buyer who becomes delinquent because of personal or financial problems.

These initial phases of the debt collection effort will vary from creditor to creditor. Most creditors have a flexible policy, keeping the account until it is determined that further collection efforts by the creditor himself would be futile.

A. Assignment to a Collection Agency

The account may then be assigned to a collection agency.[28] * * *

When the claim is assigned to a collection agency, the assignor usually feels that it is uncollectible.[29] The collection agency investigates the claim by determining the extent of the debtor's assets, what he does, and where he lives. If the agency feels initially that the account is uncollectible, it will periodically check for assets and proceed when any are discovered. Even if it determines that the debtor has few assets, it will attempt to collect the debt by making arrangements for small periodic payments.

A good number of the accounts assigned to collection agencies are "skips"; and, consequently, the agencies gear their efforts more toward finding people than do the collection departments of the assignors. Also, perhaps more importantly, the collection agency can utilize more forceful techniques of debt collection than the retail seller—particularly the small local merchant—who is vitally concerned with customer good will. * * *

26. For example, a technical training film which one large finance company shows its collectors emphasizes the following points: it is important both that collections be made and that the customer's good will be retained; if the debt was made on the basis of ability to pay, it follows that collections should be made on the same basis; the collector must find out all the facts which bear on the debtor's ability to pay and conduct himself accordingly. .

28. In the retail installment obligation categories (Categories 1, 3, and 4), a total of 118 of the 164 accounts had been assigned

to a collection agency. One creditor's attorney estimates that, depending upon the type of paper involved, between 1% and 10% of a seller's installment contract accounts must be given to a collection agency because the seller's collection resources have been exhausted.

29. The president of a large collection agency in Los Angeles estimates that these accounts are uncollectible about half the time. Further, he estimates that about one quarter of the accounts received are not processed extensively because they are too "uncollectible" to be worth the cost.

B. Resort to the Legal Process

At some point in the collection process—when it is determined that the buyer cannot be induced into settlement on the basis of personal contact—the decision may be made to institute legal proceedings. The goal of each phase of the debt collection effort, including resort to the legal process, is to induce the debtor to come in and pay the account in full, or, if this is not financially possible, to make arrangements for gradually paying off the debt. If the institution of a lawsuit itself [34] or a pre-judgment attachment levy does not induce settlement, the creditor will initiate the steps required to obtain and then execute upon a judgment in order to collect the account.[36] The costs incurred in so doing are minimized when he can rely on obtaining default judgments by clerk on a mass scale.

* * *

———

Well, none of this seems so bad, does it? So why is there any need for regulation of collection tactics? As you might suspect, not all debt collectors operate in such a civilized fashion. The following material will give you some idea of the kinds of problems which led to the adoption of the federal Fair Debt Collection Practices Act (FDCPA), which we will consider more fully in Section C of this chapter.

D. CAPLOVITZ, CONSUMERS IN TROUBLE: A STUDY OF DEBTORS IN DEFAULT

178–80 (1974) *

The distinction between harassment and legitimate collection procedures is by no means clear. To explicate the concept of harassment it is necessary to review the events that ensue when a debtor misses payments. Virtually all creditors send their delinquent debtors a series of dunning letters of increasing harshness. One collection lawyer we interviewed, whose major client was a large New York bank, pointed out that the bank's computer was used to send out the first few letters automatically. The early letters are usually polite reminders of the delinquency; subsequent letters threaten legal action, the ruining of the debtor's credit rating, and the involvement of the debtor's employer. Typical of the latter is the following:

34. One attorney, who files several thousand collection cases a year, sends a letter requesting an interview with the debtor before he files suit on the theory that a letter from an attorney will have greater effect than one from a creditor. The attorney stated that this means of collection, while only occasionally provoking a response, has substantial effectiveness in dollar volume.

36. The direct return from use of the legal system is impressively high: one creditor estimates that the chances that a debt will be paid are 90% greater with a judgment. Normally, the decision to file suit will only be made when it has been determined that the debtor has some assets, usually a job.

* Copyright © by McMillan Publishing Co., Inc. Reprinted by permission of the publisher.

We are holding you responsible for this debt and unless arrangements are made to pay it, we will notify [the name of debtor's employer] concerning this matter. They frown upon employees owing these kinds of debts.

In a number of cities, local credit bureaus offer debt collection services to their members. Debtors then receive dunning letters on the stationery of the credit bureau, letters which indicate that their credit rating will be ruined unless payment is made. The effort to intimidate delinquent debtors via dunning letters has even led to the formation of fraudulent collection firms with Washington, D.C., addresses, whose stationery contains seals that make the letters appear to be official communications from the federal government. The recipients of such letters are given the false impression that the federal government will be after them if they do not settle their debt.

The borderline between the legal and illegal is quite fuzzy in these extrajudicial collection procedures. It has been argued that the creditor's communication with the debtor's employer prior to judgment, or even the threat of such communication as in the above sample letter, denies the debtor his constitutional rights. Since many employers who receive such letters order their employee to settle the debt or face dismissal, the debtor may be forced to pay even though he has valid defenses. In short, such pressures may well deprive the debtor of his day in court. However valid this reasoning may be, the courts have yet to accept it. Debtors who have sued creditors for damages done to them because their employers were contacted have yet to win their suits, and the consensus of the courts seems to be that the creditor has a legitimate right to contact the employer.

Creditors have also been known to contact neighbors and relatives of debtors in an effort to get them to exert pressure on the delinquent debtor. And of course the creditor's representatives have been known to call debtors at all hours of the day and night and be rather insulting in the course of these conversations.

Some indication of the possibilities for harassment involved in collection procedures is provided by the manual on collection techniques produced by American Collectors Association for its members. The primer begins:

> Don't be a "tough guy." This is the one image that seems most inviting to the neophyte collector, and the one image that the collector must strive to avoid. Belligerence begets belligerence. Speak softly but imply that you are carrying a big stick and "get tough" only when it will serve a good purpose. * * * it is fundamentally true that every person has his secret Achilles heel * * * a weak spot in his armor. Once found by the collector and properly pressed, it will almost always produce payment.

The manual then goes on to enumerate some typical weak spots:

> It took you years and years of hard work and sacrifice to build up the good record you own—are you going to jeopardize it all with this one bad bill?

> Your boss pays his bills on time and I think I know how he feels about people who don't.

> Nobody wants to hire a fellow with bills in a collection agency. For one thing he is usually thinking about his bills instead of his job.

> You have to have insurance to drive your car, and insurance companies are checking people's credit ratings pretty closely before renewing policies.

The manual even covers the possibility that the debtor hangs up on the collector.

> Occasionally a debtor will hang up on you. Immediately dial again with a firm voice [sic] saying something to the effect, "If you hang up on me again, it will cost you plenty."

The manual is filled with advice to cover all sorts of situations. Even the lame, halt, and infirm are covered. Conceding that many of these debtors may be unable to pay, those who wrote the manual suggest adopting this tactic:

> There is an old saying that if you knew your neighbor's troubles, you would never trade. We all have troubles of some kind. Now about this bill. * * *

As these quotations on collection techniques issued by the collectors trade association suggest, harassment is closely connected with the collection process.

DALY, "HOW COLLECTION AGENCIES FORCE YOU OUT OF DEBT"

Village Voice, May 22, 1977.
Reprinted in the Fair Debt Collection Practices Act Hearings, Subcommittee on Consumer Affairs, U.S. Senate Committee on Banking, Housing and Urban Affairs.
95th Cong., 1st Sess., May 12–13, 1977, pp. 711–14.

Billy Maxwell of Riverdale was unemployed, two months in arrears with his rent, and three payments behind on his car loan. Last month, he saw a help-wanted ad for "investigators" who "like good money." The following morning, Maxwell put on a suit and hopped the subway to a downtown Brooklyn collection agency.

> "It can be boring," the president of the company told Maxwell at the end of the 10–minute interview. "But, once you pick up the basics, there's plenty of room for innovation. We get half of what we collect as profit. The point is to get the money." A framed emblem certifying the firm's membership in the American Collectors Association hung behind the executive's desk. Of the $7 billion of consumer credit granted in New York City in 1975, over $27.2 million was referred to ACA members for collection. The ACA's code of operations calls on members to "show due consideration for the misfortunes of consumers in debt" and "do everything reasonable to assist the consumer in the solution of any financial problems he may have."

* * *

"Eric Tibbetts," the man [at the next desk] said, holding out his hand to Maxwell, "I'll be the one who breaks you in." Tibbetts tossed a blue folder onto Maxwell's desk. Maxwell's first case was a seven-year-old finance-company account.

"We'll start you with renewals," Tibbetts said. "In this business, the two most important things to know about the guy are his phone number and where he works. You already got both. This account kicked around the finance company's own collection office until it got on the far side of the statute of limitations. You got to call the guy up and tell him to send in a dollar as a gesture of good faith. He makes any partial payment, the debt's active again. Ask for a post-dated check. We deposit it early, it comes back. Then we can call the guy and tell him that he's going to jail for passing a bad check unless he pays the full amount."

Maxwell dialed the phone number scrawled on the outside of the folder.

"I don't talk to no debt men," the debtor said, hanging up. Maxwell dialed again. There was no answer.

"You should keep trying," Tibbetts said when Maxwell asked for advice. "But, since it's your first day, we'll teach the guy a lesson." Tibbetts grabbed the yellow pages. In 10 minutes, he ordered seven pizzas, 14 Chinese dinners, 100 roses, a team of carpet cleaners, and three masseurs sent to the debtor's house.

"Maybe you should just sit tight and watch me for a few days," Tibbetts said, opening another blue folder and reaching for his telephone. "We'll do the bank gag."

"Hello," Tibbetts said in a high-pitched voice. "Mrs. Engelman? This is Mr. Waters at Flatbush Federal Savings. This week we are offering free checking to new depositors. Are you interested? Oh, you already bank at the Dime. Thank you very much."

"Now we know where she banks," Tibbetts said to Maxwell. "I'll wait a week so she won't make the connection. Then I'll call and tell her that I know she can pay her bill because she's got an account at the Dime Savings Bank. Sometimes it's good to also call the bank and say you're with Master Charge and you're doing a credit check. They'll give you the account number. If you know that, you can really put people on the edge."

"Let's skip-trace this fella", Tibbetts said, grabbing a delinquent department-store account. The debtor, Charles Evans, had run up a $438 bill before he moved to a new address and switched his telephone to an unlisted number. Tibbetts dialed the Board of Education.

"Hello," Tibbetts said. "This is Dr. Williams at Kings County Hospital. We have a young girl here named Chimira Evans. She's been hit by a car. Do you have an emergency number for her parents?" Fifteen minutes later, when he had Evan's new phone number, Tibbetts dialed 518–471–8111.

"This is central name and address," Tibbetts said to Maxwell. "You give them a number and they give you the name and address it's listed to."

Tibbetts moved on to another "skipper," Herman Kahn. A copy of a credit application provided Tibbetts with the phone number of Kahn's parents.

"This is Willie, Herman's friend from high school," Tibbetts said to Kahn's mother. "Could you tell me how to get hold of him?" Tibbetts wrote Kahn's new address on the back of a post card stamped "Interstate Delivery Service Notice to Deliver."

"The mother didn't have the guy's number," Tibbetts explained to Maxwell, "He'll call the number on the delivery notice. The girl over in the corner takes those calls. She'll say that she's having trouble locating the package and ask the guy to leave a number where she can call him back."

"Now we'll do a social security case," Tibbetts smiled. "This one's a retiree. We're not legally allowed to touch any federal money. So, with the people on social security or welfare, you got to scare them into paying," Tibbetts called the pensioner and introduced himself as "Mr. Rath of the Social Security Administration in Washington."

"Of course you know," Tibbetts said in a nasal tone, "that you are responsible for meeting your debts and obligations if you wish to continue receiving benefits."

Before breaking for lunch, Tibbetts called up a woman on welfare and threatened to instruct the Department of Social Services to classify her as "an unfit mother who can't pay her bills" and place her children in a foster home.

"Isn't some of this stuff illegal?" Maxwell asked Tibbetts over lunch at Zum Zum. Tibbetts laughed. According to Section 601 of the New York State General Business Law, it is a misdemeanor for debt collectors to make phone calls that "abuse or harass debtors," or claim or threaten "to enforce a right with knowledge or reason to know that the right does not exist," including garnishment of salaries. The law also forbids: Impersonation of "any state representative"; any attempt to collect fees "unless legally done"; disclosure of "a debtor's reputation of credit worthiness with knowledge or reason to know that the information is false"; communication "of the nature of a consumer claim to the debtor's employer prior to obtaining final judgment against the debtor"; and use of "communication which simulates in any manner legal or judicial process or gives appearance of being authorized, issued, or approved by a government, governmental agency, or attorney of law when it is not."

"Of course it's illegal," Tibbetts said.

After lunch, Tibbetts gave Maxwell a phone number. "Call every 15 minutes," he said. "Just lower your voice and say that time is getting short and they'll have to pay hundreds of dollars in court costs if they don't cough up." Tibbetts dialed the home number of a new account. He introduced himself as "Mr. Star of the Social Security

Administration" to the woman who answered the phone, and said he was "checking to make sure that our records were correct with regard to your husband's employment." Tibbetts wrote down the name of the husband's employer and reached for a directory.

"Do you know that you're employing a deadbeat?" Tibbetts asked the employer a few minutes later.

* * *

"You really should do the right thing and pay the full amount," Tibbetts said to a cab driver behind on his television payments. "You'll have a lot more self-respect if you act like a good citizen." After a dozen more calls, Tibbetts pushed his phone away, leaned back in his chair, and took two aspirins.

The following excerpt of testimony was made under oath by one Mr. Clark before a House subcommittee holding hearings on debt collection abuses. Mr. Clark identified himself as a former debt collector; he testified under the cloak of immunity, an assumed name, and a ski mask. This brief excerpt merely gives the flavor of his presentation.

Some of the other techniques that I can go into—I described to you "beating", which is continually calling and harassing a debtor. You could call and threaten a debtor with any number of things. You could threaten him with suit; you could threaten him with losing his children and putting them in orphanages; you could threaten him with going to jail; you could threaten him physically.

I remember one particular instance that a lady got me very upset, and I asked her, "Ma'am, what size shoes do you wear?"

And she told me, "I wear a size 7."

And I said, "Fine, ma'am, I am going to have a pair made out of cement for you and we'll send them over," and I just hung up on her. And late that afternoon her daughter walked in with a check to pay the bill.

You can often not get ahold of debtors, once they know your name and recognize your voice. They try to avoid you.

I had one particular woman that I talked to two times. She, apparently, knew my name. She knew the debt that I was trying to collect. So she would never speak with me on the telephone.

When I went to her house she would go upstairs and her children would tell me that she was not home.

She got me very upset, and it became a challenge to me to collect that debt. I, therefore, had to find a way—well, after thinking about this situation I called the woman up in the afternoon, and I said, "Mrs. Jones, this is 'so-and-so' from the police department, and you must get down to the local hospital now. Your son has been in an automobile accident and both his legs have been cut off."

She cried, she screamed, she got hysterical. I finally calmed her down a bit and told her to get over to the hospital immediately.

A few minutes later she came into the emergency entrance of the hospital where myself and another collector met her. We explained to her that she did not have to worry about her son, that he was not down here, and that we were just here about the bill.

Well, she thanked me, that her son had not had his legs cut off, and then she paid the bill.

Hearings on H.R. 11969, Subcommittee on Consumer Affairs, House Committee on Banking, Currency & Housing, 94th Cong., 2d Sess., March 30, 1976.

Notes

1. Why do debt collectors resort to abuse? Wouldn't it be easier, not to mention less risky, simply to use one of the many legal remedies?

2. Would you expect a creditor collecting her own debts or a professional debt collector to be more likely to use abusive techniques? Why?

3. Do you think that legal reforms will reduce or eliminate the kinds of practices described in this material? Consumer credit industry witnesses who testified after Mr. Clark argued that his practices violated dozens of existing laws, that Clark was due about fifty years in jail, and that no written laws could stop conduct such as Clark was willing to engage in. If this is true, what is the effect of reform legislation?

4. Should courts or legislatures consider the reasons a debtor defaulted when structuring rules to regulate creditor conduct? For example, should the law permit more coercive or harassing collection methods when the debtor is a real "deadbeat," and prohibit aggressive collection methods when the debtor lost her job or had a sudden illness?

5. What role should the lawyer play in the collection process? As creditor's counsel, are you under any ethical restrictions that might inhibit your use of abusive techniques, even if they are otherwise legal? What about debtors' lawyers? What do the rules of professional conduct have to say about all this? See A.B.A. Model Rules of Professional Conduct (1983):

Rule 3.1 A lawyer shall not bring or defend a proceeding, or assert or controvert an issue therein, unless there is a basis for doing so that is not frivolous, which includes a good fatih argument for an extension, modification or reversal of existing law.

Rule 4.4 In representing a client, a lawyer shall not use means that have no substantial purpose other than to embarrass, delay, or burden a third person, or use methods of obtaining evidence that violate the legal rights of such a person.

6. See generally, Leff, Injury, Ignorance and Spite—The Dynamics of Coercive Collection, 80 Yale L.J. 1 (1970); Greenfield, Coercive Collection Tactics—An Analysis of the Interests and the Remedies, 1972 Wash.U.L.Q. 1 (1972).

2. UNDERSTANDING DEBTOR DEFAULT

Law students tend to get a somewhat jaded view of reality. In law school courses, by studying appellate cases, we tend to concentrate on transactions that have broken down. It is easy to forget that most transactions do not break down, and most of the time lawyers are not needed at all. This is as true in the consumer credit area as any other area. Almost all consumers, upwards of 95%, pay their debts on time. Moreover, most of those who have problems do so for reasons they cannot control. The following material should help you understand why and how some consumers get into debt trouble. It should also help you understand and evaluate the legal system's response to these problems.

D. CAPLOVITZ, CONSUMERS IN TROUBLE: A STUDY OF DEBTORS IN DEFAULT (1974).*

Excerpts from pp. 53 through 108.

Table 4.1

MAJOR CATEGORIES OF REASONS FOR DEFAULT

Debtor's Misfortunes and Shortcomings	First Reason	Second Reason	Third Reason	Total Reasons	Total Individuals
1. Loss of Income	43%	18%	10%	24%	48%
2. Voluntary Overextension	13	23	32	17	25
3. Involuntary Overextension	5	12	7	7	11
4. Marital Instability	6	4	5	5	8
5. Debtor's Third Parties	8	4	6	6	9
6. Debtor Irresponsibility	4	2	—	4	5
Creditor May Be Implicated					
7. Fraud, Deception	14	13	15	14	19
8. Payment Misunderstandings	7	3	—	6	8
9. Partial/Late Payments	—	15	6	5	7
10. Item Returned to Creditor	*	6	14	2	4
11. Harassment by Creditor	—	1	5	1	1
12. All Other (Miscellaneous)	1	—	—	*	*
Total Per Cent	101%	101%	100%	101%	145%
N=	(1,320)	(570)	(110)	(2,000)	(1,326)

* Signifies less than ½ of one per cent.

Fully half the debtors mentioned loss of income as a reason for their default, and in most instances this was the primary reason. Closer examination shows that in a majority of these cases the vicissitudes of the job market were to blame. More than one fourth of all the debtors ended in default because they lost their jobs, were laid off temporarily, were shifted to a shorter work week, or were victims of strikes. Illness of the chief wage earner is the next largest subcategory. Sixteen percent of the debtors fell behind on their payments because illness impaired their earning power. Although these subcategories account for most of the loss-of-income cases, other factors were encountered as well * * *. Almost 5 percent of the debtors (59 cases) suffered an economic reversal because a secondary wage earner, almost invariably the wife, lost her job either because of illness or pregnancy. These cases are divided almost equally between accounts of illness to the wife and pregnancies which forced the wife to leave the labor force. * * * Included under the heading "loss of income" are 19 debtors who link their default to their being on welfare. Some of these debtors were on welfare when they made the credit purchase; others went on welfare because of illness or job loss after incurring the debt obligation. * * * Of particular interest are the 14 debtors who pointed out that their debt problems contributed to their loss of income. They had either lost jobs because of garnishments or had quit jobs for fear of garnishment, by either previous or current creditors. This type of reason understandably shows up only as a secondary one, with overextension as the primary reason.

* * *

As seen in Table 4.1, overextension as the result of excessive voluntary debts is the second most frequent reason for default, affecting approximately a quarter of the debtors. Of the 338 debtors who were so classified, approximately half mentioned their excessive bills as a secondary reason. These people were apparently able to manage their heavy debt burden until some crisis occurred that lowered their income. In almost all these cases the overextension resulted from consumer debts, but there were 11 debtors who defaulted on personal loans taken out in order to meet business debts.

Overextension, of course, refers not to the absolute amount of debt but to the ratio of debt to income. Although many of the overextended debtors had large debt obligations, some found themselves unable to keep up with even modest payments. For example, a 49–year–old white New Yorker with six children earned only $3,000–$4,000 a year as a night-time cab driver. He defaulted on a used car for which the payments were $55 a month. He also was obligated to pay $25 a month for a small loan. Although his total payments were only $80 a month, relative to his income and large family, this debt was too much for him to handle.

* * *

The notion of voluntary overextension is somewhat misleading, for it places the burden entirely on the debtor who presumably has been imprudent. But it must be remembered that even the most imprudent debtor, the one with many debt obligations, was still able to get credit at a time when he was heavily in debt. Because many merchants and lenders do not carry out careful investigations before extending credit, they encourage debtors to overextend themselves. Moreover, in a number of instances, debtors were overextended because they had been victimized by a creditor other than the one who had brought the suit.

(S., R., P. & R.) Consumer Law 2d Ed. ACB—17

Their overextension stemmed not from imprudence but from their being the victims of error and fraud by other creditors.

* * *

In Table 4.1 we saw that 11 percent of the debtors got into trouble in part because of some unanticipated financial obligation; for 5 percent, this was the primary reason for their default. These cases fall into several subtypes.

The majority involve unexpected medical bills because of illness in the immediate family or the pregnancy of the debtor's wife. Almost 8 percent of the debtors had such medical expenses, and in 2 percent of the cases these bills were related to the wife's pregnancy. It should be noted that these figures seriously underestimate the strains placed on these debtors because of illness, for they refer primarily to family members other than the chief wage earner. As seen in Table 5.1, fully 16 percent of the debtors suffered losses of income because of illness to themselves and in many of these cases medical bills stemming from the debtor's illness probably presented added strains on the family's financial resources.

* * * The defaults of about 9 percent of the debtors could be traced to family problems; in about 6 percent of the cases this was the primary reason for the default. In the great majority of these cases, the dissolution of the marriage through separation or divorce was the critical factor underlying the default, but marital strains short of separation were also a factor in some cases, and family problems other than marital strain were occasionally relevant. * * *

For 10 percent (127) of the debtors the default was linked to persons (or in a few instances, agencies) whom they involved in their debts or, more frequently, persons who involved them (the debtors in our sample) in their debts. The majority in this category were cosigners for friends or relatives who had defaulted. These cosigners posed problems both for the design of the study and for the classification of reasons for the default. We assumed that any debtor who cosigned for a friend or relative outside his immediate family would know very little about the initial transaction, * * *. As we shall see, in many instances the cosigner apparently was not presented with a choice and was immediately sued when the original debtor defaulted. In short, the category of "cosigner" covers a multitude of reasons that we know little about. * * * The 76 debtors who were sued because they were cosigners for defaulters frequently had stories which implicated not only the person who left them "holding the bag" but the creditor as well. * * *

The last major group of reasons reflecting upon the debtor rather than the creditor is debtor irresponsibility. This is perhaps the most arbitrary category. It could be argued that the 172 debtors who defaulted primarily because of voluntary overextension behaved irresponsibly and that many debtors who failed to live up to their obligation after they became separated or divorced were also irresponsible.

But in both of these types, the default stemmed primarily from inability to pay rather than unwillingness to pay. The more narrow category of debtor irresponsibility applies to 66 debtors, about 5 percent of the entire sample, and in almost all these cases this was the primary reason for the default. These cases fall into four distinct subtypes, bad faith, forgetfulness (the debtor admits that he simply forgot to pay), failure to pay while the debtor was out of town for a period of time, and refusal to pay on merchandise that was stolen or destroyed in an accident.

The largest of these categories, containing 21 of the 66 cases, is the one that fits least well under the notion of irresponsibility, for it consists of debtors who left town temporarily and failed to arrange for payments in their absence. As we shall see, in a number of these cases the debtor was called out of town suddenly because of some family crisis. Some 16 debtors gave accounts of their defaults that reflect bad faith on their part. They come closest to the credit industry's image of the deadbeat; as a group they comprise only 1 percent of the entire sample. The second type of irresponsibility consists of a rather homogeneous grouping of some 13 debtors who admit that they had been careless and had simply forgotten to make their payments. * * *

We have seen that 35 percent of the debtors gave reasons for their default that implicated the creditor in varying degrees. By far the largest category of creditor-related reasons consists of allegations of fraud and deception. Nineteen percent mentioned such wrongdoing by the seller as part of the reason for their default, and for 14 percent of all debtors it was the primary reason. The broad category of fraud covers a multitude of sins. * * * They range from complaints about defective merchandise, wrong merchandise, price and insurance deception, to allegations of being tricked into signing contracts. The largest proportion of these complaints, almost half the total, deal with defective merchandise, represented by the first three categories. Approximately 1 of every 10 debtors mentioned defective merchandise as contributing to his default; for 6 percent this was the primary reason. (These figures refer to the sum of the first three categories.) The distinction between the first two categories of defective merchandise corresponds to the legal distinction between an express and an implied warranty. If the merchandise does not perform its presumed function (for example, the automobile does not move or the toaster does not work), then the implied warranty has been violated even if no written guarantee of performance was provided (the first category). The third category differs from the first two in that the defect was not immediately apparent. The debtor in these cases had the merchandise for a short period of time only to discover that it was of such poor quality that he felt betrayed by the creditor. * * *

In 32 cases, almost 3 percent of the entire sample, the reason for the default was linked to the dealer's failure to deliver the merchandise for which the debtor thought he had contracted. In most of these cases, this was the primary reason for the default. Included here are debtors who were led to believe that they were buying one model or brand of merchandise but received another, and debtors who contracted for new merchandise but were sent used goods. Most of these cases involved purchases of furniture and appliances but a few dealt with automobiles. Some 13 debtors, about 1 percent of the entire sample, traced their default in part to the dealer's failure to deliver all the merchandise entered on the contract, or in a few cases to their being billed for merchandise that they had not ordered. * * *

In chapter 3 we saw that 45 percent of the debtors who were told a price at the time of the sale were misled about the true cost of their purchase. In about 25 percent of these cases the discrepancy was substantial, in that the total time sales price was greater by 25 percent or more than the quoted price. In spite of this widespread abuse, only 2 percent of the debtors (41 cases) mentioned price deception as a *reason* for their default, and in only a little more than 1 percent of the cases was this the primary reason. The disparity between the actual amount of deception regarding price and the role such deception played in the default is yet further evidence that many debtors were willing to meet their obligation even though they felt they had been cheated.

In chapter 3 we saw that 35 percent of those who made purchases said that they had been misinformed in some way about the transaction. Quite a number of these debtors pointed out that the dealer made false promises. Although such reports were fairly common among these debtors, only 18 of them, about 1 percent of the sample, specifically cited such false promises as a reason for their default (in most of these cases, it was the primary reason). The most common pattern here is the chain-referral scheme, under which the buyer is promised price reductions or even free merchandise in return for finding more customers. A second pattern in these cases is the "tie-in" sale, in which the buyer is supposedly given something free and need pay only for some service or supplies.

* * * Perhaps the ultimate form of deception occurred in those cases in which the debtor was unaware that he was signing an installment contract at all. * * * [S]ome 13 debtors, not quite 1 percent of the sample, had this complaint.

———

The author, now a practicing attorney, has updated his views on these problems, however.

D. CAPLOVITZ, CREDIT CARD MANIA IN AMERICA AND PERSONAL BANKRUPTCY, PAPER FOR CONFERENCE ON UNEMPLOYMENT AND CONSUMER DEBTS IN EUROPE

(Hamburg, 1989).*

THE CREDIT CARD JUNKIE

A major theme of the study I did 21 years ago was why the debtor defaulted on his installment debt. The dominant reason then was some unexpected event that interfered with the flow of the debtor's income. Almost half of the debtors we interviewed suffered a loss of income because of unemployment or illness or a strike or a change of job. Another 11 per cent had unexpected expenses that drained their income, such as an illness to a family member that resulted in large medical bills, or some accident that damaged their property and required repairs. In all, about 60 per cent gave loss of income related reasons for their default. Other unexpected events played a role, such as the break up of a marriage. This was mentioned by 8 per cent. Twenty one years ago, only about a quarter of the debtors gave as a reason for their default their having taken on more debts than they could handle, what I called voluntary overextension.

In the credit card era of today, there has been a dramatic change in the reasons for default. Today, an overwhelming majority have gotten into trouble because they used more credit than they could handle. They voluntarily got themselves deep in debt by using the many credit cards they have. Whereas loss of income was the major reason for default twenty years ago, today the major reason is what I then called voluntary overextension, that is, the irresponsible use of credit. I call these people "credit card junkies" and they are addicted to credit in much the same way an alcoholic is addicted to alcohol and a drug user is addicted to drugs. * * * Over the past fifteen years, the bankruptcy rate in America has grown from under 200,000 a year to about 600,000. As high as the bankruptcy rate is, it still represents only a tiny fraction of the millions of American consumers who are hopelessly entangled in debt. My own research back in the sixties, when we surveyed employers to find out how many garnishment orders they received each year, led me to estimate that about fifteen million Americans were deeply in debt, a number that is no doubt much higher today.

Although the undisciplined consumer must accept much of the blame for the crisis, the issuers of credit, the banks are equally at fault. When I did my research some 21 years ago, the literature produced by the credit industry stressed principles that applied to the extension of credit. This literature said that the creditors would carefully check the

* Reprinted with permission from the author.

would-be debtor's income and level of debt before extending credit. Presumably, if the debtor had a fair amount of debt already, the creditor would not issue him more credit. Such responsible behavior on the part of creditors is no longer operative in the mad world of credit today. The banks are ready to extend credit to people of low income and they never seem to deny credit to people who already have a high level of debt. * * *

* * *

Although the limit on any one line of credit may be two or three thousand dollars, these debtors owe the same bank anywhere from $10,000 to $20,000 on the different lines of credit. Banks push credit cards by sending consumers letters saying you have "pre-approved credit." * * *

———

Not all investigators agree with Caplovitz' new theories on the source of consumer credit problems.

T. SULLIVAN, E. WARREN, & J. WESTBROOK, AS WE FORGIVE OUR DEBTORS
187–88, 331 (Oxford, 1989).*

We were unsuccessful in our efforts to predict credit and debt using indicators such as income, prestige, job tenure, chapter, and joint filing for our various "junkie" groups. For example, although we know from Table 10.2 that job tenure varies among these groups, it was not a significant predictor of credit card debt. While we can identify small numbers of debtors who are heavily burdened with debt, we conclude that in many respects they resemble the other debtors.

* * * Credit card debt is a substantial portion of what typical, wage-earning consumers carry into bankruptcy, but its impact is different from what we had anticipated. The stereotypical debtors with a special weakness for credit card debts are represented, but their number is small. Out of 1202 cases, we could find only 23 debtors (less than 2%) who met all three criteria indicating abuse: high credit card debt/income ratio, high proportion of unsecured debt in credit cards, and in the top 15% of the absolute amount of credit card debt carried into bankruptcy. Other potential abusers do not meet these criteria, although they might on some normative scales be abusers in every sense of the word. On the other hand, even among the 23 debtors, including the Voelkers and Tony Allegro, there might be debtors whose tales would make us pause before we branded them abusers.

Even when we use a broader classification of abuse, looking at debtors who meet only one or two of the tests, the data in the files introduce ambiguities. A large fraction of the debtors with staggering debt/income ratios had serious income interruptions during the years before bankruptcy, suggesting that a downturn in income rather than an upswing in discretionary spending accounted for their financial circumstances. But an almost equal number of debtors with high debt/income ratios had stable incomes; they had amassed huge credit card debts on the basis of incomes far too low to repay them.

* * *

The analysis of credit card debt, for example, reveals a substantial group (about 15% of the wage earners) who owe more than half a year's income in credit card debt alone. These cases break down into two parts: those who ran up huge debts compared to existing income and those for whom income dropped or was interrupted, making their debts insupportable.

The cases in which a debtor had stable income and managed to amass credit card debts in excess of half a year's income surely represent some clear abuses. But any fingerpointing has to go both ways. Credit card issuers were willing to give out the fifth, sixth, or seventh bank card and to approve charges after debtors already owed short-term debt so large that they could not possibly pay the interest, much less the principal. * * *

Notes

1. There has been no serious attempt to update the original Caplovitz study since 1974 so we are compelled either to continue to use those findings or to replace them with speculations and anecdotal data. According to Caplovitz, funding for such studies has not been available (except, possibly, through creditors) for a decade.

2. The Sullivan, Warren and Westbrook study focuses on a different group of people—those who file for a discharge of debts in bankruptcy. Instead, the Caplovitz study dealt with those who merely default on one or more credit obligations, and who may have been considered sufficiently judgmentworthy to be worth suing. The latter is a very different group of people, and a group that is more relevant to any analysis of debt collection efforts. (From a creditor's point of view, it is the difference between a car with one or more flat tires and one which is "totalled.")

3. Some of your authors believe that the lack of reliable modern data on these problems is both surprising and sad. It may, however, be an accurate reflection of current priorities and concerns.

SECTION B. JUDICIAL CONTROLS ON COLLECTION ABUSES

Prefatory Note

The materials in this section concern the use of harassment as a collection tool. As Grant, supra p. 439, suggests, most collections are realized by exerting "unwelcome pressure" on the debtor. Thus, some *unwelcome* pressure is felt necessary to keep the credit and collection system running smoothly, and delinquencies within the 2% range found by Grant. (Although it can be higher during recessions.) Where does one draw the line between permissible and impermissible *unwelcome* pressure?

Creditor pressure often starts with standard, 30, 60 and 90 day dunning letters. These may begin by inquiring whether the debtor has forgotten to send a payment by inadvertence, but usually end by threatening to take action in court against the debtor's "credit rating," or both. Next often comes personal contacts, either by telephone or in person.

At some point, the manner, number or content of the contacts may pass the bounds of what society considers permissible for the purpose of keeping the credit system running smoothly. A possible example is the following letter, used by a small loan company in Maine, threatening imprisonment for debt:

Dear [Debtor]

I have just come across your account. I and the company will not stand for this. We are no longer going to take care to be careful with you. We have a corporation lawyer who at this time is getting ready to have you confined in the county jail until such time as someone pays the entire balance of this loan. I do not see why the company has let you get away with this so long. I would like nothing better than to see everyone like you behind bars until they paid off all of their delinquent bills. People who do not pay their obligations are nothing [word blocked out and "no good" inserted], and this is my opinion.

I hope you will enjoy sitting behind bars all summer long and if you don't pay, I hope that you will enjoy spending year after year in jail, because I will see that you are never let out. The only reason why you won't go to jail is because you start sending us payments, and continue to send them every month. I do not expect that a person like you could afford a full payment, but I expect to see $15.00 every month and we will not charge you interest.

I expect to see either a payment this week or you in jail as soon as possible.

Sincerely,

[Creditor]

The courts have invented a variety of weapons for aggrieved defaulting debtors to use against creditor pressure devices. As the following cases show, different causes of action are available in different states. Is there any similarity in the analyses of the courts, even though different causes of action are involved? Any similarity in criteria used?

CHAMPLIN v. WASHINGTON TRUST CO.
OF WESTERLY

Supreme Court of Rhode Island, 1984.
478 A.2d 985.

This litigation revolves around a single 1976 telephone call plaintiff, Barbara B. Champlin (Barbara), received from the attorney for defendant, The Washington Trust Company, of Westerly (the bank), in which the attorney sought payment on a series of notes allegedly executed by Barbara and her husband, Thomas Champlin (Thomas). Barbara and Thomas were married in 1954.

* * *

Later, in April 1974, the couple separated; divorce proceedings soon followed. Matters reached the point where a final decree of divorce was entered in the Family Court in January 1975.

* * *

Thomas, who was as unfortunate in business as he had been in matrimony, instituted bankruptcy proceedings. He was adjudged and declared a bankrupt by the United States Bankruptcy Court for the District of Rhode Island in January 1977. Among the obligations discharged by virtue of those proceedings was a series of promissory notes made payable to the bank. The notes—four in number—were actually renewals of earlier notes. Each instrument was a ninety-day note.

When no payments were made, the bank's vice president sent a letter dated December 26, 1975, to Thomas and Barbara by certified mail, asking that they contact him about the overdue notes. The letter was received by Barbara at the Post Road address in mid-January 1976, almost a year after she and Thomas had been divorced. Barbara discussed the bank's request with her father. On his advice she took no action. At that time the father was terminally ill, was hospitalized, and had become his daughter's chief adviser and confidant following the breakdown of her marriage. He served in such capacity until his death on February 1, 1976.

The bank, having had no success in collecting on the four notes, turned the matter over to its attorney, Thomas H. Eyles, for collection. He sent a letter dated January 30, 1976, to Thomas and Barbara, asking that they contact him about the four notes. The letter also informed the couple that the bank had set off whatever was in their accounts against the outstanding indebtedness.

The vice president had known Barbara's father and informed Eyles, the attorney, of his passing. In early April 1976 both the vice president and the attorney traveled to the Probate Court clerk's office in Little Compton and there obtained a copy of the father's will. Later, the vice president called Barbara, who was then working, at her place of employment, a small store in Wakefield. When Barbara came to the phone, the vice president turned the phone over to Eyles. Barbara testified that at this point in her life she was in "very bad shape" emotionally because of a lack of money, overdue mortgage payments, and the death of her father.

Eyles identified himself to Barbara as the attorney representing the bank, mentioned the notes, and then asked her what she intended to do about paying them. She responded by telling the attorney that she had never signed the notes. Eyles, however, took issue with Barbara's representation and informed her that he was aware of the provisions of her father's will and asked Barbara if she would be willing, as payment of the debt, to assign whatever interest she had in her father's estate to the bank. According to Barbara, she became "terrified" at this point and told the bank's attorney to call her attorney. Barbara testified she was quite upset by the call and was unable to return to work for about "a week or so." She described herself during this period as extremely nervous, physically ill, and unable to sleep. At no point, however, did she consult a physician.

When the jury returned after completing its deliberations, the foreman gave verbal responses to written questions with which the jury had been furnished, two of which are relevant to this appeal. The jury gave an affirmative answer to the inquiry, "Do you find defendant's conduct intentional and unreasonable in the circumstances of this case?" and awarded compensatory damages of $3,000. It gave similar response to the second question, "[W]as the conduct of defendant willful, wanton, reckless or wicked so as to merit the imposition of punitive damages because of the telephone call from Mr. Eyles to Mrs. Champlin?" and awarded punitive damages of $60,000.

The decisive question in this controversy, as we see it, is what standard of liability is to be imposed upon a creditor whose actions allegedly inflict emotional distress on a debtor? There were three theories presented for the trial justice's consideration. They are set forth in the Restatement (Second) *Torts,* §§ 46, 312, and 313 (1965). Section 46 imposes liability on one whose extreme and outrageous conduct intentionally causes severe emotional distress. Section 312 imposes liability on one whose conduct intentionally causes emotional distress; the conduct need not be extreme or outrageous, and the emotional distress need not be severe. Section 313 imposes liability on one whose conduct unintentionally causes emotional distress; as in § 312, the emotional distress need not be severe.

The bank claimed in its motions for a directed verdict at the close of Barbara's case and at the close of the presentation of all the evidence that it should be held liable only under § 46. Barbara claimed instead that the bank should be liable under either § 312 or § 313.

* * *

[This] situation demands a balancing of the interest of a creditor in collecting a debt against the interest of the debtor to be free from the infliction of emotional distress. Consequently, courts have uniformly insisted that the creditor's conduct be clearly and obviously excessive in order to sustain a claimant's recovery; "liability usually has rested on a prolonged course of hounding by a variety of extreme methods." Prosser, *Handbook of the Law of Torts,* § 12 at 57 (4th ed. 1971).

Those jurisdictions that permit recovery for emotional distress in the debt-collection context do so either under the higher threshhold of liability imposed by § 46, * * * or under an invasion-of-privacy theory. * * * We were unable to find any reported cases that used either § 312 or § 313 as the basis for holding a creditor liable for collection tactics. We join the ranks of those jurisdictions that have adopted the criteria set forth in § 46.

The higher threshhold of § 46 is required in debt-collection cases because of the belief that when a creditor or his agent is privileged to use a number of tactics to collect a debt, even though those tactics may cause the debtor to suffer emotional distress, the creditor should be held accountable only if those tactics are extreme and outrageous. In general a creditor will not be held liable when he has done no more than insist on his legal rights in a permissible way, even though such insistence is likely or even certain to annoy, disturb, or inconvenience the debtor or even cause him to suffer some emotional distress.

In the usual debt-collection case in which the debtor is permitted to recover under § 46, the creditor's action must be considered extreme and outrageous. This standard can be met by conduct of considerable duration, whether it be a long series of "dunning" letters, or a combination of letters and telephone calls. A creditor is rarely held liable for an isolated event, i.e., a single telephone call, unless that event is such that no reasonable person could be expected to endure it. Restatement § 46, comment (j).

A compilation of debtor-harassment cases can be found in Annot., 87 A.L.R.3d 786 (1979) and 46 A.L.R.3d 772 (1972). Those cases make it clear that there are four elements that must coincide to impose liability: (1) the conduct must be intentional or in reckless disregard of the probability of causing emotional distress, (2) the conduct must be extreme and outrageous, (3) there must be a causal connection between the wrongful conduct and the emotional distress, and (4) the emotional distress in question must be severe.

* * *

The extension of credit has played a significant role in the economic betterment of our citizens, whether the credit comes by way of a credit card, an unsecured note, a security interest in the family car, or a note that is secured by a mortgage on the family homestead. If credit is to continue to play the significant role that it does in our society, the financial community must be afforded reasonable latitude in the manner in which it seeks to collect overdue notes, even though there may be times when those methods might cause some inconvenience or embarrassment to the debtor. In making this statement, we would emphasize that the right to pursue the debtor is not a license to outrage the debtor.

In this case Eyles was neither abusive nor threatening. True, at the time he called, Barbara was in a weakened emotional condition, but a part of this condition was the very reason he contacted her. Her father had died, and Eyles believed she might be inheriting a portion of her father's estate, which in turn could be used to pay off the notes. Although his request for an assignment of Barbara's contingent interest in her father's estate might seem to some to be tactless, Attorney Eyles, in making the suggestion, was merely protecting the best interests of his client. We see nothing in his brief encounter with Barbara that could be classified as extreme and outrageous.

In light of what we have said, we are of the belief that the trial justice erred when he denied the bank's motion for a directed verdict.

The defendant's appeal is sustained, the judgment appealed from is vacated, and the case is remanded to the Superior Court with instructions to enter judgment for the defendant.

APPENDIX

1 Restatement (Second) *Torts* (1965):

"§ 46. Outrageous Conduct Causing Severe Emotional Distress

(i) One who by extreme and outrageous conduct intentionally or recklessly causes severe emotional distress to another is subject to liability for such emotional distress, and if bodily harm to the other results from it, for such bodily harm."

2 Restatement (Second) *Torts* (1965):

"§ 312. Emotional Distress Intended

If the actor intentionally and unreasonably subjects another to emotional distress which he should recognize as likely to result in illness or other bodily harm, he is subject to liability to the other for an illness or other bodily harm of which the distress is a legal cause,

(a) although the actor has no intention of inflicting such harm, and

(b) irrespective of whether the act is directed against the other or a third person."

"§ 313. Emotional Distress Unintended

(1) If the actor unintentionally causes emotional distress to another, he is subject to liability to the other for resulting illness or bodily harm if the actor

(a) should have realized that his conduct involved an unreasonable risk of causing the distress, otherwise than by knowledge of the harm or peril of a third person, and

(b) from facts known to him should have realized that the distress, if it were caused, might result in illness or bodily harm.

(2) The rule stated in Subsection (1) has no application to illness or bodily harm of another which is caused by emotional distress arising solely from harm or peril to a third person, unless the negligence of the actor has otherwise created an unreasonable risk of bodily harm to the other."

Problem 1

Your client, Daniel Default, bought goods on credit from Charlie Cheerful. There has been a dispute about the quality of the goods, whether Charlie should repair or replace them under the warranty; and Dan has refused to make the payments called for in the credit agreement. Yesterday, Charlie tried to telephone Dan at work, but the call was routed to the personnel manager of Dan's employer. The personnel manager stated that it was their normal policy not to allow personal telephone calls to employees during working hours. Charlie explained that he had tried to call Dan at home unsuccessfully, and that it was "necessary to contact Mr. Default at work to clear up an outstanding account." When the personnel manager still refused to permit the call to go through, Charlie called Dan a "deadbeat" and expressed the hope that the employer would discharge Dan if the debt was not paid.

(a) The employer did not in fact discharge Dan, but relations with his superiors at work "feel strained." Does Dan have a successful cause of action either for damages or to restrain such future conduct? Does it matter whether there was in fact a breach of warranty?

(b) Do your answers change if Dan is later discharged by the employer?

Cf., Harrison v. Humble Oil & Refining Co., 264 F.Supp. 89 (D.S.C. 1967).

Problem 2

Your client, Ed Easy, also bought goods on credit from Charlie Cheerful, and has not made any payments on his credit agreement since six months ago. At that time Ed became unemployed. During that six months Charlie has called Ed about two or three times a week. The calls may come at any time from 9 A.M. to 11 P.M.

When the calls began, Ed explained that he was unemployed and had no extra funds with which to make payments. Charlie advised him to cut back further his standard of living so as to have funds left over from his unemployment check with which to make payments. When Ed refused to do this, Charlie called him a "cheat" and a "deadbeat" and said he "was just trying to beat his bills." Later, when Ed pleaded again that his unemployment was the real problem, Charlie suggested that he was not trying hard enough. "If you can't get a job, I can get one for you—digging ditches." Ed then stated that he was a handicapped person, and could not dig ditches. Charlie replied that he thought Ed was "lying"; and even if he was not, he could find a job if he really tried.

Since then, the level of dialogue has gone downhill. Ed describes their content as mostly descriptions of new employment opportunities (none of them suitable for Ed) and Charlie's references to how Ed's credit rating will be destroyed and how the furniture will be repossessed (Charlie has a security interest in it). Ed received a pamphlet in the mail—"How to Prepare Your Furniture for Repossession." He describes Charlie's tone of voice as "very rough" and his language as "obnoxious," and "nasty." Does Ed have a successful cause of action either for damages or to restrain such conduct in the future? Cf., Houston–American Life Ins. Co. v. Tate, 358 S.W.2d 645 (Tex.Civ.App. 1962). Would Charlie be protected from either the damage award or the injunction by the First Amendment materials in Chapter 1?

Would it matter whether Ed had a defense to payment of the credit agreement—such as breach of warranty or usury? In other words, is a creditor with a legitimate debt privileged to be more obnoxious than a creditor with a clouded or disputed claim?

Should it matter whether Ed suffers only mental anguish from Charlie's conduct, or also suffers physical injury? The Texas Courts wrestled with this problem over a long period of time while developing the tort of "unreasonable collection practices." See Harned v. E–Z Finance Co., 151 Tex. 641, 254 S.W.2d 81 (1953); Wright v. E–Z Finance Co., 267 S.W.2d 602 (Tex.Civ.App.1954). If such a dichotomy were insisted upon how would headaches or loss of sleep be classified?

HAMILTON v. FORD MOTOR CREDIT CO.

Court of Special Appeals of Maryland, 1986.
66 Md.App. 46, 502 A.2d 1057.

Bloom, Judge.

Ford Motor Credit Company (FMCC) repossessed a motor vehicle that had been purchased by Sharon Marie Hamilton and her mother, Verna Hamilton, and financed through an installment sales contract that was assigned to FMCC. Because of FMCC's conduct before and after repossessing the vehicle, a jury in the Circuit Court for Baltimore County awarded the Hamiltons verdicts totalling $64,757.20 against FMCC and one of its employees, Bernard Alaimo. Judge John F. Fader, II, who had presided over the trial, granted a judgment N.O.V. with respect to one of the Hamilton's claims, reducing the verdict total to $12,206.20. Both Sharon and Verna appealed. FMCC and Alaimo cross-appealed, contending that the remaining verdicts resulted from errors committed by the trial judge.

* * *

We reject all of the contentions of error made by appellants and cross-appellant and affirm the judgment of the circuit court.

Facts

On November 27, 1979, Sharon Hamilton and her mother, Verna Hamilton, purchased a Ford Courier truck from Al Packer Ford in

Baltimore City. They executed a Maryland Automobile Retail Installment contract, which Sharon signed as buyer and Verna signed as cobuyer. The truck was purchased for Sharon's use and was titled in her name. The total purchase price was $9095.36 with monthly payments of $165.32. The contract was immediately assigned to FMCC.

In late 1980 or early 1981 Sharon drove to Florida to visit friends and to investigate the possibilities of working or attending school there. She was involved in an accident; the truck was damaged, and she sustained fractures of cervical vertebrae. She returned to Baltimore in March 1981, leaving the truck in Florida. Verna told an agent of FMCC about the accident and informed him that Sharon would be out of work for a while. FMCC granted the Hamiltons an extension of one month on the truck payments.

In the spring of 1981, the Hamiltons fell behind in their payments. Sharon was only working part time and largely on a volunteer basis, while Verna was devoting most of her time to caring for her husband, who had suffered a heart attack and a stroke in 1980 and was terminally ill, requiring not only the care of Verna, a trained nurse, but other family members, as well, to meet many of his basic needs. Verna and her husband received social security benefits.

FMCC representatives began calling Verna persistently to demand payment, although Verna contends that she repeatedly told them that Sharon was injured and unable to work, that her husband was ill, and that she was financially unable to make the payments. FMCC and Alaimo, however, contend that they did not learn of the condition of Verna's husband until sometime in September of 1981, shortly before the truck was repossessed.

Although various FMCC representatives telephoned Verna, the majority of the calls were made by appellee Bernard Alaimo, who had apparently been assigned the role of principal antagonist. All parties agree that Alaimo was rude and hostile to Verna when he called and that his rudeness and abruptness increased with time. He telephoned at all hours of the day and into the early evening, sometimes several times a week. After a while, he stopped introducing himself when Verna answered the phone and merely began his calls with a demand for payment. One of Verna's neighbors received several calls for Verna, though no messages were left. In the fall of 1981, Alaimo called one evening after 10:00 p.m., awakening Verna from a sound sleep. He shouted at her and, referring to Sharon's earlier assurances that she was seeking employment and would make payment soon, said, "How could you have raised such a liar? I'll be seeing you in court." On another occasion he threatened to ruin Verna's credit.

Verna's daughter Mary and another witness testified that Verna was visibly upset by these calls. Mary took a number of calls herself and once asked FMCC to stop calling because her father was ill and the calls would awaken him and upset Verna. Verna testified that she began to have considerable difficulty sleeping. She claimed that

FMCC's persistence was the cause of that condition, but there was other evidence to the effect that for several years she had suffered urinary incontinence that caused her to get up several times each night. It is clear, nevertheless, that Verna was extremely agitated, as were other members of her family. She felt harassed and abused.

Between March and October 1981, Sharon travelled back and forth to Florida several times, but the truck remained in Florida. On several occasions, representatives of FMCC demanded that Verna tell them exactly where in Florida the truck was located. Verna insisted that she was never sure exactly where her daughter was, because Sharon moved quite frequently and often stayed with friends.

The vehicle was finally repossessed in Florida on November 16, 1981. * * *

* * *

In February 1984, Sharon and her mother brought suit against FMCC and Alaimo in the Circuit Court for Baltimore County. * * * In Count Five, Verna sued FMCC and Alaimo for intentional infliction of emotional distress; and in Count Six, Verna sued FMCC and Alaimo for negligent infliction of emotional distress. * * * At the close of the plaintiffs' case, the court granted defendants' motion for judgment on the Sixth Count (negligent infliction of emotional distress) on the ground that Maryland does not recognize such a cause of action. Defendants moved for judgment on all remaining claims at the close of all the evidence; the court reserved ruling on the * * * issues of liability and damages as to the claim for intentional infliction of emotional distress. * * * The jury found for Verna on her claim for intentional infliction of emotional distress, awarding her $1.00 in compensatory damages and $52,500.00 punitive damages against FMCC and $50.00 punitive damages against Alaimo.

Judge Fader subsequently granted defendants' motion for judgment N.O.V. as to the count for intentional infliction of emotional distress on the basis that plaintiffs had failed to present sufficient proof to justify recovery on that cause of action. * * *

I. *Intentional Infliction of Emotional Distress*

This appeal directs our attention once again to the tort of intentional infliction of emotional distress.

The tort of intentional infliction of emotional distress has only recently found recognition in this State, initially by the Court of Appeals in *Harris v. Jones,* 281 Md. 560, 380 A.2d 611, *aff'g Jones v. Harris,* 35 Md.App. 556, 371 A.2d 1104 (1977). Maryland litigants have been quick to test its limits, eager to assert that its principles should be extended to the facts of their particular cases. * * * *Harris,* adopting the reasoning of the Supreme Court of Virginia in *Womack v. Eldridge,* 215 Va. 338, 210 S.E.2d 145 (1974), held that there are "four elements which must coalesce to impose liability for intentional infliction of emotional distress * * *" Those elements are:

(1) The conduct must be intentional or reckless;

(2) The conduct must be extreme and outrageous;

(3) There must be a causal connection between the wrongful conduct and the emotional distress;

(4) The emotional distress must be severe.

* * *

The Hamiltons contend that the court erred in granting appellees' motion for judgment following the return of the jury's verdict, arguing that there was sufficient evidence to go to the jury. We disagree.

The evidence which the Hamiltons presented consisted of a wide array of objectionable and harassing conduct. There were persistent phone calls, one allegedly late at night. There were repeated calls even after Verna insisted she did not know where the truck was and that she was in no financial condition to pay. There were threats to sue, threats to ruin the Hamiltons' credit, and threats to attach Verna's house and property. There were incorrect assertions that Florida law applied. There was Verna's already strained emotional state due to her husband's illness, Sharon's injuries, and her own difficulty in sleeping, all of which Verna contends appellees knew.

Yet even considering all of the evidence in the light most favorable to appellants, which we must do when reviewing the entry of a judgment notwithstanding the verdict, we conclude that the four elements set out in *Harris* were not met. We focus particularly on the second and fourth elements. The second requirement is that the conduct be extreme and outrageous. Appellees' conduct was unquestionably rude, insensitive, callous, and in poor taste. It was not, however, extreme and outrageous. To satisfy that element, conduct must completely violate human dignity. "[E]xtreme and outrageous conduct exists only if 'the average member of the community must regard the defendant's conduct * * * as being a complete denial of the plaintiff's dignity as a person.'" *Dick v. Mercantile–Safe*, 63 Md. App. at 276, 492 A.2d 674, quoting *Alsteen v. Gehl*, 21 Wis.2d 349, 124 N.W.2d 312, 318 (1963). The conduct must strike to the very core of one's being, threatening to shatter the frame upon which one's emotional fabric is hung.

Appellees' acts were examples of bad taste and poor judgment in connection with the collection of a lawful debt but did not amount to intentional infliction of emotional distress. Creditors have the right to insist on payment of just debts and may threaten legal proceedings. Appellees' persistent attempts to extract payment were unquestionably offensive to appellants, but as Professor Calvert Magruder observed, "'Against a large part of the frictions and irritations and clashing of temperaments incident to participation in community life, a certain toughening of the mental hide is a better protection than the law could ever be.'" *Harris,* 281 Md. at 568, 380 A.2d 611, quoting 49 Harv.L. Rev. 1033, 1035 (1936). Moreover, appellees were not so much unopposed invaders of Verna's psyche as they were combatants against Verna for the collection of payments. It appears that she did not meekly endure the telephone calls but responded in a hostile fashion herself, speaking loudly and hanging up on occasion, generating the "thrust and parry" this court observed in *Dick*.

Verna also failed to demonstrate that her emotional distress was severe. She produced evidence that she was upset, that she had difficulty sleeping, and that she was embarrassed. To sustain an action for intentional infliction of emotional distress, however, one must suffer an emotional response so acute that no reasonable person could be expected to endure it. One must be unable to function, one must be unable to tend to necessary matters. Verna simply produced no evidence that she could not function or tend to her everyday affairs. The tale of her frustration and anguish was not one of pain so acute that no reasonable person could be expected to endure. The absence of such evidence by itself was fatal to her claim.

Verna's emotional response to appellees' conduct was no more severe than that of the plaintiff in *Harris*, which the Court found to be an insufficient basis for recovery. Harris was humiliated; his nervous condition aggravated and his speech impediment worsened; he had to see a physician; and he felt "like going into a hole and hide [sic].'" Although Verna's distress was keen and apparently genuine, it was not disabling. Her ego was bruised and her dignity was bent, but neither was destroyed.

Appellants attempt to distinguish this case from *Harris* and its progeny that involved employer/employee relationships by arguing that an employee must expect to endure more abusive conduct by virtue of his subordinate position. This argument has no persuasive merit. Conduct that would qualify as extreme and outrageous when committed by a creditor should not have to be accepted from an employer. Moreover, *Dick v. Mercantile–Safe, supra,* dealt specifically with the relationship between debtor and creditor. We drew no distinction in that case between an employment relationship and a credit arrangement, and we find none here. In developing the tort of intentional infliction of emotional distress, whatever the relationship between the parties, recovery will be meted out sparingly, its balm reserved for those wounds that are truly severe and incapable of healing themselves.

* * *

Affirmed.

Note

Why did FMCC bother with all the harassment? Why didn't it just repossess at the beginning? Could an outrageous repossession procedure result in a debt collection tort? See Jackson v. Peoples Federal Credit Union, 25 Wash.App. 81, 604 P.2d 1025 (1979).

SHERMAN v. FIELD CLINIC

Illinois Court of Appeals, 1979.
74 Ill.App.3d 21, 29 Ill.Dec. 597, 392 N.E.2d 154.

STAMOS, PRESIDING JUSTICE.

Plaintiffs, Margaret Sherman, Raymond M. Sherman, Jr., and Deborah Billy, Margaret Sherman's minor daughter, brought this action in the circuit court of Cook County seeking recovery for damages allegedly arising out of attempts made by defendant Collection Accounts Terminal, Inc. (CAT), to collect a debt purportedly owed by plaintiffs to defendants Field Clinic and Raymond F. Cunningham, M.D., doing business as Field Clinic (the Clinic). Count I of the complaint alleged intentional infliction of severe emotional distress and sought compensatory damages. * * *

* * *

Plaintiffs' complaint in two counts, filed in conjunction with a jury demand, made the following allegations. Plaintiffs are members of a family who reside together. CAT is a collection agency which served as the agent of the Clinic for the collection of an account in the amount of $170 purportedly owed to the Clinic for medical care administered to plaintiff Margaret Sherman. During the period beginning on or about September 13, 1977, and ending on or about November 22, 1977, CAT, as the agent of the Clinic, engaged in severe harassment of plaintiffs in an attempt to collect on the account owed to the Clinic. The acts committed by CAT or its agent included the following: telephoning plaintiffs' residence 10–20 times per day 3 days per week and 5–6 times per day 2 other days per week; sending numerous letters to plaintiffs' residence; making numerous telephone calls to Mr. Sherman at his place of business, though only Mrs. Sherman was responsible for any debts due the Clinic; threatening to "embarrass" Mr. Sherman by contacting his employers and co-workers; threatening to garnish half of Mr. Sherman's wages; frequently using profane and obscene language in calls to Mr. Sherman; calling and speaking to Mrs. Sherman's 15 year old daughter, plaintiff Deborah Billy, in connection with the debt, though only Mrs. Sherman was responsible for any debts due the Clinic; frequently making threats to the daughter that Mr. and Mrs. Sherman would be sent to jail for not paying the bill; and frequently using abusive language in calls to Mrs. Sherman. Plaintiffs alleged that this extreme and outrageous conduct was wanton, malicious, and oppressive, and was intended to inflict, and did inflict, severe mental and emotional distress on the plaintiffs, wherefore plaintiffs sought compensatory damages from CAT and the Clinic.

* * *

CAT filed an answer to the complaint, admitting that it acted as the Clinic's agent in attempting to collect on the account and admitting that it was a collection agency within the meaning of the Collection Agency Act, but otherwise denying the allegations of the complaint.

The Clinic, however, filed a motion to dismiss the complaint as substantially insufficient in law in the following particulars: first, that neither count of the complaint stated a cause of action; second, that the only basis for liability alleged against the Clinic was that CAT acted as the Clinic's agent in attempting to collect on the account, and the mere allegation of an agency relationship was insufficient to state a cause of action for vicarious liability; third, that a credit agency is an independent contractor and therefore the Clinic cannot be liable for the torts of CAT; * * *.

Acting on this motion, the trial court dismissed both counts of the complaint as to the Clinic on the grounds that CAT was an independent contractor and not an agent of the Clinic, and that the tortious acts alleged were beyond the scope of their agency relationship. Plaintiffs appeal from this portion of the trial court's order. The trial court also held that Count I of the complaint stated a cause of action against CAT for intentional infliction of severe emotional distress, * * *.

The threshold issue is whether the trial court erred in dismissing plaintiffs' complaint as to the Clinic on the grounds that CAT was an independent contractor and the acts allegedly committed by CAT were beyond the scope of any agency relationship between CAT and the Clinic * * *. [The court ruled that plaintiff's allegation that CAT committed the allegedly tortious acts while acting as the clinic's agent was sufficient to establish the clinic's possible vicarious liability.]

Having found that plaintiffs' complaint sufficiently alleged the Clinic's possible vicarious liability for CAT's allegedly tortious conduct, we must now consider the issues raised by the Clinic's cross-appeal relating to whether the complaint states any cause of action in tort. The first issue is whether the trial court properly found that the complaint stated a cause of action for intentional infliction of severe emotional distress. The elements of that tort are: (1) extreme and outrageous conduct, (2) intended to cause (or committed in reckless disregard of the probability of causing), (3) and causing, (4) severe emotional distress on the part of the plaintiff. Restatement (Second) of Torts § 46 (1965).

The only element that the Clinic contends is lacking here is the first, extreme and outrageous conduct. In *Public Finance Corp. v. Davis* (1976), 66 Ill.2d 85, 4 Ill.Dec. 652, 360 N.E.2d 765, our supreme court had occasion to consider the nature and content of this element in the same setting as here, that of debt collection. Noting that the plaintiff in *Public Finance* admitted owing the debt, the court found that the collection agency's conduct was not so extreme and outrageous as to constitute a basis for recovery under the theory alleged. Except for a single impermissible act, the complaint reflected only a persistence in making telephone calls and a certain lack of sensitivity in making visits on the part of the collection agency. The court specifically noted that in cases permitting actions for severe emotional distress to proceed, the debtors had alleged "the use of abusive and vituperative language, shouting and railing at the debtor, repeated threats of arrest and ruination of credit, threats to appeal to the debtor's employer to endanger his employment and accusations of dishonesty." *Id.* at 92, 4 Ill.Dec. at 655, 360 N.E.2d 765 at 768.

In the instant case, we note that the complaint does not unequivocally affirm or deny the existence of the debt. Nevertheless, and in any event, because so many of the allegations which the court specifically noted were absent from the complaint in *Public Finance* are present here, we find that plaintiffs have adequately stated a cause of action. Unlike the plaintiffs in *Public Finance,* plaintiffs have alleged not only a veritable multitude of telephone calls, but also the frequent use of profane, obscene, and abusive language therein. They have also alleged threats to "embarrass" the purported debtor's husband with his employer, to garnish his wages, and to put him and the purported debtor in jail. Thus, the abusive and threatening language which the court in *Public Finance* repeatedly noted was absent from the complaint is present here. In addition, plaintiffs have alleged unwarranted communications with the purported debtor's husband at his place of employment and with the purported debtor's minor daughter. Similar allegations were noted by the court in *Bureau of Credit Control v. Scott* (1976), 36 Ill.App.3d 1006, 1007, 345 N.E.2d 37, in finding that a cause of action for intentional infliction of severe emotional distress had been stated. We hold that the trial court properly found that Count I of plaintiffs' complaint states a cause of action.

Notes

1. Was the conduct of CAT (in *Sherman*) worse than the conduct of FMCC (in *Hamilton*)? Can you reconcile the cases?

2. In *Sherman,* the collector threatened to have the debtor sent to jail for not paying the debt. Could that be done? See Chapter 9, Part D, infra. If not, is it improper to make the threat? Could the creditor's lawyer threaten criminal prosecution to collect a debt?

3. Would the activities of the witnesses who testified in the Congressional hearings on the FDCPA, reproduced at pages 443–447, supra, be tortious?

Problem 3

Sally Consumer owned a small dog, Rover, which was injured when it was struck by a car. She took Rover to Dr. Zorba, a local veterinarian, and Rover recovered while in the doctor's care. Dr. Zorba was fussy about his fees, however, and he demanded cash before he would release Rover. Sally offered to work out a payment schedule, but Zorba refused. Instead, he threatened to "do away with your dog" unless he got cash. Has he committed a tort?

Problem 4

In 1985, Myron Newby was treated at Swedish Hospital in Seattle. Myron and his wife, Nada, signed a note to the hospital for $23.35. In 1987, the Newbys moved to Alaska, where Mr. Newby died in 1989.

Later that year, Nada Newby found work at Presbyterian Hospital in Palmer, Alaska, as a cook. Merritt Long was a professional debt collector in Palmer. He was also on the Board of Trustees of Presbyterian Hospital. As a debt collector, he had received an assignment of the debt the Newbys owed to Swedish Hospital. Long contacted Nada Newby and told her that if she did not make arrangements to pay the Swedish bill, it would mean her job. He also presented Nada Newby's case to the Board of Presbyterian Hospital, and the Board passed a resolution which required Nada to pay her debt to Swedish Hospital within 30 days or be dismissed from the staff of Presbyterian Hospital. Thirty days later, Nada Newby was fired. Does she have a case against either Long or Presbyterian Hospital? On what theory?

FERNANDEZ v. UNITED ACCEPTANCE CORP.

Court of Appeals of Arizona, 1980.
125 Ariz. 459, 610 P.2d 461.

O'CONNOR, JUDGE.

The appellees were successful as plaintiffs in a trial to the court obtaining judgment against appellant in the amounts of $2,500.00 general damages for invasion of privacy and $750.00 for attorneys fees, plus interest and costs of suit. A timely appeal was filed by the appellant, United Acceptance Corporation.

The complaint was filed August 23, 1976, by Alvaro Fernandez and Nora Fernandez, his wife, against International Spas, Inc. and United Acceptance Corporation. Nora Fernandez had entered into a retail installment contract with International Spas, Inc. to obtain a health spa membership for $350.00 plus 18% interest. The contract price was payable in 24 monthly installments of $16.50 each with an acceleration clause in the event of a default. International Spas, Inc. agreed in the contract to "maintain facilities and personnel to serve the reasonably anticipated requests of members for service throughout the entire term of the agreement." The membership contract was subsequently assigned to United Acceptance Corporation which thereafter attempted to collect the monthly payments from Nora Fernandez. Payments were made by appellees for the months of July, August, and September, 1975, although each was made after the due date and after various written notices and telephone calls by appellant, United Acceptance Corporation. No monthly payment was received thereafter and appellant made telephone calls to Nora Fernandez' place of employment, to her residence, to her neighbors, and to her husband. Written notices were sent. Messages were left for appellee when she was not at her office. Appellees moved their residence. They also had their telephone number changed as a result of appellant's numerous calls. During November and December, 1975, appellant attempted to contact Nora Fernandez approximately every other day, without success. On January 8, 1976, Nora Fernandez telephoned appellant's office and stated she could make only small payments. She testified at trial that on January

8, 1976, appellant's representative threatened to repossess her automobile if she did not immediately pay $100.00.

* * *

At trial the evidence also showed that Nora Fernandez had used the spa facilities approximately three times weekly after June 13, 1975, and then less frequently until February, 1976. Nora Fernandez testified that she tried to use the Mesa spa facilities nearest her home and that the sauna there was inoperative much of the time during the first months of her membership. She also testified that various pieces of exercise equipment were generally in a state of disrepair. Nora Fernandez decided in November, 1975, that she would cancel her membership due to the poor condition of the facilities. She stated that when she advised International Spas, Inc. that she wanted to terminate her membership, she was told it could not be cancelled.

There was also testimony by appellees and another relative that the telephone calls made by appellant upset Nora Fernandez, and made her nervous at work.

The complaint was filed by Mr. & Mrs. Fernandez against United Acceptance Corporation, the appellant, for invasion of privacy and against International Spas, Inc. for breach of contract. United Acceptance Corporation counterclaimed for recovery of the balance due on the membership contract which was entered into by appellees and International Spas, Inc. and was then assigned to United Acceptance Corporation.

The trial court found that International Spas, Inc. breached its contract with Nora Fernandez by failing to maintain the premises in a suitable condition. The court also found that the conduct of United Acceptance Corporation constituted an invasion of the plaintiffs' privacy "by reason of undue harassment and misrepresentations." Damages were awarded to plaintiffs and against United Acceptance Corporation as indicated above. The court also found against United Acceptance Corporation on its counterclaim.

Appellant contends that there was insufficient evidence at the trial to support a finding of invasion of privacy by undue harassment and misrepresentation. We find there was sufficient evidence to support the trial court's finding.

This court has recognized the general principle that a creditor has a right to take reasonable measures to pursue his debtor and to persuade payment even though such steps may result in some invasion of the debtor's privacy.

However, unreasonable measures taken by a creditor in attempting to collect a debt may be an invasion of privacy. In *Rugg v. McCarty,* 173 Colo. 170, 476 P.2d 753 (1970), the creditor repeatedly called and wrote the debtor demanding payment. The creditor also threatened to garnish the debtor's wages, but knew or should have known that it could not garnish her wages. In finding that the creditor invaded the debtor's right of privacy, the court explained:

> When *unreasonable action* in pursuing a debtor is taken, which foreseeably will probably result in extreme mental anguish, embarrassment, humiliation or mental suffering and injury to a person possessed of *ordinary sensibilities,* under the same or similar circumstances, then such conduct falls within the forbidden area and a claim for invasion of privacy may be asserted. * * * It is not intended by this rule to curtail legitimate persuasion toward settlement of debtor accounts, as we recognize that private debt settlement is a desirable end in the field of commerce. The rule simply draws the line beyond which a creditor must employ legal remedies to collect from his debtor and may not resort to self-help by means of oppressive conduct amounting to unlawful intimidation.

476 P.2d at 755–56 (emphasis supplied).

* * *

In this case it is our opinion there is sufficient evidence on which the trial court could find that the conduct of appellant constituted an invasion of the appellees' right of privacy. An agent of appellant threatened to repossess appellees' automobile if the sum of $100.00 was not paid forthwith. The appellant knew or should have known it had no lawful right at that time to repossess appellees' automobile. In addition, a large number of telephone calls to appellee's place of employment and to neighbors were made by appellant. The trial court could have determined on the basis of these facts that the actions of United Acceptance Corporation were unreasonable and constituted an invasion of the appellee's right of privacy.

* * *

The Judgment is affirmed.

Notes

1. Is the privacy theory really any different from that of intentional infliction of emotional distress? In the *Champlin* case, supra, the plaintiff had included in her complaint a count for invasion of privacy. In a footnote, the court noted that "this facet of her appeal is moot because we are of the opinion that in establishing a violation of her right of privacy, [plaintiff] would have had to satisfy the requirements of [Restatement (Second) of Torts] § 46." 478 A.2d at 988.

2. If the two theories are basically the same, can you reconcile the cases? Was the conduct of United Acceptance Corp. in *Fernandez* any worse than the conduct of Ford Motor Credit in *Hamilton?*

3. Courts have sometimes applied yet other tort theories in debt collection cases. See, e.g., Dawson v. Associates Financial Services, 215 Kan. 814, 529 P.2d 104 (1974) (outrage); Duty v. General Finance Co., 154 Tex. 16, 273 S.W.2d 64 (1954) (unreasonable collection efforts). As a practical matter, however, the types of facts the plaintiff needs to prove to establish a claim are similar for each theory. Do you see any advantage in using one theory or another?

SECTION C. THE FAIR DEBT COLLECTION PRACTICES ACT (FDCPA)

Congress responded to repeated complaints of collection abuse by enacting the Fair Debt Collection Practices Act (FDCPA) in 1977 (effective March 20, 1978). The FDCPA was codified as Title VIII of the Consumer Credit Protection Act (CCPA), and is the only federal statute dealing specifically with debt collection problems. You will find it in your statutory supplement.

However, FDCPA applies *only* to third party collectors, and does not apply to collection efforts by the original creditors. In other words, collection tactics by original lenders and credit sellers are not restricted by this statute. It is directed primarily at the efforts of those who collect debts as their principal occupation, not those who lend or sell and then (incidentally) collect. Thus, FDCPA probably affects about 10% of collection activity.

The FDCPA is written in laundry list form; it prohibits a vast array of specific debt collection practices within a smaller number of general groupings. Read sections 805 through 808, and then read the following cases.

JETER v. CREDIT BUREAU, INC.

United States Court of Appeals, Eleventh Circuit, 1985.
760 F.2d 1168.

On Petition for Rehearing

Anderson, Circuit Judge

* * *

Appellant Jeter appeals the district court's grant of summary judgment in favor of appellee Credit Bureau, Inc. ("Credit Bureau"), in Jeter's suit under the Fair Debt Collection Practices Act ("FDCPA"), 15 U.S.C.A. § 1692. 584 F.Supp. 973. With regard to Jeter's claims under 15 U.S.C.A. § 1692e ("False or misleading representations"), we hold that the district court applied an improper legal standard and erred in granting summary judgment to Credit Bureau. We agree with the district court's grant of summary judgment in favor of Credit Bureau with regard to Jeter's claim under 15 U.S.C.A. § 1692d ("Harassment or abuse"). Thus, we affirm in part, reverse in part, and remand for proceedings not inconsistent with this opinion.

I. Facts and Procedural Background

Credit Bureau operates a debt collection agency subject to the FDCPA. Credit Bureau attempts to collect money on behalf of creditors who refer accounts (*i.e.*, alleged debts) to Credit Bureau for collection. One of Credit Bureau's clients during the time period preceding this lawsuit was Associated Consumers Club ("Associated Consumers"). Sometime prior to October 25, 1983, Jeter incurred what Associated

Consumers believed was a valid legal debt with Associated Consumers. On October 25, 1983, Jeter's account was referred by Associated Consumers to Credit Bureau for collection. On March 4, 1983, Credit Bureau sent Jeter a letter which reads as follows:

> Take notice that the above creditor claims you are indebted to him as shown.

> Although duly demanded, the same has not been paid. You have ignored our previous contacts.

> Therefore, you are hereby notified that unless satisfactory arrangements are made within five (5) days from this date, we will recommend to our client, suit and subsequent action (judgment, garnishment, levy, and/or attachment proceedings) may be instigated against you by their attorneys.

> Respond now and avoid the necessity of further action. An envelope has been enclosed for your convenience.

After March 4, and prior to April 7, 1983, neither Credit Bureau nor Associated Consumers took any further action with regard to Jeter's account. Jeter did not respond to the letter during this time period. On April 7, 1983, Credit Bureau sent Jeter another letter which reads as follows:

> This is our final notice to you before recommending that our client give the account to their attorney for legal action.

> Although it may cause you embarrassment, inconvenience and further expense, we will do so if the entire balance is not in this office within the next five days.

> To insure proper credit, please return this notice with your payment in the envelope enclosed.

> Attend to it now—This is a final notice.

Neither Credit Bureau nor Associated Consumers took any action with regard to Jeter's account subsequent to the April 7, 1983, letter.

Sometime prior to May 11, 1983, Jeter hired a lawyer, Elizabeth Leonard. On May 11, 1983, Ms. Leonard sent a letter on Jeter's behalf to Credit Bureau stating Jeter's position that she owed no money to Associated Consumers. A copy of the letter was sent to Associated Consumers. Thereafter, Credit Bureau determined that the collection of Jeter's account was impractical, closed its files, and made no further contact with Jeter.

On June 16, 1983, Jeter sued Credit Bureau in the federal district court for the Northern District of Georgia claiming violations of the FDCPA. First, Jeter claimed that as a consequence of Credit Bureau's letters and its subsequent inaction, Credit Bureau had violated 15 U.S. C.A. § 1692e(5) for "threat[ening] to take any action that cannot legally be taken or that is not intended to be taken" and § 1692e(10) for using "any false representation or deceptive means to collect or attempt to collect any debt * * *." * * *

After limited discovery, the district court, responding to Credit Bureau's motion for summary judgment and Jeter's motion for partial summary judgment, granted summary judgment to Credit Bureau on all issues. This appeal ensued.

* * *

II. APPLICABLE LEGAL STANDARD

The district court held that in determining whether the FDCPA has been violated the court was obligated to "decide whether a 'reasonable consumer' would be deceived, mislead [sic], or harassed by the letters at issue in this case." Relevant administrative adjudications and case law under the Federal Trade Commission Act ("FTC Act"), 15 U.S.C.A. § 41, et seq., upon which we rely by analogy, and persuasive authority under the FDCPA lead us to the conclusion that the district court applied an improper standard.

Section 5 of the FTC Act declares unlawful all "unfair or deceptive acts or practices in commerce." 15 U.S.C.A. § 45(a)(1). An act or practice is deceptive or unfair under § 5 if it has the tendency or capacity to deceive. The FTC Act was enacted to protect unsophisticated consumers, not only "reasonable consumers" who could otherwise protect themselves in the market place. * * *

* * * The FTC and the federal courts have consistently held that it is a deceptive practice to falsely represent that unpaid debts would be referred to a lawyer for immediate legal action. In these cases, consistent with the legal standard in other actions under § 5, the FTC has looked not to the "reasonable consumer," but to a less sophisticated consumer and whether the debt collection practice has a tendency or capacity to deceive.

The above discussion indicates that, prior to the passage of the FDCPA, the FTC had protected unsophisticated consumers from debt collection practices which have a tendency or capacity to deceive. Credit Bureau argues that the FTC jurisprudence under § 5 is irrelevant to litigation under the FDCPA. Our review of the authorities leads us to precisely the opposite conclusion. In its "findings and declaration of purpose" incorporated in the FDCPA, Congress found that despite prior FTC enforcement in the area "[t]here is abundant evidence of abusive, deceptive and unfair debt collection practices by many debt collectors. * * * Existing laws and procedures for redressing these injuries are inadequate to protect consumers." 15 U.S.C.A. § 1692(a), (b). The legislative history echoes these purposes and concerns. S.Rep. No. 95–382, 95th Cong., 1st Sess., *reprinted in* 1977 U.S.Code Cong. & Ad.News 1695, 1697 ("The committee believes that the serious and widespread abuses in this area and the inadequacy of existing State and Federal laws make this legislation necessary and appropriate"). It would be anomalous for the Congress, in light of its belief that existing state and federal law was inadequate to protect consumers, to have intended that the legal standard under the FDCPA be *less* protective of consumers than under the existing "inadequate" legislation. We are not prepared to adopt such an anomalous interpretation of the FDCPA. As the Alaska Supreme Court aptly described the FDCPA's relationship to prior consumer protection legislation:

> The [FDCPA] *expands* already existing Federal Trade Commission jurisdiction over unfair or deceptive acts and practices of collection agencies; it is not written on a clean slate. The Federal Trade Commission's prior exercise of jurisdiction in this area is entitled to great weight, and leads to the conclusion that the new Act merely supplements the [FTC Act] * * *.

State v. O'Neill Investigations, Inc., 609 P.2d 520, 530 (emphasis in original).

In light of the purposes of the FDCPA, the general FTC jurisprudence under § 5, and the prior FTC enforcement in the debt collection area, we conclude that the district court erred in judging Credit Bureau's actions by reference to the "reasonable consumer." Our position is supported by a majority of the federal courts to address this question.

* * *

III. FALSE OR MISLEADING REPRESENTATIONS?

Jeter claims that the letter sent by Credit Bureau violated 15 U.S. C.A. §§ 1692e(5) and (10). These subsections provide:

> A debt collector may not use any false, deceptive, or misleading representation or means in connection with the collection of any debt. Without limiting the general application of the foregoing, the following conduct is a violation of this section:
>
> *   *   *   *   *   *   *   *   *
>
> (5) The threat to take any action that cannot legally be taken or that is not intended to be taken.
>
> *   *   *   *   *   *   *   *   *
>
> (10) The use of any false representation or deceptive means to collect or attempt to collect any debt or to obtain information concerning a consumer.

Jeter has presented two theories for relief under subsection (5). First, Jeter claims that Credit Bureau's letters indicate that it would recommend legal action upon the expiration of the five-day period referred to in the letters or shortly thereafter and, as such, amounted to threats to take actions which were not intended to be taken. Second, Jeter claims that Credit Bureau *never* intended to recommend legal action. Jeter also maintains that the letters, individually and/or collectively, were deceptive within the meaning of subsection (10). We will discuss in turn Jeter's two theories for relief under subsection (5), and then her claim under subsection (10).

A. *Claim Under Subsection (5)*

Subsection (5) of § 1692e does not require application of the legal standard developed in Part II, *supra*. The subsection (5) issue is simply whether or not Credit Bureau *intended* to take the action threatened.

Thus, subsection (5) requires proof of a fact which amounts to a *per se* violation of § 1692e. The sophistication, or lack thereof, of the consumer is irrelevant to whether Credit Bureau "threat[ened] to take any action ＊ ＊ ＊ that [was] not intended to be taken."

First, we consider Jeter's claim that Credit Bureau falsely threatened to take legal action in the immediate or near future. It is undisputed in the record that Credit Bureau did not recommend legal action immediately upon the expiration of the five-day period after it sent the letters to Jeter or shortly thereafter. The district court's reliance on the fact that "[a]n officer of the defendant has stated that the defendant did, in fact, intend to recommend legal action," is not by any means dispositive with regard to whether Credit Bureau intended to recommend legal action upon the expiration of the five-day period. ＊ ＊ ＊ If one reads the letters literally, the alleged debtor is simply required to make payment to Credit Bureau within five days, and if the alleged debt is not paid, Credit Bureau will recommend suit sometime thereafter. However, a reasonable jury could read the letter as a threat to recommend legal action immediately upon the expiration of the five-day period or shortly thereafter. For instance, the first letter says that Credit Bureau would recommend legal action "unless satisfactory arrangements are made within five (5) days." The letter goes on to tell the alleged debtor to "[r]espond now and avoid the necessity of further action." A jury could have interpreted this language as indicative of a threat to recommend legal action immediately upon expiration of the five-day period, if Jeter had not paid the alleged debt. Similarly, Credit Bureau's second letter to Jeter states that Credit Bureau will recommend legal action "if the entire balance is not in this office within the next five days." The letter goes on to tell Jeter to "[a]ttend to it now ＊ ＊ ＊." In short, the jury could reasonably have found that Credit Bureau's reference to a five-day period preceding the recommendation of a lawsuit against Jeter was indicative of a threat to recommend legal action immediately upon the expiration of the five-day period or shortly thereafter if the alleged debt was not paid.

Thus, the jury has two tasks. First, it must ascertain the meaning of Credit Bureau's letters to determine just what was threatened. As indicated above, a reasonable jury may find that the letters evidence a threat to recommend legal action immediately upon expiration of the five-day period or shortly thereafter. If the jury so finds, it must then decide whether Credit Bureau intended to take such threatened action in this case. In this regard, the jury may consider Credit Bureau's assertion that at the times the letters were sent Credit Bureau intended to recommend legal action. Of course, the jury will have to consider the contrary evidence that legal action was not recommended shortly after the expiration of the five-day periods, and, in fact, was *never* recommended at all.

We turn now to Jeter's second claim under subsection (5): whether Credit Bureau *ever* intended to recommend legal action in Jeter's case.

Credit Bureau relies on the affidavit of its regional manager, Mel Center, which states the following three relevant facts:

> (1) That at the time the letters were sent, Credit Bureau intended to recommend legal action against Jeter; (2) That Credit Bureau does recommend that clients take legal action to collect debts that Credit Bureau has been unable to collect; and (3) That Credit Bureau has recommended that Associated Consumers take legal action to collect debts that Credit Bureau has been unable to collect.

In addition, Credit Bureau's partial responses to Jeter's interrogatories indicate that it does take legal action in cases like Jeter's involving small debts. On the other hand, Jeter presents the deposition of Michael Rogers, president of Associated Consumers. He testified that:

> (1) For the years 1981–83, Associated Consumers referred approximately 105–110 accounts to Credit Bureau for collection; (2) That Credit Bureau never recommended that Associated Consumers bring a lawsuit to collect a debt; (3) That Credit Bureau, not Associated Consumers, was the entity that brought legal action when it was deemed appropriate; (4) That Credit Bureau, not Associated Consumers, was the entity that made the determination as to whether legal action was appropriate; and (5) In 1983, Credit Bureau sued on approximately 15 Associated Consumers' accounts.

We conclude that there is a genuine issue of fact as to whether Credit Bureau ever intended to recommend legal action against Jeter.

* * *

B.   Claim Under Subsection (10)

We turn now to Jeter's subsection (10) claim. Here, the legal consequences of Credit Bureau's failure to recommend legal action within five days does require the application of the legal standard enunciated in Part II, *supra*.

We conclude that the district court erred in granting summary judgment to Credit Bureau. As we have indicated in Part III.A., *supra*, a reasonable jury could well have interpreted Credit Bureau's letters as threatening to take legal action immediately upon expiration of the five-day periods or shortly thereafter, if the debtor had not yet paid the alleged debt. Under subsection (10), we must consider whether the "least sophisticated consumer" would be deceived by Credit Bureau's letters, *i.e.*, whether the letters were a "deceptive means" to collect alleged debts, valid or invalid, by the use of false or deliberately ambiguous threats to recommend legal action. It may be, although we doubt it, that a "reasonable consumer" would have taken Credit Bureau's letters as empty threats to recommend legal action at some undisclosed time in the distant future; however, the fact that Jeter hired a lawyer and responded to the second letter seems to support the opposite view. In any event, we are confident that whether the "least sophisticated consumer" would construe Credit Bureau's letter as deceptive is a question for the jury. On remand, the jury should be instructed on the standard enunciated in Part II, *supra*, and allowed to determine whether, operating under that standard, Credit Bureau's letters were deceptive.

* * *

[The court determined that Credit Bureau's conduct did not constitute harassment or abuse under FDCPA.]

CONCLUSION

For the foregoing reasons, we affirm in part, reverse in part, and remand to the district court for proceedings not inconsistent with this opinion.

AFFIRMED in part, REVERSED in part, and REMANDED.

Notes

1. Note that the FDCPA applies only to professional debt collectors (including attorneys), and not to creditors who may themselves try to collect debts owed to them. Why? Are creditors less likely than professional debt collectors to engage in abusive collection practices? Should they be less accountable if they do engage in abusive practices?

2. Under § 814, the F.T.C. has authority to enforce the FDCPA. Even prior to the enactment of the FDCPA, the F.T.C. often prosecuted people who used abusive debt collection practices by using its authority under the F.T.C. Act. See 15 U.S.C.A. § 45; In re National Account Systems, Inc., 89 F.T.C. 282 (1977). For recent cases in which the F.T.C. has used its authority under the FDCPA, see United States v. Central Adjustment Bureau, 667 F.Supp. 370 (N.D.Tex.1986), aff'd, as modified 823 F.2d 880 (5th Cir.1987); United States v. ACB Sales & Service, Inc., 683 F.Supp. 734 (D.Ariz.1987).

3. Is it relevant to the court's decision that Jeter claimed not to be indebted to Associated Consumers? Should the standards by which a collection agency's conduct is judged under FDCPA be different for accurate and erroneous assertions of debtor default?

WEST v. COSTEN

United States District Court, Western District of Virginia, 1983.
558 F.Supp. 564.

TURK, CHIEF JUDGE.

Plaintiffs bring this class action alleging that the defendants, William C. Costen (Costen), Multi–Service Factors, Inc. (MSF), Deborah J. Kirksey (Kirksey), Janet Lee (Lee), and Virginia M. Price (Price), have violated the Fair Debt Collection Practices Act (FDCPA or the Act), 15 U.S.C. § 1692 *et seq.* The court has jurisdiction under 15 U.S.C. § 1692k(d) and 28 U.S.C. § 1331. The action is before the court on the plaintiffs' motion for partial summary judgment on the issues of liability and on the defendants' motion for summary judgment.

* * *

* * *

On August 15, 1979, six individual plaintiffs (West, Walker, Jackson, Dawson, Spangler, and Preston) filed this suit as a class action under the FDCPA seeking actual and statutory damages for themselves and their class and subclass for an alleged pattern of illegal collection practices by the defendants.

* * *

The plaintiffs are all natural persons who were living in or near Roanoke at the time of their dealings with the defendants. Except for Spangler, the plaintiffs either owed, or at one time owed, the debts which the defendants attempted to collect for various creditors. Plaintiff-intervenor Dent denies owing the debt on which collection was attempted from her and her son. The defendants' collection attempts which are the subject of the case *sub judice* all occurred between September, 1978 and January, 1980.

MSF was a Pennsylvania corporation which was licensed to do business in Virginia. Costen was the president of MSF. His job was to obtain new accounts from merchants and retailers. As part of his compensation, Costen received ten percent of the amount that MSF earned from the accounts that he personally sold. Jeffrey P. Johnson was the vice president and secretary of MSF. Karen Mayberry was MSF's treasurer. These same individuals also served as directors of the corporation.

MSF's individual collection agents were paid on a commission basis only; they received no salary. Robert Shisler, MSF's office manager, was responsible for recruiting and training new collection agents, as well as for setting and computing their commissions. MSF apparently had no formal training for its "commissioned collection agents," however. Instead, they learned their collection methods on an informal basis from other individual collectors. But MSF's collection agents were told that they must comply with the FDCPA, and FTC rules concerning debt collection practices were posted on the office walls where they worked.

Most of the debts that MSF attempted to collect were dishonored checks. After MSF obtained an account, the creditor would deliver the bad checks to the corporation. A work card was then prepared from each check. A carbon copy of the work card was kept in a master file and the hard copy was distributed to the individual collectors. However, prior to the individual collectors taking any action themselves, a secretary would send the debtors a letter advising them that they had a check outstanding, who it was to, and the amount. If the debtor did not respond to the initial letter within two weeks, the individual collectors would then attempt collections. The individual collectors would first mail printed forms demanding payment by a specified time. Then, if the forms did not work, they would make telephone calls to the debtors. MSF's collection agents sometimes made personal visits to the debtor's residence. All collection efforts were to be noted on the hard copy of the work card. If a check was paid, it would be returned to the client, along with the amount of the check less MSF's commission, and the work card destroyed. If the check could not be collected, it would be returned to the creditor and the work card destroyed.

MSF would receive between thirty and fifty percent of the amount of the check collected for its client. The person who sold the account, usually Costen, would receive ten percent of MSF's share, and the individual collector would receive twenty percent. Furthermore, as a standard practice, MSF always attempted to collect a $15 service charge on each bad check, regardless of the amount of the check. If the $15 service charge was collected in full, the individual collector received $7; the person who garnered the account (usually Costen) received $.75; the office manager received $1; and the balance would go to MSF for general operating expenses.

4. THE PARTIES' CONTENTIONS

The named plaintiffs allege that they have suffered extreme emotional distress, embarrassment, and humiliation as the results of the defendants' collection efforts. They contend that the defendants violated the FDCPA by: (1) communicating with third parties concerning the collection of debts in violation of 15 U.S.C. § 1692c(b); (2) threatening that criminal prosecution was pending or that warrants were to be issued when such was not intended or could not be done legally in violation of 15 U.S.C. § 1692e(4) and (5); (3) failing to comply with the notice and validation of debt procedures required by 15 U.S.C. § 1692g(a); (4) collecting service charges not expressly authorized by the agreement creating the debt or permitted by law in violation of 15 U.S.C. § 1692f(1); and (5) misrepresenting the amount of the debt owed and the legality of receiving service charges as compensation for collecting debts in violation of 15 U.S.C. § 1692e(2)(A) and (B).

* * *

* * * MSF is clearly a "debt collector" within the meaning of the Act because it is a "person" who uses the telephones and mails in the business of collecting debts owed or due or asserted to be owed or due another. As a corporation can act only through its agents, MSF may be held liable for the violations of its collection agents.

Kirksey, Lee, and Price are also "debt collectors" under the FDCPA because they regularly collected or attempted to collect directly debts owed or due or asserted to be owed or due another. Thus, these individual debt collectors can also be held liable for violating the provisions of the FDCPA.

* * *

8. THIRD PARTY CONTACTS

Like other sections of the FDCPA, its prohibition against certain third party contacts by debt collectors is designed to protect a consumer's reputation and privacy, as well as to prevent loss of jobs resulting from a debt collector's communication with a consumer's employer concerning the collection of a debt. For the purpose of this section only, the FDCPA defines the term "consumer" to include "the consumer's spouse, parent (if the consumer is a minor), guardian, executor, or administrator." 15 U.S.C. § 1692c(d). Thus, partial summary judgment may be granted against a debt collector for third party contacts if the undisputed facts show that the debt collector, without the consumer's consent or court permission, communicated with third parties, (not including the consumer's spouse, attorney, or parents if the consumer was a minor), about the debt.

West alleges that on July 2, 1979, Kirksey came to her house and, in the presence of a third party, threatened to have an arrest warrant issued unless West made payments on her debts. West later admitted, however, that another woman, not Kirksey, talked with her about her debts in the presence of a third party, Pat Cundiff. In addition, Kirksey did call Cundiff more than once in attempting to contact West. But the record is unclear concerning Kirksey's reasons for contacting Cundiff more than once; thus, the court is unable to conclude that Kirksey violated section 1692c(b) by failing to comply with section 1692b(3). Moreover, Kirksey testified that she would seek location information only when she talked with someone other than the consumer; she would not discuss the debt. Consequently, partial summary judgment is denied as to the liability of Kirksey and MSF to West for third party contacts.

Concerning Walker's third party contact claim, on November 11, 1978, Lee spoke with Walker's grandparents and uncle about Walker's debt. There is no evidence in the record to dispute this. Consequently, partial summary judgment is granted in favor of Walker as to the liability of Lee and MSF for unlawful third party contacts.

Jackson and Preston both allege that Price spoke to their families about their debts and made threats of criminal prosecution. Jackson stated that on December 4, 1978, Price told Jackson's sister about the debts, and that on "several occasions," Price attempted to persuade members of Jackson's family to make payments by telling them that Jackson would be imprisoned unless the payments were made. Preston testified that Price told Preston's wife than an arrest warrant would be issued if he did not pay his debts. Preston was not aware of any communication between Price and anyone other than Preston's wife about the debts, however.

Price testified that she did not recall talking with Jackson's mother about anything except trying to locate Jackson. She admitted, however, that she may have talked with a consumer's parents about the debt if they brought it up first. In light of this testimony and the specific facts in Jackson's affidavit and deposition, the court finds that it is undisputed that Price, without Jackson's consent, spoke with third parties about Jackson's debt. Accordingly, partial summary judgment is granted in favor of Jackson and against Price and MSF for unlawful third party contacts.

* * *

9. THREATS OF ARREST

* * * [A] debt collector's threat to have a consumer arrested unless a debt is paid would violate section 1692e(5) if the debt collector could not lawfully do so or did not intend to take such action. Either of these violations would violate section 1692e(4) as well. And a debt collector's representation or implication that nonpayment of a debt will result in the creditor having the consumer arrested or imprisoned would also violate section 1692e(5) if the creditor did not intend to do so or could not legally take such action. Therefore, in the case *sub judice,* partial summary judgment will be granted as to liability for violation of section 1692e(4) and (5) when there is no genuine issue of material fact as to any of these elements.

On June 18, 1979, West received a payment demand notice from MSF which was signed by Kirksey and on which was written the notation "criminal warrant pending." Furthermore, according to West, when she inquired at MSF about the debts, Kirksey told her that Kirksey would have a warrant issued for her arrest unless she paid weekly amounts towards her debts. In late June or early July, 1979, West received another notice from MSF which stated that she should call Kirksey "immediately to prevent issuance of warrant on your worthless check." Finally, West stated that Kirksey came to her home on July 2, 1979, and threatened to issue a warrant for her arrest unless she made the payments.

Kirksey does not dispute that she would call consumers and tell them that there were warrants outstanding on their dishonored checks. She admits that she wrote "criminal warrant pending" on the demand notice sent to West. But Kirksey also testified that she told consumers that their *creditors* would have them arrested if they did not pay their debts. Contrary to West's contentions, a reasonable inference may be drawn from this evidence that Kirksey did not tell West that she would have an arrest warrant issued herself unless West paid the alleged debts. So, even assuming that a debt collector cannot lawfully seek an arrest warrant against a consumer for writing a bad check, the uncertainty as to whether Kirksey threatened to personally obtain a warrant against West precludes partial summary judgment against Kirksey for violation of section 1692e(5). Furthermore, plaintiffs' motion for partial summary judgment as to Kirksey's liability under section 1692e(4) must likewise be denied. Although Kirksey's representations implied that a creditor would have West arrested unless she paid her dishonored checks, such action by a creditor is lawful and the evidence conflicts as to whether West's creditors intended to take such action. West was never arrested for the dishonored checks that Kirksey attempted to collect. Yet Kirksey knew that Kroger, one of West's creditors, had a warrant outstanding against West because she was told this by a Kroger employee. Although Kirksey attempted to collect bad checks written by West to merchants other than Kroger, a reasonable inference may be drawn from the record that Kirksey believed that

Kroger intended to have West arrested unless West paid her debt. Thus, it is not perfectly clear that Kirksey's handwritten notations violated section 1692e(4). Accordingly, partial summary judgment is denied as to Kirksey's liability to West for threats of arrest.

The facts concerning Walker's claim against Lee are undisputed. On November 18, 1978, Lee told Walker's grandparents and uncle that Walker would be arrested if the debt was not paid. Although Walker paid one debt, on November 20, 1978, Lee called her again and threatened criminal prosecution unless she paid another debt by November 22. Lee also threatened to have a warrant issued for Walker's arrest if Walker did not pay the debt by December 4, 1976. Walker was never arrested for passing bad checks, however.

Lee has failed to offer any evidence to dispute Walker's testimony. Thus, it is undisputed that Lee threatened to personally have Walker arrested unless the debts were paid. Walker was never arrested for passing bad checks and Lee has not presented any evidence that she intended to have Walker arrested. Nor is there any evidence that a creditor intended to have Walker arrested unless she paid her debts. Because there is no genuine issue that Lee threatened Walker with arrest when neither Lee nor a creditor intended to take such action, partial summary judgment is granted in favor of Walker as to Lee's liability to her under section 1692e(4) and (5).

* * *

10. VALIDATION OF DEBTS

Among other things, 15 U.S.C. § 1692g(a) requires a debt collector to give a consumer written notice, either in the initial communication or within five days thereafter, of the amount of the debt, the name of the creditor to whom the debt is owed, and

> a statement that if the consumer notifies the debt collector in writing within the thirty-day period [after receipt of the notice] that the debt, or any portion thereof, is disputed, the debt collector will obtain verification of the debt or a copy of a judgment against the consumer and a copy of such verification or judgment will be mailed to the consumer by the debt collector. * * *

If the consumer disputes the debt or requests validation in writing, the debt collector must cease collection efforts until he verifies the debt and mails the verification to the consumer. 15 U.S.C. § 1692g(b).

The named plaintiffs have presented evidence that they never received any written notice of their rights to verify or to dispute the validity of the debts. The defendants did include as Exhibit 2 to their answers to request for production of documents what appears to be a typewritten version of the notice required by section 1692g(a). But no named plaintiff ever received such a writing. Indeed, at their depositions, neither Kirksey nor Price were able to recall any forms supplied or used by MSF other than the types received by the plaintiffs. * * *

In addition, no evidence has been presented to the court that even suggests that MSF ever sent the required notice to anyone from whom it attempted to collect a debt. Defendants have produced forms that contain the required notice. But there is no evidence whatsoever that these forms were mailed to consumers either at the initial communication or within five days thereafter. On the other hand, there is ample evidence in the attachments to the affidavits of the named plaintiffs, plaintiffs' responses to defendants' request for production of documents, and the exhibits introduced at the class certification and preliminary injunction hearing that MSF regularly disregarded the requirement of written notice. Accordingly, partial summary judgment is granted in favor of the class members on the issue of MSF's liability for a pattern of violations of section 1692g(a).

11. SERVICE CHARGES

The evidence shows without question that MSF regularly collected, or attempted to collect, a $15 service charge on each bad check, regardless of the amount of the check. The plaintiffs contend that this practice violated the FDCPA by collecting an amount that was not expressly authorized by the agreements creating the debts or permitted by law, and by misrepresenting the amounts of the debts and the legality of the compensation which the defendants could receive.

A. Collection of Amounts in Addition to Principal Obligations

Section 1692f(1) provides that a debt collector may not use any unfair or unconscionable means to collect or attempt to collect any debt, such as:

> The collection of any amount (including any interest, fee, charge, or expense incidental to the principal obligation) unless such amount is expressly authorized by the agreement creating the debt or permitted by law.

(emphasis added). The court is without doubt that a service charge such as that imposed by MSF is a "fee, charge, or expense incidental to the principal obligation . . ." * * *

The lawfulness of a service charge under section 1692f(1) depends on whether the charge is "expressly authorized by the agreement creating the debt or permitted by law." Turning to the first test, the court expressly found after evidence and argument on the preliminary injunction in this case that "this charge is not expressly authorized by the agreement creating the underlying debt." Order entered January 17, 1980, p. 3. Although this finding was for the purpose of injunctive relief only, because the defendants have made no contrary representation, the court finds for the purpose of damages relief that the service charges collected by MSF were not expressly authorized by the agreements creating the underlying debts.[7]

---

7. A debt collector might argue that he was collecting a charge "expressly authorized by the agreement creating the debt" in the following situation. The debt collector enters into an agreement with a retail grocery store to provide collection service

Thus, MSF's collection of service charges is lawful under section 1692f(1) only if the charges are "permitted by law." Plaintiffs argue that because no Virginia or federal statute or other law authorizes the practice, the charges cannot be said to be "permitted by law." The defendants counter this thrust by "the fact that [the practice] is not prohibited by Virginia law." In other words, the defendants argue that the very absence of any statutory authority concerning service charges justifies the practice because such charges are at least not prohibited by law. As defendants correctly point out, resolution of this issue depends on the interpretation of the phrase "permitted by law." In turn, interpretation of this phrase can only be done in context with the entire provision.

* * *

But Virginia law neither expressly permits nor expressly prohibits a third party debt collector from collecting add-on fees. Thus, if valid under state contract law, an agreement relative to such fees would be permitted because it would not be expressly prohibited by state law. But when, as here, the agreements creating the debts did not expressly authorize the fee, the question is whether Virginia's silence on this specific issue constitutes legal permission to collect the fee. The court holds that it does not. In the context of this case, the court interprets section 1692f(1) to mean that if state law does not expressly permit or prohibit a debt collector from collecting a service charge in addition to the amount of a dishonored check, then such charge is lawful only if the agreement creating the debt expressly authorizes it. Simply stated, "permitted by law" is different from "not prohibited by law." Permission requires an affirmative authorization, not just indulgent silence. So the fact that Virginia does not expressly prohibit such charges does not mean that state law permits them in the absence of an agreement providing for such; rather, it means the contrary.[8] Therefore, the

on its past-due checks. As part of the agreement the debt collector will receive $15 for each check collected. In turn, the grocery is to post a sign notifying its customers that their checks are now being collected by the particular debt collector and that there will be a $15 service charge for all returned checks. The debt collector then attempts to collect the amount of the dishonored check plus the $15 service charge. Pursuant to the agreement between the grocery and debt collector, once the check is collected, the grocery would receive the amount of the check and the debt collector would keep the $15 service charge. Assuming that state law permitted collection fees to be added-on to the amount of the debt itself, whether the service charge had been properly provided for by the posting of a sign notifying the creditor's customers of its agreement with the debt collector would be determined under state contract law. Regardless, there is no

evidence in the case *sub judice* that MSF entered into any such agreement with its clients. * * *

8. This is consistent with the manner in which Virginia law provides for the imposition of service charges for bad checks in other situations. For instance, a state court, upon a determination that the plaintiff has prevailed in a civil action to recover the sum payable on a bad check drawn by the defendant, "shall add the following amounts, as costs, to the amount due the plaintiff for the check: (i) the sum of ten dollars to defray the cost of processing the returned check * * *." Va.Code § 6.1–118.1 (1979 Repl.Vol.). A small loan licensee is prohibited from adding additional charges for services except insurance premiums paid by the licensee and "a handling fee not to exceed ten dollars for each check returned to the licensee because the drawer had no account or insufficient

court holds that the service charges collected by Multi–Service were not "permitted by law" as that phrase is used in the FDCPA.

* * *

Accordingly, partial summary judgment is granted against MSF in favor of Walker, Preston, Jackson, and the members of the subclass for liability under section 1692f(1). * * *

* * *

12. PIERCING THE CORPORATE VEIL

* * *

Although Costen is a "debt collector" for the purpose of the court's subject matter jurisdiction over him pursuant to the FDCPA, there is no allegation or evidence that he personally violated any provisions of the Act and, unlike MSF, he cannot be held vicariously liable for the statutory violations of MSF's collection agents. An officer of a corporation cannot be held personally liable for the wrongful conduct of the corporation's employee's absent personal involvement with the conduct.

But not only was Costen MSF's President, he was also its dominant shareholder. Costen originally owned 83 of 98 outstanding shares of the corporate stock and he maintained a majority interest as more shares were issued. * * *

* * *

Thus, the court concludes that Costen has misused the corporate form and that justice requires that MSF's corporate form be disregarded and liability imposed upon Costen. Therefore, the plaintiffs' motion for partial summary judgment is granted as to issue of Costen's liability under the FDCPA. Accordingly, Costen is liable to the plaintiffs to the same extent as MSF is liable to the plaintiffs.

Accordingly, the claims for which partial summary judgment have been denied and the issues of damages remain for trial.

IT IS SO ORDERED.

Notes

1. The story of Katie West and the other plaintiffs did not end with the ruling in this case. As the court noted, Costen had filed a petition in Chapter 13 of the Bankruptcy Code on May 4, 1981, while the West suit was pending. The FDCPA suit ended in August, 1985; a judgment was entered against Costen in the amount of $9893.26 ($1500 damages and $8393.26 attorneys' fees). Meanwhile, Costen was proceeding under a Chapter 13 plan which provided payments to secured creditors, but essentially left unsecured creditors, including the West plaintiffs, little or nothing. The bankruptcy court approved a final payment under the plan, along with a discharge of unsecured claims in May, 1986. This order was

funds in the payor bank." Va.Code § 6.1–278 (1982 Cum.Supp.). * * * In light of these express statutory authorizations for the collection of service charges for bad checks in certain circumstances, the court concludes that Virginia law does not permit such charges absent either express statutory authorization or agreement between the drawer and payee. Otherwise, the above statutes would be superfluous.

approved by the District Court and the United States Court of Appeals. West and the others objected to the discharge of their judgment debt on the ground that Costen had obtained money by false pretenses or false representations. See B.C. § 523(a)(2). As the District Court noted, if Costen had filed in Chapter 7 instead of Chapter 13, this debt would not have been discharged. B.C. § 727. But under Chapter 13's more liberal discharge provision, see B.C. § 1328(a), the West judgment could be discharged. MSF, Costen's collection company, had gone out of business years before. As a result, despite the ruling in the FDCPA case piercing the corporate veil and the Court's valiant attempt to preserve some assets for the West plaintiffs, it appears that they ended up with nothing. See West v. Costen, 826 F.2d 1376 (4th Cir.1987).

2. Would the plaintiffs in either Hamilton v. Ford Motor Credit Co., p. 462, supra, or Sherman v. Field Clinic, p. 467, supra, have been entitled to recover under the FDCPA? Why or why not?

3. Reconsider the bad check charge issue. All of us have seen signs at merchant outlets proclaiming that a service charge of $15 or the like will be imposed on returned checks. Are these charges enforceable? If a merchant (or a debt collector) wanted to ensure that they were, what procedure would you suggest? Is posting a sign enough?

4. According to the court, which of the following is the correct statement of the legal principle to be used in determining whether bad check charges may be collected:

     a. All charges not expressly prohibited are permitted.

     b. All charges not expressly permitted are prohibited.

     c. All charges are expressly permitted, including those which are prohibited.

     d. All charges not expressly prohibited are mandatory.

5. What about the activities of attorneys who specialize in debt collection? Attorneys are covered by FDCPA, and may have some special problems. Read FDCPA § 812.

LITTLES v. LIEBERMAN

United States District Court, Eastern District of Pennsylvania, 1988.
90 B.R. 700.

Van Antwerpen, District Judge.

[Lieberman, a practicing attorney, brought copies of a dunning letter to a creditor. The dunning letters were to be sent to several designated debtors of the creditor, but plaintiff Littles was not one of the debtors so designated. Lieberman brought them to the creditor because of delays and secretarial problems in his own office. Lieberman's letter stated "unless I receive payment in full within one week * * * I will be compelled to proceed with suit against you," and described the effect of a Sheriff's sale. Somehow, a letter with those contents on Lieberman's letterhead was sent to Littles, but without Lieberman's authority or authorized signature. Littles commenced suit, inter alia, against Lieberman under FDCPA. The court considered Lieberman's liability under FDCPA § 812, 15 U.S.C. § 1692; as follows:]

The legislative history of this section is found at 1977 U.S.Code Cong. and Admin.News p. 1699, as follows:

"*Furnishing deceptive forms*

Another common collection abuse is known colloquially as 'flat-rating.' A 'flat-rater' is one who sells to creditors a set of dunning letters bearing the letterhead of the flat-rater's collection agency and exhorting the debtor to pay the creditor at once. The creditor sends these letters to his debtors, giving the impression that a third party debt collector is collecting the debt. In fact, however, the flat-rater is not in the business of debt collection, but merely sells dunning letters.

This bill prohibits the practice of flat-rating because of its inherently deceptive nature. The prohibition on furnishing such forms does not apply, however, to printers and custom stationery sellers who innocently print or sell such forms without knowledge of their intended use."

The practice engaged in by defendant Lieberman, as described in the testimony of Fleet manager Ronald Price, fits the description of "flat-rater". The fact that defendant Lieberman is a lawyer, rather than a collection agency, is no defense for two reasons: first, that the statute itself does not specify "collection agency"; and second, that a misrepresentation by Mr. Lieberman as an officer of the court is a greater wrong than a misrepresentation by a collection agency. Form furnishing or "flat-rating" is a practice distinct from other prohibited practices. Put simply, FDCPA makes it an offense to make false or misleading representations (§ 1692e) or to permit others to use your name in a deceptive way (§ 1692j). The key phrase in § 1692j is "knowing that such form would be used to create a false belief." The letter, particularly as used in this case, is clearly designed to create a false belief, *i.e.,* that Attorney Lieberman intends to take legal action to collect the debt. If he does not, the letter is deceptive, and violates both the letter of the act and the expressed intent of the Congress.

With regard to the question of whether the typed portion of the letter constitutes a form, the *Random House College Dictionary,* 1975, gives the following definitions of the word "form":

"a set order of words, as for use in a religious ritual or in a legal document; a typical document to be used as a guide in framing others for like cases; a set, prescribed or customary order of method of doing something."

* * *

Regarding *scienter,* we have testimony by Fleet's manager, Ronald Price, showing that defendant Lieberman gave Fleet copies of the form to be addressed to specified debtors. Defendant Lieberman's name was to be signed by a Fleet employee. No authorization by defendant Lieberman or manager Price was given for sending the letter to Clara Littles. How could defendant Lieberman be blamed for its being sent to her? Simply by giving Fleet the blank form, which included his name and letterhead, he lost control of the use of his own good name. Defendant Lieberman, as an officer of the court, owes the public a duty to control the use of his professional name. His failure to do so imputes the knowledge required by § 1692j.

Notes on the Application of the FDCPA to Attorneys

1. The definition of "debt collector" in FDCPA § 803(6) includes "any person who regularly collects or attempts to collect, directly or indirectly, debts owed or due or asserted to be owed or due another * * *" As originally written, the FDCPA expressly excluded attorneys from its coverage. However, that exclusion was deleted in 1986, and attorneys must now comply with the FDCPA in their collection work. Just how far the FDCPA reaches is explained by the following:

> "There is no question that FDCPA applicability is not limited just to attorneys who make debt collection the focus of their practices. * * * The key to this definition [of 'debt collector'] is the concept of engaging in collection activities 'regularly.'

> Both the legislative history of this amendment and the case law regarding similar provisions in the Federal Consumer Credit Protection Act demonstrates that any attorney who engages in collection activities more than a handful of times per year must comply with the FDCPA. Both sides in the floor debate conceded that the amendment would make the act apply not only to those lawyers who have collection practices but also to those 'who collect on an occasional basis' and 'the small law firm which collects debts incidentally to the general practice of law.' "

Hobbs, Attorneys Must Now Comply With Fair Debt Collection Law, X Pa. J.L.—Rptr. No. 46, at 3 (Nov. 21, 1987); quoted in Littles v. Lieberman, 90 B.R. 700 (D.Pa.1988), at 707.

> "Congress has not defined 'regularly,' but the legislative history indicates that attorneys must interpret this term broadly:

>> '[t]he requirement that debt collection be done "regularly" would exclude a person who collects a debt for another in an isolated instance, but would include those who collect [debts] for others in the regular course of business.'

> Thus, any law firm collecting debts for its clients on more than an 'isolated' basis (which theoretically could mean *once*) probably falls within the language of the statute."

Sweig, Guidelines for Consumer Debt Collection by Attorneys Under the 1986 Amendment to FDCPA, 21 New Eng.L.Rev. 697, 699 (1987).

In *Littles v. Lieberman,* supra, the court held that the FDCPA applied to an attorney with a general practice, even though that practice involved only "a minor but regular practice in debt collection." 90 B.R. at 707.

2. Do the 1986 amendments mean that the F.T.C. now has the authority to investigate a law firm whom it suspects may be violating the FDCPA? Would the F.T.C. have had that authority even before the

amendments? What would prompt the F.T.C. to undertake such an investigation? See generally F.T.C. v. Shaffner, 626 F.2d 32 (7th Cir.1980).

3. Are attorneys subject to liability under state "little FTC" acts? In most states, the supreme court has the authority to regulate the practice of law. Do you think this authority might somehow prevent or preempt the legislature from regulating the conduct of attorneys? Do you see any separation of powers or other problems here?

4. In Rhode Island, a constitutional issue involving attorneys who collect debts has come up the other way around. The practice of law is defined to include "the undertaking or acting as a representative or on behalf of another person to commence, settle, compromise, adjust or dispose of any civil or criminal case or cause of action." R.I.Gen.Laws § 11–27–2. Courts had held that this applied to persons seeking payment of debts owed others. As a result, only lawyers could do debt collection work in Rhode Island; anyone else who did it was engaged in the unauthorized practice of law. The statute was challenged by a nation-wide debt collection company and was found to be an unconstitutional burden on interstate commerce. National Revenue Corp. v. Violet, 807 F.2d 285 (1st Cir.1986).

Problem 5

Ace Debt Collectors, Inc., is a nationwide debt collection agency with offices in every state. In each of its offices it maintains copies of "attorney letters." These letters were prepared by an attorney and are on the attorney's letterhead, but they are unsigned. The office manager in each of Ace's offices decides in each case when and whether the letter should be sent, and fills in the form letter with the name and address of the particular debtor involved, the amount of the debt, and the name of the client/creditor. The content of the letter is substantially the same as that used in the Little v. Lieberman case.

a. Does use of these letters violate the FDCPA? If so, who is liable?

b. Is it ethical for an attorney to allow her name to be used in this manner? Doesn't the lawyer have some obligation to investigate the facts of each case?

c. Who is the attorney's client? If the attorney has contact exclusively with Ace, is she authorized to represent the individual creditors?

Problem 6

In 1976, W.T. Grant Company filed for bankruptcy. It sold its accounts receivable to Federal Financial Corporation, a corporation formed solely for the purpose of collecting Grant's accounts. Nationwide, there were several hundred thousand accounts, many of which were long since delinquent. One of these accounts was that of Cindy Ann Kimber. After the assignment from Grant, FFC notified Kimber that the account had been transferred and that payment was overdue. A few other reminders followed, but in 1979 all contact between FFC and Kimber ceased. In 1984, FFC referred the account to an attorney for collection. The attorney contacted Kimber in 1985, and when she refused to pay, suit was filed. Kimber's lawyer got the suit dismissed because the statute of limitations had run. Kimber then sued FFC, arguing that FFC violated the FDCPA by suing or threatening to sue on consumer debts which were time-barred.

    a. FFC argues it is not a "debt collector" within the meaning of the FDCPA. What do you think?

    b. FFC argues that there is no violation because the statute of limitations is an affirmative defense which is waived if not raised by a defendant debtor, and therefore it should not be penalized for filing a time-barred suit. What result?

    c. Is it ethical for an attorney knowingly to file a suit on a claim which is barred by the statute of limitations? Does it matter that the defendant is a consumer who is not likely to know this, and who may in fact respond to the suit by paying all or part of the debt?

    d. Given that the statute of limitations must usually be raised as an affirmative defense, is it ethical for an attorney *not* to file a time-barred suit?

Problem 7

Local Credit Bureau is both a credit reporting agency and a debt collection agency. As part of its debt collection activity, it writes collection letters to defaulting debtors on company stationery which contains its full name in the letterhead. It also uses pre-printed envelopes which contain the company name in the upper left corner. In light of FDCPA §§ 807(16) and 808(8), would you advise Local to continue this practice?

Note on State Statutes

Almost all states have statutes which deal with the problem of abusive debt collections practices. Many of these state laws are carbon copies of the FDCPA, but it would be a mistake to think that they are all alike. In fact, they vary widely, and often a consumer will have rights under a state law when she does not under the FDCPA. For example, unlike the FDCPA, many state collection laws apply to the original creditor as well as to third party debt collectors. Enforcement provisions also vary. Most allow private enforcement actions, although some are limited to administrative enforcement. A few even provide for criminal sanctions.

What of the states that have no debt collection statutes? In some cases, courts have applied general consumer deceptive practices statutes ("little FTC acts") in the debt collection context. For an illustrative case, see State ex rel. Miller v. Midwest Service Bureau of Topeka, Inc., 229 Kan. 322, 623 P.2d 1343 (1981).

Chapter 8

FORECLOSING ON SECURITY

In chapter 3, we saw that a creditor's ability to get security for a consumer loan is often restricted in consumer cases. Yet despite these restrictions, creditors often take security interests in consumer collateral, most commonly in automobiles.

When the debtor defaults under the security agreement, the creditor's remedies are spelled out in Article 9 of the Uniform Commercial Code (UCC). These remedies are supplemented in many states by special consumer statutes. In this book we will not repeat all of the material typically studied in courses in Secured Transactions and the like. (If you need review, J. White & R. Summers, Uniform Commercial Code ch. 25 (3d ed. 1988), would be a good place to start.) Instead, we will focus on issues which commonly arise in consumer cases, particularly those involving automobiles.

SECTION A. UNDER WHAT CONDITIONS CAN A CREDITOR REPOSSESS?

1. REPOSSESSION—WHEN?

Although Article 9 prescribes both the debtor's and creditor's rights after default, it does not define the term "default." Instead, the events which constitute default in a particular transaction are left to the parties to define in the security agreement. Of course, in consumer cases, this means that the creditor will dictate the terms of default. Nonpayment is the most common term, and the most common cause, of default. The typical consumer security agreement will also list other events of default, including such things as failure to insure the collateral, moving the collateral out of the state, and allowing other liens to attach.

Beyond this, the security agreement will often contain an acceleration clause coupled with a so-called "insecurity" clause. Under an insecurity clause, a creditor may declare a default and accelerate the obligation when he "deems himself insecure," even though the consumer might still be current on her payments. What justification must a creditor show before it can exercise an insecurity clause? Consider the following.

SHEPPARD FEDERAL CREDIT UNION v. PALMER

United States Court of Appeals, Fifth Circuit, 1969.
408 F.2d 1369.

GEWIN, CIRCUIT JUDGE:

* * *

The crux of the dispute in the trial of this case was whether the appellant Credit Union's seizure of the appellee Palmer's automobile was legally justifiable. Palmer had borrowed money from the Credit Union to purchase the car and the latter had taken a security interest in it. The security agreement contained the following acceleration clause:

> [I]f said mortgagee shall at any time deem said mortgagor, said chattels, said debt or said security unsafe or insecure, then upon the happening of said contingencies or any of them, the whole amount herein secured remaining unpaid, is by said mortgagor admitted to be due and payable, and said mortgagee may at said mortgagee's option (notice of which option is hereby expressly waived), foreclose this mortgage by action or otherwise, and said mortgagee is hereby authorized to enter upon the premises where said goods and chattels may be, and remove and sell the same and all equity of redemption of the mortgagor therein * * *.

Although this so-called insecurity clause is drafted in the broadest possible terms, the Texas Uniform Commercial Code makes it clear that the secured party can accelerate "only if he in good faith believes that the prospect of payment or performance is impaired." Deeming itself insecure, the Credit Union in this case seized Palmer's automobile which was still under the Credit Union's control at the time of these proceedings. The primary question in the court below was whether the creditor's action stemmed from a reasonable, good-faith belief that its security was about to become impaired.

In its instructions to the jury the district court stated in part:

> Palmer is entitled to damages unless Credit Union proves by a preponderance of the evidence that it had reasonable grounds to believe that on February 9, 1967 the debt involved herein or said security was unsafe or insecure * * *.

The court emphasized this charge by repeating the substance of it in its rather brief instructions. Moreover, the first special issue out of six submitted to the jury was couched in the same terms. The charge clearly placed the burden of proof upon the Credit Union to establish the reasonableness of its conduct. However, the Texas UCC states: "The burden of establishing lack of good faith is on the party against whom the power [to accelerate] has been exercised." The error committed here is patent. Under the Texas law, the creditor is presumed to have acted in good faith. The trial court in this case turned the presumption around when it placed the burden of proof on the creditor.

When the record on appeal discloses that an error has been committed which results in a miscarriage of justice, this court must reverse even though the party prejudiced raised no objection in the court below. * * *

* * *

Palmer was a twenty-four year-old man who had joined the Air Force on May 28, 1966 for two years of service as a registered nurse. On October 11, 1966, some four and a half months after entering the service, he applied to the Credit Union for a loan. At that time his salary was $400 per month. Other than summer and part-time work, he had worked a total period of six months before entering the service. After the approval of his application, he authorized a Class E Allotment in the amount of $110.19 to be paid to the Credit Union once a month.

Palmer submitted his resignation to the Air Force on February 2, 1967, less than four months after receiving the loan. The next day he went to the Credit Union's offices and informed the appropriate officer of his resignation and of the possibility of its being accepted. He informed the officer that he was considering moving to Dallas to work. The officer then demanded the keys to the secured car and Palmer handed them over. Palmer protested that he had always been prompt in making his payments and that his nurse's license would permit him to get a job in forty-eight of the fifty states without retesting. Nevertheless, the officer retained the car keys and subsequently drove Palmer to his home. This repossession without prior notice was clearly contrary to the Defense Department's suggested Standard of Fairness which the Credit Union had adopted.[6] Subsequently, Palmer's resignation from the Air Force was accepted and he moved to Dallas where he secured a nursing job at a substantial increase in salary. In spite of the Credit Union's retention of his car, he continued to make the monthly payments fully and promptly. On May 5, 1967, Palmer filed suit in the United States District Court for the Northern District of Texas. After a full trial, the jury answered special interrogatories to the effect that the Credit Union's action had been malicious; it awarded Palmer punitive damages in the amount of $4,225 as well as actual damages.

On these facts we cannot say that proper instructions would not have altered the outcome in some substantial way. As regards this debtor, the Credit Union's determination that it was insecure was certainly erroneous; it could hardly have asked for a more conscientious and responsible debtor. However, it takes more than mere error to show unreasonableness or bad faith, not to mention malice. Thus on

---

6. Item 9 of the Standard provided in part: If the security for your loan is repossessed and sold to satisfy or reduce your debt, the following conditions will be met:

(1) You will be given reasonable notice in writing of our intention to repossess.

(2) You will be notified after repossession of your total obligation to this credit union. This will include your loan balance, interest due to date and other costs incident to repossession and sale.

the real issues the evidence was closely divided, and we think that a jury could reasonably decide either for or against liability depending on its view of the facts. Accordingly, we are of the opinion that the district court's erroneous charge on burden of proof resulted in a miscarriage of justice.

*   *   *

Reversed.

Notes

1. Do you think correcting the instruction on the burden of proof will change the result? Did the credit union honestly believe itself to be insecure when it asked Mr. Palmer to hand over the keys? Can Mr. Palmer prove the credit union was not insecure?

2. While UCC § 1–208 seems to give the creditor almost complete discretion, in fact this section was thought to have ameliorated some of the harshness of the common law approach to insecurity clauses, which at times seemed to allow a neurotic creditor to act merely on whim. But if under § 1–208 the burden of proof is on the debtor, and "good faith" is purely subjective, has anything changed?

3. In response to the problem of insecurity clauses in consumer cases, a few states have adopted special rules which change the focus. These rules place the burden on the creditor to show "significant" and identifiable insecurity. A typical statutory provision of this type is U3C § 5.109. Please read that section before reading the following case.

MEDLING v. WECOE CREDIT UNION

Supreme Court of Kansas, 1984.
234 Kan. 852, 678 P.2d 1115.

McFARLAND, JUSTICE:

This action arises from the repossession of an automobile and is brought under the Uniform Consumer Credit Code (UCCC), K.S.A. 16a–1–101 *et seq.* Plaintiff Sandra J. Medling contends defendant Wecoe Credit Union acted unlawfully in repossessing and selling her 1979 Ford Thunderbird. The credit union counterclaimed for a deficiency judgment. Following a bench trial, the district court held in favor of defendant credit union on plaintiff's petition and on defendant's counterclaim. Plaintiff appeals therefrom.

The first issue is whether there is substantial competent evidence to support the trial court's finding [that] the December, 1979, repossession of the automobile was lawful.

*   *   *

Plaintiff challenges the sufficiency of the evidence supporting the trial court's finding the defendant credit union properly declared the consumer credit transaction loan in default on the basis the prospect of payment, performance, or realization of collateral was significantly impaired.

The May 31, 1979, security agreement herein provides, in relevant part:

"EVENTS OF DEFAULT ENTITLING SECURED PARTY (THE CREDIT UNION) TO REPOSSESS. It is agreed by the parties hereto that the following events do reasonably constitute default which entitles the credit union to repossess collateral covered by this Security Agreement.

"(1) Default for ten (10) days for failure to make any payment as required by agreement with the credit union; and failure of the debtor to cure the default within twenty (20) days following the mailing of Notice of Consumers Right to Cure Default of Required Payment in the form and manner required by law;

"(2) Subsequent defaults of any required payment;

"(3) *Significant impairment of the prospect of payment by the Debtor;*

"(4) *Significant impairment of the prospect of performance by the Debtor of any of the agreements herein;*

"(5) Significant impairment of the realization of collateral by the Debtor by any of the following acts or omissions:

"(a) Failure of the Debtor to fulfill any of his agreements provided for herein;

"(b) Any warranty, representation or statement concerning the collateral made or furnished to the credit union by or on behalf of the Debtor which proves to have been false in any material respect when made or furnished;

"(c) Loss, theft, substantial damage, destruction, sale or encumbrance to or of any collateral, or the making of any levy seizure attachment thereof or thereon;

"(d) Death, insolvency, business failure, appointment of a receiver for any part of the property of assignment for the benefit of creditors by, or the commencement of any proceedings under any bankruptcy or insolvency laws by or against Debtor or any guarantor, co-maker, endorser or surety for or with Debtor.

"REPOSSESSION AND OTHER REMEDIES. Upon any such default, or any other significant impairment of collateral not herein described, the credit union may declare all obligations secured hereby immediately due and payable and shall have the remedies of a secured party under the law of this state. * * *"

K.S.A. 16a–5–109 statutorily defines and limits default for consumer credit transactions under the UCCC as follows:

"An agreement of the parties to a consumer credit transaction with respect to default on the part of the consumer is enforceable only to the extent that

"(1) the consumer fails to make a payment as required by agreement; or

"(2) *the prospect of payment, performance, or realization of collateral is significantly impaired; the burden of establishing the prospect of significant impairment is on the creditor.*" (Emphasis supplied.)

The parties agree plaintiff was current on her payments at the time default was declared and the repossession occurred in December, 1979. The trial court found the prospect of payment, performance or realization of collateral was significantly impaired and that repossession was therefore lawful pursuant to K.S.A. 16a–5–109(2).

The facts supporting such finding are as follows. On May 31, 1979, plaintiff (then Sandra J. Fuller) obtained a consumer credit loan for $6,500.00 from defendant credit union. The loan was for the purchase of a 1979 Ford Thunderbird automobile. The loan was secured by a security agreement which listed the Thunderbird as collateral along with a 1974 pickup truck. Ronald L. Fuller, plaintiff's then husband, was a cosigner of the security agreement. The purchase of the Thunderbird increased plaintiff's existing indebtedness at the credit union to $12,440.50. Interest was 12 percent per annum. Monthly payments were increased to $327.60 commencing June 30, 1979.

In May, 1979, Sandra Medling was employed by Western Electric Company at its plant in Johnson County, Kansas. The employees of this plant had established Wecoe Credit Union for their use. * * * One of the loan features of the credit union was employees could pay off their debts to the credit union by automatic payroll deductions. Plaintiff's $327.60 monthly payments were to be paid to the credit union through this automatic payroll deduction scheme.

In August, 1979, plaintiff and Ronald Fuller were divorced. A month later, September, 1979, plaintiff married Victor F. Medling. On November 27, 1979, plaintiff went to the credit union and visited with Mr. Max Erath, President of Wecoe. Plaintiff advised Mr. Erath she would be terminating her employment with Western Electric on January 4, 1980, and would then be moving to Michigan. Plaintiff further advised Mr. Erath she should be receiving an $8,000.00 tax refund and she would apply all of this to her debt. Plaintiff also wrote out her new address for Mr. Erath in Michigan as follows:

"Sandra Medling   —268–6211
7619 Monrovia Lane
Shawnee, Kansas 66216

% Arn Haynes
200 Canter Lane
Holly, Michigan"

Mr. Erath's notes of the conversation additionally reflected:

          "11–27–79   am
                        Ext.
          Sandra Fuller 6102
Payment 327.60   Loan Bal. 11209.67
          Leaving date 1–4–80
  Plans to apply approx. $8000 before Leaving.
Who has 79 Ford   She has
   "   "   74 Chev PU   He has"

Instead of terminating her employment as of January 4, 1980, plaintiff quit her Western Electric job immediately after the November 27, 1979, conversation with Mr. Erath. Upon learning plaintiff was no longer employed by Western Electric, Mr. Erath telephoned plaintiff on December 3, 1979. Plaintiff advised Mr. Erath she would come in to discuss her loan the same day but did not appear. The following day Mr. Erath again telephoned plaintiff who advised him she would be in to discuss her loan the same day. She did not appear. This same scenario occurred on December 5 and 7, 1979. Meanwhile Mr. Erath's attempts to check out the Michigan address were unsuccessful. Additionally, there were questions relative to whether the cosigner (plaintiff's ex-husband, Ronald L. Fuller) was still employed and whether he continued to be a Kansas resident.

By December 7, 1979, although plaintiff was current on her loan payments, concern at the credit union over the loan was deepening. Among the factors causing anxiety to the credit union were:

1. Inability to get plaintiff to come in and discuss her loan, despite the four attempts.

2. Inability to get plaintiff to clarify her statements regarding a possible move to Michigan.

3. As of then, unsuccessful attempts to check out the Michigan address plaintiff had given the credit union in writing on November 27, 1979.

4. Status of cosigner's employment and whether he was still in Kansas.

5. Knowledge plaintiff was now unemployed.

6. As plaintiff had quit her employment at Western Electric, the credit union no longer enjoyed payment by automatic payroll deductions.

7. A growing fear plaintiff was about to leave Kansas with the 1979 Thunderbird which was the principal collateral securing the credit union's loan.

8. The amount of the loan was at the upper limits of the credit union's loaning policy.

The executive committee of defendant credit union conferred relative to the loan and concluded the prospect for payment, performance or realization of the collateral was significantly impaired and the Thunderbird should be repossessed. On the night of December 9/10, 1979, repossession occurred peaceably, but without consent.

*   *   *

Defendant credit union had the burden of proof under 16a–5–109(2) to establish the prospect of payment, performance, or realization of collateral was significantly impaired at the time of repossession. Plaintiff does not challenge the trial court's determination the credit union had the burden of proving "significant impairment" by the preponderance of the evidence. * * *

Plaintiff denies receiving the telephone calls from Mr. Erath on December 3, 4, 5 and 7, 1979, and relies heavily on this denial in contending the credit union failed to meet its burden of proof. In so doing, plaintiff improperly asks this court, on appellate review, to weigh the evidence.

It is undisputed that on November 27, 1979, plaintiff: (1) advised the credit union she was going to quit her job at Western Electric on January 4, 1980; (2) in fact, quit her job on November 27, 1979; and (3) was going to move to Michigan taking the automobile to an address which the credit union was unable to verify. Additionally, the trial court found that plaintiff was contacted by the credit union on December 3, 4, 5 and 7, 1979, for the purpose of having her come to the credit union to explain the obvious inconsistencies between plaintiff's stated plans and her actual conduct. On each occasion plaintiff promised to come to the credit union shortly thereafter but did not appear. Plaintiff had been divorced from the cosigner of the loan subsequent to its execution. The cosigner was not an employee of Western Electric, and the cosigner was "apparently not very reliable."

We conclude the findings of the trial court relative to this issue are supported by substantial competent evidence including the trial court's conclusion the credit union was entitled to declare a default and repossess the automobile on the basis the prospect of payment, performance, or realization of the collateral was significantly impaired.

The second issue is whether the trial court erred in not holding the repossession was unlawful for failure to give prior notice of default pursuant to K.S.A. 16a–5–110.

* * *

* * * The specific language of the statute and the Kansas Comment following the statute show there is no requirement of notice prior to repossession where the default is predicated upon substantial impairment of collateral pursuant to 16a–5–109(2) as opposed to failing to make an installment payment under 16a–5–109(1).

There are reasons why no notice is required in default for the prospect of substantial impairment situations. Where default occurs under 16a–5–109(2) the prospects of a continuing relationship between the creditor and the debtor is endangered, so such default is not subject to cure. When default is not subject to cure there is no need to give notice. As one commentator has noted, it is important to observe from the statutory language of 16a–5–110, notice is only relevant when installment default is involved.

"Equally important is the fact that the type of default contemplated involves only the failure to pay a required installment. Thus, if the debtor is in default for having allowed the insurance coverage on his secured automobile to lapse (and assuming that such a default satisfies the creditor's burden under the UCCC of demonstrating that the prospect of payment, performance or realization upon its collateral is significantly impaired), *no notice of right to cure is required."* 46 J.K. B.A. at 95. (Emphasis supplied.)

The security agreement herein provided repossession could be had without prior notice. As previously noted, 16a–5–110 does not require notice in this type of default and hence the agreement of the parties was not in violation of the UCCC. We conclude this issue is without merit.

* * *

The judgment is affirmed.

Notes

1.   At least nine states have statutes similar to U3C § 5.109. See generally Rasor, Limitations on Taking and Enforcing Security in Consumer Credit Transactions, § 20AA.05, in 1B P. Coogan, ed., Secured Transactions Under the Uniform Commercial Code (1984). Most of these statutes are written in general language, following the U3C example. Two of them, however, have provided lists of factors which constitute "significant impairment." See Ill.Rev.Stat. ch. 121½, ¶ 513 (abandonment or destruction of collateral or reasonable cause to believe the debtor has left or will leave the state); Me.Rev.Stat. tit. 9A, § 5–109 (death, insolvency or commencement of insolvency proceedings, loss or substantial damage to or destruction of uninsured collateral, sale or prior encumbrance, and lapse or termination of insurance). Does this mean that other things which might happen cannot constitute significant impairment?

2.   Would the credit union in *Palmer* have been able to show significant impairment under the U3C or a similar statute?

3.   Several states give consumer debtors the right to cure certain defaults, usually non-payment. You might think of these statutes as statutory grace periods. Most of them are similar to the U3C provision discussed in *Medling,* but a few take different forms. Wisconsin, for example, allows the debtor to cure twice; West Virginia allows it three times. The courts often say that compliance with the cure provisions is a condition precedent to a lawsuit by the creditor. See, e.g., Farmers Trust and Savings Bank v. Manning, 311 N.W.2d 285 (Iowa 1981). What happens if the creditor accelerates and repossesses before sending the proper cure notice? See Farmers State Bank v. Haflich, 10 Kan.App.2d 333, 699 P.2d 553 (1985).

DREW v. CHRYSLER CREDIT CORP.

United States District Court, Western District of Missouri, 1984.
596 F.Supp. 1371.

SACHS, DISTRICT JUDGE.

* * * On January 3, 1980 plaintiffs purchased and financed a 1975 Toyota automobile with Bethany Trust Company for a total of $2,508, payable $104.50 per month, commencing February 3, 1980. On February 21, 1980 plaintiffs agreed to purchase a new 1980 Plymouth

Champ automobile from North Belt Chrysler–Plymouth, a new car dealer in St. Joseph, Missouri, and agreed to trade their 1975 Toyota under a written agreement. Shortly thereafter, North Belt accepted, and assigned to defendant, the Retail Installment Contract of Robert and Linda Drew on the 1980 Champ.

North Belt delivered its check No. 10466 to Bethany Trust for $2,143.75 to pay off the loan on the 1975 Toyota traded in by plaintiffs; Bethany Trust released its lien on the Missouri title and delivered the title, signed by plaintiffs, to North Belt. On February 26, 1980 Bethany Trust stamped the note of plaintiffs "Paid", returned the note, and refunded $259.75 unearned finance charge on the 1975 Toyota. On February 28, 1980 the North Belt check was returned as unpaid to Bethany Trust. The new car dealer was then in dire financial straits, and defendant sued North Belt on that day for replevin and other remedies. The dealership closed its doors.

Plaintiffs, at the request of Bethany Trust, thereafter executed a guaranty on March 4, 1980 for the $2,143.75 unpaid check of North Belt and subsequently signed a note and paid Bethany Trust. Peggy Rinehart, an officer of Bethany Trust has signed an affidavit to the effect that Bethany Trust did not intend to receive the North Belt check as payment and satisfaction of the debt owed to it by plaintiffs. When the check was returned as unpaid, Bethany Trust looked to plaintiffs to make payment on their promissory note, which had been marked "paid" on the mistaken assumption that the auto dealer's check was fully funded.

Correspondence ensued between plaintiffs' and defendant's counsel. Plaintiffs sought to set off the $2,143.75 against the debt to Chrysler Credit. Defendant denied the setoff and demanded full monthly payments. Upon advice of counsel, plaintiffs paid and defendant received thirty monthly payments of $128.18. On September 3, 1982 plaintiffs tendered a check for $35.31 to defendant as full and final payment. Under plaintiffs' calculations, these payments plus the setoff amount would satisfy their debt to defendant. Defendant did not accept the check as tendered.

On November 1, 1982 defendant mailed to plaintiffs, and their attorney, a notice of intent to repossess. On November 20, 1982 defendant did repossess the 1980 Champ from plaintiffs' closed, but unlocked garage without knowledge of plaintiffs. On November 22, 1982 plaintiffs obtained the return of certain contents of the 1980 Champ. * * * Defendant mailed a notice of the sale after repossession to plaintiffs and their attorney on November 23, 1982. Neither plaintiffs nor anyone on their behalf offered to redeem or pay anything further on the 1980 Champ. Defendant's counsel wrote to plaintiffs' counsel on December 29, 1982 and March 1, 1983 to invite bids on the car. None were forthcoming.

The principal issues presently before this court are (1) whether the retail installment contract purchased by defendant from North Belt was taken subject to all claims and defenses that plaintiffs would have had against North Belt; (2) if so, whether defendant converted plaintiffs' property when it repossessed the 1980 Champ. The court answers both of these questions in the affirmative.

When defendant purchased the retail installment contract from North Belt, it was purportedly taken subject to all claims and defenses that plaintiffs would have had against North Belt. The contract was stamped with the language specified by 16 C.F.R. § 433.2 (1984):

> NOTICE: ANY HOLDER OF THIS CONSUMER CREDIT CONTRACT IS SUBJECT TO ALL CLAIMS AND DEFENSES WHICH THE DEBTOR COULD ASSERT AGAINST THE SELLER OF GOODS OR SERVICES OBTAINED PURSUANT HERETO OR WITH THE PROCEEDS HEREOF. RECOVERY HEREUNDER BY THE DEBTOR SHALL NOT EXCEED AMOUNTS PAID BY THE DEBTOR HEREUNDER.

* * *

The Drew's automobile was a consumer product * * *. Defendant took its paper subject to plaintiffs' claims against the automobile dealer.

Defendant next contends that plaintiffs did not owe Bethany Trust $2,143.75 because when the check of North Belt was delivered to Bethany Trust, Bethany Trust released its lien on the Missouri title and stamped the note of plaintiffs "Paid", returned the note and refunded the unearned finance charge. Plaintiffs counter that Bethany Trust did not intend to accept the check of North Belt as payment and satisfaction of the debt owed by plaintiffs. As the court previously noted, Peggy Rinehart, an officer of Bethany Trust, signed an affidavit that the bank did not intend to accept the check as payment in satisfaction. In *Hall v. Knapp*, the Missouri Court of Appeals stated that where a check is accepted as the "means" through which payment may be obtained and not as payment itself, the claim or debt is not extinguished by mere acceptance of the check. Where there is no agreement that the check itself shall constitute payment, a "satisfaction" does not occur until payment of the check has actually been received. Based upon the affidavits, the court must conclude that the parties did not intend the check itself to constitute payment. Thus, no satisfaction occurred. When the check of North Belt did not clear, Bethany Trust properly looked to plaintiffs to make good on the note.

Once the court has decided that plaintiffs should have been allowed the setoff against defendant's claims for payment (thereby placing defendant in violation of § 408.405), the court must then decide whether a cause of action has been created because of defendant's seizure of the car following its wrongful refusal to allow the setoff.

The Missouri Court of Appeals held in *Jones v. First Union Bancorporation,* that "[i]n order for plaintiff[s] to have a right of action for conversion, it is incumbent upon [them] to show that [defendant] had no right to repossess the automobile." If plaintiffs were indeed entitled to the setoff, defendant did not have a right to repossess the car. The same is true with respect to plaintiffs' charge of trespass. In *Baker v. Newcomb,* 621 S.W.2d 535, 537 (Mo.App., S.D.1981) (en banc), the Missouri Court of Appeals held that

> [a] party is liable in trespass even though acting under a mistaken belief of law or fact, however reasonable * * *. A party may be liable in trespass if he intends to do the act which results in the damage, although in so doing he did not intend to commit an act of trespass; may not even know that his act will constitute a trespass, and may act in good faith and through honest mistake.

(citations omitted). Moreover, since plaintiffs had been making all reasonable efforts to work out their disputes with defendant, defendant can make no argument that § 408.405 does not apply in this case.

The court finds the rest of the defendant's contentions to be without merit in this action. Accordingly, it is hereby

ORDERED that defendant's motion for summary judgment is DENIED. It is further

ORDERED that plaintiffs' motion for partial summary judgment is GRANTED. All that remains to be tried in this case is the issue of damages. A trial notice will be forthcoming.

ON MOTION TO VACATE OR ALTER JUDGMENT

* * *

Defendant next asserts that the court's "most fundamental error" in its ruling was in failing to note an alleged mathematical error in plaintiffs' final payment. If the calculations were incorrect by one payment of $128.18 this would not be dispositive. Defendant had never narrowed the controversy or indicated that it would have been satisfied with the extra $128.18 payment. On the contrary, defendant's "notice of intention to repossess" demands *two* such payments, plus "late charges", or $266.36. Def.Dep.Exh. 20, attached to Def. Motion for Summary Judgment filed Feb. 13, 1984, Doc. 34. Defendant premised its repossession on an assertion of "Total amount now due" that was excessive on any calculation, if the setoff is sound. It seems irrelevant that plaintiffs may have made a minor miscalculation.

Defendant may, however, ultimately be entitled to the $128.18 as a setoff at trial to any award of damages to plaintiffs.

Defendant continues to argue that plaintiffs are going beyond their statutory remedies in seeking more than a "defense" or "setoff against a claim by the holder or assignee." § 408.405, RSMo. But plaintiffs did initially assert their setoff rights defensively. When defendant violated their statutory rights and then engaged in a wrongful repossession, the repossession damages arise from a second violation of law and are not subject to the statutory limitation.

ORDERED that defendant's motion to vacate, alter and amend the judgment entered on October 26, 1984, or to order interlocutory appeal to the Eighth Circuit of that Order, is DENIED.

Problem 1

On June 3, Blaine purchased an automobile from Calhoun Chevrolet Co., financing it through GMAC. The credit contract included a security interest on the car and required Blaine to make a payment on the third day of each month, maintain casualty insurance on the car, and notify GMAC of any change of address. On June 4, Old Reliable Insurance Co., after reviewing Blaine's driving record, cancelled all insurance on the car. Blaine has not obtained substitute insurance. On July 1, Blaine moved from the address listed on the contract to another apartment across the street. Blaine was so busy moving that he forgot to mail the payment check until July 3. It was not delivered to GMAC until July 5.

Which, if any, of the above facts constitute a default which will allow repossession under UCC § 9–503? Cf., Pierce v. Leasing International, Inc., 142 Ga.App. 371, 235 S.E.2d 752 (1977). Which, if any, of the above facts constitute a serious threat to the creditor's security? Does the consumer have any protection under the UCC against precipitous acceleration or repossession?

Problem 2

Again Blaine purchased a car and then financed it through GMAC. The credit contract stated that "There shall be a default hereunder if creditor has reasonable cause to believe that the car is in danger of misuse or confiscation, and creditor may then repossess the car." Two months later, Blaine was arrested and charged with "criminal possession of a controlled substance." The police said the car was used to transport narcotics and threatened to confiscate it. Before conviction, trial, or even indictment, GMAC notified Blaine that it felt its security interest was in jeopardy and sought repossession. The car was released to GMAC. Does Blaine have any action to recover possession of the car?—if he is subsequently acquitted? Cf., Blaine v. General Motors Acceptance Corp., 82 Misc.2d 653, 370 N.Y.S.2d 323 (1975); UCC § 1–208.

Of course, late payment is always a default. Or is it? Consider the following.

BATTISTA v. SAVINGS BANK OF BALTIMORE

Court of Special Appeals of Maryland, 1986.
67 Md.App. 257, 507 A.2d 203.

ADKINS, JUDGE.

The basic issue presented in this appeal is: was there a jury question on the issue of whether appellee, Savings Bank of Baltimore, had waived its right to repossess the Honda automobile of appellant, Jacqueline Battista? Battista says the Bank's frequent acceptance of late payments without repossession provided sufficient evidence to take the waiver issue to the jury. The Bank argues to the contrary, emphasizing the presence of an anti-waiver provision in the installment sales agreement. There are subsidiary issues relating to the sufficiency of the evidence as to both compensatory and punitive damages if we agree with Battista that it was for the jury to decide whether the Bank wrongfully repossessed her car.

We shall outline the pertinent facts as we discuss the specific issues. First, we sketch the procedural posture of the case.

In January 1978, Battista purchased a 1978 Honda Civic from O'Donnell Pontiac, which assigned its retail installment sales agreement to the Bank. Battista made several monthly payments late. The Bank accepted these until October 1980. In that month, when Battista had not made her August or September payments, the Bank repossessed the automobile. Although the account was later brought current—in fact, advance payments were made—the Bank initially refused to return the vehicle upon Battista's request. Eventually the car was returned.

Battista then sued the Bank for conversion, negligence, and breach of contract, claiming both compensatory and punitive damages. At the close of her case, the Circuit Court for Baltimore City granted the Bank's motion for judgment on the punitive damages claim. The remainder of the case went to the jury, which brought in a verdict of $9,000 in favor of Battista and against the Bank. The Bank filed a timely motion for judgment n.o.v., the court granted it, and judgment was entered for the Bank. As to the conversion claim—the only ground for the Bank's liability asserted on appeal—the judge reasoned

> it boils down to whether or not there was evidence of conduct which insofar as the bank is concerned, whether there was evidence of conduct which presented a factual issue as to waiver or as to modification.
>
> Now, the terms of the contract are quite clear * * *. [T]he contract is quite clear that, as to when or whether a waiver or modification of the contract occurs * * *.
>
> The conduct alleged during the trial of the case as to the bank, I find to be inadequate to produce a factual issue. At best the jury, I think, was put in a position to speculate both as to damages and as to the issue of whether or not there was a waiver, and, of course, as to whether or not there was a conversion, inasmuch as the original taking was a legal one; then a conversion would not exist.

This appeal followed.

Waiver and the Conversion Claim

Battista's conversion claim was based on the theory that the Bank was not authorized to repossess her car in October 1980. If that theory is correct, there is no doubt that there was a conversion. " 'A conversion' is any distinct act of ownership or dominion exerted by one person over the personal property of another in denial of his right or inconsistent with it." The Bank, on the other hand, points to the undisputed fact that when the car was repossessed, two monthly payments were past due. The agreement provided:

> In the event of a default * * * the entire unpaid balance of the purchase price shall, at the option of the Holder [Bank], become immediately due and payable, and * * * the Holder may, with or without legal process and with or without previous notice or demand for performance *enter into the premises where the vehicle may be* * * * *and take* possession of the same * * * [emphasis supplied].

Thus, says the Bank, there was no conversion; it merely exercised its rights under the agreement.

The central issue, as we have seen, is whether there was sufficient evidence for a fact-finder to decide that the Bank had, by its conduct, waived its contractual right to repossess upon default. The legal principle is well-established:

> The creditor may have waived the right to object to the default of the debtor, in which case repossession is wrongful. Waiver of default is commonly found in the creditor's accepting late payments without protest and in failing to notify the debtor that strict adherence to the agreement terms will be required.

* * *

As we have said, Battista purchased her Honda in January 1978 from O'Donnell Pontiac. The transaction was memorialized in an agreement, on a form supplied by the Bank, and assigned by O'Donnell to the Bank. The agreement required Battista to make 42 consecutive monthly payments of $136.79 each, beginning on February 20, 1978. The amount of each payment included a sum for the purchase of credit life and credit disability insurance. The agreement included the "repossession upon default" provision we have already quoted, as well as the following:

> Failure of Holder to exercise any of the Holder's rights hereunder provided shall not be deemed a waiver thereof, and no waiver of any such rights shall be deemed to apply to any other of such rights, nor shall it be effective unless in writing and signed by the Holder.

At first all went well. Battista made payments regularly, and often on time, although some were a few days late. But in May 1979, Battista was injured in an accident, and as a consequence, disabled. She discovered that Geneva Life Insurance Company was carrying her disability credit insurance (we do not know who selected Geneva; it was not Battista) and she invoked the provisions of that insurance, by the terms of which Geneva was to make the monthly payments to the Bank.

The June 1979 payment was not paid on time and on July 10, the Bank sent Battista a notice saying it intended to repossess the car unless she made payment within ten days. Battista called the Bank, explaining that she was out of work and that Geneva would be making the payments. The Bank official to whom she spoke (Mr. Prescimone) said "we will wait awhile and see what happened." On July 18 Geneva sent the Bank a check for $136.79. The car was not repossessed.

During the summer Geneva at various times sent the Bank various checks for various amounts. These irregularities, it seems, occurred because Geneva required medical verification every 30 days that Battista's disability was continuing. Her doctor, however, did not wish to see her every 30 days, and did not wish to issue a certificate of disability when he had not seen her. As a consequence, Geneva received irregularly-timed disability certificates. Whenever it received a certificate, it sent the Bank a check, sometimes for more than a single payment. There was evidence that the Bank was aware of this circumstance. It accepted all of Geneva's checks.

On September 18, 1979, the Bank sent Battista another letter asserting that the August payment had not been made and threatening repossession unless she paid $136.79 plus late charges within ten days. Battista again phoned Prescimone and explained the situation. Geneva eventually made the payment. The car was not repossessed. This scenario was repeated following another repossession letter dated July 9, 1980. Both before and after that Geneva made its occasional payments, all of which were accepted by the Bank. The car was not repossessed.

Things came to a head in September 1980. By letter dated September 10, but apparently not mailed until September 23, the Bank demanded the August payment and again threatened repossession if payment was not received within ten days of September 10 (that critical date had passed before the letter was mailed). Battista again called the Bank "many times" and attempted to contact Prescimone, but he was never available and never responded to her messages to return her calls. On October 5 the car was repossessed. By October 16 the Bank had received enough payments to bring the account current through December 20. The Bank finally returned the car to Battista on November 25.

What legal conclusions can we draw from these facts? * * *

The Maryland cases we have cited show clearly that the principle of waiver by conduct is recognized in this State, consistent with the doctrine explained by Anderson; None of those cases, however, dealt with an agreement that, like the one before us, contained an express non-waiver provision. Nor did they consider the effect of notices of intention to repossess, such as those sent in this case.

The problem of a non-waiver agreement has been addressed in other states. Illinois and Alabama adopt the position the Bank espouses here: there can be no waiver by conduct in the face of a non-waiver agreement requiring any waiver to be in writing.

In *General Grocer Co. of Illinois v. Bachar,* 51 Ill.App.3d 907, 8 Ill. Dec. 720, 365 N.E.2d 1106 (1977), there was an agreement that provided for repossession on default in required payments and that further provided:

> No failure or delay by Lender in exercising any right or remedy hereunder or otherwise shall operate as a waiver thereof. A waiver of any such right or remedy must be in writing and shall be limited to the specific instance and to the right or remedy expressly waived * * *.

8 Ill.Dec. at 721, 365 N.E.2d at 1107. The Illinois court opined (without citation of authority, and with the comment that the defaulting debtor had offered none): "In the light of such 'non waiver' clause, which was agreed to by the [debtor], we cannot interpret the [creditor's] conduct in accepting tardy payments (whether such instances be many or few) to constitute a suspension of the terms of an agreement to make payments on a date certain." 8 Ill.Dec. at 723, 365 N.E.2d at 1109.

A more carefully-considered opinion is *Hale v. Ford Motor Credit Corp.*, 374 So.2d 849 (Ala.1979). There the conditional vendee made every monthly payment late over a period of about a year. When the holder of the security interest eventually repossessed the vehicle, the vendee sued for conversion. The security agreement provided that "[w]aiver * * * of any default shall not be a waiver of any other default" and required any waiver to be written. A closely-divided (6–3) Supreme Court of Alabama held:

> A security agreement is effective according to its terms * * *. The inadvertence of the debtor here cannot raise an estoppel against the contractual interest of the creditor under the express terms of the security agreement * * *. There having been no modification of the express agreement, the secured party, upon default, had the right to take possession of the collateral.

374 So.2d at 853 [citations omitted].

The dissenters were of the view that the conduct of a financial institution in accepting late payments over a period of time may estop it from repossessing a vehicle unless it gives prior notice of intent to do so. Here, the notices were thought to be deficient because they advised only that the car *could* be repossessed if the payments were not made.

Hale has been followed in Alabama, albeit with some reluctance. * * *

Other states have rejected the Illinois–Alabama approach. In *Smith v. General Finance Corp. of Georgia*, 243 Ga. 500, 255 S.E.2d 14 (1979), for example, the Supreme Court of Georgia held that "a provision in a contract against waiver of contractual rights may itself be found by a jury to have been waived." 255 S.E.2d at 15. In so holding, the court expressly disapproved *Fair v. General Finance Corp. of Georgia*, 147 Ga.App. 706, 250 S.E.2d 9 (1978). The latter case had held that in the face of a contractual non-waiver provision, there could be no waiver of the right to repossess by acceptance of late payments without repossession.

Similar in result to *Smith* is *Van Bibber v. Norris,* 404 N.E.2d 1365 (Ind.App.1980). In that case the conditional vendee of a house trailer was late in making 57 out of 59 monthly payments. Of these, 37 were more than ten days late. The vendor's assignee (a bank) would press for payment on each occasion; the vendee would eventually make payment; the bank would accept the payment. Eventually, after the vendee had been sued for rent by a trailer park, had tried to remove the trailer from the park surreptitously, and had been arrested, the bank repossessed. The trial court found a waiver; the intermediate appellate court affirmed, despite a contract provision that "[n]o waiver by the Sellers [the bank] of any default shall be effective unless in writing, nor operate as a waiver of any other default nor of the same default on a future occasion." 404 N.E.2d at 1374.

The appellate court concluded that a secured party that establishes a pattern of accepting late payments may not suddenly insist on timely payment and declare a forfeiture unless it first gives reasonable and specific notice of its intention to do so. As to the contractual non-waiver provision, it was not enough.

> [T]he bank's conduct in accepting fifty-seven past due payments and thirty-seven delinquent payments spoke louder than its word. The trial court was adequately justified to conclude that the bank had waived timely payments.

404 N.E.2d at 1374.

Cobb v. Midwest Recovery Bureau Co., 295 N.W.2d 232 (Minn.1980) completes our trilogy of cases permitting a finding of waiver despite a non-waiver clause. Cobb bought a Mack truck in December 1971. The installment sale contract stipulated:

> No amendment of this contract shall be binding upon the seller unless in writing and signed by its duly authorized representative. * * * Any waiver of any breach or default shall not constitute a waiver or [sic] any other or subsequent breach or default.

295 N.W.2d 232.

By November 1973, Cobb was two payments behind. He secured two extension agreements, but remained in arrears. Mack Truck sent various letters demanding payment, although it did not threaten repossession. In 1975 Mack threatened to terminate the contract unless certain payments were made. They were not made, but Mack did nothing more until March 1976, when it repossessed the vehicle. Up until then, Mack had accepted every late payment.

The Supreme Court of Minnesota carefully reviewed the authorities, noting the two divergent lines of decisions we have discussed. Citing cases from Florida, Nevada, Oregon, and Texas (in addition to the Georgia authority we have reviewed), it found an apparent majority of the states that had considered the issue in favor of permitting waiver, even in the face of a non-waiver clause. The court affirmed Cobb's recovery of compensatory damages against Mack:

We hold that the repeated acceptance of late payments by a creditor who has the contractual right to repossess the property imposes a duty on the creditor to notify the debtor that strict compliance with the contract terms will be required before the creditor can lawfully repossess the collateral.

295 N.W.2d at 237.

We believe that the decisions permitting waiver of contractual rights despite a non-waiver clause requiring a written waiver are consistent with Maryland decisions. * * * We hold, therefore, that a waiver of a contractual right to prompt payment or a waiver of a contractual right to repossess (or for that matter a statutory right to repossess; *see* § 12–624(a) of the Commercial Law Art.) may be effected by conduct, and the same is true as to the provisions of a non-waiver clause. When such a waiver has occurred, the creditor, before it can insist on future performance in strict compliance with the contract, must give plain and reasonable notice to the debtor that it intends to do so; *see* § 2–209(5) of the Commercial Law Art.[4]

When we apply this holding to the facts before us, a clear result emerges: the question of waiver was one for the jury in this case. Returning to our earlier definition of waiver, there is no doubt that the Bank was well aware of its rights to require timely monthly payments and to repossess Battista's car in the absence of such payments. There is no doubt that a number of payments were late and that the Bank did not repossess until the August and September 1980 payments were in arrears. There was evidence sufficient to support a finding that the Bank was aware of Battista's disability, of the disability insurance arrangement with Geneva, and of the reason why Geneva's payments were not always timely. Despite that evidence, the Bank accepted ten or more irregular payments from Geneva.

Given these facts or allowable inferences from facts, a reasonable jury could also find that Battista had justifiably relied on a course of conduct by the Bank; a course of conduct inconsistent with an intention to insist rigorously on the prompt payment and forfeiture provisions of the contract. As a consequence, the jury might have found (and in fact did find) waiver of those provisions by the Bank, as well as waiver of the non-waiver clause.

As we have seen, such a waiver imposes on the creditor a duty to warn the debtor that strict compliance will be required in future. It is true that each time the Bank sent a "ten-day letter" to Battista, it warned of the need for strict compliance and said it would repossess the car. But it is also true that *every* time (except the last one) the Bank sent such a letter, it thereafter did not insist on strict compliance, nor

---

4. Commercial Law Art. § 2–209(5) (part of the Uniform Commercial Code) reads:

A party who has made a waiver affecting an executory portion of the contract may retract the waiver by reasonable notification received by the other party that strict performance will be required of any term waived, unless the retraction would be unjust in view of a material change of position in reliance on the waiver.

did it repossess the car. That conduct might have constituted another waiver or the jury might have found that the Bank's retraction of waiver was not given by the reasonable notice required by § 2–209(5) or that the retraction was unjust within the meaning of that section.

The bottom line is that these matters, essentially involving intent, ordinarily are best left to the fact-finder, as many cases have held. Initially, that was done in this case. The judge erred when he changed his mind and granted judgment n.o.v. for the Bank after the jury, with a sufficient factual basis for doing so, had decided the waiver issues in favor of Battista.

* * *

CONCLUSION

We have held that the judge erred in granting the Bank's motion for judgment n.o.v. and for that reason we must reverse. We have also held that Battista's punitive damages claim was properly kept from the jury. Because of the procedural posture of this case, the Bank's argument that the jury awarded excessive compensatory damages is unavailing. Under Rule 1075 we may, "[o]n reversing a judgment * * * enter such judgment as ought to have been entered by the lower court." We shall do so.

JUDGMENT REVERSED.

JUDGMENT ENTERED IN FAVOR OF JACQUELINE BATTISTA AND AGAINST SAVINGS BANK OF BALTIMORE IN THE AMOUNT OF $9,000 WITH INTEREST AT TEN PERCENTUM PER ANNUM FROM MARCH 21, 1985, AND COSTS. APPELLEE TO PAY THE COSTS ON APPEAL.

Note

If you represented the bank at the time the "10 day" letters were written, what would you have advised the bank to put in the letters? Given the bank's behavior, could it write any letter which would undo the waiver problem? What other advice would you give?

2. REPOSSESSION—HOW?

When the debtor defaults, the creditor ordinarily has the right to repossess the collateral. The creditor may do this through self-help, without going to court, as long as the repossession can be done without breaching the peace. See UCC § 9–503. In consumer cases, the type of collateral most likely to be repossessed is the automobile. Estimates vary, but it may be that as many as 1,000,000 cars are repossessed in the United States every year. Naturally, confrontations and other problems sometime occur. What are the rights and responsibilities of the parties when this occurs?

WILLIAMS v. FORD MOTOR CREDIT CO.

United States Court of Appeals, Eighth Circuit, 1982.
674 F.2d 717.

BENSON, CHIEF JUDGE.

In this diversity action brought by Cathy A. Williams to recover damages for conversion arising out of an alleged wrongful repossession of an automobile, Williams appeals from a judgment notwithstanding the verdict entered on motion of defendant Ford Motor Credit Company (FMCC). In the same case, FMCC appeals a directed verdict in favor of third party defendant S & S Recovery, Inc. (S & S) on FMCC's third party claim for indemnification. We affirm the judgment n.o.v. FMCC's appeal is thereby rendered moot.

In July, 1975, David Williams, husband of plaintiff Cathy Williams, purchased a Ford Mustang from an Oklahoma Ford dealer. Although David Williams executed the sales contract, security agreement, and loan papers, title to the car was in the name of both David and Cathy Williams. The car was financed through the Ford dealer, who in turn assigned the paper to FMCC. Cathy and David Williams were divorced in 1977. The divorce court granted Cathy title to the automobile and required David to continue to make payments to FMCC for eighteen months. David defaulted on the payments and signed a voluntary repossession authorization for FMCC. Cathy Williams was informed of the delinquency and responded that she was trying to get her former husband David to make the payments. There is no evidence of any agreement between her and FMCC. Pursuant to an agreement with FMCC, S & S was directed to repossess the automobile.

On December 1, 1977, at approximately 4:30 a.m., Cathy Williams was awakened by a noise outside her house trailer in Van Buren, Arkansas. She saw that a wrecker truck with two men in it had hooked up to the Ford Mustang and started to tow it away. She went outside and hollered at them. The truck stopped. She then told them that the car was hers and asked them what they were doing. One of the men, later identified as Don Sappington, president of S & S Recovery, Inc., informed her that he was repossessing the vehicle on behalf of FMCC. Williams explained that she had been attempting to bring the past due payments up to date and informed Sappington that the car contained personal items which did not even belong to her. Sappington got out of the truck, retrieved the items from the car, and handed them to her. Without further complaint from Williams, Sappington returned to the truck and drove off, car in tow. At trial, Williams testified that Sappington was polite throughout their encounter and did not make any threats toward her or do anything which caused her to fear any physical harm. The automobile had been parked in an unenclosed driveway which plaintiff shared with a neighbor. The neighbor was awakened by the wrecker backing into the driveway, but did not come out. After the wrecker drove off, Williams returned to her house trailer and called the police, reporting her car as stolen. Later, Williams commenced this action.

The case was tried to a jury which awarded her $5,000.00 in damages. FMCC moved for judgment notwithstanding the verdict, but the district court, on Williams' motion, ordered a nonsuit without prejudice to refile in state court. On FMCC's appeal, this court reversed and remanded with directions to the district court to rule on the motion for judgment notwithstanding the verdict. The district court entered judgment notwithstanding the verdict for FMCC, and this appeal followed.

Article 9 of the Uniform Commercial Code (UCC) which Arkansas has adopted and codified as Ark.Stat.Ann. § 85–9–503 (Supp.1981), provides in pertinent part:

> Unless otherwise agreed, a secured party has on default the right to take possession of the collateral. In taking possession, a secured party may proceed without judicial process if this can be done without breach of the peace. * * *

In *Ford Motor Credit Co. v. Herring,* 27 U.C.C.Rep. 1448, 267 Ark. 201, 589 S.W.2d 584, 586 (1979), which involved an alleged conversion arising out of a repossession, the Supreme Court of Arkansas cited Section 85–9–503 and referred to its previous holdings as follows:

> In pre-code cases, we have sustained a finding of conversion only where force, or threats of force, or risk of invoking violence, accompanied the repossession. *Manhattan Credit Co., Inc. v. Brewer,* 232 Ark. 976, 341 S.W.2d 765 (1961); *Kensinger Acceptance Corp. v. Davis,* 223 Ark. 942, 269 S.W.2d 792 (1954).

The thrust of Williams' argument on appeal is that the repossession was accomplished by the risk of invoking violence. The district judge who presided at the trial commented on her theory in his memorandum opinion:

> Mrs. Williams herself admitted that the men who repossessed her automobile were very polite and complied with her requests. The evidence does not reveal that they performed any act which was oppressive, threatening or tended to cause physical violence. Unlike the situation presented in *Manhattan Credit Co. v. Brewer, supra,* it was not shown that Mrs. Williams would have been forced to resort to physical violence to stop the men from leaving with her automobile.

In the pre-Code case *Manhattan Credit Co. v. Brewer,* 232 Ark. 976, 341 S.W.2d 765 (1961), the court held that a breach of peace occurred when the debtor and her husband confronted the creditor's agent during the act of repossession and clearly objected to the repossession, 341 S.W.2d at 767–68. In *Manhattan,* the court examined holdings of earlier cases in which repossessions were deemed to have been accomplished without any breach of the peace, *id.* In particular, the Supreme Court of Arkansas discussed the case of *Rutledge v. Universal C.I.T. Credit Corp.,* 218 Ark. 510, 237 S.W.2d 469 (1951). In *Rutledge,* the court found no breach of the peace when the repossessor acquired keys to the automobile, confronted the debtor and his wife, informed them he was going to take the car, and immediately proceeded to do so. As the *Rutledge* court explained and the *Manhattan* court reiterated, a breach of the peace did not occur when the "Appellant [debtor-possessor] did not give his permission but he did not object." *Manhattan, supra,* 341 S.W.2d at 767–68; *Rutledge, supra,* 237 S.W.2d at 470.

We have read the transcript of the trial. There is no material dispute in the evidence, and the district court has correctly summarized it. Cathy Williams did not raise an objection to the taking, and the repossession was accomplished without any incident which might tend to provoke violence.

Appellees deserve something less than commendation for the taking during the night time sleeping hours, but it is clear that viewing the facts in the light most favorable to Williams, the taking was a legal repossession under the laws of the State of Arkansas. The evidence does not support the verdict of the jury. FMCC is entitled to judgment notwithstanding the verdict.

The judgment notwithstanding the verdict is affirmed.

HEANEY, CIRCUIT JUDGE, dissenting.

The only issue is whether the repossession of appellant's automobile constituted a breach of the peace by creating a "risk of invoking violence." *See Ford Motor Credit Co. v. Herring,* 267 Ark. 201, 589 S.W.2d 584, 586 (1979). The trial jury found that it did and awarded $5,000 for conversion. Because that determination was in my view a reasonable one, I dissent from the Court's decision to overturn it.

Cathy Williams was a single parent living with her two small children in a trailer home in Van Buren, Arkansas. On December 1, 1977, at approximately 4:30 a.m., she was awakened by noises in her driveway. She went into the night to investigate and discovered a wrecker and its crew in the process of towing away her car. According to the trial court, "she ran outside to stop them ∗ ∗ ∗ but she made no *strenuous* protests to their actions." (Emphasis added.) In fact, the wrecker crew stepped between her and the car when she sought to retrieve personal items from inside it, although the men retrieved some of the items for her. The commotion created by the incident awakened neighbors in the vicinity.

Facing the wrecker crew in the dead of night, Cathy Williams did everything she could to stop them, short of introducing physical force to meet the presence of the crew. The confrontation did not result in violence only because Ms. Williams did not take such steps and was otherwise powerless to stop the crew.

The controlling law is the UCC, which authorizes self-help repossession only when such is done "without breach of the peace ∗ ∗ ∗." The majority recognizes that one important policy consideration underlying this restriction is to discourage "extrajudicial acts by citizens when those acts are fraught with the likelihood of resulting violence."

Despite this, the majority holds that no reasonable jury could find that the confrontation in Cathy Williams' driveway at 4:30 a.m. created a risk of violence. I cannot agree. At a minimum, the largely undisputed facts created a jury question. The jury found a breach of the peace and this Court has no sound, much less compelling, reason to overturn that determination.

Indeed, I would think that sound application of the self-help limitation might require a directed verdict in favor of Ms. Williams, but certainly not against her. If a "night raid" is conducted without detection and confrontation, then, of course, there could be no breach of the peace. But where the invasion is detected and a confrontation ensues, the repossessor should be under a duty to retreat and turn to judicial process. The alternative which the majority embraces is to allow a repossessor to proceed following confrontation unless and until violence results in fact. Such a rule invites tragic consequences which the law should seek to prevent, not to encourage. I would reverse the trial court and reinstate the jury's verdict.

Notes

1. "Breach of the peace" has been left to the courts to define, and there are hundreds of cases. In consumer cases, the courts have routinely held that unauthorized entry into the debtor's residence or closed garage is a breach of the peace. Compare U3C § 5.112. By the same token, repossessions from the debtor's yard or driveway are usually allowed, absent any confrontation, despite the technical trespass. What should be the result if the creditor takes the car from an open garage or a carport?

2. Doesn't the majority opinion in *Williams* encourage debtors to use violence to try to prevent their cars from being repossessed?

3. Assume that when Cathy Williams came outside she had a gun and said to the repo men, "if you come back for my car, I'll leave you laying right where I find you." Assume the repo men leave but come back the next night and take the car. Has there been a breach of the peace? Cf., Jordan v. Citizens and Southern Nat. Bank, 278 So.Car. 449, 298 S.E.2d 213 (1982); Wade v. Ford Motor Credit Co., 8 Kan.App.2d 737, 668 P.2d 183 (1983).

Problem 3

Bill Bones bought an airplane and financed it by borrowing from Friendly Finance Co. Bones gave Friendly a security interest in the airplane, but defaulted on his payments under the security agreement. Alert, an employee of Friendly, located the airplane in a hangar at the Boise Municipal Airport. Without notice to Bones, Alert opened the hangar door, "hot-wired" the ignition switch of the airplane, started the engine, took off from the Boise airport without clearance from the tower, and flew it to Oklahoma City, where it was resold.

Was the repossession in violation of UCC § 9–503? If it was, what is Bones' remedy? Does UCC § 9–507 apply? Does it preempt other possible remedies, such as tort recoveries?

Problem 4

Daniel Default bought on credit from Charlie Cheerful three rooms of furniture for his three room apartment. He failed to make any of the payments due. After four months, Charlie "picked" the lock to Dan's apartment, entered the apartment and removed all of the furniture. Dan's landlord discovered Charlie's actions during the repossession and called the police, but they never arrived. The landlord listened further and finally determined the motives behind Charlie's actions. He did not object, but merely asked that Charlie leave the door locked when through. Charlie did.

When Dan returned to his apartment, he objected greatly, and would like to pursue "any legal remedies available." Could you help him? Cf., Cherno v. Bank of Babylon, 54 Misc.2d 277, 282 N.Y.S.2d 114 (1967).

Would it make any difference if the credit contract had the following clause: "In the event of default, Bank is authorized to repossess the collateral and to enter any premises where the collateral may be located and take the same with or without legal process."

Notes

1. When only a "technical" trespass has been involved, the courts have usually not found any breach of the peace, on a variety of grounds. See, e.g. Reno v. GMAC, 378 So.2d 1103, 27 UCC Rep.Serv. 1452 (Ala.1979); Raffa v. Dania Bank, 321 So.2d 83 (Fla.App.1975); Harris Truck & Trailer Sales v. Foote, 58 Tenn.App. 710, 436 S.W.2d 460, 5 UCC Rep. 569 (1968).

2. When self-help repossession requires entrance into a residence, courts have been quick to find a breach of the peace whenever the repossession occurs without the informed consent of the debtor. See, e.g., Girard v. Anderson, 219 Iowa 142, 257 N.W. 400 (1934).

3. "The law recognizes that personal property taken as a mortgage security, because of its transitory nature can be easily lost, strayed, converted or stolen. Realty can not stray, be converted, or stolen; hence the law of merchant recognizes the necessity of sanctioning summary methods of seizure to call in chattel mortgages. Were it otherwise, any system of credit extended upon chattels as security would be imperiled, and perhaps break down. Cautious lenders would decline to lend on so insecure a collateral; hence, we have the principal that immediately on default, the chattels are the property of the mortgagee to seize as the provisions direct, and no other or further notice is required except as the chattel mortgage, itself, covenants." Goodman v. Schulman, 144 Misc. 512, 258 N.Y.S. 681 at 683 (1932).

4. "Breach of the peace" is, however, basically a question of fact for the trier of fact, and its determination is very difficult to overturn. For an example of like facts producing unlike results, compare Speigle v. Chrysler Credit Corp., 56 Ala.App. 469, 323 So.2d 360, 17 UCC Rep.Serv. 1395 (1975) with Deavers v. Standridge, 144 Ga.App. 673, 242 S.E.2d 331, 23 UCC Rep. Serv. 834 (1978).

Note on Judicial Repossession

A decade or two ago, it was a somewhat open question whether self-help repossession under UCC § 9–503 was constitutional. Pre-judgment seizure of a debtor's property under attachment, garnishment, and similar procedures had generally been stricken down, see especially Sniadach v. Family Finance Corp., 395 U.S. 337, 89 S.Ct. 1820, 23 L.Ed.2d 349 (1969); Fuentes v. Shevin, 407 U.S. 67, 92 S.Ct. 1983, 32 L.Ed.2d 556 (1972), and many observers believed that these rulings might be extended to secured transactions. Today, however, the constitutionality of UCC § 9–503 and the process of self-help repossession is no longer in doubt. See, e.g., Adams v. Southern California First National Bank, 492 F.2d 324 (9th Cir.1973).

The issue submitted to court determination in *Adams,* supra, and similar cases, was whether self-help repossession involved "state action". The courts held that it did not. In none of those cases did the secured creditor seriously seek a court determination that self-help repossession conformed to our usual notions of due process. Thus, where the action of the creditor can be considered "federal action", such as by a federal corporation (FNMA) acting under federal regulations, the *Adams* doctrine offers no protection. See, Roberts v. Cameron–Brown Co. 410 F.Supp. 988 (S.D.Ga.1975) (non-judicial "power of sale" foreclosure of real estate subject to Fifth Amendment procedural due process requirements of notice and opportunity to present defenses.)

Despite the lack of any constitutional requirement, however, a state may prohibit self-help repossession as a matter of policy if it chooses to do so. The Model Consumer Credit Act disposes of self-help repossession without mincing words: (MCCA § 7.202)

> "No person shall take possession of collateral by other than legal process * * *, notwithstanding any provision of law or term of a writing."

The U3C does not go nearly as far; it prohibits self-help repossession of certain exempt property. U3C § 5.116. At least one state has abolished self-help repossession as well. Wisconsin Consumer Act, §§ 425.203–425.206. What is likely to be the focus of the debate in a legislature considering a similar enactment?

What would barring self-help auto repossessions cost? Two speculative analyses estimated incremental annual costs to creditors (and thus ultimately to their customers) of $143 million and $219 million. See White, "The Abolition of Self–Help Repossession: The Poor Pay Even More," 1973 Wis.L.Rev. 503, and Johnson, "Denial of Self–Help Repossession: An Economic Analysis," 47 S.Cal.L.Rev. 82 (1973). See also, Dauer & Gilhool, "The Economics of Constitutionalized Repossession: A Critique for Professor Johnson and a Partial Reply," 47 S.Cal.L.Rev. 116 (1973). A subsequent article takes issue with the conclusions of White and Johnson, supra, and concludes that the incremental costs of using "constitutionalized" repossession would be no more than 28¢ per transaction and would be more than offset by benefits to consumers who have defenses to assert, more voluntary workouts, and avoidance of confrontations between repossessors and consumers. Crandall, "Proposal for Consumer Credit Reform: A Definition of Default, A Right to Cure, and A Right to Notice and an Opportunity for a Hearing Before Repossession," 13 Gonzaga L.Rev. 1, 50–68 (1977).

However, the only analysis of actual data after enactment of such legislation is Whitford & Laufer, "The Impact of Denying Self–Help Repossession of Automobiles: A Case Study of the Wisconsin Consumer Act," 1975 Wis.L.Rev. 607.* Their conclusion, pp. 653–57, is as follows:

> The major contention of the critics of judicialized repossession has concerned the impact of that legal change on the availability of credit, particularly to the poor. The best data available to us suggest that the number of automobile loans extended has not declined substantially in Wisconsin since the Act, despite tight money conditions for most of the period studied. Because the costs of repossession have indisputably risen significantly, it is likely nonetheless that the Act has had at least marginal impact in restricting credit availability, perhaps primarily by causing an increase in required downpayments. Our informal interviews with low value used car dealers, who presumably sell disproportionately to the poor, suggested there may have been a substantial restriction of credit to their clientele—primarily in the form of higher required down payments.
>
> Even if judicialized repossession has made credit less available, especially to the poor, on the premises of welfare economics it cannot be determined whether this reduced credit availability increases or decreases resource allocation efficiency. The marginal return to society of the most risky automobile credit now extended may not exceed its marginal costs, for example because of the various externalities associated with default and repossession. A similar theoretical conclusion can be drawn about the position of the poor themselves; if there is a proclivity by consumers to undervalue long-term risks, such as those associated with default, the benefits of credit to the highest risk debtor can be less than its costs. The possibility that the poor are "better off" because of reduced credit availability is enhanced if the restriction of credit to the poor has taken the form primarily of higher downpayments, as seems likely. Then, many poor can adapt to this change simply by buying a cheaper car, thereby maintaining mobility but reducing the costs of default, since less is obligated or risked. There is some evidence that any reduced credit availability for the poor has had this effect, for example the MVD data indicating no reduction in the volume of secured credit sales of motor vehicles since the Consumer Act became effective.
>
> The critics of judicialized repossession have not predicted the magnitude and form of the reduction in credit availability in terms that permit us to test whether the magnitude of any reduction in Wisconsin is less than they expected. Nevertheless, they seem to have expected a more substantial reduction than the available data suggest has occurred. It must be noted that most of the critics were concerned

* Copyright © 1975 by the Wisconsin Law Review. Reprinted by permission of the publisher and the authors.

with evaluating the impact of litigation challenging the constitutionality of self-help repossession. As a legislative enactment, the Wisconsin Consumer Act could and did adopt a number of cost-saving procedures that could not result directly from a constitutional decision. Chief among these is the provision limiting or dispensing with the need for attorneys in repossession actions. In addition to understandably failing to account for these cost-saving procedures, however, we believe the critics underestimated the ability of creditors to avoid some potential extra costs of judicialized repossession by altering their collection procedures. In particular, since the alternative of repossession is less attractive, on theoretical grounds we would expect creditors to tighten up informal collection practices. We would also expect a reduced rate of repossession and a higher frequency of refinancing agreements.

One of the major objectives of the study was to test our hypothesis that judicializing repossession would tend to increase workouts and reduce repossessions. The hypothesis was beautifully confirmed during the first year of the Act, as the number and the rate of repossessions declined precipitously, both absolutely and relative to the experience elsewhere. During the second year, repossessions rose rapidly. At this time it is impossible to know whether the second year reflects the beginning of a continuous upward trend in repossession rates or simply a correction of creditor overreaction in the first year of the Act to the assumed difficulty of judicialized repossession. If the latter, repossessions can be expected to level off at or somewhat below the rate that would have existed in the absence of the Act, as best as it can be estimated from changes in repossession rates elsewhere. Our theoretical analysis leads us to favor the latter explanation of course—and our personal interviews with the large creditors offered some support for this explanation—but only empirical research at a later time can conclusively resolve this issue.

* * * Our results are hardly conclusive, but we remain impressed nevertheless with the possibility that judicialized repossession can enhance the general welfare by inducing greater creditor efforts at informal collection, including the arrangement of refinancing agreements. A successfully completed workout benefits everybody, largely because the extra use value of the automobile in the debtor's hands is preserved, whereas it is typically destroyed by repossession. Informal collection, refinancing agreements, and to a lesser extent even voluntary surrender, can also avoid other secondary costs typically attending repossession—such as inconvenience and possibly loss of job—costs that might otherwise be borne by parties external to the transaction.

Voluntary Surrender: The New Battlefield

Even when the law abolishes self-help repossession, or loads it down with cure periods, have we merely shifted the pressure point in the continuing battle between unpaid creditor and consumer? Even the strongly pro-consumer MCCA, as well as the Wisconsin Consumer Act, would permit a consumer to give up collateral by "voluntary surrender." This raises the question of how much pressure or persuasion the creditor can bring to bear to induce a surrender which can fairly be said to be voluntary on the consumer's part. Keep in mind the creditor's desire to act quickly against depreciating collateral.

WACHAL v. KETTERHAGEN MOTOR SALES

Wisconsin Supreme Court, 1978.
81 Wis.2d 605, 260 N.W.2d 770.

FACTS

Plaintiff-respondent John J. Wachal brought this action against defendant-appellant Ketterhagen Motor Sales, Inc., for wrongful repossession of collateral under secs. 425.301(2), 425.305 and 425.308, Stats., sections of the Wisconsin Consumer Act which became effective on March 1, 1973.

On July 12, 1974, plaintiff bought a used Ford Torino station wagon from defendant in Whitewater, Wisconsin, agreeing to make a down payment and to pay monthly installments of $89.12 to defendant. The defendant assigned the conditional sales contract to the Commercial Bank of Whitewater with full recourse. The plaintiff missed three of the first five monthly payments and failed to obtain insurance on the station wagon as the sales agreement required.

On October 9, 1974, the plaintiff notified the Commercial Bank in writing that because of financial difficulties he could not make an October payment. The plaintiff received past due notices dated October 19 and November 15 from the bank. He also received a Notice of Consumer's Right to Cure Default, dated December 9, 1974. A Commercial Bank loan officer communicated with the plaintiff regarding his default in August, October, November and December.

On December 11 and 12, 1974, Joseph Ketterhagen, Jr., the secretary-treasurer of the defendant corporation, met the plaintiff in the parking lot of the Carnation Milk Company where the plaintiff was employed. Testimony as to what took place during these meetings between plaintiff and the officer of the defendant corporation will be reviewed in the opinion herewith. On December 13, 1974, while the plaintiff was at work, the officer of the defendant corporation brought a set of keys to the plaintiff's residence and repossessed the station wagon.

* * *

ROBERT W. HANSEN, JUSTICE.

This is the first appeal to this court involving the application of the Wisconsin Consumer Act, * * *. All issues raised by the appellant stand or fall on the answer to the question: Did the plaintiff "surrender" the station wagon to the defendant within the meaning of sec. 425.206(1)(a), Stats.?

Supplanting with respect to consumer credit transactions the provisions for repossession of collateral in the Uniform Commercial Code, the Wisconsin Consumer Act provides, subject to certain exceptions, that: "[N]o creditor shall take possession of collateral by means other than legal process in accordance with this subchapter." One exception to this requirement exempts cases where "(a) The customer has surrendered the collateral." If a merchant repossesses collateral other than in a "surrender" or through the prescribed legal processes, the creditor incurs substantial penalties, statutorily specified. * * *

As to the "voluntary surrender" of collateral, the Act provides: "Notwithstanding * * * any other law, the customer shall have the right at any time to voluntarily surrender all of his rights and interests in the collateral to the merchant." The Act defines a "voluntary surrender" as follows: "The surrender of collateral by a customer is not a voluntary surrender if it is made pursuant to a request or demand by the merchant for the surrender of the collateral, or if it is made pursuant to a threat, statement or notice by the merchant that the merchant intends to take possession of the collateral." The parties agree that if the surrender here was voluntary, the plaintiff's action for wrongful repossession of the collateral would fail, and it is clear that it would. * * *

As might be expected, the evidence presented at trial concerning the circumstances surrounding the repossession of the station wagon is in conflict. Particularly sharp is the conflict in the testimony as to what was said by each party during the two conversations in the parking lot at the plaintiff's place of employment. For the defendant corporation, its secretary-treasurer, Joseph Ketterhagen, Jr., testified that, when he met the plaintiff in the parking lot for the second time on December 12th, the plaintiff told him that the paycheck from which he had promised a payment had been garnisheed. The corporate officer testified he then said, "Well, Mr. Wachal, we can't go on this way. Something has to be done" and that Mr. Wachal replied, "Well, you will have to take the car" and added, "Would you do me a favor and give me a day to clean it out?" If this was all that transpired prior to the repossession, a finding of a "voluntary surrender" of the station wagon by the plaintiff would have been supported by the evidence.

The plaintiff, however testified that Mr. Ketterhagen met him in the parking lot after work on December 11th, asked him if he had some money to pay on the station wagon and warned him, " * * * if I * * * couldn't get a payment to him, he would have to take the car." The plaintiff also testified that he told Mr. Ketterhagen that he would get paid the next day and would try to make a payment out of that check. According to the plaintiff, Mr. Ketterhagen then asked him where he lived and where he kept the station wagon and told him that he would come back again the next day for the payment. The plaintiff testified that the next day Mr. Ketterhagen met him again in the parking lot but, because his wage check had been garnisheed, he told Mr. Ketterhagen that he could not make a payment on the station wagon. Plaintiff further testified that Mr. Ketterhagen then told him, "Well, he said he had no alternative. He would have to come and get the car." Plaintiff testified that he told Ketterhagen, " * * * if he had to come and get it that I would have to have time to get it cleaned out to get my personal things out and stuff like that."

In its memorandum opinion the trial court placed heavy stress on the circumstances surrounding the actual taking of the station wagon by the defendant's officer on December 13, 1974. On that date, while the plaintiff was at work, the officer went to the plaintiff's residence where he knew the car was parked and took with him a duplicate set of keys. The wife of the plaintiff refused the officer's request that she turn over the keys to the car. While there is no evidence that the plaintiff directed his wife to refuse to surrender the keys, it was conceded by the defendant at trial and the trial court so found that the defendant's officer used a duplicate set of keys to drive the station wagon away and that the personal effects of the plaintiff were not removed from the car. The trial court concluded that "the surrender of the vehicle was not 'voluntary' on the part of the plaintiff. [The car] was, I believe 'snatched' in the very manner condemned by the drafters of the comparatively new Consumer Code." That is strong language. But it is clear that the circumstances surrounding the actual taking strongly support the trial court's holding that the taking here was not a "voluntary surrender" as it is defined by the Act. On these facts and this record the judgment in favor of the plaintiff is affirmed.

Problem 5

Bud Genius, a resident of Wisconsin, is four days late with his stereo payment. The credit manager for General Electric Credit Company, which holds his contract, calls Bud and says: "Look, Bud, you've been late with several other payments before. You're working on your Ph.D. in history, and we know there are no jobs in that field, so you are not likely to have any steady income in the near future. Why don't you just let us take back the stereo and try to get the best possible resale price on it now before the new models come out. I've got a guy on his way over to your place right now, and I hope you'll be reasonable and save us both a lot of time, trouble and expense by surrendering the stereo."

When the GECC man arrives, Bud lets him take the stereo away. Has GECC violated the Wisconsin Consumer Act (which is modeled on the MCCA)?

If Bud lived in a state which had enacted the U3C, would GECC have violated that statute? See U3C § 5.111(3).

Problem 6

Donna Homa bought a new Ford from East Towne Ford, Inc. The purchase was financed by Ford Motor Credit Co. After having missed five payments in a row, she took the car to East Towne Ford for repairs. While she was waiting, the business manager initiated a discussion with her about her missing payments, gave her a voluntary surrender form and asked her to read and sign it. She did so. On the form, above the signature line, was a statement which read: "You have the right to a hearing on the issue of default before repossession." Has East Towne Ford violated the Wisconsin Consumer Act? See Homa v. East Towne Ford, Inc., 125 Wis.2d 73, 370 N.W.2d 592 (App.1985).

CHRYSLER CREDIT CORP. v. McKINNEY
Supreme Court of Alabama, 1984.
38 U.C.C.Rep.Serv. 1409.

SHORES, J. Defendant Chrysler Credit Corporation appeals from a judgment entered against it and in favor of the plaintiffs in the amount of $20,000. We affirm.

In July 1980, Jimmy McKinney bought a Dodge Mirada from Countywide Dodge for his wife's use. He negotiated and executed on behalf of McKinney Ceramic Tile Co., Inc., of which he was president and majority stockholder, a retail installment contract financing the automobile with Chrysler Credit Corporation. McKinney made only two payments pursuant to this agreement, because Countywide Dodge failed to repair the car to his satisfaction.

McKinney returned the car to Countywide Dodge on numerous occasions for repairs. The dealership successfully repaired most of the defects, but never succeeded in repairing a leak in the roof of the automobile. This leak was so bad that at times, after a rainshower, two inches of water was left standing in the front floor. Because of this repeated leaking, the car's interior had an offensive odor, and the leather interior was damaged.

Mr. McKinney visited the dealership time after time and, at one point in September, explained the problem to the owner of Countywide Dodge, who assured him it would be repaired. It was not. He then wrote letters to the dealership, Chrysler Corporation, and Chrysler Credit Corporation, notifying them that he would make no more payments on the vehicle until the leak was repaired. He received no responses to these letters. Chrysler Credit later telephoned him about his failure to make the payments on the vehicle. Once again, he discussed the leak in the roof and was assured that it would be repaired. Soon thereafter, James Smith, a repossession agent of Chrysler Credit, contacted Mrs. McKinney about the car and the McKinneys' failure to make the payments on the note. Mrs. McKinney met Smith at a restaurant to discuss the matter. After a conversation, wherein Mrs. McKinney detailed to Smith the problem with the car, she and Smith reached an agreement. Mrs. McKinney testified as follows concerning the agreement:

> "He [Smith] told me that everything was fine, that all he had to do was to get me to take the car into the lot and it would be fixed. You know, they would fix the leak in it. And, if they fixed the leak in it, then we would bring up the payment, which I agreed to."

Mrs. McKinney called their attorney from the restaurant. He spoke with Smith and confirmed the agreement not to repossess the car unless and until the McKinneys failed to bring the payments up to date following the repair of the vehicle's roof.

Mrs. McKinney and Smith then left the restaurant and drove to the dealership, where Mrs. McKinney surrendered the automobile to the dealership for repairs. The owner of the dealership confirmed the agreement to catch up the past due payments when the car was repaired.

A few days later, Chrysler Credit sent repossession notices to the McKinneys, advising them that the automobile had been repossessed and would be sold within five days after the receipt of those notices. The attorney for the McKinneys corresponded with Chrysler Credit, informing them of the agreement that repossession would not occur unless the repairs were made and the payments were not then brought up to date. Chrysler Credit did not respond to this letter.

The day after the repossession took place, Chrysler Credit called upon Countywide Dodge to pay off the McKinney account, pursuant to its recourse agreement, which it did.

Following these events, Countywide again made numerous attempts to repair the leaking roof in the car. Several times Mr. McKinney went in to the dealership and, each time, the roof leaked when tested. Later, Mr. McKinney was told to remove his personal belongings from the vehicle because it was no longer his car and was being sold. Thereupon Mr. McKinney filed suit against Chrysler Credit, Chrysler Corporation, and Countywide Dodge.

The trial court granted Countywide's motion for directed verdict at the close of the plaintiffs' case. The jury returned a verdict against Chrysler Corporation and in favor of the plaintiffs for breach of warranty. That verdict is not an issue in this appeal. The jury also returned a verdict against Chrysler Credit Corporation for $20,000.00 on a conversion claim.

Only Chrysler Credit appealed. It argues that a conversion of the plaintiffs' vehicle never took place because the McKinneys were in default, and Chrysler Credit, acting within its rights under § 7-9-503, Ala. Code 1975, was entitled to possession. * * * Section 7-9-503 gives the secured party the right to possession upon default, but it does not authorize repossession by trick or fraud.

The evidence in this case would permit a jury to find that Mrs. McKinney was tricked into surrendering the automobile to the repossession agent of Chrysler Credit and the Dodge dealer. The evidence also supports a finding that Chrysler Credit fraudulently led Mrs. McKinney to believe that the car would not be repossessed unless the McKinneys failed to make the necessary payments after the car was repaired. The jury could find that Chrysler Credit breached the agreement and two days later sent the McKinneys repossession notices.

The facts here are very similar to those considered in Ford Motor Credit Company v. Byrd, 351 So.2d 557 (Ala.1977), where the court held that a repossession by trick, artifice, or fraud is wrongful and will support an action for conversion of the chattel.

In Byrd, the owner/debtor was persuaded to take his car to the dealership in order to establish whether he was in fact in default. Once the car was on the dealer's lot, and while the owner was inside reviewing his account, the car was taken and locked in a storage area, without the knowledge of the owner.

Self-help repossession is not permitted in all circumstances. As this court set out in Byrd:

"We cannot interpret § 9–503 to permit obtaining possession through trick, without knowledge on the part of the debtor. To interpret § 9–503 to allow repossession in these circumstances would encourage practices abhorrent to society: fraud, trickery, chicanery, and subterfuge, as alternatives to employment of judicial processes that foster the concept of ours being a government of laws and not of men." 351 So.2d at 559.

As Byrd held, a repossession by artifice, trick, or fraud will support an action for conversion. The evidence clearly supports the jury's finding of wrongful repossession and conversion.

Chrysler Credit maintains that a repossession and sale never actually took place. However, all the records are marked with the large stamp, "REPO"; Chrysler Credit was billed for the "repossession of Jimmy McKinney" by its agent, Smith; and Chrysler Credit proceeded to demand a repurchase of the McKinneys' note by the dealership, Countywide. Chrysler Credit acknowledged the receipt of the money for the repurchase of the McKinneys' note on November 26, 1980, the day after the repossession took place. This evidence supports the jury's verdict that a repossession and sale of the collateral, in violation of the McKinneys' right of title and possession, took place.

* * *

Chrysler Credit also argues that the trial judge erred in giving plaintiffs' requested charges numbers one and two, which read:

Charge # 1:

"I charge you ladies and gentlemen of the jury that the plaintiffs in this case were entitled to withhold payment to Chrysler Credit Corporation in the event you find from the evidence that the automobile in question was substantially defective and that the selling dealer failed to repair the defect within a reasonable time after notice of the defect."

Charge # 2:

"I charge you ladies and gentlemen of the jury that if you find from the evidence that the automobile in question contained a substantial defect which was not repaired after notice to the selling dealer within a reasonable time, then you may conclude that the Plaintiffs in this case were justified in withholding payments to Chrysler Credit Corporation."

We find no error in the judge's instruction to the jury.

The plaintiffs properly withheld payment on the automobile until all the defects which impaired the value of the vehicle to them were repaired. Certainly, a substantial defect existed in the McKinneys' automobile and, until that defect was cured or repaired, the McKinneys had the right under their installment contract to withhold payment on the vehicle. That contract was assigned to Chrysler Credit and contained a provision which read: "Any holder of this consumer credit contract is subject to all claims and defenses which the debtor could assert against the seller of goods or services obtained pursuant hereto or with the proceeds hereof." Countywide Dodge had failed to honor its commitment to repair the vehicle, thereby subjecting Chrysler Credit to the McKinneys' right to withhold payment. The judge's instructions to that effect were properly given.

* * *

The judgment of the trial court is hereby affirmed.

Affirmed.

Notes

1. Three months after this opinion was handed down, the Alabama Supreme Court withdrew the opinion and remanded the case for a new trial because one of the jurors was not qualified. See Chrysler Credit Corp. v. McKinney, 456 So.2d 1069 (Ala.1984).

2. Would the result have been different if the security agreement had contained a clause which stated "no modification of any of the terms of this agreement shall be valid unless made in writing and expressly assented to by the seller"?

Problem 7

While he was behind on his payments to Big Bank, Woodstock took his car to Linus's garage for repair. Lucy, an officer of Big Bank, traced the car to the garage and went to repossess it. Linus told Lucy that she could not have the car unless she paid the repair bill. Lucy agreed, paid Linus, and took the car. Is Big Bank liable for wrongful repossession?

SECTION B. LIQUIDATING THE COLLATERAL AND SEEKING A DEFICIENCY

For the creditor, repossessing the collateral is merely the first step. The creditor does not really want to keep the collateral; he wants money. The normal method of turning the collateral into money is to resell it, either at a public or a private sale. From your courses in commercial transactions, you will recall that resales of collateral are governed by Article 9 of the UCC. Under § 9–504(3), the creditor has great latitude in choosing the specific means for conducting the sale; the primary restriction is that all aspects of any sale must be "commercially reasonable." These restrictions are basically the same for consumer cases as for large commercial cases; we will not review all of that law here. (If you need review, see White & Summers, Uniform Commercial Code § 25–9 et seq. (3d ed. 1988)).

From the consumer perspective, a more important issue is the debtor's liability for the deficiency. Under UCC § 9–504(2), if the resale of the collateral does not bring enough money to cover the outstanding indebtedness, the debtor remains liable for the balance. Naturally, the manner of resale can have a significant effect on this. For example, the creditor might fail to resell the collateral in a commercially reasonable manner. This might produce a return which is less than the fair value of the collateral, and this, in turn, would increase the deficiency. Likewise, the creditor might sell the collateral at wholesale, where a sale at retail might have produced a much higher price. Does the consumer have a right to complain about these allegedly improper resales?

IMPERIAL DISCOUNT CORP. v. AIKEN

New York City Civil Court, Kings County, 1963.
38 Misc.2d 187, 238 N.Y.S.2d 269.

FRANK COMPOSTO, JUDGE.

This is an action on a retail installment contract by Imperial Discount Corporation, an alleged purchaser for value of said contract. After a hearing held on this inquest, the plaintiff's complaint is dismissed.

Despite the fact that there is no appearance on behalf of the defendant, the Court deems itself duty-bound to require of the plaintiff that minimum measure of proof to sustain its cause of action. While the Court will sustain a recovery to which a plaintiff is justly and fairly entitled, it will not grant judgment where, as here, plaintiff has failed to prove to the satisfaction of the Court that it met the statutory prerequisites.

The defendant, owner of a 1955 Oldsmobile, purchased a Delco battery on credit from a retail auto store for $29.30. In order to be permitted to pay by weekly installments, he agreed to a "credit service charge of $5.70." He thus started his journey into the cavernous depths of indebtedness with his 1955 Oldsmobile, a new Delco battery and a debt of $35.00, attested to by his signature on the aforesaid retail installment contract with its inevitable fine print and legalistic verbiage.

He failed to make due and timely weekly payments, and there came a time when a summons and verified complaint of eight paragraphs was served upon him in this case. * * *

Paragraph third of the complaint relates to the purchase by defendant "of certain goods, wares, and merchandise (the battery), at the agreed and stated price of $35.00, no part of which has been paid, excepting the sum of $23.25, leaving a balance due and owing of *$11.75."*

Paragraph fourth alleges the defendant owes late charges of twenty-five cents.

Paragraph fifth alleges defendant owes plaintiff's attorney fees of $16.80.

Paragraph sixth alleges the defendant owes plaintiff repossessing charges of $45.00. The retail installment contract had a provision that "The buyer hereby mortgages the motor vehicle hereinafter described as additional security for the payment of the time balance set forth above, together with any other motor vehicle hereinafter acquired in replacement thereof." Plaintiff caused the defendant's automobile to be repossessed, and as alleged in paragraph seventh, the repossessed automobile was sold at public auction, and the defendant owes auctioneer's fees of $35.00 and storage charges of $70.00, based on a charge of $2.50 per day for 28 days.

Paragraph eighth is the only paragraph in which the defendant may find a modicum of comfort. It does not allege he owes for any item of damage—in fact, he is given credit for $50, the amount for which his repossessed automobile was sold. Then follows the allegation "That pursuant to the said chattel mortgage and installment contract, there is presently due the total of $128.80."

When the defendant's journey, which started with an indebtedness of $35.00, of which $23.25 had been paid, leaving a balance of $11.75, reached its unsought destination in this court, the defendant was *sans* his battery, *sans* his automobile, and confronted with a demand for "judgment for $128.80, together with interest, costs, and disbursements of this action." The futility of trying to free himself of the engulfing accumulation of charges must have so overwhelmed the defendant that he failed to answer the summons and complaint, and thus this inquest.

The defendant must now have realized the import of the despairing observation that "For want of a nail, a shoe was lost; for want of a shoe, a horse was lost; for want of a horse, a kingdom was lost." For want of $11.75, this defendant lost the battery, lost his 1955 Oldsmobile, and is subject to a judgment for $128.80.

The proof offered by plaintiff fails to satisfy the Court that it complied with all the prerequisites of the applicable law; but transcending questions of proof, the conscience of the Court is shocked by the mountainous pyramiding of charges imposed on a defaulting installment buyer, which are seemingly sanctioned by the Retail Instalment Sales Act. Apparently this is not an isolated case. The Court is of the opinion that the Legislature never contemplated such oppressive, confiscatory, and unconscionable results. If this is an example of the practical working of the aforesaid law, then clearly the need for remedial legislation is manifest.

Judgment on inquest denied, complaint dismissed.

Notes

1. The court says that the creditor failed to meet the statutory prerequisites for judgment. How? Did the creditor fail to comply with the requirements of Article 9? Did it do anything illegal? What is the basis for the court's ruling?

2. Would the result be the same under the U3C? See especially §§ 3.301 and 5.103.

Problem 8

You are local counsel for Farmer's Credit Co. They repossess and resell about a hundred cars and tractors a month. They wish you to draft guidelines to govern their resale procedures, and to draft them in such a way that there will be no violations of any statute.

In particular they wish to know (1) whether they can continue to sell at both public and private sale; (2) at what point in time they must decide whether a repo will be sold at public sale or at private sale; (3) to whom notices must be sent; (4) how the notices will read (Please draft samples); and (5) when they must be sent. For each type of sale they also wish to know (1) where, when and under what conditions they must be held; (2) whether advertising is necessary in addition to all the notices which were sent out; (3) whether Farmer's can purchase the repo itself; and (4) at what price it may so purchase the repo.

Read carefully UCC § 9–504. There is no section in the U3C which similarly governs the method of resale.

Problem 9

Farmer's financed the purchase of a used tractor by Cecil Goodin from Daring Dealers for $4000. When Goodin fell behind in his payments, Farmer's repossessed the tractor without breach of the peace. Farmer's decided to sell the tractor at public sale, and followed exactly the guidelines you developed in Problem 1. It notified, not only Goodin, but also everybody else they could think of. They advertised in six separate local newspapers. But, alas! At the time and place of the public sale, no one appeared except Farmer's, and it did not want to buy. After the sale had been held open for one hour, an agent of Daring Dealers appeared and bid $250. The sale was held open for another two hours, but no other bidders appeared, and the tractor was then sold to Daring for $250.

Goodin can present the following evidence: Daring "overhauled" the tractor at a cost of $1000, and is now attempting to resell it for $4000. Father Tuck, a local priest and noted agronomist, is willing to testify that the tractor was worth at least $3000 at the time of the sale, before the overhaul; and he would have bid that price if he had been present at the public sale. Has your client violated Article 9 by allowing the tractor to be bid in at $250? Cf. Goodin v. Farmers Tractor & Equipment Co., 249 Ark. 30, 458 S.W.2d 419 (1970). Is UCC § 9–507 controlling in this case?

Problem 10

(a) Mallicoat purchased a car from Hull–Dobbs for $600. He paid $250 down, and financed the remaining $350 through Volunteer Finance Company. The $350, plus a finance charge of $227, created a principal balance of $577 to be paid in 15 monthly installments of $38.47 each. The credit contract granted a security interest in the car to Volunteer. After paying one installment Mallicoat refused to make additional payments, claiming the car was defective. Volunteer repossessed. It then sent a registered letter to Mallicoat stating that the car would be sold to the highest bidder, but no mention was made of the time and place of sale. The letter was returned to Volunteer as unclaimed.

Two weeks later there was a public sale at which the car was sold to Beeler Motor Co. for $150, which was probably a fair price for the car. Volunteer now seeks a deficiency judgment. How would you decide the claim? Volunteer claims that notice is not important if a fair price is realized. Mallicoat claims that inadequate notice was given, and no notice received. Which argument should prevail? If Mallicoat prevails, which is the more appropriate remedy—the 9–507 penalty of the UCC, or the "no deficiency judgment" of *Hansen?* Compare Mallicoat v. Volunteer Finance & Loan Corp., 57 Tenn.App. 106, 415 S.W.2d 347 (1966) with Barker v. Horn, 245 Ark. 315, 432 S.W.2d 21 (1968).

(b) Would it make a difference if the car was *voluntarily surrendered* to Volunteer by Mallicoat, rather than repossessed? Compare Nelson v. Monarch Investment Plan, 452 S.W.2d 375 (Ky.1970), with Moody v. Nides Finance Co., 115 Ga.App. 859, 156 S.E.2d 310 (1967).

SAVOY v. BENEFICIAL CONSUMER DISCOUNT CO.

Supreme Court of Pennsylvania, 1983.
468 A.2d 465.

FLAHERTY, J. This is an appeal from an order of the Superior Court which reversed and vacated an order of the Court of Common Pleas of Delaware County awarding a deficiency judgment to the appellant, Beneficial Consumer Discount Company (hereinafter Beneficial), following repossession and resale of a vehicle in which Beneficial held a security interest. Beneficial had loaned to the appellee, Julia Savoy, the sum of $4,752.00, with repayments to be made in monthly installments. To secure repayment, Beneficial obtained a security interest in a 1964 Cadillac owned by Savoy. A default in payment occurred in October, 1968, and, as a result of this and of subsequent defaults, the vehicle was repossessed. In January, 1969, it was resold by Beneficial to a used car dealer, via an unadvertised private sales offering, at a bid price of $250.00. Beneficial credited the sale price, less expenses, to the amount owed by Savoy, and the instant action was commenced to recover the balance remaining due on the loan.

The trial court held that resale of the Cadillac for the price of $250.00 was not commercially reasonable, and, hence, rejected Beneficial's computation of the remaining loan deficiency. Rather, the court took judicial notice of the Redbook value of the vehicle and reduced the original deficiency by that amount, awarding judgment for the resulting balance. Savoy took an appeal from the deficiency judgment to the Superior Court, which held that the lower court erred in taking judicial notice of the Redbook value of the vehicle and further held that, when there has been a commercially unreasonable disposition of collateral by a secured creditor, a presumption arises that the value of the collateral was equal to the amount of the indebtedness. On grounds that Beneficial had not sustained its burden of rebutting that presumption, Superior Court vacated the deficiency judgment. We affirm.

The Uniform Commercial Code confers upon a secured party the right, upon default, to dispose of collateral by sale or lease, subject to the requirement that "every aspect of the disposition including the method, manner, time, place and terms must be *commercially reasonable*." 13 Pa CSA § 9504(c) (emphasis added). When a private sale of repossessed collateral has been made, and the debtor raises the question of the commercial reasonableness of that sale, the great weight of authority holds that the burden of proof on this issue is shifted to the secured party seeking a deficiency judgment to show that, under the totality of circumstances, the disposition of collateral was commercially reasonable.

The trial court determined that Beneficial did not sustain its burden of showing that the $250.00 price obtained upon resale, in January, 1969, of the 1964 Cadillac in question was commercially reasonable. Beneficial proffered the Redbook, of which judicial notice was taken, but which tended to indicate, as discussed infra, that Cadillacs of the 1964 model year may have had, at approximately the time of the instant resale, values substantially in excess of $250.00. Beneficial entered into evidence a business record showing that a total of three separate bids were received from used car dealers in response to its private sales offering of the Cadillac. The actual amounts of those bids, however, were excluded on grounds they constituted hearsay evidence of value. Significantly, Beneficial did not submit *any* evidence relating to the condition of the automobile at the time of resale. In short, Beneficial failed to establish reasonableness of the resale price procured.

When there has been a commercially unreasonable disposition of collateral, the issue arises as to the effect of that disposition upon a creditor's entitlement to recovery of remaining debt. It is the view in certain jurisdictions that when a sale is found to have been commercially unreasonable, the creditor should be barred entirely from obtaining a deficiency judgment against the debtor. Other courts have held that failure to establish commercial reasonableness of the resale price creates a presumption that the value of the collateral equalled the indebtedness secured, thereby extinguishing the indebtedness unless the secured party rebuts the presumption. We believe that the latter approach, which was adopted by Superior Court in the instant case, is the more enlightened and equitable. The former approach, foreclosing a creditor from the possibility of securing any deficiency judgment, would provide the debtor with a windfall relief from his obligation while extinguishing a creditor's right to recover sums truly owed. Further, in conjunction with the rebuttable presumption now adopted, the debtor's interests are adequately protected by Code provisions allowing the debtor a right to recover any losses caused by a secured party's failure to comply with the requirement that collateral be disposed of in a commercially reasonable manner. 13 Pa CSA § 9507(a).

The issue that remains, therefore, is whether Beneficial sustained its burden of rebutting a presumption that the value of the 1964 Cadillac equalled the amount of the indebtedness. As discussed previously, Beneficial failed to enter into evidence proof that the value of the automobile corresponded to the price procured for it, viz. $250.00. Were it not for the fact that the trial court took judicial notice of a Redbook value for Cadillacs of the same model year, there would have been no basis for a conclusion that the value of the automobile was less than the amount of the indebtedness.

The trial court took judicial notice that the Redbook indicated a *wholesale* value for the particular Cadillac model as between $1,100.00 and $1,500.00 as of January, 1968, which was one year prior to the sale of collateral now in question. The court surmised that, due to the passage of that year, the *retail* value at the time of sale in January, 1969 should have been $1,500.00, which figure the court regarded as the vehicle's commercially reasonable value. We believe that, under the circumstances, it was error for judicial notice to have been accorded to the Redbook value of the collateral.

As this court stated in Albert Appeal, 372 Pa 13, 20, 92 A2d 663, 666 (1952), "The doctrine of judicial notice is intended to avoid the necessity for the formal introduction of evidence in certain cases when there is no real need for it,—where a fact is so well established as to be a matter of common knowledge." The value, however, of a given automobile at a particular time, when, as in the present case, there has been admitted no evidence as to its *condition*, is not an incontestable fact or a matter of common knowledge. In the absence of information regarding a vehicle's condition, there is no basis for comparison of its value with values of vehicles described in Redbook listings.

Hence, the trial court erred in concluding that the value of the collateral disposed of by Beneficial was other than, as is to be presumed where there has been a commercially unreasonable disposition of the same, an amount equal to the indebtedness. Beneficial's entitlement to a deficiency judgment has been extinguished by its failure to rebut the presumption as to the value of the collateral. Superior Court, therefore, properly reversed the order of the trial court and vacated the deficiency judgment.

Order affirmed.

FIRST STATE BANK OF MORRILTON v. HALLETT

Supreme Court of Arkansas, 1987.
291 Ark. 37, 722 S.W.2d 555.

HOLT, JR., C.J. The appellant, First State Bank (FSB), concedes it failed to give the appellee, Edith Hallett, proper notice before it sold her collateral which it repossessed when she defaulted on a promissory note. FSB nevertheless sought a deficiency judgment against Hallett for the balance owed on the note. The trial court granted Hallett's motion for summary judgment, dismissing the FSB claim. The issue on appeal is whether the failure of FSB as a secured party, to give proper notice to debtor Hallett of the time and place of the sale of repossessed collateral, as required by Ark.Stat.Ann. § 85–9–504(3) (Supp.1985), absolutely bars FSB's right to a deficiency judgment. We hold that it does and affirm the trial court. * * *

Hallett gave FSB a promissory note in the amount of $11,342.90, secured in part by a security interest in a 1983 pickup truck. Hallett defaulted. FSB repossessed the truck and sold it without written notice to Hallett of the sale date. A deficiency of $4,057.40 remained on the note. The trial court granted Hallett's motion for summary judgment because FSB had not complied with § 85–9–504(3)'s guidelines for the disposition of repossessed collateral. * * *

The trial court's ruling complies with our most recent decision, Rhodes v. Oaklawn Bank, 279 Ark. 51, 648 S.W.2d 470 (1983). In Rhodes, we reversed a deficiency judgment in favor of the secured party, and held:

> "When a creditor repossesses chattels and sells them without sending the debtor notice as to the time and date of sale, or as to a date after which the collateral will be sold, he is not entitled to a deficiency judgment, unless the debtor has specifically waived his rights to such notice."

FSB does not attempt to distinguish Rhodes, but rather argues that it should be overruled in favor of an earlier line of cases which took a different approach to this issue. Those cases did not bar a deficiency judgment altogether, but instead "indulg[ed] the presumption in the first instance that the collateral was worth at least the amount of the debt, thereby shifting to the creditor the burden of proving the amount that should reasonably have been obtained through a sale conducted according to law." We think Rhodes represents the right approach and, although it did not expressly overrule these cases, its effect was to change our law.

Creditors are given the right to a deficiency judgment by Ark.Stat. Ann. § 85–9–502(2) (Supp.1985): "If the security agreement secures an indebtedness, the secured party must account to the debtor for any surplus, and unless otherwise agreed, the debtor is liable for any deficiency." As stated, § 85–9–504(3) requires the creditor to send reasonable notification to the debtor before he disposes of this type of collateral. If the creditor does not dispose of the collateral in accordance with the code provisions, Ark.Stat.Ann. § 85–9–507 (Supp.1985) gives the debtor "a right to recover from the secured party any loss caused by a failure to comply with the provisions of this Part [§§ 85–9–501—507]."

There is a split of authority nationwide on the correlation of these provisions of the code. A group of cases follows the position that § 85–9–507 gives the debtor a defense to a deficiency judgment when the creditor has failed to give proper notice, and that the deficiency judgment is reduced by the damages the debtor can prove. Our previous cases, as represented by Norton, supra, followed this approach with the presumption in favor of the debtor that the collateral and the debt were equal and the burden placed on the creditor to prove a deficiency. The apparent majority position, however, with which we concur, is that § 85–9–507 is not applicable to the creditor's action to recover a deficiency judgment, but is a separate affirmative action by the debtor to recover damages. The creditor's right to a deficiency judgment is not merely subject to whether the debtor has a right to damages under § 85–9–507, but instead depends on whether he has complied with the statutory requirements concerning disposition and notice.

This view was explained in Atlas Thrift Co. v. Horan, 27 Cal.App. 3d 999, 104 Cal.Rptr. 315 (1972), quoting Leasco Data Processing Equip. Corp. v. Atlas Shirt Co., 66 Misc.2d 1089, 323 N.Y.S.2d 13 (1971):

"The plaintiff's contention that a secured creditor's right to a deficiency judgment under the described circumstances is limited only by the remedies set forth in 9–507 seems to me a tenuous one indeed, apart from the fact that no such effect was ever accorded the corresponding section in the Uniform Conditional Sales Act. * * *

"Preliminarily, it may be noted that Section 9–507 makes no direct allusion to the circumstances under which a right to a deficiency judgment may arise.

"More significant is the special nature of the language used: 'the debtor or any person entitled to notification * * * has a right to recover from the secured party any loss caused by a failure to comply with the provisions of this Part.' If this were intended to authorize a defense to action for a deficiency judgment, it is hard to envisage language less apt to that purpose. The words used plainly contemplate an affirmative action to recover for a loss that has already been sustained—not a defense to an action for a deficiency. The distinction between an affirmative action and a defense is a familiar one, phrases that articulate the different concepts are familiar in the law, and it is unlikely that the experienced authors of the [Uniform Commercial Code] intended by the above language to provide a limited defense to an action for a deficiency judgment based on a sale that had violated the simple and flexible statutory procedure.

"It seems far more probable that this latter section has nothing whatever to do with defenses to an action for a deficiency, since it was never contemplated that a secured party could recover such a judgment after violating the statutory command as to notice."

The Horan court concluded: "The rule and requirement are simple. If the secured creditor wishes a deficiency judgment he must obey the law. If he does not obey the law, he may not have his deficiency judgment."

When the code provisions have delineated the guidelines and procedures governing statutorily created liability, then those requirements must be consistently adhered to when that liability is determined. Here, FSB failed to comply with the code's procedures for disposition of collateral, and is therefore not entitled to a deficiency judgment under the code.

Affirmed.

HAYS, NEWBERN, and GLAZE, JJ., dissent.

Problem 11

Bill Bones owned a cottage on Lake Erie. Bill bought a sailboat on credit from Sam Silver for $8000. Bill made a down payment and signed a security agreement naming Silver as the secured party, and requiring 48 monthly payments of $200. Silver assigned this security agreement to Charlie Cheerful, promising to repurchase the contract if Bill should default.

The boat was delivered and Bill enjoyed the summer immensely and the June, July, and August payments were made on time. After Labor Day, Bones returned to the city. The monthly payments combined with the costs of storing the boat for the winter were too much. Bill defaulted on his September payment. On October 5, Charlie repossessed by convincing the owner of the storage dock that he was entitled to the boat. Charlie hooked the boat on a truck and drove away.

On October 7, Charlie notified Bill that the boat had been repossessed; that, unless Bill paid the September and October payments and $350 repossession costs before October 12, the boat would be sold as soon as possible after that date; and that Bill would be held accountable for any deficiency.

The letter arrived at Bill's home on October 8, but Bill was out of town on business. His wife did not know the boat had been taken from its winter storage dock and did not open the envelope. Bill returned home on October 11, read the letter, called Charlie and said that he would pay tomorrow. Bill did not show up on the 12th or the 13th. On the 14th Charlie delivered the boat to Boat Auction Co. which sold the boat at a regularly scheduled auction on October 16 for $5,500 cash. The auction was advertised twice each week in the classified section of the local newspaper. On October 15 and 16 the ad read: "All kinds of marine equipment for sale. Some new. Some repossessed. Some used. All at huge savings. Boat Auction Co. Pier # 1. Next auction: October 16 at 10:00 A.M." These auction sales were well known to the local boat enthusiasts and were often accompanied by spirited bidding. Indeed, in this case you are told by an appraiser that $5,500 was a fair price to have been paid for this particular boat.

Charlie sued Silver for the difference between the unpaid purchase price and the $5,500 received. In turn, Silver sued Bill for the deficiency.

(a) How would this controversy be resolved if the only controlling law were the Uniform Commercial Code?

(b) What decision if U3C 5.103 were in effect?

RANDOLPH v. FRANKLIN INVESTMENT CO.

District of Columbia Court of Appeals, 1979.
398 A.2d 340.

FERREN, ASSOCIATE JUDGE:

On January 27, 1977, a division of this court affirmed a $750 deficiency judgment against appellants, Joseph and Antoinette Randolph. The appellee finance company, Franklin Investment Co., Inc. (Franklin), had repossessed their automobile, resold it, and then sued to recover the difference between the proceeds of the sale and the balance due on the Randolphs' note. We vacated the division's opinion and granted the petition for rehearing en banc because of the "exceptional importance," D.C.App.R. 40, of resolving certain issues inherent in automobile financing transactions under District of Columbia law. We conclude that the decision of the trial court must be reversed and the deficiency judgment disallowed because Franklin resold the auto without the requisite notice to the Randolphs. We further conclude that the case must be remanded to the trial court for entry of an order granting the Randolphs leave to file their counterclaim, which the motions judge had declined to permit.

On November 15, 1968, the Randolphs entered into a contract with G.B. Enterprises, t/a Lee Ford, for the purchase of a 1965 Pontiac. After making a $300 cash downpayment, appellants owed a balance of $1,445 to which an insurance charge of $175.32 and a finance charge of $453.52 were added, leaving a total time-price balance of $2,073.84. The contract called for payment of 51 biweekly installments of $39.88, commencing November 30. On the date the contract was signed, Lee Ford assigned it and the accompanying promissory note, without recourse, to Franklin for $1,445 in cash.

During the first nine months of the contract, appellants were consistently late in making payments. Joseph Randolph testified that his paydays fell on different dates, and that when he had to be late with a payment he would call Franklin to explain that he had not been paid at work. Franklin admitted to accepting 17 consecutive late payments beginning with the first on December 3. Franklin assessed delinquency charges for twelve of these payments. On August 19, 1969, appellants submitted a payment which, under the original contract schedule, had fallen due on July 26. After receiving neither of the August payments nor the one falling due on the first Saturday of September, Franklin arranged for repossession of the car sometime between Monday, September 8, and Wednesday, September 10.

After an advertised public sale on September 26 at which no bids were submitted, the car was sold as scrap for $125 some four months later at a private sale in January 1970. There is a dispute as to whether the Randolphs had been notified about the public sale, but Franklin concedes that the Randolphs did not receive notice of the second, private sale.

In Franklin's action for a deficiency judgment, the trial court took evidence on the value of the automobile at the time of resale. The Randolphs testified that prior to repossession, the automobile was in excellent working condition. One of Franklin's vice-presidents then testified that he had not seen the car between its repossession and resale, but that the wholesale value of a 1965 Pontiac like the Randolphs' would have been between $375 and $800 at the time of the January 1970 resale. On the basis of this evidence, the trial court implicitly valued the Pontiac at $503, for it offset $378 against the claimed deficiency of $1,128 (net of the $125 sale proceeds) and awarded Franklin a judgment of $750.

* * * Franklin concedes that it did not notify the Randolphs of the proposed private sale. We conclude, contrary to the division's opinion, that Franklin's failure to give the required notice of the private sale was not cured—and legally could not be cured—by the trial court's determination of the reasonable value of the car (for which the Randolphs were given credit) at the time of the sale. Assuming, without deciding, that a creditor may pursue a deficiency judgment in this situation—contrary to the Randolphs' contention—we hold that by failing to give the required notice [of] the private sale, the creditor, Franklin, is not entitled to a deficiency judgment; its recovery is limited to the proceeds of the private sale.

A creditor's obligation to give the debtor notice of repossession and resale of collateral, as well as its responsibility to carry out this remedy in a prescribed fashion, is governed by the Uniform Commercial Code (UCC), and by the regulations promulgated by the District of Columbia Council pursuant to the Motor Vehicle Financing Act, D.C.Code 1973, § 40–902(e)(1). The UCC provides that following repossession, a secured party electing to dispose of the collateral must do so in a "commercially reasonable" manner, having sent the debtor reasonable advance notice of sale:

[The court quoted UCC § 9–504(3)]

* * *

The rules of court incorporate these creditor responsibilities. Super.Ct.Civ.R. 55–II(b) bars recovery of a deficiency judgment after repossession of personal property unless the plaintiff-creditor has "complied with applicable law" and the property has been "resold for a fair and reasonable price." We have to determine, therefore, how literal the creditor's compliance must be with the applicable statutes and regulations, in order to permit a deficiency judgment in Superior Court.

* * * Because Rule 55–II(b) denies the trial court authority to grant a deficiency judgment unless the plaintiff-creditor has "complied with applicable law," and because, as elaborated below, we conclude that the UCC and Title 5AA regulations preclude a deficiency judgment when proper notice of a public or private sale has not been given, we find no legal basis for the court to award a deficiency judgment when only the second requirement of the rule, resale at "a fair and reasonable price," is met.

Franklin argues, to the contrary, that the object of Rule 55–II(b) and of the notice requirements of the UCC and Title 5AA regulations is to insure that debtors whose property is repossessed are credited with no less than the fair market value of this collateral in any subsequent action for a deficiency judgment. It follows, according to Franklin, that the trial court fully accomplished the purpose of the UCC, the Title 5AA regulations, and, as a result, Rule 55–II(b) by finding the fair market value of the 1965 Pontiac, crediting the Randolphs with it, and thus properly limiting the deficiency judgment. In Franklin's view, therefore, the trial court rendered any breach of the notice requirements harmless—and thus immunized its decision from reversal.

Franklin's argument is unpersuasive. There are solid reasons why failure to give notice can never (in the absence of actual notice) be deemed harmless. In the first place, the UCC, § 28:9–506, and the regulations, 5AA DCRR § 5.2(b) and (c), guarantee a debtor the right to redeem the collateral at any time before the secured party has arranged for its disposition, provided that the debtor tender the balance due plus the expenses of retaking the property. Without appropriate notice of the date on or after which the creditor has scheduled sale of the property, the debtor will not have a clear idea of the time he has available to make the arrangements necessary for redemption. Moreover, unless the debtor has knowledge of the location where the property is stored, his redemption efforts may be hampered. The debtor, for example, may attempt to refinance the property by borrowing from friends, if not a financial institution. Such third parties may demand their own security interest in the property and may therefore desire to inspect it before committing themselves to any arrangement.

Second, even when redemption is not a realistic possibility, the debtor still has an important interest in knowing when and where the disposition of the collateral is to take place. Although the UCC requires a creditor to dispose of the collateral in a "commercially reasonable" fashion, § 28:9–504(3), and Rule 55–II(b) requires the creditor to demonstrate that a "fair and reasonable price" was received for the property, it is likely—as a practical matter—that the debtor, absent notice of the time and place of sale, will be severely disadvantaged in defending against the deficiency action. Simply put, he will be hard pressed to produce evidence, even if available, to rebut the contention that the creditor disposed of the property at a reasonable price.

It is true, of course, that under the UCC and District regulations, in the event of a private sale—as eventually occurred in the present case—the creditor is only required to notify the debtor 10 days in advance "of the time after which such private sale may be held." It follows, therefore, that absent a requirement of notice of the exact time and place of sale (in contrast with the notice required for a public sale or auction), notice of the time left prior to private sale is especially significant, for the debtor's option at that point is virtually limited to redemption; *i.e.,* unless the vehicle has remained until time of sale at "the exact address where the motor vehicle is stored" upon repossession, and the debtor has been able to watch over it until the sale takes place, the opportunity to monitor the private sale is not likely to be available.

It is no answer to say that the UCC's requirement of "commercial reasonableness," enforcible by the courts, will assure that the debtor receives credit for the full value of the collateral upon resale, as the questionable quality of evidence at the trial of this case attests. Given the availability of a deficiency judgment, as well as the requirement that the debtor receive any surplus upon resale, a secured creditor does not necessarily have an incentive to achieve the highest possible resale price (unless, perhaps, he knows the debtor is judgment proof). But even more to the point, when the creditor and his prospective purchaser are not dealing at arms length—*e.g.,* they are jointly owned or otherwise repeatedly deal with one another—there may even be perverse incentives for the creditor to minimize the price he receives in disposing of the collateral, in order that his affiliate can maximize the profit on a subsequent sale back to the public while the repossessor is made whole by the deficiency judgment. Studies have shown that this practice has been common in the District of Columbia. *See* Firmin & Simpson, *Business as Usual: An Empirical Study of Automobile Deficiency Judgment Suits in the District of Columbia,* 3 Conn.L.Rev. 511, 517 (1971).[10]

10. In cases where the auto dealer transfers the debtor's note to the finance company without recourse, it apparently was common in the District of Columbia not many years ago for the finance company to resell the repossessed automobile to the original dealer at a price well below the market value quoted by the National Automobile Dealers' Association, thereby facilitating an unnecessarily high deficiency claim and an inflated profit on the second resale. *See* Firmin & Simpson, *supra* at 517–19. In other instances, the auto dealer may transfer the debtor's note to the finance company with recourse, resulting, upon default, in the dealer's accepting reassignment of the note. *See* Corenswet, *I Can Get It For You Wholesale: The Lingering Problem of Automobile Deficiency Judgments,* 27 Stan.L.Rev. 1081, 1081–82 (1975) (Alameda County, California Study); Comment, *Remedies for Failure to Notify Debtor of Disposition of Repossessed Collateral Under the U.C.C.,* 44 U.Colo.L.Rev. 221, 225 (1972) ("Colo."). In that case, the dealer itself undertakes repossession and

In our review of the case law from other jurisdictions we have found two sharply contrasting lines of authority. The first establishes a rule requiring strict compliance with the UCC. A creditor who fails to comply with the statutory requirements for notice of resale is not entitled to a deficiency judgment. Because of the substantial prejudice to debtors in the absence of notice of resale, especially when compared to the ease with which any creditor can comply with the notice requirements, we adopt this strict rule. The second line of authority was followed by the trial judge and the division of this court. It would permit a creditor to obtain a deficiency judgment, despite failure to comply with notice requirements, if the creditor carries the burden of demonstrating that, irrespective of the actual proceeds on resale, "the fair and reasonable value of the security [was] credited to the debtor's account." *Conti Causeway Ford v. Jarossy,* 114 N.J.Super. 382, 276 A.2d 402, 404–05 (1971), *aff'd,* 118 N.J.Super. 521, 288 A.2d 872 (1972). We reject this approach. The trial court's judgment granting Franklin a $750 deficiency judgment accordingly must be reversed.

We turn, finally, to the motions judge's denial of the Randolphs' motion for leave to file a counterclaim. Approximately one month prior to trial—and two months after the trial date had been scheduled—the Randolphs sought leave to file an amended answer and a counterclaim. The amended answer alleged defenses of usury, as well as violations of the regulations on repossession and resale and of Rule 55–II(b) on deficiency judgments. The proffered counterclaim virtually mirrored the amended answer; the Randolphs affirmatively sought return of all illegal payments, as well as damages for wrongful, willful, and malicious repossession and resale.

The interrelatedness of defensive and affirmative relief is evident in the context of a secured creditor's action for a deficiency judgment under UCC § 9–504(2) and the debtor's corresponding right to recover under § 9–507(1) for the secured party's failure to comply with the UCC's repossession and resale provisions. Although § 9–507(1) provides for an affirmative debtor's remedy, not a defense to a deficiency judgment, it is commonly used to achieve a setoff, as well as a surplus for the debtor after setoff. *See Mallicoat v. Volunteer Finance & Loan Corp.,* 415 S.W.2d 347 (Tenn.1966); *Conti Causeway Ford v. Jarossy, supra.* It appears wholly at odds with the regulatory scheme, therefore, to permit a debtor to file an amended answer, based on the creditor's alleged violations of statutes and regulations, while denying the debtor the right to assert a compulsory counterclaim (which otherwise will be forever lost) based on the very same facts and provisions of law.

suit for a deficiency judgment after resale—again, not uncommonly resulting in a price below market value. *See* Corenswet, *supra* at 1081–82. *See generally* Hersbergen, *The Improvident Extension of Credit as an Unconscionable Contract,* 23 Drake L.Rev. 225, 256–59 (1974) (Des Moines, Iowa Study); White, *Representing the Low Income Consumer in Repossessions, Resales, and Deficiency Judgment Cases,* 64 Nw.U.L.Rev. 808 (1970); Shuchman, *Profit on Default: An Archival Study of Automobile Repossession and Resale,* 22 Stan.L. Rev. 20, 26–28 (1969).

Accordingly, we hold that the case must be remanded to the trial court for entry of an order permitting the Randolphs to file their counterclaim. In doing so, however, we should make two final observations.

We essentially are remanding to permit the Randolphs to pursue affirmative relief under UCC § 9–507(1). We sustain the division's view that the transaction was not usurious; thus, there is no longer a basis for the Randolphs' usury count in the proffered counterclaim seeking return of payments made.

* * *

Finally, under UCC § 9–507(1), remedies are theoretically available for wrongful repossession as well as wrongful resale. Although presumably this can lead to only one recovery, there is a theoretical possibility that the value of the automobile at the time relevant to a wrongful repossession action will differ from the value at the time relevant to a wrongful resale action. In reversing Franklin's judgment for a deficiency because of resale without the required notice to the Randolphs, we did not have to deal with their claim that repossession also had been wrongful. Now, however, we must consider whether to reach that issue, in view of our reinstatement of the counterclaim.

There is nothing in this record to indicate that the Randolphs' 1965 Pontiac had different values at the times of repossession and resale, four months apart. Moreover, the possibility that the Randolphs can prove a loss, based on a value of the auto in excess of the $1,128 balance due on their debt at the time of repossession, is highly speculative. Possibly, in fact, the Randolphs will ask for the formula remedy under § 9–507(1), arguing that it is available irrespective of any proved loss. Under the circumstances, therefore, we conclude that reinstatement of the counterclaim does not oblige us to consider the repossession issue.

Franklin's deficiency judgment is accordingly reversed, and the case is remanded to the trial court for entry of an order granting the Randolphs leave to file their counterclaim.

So ordered.

[The dissenting opinion of Judge Reilly is omitted.]

Notes

1. The approach taken in *Savoy* as to the burden of proof has been widely adopted; the creditor normally has the burden of proving that the resale was commercially reasonable. As for the consequences if it is not, most American jurisdictions today follow the *Savoy* rule that there is a rebuttable presumption that the collateral was worth the balance outstanding on the loan at the time of the resale. This presumption produces a zero deficiency, but the creditor can recover a deficiency if he can show that the resale brought full value for the collateral despite noncompliance with the UCC. See, e.g., Emmons v. Burkett, 256 Ga. 855, 353 S.E.2d 908 (1987). As demonstrated by *Hallet* however, the view is not unanimous, however, and many jurisdictions deny a deficiency judgment to the errant creditor.

Further, many states have special rules like that in *Randolph*, which deny deficiencies when the creditor screws up, and sometimes even when he doesn't. See U3C § 5.103.

2. Despite the efforts of the trial court in *Savoy*, the case law is nearly unanimous that the creditor is not obligated to resell at retail. Yet, can't it be argued that, in cases in which the creditor is himself a retail seller, it is not unreasonable to expect the creditor to use that market? What do you suppose ultimately happens to these cars? See Ford Motor Credit Company v. Jackson, 126 Ill.App.3d 124, 81 Ill.Dec. 528, 466 N.E.2d 1330 (1984).

3. Cases involving deficiency judgments tend to be viewed on a one-at-a-time basis. Either this creditor in this case complied with Article 9 or he did not; either he is entitled to a deficiency or he is not. And even the math is done on a case by case basis: the debt was $8,000; the resale brought $5,000; the deficiency therefore equals $3,000. But automobile creditors who deal with hundreds or even thousands of these cases each year are likely to have a different perspective. Few debtors bother to challenge resale practices; in fact, most debtors may have little interest in the case after the car is repossessed. They may be relieved when the creditor does not come after them for the deficiency. But practices commonly followed in the automobile industry indicate that debtors may have more at stake than they realize. The following material is designed to give you a more sophisticated perspective on all of this.

FEDERAL TRADE COMMISSION, BUREAU OF CONSUMER PROTECTION, CREDIT PRACTICES, STAFF REPORT AND RECOMMENDATION OF PROPOSED TRADE REGULATION RULE

260–94 (1980).

Most repossessions in the United States involve automobiles, mobile homes and similar large ticket items, with automobiles playing a dominant role. It has been estimated that as many as one million automobiles are repossessed each year.

* * *

According to the National Consumer Law Center, prejudgment loss of possession of an auto in a secured transaction resulted 75% of the time when there was a default. * * *

Most repossessed collateral is sold by the repossessing creditor for less than wholesale. The result is that consumers subject to repossession not only lose their property, but are left owing large deficiencies. This is true despite the fact that most repossessed collateral consists of items such as automobiles for which there exist readily available retail markets.

* * *

In this connection, the National Consumer Law Center's survey of 105 legal services offices in the United States is further evidence, on a nationwide scale, of the plight of consumers whose property is repossessed. In the area of repossessions, this study reports that:

"67% of the motor vehicle sales brought prices below fair *wholesale* market value * * *."

These figures translate into deficiency balances which the NCLC survey reports are pursued 71% of the time. Moreover, the NCLC reports that the "commercially reasonable" resale standard was a factor in judicial evaluations of repossession and deficiency judgments in only 13% of the reporting jurisdictions.

The consumer injury associated with low prices received for repossessed collateral is apparent. Consumers lose the use of property which is generally only replaceable by them at retail. They end up owing their creditor substantially more than they would if the property were sold in the retail market. The studies on this record all reveal that a retail price for collateral would, in most cases, eliminate any deficiency balance.

The large deficiencies resulting from current repossession sales practices are revealed in statistics supplied by creditors. Large banks responding to an American Bankers Association survey reported deficiencies averaging $1,165 or 45.8% of the amounts owed at the time of repossession. Ford Credit reported deficiencies in the first six months of 1977, averaging $780. In a sample of 38 repossessions sold in September of 1977, Security Pacific Bank reported deficiencies averaging $1,827 or over 40% of the balance owed.

In addition to the loss of their property, consumers experience the threats and costs associated with efforts to collect deficiency balances. While many creditors insisted that deficiencies are difficult or impossible to collect, this record contains abundant evidence that collection efforts are made.

* * *

This record shows that consumers are rarely in a position to challenge the amount of deficiencies assessed against them. The vast majority of judgments are taken by default, with no appearance by the consumer. While in rare cases a court may set aside a particularly self-serving resale, most of the time the consumer is at the mercy of his creditor when his property is sold. In this connection, creditor threats to enforce deficiency claims occur frequently with disruptive and harmful effects on those who receive them.

* * *

The evidence discussed in the previous section demonstrates that most deficiencies are assessed on the basis of sales of collateral at less than wholesale prices. However, the record also establishes that most expensive repossessed collateral, and in particular most repossessed automobiles, can be sold at retail, and that the resulting higher prices would reduce deficiencies. In some instances, deficiencies would be eliminated, and surpluses would be created. To evaluate the evidence on this subject, it is necessary to examine the market for repossessed cars in some detail.

[Earlier], we noted that about one third of all car repossessions are a result of loan transactions. In such transactions, the repossessing creditor is usually responsible for sale of the collateral. In half of all sales finance transactions, the creditor to which the finance contract was assigned is similarly responsible for sale of the collateral. In the remainder of sales finance transactions, a different system is used. The dealer and the creditor enter into what is often called a recourse arrangement.

Here a dealer and a creditor agree that in the event of a default, the dealer will "buy back" the contract from the creditor to whom it was assigned. The dealer pays off the amount due on contract and receives possession of the security, which he then sells. As noted above, indirect paper accounts for over two-thirds of all repossessions and one-half of all auto financing. One-half of the indirect paper transactions in the market are recourse transactions. Thus, while a majority of repossessed cars are sold by the repossessing creditors (in loan transactions and non-recourse sales), approximately one-third are currently sold by dealers as a result of recourse arrangements.

Record data covering in excess of 1,000 repossession sales by 28 dealers shows that the vast majority of recourse repossessions are currently sold at retail from the dealer's used car lot.

* * *

Repossessions sold by creditors other than dealers are ordinarily wholesaled. However, except in the case of total wrecks, the wholesale purchaser is usually a dealer who subsequently retails the car to a consumer.

Thus, the current experience shows that repossessed cars are retailed in the same manner as other used cars, either by the repossessing party or the dealer who purchases from the repossessing party. This fact raises two questions relevant to the evaluation of current practices. First, can repossessions that are now retailed only after a wholesale disposition be retailed directly, so that consumers subject to repossession can get the benefit of the retail price? Second, taking into account possible increased sales costs, do retail sales in fact result in smaller deficiencies? The record contains substantial evidence on both of these issues.

The record shows that two-thirds or more of repossessions involve sales finance transactions. In sales finance transactions, recourse agreements provide a method by which repossessed cars are directly placed in dealerships for retail sale. The practicality of this method is demonstrated by its widespread current use. Participants in the proceeding identified no economic differences between recourse and nonrecourse transactions which would prevent a shift from one form of financing to the other. Current patterns of usage are based largely on regional custom.

* * *

The record also contains evidence that many repossessed cars can be retailed directly by creditors. Many creditors already do this. Moreover, many creditors sell as many cars each year as a typical used car dealer, so that it would be feasible for them to establish the same sort of retail sales facilities. Security Pacific Bank sells almost 1,000 repossessions each year, primarily from a centralized lot with full-time mechanics. Security Pacific claimed it "does not have the repossession volume to make a retail used car operation viable." Yet many retail used car dealers sell 100 or fewer cars each year. By comparison, banks with a deposit size of over $500 million annually average 75 repossessions on loan transactions and 146 on non-recourse sales finance. Banks of this size hold 25% or more of all automobile credit in the United States. Finance company automobile credit is almost entirely in the hands of the automobile manufacturers' finance subsidiaries, each of which sells thousands of repossessed cars per year.

It thus appears that a majority of repossessed automobiles can be retailed directly. For those repossessions which are now handled on a recourse basis and sent directly to car lots, this would require no changes in existing ways of doing business. For many other repossessions, only moderate changes would be necessary.

* * *

This record reflects the fact that when a creditor repossesses a consumer's property, the interests of the creditor and those of the consumer do not coincide. The creditor does not necessarily have an incentive to obtain the highest possible price for the collateral. There are a number of reasons for this, including the fact that Article 9 of the U.C.C., which requires that any surplus be repaid to the consumer, imposes a ceiling on the return available to a creditor in a repossession sale. At the same time, the fact that deficiencies can be collected from consumers in many cases tends to mitigate any necessity of maximizing the repossession sales price. Moreover, any loss to a creditor in the form of an uncollected deficiency is mitigated by immediate tax benefits, which tend to reduce the amount of the actual loss by 50%.

The problems are different in the household goods market where there is no recognized market for the resale of household goods. Here, the creditor's repossession cost is low, but the benefits from repossession are also low. The costs to the consumer flowing from the loss of household necessities are devastating. In this context, what is very inexpensive for a creditor is very costly for a consumer and hence reflects a fundamental conflict of interests.

In the area of high priced collateral, creditors will invest in a repossession sales effort only to a point where the net return from the repossession sale equals the net return from resources invested in the collection of deficiencies. Thus, where the right to collect deficiencies exists, a lesser sales effort is a reasonable expectation. While this does not mean that creditors do not make some effort to sell repossessed collateral, the record demonstrates that creditors do not invest their resources in maximizing the sales price.

Many creditors testified that they preferred to devote their attention to credit activities and not to car sales, where repossessions must be sold:

> We want to be in banking and not in automobile vending.

An excerpt from a finance company procedural manual illustrates the connection between creditors' incentives and low prices for repossessed collateral:

> Selling repossessed cars is not our primary business—it is merely one problem in our financing operations. Make it clear to your prospects that because selling used cars is only a sideline of our main business, we cannot permit them to accumulate. So we set our own prices below the market to insure rapid turnover. Also bring out that we are merely trying to reduce our losses, not make a profit.

This policy reflects the fact that higher returns are available to the creditor when resources are devoted to activities other than U.C.C. sales. It ensures that collateral is sold as quickly as possible, despite the fact that this precludes a retail sale for a higher price.

Both the desire to concentrate on credit activities and the desire to liquidate collateral quickly are understandable business motivations. Nevertheless, they are inconsistent with maximization of sales prices and result in a divergence of interest between the creditor and the debtor whose collateral has been seized.

Creditor incentives are also affected by certain creditor-dealer agreements where a creditor conducts the sale but any loss is paid by the dealer who, in turn, may proceed against the consumer for a deficiency. In such cases, there is no creditor incentive to maximize the resale price. A similar situation may obtain in certain recourse sales where a dealer purchases the car from the creditor for less than its wholesale price and, at the same time, pays the creditor the difference between the "sale" price and the amount owed. The creditor is made whole. The dealer has an incentive to set the lowest possible price in order to maximize the "deficiency" which he will be entitled to collect. While the total amount paid by the dealer is the same, the "price" paid for the automobile determines the consumer's liability.

The conflicting interests discussed above take a more extreme form where creditors and sellers are able to maximize mutual profits by working cooperatively. Many repossession sales are characterized by self-dealing, collusion, and similar practices. Because of the clandestine nature of these practices, it is impossible to quantify their prevalence. However, their role in the market is significant * * * General Motors Acceptance Corporation engages in self-dealing and accounts for 10% or more of all repossessions in the United States.

Following purchase of the vehicle by GMAC, recourse cars were returned to the originating dealer who paid off GMAC based on the outstanding balance and not based on the "public sale" price GMAC charged itself. Non-recourse cars were resold by GMAC to third parties in a private sale. However, in all cases where a deficiency was permitted, it was assessed on the basis of the sale by GMAC to itself. Thus, in recourse transactions consumers were deprived of the benefit of a subsequent retail sale from the dealer's lot.

A New Idea for Valuation—The Dutch Approach

Dutch Civil Code § 1576 provides that the debtor in a hire-purchase transaction (their functional equivalent to an Article 9 secured transaction) has a right to re-purchase the collateral for 14 days after the creditor has repossessed. After the first repossession, the debtor need only bring the scheduled payments current in order to re-acquire possession of the collateral. After a second repossession, the debtor must satisfy the total obligation in order to re-acquire possession. However, a practice has grown up that the creditor places a valuation on the collateral (by appraisal or otherwise) soon after repossession, sends this valuation to the debtor, and permits the debtor to re-acquire the collateral for this stated "valuation price" during the 14 day period, and thereafter until actual redisposition by the creditor.

In the proposed Dutch Consumer Credit Act, currently under consideration by the government, the current practice described above, will be drafted into the statutory scheme. After repossession, the creditor will be required to place a valuation on the collateral, to notify the debtor of this valuation, and to permit the debtor to redeem the collateral for this "valuation price" for 14 days after notification, and thereafter until redisposition. Further, while the creditor may eventually resell the collateral at a price which is higher or lower than the valuation price, any deficiency sought by the creditor must give to the debtor a credit for the repossessed and resold collateral of at least the amount of the "valuation price."

The theory is that the debtor's redemption rights will keep the creditor from setting the "valuation price" too low. And, the limits on any later deficiency will keep the creditor from setting it too high. Thus, theoretically the creditor should make the most accurate valuation possible.

Is this an idea which would be useful in American consumer credit secured transactions?

IN RE FORD MOTOR CO.

Federal Trade Commission
94 F.T.C. 607 (1979).
vacated sub nom. Ford Motor Co. v. FTC, 673 F.2d 1008 (9th Cir.1982)
cert. denied sub nom. FTC v. Francis Ford, Inc., 459 U.S. 999.

DIXON, COMMISSIONER:

This case involves the alleged failure of a large Portland, Oregon automobile dealer to refund to its customers surpluses resulting from the repossession and resale of those customers' cars. The complaint was issued on February 10, 1976, and charged Ford Motor Company, Ford Motor Credit Company, and Francis Ford, Inc. with violation of Section 5 of the Federal Trade Commission Act (15 U.S.C. 45) by virtue of alleged failures to refund surpluses. On March 17, 1978, the case was withdrawn from adjudication with respect to Ford Motor Company and Ford Motor Credit Company, which had signed consent agreements (subsequently accepted and made final by the Commission) in disposition of the charges of the complaint. Proceedings as to the remaining respondent, Francis Ford, continued with hearings before Administrative Law Judge (ALJ) Lewis Parker. He entered an initial decision on January 4, 1979, that largely sustained the complaint, although not entirely to the satisfaction of complaint counsel who, along with respondent Francis Ford, have brought this matter to the Commission on cross appeals.

* * *

A. BACKGROUND

Francis Ford is one of the two highest-volume Ford dealers in the Portland, Oregon, area, with sales of roughly 2400 vehicles per year, and revenues in excess of $13 million during each of the two years preceding issuance of the complaint. About 70 percent of Francis Ford's retail sales of motor vehicles are financed in whole or in part, either through Ford Motor Credit Co. or the United States National Bank of Oregon.

When a customer purchases a car on credit, he or she will typically execute an installment contract that calls for monthly installment payments and grants a security interest in the automobile as protection against nonpayment. The contract is then assigned by Francis Ford to the lending institution. By agreement with both Ford Motor Credit Co. and U.S. National Bank of Oregon, each retail installment contract assigned to these institutions is deemed to be assigned on a "repurchase" basis unless otherwise specified. Under its repurchase agreements, Francis Ford is obliged, in the event that a customer defaults and the lender repossesses the car, to pay to the lender the outstanding balance on the loan, in return for which Francis Ford receives back the repossessed car.

B. THE GENERAL DUTIES OF A SECOND [SIC] PARTY WITH RESPECT TO REPOSSESSED COLLATERAL

The duties of Francis Ford with respect to repossessed collateral are governed by the Uniform Commercial Code, * * *.

* * *

A principal duty of a secured party, and the one at issue here, is the obligation to account to the debtor for any surplus realized on the repossessed collateral:

> If the security interest secures an indebtedness, the secured party must account to the debtor for any surplus, and, unless otherwise agreed, the debtor is liable for any deficiency. * * * UCC § 9–504(2); ORS § 79.5040(2).

* * *

D. COMPUTATION OF SURPLUSES: FRANCIS FORD'S PRACTICE

Having carefully reviewed the testimony of all witnesses in this case, it remains somewhat unclear to us precisely how (or whether) Francis Ford attempted to determine the possible existence of surpluses when it obtained repossessed automobiles. It seems clear that no effort was routinely made to compare the proceeds of an actual resale of the collateral with the debtor's indebtedness and expenses incident to the resale, however they might be calculated.

Two other possibilities as to how Francis Ford dealt with its legal obligations under the UCC prior to the trial in this case are suggested by the record. Some of the testimony indicates that Francis simply regarded its own repurchase of a repossessed car from the finance company as constituting a proper UCC sale for purposes of determining the proceeds. By definition, this method would always result in the "proceeds" equalling or falling short of the indebtedness, since the price at which Francis Ford repurchased from the finance company would be essentially the amount owed by the defaulting consumer to the finance company. Thereafter, Francis Ford would regard the repossessed vehicle as its own, and any resale would be treated as would the resale of any used car.

* * *

This approach to the determination of surpluses is plainly unlawful under the Uniform Commercial Code, which specifies that:

> A person who is liable to a secured party under a guaranty, indorsement, repurchase agreement or the like and who receives a transfer of collateral from the secured party or is subrogated to his rights has thereafter the rights and duties of the secured party. *Such a transfer of collateral is not a sale or disposition of the collateral under this Article.* [§ 9.504(5); ORS § 79.5040(5), emphasis added.]

Alternatively, Francis Ford suggests that its practice was to assign an estimated wholesale valuation to each repossessed automobile at the time it was repurchased from Ford Motor Credit or United States National Bank of Oregon. This wholesale valuation was treated as constituting the "proceeds" from the repossessed vehicle, and in Francis Ford's view, such "proceeds" never exceeded the amount owed by the customer. Francis Ford's wholesale valuation, however, appears to have been based upon a subjective assessment by its own officials, rather than upon the results of an arms-length market transaction, or even upon the estimation of a market reporter, such as the Kelly Blue Book, although Francis Ford argues that it used the blue book plus the judgment of its own used car manager.

Testimony of Francis Ford officials further indicates that they approached whatever subjective valuation of the proceeds they may have undertaken with the attitude that a surplus simply could not occur.

* * *

This is certainly the case if, as a Francis official repeatedly testified, it was Francis' practice to value repossessed vehicles at the *lower* of wholesale value or cost.

Based upon our review of the testimony, we doubt that Francis Ford made any serious attempt to determine whether a surplus might exist with respect to the repossessed cars it repurchased from its lenders. Assuming, however, *arguendo,* that it did in fact attempt to measure surpluses by means of comparing its used car manager's estimate of wholesale value with the amount of indebtedness, it is obvious that this method, also, is impermissible under the law. As Judge Parker found, the UCC clearly contemplates that the proceeds from a repossessed vehicle will be determined upon the basis of an actual marketplace *sale* of the repossessed collateral.

* * *

The practical wisdom of this plain legal requirement is apparent. To allow determination of an automobile's wholesale value to be based upon a subjective appraisal by the very party obliged to refund any surplus resulting from that appraisal is much like assigning Count Dracula to guard a blood bank. The intolerable conflict of interest that results can be predicted to deprive the debtor of any realistic opportunity to obtain credit for the fair value of the repossessed collateral. Even one of respondent's expert witnesses, who argued that the proceeds should be measured by a wholesale rather than a retail valuation of the repossessed collateral, acknowledged that such wholesale valuation should be the result of a commercially reasonable, arms-length marketplace transaction, in order to avoid so-called "low-balling" by the used car dealer.

Since the only marketplace transaction that occurred with respect to repossessed collateral at Francis Ford was the dealership's resale of the collateral at retail, it is that sale by which the existence of any surpluses must be calculated.

* * *

We conclude, therefore, that Francis Ford has systematically failed to account for, and to refund to consumers, surpluses to which they are entitled under state law. We further conclude that this practice is an unfair practice under Section 5 of the Federal Trade Commission Act.

* * *

Notes

1.   The general assumption of most people is that automobile repossessions and resales invariably result in deficiencies rather than surpluses. Do the FTC Staff Report and the *Ford* case make you rethink that assumption?

2.   The *Ford* case was the upshot of several FTC actions to try to stop creditors from keeping surpluses for themselves. The consent agreement with Ford, mentioned in the opinion, can be found at 44 Fed.Reg. 62481 (Oct. 31, 1979). Similar agreements were reached with Chrysler, 45 Fed. Reg. 70882 (Oct. 27, 1980) and General Motors, 45 Fed.Reg. 14870 (March 7, 1980). Before you get too excited about these developments, however, you should know that the Ninth Circuit Court of Appeals set aside the FTC's opinion in the *Ford* case. The court held that the FTC had exceeded its authority when it used the process of adjudication to establish a rule of general application. Does this mean that the FTC opinion in *Ford* is of no value to consumer lawyers in future cases?

3.   During the 1970s, the FTC was moving on two fronts at once. Not only was it adjudicating cases against automobile dealers like Francis Ford and automobile manufacturer finance subsidiaries like Ford Motor Credit Company, it was also drafting a proposed trade regulation rule to deal with the problem of deficiencies. Parts of these proposals finally became the FTC Credit Practices Rule which is now in effect. The original draft of this rule contained a provision (which was not adopted) that would have prohibited recovery of any deficiency unless the debtor was credited with the fair market *retail* value of the collateral. This rule would have applied not only in cases involving recourse agreements like that between Francis Ford and FMCC, but in other cases as well. What do you think of such a rule? Would it be likely to produce surpluses, or at least reduce deficiencies, in consumer repossessions? Might it cause any problems? Consider the following:

a.   A dealer repossesses a car. Because the debtor must be given credit for retail value, the dealer figures he might as well try a retail sale. He places the car in the used car area of his lot, along with the other used cars.

What happens if no one buys the car?

b.   If the dealer sells the car from his lot, and he otherwise has an adequate supply of cars to satisfy all customers, is he losing one sale (and therefore one profit)? I.e., wouldn't the customer have purchased a car anyway, and won't that car now remain unsold?

4.   As we saw earlier, courts generally permit wholesale value (or less) in repossession resales. Massachusetts, however, has adopted a retail standard in certain consumer retail installment sales. No deficiency is allowed if the unpaid balance at the time of default was $1,000 or less. (Compare U3C § 5.103.) In other cases, the creditor may recover a defi-

ciency measured by deducting the fair market value of the collateral, *not* the resale price, from the unpaid balance. The value of the collateral is presumed to be the estimated retail value published in sources like the blue book for automobiles. See Mass.Gen.Laws Ann. ch. 255, § 13J, and ch. 255D, § 22.

5. There have been several studies of the problem of deficiencies in consumer cases, especially in the automobile industry. Besides the FTC study reprinted earlier, the following are quite useful: White, Consumer Repossessions and Deficiencies: New Perspectives From New Data, 23 Boston Col.L.Rev. 385 (1982); Shuchman, Profit on Default: An Archival Study of Repossession and Resale, 22 Stan.L.Rev. 20 (1969); Note, Business as Usual: An Empirical Study of Automobile Deficiency Judgment Suits in the District of Columbia, 3 Conn.L.Rev. 511 (1971); Note, I Can Get It For You Wholesale: The Lingering Problem of Automobile Deficiency Judgments, 27 Stan.L.Rev. 1081 (1975). See also Reed, Anatomy of a Deficiency Action: A Case History in Recovery of Deficiency Balance After Repossession of an Automobile, 82 Conn.L.J. 37 (1977).

Note on Alternative Remedies

If Silver sells Bones a car for $5000 on credit and retains a security interest, and Bones then defaults, what remedy has Silver? Logically, there are at least four alternatives: (1) we can allow Silver to retake his car and require him to be satisfied with that; (2) we can permit him to ignore the car and sue for the balance due; (3) we can allow him to retake the car and give the buyer credit for its value, and then let him sue for any balance still due; or (4) we can both let him retake the car and also sue for the entire balance due, with no credit for the value of the retaken car.

Which is permitted at law? Over the full course of history, we have permitted each of the four—even including (4), which would be regarded as unconscionable by today's standards. But over the last 50 years, the choice has boiled down to a conflict between two approaches. On the one hand, courts construing common-law "conditional sale" agreements often required the seller to choose either (1) or (2). On the other hand, the approach of UCC Article 9 permits (3).

The thinking behind (3) had its genesis in the law of real property mortgages and pledges, where it developed into a notion that the creditor might be *required* to give the debtor credit for the value of the secured property, in order to assure that the debtor ended up with any excess value over and above the debt. However, "Sad experience has taught us that a power of sale, coupled with a right to a deficiency judgment, can be harder on the debtor than strict foreclosure ever was. The surplus to be returned to the debtor after the sale is a glittering mirage; the deficiency judgment is the grim reality." G. Gilmore, Security Interests in Personal Property 1188 (1965).

This fact gives the thinking behind the conditional sale formulation some real content. If the creditor is restricted to a choice between (1) and (2), he is likely to choose the easy, expeditious (1), even if the property to be taken does not equal the full value of the debt. On the other hand, if he has (3), he can have the best of both worlds—repossession for the easy, expeditious beginning, and resale and deficiency for the remainder.

After the UCC adoption of approach (3), the U3C re-adopted the older approach requiring the seller to choose between (1) and (2). Utah enacted the original (1969) version of the U3C, and the following case resulted:

PEOPLES FINANCE & THRIFT CO. OF OGDEN v. PERRY

Supreme Court of Utah, 1973.
30 Utah 2d 282, 516 P.2d 1400.

TUCKETT, JUSTICE:

The plaintiff initiated these proceedings in the court below seeking to recover the balance due on a promissory note and to foreclose its interest in a security agreement covering a Chevrolet truck. The court awarded judgment on the note but decided that the plaintiff was not entitled to foreclose its interest in the security. The court in effect ruled that the plaintiff had to elect either to take a money judgment or possession of the security. Plaintiff is here seeking a reversal of that part of the court's decision which denied the plaintiff the right to sell the truck at a private or public sale pursuant to the terms of the security agreement and for a deficiency judgment awarded if the sale did not satisfy the judgment.

The decision of the lower court is correct if the transaction falls within the provisions of [U3C] Section 5–103, pertinent parts of which are as follows:

> (2) If the seller repossesses or voluntarily accepts surrender of goods which were the subject of the sale and in which he has a security interest and the cash price of goods repossessed or surrendered was $1,000 or less, the buyer is not personally liable to the seller for the unpaid balance of the debt arising from the sale of the goods, and the seller is not obligated to resell the collateral.

* * *

> (6) If the seller elects to bring an action against the buyer for a debt arising from a consumer credit sale of goods or services, when under this section he would not be entitled to a deficiency judgment if he repossessed the collateral, and obtains judgment

> (a) he may not repossess the collateral, and

> (b) the collateral is not subject to levy or sale on execution or similar proceedings pursuant to the judgment.

The facts surrounding the transaction here under consideration are generally not in dispute. On February 3, 1972, the defendant Robert J. Perry borrowed money from the plaintiff in order to purchase a Chevrolet truck. The defendant Douglas Higgins cosigned the note with Perry. Perry also executed a security agreement on the truck he was purchasing with the proceeds of the loan. The loan was made to

Perry prior to the purchase transaction. A consumer credit sale is defined by [U3C] Section 2–104, in the following language:

> (1) Except as provided in subsection (2), "consumer credit sale" is a sale of goods, services, or an interest in land in which

> (a) credit is granted by a seller who regularly engages as a seller in credit transactions of the same kind,

* * *

It is the plaintiff's contention that the transaction with the defendants was a consumer loan. The term "consumer loan" is defined by [U3C] Section 3–104, in the following language:

> (1) Except with respect to a loan primarily secured by an interest in land (section 70B–3–105), "consumer loan" is a loan made by a person regularly engaged in the business of making loans in which

> (a) the debtor is a person other than an organization;

> (b) the debt is incurred primarily for a personal, family, household, or agricultural purpose;

> (c) either the debt is payable in installments or a loan finance charge is made: * * *

The word "loan" is defined by [U3C] Section 3–106, as follows:

(1) the creation of debt by the lender's payment of or agreement to pay money to the debtor or to a third party for the account of the debtor;

(2) the creation of debt by a credit to an account with the lender upon which the debtor is entitled to draw immediately;

(3) the creation of debt pursuant to a lender credit card or similar arrangement; and

(4) the forbearance of debt arising from a loan.

The restrictions of [U3C] Section 5–103 apply only to consumer credit sales and not to consumer loans. The facts in the instant case show that the plaintiff was engaged in lending money but there is nothing to show that the plaintiff was regularly engaged "as a seller in credit transactions of the same kind." The fact that the loan was arranged for by Perry in advance of the transaction and the proceeds of the loan in the form of a check drawn by the plaintiff were payable to Perry and to the automobile dealer, would not tend to show that the transaction was other than a loan. The facts surrounding the sale would not tend to show that the plaintiff and the defendant Perry were engaged in the sales transaction as joint venturers. We are of the opinion that the transaction was a consumer loan rather than a consumer sale. While the effect of our decision may tend to create a loophole whereby those engaged in the sales of goods may escape the restrictions of Section 70B–5–103, we believe it is a matter for the legislature to deal with rather than the courts.

That part of the judgment of the court below which required the plaintiff to make an election to either repossess the security or to reduce the promissory note to judgment, is reversed. No costs awarded.

CALLISTER, C.J., and HENRIOD and ELLETT, JJ., concur.

CROCKETT, JUSTICE (dissenting).

Section 70B–5–103, was enacted for the purpose of preventing oppressions which often result in connection with the repossession of goods sold under title-retaining sales agreements and the persistence in further collection on the purchase price, costs and attorneys' fees as provided in such agreements. The remedies provided therein are usually in fine print, unwittingly agreed to by purchasers who are uninformed, and/or in many instances unable to bargain at arm's length anyway. The statute is purposed to minimize injustices by giving the seller his option; to repossess the goods and keep what has been paid thereon; or to sue for the purchase price, but not to allow him both.

The trial court correctly saw through the instant transaction as but a subterfuge to avoid the effects of the statute just referred to. It is plainly apparent that the plaintiff was fully aware of and participating therein from the fact that the plaintiff made its check not to Perry as it would have done under a separate, independent and unrelated loan, but made it to Perry *and* the automobile dealer. Thus the trial court was correct in determining that plaintiff was particeps to the "consumer credit sale"; and in concluding that its rights are governed by said Section 70B–5–103. The main opinion is correct in characterizing itself as a "loophole" through which those engaged in the business can circumvent what the legislature intended as a salutary effect of that statute. I decline to join therein. I would affirm the judgment.

Notes

1. What is the "loophole" the majority thinks it is creating? Did the court create it, or did the drafters? If the latter, did they do it on purpose? What purpose? Reconsider the direct loan problem we studied in Chapter 6, supra. Are the situations similar? Is there a greater danger for consumer abuse in the holder in due course setting than in the deficiency setting?

2. Utah enacted the original version of the U3C. The 1974 revision of the U3C added a provision to address the deficiency problem in certain consumer loans. See U3C § 5.103(4). Would this provision have applied in *Perry?* Does it close the "loophole"?

3. Over half the states have some statutory provision which restricts or eliminates the creditor's ability to recover a deficiency in some consumer cases. These statutes vary in their approaches to the problem and in the types of consumer transaction covered. Some, like Utah's, apply only to sales; others apply also to loans. Most set dollar limits, but some measure the amount at the time of default rather than the time of the original sale or loan. Why distinguish between sales and loans? Is there a significant

difference in the need for protection? Why set dollar limits? Is there a greater danger of abuse in small transactions?

4. Assume you are a law clerk for the firm that represents Walker–Thomas Furniture Company. Your boss says she knows you're up on all these newfangled consumer laws, and she asks you to suggest ways to beat each of the three statutory approaches suggested above. Or, if you can't "beat" them, at least suggest how the company can adjust its practices to live with them. What will you say?

Problem 12A

Bill Bones bought a VCR on credit from Sam Silver for $1200. Silver obtained a signed security agreement from Bones. Bones defaulted and Silver repossessed the VCR without breaching the peace. Silver was not able to resell the VCR for more than $300, and he sold it for that amount in a commercially reasonable manner. May Silver recover the deficiency from Bones in a jurisdiction enacting the U3C? See U3C, § 5.103.

Problem 12B

Same facts as Problem 12A, but they occur in a jurisdiction which has enacted the Model Consumer Credit Act. See MCCA § 7.208(1), below. How different is the underlying principle of the MCCA from that of U3C § 5.103?

MCCA § 7.208   Prohibition of Deficiency; Right to Surplus

(1) If the creditor takes possession of collateral pursuant to an action authorized by this Part, or by the acceptance of the voluntary surrender of the collateral by the consumer, the consumer is not personally liable to the creditor for any unpaid balance of the obligation.

(2) If the consumer has paid at least fifty (50) percent of the cash price of the goods, the creditor shall sell the collateral at a public sale within ninety (90) days after he takes possession of the collateral. The proceeds of the sale shall be applied pursuant to the requirements of [Section 9–504(1) of the Uniform Commercial Code] with the exception that attorneys' fees and legal expenses incurred by the creditor shall not be included as expenses of the creditor.

* * *

(4) The consumer is not liable for any deficiency, but is entitled to any surplus which remains after distributing the proceeds. In a proceeding for a surplus, it is presumed that the collateral was in average condition at the time of surrender and that it was sold for its fair market value. The fair market value of the collateral is a question of the trier of fact. Periodically published trade estimates of the retail value of goods are presumed, to the extent they are recognized in the particular trade or business, to be the fair market value of the collateral.

Problem 13

Bill Bones bought a VCR on credit from Sam Silver for $1200. Bones borrowed the $1200 from Charlie Cheerful, who made the check out to both Bones and Silver. Cheerful obtained a signed security agreement from Bones. Bones defaulted and Cheerful repossessed the VCR without breaching the peace. Cheerful was not able to resell the VCR for more than $300, and he sold it for that amount in a commercially reasonable manner. May Cheerful recover the deficiency from Bones in a jurisdiction enacting the U3C? Is there any difference in Bones' susceptibility to abuse between the transactions in Problems 12A and 13? Is there any difference in these transactions from his perspective?

Problem 14

Beth Byer bought a car for $3000. First Bank loaned her $2700, and took a security interest in the car. Six months later, Beth lost her job and stopped making payments. The balance outstanding was then $2500. First Bank repossessed the car, which was then worth about $2000 retail, and would probably bring about $1400 at a wholesale auction sale of repossession. Will there be any surplus to protect for Beth? Is there a possible deficiency? As counsel to First Bank, would you advise it to "accept the collateral in discharge of the obligation," or resell and pursue a deficiency judgment against Beth when she is employed again? Is there any UCC provision to prohibit a deficiency judgment? Cf., UCC § 9–505.

Is there any U3C provision to prohibit a deficiency judgment? See U3C § 5.103. Is there a great need to protect a possible surplus? Have the U3C draftsmen given the consumer a protection she does not need, while leaving her vulnerable where she needs protection the most?

Why, at the least, did the Uniform Commissioners not add U3C § 5.103 to the 1972 Revisions of UCC Article 9?

Problem 15

Assume that in Problem 12A, George Generous cosigned Bill Bones' note. May Silver recover the deficiency from Generous? See Americana State Bank v. Jensen, 353 N.W.2d 652 (Minn.App.1984).

Problem 16

Assume that in Problem 12A, the debt carried finance charges of $551, so that Bones' total obligation to Silver was $1751. May Silver recover the deficiency under U3C § 5.103 See Shakopee Ford, Inc. v. Wittenberg, 371 N.W.2d 56 (Minn.App.1985).

Chapter 9

THE CREDITOR GOES
TO COURT

SECTION A. DEFAULT JUDGMENTS
(AND HOW TO GET THEM)

The consumer in default always has the last ditch opportunity to defend himself in court. Right? Wrong!

COMMITTEE REPORT, "DOES A VENDEE UNDER AN INSTALLMENT SALES CONTRACT RECEIVE ADEQUATE NOTICE OF A SUIT INSTITUTED BY A VENDOR?"

Ass'n of the Bar of the City of New York, Record 263–67 (1968).

This report does not touch on all the problems of the low income consumer. It seeks to explore only two problems: (1) the inadequacies connected with notice to defendants, and, more particularly, service of the initial papers in an action against a vendee who has failed to meet the payments under an installment sales contract, and (2) the institution of lawsuits by third parties with inconvenient or improperly laid venue.

THE BACKGROUND

1. Inadequate Service

Every year hundreds of thousands of default judgments are entered in the courts of New York. Studies undertaken by The Legal Aid Society, the legal office of Mobilization for Youth, CORE, the Civil Rights Bureau in the office of the Attorney General of the State of New York, and other groups have brought to light a shocking absence of notice to the defendants in such cases, particularly in the areas of consumer installment credit sales and landlord-tenant cases.

The Civil Rights Bureau of the New York State Attorney General's office examined approximately 1000 files of cases in which default judgments had been entered in the Civil Court of the City of New York

559

and concluded that serious deficiencies were present. In those cases the process server's affidavit indicated that he had made personal service on the defendant at his residence. However, when the Bureau attempted to locate the defendants but a few weeks after such service, letters sent to them were returned by the Post Office as undeliverable. A significant number of defendants who were located denied that personal service had ever been made. Other studies uncovered instances in which defendants were alleged to have been served at a given address when in fact such defendants were dead, in the hospital, in jail, or away in the military service, or the address to which the service was made turned out to be an empty lot, an excavated or abandoned building. * * *

Effective personal service is immensely difficult and expensive, and, when juxtaposed with the relatively small amount to be collected on any single installment sales contract, encourages fraud. Slum dwellers are frequently difficult to locate. Often, they neglect to notify the seller of a change in address. The difficulty of service is illustrated by the fact that when one recent study of 300 default judgments was attempted about a year after the judgments, a staff of interviewers could locate only 10% of the defendants. No one is receptive to a process server, particularly people with outstanding overdue bills. Often, true personal service requires real detective work. Fees in such situations may range as high as $100 or more. Obviously, in such cases a number of calls would have to be made and even then the chances of success are minimal. However, the rules of the Civil Court—where most actions on installment sales contracts are instituted—provide that a party can recover only $2.50 as costs in the event judgment is entered. Therefore, the amount of a small claim will not justify an expenditure of substantial sum for service of process.

Collection agencies in these cases turn process over to service agencies which employ individual process servers. Ofttimes, such individuals are transients who work only intermittently. * * *

The work is difficult, unattractive, and often downright risky. The making of false affidavits of service is encouraged by the method of payment. Process service agencies pay a process server on the basis of the number of services he completes. Thus, a process server has to serve as many as possible as quickly as possible in order to make even a minimum living. The results are carelessness, a lack of genuine effort to serve, and fraud.

Law enforcement agencies must take an active part in discouraging these practices. Efforts have been made in the past to amass the kind of evidence necessary for a perjury prosecution; they have been uniformly unsuccessful. * * *

2. Inconvenient or Improper Venue

Default judgments result not only because of inadequate service, but because sellers in retail installment situations as a matter of commercial practice assign contracts to third parties, usually finance companies who in case of the purchaser's default bring actions in courts remote from the vendor as well as the purchaser. The purchaser under an installment sales contract is frequently unskilled. He can generally ill afford to spend any time away from his job. He can hardly take a whole day to journey to a distant county. Information was presented to the Committee which tended to support the proposition that, on a more than casual basis, this knowledge is exploited by the vendor.

Whether default judgments obtained in such cases suffer from a jurisdictional defect or whether the venue is waivable depends on the court and the locale. In either case the deficiency can be remedied only if the purchaser-defendant avails himself of legal counsel prior to the time that a judgment is obtained against him and an income execution levied.

CONCLUSIONS

The majority of the Committee favored the following legislative and Association action:

1. "Sewer Service"

The Committee approved the proposition that service of process be made by registered or certified mail to the addressee only with the understanding that in the absence of a return from the Post Office with proof of service, personal service in accordance with present legislation still had to be attempted. The courts would be empowered to alter this procedure where a mailing would take too long, e.g., where the use of a provisional remedy is sought. Other suggestions, as for instance the licensing of all process servers or requiring that all process be served exclusively by court officers, were found to be appealing but deserving of further study, therefore, not practical for immediate action.

2. Inconvenient or Improper Venue

The Committee urges that legislation be enacted which will add the following language as subsection 8 of § 402 of the *N.Y. Personal Property Law:*

> "Seller agrees that actions based on this instrument must be instituted in the county in which the purchaser resides, or resided at the time the contract was executed, or the county where the purchaser executed the agreement.
>
> The parties agree that legal proceedings instituted elsewhere will be void and of no effect."

* * *

4. Disciplinary Action Regarding Attorneys Who Utilize "Sewer Service" Operations

The staff of the Committee on Grievances of The Association of the Bar of the City of New York was contacted and indicated their interest in this problem. Certain material was submitted to them by the Committee on Legal Assistance. With the aid of that material, they conveyed their ability and desire to reactivate certain investigations. These investigations concerned attorneys who dealt with certain process servers on an assembly-line basis and were responsible for a vast number of default judgments and were to be directed towards discovering whether there was knowledge on the part of these attorneys that personal service had not been made, regardless of the process server's affidavit to the contrary.

It was understood that the staff of the Committee on Grievances would review certain court records and bring any useful evidence which they might discover to the Grievances Committee of the Association. In any event, the staff would report their findings to the Executive Committee of The Association of the Bar of the City of New York.

Notes

1. In United States v. Barr, 295 F.Supp. 889 (S.D.N.Y.1969), process servers, who were private individuals and not officials of the State of New York, were indicted under 16 U.S.C.A. § 242 for willfully, under color of state law, subjecting persons to deprivation of the federal constitutional right to due process of law. Defendants were charged with causing default judgments to be entered in state courts by signing affidavits of service of summonses and complaints which had not in fact been served.

Defendants moved to dismiss the indictments contending that their conduct involved no "state action." The motion to dismiss was denied: they were held to have acted under color of state law because they performed "the function of the sheriff, when serving a summons," and because their false affidavits triggered the state's judicial machinery to issue default judgments. They were also held to have induced court clerks, who *were* state officials, to act on the basis of their affidavits.

2. Sewer service is one method of obtaining a default judgment, for if the defendant is not aware that he is being sued, he will default in answering. *Barr* shows one method of counter-attack, but it depends upon both massive fact-gathering and also persuading a busy prosecutor to expend time and effort on the problem. A better counter-attack might be to design a better system of notifying defendants. What basic features should such a system have?

3. What is the difference, so far as "acting under color of state law," between a private person who serves summonses and a private person who repossesses property which has reverted to a creditor after default?

4. In 1973, New York responded to the recommendations of the Bar committee by adding § 503(f) to the rules governing civil practice. This provision basically requires actions in consumer credit transactions to be brought in the county of the debtor's residence. N.Y.—McKinney's Civ. Prac.Law and Rules § 503(f). See Empire Nat. Bank v. Olori, 87 Misc.2d 320, 384 N.Y.S.2d 948 (1976).

SPIEGEL, INC. v. F.T.C.

United States Court of Appeals, Seventh Circuit, 1976.
540 F.2d 287.

BAUER, CIRCUIT JUDGE.

Essentially the question before us is whether the Federal Trade Commission ("FTC") has the power to prevent large retail businesses from suing customers for delinquent credit accounts in a court distant from the consumer's residence. The FTC ordered that petitioner Spiegel "cease and desist from instituting suits except in the county where the defendant resides at the commencement of the action, or in the county where the defendant signed the contract sued upon." Spiegel brings this appeal of the Commission's order.

There is no dispute as to the facts of the case. Spiegel admitted all of the material facts contained in the FTC complaint. The complaint charges that Spiegel violated Section 5 of the Federal Trade Commission Act, 15 U.S.C. § 45, which prohibits unfair business practices, by instituting collection suits in the Circuit Court of Cook County, Illinois, against retail credit mail order purchasers who reside in states other than Illinois.

Spiegel is a Delaware corporation with its office and principal place of business in Chicago, Illinois. It is a catalog retailer engaged in the advertising, offering for sale, and distribution of clothes, household goods, appliances, tools, tires, and various other articles of merchandise. In the course of its mail order business, it receives orders in Illinois from purchasers in various states and ships products to them in their home states. It regularly extends credit to consumers in order to facilitate purchase of the products.

Previously, in the course of its collection of retail credit accounts, Spiegel regularly used Illinois courts to sue allegedly defaulting retail mail order purchasers who resided outside of Illinois. The practice of filing suits in Illinois was terminated in February 1973 because this collection method proved unsatisfactory to Spiegel.[3] In filing these collection suits Spiegel used the Illinois long-arm statute to establish jurisdiction. Spiegel voluntarily dismissed those actions where the defendant raised an objection to the inconvenience of the forum. Of course, in order to object the consumer had to travel to the Illinois court or obtain local counsel, an act which was often impractical considering the amount in dispute in most cases.

Many of the customers sued by Spiegel live outside the State of Illinois. They received Spiegel's catalogs and advertising material in

---

3. According to Spiegel's brief this was due to the fact that judgments in Illinois, as in many other states, are not self-executing and require supplementary proceedings in other jurisdictions in order to collect the judgment. A defendant may raise the issue of lack of personal jurisdiction in his home state to enforce a judgment obtained in another jurisdiction. *See also Hanson v. Denckla,* 357 U.S. 235, 255, 78 S.Ct. 1228, 2 L.Ed.2d 1283 (1958).

their homes and executed the contract to purchase in their home states. Almost all of them have no pertinent contact within the State of Illinois other than their dealings with Spiegel.

The administrative law judge determined that the distance, cost and inconvenience of defending such suits in Illinois placed a virtually insurmountable burden on the out-of-state defendants to appear, answer and defend. Subsequently the Commission concluded that Spiegel's collection practices through the use of the Illinois courts was offensive to clearly articulated public policy and oppressive and injurious to consumers.

On appeal Spiegel principally argues: that its conduct was legal and appropriate under Illinois law; that its conduct does not amount to a violation of Section 5 of the Act; that the Commission exceeded its authority in deciding the case on the basis of consumer's due process rights; that the Commission's order is burdensome and unwarranted since Spiegel has represented that it has stopped suing its customers in distant courts.

Under Illinois law Spiegel's conduct may have been perfectly proper. Whether it is unfair to hold a consumer answerable in a foreign forum for a mailorder credit account in arrears is a difficult jurisdictional question. It is clear, however, that in some cases jurisdiction would be proper.

* * *

Assuming *arguendo* that jurisdiction under Illinois law is proper, we still believe that the FTC has the power to enjoin Spiegel from bringing the suits. In *Federal Trade Commission v. Sperry & Hutchinson Co.*, 405 U.S. 233, 92 S.Ct. 898, 31 L.Ed.2d 170 (1972), the Supreme Court left no doubt that the FTC had the authority to prohibit conduct that, although legally proper, was unfair to the public.

* * *

In determining whether Spiegel's challenged practices are unfair under Section 5 of the Act, the Commission remained faithful to its previously announced criteria. A practice is unfair when it offends established public policy and when the practice is immoral, unethical, oppressive, unscrupulous or substantially injurious to consumers.

In this case, since the facts are not in dispute, the Commission only had to determine whether Spiegel's policy of using state long-arm statutes against distant mail order customers violated public policy and was injurious to consumers. In making that determination the Commission concluded:

> "[S]piegel's practice of suing its out-of-state mail order customers in Illinois courts is patently offensive to clearly articulated public policy, intended to guarantee all citizens a meaningful opportunity to defend themselves in court.
>
> *   *   *   *   *   *   *   *   *
>
> [R]espondent's use of the Cook County forum, * * * forces the consumer who wishes to defend to appear in a courtroom hundreds or

thousands of miles from home, at a cost in travel alone which may exceed the amount in controversy. The option of hiring a lawyer who would be able to file a motion contesting jurisdiction is likely to be equally unviable. Nor do we think it lessens the damage done to argue that judgments unfairly obtained by Spiegel would be rejected if it attempted to collect on them. Affirmative efforts to defend a collection suit can also impose costly and unaccustomed burdens on the consumer, and in any event there are many injurious uses which can be made of improper judgments, short of execution, such as sullying credit records * * *"

* * *

* * * The record clearly shows that Spiegel's customers are out-of-state mail order purchasers, almost all of whom received Spiegel's catalogs or other advertising matter and executed purchase orders or contracts in their home states, and had no pertinent contacts with the State of Illinois other than their dealings with Spiegel.

Similarly, it was reasonable for the Commission to conclude that Spiegel's suits involve relatively small amounts, since it is unlikely that many, if any, mail orders of the types of merchandise described in the complaint involve transactions valued in "thousands of dollars," as Spiegel now argues on appeal. It is equally unlikely that the suits involve cumulations of numerous small debts, since neither Spiegel nor any other rational mail order retailer would long continue to extend credit to distant consumer accounts already believed to be in default.

The Commission's observations concerning the difficulties and costs which stand in the way of consumers who wish to defend against suits in a distant forum are matters of common knowledge. Where suits involve relatively small debts, the choice of retaining counsel is not a practical alternative, even in one's home town, and since travel costs alone may exceed the amount in controversy, a *pro se* appearance in an out-of-state forum is virtually foreclosed by economic considerations.

* * *

The order of the Commission is enforced as modified.

Notes

1. Would the result be the same under the F.T.C.'s present market-oriented, cost-benefit approach to "unfairness"? Recall the material on the unfairness cases discussed in Chapter 1, supra at page 64.

2. If the Cook County court entered a judgment for Spiegel in an individual case against a debtor in Kansas, would a Kansas court have to give "Full Faith and Credit" to the Illinois judgment? Could the debtor raise the inconvenient forum issue in the Kansas court?

3. How adequate are the U3C provisions dealing with these matters? See U3C §§ 5.113–5.115. Is one state's laws likely to have much impact on the problem? The federal Fair Debt Collection Practices Act prohibits debt collectors from suing consumer debtors in inconvenient forums. FDCPA § 811. Does this provision adequately deal with the problem raised in

Spiegel? Would it have prevented Spiegel from suing a Wyoming debtor in Chicago? Recall the definition of "debt collector" in FDCPA § 803(6).

Problem 1

Paragon Homes of Midwest, Inc., is an Indiana corporation in the home improvement business. It is licensed to do business in Wisconsin, but it does not do any business in New York. A provision of Paragon's standard form contract states that "This agreement shall be deemed to have been made in Nassau County, New York, and the parties hereby submit to the jurisdiction of the Supreme Court, Nassau County, and hereby appoint the United States Corporation Company as agent for the purpose of accepting service of any process relating to any action arising under this contract." Paragon sues a Wisconsin consumer in New York under the authority of this provision. Does the New York court have jurisdiction? If so, should it exercise it? See Paragon Homes of Midwest, Inc. v. Crace, 4 U.C.C.Rep. 19 (Supreme Court, Nassau County, 1967) (Unpublished Case).

Note on "Confession of Judgment" Clauses

At one time, it was commonplace in some states for consumer contracts to contain "confession of judgment" or "warrant of attorney" clauses. (These contracts are also known as "cognovit notes.") These provisions authorize the creditor, on the debtor's default, to have judgment entered immediately against the debtor. The entry of judgment may be accomplished without notice to the debtor and without opportunity to challenge the debt or raise any defense. The value of these clauses is obvious: not only do they permit prompt levy on the debtor's assets, they give the creditor immense leverage in later settlement negotiations.

Today, most states either outlaw confessions of judgment or severely restrict the circumstances under which they can be used. See, e.g., U3C § 3.306. In addition, the FTC Credit Practices Rule makes it an unfair credit practice for creditors to include these clauses in consumer contracts. See § 444.2(a)(1). As the following case demonstrates, however, confessions of judgment have not entirely disappeared.

PATTON v. DIEMER
Supreme Court of Ohio, 1988.
35 Ohio St.3d 68, 518 N.E.2d 941.

Plaintiff-appellant, Richard F. Patton, is an attorney engaged in the practice of law in the state of Ohio. On February 4, 1977, appellant obtained a final decree of divorce on behalf of defendant-appellee, Julie Ann Diemer, from her former husband, Thomas E. Diemer. From July 30, 1977 through December 5, 1984, appellant provided 494¾ hours of post-decree legal services to appellee. During the course of his post-decree representation of appellee, appellant sought from Thomas Diemer an award of attorney fees. On December 5, 1984, a hearing was held before a referee appointed by the Cuyahoga County Court of Common Pleas upon the application for attorney fees. Prior to the hearing, appellee signed a cognovit note for the attorney fees due, payable to appellant in the amount of $50,448.60. The note contained a warrant of attorney to confess judgment which allowed execution thereon without prior notice to the debtor.

On March 6, 1985, appellant instituted the present action on the cognovit note in the Cuyahoga County Court of Common Pleas. Judgment was entered thereon at that time in the amount of $51,609.61. Appellee received notice of this judgment on March 15, 1985. No appeal therefrom was pursued. * * *

On February 27, 1986, appellee filed what was captioned as an Amended Motion for Relief from Judgment, pursuant to Civ.R. 60(B). This motion was opposed by appellant. On April 22, 1986, the court of common pleas granted the motion. Upon appeal, the court of appeals affirmed the judgment of the common pleas court.

The cause is now before this court pursuant to the allowance of a motion to certify the record.

SWEENEY, JUSTICE.

* * *

R.C. 2323.13(E) specifically precludes the use of a warrant of attorney to confess judgment where the underlying action involves a consumer transaction. It provides in relevant part:

"*A warrant of attorney to confess judgment contained in any instrument executed on or after January 1, 1974, arising out of a consumer loan or consumer transaction, is invalid and the court shall have no jurisdiction to render a judgment based upon such a warrant.* An action founded upon an instrument arising out of a consumer loan or a consumer transaction as defined in this section is commenced by the filing of a complaint as in any ordinary civil action." (Emphasis added.)

R.C. 2323.13(E)(2) defines the term "consumer transaction." It provides:

"As used in this section:

" * * *

" * * * (2) *'Consumer transaction' means* a sale, lease, assignment, award by chance, or other transfer of an item of goods, *a service,* franchise, or an intangible, *to an individual for purposes that are primarily personal, family, educational, or household.*" (Emphasis added.)

The definition of "consumer transaction" contained within R.C. 2323.13 clearly encompasses the attorney-client relationship. Legal representation is undoubtedly a "service * * * to an individual for purposes that are primarily personal, family, educational, or household." Consequently, the attorney-client relationship is a "consumer transaction" as defined by R.C. 2323.13.

* * *

A warrant of attorney to confess judgment which has as its basis a consumer transaction is rendered wholly invalid by operation of R.C. 2323.13(E). More significantly, a common pleas court lacks jurisdiction to render judgment upon a warrant of attorney pursuant to R.C. 2323.13 where the relationship giving rise to the claim for relief involves a consumer transaction.

It is therefore apparent that the common pleas court lacked jurisdiction to render the March 6, 1985 judgment. * * * It was therefore within the inherent power of the trial court to vacate the March 6, 1985 judgment and to reinstate the cause for trial.

Accordingly, the judgment of the court of appeals is affirmed.

Judgment affirmed.

Notes

1. The Ohio statute is typical of state laws on the subject. Would the FTC Rule have prohibited the clause used by Richard Patton? Did Mr. Patton violate any ethical obligation toward his client by having his client sign a cognovit note?

2. Under California law, judgments by confession are allowed "only if an attorney independently representing the defendant signs a certificate that the attorney has examined the proposed judgment * * * and has advised the defendant to utilize the confession of judgment procedure." Cal.Code Civ.P. § 1132(b). Does this procedure avoid the dangers inherent in other confessions of judgment? Is it permissible under the FTC Rule? Why would an attorney advise a defendant to confess judgment? See Wax v. Infante, 138 Cal.App.3d 138, 187 Cal.Rptr. 686 (1982).

3. Confessions of judgment have been subjected to constitutional attacks, but they have usually survived on the theory that they are valid waivers of constitutional rights. See Swarb v. Lennox, 405 U.S. 191, 92 S.Ct. 767, 31 L.Ed.2d 138 (1972); North Penn Consumer Discount Co. v. Schultz, 250 Pa.Super. 530, 378 A.2d 1275 (1977).

SECTION B. SEIZING THE DEBTOR'S PROPERTY

A judgment is one thing; actually collecting the money from the debtor is another. By itself, a judgment is nothing more than a piece of paper telling the creditor what he already knew—that the debtor owes him some money. However, it is a piece of paper with some value. With it, the creditor may initiate a series of judicially-aided procedures which ultimately lead to seizure of some of the debtor's property. The most common of these procedures are garnishment and execution. We will look briefly at each of them in this section.

You should understand that these remedies are likely to be used only by unsecured creditors. Secured creditors ordinarily may repossess their collateral after default. We studied this process in Chapter 8.

Unsecured creditors, on the other hand, need to go to court and get a judgment before they can take any of the debtor's property.

You should also recognize that, while these remedies may sound good on paper, there are important legal and practical limitations on their exercise. For one thing, not all of the debtor's property is available for seizure by the creditor. All states have "exemption" laws which list certain property creditors may not reach through judicial collection remedies. The lists vary widely among the states, although all states include certain personal property such as household goods, and most states recognize a homestead exemption of a certain value. As a result, in many consumer cases the debtor may not have any property the creditor can take.

Another important limitation is the availability of bankruptcy. If the debtor files bankruptcy, the creditor will ordinarily be unable to continue any collection process he may have started. Worse, he may even have to give back property he has already seized. (The "automatic stay" and "preference" rules which apply in these circumstances are normally studied in courses in bankruptcy law or debtors' and creditors' rights. See Bankruptcy Code §§ 362 and 547.) To add insult to injury, even if our creditor surmounts these hurdles, the debtor's secured creditors are likely to end up with all the assets anyway.

Beyond all this, there are constitutional limitations on the exercise of these remedies. We will look at the constitutional issues later in this section, at page 583.

Despite all these difficulties, however, creditors armed with judgments do sometimes succeed in reaching some of the debtor's property through these judicial collection devices. The following material addresses some of the issues lawyers may face in consumer transactions where this occurs.

1. GARNISHMENT OF THE CONSUMER'S WAGES

Prefatory Note

The unsecured judgment creditor's favorite collection device is the garnishing of the consumer debtor's paycheck. Whether the creditor has gotten a deficiency judgment after foreclosing on collateral, or whether the consumer's non-appearance has produced a default judgment, the consumer's week-to-week earnings are a fruitful source of further recovery. (At least this is true where it was not the loss of a job that precipitated the consumer's default in the first place.)

Garnishment is a statutory proceeding in which any property of a debtor, including property held by a third person, is applied to pay a creditor. Wage garnishment orders an employer to withhold wages due a debtor-employee and pay the funds to his creditor. State legislatures have enacted protections ranging from prohibition of wage garnishment to limitations which permit the debtor to exclude a stated percent or dollar amount from the garnishment order for his and his family's support.

In extending credit, the creditor usually relies principally on the consumer's wage earning ability; and so creditors consider garnishment to be an important remedy, since it is the method which permits them direct access to his earnings. However, wage garnishment is not simply a two party transfer from consumer to creditor—it involves a third party, the consumer's employer. Employers dislike garnishment orders because of the extra bookkeeping involved. In many states such orders affect only funds already earned and still unpaid, so the order is repeatedly served immediately before payday—so the computer-processed paycheck must be thrown out and new checks processed by hand.

As part of the CCPA, federal legislation limits the amount of a consumer's disposable earnings which may be garnished to 25%, and also creates a minimum weekly dollar exemption of 30 times the minimum wage. The federal law permits states to exempt greater amounts, or prohibit garnishment altogether. In addition, the federal law provides that no employer may discharge any employee because of garnishments arising out of a single debt. The federal provisions restricting garnishment are in 15 U.S.C.A. §§ 1672, 1673, 1674 (CCPA §§ 302, 303, 304). The U3C contains virtually identical provisions in §§ 5.105 and 5.106, and in addition flatly prohibits prejudgment garnishment.

As to garnishment methods, the Supreme Court has held that a garnishment cannot be obtained against a debtor residing in the state where the garnishment is sought simply on petition of one party—the creditor—before judgment. The Court in Sniadach v. Family Finance Corporation held that the temporary withholding of a resident debtor's wages under a garnishment order without opportunity for the debtor to be heard or to present any available defense to the creditor's claim was violative of procedural due process granted under the 14th Amendment. Justice Douglas, writing for the majority, held that such prejudgment garnishment affords "enormous" leverage to creditors and "may as a practical matter drive a wage-earning family to the wall." Prejudgment garnishment of out-of-state debtors is apparently still permitted.

National Commission on Consumer Finance (NCCF) Report

33–34 (1972)

The Commission believes that Title III of CCPA was a giant step toward more effective and equitable consumer protection. It put limits on garnishment where none—or almost none—existed in many states, and it geared those limits to the minimum wage, not to an inflexible dollar amount. It provided a debtor-employee with some measure of job security in the event of garnishment for one debt. But the Commission feels that the CCPA protections should be further improved.

A wage earner working a full 40–hour week at the minimum hourly rate earns, by standards recognized by Congress, the minimum amount necessary to support a family at a bare subsistence level. To exempt from garnishment an amount based on a 30–hour workweek seems unreasonable. It does not afford those employees earning the minimum wage with adequate means to provide basic necessities. For this reason the Commission recommends that the exempted portion of an employee's salary be increased to 40 times the Federal minimum wage.

The Commission recommends that an employee should not be subject to discharge for garnishments or attempted garnishments by any number of creditors because the loss of employment causes further hardship on the debtor and his family and virtually guarantees inability to satisfy any obligations. Furthermore, the Commission feels that creditors should not be able to garnish indiscriminately the nonexempt portion of the debtor's disposable income. In given circumstances, such as illness in the family and previous unemployment, garnishment of the nonexempted portion of the debtor's salary may make it impossible for him to provide for himself and his family. Under such extraordinary circumstances, the Commission believes the debtor should have an opportunity to present the facts to a court and let the court, if it deems proper, adjust the amount of the garnishment.

Because garnishment is one of the most common and effective means by which a creditor can enforce a judgment against a defaulting debtor, it was deemed an essential collection device by both secured and unsecured creditors in the Commission's Survey. It was considered the most essential remedy by creditors extending unsecured credit, and in secured transactions it was ranked second only to the right to take a security interest. The cross-state econometric model indicated that in states where garnishment was either prohibited or restricted beyond limitations imposed by the CCPA, the availability of credit was substantially curtailed, and charges for credit were apparently increased. These findings lead the Commission to recommend that garnishment be allowed in all states subject to the restrictions discussed.

LONG ISLAND TRUST CO. v. UNITED STATES POSTAL SERVICE

United States Court of Appeals, Second Circuit, 1981.
647 F.2d 336.

KEARSE, CIRCUIT JUDGE:

Plaintiff-appellant Long Island Trust Company ("Long Island Trust") appeals from a judgment of the United States District Court for the Eastern District of New York, George C. Pratt, *Judge,* dismissing its complaint against defendant-appellee United States Postal Service ("USPS") challenging USPS's refusal to honor an income garnishment served by Long Island Trust with respect to a USPS employee. The district court granted summary judgment on the ground that the employee's wages were already subject to garnishment for family support in excess of 25 percent of his weekly disposable earnings, and the Consumer Credit Protection Act of 1970 (the "Act"), 15 U.S.C. § 1671 *et seq.* (1976 and Supp. III 1979), prohibits further garnishment by a judgment creditor. We affirm.

FACTS

The facts are not in dispute. On August 15, 1978, Long Island Trust recovered a judgment in the amount of $914.38 against one Donald Cheshire, Jr. On October 20, the judgment remained unsatisfied to the extent of $607.50, and Long Island Trust caused an income execution to be served on USPS, Cheshire's employer, directing that 10 percent of Cheshire's bi-weekly wages be paid to the county sheriff for the benefit of Long Island Trust. USPS refused to comply with the income execution, claiming that more than 25 percent of Cheshire's disposable income was already being withheld for court ordered support payments under New York Pers.Prop.Law § 49–b (McKinney Supp. 1980), and that any further deductions from Cheshire's wages were barred under the Consumer Credit Protection Act.

Long Island Trust commenced the present proceeding pursuant to N.Y.C.P.L.R. § 5231(e) (McKinney 1978) to recover the accrued installments from USPS. USPS moved for summary judgment on the basis of the fact that $214 of Cheshire's bi-weekly disposable income of $508, or 42 percent, was already being garnished pursuant to orders of support issued by the Nassau County Family Court. It argued that the Consumer Credit Protection Act prohibits garnishment on behalf of a judgment creditor where the employee's disposable income is already garnished to the extent of 25 percent or more. Long Island Trust did not dispute the facts, but argued that both New York law and the Act allow simultaneous garnishment for family support and payment of judgment creditors, even when the amount of the support garnishment exceeds 25 percent.

The district court adopted the interpretation of the Act pressed by USPS, and entered judgment dismissing the action.

* * *

New York law provides that as between garnishments of the same type, the prior in time is to be satisfied first. As between creditor garnishments and support order garnishments, New York gives priority to those for support, regardless of the timing of those garnishments. On either basis in the present case, the support order garnishments of Cheshire's wages have priority over Long Island Trust's income execution.

Turning to the language of the Act, we read § 1673 as placing a ceiling of 25 percent on the amount of an employee's disposable earnings that is subject to garnishment, with the exception that the ceiling may be raised as high as 65 percent if the garnishment is to enforce family support orders. Thus, when garnishments are sought only by creditors, no more than 25 percent of disposable earnings may be withheld for that purpose; when the garnishments are sought only to enforce support orders, as much as 65 percent of disposable earnings may be withheld for that purpose. The interrelationship, however, between the general rule and the exception, when both creditor and support garnishments are sought, is less clear. Long Island Trust contends that the Act was designed to promote the "orderly payment of consumer debts". It argues, from this premise, that support garnishments should be considered entirely independently of creditor garnishments, and that the Act should be construed as reserving 25 percent of the employee's earnings for attachment by creditors and leaving 75 percent for personal and family expenses, including the satisfaction of family support orders. We find no basis for this argument either in the language of the statute or in its legislative history.

To begin with, Long Island Trust's notion of the principal purpose of the Act is untenable. In passing the Consumer Credit Protection Act, Congress acted principally not to protect the rights of creditors, but to limit the ills that flowed from the unrestricted garnishment of wages. It was concerned with the burgeoning number of personal bankruptcies (208,000 in 1967, as contrasted with 18,000 in 1950), which it felt put an undue burden on interstate commerce. And it observed that the number of personal bankruptcies was vastly higher in states that had harsh garnishment laws than in states that did not allow garnishment, a disparity that tended to destroy the uniformity of the bankruptcy laws. The Act was thus designed to curtail sharply the rights of creditors to garnish employee wages, * * *. Even as enacted, the Act provides that in any state that provides stricter laws against garnishment, the Act will yield to state law. 15 U.S.C. § 1677. Thus, so far from placing principal emphasis on creditor protection, the Act only restricted, and in no way expanded, the rights of creditors.

As originally passed, the Act provided that support order debts were not subject to the 25 percent restriction, but it did not limit the amount of an employee's earnings that could be garnished to enforce a support order. Nothing in the legislative history stated expressly that when 25 percent or more of an employee's earnings had been garnished for support no further garnishments could occur. Nor was there any suggestion that Congress envisioned that support order garnishments were to be permitted as an addition to the general 25 percent limitation. The descriptions of the support order exception stated simply that "Section [1673(b)] excepts from this prohibition debts due for the support of any person * * *," H.R.Rep. Reprint at 1989, and "[t]he restriction on garnishment provided for in the bill does not apply to any debt due to a court order for the support of any person * * *." *Id.* at 1978. The express goal of the statute as a whole, however, was to "*restrict* [ ] the availability of garnishment as a creditors' remedy," *id.* at 1989 (emphasis added), and it is this overall goal that we must bear in mind.

In 1977, Congress amended the Act to limit the amount of earnings that could be garnished to enforce a support order. Senator Nunn, the sponsor of the amendment, described the need for such a restriction as follows:

> There is no limit in Federal law on the percentage of wages or other employment-related income which may be garnished for child support or alimony under court order. Many States allow garnishment of 100 percent of earnings * * *. Because of the arrearages that have resulted through incomplete payments (or no payments) of child support and alimony orders, the wages or the annuities of a number of people have been garnished at 100 percent for periods of many months and even years. This has sometimes caused the second families of the fathers in these cases to face financial ruin.

123 Cong.Rec. 6728 (1977). Thus the Act was amended to place the current 50–65 percent ceiling on garnishments to enforce orders of support, giving further proof of Congress's primary concern for the financial well being of the employee.

Given the overall purpose of the Act and the priority accorded in New York to garnishments for support, we find no merit in Long Island Trust's argument, that 25 percent of an employee's disposable earnings are reserved for creditors and that up to 65 percent *more* may be garnished to enforce a support order. * * * And in view of Congress's overall purpose of restricting garnishments in order to decrease the number of personal bankruptcies, it would be unjustifiable to infer that the general ceiling and its exceptions were intended to be cumulated to allow garnishments of disposable income to the total extent of 90 percent. Thus, we hold that where, as here, support garnishments have priority and result in the withholding of 25 percent or more of an employee's disposable earnings, creditor garnishment is impermissible under the Act.

* * *

We are mindful of the argument that the statute as thus construed may help debtors to evade payment of their just debts if they collusively procure orders of support that exceed the general statutory maximum of 25 percent. This possibility is lessened in New York by the state's requirement of full financial disclosure by the parties to a support proceeding, and by the New York courts' responsibility to determine both the needs of the family and the means of the wage earner. More importantly, the point that garnishment restrictions may have the effect of assisting debtors to avoid payment of their debts was considered, and indeed vigorously debated, in Congress prior to the passage of the Act. Thus, even had New York not so clearly mandated safeguards against collusion, we would hardly feel free to tamper with the way in which Congress has chosen to balance the interests of the debtor, his family, and his creditors.

Finally, we point out that this interpretation of the Act does not leave Long Island Trust powerless to collect on its judgment. N.Y.C.P.

L.R. Article 52 provides a variety of means for the enforcement of money judgments. * * *

The judgment dismissing the complaint is affirmed.

Problem 2

Bob Crachit works as a clerk in the office of a local bank. He earns $400 per week in wages, but his take home pay is only $188 because of the following deductions: taxes—$60; social security—$20; health insurance plan—$30; retirement plan—$25; contribution to local public television station—$2; court ordered child support—$75. Marley Finance Co. has a judgment of $2500 against Crachit. How much of Crachit's income may Marley garnish?

Problem 3

Dianne Allen worked for Southern California Gas Co. (SCG). SCG received a notice of garnishment concerning a debt Ms. Allen owed to Ace Finance Co. In compliance with the garnishment order, SCG began withholding funds from her paycheck and sending the money to Ace. A month later, SCG received a garnishment notice concerning a debt Ms. Allen owed to Local Department Store. However, Ms. Allen immediately contacted Local and arranged a release of the garnishment before any money was actually withheld from her paycheck. Nevertheless, a week later, she was fired.

   a. Did SCG violate the federal garnishment laws? See especially CCPA § 304.

   b. If so, what is Dianne Allen's remedy? May she sue SCG for reinstatement and back pay? See Donovan v. Southern California Gas Co., 715 F.2d 1405 (9th Cir.1983).

2. JUDGMENT AND EXECUTION LIENS

D. EPSTEIN, DEBTOR–CREDITOR LAW IN A NUTSHELL

45–48, 51–52 (3d ed. 1986).*

Many states statutorily provide that the rendition of a judgment itself creates a lien [usually on realty only, see below]; no additional judgment creditor action is required to create a judgment lien. Other states have statutes that provide that a judgment lien arises only after the "docketing" of the judgment in a county in which the debtor has property. (Docketing is usually accomplished by the county clerk's making an entry of the judgment under the last name of the judgment debtor in the appropriate docket book.) In such states, a judgment rendered by a state court in County X, cannot create a lien on property in County Y until the judgment is docketed in County Y.

* * *

The judgment lien operates as a general lien on all of the debtor's property subject thereto, not as a specific lien upon particular property. In Alabama, Georgia, and Mississippi, the judgment lien reaches both real and personal property; California now provides for judgment liens on "business personal property." In all other states that recognize the judgment lien, it is limited to real property—not a specific piece of real property, but all real property of the debtor or, in states that require docketing, all real property of the debtor in counties in which the judgment has been docketed.

* * *

The jurisdictions vary considerably with respect to the proper method of enforcement of judgment liens. In some jurisdictions, fore-closure proceedings is the only method; in other states, levy and sale under a writ of execution is required; and some states permit a choice between foreclosure actions and a writ of execution.

* * *

Today, the law of execution is statutory. Most statutes provide for a single writ of execution by which a judgment creditor can have the judgment debtor's property seized and sold in satisfaction of the judgment. In most states a writ of execution can reach both personalty and realty; in a very few states a writ of execution does not reach realty; in still others, the judgment creditor is statutorily required to look first to the personal property of the debtor.

As execution is statutory, the exact procedure varies somewhat from state to state. A writ of execution is issued by the clerk of the court in which the judgment was rendered. Issuance of the writ is a ministerial act and involves neither a hearing nor discretion on the part of the clerk. The writ is directed to the sheriff or some other statutorily authorized official; it orders the official to levy on the property described in the writ and, usually after appraisal and due notice, to sell such property at public sale. As with attachment, there are problems as to what constitutes an effective levy and problems of liability for an improper levy. The writ specifies a "return date"; by that date, the sheriff or other official must return the writ to the issuing clerk with an endorsement stating the property seized and sold or the impossibility of finding leviable assets. The latter form of return is often referred to as return *nulla bona*. If the return is *nulla bona*, a second (*alias*) and further (*pluries*) writs may issue.

What problems might arise in this process? Consider the following.

MIEBACH v. COLASURDO

Washington Supreme Court, 1984.
102 Wash.2d 170, 685 P.2d 1074.

DOLLIVER, JUSTICE.

Defendant Valeria Colasurdo seeks reversal of the decisions rendered by the trial court and Court of Appeals which quieted title to her residence in plaintiff William Miebach. In February 1974, Valerie Shearer, daughter of Valeria Colasurdo, executed an installment note in favor of Group Health Credit Union for $1,300 to purchase a Mercedes automobile. Valeria Colasurdo and her husband, Dominic, signed the note as comakers. The note provided that each maker was bound as principal, not as surety, and waived any right to presentment, demand, protest, notice of nonpayment, objection to assignment of the note for collection or to suit thereon. Shearer made two payments to the credit union. Thereafter, the credit union assigned the note to Washington Credit, Inc., a collection agency.

After Washington Credit received a few payments from Shearer, further collection efforts failed. Washington Credit filed suit in Seattle District Court in June 1977 to collect the amount due. Shearer was personally served. The Colasurdos were served by substitute service upon their 15–year–old foster daughter, Samatra Phillips, who was then residing at the Colasurdos' home. Valeria Colasurdo testified she never received this notice. Neither Shearer nor the Colasurdos appeared. A default judgment was entered against the parties, jointly and severally, in August 1977 in the amount of $1,150.24.

Following the filing of the judgment, a praecipe for a writ of execution was issued to Gary Culver, Washington Credit attorney, in June 1978. Culver testified he drove by the Colasurdo residence in an attempt to locate personal property. Pursuant to his usual practice, he searched for personal property (*e.g.,* boats, cars) outside of the house, but made no other inquiry. Unable to locate any personal property, Culver wrote to the sheriff's office requesting the sheriff to levy upon and sell at an execution sale the Colasurdo residence. At that time, the sheriff would rely on an attorney's statement and not independently verify the existence of any personal property.

In June 1978, the sheriff recorded a writ of execution against the Colasurdo residence. Pursuant to former RCW 6.24.010(2), a notice of the sheriff's sale was posted on the Colasurdo property and published for 5 consecutive weeks in the Daily Journal of Commerce. While admitting she saw the posted notice, Valeria Colasurdo testified she knew of no outstanding debts and believed if there was any problem her daughter would take care of it. Moreover, she considered the notice to be a "scare tactic" used by the finance company towards Valerie and believed if there was a problem involving her home, her mortgage company would personally contact her.

Neither Shearer nor the Colasurdos attended the July 1978 sheriff's sale. At the time of the sale the home had a fair market value of $106,000, in which the Colasurdos had a $77,000 equity. The residence was sold to Washington Credit, the only bidder, for $1,340.02, in full satisfaction of the default judgment. No objections were filed and an order confirming the sale was entered on September 21, 1978. In December 1978, Washington Credit assigned its interest obtained by the sheriff's certification of purchase to Master Mortgages, Inc., for $850. Master Mortgages was a real property holding company solely owned by Gary Culver. Neither Shearer nor the Colasurdos paid the judgment during the 1–year redemption period. The property was conveyed by sheriff's deed to Master Mortgages in August 1979.

In August 1979, plaintiff Miebach, a real estate investor, contacted Culver to inquire generally about the ramifications of sheriff's sales. The two met several times over the next few weeks, during which Miebach expressed interest in purchasing the Colasurdo residence. Miebach knew the property had been sold as a result of a judgment against the Colasurdos. He also knew the Colasurdos were in possession and that improvements were being made to the premises. Miebach believed he only needed to institute an unlawful detainer action. In deciding to purchase the property, Miebach relied on his search of the records and title insurance.

In September 1979, Master Mortgages conveyed the property by special warranty deed to Arctic Trading Company for $15,000. Arctic Trading shared office space with Master Mortgages. Culver then acted as Arctic's attorney and received one-half of its sale profits. In October 1979 Arctic, represented by Culver, conveyed the Colasurdo property by special warranty deed to Miebach for $80,000. On October 31, 1979, Miebach served upon the Colasurdos a 3–day notice to vacate. Valeria Colasurdo testified this was the first time she learned Washington Credit had sued her. The Colasurdos did not vacate the premises. Thereafter, Miebach brought an unlawful detainer action. The Colasurdos answered, asserted legal and equitable defenses, and later brought a separate action to vacate the default judgment and set aside the sheriff's sale. By stipulation, the two actions were consolidated by the trial court.

* * *

At trial, testimony addressed whether the 15–year-old foster daughter, Samatra Phillips, was a "person of suitable age and discretion" with whom to leave the complaint and notice. The trial court held Valeria Colasurdo failed to show by clear and convincing evidence that Phillips was not a person of "suitable discretion" and thus the substituted service on the Colasurdos was valid. The court found Valeria Colasurdo had actual and constructive notice of the sheriff's sale, but took no action; the order of confirmation of sale cured all irregularities and no jurisdictional defects were found; and all conveyances were in accordance with Washington law. Miebach was deemed a bona fide purchaser. With a "heavy heart" the court rendered judgment for Miebach and dismissed Colasurdo's action.

Colasurdo appealed. Court of Appeals, Division One, affirmed in a 2 to 1 decision. The majority held Colasurdo failed to sustain her burden to vacate the judgment or challenge service and notice requirements. Specifically, Colasurdo was found to have waived her right to object to any irregularities with the sheriff's sale as the order of confirmation was entered in September 1978 and she did not move to set it aside until January 1980. The majority affirmed the trial court's determination that Miebach was a bona fide purchaser, thus foreclosing equity intervention. Judge Williams, dissenting, examined Miebach's actions and concluded he was not a bona fide purchaser. He recognized the gross inadequacy of the purchase price—less than 2 percent of fair market value. Lastly, he viewed the execution sale as being "tainted by unfairness because no true effort was made to satisfy the debt from Colasurdos' personal property. Equity requires that this sale be set aside."

* * *

While our determination of what is sufficient to put an ordinary prudent person upon inquiry notice has varied, a review of the record persuades us Miebach was not a bona fide purchaser. At trial Miebach testified he had been an investor for 23 years and had "ventured into real estate." After the purchase of the Colasurdo home, he had made other sheriff sale investments. One involved a default judgment taken by Washington Credit for an unpaid candy bill of $205.20. *Robeson v. Helland,* 32 Wn.App. 487, 488, 648 P.2d 461 (1982). The Robesons' Bellevue home was sold at a sheriff's sale to the minor children of Gary Culver. Miebach later acquired title for $33,000. Six days later he deeded the property to another party for $41,000. In another, a $80,000 home was sold to satisfy a $1,295.12 debt owed to Washington Credit. *Washington Credit, Inc. v. Houston,* 33 Wn.App. 41, 650 P.2d 1147 (1982), *dismissed and mandated,* 100 Wn.2d 1010, 650 P.2d 1147 (1983). Title was later transferred to Master Mortgages, who conveyed to Miebach.

Miebach had within his knowledge sufficient facts to put an experienced businessman, as himself, on inquiry notice. When deciding to purchase the Colasurdo residence, he drove by twice and once looked around the house. After knocking on the door, he determined no one was home. He did notice a sign inside the door referring to a permit, allowing for improvements on the property. By examining the records, Miebach was also aware the property had been sold at less than 2 percent of its fair market value. The suspicions of an ordinary prudent person in Miebach's position would have been aroused by these circumstances. The lone fact Miebach believed the Colasurdos were "holding over", in light of the other circumstances in the case, does not persuade us, as it did the Court of Appeals, he had no notice of the Colasurdos' equitable claim. The actions taken by Miebach do not conform with our view of those to be taken by an ordinary prudent investor.

If Miebach had made a reasonably diligent inquiry, he would have discovered the Colasurdos were aware of neither the default judgment nor the sheriff's sale.

* * *

We hold Miebach had constructive if not actual notice of the Colasurdos' claim of right to or equity in their residence before he acquired title. He was not a bona fide purchaser.

Without the intervening rights of a bona fide purchaser, "[t]here is no question but that equity has a right to step in and prevent the enforcement of a legal right whenever such an enforcement would be inequitable."

Generally, "mere inadequacy of price, unless so gross as to shock the conscience, is not enough to set aside a judicial sale * * *" However, "when there is a great inadequacy, slight circumstances indicating unfairness will be sufficient to justify a decree setting the sale aside" on equitable grounds. *Roger v. Whitham*, 56 Wash. 190, 193, 105 P. 628 (1909).

In *Roger,* this court voided a foreclosure sale where a home valued at over $3,000 was sold for $111.32. In *Lovejoy,* parcels of real estate worth in excess of $4,000 were sold at a sheriff's sale for $87.92. The court strongly disapproved the judgment creditor's refusal to collect a debt of $63.15 out of personal property. The sale was set aside because of the

> obviously studied course of the judgment creditor in refusing or failing to pursue those plain, simple and adequate ways to collect, constitute in part that unfairness which coupled with the shockingly inadequate price for which they purchased at the execution sale, fully warranted respondents in their appeal to a court of equity for relief * * *.

Lovejoy v. Americus, supra, 111 Wash. at 575, 191 P. 790.

Here, too, there was no true effort to satisfy the default judgment from personal property or even to discover what personal property might be available. Now, however, a statute requires the judgment creditor to exercise due diligence to ascertain if the judgment debtor has sufficient nonexempt personal property to satisfy the judgment with interest. Due diligence

> includes but is not limited to the creditor or the creditor's representative personally visiting the premises, contacting the occupants and inquiring about their relationship to the judgment debtor, contacting immediate neighbors of the premises, and searching the records of the auditor of the county in which the property is located to determine if a declaration of homestead or nonabandonment has been filed by the judgment debtor.

RCW 6.04.035(2). The statute sets forth the standards required to eliminate any possibility one's home will be sold to satisfy a small debt.

Although these are statutory requirements, they are also standards which will be imposed by this court even in the absence of a statute. While the parties complied with the then-existing notice requirements of RCW 6.24.010 (sheriff's sales) and RCW 6.24.140 (redemption), this is not enough. We will not allow Valeria Colasurdo's home to be taken for a pittance when surrounded by the circumstances of inequity in this case. The sheriff's sale is set aside.

* * *

Notes

1. How low a price is too low? Are standards such as "shock the conscience" or "gross inadequacy" appropriate, or should a court set aside all sales below some stated percentage of the property's value? If you think the latter approach is better, what percentage would you use?

2. Is low price by itself ever enough to set aside the sale, or must there always be some other factors which contribute to the low price? The traditional rule in most jurisdictions is that stated by the court in *Miebach.* The Washington court followed this approach in a recent case involving a sheriff's sale of commercial property on facts remarkably similar to those in *Miebach*—the sale price was $14,125.85; the value was $290,000; and the buyers were experienced investors who knew they were buying property which was being sold to satisfy a judgment. Casa del Rey v. Hart, 110 Wash.2d 65, 750 P.2d 261 (1988). Courts in a few other jurisdictions have held that inadequate price alone is enough. The Pennsylvania courts have long followed this approach. For a recent example, see Scott v. Adal Corp., 276 Pa.Super. 459, 419 A.2d 548 (1980). Sometimes you will even see more extreme approaches to the problem. In Huff v. Huff, 622 S.W.2d 731 (Mo. App.1981), a sheriff's sale brought $500 for a piece of property worth $25,000. The court said the price was so grossly inadequate as to constitute fraud.

3. In *Miebach,* what happens next? The court set aside the sale, but isn't the judgment against Ms. Colasurdo still in effect? What should she do now? What should Washington Credit do now?

4. While the principal case was on appeal, Valeria Colasurdo sued the sheriff who conducted the execution procedures. She argued that he was negligent in conducting the sale without making an independent determination that there was no personal property which could have been seized. In fact, she said, there were several bank accounts, three cars, and other personal property, and they did not have to resort to taking her house. The court held that the sheriff had no such duty; his reliance on the attorney's report was enough. Colasurdo v. Waldt, 49 Wash.App. 257, 752 P.2d 920 (1987).

5. Do you feel sorry for William Miebach? Didn't he just lose his $80,000 investment? Do you think he thought about this possibility? See Miebach v. Safeco Title Insurance Co., 49 Wash.App. 451, 743 P.2d 845 (1987).

6. Most attorneys dislike collection work because the fees are low and the work has almost no intellectual challenge. Consider Gary Culver's

position in all of this. Hasn't he figured out a way to make collection work pay? How much money did he make as a result of handling this $1150 collection for Washington Credit? Didn't he, in effect, become the buyer at the execution sale? Is that proper? Might he have a duty to account to his client, Washington Credit, for the profits he received on the resale? How many parties did he represent or advise in this string of transactions? Do you think he violated any ethical rules? Do you think his behavior was proper?

Problem 4

Was the low price really the crucial element in *Miebach*?

Carol Calm is a Seattle homeowner, and the mother of two daughters, Amy and Beth. When Amy bought a car from Francis Ford, she needed a cosigner to qualify for the necessary credit. Carol signed the $12,000 credit agreement as a comaker. Later, Carol and Amy became estranged, and Amy moved across town without leaving a forwarding address, ceased all communication with Carol, and stopped making the installment payments. After two missed payments, and its dunning notices were returned unopened, Francis Ford sued Amy and Carol for the outstanding balance ($10,000) in Seattle District Court. Amy was personally served, but Carol was served by substitute service on 15–year old Beth. Beth, however, forgot to give Carol the papers or any message about them. Since neither Amy nor Carol appeared, the court entered a default judgment against both of them.

Following the filing of the judgment, a praecipe for writ of execution was issued to Gary Culver, an attorney. Culver drove by Carol's home, did not see any boats or cars there, and then wrote the sheriff's office stating that he was unable to locate any personal property, and requesting the sheriff to levy upon and sell Carol's home. The property was then worth about $110,000.

The sheriff recorded a writ of execution, and posted a notice of sheriff's sale, on Carol's property, and also published the requisite newspaper notices. Carol ignored all notices. At the sheriff's sale, only Culver was present. He had learned something from dealing with the Colasurdos, and bid $100,000 for the property, but expressly made $90,000 conditional and not due or payable until the 1 year redemption period had run. The sheriff took the $10,000, paid Francis Ford in full, obtained an order confirming the sale. One year later, when neither Amy nor Carol had paid the judgment, the sheriff collected $90,000 from Culver and issued a certification of purchase to Culver.

The sheriff is now standing on Carol's doorstep with $90,000 in one hand and a 3–day notice to vacate her home in the other. She wants to know whether the default judgment can be vacated and the sheriff's sale set aside. What is your advice, counsellor? What theories were used in *Miebach*, and are they still available when the price paid is raised?

Would your answer change if Culver had sold his interest to Miebach for $105,000 and Miebach was seeking to oust Carol?

Note on the Constitutionality of Post–Judgment Seizure

A couple of decades ago, it was commonplace for creditors to seize a debtor's property even before getting a judgment against the debtor. Seizure of wages through pre-judgment garnishment was common, as was pre-judgment seizure of other assets through a procedure known as attachment. In a series of cases beginning with Sniadach v. Family Finance Corp., 395 U.S. 337, 89 S.Ct. 1820, 23 L.Ed.2d 349 (1969), however, the Supreme Court has ruled that a debtor's property generally may not be seized without notice and an opportunity to be heard. As a result, most procedures allowing pre-judgment seizure have fallen into disuse. See also Fuentes v. Shevin, 407 U.S. 67, 92 S.Ct. 1983, 32 L.Ed.2d 556 (1972).

These cases did not affect post-judgment collection procedures, because obviously the availability of a trial gave the debtor the due process protections missing from most pre-judgment remedies. In recent years, however, even post-judgment seizure has come under constitutional attack.

DIONNE v. BOULEY

United States Court of Appeals, First Circuit, 1985.
757 F.2d 1344.

LEVIN H. CAMPBELL, CHIEF JUDGE.

[Rose Dionne challenged a Rhode Island post judgment procedure which allowed any judgment creditor "who was unable to execute his judgment to file a second debt on judgment action against the debtor and to attach the debtor's property as security for this second suit. Dionne's bank account was attached pursuant to a suit of this nature filed by the creditor," who "sought another money judgment in the amount of $551.80 plus costs of $50. Dionne was served with process in this second action on August 17, 1982. That same day, she received notice from her bank that one of her checks had been returned for insufficient funds and that the bank was imposing a $5 service charge for the check's return. On calling the bank to inquire about this, Dionne was told that her funds had been attached."]

[Dionne's bank account consisted mostly of social security benefits which were not subject to "garnishment, attachment or other legal process" under federal law. Dionne was not given notice of any procedures through which she could challenge the attachment or raise a claim of exemption.]

According to the parties' stipulations it was the practice of the state district court to issue blank writs of attachment upon request, with the name of the clerk and the seal already affixed, to creditors or their attorneys. No motion to attach was required with these, the writ being simply served directly on the trustee (i.e. bank, employer). The parties also stipulated that there was no required hearing or notice of any possible hearing, either before or after the writ of attachment was issued and served, and that there was no notice to the judgment debtor of any possible defenses or exemption claims.

A short time after learning of the attachment, on September 14, 1982, Dionne brought this action in the federal district court challenging the constitutionality of the postjudgment garnishment procedure in the state district court system. She asserted causes of action under 42 U.S.C. § 1983 for alleged violation of the due process and supremacy clauses of the federal Constitution. Dionne criticized the state's failure to have provided her with a prompt notice of the attachment that would have informed her of the existence of the state and federal exemptions and the means for her to claim them. She further criticized the lack of any specific provision in Rhode Island law for a hearing, either prior to the attachment or immediately following the issuance and service of the writ, at which any exemptions could be claimed. She requested declaratory and injunctive relief, and class certification.

* * *

Thereafter, Dionne moved for summary judgment, most of the above facts having been previously stipulated by the parties. On March 23, 1984, the district court issued its opinion and order, declaring the challenged procedure unconstitutional and issuing the requested injunction. Defendant appeals from the judgment below asserting that the case was moot, that the district court should have abstained, and that the challenged procedures are not unconstitutional. * * *

* * *

IV.   DUE PROCESS

There is no dispute that Dionne was entitled to the exemption created by Congress in 42 U.S.C. § 407 with respect to the social security funds she had deposited in her attached bank account. It is also clear that Dionne's interest in retaining her exempt social security funds free from attachment was the kind of property interest that is entitled to due process protection. The question is simply whether Rhode Island post-judgment garnishment procedure, as currently set out in state law, affords Dionne appropriate notice and a sufficient opportunity to assert her exemption claim. We agree with the district court that it does not.

In *Mathews v. Eldridge*, 424 U.S. 319, 96 S.Ct. 893, 47 L.Ed.2d 18 (1976), the Court said that,

> identification of the specific dictates of due process generally requires consideration of three factors: First, the private interest that will be affected by the official action; second, the risk of an erroneous deprivation of such interest through the procedures used, and the probable value, if any, of additional or substitute procedural safeguards; and finally, the Government's interest, including the function involved and the fiscal and administrative burdens that the additional or substitute procedural requirement would entail.

424 U.S. at 335, 96 S.Ct. at 903.

Applying this standard, the district court found that the process afforded by Rhode Island was inadequate since it failed to provide the judgment debtor with prompt and adequately informative notice, advising her not only that her property had been attached but of the relevant exemptions and of the means available for asserting them. Current state procedure also lacks express provision for a prompt post-attachment hearing at which to assert any exemption. The district court concluded that any burden imposed on creditors and on the state courts by procedures of this type was outweighed by the interest of a judgment debtor, like Dionne, in avoiding or, at least, minimizing, the serious consequences of an erroneous deprivation of her property.

* * *

We thus turn to the question of the adequacy of present Rhode Island procedures in protecting the debtor against the risk of wrongful attachment of otherwise exempt property.

As we have seen, Rhode Island law is silent as to any right of a judgment debtor to be heard after an attachment is made. It is even unclear if the debtor must be notified of the bare fact of the attachment, and even if he is so notified (as occurred here) any notice would be limited to that fact alone, and would not enlighten the debtor as to his rights and remedies. While it is not unusual for people to need a lawyer's help to understand their situation and any available remedies, we think that due process in this context—which involves destitute people whose property has suddenly been seized as well as exemptions pertaining to life's basic necessities—requires that Rhode Island provide and spell out procedural rights and remedies more clearly than it has yet done.

* * *

In sum, we are in general agreement with the district court's conclusion that Rhode Island has not provided judgment debtors whose property it permits creditors to seize unilaterally by writ of attachment with sufficient, defined procedural process to meet the requirements of the due process clause of the fourteenth amendment.

* * *

The judgment of the district court, as modified by this opinion in respect to the lack of any need to list all federal and state exemptions in the required notice, is affirmed.

Note

How should the Rhode Island legislature respond to this decision? The New York post-judgment collection procedure was held unconstitutional in Deary v. Guardian Loan Co., 534 F.Supp. 1178 (S.D.N.Y.1982). After this decision was handed down, the New York legislature amended its laws by requiring that the following notice be given to the debtor:

NOTICE TO JUDGMENT DEBTOR

Money or property belonging to you may have been taken or held in order to satisfy a judgment which has been entered against you. Read this carefully. YOU MAY BE ABLE TO GET YOUR MONEY BACK

State and federal laws prevent certain money or property from being taken to satisfy judgments. Such money or property is said to be "exempt". The following is a partial list of money which may be exempt:

1. Supplemental security income (SSI);

2. Social security;

3. Public assistance (welfare);

4. Alimony or child support;

5. Unemployment benefits;

6. Disability benefits;

7. Workers' compensation benefits;

8. Public or private pensions; and

9. Veterans benefits.

If you think that any of your money that has been taken or held is exempt, you must act promptly because the money may be applied to the judgment. If you claim any of your money that has been taken or held is exempt, you may contact the person sending this notice.

Also, YOU MAY CONSULT AN ATTORNEY, INCLUDING LEGAL AID IF YOU QUALIFY. The law (New York civil practice law and rules, article four and sections fifty-two hundred thirty-nine and fifty-two hundred forty) provides a procedure for determination of a claim to an exemption.

N.Y.Civ.Prac.Law and R. § 5222 (McKinney). Assuming these procedures are followed by creditors, is the New York approach constitutional? See McCahey v. L.P. Investors, 774 F.2d 543 (2d Cir.1985).

Problem 5

Using the criteria stated in *Dionne*, consider again the Washington State post-judgment execution procedure set forth in *Miebach* and Problem 4. Does that process meet the constitutional dictates of due process? Are there significant risks of erroneous deprivation of the debtor's home? Note that the state court focused on a different problem in *Miebach*, due to other principles it found to be established in state law.

SECTION C. SEIZING THE DEBTOR—
IMPRISONMENT FOR DEBT

(Consumers Put in Jail Because They Can't Pay Their Bills?
Impossible! * * * Or Is It?)

Everyone knows that imprisonment for debt is a thing of the past, something that belongs to common law England and the novels of Charles Dickens. Right? Wrong! Nearly all states have constitutional provisions which purport to ban imprisonment for debt. However, these provisions nearly always contain exceptions which allow imprisonment for certain categories of civil debts. As a result, today in the

United States people are routinely jailed or credibly threatened with jail for non-payment of civil obligations.

This section explores the use of incarceration as a debt collection tool. The state always seems to be sympathetic to the problems of the unpaid creditor. The inventive minds of state officials have found several methods of incarcerating non-paying debtors. Today, our legal system recognizes three basic processes through which debtors may be imprisoned for civil debts. The first is a procedure known as "body execution"; the second is the judicial contempt power; and the third is the use of criminal laws. The latter two procedures are much more common than the first, although, as we will see, all are still commonly used today.

1. BODY EXECUTION

The body execution procedure has a long common law history. You may think of it as basically a corporal counterpart to the ordinary collection process of property execution, (except that the creditor does not get to sell the debtor). A special post-judgment writ, *capias ad satisfaciendum,* existed for the purpose, under which the sheriff was instructed to seize and incarcerate the debtor. At common law, the debtor usually (but not always) could secure his release by paying the debt. The case of Landrigan v. McElroy, below, demonstrates that body execution and similar procedures are still with us. See also Security Savings Bank v. Mueller, 308 N.W.2d 761.

LANDRIGAN v. McELROY
Supreme Court of Rhode Island, 1983.
457 A.2d 1056.

WEISBERGER, JUSTICE.

The defendant appeals from a Superior Court order granting the plaintiff's motion for a body execution pursuant to G.L.1956 (1969 Reenactment) § 9–25–15. The defendant contends that the body execution statute contravenes the Fourteenth Amendment to the Constitution of the United States. We agree that a portion of the statute is unconstitutional. Accordingly, we sustain the defendant's appeal, vacate the order that granted the plaintiff's motion for a body execution, and remand the case to the Superior Court.

The facts that led to the issuance of the body execution in this case are undisputed. A civil action for assault and battery in the Superior Court resulted in a jury verdict for plaintiff. Judgment was entered in the amount of $42,029.28 plus interest on December 3, 1976. The trial justice denied defendant's motion for a new trial, and defendant appealed to this court. On February 22, 1979, we summarily denied and dismissed defendant's appeal. The plaintiff then requested that the clerk of the Superior Court prepare an execution on the judgment. During March and April of 1979 two executions were issued, but both were returned unsatisfied.

Thereupon, plaintiff moved pursuant to § 9–25–15 for an execution against the body of defendant.[1] Arguing that the body execution statute was unconstitutional, defendant objected. After a hearing, a Superior Court justice granted plaintiff's motion and on April 29, 1980, ordered that an execution issue against the body of defendant. On the same day, a stay pending appeal to this court was granted.

The arguments of defendant on appeal can be summarized as follows: (1) section 9–25–15 denies defendant the equal protection of the laws by depriving him of his fundamental right to physical liberty without a compelling state interest, [and] (2) the issuance of a body execution without a prior hearing concerning defendant's ability to pay the tort judgment does not comport with the requirements of procedural due process * * *.

HISTORY OF THE BODY EXECUTION STATUTE

Imprisonment for debt is an ancient remedy. Indeed, under Roman law creditors could seize and imprison even insolvent debtors and sell them into slavery; if more than one creditor had a claim against a debtor, they could partition the debtor's body into proportionate shares. At common law, the writs of *capias ad respondendum and capias ad satisfaciendum* authorized the arrest of the debtor at the initiation of the lawsuit or after judgment had been rendered respectively. Vestiges of these procedures existed in colonial America and in the United States during the post-Revolutionary War period. In response to abusive utilization of body execution statutes by creditors during the late-eighteenth and nineteenth centuries, state legislatures enacted statutory and constitutional provisions that limited or entirely prohibited imprisonment for debt. The Constitution of the State prohibits, absent a strong presumption of fraud, continued imprisonment of a judgment debtor "after he shall have delivered up his property for the benefit of his creditors * * *." Moreover, once a contract judgment debtor is imprisoned pursuant to a body execution, he or she may obtain release almost immediately by taking the "poor debtor's oath."[3] In addition, the creditor for whose benefit the debtor is imprisoned must pay in advance for the prisoner's board.

Section 9–25–15 must be examined in light of these limitations and its own legislative history. The body execution statute originated in the Court and Practice Act of 1905. * * * In 1961 the Legislature amended the statute to enable judgment creditors to obtain through ex

---

1. General Laws 1956 (1969 Reenactment) § 9–25–15 provides in part:

"An execution, original, alias, or pluries, may issue against the body of a defendant not exempt from arrest in an action * * * sounding in tort in which the title to real estate was not in dispute * * * provided, however, that no execution, original, alias or pluries, shall issue against the body of a defendant

unless so ordered by a justice of the superior court or a justice of a district court upon the written ex parte motion of a party named in the action."

3. The defendant in this case, however, is a debtor on a tort judgment. He therefore would not be subject to discharge pursuant to the "poor debtor's oath" until six months after imprisonment.

parte motion execution against the bodies of judgment debtors. Clearly, this amendment was intended "to deprive judgment creditors of arbitrary power to issue, through their counsel, body executions against judgment debtors and to require submission of the petitions to judicial scrutiny." *Martin v. Estrella,* 110 R.I. 368, 370, 292 A.2d 884, 886 (1972). We have held, however, that once a judgment creditor sets forth one of the statutory grounds for issuance of a body execution, the trial justice has no choice but to grant the creditor's motion. As will become evident, our decision today overrules *Martin v. Estrella* to the extent that the court's opinion in that case deprives a trial justice of *any* discretion to deny a motion for a body execution.

THE CONSTITUTIONAL VALIDITY OF § 9–25–15

The defendant bases his equal-protection challenge to § 9–25–15 on the doctrine enunciated by the United States Supreme Court in *Williams v. Illinois,* 399 U.S. 235, 90 S.Ct. 2018, 26 L.Ed.2d 586 (19.'0), and *Tate v. Short,* 401 U.S. 395, 91 S.Ct. 668, 28 L.Ed.2d 130 (1971). In both cases the Court addressed the constitutionality of imprisoning a defendant beyond the statutorily authorized term solely because the defendant was unable to pay a fine that accompanied his sentence. The Court determined that such imprisonment constituted invidious discrimination in violation of the equal-protection clause. These cases make clear that the state cannot imprison an individual solely because of a lack of money.

The defendant points out that a federal district court relied on *Williams* and *Tate* to strike down, as facially repugnant to the equal-protection clause, the body execution statute of another state. In *Abbit v. Bernier,* 387 F.Supp. 57 (D.Conn.1974), the court found that even though the Connecticut statute did not expressly exclude a preincarceration hearing to determine ability to pay, the state courts, implemented the statute without providing for such hearings. Consequently, the court struck down the statute as unconstitutional. Subsequently, a Connecticut state court found that the *Abbit* court erroneously concluded that court practices in the state did not include a hearing to determine the judgment debtor's ability to pay. Accordingly, the state court upheld the body execution statute by interpreting it as requiring such a hearing.[6]

The body execution statute at issue in *Abbit* * * * was silent concerning a preincarceration hearing to determine the judgment debtor's ability to pay. The "ex parte" amendment to our statute, on the other hand, implicitly excludes such a hearing. Moreover, this court's interpretation of that amendment in *Martin v. Estrella* deprives a trial justice of any discretion to deny issuance of a body execution once a creditor sets forth the existence of a statutory ground. We are of the opinion, therefore, that § 9–25–15 is incapable of an interpretation

---

6. Subsequently, the Connecticut Legislature repealed the body execution statute.

upholding its validity as long as the "ex parte" languge is an effective part of the statute.

The body execution statute does not expressly create two classifications of tort judgment debtors, namely, those debtors who are able to pay but refuse to do so and those who are unable to pay. As the Court stated in *Williams,* however, "a law nondiscriminatory on its face may be grossly discriminatory in its operation." By failing to provide for a preincarceration hearing to determine ability to pay, the statute in effect enables only tort judgment debtors who are able to pay to obtain immediate release from imprisonment. These individuals need only comply with the judgments and executions against them. On the other hand, tort judgment debtors who are unable to pay must remain in prison for at least six months. They are, therefore, incarcerated solely because of their lack of money. This disparate treatment is precisely the type of invidious discrimination prohibited by the Court in *Williams* and *Tate.*

Moreover, imprisoning a tortfeasor who is unable to pay a judgment does not implement the governmental interest in enforcing judgments and executions. Supplemental proceedings in aid of execution more effectively further this interest because such proceedings enable a creditor to obtain satisfaction of a judgment on an installment payment basis. In short, imprisoning debtors who are unable to pay judgments against them does not have a rational connection with enforcement of the obligation to pay. This court will not attribute to the Legislature an intent that would result in absurdities or would defeat the underlying purpose of legislation.

We hold that the ex parte hearing provision of the 1961 amendment to § 9–25–15 is unconstitutional as violative of the equal-protection clause. We assume, however, that the Legislature would prefer that this court strike down only the unconstitutional portion if such a construction is reasonably possible. Accordingly, we shall sever the ex parte hearing portion of the 1961 amendment to § 9–25–15 from the rest of the statute, strike down this element as unconstitutional, and interpret the remaining portion of the statute as requiring a hearing to determine the judgment debtor's ability to pay. * * *

* * *

* * * Henceforth, the body execution statute will be enforced only against judgment debtors who fail to demonstrate in a preincarceration hearing that they are unable to pay the jugdment against them. The issuance of body executions will therefore be subject to more meaningful judicial scrutiny with the benefit of an adversary rather than ex parte hearing as a condition precedent.

DUE–PROCESS REQUIREMENTS

* * *

Procedural due process requires that no deprivation of life, liberty, or property should occur without a prior hearing. * * *

In *Mills v. Howard,* we noted that "[t]he opportunity for a pre-incarceration hearing becomes all the more significant when it is recalled that one's indigency can be a proper defense to an action seeking enforcement of an order or decree calling for the payment of money." This determination was made in the context of a due-process challenge to the Family Court's issuance of a body execution pursuant to G.L.1956 (1969 Reenactment) § 15–5–16. Although this statute and its successor, G.L.1956 (1981 Reenactment) § 15–5–16.3, apply only to the enforcement of orders awarding alimony and child support, their implementation has effects not unlike those caused by the implementation of the statute under review in this case. The opinion of the court in *Mills v. Howard* is therefore very persuasive.

Accordingly, we hold that due process requires that a hearing take place after reasonable notice to determine the defendant's ability to pay the judgment against him prior to the issuance of a body execution. At this hearing, the defendant has the burden of raising the issue of ability to pay and of demonstrating such an inability by a fair preponderance of the evidence. If the trial justice determines that the defendant is unable to pay the judgment, he must refuse to issue the body execution. Rather he may order partial payments or take whatever other action is appropriate under the circumstances.

For the reasons stated, the appeal of the defendant is sustained. We vacate the order below which granted the plaintiff's motion for a body execution and remand the case to the Superior Court for proceedings consistent with this opinion.

Notes

1. Where allowed, imprisonment through body execution is used by creditors with some frequency. In Desmond v. Hachey, 315 F.Supp. 328 (D.Me.1970), the court noted that the records showed that just two of Maine's "disclosure commissioners" had issued 470 writs of capias to incarcerate in a three year period, which had resulted in "a total of 179 debtors spent 1,754 days in debtors' prison" during the period. Id., at n. 6.

2. Other recent cases have successfully challenged body execution statutes on constitutional grounds. See, for example, Kinsey v. Preeson, 746 P.2d 542 (Colo.1987), in which the Colorado statute was held to violate the equal protection clause of the Fourteenth Amendment by discriminating on the basis of indigency. See also Palumbo v. Manson, 35 Conn.Sup. 130, 400 A.2d 288 (1979).

3. In Maine, although Desmond v. Hachey, supra, struck down one body execution process, the current statutory procedure permits a court to order the debtor to make installment payments on a debt. If the debtor fails to comply with the order, the creditor may obtain an order of civil arrest against the debtor. A hearing is required to inquire into the debtor's ability to pay. See 14 M.R.S.A. §§ 3127, 3134, and 3135. For a discussion of the constitutional limitations on these procedures, see Wells v. State, 474 A.2d 846 (Me.1984).

4. Does due process adequately answer all the objections to imprison-ment for debt? After *Landrigan*, has debtor imprisonment been outlawed in Rhode Island? Why should we allow a debtor to be incarcerated for non-payment even *after* a hearing?

5. In many states, body execution is available only to collect debts arising out of torts, and is often limited to intentional torts involving malice or the like. See, e.g., Windham Distributing Co., Inc. v. Davis, 72 N.C.App. 179, 323 S.E.2d 506 (1984). Why should body execution be prohibited for contract debts but not for tort debts?

6. The New Jersey execution statutes contain a special rule which prohibits females from being arrested or imprisoned in any civil action. N.J.Stat.Ann. 2A:15–40. In South Carolina, females may not be arrested in civil actions except for willful injury. Are these provisions constitutional? If not, what should be done about it?

2. CONTEMPT

The second process commonly used to imprison debtors is the judicial contempt power. The creditors most likely to use this tech-nique are probably ex-spouses to whom alimony or support payments have not been made. These procedures are usually held not to consti-tute unlawful imprisonment for debt on the dubious ground that the debtor goes to jail not for failing to pay, but for failing to obey a court order. See McCrary v. McCrary, 723 P.2d 268 (Okl.1986). Similar contempt procedures are sometimes used in ordinary civil cases. The court may order the defendant to make installment payments on a debt, for example, and then hold him in contempt if he misses pay-ments. See Wells v. State, 474 A.2d 846 (Me.1984) (commitment order set aside because certain procedures were not followed).

In ordinary consumer debt cases, the most common use of the contempt power to put debtors in jail is through post-judgment discov-ery procedures under which debtors may be hauled into court to answer questions about their assets. Procedures for examining judgment debt-ors are commonly known as "supplementary proceedings." They are available in almost all states. In some states, the creditor must first attempt to recover the debtor's property through the use of ordinary execution procedures; in others, the creditor may go directly after the debtor. For a typical case, see Early Used Cars, Inc. v. Province, 218 Va. 605, 239 S.E.2d 98 (1977).

Supplementary discovery proceedings are effective because they rely on the threat of contempt. In the hands of aggressive creditors, they can become a formidable tool. For example, at one time, 400 debtors a year were jailed in Maine through the use of supplementary proceedings.

The New York procedure is typical of that used in other states. The following article, based on an empirical study, describes how it works.

ALDERMAN, "IMPRISONMENT FOR DEBT: DEFAULT JUDGMENTS, THE CONTEMPT POWER & THE EFFECTIVENESS OF THE NOTICE PROVISIONS IN THE STATE OF NEW YORK"

24 Syracuse L.Rev. 1217, 1222–25, 1229 (1973).*

A. The Statutory Scheme

A money judgment is a special kind of debt which affords the judgment creditor remedies not available to other creditors. However, even money judgments do not collect themselves. In order to enforce his judgment the creditor either must locate and attach the debtor's assets, or, assuming no attachable assets, compel payment from the debtor himself.

In order to assist the judgment creditor in his search for assets, New York allows the judgment creditor to compel the judgment debtor to disclose the nature, value and location of all his assets. Section 5223 * * * provides that the disclosure shall be effectuated "by serving upon any person a subpoena. * * * [F]ailure to comply with the subpoena is punishable as a contempt of court."

Although three types of subpoenas are statutorily authorized, the most commonly used forms are (1) the subpoena requiring attendance of the debtor for the taking of a deposition, and (2) the information subpoena, which is accompanied by written questions to be answered and returned by the debtor. Upon service of either of these subpoenas the judgment debtor must, under penalty of contempt, comply with its directions. Assuming proper service by the judgment creditor and compliance by the judgment debtor, assets will be disclosed and the judgment satisfied. Alternatively, a disclosure of no attachable assets will temporarily appease the judgment creditor or force him to look elsewhere to satisfy the judgment. In the event that the judgment debtor fails to comply with the judgment creditor's subpoena, however, the CPLR provides that the debtor may be found in contempt and punished accordingly. * * * While the court has the power to punish the judgment debtor summarily, the practice generally followed in the case of nondisclosure is the issuance of a show cause order and a subsequent hearing to determine the guilt or innocence of the alleged contemnor.

In the event that the judgment debtor fails to appear at the show cause hearing he will be adjudged in contempt in absentia, the burden of proof having shifted to the debtor to show cause why he should not be held in contempt. After return of the show cause order and a determination that the judgment debtor is in contempt, the debtor may be fined an amount sufficient to indemnify the aggrieved creditor, or to pay him an amount not exceeding costs plus $250. Immediately thereafter a commitment order will issue, directing that the judgment debtor stand committed to the local jail until such time as the fine is paid. The judgment debtor may then remain incarcerated, without the assignment of counsel or judicial review, for up to 90 days. The fine, when paid, is remitted directly by the court to the judgment creditor and is applied to the debt.

B. THE PROBLEM REDEFINED: THE HYPOTHESIS

* * * Most of the judgments won by creditors in the course of this study were rendered by default and were for relatively small amounts, reinforcing the hypothesis that many of the debtors involved in this process were of low income. Further investigation disclosed that not infrequently allegedly contumacious debtors expressed no knowledge of the contempt hearing and claimed total innocence to the charges. This finding prompted a question which became the focus of further inquiry: was the present statutory scheme sufficient to ensure that only the truly recalcitrant judgment debtors were punished, or were contempt proceedings being used by creditors as an alternative method of collection against low income judgment debtors generally, without regard to their contamacious attitude or lack of it? Based upon these initial findings and field observations by individual researchers, two hypotheses were framed for testing in the major study. These were:

(1) The show cause hearing prior to a determination of contempt fails to afford the debtor meaningful notice and opportunity to be heard; and

(2) the subsequent incarceration of the judgment debtor therefore violates his constitutional rights.

E. DATA

For the two month period under consideration a total of 467 cases appeared on the calendar of Onondaga County Court, Motion Term, all but 12 of which were concerned with contempt proceedings and the enforcement of money judgments. A profile of the study population reveals that 296 of the cases (63.4 percent) were instituted to enforce, through the contempt power, debtor compliance with information subpoenas. In 93 of these disclosure cases, the judgment debtor was being fined for a repetitive failure to comply with the judgment creditor's requests for disclosure. Forty-seven cases (10.6 percent of the total) were instituted either to obtain or to enforce an installment payment order. In only 32 cases (6.9 percent) did the judgment debtor appear at the show cause hearing. In all cases in which the judgment debtor appeared the court granted either an adjournment or discontinuance.

Note

In Desmond v. Hachey, 315 F.Supp. 328 (D.Me.1970), the court held that the procedure then used in Maine, which permitted the summary arrest and incarceration of a debtor who failed to appear at a hearing to inquire into his assets, was a violation of due process. Would this decision be useful precedent in challenging the validity of the New York statute? Would the answer depend on how the New York statutory scheme is used in fact? (On this point, see the rest of the Alderman article). For the reaction of a federal bankruptcy court as to whether a New York court's use of the described contempt procedures was "to uphold its dignity or * * * was a circumvented method of collecting a judgment," see Guariglia v. Community Nat. Bank & Trust Co., 382 F.Supp. 758 (E.D.N.Y.1974).

The New York statute discussed by Alderman was the subject of another judicial challenge which escalated into a landmark Supreme Court decision on the "abstention" doctrine. Meanwhile the New York contempt procedures continue as they were. Juidice v. Vail, 430 U.S. 327, 97 S.Ct. 1211, 51 L.Ed.2d 376 (1977).

3. CRIMINAL LAWS

The criminal laws are the third technique through which debtors may be put in jail. In all states, non-payment of at least some types of debts has been criminalized. The effect of these laws is to create special classes of creditors which are able to use the state as unpaid collection agents.

The most common example of criminalizing civil debt is the use of bad-check laws. The following case is a good example for study.

STATE EX REL. RICHARDSON v. EDGEWORTH
Supreme Court of Mississippi, 1968.
214 So.2d 579.

Ethridge, Chief Justice.

This suit was brought in the Circuit Court for the First Judicial District of Hinds County by Evelyn Taylor Richardson, administratrix of the estate of Billy Joe Richardson, deceased (appellant), against two justices of the peace of Hinds County, Homer Edgeworth and James L. Barlow, their deputy sheriffs and surety companies (appellees), for the wrongful death of Richardson by suicide, allegedly caused by the intentional abuse of legal process by the defendants. At the close of plaintiffs' case, the circuit court gave a directed verdict for defendants. We reverse and remand the case to the circuit court for a full trial on the merits, and hold that the testimony for plaintiffs, if accepted by the jury, shows that: (1) Defendants intentionally abused the criminal processes of the justice of the peace courts for the purpose of inflicting upon Richardson sufficient emotional distress to cause him to pay a civil debt and the court costs collected by defendants. (2) These intentional torts were substantial factors producing the single result of Richardson committing suicide while under an irresistible impulse, and each are jointly and severally liable.

* * *

On July 6, 1966, at 11 p.m., Deputy Sheriff Albert Sullivan, who was attached to the office of Justice of the Peace James L. Barlow, went to the Richardson home and informed him that he had three criminal warrants for his arrest. The first, issued by Barlow, stemmed from a criminal affidavit signed in blank by Mrs. Flowers, for Flowers Minnow Farm, for collection of a $10 check drawn by Richardson. Mrs. Flowers had called Barlow's office, informing him that she had a check for collection. A constable picked it up and had her sign the blank criminal affidavit, without appearing before Barlow. The second warrant resulted from a criminal affidavit signed on behalf of a cleaning establishment by Mrs. Lelia Smith, for the collection of a $3.00 check drawn by Richardson. She also did not sign the affidavit before Barlow. The third warrant was based upon an affidavit signed for a store by H.L. Duke for collection of a $1.00 check drawn by Richardson. Once again, the criminal affidavit was signed in blank and without Barlow's presence. See Miss.Code 1942 Annot. § 2153 (Supp.1966) (false pretense, "bad check" law).

Sullivan served the three criminal warrants on Richardson, and, since neither Billy Joe nor his wife had the money necessary to pay the checks, costs and fines, Sullivan took them in his car to the office of Barlow, where Billy Joe was allowed to call an officer of his employer, Mississippi Bearings, Inc., who subsequently loaned him the money to pay the demands made by Sullivan. Sullivan drove the Richardsons from Barlow's office to the office of the employer, where the loan was made and the money was paid. Barlow issued a receipt showing that he had received $107 from Mississippi Bearings, Inc. The receipt listed three numbers corresponding with the criminal docket and page number of each of the above items. These pages on Barlow's justice court docket revealed that for each warrant Richardson had been required to pay a fine of $25.00, an officer's fee of $4.00, and mileage for conveying a person to jail of $2.00, plus the amount of each check involved. From the $107.00 collected from Richardson, Barlow paid Mrs. Flowers $10.00, the store $1.00, and the cleaners $3.00, the amounts of the respective checks. Sullivan received three mileage payments of $2.00 each, even though he had served all three warrants on one trip and had not taken Richardson to jail. Sullivan made no return on two of these bench warrants.

A few days later, written notice was received by the Richardsons at their home advising them to come to Barlow's office. On July 11, 1967, they went to his office and were told to pay two checks. Richardson remained at Barlow's office while Mrs. Richardson sought to borrow the money from a physician under whom she worked at the hospital. Had she failed, her husband would have been taken to jail. * * *

* * * On July 26, 1966, the Richardsons appeared at Barlow's office and were informed that he had four checks for collection. Richardson was given the alternative of paying them or going to jail. The first of these four checks was picked up from J.E. Farmer at his barber

shop by George Warren, another deputy sheriff working out of Barlow's office. This check, made by Richardson for $2.25, was taken to Barlow's office, where, without authority from Farmer, Sullivan signed a criminal affidavit for its collection. Richardson was required to pay a $25.00 fine, $4.00 officer's fee, $2.00 mileage, and the amount of the check, $2.25.

* * * The third check was given to Wayne Spradling's Service Station by Richardson in the amount of $5.00. A warrant was issued by Barlow on a criminal affidavit which had not been signed by Spradling. It was in blank, but Barlow notarized it anyway. The check had been turned over to Barlow's other deputy, George Warren, and Spradling did not appear before Barlow to sign it. As on other occasions, Richardson was required to pay a $25.00 fine, $4.00 officer's fee, $2.00 mileage, plus the amount of the check, in this instance $5.00. No return was made on the special bench warrant issued for the arrest of Richardson. * * *

* * *

In the meantime, economic pressures on the Richardson family became very intense. As a result of the July 6 incident, when Billy Joe had to borrow money from his employer, the employer fired him. Billy Joe got a job as a commission salesman, but was earning practically nothing. * * * According to the calculations of Mrs. Richardson and her husband, they had not overdrawn his checking account. Four night deposits which they had made had not been credited to his account. All of these factors placed them in such a dire financial condition that they had had difficulty buying food.

On July 28, 1966, around 1:30 a.m., Deputy Sheriffs John Grant and Harvey Ray awakened Mr. and Mrs. Richardson. Grant informed them that he was a deputy sheriff, working out of Justice of the Peace Edgeworth's office, and that he had two warrants for the arrest of Billy Joe. The first was issued from a criminal affidavit signed by Mrs. Mitchell on behalf of a grocery store. It was presented to her at the store, where she signed it in blank, not before Edgeworth, and gave it to Deputy Grant along with Richardson's check. On several prior occasions she had signed blank affidavits for the collection of checks by Edgeworth, and in this particular instance, her intention was the same. Mrs. Mitchell testified that Justice of the Peace Edgeworth had called her by telephone before the trial and told her that, if she did not testify that she had signed the affidavits in his office, he would make a liar out of her. Nevertheless, she said that she did not sign the affidavit before him.

* * *

In the dark of this early morning hour, when Grant told the Richardsons that he had two warrants for Billy Joe's arrest, Mrs. Richardson, who was pregnant, fainted. Grant told him that $70 would be required to pay the two checks. This demand was made on the following basis:

Total of two checks	$10.00
Two fines of $25.00 each	50.00
Two court costs of $4.00 each	8.00
Mileage charge	2.00
Total	$70.00

Billy Joe asked Grant if he could try to borrow the money and Grant permitted him to do so. [He tried, but was unable to borrow the $70.] Billy Joe then asked Grant if he could go in his house to get some socks. With permission, Richardson went in the house, and after a short interval of time there was a gunshot. Mrs. Richardson and Grant ran inside and found Billy Joe lying on his back across the bed, without shoes and with his feet on the floor. There was a large wound in the pit of his stomach, and a shotgun was lying on the floor beside the bed. He died within a few minutes. * * *

Dr. Oscar E. Hubbard, a professor of psychiatry at the University of Mississippi Medical School who had many years of experience in the practice of psychiatry, testified for the plaintiffs. A detailed hypothetical question was propounded to him. He stated that it was his opinion, with reasonable medical certainty, that the criminal charges brought by Barlow and Edgeworth and the arrests by Sullivan and Grant proximately caused or contributed to Richardson's suicide. Dr. Hubbard further stated that Richardson had a psychoneurotic disorder which consisted of a phobic concern about being sent back to jail. Upon Grant's demand Billy Joe was caught between being jailed once more, or borrowing the necessary money. After his frantic but fruitless search for money, he found himself getting closer and closer to being locked up, with all of his avenues of escape closed. Thus, Dr. Hubbard said, Richardson was seized by an irresistible or uncontrollable fear, and without being able to reason with himself as to the consequences, he killed himself. His fear of prison under these pressing emotional circumstances manifested itself as an uncontrollable impulse. Dr. Hubbard thought that it was under this mounting pressure from his unreasoning fear of having to return to jail, that Richardson panicked and impulsively killed himself. In short, he had an uncontrollable impulse to commit suicide which must have arisen at the approximate time Richardson returned to his room and committed the act. Dr. Hubbard thought that the actions of Barlow and Edgeworth and the deputies contributed to and were causes of the uncontrollable impulse and resulting suicide.

At the close of plaintiffs' case the circuit judge sustained the motion of defendants for a directed verdict. However, he concluded that the two justices of the peace had permitted and perhaps encouraged the use of criminal processes of the courts solely for the collection of civil debts. There were many irregularities practiced by defendants, including: (1) Permitting people to sign criminal affidavits without advising them of the criminal nature of the documents; (2) failing to require affiants to appear before the justice of the peace for sworn statements; (3) permitting criminal affidavits to be signed in blank; (4) charging excessive mileage; (5) soliciting collection of accounts, through their deputy sheriffs and constables; and (6) using the criminal process for the collection of civil debts alone.

* * *

The two justices of the peace and their deputies committed intentional torts—the abuse of process. Its elements are that the defendants made an illegal, improper, perverted use of the process, they had an ulterior motive or purpose in doing so, and damages resulted to plaintiffs from the irregularities. Plaintiffs' evidence would support a jury finding that Richardson committed suicide while acting under an irresistible impulse in a moment of temporary mental derangement substantially caused by these acts. Where a defendant has committed an intentional tort, questions of whether the deceased was induced to take his life by an irresistible impulse and whether the intentional tort was a substantial factor in causing the suicide are ordinarily issues for the jury. Since plaintiffs' evidence supports those factors, we do not reach the additional issues considered in Tate v. Canonica, which allowed recovery for suicide caused by an intentional tort if the mental stress which the defendant inflicted was a substantial cause of the suicide, even if the decedent was aware of his act and was not responding to an irresistible impulse.

In short, the defendants' intentional conduct is a legal cause of harm to plaintiffs if their individual acts were substantial factors in bringing about the harm. Restatement, Torts §§ 279, 280 (1938); Restatement, Second, Torts, § 455 (1965). * * *

* * *

* * * In the instant case, the consecutive wrongs of Barlow and Sullivan, and then Edgeworth and Grant, were not negligent but intentional torts. The jury would be justified in finding that both of them contributed to the delirium or insanity which made it impossible for Richardson to resist an impulse caused by that condition depriving him of his capacity to govern his conduct in accordance with reason. * * *

A justice of the peace is a judicial officer. A justice of the peace court is a judicial body. This officer and this court have no constitutional right or power to serve as a collection agency for creditors. A creditor may properly file his claim for a civil debt against the debtor in a justice of the peace court. But the justice of the peace serves only as a judicial officer to determine the validity of the claim. He is not a collection bureau. If he acts as a collection bureau, or if he utilizes the criminal processes of the court to collect a civil debt, he is perverting the functions of this small claims court and bringing disrespect upon the entire judicial process.

The judgment of the circuit court is reversed, and the case is remanded for a new trial.

Query: Is the holding in this case with respect to the Justices of the Peace affected by the Supreme Court's decision in Stump v. Sparkman, 435 U.S. 349, 98 S.Ct. 1099, 55 L.Ed.2d 331 (1978), where judicial immunity was accorded a judge who, *ex parte,* ordered the sterilization of a 15–year-old girl?

Problem 6

You have become counsel to the Sheriff's Department. In this locale creditors have, in the past, filed criminal affidavits whenever their customers' checks have "bounced". How would you advise the Department to handle such matters in the future? Upon whose orders should deputies act? Should they refuse to accept full payments, or "restitution", offered by the consumers? If no "restitution" is offered, what should their action be after serving the warrant?

Notes

1. It is easy to imagine that such practices are limited to a single state, but the cumulation of the effects of all the different devices raised in Section C should evidence that seizure of the debtor through some device is widespread. For one more variation on a theme, see "Old Company Store Is Gone, but Georgia Has Pseudo–Check," Wall Street Journal, Dec. 6, 1977, p. 1. It details a system in which consumers are allowed to sign checks for goods or services although they have no bank account. The businessman keeps the check, and tears it up when the consumer pays cash, or swears out a warrant charging the consumer with writing a fraudulent check if the consumer doesn't, or can't, pay.

In one instance, Mabel Edith purchased $36.59 of groceries from Juanita Culpepper, and "paid" for them by writing a check, although she didn't have a bank account, and used a counter check form. When she didn't pay, she was arrested by a "gun on hip" deputy sheriff. She entered a plea of guilty (as nearly all other users of the pseudo-check system do) and was fined $60 plus the $36.59. If she had not arranged bail, she would also have been charged a $2 "turnkey" fee and $3 a day for meals. She also received a one-year suspended sentence to assure that she paid the fine. In another, Betty Jean Roberts wrote a $12 check to Dr. Guy Mann, but wrote on the bottom: "Will pick up check Sunday." Even though it was obviously not intended to be cashed, it was, and she is now paying a $65 fine in addition to the $12. "It is difficult to tell how widespread the system is, but lawyers here say it is fairly common in rural areas," reports the Journal.

2. These misdirected criminal cases can be dismissed if the defendant has a lawyer, but the consumers involved in them are often poor and have no attorney. Anyway, a lawyer would charge $150, and does not give credit.

Thus, the question remains, how to stop the system of arrests and prosecutions. There are several public agencies or offices involved in the system. The merchant will avoid using small claims court if it can be done by swearing out a warrant. The justice of the peace who issues the warrant is supposed to determine "probable cause" before doing so. The sheriff will often also be contacted directly by the merchant who shows him a check stamped "no account". The district attorney is responsible to prevent use of criminal courts to collect debts. And the trial judge often finds that the defendants involved plead guilty.

In *Richardson,* the device used to try to halt the system was an action for "abuse of process." Would the facts in the Georgia situation meet the requirements for such an action? See Restatement, Torts (Second) § 455 (1965). Are there other devices available to use against this system?

3. When a merchant takes a check knowing that there is no bank account, is fraud involved? Reread the deceit materials in Chapter 1. How can the sheriff or justice of the peace tell whether the problem involves fraud, for which a criminal sanction is appropriate, or merely a credit transaction, for which the appropriate remedy is a civil action?

4. Bad check laws are not the only use of the criminal law to collect civil debts. For example, in many states it is a crime for debtors to sell property which is subject to a security interest without the creditor's permission. See, e.g., Kan.Stat.Ann. § 21–3734. A few states now have statutes which make it a crime to fail to return rental property within a given period, such as 72 hours, after demand. Laws of this type usually, but not always, survive constitutional challenge. In State v. Madewell, 63 N.J. 506, 309 A.2d 201 (1973), a rental property return law was held to violate the prohibition against imprisonment for debt. The court said it was nothing more than a civil debt collection device in the guise of a criminal law. Could bad check laws be challenged on the same ground?

5. In many states, failure to pay a tax is a crime. Would this law violate a prohibition against imprisonment for debt? Is a tax a civil debt? Are the policies different when the state is the creditor? See State v. Higgins, 254 Ga. 88, 326 S.E.2d 728 (1985).

6. Are you surprised to learn that imprisonment is still available as a collection device for many types of civil debts? Do you think it should be? Why or why not?

Query: What do creditors gain by instigating procedures that may result in the incarceration of the consumer debtor? If the consumer can't pay his bills on time anyhow, it would seem the chances of paying those bills from jail are nil.

SECTION D. THE FEES OF THE CREDITOR'S ATTORNEY

MARINE MIDLAND BANK v. ROBERTS

Civil Court of the City of New York, Kings County, 1980.
102 Misc.2d 903, 424 N.Y.S.2d 671.

ANNE G. FELDMAN, JUDGE.

Plaintiff brings the underlying actions to enforce attorneys' fees provisions in three contracts: two retail installment contracts for the purchase of automobiles and one retail installment credit card agreement.

The facts in each case are identical. The debtor/defendant defaulted on his payments and, in accordance with the acceleration clause in each contract, the entire balance became immediately due. When these amounts remained unpaid, plaintiff's attorney served summonses and complaints on the debtors and obtained default judgments against them. The Clerk of this Court has already entered judgments on the liquidated amounts due under the contracts, but plaintiff's attorney has not yet acted to enforce these judgments.

Nonetheless, plaintiff seeks now to recover attorneys' fees under the provision in each contract which requires the debtor to pay legal fees, calculated as a percentage of the amount due upon default, on matters referred to attorneys for collection.

Courts have long recognized as lawful a contractual provision for attorneys' fees calculated as a specific percentage of the unpaid debt.

Section 302(7) of the Personal Property Law, which governs the retail installment contract for the purchase of an automobile, permits a contract to provide for the payment of attorneys' fees "not exceeding fifteen percent of the amount due and payable under such contract."

Similarly, section 413(5) of the Personal Property Law, which governs the retail installment credit card agreement, permits the contract to provide for the imposition of attorneys' fees, not exceeding twenty percent of the amount due and payable under the contract.

These statutory percentages are not fixed fees, however, since the public policy of our state "condemns the contractual imposition of a penalty." (*First National Bank of East Islip v. Brower*, 42 N.Y.2d 471, 398 N.Y.S.2d 875, 368 N.E.2d 1240 (1977)). The Personal Property Law merely sets maximum limits on the attorneys' fees which may be imposed, based upon the reasonable value of the necessary services "actually rendered". The party seeking attorneys' fees must demonstrate to the Court the quality and quantity of the services rendered so that the Court, consistent with its traditional and inherent power to regulate the practice of law, including the collection of attorneys' fees, may determine on a *quantum meruit* basis the reasonable fees to be awarded.

The relevant factors in determining the value of legal services are the nature and extent of the services, the actual time spent, the necessity therefore, the nature of the issues involved, the professional standing of the counsel and the results achieved.

The testimony at the inquest revealed that the legal services provided thus far have been minimal and have been identical in each case regardless of the amount of attorneys' fees sought. This Court, however, recognizes that in actions of this type, particularly where default judgments are obtained, the bulk of necessary legal services are expended in collecting the judgment. That process may be, as in most cases, "routine and perfunctory," or may involve substantial time and skill.

Counsel for plaintiff admits the impossibility at this juncture of fixing precisely the time or services which will be required to enforce the judgments. He urges, therefore, that the Court, in determining the attorneys' fees on a *quantum meruit* basis, accept his estimate of the services he expects will be reasonably necessary to satisfy the judgment as evidence in the determination of attorneys' fees.

This Court rejects plaintiff's contention as inconsistent with the doctrine of *quantum meruit* and will permit an award only for work already actually performed.

* * *

The Court, therefore, awards plaintiff $100.00 in each case as fair and just compensation for the services rendered in obtaining the default judgments. This award is made without prejudice to subsequent actions to recover reasonable compensation for legal services actually performed by counsel in enforcing the judgments.

Notes

1. Should the creditor's right to collect attorney's fees from the consumer debtor depend on whether a licensed attorney is actually employed to collect the debt? Suppose the collection work is done by in-house personnel, including law clerks and paralegals? See U3C § 2.507. Why do you suppose the U3C drafters were so indecisive?

2. Isn't turnabout fair play? Should victorious consumer litigants be entitled to *their* attorney's fees from creditors who violate the law? More on this in Part IV, but see U3C § 5.201(8); TILA § 130(a)(3).

Problem 7

Harry is a judge who also teaches a course in "real courtroom evidence." In other words, he is a busy man. Harry bought a refrigerator from Sam Silver on credit for $800. He signed a printed form credit contract which granted Sam a security interest to cover the refrigerator. In the credit contract, Harry also promised to pay "any costs of collecting the debt, including attorneys' fees of 15% of the outstanding balance upon referral to an attorney who is not a salaried employee of the creditor."

Harry was so busy that he forgot to make payments. So, one day he received a call from an employee of Caroline, a local collection attorney. She reminded him of his failure to pay, and demanded immediate payment in full. Harry, chagrined at his default, said he would pay in full and would immediately mail a check for $800. Caroline's employee said that that would not be satisfactory, for now he owed $920—an $800 outstanding balance and $120 attorney's fees. Harry now consults you. What, if anything, can you do to help him? Cf., Consumers Time Credit, Inc. v. Remark Corp., 259 F.Supp. 135 (E.D. Pa.1966).

NCCF Report

25–26 (1972)

Attorney's Fees

In many states, creditors are able to include in consumer credit notes and contracts a clause providing for payment by the debtor of attorneys' fees if the debtor defaults on the contract. This is usually expressed as a percentage of the amount in default irrespective of the actual amount of attorneys' fees incurred by the creditor. Other states, however, prohibit such contractual provisions. The prohibition is most common in small loan laws. Section 2.413 of the [1968] Uniform Consumer Credit Code (UCCC) provides alternatives,—one authorizing, one prohibiting attorneys' fees.

Consumer credit contracts or agreements should be able to provide for payment of reasonable attorneys' fees by the debtor in the event of default if such fees result from referral to an attorney who is not a salaried employee of the creditor; in no event should such fees exceed 15 percent of the outstanding balance. However, the agreement should further stipulate that in the event suit is initiated by the creditor and the court finds in favor of the consumer, the creditor should be liable for payment of the debtor's attorney's fees as determined by the court, measured by the amount of time reasonably expended by the consumer's attorney and not by the amount of the recovery.

The Survey showed that many creditors believed attorneys' fees were useful to collection activities and that they often relied on that provision. *But, in view of the Survey finding that major reasons for default stem from situations beyond the debtor's control, the Commission finds it in the best interest of all to limit recovery to 15 percent of the outstanding balance owed at default.*

The Commission recommends allowing attorneys' fees provisions in consumer credit notes and contracts because such fees should be borne directly, but to a reasonable extent, by the debtor. Costs of collecting from defaulting debtors should not be borne indirectly by all the creditor's customers in higher rates of charge to cover higher overhead. (Emphasis added.)

Query: Some creditors object to any limitations on their attorneys' fees on the ground that *someone* has to pay them, and that it is better to have them borne by those individuals who default than by the general population of borrowers. Consumers respond that if creditor attorneys are not subsidized by consumers, those attorneys will perform their tasks more efficiently. Did the Commission's Report seriously consider either argument? What, if anything, does the emphasized language in the third paragraph mean?

SECTION E. AN EVALUATION OF THE EFFECTS OF COERCIVE COURT ACTIONS

In this and the previous two chapters, we have studied several alternative methods a creditor may use to try to force consumer debtors to part with their money. Why does a creditor choose one method instead of another in a particular case? Does the legal system, either wittingly or unwittingly, tend to steer creditor collection activity into one or another direction? If so, is it the right direction? Where and how should the debt collection system be improved? Evaluate the following proposals.

WHITFORD, A CRITIQUE OF THE CONSUMER CREDIT COLLECTION SYSTEM

1979 Wis.L.Rev. 1047, 1116–36.*

IV. REFORMING THE SYSTEM

* * *

A. *Encouraging More Informal Bargaining and Settlement*

The fundamental issue regarding moderate reform of the consumer credit collection system is whether the incidence of coercive execution should be increased or decreased. It is not clear which approach would best reduce creditors' collection costs. Because creditors sometimes initiate execution when it would be more cost effective to pursue further informal settlement opportunities, discouraging coercive execution might actually reduce creditor collection costs. But even if creditor collection costs should increase, discouraging coercive execution may be desirable from a wealth maximization perspective. Such discouragement should reduce many of the costs of execution, especially secondary costs, which are not borne by creditors. On the other hand, discouraging coercive execution will induce increased creditor efforts at informal settlement. These increased efforts raise new costs to consider, such as invasion of privacy and emotional injury from harassment.

Balancing all these factors, my guess is that society as a whole would be better off with less coercive execution. I recognize that decreasing the incidence of coercive execution will lead to increased reliance on informal collection practices. But many of the harms resulting from such practices, particularly emotional injury, are at least equally, if not more serious consequences of coercive execution.

* * *

The next subsections discuss different ways of discouraging coercive execution, particularly execution for the primary purpose of gaining bargaining leverage. No effort will be made to canvas all possible techniques; nor is it my position that there is a single best technique.

Rather, I see a reform program as including a number of complementary techniques.

1.   REQUIRING MEDIATION

Professor Leff has suggested that the incidence of coercive execution would be decreased by the establishment of a state subsidized mediation service specializing in creditor-debtor problems. His proposal was derived from his perception that one reason for excessive execution is that creditors and debtors often misperceive the likely outcome of coercive execution. The principal purpose of a mediation service would be to cure this information problem by providing debtors and creditors with disinterested estimates of the likely outcome.

* * *

2.   CHANGING THE PRIORITY RULES

The rules governing priorities between unsecured creditors encourage coercive execution. The obvious solution is to change the priority rules so the first creditor to initiate coercive execution does not by that action necessarily obtain an advantage over other creditors. Two such proposals have previously been made. In the 1930s, Dean Wesley Sturges suggested a system that would determine priority among unsecured creditors by date of credit extension. A more recent proposal borrowed on the innovation of Article 9 of the Uniform Commercial Code in suggesting creation of a filing system for unsecured creditors, with priority determined by date of filing.

Both proposals were motivated largely by a desire to discourage overextension of credit to consumers rather than to affect collection practices.

* * *

3.   CREATING COST BARRIERS TO EXECUTION

A classic American way to discourage undesired conduct is to tax it. Of course, any tax on coercive execution, even though payable initially by creditors, will be passed on to debtors, most likely in the form of higher interest rates or reduced credit availability. Nonetheless, a lowering of the incidence of coercive execution should result, provided the tax is initially paid by creditors. A creditor able to resolve a higher percentage of collection problems informally would then have lower costs than competitors because of lower execution taxes and consequently would have a competitive advantage.

Politically, it seems unlikely that a tax on coercive execution will ever be adopted. A similar effect could be obtained, however, simply by limiting the proportion of present costs of coercive execution that creditors can transfer to debtors. To some extent this is already happening as states increasingly invalidate contract provisions requiring debtor reimbursement of creditor attorney fees incurred in collection.

* * *

B. Reducing the Costs of Execution

*   *   *

Though perhaps unintentionally, a state's laws governing coercive execution will tend to channel coercive execution into one or very few forms of execution, by making some forms more efficient than others to creditors. This point is illustrated by Professor Caplovitz in his famous study of judgment debtors. He reported that in New York, where wage garnishment was a cheap and simple form of execution, repossessions under security interests occurred less frequently than in Detroit, where wage garnishment was more cumbersome. Though such correlations cannot in themselves prove a causal relationship, a presumption of cause and effect is inituitively sensible and consistent with the data.

*   *   *

1. THE UNEASY CASE FOR INCOME EXECUTION

The two usual forms of execution are wage garnishment and property execution, including repossession. As between the two, strong arguments exist in favor of channeling execution towards wage garnishment. The strongest argument derives from the "lost value" phenomenon that characterizes all property execution. Some of this lost value could be avoided by improvements in the procedures for property execution, but much of the lost value is simply inevitable. Typically, the goods seized through property execution have a significantly higher value in a debtor's hands than they have in the market. Under income execution, on the other hand, the ratio between value lost to the debtor and the amount of debt paid is potentially close to one. Income execution also provides a certain element of justice, or at least realized expectations; even in secured credit situations, creditors and debtors alike expect repayment from future income.

The potential efficiency of wage garnishment is often not realized today, partly because of unnecessarily high court costs. More troublesome are the substantial secondary costs historically associated with wage garnishment, typically because of adverse reaction by the debtor's employer. The seeming intractability of these costs has caused a number of commentators to recommend abolition of wage garnishment.

The secondary costs resulting from garnishment are of a different order than the secondary costs resulting from property execution. Much of the lost value resulting from property execution is a true loss, since the goods are taken from the person who can put them to their highest use. But if a garnishment victim loses his or her job, presumably that job will be filled by somebody else. Strictly from a wealth maximization point of view, it will often be a matter of indifference to society who holds the job. If the productivity of the garnishment victim significantly exceeds that of the replacement, it is unlikely the employer would have dismissed the former in any event. And whatever happens, one worker remains unemployed.

There is still reason, however, to be concerned about secondary costs to the garnishment victim. First, if such costs are substantial and are likely to be incurred, the threat of wage garnishment becomes an extremely effective *in terrorem* leverage device—one quite capable, for example, of persuading debtors to abandon defenses. Unless such effects of wage garnishment can be avoided, perhaps garnishment should be abolished as a form of coercive execution no matter how efficient it is in converting a debtor's assets into debt retirement.

* * *

Earlier, I described the limited effectiveness of existing statutes designed to control secondary costs by prohibiting employers from dismissing debtors because of garnishment. The fundamental fault is that the legislation does nothing to ameliorate those factors that traditionally have made it in an employer's interest to dismiss or take other adverse action against a garnished employee. The cost of garnishment to the employer has been primary among these factors. Consequently, it would almost certainly be more effective in limiting secondary costs simply to pay an employer a sufficient fee to cover its costs in complying with a garnishment order.

* * *

A solution to this conundrum would be to reduce the costs of employer compliance with a garnishment order. In most jurisdictions today a creditor must initiate a separate garnishment proceeding each pay period, and the employer often learns of the garnishment only shortly before payday. As a result, the employer must make separate calculations of the amount subject to garnishment for each pay period, often on very short notice, at considerable bookkeeping expense. One measure to reduce these costs would be to require that an employer receive notice of garnishment at a certain interval before payday. For example, garnishment orders might be effective only as to paychecks issued seven days after service on an employer, in order to avoid bookkeeping expenses attributable to the need to make sudden adjustments. Another cost-saving measure, already adopted in some jurisdictions, is a "continuous garnishment" system. Under a continuous garnishment system, an order requires an employer to deduct an appropriate amount each pay period until the entire debt is retired. Such "continuous garnishment" enables the employer to make only a single set of calculations, treating garnishment like any other payroll deduction. Moreover, a creditor seeking to collect an entire debt through garnishment need bring only one garnishment action, saving court costs.

* * *

In summary, the case for wage garnishment as the least undesirable form of coercive execution is uneasy. Because of the lost value principle, garnishment does offer the promise of avoiding the waste of debtor assets that characterizes most property execution. Yet substantial secondary costs may outweigh that apparent advantage. My tentative conclusion is that wage garnishment should be the favored form of coercive execution, providing it proves possible to limit the effects of garnishment on job security.

* * *

2.   THE PROBLEM OF SECURITY INTERESTS

A creditor can have several motives for demanding collateral for a credit extension. In insolvency, a properly perfected security interest provides the secured creditor with priority rights in the collateral over other creditors. Security interests also help creditors avoid exemption laws, since collateral can be repossessed even where otherwise exempt from execution. Finally, security interests commonly provide the creditor with a cheaper form of coercive execution than would otherwise be available. Moreover, because repossession is generally cheap and easy, threats to repossess are inherently credible; the presence of security interests can therefore enhance a creditor's informal bargaining power.

I have argued that, in general, income execution should be preferred over property execution. This argument applies to secured as well as unsecured credit. Lost value can result from repossession of collateral as much as from the kinds of property execution available to unsecured creditors. This reasoning suggests that repossession under security interests should be limited to situations in which a creditor can show a special need, such as situations where income execution cannot provide adequate relief. Such restrictions on repossession would not interfere with a secured creditor's desire to obtain priority over other creditors where such priority is needed, usually in insolvency cases. Security interests would also remain a way to avoid exemption laws. Although security interests would no longer provide a particularly advantageous form of coercive execution, the current availability and ease of repossession of collateral may encourage quick resort to coercive execution, a result I have argued is generally undesirable.

Note

For a different perspective on these issues, see Scott, Rethinking the Regulation of Coercive Creditor Remedies, 89 Colum.L.Rev. 730 (1989).

Problem 8

You are counsel for a legislative committee in your state. The committee is considering legislation on various consumer matters, including the collection system. You have been asked to recommend changes in the present system which would fulfill the twin goals of increased consumer protection and reduced collection costs. Are these goals compatible? What will you recommend? Be as specific as possible.

For example, in Chapter 7, Section A.2., the original Caplovitz study of debtors in default breaks down into various categories, those consumers who are subject to coercive collection techniques, both judicial and "self-help". The categories were products of debtor self-identification and included those with interruption of income, voluntary overextension, unexpected bills due to illness, marital breakup, creditor fraud and defective merchandise. That set of categories may not be complete, however, for there may also be new categories as suggested by Caplovitz's 1989 paper, and there may also be a set of categories from the creditors' perspective. For each of the categories you adopt, what coercive collection techniques are likely to be effective? Cost efficient? Appropriate?

Part III

REGULATION OF PRICES
AND ALLOCATION OF
RESOURCES

While the state has not generally regulated the prices of goods and services in our legal system, regulation of the price of money has been the norm in the U.S. Further, this form of regulation has usually been expressed in statutes and in state constitutions. It has also almost always been exact in nature, defined not by flexible standards such as unconscionability, but by precise mathematical limits. State control of the price of money did not originate with our society; in fact, interest rate regulation can be traced to the earliest historical times. We will explore that history and its modern counterparts in the next chapter.

Meanwhile, a paramount question which the student should keep in mind in this part of the text is why we regulate the price of money at all. How is money different, if at all, from other commodities which are left unregulated? Is all this regulation merely a hangover from ancient law and religious taboos, or is there some folk-wisdom represented by the nearly unanimous adoption of these regulations? Another important question is what effect does rate regulation have on the availability of credit, especially to the poor.

In Part III, first in Chapter 10, we will explore the regulation of the prices of goods and services, primarily to establish a foundation indicating how little of such regulation is done by courts or legislatures. In Chapter 11, we will examine the contrasting plethora of methods used by state governments to regulate interest rates (the price of money borrowed). In this examination, distinctions must be made between lender credit (what you get from a bank or finance company) and seller credit (what you get from Sears or directly from an auto dealer). Distinctions must also be made between Nineteenth Century usury laws and Twentieth Century statutes, such as Retail Installment Sales Acts.

The states are not, however, the only jurisdiction to enact laws in this area. The federal government has also enacted statutes intended to "override" state law, and these statutes will be examined in Chapter 12.

Chapter 13 attempts a coordinated evaluation of the effects of interest rate ceiling legislation on the price of credit, the availability of credit and competition among creditors.

Finally, Chapter 14 examines the separate problem of the regulation of rates (prices) for credit insurance. This area presents unique issues for analysis because of the existence of "reverse competition" in a system which pretends to be regulated by market forces.

Chapter 10

REGULATING THE PRICES OF GOODS AND SERVICES

Prefatory Note

By and large, common law jurisdictions have not attempted to regulate prices, except in emergencies. Instead, our society has relied on economic market mechanisms, rather than on bureaucratic mechanisms, to hold down the price of goods and services. In times of emergency, price controls have been used, but with a mixed record. They are more likely to be effective in times of war than in times of peace. The latest peacetime use of price controls in the U.S., for example, in 1971–72, cannot be termed a success.

There are two exceptions to this general unwillingness of the state to attempt to control prices. The first is rate regulation of public utilities such as electricity, natural gas, water, local telephone service, and the like. Discussion of this form of price control is beyond the scope of this book.

The second exception is the doctrine of unconscionability. This doctrine originated in equity, where courts sometimes denied specific performance in cases where the price was considered to be too high. See, e.g., Ballentyne v. Smith, 205 U.S. 285, 27 S.Ct. 527, 51 L.Ed. 803 (1907); Mangold v. Bacon, 237 Mo. 496, 141 S.W. 650 (1911). Today, this doctrine survives not only as an equitable device, but also in such statutes as the Uniform Commercial Code, § 2–302, the U3C, §§ 5.108 and 6.111, and "little FTC acts," see UCSPA § 4. While price unconscionability is more likely to be argued in consumer cases, it is not limited to those cases. See, e.g., Miami Tribe v. United States, 281 F.2d 202 (Ct.Cl.1960).

The leading UCC case involving a consumer is American Home Improvement, Inc. v. MacIver, 105 N.H. 435, 201 A.2d 886 (1964). In MacIver, the seller sued for payment under a contract for installation of windows and home siding. The court found that the value of the goods and services under the contract was $959, but that the consumer would have had to pay an additional $800 commission and another

$809.60 interest and carrying charges. This, said the court, was too much; the contract was unconscionable and could not be enforced. The court did not consider whether the seller's profit was excessive, nor did it look at the practices of other home improvement merchants. In fact, volumes have been written about the court's economics, or lack thereof, but this case clearly re-established in a modern setting the idea that courts may review prices, at least in a limited set of circumstances.

Another widely-cited case, Frostifresh Corp. v. Reynoso, 52 Misc.2d 26, 274 N.Y.S.2d 757 (Dist.Ct.1966), rev'd on issue of relief, 54 Misc.2d 119, 281 N.Y.S.2d 964 (1967), involved the purchase of a freezer by a Spanish-speaking consumer. The contract was printed in English, and the seller neither translated nor explained it. The wholesale cost to the seller was $348, the retail cash price was $900, and the total credit (time) price to the consumer was $1,145.88. The court found the contract unconscionable.

While the doctrine of price unconscionability seems firmly established, there are only a small number of cases which apply it. *Jones,* below, is representative of those cases, most of which date from 1965–1975. In recent years, there have been few cases in which the argument has been raised, and even fewer in which it has been successful. Recall the discussion of the unconscionability issue in Remco, Inc. v. Houston, supra at page 159. Perhaps this reflects the general reluctance of the courts, as arms of the state, to interfere with the price-setting function of the market. For a more detailed discussion of price unconscionability, see J. White and R. Summers, Uniform Commercial Code § 4–5 (3d ed. 1988).

JONES v. STAR CREDIT CORP.

Supreme Court of New York, Nassau County, 1969.
59 Misc.2d 189, 298 N.Y.S.2d 264.

SOL M. WACHTLER, JUSTICE.

On August 31, 1965 the plaintiffs, who are welfare recipients, agreed to purchase a home freezer unit for $900 as the result of a visit from a salesman representing Your Shop At Home Service, Inc. With the addition of the time credit charges, credit life insurance, credit property insurance, and sales tax, the purchase price totalled $1,234.80. Thus far the plaintiffs have paid $619.88 toward their purchase. The defendant claims that with various added credit charges paid for an extension of time there is a balance of $819.81 still due from the plaintiffs. The uncontroverted proof at the trial established that the freezer unit, when purchased, had a maximum retail value of approximately $300. The question is whether this transaction and the resulting contract could be considered unconscionable within the meaning of Section 2–302 of the Uniform Commercial Code [The court quoted UCC § 2–302.]

* * *

Section 2–302 of the Uniform Commercial Code enacts the moral sense of the community into the law of commercial transactions. It authorizes the court to find, as a matter of law, that a contract or a clause of a contract was "unconscionable at the time it was made", and upon so finding the court may refuse to enforce the contract, excise the objectionable clause or limit the application of the clause to avoid an unconscionable result. "The principle", states the Official Comment to this section, "is one of the prevention of oppression and unfair surprise". It permits a court to accomplish directly what heretofore was often accomplished by construction of language, manipulations of fluid rules of contract law and determinations based upon a presumed public policy.

There is no reason to doubt, moreover, that this section is intended to encompass the price term of an agreement. In addition to the fact that it has already been so applied, the statutory language itself makes it clear that not only a clause of the contract, but the contract in toto, may be found unconscionable as a matter of law. Indeed, no other provision of an agreement more intimately touches upon the question of unconscionability than does the term regarding price.

Fraud, in the instant case, is not present; nor is it necessary under the statute. The question which presents itself is whether or not, under the circumstances of this case, the sale of a freezer unit having a retail value of $300 for $900 ($1,439.69 including credit charges and $18 sales tax) is unconscionable as a matter of law. The court believes it is.

Concededly, deciding the issue is substantially easier than explaining it. No doubt, the mathematical disparity between $300, which presumably includes a reasonable profit margin, and $900, which is exorbitant on its face, carries the greatest weight. Credit charges alone exceed by more than $100 the retail value of the freezer. These alone may be sufficient to sustain the decision. Yet, a caveat is warranted lest we reduce the import of Section 2–302 solely to a mathematical ratio formula. It may, at times, be that; yet it may also be much more. The very limited financial resources of the purchaser, known to the sellers at the time of the sale, is entitled to weight in the balance. Indeed, the value disparity itself leads inevitably to the felt conclusion that knowing advantage was taken of the plaintiffs. In addition, the meaningfulness of choice essential to the making of a contract, can be negated by a gross inequality of bargaining power.

There is no question about the necessity and even the desirability of instalment sales and the extension of credit. Indeed, there are many, including welfare recipients, who would be deprived of even the most basic conveniences without the use of these devices. Similarly, the retail merchant selling on instalment or extending credit is expected to establish a pricing factor which will afford a degree of protection commensurate with the risk of selling to those who might be default prone. However, neither of these accepted premises can clothe the sale of this freezer with respectability.

* * *

Having already paid more than $600 toward the purchase of this $300 freezer unit, it is apparent that the defendant has already been amply compensated. In accordance with the statute, the application of the payment provision should be limited to amounts already paid by the plaintiffs and the contract be reformed and amended by changing the payments called for therein to equal the amount of payment actually so paid by the plaintiffs.

Problem 1

Educational Services Co. sells educational books from door to door. It instructs its salesmen not to use high pressure tactics, and in general they do not use them. All relevant licensing and other regulations are complied with, including the contract providing a three-day cancellation period. The company sells a "basic educational package", consisting of twenty volumes, for $270 on an 18–month credit contract. Of that price, the salesman receives $38. An accurate TIL disclosure statement is given each customer.

Ima Victim purchased the basic education package, received the books, waited two weeks, then started reading them. She is unhappy with the books, and wants out of the contract. In particular, she has now noticed that several local stores sell the exact same books for a total of $104 cash. The wholesale price for these books totals $34. Is the contract of Educational Services "unconscionable" because of its price *alone*? Cf., Kugler v. Romain, 58 N.J. 522, 279 A.2d 640 (1971).

Notes

1. Consider the following language from *Kugler,* above:

"The Attorney General's claim was that there was one illegal aspect of the sales contract which was common to every transaction, namely the fixed price. This price for the package of books and materials, which the testimony showed was about two and a half times a reasonable price in the relevant market, was found by the trial court to be exorbitant. As we have already noted, the Attorney General pointed out that in addition to being excessive in relation to defendant's cost, the books had very little and in some cases no value for the purpose for which the consumers were persuaded to buy them. Consequently he urged that under the circumstances the price was unconscionable under Section 2–302 of the Uniform Commercial Code and, as such, was within the proscription of Section 2 of the Consumer Fraud Act. More particularly, he contends that on the uncontradicted and common facts of each transaction, the unconscionable price must be equated with the deception, fraud, false pretense, misrepresentation or knowing material omission condemned by Section 2. If the contention is sound, then it should follow that every consumer who executed the form agreement for the educational package described above at the price fixed by defendant ought to be considered similarly situated, and the Attorney General would therefore be entitled to a judgment invalidating the contract for the entire class of such consumers.

"As already noted, however, the trial court declined to hold that the price, per se constituted a violation of Section 2 in the absence of some comitant deceptive practice perpetrated by the seller. ＊ ＊ ＊

"Here the facts reveal that the seller's price was not only roughly two and one half times a reasonable market price, assuming functional adequacy of the book package for the represented purpose, but they indicate also that most of the package was actually practically worthless for that purpose. Such price-value disparity clearly constitutes unconscionability ＊ ＊ ＊."

Does the court say anything about the unconscionability of contracts which exhibit only high prices? Or, is the court saying that some combination of high prices and deception is required for a finding of unconscionability? The necessity for both "procedural" unconscionability—duress or deception of some sort—*and* "substantive" unconscionability—overly harsh terms—has been widely debated. See, e.g., Leff, "Unconscionability and the Code—The Emperor's New Clause." 115 U.Pa.L.Rev. 485 (1967); Ellinghaus, "In Defense of Unconscionability," 78 Yale L.J. 757 (1969), Spanogle, "Analyzing Unconscionability Problems," 117 U.Pa.L.Rev. 931 (1969). Or, does the court take no position on the issue, believing it does not need to?

2. In Problem 1, what is a reasonable market price for the books? Note the variety of choices: wholesale, wholesale plus a reasonable markup, retail at a store, retail at a store plus some reasonable additional markup for door to door selling, retail at a store plus salesman's commission, or prices charged by other door to door salesmen. What is the "relevant market"—wholesale, store retail, or home solicitation sales?

3. If, as the *Kugler* court states, the problem lies in charging two and a half times the reasonable market price, are the retail stores in Problem 1 charging unconscionable prices ($104) in that they charge three times the wholesale price ($34)?

4. How does one prove prices are "too high"? Cf., Tashof v. Federal Trade Comm., 437 F.2d 707 (D.C.Cir.1970). Suppose the evidence shows that while prices in the suburbs are lower, prices in the inner-city ghetto neighborhood are all about as high as the seller's in a particular case; is that relevant? Would you allow the store to prove that its higher prices were due to (a) high collection costs because of a high ratio of defaulting buyers; (b) high pilferage or vandalism costs (perhaps in the form of high insurance costs); (c) "inefficient" business practices, such as processing one's own credit rather than farming it out? Would you allow the ghetto merchant to introduce his income tax return to prove he really wasn't getting rich at it?

5. Professor Kripke has suggested the possibility of a duty to disclose high prices, on an analogy to theories by which the courts have imposed such a duty on dealers in securities. He asks whether such a "duty" might be based on the fact that "the dealer or salesman emphasizes his common

color or language with the customer, insists on a first-name basis, etc."
See Kripke, Consumer Credit 229 (1970).

6. Note that many of the "high-price" cases, like *MacIver, Jones* and
Kugler, are also home-solicitation sales cases. Are these courts saying that
door-to-door sellers are under a duty to disclose disparity between their
prices and others, perhaps because buyers confronted with a single salesman in their own home cannot comparison shop? Or, are they saying that
the cost of salesmanship is a cost that society need not bear? Are they
saying both? Scrutinize again the court's figures in *MacIver.*

7. When all is said and done, is "unconscionability" a useful or
adequate and appropriate vehicle for controlling excessive prices? Is it
likely to be effective? Would it be preferable to pass a statute saying that
any price which is more than two or two and a half times the prevailing
price is unlawful? Why do we usually not enact statutes that set the
maximum prices at which various goods or services may be sold?—or
statutorily fix the seller's profit margin? (Isn't one or the other of these
just what usury statutes do? Hold this question over to the next chapter,
on interest rates.)

Note on Comparative Law

In certain civil-law systems, a doctrine that has its roots in the
legislation of imperial Rome provides a remedy for certain instances of
gross disparity between value and price. The doctrine is described by the
phrase "laesio enormis" (enormous injury) or simply "lesion." As defined
by the Justinian Code, the doctrine allowed rescission for land contracts
where the disparity of price and value was on the order of 2:1. It appears
today in disparate guise in the laws of several European countries and of
Louisiana. Planiol, in his Traite Elementair De Droit Civil, says:

> "The owner who consents to sell at an enormous loss should be
> considered as having dealt under some sort of violence; he has sold his
> property for almost nothing because he was in pressing need of money.
> His consent was not free. If a proprietor wishes to give away his
> property, he should do so in the form of a donation; if he wishes to sell
> it, he should get a sufficient price; when he contents himself with an
> insignificant price it is because he was deceived or was forced by need.
> * * * It is evident, therefore, that the authors of the Code [i.e., the
> Code Napoleon—ed.] assimilated the lesion in sales to a vice of con-
> sent." Vol. 2 Part 1 § 1588, pp. 879–80 (11th Ed., 1939, Translated by
> the Louisiana State Law Institute with the authority of the Librairie
> Generale de Droit et de Jurisprudence, Paris, 1959).

How do these reasons compare with the reasons in the "too-high price"
opinions of American courts?

Prefatory Note

The flurry of price-unconscionability cases around 1970 seems to
have died off, at least as to cases concerning the price of goods. There
may be developing, however, a new series of cases involving the price of
services. *Murphy* provides the transition, and *Perdue* is the new
leading case.

MURPHY v. McNAMARA

Connecticut Superior Court, New Haven, 1979.
36 Conn.Sup. 183, 416 A.2d 170, 27 U.C.C.Rep.Serv. 911.

BERDON, J.

* * *

The plaintiff is a recipient of welfare and has four minor children ranging in ages from five to sixteen. The defendant is in the business of renting and selling television and stereo sets. The plaintiff saw an advertisement placed by the defendant in a local newspaper offering color television sets and stereos. The advertisement stated in part the following:

> "Why buy when you can rent? Color TV and stereos. *Rent to own!* Use our Rent-to-own rental plan and let TV Rentals deliver either of these models to your home. We feature—Never a repair bill—No deposit—No credit needed—No long term obligation—Weekly or monthly rates available—Order by phone—Call today—Watch color TV tonight."

As a result of this offer, the plaintiff called the defendant on January 8, 1979. The next day she entered into an agreement with the defendant which purported to provide for a lease of a twenty-five inch Philco console color television set. The agreement provided for weekly payments of $16.00, and if the plaintiff paid said sum for 78 successive one-week terms, she would become the owner of the television set. The agreement also contained the following clause:

> "Termination by Renter: Renter, at its option, may at any time terminate this agreement by return of the property to owner in its present condition, fair wear and tear excepted and by payment of all rental payments due through the date of return."

The plaintiff entered into the transaction with the defendant because she was persuaded through the advertisement that she could obtain the ownership and use of the television set without establishing credit. Upon delivery of the set, she paid $36.00 to the defendant which represented $16.00 for the first week's rent and a $20.00 delivery charge. At no time did the defendant advise the plaintiff of the total amount she would be required to pay in order to own the set under the terms of the agreement, which sum amounted to $1,268.00 (including the delivery charge). The retail sale price for the same set was $499.00.

From the period of January 9, 1979 to July 3, 1979, the plaintiff made payments which totaled $436.00. On or about that date, she noticed a newspaper article which criticized the lease plan and she realized the amount she would be required to pay for the television set under the agreement. She stopped making payments and consulted an attorney.

* * *

The plaintiff first argues that the transaction which she entered into with defendant was not a lease but in fact a conditional sale. It is clear the parties intended a sale and this intention controls the transaction. "Regardless of what name the parties give to a transaction, the courts, in general, look beyond the form to the substance, and when one who is called a lessee may become the owner of the leased property at the end of a lease term on full payment of the stipulated rent or by the payment of a small additional amount, the transaction is generally held to be a conditional sale, even though it is couched in the terms of a lease." Tishman Equipment Leasing, Inc. v. Levin, 152 Conn 23, 28 (1964).

* * *

In evaluating the claim that the bargain was unconscionable, the impact upon the plaintiff must be considered. The plaintiff, a welfare recipient, was lured to the defendant because of the "no credit needed" representation and that she would eventually own the television set. Clearly, the plaintiff did not have equal bargaining power with the defendant; the plaintiff was at a disadvantage because her economic circumstances required an extension of credit in order to make the purchase. Furthermore, no attempt was made to advise her that she would be paying $1,268.00 for a television set that sold at retail for $499.00.

* * *

An excessive price charged a consumer with unequal bargaining power can constitute a violation of § 2–302 of the Uniform Commercial Code. In the case of Jones v. Star Credit Corp., the plaintiffs, welfare recipients, purchased a home freezer unit for $900.00. The freezer had a retail value of approximately $300.00. The court held the contract was unconscionable under § 2–302 of the Uniform Commercial Code and reformed the contract by excusing further payments over the $600.00 already paid by the plaintiffs.

There have been similar holdings by other courts. E.g., Toker v. Westerman, two and one half times the reasonable retail value; Toker v. Perl, price two and one half times the value; Frostifresh Corp. v. Reynoso, price over three times the value; American Home Improvement, Inc. v. MacIver, requiring substantial interest payments; see Fairfield Lease Corp. v. Pratt, a one-sided lease agreement. * * *

* * *

In sum, the ex parte injunction against the defendant is modified and shall continue in force from this date until further order of the court (without bond) as follows:

(a) The defendant is enjoined from attempting to gain possession of the television set through self-help. If the defendant seeks a prejudgment remedy pertaining to the television set which is the subject matter of this suit, he shall disclose to the judicial authority a copy of this memorandum of decision; and

(b) The defendant is enjoined from threatening the plaintiff or initiating a criminal complaint against the plaintiff based upon section

53–129b of the General Statutes regarding the television set which is the subject matter of this suit.

Note on Regulating the Price of Services

1. Should a judge have the power to set the prices which can be charged by purveyors of services? For example, should courts judge how much a bank can charge for its checking account services? Or, for another example, should courts (or legislatures) judge how much attorneys can charge for their services? Can you make a persuasive argument to regulate one of these sets of prices, and not the other?

2. United States courts will, upon occasion, review the fees charged by attorneys. An example is Newman v. Silver, 553 F.Supp. 485 (S.D.N.Y. 1982) in which a client, who plead guilty to turning odometers back, sued his attorney—to whom he had paid $181,000. The court concluded (with multiple citations omitted):

> * * * It is recognized that contracts for compensation of an attorney by his client are not generally subject to revision by a court. The court, however, does retain the traditional authority to supervise the charging of fees for legal services pursuant to the court's inherent power to regulate the practice of law. Courts have the power to examine the agreement to make sure it is not unreasonable or oppressive where it was wrongfully procured, and have not hesitated to find agreements for compensation of attorneys invalid because they were unconscionable or "out of proportion to the value of the attorney's services."

> Indeed the practical effect of a legal fraud can be found from the amount of the fee alone. In discussing the unconscionability of a contingency fee the court stated:

>> [T]he amount of the fee standing alone and unexplained, may be sufficient to show that an unfair advantage was taken of the client, or in other words, that a legal fraud was perpetuated upon him.

> Although discussion of unconscionability most frequently arises in the context of a contingency fee arrangement, the doctrine is equally applicable under a contract based upon hourly rates, and therefore is also applicable to an unspecified fee arrangement as occurred in this case.

> Under the facts and circumstances presented at trial, I conclude that Silver's actions evidence a breach of his duty of utmost fairness and loyalty owned to Newman. Without establishing a clear agreement on the price for his legal services, Silver over a period of time demanded and received what amounted to an exorbitant sum of his services. This is particularly evident, given the finding that his only services consisted of conferring with his client, reviewing some documents, arranging for and making improper overtures toward Judge Motely, copying verbatim and resubmitting a motion that had been submitted by prior counsel, conferring with the FBI, and representing Silver upon his plea of guilty and upon his sentence. There was no evidence of independent investigation, research or other work product

by Silver. * * * The amount of the fee charged, particularly in light of the services rendered and the absence of a specific contract was sufficient to show that unfair advantage was taken. In substance a legal fraud was perpetrated on Newman by his attorney for which recovery should be granted.

* * *

* * * I conclude that on a quantum meruit basis Silver was entitled to at most a reasonable fee in the amount of $11,700.00. Newman, therefore, is entitled to recover $169,300.00 which represents the difference between the reasonable fee and the $181,000.00 net amount that Silver received.

This aspect of the trial court's opinion was affirmed in Newman v. Silver, 713 F.2d 14 (2d Cir.1983), but the case was remanded for further proceedings on possible fee-splitting by the attorney.

3. On the constitutionality of price regulation, see Drobak, Constitutional Limits on Price and Rent Control: the Lessons of Utility Regulation, 64 Wash.U.L.Q 107 (1986).

Problem 2

Harry bought a Mercedes from Sam Silver on credit for $40,000. The credit agreement did not require Harry to pay collection costs if he defaulted. However, when Sam assigned Harry's contract to Friendly Finance Company, the assignment did state that Sam would "pay any costs of collection, including attorneys' fees of 15% of the outstanding balance."

Harry forgot to make any payments. So, one day he received a call from an employee of Caroline, a local collection attorney. She reminded him of his failure to pay, and demanded payment in full. Harry, chagrined at his default, said he would immediately mail a check for $40,000 and he did. Caroline's employee received Harry's check, cashed it, then credited Sam's account for $34,000 ($40,000 − 15%). Sam consults you. He thinks Caroline's charge of $6,000 is a little high. Caroline's employee spent a total of less than 10 minutes on the collection, and Caroline herself spent no time at all on the collection. Please advise Sam. Can any of the doctrines in this Chapter be used to reduce Caroline's fee?

Note on Comparative Law II

Although most American attorneys consider that a "market economy" includes the freedom to price legal services without governmental regulation, that is not always true. One example is Germany, certainly a nation with a "market economy." However, the maximum fees chargeable by a German attorney are set by a governmentally-ordered schedule. A corollary of the established fee schedule is that most German consumers have "legal insurance" and can use legal representation with greater ease than can American consumers. Is this system preferable—from the consumer's viewpoint?

PERDUE v. CROCKER NATIONAL BANK

Supreme Court of California, In Bank, 1985.
38 Cal.3d 913, 216 Cal.Rptr. 345, 702 P.2d 503.

BROUSSARD, JUSTICE.

Plaintiff filed this class action to challenge the validity of charges imposed by defendant Crocker National Bank for the processing of checks drawn on accounts without sufficient funds. (The parties refer to such checks as NSF checks and to the handling charge as an NSF charge.) He appeals from a judgment of the trial court entered after that court sustained defendant's general demurrer without leave to amend.

On July 3, 1978, plaintiff filed suit on behalf of all persons with checking accounts at defendant bank and a subclass of customers who have paid NSF charges to the bank. The complaint first alleges a contract under which the bank furnishes checking service in return for a maintenance charge. It then asserts that "It is the practice of defendants to impose and collect a unilaterally set charge for processing checks presented against plaintiffs' accounts when such accounts do not contain sufficient funds to cover the amount of the check." "Defendants have at various times unilaterally increased the NSF charge to an amount the defendants deemed appropriate, without reference to any criteria, and defendants imposed and collected the said increased amount without any explanation or justification by defendants to plaintiffs." At the time of filing of the suit, the charge was $6 for each NSF check, whether the check was honored or returned unpaid, even though "the actual cost incurred by the defendants in processing an NSF check is approximately $0.30."

The bank requires each depositor to sign a signature card which it uses "to determine and verify the authenticity of endorsements on checks". In extremely small (6 point) type, the signature card states that the undersigned depositors "agree with Crocker National Bank and with each other that . . . this account and all deposits therein shall be . . . subject to all applicable laws, to the Bank's present and future rules, regulations, practices and charges, and to its right of setoff for the obligations of any of us." The card does not identify the amount of the charge for NSF checks, and the bank does not furnish the depositor with a copy of the applicable bank rules and regulations.

On the basis of these allegations, plaintiff asserts five causes of action: (1) for a judicial declaration that the bank's signature card is not a contract authorizing NSF charges; (2) for a judicial declaration that such charges are oppressive and unconscionable; (3) to recover damages for unjust enrichment derived from the bank's collection of illegal NSF charges; (4) to enjoin alleged unfair and deceptive practices—the bank's failure to inform customers of the contractual nature of the signature card, and its practice of waiving NSF charges as to certain preferred customers; and (5) to recover the difference between the NSF charges and defendant's actual expenses in processing NSF checks on the theory that the charges represent an unreasonable attempt to fix liquidated damages.

Defendant filed general and special demurrers to each of the asserted causes of action. The superior court sustained the general demurrers and, taking notice of the fact that plaintiff had filed three previous complaints in another action raising similar issues, denied leave to amend. Plaintiff appeals from judgment for defendant.

* * *

I. PLAINTIFF'S FIRST CAUSE OF ACTION: WHETHER THE SIGNATURE CARD IS A CONTRACT AUTHORIZING NSF CHARGES.

The complaint alleges that "The signature card prepared by the defendants does not identify the amount of any charge to be paid by the plaintiffs for processing NSF checks and is not an agreement for such payment. The card does not constitute mutual assent to NSF charges in any particular sum or at all and accordingly is not a contract conferring authority to do the acts complained of herein." "Based upon the language of the signature card, the plaintiffs believed and expected that the signature card was intended as a handwriting example for purposes of identification and verification only." Plaintiff therefore seeks a judicial declaration "as to whether the signature card is a valid or enforceable contract and * * * a lawful basis for the imposition of the NSF charge."

The cases unanimously agree that a signature card such as the Crocker Bank card at issue here is a contract. * * *

* * *

* * * We conclude that plaintiff here is not entitled to a judicial declaration that the bank's signature card is not a contract authorizing NSF charges. To the contrary, we hold as a matter of law that the card is a contract authorizing the bank to impose such charges, subject to the bank's duty of good faith and fair dealing in setting or varying such charges. Plaintiff may, upon remand of this case, amend his complaint to seek a judicial declaration determining whether the charges actually set by the bank are consonant with that duty.

II. PLAINTIFF'S SECOND CAUSE OF ACTION: WHETHER THE BANK'S NSF CHARGES ARE OPPRESSIVE, UNREASONABLE, OR UNCONSCIONABLE.

Plaintiff's second cause of action alleges that the signature card is drafted by defendant bank which enjoys a superior bargaining position by reason of its greater economic power, knowledge, experience and resources. Depositors have no alternative but to acquiesce in the relationship as offered by defendant or to accept a similar arrangement with another bank. The complaint alleges that the card is vague and uncertain, that it is unclear whether it is intended as an identification card or a contract, that it imposes no obligation upon the bank, and permits the bank to alter or terminate the relationship at any time. It then asserts that "The disparity between the actual cost to defendants and the amount charged by defendants for processing an NSF check unreasonably and oppressively imposes excessive and unfair liability upon plaintiffs." Plaintiff seeks a declaratory judgment to determine the rights and duties of the parties.

Plaintiff's allegations point to the conclusion that the signature card, if it is a contract, is one of adhesion. The term contract of adhesion "signifies a standardized contract, which, imposed and drafted by the party of superior bargaining strength, relegates to the subscribing party only the opportunity to adhere to the contract or reject it." The signature card, drafted by the bank and offered to the customer without negotiation, is a classic example of a contract of adhesion; the bank concedes as much.

In *Graham v. Scissor–Tail, Inc., supra,* 28 Cal.3d 807, 171 Cal.Rptr. 604, 623 P.2d 165, we observed that "To describe a contract as adhesive in character is not to indicate its legal effect. * * * [A] contract of adhesion is fully enforceable according to its terms [citations] unless certain other factors are present which, under established legal rules— legislative or judicial—operate to render it otherwise." "Generally speaking," we explained, "there are two judicially imposed limitations on the enforcement of adhesion contracts or provisions thereof. The first is that such a contract or provision which does not fall within the reasonable expectations of the weaker or 'adhering' party will not be enforced against him. The second—a principle of equity applicable to all contracts generally—is that a contract or provision, even if consistent with the reasonable expectations of the parties, will be denied enforcement if, considered in its context, it is unduly oppressive or 'unconscionable.' "

* * *

Plaintiff bases his claim of unconscionability on the alleged 2,000 percent differential between the NSF charge of $6 and the alleged cost to the bank of $0.30. The parties have cited numerous cases on whether the price of an item can be so excessive as to be unconscionable. The cited cases are from other jurisdictions, often from trial courts or intermediate appellate courts, and none is truly authoritative on the issue. Taken together, however, they provide a useful guide to analysis of the claim that a price is so excessive as to be unconscionable.

To begin with, it is clear that the price term, like any other term in a contract, may be unconscionable. Allegations that the price exceeds cost or fair value, standing alone, do not state a cause of action. Instead, plaintiff's case will turn upon further allegations and proof setting forth the circumstances of the transaction.

The courts look to the basis and justification for the price, including "the price actually being paid by * * * other similarly situated consumers in a similar transaction." The cases, however, do not support defendant's contention that a price equal to the market price cannot be held unconscionable. While it is unlikely that a court would find a price set by a freely competitive market to be unconscionable, the market price set by an oligopoly should not be immune from scrutiny. Thus courts consider not only the market price, but also the cost of the goods or services to the seller, the inconvenience imposed on the seller and the true value of the product or service.

In addition to the price justification, decisions examine what Justice Weiner in *A & M Produce* called the "procedural aspects" of unconscionability. Cases may turn on the absence of meaningful choice, the lack of sophistication of the buyer and the presence of deceptive practices by the seller.

Applying this analysis to our review of the complaint at hand, we cannot endorse defendant's argument that the $6 charge is so obviously reasonable that no inquiry into its basis or justification is necessary. In 1978 $6 for processing NSF checks may not seem exorbitant, but price alone is not a reliable guide. Small charges applied to a large volume of transactions may yield a sizeable sum. The complaint asserts that the cost of processing NSF checks is only $0.30 per check, which means that a $6 charge would produce a 2,000 percent profit; even at the higher cost estimate of $1 a check mentioned in plaintiff's petition for hearing, the profit is 600 percent. Such profit percentages may not be automatically unconscionable, but they indicate the need for further inquiry.

Other aspects of the transaction confirm plaintiff's right to a factual hearing. Defendant presents the depositor with a document which serves at least in part as a handwriting exemplar, and whose contractual character is not obvious. The contractual language appears in print so small that many could not read it. State law may impose obligations on the bank (e.g., the duty to honor a check when the account has sufficient funds) but so far as the signature card drafted by the bank is concerned, the bank has all the rights and the depositor all the duties. The signature card provides that the depositor will be bound by the bank's rules, regulations, practices and charges, but the bank does not furnish the depositor with a copy of the relevant documents. The bank reserves the power to change its practices and fees at any time, subject only to the notice requirements of state law.

In short, the bank structured a totally one-sided transaction. The absence of equality of bargaining power, open negotiation, full disclosure, and a contract which fairly sets out the rights and duties of each party demonstrates that the transaction lacks those checks and balances which would inhibit the charging of unconscionable fees. In such a setting, plaintiff's charge that the bank's NSF fee is exorbitant, yielding a profit far in excess of cost, cannot be dismissed on demurrer. Under Civil Code section 1670.5, the parties should be afforded a reasonable opportunity to present evidence as to the commercial setting, purpose, and effect of the signature card and the NSF charge in order to determine whether that charge is unconscionable.

III. Plaintiff's Fourth Cause of Action: Whether the Bank
has Performed Acts of Unfair Competition.

* * *

Neither allegation is clear and precise. After reading paragraph 38, we are uncertain whether plaintiff contends that the signature card itself is deceptive, or whether he contends that the bank employs misrepresentations or other deceptive practices in presenting the card to the depositor. If the latter is plaintiff's contention, the complaint should set out the challenged representations or practices.

* * *

In conclusion, the superior court properly sustained a demurrer to plaintiff's fourth cause of action, but erred in denying leave to amend. Plaintiff should be permitted to amend to set out the alleged deceptive practices employed by defendant. The trial court would be within its discretion in denying leave to amend to claim unlawful discrimination in waiving NSF charges, but since plaintiff must be allowed to amend on the deceptive practices issue, the court may choose to permit amendment as to the waiver issue as well.

IV. Plaintiff's Fifth Cause of Action: Whether the Bank's
Charge for NSF Checks is an Unlawful Penalty.

Paragraph 42 of the complaint states that "[c]ausing NSF checks to be presented for payment is a breach by plaintiffs of their contractual obligations to defendant * * *" The NSF charge collected by defendants, however, "is a penalty and is not imposed to compensate defendants for damages incurred by plaintiffs' breach", and therefore violates Civil Code sections 1670 and 1671. The complaint concludes that "[p]laintiffs are entitled to recover the difference between the unlawful charges collected and defendants' actual damages * * *."

By these allegations, plaintiff seeks to invoke the rule that a contractual provision specifying damages for breach is valid only if it "represent[s] the result of a reasonable endeavor by the parties to estimate a fair average compensation for any loss that may be sustained."

An amount disproportionate to the anticipated damages is termed a "penalty." A contractual provision imposing a "penalty" is ineffective, and the wronged party can collect only the actual damages sustained.

Two Court of Appeal decisions have addressed plaintiff's contention and concluded that the writing of an NSF check is not a breach of contract, and thus the fee charged for processing the check is not a penalty.

* * *

* * * We conclude that the court correctly sustained the demurrer to plaintiff's fifth cause of action without leave to amend.

V. WHETHER CALIFORNIA LAW, AS APPLIED TO NSF CHARGES
IMPOSED BY NATIONAL BANKS, IS PREEMPTED BY FEDERAL LAW.

* * *

In sum, the controlling doctrines of California law do not facially
conflict with any federal statute or regulation. Neither does it appear
from the pleading that the application of these doctrines to national
bank contracts will impair the efficiency or viability of national banks,
or frustrate the purpose of legislation regulating (or deregulating) those
banks. Although conceivably information not contained in the pleadings might lead to a different conclusion, such information is not before
us in reviewing a judgment upon demurrer. We cannot presume,
without evidence, that prohibiting a national bank from setting unreasonable prices or enforcing an unconscionable contract will render that
bank less efficient, less competitive or less able to fulfill its function in
a national banking system.

VI. CONCLUSION.

Plaintiff's second and third causes of action state grounds for relief
without need for further amendment; his first and fourth causes of
action can be amended to state such grounds. The fifth cause of action
alone is fatally defective. We conclude that the trial court erred in
sustaining defendant's demurrer without leave to amend and in entering judgment for defendant.

The judgment is reversed, and the cause remanded to the superior
court for further proceedings consistent with this opinion.

Notes

1. The following regulation was issued by the Comptroller of the
Currency shortly before oral argument in the *Perdue* case:

(b) Establishment of deposit account service charges, and the
amounts thereof, is a business decision to be made by each bank
according to sound banking judgment and federal standards of safety
and soundness. In establishing deposit account service charges, the
bank may consider, but is not limited to considering:

(1) Costs incurred by the bank, plus a profit margin, in providing
the service;

(2) The deterrence of misuse by customers of banking services;

(3) The enhancement of the competitive position of the bank in
accord with the bank's marketing strategy;

(4) Maintenance of the safety and soundness of the institution.

(c) A national bank may establish any deposit account service
charge pursuant to paragraphs (a) and (b) of this section notwithstanding any state laws which prohibit the charge assessed or limit or
restrict the amount of that charge. Such state laws are preempted by

the comprehensive federal statutory scheme governing the deposit-taking function of national banks.

12 C.F.R. § 7.8000 (1989).

   A.   Does Crocker's bad check charge comply with these guidelines? How can you tell?

   B.   Does subsection (c) preempt all state law and therefore preclude the California Supreme Court from finding Crocker's bad check charge to be unconscionable? If you represented the plaintiffs, what argument could you make?

2. If you represented the plaintiffs on remand, what evidence would you want to introduce to establish that the bad check fee is unconscionable? Where would you get that evidence? What if you represented the bank?

3. If the plaintiffs win on remand, can they get damages? Restitution? If not, what remedy should they receive? Does this help them? Does it help their lawyers? See also Best v. United States National Bank, 303 Or. 557, 739 P.2d 554 (1987).

Problem 3

You represent the largest bank in the town in which you practice. In light of the *Perdue* case, the bank's president has asked you to review all charges and fees the bank imposes on its customers. These include monthly and per-check service charges on checking accounts, charges for using the bank's debit card in its "Insta-cash" machines and other locations, processing fees for automatic deposits and withdrawals, and other similar charges. The president wants to know if any of these charges are vulnerable to attack on unconscionability or other grounds. What will you tell her? What other information will you need to know before you can give proper advice? Among other things, would you advise the bank to disclose all charges in the deposit agreement? Why? Would that avoid the unconscionability argument? Would it preclude the bank from later amending its charges?

Chapter 11

STATE REGULATION OF THE COST OF CREDIT

SECTION A. HISTORICAL INTRODUCTION

Some understanding of historical context is always important in the study of law, but it takes on special significance in the area of interest rate regulation. The doctrine of usury and the regulation of interest rates by the state can be traced several thousand years. In fact, Western society has seen very few historical periods in which interest rates were left to the free market. To law students, the current debate over whether to raise or lower interest rate ceilings may seem new, but in reality it has been going on a long time. This section will provide a brief historical survey of this fascinating and complex subject.

Earliest societies. Lending, including consumer lending at interest, is far older than coinage or even writing. Primitive pastoral societies are known to have engaged in loan transactions involving working capital (grain, tools, etc.) as well as consumer goods (food, clothing, etc.). The earliest literate societies often adopted written laws, typically derived from ancient custom, which contained provisions regulating interest. For example, several rules on lending practices are contained in the Biblical texts of the Hebrew laws. Exodus 22:25 says: "If you lend money to any of my people with you who is poor, you shall not be to him as a creditor, and you shall not exact interest from him."

Biblical texts are not the only sources of early written laws. Surviving records from the Sumerian period, about 3000 B.C., show many commercial loans with interest. Around 1800 B.C., the Babylonian king Hammurabi created a legal code which contained many rules on lending, including the earliest surviving law establishing interest rate ceilings. Interest was permitted, but was limited to 33⅓% on loans of grain and 20% on loans of silver. These rates reflect customary levels during this period.

Greece and Rome. In early Greece, there were no interest rate ceilings. Rates were controlled entirely by the market. This apparently worked; commercial rates in Athens dropped from the range of 16% to 18% in the fifth century B.C. to about 6% to 10% in the first and second centuries. However, at the same time (as is true today), rates for consumer loans were much higher, typically around 36%.

In Rome, laws regulating credit and setting maximum interest rates appeared as early as the fifth century B.C. in the famous Twelve Tables (c. 443 B.C.). The Twelve Tables reduced the prevailing rates by setting the limit at 8⅓%. The limit was raised in the first century B.C. to 12%, where it remained until Rome was sacked in 410 A.D. Of course, actual rates during these periods could be lower than the legal limit.

The Christian Influence. The early Christian church not only condemned what we would call "usury," or excessive interest, but also any form of interest. As a result, and because of the strong church influence over civil authorities, usury was generally prohibited during the Middle Ages. In fact, in 800 Charlemagne made interest illegal throughout the Empire. This prohibition remained in effect through the 12th or 13th century.

English law. During the Middle Ages, England followed the pattern established in Europe; interest was prohibited by both church law and civil law. This pattern remained right up to the end of the 15th century. A statute in 1487, for example, declared void all contracts providing for interest. A half century later, however, attitudes had changed, and in 1545, a law was passed which allowed interest of up to 10%. Later, the maximum legal rate was lowered to 5%. 12 Anne.Stat. 2, c. 16 (1713). This latter statute was the forerunner of modern American statutes. England repealed its usury laws in 1854, while their American offspring remained.

Today, there are no general usury ceilings in England, although there may be mechanisms to deal with extremely oppressive lending practices. Under the Consumer Credit Act of 1977, the court can interfere in certain consumer transactions if the rate of return is so exorbitant as to be "extortionate." There are no numerical guidelines or presumptions, however, and courts must decide cases on an individual basis.

The American experience. The American colonies basically followed the English model. Massachusetts adopted a usury law (at 8%) in 1641, and during the 17th and 18th centuries, the other colonies and states followed suit and adopted usury ceilings of their own. Rates varied from 5% to 8%, although the most common limit was 6%. Massachusetts also became the first state to follow the English pattern to the end; it repealed its general usury law in 1867. Only a few other states followed suit. By the turn of the 20th century, a few Western states allowed interest at rates of 10% or 12%, but usury ceilings in most states remained at 6%.

The Twentieth Century. The low usury ceilings prevalent at the turn of the century simply did not allow for profitable legal lending to consumers. This left the consumer market largely to illegal lenders. In fact, during this period, loan sharks were probably the most common source of small-scale consumer credit. Two processes developed to circumvent these price ceilings: one for lender credit and the other for seller credit.

Regulation of Lender Credit. The standard approach by most states was to enact numerous exceptions to their general usury statutes which permitted various forms of cash credit that could not otherwise have been accommodated. These exceptions opened up *legal* alternatives to the unregulated *illegal* lending that flourished in America in the late 1800s and early 1900s in spite of the usury laws.

As always throughout history, a group of cleverly structured financial transactions appeared which legitimate lenders could use to get around the usury laws. In the consumer area, one of the most important was the so-called Morris plan loan. These were created in 1910 (by a lawyer named Arthur Morris), and operated through Morris Plan Banks, also known as industrial banks. Under these plans, a lump-sum, single-payment loan was made for a definite period, say a year, at the highest lawful rate. At the same time, but as a separate transaction, the consumer would agree to make monthly or weekly deposits into a special account at the bank. These deposits would be made during the entire term of the loan transaction, and their total always equaled the amount needed to pay off the original loan (plus interest). The overall effect, of course, was to create an installment loan at effective rates nearly double the usury ceiling. Morris plan loans are still available in about half the states, but modern banking and usury laws have diminished their importance.

Small loan or consumer finance companies are also basically products of the 20th century. The major impetus for their development came from studies produced by the Russell Sage Foundation between 1905 and 1908. These studies concluded that the best way to deal with the loan shark problem was to raise the usury limits high enough so that legitimate lenders would enter the market. This led to the Uniform Small Loan Act in 1916, and all states (except Arkansas) ultimately enacted some sort of small loan act. These acts were seen as exceptions to the general usury laws. They all required consumer lenders to obtain licenses, and in exchange they allowed small consumer loans to be made at much higher rates.

In one sense, small loan acts helped to establish a pattern that came to dominate early Twentieth Century rate regulation legislation. Such legislation is often sponsored by the credit industry. This may seem surprising at first, but it should be less so if the matter is viewed historically. Each segment of the lending industry has often sponsored its own laws, usually seeking special treatment or exceptions to the general usury limits. One result of this activity is that the lending industry is highly fragmented; many segments do not directly compete with each other. These divisions reflect differences in the markets which lenders have carved out for themselves, sometimes encouraged by the various exceptions and special rules found in the usury laws. Banks, for example, are rarely regulated by the same laws (usury or otherwise) as are small loan companies, and the two rarely compete directly for their respective shares of the consumer loan market. In fact, each type of lender often has its own regulatory statute, interest rate ceilings, restrictions on required and permissible contract provisions, and licensing requirements. By the mid-20th century, so many exceptions and special rules had appeared that it sometimes seemed that as many transactions were excluded as were governed by the general usury laws. Of course, most of the excluded transactions are subject to statutes, including interest rate ceilings, of their own. Today, the most descriptive characteristics of state usury laws are probably complexity and disarray. In part, of course, this hodge-podge reflects the general lack of uniformity in the law of consumer credit which we have seen throughout this book. Yet, in large part, it also reflects the historical pattern of the usury laws.

Regulation of Seller Credit—The Time–Price Doctrine. The most remarkable division within the credit market is between lenders of money and credit sellers of goods, a division which was produced by the time-price doctrine.

> Essentially, this was a legal principle permitting a seller of goods and services freely to establish two prices, a cash price and a time, or credit, price. Under common law the differential was not considered interest subject to general usury statutes. So, sales credit—credit extended in conjunction with the sale of merchandise—became exempt from general usury statutes which facilitated its growth. Since 1935 many states have enacted legislation limiting the time-price differential on the credit sale of motor vehicles and other consumer goods as well as on revolving credit. NCCF Report, at 93 (1972).

Throughout history, creditors have always been on the lookout for ways to restructure their lending transactions into forms which were not affected by the usury laws. The judicially developed "time-price doctrine," for example, exempted credit sales from usury laws, and this prompted many creditors to create artificial sales to take advantage of this rule. However, such attempts to reshape the transaction to avoid application of the usury laws is little different from attempts during the Middle Ages to recast loan transactions in the form of partnerships or annuities. These devices permitted a profitable rate of return without running afoul of prohibitions against interest on loans.

Creditors today are not much different; new devices constantly appear which attempt to avoid the effects of usury or other restrictive laws. Perhaps the most pervasive current example in the consumer area is the lease, or rent-to-own contract. These transactions are designed to fall neatly between the legislative cracks: on paper, at least, they are not loans, so are not covered by traditional usury laws; nor are they sales, and so are not covered by modern retail installment sales acts. There is another historical parallel here: just as legislatures once responded to the credit sale problem by enacting retail installment sales acts, so are they in recent years responding to the rent-to-own problem with special consumer lease laws. We will explore these transactions in more detail in section C of this chapter.

Note

As this discussion shows, attitudes towards usury, as much as economic cycles themselves, have waxed and waned through the centuries. The debate today is carried on in terms that are not really much different than those of 500 or 1500 years ago. Economic, social, and moral arguments are all mustered in support of both positions.

National Commission on Consumer Finance (NCCF) Report

91–94 (1972)

Basically, there are two conflicting views on how to assure reasonable rates for consumer credit transactions. Some support "free rates," arguing that prices of credit should be established by the market unhindered by direct government interference. Others support "decreed rates," opting for price ceilings on consumer credit. Spokesmen for the two viewpoints are both numerous and dedicated. Economist Dr. Milton Friedman leaves no doubt as to his position:

* * * I know of no economist of any standing * * * who has favored a legal limit on the rate of interest that borrowers could pay or lenders receive—though there must have been some * * *. Bentham's explanation of the "mischief of the anti-usurious laws" is also as valid today as when he wrote that these laws preclude "many people, altogether, from the getting the money they stand in need of, to answer their respective exigencies." For still others, they render "the terms so much the worse . . . While, out of loving-kindness, or whatsoever other motive, the law precludes a man from borrowing, upon terms which it deems too disadvantageous, it does not preclude him from selling, upon any terms, howsoever disadvantageous." His conclusion: "The sole tendency of the law is to heap distress upon distress."

But economist Leon Keyserling does not agree:

I find it deplorable that we feel bound to set an 18 percent interest rate ceiling for these people, which is three times the rate at which (as I have cited) a powerful corporation can borrow money on bonds while many of our greatest corporations finance themselves and do not have interest costs of large significance. I think the ceiling should be very much lower * * * I am not going to take the position that even 12 percent is a conscionable interest rate for the kind of people borrowing money for these kinds of purposes. They ought to be able to borrow for much less, even if this requires new public programs.

These differing viewpoints have existed for centuries.

Notes

1. Today in the United States, we seem to be in the midst of another anti-usury cycle, reminiscent of ancient Greece or Benthamite England in the mid–1800s. State laws limiting the cost of credit have come under heavy attack. During the late 1970s and early 1980s, inflation, high operating costs, and competition for the depositor's dollar made it difficult for creditors to offer consumer credit within the constraints of state usury laws. Banks were often reluctant to make auto loans, for example, or to extend credit card lines at rates of 18%, when their "prime" rates for commercial customers were over 20%.

The economic pressure on interest rates has eased since those days, but the pressure on the usury laws themselves has continued unabated. During the 1980s, several states abolished their rate ceilings for some or all types of loans. Many others replaced their traditional strict usury ceilings with floating rate ceilings for certain transactions. One interesting by-product of this activity is that a number of major banks have moved their credit subsidiaries to states with higher ceilings or no ceilings. One of your co-authors, for example, has a VISA card issued by a Detroit bank through a Delaware subsidiary.

2. Another important indicator of the current anti-usury trend is the phenomenon of federal preemption of state usury laws. Between 1974 and 1980, Congress enacted a series of laws which temporarily or permanently preempted state usury laws for certain types of loan transactions. In addition, Congress has itself set interest rate ceilings for federally chartered lending institutions. We will consider these developments in detail in Chapter 12.

3. The question remains, however—why do we have usury statutes at all? We do not have price controls on sales or rentals of goods or realty. When we have had such price controls, they often were a disaster. Why have price controls on rentals of money? How is this different from renting a car?

Try to articulate what goals you would hope to accomplish by creating a usury ceiling. For each goal, try to articulate exactly how the usury ceiling achieves that goal. Then articulate any problems created by accomplishing that goal. This material attempts to examine whether any goals can be effectuated, and the societal price which must be traded off if they are.

4. One goal which might be suggested is to limit "high" profits of lenders who charge "high" rates. With that concept in mind, read the FTC Economic Report on D.C. Retailers, below, in Chapter 13.

Problem 1

Assume that in your home state you wish to borrow $1,500. What different types of lenders are available to make you such a loan? Are they all governed by the same rate ceiling statute? Ascertain the following, on the assumption you will repay the loan in twelve equal monthly installments:

(a) What is the applicable interest rate ceiling (if any) for each type of lender?

(b) What additional charges may each creditor impose (legally, but above and beyond the maximum "interest" charge)? What are these charges for?

(c) If you repaid the loan in full after the sixth month, would you be entitled to a rebate or credit for any of the interest or other charges? How much?

Problem 2

(For students willing to do a bit of field research—over a long weekend, perhaps):

Ascertain what are the *lowest* rates at which a one-year $1,500 loan is actually available in your home state. Is it available at less than the applicable rate ceiling? This will involve checking with a variety of possible lenders—banks, credit unions, small loan or finance companies. Would you in fact qualify for the loan at those rates? How often, and from what types of lenders was credit available at less than ceiling rates?

SECTION B. MODERN INTEREST RATE CEILING STATUTES

1. REGULATION OF LENDER CREDIT

As we have seen, the larger debate over whether usury laws are good or bad in general, or whether they help or hurt the consumer in particular, has been going on for centuries. The contemporary aspects of this debate will be examined in Chapter 13. Meanwhile, these larger issues have partly overwhelmed the more traditional technical and computational issues which have dominated litigation under traditional usury laws. As the following materials demonstrate, however, these issues continue to be important, and students should have some understanding of the technical aspects of modern laws which establish maximum interest rate ceilings.

PALMER v. BANK OF LOUISVILLE AND TRUST CO.

Court of Appeals of Kentucky, 1985.
682 S.W.2d 789.

DUNN, JUDGE.

Appellants, all consumer borrower customers of the appellee bank, appeal from the summary judgment of the Jefferson Circuit Court entered against them in favor of the bank in this consolidated action against it testing the validity of charges for real estate title search fees, appraisal fees, and title insurance fees incidental to their second mortgage loans measured by the limitations in KRS 287.215(2) and seeking to enforce those limitations.

KRS 287.215(2), part of the statute which governs certain installment loans made by Kentucky banks, in pertinent part provides:

> In addition to the charge permitted by this section, no further amount shall be directly or indirectly charged, contracted for or received on any such installment loan, except lawful fees actually paid to a public officer for filing, recording or releasing any instrument securing the loan and delinquent charges hereinafter set out, and except an investigation fee not exceeding one dollar ($1.00) for each fifty dollars ($50.00) or fraction thereof upon the first eight hundred dollars ($800.00) of the principal amounts of such loans.

Appellants argue that the charges in question, which in each instance were listed on the face of the note as "charges to the borrower" and which were included in the total amount borrowed, were statutorily impermissible, and under KRS 287.215(10), if charged willfully, the loan is void and the bank is prevented from collecting interest. We disagree completely.

Each loan in question was secured by real estate as collateral. The bank, in making the loans, not only had the right, but also had the duty, to insist that the loan be secure. Towards this end it could almost arbitrarily require that all or any of the requirements of satisfactory appraisal, title examination or title insurance be provided before lending the money. But it did not do so as evidenced by different requirements for each of the appellants. For appellant Beason's loan, all three were required; for the appellants Palmer's and Steiner's loans, only appraisal and title examination were required; while for the appellant Mullins' loan, all [that] required was a title examination. Each loan, considered on its own circumstances, dictated what was necessary to afford reasonable security measures in advance of the loan.

The title and appraisal services for the appellants were provided by independent attorneys and appraisers and the charges were paid directly to them by the bank from the loan proceeds. It retained none of the charges nor did it benefit from them, despite appellants' argument to the contrary that it did so indirectly from collecting interest on the charges part of the loans. This inconsequential benefit is too remote to fall within the spirit of the act and the abuses it seeks to prohibit.

There is no Kentucky case construing KRS 287.215(2) in this regard, but in connection with an analogous statute concerning prohibited charges, *Mills v. Parrott*, Ky., 237 S.W.2d 851 (1951), held that under KRS 288.150(2), the small loans statute, the prohibition that "no further charge or amount whatsoever for any examination, service, brokerage commission, expense, fee or bonus or any other thing shall be directly or indirectly charged * * *" was not violated by a small loan company in disbursing proceeds for credit life insurance to the insuring company, since it received no direct or indirect benefit from it.

* * *

* * * The Kentucky Department of Banking, which annually audits and examines Kentucky banks and is the state statutory regulatory authority for the banking industry, has consistently interpreted KRS 287.215 to permit such disbursements of such fees and charges to third parties and has issued official policy guidelines to that effect.

We agree with the bank that the terms of the statute are ambiguous, as evidenced by the diverse points of view concerning it in this very litigation, in the sense reasonable differences of opinion exist as to its meaning. We can, and do, therefore, give weight to the Kentucky Department of Banking's interpretation permitting disbursements to a third party.

In summary of this issue, we hold that charges for appraisal fees, title examinations, and title insurance and which are disbursed to third parties, are not prohibited by KRS 287.215(2). The statute applies only to fees and charges received and retained by the lender.

* * *

There being no issue concerning the material facts attendant to this issue before the trial court, we affirm its summary judgment in the bank's favor.

Notes

1. Consider what the expenses of a lender are. There is, of course, the cost of money (in effect, the borrower is renting money from the lender) and the risk of loss if the loan becomes uncollectable. However, there are also costs of initiating and maintaining the loan. E.g., lenders advertise, rent offices and computers, hire employees, retain lawyers to draft contracts and disclosure forms, and so on. Further, do all borrowers pay on time? The major cost associated with default is likely not to be those loans written off as uncollectible, but rather the cost of prodding slow and irregular payers, and potential uncollectibles, into getting back on track.

2. Which of the expenses of a lender should be covered by "interest" or "the finance charge", and which should be covered by some other type of charge? Note that a finance charge, once the rate has been established, varies directly with the size of the loan and also varies directly with the duration of the loan. Of the expenses noted above, which of them vary directly with the size of the loan, which with the duration of the loan, and which with both? For those expenses which do not vary directly with both, how can the lender be expected to cover them through the use of a finance charge calculated upon a rate per dollar amount per time?

3. Would it be preferable to allow the lender to charge separately for those expenses which do not relate directly to a rate per amount per time? Concerning the expenses of collecting payments from those who do not pay on time, the law generally permits default, delinquency and deferral charges. See U3C §§ 2.203, 2.204, 3.203, 3.204.

CUEVAS v. MONTOYA

Court of Appeals of Washington, 1987.
48 Wash.App. 871, 740 P.2d 858.

McINTURFF, CHIEF JUDGE.

Daniel and Shirley Cuevas sued Richard Montoya, claiming he charged them excessive attorney fees, usurious interest rates and violated the Consumer Protection Act. Mr. Montoya answered, claiming that the Cuevases owed him attorney fees, and sought collection on a promissory note. The two actions were consolidated. The Superior Court reformed a statutory warranty deed to a mortgage and awarded Mr. Montoya judgments for attorney fees, the balance due under the promissory note and attorney fees to collect on the promissory note.

* * * Mr. Montoya performed legal services for Mr. and Mrs. Cuevas from 1981 through 1983. He represented Mr. Cuevas on several matters.

Mr. Montoya made loans to the Cuevases out of his "earned fees" in his trust account. Additionally, Mr. Montoya borrowed money from Security Bank on two occasions, which he then loaned to the Cuevases. On January 15, 1982, Security Bank loaned Mr. Montoya $3,000 at 18 percent interest. A collection account was created; the collection agreement provided that Shirley Cuevas was to make payments to be applied on Mr. Montoya's loan account. Security Bank charged $104 as a setup fee, which Mr. Montoya claims should be reimbursed by the Cuevases and is included in his claim for fees. The Cuevases signed a promissory note for $3,000 at 18 percent interest, payable to Mr. Montoya. The usury ceiling in January 1982 (at the time the $3,000 loan was made) was 15.55 percent.

In the second loan transaction, Mr. Montoya borrowed approximately $8,000 from Security Bank, securing it with property Mr. and Mrs. Cuevas had deeded to him by warranty deed. He indicated the loan was for operating capital. The interest rate charged on the loan was adjusted monthly at the prime rate plus 2.5 percent; at no time during the loan did the bank charge less than 13 percent. Mr. Montoya prepared a promissory note for $8,300 dated April 1, 1983, which Shirley Cuevas signed, providing for interest of 12 to 13 percent. The usury ceiling on April 1, 1983 was 12.67 percent. The Cuevases made two payments. Mr. Montoya charged the Cuevases attorney fees for his time related to the loan transactions. Plaintiff's brief, at 12–15, states Mr. Montoya's attorney fees on the $3,000 loan were $399 and on the $8,000 loan were $742.

Mr. Montoya presented billings at trial for the time representing the Cuevases. The total attorney fees and loan balances Mr. Montoya claimed due at the time of trial was $8,390.42. The court reduced this to $8,075.42, subtracting a charge for representation of another person which the trial court held unenforceable under the statute of frauds.

First, the Cuevases contend the loans made by Mr. Montoya to the Cuevases were usurious. This discussion involves three sub-issues:

A. *Were the stated interest or actual interest charges usurious?*

RCW 19.52.020(1) sets the maximum legal rate of interest. It also forbids anyone from directly or indirectly taking or receiving any greater interest for the loan.

The party asserting usury must prove five elements by a preponderance of the evidence:

> (1) a loan or forbearance; (2) money or its equivalent as the subject of the loan or forbearance; (3) an agreement that the principal shall be repayable absolutely; (4) the exaction of a rate of interest in excess of that allowed by law for the use of the money loaned or for the benefit of the forbearance; (5) an intention to violate the law.

The intent necessary to establish usury is not intent of a culpable nature, but simply intent to enter a transaction which in fact carries an unlawful rate of interest. The plaintiff need not show defendant intentionally violated the usury laws, only that the extraction of the unlawful interest was not the result of mistake or oversight.

* * *

The trial court concluded that "by the time plaintiffs paid defendant the effective interest rate was less than 12 percent", therefore, there were no usurious charges on the loan. The record shows three payments totalling $3,000 were made to the collection account and the total interest paid was $327.40. Mr. Montoya's bill, however, showed he charged the Cuevases $540 in interest on the $3,000 note, despite the fact they repaid $2,000 of the loan within 5 months after they took it out. The sum of $540 equals interest at 18 percent on $3,000 for 1 year. Subsequently, Mr. Montoya testified that the amount of interest he actually collected was the approximately $330 paid to his collection account. Assuming $330 is the actual interest assessed, it is at an 18 percent annual rate for the amount of time the loan was actually outstanding.[1]

Mr. Montoya made a second loan for $8,300 to the Cuevases on April 1, 1983. The promissory note provided for interest at "12 to 13 percent per annum", plaintiffs to pay the variable interest charged on Mr. Montoya's loan by Security Bank. The usury ceiling at the time the loan was made was 12.67 percent. There was evidence in the record that at no time was the interest charged by Security Bank less than 13 percent. The Cuevases paid two payments to Mr. Montoya at the usurious rate and were found liable for all principal and interest paid by Mr. Montoya to Security Bank.

1. The $3,000 promissory note was dated January 11, 1982. From Janet Twombley's testimony regarding the collection records, a payment was made on May 14, 1982 composed of $176.02 interest and $1,823.94 principal. A second payment was made on January 28, 1983 composed of $150.21 interest and $850.34 principal. A third payment was made February 16, 1983 composed of $2.89 interest and $325.92 principal. By our calculations, $176.06 interest on $3,000 for 4 months is approximately 18 percent.

We hold usurious interest rates are stated on the face of both promissory notes. Additionally, payments made by the Cuevases included interest computed at usurious rates. Therefore, the judgment of the trial court enforces usurious interest rates.

B. *Should the trial court have treated the loan setup costs and attorney fees as interest in analyzing whether the loans were usurious?*

Mr. Montoya charged the Cuevases $399 in attorney fees to set up the $3,000 loan and claims he should be reimbursed for a $104 setup fee for the collection account at the bank regarding this loan. Mr. Montoya charged the Cuevases $742 in attorney fees to set up the $8,000 loan. The Cuevases claim these charges should be categorized as interest in determining if the loans were usurious.

Under RCW 19.52.020, a setup charge is exempt from characterization as interest only if made in connection with a loan of $500 or less. *Aetna Finance Co.,* 38 Wash.App. at 926, 691 P.2d 581. "Charges for making a loan and for the use of money are interest; charges are not interest if they are for services actually provided by the lender, reasonably worth the price charged, and for which the borrower agreed to pay." *Aetna Finance Co.,* at 926, 691 P.2d 581, charges for the administrative services described as "preparing the loan documents, arranging and paying off the [loans], * * * arranging the payment of the truck, recording fees and loan disbursement" were held to be setup charges normally incidental to making a loan, thus treated as *interest.*

Under *Aetna Finance Co.,* the trial court should have classified as interest the attorney fees Mr. Montoya charged the Cuevases relative to the loans because they amount to charges for services normally incidental to making a loan. Additionally, the setup fee Mr. Montoya passed on to the Cuevases on the $3,000 loan should have been treated as interest under the *Aetna Finance Co.* rule. To the extent these charges exceed allowable interest charges under the usury statute, they are not recoverable by Mr. Montoya.

C. *Was Mr. Montoya Entitled to an Award of Attorney Fees Under the Promissory Note?*

RCW 19.52.030(1) provides that "[i]f a greater rate of interest than is allowed by statute shall be contracted for or received or reserved * * * the creditor shall *only* be entitled to the principal less twice the amount of the interest paid, and less the amount of all accrued and unpaid interest". (Italics ours.) In *Aetna Finance Co.,* at 929, 691 P.2d 581, the court stated "under RCW 19.52.030(1), a lender who sues to enforce a usurious loan contract may not recover attorney's fees or costs, notwithstanding contrary contract terms." The usurer is entitled to recover only the principal, less the penalty for usury.

The trial court's award to Mr. Montoya of $1,751.25 for attorney fees under the promissory note is therefore reversed.

Second, the Cuevases contend the loans Mr. Montoya made to the Cuevases violate the Consumer Protection Act. RCW 19.52.036 declares that entering or transacting a usurious contract is an unfair trade or practice for the purpose of application of the Consumer Protection Act found in RCW 19.86.

To make out a private claim under the Consumer Protection Act, the plaintiff ordinarily must show five essential elements: (1) the act or practice is unfair or deceptive; (2) it occurred in trade or commerce; (3) the act affected the public interest; (4) it resulted in injury to plaintiff's business or property; and (5) there was a causal link between the unfair or deceptive act and the injury suffered.

However, when usury has been shown, the plaintiff need not show the first two elements of a private claim under the Consumer Protection Act because the usury statute expressly declares the Consumer Protection Act is violated by entry into a usurious contract.

The Cuevases still must prove the last three elements of a private cause of action. Here, the Cuevases showed injury to their property—the unlawful interest is a financial injury. The usurious loan terms were the cause of the Cuevases' financial injury. The public interest requirement may be satisfied per se by showing that a statute has been violated which contains a specific legislative declaration of public impact. The usury statute, RCW 19.52.005, contains a declaration of policy which meets the per se public interest requirement:

> RCW 19.52.005, 19.52.020, 19.52.030, 19.52.032, 19.52.034, and 19.52.036 are enacted in order to protect the residents of this state from debts bearing burdensome interest rates; and in order to better effect the policy of this state to use this state's policies and courts to govern the affairs of our residents and the state; and in recognition of the duty to protect our citizens from oppression generally.

Thus, the Cuevases have shown all five elements of a private consumer protection action.

The Consumer Protection Act provides penalties including recovery of actual damages, costs of the suit including reasonable attorney fees and discretionary triple damages not to exceed the lesser of $10,000 or three times the actual damages sustained. RCW 19.86.090. In 1983, the limit on treble damages was increased from $1,000 to $10,000; *Swain v. Colton,* 44 Wash.App. 204, 206, 721 P.2d 990 (1986) held the amendment applied prospectively only. The effective date of the amendment was July 24, 1983. Laws of 1983, ch. 288, § 3, at 1403.

Mr. Montoya made the $3,000 loan to the Cuevases on January 11, 1982, and the $8,300 loan on April 1, 1983. Therefore, the preamendment $1,000 limit on treble damages is applicable to these loans.

Given our holding that the loans made by Mr. Montoya are usurious, the Consumer Protection Act is applicable. On remand, damages, attorney fees and costs should be awarded to the Cuevases under the Consumer Protection Act.

* * *

Accordingly, we reverse the trial court judgments in favor of Mr. Montoya. We hold the promissory notes violated the usury laws and the consumer protection statute; thus Mr. Montoya is not entitled to the $1,751.25 attorney fees previously awarded under the promissory note.

* * *

In summary, the Cuevases will be entitled to judgment against Mr. Montoya for attorney fees, costs and damages. Mr. Montoya will be entitled to judgment against the Cuevases in quantum meruit for the value of his services, except those to enforce the promissory notes and those treated as interest under the usury statute and thereby disallowed.

* * *

Notes

1. Was it ethical for Mr. Montoya to loan money to his clients? Rule 1.8 of the Model Rules of Professional Conduct says:

(a) A lawyer shall not enter into a business transaction with a client or knowingly acquire an ownership, possessory, security or other pecuniary interest adverse to a client unless:

(1) the transaction and terms on which the lawyer acquires the interest are fair and reasonable to the client and are fully disclosed and transmitted in writing to the client in a manner which can be reasonably understood by the client; and

(2) the client is given a reasonable opportunity to seek the advice of independent counsel in the transaction; and

(3) the client consents in writing thereto.

Were the terms of these loans "fair and reasonable"? Could Mr. Montoya have been subjected to disciplinary proceedings for his behavior in this case?

2. Creditors have long sought ways to restructure or add extra charges to loan transactions in order to avoid the usury laws, but few creditors would blatantly state a rate above the lawful limit. Why do you suppose Mr. Montoya did this? Was it just ignorance of the usury laws? If Mr. Montoya had gone to another lawyer who set up the transaction in this manner, would he have a claim against the other lawyer for malpractice?

3. As noted earlier, one device creditors have long used to avoid the effects of usury laws is to add on additional charges such as commissions or service charges. Courts, in turn, have typically responded skeptically to these sorts of charges, often holding them to be forms of hidden interest. In this respect, Cuevas is typical. What is the rationale for treating the $104 "setup" fee and the $742 attorney fees as "interest"? Since the stated rate already exceeded the usury limits, did it make any difference in this case? In Aetna Finance Co. v. Darwin, relied on by the court in Cuevas, the court held that a $1,000 "loan funding fee" was really a form of interest. In many states, there are now special statutes which list the types of additional fees and charges which creditors may or may not

impose. The Washington statute cited in Cuevas, for example, permits a setup charge of up to 4% of the loan or $15, whichever is smaller, for loans under $500. In these cases, the statute expressly states that the setup charge is not to be considered interest. (How did Mr. Montoya possibly hope to succeed in his argument that a $104 fee on a $3,000 loan was not interest?) See also U3C § 2.501.

4. Would the setup fee have been considered a "finance charge" under the TILA? See Reg. Z § 226.4. Are state courts bound by the TILA's definition of finance charge in their determinations of whether particular charges are "interest" under state usury laws? If not, might they look to the TILA for guidance? Are the issues the same?

5. What was the consequence to Mr. Montoya of having violated the usury laws? Penalties for usury vary widely among the states. In a few states, usury makes the entire underlying transaction void; the creditor may not even collect the principal. The Washington statute quoted in Cuevas is more typical; the creditor in most states is prohibited from collecting interest and may suffer an additional monetary penalty as well. There are other patterns. Also, in some states usury over a certain amount may be criminal. In Washington, for example, rates over 45% make a lender liable for an extortionate extension of credit, a misdemeanor. West's Rev.Code Wash.Ann 9A.82.020 (repealed effective July 1, 1995). See also U3C § 5.107. Extortion in consumer transactions is also a crime under federal law. 18 U.S.C.A. § 892.

6. The idea that a usurious loan may make the lender liable under a "little FTC" or deceptive practices statute is somewhat novel. Was the Washington court's application of this statute correct? If so, does this create a whole new line of attack on usurious loans across the country, or is there something unique about the Washington statutes? Can you think of an argument against applying a deceptive practices statute to the usury setting?

Problem 3

Lucy and Linus requested a loan of $39,500 from Ace Finance. The loan was to be used for home improvement and to purchase a pickup truck for personal use. The usury laws limited interest to 12% on loans under $50,000, but there was no limit on loans over $50,000. Ace was unwilling to loan any money to Lucy and Linus at 12%, but it did agree to lend them $51,000 at 20%. Under the terms of the loan, Ace distributed $16,000 to the truck dealer and $23,500 to the home improvement contractor. It also applied $5,000 to pay off the balance of an old loan they had with Ace, $150 for title insurance on the property put up as security, $15 for recording fees, and kept $1,020 as a 2% loan funding fee. It then gave the balance of the loan amount, $5315, to Lucy and Linus in cash. When Lucy and Linus defaulted and Ace sued on the note, usury was raised as a defense. What result?

Problem 4

In many states, corporations may not raise usury as a defense. Assume that state law sets a usury ceiling of 7% on consumer loans, and that loans to corporations are not subject to this ceiling. Florence and Elmer Allan wanted to borrow $7500 for personal purposes, but the going market rate was much higher and no one would lend to them at 7%. Ace Finance, however, told them that it would make the loan if they would incorporate. Ace referred the Allans to its attorney, Robinson, who prepared the incorporation papers. A few weeks later, the loan was made at a rate of 18%.

    (a) If the Allans are sued, may they raise usury as a defense?

    (b) Is Robinson guilty of any ethical violations? Would it make any difference if he collected a fee or salary from Ace? What if the amount of his fees were deducted from the loan proceeds?

See Allan v. M & S Mortgage Co., 138 Mich.App. 28, 359 N.W.2d 238 (1984).

UNITED KANSAS BANK & TRUST CO. v. RIXNER

Court of Appeals of Kansas, 1980.
4 Kan.App.2d 662, 610 P.2d 116, aff'd, 228 Kan. 633, 619 P.2d 1156.

MEYER, JUDGE:

This suit to recover on a promissory note was brought by the Santa Fe Trail State Bank (appellant) against the appellees Richard D. Rixner (Rixner) and Daniel S. Frackowiak (Frackowiak).

Appellees executed a promissory note in the amount of $5,039.76 to Superior Trailer Sales Co., assignor of appellant. The note evidenced a loan of $4,500.00 with a finance charge of $539.76, payable in twelve monthly installments of $419.98 each. This resulted in an annual percentage rate of 21.45%.

Rixner and Frackowiak defaulted and appellant sued on the note. The agreement executed in conjunction with the note contained a form clause which stated that the loan was subject to the Uniform Consumer Credit Code (UCCC). Frackowiak filed a counter-claim alleging violations of the UCCC, specifically charging an interest rate over the maximum limit and making a "supervised loan" when the lender was not qualified as a "supervised lender." Frackowiak filed a motion for summary judgment in which defendant Rixner joined. Summary judgment was granted in favor of Frackowiak and Rixner. The judgment voided the agreement and awarded attorney fees to Frackowiak's attorney. The court, however, declined to impose any penalty or to award a refund of payments made, and also declined to award attorney fees to Rixner's attorney.

*   *   *

Appellant next complains that the court erred in granting summary judgment.

The first question which must be determined is whether the UCCC applies to the transaction. The appellant argues that the clause in the contract which stated, "[t]his loan is subject to the provisions of sections 1 through 131 of the Kansas Uniform Consumer Credit Code applying to consumer loans," was not binding.

The loan was admittedly taken for a business purpose and, therefore, would not qualify as a consumer loan under K.S.A. 16a–1–301(14) (a)(ii). Parties can contract, however, to have their transaction subject to the UCCC. If they so contract, the action is a consumer credit transaction for the purposes of K.S.A. 16a–1–101 through 16a–9–102 of the act.

* * *

We also conclude that the trial court was correct in its conclusions of law that the transaction violated the UCCC provision regarding supervised loans and an interest rate above the maximum credit rate ceiling.

Under K.S.A. 16a–1–301(40), a "supervised loan" means a consumer loan in which the rate of the finance charge, calculated according to the actuarial method, exceeds twelve percent (12%) per year. K.S.A. 16a–2–301 provides that:

> "Unless a person is a supervised financial organization or has first obtained a license from the administrator authorizing him to make supervised loans, he shall not engage in the business of
>
> (1) making supervised loans; or
>
> (2) taking assignments of and undertaking direct collection of payments from or enforcement of rights against debtors arising from supervised loans * * *."

K.S.A. 16a–5–201(2) provides:

> "If a creditor has violated the provisions of this act applying to authority to make supervised loans (section 16a–2–301), the loan is void and the consumer is not obligated to pay either the amount financed or finance charge. If he has paid any part of the amount financed or of the finance charge, he has a right to recover the payment from the person violating this act or from an assignee of that person's rights who undertakes direct collection of payments or enforcement of rights arising from the debt."

Since the annual percentage rate of 21.45 percent was over 12 percent per year, the creditor was making a "supervised loan" and, therefore, was required to be licensed as a supervised lender. Since he was not licensed, he violated K.S.A. 16a–2–301 and became subject to the penalty provision under K.S.A. 16a–5–201(2). Therefore, the loan is void and the appellees have a right to recover the $419.98 payment made to appellant.

* * *

Further, there was a violation of K.S.A.1979 Supp. 16a–2–401. K.S.A.1979 Supp. 16a–2–401(1) sets the maximum limit for consumer loans. It provides:

> "With respect to a consumer loan, including a loan pursuant to open end credit, a lender may contract for and receive a finance charge, calculated according to the actuarial method, not exceeding eighteen percent (18%) per year on the unpaid balances of the amount financed not exceeding one thousand dollars ($1,000) and fourteen and

forty-five hundredths percent (14.45%) per year on that portion of the unpaid balance in excess of one thousand dollars ($1,000)."

Since the lender in this case was not a supervised lender, he would not qualify for the rates set out in subsection (2).

The annual percentage rate of 21.45% on the balance of $4,500.00 exceeded the statutory maximum and, therefore, was in violation of said section.

* * *

Rixner cross-appeals from the trial court's refusal to consider his motion for attorney fees. The statute which awards attorney fees (K.S.A. 16a–5–201[8]) is also mandatory.

> "In an action in which it is found that a creditor has violated any provision of sections 1 through 131 [16a–1–101 through 16a–9–102] of this act, the court *shall* award to the consumer the costs of the action and to his attorneys their reasonable fees." (Emphasis added.)

It may well be that the trial court may find that the attorney for Rixner performed less work than did the attorney for Frackowiak, and, therefore, is not entitled to as large a fee. Nevertheless, it is incumbent upon the trial court to receive evidence as to Rixner's attorney's work in relation to this case and to grant a fee for the proper worth of those services.

The motion to tax attorney fees as costs on appeal filed by the attorney for Frackowiak is considered, and said attorney is awarded the sum of $750.00 for his services on appeal, same to be paid by appellant.

Affirmed in part; reversed in part; and remanded for further proceedings in harmony with this opinion.

Notes

1. Note that the Kansas penalty provision (§ 5–210(2)) is a non-uniform provision which is considerably more favorable to the aggrieved consumer than is the uniform provision.

2. The basic structure of the statute (and therefore the industry) is typical, however, in that it divides the lending industry into different "segments" of the industry. In this instance, the "segments" are "supervised lenders" and unsupervised lenders, each of which has its own maximum interest rate limits. A lender therefore needs to compete only with other lenders within its own segment, and inter-segment competition is rare.

3. Under the U3C, the segmentation of the lender market is limited. It was great step forward from the prior law in which that same industry was divided into small loan companies, industrial loan companies, credit unions, savings and loan associations, savings banks, commercial banks, "small, small loan companies," pawnbrokers, etc., *each* of which could have its own set of different interest rate ceilings, and therefore its own market segment.

4. For a case in which a borrower who paid more than 10% interest to a lender "not licensed to make supervised loans" under the U3C, and did not obtain a summary judgment, see Rea v. Wichita Mortgage Co., 747 F.2d 567 (10th Cir 1984). The lender asserted that it had relied on the erroneous advice of legal counsel and believed that it did not need a license to make supervised loans. The appellate court held that such assertions raised issues of fact concerning the "bona fide error defense," and could not be decided on summary judgment.

2. REGULATION OF SELLER CREDIT

Most early time-price cases involved the sale of land. Only two parties, the seller and buyer, were involved, and the credit terms rarely involved installment credit as we know it today. In this setting, the doctrine, although often criticized for its artificial distinctions, worked reasonably well. That is, it was usually easy to tell whether a particular transaction was a loan of money or a sale of property.

However, most modern seller credit transactions involve sales of goods, either through closed-end or open-end credit plans. The closed-end transactions were litigated first, and the time-price doctrine applied without much analysis, see e.g., Morris v. Capitol Furniture and Appliance Co., 280 A.2d 775 (D.C.App.1971), except for a celebrated Arkansas case, Hare v. General Contract Purchase Corp., 220 Ark. 601, 249 S.W.2d 973 (1952).

The open-end credit sales transaction posed a greater intellectual challenge to courts in applying the time-price doctrine to a sale in which there was no stated, or even calculable, "time price." After all, the "credit buyer" who used a credit card could pay in full during the "free ride" period, and pay only the "cash price." Alternatively, the credit card buyer could stretch out the payments almost indefinitely by making new purchases and small payments, and, eventually pay more than double the cash price. The courts, however, ignored the intellectual challenge and applied the time price doctrine without analysis, see, e.g., Kass v. Garfinckel, 299 A.2d 542 (D.C.App.1973), except (again) in Arkansas. Sloan v. Sears, Roebuck and Co., 228 Ark. 464, 308 S.W.2d 802 (1957).

When the Nebraska Supreme Court, in Lloyd v. Gutgsell, 175 Neb. 775, 124 N.W.2d 198 (1963), ruled that the state's constitutional usury limit could not be avoided by use of the time-price doctrine, a change in the state constitutional provision was required, and was made.

A similar pronouncement by the Tennessee Supreme Court caused consternation in that state. In Cumberland Capital Corp. v. Patty, 556 S.W.2d 516 (Tenn.1977), the court ruled that the state constitution's "ten percent" meant simple interest, not an add-on or discount computation, and state laws that permitted such computations were declared unconstitutional. Again, a state constitutional amendment quickly followed.

The time-price doctrine is still alive and well in many jurisdictions, however. See, e.g., Foreign Commerce, Inc. v. Tonn, 600 F.Supp. 133 (D.V.I.1984), for a recent successful use of this defense to a usury claim.

The Displacement of the Time–Price Doctrine—A Note on Retail Installment Sales Acts

The judicially-created time-price doctrine has not been judicially struck down in most jurisdictions. However, it does leave a problem. Where the doctrine is accepted, there is no limitation on the rate or amount which a credit seller may impose for selling on time. The resolution of that problem was the wholesale enactment of Retail Installment Sales Acts (RISA's) by states during the 1940's and 1950's. These statutes are the de facto replacement of the time price doctrine, which operates now only in the interstices of those statutes. Some RISA's cover only motor vehicles sales, but most cover sales of all goods. Some cover only the traditional installment sale, but most now cover revolving charge accounts of merchants, and many also cover bank revolving charge accounts. Some cover all purchases, but most are limited to consumer purchases. The current status of state legislation may be found in the CCH Consumer Credit Guide, Compilation of State Laws. For an earlier review of their origins, see B. Curran, Trends in Consumer Credit Legislation 83, 92–123, 254–55 (1965). The U3C retains much of the coverage of the old RISAs, including the regulation of rates in credit sales.

IN RE STEWART

United States Bankruptcy Court, E.D. Pennsylvania, 1988.
93 B.R. 878.

SCHOLL, BANKRUPTCY JUDGE.

A. INTRODUCTION

The instant little adversarial proceeding presents to us a glimpse of the dark side of the marketplace, revealing that, as in the 1960's, the poor may still pay far more for everyday consumer goods than more affluent members of the community. See D. CAPLOVITZ, THE POOR PAY MORE, 81–104 (1967); and W. MAGNUSON & J. CARPER, THE DARK SIDE OF THE MARKETPLACE, 32–41, 75–76, 118–20 (1968). As described in those documentaries, describing the lot of low-income consumers in the 1960's, we find that merchants who charge—and get—exorbitant prices for consumer goods and finance companies which protect them through probable feigned innocence of the merchants' activities are alive and well in the late 1980's. It also exemplifies that consumer protection legislation of the 1970's is available to protect disadvantaged consumers from some of the practices recognized as unfair in the 1960's, but that new devices contrived by ghetto merchants to circumvent such remedial legislature require a liberal interpretation of such legislation to blunt such exploitation.

* * *

C. FINDINGS OF FACT

1. In early February, 1987, the Debtor called the Seller on the telephone in response to an advertising circular concerning availability of appliances and furniture on credit at the address of a store known as "M. London," located at 500 West Girard Avenue in a low-income neighborhood of Philadelphia.

2. The Debtor, as mentioned above, an elderly part-time minister with limited income, informed the Seller via the telephone that he was interested in purchasing a 25–inch color TV and a VCR on credit. The Seller proceeded to elicit from him all of the information necessary to fill out a credit application in the telephone conversation.

3. Several days later, on February 27, 1987, the Seller went to the home of the Debtor and his wife with a blank two-page installment sale contract form provided by the Finance Company and bearing its name. The Finance Company had, in conversations with the Seller, already orally approved the Debtor's credit application as the result of its oral review of the contract terms with the Seller. However, it indicated that it was concerned only with whether the Debtor was a good credit risk for the amount of credit in the contract, not whether the prices charged for the goods purchased were reasonable.

4. The Debtor's elderly wife, being homebound, signed the blank contract at the home. The Seller then drove the Debtor to the M. London store where the Debtor picked out the particular TV and VCR that he desired to purchase. Thereafter, the Seller completed the installment sale contract, and it was then signed by him and the Debtor.

5. Prior to the execution of the contract, the Seller never quoted Plaintiff any prices for the TV and VCR, and none of the items in the M. London showroom had price tags. However, as the Seller admitted, M. London would have charged any customer only $867.00 for the TV and VCR in issue, and the Seller paid M. London only $867.00 for the items that he sold to the Debtor.

6. The Seller testified that he was provided with a rent-free office at the M. London store, shared a telephone with the store, sold only items which M. London carried, and sold these items only on credit. Also, the store provided free delivery and installation services to the Seller's customers as well as its own.

7. The contract disclosed a cash sale price of $2,090.00, and recited that the Debtor had made a downpayment of $190.00. In fact, the Debtor made no such downpayment and the total price, which also included a $19.95 TV antenna, was $1,900.00. After addition of $117.90 for credit life and disability insurance, the total sum of $2,017.90 was financed at an annual percentage rate (hereinafter "APR") disclosed as

eighteen (18%) percent per year, over 36 months, resulting in a disclosed finance charge of $607.94. With respect to payment terms, the contract called for 36 payments of $72.94 each, or total payments of $2,625.84.

8. As was contemplated by the contract form and prearranged by those parties, the Seller immediately thereafter assigned the contract to the Finance Company.

* * *

10. The Debtor reasonably concluded that he was dealing directly with the M. London store and he had no knowledge that M. London was selling these items at retail for only $867.00. He recognized that the prices which he paid under the contract were very high, but he believed that his only option was to purchase similar items from a "rent-to-own" company, whose prices he had discovered were even higher than those which he agreed to pay to the Seller pursuant to the instant contract.

11. The Debtor, though intending to pay for these items per the contract, had made only six (6) payments on the contract, for a total of $437.64, when he encountered financial difficulties. He has retained the goods, subject to a purchase money security interest in favor of the Finance Company. Neither the Finance Company nor the Debtor, on its behalf, has filed a Proof of Claim in the Debtor's Chapter 13 case.

D. Conclusions of Law

1. *A "Hidden Finance Charge" of $1,344.01 was Imposed Upon the Debtor in the Instant Transaction*

The sole issue raised in the Debtor's original Complaint and the centerpiece of all of the claims articulated in his Amended Complaint is the contention that the "real" cash price in the transaction was $867.00, not $1,900.00 as disclosed in the contract. Under the GSISA [Pennsylvania Goods and Services Installment Sales Act], which the parties do not dispute applies to this transaction, the maximum permissible finance charge is simple interest, or interest expressed as an annual percentage rate (hereinafter "APR") of eighteen (18%) percent per annum. On an obligation of $867.00, paid over 36 months, the maximum permissible finance charge under 69 P.S. § 1501(a) would be $262.40. The maximum permissible charge of an obligation in the amount of $984.90, the sum of $867.00 and the $117.90 for credit life and disability insurance included in the contract in issue, would be $296.95.

By way of contrast, the Debtor here was charged a disclosed finance charge of $607.94. This charge was imposed by calculating the amount financed as $2,017.90. We believe that the facts establish that the difference between the articulated unpaid balance of the cash price ($1,900.00) and the "real" cash price ($867.00) was a $1,033.00 "hidden" finance charge. The actual finance charge was therefore $607.94 plus $1,033.00 or $1,640.94, an increment of $1,343.99 over $296.25, the actual maximum permissible finance charge under 69 P.S. § 1501(a).

The Finance Company contends that these additional charges to the Debtor were not "hidden." It argues that the total figure of $1,900.00, further increased by the erroneous statements that the cash price was $2,190.00 and that the Debtor made a $190.00 downpayment, are clearly stated on the contract. The Debtor was not, argues the Finance Company, overcharged or at least overcharged unwittingly. Even if the price was unreasonably high, the Debtor was merely paying a sum of which he was well aware and voluntarily agreed to pay for the TV and the VCR.

Further, the Finance company argues that the Debtor is requesting this court to regulate the price that a retailer may charge to a customer. If the customer agrees, as did the Debtor here, the Finance Company contends that there should be no limits on what a retailer may charge.

* * *

The flaw in the Finance company's reasoning is failing to recognize that consumer protection laws must be read with a built-in agenda of protecting the unwary and the disadvantaged consumer from entering into transactions which the legislation has deemed constitute over-reaching and hence prohibiting certain practices as a matter of public policy. Such legislation was not, generally, drafted to protect lenders, who have far more resources and leverage in controlling the terms of the marketplace than do low-income consumers. Thus, the grotesque but we suspect all too common pricing scheme of the Seller exemplified by the facts of this case must be approached from the vantage point of not what a consumer residing in an inner-city neighborhood, in desperation due to lack of alternatives, might be willing to pay for a small share of "the good life," but what the legislature has deemed is the maximum that can be charged to any consumer in such a transaction and no more.

The Debtor is not arguing that the price should be regulated. The Seller has candidly told us that the M. London store, itself a ghetto merchant unlikely to be a fertile place for bargains, was selling the items purchased by the Debtor for an $867.00 retail price. The only difference between a consumer's dealing with M. London and the same consumer's dealing with the Seller here is that the latter provided convenient credit terms. It is therefore clear, under these facts, that the additional price charged by the Seller over that charged for the same goods by M. London is, in actuality, a finance charge.

Finally, we can shed no tears for the Finance Company. Were it not for the "hear no evil, see no evil" attitude of the Finance Company, which supplied forms and, in one sense, provided credit directly to the Debtor through the mere medium of the Seller as its agent, the scheme of the Seller could not have been successfully financed. In light of the facts that the Seller used the Finance Company's forms and was able to get it to approve credit in this transaction with a mere telephone call, it is obvious that the Seller and Finance Company deal extensively with one another. We can therefore safely assume that the figurative slap on the wrist of this decision has been more than offset by a number of low-income consumers who have ignorantly plodded their way through payment of almost $3,000.00 for goods which a higher-income consumer could purchase at less than a quarter of this sum.

Our conclusion that the hidden finance charge imposed here is impermissible has been roundly supported by the small body of law which has developed when low-income consumers have found their way to legal help able to scratch beneath the surface of an opportunistic but apparently legal transaction and present the difficult proof that the "real" value of a product is far less than the articulated sale price, and that the price is inflated solely as a charge for the seller's liberal credit policies and hence is in fact a cost of credit.

[The court then discussed a series of cases which consider the "hidden finance charge" issue under TILA, including Yazzie v. Reynolds, supra at Chapter 2, Section B.5., and cases discussed therein. It concluded this sale included a hidden finance charge under TILA criteria.]

We therefore have no difficulty in concluding that at least $1,343.99 of "hidden" finance charges were imposed upon the Debtor in this transaction. The extensive overreaching presented by this transaction, exemplifying a target of the works of Caplovitz and Magnuson and Carper, can thus be translated into a series of illegal as well as unconscionable acts.

The conclusion that a "hidden finance charge" exists which was not disclosed as such opens a Pandora's box of claims, most of which are aptly raised by the Debtor in the Amended Complaint in the proceeding in issue. *Mourning,* the health spa cases, and the auto sales cases cited above were all TILA cases. The gross mis-statement of the amount financed and the finance charge is, under the direct authority of many of those cases, clearly a violation of the TILA giving rise to a statutory penalty of $1,000.00. The APR computed on the "true" basis of a transaction reflecting a finance charge of $1,640.94 and an amount financed of $984.90, computes to an APR of over eighty (80%) percent in the transaction rather than the eighteen (18%) percent APR disclosed. Furthermore, the failure to disclose an excess finance charge of $1,343.99 which we hold was actually imposed in the transaction gives rise to an additional claim for actual damages in that amount under 15 U.S.C. § 1640(a)(1). Thus, TILA liability of $2,343.99 attaches. In addition, costs and attorney's fees must be provided to the Debtor's counsel pursuant to 15 U.S.C. § 1640(a)(3).

With respect to the GSISA, the actual "service charge" is clearly in excess of the eighteen (18%) percent APR maximum rate allowed in that statute. Although the Pennsylvania consumer credit laws are notable for their absence of remedies, the GSISA does contain a provision barring collection of any finance charges imposed in the transaction if that Act has been violated in the transaction. 69 P.S.

§ 2202. However, it is difficult to measure the damages under § 2202, since this would oblige us to determine how much of the $437.64 paid by the Debtor was attributable to finance charges. We believe that the most reasonable way to determine this is to divide the actual finance charges ($1,640.94) by the total of payments ($2,625.24) to determine the percentage of the payments made which was actually attributable to finance charges (62.53 percent), and multiply this percentage by the payments made ($437.64). The resulting figure is $273.66.

* * *

From the foregoing discussion, it can clearly be seen that the damages for which the Seller would otherwise be liable would greatly exceed the $2,500.00 which he wisely agreed to pay to the Debtor in satisfaction of all of the liability which would otherwise attach.

However, this resolution does not impact on the liability of the Finance Company. The settlement of the Debtor's claim against the Finance Company, even assuming that it is a joint tort-feasor with the Seller, does not, in the absence of a release specifically so providing, discharge the Finance Company, but merely reduces the Debtor's claim against it in the amount of the consideration of $2,500.00 paid by the Seller. * * *

* * *

ORDER

AND NOW, this 8th day of December, 1988, after a trial of this proceeding on June 23, 1988, and upon consideration of the submissions of the parties thereafter, it is hereby ORDERED as follows:

1. Judgment is entered in favor of the Plaintiff, ALFRED STEWART, and against the Defendant, LOUIS ABRAHAMSEN, t/a CENTURY CARPET & CONTRACTORS, in the amount of $6,649.62. However, this judgment will be satisfied upon the payment of $2,500.00 by the said Defendant to the Standing Chapter Trustee in accordance with the parties' Stipulation of October 31, 1988.

Notes

1. Once a state has enacted a Retail Installment Sales Act (RISA), the credit seller's credit charges are limited by the RISA. The time-price doctrine may protect the credit seller from usury statutes, but RISAs are drafted without using the concept of usury, and do define "consumer credit sale" so as to include such transactions. See, e.g., U3C § 1.301(12).

2. The U3C interest rate limits are stated in U3C §§ 2.201 (closed-end) and 2.202 (open-end). They are separate and distinct from the U3C limits on lender credit, so that sales credit and loan credit (§ 2.401(1)) and supervised loan credit (§ 2.401(2)) are still three different "market segments", even under the U3C. Can the preservation of this distinction be defended?

Problem 5

Suppose Mr. Stewart and the M. London store were in a U3C state, and Seller and Mr. Stewart carried out a transaction identical to the one in the preceding case. Would Seller have violated the U3C § 2.201 interest rate regulations? Useful definitions to analyze include "consumer credit sale" (§ 1.301(12)), "finance charge" (§ 1.301(20)) and "amount financed" (§ 1.301(5)). If these definitions are the same as the definitions in TILA, then the analysis is straightforward and has already been done twice: once in Chapter 2 (*Yazzie*) and once in Chapter 11 (*Stewart*). And, no one would confuse the public by proposing definitions different from those in TILA, would they?

Incidentally, once you have figured out the dollar amounts of the amount financed and finance charge, how difficult is it to determine whether the rate ceilings in § 2.201 are violated or not?

Problem 6

Fleur D. Lee lives in a state which has enacted the U3C. As it is allowed to do under § 2.202, the Cardinal Bank charges 2% a month (24% APR) on all MasterCard sales balances under $500. Fleur bought a compact disc player from Wheaton Plaza Hi Fi for a total price of $300.46, and charged it on her Cardinal Bank MasterCard. However, as is typical in these types of credit card plans, the bank paid Wheaton only $279.42 for the charge slip. The 7% reduction is a "merchant discount" charged by the bank to cover its costs of handling the paperwork, advancing credit to the merchant, and collecting from the cardholder. Has Cardinal violated the U3C rate ceilings by imposing this merchant discount? See §§ 1.301(20) and 2.202. If so, what is Fleur's remedy? See U3C § 5.201(2), (3), (7), and (8). Are these provisions likely to induce test litigation? Would you represent Fleur on a contingent fee basis?

Problem 7

Piggy Bank, which does business in a U3C state, offers VISA cards to its customers. It is concerned that its VISA revenues are not covering the expenses of operating the program. It cannot raise its rates because they are already at the statutory ceiling. The bank vice president has asked you whether it can legally do any of the following things:

(a) Eliminate the free ride period so that all credit card purchases would accrue finance charges from the date of the transaction;

(b) Impose a minimum 50 cent monthly charge on all accounts which were used during the preceding billing period, whether or not the balance was paid off at the first billing (see U3C §§ 2.202, 2.401, 1.301(12) and (15));

(c) Impose a flat $15 annual membership fee on all cardholders. See U3C § 2.501; Key v. Worthen Bank & Trust Co., 260 Ark.

725, 543 S.W.2d 496 (1976). Is there any difference between an annual membership fee and a 50 cent monthly minimum charge?

Notes

Most Retail Installment Sales Acts (RISAs) have displaced the time price doctrine where they are applicable, and most states have enacted RISAs. So, the time-price doctrine is dead, right? Before jumping to that conclusion, you should be aware that most RISAs do not apply to credit sales of realty, and some do not cover seller credit card and other open-end credit transactions. Thus, as the following case shows, this particular form of metaphysics sometimes arises still.

BOERNER v. COLWELL CO.

Supreme Court of California, 1978.
21 Cal.3d 37, 145 Cal.Rptr. 380, 577 P.2d 200.

MANUEL, JUSTICE.

Plaintiff Florentine Boerner and eight other named plaintiffs commenced this class action against defendant The Colwell Company (Colwell), alleging in substance that certain transactions involving its purchase of installment contracts for the construction of vacation homes constituted usurious loans to the purchasers of such homes (including plaintiffs) and seeking appropriate equitable and monetary relief. Pursuant to stipulation of the parties the cause was bifurcated for trial, the issue of defendant's liability to be tried first to the court sitting without a jury, and certain other issues, including those relating to the class action aspects of the matter, to be reserved for any necessary subsequent proceedings. The trial court, following trial of the liability issue, entered judgment for defendant Colwell, finding and concluding in essence that the contracts constituted bona fide credit sales from the building contractors to the purchasers followed by valid assignments to Colwell and that the transactions as a whole did not constitute loans subject to the usury laws. Plaintiffs appeal from the judgment.

I

The evidence, which is essentially uncontradicted, established the following: Colwell is a mortgage banking firm. Since 1961 it has had an installment contract department engaged in the purchase of installment contracts for the sale of mobile homes, vacation homes, and home improvements. Transactions in the latter two categories are handled in essentially the same fashion. When contacted by a builder interested in arranging for the purchase of its contracts, and when satisfied with the builder's qualifications and general business reputation, Colwell and the builder sign an agreement detailing the conditions on which the builder's contracts will be accepted for purchase. Colwell then provides the builder with a series of forms—an individual set of which includes a credit application, a lien contract and deed of trust, and a truth-in-lending disclosure statement. It also advises the builder of the finance charge rate to be included in a contract if it is to be accepted for assignment.

When a builder using the Colwell service enters into a vacation home construction contract with a landowner wishing financing, the forms provided by Colwell are filled out and executed by both parties to the contract. These forms, along with the construction contract and the plans and specifications, are submitted to Colwell, which then undertakes a credit check, makes a "desk appraisal" of the value of the real property including the contemplated improvements, and orders a preliminary title report. If these investigations yield results acceptable to Colwell, it informs the builder and the landowner that it has accepted the contract for purchase and records the assigned lien contract and deed of trust. The price paid is the cash price reflected in the construction contract less a small charge for the builder's use of Colwell's "voucher system," a system developed by it to avoid mechanic's liens and disputes over payment. The buyer, however, at this point becomes bound to pay Colwell the deferred purchase price (cash price plus finance charge), in monthly installments as reflected in the assigned lien contract—payment being secured by means of the assigned trust deed.

The evidence further showed that plaintiff Boerner and her husband (now deceased) contracted with FWF Construction Company for the construction of a vacation home on their property; that the eight other named plaintiffs (hereinafter the Wards) contracted with Nordic Mountain Homes for the construction of a vacation home on property which they owned jointly; that in each case the buyer desired financing and requested that the builder arrange it if possible; that in each case the builder arranged to have the construction financed by defendant Colwell in accordance with the procedure outlined above; and that in each case the annual percentage rate payable under the assigned lien contract and deed of trust was in excess of 10 percent.

On the basis of these facts the trial court found and concluded that the transactions taking place between plaintiffs and their respective builders were bona fide credit sales and "not parts of loan transactions clothed in the form of credit sales"—and that the respective assignments of the builder's rights to Colwell were "an assignment of rights under a credit sale and were not loans by [Colwell] in the form of assignments." Accordingly, judgment on the complaint was entered for defendant Colwell.

II

* * *

Although the constitutional and statutory provisions dealing with usury speak only in terms of a "loan" or a "forbearance" of money or other things of value, the courts, alert to the resourcefulness of some lenders in fashioning transactions designed to evade the usury law, have looked to the substance rather than the form of such transactions in assessing their effect and validity, and in many cases have struck down as usurious arrangements bearing little facial resemblance to what is normally thought of as a "loan" or a "forbearance" of money. In all such cases the issue is whether or not the bargain of the parties, assessed in light of all the circumstances and with a view to substance rather than form, has as its true object the hire of money at an excessive rate of interest. The existence of the requisite intent is always a question of fact.

One area of great concern in this respect—to the commentators as well as to the courts—has been that of credit sales. It has long been the law in this jurisdiction, as well as in the vast majority of other jurisdictions, that a bona fide credit sale is not subject to the usury law because it does not involve a "loan" or "forbearance" of money or other things of value.

* * *

We do not, however, understand plaintiffs to here mount a broadside attack upon the so-called time-price doctrine as an "exception" to the laws *governing* usury. Their position, as we perceive it, is simply that granting the nonapplicability of usury laws to bona fide credit sales, the transactions here in question—viewed from the standpoint of substance rather than form—must nevertheless be held to be usurious loans. We proceed to an examination of this contention.

III

* * *

Plaintiffs, in their effort to demonstrate error in the trial court's finding that bona fide credit sales rather than usurious loans were here involved, direct our attention to a number of aspects of the subject transactions which in their view compel a contrary determination. Thus they urge that here there was no "transfer of * * * property * * * for a price" because at the time of the subject transaction the "property" in question (i.e., a completed vacation home) was not in existence. It is clear, however, that contracts of the type here in question—calling for the provision of materials and labor in the construction of specified improvements to real property—result in a transfer of "property" within the meaning of the credit-sale doctrine. Equally without significance is the fact that one of the documents executed by the parties, namely the construction contract, failed to establish and set forth separately stated cash and credit prices; our consideration of the parties' transactions from the standpoint of substance rather than form requires that we consider together all of the documents which they executed to memorialize them, and both the lien contract/deed of trust and the truth-in-lending disclosure statement clearly indicate both the cash and credit prices. Similarly, the fact that the parties, in several of the documents generated by the transactions—notably the credit applications and various letters written by Colwell—referred to them as "loans" is not a matter to be viewed as dispositive if, in light of all of the other circumstances, it appears that the substance of the bargain was otherwise. By the same token the statement of finance rates and charges in terms of a percentage of cash price is not necessarily indicative of a "loan" at "interest."

* * *

We are thus brought to what we deem to be the most troublesome aspect of the subject transactions from the point of view of assessing their true substance: the role of the third-party financing institution. If it be granted—as we think it must—that these transactions would be regarded as bona fide credit sales had there been no assignment of the contracts from the respective builders to Colwell, must this characterization be altered in light of the assignments and the circumstances out of which they arose?

We think it clear from our *Morgan* decision that the fact of assignment *in and of itself* has no significant effect on the characterization of the transaction according to its substance, for that case like *this one* involved the *assignment* of a credit sale contract for the construction of a residence from the builder to a financing institution. There, however, our opinion reflects no significant involvement of the financing institution in the development and consummation of the bargain between the buyer and the builder, and the only indication relating to temporal sequence is our observation that the assignment occurred "[w]ithin three months thereafter. * * *" (69 Cal.2d at p. 886, 73 Cal.Rptr. 398, 447 P.2d 638.) Here, on the other hand, the financing institution occupied a central position in shaping the transactions from the outset. The buyers having determined that they would go forward with the contemplated construction of their vacation homes only if financing could be obtained, the builders set in motion a procedure whereby, in accordance with prior arrangements made by them with Colwell, the feasibility of financing *by Colwell* could be determined. Under this procedure the parties were supplied with forms developed and supplied *by Colwell* which essentially set forth the terms under which *Colwell,* through the device of contemporaneous assignment at a prearranged discount, would agree to finance the contemplated purchase and sale. Included among these terms was the finance charge to be paid by the buyers. *Colwell,* not the builders, passed upon the question of the buyer's credit reliability, and only when *it* determined that such credit reliability was acceptable *to it* did it agree to participate in the transactions as the financing agent.

* * *

The question before us, therefore, resolves itself to this: Does the mere participation by a nonexempt financing institution in a transaction such as that before us—no matter how well-intentioned and no matter how fully disclosed to the contracting parties—operate to convert what would otherwise be regarded as a bona fide credit sale (such as, for example, in the case where the builder is able to finance the sale itself without institutional assistance) into a "loan" subject to the usury laws?

Under the law of this and the significant majority of other jurisdictions the answer is clearly no.

* * *

We conclude that the participation by Colwell in the shaping of the contracting parties' bargain—in the manner and mode revealed by this record—does not operate to convert the resulting transactions, including the contemplated assignment, into usurious loans. While the relative "closeness" of the relationship between the seller and the financing institution may have a significant effect on whether the latter's rights are to be considered subject to the defenses and claims of the purchasers, we hold that it is without significance in itself in the determination whether the subject transactions, considered from the point of view of substance rather than form, are to be characterized as usurious loans rather than bona fide credit sales.

* * * In any event, it is our view that the instrument of the usury laws has no place in the field of bona fide credit sale financing, and that its use must be limited to those cases in which the record clearly reveals that the substantial intent of the parties was to effect the hire of money at an excessive rate of interest rather than to finance a bona fide sale of property. This is not such a case.

The judgment is affirmed.

TOBRINER, CLARK and RICHARDSON, JJ., concur.

MOSK, JUSTICE, dissenting.

I dissent.

* * *

All of the facts in this case indicate that the transactions were loans, not credit sales. Thus: the builders informed plaintiffs that construction of the vacation homes was contingent upon plaintiffs' obtaining financing; the builders did not offer to finance the construction, or to extend credit to plaintiffs; they agreed to build the homes only if plaintiffs could provide the necessary funds; to this end, the builders put plaintiffs in contact with defendant; plaintiffs applied for credit to defendant, not to the builders, and it was defendant who passed upon plaintiffs' credit and determined whether or not to finance the construction on their behalf; defendant supplied the builders with the forms to be used in entering into credit sales of materials and labor to plaintiffs; defendant dictated the finance charge which the builders must levy if defendant were to purchase the contracts; defendant had no property or services to sell; its sole function was to furnish the money, without which the builders would not commence the construction called for by the contracts; upon assignment of the contracts to defendant, the builders looked to defendant for payment of the cost of construction; by the assignment, plaintiffs became bound to pay defendant the cash price of the construction, plus the finance charge.

These facts indicate that, as between plaintiffs and defendant, the transactions, in substance, created an obligation on defendant's part to pay the cash price to the builders on plaintiffs' behalf, and an obligation on plaintiffs' part to pay an equivalent sum to defendant, plus the finance charge. Therefore, the transactions were loans. A similar conclusion was reached in *National Bank of Commerce of Seattle v. Thomsen* (1972) 80 Wash.2d 406, 495 P.2d 332, wherein the court stated (at p. 338): "It is correct that one who sells goods or services on credit is not a lender of money. But a third party who pays the seller on behalf of the purchaser is, insofar as his relations with the purchaser are concerned, a lender of money. In a case such as this, where the purchase is financed from the beginning, there is never a true *conditional* sale. The sale is complete as far as the vendor is concerned. He does not extend credit to the purchaser; rather, he is paid in full at the time of purchase. The 'conditional sale contract' is then but a security device to protect the party who finances the purchase." (Italics in original.)

* * * [T]he evidence in this case is subject to only one reasonable inference, *viz.:* the transactions in question were loans, not credit sales. It follows that the "finance charge" is interest. Since that interest in each of transactions exceeds 10 percent per annum, it is usurious.

*   *   *

Notes

1. Under the time-price doctrine, the difference between the cost if you pay cash and the cost if you buy on credit is not "interest" and therefore is not subject to laws setting ceilings on interest rates. Does that sound like advanced metaphysics? The explanation is more economic than legal. Companies named Singer and Ford wanted mass markets for relatively expensive products. Merchant credit was needed and could not be provided at 6% simple interest, the typical rate at the time. It was also believed that merchants, unlike bankers and other lenders, were amateurs at credit transactions and did not need regulation. Which, if any, of these arguments do you find persuasive?

2. Which opinion do you think is more persuasive? Was the transaction in Boerner a loan or a sale? How can you tell? Note how the way the court framed the issue seemed to lead it to its conclusion: Since the deal would clearly be a sale if the builder had extended credit itself, obviously an assignment to, or "mere participation" by, a lender would not make it a loan. But can't that argument be worked both ways? What if the buyers had gone to Colwell and borrowed the money directly? That would clearly be a loan. Should the result be different simply because the lender paid the loan proceeds to a third party? Does the distinction between a loan and a sale have any meaning in this setting?

3. Under the time-price doctrine, there is no limit on the rate or amount a credit seller may impose. Does this pose a problem? One resolution was the wholesale enactment of Retail Installment Sales Acts (RISAs) by the states during the 1940s and 1950s. These statutes set limits on the rates credit sellers may charge, and so in effect replaced the doctrine, at least for transactions covered by the statutes. Some RISAs

cover only motor vehicle sales, for example, but most cover sales of all goods. Most are also limited to consumer transactions. The time-price doctrine, however, continues to operate in transactions not covered by RISAs. The California RISA, known as the Unruh Act, for example, does not cover land transactions such as that involved in Boerner. Several states now have special laws which apply to certain transactions involving land. See, e.g., the Michigan Home Improvement Finance Act, Mich.Comp. Laws Ann. § 445.1101 et seq.

Problem 8

Benny Kass uses his MasterCard, issued by First Bank, to purchase goods at Garfinckel's in the District of Columbia. [D.C. has not enacted the U3C.] Since he did not pay the charges in full within the "free ride" period, First charged him 1½% a month on the outstanding balance. The D.C. usury law still had an 8% ceiling. Is the bank protected by the time-price doctrine? Would it make any difference if Benny had used Garfinckel's own card instead? Should it? Compare Kass v. Garfinckel, 299 A.2d 542 (D.C.App.1973), with Kass v. Central Charge Service, Inc., 304 A.2d 632 (D.C.App.1973). What sort of statutory solution would you recommend to avoid this problem?

SECTION C.   HIDDEN COSTS IN NON–CREDIT TRANSACTIONS: LEASES AND RENT–TO– OWN CONTRACTS

As noted earlier, one of the classic ways which suppliers often used to avoid the usury laws was to structure transactions into forms which were not covered by those laws. Today, it is quite common for a credit sale transaction to be restructured in the form of a lease. This practice is common both in the commercial and the consumer areas. In the commercial area, parties may wish to use the lease form for business reasons such as tax or accounting purposes. In the consumer area, on the other hand, the lease form is nearly always used in an attempt to avoid the effects of a consumer protection law designed for sales transactions, such as a disclosure law or a RISA. Recall our discussion in chapter 2 of the difficulty in applying the federal Truth in Lending Act to leases. The issues are similar in the usury area. A RISA may set a rate limit on credit sales, for example; but a "lessor" of goods, if he can convince a court that the lease is not a "sale," will not be bound by it.

In recent years, the rent-to-own form of consumer lease has gained prominence. These contracts normally produce astonishingly high rates of return to the supplier, rates which are nearly always hidden from the consumer.

NATIONAL CONSUMER LAW CENTER, USURY AND CONSUMER CREDIT REGULATION
129–30 (1987).*

Perhaps the most important example of the use of leases to conceal consumer credit sales is the "Rent-to-Own" (RTO) leasing industry. RTO businesses are essentially appliance and furniture retailers which arrange lease agreements rather than typical installment sales contracts for those customers who cannot purchase goods with cash. These lease agreements contain several special features. First, the lease agreements contain purchase options which typically enable the lessees to obtain title to the goods in question by making a nominal payment at the end of a stated period, such as 18 months. Second, the leases are short term, so that "rental payments" are due weekly or monthly. Third, the leases are "at will." In other words, the leases theoretically need not be renewed at the end of each weekly or monthly term.

The RTO industry aims its marketing efforts at low-income consumers by advertising in minority media, buses, and in public housing projects, and by suggesting it has many features attractive to low-income consumers: quick delivery, weekly payments, no or small downpayments, quick repair service, no credit checks, and no harm to one's credit rating if the transaction is cancelled. Most RTO customers enter into these transactions with the expectation of buying an appliance and are seldom interested by the rental aspect of the contract. This attitude is encouraged by RTO dealers who emphasize the purchase option in their marketing even while they are minimizing its importance in the written contract. Of course, if and when a transaction is challenged in court, a RTO dealer will point to the rental provisions of the contract and claim that statutes which control traditional retail installment sales are irrelevant to RTO agreements.

The chief problem with RTO contracts is not only that these supposed leases are used to mask installment sales, but also that these sales are made at astronomic and undisclosed effective interest rates. Under most RTO contracts, the customer will pay between $1000 and $2400 for a TV, stereo, or other major appliance worth as little as $200 retail, if used, and seldom more than $600 retail, if new. This means that a low-income RTO customer may pay $1\frac{1}{2}$ to 12 times what a cash customer would pay in a traditional retail store for the same appliance.

The finance charge and interest rate or annual percentage rate (APR) of an RTO contract depends on the retail cash value of the appliance (especially whether new or used) and the timing, amount, and number of payments. The following chart illustrates the APR computations, assuming payments in arrears.[176]

176. Payments in advance are called "annuity due" transactions, as contrasted with "ordinary annuities" as used in Truth

Amount Financed	Weekly Payment	52 Weeks Finance Charge	APR	78 Weeks Finance Charge	APR	104 Weeks Finance Charge	APR
200	$16	$632	408%	$1048	415%	$1464	416%
	$18	$736	462%	$1204	467%	$1672	468%
300	$16	$532	254%	$ 948	272%	$1364	276%
	$18	$636	294%	$1104	309%	$1572	311%
400	$16	$432	168%	$ 848	197%	$1264	204%
	$18	$536	201%	$1004	226%	$1472	231%
500	$16	$332	111%	$ 748	148%	$1164	159%
	$18	$436	140%	$ 904	173%	$1372	182%
	$20	$540	168%	$1060	197%	$1580	204%
600	$16	$232	68%	$ 648	113%	$1064	128%
	$18	$336	95%	$ 804	135%	$1272	147%
	$20	$440	121%	$ 960	156%	$1480	167%
700	$18	$236	60%	$ 704	106%	$1172	122%
	$20	$340	84%	$ 860	125%	$1380	139%
	$22	$444	107%	$1016	144%	$1588	156%

For example, in the Boston area, a 19″ brand name, new color TV with standard features may sell for less than $300. A 25″ table model, color television may sell for less than $500 and a 25″ console television may sell for less than $600. Remote control and other options may add $60 to $70 to the price. Therefore, if an RTO customer leases a new 19″ color TV (worth $300) for $16.00 per week for 52 weeks, the APR would be about 254%. However, if the customer leased a *used* 19″ color TV (worth about $200 or less) for the same payment terms, the APR could be 408% or more.

HAWKES TELEVISION, INC. v. MAINE BUR. OF CONS. CREDIT PROT.

Supreme Judicial Court of Maine, 1983.
462 A.2d 1167.

GODFREY, JUSTICE.

The plaintiff Hawkes Television, Inc. ("Hawkes") appeals from a judgment in Superior Court, Cumberland County, holding that the company's "rent to own" program violates the Maine Consumer Credit Code. Hawkes also moves to dissolve an injunction issued by the Superior Court pending appeal. We reverse the judgment of the Superior Court and grant the motion to dissolve the injunction.

in Lending's Regulation Z, Appendix J. For example, the top line of the chart shows different APRs if RTO payments are made at the beginning of each week: 52 weeks at $16 bears an APR of 445%, 78 weeks at $16 amounts to 451% APR, and 104 weeks yields 452%, because the time value is different. The entire chart would show greater APRs for payments in advance. Because RTO dealers usually demand payments at the beginning of each week, the astronomic A.P.R.'s in this chart are probably understated.

In August, 1981, the defendant Maine Bureau of Consumer Credit Protection ("Bureau") examined the records of Hawkes to determine compliance with the Maine Consumer Credit Code, M.R.S.A. tit. 9–A ("Code"). Hawkes is a Maine corporation that sells, rents and repairs televisions and stereo equipment from a store in Westbrook. At the time of the examination, Hawkes operated a "rent to own" program under which consumers could purchase television sets and stereo systems by making weekly "rental" payments to Hawkes, typically for 104 weeks. Under the terms of the rental agreement at issue, customers may rent a Curtis Mathes television set for a fixed weekly payment, which varies according to the type of unit rented, plus a $25 processing fee to be paid in advance. At the end of each week, the agreement automatically terminates, and the customer must return or have Hawkes retrieve the set unless he renews the agreement by paying another week's rent. If the customer makes 104 consecutive weekly payments, he becomes owner of the set without paying any additional consideration. Otherwise, Hawkes retains title to the set. It may be used only at the location specified in the rental agreement. If the customer moves, he must notify Hawkes, which will move the set to the new premises without charge. The minimum rental period is one week. The Hawkes agreement is of a type generally known as a "rental purchase contract."

A customer who completes a typical rental contract ($17 per week for 104 weeks for a 25–inch color console) pays $1,768 to own the television. The cash price for a comparable model sold by Hawkes is $939. In other words, customers who "rent to own" that model pay the equivalent of an annual interest rate of 70.52 percent over the two years of the contract. The only difference in servicing costs between a rental and a cash-sale television set is that all house calls after 90 days on the sales televisions are subject to a fee of fifteen to twenty dollars. While Hawkes prominently advertised the weekly rent necessary to obtain the unit, nowhere did the store disclose the two-year rent total. Hawkes concedes that its rental purchase contract, if treated as a consumer credit sale under the Code, would violate the Code's usury provisions.

Advertising for the rental program was aimed at and attracted customers who could not obtain more traditional credit. The advertisements promoted the program as a method of owning a television set without undergoing a formal credit check. Most rental customers intended to complete the 104–week payment schedule and 65 percent of them did in fact accomplish that goal.

* * *

The Superintendent charges that the Hawkes rent-to-own agreement violates Code provisions limiting the amount of finance charge that a seller may contract for and receive in a "consumer credit sale."

[The court quoted the statutory definitions of the terms "consumer credit sale," "credit," and "sale of goods." In Maine, these terms conform to the definitions found in U3C § 1.301.]

The narrow issue is whether the Hawkes rental agreement constitutes a "consumer credit sale" within the meaning of subsection 1–301(11) of the Code. If so, it violates the Code's usury provisions; if not, those provisions are inapplicable.

Most of the arguments of counsel have addressed whether the Hawkes agreement constitutes a "sale of goods" within the meaning of subsection 33 of section 1–301. If that were the crucial question in this case, we might be able to affirm the decision of the Superior Court. However, other definitions require reversal. Subsection 11 requires that a "consumer credit sale" be one in which the seller grants credit for "the debt," and the definition of "credit" in subsection 15 confirms the inference from subsection 11 that a debtor-creditor relationship between consumer and seller must be created by the sale. Hawkes extends no credit to its rental customers. Without doing violence to the statutory language, we cannot hold that the Hawkes rental lessees are debtors of Hawkes in the sense of the Code or that Hawkes has extended them credit.

It is apparent that a Hawkes rent-to-own customer pays dearly for the privilege of renting his television set. In that respect his condition resembles the plight of a victim of usury. Nevertheless, the Code definition of "consumer credit sale" cannot possibly bear the meaning the Superintendent has assigned to it to bring the Hawkes rent-to-own agreements within the reach of the Code. It is true that the Code must be liberally construed and applied to promote its underlying purposes and policies, 9–A M.R.S.A. § 1–102(1). Yet, if the Hawkes agreements cannot come within the scope of the definitional language by any rational interpretation, the fact that the Code must be given a liberal construction does not avail. If the definitional provisions of the Code even left some doubt about the applicability of the Code, the Superintendent's interpretation would be entitled to due deference. Here section 1–301 leaves no room for doubt. This was not a credit sale under the Code. The mandate for liberal construction does not give the Superintendent or the courts authority to enlarge the coverage of the statute.

The entry is:

Judgment reversed.

Motion to dissolve the injunction granted.

All concurring.

Notes

1. The cases are by no means uniform; there are cases holding that rent-to-own contracts are disguised credit sales. The result often depends on the purpose for which the inquiry is made. For example, as we saw in chapter 2, current definitions under the TILA mean that no rent-to-own contract will be held to be a sale for TILA purposes. On the other hand, the same contract may be held to be a credit sale for purposes of applying

Article 9 of the Uniform Commercial Code or the federal bankruptcy law. See, e.g., Sight & Sound of Ohio, Inc. v. Wright, 36 B.R. 885 (S.D.Ohio 1983); In re Puckett, 60 B.R. 223 (Bkrtcy.Tenn.1986). There are fewer cases raising the issue in the usury context. If a lease is really a sale for one purpose, should that be determinative of its status for other purposes? Aren't the economic realities of the transaction the same regardless of the legal question presented by a particular dispute? But are the issues and underlying policies the same under Article 9, for example, as they are under a usury or disclosure law?

2. As noted in chapter 2, several states have responded to the gap left by the federal TILA and state RISAs by enacting separate legislation to regulate consumer leases. Maine and Iowa both have the U3C, and both states have addressed the rent-to-own problem. Yet their approaches differ in significant ways.

In 1983, the same year the Hawkes case was decided, Maine amended the definitions of the terms "credit" and "sale of goods" in its U3C. The following language was added to the definition of "credit":

"∗ ∗ ∗ or to obtain possession of property or the benefit of services and defer payment therefor pursuant to an agreement which includes, but is not limited to, a sale of goods, a sale of an interest in land, a sale of services or a loan."

Me.Rev.Stat.Ann. tit. 9–A, § 1–301(15). At the same time, the definition of "sale of goods" was amended by adding the following language at the end of the original definition:

". . . including any optional renewals thereof."

Me.Rev.Stat.Ann. tit. 9–A, § 1–301(33). Pennsylvania and North Carolina have taken similar approaches.

Do you see how these new definitions will bring rent-to-own contracts within the Maine U3C? Yet, a few questions remain. Now that rent-to-own contracts are covered, for example, how do you determine whether the interest rate ceilings are being exceeded? Do you start with the comparable cash price for each item rented, and then assume that the difference in total payments is a finance charge? Will it always be possible to determine how much the finance charge is? If not, how can you calculate the effective rate of return? Might this amendment drive rent-to-own suppliers out of the state? Why? If it did, would that be a good thing or a bad thing?

Iowa responded in 1987 to the problems generated by the rent-to-own industry. However, unlike Maine, Iowa chose not to bring these transactions within the concept of "credit sale." Instead, it added a new Part 6, entitled the "Consumer Rental Purchase Agreement Act," to Article 3 of its U3C. Iowa Code Ann. § 537.3601 et seq. This approach accepts the premise that rent-to-own agreements are somehow fundamentally different from credit sales. As a result, while a separate set of consumer protection provisions now applies, rent-to-own transactions remain outside the reach of the Iowa U3C interest rate rules. Several other states have followed this approach.

Iowa did adopt one interesting and unique provision, however, which will have the effect of limiting the rate of return in rent-to-own transactions. First, it allows the lessee to acquire ownership of the property at any time after making the first payment by tendering 50% of the amount of the remaining payments due under the lease. This rule is similar to the rules we studied earlier which required creditors to rebate unearned interest on prepayment. Perhaps more significantly, the law also permits the lessee to acquire ownership of the property when 50% of all payments made under the lease equals the cash price of the property. In effect, this prevents the lessor from obtaining more than a 100% return over the term of the lease. See Iowa Code Ann. § 537.3608.

The new Iowa rule raises some interesting questions. For example, what effect will this rule have on the actual rate of return? Won't that depend on the length of the contract? How would this provision have helped the consumers in the *Hawkes* case or in the *Remco* case, supra page 159? Under the Iowa rule, would the RTO consumer in *Remco* already have become the owner of the TV set at the time she defaulted? If not, how much more would she have had to pay? Was the overall return on the contract within the Iowa limits?

How effective do you think Iowa's prepayment rule will be? Are consumers who purchase goods from rent-to-own suppliers likely to prepay? And even if a consumer does manage to prepay, won't the effective return still be very high during the period the consumer had the actual use of the money?

Problem 9

You are counsel to Ace Rent–To–Own Company. Ace has branches in several states, and wants to expand its operations into Maine and Iowa. Its standard contract has always looked like the one used in the Hawkes case (and the one used in the Remco case, supra at page 159). What changes will Ace have to make in its Maine operations in order to comply with the Maine U3C? What changes will it have to make in Iowa? (The Iowa statute does more than deal with the problem of prepayment and ownership; it also has several requirements concerning disclosure, format, permitted charges, renegotiation, advertising, default and cure, and much more.)

Problem 10

Mr. and Mrs. Williams needed $1342.52 to cure overdue mortgage payments. Bantuelle agreed to supply the money under a contract in which he purchased their home (worth between $25,000 and $30,000) for $1342.52, but gave the Williamses an option to repurchase the home for $2342.52 within 60 days. When they couldn't pay at the end of the 60–day period, Bantuelle demanded their eviction. They countered with a claim that the transaction was really a disguised mortgage loan, that the $1,000 difference was interest, and that the effective rate of return made the deal usurious. Bantuelle argued that the transaction was a sale and repurchase agreement and therefore the usury law did not apply. What result? See Bantuelle v. Williams, 667 S.W.2d 810 (Tex.Civ.App.1983).

Chapter 12

FEDERAL REGULATION (AND DEREGULATION) OF THE COST OF CREDIT

As in many other areas of law and life, the federal government has, especially during the past decade or so, become increasingly involved in the business of consumer interest rate regulation (and deregulation). While this makes it far more difficult to understand the impact of state usury laws, your study of the regulation of the costs of credit would be incomplete without some exploration of these federal efforts. This chapter is devoted to that subject.

SECTION A. FEDERAL PREEMPTION OF STATE USURY LAWS

1. FEDERALLY CHARTERED INSTITUTIONS

There are several important ways in which federal law affects interest rates on consumer loans. The most important arises out of the fact that many lending institutions are chartered by the federal government, and, as such, they are instrumentalities of the federal government. Federally chartered lending institutions include national banks, federal savings and loan associations, and federal credit unions. Because of this status, Congress has always had the power to regulate these institutions in any way it wanted, including the setting of interest rate ceilings on loans. When Congress does this, of course, any conflicting state laws are preempted. In fact, Congress has long exercised this power.

With respect to national banks, Congress has traditionally deferred to state usury law. The National Bank Act of 1864 allowed national banks to charge interest at the rate permitted by state law in the state where the bank was located. The original intent of this rule was to allow national banks to compete on equal terms with state banks. See generally Tiffany v. National Bank of Missouri, 85 U.S. (18 Wall.) 409, 21 L.Ed. 862 (1874). This rule has remained basically unchanged to this day; the present version can be found at 12 U.S.C.A. § 85. As an alternative rate, national banks are permitted to charge interest at rates up to 1% above the federal reserve discount rate for 90–day commercial paper. This alternative rate favors national banks when state usury limits are extremely low. In addition, the so-called "most favored lender" doctrine allows national banks, under some circumstances, to borrow state law rates which apply to other institutions when those rates are higher than the rates national banks could otherwise charge for similar loans. See the Equitable Trust case, infra at page 675.

The pattern thus established was compatible with state regulation of interest rates. From 1978 to 1980, however, three important events disturbed that traditional pattern. First, in Marquette National Bank v. First of Omaha Corp., below, national banks were allowed to "export" the rates of their "home office state" into other states in which the banks do business, thereby making the home state rate in effect preempt the rate ceilings of the borrower's state. Second, in 1980, Congress preempted all state usury laws for federally insured state banks. (Almost all state banks are federally insured.) Third, also in 1980, Congress preempted all state usury laws governing home mortgage loans for all institutions, not just banks, and not just federal institutions. We will examine each of these federal actions.

MARQUETTE NATIONAL BANK v. FIRST OF OMAHA CORP.

Supreme Court of the United States, 1978.
439 U.S. 299, 99 S.Ct. 540, 58 L.Ed.2d 534.

MR. JUSTICE BRENNAN delivered the opinion of the Court.

The question for decision is whether the National Bank Act, Rev. Stat. § 5197, as amended, 12 U.S.C. § 85, authorizes a national bank based in one State to charge its out-of-state credit-card customers an interest rate on unpaid balances allowed by its home State, when that rate is greater than that permitted by the State of the bank's nonresident customers. The Minnesota Supreme Court held that the bank is allowed by § 85 to charge the higher rate. Minn., 262 N.W.2d 358 (1977). We affirm.

I

The First National Bank of Omaha (Omaha Bank) is a national banking association with its charter address in Omaha, Neb. Omaha Bank is a card-issuing member in the BankAmericard plan. This plan enables cardholders to purchase goods and services from participating merchants and to obtain cash advances from participating banks throughout the United States and the world. Omaha Bank has systematically sought to enroll in its BankAmericard program the residents, merchants, and banks of the nearby State of Minnesota. The solicitation of Minnesota merchants and banks is carried on by respondent

First of Omaha Service Corp. (Omaha Service Corp.), a wholly owned subsidiary of Omaha Bank.

Minnesota residents are obligated to pay Omaha Bank interest on the outstanding balances of their BankAmericards. Nebraska law permits Omaha Bank to charge interest on the unpaid balances of cardholder accounts at a rate of 18% per year on the first $999.99, and 12% per year on amounts of $1,000 and over. Minnesota law, however, fixes the permissible annual interest on such accounts at 12%. To compensate for the reduced interest, Minnesota law permits banks to charge annual fees of up to $15 for the privilege of using a bank credit card.

The instant case began when petitioner Marquette National Bank of Minneapolis (Marquette) itself a national banking association enrolled in the BankAmericard plan, brought suit in the District Court of Hennepin County, Minn., to enjoin Omaha Bank and Omaha Service Corp. from soliciting in Minnesota for Omaha Bank's BankAmericard program until such time as that program complied with Minnesota law. Marquette claimed to be losing customers to Omaha Bank because, unlike the Nebraska bank, Marquette was forced by the low rate of interest permissible under Minnesota law to charge a $10 annual fee for the use of its credit cards.

* * *

The District Court of Hennepin County granted plaintiffs' motion for partial summary judgment, holding in an unreported opinion that "nothing contained in the National Bank Act, 12 U.S.C. § 85, precludes or preempts the application and enforcement of Minnesota Statutes, § 48.185 to the First National Bank of Omaha's BankAmericard program as solicited and operated in the State of Minnesota." The court enjoined Omaha Service Corp., "as agent of the First National Bank of Omaha," from "engaging in any solicitation of residents of the State of Minnesota or other activity in connection with the offering or operation of a bank credit card program in the State of Minnesota in violation of Minnesota Statutes, § 48.185."

On appeal, the Minnesota Supreme Court reversed. * * *

* * *

Omaha Bank is a national bank; it is an "instrumentalit[y] of the federal government, created for a public purpose, and as such necessarily subject to the paramount authority of the United States." *Davis v. Elmira Savings Bank,* 161 U.S. 275, 283, 16 S.Ct. 502, 503, 40 L.Ed. 700 (1896). The interest rate that Omaha Bank may charge in its Bank-Americard program is thus governed by federal law. The provision of § 85 called into question states:

> "Any association may take, receive, reserve and charge on any loan or discount made, or upon any notes, bills of exchange, or other evidences of debt, interest at the rate allowed by the laws of the State, Territory, or District *where the bank is located,* * * * and no more, except that where by the laws of any State a different rate is limited for banks

organized under State laws, the rate so limited shall be allowed for associations or existing in any such State under this chapter." (Emphasis supplied.)

Section 85 thus plainly provides that a national bank may charge interest "on any loan" at the rate allowed by the laws of the State in which the bank is "located." The question before us is therefore narrowed to whether Omaha Bank and its BankAmericard program are "located" in Nebraska and for that reason entitled to charge its Minnesota customers the rate of interest authorized by Nebraska law.

There is no question but that Omaha Bank itself, apart from its BankAmericard program, is located in Nebraska. Petitioners concede as much. The National Bank Act requires a national bank to state in its organization certificate "[t]he place where its operations of discount and deposit are to be carried on, designating the State, Territory, or district, and the particular county and city, town, or village." Rev.Stat. § 5134, 12 U.S.C. § 22. The charter address of Omaha Bank is in Omaha, Douglas County, Neb. The bank operates no branch banks in Minnesota, nor apparently could it under federal law.

The State of Minnesota, however, contends that this conclusion must be altered if Omaha Bank's BankAmericard program is considered: "In the context of a national bank which systematically solicits Minnesota residents for credit cards to be used in transactions with Minnesota merchants the bank must be deemed to be 'located' in Minnesota for purposes of this credit card program."

We disagree. Section 85 was originally enacted as § 30 of the National Bank Act of 1864, 13 Stat. 108. The congressional debates surrounding the enactment of § 30 were conducted on the assumption that a national bank was "located" for purposes of the section in the State named in its organization certificate. Omaha Bank cannot be deprived of this location merely because it is extending credit to residents of a foreign State. Minnesota residents were always free to visit Nebraska and receive loans in that State. It has not been suggested that Minnesota usury laws would apply to such transactions. Although the convenience of modern mail permits Minnesota residents holding Omaha Bank's BankAmericards to receive loans without visiting Nebraska, credit on the use of their cards is nevertheless similarly extended by Omaha Bank in Nebraska by the bank's honoring of the sales drafts of participating Minnesota merchants and banks. Finance charges on the unpaid balances of cardholders are assessed by the bank in Omaha, Neb., and all payments on unpaid balances are remitted to the bank in Omaha, Neb. Furthermore, the bank issues its BankAmericards in Omaha, Neb., after credit assessments made by the bank in that city.

* * *

Since Omaha Bank and its BankAmericard program are "located" in Nebraska, the plain language of § 85 provides that the bank may charge "on any loan" the rate "allowed" by the State of Nebraska.

Petitioners contend, however, that this reading of the statute violates the basic legislative intent of the National Bank Act. At the time Congress enacted § 30 of the National Bank Act of 1864, 13 Stat. 108, so petitioners' argument runs, it intended "to insure competitive equality between state and national banks in the charging of interest." This policy could best be effectuated by limiting national banks to the rate of interest allowed by the States in which the banks were located. Since Congress in 1864 was addressing a financial system in which incorporated banks were "local institutions," it did not "contemplate a national bank soliciting customers and entering loan agreements outside of the state in which it was established." Therefore to interpret § 85 to apply to interstate loans such as those involved in this case would not only enlarge impermissibly the original intent of Congress, but would also undercut the basic policy foundations of the statute by upsetting the competitive equality now existing between state and national banks.

We cannot accept petitioners' argument. Whatever policy of "competitive equality" has been discerned in other sections of the National Bank Act, § 30 and its descendants have been interpreted for over a century to give "advantages to National banks over their State competitors." *Tiffany v. National Bank of Missouri,* 18 Wall. 409, 413, 21 L.Ed. 862 (1874). "National banks," it was said in *Tiffany,* "have been National favorites."

* * *

Petitioners' final argument is that the "exportation" of interest rates, such as occurred in this case, will significantly impair the ability of States to enact effective usury laws. This impairment, however, has always been implicit in the structure of the National Bank Act, since citizens of one State were free to visit a neighboring State to receive credit at foreign interest rates. This impairment may in fact be accentuated by the ease with which interstate credit is available by mail through the use of modern credit cards. But the protection of state usury laws is an issue of legislative policy, and any plea to alter § 85 to further that end is better addressed to the wisdom of Congress than to the judgment of this Court.

Affirmed.

Problem 1

Citibank is a large New York City bank. It has issued many credit cards to consumers in New York state, and has also issued many others to consumers in other states. Suppose New York state legislation restricts interest rates on bank credit cards to 1.5% per month, but Citibank wants to charge more than that. South Dakota offers to repeal all interest rate legislation if Citibank will move its credit card processing operations to South Dakota. Citibank obtains a charter for a subsidiary national bank (actually a non-bank bank) whose "home state" is South Dakota, and all interest rate legislation in South Dakota is repealed.

Andy lives in New York City, and obtains a Citibank Mastercard. Andy thought he was dealing with his branch of a New York bank, but his card was issued (and his application processed) by the South Dakota subsidiary bank. Andy sees that he is being charged 2% per month on his Citibank card, and he consults you as to whether he has a cause of action against Citibank for a violation of New York Law. What is your response?

If you believe that Andy has no cause of action due to this charge, Andy has one further question: Why doesn't New York law, enacted to protect New York consumers, protect him, since he is a New York consumer? What is your response?

Notes

1. In 1980, Congress extended the reach of federal law by preempting all state usury laws for federally insured state banks. (Almost all state banks are federally insured.) Federal law now permits these banks to charge interest on loans at rates up to 1% above the federal reserve discount rate for 90–day commercial paper, the same as that allowed for national banks. See 12 U.S.C.A. § 1831d.

2. Federal savings and loan associations are heavily regulated by federal law, and nearly all attempts at state regulation have been held preempted. See, e.g., Fidelity Federal Savings & Loan Ass'n v. de la Cuesta, 458 U.S. 141, 102 S.Ct. 3014, 73 L.Ed.2d 664 (1982), holding that federal S & Ls could use "due-on-sale" clauses in their mortgage contracts despite a state rule to the contrary. On the other hand, until 1980, Congress had said that federal S & Ls were subject to state usury laws, at least for home mortgages. 12 U.S.C.A. § 1425. In 1980, however, Congress reversed its position and preempted state usury ceilings for all federally insured savings and loan associations, including state S & Ls, and set its own ceiling of 1% above the discount rate for 90–day commercial paper. This matches the ceiling set for federally insured banks.

3. Unlike the experience with federal savings and loans, Congress has traditionally set interest rate ceilings for federal credit unions. See 12 U.S. C.A. § 1757(5)(A)(vi), which sets the ceiling at 15% a year, but allows the National Credit Union Administration Board to set higher temporary rates. Since 1980, this administratively imposed ceiling has always been above 15%. (It was 21% for a few years, and most recently has been set at 18%. 12 C.F.R. § 701.21(c)(7) (1989).) In 1980, at the same time Congress was freeing federally insured banks and savings and loans from state usury laws, Congress also preempted state law for federally insured credit unions (including state credit unions) and set the ceiling at (you guessed it) 1% above the discount rate for 90–day commercial paper. 12 U.S.C.A. § 1785(g).

4. As you can see, 1980 was something of a banner year for federally chartered and federally insured lending institutions. As part of a larger, general movement toward deregulation of the financial services industry, these institutions were basically freed from all state usury laws.

Note on Federal Preemption of State Law Other Than Interest Rate Ceilings

The movement toward greater federal preemption of state law is not limited to usury laws. Especially in the mortgage lending industry, there has been increasing movement toward preempting other state law restrictions on lending practices. This is not only true for federally chartered lenders, but also for state institutions. A small example is the 1982 Depository Institutions (Garn-St. Germain) Act, 12 U.S.C.A. § 1701j–3, which preempted state law concerning so-called "due on sale" clauses. With respect to federally chartered lenders, this act did little more than codify the result of the de la Cuesta case, noted above. However, this act went further and preempted state due-on-sale restrictions for non-federal lenders as well. See Western Life Ins. Co. v. McPherson K.M.P., 702 F.Supp. 836 (D.Kan.1988).

A more far-reaching piece of federal legislation in this area is the Alternative Mortgage Transaction Parity Act of 1982, 12 U.S.C.A. § 3800 et seq. In prior years, federal mortgage regulations had liberalized the practices of federal lenders, especially by permitting various forms of adjustable rate and other non-traditional loans. As a result, these lenders were thought by Congress to have an unfair advantage over state lenders. The AMTPA was designed to eliminate this discriminatory advantage. It specifically preempts state law and frees state housing lenders to use adjustable rate and other forms of "alternative mortgage transactions." However, if these lenders wish to take advantage of this preemption, they must comply with the federal regulations which apply to federally chartered lenders who make similar loans.

A similar form of federal preemption is found in the federal regulations concerning mobile home loans. These regulations, however, are specifically tied to a federal usury preemption, and we will consider it in more detail below. See Section B of this Chapter.

2. THE "MOST FAVORED LENDER" DOCTRINE

ATTORNEY GENERAL OF MARYLAND v. EQUITABLE TRUST CO.

Court of Appeals of Maryland, 1982.
294 Md. 385, 450 A.2d 1273.

RODOWSKY, JUDGE.

This case involves the interplay between (1) the National Bank Act's "most favored lender" doctrine, (2) the Maryland Consumer Loan Law (MCLL), Md.Code (1975, 1982 Cum.Supp.), §§ 12–301 et seq. of the Commerical Law Article (CL) and (3) the Retail Credit Accounts Law (RCAL), Md.Code (1975, 1982 Cum.Supp.), CL §§ 12–501 et seq. The context of the controversy is (1) bank financing of purchases, made by the holders of bank issued credit cards, from retail merchants that participate in the credit card plan, and (2) unsecured cash advances made to those credit cardholders by or for the card issuing bank.

Federally chartered banks and federally insured, state chartered banks brought this action seeking a declaratory judgment. The basic issues before this Court are:

    1. Do the plaintiff banks have a right, conferred by federal law, to utilize the rates of interest provided by MCLL when assessing finance charges on outstanding balances that represent purchases of goods and services by holders of credit cards issued by the banks; and

    2. In utilizing MCLL rates of interest, either when financing credit card purchases, or when making cash advances, must the plaintiff banks comply with any provisions of MCLL other than provisions fixing the maximum rate of interest and the maximum loan amount?

The trial court decreed that the banks could apply MCLL rates to credit card purchase balances. As to the second issue, the trial court held that a number of additional MCLL provisions must be complied with in order for the banks to utilize MCLL rates in their sales and loan credit plans. Both sides appealed. Certiorari was issued by this Court prior to consideration of the cross-appeals by the Court of Special Appeals. For reasons hereinafter stated, we shall reverse the judgment of the trial court on the first issue and shall affirm in part, reverse in part, and vacate in part on the second issue.

    First National Bank of Maryland and Maryland National Bank, which are national banking associations, and The Equitable Trust Company, Provident Savings Bank of Baltimore, The Savings Bank of Baltimore and Suburban Trust Company, which are state chartered banks, were plaintiffs below (Plaintiffs, or, the Banks). Each of the state Banks is insured under the Federal Deposit Insurance Act, 12 U.S.C. §§ 1811 *et seq.,* as amended by § 521 of the Depository Institutions Deregulation and Monetary Control Act of 1980 (DIDA), 94 Stat. 132, 164, 12 U.S.C. § 1831d. Defendants below were the Attorney General of Maryland, the Commissioner of Consumer Credit and the Deputy Bank Commissioner (the State).

    As initially held in *Tiffany v. National Bank,* 85 U.S. (18 Wall.) 409, 21 L.Ed. 862 (1874), § 30 of the National Bank Act of 1864, 13 Stat. 99, 108, which, as amended, is now 12 U.S.C. § 85, confers on national banks the same status as to permissible interest rates as is enjoyed by the "most favored lender" under applicable state law. In *Marquette National Bank v. First of Omaha Service Corp.,* 439 U.S. 299, 314 n. 26, 99 S.Ct. 540, 548 n. 26, 58 L.Ed.2d 534, 545 n. 26 (1978), the Supreme Court stated that the " 'most favored lender' status for national banks under *Tiffany* has since been incorporated into" an interpretive ruling of the Comptroller of the Currency found at 12 CFR § 7.7310(a). It reads:

    § 7.7310 Charging interest at rates permitted competing institutions; charging interest to corporate borrowers.

(a) A national bank may charge interest at the maximum rate permitted by State law to any competing State-chartered or licensed lending institution. If State law permits a higher interest rate *on a specified class of loans,* a national bank making *such loans* at such higher rate is subject only to the *provisions of State law relating to such class of loans that are material to the determination of the interest rate.* For example, a national bank may lawfully charge the highest rate permitted to be charged by a State-licensed small loan company or morris plan bank, without being so licensed. [Emphasis added.]

The first issue in this case essentially involves what constitutes a "specified class of loans" and the second issue is concerned with which provisions of MCLL are "material to the determination of the interest rate" relating to a specified class of loans. As the case comes to us, the answers to the issues framed will be the same for all Plaintiffs. The trial court declared that the state chartered Plaintiffs enjoy the most favored lender doctrine, pursuant to DIDA, to the same extent as national banks. This holding by the trial court is not challenged by the State on this appeal.

MCLL rates may be applied by national banks to certain unsecured cash advances effected by use of their credit cards as a consequence of the holding in *Commissioner of Small Loans v. First National Bank,* 268 Md. 305, 300 A.2d 685 (1973). There we affirmed a declaratory judgment that 12 U.S.C. § 85 constituted authority for national banks located in Maryland to charge interest on credit card loans of the amount dealt with in the Maryland Small Loan Act at the same rates of interest permitted to be charged by lenders licensed under that act. By Ch. 693 of the Acts of 1977 the Small Loan Act was repealed and its subject matter consolidated into MCLL. *Commissioner* did not involve whether small loan rates could be applied in the financing of credit card purchases, or reach the question of how much of the Small Loan Act applied to national banks that would utilize small loan rates on cash advances.

I

Do the Banks have the right under the most favored lender doctrine to use MCLL rates for sales transactions? In the terminology of 12 CFR § 7.7310 the inquiry is whether third party financing of purchases under an open end credit plan is a loan of the same class as the making of a cash advance under MCLL. * * *

* * *

Within the Maryland classifications of the types of credit transactions that are regulated as to rate of interest or finance charge, the extension of credit for financing purchases made pursuant to a three party, open end, credit plan is a RCAL transaction. In that class of transaction, all those who extend credit are limited to the same ceiling of 2% per month. No person, under Maryland law, can extend that type of credit at a higher rate. Under Maryland law, a corporation which is licensed to make loans under MCLL and which also happens to be in the business of acting as a financial institution under RCAL may not charge the higher MCLL rates to finance purchases under its three party, open end, sales credit plan. The national bank that acts as a financial institution in three party, open end, sales credit is, under Maryland law, subject to no rate limitation more restrictive than that of any other person engaged in that type of transaction. No one financing purchases under a credit card plan is treated more favorably by Maryland law in relation to the permissible interest rate than national banks are treated.

* * *

We think that the better reasoned decisions proceed by a two step analysis in determining the applicable rate of interest where state law has a variety of rates for different transactions, and usurious interest is claimed to have been charged. First the court looks to the state statute that is designed to regulate the rate on the specific type of transaction involved. If the rate charged by the national bank exceeds that rate, and there is another statute, regulating the same class of transaction, the court looks to the other statute to determine if there is a type of lender on that class of loan who is permitted a higher rate. If there is, the national bank may permissibly utilize that higher rate when making that class of loan.

Acker v. Provident National Bank, 512 F.2d 729 (3d Cir.1975), illustrates the importance of first determining the applicable state rate. Credit cardholders in that case sought damages under 12 U.S.C. § 86 on the ground that the defendant national banks had violated 12 U.S.C. § 85 by charging usurious interest on credit card purchases. Cash advances were not involved in the plaintiffs' transactions with the defendants. As its starting point the court stated that the National Bank Act in effect " 'defers' to the laws of the state in which a national bank is located to establish the interest rate which the national bank can charge." The difficulty was that there were two different Pennsylvania statutes, each of which was arguably applicable to the bank-operated credit card purchase plans. A section of the Banking Code established a 12% per annum rate for "installment loan[s]," for which the plaintiffs contended. The Goods and Services Installment Sales Act permitted 15% per annum, the rate used by the defendants. The court was "satisfied that bank-operated revolving credit card plans *in Pennsylvania* are not 'loans' governed by the Bank Code." *Id.* at 734 (emphasis in original; footnote omitted). It concluded that "the Pennsylvania legislature intended the fifteen percent (15%) rate of the Sales Act to apply to both retail sellers and financing agencies (including banks) * * *." *Id.* at 738. If the most favored lender doctrine made installment loans and credit card sales financing fungible, the fact that the rate was higher under the Sales Act would have automatically resolved the issue presented. The Third Circuit, however, found it necessary to determine, by applying state law, the appropriate classification for credit card purchase financing as a distinctly regulated type of transaction.

* * *

If the most favored lender doctrine obliterates state law non-discriminatory classifications of transactions, then consequences result which could never have been intended by Congress. For example, a middle-aged married couple in Maryland, whose children are raised, and who own their own home clear of any liens, might borrow money on a first mortgage for the purpose of completely refurnishing the house. Under the conditions specified by Md. CL § 103(b), there is no limit on the rate of interest in such a transaction. The couple might instead choose to buy the furniture under a credit card plan, particularly if their credit limit is high. If, under federal law, the possibility that loan proceeds might be used to purchase goods makes the highest loan rate also applicable to credit card purchase transactions, then the MCLL rate would not be the legal limit. Under the logical extension of Plaintiffs' argument, there would be no limit because there is no limit on residential mortgage loans and because the proceeds of a residential mortgage loan might be used to make purchases.

DIDA, however, makes clear that no such far-reaching result was ever intended. Part of DIDA, 94 Stat. 161, amends the National Housing Act by adding 12 U.S.C. § 1735f–7 note. This section preempts state law establishing an interest ceiling on certain "federally related" loans secured by a first lien on residential real property, and in effect legislates that there be none. Such federally related loans may be made by federally chartered and federally insured, state chartered, savings and loan associations. DIDA also enacted 12 U.S.C. § 1831d under which the state chartered, federally insured, Banks claim the benefit of the most favored lender doctrine. Undoubtedly Congress would be shocked to find that the combination of these provisions has preempted all state interest and finance charge limitations on national banks, and on federally insured state banks, throughout the entire United States, simply because certain savings and loans, on what was thought to be but one class of loan, have no rate limit at all.

Here, Maryland law treats equally all those who finance credit card purchases. There is no need to look beyond RCAL to any other rate law, in order to protect national banks doing RCAL lending, because no lender is permitted in Maryland to transfer a higher rate into RCAL. Unsecured cash advances and credit card purchase financing are, in Maryland, different classes of "loans" within the meaning of 12 U.S.C. § 85, as interpreted in 12 CFR § 7.7310(a). This Court rejects the notion that different types of transactions in which credit is extended all become a single class of loan under 12 U.S.C. § 85, because of the common denominator of credit.

We reverse on the first issue and remand for the entry of a judgment declaring that the Plaintiffs may not charge rates in excess of those permitted by RCAL on purchase transactions financed under their credit card plans.

II

Plaintiffs also contend that the only provisions of MCLL with which they are required to comply in their credit card operations are those that fix the numerical rate (§ 306(a)(2)–(7)) and that fix the maximum amount of loan (§ 303(a)). * * *

* * *

12 CFR § 7.7310(a) provides that a national bank making loans at a higher rate permitted by state law on a specified class of loans "is subject only to the provisions of State law relating to such class of loans that are material to the determination of the interest rate."

Plaintiffs' position is that the only provisions material to the determination of the rate are the numerical rate itself and any dollar amount of principal to which a specific rate is limited by state law. The Banks rely heavily on a sentence appearing in *Evans v. National Bank*, 251 U.S. 108, 111, 40 S.Ct. 58, 59, 64 L.Ed. 171, 175 (1919) which states that the National Bank Act "adopts usury laws of the States only insofar as they severally fix the rate of interest." The Court cited three decisions in support of its statement. Two of the cited cases stand for the generally accepted proposition that the penalties for violation of the usury provisions of 12 U.S.C. § 85 are established by 12 U.S.C. § 86, and not by state law. * * *

* * * *Citizens' National Bank v. Donnell,* 195 U.S. 369, 25 S.Ct. 49, 49 L.Ed. 238 (1904) affirmed a Missouri Supreme Court judgment by which interest was forfeited on a loan made by a national bank, because the interest had been compounded more than once a year in violation of Missouri statute. It was argued by the bank that compounding did not affect the rate of interest so that compounding was not prohibited by the National Bank Act's incorporation of state law. It was also argued that if the amount charged as a result of compounding were less than the maximum amount that might otherwise have been charged, there was no violation. Justice Holmes for the Court said:

The rate of interest which a man receives is greater when he is allowed to compound than when he is not, the other elements in the case being the same. Even if the compounded interest is less than might be charged directly without compounding, a statute may forbid enlarging the rate in that way, whatever may be the rules of the common law. The Supreme Court of Missouri holds that that is what the Missouri statute has done. On that point and on the question whether what was done amounted to compounding within the meaning of the Missouri statute, we follow the state court. * * *

Consequently, the national bank that takes a most favored lender's rate may not take only the numerical rate. It must also take the method of calculating that rate, except that the discounting of some loans, the class of which is unresolved, is permitted by supervening federal law. Nor may the national bank enlarge the rate charged, in a way prohibited by state law, even if the resulting charge is within the legal limit if done directly.

But rejecting Plaintiffs' numerical rate argument does not resolve the matter. Essentially we are in virgin territory, from the standpoint of precedent, when deciding what parts of MCLL, a closed end loan statute, are material to open end cash advances.

As we see it, 12 U.S.C. § 85 is the usury statute for national banks. By using that statute, and the state law which is brought into it, a court is to decide, in a specific case based on a specific transaction, whether the state interest limitations incorporated by reference in § 85 have been violated. Provisions are "material to the determination of the interest rate" if they are material to a judicial determination of whether or not the interest charged in a given transaction is unlawful. We shall apply this general principle to the specific sections of MCLL which are the subject of Plaintiffs' cross-appeal.

Section 313(a)(1) presents a fundamental concept of MCLL. It is prohibited for a lender "[d]irectly or indirectly" to "contract for, charge, or receive any interest, discount, fee, fine, commission, charge, broker-age, or other consideration in excess of that permitted by" MCLL. * * *

Section 303(a) is recognized by all as material because it establishes a $6,000 maximum loan amount.

Section 303(b) in its entirety is material. It in general makes the furnishing of consideration in exchange for an assignment of wages a loan for MCLL purposes, and declares that interest on the loan is to be measured by the difference between the wages assigned and the consideration paid for the assignment.

Section 303(c)(1) is material. The subject is an ostensibly un-secured loan which is, in reality, secured. For security purposes a lender pretends to purchase property from the borrower which the borrower is permitted temporarily to keep in his possession. If the lender recovers the property, as "owner" and "buyer," but does not credit the loan balance with the amount realized on the security, interest charged at an apparently lawful rate on a balance which should have been lower because of the deserved credit, can exceed the maximum and be usurious. * * *

Section 306(b) is material. It provides that if "any principal balance remains unpaid 6 months after the loan matures as originally scheduled or deferred," the interest drops to 6% per annum, simple interest. * * *

This brings us to § 306(e) which fixes the maximum duration for MCLL loans of various principal balances. It is the most hotly con-tested feature of this aspect of the case between the parties. This is because, in a revolving account, the lender does not currently program, in his computerized record of the borrower's account, to track how long a given cash advance has been outstanding. Lenders currently do not keep cash advances segregated, one from another, in their records for the purpose of applying principal payments to the oldest incurred portion of the total principal balance that is brought forward into a new billing period. The problem arises from the fact that MCLL contemplates closed end lending and the Plaintiffs seek to apply MCLL to open end transactions.

The Plaintiffs say that forcing their open end cash advance plans into the mold of MCLL provisions establishing a maximum term will destroy their right to be treated equally with the most favored lender and thereby violate 12 U.S.C. § 85. Based on sufficient evidence, the trial court concluded that tracking of the dates of cash advances in relation to a maximum maturity date can reasonably be accomplished, so that the factual predicate for Plaintiffs' argument is missing.

We agree with the trial court's conclusion that a given cash advance in open end credit has a maturity date for MCLL rate borrowing purposes, because one can calculate from the plan's minimum payment requirements when the cash advance will be paid in full, if a given debit to principal is considered separately from any later, additional debits to loan principal. ∗ ∗ ∗

∗ ∗ ∗

Section 309 makes the MCLL lender subject to claims or defenses which the borrower may have against a seller of goods under the circumstances therein provided. A claim or defense which prevails because of rights conferred by § 309 may result in a reduction of principal and, as a consequence of that reduction, result in a reduction of the amount of interest paid. However, it has nothing to do with the rate of interest charged, or in determining whether interest has been charged at an unlawful rate. It is not material to the rate of interest.

∗ ∗ ∗

The remaining issue deals with the "interchange fee" which operates at least within the VISA credit card system of which some of the Plaintiffs are members. As described in the evidence, the fee comes into play when the cardholder makes a purchase from a merchant who participates in the plan of a bank which is not the bank issuing the card to the cardholder. As we read the evidence, and as the briefs of all parties treat the fee in such a transaction, it is paid by the merchant signing bank to the card issuing bank. However, the trial court opinion describes the operation of the fee in such transactions as paid by the card issuing bank to the merchant signing bank. The State had argued below that the interchange fee received by a Maryland card issuing bank should be deemed an indirect fee within the meaning of § 313(a)(1). The trial court held that the interchange fee is not material to the rate and the State has appealed from that declaration. There is no direct evidence that the interchange fee applies on cash advances. ∗ ∗ ∗ Because the total emphasis in the testimony and in the trial court's opinion was on sales transactions with respect to the interchange fee, and because the master agreement governing the relationship between banks participating in the VISA system is not in the record, we are unable meaningfully to review the trial court's determination on this point. We shall therefore vacate that portion of the trial court's judgment which declares that the interchange fee is not material to the rate, without affirmance or reversal, and remand that point for such further proceedings as may be required.

JUDGMENT OF THE CIRCUIT COURT OF BALTIMORE CITY AFFIRMED IN PART, REVERSED IN PART AND VACATED IN PART AND CASE REMANDED FOR FURTHER PROCEEDINGS AND FOR THE ENTRY OF A DECLARATORY JUDGMENT CONSISTENT WITH THIS OPINION. COSTS OF THIS APPEAL TO BE PAID 95% BY THE PLAINTIFFS BELOW AND 5% BY THE DEFENDANTS BELOW.

Note

Application of the "most favored lender" doctrine is complex, and it continues to generate litigation. For some recent applications, see VanderWeyst v. First State Bank of Benson, 425 N.W.2d 803 (Minn.1988), cert. denied, 488 U.S. 943, 109 S.Ct. 369, 102 L.Ed.2d 359 applying the doctrine to a case involving an agricultural loan; Gavey Properties/762 v. First Financial Savings & Loan Ass'n, 845 F.2d 519 (5th Cir.1988), involving a commercial loan. For a more detailed analysis, see Arnold and Rohner, The "Most Favored Lender" Doctrine for Federally Insured Financial Institutions—What Are Its Boundaries?, 31 Cath.U.L.Rev. 1 (1981).

Problem 2

The legislature of your state thinks that the most favored lender doctrine puts national banks at too great an advantage over state banks, so it enacts a so-called "parity" statute under which the state banking laws are amended to provide that state banks may charge interest "at the rate permitted to national banks." First State Bank, relying on this law, makes a loan at 10%, well above the general usury limit of 7%. When sued for violating the usury laws, it makes the following argument: "The most favored lender doctrine permits national banks to charge the highest state law rate permitted to a state lender making similar loans. State credit unions may charge up to 15% on loans of this type. Therefore, national banks may charge up to 15%, and under the new state law we may also charge up to 15%. Therefore, the loan is not usurious." What do you think of the argument? See First Bank of Cadillac v. Miller, 131 Mich.App. 764, 347 N.W.2d 715 (1984).

SECTION B. HOME MORTGAGE LOANS

In 1980, Congress enacted federal usury override legislation which targeted a specific type of loan (residential mortgages) rather than a specific type of lending institution. Following is an excerpt from the relevant statute. Apply it to the materials which follow.

PUBLIC LAW 96–221, 94 Stat. 161 (1980) codified at
12 U.S.C.A. § 1735f–7 (Note)

TITLE V—STATE USURY LAWS

PART A—MORTGAGE USURY LAWS

MORTGAGES

Sec. 501. (a)(1) The provisions of the constitution or the laws of any State expressly limiting the rate or amount of interest, discount points, finance charges, or other charges which may be charged, taken, received, or reserved shall not apply to any loan, mortgage, credit sale, or advance which is—

(A) secured by a first lien on residential real property, by a first lien on all stock allocated to a dwelling unit in a residential cooperative housing corporation, or by a first lien on a residential manufactured home;

(B) made after March 31, 1980; and

(C) described in section 527(b) of the National Housing Act (12 U.S.C. 1735f–5(b)), except that for the purpose of this section—

(i) the limitation described in section 527(b)(1) of such Act that the property must be designed principally for the occupancy of from one to four families shall not apply;

(ii) the requirement contained in section 527(b)(1) of such Act that the loan be secured by residential real property shall not apply to a loan secured by stock in a residential cooperative housing corporation or to a loan or credit sale secured by a first lien on a residential manufactured home;

(iii) the term "federally related mortgage loan" in section 527(b) of such Act shall include a credit sale which is secured by a first lien on a residential manufactured home and which otherwise meets the definitional requirements of section 527(b) of such Act, as those requirements are modified by this section;

(iv) the term "residential loans" in section 527(b)(2)(D) of such Act shall also include loans or credit sales secured by a first lien on a residential manufactured home;

* * *

(b)(1) Except as provided in paragraphs (2) and (3), the provisions of subsection (a)(1) shall apply to any loan, mortgage, credit sale, or advance made in any State on or after April 1, 1980.

(2) Except as provided in paragraph (3), the provisions of subsection (a)(1) shall not apply to any loan, mortgage, credit sale, or advance made in any State after the date (on or after April 1, 1980, and before April 1, 1983) on which such State adopts a law or certifies that the voters of such State have voted in favor of any provision, constitutional

or otherwise, which states explicitly and by its terms that such State does not want the provisions of subsection (a)(1) to apply with respect to loans, mortgages, credit sales, and advances made in such State.

* * *

(c) The provisions of subsection (a)(1) shall not apply to a loan, mortgage, credit sale, or advance which is secured by a first lien on a residential manufactured home unless the terms and conditions relating to such loan, mortgage, credit sale, or advance comply with consumer protection provisions specified in regulations prescribed by the Federal Home Loan Bank Board. Such regulations shall—

(1) include consumer protection provisions with respect to balloon payments, prepayment penalties, late charges, and deferral fees;

(2) require a 30–day notice prior to instituting any action leading to repossession or foreclosure (except in the case of abandonment or other extreme circumstances);

(3) require that upon prepayment in full, the debtor shall be entitled to a refund of the unearned portion of the precomputed finance charge in an amount not less than the amount which would be calculated by the actuarial method, except that the debtor shall not be entitled to a refund which is less than $1; and

(4) include such other provisions as the Federal Home Loan Bank Board may prescribe after a finding that additional protections are required.

* * *

(f) The Federal Home Loan Bank Board is authorized to issue rules and regulations and to publish interpretations governing the implementation of this section.

(g) This section takes effect on April 1, 1980.

SMITH v. FIDELITY CONSUMER DISCOUNT CO.

United States Court of Appeals, Third Circuit, 1990.
898 F.2d 907.

STAPLETON, CIRCUIT JUDGE:

This appeal requires us to answer a discrete, but important, legal question: Does § 501(a) of the Depository Institutions Deregulation and Monetary Control Act of 1980 ("DIDMCA"), 94 Stat. 165, *codified as amended*, 12 U.S.C. § 1735f–7a(a)(I), preempt a state usury law's application to loans secured by first liens on residential property that were obtained by borrowers to finance the purchase of used cars? We hold, as did the district court, 686 F.Supp. 504, that it does.

* * *

I.

* * *

The plaintiffs' claims arose from loans extended to them, or their relations, by defendant Fidelity Consumer Discount Corporation ("Fidelity"), a wholly-owned subsidiary of Equitable Credit and Discount Company ("Equitable"). In each of the loan transactions, Fidelity gave credit to a borrower to buy a used car and received as security a first lien on the borrower's (or a cosigner's) home.

* * *

The sole issue presented by this claim is whether the district court correctly held that § 501(a) of DIDMCA preempts Pennsylvania's usury laws with respect to these transactions. It is undisputed that, absent preemption, Fidelity will have violated these statutes, the most generous of which allows lenders to charge up to 24% interest per annum. In this case, Fidelity wrote loans with disclosed annual interest rates ranging from approximately 31% to 41%. Moreover, Fidelity required, as a condition of extending credit, that the borrowing parties satisfy all existing liens on their homes, accomplished in one case by lending the borrower additional money at interest rates higher than the outstanding loans, to enable Fidelity to obtain a first lien on the borrower's or cosigner's home.

II.

This is the kind of case in which we need to remain mindful of Lord Campbell's admonition that "it is the duty of all courts of justice to take care, for the general good of the community, that hard cases do not make bad law." *East India Company v. Paul,* 7 Moo.P.C.C. (1849). However we may feel about the defendants' interest rates and business practices, it is our duty to give effect to that construction of § 501(a)(1) of DIDMCA that is most consonant with its text, its legislative history and the interpretations of the agency entrusted to administer DIDMCA.

* * *

A.

[The court quoted portions of section 501.]

* * *

A literal reading of the phrase "any loan * * * secured by a first lien on residential property" clearly encompasses the transactions in this case. In each case, Fidelity obtained a first priority security interest against the borrowers' real property. This much is beyond dispute. Hence, plaintiffs bear the heavy burden of demonstrating that giving effect to the plain meaning of subsection (A) "would produce results demonstrably at odds with the intention of the drafters." *Ron Pair Enterprises, Inc.,* 109 S.Ct. at 1031.

B.

The plaintiffs' chief argument is that Congress' intent was to limit the preemptive force of § 501(a) to purchase money mortgages. They base this argument primarily on the legislative history of this section.

DIDMCA was passed at a time when inflation and interest rates were soaring; in this context, state usury laws decreased the availability of home mortgage loans and hindered the ability of financial institutions to pay market rates of interest to depositors since usury laws limited them to lending at rates well below those that the market would have dictated. Thus, the Senate Report that accompanied the bill containing what became § 501 of DIDMCA found:

> that where state usury laws require mortgage rates below market levels of interest, mortgage funds in those states will not be readily available and those funds will flow to other states where market yields are available. This artificial disruption of funds availability not only is harmful to potential homebuyers in states with such usury laws, it also frustrates national housing policies and programs. * * *

> The committee believes that this limited modification in state usury laws will enhance the stability and viability of our Nation's financial system and is needed to facilitate a national housing policy and the functioning of a national secondary market in mortgage lending.

> In addition to the adverse effects of usury ceilings on credit availability, mortgage rate ceilings must be removed if saving and loan institutions, as directed by other provisions of [the Act], are to begin to pay market rates of interest on savings deposits. Without enhancing the ability of institutions to achieve market rates on both sides of their balance sheets, the stability and continued viability of our nation's financial system would not be assured. Thus, Federal preemption of State usury ceilings would not only promote national home financing objectives but would provide the resources with which savers could be paid more interest on their savings accounts.

S.Rep. No. 868, 96th Cong. 2d Sess. 19 (1980), *reprinted in,* 1980 U.S. Code Cong. & Admin.News 236, 254–255 (emphasis added). * * * These concerns about the health of financial markets and the health of the housing industry, though interrelated, are distinct.

If Congress' sole interest had been in promoting the greater and more evenly distributed availability of purchase money mortgages, plaintiffs would have a stronger, but by no means compelling, argument that a plain meaning reading of subsection (A) is at variance with Congress' intent. However, Congress also wished to provide lending institutions with revenues from which to pay depositors market rates of interest. This purpose is rationally advanced by allowing these institutions to provide credit at market rates to any borrower willing to use her home as collateral, whether the proceeds of the loan are to be used to purchase a new home, improve an existing one, or for some other purpose.

Had Congress chosen to preempt state laws only insofar as they inhibited the availability of purchase money mortgages, it could have easily done so. Indeed, as originally enacted by Congress, the statutory provision we are here called upon to construe provided for a usury exemption for:

> [A]ny loan * * * secured by a first lien on residential real property, by a first lien on stock in a residential cooperative housing corporation

*where the loan * * * is used to finance the acquisition of such stock,* or by a first lien on a residential manufactured home.

DIDMCA, Pub.L. No. 96–221, § 501(a)(1)(A), 94 Stat. 132, 161 (emphasis added). Thus, Congress focused specifically on the distinction between loans secured by first liens and purchase money loans so secured, and with respect to loans secured by first liens on cooperative housing stock, decided originally to preempt state usury laws only when the loans were purchase money loans. Congress did not similarly restrict the preemptive force of § 501 with respect to loans secured by first liens on residential real property or residential manufactured homes. Moreover, § 501(a)(1)(A) was ultimately amended to remove the language restricting usury preemption in the cooperative housing context to cases where the loan is used to finance the acquisition of the cooperative housing stock.

Congress could have provided for the preemption of state usury laws with respect to any loan "secured by a first lien on residential real property *used to finance the acquisition of such property."* We think its failure to do so in this context can hardly have been inadvertent. In short, we believe that if Congress had intended to limit the preemptive effect of § 501 in this manner, it "would have so stated in the language of the provision."

* * *

The unqualified statutory language is not limited by any reference to the purpose of a loan. We decline plaintiffs' invitation to reach such a limitation into the statute not only because there is no affirmative support for it in the legislative history, but also because we believe that doing so would create undesirable uncertainty in the nation's financial markets. It is in the best interests of all participants in such markets, lenders, borrowers and depositors alike, that financial institutions be able to plan their lending practices in reliance upon a predictable and clear interpretation of § 501. We believe that considerable mischief would be created if courts abandoned the unqualified language of the statute and attempted to divine, on a case-by-case basis, what loans falling within the literal words of § 501 Congress might not deem worthy of the shelter provided by that section.

As the legislative history does not convince us that there existed a clearly expressed congressional intent contrary to the plain words of subsection (A) of § 501(a)(1) of DIDMCA, we conclude that the transactions here were loans secured by a first lien on residential real property for purposes of that subsection, and that the Pennsylvania usury laws are preempted.

* * *

The judgment of the district court will be affirmed.

Notes

1. The 1980 Depository Institutions Deregulation and Monetary Control Act (DIDMCA) was not the first federal preemption of state usury laws.

Between 1974 and 1983, Congress enacted a series of laws which temporarily preempted all state usury laws for certain business and agricultural loans. In 1979, Congress preempted state usury laws for FHA- and VA-insured mortgage loans. See 12 U.S.C.A. § 1735f–7; 38 U.S.C.A. § 1828. The DIDMCA extended this exemption in 1980 to all home mortgage loans. In Doyle v. Southern Guar. Corp., 795 F.2d 907 (11th Cir.1986), cert. denied, 484 U.S. 926, 108 S.Ct. 289, 98 L.Ed.2d 249 (1987), the court held that a mobile home lender who complied with the VA and FHA exemption rules need not also comply with the DIDMCA rules in order to exempt itself from state usury law.

2.   During the first three years, under 501(b)(2), states were permitted to opt out and reinstate their own usury laws for mortgage loans. Fourteen states (Colorado, Georgia, Hawaii, Idaho, Iowa, Kansas, Massachusetts, Minnesota, Nebraska, Nevada, North Carolina, South Carolina, South Dakota, and Wisconsin) and Puerto Rico did so, and one state (Maine) opted out for certain supervised lenders.

3.   Does the ruling in Smith allow an unscrupulous creditor to manipulate the consumer into paying extremely high rates? How is it that Fidelity was able to get a *first* mortgage here? Isn't it likely that the average consumer's home is already burdened with a first mortgage loan, and that the most a lender in Fidelity's position could get would be a second mortgage? In Smith, all of the consumer borrowers were elderly, and all had owned their homes for nearly 30 years or more at the time the loans were made, long enough to have paid off, or nearly paid off, the original mortgages. (As the court noted, Fidelity advanced enough to one of the borrowers to pay off an outstanding lien on the home.) As a result, it was able to put itself in the first mortgage position and use the usury preemption provision. The facts are spelled out in more detail in the district court opinion, Laubach v. Fidelity Consumer Discount Co., 686 F.Supp. 504 (E.D.Pa.1988).

4.   Does any usury law apply to the transaction in Smith?

MOYER v. CITICORP HOMEOWNERS, INC.

United States Court of Appeals, Eleventh Circuit, 1986.
799 F.2d 1445, reh. denied, 804 F.2d 681.

TJOFLAT, CIRCUIT JUDGE:

This interlocutory appeal is from a decision of the district court holding the interest rates of three retail installment contracts for the purchase of mobile homes usurious under Georgia law. As to two of the contracts, the court rejected the lenders' argument that federal law preempted Georgia law and authorized the interest rates charged. With respect to the third contract, the court refused to apply South Carolina's usury law, which also would have authorized the interest rate charged. We disagree with the district court's treatment of the federal preemption issue and accordingly reverse its decision on this point. We affirm, however, the court's application of Georgia law to the third contract.

I.

In the late 1970's, the interest rates permitted under the usury laws of many states were so far below the interest rates called for by free market forces as to make housing unavailable to many who needed mortgage financing. In an effort to cure this problem and to permit financiers to charge the interest rates commanded in the free market, Congress, in 1980, enacted the Depository Institutions Deregulation and Monetary Control Act, Pub.L. No. 96–221, tit. V., § 501, 94 Stat. 161 (1980) (codified at 12 U.S.C. § 1735f–7 note (1982)) (DIDMCA). Section 501(a)(1) of DIDMCA expressly preempts all state laws that limit the interest rate chargeable in connection with loans creating first liens on residential real property and mobile homes, provided that the terms and conditions of such loans comply with regulations promulgated by the Federal Home Loan Bank Board (Bank Board).

A.

In 1981, two married couples from Georgia, the Sanderses and the Harrisons, purchased mobile homes from a dealer in Thomson, Georgia. They paid part of the purchase price in cash and financed the balance, giving the dealer a first lien on the purchased mobile homes by executing a retail installment contract. The contracts provided for interest rates in excess of the rate allowed by the Georgia Motor Vehicle Sales Finance Act, O.C.G.A. §§ 10–1–30 to 10–1–38 (1982) (MVSFA). The dealer sought to avoid the application of MVSFA by having the buyers execute retail installment contracts that recited that they were made in compliance with federal law, presumably DIDMCA. The dealer assigned the contracts to Citicorp Homeowners, Inc., which, in turn, assigned them to Citicorp Acceptance Co., Inc. (collectively, "Citicorp").

B.

In June 1981, the Moyers, citizens of South Carolina, entered into a retail installment sales contract with an Augusta, Georgia dealer for the purchase of a mobile home. The contract provided for an interest rate in excess of that allowed by MVSFA but permitted under South Carolina law. Apparently in an effort to ensure that South Carolina's usury law would govern the transaction, the dealer had the Moyers execute a form contract that conformed to South Carolina law. The contract provided, however, that it would be governed by the law of the state of the dealer's residence; in this instance, the dealer resided in Georgia. Nothing in the contract indicated that it had been drafted so as to comply with DIDMCA. After the contract was executed, the dealer assigned it to Citicorp.

II.

On March 22, 1983, the Sanderses, Harrisons, and Moyers (collectively "buyers" or "debtors"), invoking the district court's diversity jurisdiction, 28 U.S.C. § 1332 (1982), joined forces and filed this class action suit against Citicorp in the United States District Court for the Southern District of Georgia. They alleged that the interest rates they were paying Citicorp violated Georgia's usury law, MVSFA, and asked the court to enjoin Citicorp from collecting the interest due under their contracts. They also sought the recovery of the penalty provided in section 10–1–38(c) of MVSFA: "double the time price differential and any delinquency charge and any attorneys' fees and court costs charged and paid with respect to such" contracts. The debtors sought the above relief in behalf of all persons who had executed similar contracts assigned to Citicorp.

Citicorp, in its answer, alleged that the Sanders and Harrison contracts complied with DIDMCA and the regulations promulgated by the Bank Board; consequently, the interest charged was permissible. As for the Moyer contract, Citicorp alleged that South Carolina law, which allowed the contracted interest rate, controlled.

* * *

A.

1.

To avoid a state's usury laws, a lender must provide in his loan statement that "debtor may prepay in full or in part the unpaid balance of the loan at any time without penalty." 12 C.F.R. § 590.4(d) (1985). "The right to prepay shall be disclosed in the loan contract in type larger than that used for the body of the document." *Id.* The debtors' right to prepay without penalty is set out on the face of the Sanders and Harrison contracts. The district court, however, found that words in both the body of the documents and the prepayment clause were of the same *point* type size and accordingly ruled that the contracts did not satisfy section 590.4(d). We view the district court's interpretation of the regulation as unduly narrow.

As we noted in our en banc decision in *Grant v. General Electric Credit Corp.,* 764 F.2d 1404, 1408 (11th Cir.1985) (en banc) (per curiam), the Bank Board's originally proposed version of section 590.4(d) required that the prepayment clause be "conspicuously disclosed in the loan contract." 45 Fed.Reg. 31,124 (1980). The Board eventually employed the current type-size language because it believed that the "conspicuously disclosed" standard "may be potentially troublesome." 45 Fed.Reg. 43,684 (1980). It is clear that the current regulation is intended to require a creditor to set out the prepayment clause in such a way as to bring the clause to the debtor's attention. The Bank Board determined that larger type would accomplish this result. Nothing in the language or history of section 590.4(d), however, suggests that the prepayment clause be in a larger *point* type than the type used in the body of the document. The type in the prepayment clause of the Sanders and Harrison contracts, while perhaps of the same point type as the type used in the body of the contracts, is still "larger" than the type in the body of the contracts for the purposes of section 590.4(d).

The disclosure clause is printed in boldface type; each letter of the clause is wider than those appearing in the body of the contracts. In addition, most of the initial letters of each word in the clause are capitalized, in contrast to the initial letters of the words in the body of the contracts which are only capitalized if they begin a sentence or certain significant terms. These distinguishing factors serve to bring the prepayment clause to the attention of the debtor; we therefore hold that the Sanders and Harrison contracts satisfy section 590.4(d).

2.

Section 590.4(h)(1) provides that "no action to repossess or foreclose, or to accelerate payment of the entire outstanding balance of the obligation may be taken against the debtor until 30 days after the creditor sends the debtor a notice of default." We have noted in *Quiller v. Barclays American/Credit, Inc.*, that the regulation does not require that a contract contain a clause expressly guaranteeing the debtor thirty days' notice prior to acceleration or foreclosure. Where a contract contains terms that are inconsistent with the notice requirement of section 590.4(h), however, the contract is not in compliance with the regulation and cannot qualify for federal preemption under DIDMCA. We must therefore examine the Sanders and Harrison contracts to determine whether they contain terms inconsistent with the thirty-day notice requirement of section 590.4(h).

The documents in question twice refer to the buyers' right to be notified and to cure in the event of a default. On the face of each contract is the following provision concerning the seller's right of acceleration: "Seller may, Subject to Buyer's Right of Notice and Right to Cure, accelerate the unpaid balance of the Total of Payments less earned charges computed according to the pro rata method upon default in payment of all installment or other obligations provided herein." * * * The district court held that this provision is inconsistent with the notice requirement of section 590.4(h). We find no such inconsistency.

The notice provision on the face of the contracts is in harmony with section 590.4(h), for it clearly requires as a condition precedent to the seller's right to accelerate that the buyer be given notice and the opportunity to cure. Further, there is nothing in the provision that suggests that such rights are not those enumerated in the federal regulations. Nor is the provision on the back of the contracts inconsistent with section 590.4(h). Like the one on the face of the contracts, this provision expressly conditions the seller's rights of acceleration and forfeiture on the satisfaction of the buyers' right of notice and right to cure. * * * Accordingly, we hold that the Sanders and Harrison contracts satisfy section 590.4(h).

B.

Citicorp concedes that the Moyer contract does not satisfy the requirements of DIDMCA and that as a result the contract is subject to state law. Citicorp justifies the interest rate it has been collecting by relying on South Carolina law, which allows the rate. It contends that the trial court erred in applying Georgia rather than South Carolina law to the contract. We find no trial court error.

The contract was executed and made payable in Georgia. In addition, the contract contained a choice of law provision indicating that the contract shall be construed in accordance with the laws of the state in which the seller's place of business is located. The Moyers purchased their mobile home from a Georgia dealer. To get around this choice of law provision Citicorp relies on a choice of law rule that, it contends, Georgia courts have applied in usury cases. It argues that in such cases a contract will be upheld against the charge of usury if it provides for a rate of interest that is permissible in a state with which the contract has a substantial relationship. *See* Restatement (Second) of Conflict of Laws § 203 (1971). The Moyer contract, Citicorp maintains, has a substantial relationship with South Carolina, a state that would enforce the contract; therefore, its laws should govern the contract.

Citicorp does not persuade us. Even were we to assume that the Georgia courts would apply the Restatement rule, it does not follow that South Carolina law should govern the contract at hand. Citicorp ignores the crucial fact that the contract, which it drafted, in effect calls for the application of Georgia law. Given this choice of law provision, we find it difficult to accommodate Citicorp's argument that South Carolina law should be applied.

* * * We, therefore, see no reason not to enforce the contract's choice of law provision.

III.

In conclusion, we hold that federal law preempts the application of MVSFA to the Sanders and Harrison contracts and reverse the district court's ruling to the contrary. We affirm the court's determination that Georgia law governs the enforcement of the Moyer contract.

Notes

1. The regulations which control whether creditors qualify for the usury preemption on mobile home loans are found in 12 C.F.R. Part 590. The substantive contract rules are contained in § 590.4. They contain provisions for prepayment penalties, refunds of precomputed finance charges on prepayment, balloon payments, late charges, deferral fees, and pre-foreclosure or repossession notices. They do not, however, establish any maximum interest rate ceilings, and expressly state that no state interest rate legislation shall apply to first mortgages on mobile homes. See 12 C.F.R. § 590.4(b)(1). These rules in § 590.4 read a lot like a mini-consumer credit code. Compare, for example, the substantive rules in U3C Article 2, Part 5; Article 3, Part 3; and Article 5, Part 1. Also compare the FTC Credit Practices Rule. Why duplicate rules found in other

sources? For a more recent case applying the DIDMCA mobile home rules, see *Atkinson v. General Electric Credit Corp.*, 866 F.2d 396 (11th Cir.1989).

2. In *Moyer,* was it disingenuous for the creditor to argue that Georgia law was preempted for two of the contracts but that South Carolina law controlled the third? Why did the creditor make this argument? Did it surprise you to see a conflicts of law dispute in a usury case? How often do you think this occurs?

3. If Congress thought it was important that mobile home loan contracts comply with these substantive consumer protection rules, why didn't it just enact them directly? I.e., why limit their application only to those loans for which creditors want to escape state usury laws? When market rates are lower and creditors are willing to lend within the limits of state law, presumably they will not have to comply with these rules. Is that a loophole Congress should worry about? For that matter, why should these rules be limited to mobile home loans? If these substantive restrictions are good for the purchasers of mobile homes, shouldn't they also be good for the purchasers of cars or appliances?

4. No new federal preemptions of state usury laws have been enacted since 1980, but bills are periodically introduced into Congress which would take federal preemption much further than it has gone to date. Some of these bills would preempt state laws for all loans; others would apply to all consumer loans. Some are more limited, and would preempt state laws only for a particular class of loans, such as credit card transactions. At least one of your authors believes that the principal reason none of these proposals has been enacted is that the general economic pressure on interest rates eased considerably during the late 1980s. This author believes that when rates rise again and begin to push past state ceilings, we will hear a new outcry for federal preemption.

Notes on Variable Rate Contracts

1. Several home mortgage lenders have instituted home mortgages having a "variable interest rate"—one in which the interest rate can go up or down if interest rates generally go up or down after the loan is made. Variable rate loans have become big business; it has been estimated that as much as 60% of all residential mortgages contain variable rate features. In these types of contracts, both the lender and the consumer are gambling about future financial rates. As we saw in chapter 2, the primary approach to these problems by the federal government has been through mandatory disclosure. Yet, because of their complexity, these contracts raise several problems which invite us to consider whether there should be some form of substantive regulation. For example:

(a) The rate variations need to be governed by an index which relates to the lender's costs, but cannot be controlled directly or indirectly by the lender. Should use of a particular index, or a particular type of index, be mandated?

(b) If the rate goes up, either the consumer's monthly payments will rise, or the duration of the mortgage will be longer. If of a variable duration, the mortgage can become of infinite duration. One study used a hypothetical borrower who started with a variable mortgage in 1960 which was supposed to be paid in 28 years, but could be lengthened if interest rates went up. In 1971, after paying for eleven years, the buyer would still have had to pay for 31 more years because interest rates had risen so much. With a 7%, 30–year mortgage, having a fixed monthly payment, if the rate rises to 8%, the entire payment would go to interest and it could *never* be paid off—the consumer would be on a never-ending, interest paying treadmill. The lender would then effectively own the property, and our public policy promoting home ownership would be effectively defeated. If, on the other hand, the mortgage varies the amount of the monthly payment, should the monthly payment be allowed to increase faster than the debtor's income? How quickly can most consumers pay any significant increase in their monthly bill?

(c) Since the lender, which is normally a bank or savings and loan, has a partial, state-created monopoly and is more aware of trends in the financial market, should the borrower be given a choice between fixed and variable rate contracts? If the lenders know more about future interest rates than the consumer does, are they likely to offer variable rates only when rates are low and not when they are high? (Most economists think that interest rates will go up more than down during the next 30 years.)

To date, few of these questions have been answered by legislation, although present federal regulations require that adjustments of variable rate mortgages correspond to an interest rate index which is "readily available to and verifiable by the borrower and is beyond the control of the [lender]." 12 C.F.R. § 545.33(e) (1989); see also 12 C.F.R. § 34.7 (1990).

2. In 1987, Congress enacted the Competitive Equality Banking Act. Among other things, this act requires that all adjustable rate mortgages "include a limitation on the maximum interest rate that may apply during the term of the mortgage loan." 12 U.S.C.A. § 3806. Under Regulation Z, this maximum rate must be disclosed in the contract. Reg. Z § 226.30. Note that this assumes that there is a maximum rate, or "lifetime cap," as it is known in the industry. Note, too, that while this rule thus requires creditors to "cap" variable rate loans, it does not impose a ceiling or otherwise state what the cap must be.

3. What are the advantages to consumers of rate caps? Should there be "payment caps" as well? What would be their advantages? What are the disadvantages of rate and payment caps?

4. Variable rate contracts should be distinguished from the graduated payment mortgage, which has a fixed interest rate and total finance charge, but allows installment payments to increase according to a predetermined schedule. Its purpose is to allow lower payments when first purchasing a home. The later, higher payments recognize the potential for salary increases.

5. Should lenders be required to give consumers a choice between variable rate mortgages and standard fixed rate mortgages? Is there a justification for a denial of this consumer choice? If lenders are required to offer choices, how many alternative types of mortgages should they be required to maintain? (Present lending practices include such exotic

mortgage devices as wraparound mortgages, graduated payment mortgages, growth equity mortgages, reverse annuity mortgages, and no doubt others.)

6. Variable rate credit outside the mortgage area is still very rare, though not unheard of. See, e.g., Sale, "Floating Rate Instalment Loans: An Option for Increased Profitability," J. Retail Banking, Sept. 1980, p. 1. The following case summary involves an unusual situation but is instructive on disclosure and other problems that lurk in these variable rate transactions.

Moore v. Canal National Bank, 409 A.2d 679 (Me.1979):

Moore, who worked at Canal Bank, got an auto loan from the bank at a "preferred" employee rate of 7.5%. The loan agreement signed by Moore contained this proviso:

If I terminate my employment before the loan is paid out, I agree to sign a new note rewritten at current rate.

When Moore left the bank's employ, she signed a new note at 12%. Her subsequent suit against the bank alleged that the transaction violated the Truth in Lending Act in that the bank did not disclose the variable rate feature in the same document with the other TIL disclosures. She also asserted that the increase in rate violated Maine Consumer Credit Code § 2.504 which prohibits any "refinancing" with a rate increase of more than ¼%. *Held:* The bank's disclosure of the possible rate adjustment separately from the other disclosures did violate Old Reg. Z. As for the alleged violation of the Maine law, this was not a "refinancing" within the state provision. There was no element of new bargaining when Moore left her job at the bank and triggered the rate-adjustment provision. The statutory prohibition was aimed at "flipping" abuses, absent here. The court emphasized:

In practical effect, to hold that the "refinancing" referred to in section 2.504 includes a transaction of the kind here in question would render variable-rate loans nearly useless as a financing device—a drastic result that could not be justified in the absence of some manifestation of legislative disapproval of variable-rate loans elsewhere in the consumer credit laws and regulations.

Query: If a variable rate feature can be tied to the consumer's satisfactory employment with the creditor, could it not also be tied to the consumer's satisfactory repayment to the creditor? Why couldn't a lender in Maine say, for example, that the rate is 10% but increases to 15% if the consumer becomes delinquent and needs to extend the repayment period? Is such a practice authorized by the *Moore* holding?

Chapter 13

AN EVALUATION OF THE ECONOMIC CONSEQUENCES OF INTEREST RATE REGULATION AND DEREGULATION

SECTION A. COMPETITION AND FREE ENTRY

Rate ceilings do not exist in a vacuum. Before one can evaluate the desirability of rate ceilings, one needs to know how easy it is for creditors to enter and compete in the credit market. Theoretically, consumers benefit from open competition among large numbers of suppliers, since competitive forces will keep prices down. If this is true, rate ceilings would seem to be justified only if it can be shown that the free market is not operating effectively in the consumer credit area. The empirical data on this point is mixed. Several studies were done in the 1960s, and they seemed to point in both directions at once. Competition for new auto loans, for example, was apparently producing the desired results; rates generally stayed below the applicable rate ceilings. (Recent experience also suggest that this remains the case.) The same has generally been true for home mortgage loans, home improvement loans, and mobile home loans. On the other hand, finance company loans have tended to stay at or near the ceilings, as have most rates for credit cards. This would seem to justify regulation of small consumer loans, and perhaps credit card loans as well.

In the United States, the market for small consumer loans has never quite been free. The very first small loan acts, in the late 1910s, contained licensing requirements which were barriers to free entry into the market. At first, these laws were considered exceptions to the existing usury laws. They permitted small loan companies to charge rates well above the ceilings for other loans, but the trade-off for these higher rates was a set of restrictions on the freedom of creditors to engage in the small loan business. This remains the pattern today.

Similar licensing requirements, usually under separate statutes, have developed for other types of consumer lenders. The legislation which creates these licensing requirements normally contains interest rate ceilings applicable only to licensees, and the rates are usually different for each group. This pattern has contributed significantly to the segmentation of the industry. Further, partly because of this pattern, creditor competition is primarily intra-segment, rather than inter-segment. Thus, competition between creditors is limited both by the segmentation of the credit industry and the size of the segments, and both of these anti-competitive factors are caused in large part by the barriers to entry erected by the usury laws. Comparable licensing standards also exist in the case of applications for state or federal charters to operate depository institutions (banks, savings and loan associations, and credit unions). Curiously, no similar licensing requirements have ever developed for retail stores offering "sale" credit.

Current licensing requirements are of two basic types. The least restrictive laws are those which require merely that the applicant demonstrate the appropriate financial responsibility and meet the most basic standards of character and fitness. This was the pattern of the earliest small loan laws. Its intent was to weed out those lenders who would abuse the consuming public by not conducting their businesses honestly. (I.e., it was designed to eliminate the loan shark.)

Later drafts of the uniform small loan act included more restrictive requirements. During the late 1920s, it was thought that competition got out of hand in the form of excessive borrowing and over-lending. Paternalistic lawmakers thought the public was not well served by this state of affairs, and so they began to add requirements to these laws. Under the new regime, applicants for lending licenses had to demonstrate that their entry into the market would promote the "convenience and advantage" of the community. This type of restriction directly affects competition by keeping many lenders out of the market. In fact, in states with convenience and advantage qualifications, the regulation of small loan companies begins to take on many of the characteristics of public utility regulation.

The type of licensing statute a state elects to use can have an important impact in the market. New Jersey, for example, has long required a showing of convenience and advantage. See N.J.Stat.Ann. 17:10–5(b). In Family Finance Corp. v. Gaffney, 11 N.J. 565, 95 A.2d 407 (1953), this rule prevented a finance company from doing business in one New Jersey community. The company was "found to be qualified as to financial responsibility and character, but the license was denied on the ground that the issuance of another license in Hoboken would not promote the convenience and advantage of the community." 95 A.2d at 408. At the time, there were already two small loan licensees doing business in Hoboken. The New Jersey Supreme Court upheld the denial. (Do you agree? Was the "convenience and advantage" of the people of Hoboken well served by preventing Family Finance Corp. from operating there?)

The National Commission on Consumer Finance made the relationship between rates and market entry barriers a cornerstone of its 1972 Report. Noting that low rate ceilings may either restrict the supply of credit to some credit-worthy borrowers, or force low risk borrowers to subsidize higher risk borrowers, the Commission related these inequities to competition in the credit market.

NCCF REPORT

91–94, 147, 149 (1972)

Review of the sequential development of legislation affecting the rates charged for various forms of consumer credit in the United States indicates that most states have chosen to enact a great variety of rate ceilings on most forms of credit. In contrast to the approach adopted by most other developed countries, the states generally have adopted a decreed-price approach to the problem of assuring reasonable rates on consumer credit transactions. These varying rate structures have created substantial barriers to entry and diminished competition.

A compilation of consumer credit legislation reveals the present hodgepodge of legislation characteristic of most states. As one example, New York has separate statutes regulating instalment loans by commercial banks, loans by industrial banks, bank check-credit plans, revolving charge accounts, motor vehicle instalment sales financing, instalment financing of other goods and services, insurance premium financing, loans by consumer finance companies, and loans by credit unions. The general usury rate is 6 percent: (currently 7½ percent under special rule of the Banking Board), and criminal penalties apply if interest is over 25 percent. But the decreed maximum rates to obtain $500 of credit, repayable monthly over 12 months, range widely: bank personal and improvement loans, 11.6 percent; industrial banks, 14.5 percent; used cars up to 2 years old, 17.7 percent; used cars over 2 years old, 23.2 percent; small loan companies, 24.8 percent; other goods, 18.0 percent; retail revolving credit 1½ percent on monthly balances up to $500 and 1 percent monthly on balances in excess of $500.

The variety of rate ceilings that has developed on an ad hoc basis creates barriers to competition among segments of the consumer credit industry. Given a maximum rate of 11.6 percent in New York, commercial banks will not enter the $500–loan market served by consumer finance companies at 24.8 percent.

The Commission has noted the recent rush by banks or bank holding companies to acquire finance companies. For example, Bankers Trust New York Corp., the parent corporation of Bankers Trust Company, agreed to acquire Public Loan Company, a New York based firm with 61 offices located primarily in New York and Pennsylvania where banks are limited to a maximum of 6 percent discount on instalment loans (11.6 APR on a 12–month loan). By purchasing the finance company through its holding company, Bankers Trust will enter a consumer credit field previously denied it, in effect, by statute. Cash borrowers in the two states would have been significantly better off if banks had always been able to charge the same rates permitted licensed lenders. The added competition could only benefit cash borrowers.

Market segmentation created by rate ceilings has been made even sharper by other restrictions on various classes of credit grantors. For example, licensed lenders in New York may lend no more than $1,400 to any one borrower, whereas banks may make consumer loans as high as $5,000. Such artificial market segmentation is blatantly anticompetitive and fosters market domination by relatively few firms.

*   *   *

This situation could be changed by eliminating rate ceilings and relying on competition to ensure that borrowers pay reasonable rates for the use of credit. But * * * competition cannot be relied upon at this point in time to establish rates at reasonably competitive levels in many states. Raising rate ceilings in some areas where markets are highly concentrated would merely allow suppliers to raise prices, accept somewhat higher risks, but remain secure within the legal or other barriers which assure them that their market power and monopoly profits will not be diluted.

*   *   *

*   *   * policies designed to promote competition should be given the first priority, with adjustment of rate ceilings used as a complement to expand the availability of credit. As the development of workably competitive markets decreases the need for rate ceilings to combat market power in concentrated markets, such ceilings may be raised or removed.

Notes

1. The NCCF Report also made extensive recommendations to encourage freedom of entry, among them recommendations for federal chartering of finance companies (which are now exclusively state-licensed), and for using only "good character" as a criterion for issuing small loan licenses.

2. The U3C was a product of the same time and similar analysis. It represented a sharp break from earlier state licensing standards for small loan companies, and follows the pattern suggested by the NCCF. U3C § 2.302 sets out requirements for financial responsibility, character, and fitness, but intentionally rejects any test of "convenience and advantage." In general, however, states have not responded to the NCCF recommendations by deregulating the industry or easing entry requirements.

3. Another "competition" question arises out of the recent phenomenon of bank holding companies acquiring small loan companies. There are some inducements to such mergers and acquisitions on both sides: the

banks are often anxious to gain a foothold in the lucrative high-rate small loan field; and in a tight money market, many finance companies are hard-pressed for working capital and need the source of funds a bank affiliation would provide. Such acquisitions require prior approval by the Federal Reserve Board under standards which include a "benefits to the public" criterion.

The NCCF recommended the prohibition of "the acquisition of finance companies by banks when banks are permitted to establish de novo small loan offices."

One recent and instructive merger case, in which the "benefits to the public" issue was thrashed out, involved an application by a Pittsburgh bank holding company to acquire ownership of Local Loan Company, a chain of 124 loan offices mostly on the west coast. The Reserve Board approved the merger on several grounds: (1) Mellon was committed to the aggressive marketing of small loan services, introducing new services, and expanding into new markets; (2) the present "conservative and non-expansionary" management of Local Loan were content with lower-than-average earnings and had not done anything expansive in years; and (3) affiliation of Mellon and Local would provide Local with access to a broad range of financial services—operating capital, marketing and financial analysis, and the like. See Mellon National Corporation, Federal Reserve Board Order Approving Acquisition of Local Loan Co., 62 Fed.Res.Bull. 702 (1976).

Query: Is it obvious that aggressive expansion of Local Loan Company, with Mellon Bank backing, is good for consumers? How?

4. The following article summarizes this approach to the problems of interest rate regulation.

WARREN, "CONSUMER CREDIT LAW: RATES, COSTS AND BENEFITS"

27 Stan.L.Rev. 951, 964–68 (1975).*

[Professor Warren was the co-reporter draftsman for the Uniform Consumer Credit Code from 1964–74.]

VI. RATE REGULATION REFORM

In 1964 the National Conference of Commissioners on Uniform State Laws, fresh from its triumphs in obtaining general enactment of the Uniform Commercial Code, undertook to draft a Uniform Consumer Credit Code and to grapple with the anticompetitive nature of the consumer credit industry. Utilizing professional economic assistance at each step of their project, they set out to do what no other group had done in this country—to develop a set of rate-ceiling provisions that were as rational from an economic viewpoint as possible within the constraints of the political process. Their approach was an attempt to reconcile the economizing mode, in which market forces set the price of credit, with the sociopolitical mode, in which rate ceilings would continue to fulfill some function in safeguarding consumers.

The mechanics of the U3C provisions on rates are simple. First, residual usury laws are repealed, and rate ceilings apply only to consumer transactions—in commercial transactions businessmen are free to contract for any rate of charge they desire. Second, relatively high rate ceilings are placed on all consumer credit extensions. A bifurcated rate system is employed. A graduated rate is first applied, permitting 36 percent on the first $300, 21 percent on the next $700, and 15 percent on that portion of the loan exceeding $1000. However, a superordinate basic rate is applied, assuming that the ceiling rate never drops below 18 percent. Third, artificial barriers to competition are removed. Any creditor can make a credit extension of any size to any consumer for any purpose, the only limitation being that lenders transacting business at rates above 18 percent must be licensed. Sellers, their assignees, and seller credit card issuers need not be licensed. Convenience and advantage standards are abolished, and no minimum dollar amount is set for a showing of financial responsibility by licensees. Thus the Commissioners conceive the proper function of rate regulation to be to set ceilings which satisfy the sociopolitical interest in preventing "gouging" when competition is not effective to keep rates down, but which allow market forces to allocate credit free of anticompetitive barriers. This pattern of regulation has been substantially endorsed by the 1972 Report of the National Commission on Consumer Finance.

During the late 1960's another group entered the field of consumer credit reform: the National Consumer Law Center (NCLC), an Office of Economic Opportunity research and drafting operation, which published its National Consumer Act in 1970 and its Model Consumer Credit Act in 1973. An important asset of the NCLC is the close communication it has maintained with legal services attorneys in the consumer credit field, and perhaps its major contributions have been in redefining areas of consumer abuse and proposing legal remedies for dealing with them. The two NCLC statutes can be looked upon as authoritative statements of what the consumer establishment wants by way of a credit regulation statute.

The NCLC, however, does not view consumer credit from an economic perspective. Its model legislation takes no position on such a basic issue as usury laws, and its posture on barriers to market entry through restrictive licensing seems equivocal. One can only speculate about why the NCLC has proposed model legislation dealing in such detail with the symptomatic abuses in the consumer credit field, while largely ignoring the underlying defect which has contributed so directly to the continuance of those abuses, that is, the imperfection of the consumer credit market. The NCLC measures are peculiarly lawyers' statutes; their emphasis is on providing effective legal remedies for consumers represented by attorneys. There is no evidence of any significant professional economic input with respect to the drafting or consideration of these two acts, nor any reason to believe that the NCLC saw need for such input.

The dismaying fact is that after decades of experience with rate regulation in the area of consumer credit, there is still no consensus among interested parties on what approach to the problem is best. Moreover, the dry pages of a law review article are completely inadequate to portray the depths of distrust and bad feelings between consumer and creditor groups on this issue. Their standoff on rate regulation reform leaves undisturbed the present segmented, totally illogical patchwork of rate-ceiling laws in most states.

The dilemma facing lawmakers on the rate regulation issue today is similar to that a cartographer would confront were he to attend a meeting of the American Geographic Society only to find that one group in attendance believes the world to be flat (populist consumer groups who believe flat 10 to 12 percent across-the-board rate ceilings should be applied); another group sees the world as perfectly round and inexorably governed by the laws of the universe (economists who believe rates should be controlled only by market forces); still another group thinks the world is round in the middle and flat on both ends (U3C position that the market should be permitted to operate within high-rate ceilings); and, finally, yet another group, busily engaged in mapping the world, takes no interest in its shape (the NCLC which makes no proposals on rate ceilings). One would be tempted to call out for the coming of a consumer Galileo but for the inevitability of the heresy trial.

＊　＊　＊ The consumer credit industry has long since outlived its reputation as a shady, backstairs operation, but in terms of rate regulation there has been little change in legislative attitudes over the past 60 years. The social trends outlined above promise increasing stability in consumer credit consumption. If lawmakers can abandon more than a half century of misguided rate regulation and concentrate on the considerable task of making the consumer credit market more competitive, they are likely to find that desirable results will follow. With only a moderate level of governmental intervention (largely in the fraud and overreaching areas), consumers will be able to shop for credit as wisely as they bargain for other services. Rate ceilings will become increasingly irrelevant, and our national paranoia about the price of credit will be relieved.

Notes

1. As other parts of Professor Warren's article indicate, the U3C drafters deliberately incorporated both reforms of creditor practices, to protect debtors more, and an increase in interest rate ceilings. Thus, there was an attempt to create a "rate and reform package." Although the U3C has not been adopted widely, since 1969, state legislatures have widely adopted the interest rate ceiling structure of the U3C—but without the

"reform" half of the package. Compare 1 CCH–CCG ¶¶ 505, 520, 540 with
B. Curran, Trends in Consumer Credit Legislation 158–166, 270–77 (1965).
On the other hand, several federal reforms, including the FTC Holder in
Due Course Rule and the Credit Practices Rule, adopt some of the proposed
reforms, without altering rate ceilings. What do these facts suggest about
relative political strengths of creditors and consumers at different levels of
government?

2. As to current "backstairs operations" of the consumer credit industry, see Commonwealth v. Beneficial Finance Co., infra, Chapter 19.

Argumentative Observations

1. How relevant to ordinary people is all this stuff about potential
competition between creditors, anyway? Low income consumers don't
"shop" for better interest rates, and it would not do them much good to
do so anyway. Middle-income people don't shop for credit either—at
least not very much. How about you? Have you asked more than one
creditor what his "prices" are, in the same way you would naturally
ask in buying food, or a stereo, or a car? Why not?

How easy or difficult is it to shop for credit? There are both
mechanical and psychological barriers. As an example of the former,
how often are rates advertised? (Note that there is a major exception
for auto loans.) As an example of the latter, how certain are you that a
particular lender will lend you money? Are you as certain about that
as you are that a store will sell you goods it has in stock? Do you think
your chances of getting the loan might be hurt by telling the lender
that you are "shopping"? Do these answers have anything to do with
competition or the lack of it?

2. On the other hand, perhaps all this competition stuff may not
be merely neutral, meaningless abstraction. It may have very negative
effects. With limited entry, there may be so few competitors that none
need compete, and all may charge high interest rates without fear.
How many competitors are there in the franchising of universally-
acceptable bank credit cards? Are you aware of competitive differences
in the terms they offer consumers? Do these implications provide an
argument for usury laws?

SECTION B. THE EFFECT OF RATE
CEILINGS ON PROFITS AND AVAILABILITY
OF CREDIT

Prefatory Note

If we continue to have rate ceilings at all, where should they be set
so as to protect consumers from over-reaching while also giving the
creditor a fair return? What happens if rate ceilings are set low—are
consumers protected in fact, and from what? What are the creditor's
costs of extending credit?

The materials in this Section address these issues. The excerpts from the 1972 Report of the National Commission on Consumer Finance lay out the traditional analysis of the rationale for rate ceiling legislation, then state its own findings in relation to those identified purposes. Later materials in the Section explore other ramifications, both economic and non-economic, of interest rate ceiling legislation.

After reading these materials, the student should be prepared to make her own evaluation of usury laws. In addition, she should be prepared to offer her own answer to the key question in this area: Why regulate interest rates at all?

NCCF REPORT

95–108 (1972)

PURPOSE OF RATE CEILINGS ON CONSUMER CREDIT

Although the Biblical tenets against taking *any* return for the use of credit have largely been rejected in today's society, other reasons have been advanced to justify placing upper limits on rates charged for the use of credit-rate ceilings. These reasons include:

1. To redress unequal bargaining power.

2. To avoid overburdening consumers with excessive debts.

[3]. To assure that consumers pay fair rates for credit.

* * *

To redress unequal bargaining power

Advocates of low rate ceilings on credit often argue that the unequal bargaining power of debtors versus creditors will allow creditors to charge what the traffic will bear—the ceiling rate. Support for rate ceilings is usually based on the assumption that most consumers are not knowledgeable about the complexities of finance charges, are incapable or unwilling to use Truth In Lending information, and do not shop for credit.

* * *

Do rates rise to rate ceilings? Staff studies show that assertions that rates always rise to the ceiling are incorrect except when the price ceiling is set at or below the market rate for the particular form of credit placed under price control.

* * *

Do rates rise for other reasons? Commission studies have provided some support for the notion that consumers are not wholly knowledgeable about finance charges and APR's, nor do they appear to shop as intensively for credit as they do for the goods financed. Rates can be higher in some consumer credit markets because ignorance and inertia among borrowers combine with the absence of competition among suppliers. As a result, unequal bargaining power may exist, and the absence of alternative credit sources leads to higher rates or restricted credit availability (or both) in such consumer credit markets. Yet

(S., R., P. & R.) Consumer Law 2d Ed. ACB—25

*   *   * the use of rate ceilings to correct instances of unequal bargaining power and an absence of alternative credit sources is largely ineffective. On balance, rate ceilings appear less desirable than policies to make competition workable.

To avoid overburdening consumers with excessive debts

On the theory that consumers cannot estimate how much debt they can carry when acquiring a good or service, some argue for rate ceilings on credit to prevent consumers from becoming overburdened with debts and subject to abusive collection tactics. They contend that credit grantors who are permitted high rates will entrap unwary consumers, overload them with debt, and then use harsh tactics to collect. The theory is sustainable if it can be shown that consumers who would pay rates above ceiling are those who would become overindebted. Generally, it is assumed that they would be.

*   *   *

What debts are excessive? A discussion turning on excessive use of consumer credit should establish what is meant by "excessive." For some, it means a consumer used credit, possibly at a fairly high APR, to acquire something—a color TV set, or a big car—that the critics consider unwise because of the consumer's economic or social status. To prevent this "prodigal" from such an unwise decision, a low rate ceiling might force down the permitted APR to the point that he is denied credit. The Commission finds it repugnant to force a denial of credit on many *creditworthy* borrowers by the imposition of another's value system.

Another meaning of "excessive" is simply an accumulation of debt that a consumer is unable to repay in accordance with the terms of his credit agreements. This sensible definition avoids imposing one individual's value system upon another.

Do rate ceilings prevent excessive debt? A basic tenet of our economic system is that most consumers and creditors are rational. Banks and finance companies responding to a Commission survey reported that unemployment and illness were the first and third most important reasons, respectively, for debtors' failures to meet their obligations. At the time they obtained credit these consumers made rational decisions that were later upset by unexpected events. Lowered rate ceilings would not have prevented them from wanting to use credit.

The second most important reason cited was "overextension of credit." This represents an error in judgment by both creditor and consumer; both incorrectly estimated future cash flows to meet the promised payments. Although it is in the self-interest of each party to avoid such errors, they do occur. How does lowering the rate ceiling affect mutual errors of judgment? Governmental lowering of rate ceilings forces lenders offering cash credit to take less risk, narrowing the market they are willing to serve. Consumers are not so constrained; they are even more eager to take on obligations at the lower rate. But because the lender makes the ultimate decision to accept or reject a consumer's promise to pay, he will deny more applications at the lower rates, assume less risk, and limit overextensions of *cash* credit.

* * *

But overextension of cash credit is only a part of the problem. A consumer with less than a prime credit rating who wishes to borrow cash to shop for a TV set may be rejected by all cash lenders because they cannot afford to serve him. But he can still obtain credit at credit retailers if they can merely transfer part of the finance charge into the cash price of the goods and services sold. Even if the ceiling price for credit were set at *zero percent,* consumers could still become overburdened by purchasing goods and services on credit. They do so today from some credit retailers who make no explicit charge for the use of credit. In such situations, a rate ceiling does not prevent consumers from becoming overextended when they are tempted to buy beyond their means. It merely narrows the range of credit sources available and puts the credit retailer in a more powerful bargaining position relative to the consumer who desires credit.

* * *

To assure that consumers pay fair rates for credit

The most compelling problem to be considered is whether rate ceilings assure that consumers pay "fair" rates for credit. The crucial questions deal with whether rates are fair for some, for all, and for whom if not for all. Additionally, there is an immediate problem in judging the fairness of rates without judging the associated terms under which credit is granted. This package—the credit offer function—is complex with features having differing values to different consumers. These features should properly be taken into account in determining if a consumer is paying a fair rate. Finally, there exists no generally acceptable standard for what is a fair rate. Notwithstanding this complexity, it is possible to consider the impact of rate ceilings in terms of a two-dimensional credit offer function: rate and risk. The underlying assumption, of course, is that consumers who pose a high risk to the credit grantor must pay higher rates, other things being equal.

* * *

Thus, rate ceilings may allow some better credit risks to pay less in imperfectly competitive markets, but only at the expense of the higher risk borrowers who are excluded from the market. As noted before, rate ceilings may cause a transfer of credit costs to cash price in sales credit.

It would be fallacious to assume that higher risk consumers thus denied legal cash loans would forego their desired credit-financed consumption. Some will turn to sales credit where some portion of the finance charge may be buried in the cash price of the good or service. Others may turn to the illegal loan market.

* * *

The difficulty is that most consumers forced from the legal cash loan market into the hands of loan sharks are represented in no statistical sample, pay rates that are unreported and undisclosed, and must remain mute when legislatures lower price ceilings on consumer credit in well-intended efforts to afford greater "protection" to some other borrowers. Without presuming to pass on constitutional issues, the Commission must at least raise the question of whether it is desirable for the state to deprive one group of consumers access to cash credit by rate ceilings while permitting more affluent consumers to obtain cash credit.

* * *

MICKENS, USURY DEVELOPMENTS IN 1981
15 Clearinghouse Review 806, (January, 1982).*

New York, which eliminated its interest rate ceilings on consumer credit effective December 1, 1980, provides a perfect example of the kinds of creditor abuses that can be expected after elimination of state interest rate ceilings. Consumer credit costs have increased significantly since usury ceilings were removed. One furniture store that was randomly audited was charging over 200 percent annual percentage rate (APR). In February 1981 (just 3 months after the ceilings were lifted) the New York State Banking Department completed a study to see how much consumer credit interest rates had increased after the state's usury ceilings had been removed. It found substantial rate jumps in the markets that have always needed regulation most. Finance companies' rates had risen by almost one third (from 19 to 25 percent), while used car financing had become much more expensive (increasing from 20 to 24 percent). Ironically, finance companies now charge the same average APR, 24 percent, for both secured and unsecured credit!

Bank rates in New York have also increased. Revolving bank credit cards increased (from roughly 16.5 percent, under a two-part rate structure) to as much as 19.8 percent. * * * Used car loans from banks moved from 13 to 18 percent, a greater relative increase than that of the finance companies for this kind of lending. Second mortgage "home improvement" loans now cost over 18 percent, up from just under 13 percent before deregulation.

In spite of the above increases, only 8 of 19 large commercial banks reported increases in availability of consumer credit; the magnitude of the increase was not reported. * * * All six of the auto dealers polled reported no change in credit policy or any increases in the volume of financing since the rate ceilings had been removed. * * *

The note below states the traditional economic attack on all interest rate ceiling legislation.

NOTE, USURY LEGISLATION—ITS EFFECTS ON THE ECONOMY AND A PROPOSAL FOR REFORM

33 Vand.L.Rev. 199, 212–14 (1980).*

A. The Effect of Usury Ceilings on the Economic Function of Interest Rates

To gauge the effectiveness of the present system of usury legislation, it is necessary to examine the economic function of interest rates in the credit market. Interest is the cost imposed on a borrower for the present use of capital over a specified period of time. This cost, like the cost of other goods and services, is a function of the intersection of the demand for credit with the supply in the credit marketplace. Unlike other goods and services, the price of which is paid in full at the time of the exchange, the cost of credit includes the element of uncertainty of non-repayment of both principal and interest. This element of uncertainty is a cost that lenders must consider in establishing the rate for a particular loan. Consequently, the calculation of market rate includes a base charge of the cost of "riskless" credit and additional charges sufficient to cover the risk expense. When the market rate for credit for a particular transaction is below the usury ceiling, the statute has no effect because market forces determine the cost of the credit. When the market rate exceeds the ceiling and the transaction is not exempted, however, lenders are unable to earn the market determined return on loans made. Consequently, these lenders have no incentive to lend because a market analysis reveals that there is either no profit or less than market return to be earned from the transaction. The practical result is that less credit is available on the controlled market. Lenders with flexible portfolios will choose to invest in uncontrolled investments or loan in states without effective usury restrictions. * * *

* * *

When the usury ceiling is in effect, however, the law interferes with the allocation role of interest rates; the ceiling restricts the freedom of borrowers to express their choice with dollars. As the return on loans drops below market rates, lenders will attempt to maximize profits by adopting methods to allocate credit that will minimize their risk and costs. Termed non-price rationing devices because the credit is allocated according to factors other than cost, lenders will ration credit based on the contract terms or on borrower characteristics. An example of nonprice rationing criteria based on contract terms is the shift to requirements of larger loans, higher loan fees, higher down payments, and shorter maturities because of the lower costs involved in proportion to the rate of return. A lender must derive all of his profit from the price he charges for the loan. If the price is fixed, he will attempt to minimize his costs within this profit margin. The most extensively used nonprice rationing criteria are those relating to the borrower's wealth and the risk of nonpayment he presents. Factors such as wealth, income, available collateral, and the relationship between the parties will determine the risk. As a consequence of the use of these criteria, the prospective borrowers who are first excluded from the legal credit market and denied the ability to borrow at any price are those borrowers who are in the market for small loans and are not competitive in the nonprice rationing system. Generally this is the segment of the population with poor credit ratings, low incomes, and high rates of unemployment. Ironically, this class includes those unsophisticated borrowers that the usury laws were designed to protect.

* * *

Notes

1. Several empirical studies support the conclusions reached in the above excerpt. See, e.g., An Empirical Study of the Arkansas Usury Law: With Friends Like That . . .", 1968 U.Ill.L.F. 544; Lynch, Consumer Credit at Ten Percent Simple: The Arkansas Case, 1968 U.Ill.L.F. 592; Crafton, An Empirical Test of the Effects of Usury Laws, 23 J.L.Econ. 135 (1980); Boyes and Roberts, Economic Effects of Usury Laws in Arizona, 1981 Ariz.St.L.J. 35. Do these studies make the case for repealing the usury laws?

2. Is it necessarily undesirable to have cash buyers subsidize credit buyers? If cash buyers were mostly high-income consumers and credit buyers were mostly low-income consumers, would it be an irrational policy decision by a legislature to try to have one subsidize the other? Compare the effect of the "free ride" period available on most credit cards, in which those who must use the true credit feature of credit cards subsidize those who can afford to take advantage of the free ride by paying in full every month, typically middle- and upper-income consumers. Is the credit card subsidy more, or less, defensible than the usury subsidy?

3. Can a nation-wide merchandiser like Sears or Penney's charge different prices in states which have low usury ceilings? Is it likely to do so? For that matter, can a nation-wide finance company like Associates or Beneficial charge different rates in different states? If you were Sears' or Beneficial's attorney, how would you advise it to operate in states with low usury ceilings? Would you favor enactment of the U3C?

4. Those who advocate abolishing usury laws focus almost exclusively on the economic effects of those laws. What are the economic effects of such laws? Do they conform to the traditional analysis?

Prefatory Note

The materials which follow touch on these issues. The first item, excerpted from the FTC's Economic Report on the practices of District of Columbia retailers, reflects the Commission's findings in a study of D.C. merchants who sold goods on credit. The merchants studied included some who dealt with middle-class consumers and some who dealt with low-income consumers.

The second item addresses the consequences of setting relatively low rate limits on the availability of credit. Maine tried to limit interest rates in an unusual way, through legislation which prohibits "flipping" by high-rate lenders, and inhibits long-term lending by them.

The practical effect on price, abuses and availability of credit of the D.C. and Maine approaches to rate regulation should be contrasted. In addition, we are still asking the question: Why regulate interest rates at all?

Credit in the District of Columbia

Prefatory Note

Occasionally the effects of a jurisdiction's restrictive rate policy can be quite visible. Washington, D.C., for example, has no special small-loan legislation, and thus no small loan companies. But Maryland small loan vendors are clustered along all the major arteries into the city—just *outside* the city limits.

In 1968, the FTC undertook to study retailers in the District of Columbia, both those who dealt with middle-class consumers and those who dealt with low-income consumers. The retailers involved sold goods on credit to D.C. buyers. The excerpts reprinted below deal with the Commission's findings concerning the (1) differences in the prices charged for merchandise by the different types of retailers, (2) the differences in rates of interest charged, (3) the differences in net profits realized, and (4) the availability of credit to different income persons from different types of retailers.

Would you have predicted each of the findings of the study? Can you explain any of the apparent discrepancies? (Especially the profit margins of retailers who deal with low-income consumers. Where do the funds from their high prices go?)

FEDERAL TRADE COMMISSION, ECONOMIC REPORT ON INSTALLMENT CREDIT AND RETAIL SALES PRACTICES OF D.C. RETAILERS

(1968), pp. 16, 20–21, 28, 42–44.

OVERALL NET PROFIT COMPARISONS

The previous section compared profits for a selected sample of 10 low-income market and 10 general market retailers. Less extensive data on income and profits were obtained from other retailers. Almost half the retailers surveyed submitted profit and loss statements and balance sheets. The companies included corporations, partnerships, and proprietorships. There was a considerable amount of variation in the accounting methods used and in individual firm returns. Nevertheless, it is possible to make some overall comparisons of net profits for each group of retailers. Low-income market retailers reported the highest net profit after taxes on net sales, 4.7 percent (table II–6). Among the general market retailers, department stores were highest with 4.6 percent. Furniture and home-furnishings stores earned a net

TABLE II–6.—*Net profit after taxes as a percent of sales and rates of return after taxes for District of Columbia retailers surveyed, 1966*

Type of Retailers	Net profit after taxes as a percent of sales	Percent rate of return after taxes on stock-holders' equity
Low-income market retailers	4.7	10.1
General market retailers:		
Appliance, radio, and television stores	2.1	20.3
Furniture and home-furnishings stores	3.9	17.6
Department stores	4.6	13.0

Source: FTC Survey.

TABLE II–4.—*Comparison of reported wholesale and retail prices for best-selling products, low-income market and general market retailers*

Products	Wholesale cost		Retail price [1]	
	Low-income market retailer	General market retailer	Low-income market retailer	General market retailer
Television sets:				
Motorola portable	$109.00	$109.50	$219.95	$129.95
Philco portable	108.75	106.32	199.95	129.95
Olympic portable	[2] 90.00	85.00	249.95	129.95
Admiral portable	94.00	91.77	249.95	129.99
Radio: Emerson	16.50	16.74	39.95	25.00
Stereo: Zenith	32.99	32.99	99.95	36.99
Automatic washers:				
Norge	144.95	140.00	299.95	155.00
General Electric	183.50	160.40	339.95	219.95
Dryers:				
Norge	80.00	87.00	249.95	102.45
General Electric	206.90	205.00	369.95	237.76
Admiral	112.00	115.97	299.95	149.95
Vacuum cleaners:				
Hoover upright	39.95	39.95	79.95	59.95
Hoover canister	26.25	24.55	49.95	28.79

1. Retail prices are cash and do not include separately imposed finance charges.
2. Reported as approximate wholesale cost.

profit after taxes of 3.9 percent; and appliance, radio, and television retailers were last in order of profitability with 2.1 percent profit after taxes on sales.

Low-income market retailers reported an average rate of return after taxes on net worth of 10.1 percent. Rates of return on net worth

FIGURE III–1.—Distribution of Effective Annual Rates of Finance Charges on Installment Contracts of Low–Income and General Market Retailers, 1966.

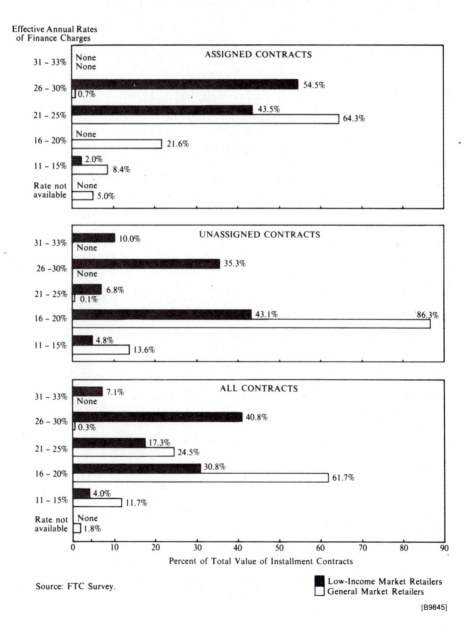

Source: FTC Survey.

Low-Income Market Retailers
General Market Retailers

[B9845]

varied considerably among general market retailers. Appliance, radio, and television retailers reported the highest rate of return after taxes, 20.3 percent of net worth. Next in order were furniture and home-furnishings retailers with 17.6 percent, and department stores with 13 percent return on net worth.

Data on profits reported above are limited and to some extent inconclusive. It does not appear, however, that low-income market retailers made profits which were substantially higher on the average than general market retailers. The high prices charged by low-income market retailers must have been accompanied in many instances by substantially higher costs arising from their method of doing business. Some of these costs probably arose from greater losses on credit sales. To some extent, costs may have been higher because of smaller volume and generally more costly and less efficient store operation.

CREDIT AVAILABILITY

The family, occupation, and income characteristics outlined in the preceding pages are central considerations in the granting of credit to any prospective customer. As a group, the customers included in the sample would be judged marginal risks by most prospective credit grantors. In fact, a review of credit references noted in the 486 contracts subjected to detailed analysis revealed that 70 percent indicated either no credit references or credit references from low-income market retailers only (table IV–9). For those with monthly incomes of less than $300, the figure was 78 percent. Except for limited purchases, customers in this group for the most part would be considered unqualified to receive credit from general market retailers.

TABLE **IV–9.**—*Credit references of customers* [1] *(classified by income groups of customers)*

Type of credit reference	Monthly income groups of customers						Total number of customers	Percent of total
	Less than $300	Percent of group total	$300 to $499	Percent of group total	$500 and over	Percent of group total		
No credit references submitted	99	53.0	91	49.7	44	37.9	234	48.1
Credit obtained only from other low-income market retailers	46	24.6	36	19.7	22	19.0	104	21.4
Subtotal	145	77.6	127	69.4	66	56.9	338	69.5
Credit obtained from other types of retailers and financial institutions	42	22.4	56	30.6	50	43.1	148	30.5
Total	187	100.0	183	100.0	116	100.0	486	100.0

1. Credit reference data obtained from credit applications submitted by customers to one low-income market retailer. Source: Bureau of Economics, Federal Trade Commission.

Access to alternative credit sources increases with higher income, even for the group included in the study sample. Only 22 percent of individuals with income below $300 per month had established credit at retail and financial establishments other than low-income market retailers; on the other hand, 43 percent of those with income exceeding $500 per month had such credit. For those with incomes in the $300 to $500 bracket, the figure was 31 percent (table IV–9).

Somewhat surprising, however, is the high proportion of customers with income above average for the sample who had established credit only with low-income market retailers. Though some may still have failed to qualify for credit elsewhere due to heavy indebtedness, numerous dependents, or uncertain job status, others surely could have qualified as acceptable credit risks of general market retailers. Apparently, certain customers continued to buy at high-price, high-margin stores because of inadequate knowledge concerning alternative buying opportunities. Still others bought from such stores because of personal relationships maintained by the retailer. Personal selling is an important part of the marketing effort of these high-price retailers. Continuing contact with customers is maintained through the use of outside salesmen or as a result of frequent visits by customers to make installment payments. Upon each visit the customer may be subjected to additional sales persuasion.

Overcommitment in Maine: A Statutory Study

The original purpose of small loan acts was to provide a high risk source of credit for emergencies, to keep necessitous consumers from loan sharks. They were given high interest rates to compensate them for lending to high-risk borrowers. In 1967, the Maine Legislature found that some consumers had been paying 36 percent simple annual interest for over 14 years, and decided to inhibit the use of such loans as a source of continuing credit. The new Maine law required that the high interest rate may be maintained on any such loan for only three years. Then, whether it has been renewed, refinanced, consolidated ("flipped") or not, the interest rate reduces to 8 percent simple interest. Under this law, 36 percent interest loans could no longer be used as a continuing line of credit. The purpose of the statutory reform was to return the small loan in Maine to its original purpose, to provide temporary high risk emergency credit.

Maine law, therefore, represents a unique approach to the problem of the overcommitted consumer. It seeks to provide sufficient credit availability to the majority of consumers that they are not driven to illegal sources of credit, and it also seeks to reduce improvident loans by inhibiting creditors from overselling their product. To accomplish both these results it provides a two-track system of credit availability. High interest rate loans can provide credit for emergencies, such as medical care, but only on a temporary basis (3 years), and the high interest can protect the creditor from risk of default. However, the current Maine law also inhibits the use of high rates for continuing line of credit. This division of rate ceilings on loans according to the duration of the loan was an attempt to restrict both the amount of high-cost, high-risk loans, and the probability of overcommitment inevitably present in any high-risk loan. However, continuing credit was available at rates up to 18% APR. It was also an attempt to induce lenders to differentiate between two types of potential customers: those with whom they wish to establish a long-term relationship at 18% APR or less; and those deemed not so creditworthy, but who would be eligible for shorter term loans at small loan company rates.

The substance of the earlier provision was retained in 1974 when Maine enacted its Consumer Credit Code by a non-uniform amendment, § 2.308(3):

> (3) No consumer loan on which the annual percentage rate disclosed is greater than 18% may provide for a greater rate than 8% per year on the unpaid balances of the principal remaining unpaid at the expiration of 37 months on the original loan, including any additional amounts borrowed, any deferral, renewal, refinancing, consolidation or extension of the contract made within the 37 months; and thereafter the unpaid principal balance shall not be directly or indirectly renewed or refinanced by the lender who made the loan, nor shall that lender grant any additional loan to the consumer until the unpaid balance has been paid in full.

Some of the underlying considerations for the non-uniform Maine amendment are illustrated in the following discussion of Maine's comparably non-uniform § 2.504.

BAR HARBOR BANK & TRUST CO. v. SUPERINTENDENT OF BUREAU OF CONSUMER PROTECTION

Supreme Judicial Court of Maine, 1984.
471 A.2d 292.

NICHOLS, JUSTICE.

The Plaintiff, Bar Harbor Banking and Trust Company, appeals from an order issued by the Superior Court, Hancock County, affirming (with one modification) a decision and order of the Superintendent of the Bureau of Consumer Credit Protection. In that decision and order, dated April 9, 1980, the Superintendent found that the Plaintiff had violated section 2–504 of our Consumer Credit Code with respect to thirty-seven loans. We uphold the Superintendent's interpretation of section 2–504 and, accordingly, we affirm the judgment below.

After conducting an examination of about 320 loans extended by the Plaintiff, the Bureau of Consumer Protection on October 3, 1979, issued a report concluding that the Plaintiff had committed thirty-nine violations of section 2–504 of the Consumer Credit Code. At the time of the examination, this section read in pertinent part:

§ 2–504.   Finance charge on refinancing

Subject to Section 2–308 with respect to a consumer credit transaction, the creditor may by agreement with the consumer, refinance the unpaid balance and may contract for and receive a finance charge based on the amount financed resulting from the refinancing at a rate not exceeding by ¼% per year the rate charged in the original agreement and stated to the consumer pursuant to the provisions on disclosure. This section shall not apply to consumer loans in which the principle [sic] thereof is payable in a single payment on demand or at a specific time and the finance charge, calculated according to the actuarial method does not exceed 12¼% per year.[2]

9–A M.R.S.A. § 2–504 (1979), *amended by* P.L.1979, ch. 660, §§ 7, 8, P.L.1981, ch. 235 § 3. The Plaintiff cured two of the alleged violations, leaving a remainder of thirty-seven alleged violations.

On January 23, 1980, the Superintendent held an administrative hearing pursuant to 9–A M.R.S.A. § 6–108 concerning the Plaintiff's alleged violations. A Bureau examiner testified that the alleged violations all involved single payment notes on which the annual percentage rate was increased from under 12¼% to over 12¼%. The Plaintiff's president urged that these transactions were "renewals," not "refinancings" within the meaning of section 2–504.

In her decision and order the Superintendent concluded that the Plaintiff had violated section 2–504. She ordered it to refund to the customers concerned the difference between the finance charges imposed on them and the maximum finance charges permitted by the statute, plus interest earned on such charges. In addition, the Superintendent ordered the Plaintiff to reform all outstanding consumer loans refinanced in violation of the statute and to cease and desist from increasing the interest rate by more than ¼% for single payment loans when the rate resulting from refinancing exceeds 12¼%.

The Plaintiff sought review of the Superintendent's decision in Superior Court pursuant to M.R.Civ.P. 80B. On May 26, 1983, that court affirmed the decision.

On appeal here the Plaintiff contends that section 2–504 does not apply to the transactions at issue because they were "renewals," while the section speaks only of "refinancing." The distinction, in the Plaintiff's view, is that a refinancing occurs before the maturity date of the initial loan and a renewal occurs on or after such date. The Superintendent, on the other hand, regards a renegotiated loan as a "refinancing" regardless of whether it occurred before or after the maturity date of the initial loan.

The question posed for us is which of these competing interpretations of the term "refinancing" better accomplishes the purposes of the statute. There is no definition of "refinance" in the Code itself.

2. The first sentence was subsequently amended by substituting "1%" for "¼%." P.L.1981, ch. 235 § 3.

We had occasion to interpret section 2–504 in *Moore v. Canal National Bank*, 409 A.2d 679 (Me.1979). That case involved a variable-rate loan, where it was agreed *ab initio* that the loan would be paid off in installments and that the interest rate on these installments would vary. After examining the language and the legislative history of the provision, we concluded that refinancings "denote a transaction requiring some element of new bargaining between the parties." We found the purpose of the section to be the deterrence of "flipping," the practice whereby lenders take advantage of embarassed debtors by conditioning the renegotiation of a loan repayment on a considerable increase in the finance charge. We stated at that time:

> Section 2.504 is designed to cover primarily the common situation in which a consumer-debtor, unable to meet payments due under a loan, seeks to negotiate a refinancing that will reduce the size of each payment, or lengthen the payment intervals, and extend the period of the loan. In that type of case the object of the Maine version of section 2.504 is clearly to limit to ¼ per cent any increase of the annual percentage rate to prevent undue exploitation by the creditor of the debtor's necessity.

Id. at 687. This rationale for restricting finance charges applies with equal force to single payment and installment notes and to renegotiation transactions both before and after the loan's maturity date.

The Consumer Credit Code is to "be liberally construed and applied to promote its underlying purposes and policies." 9–A M.R.S.A. § 1–102(1). One such purpose, as elucidated in *Moore, supra,* is to prevent "flipping" when a debtor seeks to arrange an alternate scheme for repayment. This purpose would be thwarted if "flipping" were to be permitted in every instance where the alternate arrangement had been made at or after the original maturity date. To avoid that result, we need not strive to "liberally construe" the term "refinancing," however. We simply may choose the ordinary, dictionary meaning over the Plaintiff's novel, unsupported definition.

The Plaintiff cites only two cases to support the definition which it urges: * * * These cases are not on point, nor do they make the distinction that the Plaintiff advocates. In fact, they do not interpret "refinancing" at all. Other courts have defined "refinancing" broadly, with no indication that it is limited to transactions prior to the original loan's maturity date.

There was testimony at the hearing that the banking industry generally regards "refinancing" and "renewal" to be synonymous. The Plaintiff asserted to the contrary but offered no support. Accordingly, we adopt the Superintendent's interpretation of "refinancing" as embracing the transactions involved in this appeal.

The Plaintiff next contends that it is unreasonable and contrary to the legislative intent for the Bureau to interpret section 2–504 to apply to any refinancing in which the *resulting* interest rate, rather than merely the interest rate in the initial transaction, exceeds 12¼%.

Section 2–504 expressly limits its application to loans on which the finance charge exceeds $12\frac{1}{4}\%$ per annum, if the loan is secured by a single payment time note. All but three of the Plaintiff's contested loans were so secured, and on all the loans the initial finance charge was less than $12\frac{1}{4}\%$, while the finance charge after refinancing was greater than $12\frac{1}{4}\%$. The Plaintiff interprets the "$12\frac{1}{4}\%$" limitation as applying to the initial loan.

As the Superintendent observed in her decision and order, "[t]he Bureau has a long-standing history of interpreting the [$12\frac{1}{4}\%$] exception * * * to apply to the resulting refinanced loan and *not* the original loan being refinanced." The construction of a statute by an agency charged with enforcing it is entitled to great deference. We shall accept the agency's construction, especially if, as here, it is long established or contemporaneous with the statute, unless it clearly violates the legislative intent.

It is not clear from the language of the statute whether the "finance charge" referred to means only the initial charge or any subsequent finance charge as well. Nor is the available legislative history helpful in deciphering the Legislature's intent with respect to this provision.

Accordingly, we conclude that this is a matter in which deference to the expertise of the Bureau is appropriate.

The entry must be:

Appeal denied.

Judgment affirmed.

Problem 1

During the 1980s, the use of five-year automobile loans became prevalent. Before 1970, the three-year loan was the norm, and even four year loans were almost unknown. But by 1980, four year loans comprised more than half the automobile financing by some creditors, and ever-increasing length seems to be the trend. Automobile dealers like the current five-year loans because, as car prices rose with inflation, the dollar amount of installment payments did not rise as quickly if spread over a five year period.

Is the lengthening of normal payment schedules misleading under FTC Act § 5? See the materials in Chapter 1. Or, does TIL pre-empt any such analysis by authorizing any financing pattern so long as it is properly disclosed?

Does the Maine non-uniform amendment to the U3C, discussed above, prohibit such four or five year loans? See U3C § 1.301(15). Note that, if applicable, the amendment regulates only those loans whose original APR is greater than 18%.

Would the amendment regulate a five year credit sale by the dealer himself? See U3C § 1.301(12). Why should the provision apply only to consumer loans? Recall that, so long as the prices of cars are not regulated, regulation of the price of seller credit is only partially effective. The seller, unlike the lender, can avoid much of the economic impact of interest rate ceilings by raising the prices of cars.

What has been the effect of this statutory revision on credit availability in Maine?

In 1972, Professor George J. Bentsen undertook to examine the effects of the amendment to the Maine Small Loan Act. In this study he found that:

1. Outstanding loans from small loan companies had decreased:

(in millions of dollars)

1968	1969	1970	1971
$27.6	$21.9	$16.7	$10.8

However, bank and credit union loans increased markedly.

2. Outstanding "aggregate consumer personal loans" from all lenders (but not including credit sellers) had increased.

(in millions of *constant* dollars)

1968	1969	1970	1971
$204	$211	$213	$225

3. A majority of his sample of small loan company borrowers wanted funds for the purpose of consolidating their present debts.

4. As the small loan companies reduced their business, some of their previous customers were rejected when they applied for a new loan or renewal. Of those rejected, 50% were able to borrow from other lenders, and an undetermined additional percentage subsequently obtained credit from credit sellers. Of those who used other lenders, 54% were successful in obtaining credit from lower priced lenders, such as banks and credit unions, and 40% used another small loan company.

5. Of those, less than 50%, who did not obtain funds from other lenders, 77% of them continued to pay their debts regularly, while almost all of the balance missed some payments but also paid their debts. Only one person (out of 250) declared bankruptcy.

6. Of those who used other lenders, 74% of them reported they felt "better". Almost all of those who reported they felt "worse" had gone to another small loan company. Their predominant response was that it was still "too easy" for them to obtain money—they were "still under the burden" of the loan company.

7. Of those who did not use other lenders, 36% of them reported "feeling better", 36% reported "feeling worse", and 28% felt about the same. Those who felt worse represent about 2% of total borrowers in the state. Two-thirds of those who felt worse continued to pay their debts regularly.

See Bentsen, An Analysis of Maine's "36 Month Limitation" on Finance Company Small Loans, in National Commission on Consumer Finance, II Technical Studies 159 (1973).

Counterpoint

One of your editors (who was not present in Maine at the time of the legislative activity described above) is dubious of the conclusions to be drawn from the Maine experience. The substantial decline in small loan companies' holdings and the resulting departure of most of those companies from the state may be a "good thing" only for the banks and retail creditors who remain—and who can charge rates on new transactions higher than the departed finance companies can after the 37 month period has run. Even if the Maine statute works as designed, it amounts to overt credit allocation and may impose needless inconvenience and financial hardship on those customers who genuinely want and need longer term credit. Is it government's role to tell borrowers that, despite their willingness to pay, certain types of credit are off-limits?

Notes

1. "The decisions to keep interest rate ceilings at approximately their previous level, and to retain the 37–month limitation on high-interest loans, were both deliberate. The legislature was seeking to keep the amount of credit available to Maine consumers approximately the same when the M3C is effective. This availability of credit is related to the interest rates which may be charged, and the legislature seems to have indicated that it is satisfied with present availability, although it was urged both that credit was too restricted and that it was too easily available." Spanogle, Changes in the Present Law under the Maine Consumer Credit Code, 25 Maine L.Rev. 173, 188 (1974).*

2. Do those who advocate abolishing usury laws focus too much on the economic effects and too little on other social consequences? The following article presents some arguments on the other side.

WALLACE, "THE USES OF USURY: LOW RATE CEILINGS REEXAMINED"
56 B.U.L.Rev. 451, 495–96 (1976).**

[Professor Wallace suggests four possible purposes for such ceilings:

(a) To protect consumers from the hardships associated with default on high risk credit—repossession, harassment, garnishment and attendant psychic harms;

(b) To provide a kind of controlled disintermediation—i.e., to encourage extensions of credit in one area, such as housing, by putting tight ceilings on credit rates for other purposes;

(c) To prevent overpricing, discriminatory pricing, and deception by creditors;

(d) To reform the basic liability rules in consumer credit in the direction of a kind of "no fault" system where consumers are covered by insurance which protects them from all but negligent defaults.]

IV. Conclusion

Recently, there has been much criticism and little defense of low consumer credit rate ceilings. The result has been an unbalanced view of the issues involved. An overview of the potential of lowered ceilings suggests several uses that appear to deserve thorough consideration before a state or the nation elects a high ceiling policy. Furthermore, close examination of one use—protecting high risk debtors from the psychic harm associated with default—suggests that a moderately low ceiling applied to all forms of consumer credit provides a significant improvement in the distribution of benefits within society. There will, of course, be those who disagree. When considerations of social policy turn on the degree of psychic harm which one or another class must bear, empirical evidence can only help uncover the right decision, it cannot identify it with certainty. A conclusion in favor of a particular alternative must instead turn on the exercise of careful judgment, informed by the available evidence and shaped by the relevant ethical considerations. My purpose has been to show those who set rate ceiling policy that a reasonable judgment can be made to use lowered ceilings for protective purposes. A fair evaluation of the empirical evidence and relevant ethical considerations supports, on balance, lowered ceilings instead of the high ceiling alternative generally proposed. Of course, those who assess differently the real world—the workings of the credit industry, the motivations of credit users and the effectiveness of government regulation—will dispute this conclusion. The available empirical evidence certainly does not preclude differences on this basis, and I would prefer more evidence correlating default harm with high risk credit before advocating wide adoption of lowered ceilings.[185] But in my judgment the most reasonable conclusion is that the psychic harm caused by default will have great impact on high risk debtors if they do borrow and default, while losing the benefits of credit and suffering pain and embarrassment when it is denied will have a relatively slight effect.

Differing interpretations of the evidence should not be exaggerated, however. The disagreement over rate ceiling policy arises from a basic difference as to the ethical considerations which should be brought to bear on the decision. In this respect, the argument for lowered ceilings appears to rest on stronger grounds than that advanced by its critics. The ethical justification for lowered ceilings begins from the premise that any program designed to improve the distribution of benefits and burdens in the society must at a minimum favor those who are the

185. After the time taken by the National Commission to produce so unclear a view of the rate ceiling question at such great expense, Congress and the states will probably be reluctant to fund further study. The empirical limitations that I have acknowledged can thus be expected to continue.

least advantaged.   Lowered ceilings appear to satisfy this criterion. They will protect two classes of debtors, both of which now use high risk credit but are unaware of the risks they run when they do so, at the expense of a [more knowledgable] third class which seems likely to be better off than the others.   In contrast, the ethical position of those who oppose lowered ceilings remains obscure.   On the surface the critics argue that low ceilings will intolerably impair individual liberty and must therefore be rejected.   Yet close analysis demonstrates little, if any, impairment of the liberty of the two classes of debtors who are to be protected.   Although the freedom of the third class to use credit is in fact impaired, any program to improve distribution will probably encroach somewhat on the freedom of others to do what they want.   Few will disagree that some limited encroachment on freedom is acceptable if a significant improvement in distribution results.

Some critics have also premised their position on a version of utilitarianism.   They argue that high ceilings will maximize the sum of social satisfaction, but they fail to inquire whether those less well off at the start are those who end with the greatest improvement.   A high ceiling program would favor the third class of debtors—those who are aware of the risks of high risk credit and want to use it—at the expense of the first two classes.   It is difficult to see how social conditions are improved when the effect of a program is to worsen the lot of the least advantaged classes affected.   If the critics have an ethical justification for high ceilings which rests on a different foundation, they have failed to explain it.

Reformers have tended to decide questions of social organization involving the marketplace by an easy reliance upon the standard wisdom that an unregulated market, on balance, will produce the best result.   Thus, they first suggest solving a social problem in the marketplace by increasing the conformance of the real market to the intellectual model of the unregulated market.   Yet defining the best social organization is an ethical question, and the ethical underpinnings of the results of the unregulated market seem increasingly out of tune with the ethical views of the dominant culture.   When the market exposes individuals to risk of severe physical or psychic harm, ethical concerns will likely reject reliance on the unregulated market.   The Consumer Product Safety Commission's authority to ban unsafe products is one demonstration of this rejection.   Therefore, it is no surprise that a close examination of the consumer credit system leads in a similar direction.   Rate ceilings will be, in effect, a ban on unsafe credit.   What should surprise is the failure to notice the similarity between banning unsafe products and banning unsafe credit.   But the model of the unregulated market seems to hold an almost magic fascination; unfortunately, the magic tends to bewitch rather than clarify.   Although economic analysis helps identify a reform program's cost and benefits, it also tends to obscure the relevant ethical questions. The only antidote is to inquire continually whether the market will reach an ethically justifiable result.   When that question is asked about consumer credit, the answer suggests lowered rate ceilings, inconsistent though they may be with the very essence of an unregulated market.

Problem 2

Sam Silver, a merchant who has sold goods only for cash all his life, has now decided to accept MasterCard and VISA cards. However, on the credit card sales, he will receive only 95% of the face amount of the charge from his bank. Must he raise the prices of his goods by 5% to maintain his same profits? (Or, if only half of his customers use credit cards, must he raise his prices 2.5%?)

If your answers to the above questions are "Yes", how can Master-Card possibly sell their system to any merchant? Have our simplistic economics overlooked anything—such as potentially increased sales?

Are there any similar problems of over-simplification in the preceding studies of D.C. or Maine?

MORRIS, CONSUMER DEBT AND USURY: A NEW RATIONALE FOR USURY

15 Pepperdine L.Rev. 151, 152–56, 169–71, 177–78 (1988).*

This article examines usury as a macroeconomic tool accommodating individual appetites for consumer indebtedness and society's need for economic development. Usury laws are not simply the means of protecting individuals from indebtedness, or of protecting the individual consumer's interest, but they are also a "means of economic policy employed * * * in fighting inflation." This second application of usury, as a macroeconomic tool, and not simply a microeconomic tool, is the most important use of usury in our post-industrial economy, particularly as we struggle with the problems of developed economies, declining employment prospects, high consumer demand for products and services and widespread, convenient credit opportunities. While much criticism has been directed at usury laws as an anticompetitive form of consumer protection, this article argues that even assuming anticompetitive effects exist, they are not dispositive of the merits of usury. In addition, this paper urges reconsideration of usury laws as a means of protecting society from the negative effects of enormous consumer indebtedness.

II. Usury as a Macroeconomic Tool

* * *

In American society, while we continue to have usury laws, they have been greatly undermined by accommodating the business world's need for capital to grow and expand. This has been compounded by the view of usury as a form of microeconomic governmental interference justified only by paternalism. The tension between economic development and usury laws in American society is evidenced by the numerous statutory and judicial exemptions in state usury laws to accommodate businesses that depend upon consumer credit for their viability. Indeed, most modern societies have retained usury laws despite this tension between economic growth and fears about the dangers of excessive personal indebtedness despite the fact that debt slavery and most of the other cruel aspects of debt oppression have been outlawed. While the relationship between consumer debt and economic development is apparent and has been understood since the 14th century revival of trade, it is no longer clear whether usury has any legitimate protective application in societies without debt slavery. While it probably served to moderate the political and social unrest caused by widespread debt oppression in ancient civilizations, it remains to be seen whether usury has come to serve any important social objective in our time or whether it is outmoded and unjustifiable as microeconomic paternalism.

We are in the midst of an antiregulatory trend in public administration, and in that spirit usury has been uniformly criticized in law review literature as anticompetitive and amounting to the unnecessary regulation of lenders. Meanwhile, courts and legislatures are in the process of disassembling most usury regimes on a piecemeal basis. Before the criticism of usury becomes overwhelming, usury should be reconsidered to examine its purpose and relevance to modern economic lives. Although it does depress competition, anticompetitive effects are not dispositive of the possible merits of usury. Usury may still be a good way for society to moderate competing interests in the use of credit and the accumulation of debt in society.

* * *

III. USURY AS CONSUMER PROTECTION

To the extent that usury prescribes the rate of interest lenders may charge borrowers, usury paternalistically substitutes government judgment for that of the parties to the transaction, displacing the market dialogue by eliminating bargaining at least on that term. Viewed on a larger scale, however, usury has another important market effect: its effect on the supply of credit. Usury is a mechanism for controlling the amount of credit in society. By controlling lender incentive to lend by limiting profits from lending, usury laws counterbalance forces increasing the supply of credit. As such, it is a proxy for society's interest in controlling the amount of credit more than society's interest in controlling lender profit.

A. Paternalism for the Incapacitated Borrower

Beyond the larger social interest at stake, the paternalism of usury serves a compelling interest in the case of at least one type of borrower, the incapacitated borrower. Where incapacitation affects the borrower's ability to participate in the marketplace effectively, paternalism remains a compelling reason for structuring lender-borrower relationships according to an objective standard. Although paternalism in legal regulation is no longer considered a compelling rationale for regulation, protecting the vulnerable is the traditional consumer protection rationale. Incapacitated borrowers are susceptible to making mistakes in bargaining transactions, for which they must bear the consequences. Based on the belief that incapacitated borrowers will make irrational decisions about credit, or will be unable to evaluate information or will misestimate risks attendant on the credit transaction, government substitution of judgment is a direct appeal to public moral values, limiting the degree to which vulnerability can be used against the borrower. These are moral values which are themselves important, even apart from efficiency concerns.

There are a number of different kinds of incapacity affecting borrowers, especially modern borrowers. One type of phenomenon that will cause the borrower to be unable to evaluate information is "bounded rationality," a limitation on the ability of any human being to process many pieces of information. Any typical credit transaction involves many considerations along with the applicable interest rate—things which may be related to the cost of credit. Depending on the product or services being purchased on credit, the transaction can become very complicated in the number of terms to be negotiated and their interrelationship. Because of complications inherent in any credit purchase, borrower search, shopping and bargaining strategies tend to reflect self-imposed limitations on information, limiting consumer ability to bargain on all terms using all relevant information.

* * *

Another modern phenomenon that leads to irrational decisions about the use of credit is a compulsive disorder called credit binging or credit abuse. This disorder is growing among well-educated, upwardly mobile young adults who use credit to subsidize a standard of living to which they are accustomed or to which they aspire, but which their current income will not support. The credit abuser uses the pleasure of purchasing goods to overcome feelings of boredom, anxiety, anger, fear, or loneliness. This compulsive behavior has prompted the formation of self-help groups, and has attracted public attention in the media. This disorder incapacitates more borrowers than the traditional types of incapacity such as mental illness, senility, and occasional illiteracy.

Protection of the vulnerable is one of the oldest motivations for consumer protection. Legitimate exercise of paternalistic power recognizes that information is of no use to an illiterate or mentally incompetent person. In order to protect these persons from the consequences of their own actions, a civilized society imposes limits on the ability of others to take advantage of such handicaps. Usury laws which regulate the lender-borrower relationships limit the ability of lenders to take advantage of borrowers who are handicapped in ways that prevent borrowers from fully participating in the bargaining phase of an extension of credit. Usury laws do this by setting objective standards of conduct for lenders. Many of the borrowers assisted by this paternalism might also benefit from a market perfecting strategy like consumer information, but many borrowers who make irrational decisions will not be able to benefit from a market perfecting strategy that refocuses responsibility for mistakes in the bargaining process on them.

Paternalism is a legitimate restraint on lender conduct in order to protect vulnerable people; therefore, usury should not be discarded in its entirety as inappropriately paternalistic. Before policy-makers commit themselves to a choice that excludes limits on interest rates, they should obtain more empirical data on the numbers of borrowers who may be affected by an inability to negotiate credit in their own best interests. These people are incapacitated in terms of the normative model of consumer behavior. Lender marketing and negotiating behavior with respect to these people is the most important factor to control in avoiding problematic debt situations with these borrowers. Usury laws provide objective, self-executing controls on lender behavior.

* * *

Society has a clear interest in limiting exploitation as an exploitative society is in danger of instability by its exploited members. Society also has an interest in both debt and credit as they promote economic development and affect employment, savings, and a host of other factors connected with domestic stability. The structure of lender-borrower relationships should protect society's interest in indebtedness and credit. The question of whether the unregulated market is the best way to structure these relationships is of current importance as lenders seek more freedom from regulation in an era of increased competition and seek to market more credit to a population squeezed by diminishing employment opportunities and diminishing standards of living.

* * *

The tension between these policy concerns, economic development and protection from destabilization, continues in American society today, mainly in terms of the debate over who should structure the relationship between lenders and borrowers, the government or an idealized "free market." Indeed, the constituency pressing for the abolition of usury laws in both state and federal legislatures is composed of lenders and businesses dependent upon consumer credit for profitability. They, like Bentham, are obviously much more concerned with the role consumer debt plays in economic development and growth than with the potential for injury from widespread indebtedness and an oversupply of credit.

* * *

IV. CREDIT AND THE THREAT OF RECESSION

* * *

A. Unemployment and Consumer Debt

During recession, employment diminishes and salaries tend to decline, a trend that is already part of our long term economic prognosis. Even apart from a recession, the trend toward redesign of full time employment into part-time work, growth of part-time and seasonal work and the spread of wage freezes and wage reductions from one industry to another, foreshadow a decline in annual salaries and decline in the average American standard of living. Meanwhile, recent studies report that consumers, most of whom depend upon steady employment and rising income levels for repayment of debt, have undertaken the highest debt load in American history with fewer savings than ever to meet emergencies, or even temporary interruptions in cash flow.

Modern borrowers (and thus modern lenders) need employment income in rising amounts to avoid default. * * * As our consumer debt grows, American borrowers (individually and American lenders in the aggregate) become more dependent on continued employment. With consumer debt approaching one trillion dollars, unemployment and underemployment pose the real danger to society that large numbers of borrowers will default on credit obligations even apart from some event which could trigger a recession.

While default does not reduce modern debtors or their families to slavery, the event can be devastating to individuals and their families, as well as costly to society in quantifiable and nonquantifiable ways.

* * *

B. The Crisis of Credit

Today, institutional pressures to increase consumer debt outweigh borrower incentive to refrain from indebtedness. Lenders, pushed by new competition from any business that has enough market power to raise and lend money, are under enormous pressure to sell credit and expand their portion of consumer debt in order to maintain profits. Market segmentation between lenders had protected profitability for many years. Banks were the most selective lenders charging lower rates to their customers than small loan companies which served different borrowers at higher rates permitted by law. Deregulation and new competition have fostered an intense competition between these lenders resulting in more credit being made available to more borrowers than ever before. This increased competition has caused an expansion of the pool of available consumer credit and may be the single most influential factor leading to problematic debt in our society today. Under deregulation, banks marketing credit have extended more credit in the form of credit cards to consumers than ever before. Lenders granting credit to borrowers in record numbers and at record rates may have overwhelmed rational, information-seeking behavior of borrowers. Borrowers often fail to consider important credit characteristics such as term and rates, assuming that if they can obtain credit in the judgment of the lender, they must be able to afford the repayments. This abdication in the normative borrower dialogue makes the granting of credit by lenders the single most important contributing factor to problematic debt.

* * *

V. AN OVERABUNDANCE OF CREDIT: MARKET
FAILURES AND OVERSUPPLY

Usury laws benefit four groups of consumer borrowers, each of whom does not, or cannot, participate fully in the marketplace. Their failure to participate in the market causes a market failure which, in each case discussed below, causes them to borrow more credit than they want or need. This superabundance of credit contributes to a staggering internal consumer debt. Usury affects lender behavior by diminishing the amount of credit available.

Usury laws benefit uninformed borrowers who borrow more credit than they want because they do not fully understand the risks. Usury laws also benefit the incapacitated borrowers who borrow more credit than they want because they do not understand the risks. Usury laws also benefit high risk borrowers who borrow more than they may want or need because they have no choices. Finally, usury laws benefit credit card borrowers who borrow more credit than they want or need because they choose convenience instead of the process of bargaining and shopping for each extension of credit. Usury laws do not benefit the cash-paying consumer or the low risk borrower who has alternative sources of low rate credit and access to adequate information.

* * *

C. Society's Interest in Controlling The Credit Supply

Society's interest lies not necessarily in control of any of these individual consumer transactions, but rather in controlling the aggregate of them. Society's interest is complicated by the fact that debt is necessary for economic growth, but irresponsible growth can lead to social factors which undermine long term stability. Usury laws are a useful and reasonable tool for limiting consumer debt in society's best interest by balancing the need for economic development with the risk of destabilizing effects on society. Uniform and effective usury laws could be an important counterweight to the forces of oversupply. Deregulation and competition only contribute to the dangers to society from irresponsible growth. Indeed, the legal criticism of usury as anticompetitive ignores the broad trends of our present economic condition which have caused the consumer debt to balloon in the last forty years. Anticompetitiveness alone does not mean that usury is mismatched to its protective task. While economists discount the relationship of consumer debt to recession by noting that consumer debt will not lead to recession, there is little doubt that *in* a recession all consumers suffer, overleveraged consumers suffer most, and the more overleveraged our population is, the more our society will suffer. The forces which contribute to the oversupply and overleveraging of consumers in our economy make our population as a whole more vulnerable to hardship.

Usury is a recognized tool of *national* economic policy, not simply the domain of state police power. Modern European nations rely on usury laws as a tool of national policy, not intended merely for the protection of individual consumers. As a value moderating the supply of consumer credit in society, national usury laws can moderate the competing interests in indebtedness and offer consumers and society protection in a time of diminished employment or recession which is the major problem of post-industrial development.

Note

With all the fuss over usury laws, one would assume that interest rates are pretty important to consumers. But are they? The NCCF noted that interest rate "is only one of a number of features embodied in an offer of credit, just as price is only one of the considerations in the purchase of an automobile." NCCF Report, 95. Other credit features include maturity date, down payment, security, amount of monthly payment, availability of irregular payment plans, location, collection methods, prepayment penalty, and delinquency and deferral charges. Perhaps the most important feature to many consumers is whether the loan will be approved at all. Which consumers would you expect to be more concerned with interest rates, relatively poor consumers or relatively affluent consumers? Why? How does this affect your evaluation of the desirability of rate ceilings?

Problem 3

You are counsel for a group that advocates consumer rights. A bill is currently before the legislature in your state which would abolish interest rate ceilings for all consumer loans. The group has asked you to testify on this bill and to take a strong pro-consumer stand. Will you testify in favor of or against the bill? Why? What will you say?

Chapter 14

CREDIT INSURANCE

Prefatory Note

As was indicated in the preceding chapters, one way a lender can raise his revenue and profits is to tie a second service to his lending service. The most widely adopted tie-in sale is of credit insurance. It may insure the life of the debtor or provide him with disability, accident, health, or even unemployment insurance. It may also insure the collateral for the loan against fire, accident or other hazards.

In all forms of credit insurance, the consumer debtor is the insured, and the creditor is the beneficiary. Policies are normally written in group form, with the creditor acting as policyholder. The creditor in turn normally issues a certificate to the consumer reflecting his enrollment in the group policy. The creditor also arranges the insurance and pays the premium to the insurance company, but this cost is universally passed on to each individual consumer.

Credit insurance is big business. Each year, consumers spend well over $1 *billion* to insure their debts. It is also a highly profitable business, and not only for the insurance companies. Creditors, too, take a healthy slice of the credit insurance pie. Up to one-third or even as much as one-half of some creditors' incomes is due to commissions or other compensation from selling credit insurance. In fact, there are cases in which a creditor's profit from selling credit insurance exceeds that from selling its main product.

Today, credit insurance is regulated in all states by statute and by administrative regulations of various types. In most states, the relevant statute is a version of the model act promulgated by the National Association of Insurance Commissioners (NAIC), "the NAIC Model Bill to Provide for the Regulation of Credit Life Insurance and Credit Accident and Health Insurance" (hereafter, the NAIC Model Act). The most recent version of this act appeared in 1977, and at least 30 states have adopted it or something very much like it. U3C states, of course, use the U3C; Article 4 of the U3C applies to credit insurance. Administrative regulations commonly set maximum rates and the like.

The premium rates for such insurance are very high. The National Association of Insurance Commissioners has adopted a 60% loss ratio as a *goal* to be striven for. (That means for each $1.00 of premiums paid in, 60¢ is paid out in losses while 40¢ can be kept by the insuror for administrative expenses and profits.) Many experts believe that 75% or 80% would be a more appropriate level, and that loss ratios below this level produce windfall profits. Despite the NAIC suggestions, however, most states allow companies to maintain loss ratios considerably below this level. In fact, over half the states permit a loss ratio of 50%, and in many states even that goal has not been reached. The profits are also high.

Direct regulation of premium rates and coverages is always the prerogative of the state insurance commissioner. Otherwise, the treatment of credit insurance in consumer legislation has been equivocal. Both the U3C and the Truth in Lending Act exclude premiums from the finance charge if the coverage is not required and is specifically assented to, or, in the case of property insurance, could be obtained elsewhere. See U3C § 2.501(2); Reg. Z § 226.4(d)(1) and (2). The U3C's only attempt to control excessive premiums is in § 4.203(2) which directs the state insurance commissioner to disapprove rate schedules which are "unreasonable in relation to the benefits provided."

There is a long history of abuses in credit insurance terms. The insurance has been written for greater amounts or longer durations than the credit extension it secures. Upon refinancing or consolidation ("flipping"), the old insurance may not be cancelled (providing double coverage) or unearned premiums may not be rebated. The consumer's acquiescence in accepting insurance may be voluntary in form only— creditor suggestions are at least subtly coercive. Alternatively, a lender may not even seek the consumer's acquiescence, but merely announce the "optional" insurance to be included. (This practice is called "packing".) Valid claims may not be paid. But the greatest abuses seem to be in the pricing of this product.

One major factor which produces high rates for credit insurance is the "reverse competition" phenomenon. As will become immediately apparent from the cases below, creditors get a double benefit when a debtor buys credit insurance. First, they become beneficiaries on an insurance policy paid for by the consumer. Second, and more important, they get to collect a commission for selling that very policy. This commission is normally a percentage of the premium; 40 to 50% is typical. The effect of this practice is to make creditors look for insurance companies who charge the highest rates for the same coverage, because their commissions will be higher. This turns the normal market forces upside down. According to classic economic theory, competition is supposed to drive prices down. Here, competition drives prices up.

These practices are widespread and widely tolerated. Is it legal for a lender to be the debtor's creditor, his insurance broker, and the beneficiary of his credit insurance—all at the same time? Such circumstances would seem to create both fiduciary relationships and conflicting interests.

SPEARS v. COLONIAL BANK OF ALABAMA

Supreme Court of Alabama, 1987.
514 So.2d 814.

PER CURIAM.

This case originated as a class action against Colonial Bank of Alabama and Colonial Banc Corporation (both hereinafter referred to as "Colonial Bank"), and Jim Burke Buick, Inc. ("Jim Burke"), for alleged violations of the Alabama Mini–Code (Code 1975, § 5–19–1, *et seq.*); for alleged improper credit of insurance premium refunds; and for alleged conversion. The named plaintiffs, Kennie J. Spears and Handy Wilson, Jr., sought to represent a class of all individuals who had purchased automobiles from Jim Burke, the purchases of which, along with premium payments for credit life and credit disability insurance, were financed by Colonial Bank.

The plaintiffs allege that Jim Burke required them to purchase credit life and disability insurance in order to purchase the automobiles, and that the price of this insurance exceeded the premium charged by the insurance company, all in violation of § 5–19–20. In essence, they contend that Jim Burke's receipt of a commission of 50 percent of the premium from each sale of credit insurance was in violation of the Mini–Code.

* * *

Colonial Bank and Jim Burke filed motions for summary judgment on each of the plaintiffs' claims and a motion to dismiss all class-action claims. The circuit court entered two separate orders on the defendants' motions.

> The first order dealt with only one issue: "Whether or not Jim Burke Buick was entitled to charge or receive a commission on the credit life insurance, credit disability insurance, and property insurance it sold to the named Plaintiffs in conjunction with loans the named Plaintiffs obtained from the Defendants."

The trial court ruled that § 5–19–1, *et seq.,* does not "prohibit car dealers or other companies making loans covered by such sections from receiving commissions on the various types of insurance allowable under § 5–19–20, so long as all other provisions of those sections are met."

The court held that the premiums charged to the named plaintiffs were within the amounts allowed by the applicable statutes, rules, and regulations. It found, therefore, that Colonial Bank and Jim Burke were entitled to summary judgment on this theory of the plaintiffs' claims. The court also found that Colonial Bank's and Jim Burke's motions to dismiss all class-action claims were due to be granted, because the only issue supportive of the class certification was decided adversely to the plaintiffs by summary judgment.

* * *

We hold that the trial court did not err in its determination that § 5–19–20(a) does not prohibit Jim Burke, as a creditor, from receiving a commission on its sale of insurance to the plaintiffs, as debtors.

Jim Burke had arrangements with various insurers, whereby, for every policy sold to its customers, it would remit the entire premium to the insurer.[3] Thereafter, for each credit life and disability policy sold, the insurer would compensate Jim Burke by payment of a sum equal to 50 percent of the premium costs, a payment which plaintiffs contend is more correctly characterized as an illegal kickback, rather than a commission. They contend that § 5–19–20(a) prohibits a creditor from charging more than the actual coverage costs, and that only 50 percent of the premium actually paid represented the full amount charged by the insurer.

Colonial Bank states, and the record bears out, that, while its loans to the plaintiffs included the premium payments, it did not receive a commission. Jim Burke argues that the Mini–Code, and regulations promulgated pursuant thereto, permit receipt of a commission on the sale of credit insurance. It contends that the plaintiffs' definition of "premium," which would exclude commissions made thereon, is strained. Further, Jim Burke points out that § 5–19–21 provides that an "administrator is authorized and empowered to make such reasonable rules and regulations as may be necessary for the execution and enforcement of the provisions of this chapter," and that the insurer and Jim Burke relied on these rules and regulations in setting rates for credit insurance.

The plaintiffs urge us to consider this case in light of the underlying tenor of the Mini–Code, which is that of consumer protection. The plaintiffs' premise is correct. *Derico v. Duncan,* 410 So.2d 27, 31 (Ala. 1982) ("the provisions of Code 1975, § 5–19–1, *et seq.,* 'Consumer Finance,' known collectively as the Mini–Code, are regulatory in nature and are for the protection of the public, specifically, the consumer/debtor"). Thus, construction of the statute in this case must be made with the protection of the consumer in mind.

Section 5–19–20 provides, in pertinent part:

"(a) With respect to any credit transaction, the creditor shall not require any insurance other than insurance against loss of or damage to any property in which the creditor is given a security interest or insurance insuring the lien of the creditor on the property which is collateral for said transaction. Credit life and disability insurance may be offered and, if accepted, may be provided by the creditor. *The*

---

3. All life insurance procured by Jim Burke on behalf of its customers was placed with one company, Volunteer State Life Insurance Company, while two companies, MIC and Autry Insurance Agency, handled the property insurance of Jim Burke's customers.

charge to the debtor for any insurance shall not exceed the premium charged by the insurer. Insurance with respect to any credit transaction shall not exceed the approximate amount and term of the credit." (Emphasis added.)

The key to this Court's consideration of whether § 5–19–20 was violated is a determination of the meaning of "premium." There being no definition of "premium" in the Mini–Code, we look to the case law. In *Reid v. United Security Life Ins. Co.*, 290 Ala. 253, 256, 275 So.2d 680 (1973), the Court defined "premium" as "the amount paid to the insurer by the insured for the insurance," and the Court added, " 'Premium' has been defined as the sum which the insured is required to pay, and in its proper and accepted sense it means the amount paid to the company as consideration for insurance." Thus, because it is a cost of procuring the insurance, a premium may include the commission paid to the seller of the insurance.

The Alabama State Banking Department has promulgated rules and regulations establishing and authorizing the maximum single premium rates for credit life insurance and credit disability insurance. The superintendent of banks of the state banking department is empowered to make such rules and regulations as are reasonably necessary for the execution and enforcement of the provisions of the Mini–Code, pursuant to § 5–19–21. All parties agree that the premiums charged to the plaintiffs for the various insurance coverages were within the lawful maximum rates established by the state banking department.

Because the premiums charged to the plaintiffs, as debtors, were within the maximum lawful rates, there has been no cognizable violation of the Mini–Code, nor of the rules and regulations promulgated pursuant thereto. Absent any evidence to support the claim that § 5–19–20(a) was violated, we find no error requiring reversal of the defendants' summary judgment on the payment-of-commissions issue. Thus, it is axiomatic that the trial court did not err in granting the defendants' motions to deny class certification on this theory of the plaintiffs' claims.

Affirmed.

Maddox, Almon, Shores, Adams and Steagall, JJ., concur.

Jones, J., concurs specially.

Beatty, J., recused.

Jones, Justice (concurring specially).

I concur in the opinion affirming the summary judgment on the plaintiffs' claims based on the defendants' alleged violations of the Mini–Code. I write separately to express my concern that we may have overly narrowed the intended scope of the trial court's ruling.

* * *

The plaintiffs' arguments as to the problems inherent in the sale of credit insurance are well taken. The fact that the creditor is allowed compensation under the language of § 5–19–20 results in a clear probability of expensive credit insurance for the consumer. As pointed out in Fonseca, *Handling Consumer Credit Cases* § 12:10, pp. 494–99 (1986), because insurers compete against each other to place their business with creditors, the creditor is in a position to choose the insurer that offers it the highest compensation for every dollar of insurance sold. "Since Consumer has no voice in determining these rates, and since he is a non-shopping 'captive' in the sense that the sale of insurance will only come up as an incidental matter after the credit transaction is completed, the premium rate has been set high by 'reverse competition.'" Fonseca, at 495–96.

These observations notwithstanding, however, Jim Burke's liability, if any, under general agency law, can only be determined once its status as an insurance "agent" or as an insurance "broker" is ascertained.

* * *

Generally, agents and brokers have been distinguished by the fact that an insurance agent is "one employed by an insurance company to solicit risks and effect insurance," while a broker "is one who acts as a middleman between [the] insured and the company; one who solicits contracts from the public under no employment from any special company, but [who,] having secured an order[,] places the insurance with the company selected by [the] insured, or, in the absence of any selection by him, with the company selected by such broker." 44 C.J.S. *Insurance* § 136, at 797 (1945).

The question of whether a person is an insurance agent or is a broker is generally determined by his acts. But categorizing the creditor that procures credit insurance for its customers, primarily to protect the *creditor* from loss, is not so easily done. The creditor that procures such insurance presents a unique situation.

* * *

[The] description of "broker" aptly describes an entity in Jim Burke's unique position. Clearly, the bargaining power of potentially thousands of customers each year puts Jim Burke in a situation where it can obtain the "most favorable terms from competing [insurance] companies." While brokers generally seek to obtain the most favorable terms for their *clients,* the *creditor*/broker uses the competition between insurance companies to obtain the highest compensation for *itself.* This "reverse competition" results in a high premium rate for the consumer because he has no voice in determining rates, but obtains insurance only as an incident to the purchase of retail merchandise.

Notes

1. Regardless of whether it is an insurance broker or an agent, doesn't Jim Burke owe its customer good faith, loyalty, and a duty to exercise reasonable skill, care, and dilligence to protect the customer's interests? If Jim Burke is a broker, it is clear that the insured (consumer)

is its principal, and is owed such duties. That should ordinarily include advice as to the price of insurance, and the availability of any less expensive comparable insurance. Do you believe that Jim Burke did any of that? Should an insurance agent owe any less duty to the purchaser of the insurance?

Would a cause of action based on breach of fiduciary duty provide avenue for recovery by plaintiffs?

2. In 1968 Montgomery Ward began providing credit life and disability insurance to all its charge account customers. Taking no chances, they simply began adding the premium to every customer's monthly bill, but they did tell cardholders they could cancel the insurance if they specifically wrote a letter to that effect!

For the denouement of this marketing effort, see Holstein v. Montgomery Ward & Co., Circuit Court of Cook County, Illinois, CCH–CCG ¶ 99,966 (1969); Id. ¶ 99,608 (1970).

3. "Credit insurance is a national scandal. I know of no other product where the public is so blatantly abused by what are supposed to be responsible financial institutions." These words were spoken not by a consumer advocate, but by the insurance commissioner of the State of Tennessee. See, Bogdanich, "Unwanted Extras: Irate Borrowers Accuse ITT's Loan Companies of Deceptive Practices" Wall St.J., Feb. 26, 1985, p. 1, c. 6.

Problem 1

Mary Mason borrowed $200 from Service Loan Co. The finance charge was $17 (the maximum under the applicable rate ceiling) and credit life insurance was $2.19, for a total of $219.19 to be repaid in 12 monthly installments. Mary signed the part of the form requesting credit life insurance, but does not remember making a conscious choice. "I signed where I was told to."

The applicable statute reads: "A lender may accept as security for loans hereunder, reasonable insurance on the life of the debtor; provided, however, that any such insurance shall be reasonably related to the amount and term of the loan, and the amount of insurance required as security for a loan shall not exceed the amount of the loan, including charges, to be secured." The statute also allows lenders to charge "$1.00 per $100 per year for credit life insurance."

Mary's policy insured her life for $219 for the one-year term of the loan. Thus, the amount of the credit insurance did not exceed the amount of the loan at the time it was made, but it did exceed the amount of the declining balances as Mary made her monthly payments. This is called "level term" insurance.

After Mary has paid six monthly installments, she consults you. Has the loan company violated the applicable statutes? (Although the amount is small, there is a potential class action.) Cf., Mason v. Service Loan & Finance Co., 128 Ga.App. 828, 198 S.E.2d 391 (1973). Would it make a difference if a violation of the statute voids the loan as to both principal and interest? Would your answer change if the insuror is wholly-owned by the lender and earns $0.75 profit on each premium $1, which is half the profits of the parent company?

Notes

1. Why would a consumer *want* to take out "level term" life insurance when she would be paying down the balance month by month? Isn't the consumer's only concern making sure that the debt is paid off if she dies?

2. Why would the creditor want to *sell* level term insurance, at twice the premium of declining term? Doesn't the creditor risk scaring off customers by adding the higher premium? Is the creditor altruistically looking out for the debtor's survivors? Or does he have other motives?

3. Normal market mechanisms are inoperative here. The insuror is chosen by the creditor, not by the debtor who must ultimately pay the bill. Thus, the creditor may not be interested in the lowest price, but in other attributes of the insurance "package". For example, if the insuror is able to pay a sales commission to the creditor for selling its insurance, the creditor may select the insuror which offers the highest commission—and that may be the insurance with the highest price.

> "In the sale of other forms of insurance, competition produces reasonable rates because the purchaser is seeking the best possible benefits and the lowest possible rates. Under these circumstances there is little or no need for rate regulation. In the case of credit insurance, however, while the debtor usually pays for the insurance, he is not the real purchaser. The insurance charge is included as an incidental part of the credit transaction and because the costs are passed on to the debtor, there is no incentive on the part of the creditor to hold down the cost. In fact, the situation is often just the reverse. When the creditor pays a higher premium for credit insurance and passes it on to the debtor, he stands to gain more in the form of either a commission or a dividend or retrospective rate credit, based on the experience of his case."

Kenneth C. Nichols, Senior Vice President of the Prudential Insurance Company of America, Consumer Credit Industry Hearings, Subcommittee on Antitrust and Monopoly, Senate Committee on the Judiciary, 90th Cong., 1st Sess., Nov. 27–30, 1967, pp. 2348–49. See also, Comment, 10 B.C. Ind. & Comm.L.Rev. at 446, 453–55.

4. On the other hand, state usury laws may regard such an insurance commission as a disguised form of interest payment, and the commission may put the creditor in violation of the usury laws. This is the problem in *Tew,* infra. Thus, a great deal of effort has been invested by small loan companies in separating returns on insurance from returns on loans. One method uses a wholly-owned insurance company as the credit insuror, but this veil can easily be pierced. *Cope* illustrates a more subtle approach, using reinsurance and a "front man."

TEW v. DIXIELAND FINANCE, INC.

Supreme Court of Mississippi, 1988.
527 So.2d 665.

PRATHER, JUSTICE, FOR THE COURT:

Among other questions, this appeal addresses whether a small loan company, unlicensed to sell insurance, may receive a commission on the sale of credit life and disability insurance without violation of the Mississippi statutes.

Dixieland Finance, Inc., a small loan company, filed suit against a borrower, William Archie Tew, who had defaulted on a promissory note. The borrower counterclaimed alleging that the loan company had overcharged the borrower on premium payments made on credit life and credit disability insurance. From a verdict in favor of the loan company, the borrower appeals and raises the following issues:

(1) May a small loan company solicit and sell credit life and credit disability insurance? and

(2) May a small loan company, not licensed to sell insurance, receive commissions on the sale of credit life and credit disability insurance?

I.

FACTS

Dixieland Finance, Inc. (Dixieland), a Mississippi corporation, is a small loan business licensed by the Mississippi Department of Banking and Consumer Finance and is located in Collins, Mississippi. William Archie Tew (Tew) was a customer of Dixieland and had negotiated a series of loans with Dixieland beginning in 1978.

The series of loans negotiated by Tew was the result of Mr. Tew's inability to completely repay the amounts he owed. For instance, whenever Tew fell behind on his payments, Dixieland allowed Tew to negotiate a new loan and use the proceeds of the new loan to repay the former loan. Through this renewal process, Tew fell deeper and deeper into debt.

With each new loan transaction, Tew procured, through Dixieland, credit life and credit disability insurance. The purpose of this insurance was to pay off Tew's financial obligation to Dixieland if Tew died or became disabled.

During the course of its business relationship with Tew, Dixieland utilized a procedure by which it collected the credit life and credit disability insurance premiums, retained fifty percent of the gross premiums as commissions, and forwarded the remaining fifty percent to the Central Life Insurance Company of Jackson, Mississippi.

The final promissory note payable to Dixieland by Tew was executed March 23, 1984 and was for a principal amount of $1,626.36. The note provided for an initial payment of $119.11 followed by twenty monthly payments of $105.00. The annual percentage rate on the note was 35.32% and the total of all payments, including the finance charges, was $2,219.11.

Tew made only two payments of $105.00 each on the March 23, 1984 note before defaulting. Instead of renewing the loan as it had done before, Dixieland turned the account over to its attorney for collection. A complaint was filed January 9, 1985 in the Circuit Court of Covington County demanding a total of $2,446.19.[3] Also, an additional ten percent per annum interest rate began to accrue from the date the debt was accelerated. By the date of the trial, Tew owed $2,536.69.[4]

Tew counterclaimed alleging that Dixieland's method of retaining commissions from the sale of credit life and credit disability insurance was violative of the Mississippi Small Loan Regulatory Law codified at Miss.Code Ann. § 75–67–101 through –135 (1972 & Supp.1987). As a result of Dixieland's alleged statutory violations, Tew claimed that he was entitled to have voided all the financial agreements, contracts, and promissory notes he had executed with Dixieland, and that he was entitled to the return of all monies, including principal, interest, and other charges paid by him to Dixieland. This suit was tried July 8, 1985 and ended with a decision in favor of Dixieland for $2,536.69. From that decision, Tew perfects this appeal.

The resolution of the issues of this appeal require attention to three Mississippi statutory enactments: (1) the Small Loan Regulatory Law, Miss.Code Ann. § 75–67–101 et seq., (2) the Regulation of Agents for Life, Health, or Accident Insurers, Miss.Code Ann. § 83–17–101, et seq., and (3) Credit Life and Credit Disability Insurance, Miss.Code Ann. § 83–53–1 et seq.

II.

WAS IT ILLEGAL FOR DIXIELAND TO RETAIN COMMISSIONS FROM CREDIT LIFE AND CREDIT DISABILITY INSURANCE WRITTEN BY ITS EMPLOYEES?

A.

The Controlling Statutes

At no time during its business dealings with Tew was Dixieland a licensed insurance agent. However, at all times relevant to this case, Dixieland employed insurance agents licensed to write credit life and credit disability coverage. It was the understanding of the president and employees of Dixieland that credit life and credit disability insurance could be written so long as an employee of Dixieland was a licensed insurance agent.

3. Accelerated balance less
   unearned finance charge $1,834.64
   Attorney's fee   611.55
                              ─────────
                              $2,446.19

4. Original accelerated balance
   plus attorney's fee $2,446.19
   Additional interest   90.50
                              ─────────
                              $2,536.69

Also, Mr. John T. Miller, an examiner with the Mississippi Department of Banking and Consumer Finance, testified that the writing of credit life and credit disability insurance by finance companies and the receiving of commissions therefrom by the finance companies is a common practice in Mississippi. Furthermore, Mr. Miller testified the practice of small loan companies accepting commissions from the sale of credit insurance was accepted by the Department of Banking and Consumer Finance.

*   *   *

C.

Was Dixieland's Receipt of Commissions Violative of the Statute, Miss.Code Ann. § 83–17–105?

*   *   * However, a creditor cannot be licensed as an agent to write credit life and disability insurance if the creditor is a corporation. Miss.Code Ann. § 83–17–101(a) (Supp.1987) allows only "individuals, partnerships, and any corporation incorporated pursuant to Title 79, Chapter 9, Miss.Code of 1972, being the Mississippi Professional Corporation Law" to be licensed as an agent to write credit life and disability insurance. *   *   * Accordingly, the Department of Insurance cannot license a corporate creditor to write credit life and disability insurance.

Nevertheless, it has long been recognized in Mississippi that a corporate creditor is entitled to receive a commission for the sale of credit life and disability insurance. Effective February 25, 1969, the Department of Insurance issued a regulation to prohibit creditor group policyholders or agents from withholding a commission in excess of fifty percent of the insurance premium paid by the borrower. *   *   * This recognition that creditors can receive compensation for the sale of credit life and disability insurance was codified by the Legislature in Miss.Code Ann. § 83–53–25 (Supp.1986) which regulates the commission that a creditor can receive for the sale of credit life and disability insurance. Section 83–53–25 provides:

(1) No one shall pay, accrue, credit or otherwise allow, either directly or indirectly, any compensation to any *creditor,* person, partnership, *corporation,* association or other entity in connection with any policy, certificate or other contract of credit life insurance or credit disability insurance which exceeds fifty percent (50%) [45% from and after July 1, 1987] of the premium rates approved for such policy, certificate or contract. [Emphasis added.]

By virtue of these regulations and statutes it is apparent that the Legislature and Department of Insurance have recognized that creditors may, and that many in fact do, receive commission payments from the sale of credit life and disability insurance.

However, regulations ignore the inconsistency of the provisions with Miss.Code Ann. § 83–17–105 (Supp.1987) which prohibits the payment of any commission to any person who is not a licensed agent. This Court therefore holds that the receiving of such commission by

Dixieland from its sale of insurance is in violation of the Miss.Code Ann. § 83–17–105 requiring him to be a licensed agent to receive commissions.

III.

DID DIXIELAND OVERCHARGE TEW ON PREMIUMS FOR CREDIT LIFE AND CREDIT DISABILITY INSURANCE?

* * *

Dixieland did not require each borrower to buy credit insurance, but made credit insurance available for those who wanted it. As previously mentioned, Dixieland's practice was to collect the credit insurance premiums, keep 50% of the premiums, and forward the remaining 50% to Central Life Insurance Company of Jackson. It is undisputed that the entire premium collected by Dixieland was always in compliance with the maximum premiums prescribed by the comptroller.

Tew contends that Dixieland was authorized to charge for credit insurance *only the amount Dixieland actually paid* for the insurance. In other words, Tew contends Dixieland could only charge its customers the actual cost of the insurance to Dixieland.

As authority, Tew cites Miss.Code Ann. § 75–67–121 (1972), which reads in part:

> Any licensee hereunder may charge any borrower on loans of one hundred dollars ($100.00) or more * * * the *actual cost of any premium* paid for life, health and/or accident insurance on any borrower where the amount of insurance required is not in excess of the amount of the loan and the premium therefor is in keeping with that usually and customarily paid for like insurance. [Emphasis added.]

Therefore, this Court must determine whether a licensee under Miss.Code Ann. § 75–67–121 (1972) of the Small Loan Regulatory Law may charge the maximum prescribed rates, including commissions, or whether the licensee may only charge the cost of the insurance to the licensee.

* * *

As authority for his proposition that "actual cost of any premium" means only the amount Dixieland had to pay for the credit insurance, Tew cites *Bailey v. Defenbaugh & Co. of Cleveland, Inc.*, 513 F.Supp. 232 (N.D.Miss.1981). *Bailey* is analogous to the instant case in that borrowers from a small loan company procured credit insurance through the loan company, which retained 50% of the insurance premium as a commission. The United States District Court, Northern District of Mississippi, exercised jurisdiction to construe Mississippi law pendant to its jurisdiction under the federal Truth in Lending Act. The Court in *Bailey* held that the loan company was limited to charge only the amount it actually paid for the insurance.

Section 75–67–121 not only allows a licensee to charge the actual cost of any premium paid for credit insurance, it requires "the premium therefor [to be] in keeping with that *usually and customarily paid for life insurance.*" (Emphasis added.) At the time Tew executed the March 23, 1984 note, the maximum rates for credit insurance were regulated by the comptroller. Furthermore, John T. Miller, an examiner with the Department of Banking and Consumer Finance, testified it was the custom and practice of sellers in Mississippi to charge the maximum amount for credit insurance.

The word "premium" is not defined in the Act. Nevertheless, it is almost universally understood that an insurance premium paid includes the commission. The Supreme Court of Alabama recently addressed a similar issue under the Alabama small loan laws to determine whether a creditor could retain the commission portion of the insurance premium paid by the borrower for credit insurance. Because the word "premium" was not defined by statute, the Court looked to the common law to determine its meaning. The Court stated:

> In *Reid v. United Security Life Ins. Co.*, 290 Ala. 253, 256, 275 So.2d 680 (1973), the Court defined "premium" as "the amount paid to the insurer by the insured for the insurance," and the Court added, " 'Premium' has been defined as the sum which the insured is required to pay, and in its proper and accepted sense it means the amount paid to the company as consideration for insurance." *Thus, because it is a cost of procuring the insurance, a premium may include the commission paid to the seller of the seller of the insurance.* [emphasis added].

Spears v. Colonial Bank of Alabama, 514 So.2d 814, 816 (Ala.1987) (emphasis added). Because the commission retained by the creditor in *Spears* was part of the cost of the insurance premium charged to the borrower and the insurance premium was within the amount allowed to be charged, the Alabama Supreme Court found there was no violation of the Alabama small loan law.

This same principle is applicable to the Mississippi Act as both the industry and the Department of Banking have always considered the "premium" to include the commission. Well-settled rules of statutory construction support the interpretation by the industry.

For those reasons, this Court holds a licensee under § 75–67–121 may legally charge premiums up to the statutorily regulated maximum regardless of the commissions the licensee receives from the insurance company. The statute allows a licensee to collect the total cost of the premiums, not just the cost of the premiums less any commission the licensee receives.

*   *   *

CONCLUSION

This Court's conclusions may be summarized as follows:

(1) Dixieland violated Miss.Code Ann. § 83–17–105 (Supp.1987) by acting as an insurance agent without a license and by accepting commissions from the sale of credit life and credit disability insurance.

(2) Miss.Code Ann. § 83–17–133 (Supp.1987), which prescribes the penalties for violations of § 83–17–105, does not prohibit a private right of action in favor of Tew.

(3) Dixieland did not violate Miss.Code Ann. § 75–67–121 (1972) by overcharge on the sale of credit life and credit disability insurance.

(4) Dixieland should be allowed to recover its award of $2,536.69 plus accrued interest.

However, this Court must address the conflict existing between the statutes and the insurance regulations while at the same time recognizing the sanctioned practices that are widespread in the credit insurance industry. Because of the reliance placed on the Department of Insurance regulations, this Court holds that the mandate of this opinion prohibiting an unlicensed agent from collecting commissions shall be prospective, effective on and after July 1, 1989, to permit the Legislature and Executive Departments to adjust to this decision.

* * *

Affirmed.

Notes

1. In some states, most notably Arkansas, excessive credit insurance costs have been held to be disguised interest and to violate the usury laws. See, e.g., Robinson v. Rebsamen Ford, Inc., 258 Ark. 935, 530 S.W.2d 660 (1975). How would you go about calculating what portion of an insurance premium was "excessive" and therefore usurious?

2. Mr. Robert Sable, executive director of the National Consumer Law Center, has stated that the problem of high cost in credit insurance could be solved if creditors were simply prohibited from imposing a separate charge for insurance in consumer credit contracts. "By prohibiting a separate charge, nearly every problem in credit life insurance would disappear." Credit Life Insurance: Hearing before the Subcommittee on Antitrust, Monopoly, and Business Rights of the Committee on the Judiciary, United States Senate, 96th Cong., 1st Sess., serial no. 96–44, at 57 (1979). How can this be so? Is the remedy to the abuses of the credit insurance industry really that simple?

Problem 2

Oliver borrows $2500 for three years on a monthly installment basis from Ace Finance Co. The finance charge disclosed on the TILA statement is $600, and there is an insurance premium of $93 which is added to the amount financed. May Ace insure this loan for $3100? For $3193? If Oliver dies the day after the loan is made, and has not made any payments, how much will the pay off be? See NAIC Model Act §§ 2(B)(5) and 4(A). See also Winkle v. Grand National Bank, 267 Ark. 123, 601 S.W.2d 559 (1980).

Problem 3

Suppose the loan in problem 2 is a joint loan to Oliver and Harriet. A joint credit insurance policy is available at a lower cost than two individual policies, but Ace does not disclose this and sells Oliver and Harriet each a policy at the usual cost. Do they have any basis for complaint against Ace?

COPE v. AETNA FINANCE CO.

United States Court of Appeals, First Circuit, 1969.
412 F.2d 635.

COFFIN, CIRCUIT JUDGE.

This is an appeal from the district court's order allowing the claim of appellee, Aetna Finance Company of Maine, in proceedings under Chapter XIII of the Bankruptcy Act.

The facts are clearly set forth in an earlier order by the district court, and are summarized as briefly as possible hereafter. On December 7, 1963, the debtors, Robert R. and Gail L. Richards, filed petitions for wage earner plans under Chapter XIII of the Bankruptcy Act. In the schedules attached to their petitions, the debtors listed a debt to appellee in the amount of $957.22, secured by a chattel mortgage on household goods, with the notation that the debt was disputed as being in violation of the Maine Small Loan Law.

* * *

The referee found that the debtors were charged an amount for credit insurance which was in excess of any amounts authorized to be charged for credit insurance under the Maine Credit Insurance Law. The referee then concluded that Aetna's loan was void under the Small Loan Law and he disallowed the claim. The basis of the referee's order was twofold: (1) that the amount charged was unauthorized; and (2) that Aetna had failed to establish that its claim was free from usury as required by § 656(b) of the Bankruptcy Act.

The district court, on July 20, 1967, reversed the referee's order on both points. First, it held that the section of the Maine Credit Insurance Law dealing with authorized premiums, § 1208(1), was directed at insurers and did not impose any responsibility on the creditor for an unauthorized charge.[4] Secondly, the district court held that § 656(b) was applicable only *before* confirmation and hence could not be invoked with respect to Aetna's claim.[5]

Upon remand, with the district court sitting in place of the referee, evidence was presented to determine whether Aetna had charged the debtors an amount in excess of the premium charged it by the insurer.[6]

---

4. § 1208(1) of the Maine Credit Insurance Law provides that:

"1. Rates filed. Any insurer may revise its schedules of premium rates from time to time, and shall file such revised schedules with the commissioner. No insurer shall issue any credit life insurance policy or credit accident and health insurance policy for which the premium rate exceeds that determined by the

schedules of such insurer as then on file with the commissioner."

5. Since our decision does not in any way turn on the application of § 656(b), we pass this issue.

6. § 1208(4) of the Maine Credit Insurance Law provides that:

"The amount charged to a debtor for any credit life or credit health and accident

The district court found that Aetna had not in fact charged the debtors more than the amount charged Aetna by the insurer. It also concluded that even had Aetna charged the debtors more than it had been charged, there would have been no violation of the Maine Small Loan Law because of the exemption granted by § 1209 of the Maine Credit Insurance Law.[7] The district court then allowed Aetna's claim in full.

* * *

* * * The half century old Small Loan Law, contains a stark, blanket proscription against a creditor imposing on a debtor any "other charge or amount whatsoever" in addition to interest. If excess charges are made, "the contract of loan shall be void". The Credit Insurance Law was enacted in 1961 and was designed to provide comprehensive regulation of the sale of credit insurance. It expressly permits the lender to require a debtor to obtain credit insurance as a precondition to a loan, and the lender is permitted by § 1209 to market the insurance without running afoul of the provisions of the Small Loan Law. In return for these privileges, the law also imposes certain obligations on the insurer and the lender. Section 1208(1) enjoins the insurer from charging premiums in excess of those authorized by the Maine Insurance Commission. Section 1208(4) prohibits a lender from charging the debtor more than the lender was charged by the insurer. Section 1214 empowers the Maine Insurance Commissioner to impose sanctions for violations of his orders, ranging from civil penalty to revocation of license.

In the ordinary situation, where an insurer establishes a premium rate conforming to the requirements of § 1208(1), and where the creditor merely passes on the premium so charged to the borrower in accordance with § 1208(4)—even though the premium may include some amount for "cost and compensation to the creditor" under the authority of § 1207(2), there is no problem of violation of the Small Loan Law. There might even be no problem for the creditor if the insurer imposed on it a higher than authorized premium charge. The district court may well be correct in saying that such an infraction of the Credit Insurance Law is solely within the sanctioning power of the Insurance Commissioner and that § 1208(1) does not "attribute to the

insurance shall not exceed the premiums charged by the insurer, as computed at the time the charge to the debtor is determined."

7. § 1209 of the Maine Credit Insurance Law provides that:

"All policies of credit life insurance and credit accident and health insurance shall be delivered or issued for delivery in this State only by an insurer authorized to do an insurance business therein, and shall be issued only through holders of licenses or authorizations issued by the commissioner. The premium or cost of such insurance when issued through any creditor shall not be deemed inter-

est, or charges, or consideration, or an amount in excess of permitted charges in connection with the loan or other credit transaction, and any benefit or return or other gain or advantage to the creditor arising out of the sale or provision of such insurance shall not be deemed a violation of any other law, general or special, of the State of Maine. The insurance premium or other identifiable charge for such insurance may be collected from the insured or included in the finance charge or principal of any loan or other credit transaction at the time such transaction is completed."

creditor accountability for the sins of the insurer." 272 F.Supp. at 487. We agree that the statutory scheme of the Credit Insurance Law clearly distinguishes between the obligation of the insurer and that of the creditor. The underlying assumption is that separate entities, making separate and independent decisions, shall be separately responsible for decisions within their sphere of responsibility.

The case before us, however, is not the ordinary situation contemplated by the statute. In this case the court observed "that this record reveals abuses on the part of the lenders and insurers involved which cry out for immediate and effective regulatory action." 291 F.Supp. at 541. Footnoting this observation was the finding: "There can be little doubt on this record that Aetna of St. Louis, American Universal and Old Republic acted jointly to fix premium rates to be charged Aetna debtors which would provide a substantial profit to American Universal as reinsurer." 291 F.Supp. at 541, n. 10.

The interrelationship of the various parties relevant to this finding is pertinent to our decision. Aetna of Maine was a wholly-owned subsidiary of Aetna of St. Louis, with the same officers and directors. The latter also was the sole owner of American Universal Life Insurance Company of St. Louis, which shared at least some of the officers and directors of Aetna of St. Louis. Old Republic was a large, independent credit insurance company, Aetna of St. Louis being one of some 750 accounts.

Old Republic, having a license to issue insurance in Maine, which American Universal lacked, also had the benefit of knowledge of insurance laws in the various states, the ability to devise and supply appropriate forms, rate charts, and policies, and useful actuarial and legal competence. It was these services that Old Republic largely supplied, its insurance risk being completely covered by American Universal under reinsurance treaties.

Despite deposition testimony of a former employee of Old Republic that rates were fixed solely by Old Republic, the record indicates that Old Republic, after compiling rates which would produce various loss ratios, looked to American Universal to pick the loss ratio it desired. The life insurance premium chosen was at the rate of $1.00 per hundred of outstanding indebtedness a year, although expert testimony indicated that the "commonly prevailing rate" at the time throughout the country was less than half as much and Aetna had previously paid for coverage of its Maine borrowers at a cost of approximately 50 cents a hundred. American Universal showed a before-tax net income of $1.4 million on total 1962 premium income of $2.2 million, or 63 percent.[14] Its net income attributable to sales of credit insurance in Maine was $59,647.68.

14. As the district court observed, "The circumstances of this case thus provide a graphic illustration of the economic phenomenon of 'reverse competition', a long deplored feature of credit insurance transactions in many states." 291 F.Supp. at 541, n. 10. That is, instead of incentive on the part of sellers of insurance to minimize prices, the captive status of the small loan customer and the prevalence of insurance companies affiliated with lenders provide an incentive to maximize the gain from

Under these circumstances, the district court's finding that Aetna of St. Louis, American Universal, and Old Republic jointly fixed the premium rate has in reality made irrelevant the literal application of §§ 1208(1) and (4). For here, instead of an "insurer" unilaterally establishing a rate and a "lender" merely passing it on to a borrower, Aetna of St. Louis and American Universal, the parent and sister, respectively, of Aetna of Maine, participated in the making of both decisions. Indeed the situation is in essence as if Aetna of St. Louis had commanded its wholly-owned insurance subsidiary to set a rate and its own wholly-owned loan company to pass it on. For all practical purposes, the lender is setting the rate under the guise of insurer. Not only this, but there is a possibility, which we discuss infra, that the rates so fixed were unauthorized. Were this to be proven, we would see no difference between such a situation and one where Aetna of Maine added a charge to the premium and passed it on to the borrower. The fact that Aetna of St. Louis could so control the setting of the original premium that there was no necessity of Aetna of Maine's taking the second step of adding to it cannot be a basis for different legal consequences. We would not easily believe that the Maine Legislature intended to permit any such facile evasion of the regulatory scheme of the Credit Insurance Law. Assuming that the premiums were unauthorized, therefore, we would hold that Aetna of Maine, despite the surface appearance of compliance with § 1208(4), in reality violated it because of its complicity in the centralized decision making which rendered § 1208(4) irrelevant.[15]

[The court then held that an excess charge violation of the state Credit Insurance Law was also an excess charge violation of the state Small Loan Act, which voided all small loans having excess charge violations.]

We hold, therefore, that if the rates nominally set by Old Republic, but in reality fixed jointly with the lender's parent which shared in the profits, were in fact in excess of those authorized at the time, Aetna's claim must be disallowed.

[The court then decided that, on the record before it, it was not clear whether the rates charged were unauthorized by state law.]

Remanded for further proceedings consistent with this opinion.

Notes

1. Pay close attention to what the court has said and what it has not said:

Because of the close relationship between Aetna of Maine, Aetna of St. Louis, and American Universal—two being subsidiaries of the other—

credit insurance, the premium not being a cost to the lender but an opportunity for profit for the lender's affiliate.

15. We note also that the Maine Legislature was not oblivious to the problems posed by distinguishable corporate entities. In § 1202(2)(C), it defined "creditor" as "The lender of money * * * and an affiliate".

Aetna of Maine (the lender) would be liable for violating the Credit Insurance Law if the premiums charged were unauthorized. In addition, if the premiums were unauthorized, Aetna of Maine's share of those premiums would constitute usurious interest under the Small Loan Law.

But what if the premium rate being charged ($1 per hundred) were found to be *authorized?* According to a deleted portion of the opinion, the insurance commissioner had set a prospective rate limit of 64¢ per $100 of debt. Presumably insurance companies can make a profit at that level. If Aetna however can collect $1 per hundred for the same insurance coverage, where does the extra 36¢ go?

Note American Universal's loss ratio for 1962: Total income, $2.2 million; net income, $1.4 million—loss ratio 37%.

2. Evaluate the provisions of Article 4 of the U3C on insurance. They do not set maximum premiums or loss ratios, nor do they prohibit the payment of "commissions" or "experience rebates" to the creditor who sells the insurance. § 4.107. Level term life insurance, as in Problem 1, supra, is prohibited. § 4.202(1). Other provisions require rebates of unearned premiums in the event of prepayment (§ 4.108), and set special unconscionability guidelines (§ 4.106).

Are these sufficient safeguards against reverse competition and excessive premiums? Against deceptive sales techniques?

3. The suggestion has been made that creditors who tie-in insurance sales should be charged with a "fiduciary" responsibility with respect to that insurance, since they are acting ostensibly on the consumer debtor's behalf and for his protection. What are the implications of this notion? Could the creditor still earn commissions on insurance sales?

4. Would it make sense for credit insurance premiums to be included as part of the finance charge for disclosure (TIL) and rate ceiling purposes? Wouldn't this discourage overpricing? Alternatively, would it be feasible to require creditors to include within the finance charge that portion of the insurance premium they get to keep?

5. Recall the controversy over disclosure of credit insurance premiums under the Truth in Lending Act, in Chapter 2, supra. Are you now more, or less, satisfied with TIL's disclosure rules in this area?

If the lender is really selling a separate insurance package, should the lender have to make separate *credit sale* disclosures as to that insurance, under Reg. Z § 226.18(n)? Probably no creditor in the country does so. But see Cody v. Community Loan Corp. of Richmond County, 606 F.2d 499 (5th Cir.1979) (CCH–CCG ¶ 97,814).

Problem 4

You have just graduated from law school and are getting ready to buy a car. You are trying to decide whether credit insurance is a good idea, assuming you can obtain it from the least expensive insurer rather than the most expensive insurer. Assume that your loan will be in the amount of $10,000 for four years. Should you insure the loan? Why? In whose favor are the actuarial odds on this insurance?

*

Part IV

WEAPONS FOR ENFORCEMENT

None of the substantive measures discussed in Parts I, II, and III can be very helpful to the public unless they can readily be enforced. In fact, many of the early consumer protection statutes failed to provide such enforcement. More recent statutes are more likely to have effective enforcement provisions, and this development has created a subspecialty within consumer protection: the development of appropriate enforcement mechanisms. It is for this reason that your authors have decided to present the enforcement materials separately in Part IV, to allow separate evaluation of different mechanisms for ensuring compliance with consumer protection rules.

How can a statute be unenforceable? One obvious method is to provide no enforcement mechanism at all, but this happens rarely. A more usual method is to place no sanction on the violator, other than a duty to return any ill-gotten gains when (seldom) caught. In practice, the FTC did this for years. A less obvious method is to provide *only* a criminal law sanction, and require that it be enforced by an official who is not usually involved in criminal proceedings. At the state level, Small Loan Acts frequently have this as their only sanction. At the federal level, Title III of the CCPA, which restricts creditor garnishment of wages, is an example. Other methods include limiting the persons who can seek enforcement (to aggrieved consumers only, or to public agency regulators, or to federal regulators only) or to limit the enforcement mechanisms (to cease and desist orders only, or to fines only, or to restitution only, etc.).

The major problem in providing *effective* enforcement mechanisms is that they must be used in such a wide variety of situations—from those involving deliberate, wide-spread, significant violations of consumer interests to those involving inadvertent (if perhaps careless), isolated infractions of marginal interests. Thus, both flexibility and discretion seem to be necessary.

To illustrate the need for this flexibility, we have used a warfare or battlefield analogy. We start in Chapter 15 by looking at where enforcement or relief should be sought. Is it available only in federal court, or only in state court, or both? If in a state court, which state(s)?

Or is it available only through administrative agency proceedings? And, in all situations, how much have federal rules preempted state rules?

In Chapter 16, we proceed to look at the effective resolution of individual disputes. In one sense, the idea of using $20,000 in total resources to resolve a $100 dispute seems silly—unless it is *your* $100. Nevertheless, one primary contact of most people with the court system is the resolution of such small disputes, and its failure to resolve such disputes, despite the cost, would be a subtle poison, reducing general satisfaction with the legal system. In addition, there are alternative dispute resolution mechanisms—direct consumer-merchant negotiations, mediation and arbitration—and they are regulated by both federal and state governments. If attorneys get involved, there is also the issue of who should bear the cost of the *successful* consumer's attorney.

The consumer's resources are often limited, so Chapter 17 looks at his reinforcement with the resources of a public agency; which can be state, local or federal. Each agency has a different array of powers and sanctions, so we can present only illustrative examples: for a state agency, the California Attorney General; and for a federal agency, the FTC. For each, we examine their ability to stop violations, to redress past violations, and to deter violations.

Enforcement by public agencies alone is never sufficient, however, because such agencies can become overly cautious, underfunded, or co-opted by the industry they regulate. Private enforcement through multiple individual actions has always been considered inefficient and burdensome on the court system. Thus, in Chapter 18 we examine the "heavy artillery" of class actions and private attorneys general to enforce consumer protection doctrines.

Finally, in Chapter 19 we look at mechanisms which, like nuclear weapons, have the potential to deter violations. The classic Common Law deterrents are punitive damages in civil actions, and fines and prison in criminal actions. In consumer credit, however, where a license is required to do business and a regulator can deny or revoke such a license on "character and fitness" considerations, the revocation of the creditor's license (thus terminating the business) may be the most feared sanction.

Chapter 15

APPROPRIATE BATTLEGROUNDS: PROBLEMS OF FEDERALISM

As the reader can tell from the variety of statutes and caselaw encountered thus far, consumer protection laws emanate from state legislatures, from the federal Congress, from municipalities, and from administrative agencies. This array of legal rules is not only bewildering in itself, but it also creates some special frictions. Do federal laws displace state laws on the same subject, and if so, to what extent? Are states inhibited from enacting broad reforms by the existence of narrow, weaker federal laws?

In general, a federal law will not preempt comparable state law unless the federal statute explicitly says so, or the legislative history indicates that that was the congressional intent. Most recent consumer laws enacted by Congress have contained limited preemption provisions, and it has fallen to the courts and the enforcement agencies to spell out the extent of the displacement. At the same time, several federal statutes expressly authorize states to seek exemptions from the federal act—thus creating a kind of *state* preemption of federal laws.

SECTION A. FEDERAL PREEMPTION OF STATE REFORMS

One of the major consumer protection reforms of the 1980s was the wave of state "lemon laws," which in essence enhanced the remedies available to consumers for breaches of new car warranties. See supra Chapter 6, pages 400–406. Many of these state laws provide that consumers must use the manufacturer's informal dispute resolution mechanisms before being permitted to invoke the lemon law remedies of refund or replacement of the vehicle, *if* that mechanism complies with the FTC's "Rule 703" promulgated pursuant to the Magnuson–Moss Warranty Act, Section 110(a)(2), 15 U.S.C.A. § 2310(a)(2); 16 C.F.R. Part 703.

The enactment of state lemon laws with such provisions spurred the development of informal dispute resolution mechanisms by most of the major automobile manufacturers. In many cases, however, state consumer protection agencies did not believe these mechanisms were in strict compliance with the federal regulation. Furthermore, some state agencies felt the FTC was somewhat lax in its enforcement of Rule 703. As a result, several state legislatures proceeded to amend their lemon laws to provide for a variety of informal dispute resolution mechanisms, including: (1) state-certification of the mechanism's compliance with the state standards, (2) state-run arbitration programs, or (3) direct state regulation of the manufacturer's mechanisms. Faced with these tougher state laws on dispute resolution, the manufacturers went to court arguing that the Magnuson–Moss Act and the FTC regulation had preempted the stronger state laws. These arguments have usually been unsuccessful.

AUTOMOBILE IMPORTERS OF AMERICA, INC. v. STATE OF MINNESOTA

United States Court of Appeals, Eighth Circuit, 1989.
871 F.2d 717.

HEANEY, SENIOR CIRCUIT JUDGE.

The appellants, an organization of foreign automobile manufacturers ("Automobile Importers"), brought suit in the United States District Court for the District of Minnesota, challenging a Minnesota consumer law. * * * The district court held that the Minnesota law is not preempted by the Magnuson–Moss Warranty Act. The plaintiffs appeal that decision to this Court. We affirm.

* * *

In 1987, the Minnesota Legislature amended the Minnesota lemon law. Appellants challenge three aspects of the Minnesota law as being preempted by federal law: the requirement that automobile manufacturers doing business in Minnesota participate or operate such a mechanism; the provision of the law that permits either party, without the other's consent, to make oral presentations; and the provision allowing a consumer to be charged a fee for the mechanism.

* * *

A. COMPREHENSIVENESS OF THE FEDERAL SCHEME

A state law is preempted when the federal regulatory scheme is sufficiently comprehensive to make reasonable the inference that Congress "left no room" for supplementary state regulation. In other words, the regulation must be sufficiently pervasive to demonstrate an intention on the part of Congress that it wished to displace state law.

Automobile Importers argue that such an intention can be inferred from the legislative history of the Magnuson–Moss Act. They argue that a compromise was struck in Congress between the interests of the warrantors and the interests of consumers, and that permitting Minnesota's private dispute resolution mechanism to stand upsets that compromise. Such a compromise may have well occurred, * * * but

Automobile Importers fail to provide sufficient evidence to support their assertion that an aspect of this compromise was the preemption of supplemental state regulation in the area of private dispute resolution mechanisms.

* * *

* * * [T]o infer preemption in an area traditionally regulated by the states—consumer protection through warranty law—requires a "clear statement" of occupation. We find no "clear statements" of congressional intent to preempt here. The six pages of regulations are far from pervasive. The special competence of the FTC to deal with unfair trade practices is unpersuasive in light of the states' traditional role in this area. The fact that Congress gave some regulatory authority to the FTC over informal dispute resolution mechanisms fails, without any other supporting evidence, to demonstrate that Congress mandated national uniformity regarding such mechanisms.

The language, structure and history of the Act emphasize its supplemental, rather than preemptive nature. Congress authorized the FTC to adopt only "minimum requirements," implying that it intended to leave room for further state regulation. The Act's structure is supplemental: a broad savings clause followed by language creating specific, narrow areas of preemption. [Magnuson–Moss Act Sec. 111(b) & (c), 15 U.S.C. Sec. 2311]. By explicitly delineating a limited area of preemption, Congress intended to permit supplemental state regulation in areas outside of that delineation. Congress could have easily included informal dispute resolution mechanisms in its list of areas specifically preempted, but it failed to do so. The savings clause—"any right or remedy of any consumer under State law"—confirms Congress' intention to permit supplemental state regulation. Moreover, the legislative history supports the view that Congress found it necessary only to supplement present state law and not replace it. Finally, the FTC, in an informal opinion letter to the Attorney General of Kentucky, confirmed the view that the Magnuson–Moss Warranty Act was intended merely to supplement state law.

* * * Congress has not fully occupied the area of informal dispute resolution mechanisms.

B. Physical Impossibility

Compliance with both the Minnesota law and federal law is possible. Minnesota requires automobile manufacturers to establish or participate in an informal dispute resolution mechanism satisfying FTC requirements. Federal law makes warrantors' participation in such mechanisms optional. Strictly speaking, compliance with both laws is not a physical impossibility. When an automobile manufacturer complies with Minnesota's law by providing an informal dispute mechanism, that manufacturer is not violating federal law.

In addition, 16 C.F.R. § 703.5(f) provides that an informal dispute resolution mechanism may allow an oral presentation by a party to a dispute only if both the warrantor and the consumer expressly agree to the presentation. Minn.Stat. § 325F.665, subd. 6(e) provides that Minnesota's required informal dispute resolution mechanism shall allow each party to appear and make an oral presentation in Minnesota unless the consumer agrees otherwise. Again, compliance with both laws is not impossible. If the warrantor and the consumer abide by the Minnesota rule, then the FTC rule is not violated. The appellants provide no evidence that the FTC intended to prevent states from requiring oral presentations.

Finally, Minn.Stat. § 325F.665, subd. 6(i) provides that a consumer may be charged a fee for participating in a dispute mechanism, while 16 C.F.R. § 703.3(a) provides that a consumer shall not be charged any fee for use of such mechanisms. Compliance with both laws is possible even though the state has provided an option where the federal government has not.

C. COMPLIANCE WITH STATE LAW DOES NOT FRUSTRATE THE PURPOSES OF FEDERAL LAW

State legislation is preempted if compliance with the state law frustrates the purposes and objectives of federal law. To determine this, we must analyze separately each aspect of the state law complained of by the appellants. The purpose of the Magnuson–Moss Warranty Act is to enhance consumer protection, and the specific goal of section 110 is to encourage warrantors to use informal dispute resolution mechanisms.

1. Required Participation in a Dispute Mechanism

The appellants argue that *Fidelity Federal Sav. & Loan Ass'n. v. de la Cuesta,* 458 U.S. 141, 102 S.Ct. 3014, 73 L.Ed.2d 664 (1982), stands for the proposition that a state law limiting the availability of a federally-created option frustrates Congress' objectives and purposes.

In *Fidelity Federal,* the Supreme Court in 1982 concluded that limitations placed on "due-on-sale" clauses in loan instruments by the California Supreme Court are preempted by Federal Home Loan Bank Board (Board) regulation permitting federal savings and loan associations to use "due-on-sale" clauses in their mortgage contracts. Id. at 159, 102 S.Ct. at 3025.

* * *

The circumstances underlying *Fidelity Federal,* however, are dissimilar to the instant case. Initially, the history of the two is quite different. The Federal Home Loan Bank Board's decision to adopt a regulation pertaining to "due-on-sale" clauses was in response to certain states limiting the rights of federal savings and loan associations. Here, the impetus was the inadequacy of current state consumer remedies. No state had previously required warrantor participation in dispute resolution mechanisms; so, section 110 and Rule 703 were not, unlike the Board's rule in *Fidelity Federal,* adopted to preempt a particular state action. In addition, the Federal Home Loan Bank

Board clearly expressed the policy that it was important that savings and loans have the "flexibility" given by the option of whether to have "due-on-sale" clauses in a particular loan instrument. No such congressional policy of "flexibility" exists in the adoption of the Magnuson–Moss Warranty Act.

Since *Fidelity Federal* is distinguishable from this case and there is no frustration of either the broad goal of enhancing consumer protection or the specific goal of encouraging warrantor participation in informal dispute resolution mechanisms, the Minnesota law requiring automobile manufacturers' participation in informal dispute resolution mechanisms is not preempted.

2. *Oral Presentation without the Consent of Both Parties*

Congress and the FTC failed to provide a purpose for making oral presentations optional of both parties. It cannot be said that the Minnesota law permitting oral presentations at the option of the consumer frustrates the goals of enhancing consumer protection and encouraging warrantors to establish informal dispute resolution mechanisms because automobile manufacturers operating in Minnesota are required to establish such mechanisms.

3. *Consumer Fees*

Minn.Stat. § 325F.665, subd. 6(i) provides that a consumer may be charged a fee for participating in a dispute mechanism, while 16 C.F.R. § 703.3(a) provides that a consumer shall not be charged any fee for use of such mechanisms. Since the maximum fee that can be charged to a consumer is equal to the filing fee for use of conciliation court—in Hennepin County, $15.00, and in St. Louis County, $18.00—the effect of this requirement on the use of resolution mechanisms by consumers, is de minimis and not sufficient to deter consumers from using such mechanisms. Therefore, this fee aspect of the Minnesota law is not preempted.

IV. CONCLUSION

By enacting the Magnuson–Moss Warranty Act, Congress has increased the economic strength of consumers without fully occupying the area of consumer protection, an area traditionally reserved for the states. Congress intended state regulation, like the Minnesota lemon law, to operate with the Warranty Act in a mutually supplementary manner. The Minnesota law does nothing to defeat this result. For these reasons, we affirm the district court.

Notes

1. The Second Circuit was faced with a similar issue in a case challenging the New York lemon law's provisions on manufacturer-sponsored informal dispute resolution systems. Motor Vehicle Manufacturers Ass'n v. Abrams, 899 F.2d 1315 (2d Cir. 1990). The Second Circuit upheld the New York law, for reasons similar to those expressed by the Eighth

Circuit opinion in the *Automobile Importers of America* case, supra. The Second Circuit concluded that far from intending to occupy the field, Congress intended the federal Magnuson–Moss Act to "supplement, not supplant, the rights and remedies provided by state law," 899 F.2d at 1319, although it conceded that "[w]e do not suggest that the act is crystal clear on the issue of preemption." Id. at 1321. The court noted that the manufacturers might well be correct that "lack of uniformity in this area is undesirable," but bowed to the judgment of Congress and the FTC on the matter. Id. The court also noted that the differences between the New York lemon law and the FTC regulation "are obviously not earth-shattering," and that it would not be physically impossible for a manufacturer to comply with both sets of requirements. Id. at 1323.

If more states were to enact laws like New York's and Minnesota's, will automobile manufacturers be faced with a hopeless maze of conflicting regulations? Is that really what Congress intended with the broad "savings clause" of Magnuson–Moss? On the other hand, did Congress intend that the FTC rule should thwart the states' attempts to enhance consumer protection with respect to new car warranties? Is the Congressional intent on this matter ambiguous? If so, what is the basis for the decisions in these two cases?

2. In 1983, the FTC settled a case against General Motors that had accused GM of concealing from consumers some serious defects in a large number of GM vehicles. As part of the consent agreement, GM was required to set up a national third-party arbitration program to settle individual complaints relating to these defects. In re General Motors, 102 F.T.C. 1749 (1983). In 1986, New York amended its lemon law to place certain restrictions on manufacturers' arbitration programs involving new and used vehicles. Since GM had established an informal dispute resolution mechanism within the state of New York pursuant to the FTC consent order, it would also have to comply with the New York law.

In a 1990 opinion, a panel of the Second Circuit Court of Appeals held that the FTC's consent order did not preempt the allegedly conflicting portions of the New York lemon law. General Motors Corp. v. Abrams, 897 F.2d 34 (2d Cir. 1990). The majority acknowledged that "an FTC consent order may in some circumstances preempt state law, [but] we do not believe the agreement entered into by GM and the Commission was intended to have this effect on the provisions of the state Lemon Law at issue." Id. at 37. In a strong dissent, Judge Winter argued that the lack of preemption would put GM in an untenable position. The consent order mandates GM's use of the Better Business Bureau's dispute resolution program, under which lay arbitrators are allowed to "issue decisions based solely on their view of common sense and equity." Id. at 45, Winter, J., dissenting. Judge Winter argued that since the state law "commands that the arbitrators be trained in the Lemon Law and follow it," then GM may not be able to follow both the consent decree and the lemon law "unless the BBB, which is not under any legal duty to comply with the Lemon Law, voluntarily cooperates both in revising the standards followed by its arbitrators and in allowing its arbitrators to be retrained." Id. at 46.

3.   In Wolf v. Ford Motor Company, 829 F.2d 1277 (4th Cir.1987), the court held that a consumer's common law fraud action against Ford Motor Company was preempted by the Magnuson–Moss Act. Ford had represented that its Consumer Appeals Board was an independent and impartial apparatus for resolving disputes between Ford and its customers. The consumer claimed this was a fraudulent misrepresentation. This cause of action was dismissed by the trial court because "it would require the factfinder to determine, under the guise of a fraud claim, whether the Ford Consumer Appeals Board has complied with FTC Rule 703." The Fourth Circuit affirmed, citing the "congressional intent to reserve to the federal regulatory body the authority to supervise whether the mechanisms are created and operated fairly." Id. at 829 F.2d 1279. The Fourth Circuit also stated flatly that: "The FTC regulations are extensive and address all facets of the mechanisms' operation. They leave no room for state regulation." Id.

4.   The Texas lemon law set up the state Motor Vehicle Commission as a dispute resolution mechanism and requires that consumers exhaust this administrative remedy before going to court with their lemon law claims. Vernon's Ann.Tex.Civ.St. art. 4413(36), § 6.07(e). In Chrysler Corp. v. Texas Motor Vehicle Commission, 755 F.2d 1192 (5th Cir.1985), the Fifth Circuit held that the Texas dispute resolution system was not preempted by the Magnuson–Moss Act, on the basis that Congress meant to preserve, not preempt, concurrent state remedies for consumers. Does this mean that a Texas consumer would have to use the manufacturer's dispute resolution system to preserve her Magnuson–Moss claims and then also use the state run arbitration system to pursue her state lemon law claims? Was it really that helpful to consumers that the Texas arbitration provision was not preempted?

5.   In 1989, the FTC called for public comment on whether or not it should amend Rule 703. The notice was in response to a petition filed by the Motor Vehicle Manufacturers Association of the United States and the Automobile Importers of America. The manufacturers would like the FTC to institute a national certification program for informal dispute resolution mechanisms, and preempt any state law provisions that provide different requirements from Rule 703. Federal Trade Commission, Advance Notice of Proposed Rulemaking, 54 Fed.Reg. 21,070 (May 16, 1989). How should the FTC come out on these issues? What data will be crucial in determining the outcome?

Problem 1

The Fair Credit Reporting Act provides that concurrent state regulation is permitted as long as the state law is not "inconsistent" with the FCRA. See FCRA § 622, 15 U.S.C.A. § 1681t. See also discussion of the substantive provisions of the FCRA, supra Chapter 4, pages 228–264. Under this standard, which of the following provisions of a state credit reporting law would be preempted:

(1) A requirement that the sources of information acquired solely for the preparation of an investigative consumer report must be disclosed to the consumer.

(2) A requirement that consumer reporting agencies provide an actual copy of consumer reports to the consumer on request.

(3) A requirement that medical information in a consumer report be disclosed to the consumer.

(4) A prohibition against charging consumers for disclosures.

What standard should be used in determining whether or not the state law is "inconsistent"? See Retail Credit Co. v. Dade County, Florida, 393 F.Supp. 577 (S.D.Fla.1975) (whether the local law "frustrates the effectiveness or purpose of the FCRA" and whether it "denies a right or benefit conferred by the FCRA"); Equifax Services, Inc. v. Cohen, 420 A.2d 189 (Me.1980), cert. denied 450 U.S. 916, 101 S.Ct. 1360, 67 L.Ed.2d 342 (1981) (whether Congressional purposes were being thwarted); Credit Data of Arizona, Inc. v. State of Arizona, 602 F.2d 195 (9th Cir.1979) (whether compliance with the state law would trigger a federal enforcement action).

Is the FCRA's preemption provision significantly different from the equivalent provision in the Magnuson–Moss Act (§ 111(b)(1), 15 U.S. C.A. § 2311)?

Problem 2

The Fair Credit Billing Act provides that in order to trigger a creditor's responsibility to investigate an alleged credit card billing error the consumer must send a written notification to the specified address within a certain time period. Reg. Z § 226.13(b). Suppose a particular state has enacted a "little FCBA" which requires customers to send notification of billing errors by registered or certified mail. Is this state law provision preempted? See FCBA § 171; Reg. Z § 226.28(a)(2).

Problem 3

The Magnuson–Moss Warranty Act expressly preempts state laws which relate to the labeling or disclosure of warranties, and which are "not identical to" the federal requirements. This general preemption is qualified in section 111(c) as follows:

"(2) If, upon application of an appropriate state agency, the Commission determines * * * that any requirement of such state covering any transaction to which this title applies (A) affords protection to consumers greater than the requirements of this title and (B) does not unduly burden interstate commerce, then such State requirement shall be applicable to the extent specified in such determination for so long as the State administers and enforces effectively any such greater requirement."

The State of California has petitioned the FTC for a ruling that certain provisions of its statutory warranty laws are not preempted by Magnuson–Moss. The following requirements are at issue:

(a) California law requires that a warrantor disclose the identity of any repair facilities in the State either by giving the customer a list, by giving the name, address and toll-free phone number of a central directory of such facilities, or by maintaining a list at the seller's premises.

(The MMWA requires only that the warrantor disclose its mailing address or that of the person responsible for warranty repairs.)

(b) California law specifies that a written warranty on a mobile home be entitled "Mobilehome Warranty".

(MMWA requires that warranties be labeled either "full" or "limited".)

(c) California's mobile-home law requires disclosure of the address and phone number of the place where consumers can get information on warranty performance.

(MMWA requires only the address.)

(d) The California code requires mobile home sellers to display signs stating the existence of a one-year warranty and a sample copy.

(MMWA requires sellers to make their warranty provisions available to customers, but allows the seller to do this in any of four different ways.)

How should the Commission respond to California's petition? See, F.T.C. Findings and Determination on Applicability of Certain Provisions of California State Law, 42 Fed.Reg. 54004 (1977).

Problem 4

Regulations applicable to national (i.e., federally chartered) banks provide (12 C.F.R. 7.7310) that "a national bank may charge interest at the maximum rate permitted by State law to any competing State-chartered or licensed lending institution."

In a given state, assume that small loan companies are authorized to charge up to 36% on certain loans. State banks, however, are limited to a rate of 18%. Can a national bank in that state charge at the 36% rate? What justification could be afforded for permitting it to do so? See United Missouri Bank of Kansas City, N.A. v. Danforth, 394 F.Supp. 774 (W.D.Mo.1975).

SECTION B. EXEMPTIONS FOR STATES

1. Section 123 of the Truth in Lending Act states that the Federal Reserve Board shall provide an exemption for credit transactions that occur within a state that imposes "requirements substantially similar" to those of the federal Truth in Lending Act, if there is "adequate provision for enforcement" of the state law. TIL § 123, 15 U.S.C.A. § 1633. Similar exemption provisions exist for Fair Credit Billing, FCBA § 171(b), 15 U.S.C.A. § 166j(b), and for Equal Credit Opportunity, ECOA § 705(g), 15 U.S.C.A. § 1691(d).

2. Only five states—Connecticut, Massachusetts, Oklahoma, Maine and Wyoming—have been granted exemptions under Truth in Lending. No exemptions have been granted under similar provisions in the FCBA or the ECOA. Why do you suppose so few states have sought the exemption? What inducement is there for a state to seek an exemption? What reasons for *not* doing so?

3. Will an individual plaintiff still have the right to sue for violations of Truth in Lending in federal court in the exempt states? The Second Circuit settled the matter in the affirmative in the case of Ives v. W.T. Grant Co., 522 F.2d 749 (2d Cir.1975). Plaintiff filed in federal court alleging violations of the Connecticut Truth-in-Lending Act. There was no diversity of citizenship between the parties. The district court held it had jurisdiction over the state law claims by virtue of the federal Truth in Lending Act. The Second Circuit affirmed.

The *Ives* court found that when Connecticut was granted a Truth in Lending exemption in 1970 by the Federal Reserve Board, the Connecticut disclosure requirements became the disclosure requirements of the federal Act, so that "federal courts continue to have jurisdiction over any civil suit claiming violation of Connecticut disclosure requirements." The Second Circuit reasoned that while the exemption provision was meant to transfer *administrative* enforcement authority from the federal to the state government, it did not eliminate the federal court's civil liability jurisdiction. "Federal court jurisdiction * * * is not the type of federal involvement that interferes with a state's control of its own law," according to the *Ives* court. It also deferred to the judgment of the Federal Reserve Board which in an amicus brief had stressed the importance of private enforcement in Truth in Lending. Said the court:

> Keeping in mind this emphasis on private enforcement, we believe that having a choice of forums—state or federal—can only serve to encourage civil actions to insure compliance. Maintenance of a federal forum is particularly appropriate because of its often more liberal and modern procedures. Therefore, we would be loath to overturn an administrative interpretation that retained that forum, made by the very agency charged with the interpretation of the statute. Thus, we agree with the position taken by the Board that the exemption granted to the State of Connecticut did not affect the jurisdiction of the court below to hear this suit under 15 U.S.C.A. Sec. 1640.

Is there a more substantive—constitutional—difficulty with the *Ives* holding? Absent diversity of citizenship, where is the "federal question" which must serve as the basis for federal court jurisdiction now that Connecticut's disclosure law has been exempted?

If Congress (and the Federal Reserve Board) can go this far in creating federal court jurisdiction, could they simply make any violation of state consumer protection laws actionable in federal court? If they could, would it be wise?

After *Ives,* Congress codified the holding with regard to ECOA exempt states.   ECOA § 705(g).

Problem 5

The Maine Consumer Credit Code provides that any violation of the federal Truth in Lending Act is also a violation of state law.   TIL's minimum award is $100, while the minimum recovery for a violation of state law is $250.   If a creditor violates TIL, for which minimum recovery is he liable?   Does it matter whether the action is brought in federal court (as a violation of federal law) or in state court (as a violation of either federal (TIL § 130(e)) or state law)?   Could the consumer recover *both* minimum awards?

SECTION C.   EXTRA–TERRITORIAL REACH OF STATE LAWS

Not all the friction in our federal system of lawmaking is between laws enacted at the federal and state levels.   A state with strong consumer protection policies is understandably anxious to protect its citizens from rip-offs by merchants or creditors located outside the state boundaries but dealing with those citizens.   Creditors who operate largely by mail, or out of a fixed location in one jurisdiction, will equally understandably want to retain the benefits of the law of that jurisdiction.   The materials below touch on these matters.

BURR v. RENEWAL GUARANTY CORP.
Arizona Supreme Court, 1970.
105 Ariz. 549, 468 P.2d 576.

LOCKWOOD, CHIEF JUSTICE.

Plaintiff, Renewal Guaranty Corporation, hereinafter referred to as "the lender" sued James H. Burr and his wife, hereinafter referred to as "Burr", on a promissory note.   The defense was usury.   The trial court, sitting without a jury, gave judgment for the lender, and Burr appealed.

The facts are not in dispute.   The lender is a Colorado corporation, duly registered under the Money Lender's Act of Colorado, which permits it to charge 24% per year interest on loans.   It specializes in loans to life insurance salesmen secured by commissions earned by them but not yet due from their companies.   The lender advertises in trade journals and other periodicals which are read nationwide by life insurance salesmen, including those residing in Arizona.

Burr read one of the lender's ads, and applied for a loan.   The lender checked Burr's credit, and assured itself that Burr had future commissions coming.   A note was prepared in Colorado and sent to Burr, together with an assignment of his commissions.   Burr signed both documents in Arizona, and returned them to the lender, which then mailed its check to Burr.   The note was for $4,800, bore interest at the rate of 1½% per month, was specifically made payable at the lender's office in Denver, Colorado, in installments, and provided that "the construction and enforcement of this note shall be governed by the laws of the State of Colorado." Burr defaulted on his payments.

The parties agree that if the maximum permissible interest rate is governed by the laws of Arizona, the note is usurious, but if it is governed by the laws of Colorado, then it is not. The issue, therefore, involves principles of conflict of laws.

Burr contends that since the contract was made in Arizona, it must be interpreted by Arizona law. However, we believe otherwise. It is true that Burr signed the note in this state, but the note was prepared in Colorado and sent here for him to sign. When signed, it was returned to the lender. When the latter received it, there was not yet a contract. The lender could not sue on the note, for it had not yet parted with the consideration. The note became an enforceable promise to pay when the lender sent its check to Burr. We believe that the contract, evidenced by the note, was made in Colorado.

In Seeman v. Philadelphia Warehouse Co., 274 U.S. 403, 47 S.Ct. 626, 71 L.Ed. 1123 the United States Supreme Court said in 1927:

> "Respondent, a Pennsylvania corporation having its place of business in Philadelphia, could legitimately lend funds outside the state, and stipulate for repayment in Pennsylvania in accordance with its laws, and at the rate of interest there lawful, even though the agreement for the loan were entered into in another state, where a different law and a different rate of interest prevailed. In the federal courts, as was said in Andrews v. Pond, 13 Pet. 65, 77–78 (10 L.Ed. 61): 'The general principle in relation to contracts made in one place, to be executed in another, is well settled. They are to be governed by the law of the place of performance, and if the interest allowed by the laws of the place of performance is higher than that permitted at the place of the contract, the parties may stipulate for the higher interest without incurring the penalties of usury.'"

Seeman, supra, is cited in Pioneer Credit Corporation v. Carden, 127 Vt. 229, 245 A.2d 891 (1968) as authority for the statement that:

> "Absent a purposeful scheme to evade our usury laws, '(a) contract to be usurious by our law must not only be made here, but to be performed here.'"

The Restatement of the Law, Second, on Conflict of Laws, now in printing, Chapter 8 (Contracts) § 203(2) states the rule succinctly:

> "The validity of a contract will be sustained against the charge of usury if it provides for a rate of interest that is permissible in a state to which the contract has a substantial relationship and is not greatly in excess of the rate permitted by the general usury law of the state of the otherwise applicable law * * *."

This Court has already approved the rule applying the law of the state having the most significant relationship, in conflict of laws as applied to tort cases. Schwartz v. Schwartz, 103 Ariz. 562, 447 P.2d

254. It is our considered opinion that the Restatement, Second, supra, with reference to usury, represents the better and most modern statement of the correct rules to apply. Those rules represent an enlightened approach to the whole field of conflicts, based upon logic and reality rather than upon ancient unrealistic maxims.

We agree with the principles set out above, and we hold that the note in the instant case is governed by the laws of the State of Colorado and is therefore not usurious. The lender is regulated by the laws of that state, which permit it to charge interest at the rate of 24% a year. Despite this permission, the lender has charged only 1½% per month, which is ½% less than the maximum. There is no proof of bad faith and no indication that it chose the laws of Colorado in order to escape Arizona's usury laws.

[Affirmed.]

Note

The cases usually state the Restatement distinction in terms of sustaining the validity of a contract against a general usury statute, but not against a more specific interest rate regulation statute, such as a small loan act. See, e.g., Oxford Consumer Discount Co. of North Philadelphia v. Stefanelli, 55 N.J. 489, 262 A.2d 874 (1970), appeal dism'd, 400 U.S. 808, 91 S.Ct. 45, 27 L.Ed.2d 38, amended, 400 U.S. 923, 91 S.Ct. 183, 27 L.Ed.2d 182. The distinction may also be explained as a reluctance to enforce 19th Century general usury legislation, on the ground of its obsolescence.

ALDENS, INC. v. PACKEL

United States Court of Appeals, Third Circuit, 1975.
524 F.2d 38, cert. denied, 425 U.S. 943, 96 S.Ct. 1684, 48 L.Ed.2d 187 (1976).

GIBBONS, CIRCUIT JUDGE.

* * *

Aldens is an Illinois corporation operating a mail order business. By catalogs and flyers mailed from its headquarters in Chicago, it solicits orders in fifty states, including Pennsylvania. It has no tangible property in Pennsylvania. It employs no agents, salesmen, canvassers or solicitors in Pennsylvania. It has no Pennsylvania telephone listing and except for its mail order catalogs and flyers it does not advertise by use of any Pennsylvania media. It does not use any Pennsylvania credit verification sources to check on the credit of its Pennsylvania customers, although a Chicago credit reporting agency to which it resorts does inquire of credit bureaus in Pennsylvania for such information. All merchandise orders are filled from outside Pennsylvania and shipped F.O.B. from a point of origin in another state. The customers pay the shipping, handling and transportation costs. Aldens is neither required to collect nor to remit Pennsylvania use taxes nor to qualify nor to register to do business in Pennsylvania. It accepts or rejects all orders for merchandise in Chicago. Only the Chicago office grants credit, and all credit application forms and credit agreements are mailed by Pennsylvania residents seeking credit to Chicago. Aldens' credit agreement, which is used nationwide, provides for a monthly service charge of 1.75% on balances of $350.00 or less, which is an annual percentage rate of 21%, and for a monthly service charge of 1% (12% annually) on that portion of the balance which exceeds $350.00. Payments are received in Chicago and credited to customers' accounts there. Aldens' credit agreements provide for the retention of a purchase money security interest in merchandise sold on credit, but it does not file any security interest document, does not enforce any security interests, and has a security interest in merchandise unpaid for only to the extent provided by law. The Aldens agreement complies with the Federal Truth in Lending Act, and applicable truth in lending regulations of the Board of Governors of the Federal Reserve System. The agreement also complies with applicable Illinois law. It does not comply with Pennsylvania law.

Aldens' annual sales to Pennsylvania customers approximate $14,900,000, which represents about 7.6% of its annual sales. Approximately 73% of the $14,900,000 represents credit sales to some 90,000 Pennsylvania credit customers whose average balance is about $169.00. Were Aldens to comply with the Pennsylvania Goods and Services Installment Sales Act it would incur additional annual costs and expenses and would sustain annual revenue losses attributable to such compliance as follows:

> "a. Approximate additional costs of preparing catalogs, advertising materials, and credit agreements containing Pennsylvania credit terms; special computer processing and handling costs for Pennsylvania customers in setting up accounts and producing monthly billing statements $ 53,000
>
> b. Approximate loss of finance and service charge revenue from Pennsylvania customers $750,000
>
> Total $803,000"

* * *

Pennsylvania contends that its Goods and Services Installment Sales Act applies to Aldens' credit sales to Pennsylvania residents because 69 P.S. § 1103 provides:

> "For the purposes of this act a retail installment contract, contract, retail installment account, installment account, or revolving account is made in Pennsylvania and, therefore, subject to the provisions of this act if either the seller offers or agrees in Pennsylvania to sell to a resident buyer of Pennsylvania or if such resident Pennsylvania buyer accepts or makes the offer in Pennsylvania to buy, regardless of the situs of the contract as specified therein.
>
> "Any solicitation or communication to sell, verbal or written, originating outside the Commonwealth of Pennsylvania but forwarded to and received in Pennsylvania by a resident buyer of Pennsylvania shall be construed as an offer or agreement to sell in Pennsylvania.

"Any solicitation or communication to buy, verbal or written, originating within the Commonwealth of Pennsylvania from a resident buyer of Pennsylvania, but forwarded to and received by a retail seller outside the Commonwealth of Pennsylvania shall be construed as an acceptance or offer to buy in Pennsylvania."

Aldens contends that Pennsylvania cannot, consistent with the federal constitution, apply its consumer credit law to the transactions in question, which, it says, are Illinois contracts performed entirely outside Pennsylvania and in interstate commerce. Aldens contends, in other words, that § 1103 is a Pennsylvania choice of law rule setting forth a choice of law which that state cannot constitutionally make.

* * *

A. *The Due Process Limitation.*

The due process clause of the fourteenth amendment limits the power of a state to export its sovereign decisional authority, including its authority to make choices of law, to transactions with which it has an insufficient minimum interest. The contours of this limitation have been defined for the most part in cases involving attempts at extraterritorial service of process, but it has been applied in contexts outside the extraterritorial service of process area as well.[2] The "long arm" cases are the more recent, and in these the Supreme Court made an interest analysis which focused upon the interest of the state which would or would not suffice to justify *any* exercise of its sovereignty in connection with the transaction in dispute. Since McGee v. International Life Insurance Co., 355 U.S. 220, 78 S.Ct. 199, 2 L.Ed.2d 223 (1957), it has been clear that the due process clause defines a rather low threshold of state interest sufficient to justify exercise of the state's sovereign decisional authority with respect to a given transaction. Aldens urges that Pennsylvania's interest in the Illinois contracts with Pennsylvania residents is insufficient to meet the due process threshold bar. We disagree. We think it clear beyond question that Pennsylvania has a substantial interest in the rates paid by its residents to foreign companies for the use of money and in the contracts setting those rates. The stipulated facts establish that Aldens would obtain $750,000 a year more in interest than a Pennsylvania seller could lawfully obtain on identical transactions if it did not comply with the Pennsylvania Act. * * * It suffices to hold that Pennsylvania's interest in the rates which its residents pay for the use of money for purchase of goods delivered into Pennsylvania is substantial enough to satisfy any due process objection to its attempt at regulating the subject matter. To the extent that any of the cases referred to in footnote 2, supra, may suggest otherwise they must be deemed to have been limited by the

---

2. See, e.g., Hartford Accident & Indem. Co. v. Delta & Pine Land Co., 292 U.S. 143, 54 S.Ct. 634, 78 L.Ed. 1178 (1934); New York Life Ins. Co. v. Dodge, 246 U.S. 357, 38 S.Ct. 337, 62 L.Ed. 772 (1918); Allgeyer v. Louisiana, 165 U.S. 578, 17 S.Ct. 427, 41 L.Ed. 832 (1897), all invalidating on due process grounds the application of forum law to contracts made elsewhere by forum residents.

more recent interest analysis approach of cases such as McGee v. International Life Insurance Co., supra.

[The court then distinguished National Bellas Hess v. Dept. of Revenue, 386 U.S. 753, 87 S.Ct. 1389, 18 L.Ed.2d 505 (1967), holding that state taxation of interstate commerce is subject to more careful scrutiny than state regulation of such commerce under the police power.]

B. *The Full Faith and Credit Limitation.*

The full faith and credit clause contains another limitation on the authority of one state to disregard the public acts of a sister state. Its limitation applies, even to a state with a sufficient interest in the transaction to satisfy the due process threshold, when, upon an analysis of competing factors, a sister state has a greater interest in regulating the transaction. To a certain extent the considerations relevant under the due process clause and under the full faith and credit clause overlap. This is because those considerations on which Pennsylvania relies to overcome the due process limitation are placed on the scale when balancing its interest in applying its public policy against Illinois' interest. We must, therefore, first identify the competing interests and then attribute to them appropriate values. Since we have said already that Pennsylvania has a substantial interest in the rate paid by its residents for the use of money, we will turn to the competing interest of Illinois in the transaction.

Illinois affords to persons or corporations doing business there a law of contracts which sanctions the enforcement of contractual undertakings. But, granting that the contracts in issue here are substantially Illinois contracts, it does not follow that Illinois has an interest in every consequence that flows from them. Although in enacting § 1103 Pennsylvania speaks in terms of redefining the place of contracting, it does so only for the purpose of the Pennsylvania Goods and Services Installment Sales Act. Except to the extent that it requires compliance with that Act it gives full faith and credit to the Illinois law of contracts. If there is any conflict with an Illinois public act, it is only in connection with the regulation of the time-price differential charges by Illinois sellers to Pennsylvania buyers. Illinois also limits interest rates in consumer credit transactions, but it does so only by prohibiting exactions in excess of certain statutory maximums; the governing statute allows any rate to be taken in connection with an Illinois contract not in excess of the rate allowed by Illinois law.[6] Illinois has

6. "When any written contract, wherever payable, shall be made in this state, or between citizens or corporations of this state, or a citizen or a corporation of this state and a citizen or corporation of any other state, territory or country (or shall be secured by mortgage or trust deed on lands in this state), such contract may bear any rate of interest allowed by law to be taken or contracted for by persons or corporations in this state, or allowed by law on any contract for money due or owing in this state; provided, however, that such rate of interest shall not exceed 8% per annum, except as expressly authorized by this Act or other laws of this State. * * *" 74 Ill.Rev.S. § 8 (Supp.1975).

manifested no interest in requiring that firms headquartered there obtain the maximum interest allowed under its law. If Illinois actually specified the terms on which Illinois sellers could contract, as in Order of United Commercial Travelers v. Wolfe, supra, we would be faced with a full faith and credit issue requiring a delicate balancing of competing interests. In this case, however, there is no conflict between Illinois policy and Pennsylvania policy and no public act of Illinois to which Pennsylvania has not but should give full faith and credit. Thus, the full faith and credit clause does not prevent application of Pennsylvania law.

C.   *The Commerce Clause Limitation.*

As we have seen the due process clause requires the identification of *any* Pennsylvania interest sufficient to justify the exercise of Pennsylvania sovereignty with respect to a given private transaction. The full faith and credit clause, on the other hand, requires a balancing of the possible competing interests of separate state sovereignties. Under the commerce clause our attention shifts to conflicts between local and national interests.

Classifying the Supreme Court's commerce clause adjudications for the purpose of analytical application may seem to many an exercise in futility. In this area of constitutional law, perhaps more than in any other, the political philosophy of the Court's majority at a given moment has influenced not only the outcome, but the reasoning of the decisions. Thus an opinion from one era may reflect an evaluation of the relative weight to be given to local versus national interests that a later court has rendered obsolete. Complicating the picture further, the Court's majority has not always been consistent in its perception of the extent to which Congress rather than it should determine where the national interest lies. Nevertheless, some analytical framework must be attempted or we will be reduced to the even more futile exercise of color-matching the stipulated facts in this case to the commerce clause cases which appear to glow with the most nearly similar hue. We suggest, then, that the commerce clause limits the power of a state to impose its choice of law on any transaction that is within the broad ambit of congressional power to regulate interstate commerce, and

(1) is one in which Congress has made its own choice of law, or

(2) is one in which Congress has made no specific choice of law, but

(a) despite this inaction the nature of the subject matter requires a uniform national rule, or

(b) the choice of law made by the state discriminates against persons engaged in interstate commerce in favor of local interests, or

(c) a non-discriminatory state choice of law, in an area where national uniformity may not be essential, imposes a

burden on interstate commerce in excess of any value attach-
ing to the state's interest in imposing its regulation.

If the state choice of law does not run afoul of any of the foregoing
categories it is valid under the commerce clause whether it is called a
"police" regulation or a "tax" case, a regulation "of commerce," or if it
goes by any other name. The label is not, or should not be, significant.
What is, or should be, significant is the identification of factors which
will place the case in one or another of the analytical categories, or in
none.

In this case we can eliminate category (1), for although Congress
has acted comprehensively in the field of retail installment credit in
the Federal Truth in Lending Act, it has not seen fit to regulate
interest rates in that field. It has, moreover, expressly deferred to
state authority. * * * [A]t a minimum it is a congressional recognition that the maximum level of interest rates in consumer credit
transactions is not a subject matter requiring a uniform national rule.
In face of this express congressional recognition that national uniformity is not required it would not, we suppose, be open to the Court to hold
otherwise.

Aldens urges that the Pennsylvania statute falls within category
2(b) in that it discriminates against interstate commerce. The full
flavor of the argument is best captured by a quotation:

"The Pennsylvania Act discriminates against interstate commerce in
the sense that it benefits Pennsylvania companies making sales in
Pennsylvania to non-Pennsylvania residents by leaving those in-state
sales totally unregulated and burdens non-Pennsylvania companies
making sales outside Pennsylvania to Pennsylvania residents by regulating the terms and conditions of those out-of-state sales * * *."

This argument is extremely fanciful. Pennsylvania makes no
effort to regulate the time-price differential charged by anyone to a
resident of another state. It explicitly negates any such effort by
exempting transactions by Pennsylvania sellers with residents of other
states. Thus Pennsylvanians and Illini stand in exactly the same
position in selling to Delawareans. It also places Pennsylvanians and
Illini exactly on a par in selling to Pennsylvanians. No local interest is
given an advantage within or without Pennsylvania. If Aldens wants
to sell to a Pennsylvanian it can only do so on the same terms as a
Pennsylvania mail order seller, who is engaged in interstate commerce.
There is no discrimination.

Finally Aldens urges that the Pennsylvania act falls within category 2(c) by placing a direct burden on interstate commerce which cannot
be justified by any interest of the Commonwealth. To put this argument in perspective we refer back to the discussion of the discrimination contention directly above. A mail order house located in Philadelphia, buying merchandise in interstate commerce, for resale in
Pennsylvania, is in any realistic economic sense, engaged in interstate
commerce just as much as is Aldens. Pennsylvania's regulation of the

time-price differential in mail order sales by the Philadelphia mail order house, therefore, imposes on interstate commerce the same burden as in the case of sales by Aldens. Thus the decisive issue with respect to category 2(c) is not whether § 1103 is valid as applied to Aldens, but rather whether Pennsylvania can regulate the time-price differential on any consumer credit transaction in the stream of interstate commerce. The burden on interstate commerce does not depend upon the happenstance of respective locations of buyer and seller. The fundamental issue is whether the national interest in the free movement of money, credit, goods and services outweighs the valid local interest in restricting maximum interest rates on consumer "loans" and setting uniform contract terms for such transactions. Before the emergence of a national currency and a national monetary policy, and especially before the emergence of national concern over consumer protection in interstate commerce, the issue would not have been seriously debated. But even in the period since these developments, no case that we have been referred to has even so much as hinted that usury laws and related contract laws are not appropriate matters for local regulation. This despite the facts that such laws do burden interstate commerce, and that the burden is increased by the lack of uniformity.[15] Considering, however, the historical recognition that the states may, despite the burden on commerce, enact varying usury laws and varying contract laws, any judgment that the present proliferation of regulations of consumer credit transactions has burdened commerce unduly must be made by Congress. Here the legislative judgment made in § 1610(b) of the Truth in Lending Act once more becomes significant. Congress has deferred to the states on the matter of maximum interest rates in consumer credit transactions. Since it has

15. The extent of disparity in state treatment is described in Aldens' brief:

"Of the 47 jurisdictions which regulate finance charges on revolving credit accounts, 42 regulate only transactions entered into within the regulating state in terms of traditional contract law. The statutes in a number of states affirmatively restrict their application to in-state transactions: Many other jurisdictions have no specific provision concerning the application of their regulations, but make them applicable to in-state transactions by the normal common law principles: Colorado, Idaho, Indiana, Kansas, Oklahoma, South Carolina and Utah, although recognizing the legality of out-of-state credit agreements with finance charges in excess of those permitted under their own laws, deny enforcement in their courts of so much of the finance charges as exceed the locally permitted rates.

"By contrast, three states have enacted statutes which apply not only to

the traditional agreement made within the state, but—at least under certain circumstances—also to revolving credit charge sales made to buyers residing in the state even though under traditional legal concepts the contract would be held to have been made in another state: Effective January 1, 1975 a fourth state will join this group. These states seek to give their residents protection even in interstate transactions, but do not at the same time try to free in-state companies from following the state regulations when they deal with out-of-state buyers.

"Only Massachusetts may conceivably have sought the same ends as the Pennsylvania Act, although the Massachusetts statute is plainly different on its face from Pennsylvania's. Indeed, the Massachusetts statute, based as it is on the place where the buyer signs the credit agreement, has a totally unpredictable scope given today's mobile population.

" * * * "

done so we decline to hold that the burden imposed by Pennsylvania on Aldens' interstate commerce by virtue of § 1103 is so great that it outweighs the Commonwealth's interest in regulating the rates which its resident consumers may pay for the temporary use of money or the terms on which they may contract for such use.

* * *

Those state statutes closing the courts to foreign corporations which fail to qualify locally are paradigms of our category 2(c). The state has an interest in requiring local qualification, and if there are sufficient local contacts by the foreign corporation the state may enforce that interest by imposing the severe sanction of closing local courts. But where, as in *Allenberg Cotton,* supra, local presence has virtually no intrastate aspect, the burden on interstate commerce from the imposition of the sanction outweighs the state's interest. Striking that balance is always a matter of federal law. But it is federal law on which the Court has received no instruction from Congress, and in which the Court proceeds on a case-by-case basis. The most significant difference between cases involving state statutes closing the door to foreign corporations and this case is that here Congress has expressly deferred to the states on the matter of consumer credit interest rates. Congress having used the legislative scales, there is no need and there may be no room for the kind of judicial weighing which produced one result in Eli Lilly & Co. v. Sav–On–Drugs, Inc., 366 U.S. 276, 81 S.Ct. 1316, 6 L.Ed.2d 288 (1961) and another in *Allenberg Cotton,* supra. Even if Congress had not done so, *Allenberg Cotton* is in any event distinguishable from this case because of the significant local impact of the time-price differential paid by Pennsylvania residents and the relatively slight burden on interstate commerce from Pennsylvania's regulation of that differential.

We conclude then, that the district court properly granted the Attorney General's motion dismissing Aldens' complaint, because § 1103 conflicts with no provision of the federal constitution.

Notes

1. At least four other cases have come to the same conclusion. Aldens, Inc. v. LaFollette, 552 F.2d 745 (7th Cir.1977), cert. denied, 434 U.S. 880, 98 S.Ct. 236, 54 L.Ed.2d 161 (Wisconsin interest rate ceiling was applicable to sales to its residents by out-of-state mail order firm); Aldens, Inc. v. Ryan, 571 F.2d 1159 (10th Cir.1978) (Oklahoma Credit Code was applicable); Aldens, Inc. v. Miller, 610 F.2d 538 (8th Cir.1979) (Iowa Consumer Credit Code applicable); Whitaker v. Spiegel, Inc., 95 Wash.2d 661, 623 P.2d 1147, as modified, 637 P.2d 235 (1981) (Washington state usury limit applicable to out-of-state seller).

Are *Aldens* and *Burr* reconcilable? Do they in fact address the same issue?

2. Contrast with the holding in *Aldens* that in Marquette Nat. Bank v. First of Omaha Service Corp., 439 U.S. 299, 99 S.Ct. 540, 58 L.Ed.2d 534

(1978). In *Marquette,* the Supreme Court agreed that a national bank located in Nebraska could charge its Minnesota credit card customers the prevailing Nebraska rate despite a lower ceiling in Minnesota. This result, said the Court, was required by the supervening provisions of the National Bank Act, 12 U.S.C.A. § 85, permitting a federally-chartered bank always to charge the highest rate of its state of location—Nebraska in this case.

3. Several cases have held that out-of-state debt collectors can be required to be licensed in the state where they contact debtors, without imposing an undue (unconstitutional) burden on interstate commerce. Silver v. Woolf, 538 F.Supp. 881 (D.Conn.1982); Commonwealth v. Allied Bond and Collection Agency, 394 Mass. 608, 476 N.E.2d 955 (1985).

4. A Georgia-based direct mail marketer asserted that an investigation of its activities by the Kansas Attorney General, alleging fraudulent vacation "giveaways" in violation of the Kansas Consumer Protection Act (KCPA), was unconstitutional. A U.S. district court rejected this argument. Conte & Co., Inc. v. Stephan, 713 F.Supp. 1382 (D.Kan.1989). The court first noted that the federal postal fraud statute does not preempt state anti-fraud statutes:

> Thus, while the state may not regulate the mail, it may prevent unfair trade practices from occurring within its boundaries. The state has chosen here through the KCPA to augment the federal laws by providing additional safeguards. We find nothing in the federal statutes on the United States mails to preclude the passage and implementation of legislation such as the KCPA.

Id., 713 F.Supp. at 1386. The court also found there were sufficient minimum contacts with the state of Kansas to justify the assertion of jurisdiction over the Georgia company without violating the due process clause of the 14th amendment. *Id.* at 1388.

Problem 7

Careful Credit, Inc., a small loan company licensed under the U3C by the State of Indiana to charge rates up to 36%, contacts Charlie Consumer, a Wisconsin resident, in Wisconsin. Careful is not licensed as a small loan company in Wisconsin, and proposes making debt consolidation loans at rates higher than the rates allowed under Wisconsin ceilings. Over half of the loan volume of such creditors is for debt consolidation, so Careful's letter is pitched for such purposes. It states that, if Charlie will list all his outstanding creditors in his loan application, he can consolidate his debts through Careful into one monthly payment. Careful will pay each of the consumer's existing creditors directly, and Charlie will not be bothered by them again. If Charlie follows these instructions, which law governs—Wisconsin or Indiana? See U3C § 1.201(1) and (2).

Problem 8

Barbara Buyer, a New York resident, has a credit card from Super Sales Store, Inc., a nationwide retailing chain whose main office is located in New York City. Barbara purchases goods from a Super Sales Store in New York, receives her monthly bills from a New York office, and returns her monthly payments to a New York City post office box. However, when Barbara first applied for a credit card from Super Sales, she put her application into a postage-paid business return envelope which had an Indiana post office box address. Which law governs the relationship between Barbara and Super Sales, New York or Indiana (U3C)?

See U3C § 1.201(1). Does this section allow the creation of "creditor havens" (akin to Nevada for divorces) which have the least effective consumer protection laws?

Note

The basic approach of traditional choice of law cases which look to the law of the state in which the contract is made, is preserved in the U3C, but with a few exceptions. As the cases show, the place of making the contract can easily be controlled by the creditor, allowing the creditor to choose a state with high rate ceilings or lax enforcement. *Aldens* indicates that a state can constitutionally enact legislation which avoids these principles, and resists the assertion of extra-territorial application of the law of the creditor's state. However, there is a different problem when the legislation of a state is more neutral, and it is the *courts* of the consumer's state which are asked to use avoidance principles to resist the application of the law of the creditor's state (such as the U3C). Even interest analysis may not aid such a court, for this concept has been used to apply the law of the creditor's place of business. Crisafulli v. Childs, 33 A.D.2d 293, 307 N.Y.S.2d 701 (1970). Further, the use of avoidance principles would necessarily be based upon the application of public policies to protect resident consumers, but it has been stated that "public policy per se plays no part in the choice of law problem." Pioneer Credit v. Catalano, 51 Misc.2d 407, 273 N.Y.S.2d 310 (1966); Kinney Loan & Finance Co. v. Sumner, 159 Neb. 57, 65 N.W.2d 240 (1954). Do you agree? Should the courts in the consumer's state refuse to consider avoidance principles and look only at the technicalities of the competing statutes?

Chapter 16

SMALL ARMS FIRE:
THE PRACTICAL RESOLUTION OF
INDIVIDUAL DISPUTES

Prefatory Note

This chapter concerns the practical problems faced by consumers as they attempt to resolve disputes over consumer goods and services. For instance, you have a car (or a $50 telephone answering machine) which doesn't run "right" and the dealer isn't being cooperative. It is the kind of problem which will not bankrupt the individual, but it is continually annoying. It is also often not of sufficient economic value to bring to an attorney, unless he is part of a pre-paid legal system. However, whether attorneys are involved or not, consumer complaint resolution is an important part of the total legal system. And, as we have seen in Chapter 6, an inappropriate consumer response (such as ceasing payments without effective notice) can create enormous problems for the consumer. What are appropriate responses? Are any of them effective?

1. Usually, the first consumer response is to complain to the merchant directly to seek repair or a refund (although a surprising number of consumers simply suffer their losses silently). In a majority of cases, unless the consumer has dealt with a deliberate rip-off artist, this will obtain some relief, but can sometimes require the consumer to conduct complex personal negotiations.

2. The second step is usually to seek help from an industry-sponsored informal dispute resolution mechanism. The oldest of these is the Better Business Bureau (BBB) program. In the 1980s, most car manufacturers began to offer such programs, spurred on by state lemon laws which required consumers to pursue this option before claiming a refund or replacement vehicle in court. A few pioneering state governments have also set up their own consumer dispute resolution systems.

3. Some consumers eventually use the legal system for dispute resolution, either by choice or because they are sued. A few can use the shield of unconscionability, but a sword would be more useful.

Statutes like the Truth-in-Lending Act and the Magnuson–Moss Warranty Act provide some weapons for consumers on the attack, such as statutory damages and attorney's fees.

4. Statutory provisions for the award of attorney's fees to the successful consumer plaintiff are obviously intended to make it easier for consumers to obtain legal counsel and access to the courts. There are some pitfalls for the eager attorney seeking to claim such fees, however.

The materials in this chapter consider these approaches, and the problems with each of them.

SECTION A. THE CONSUMER COMPLAINS DIRECTLY TO THE MERCHANT OR CREDITOR

BEST AND ANDREASON, "CONSUMER RESPONSE TO UNSATISFACTORY PURCHASES: A SURVEY OF PERCEIVING DEFECTS, VOICING COMPLAINTS, AND OBTAINING REDRESS"

11 Law & Soc.Rev. 701, 728–29 (1977).*

At the problem perception stage, individuals of low socioeconomic status notice fewer problems. Similarly, low household interest in consumer affairs is linked to low problem perception rates. For all households, simple manifest problems are perceived more strongly than judgmental problems. And almost all consumers are reluctant to acknowledge that they have suffered more than an average amount of trouble with purchases.

At the complaint voicing stage, buyers suppress complaints concerning about two-thirds of the problems they perceive. Not all suppressed complaints are associated with complete inaction. In some instances, buyers may exit; however, these exit actions do not serve to compensate the buyer for the loss incurred nor to inform the appropriate business about its failure. Buyers do present roughly one-third of perceived problems to complaint processors, but these do not accurately represent the full range of consumer problems. Compared with perceived problems, voiced complaints overrepresent problems that are simple, that involve high cost, and that are experienced by high socioeconomic status households. The data show, too, that third parties deal with only a small segment of the problems people perceive and the complaints people voice. This provides an illustration of Stewart Macaulay's thesis in a consumer setting, although it may be more accurate to say that only a small number of cases reach third parties than to say that involvement of third parties is particularly likely to occur in certain kinds of cases. Because of the pattern of third-party use, businesses are able to impose their own unreviewed standards for decision-making on almost all the complaint cases they handle.

The data on response to complaints show that overall, somewhat more than half are resolved to the satisfaction of consumers. Complaints concerning services do not produce as many favorable outcomes as those concerning products, and there is a similar disparity between complaints about judgmental and manifest problems.

Buyers thus provide business with a subsidy in the form of up to a two-thirds discount on requests for redress, and many voiced complaints are not resolved to the buyer's satisfaction. Perhaps our society is so organized that it can easily tolerate the existence of many unresolved grievances. On the other hand, feelings of powerlessness in the marketplace may contribute to social distress.

Note

In this field, there are numerous surveys with, predictably, a wide variety of results. See, e.g., King & McEvoy, A National Survey of the Complaint–Handling Procedures Used by Consumers, King Research, Inc. (1976). There is one survey which finds an 82% affirmative response to the question: "Were you satisfied with the results of your complaint?" However, it was a survey of the customers of only one store in Denver which dealt with white, middle class buyers of "a leading brand" of TVs and washer-dryers. Further, the question asked could not elicit any information about unperceived or unvoiced complaints. Ross & Littlefield, "Complaint as a Problem–Solving Mechanism," 12 Law & Soc.Rev. 199 (1978).

Problem 1

Saul Brenner took his car to Kramer Auto Service for repairs. The repairs to be made were agreed upon and estimated to cost $25. When Brenner returned for the car, the bill read $51.02. Kramer had performed additional services and, of course, demanded to be paid for them. Brenner objected that the extra services were not needed, but Kramer became obdurate and gave Brenner an option: either Brenner paid, or Kramer would keep possession of the car. Brenner paid by using his VISA card. What can Brenner do now to resolve this dispute? Complaining directly to the merchant is not likely to be effective; and if he has already paid, the burden of initiating litigation is on him. But, does Brenner have a self-help remedy under Federal statutes? Under Federal regulations? See Fair Credit Billing Act (CCPA) §§ 161, 170; Reg. Z § 226.12(c). If Brenner is a person who always pays within 30 days, how much of his VISA card account billing would you advise him to pay to avoid finance charges?

Note on Creditor Self–Help

Seventy-four-year-old Nina Maddox of Annapolis, Maryland, received a bill from C & P Telephone for $33,000 for long distance calls—4,000 calls to "900 numbers" in the Los Angeles area (apparently, mostly to matchmaker services or dial-a-sexy-story tapes). The calls were made in rapid succession, one after the other, for 18 or 20 hours at a time. Both Nina and C & P agree that a machine made the calls, not a person; and computer hackers have been "hanging" people like Nina for many months, usually with calls to sex tapes.

Nina says she did not make the calls, and denies liability for them. C & P simply responds that Nina is still responsible for paying the bill. Nina hired an attorney who wrote a letter to C & P, but C & P responded with a letter threatening to cut off Nina's phone service. After some further discussions, C & P offered to settle for only $3,000, but it figured it had met her more than halfway—and it even offered to let her make installment payments. When Nina refused to pay for any calls she had not made, C & P again threatened to cut off her telephone service. If you represent Nina, what can you do?

[Adapted from "Bob Levey's Washington" in the September 6, 1990, Washington Post, page C16.]

SECTION B. INFORMAL DISPUTE RESOLUTION MECHANISMS

Prefatory Note

Before a consumer gets to court with a complaint, he is likely to encounter the opportunity to submit his dispute to a nonjudicial forum, now fashionably known as "alternative dispute resolution" or ADR. Such systems may be informal, industry-sponsored programs, such as that of the Better Business Bureau. Formal arbitration and the use of professional mediators are also becoming increasingly popular to hammer out settlements in cases where a complaint has already been filed in court. In many jurisdictions, the courts may order mediation or even a mini-jury trial for certain types of disputes.

The goal of most of these programs is to help the parties work out a mutually agreeable settlement without incurring the expense of full-blown litigation. For instance, the defendant banks and the consumer class in the *Perdue* case, supra Chapter 10, pages 623–629, agreed to retain a neutral, independent facilitator because the traditional one-on-one settlement negotiation model seemed doomed to failure due to the adversarial positions of the parties. They succeeded in reaching a settlement agreement that avoided further years of litigation in a complex consumer class action. See Lundquist, Alternative Dispute Resolution as a Settlement Strategy in the Wake of Perdue v. Crocker National Bank, 43 Bus.Law. 1095 (1988). Thus, consumer disputes ranging from a problem with a $100 lawnmower to a complex class action suit can potentially benefit from alternative dispute resolution.

ADR promises to provide a speedier, more efficient way to resolve disputes, but are there some hidden costs? Will the party with less bargaining power, such as the consumer, be coerced into making a settlement that is not necessarily in his best interests? Will the third party mediators apply legal standards or simply work out disputes according to their own rough sense of justice? Are these procedures in fact reducing the load on the judicial system and making dispute resolution more accessible or do they simply add another obstacle on the path to a judicial remedy?

Industry–Provided Dispute Resolution Mechanisms

MINDELL, REPORT ON 1986 CHANGES IN LAWS AFFECTING CONSUMER PROTECTION

196 New York Law Journal, Aug. 20, 1986, at 1, col. 3.*

Pursuant to subdivision (g) of § 198–a, [New York Lemon Law] if a manufacturer has established a dispute resolution mechanism which complies in all respects with the Federal Trade Commission's (FTC) regulations issued pursuant to the federal Magnuson–Moss Warranty Act, as set forth in 16 CFR § 703, a consumer must first resort to such procedure before seeking in court the statutory remedies of refund or replacement. For example, General Motors, American Motors, Honda, Nissan and several other makers of foreign autos use the Better Business Bureau program, while Ford and Chrysler have their own mediation-arbitration boards.

Since the effective date of the "New–Car Lemon Law," Sept. 1, 1983, thousands of New York consumers have sought the assistance of these panels in an effort to resolve disputes concerning defective new cars. A substantial number of consumer complaints have been generated as a result of such recourse. Consequently, our office conducted a thorough evaluation of these procedures as they relate to lemon-law cases. This review had a twofold purpose: first, to determine if the procedures comply with Rule 703 (to date, the FTC has not certified officially any program, although it is authorized by Magnuson–Moss to do so); and second, to determine if the arbitration decisions are consistent with the "New–Car Lemon Law" (§ 198–a).

The evaluation by this office revealed substantial noncompliance with the requirements of Rule 703. In addition, it found that numerous arbitration decisions have failed to follow the guidelines of subdivision (c) of § 198–a. That subdivision, as amended, requires that, in buy-back cases, the manufacturer must refund to the consumer (i) the full purchase price, or lease price, including trade-in allowance, and (ii) all license fees, registration fees and any similar governmental charges. The dealer may deduct an allowance for the purchaser's use in excess of the first 12,000 miles of operation.

Manufacturer's Position

Many arbitration decisions, which fail to apply statutory remedies, may be attributed to an arbitrator's lack of familiarity with the law. But it has been the general position of the manufacturers that the arbitration awards in their dispute settlement procedures need not be consistent with that law. Indeed, some manufacturers have agreed not to assert a consumer's failure to use the program as a basis for dismissal of lemon-law actions and have labeled their programs as purely "voluntary" in nature. But even if consumers can by-pass arbitration and proceed directly to litigation with the manufacturer's prior consent, this wholly unrealistic scenario defeats the very purpose of the law. Few consumers can bear the additional delays and expense attendant to litigation. Consequently, the vast majority of consumers must be content with an arbitration award, and for this reason that award should conform to the law.

Another fundamental concern of the Attorney General's Office regarding the Chrysler and Ford arbitration programs as they function in New York relates to their failure to afford consumers the opportunity to attend and make an oral presentation at arbitration meetings. To the contrary, decisions are made on the written record at a hearing at which the parties to the dispute are not present. While not required by Rule 703, we believe that these programs work to the serious disadvantage of consumers by not permitting oral presentations.

The Department of Law's recent analysis of the Better Business Bureau's Auto Line dispute resolution program revealed a high degree of success with the oral presentation approach. Based upon this experience, our office is convinced that oral presentations enable consumers to present their case more effectively, to learn of and rebut the manufacturer's contradictory information and to supply missing or new documentation. Oral presentations offer the benefit of counteracting any pressure on arbitration board members to decide cases quickly rather than thoroughly. Moreover, they also deter any tendency on the part of the board members to avoid a full consideration of each case on the merits in an effort to compromise. Finally, the use of oral presentations at board hearings would serve to remove the appearance of bias and secrecy.

Note

The 1986 amendments to New York's Lemon Law require arbitrators to be trained in and to apply Lemon Law remedies, and oral presentations must be permitted at the request of the consumer.

LERNER, ARBITRATION AS LEMON AID

192 New York Law Journal, Sept. 13, 1984, at 1, col. 1.*

CONNECTICUT

* * * The State Attorney–General focused on the national procedures of certain manufacturers administered by the Better Business

Bureau and, on December 13, 1985, reported that ". . . the Better Business Bureau is bringing its arbitration program into compliance in all but two types of the areas cited in an October report. * * *"

* * *

A summary of the problem areas outlined in the October report, together with a review of the progress made since that time, follows:

"1. Failure to clearly state consumers' rights and obligations in written operating procedures (i.e., performance deadline by manufacturer, specification of consumer-caused delays, choice of oral or written proceedings). PROGRESS: Some specific changes have already been made: the rest have been agreed upon.

"2. Requirement of mediation with manufacturer prior to arbitration. PROGRESS: Mediation will continue to be part of the BBB program, giving the consumer the option of negotiating with the manufacturer's representative, but not requiring it.

"3. Failure to meet forty-day deadline. PROGRESS: The FTC is currently considering the BBB's request for an exemption from the forty-day deadline extending to 60 days the time within which a dispute must be resolved. The BBB has given assurances that they can complete the procedure within 60 days and the FTC is likely to grant the BBB's request.

"4. Failure to adequately provide for written as well as oral proceedings. PROGRESS: Written procedures and forms have been changed to give consumers a clear explanation of options for oral, written or telephone procedures.

"5. Failure to consider consequential damages in the arbitration process. PROGRESS: While the Attorney General believes that consequential damages must be included, there is a remaining question as to the scope of such damages. Therefore, questions are being submitted to the Federal Trade Commission for a formal advisory opinion on the matter.

"6. Insufficient training of arbitrators. PROGRESS: BBB has agreed to develop a training manual and expand the training program for arbitrators.

"7. Lack of participation by neutral technical experts. PROGRESS: The issue of technical experts will be submitted to the FTC for a formal advisory opinion."

* * *

MASSACHUSETTS

* * *

Arbitration is not required under the [Massachusetts] Lemon Law.

* * *

On June 20, 1984 the State of Executive Office of Consumer Affairs and Business Regulation reported on six months' experience with the law. It noted in part:

"The biggest problem with the law so far is the non-participation of auto manufacturers in arbitration prescribed by the law." This is particularly distressing because "it was the manufacturers who wanted arbitration included in the law in the first place."

The Report concluded that the arbitration provision of the lemon law was not working. "The intent of the law that there should be a speedy, fair way to resolve lemon disputes has not been realized. * * *"

* * *

GUARE, VERMONT HARVESTS ITS LEMON CROP (LETTER TO EDITOR)
Wall Street J., November 5, 1986, at 31, col. 2.

* * *

In Vermont, the General Assembly concluded in 1984 that the Arbitration offered by the Better Business Bureau, car manufacturers, et al. did not work. Since 1984, Vermont has had a lemon law operated by a five-member board appointed by the governor. Through September 1986, the board has heard 101 cases, and awarded 32 refunds and 10 replacement vehicles. There have been 10 appeals to the superior court. One superior court decision has been appealed to the Supreme Court.

Paul H. Guare
Clerk, Motor Vehicle Arbitration Board

MOUNTCASTLE v. VOLVOVILLE, USA, INC.
Supreme Court of New York, Nassau County, 1985.
130 Misc.2d 97, 494 N.Y.S.2d 792.

ELI WAGER, JUSTICE.

Defendant Volvo of America Corporation (Volvo) seeks an order dismissing this action pursuant to CPLR 3211(a)(5) on the grounds of arbitration and award. The case is novel in that it involves the interpretation of the recently enacted "Lemon Law" which relates to the protection of consumers in the purchase of defective automobiles.

The facts of this case are essentially undisputed. Plaintiffs purchased a new 1984 automobile in August of 1984 from the defendant Volvoville, USA, Inc., a factory authorized dealer of defendant Volvo. On September 13, 1984 the plaintiffs brought the vehicle to defendant Volvoville for repairs to the braking system. The car was returned to the consumer as repaired but had to be returned to the repair shop on September 15, 1984 for the same problem. The vehicle was returned to Volvoville repeatedly, on September 21, 1984, October 6, 1984 and October 18, 1984 as a result of the reoccurrence of the same braking problem. In mid October 1984 plaintiffs exercised their rights under General Business Law section 198–a (the New York "Lemon Law"), and demanded a refund of the purchase price of the car or a new car as a result of the continuing problems with the automobile and the dealer's inability, after more than four attempts, to repair it.

Although no informal dispute settlement procedure, as contemplated by General Business Law section 198–a(g), existed for Volvo at the time the problems with this vehicle occurred, subsequently in November of 1984 they agreed to establish an informal dispute settlement procedure consisting of non-binding arbitration through the Long Island Better Business Bureau.

Plaintiffs and defendant Volvo only participated in the non-binding arbitration, which resulted in a determination by the arbitrator directing that, upon the consumer's acceptance of the decision, the manufacturer of the vehicle (Volvo) would pick up the vehicle and have one final opportunity to repair the braking problem. Should the final repair attempt be unsuccessful, Volvo was directed to refund to the consumer the full purchase price of the automobile.

The Better Business Bureau advised the plaintiffs of the arbitrator's decision, its non-binding nature, and requested an acceptance or rejection of the decision and award. By letter dated April 16, 1985, plaintiffs rejected the arbitrator's decision.

Defendant Volvo now moves for a dismissal of the action pursuant to CPLR 3211(a)(5) alleging arbitration and award.

Defendant Volvo bases the instant motion to dismiss on two theories. First, that they were never notified by their dealership about the problems being experienced with respect to this automobile and second, that as a result of their participation in the non-binding arbitration, and the rendering of an award, they fall into the category of litigants entitled to a dismissal on the basis of arbitration and award. * * *

* * *

General Business Law section 198–a(b) provides that, with respect to a defect in a purchased automobile, " * * * the consumer shall during [the warranty] period report the nonconformity, defect or condition to the manufacturer, its agent or its authorized dealer. If the notification is received by the manufacturer's agent or authorized dealer, the agent or dealer shall within seven days, forward written notice thereof to the manufacturer * * *." * * *

Given the relationship of the factory authorized new car dealer and the manufacturer and the requirements of section 198–a(b) of the General Business Law, the failure of the dealer to properly notify the manufacturer cannot serve to free the manufacturer from its responsibility to the consumer-plaintiffs in this action. The "Lemon Law" statute, by its express language (General Business Law § 198–a[b]), precludes this result. * * *

* * *

Volvo of America's demand for a dismissal on the basis of arbitration and award (CPLR 3211[a][5]) fails in the face of the express language of the "Lemon Law". General Business Law section 198–a(h) specifically provides that "[i]n no event shall a consumer who has resorted to an informal dispute settlement procedure be precluded from seeking the rights or remedies available by law." While it is clear that use of the informal dispute settlement procedure is a condition precedent to entitlement to the benefits provided by General Business Law section 198–a(c) (see 198–a[g]), it is equally clear that the settlement procedure award may be rejected by the consumer. The dispute resolution procedure is expressly termed "informal" by the statute itself and the procedure and decisions reached are not to be "legally binding on any person" (C.F.R. § 703.5[j] as implemented by General Business Law § 198–a[g]; see also Attorney General's memorandum to the Governor dated June 23, 1983, p. 3).

Accordingly, the informal dispute resolution procedure resorted to in this case and the resultant award, in the face of plaintiffs' rejection of the decision, do not form the basis for a dismissal of this case pursuant to CPLR 3211(a)(5).

Accordingly, defendant Volvo of America's motion to dismiss is denied.

Problem 2

Robbin Hood bought a new car in New York from Dale Dodge Dealers and received a one year "Limited Warranty" from Chrysler under Magnuson–Moss. The sale was also subject to New York's "Lemon Law."

After 30 days, the clutch in the new car failed to operate properly. Hood took the car to Dale, who "repaired" the clutch. Although the clutch operated properly when it left the dealership that day, it failed again within 10 days. Dale "repaired" again, but it failed for a third time five days later. Dale "repaired" it a third and a fourth time, but it failed a fifth time 15 days later. Hood had the car towed to the dealership once again.

At this point, Dale began to believe something serious was wrong, so it called Chrysler to ask for instructions. The Chrysler representative told Dale that clutches were not covered by Chrysler's limited Warranty, and that the Dealership Service Manual stated that point very clearly. The Chrysler representative stated that she did not care what Dale did with, or to, Hood's car, but that Chrysler would not pay for any of it—and also would not reimburse Dale for past services provided to Hood for the failed clutch.

Dale then contacted Hood and explained that clutches are not covered by Chrysler warranties, so that any repairs would be at his expense. Dale also explained that past services had been at Dale's expense, and that all the bills ($600) from the three prior repair attempts would have to be paid before Hood could get his car back. To date, Hood has not done so, and Dale still has possession of the car.

Hood has tried to negotiate with Dale and with the Chrysler representative, but they have made no adjustment in their demands.

Meanwhile, he is walking. He visited your office to seek legal counsel, and you advised him of the arbitration program sponsored by Chrysler. Since this was a low-budget case, you suggested that Hood might well want to try arbitration first, because it would involve no attorney fees. At that time, you were aware that the Chrysler arbitration program did not meet FTC Guidelines under Magnuson–Moss, but that did not seem critical.

Hood took your advice and filed a proper complaint with the Chrysler arbitration program. He then prepared his case and asked for an arbitration hearing. He was granted the hearing.

On the morning of the hearing, he overheard the arbitrator, William Scarlet, and the Chrysler representative talking to each other. It was obvious that the Chrysler representative had previously appeared before Scarlet at least six times, and had previously handled at least 100 arbitrations. The Chrysler representative had also brought an experienced mechanic with her to be an "expert witness" on Chrysler's behalf. Finally, Scarlet thanked the Chrysler representative for Chrysler's reimbursement to Scarlet of Scarlet's travel expenses of $75. Hood knows where Scarlet lives, and it is about 10 miles from the hearing site.

After overhearing this conversation, Hood becomes concerned and calls you for advice.

(a) Hood states that he has not yet signed any paper which binds him to arbitrate. He now wants to "walk away" from the arbitration process, and use the courts instead. Can he do that? Is there any requirement that he arbitrate before going to court?

(b) If Hood continues the arbitration process, and the arbitrator rules against him, can he still pursue his legal remedies in court? If he later sues in court, will the arbitration findings and decision be admissible against him? Will they be binding on the court?

(c) Would you advise Hood to continue the arbitration process or not? Does it seem unreasonably biased against him? Why, or why not?

(d) If Hood's primary concern arises from Scarlet's statements, can Hood ask Scarlet to disqualify himself due to Chrysler's payments or previous association with Chrysler's representative? If so, what is the likelihood that Scarlet's replacement will create an improvement in these aspects?

Problem 3

Same facts as Problem 2. This time, however, you are the arbitrator, and Hood has continued the arbitration process. Hood presented evidence that Dale tried to fix the clutch four times, and failed four times. He wants to cancel the sale and get his money back. He also presented evidence of his cost of renting a substitute car from Hertz while Dale kept possession of his new car.

The Chrysler representative has presented evidence that Chrysler has never considered the clutch to be a "covered item" under the "Limited Warranty", that the Dealership Service Manual has so stated for the past 25 years, and that it has been a custom of Chrysler, continuously and rigorously, not to pay for any clutch repairs. Chrysler defends this practice on the ground that clutches are easily abused and that after a failure it is impossible to determine whether that failure was caused by a defect or driver abuse, and therefore any failure of a clutch is considered a product of driver abuse. The "expert witness" testifies that all of the above is true.

You, as arbitrator, must now decide this dispute.

(a) Must you follow state law? For example, must you follow all the warranty rules established by UCC Article 2, including its definitions of what is warranted (UCC §§ 2–313–315), and its notification requirements (UCC § 2–607)? More importantly, must you follow the same rules on burden of proof of a defect that a court should use, and insist that Hood prove what was wrong with the clutch, rather than merely assert that it failed?

(b) Must you follow state law, revisited. For example, if the clutch has failed to be repaired 4 times, and you find that the clutch problem is due to manufacturer's defect and not driver abuse, must you order a "buy-back"? Or, can you limit your order to a requirement that Chrysler provide Hood with a replacement equivalent car? Or install a replacement clutch? Or, pay the bill of an independent mechanic to replace the clutch?

Does it make any difference that Chrysler received notice of this problem only after the last clutch failure, and has not yet had any opportunity to repair the defect? Should an arbitrator have flexibility in designing the order given in this type of situation?

Note on Arbitrator Training

In response to complaints that arbitrators did not know and did not apply the New York Lemon Law in making awards, the Better Business Bureau of Western New York sent a communication to all of its arbitrators. The critical passages of that communication are set out below. Would they induce you, as the arbitrator, to change your analysis in Problem 3?

WHAT ARE THE ARBITRATOR'S OBLIGATIONS UNDER THE LAW?

To be trained in arbitration; to be familiar with the Lemon Law; to apply the Lemon Law.

WHAT IS THE LEMON LAW "BILL OF RIGHTS"?

A summary of the consumer's rights under the law, which must be furnished to arbitrators and consumers coming to arbitration.

NEW CAR LEMON LAW BILL OF RIGHTS

(1) In addition to any warranties offered by the manufacturer, your new car is warranted against all material defects for eighteen thousand miles or two years, whichever comes first.

(2) You must report any problems to the manufacturer, its agent, or authorized dealer.

(3) Upon notification, the problem must be corrected free of charge.

(4) If the same problem cannot be repaired after four or more attempts, or if your car is out of service to repair a problem for a total of thirty days during the warranty period, you may be entitled to either a comparable car or a refund of your purchase price, plus license and registration fees, minus a mileage allowance only if the vehicle has been driven more than 12,000 miles.

(5) A manufacturer may deny liability if the problem is caused by abuse, neglect, or unauthorized modifications of the car.

(6) A manufacturer may refuse to exchange a comparable car or refund your purchase price if the problem does not substantially impair the value of your car.

(7) If a manufacturer has established an arbitration procedure, the manufacturer may refuse to exchange a comparable car or refund your purchase price until you first resort to the procedure.

(8) If the manufacturer does not have an arbitration procedure, you may resort to any remedy by law and may be entitled to your attorney's fees if you prevail.

(9) No contract or agreement can void any of these rights.

(10) As an alternative to the arbitration procedure made available through the manufacturer, you may instead choose to submit your claim to an independent arbitrator, approved by the attorney general. You may have to pay a fee for such an arbitration. Contact your local consumer office or Attorney General's office to find out how to arrange for independent arbitration.

Note on State–Sponsored Dispute Resolution Mechanisms

State-sponsored dispute resolution mechanisms provide an alternative in some states to the mechanisms provided under the auspices of the manufacturer. For instance, the New York Lemon Law 1986 amendments give consumers the option of submitting their claims to an independent arbitrator approved by the attorney general, in lieu of the manufacturer's arbitration procedure. Manufacturers are required to submit to the state-sponsored binding arbitration, if the consumer elects this procedure. Unlike the manufacturer proceeding, the state-sponsored program is binding on both parties. N.Y.—McKinney's General Business Law. § 198–a(k). Connecticut, the District of Columbia, Massachusetts, Montana, Texas, Vermont and Washington also offer state run dispute resolution programs.

The New York Lemon Law also contains several restrictions on the manufacturers' voluntary arbitration programs, which were upheld against a federal preemption challenge by the manufacturers' trade association. Motor Vehicle Mfrs. Ass'n v. Abrams, 899 F.2d 1315 (2d Cir. 1990), noted in Chapter 15, supra. The independent arbitration procedure, however, has been upheld in a New York court. Motor Vehicle Manufacturers Ass'n v.

State, 75 N.Y.2d 175, 551 N.Y.S.2d 470, 550 N.E.2d 919 (1990). Both of these rulings are subject to appeal.

Why do you suppose the New York and other state legislatures felt it was necessary to set up an independent arbitration procedure?

SECTION C. THE CONSUMER GOES TO COURT

The materials above describe non-judicial machinery for enforcing consumer rights. In many cases, of course, attempts at amicable settlement will fail, or alternative dispute resolution programs will not be available. The consumer may find himself the defendant in a lawsuit in some cases, or to assert an affirmative claim, the consumer may have to go to court. This presents real economic barriers for the consumer where the stakes are only the modest sums represented by a defective microwave oven, or a 2% overcharge on a small loan. How can the law assure vindication—in court if necessary—for consumer claims which are small in amount and would be dwarfed by the attorney's fees, court costs, lost wages and similar expenses involved in pursuing them?

1. THE SHIELD OF UNCONSCIONABILITY

Throughout the earlier materials, we have considered the utility of the unconscionability doctrine in the context of whether it was better to approach abuses of consumers using a general doctrine such as unconscionability or a specific technical provision describing the particular abuse. For example, in *Williams v. Walker–Thomas Furniture*, supra Chapter 3, pages 209–212, the court used the doctrine of unconscionability to strike down a cross-collateral clause, whereas in some U3C states there is now a specific provision restricting the use of such clauses. In *Remco Enterprises, Inc. v. Houston*, supra Chapter 2, pages 159–161, the court rejected the defendant's unconscionability argument with regard to the price of a "rent-to-own" television set because the admittedly hefty markup did not "shock the conscience" of the court. Finally, in *Perdue v. Crocker National Bank*, supra Chapter 10, pages 623–629, the California Supreme Court held that class plaintiffs had stated a cause of action when they alleged that a bank's charges for processing checks for accounts that did not have sufficient funds (NSF charges) were unconscionably high.

The bottom line of all this is whether a general prohibition against unconscionability can be used as a sword by consumers, or only as a shield against the enforcement of unfair contract provisions. The earliest formulation of the doctrine occurred in common law and later in the UCC. See UCC § 2–302. To analyze the enforceability of the UCC (and common law) doctrine, consider the following:

Problem 5

As was discussed in Chapter 6, the UCC states that any limitation on remedy which limits consequential damages for injury to the person in consumer goods sales is "prima facie unconscionable." UCC § 2–719(3). However, for years after the general enactment of the UCC, until enactment of Magnuson–Moss, most automobile and other manufacturers continued to exclude such damages in their standard forms.

(a) Robbin Hood bought a new car from Dale Dodge Dealers on credit. The contract of sale contained a "standard warranty" which warranted the car "to be free from defects in material and workmanship for 12 months or 12,000 miles, whichever comes first." The contract also contained the following clause: "Seller's obligation under this warranty is limited to repair or replacement of defective parts without charge to Buyer."

Thirty days after the sale, as Hood was driving on the expressway, a cotter pin in the steering mechanism broke; Hood could not control the car; and it crashed into a bridge abutment. Hood was physically injured and the car was damaged. Dale is willing to stipulate that the cotter pin was defective, and is willing to repair the car; but Dale & Dodge both pointed to the limitation on remedy clause and refused to do more. Hood accepted the offer and signed a release of all claims in exchange for repair of the car. Can you now obtain redress for his personal injuries? Would it be easy to do so?

(b) Whether you can obtain redress for Hood or not, is there anything in the UCC which allows you to stop Dale, or Dodge, from continuing to use a contract clause which is "prima facie unconscionable"?

(c) Whether you can obtain redress or enjoin further usage or not, is there any penalty attached to the use by Dale, or Dodge, of a contract clause which is "prima facie unconscionable"? Is there any real need for a deterrent in such a case?

FROSTIFRESH CORP. v. REYNOSO

New York District Court, Nassau County, 1966.
52 Misc.2d 26, 274 N.Y.S.2d 757.

[Plaintiff sold a refrigerator-freezer to defendant for $1146 ($900 price plus $246 finance charge). Defendant protested to the salesman that he had only one week left on his job and couldn't afford the appliance, but the salesman distracted him with a referral sale scheme and deluded him into believing it would cost nothing. The oral negotiations were in Spanish; but the written contract was entirely in English, and was neither translated nor explained. The cost of the appliance to plaintiff was $348.

Defendant paid $32 and defaulted. Plaintiff sued for the $1114 balance still outstanding plus $227 attorney fees plus a $23 late charge. At trial, the court requested evidence on the commercial setting, purpose and effect of the contract to determine whether it was unconscionable. The court then found the defendants were handicapped by not knowing the nature or terms of a contract submitted to them in a foreign language, and held the contract price and terms "shocking to the conscience."]

The question presented in this case is simply this: Does the court have the power under section 2–302 of the Uniform Commercial Code to refuse to enforce the price and credit provisions of the contract in order to prevent an unconscionable result.

It is normally stated that the parties are free to make whatever contracts they please so long as there is no fraud or illegality.

However, it is the apparent intent of the Uniform Commercial Code to modify this general rule by giving the courts power "to police explicitly against the contracts or clauses which they find to be unconscionable. * * * The principle is one of the prevention of oppression and unfair surprise."

The comment cites Campbell Soup Company v. Wentz, 3 Cir., 172 F.2d 80, to illustrate the principle. It is interesting to note that the Wentz case involved oppression with respect to the price Campbell Company agreed to pay for carrots, the price specified in the contract being $23.00 to $33.00 a ton. In the particular case Wentz, the farmer, refused to deliver carrots at the contract price, since the market price at such time had increased to $90.00 a ton. The Court of Appeals said "We think it too hard a bargain and too one-sided an agreement to entitle the plaintiff to relief in a court of conscience" (p. 83).

In the instant case the court finds that here, too, it was "too hard a bargain" and the conscience of the court will not permit the enforcement of the contract as written. Therefore the plaintiff will not be permitted to recover on the basis of the price set forth in the retail installment contract, namely $900.00 plus $245.85 as a service charge.

However, since the defendants have not returned the refrigerator-freezer, they will be required to reimburse the plaintiff for the cost to the plaintiff, namely $348.00. No allowance is made on account of any commissions the plaintiff may have paid to salesmen or for legal fees, service charges or any other matters of overhead.

Accordingly the plaintiff may have judgment against both defendants in the amount of $348.00 with interest, less the $32.00 paid on account, leaving a net balance of $316.00 with interest from December 26, 1964.

FROSTIFRESH CORP. v. REYNOSO

Supreme Court of New York, Appellate Term, Second Department, 1967.
54 Misc.2d 119, 281 N.Y.S.2d 964.

PER CURIAM.

Judgment unanimously reversed, without costs, and a new trial ordered limited to an assessment of plaintiff's damages and entry of judgment thereon.

While the evidence clearly warrants a finding that the contract was unconscionable we are of the opinion that plaintiff should recover its net cost for the refrigerator-freezer, plus a reasonable profit, in addition to trucking and service charges necessarily incurred and reasonable finance charges.

Notes

1. What should the trial judge do upon remand? What further evidence would you need? How would you calculate seller's recovery now?

2. Would the *Frostifresh* case have been better from the consumer's standpoint if it had been brought as a referral sale violation under the specific coverage of RU3C § 3.309, or as an unconscionability case under U3C § 5.108(2) and (4)?

BEST v. UNITED STATES NATIONAL BANK OF OREGON

Court of Appeals of Oregon, 1986.
78 Or.App. 1, 714 P.2d 1049; aff'd, 303 Or. 557, 793 P.2d 554 (1987).

RICHARDSON, PRESIDING JUDGE.

This is a class action challenging the validity of defendant bank's service charge for processing checks drawn against non-sufficient funds (NSF charge). Plaintiffs brought this action on behalf of themselves and other persons similarly situated. * * * The trial court granted the bank's motion for summary judgment against those claims. Plaintiffs appeal and the bank cross-appeals. We affirm in part and reverse in part.

* * *

We next consider plaintiffs' unconscionability claim. They allege that the NSF charge was unconscionable, because it greatly exceeded the bank's cost of processing NSF checks. They sought restitution of the NSF charges they had paid. The trial court ruled that, under *Rosboro Lumber Co. v. EBI,* 65 Or.App. 679, 672 P.2d 1336 (1983), *rev'd on other grounds,* 297 Or. 81, 680 P.2d 386 (1984), the doctrine of unconscionability is not a basis for affirmative relief.

Plaintiffs cite Uniform Commercial Code § 2–302 (ORS 72.3020) and Restatement (Second) Contracts, § 208 (1979), as the bases of their claim. They contend that the result will be the same whether their claim is analyzed under the UCC or the Restatement. Whether or not that is true, UCC § 2–302 does not apply in this case, because UCC Article 2 is limited to transactions in goods. UCC § 2–102 (ORS 72.1020). However, because the Restatement follows UCC § 2–302, *see* Reporter's Note to § 208, and UCC § 2–302 has been influential in nonsales cases, *see* Comment *a* to § 208, cases decided under that section are helpful in analyzing plaintiffs' claim.

In *Rosboro Lumber,* the plaintiff sought restitution of workers' compensation insurance premiums it had paid to the defendant, on the basis, *inter alia,* that the defendant had engaged in unconscionable conduct. We analyzed that claim under the Restatement and held that, "although unconscionability may be a defense to the enforceability of a contract, it is not a basis for affirmative relief." We affirmed the dismissal of the plaintiff's unconscionability claim.

Rosboro Lumber is clearly on point and adverse to plaintiffs' claim. They offer a number of suggestions to avoid its holding. First, they point out that the emphasized portion of the following passage from Dobbs on Remedies 707 (West Ed.1973), which we quoted in *Rosboro Lumber,* 65 Or.App. at 682, 672 P.2d 1336, supports their claim for restitution:

> " * * * [T]he remedy [for unconscionability] remains essentially defensive, for the plaintiff does not recover damages; he will only be relieved of the contractual obligation, *or, possibly, if he has already paid an unconscionable sum, will be allowed restitution to the limits of conscionability.*" (Emphasis supplied.)

Dobbs, however, cites no authority for that assertion and, as discussed below, we have found none. Furthermore, the *holding of Rosboro Lumber* is that the doctrine of unconscionability is not a basis for restitution.

Second, plaintiffs cite *Zemp v. Rowland,* 31 Or.App. 1105, 572 P.2d 637 (1977), *rev. den.* 282 Or. 537 (1978), for the proposition that unconscionability is a basis for restitution. There, the plaintiffs brought an action against their landlord to recover a nonrefundable fee that they had paid under a provision of their lease. They alleged that the provision was unconscionable under the Oregon Residential Landlord and Tenant Act. We held that the provision was not unconscionable. We did not hold that restitution would have been available had we found the provision unconscionable. *Zemp* is inapposite.

Finally, plaintiffs urge us to overrule *Rosboro Lumber.* We decline to do that. We have found no authority anywhere that the doctrine of unconscionability is a basis for restitutionary relief. In *W.L. May Co. v. Philco–Ford Corp.,* 273 Or. 701, 707, 543 P.2d 283 (1975), decided under UCC § 2–302, the court noted that "[n]ormally, the doctrine [of unconscionability] is asserted as an affirmative defense, and it does not appear that it was originally intended as a basis for damage recovery." However, the court expressly left unanswered the question of whether UCC § 2–302 could be used offensively. 273 Or. at 709, n 2, 543 P.2d

283. Cases from other jurisdictions uniformly hold that UCC § 2–302 is not a basis for an award of damages.

At least one other court has specifically denied restitution in a non-UCC case. In *Bennett v. Behring Corp.*, 466 F.Supp. 689 (S.D.Fla.1979), *appeal dismissed* 629 F.2d 393 (5th Cir.1980), property owners brought an action against a developer and others alleging, *inter alia*, that a provision in their deeds requiring them to lease certain recreational facilities was unconscionable. They sought the return of the amounts they had paid under that provision. The court held that the provision was not unconscionable, but it also stated that unconscionability is not a basis for affirmative relief:

> "Plaintiffs [sic] attempt to obtain a judgment for money damages for sums previously collected by [the defendant] under the recreation leases must fail in any event, regardless of a finding of unconscionability. While plaintiffs may be able to recover monetary damages for fraud and/or intentional misrepresentations, as alleged in Counts I and VI, the equitable theory of unconscionability has never been utilized to allow for the affirmative recovery of money damages. ∗ ∗ ∗

> "The Court finds that neither the common law of Florida, nor that of any other state, empowers a court addressing allegations of unconscionability to do more than refuse *enforcement* of the unconscionable section or sections of the contract so as to avoid an unconscionable result. ∗ ∗ ∗" 466 F.Supp. at 700. (Emphasis in original; citations omitted.)

Because the doctrine of unconscionability is not a basis for affirmative relief, the trial court was correct in granting the bank's motion for summary judgment against the unconscionability claim.

Notes

1. In addition to price unconscionability, courts have also considered so-called "procedural" unconscionability. In this type of unconscionability case, the court may consider the absence of meaningful choice on the part of the buyer, or the presence of terms which are unreasonably favorable to the seller/creditor (*Williams v. Walker–Thomas*, supra Chapter 3, pages 209–212). The court may also consider the lack of sophistication of the buyer or the use of deceptive practices by the seller (*Frostifresh Corp. v. Reynoso*, supra pages 789–791).

2. The shield of unconscionability has been applied not only to the benefit of ordinary consumers, but to businesses as well. For instance, in A & M Produce Co. v. FMC Corporation, 135 Cal.App.3d 473, 186 Cal.Rptr. 114 (1982), a California appellate court ruled that the disclaimer of warranties and exclusion of consequential damages in a contract for the sale of a $32,000 agricultural weight-sizing machine was unconscionable. In the course of affirming a $255,000 judgment (plus $45,000 attorney's fees) for the buyer, the court noted:

> [T]his contract arises in a commercial context between an enormous diversified corporation (FMC) and a relatively small but experienced

farming company (A & M). Generally, " * * * courts have not been solicitous of businessmen in the name of unconscionability." * * * This is probably because courts view businessmen as possessed of a greater degree of commercial understanding and substantially more economic muscle than the ordinary consumer. Hence, a businessman usually has a more difficult time establishing procedural unconscionability in the sense of either "unfair surprise" or "unequal bargaining power."

Nevertheless, generalizations are always subject to exceptions and categorization is rarely an adequate substitute for analysis. With increasing frequency, courts have begun to recognize that experienced but legally unsophisticated businessmen may be unfairly surprised by unconscionable contract terms (citations omitted) and that even large business entities may have *relatively* little bargaining power, depending on the identity of the other contracting party and the commercial circumstances surrounding the agreement. * * *

Id. 135 Cal.App.3d at 489, 186 Cal.Rptr. at 124.

2. THE CONSUMER GOES ON THE OFFENSIVE

As the following cases show, many consumer protection statutes provide more than a shield to the aggrieved consumer. They also offer monetary recoveries and attorney's fees to the prevailing consumer, thus providing a deterrent to violations of the statute, as well as giving the consumer the economic wherewithal to pursue the lawsuit.

As demonstrated by the *Harrell* case, the Magnuson–Moss Warranty Act permits the consumer to sue for ordinary breach of warranty under the federal Act, thus entitling the consumer to attorney's fees. Magnuson–Moss Act § 110(d), 15 U.S.C.A. § 2310(d).

The Truth in Lending Act was an archetype of the statutory damages/attorney's fees approach to encouraging private enforcement of the statute. The 1980 Simplification Act reduced the likelihood of consumer recovery for some of the more trivial types of disclosure violations. However, as *Aquino* illustrates, the remedies still survive for certain violations of Truth in Lending, such as failure to accept a consumer's cancellation of the credit contract under TILA § 125.

VOLKSWAGEN OF AMERICA v. HARRELL

Supreme Court of Alabama, 1983.
431 So.2d 156.

JONES, JUSTICE.

Plaintiffs/Appellees Curtis G. Harrell and Diane C. Harrell initiated this cause on November 19, 1981, seeking compensatory damages from Defendant/Appellant Volkswagen of America, Incorporated. The crux of Plaintiffs' complaint was premised upon allegations of breach of a new vehicle limited written warranty by Defendant in its sale to Plaintiffs of a 1981 Volkswagen "Vanagon" camper.

Plaintiffs further demanded that attorneys' fees of "a sum equal to the aggregate amount of costs and expenses, including reasonable attorney's fees," be awarded pursuant to 15 U.S.C. § 2310(d)(2) (1976) (Magnusson–Moss Federal Warranty Act).

Volkswagen denied Plaintiffs' allegations and submitted in defense, *inter alia,* that the warranty issued Plaintiffs limited their recovery, if any, to "repair" or "replacement" of defective parts, if the vehicle were presented for repairs to an authorized Volkswagen dealership during its effective warranty tenure.

* * *

The jury returned a verdict for Plaintiffs in the amount of $10,000. After an evidentiary hearing concerning attorneys' fees, costs and expenses, the trial court awarded Plaintiffs' counsel fees of $8,650.85, plus costs of $487.87, for a total award of $9,138.72. Judgment was thereafter entered against Defendant for $19,138.72.

We affirm.

The Harrells purchased a 1981 Volkswagen (VW) "Vanagon" camper on April 1, 1981, from Ted Avrett Volkswagen, Inc. in Enterprise, Alabama, for $14,714.20. * * *

From the date of purchase in April of 1981 until mid-August of that year, the vehicle was relatively trouble-free, save for a minor oil consumption problem. This trouble was apparently rectified; and, shortly thereafter, the Harrells embarked on a camping sojourn to Washington State. While in Washington, the van lost power and subsequently quit running. Unable to locate an authorized Volkswagen representative in the immediate area, Mr. Harrell purchased and installed certain ignition parts, hoping that with these parts they might reach Yakima, Washington, and the nearest authorized VW dealer. Once in Yakima, the Harrells were informed that it would be at least one and one-half weeks before the VW dealer could service his vehicle. As a result, they visited Kinetic Engineering, an "independent" garage, for a diagnostic check of their engine. This process included a timing check, as well as removal of spark plugs to measure compression. Kinetic also installed a set of points on the engine. The total charge for this service was $21.40.

After reaching Seattle, Mr. Harrell visited Freeway Volkswagen, an authorized dealership, in an effort to eradicate the trouble. Freeway kept the camper seven days, doing extensive repairs to the engine, during which time the Harrells incurred additional expenses for a replacement vehicle, food, and lodging. The service order prepared by Freeway Volkswagen bore the stamped notation "Important—Return car at 1000 miles for cylinder head retorque."

Leaving Seattle, the Harrells incurred their next major problem in Oregon, where the muffler fell off. After leaving Oregon, and while the Harrells were in Arizona, the engine again commenced to lose power.

This was followed by a renewed tapping noise. These were the same two problems initially experienced in Washington.

When the Harrells reached El Paso, Texas, the vehicle was again turned in to an authorized VW dealership for a period of five days. While in El Paso, Mr. Harrell was informed by the VW mechanic that improper "pushrods" had been installed in Seattle, and that this was the primary cause of his subsequent troubles.

Before trial, it was Volkswagen's contention that improper repairs (*i.e.*, installation of pushrods) by a "non-authorized shop" in Washington State had caused the subsequent problems during the trip to El Paso. This position was expressed in certain of Volkswagen's interrogatory answers to Question Three that were read to the jury:

> "Bob Hoy Volkswagen [the WV dealer in El Paso] removed and replaced the hydraulic lifters, disassembled and cleaned them since they were contaminated from damaged pushrods which were installed by an independent non-authorized repair shop not authorized by VWoA to perform any repairs. This non-authorized shop to which the Plaintiff had taken the vehicle had installed solid lifter pushrods instead of hydraulic lifter pushrods which were the appropriate components. These parts were inappropriate being of different lengths than the authorized parts which should have been installed. As a result they were not suited for the purpose intended, and, therefore, they deteriorated and particles of the pushrods contaminated other parts of the engine."

The only "non-authorized shop" that serviced Plaintiffs' vehicle was Kinetic Engineering in Yakima, Washington. Kinetic's services included no internal work on the engine, but only compression checks, tuning, and installation of ignition parts. The only garage to have performed "extensive" repairs on the camper before it reached El Paso was Freeway Volkswagen.

[The court then recited the additional and repeated troubles which the Harrells had with the van and with Volkswagen during the remainder of their trip and thereafter.]

Incidental and Consequential Damages

Plaintiffs' warranty herein provided in part:

> "7. VWoA is not responsible for loss of time, inconvenience, loss of use of the vehicle or other consequential damages."

The trial court allowed Plaintiffs to introduce evidence of $620.18 in consequential damages, occasioned by problems with their vehicle during the warranty period. These damages included motel bills, food bills, rental car expenses, taxi fares, and other charges. In *Winchester v. McCulloch Brothers Garage,* 388 So.2d 927, 928 (Ala.1980), this Court held that if a jury finds that the limited warranty has "failed of its essential purpose," it may then award damages under the general remedy provisions of the Uniform Commercial Code.

We know of no better example of a limited warranty "failing of its essential purpose" than that exhibited by the facts before us. Here, we do not have a case of an isolated incident of misfortune; rather, Plaintiffs purchased an expensive recreational vehicle which Defendant, or its agents, after repeated attempts, did not repair. Indeed, the last-quoted sentence from paragraph 7 of the written warranty recognizes that "[s]ome states do not allow the exclusion * * * of * * * consequential damages * * *." The legislatively pronounced public policy, as interpreted by *Winchester,* demonstrates that, "in a proper case," Alabama is one such state.

A contract limitation of remedies to repair or replacement is allowed under proper circumstances. Such a limitation, however, will not be allowed "where circumstances cause an exclusive or limited remedy to fail of its essential purpose," Code 1975, § 7–2–719(2); nor will such a limitation be allowed if "the limitation or exclusion is unconscionable," Code 1975, § 7–2–719(3). *Burbic Contracting Co., Inc. v. Cement Asbestos Prod. Co.,* 409 So.2d 1 (Ala.1982). Situations will arise "where an apparently fair and reasonable clause because of circumstances fails in its purpose or operates to deprive either party of the substantial value of the bargain." Official Comments, Code 1975, § 7–2–719. In those cases, the limitation of remedies will not be allowed.

The case before us is one of those situations in which the limited remedy, provided in the written warranty, has failed of its essential purpose. The *Burbic* Court stated:

> "A limitation of remedies to repair or replace goods fails in its essential purpose if the seller does not provide goods which conform to the contract within a reasonable time." 409 So.2d at 5.

Here, the Defendant, through its authorized dealerships, was given four opportunities to repair or replace defective parts. Defendant failed to fix the various defects in the Volkswagen during a four-month period prior to the time this suit was filed. This, then, is one of those cases in which a limitation of remedies will not be upheld; therefore, the Plaintiffs are entitled to the remedies outlined in Code 1975, §§ 7–2–714 and –715.

The Trial Court's Award of Attorneys' Fees

Volkswagen next complains that the $9,138.72 ($8,650.85 attorneys' fees and $487.87 expenses) awarded Plaintiffs, in addition to their judgment for $10,000, evidenced a clear abuse of discretion by the trial court.

We note with particular interest Defendant's lack of explanation as to why the trial court threatened it with a $100-a-day fine unless it responded to certain items of Plaintiffs' requested discovery by April 13, 1982. Additionally, Defendant refused, absent a court order, to produce its own brochure on its van, to admit the genuineness of its own warranty document, and to state its suggested retail price for the vehicle. All of these, as we see them, were unjustifiable attempts to retard what was proper discovery by Plaintiffs' counsel. Such delaying tactics necessitated that Plaintiffs file a total of five motions for relief under ARCP 37.

Plaintiffs' demand for attorneys' fees and expenses was supported by affidavit, as well as by expert testimony, to the effect that the amounts requested were fair and reasonable. Considering all the circumstances, we think these amounts were not excessive.

Affirmed.

AQUINO v. PUBLIC FINANCE CONSUMER DISCOUNT CO.

United States District Court, Eastern District of Pennsylvania, 1985.
606 F.Supp. 504.

[Aquino purchased a used car from Sheehy Ford, financed by a $5,000 loan from Public Finance. The loan was secured by security interests on Aquino's car and household goods, and also by a mortgage on Aquino's home, so she was entitled to a notice from Public of her right to rescind under TILA § 125(a) which specified the precise date upon which the three day rescission period expired. Although Public did provide the proper notice form, it did not fill in the necessary date when the three day rescission period would expire.]

[Public repossessed the car. A month later, Aquino demanded rescission of the loan, which the court held she still had a right to do, since Public had never made the necessary disclosure of the specific date on which the rescission period expired. Public, however, waited five months after this demand to acknowledge Aquino's right to rescind and to cancel the mortgage on her home. Aquino sued, charging Public violated TILA. At trial, Public still had not cancelled its security interest in her household goods or returned any of Aquino's payments. The court first held that Public's failure to terminate the home mortgage within 20 days was a violation of TILA § 125(b). The court then turned to the question of plaintiff's recoveries for a violation of TILA.]

IV. Statutory Damages and Attorney's Fees

Section 130(a) of the TILA clearly states that any creditor who violates § 1635(b) is liable for statutory damages and attorney's fees. Since the finance charge for this transaction was well over $500.00, Aquino is entitled to the maximum damage award of $1,000.00. Independent of Aquino's entitlement to statutory damages, an award of attorney's fees is mandated since her right to rescind was acknowledged by Public only after she filed this lawsuit.

Despite the clear language of § 1640(a), Public claims that Aquino is not entitled to an award of damages. In October, 1982, Aquino instituted suit against Public seeking damages under § 1640(a) for alleged disclosure violations of the TILA. That suit was settled out of court. Aquino later rescinded the transaction and filed this suit after

Public failed to honor her notice of rescission. Public argues that because Aquino has already recovered damages under § 1640(a) for a disclosure violation, she is barred from recovery under the same section for Public's failure to honor her rescission demand. In support of its position Public points to §§ 1640(d) and (g) and argues that both subsections show that an obligor is only entitled to one statutory damage award per transaction.

The meaning of subsection [(d)] seems clear. If two or more obligors, such as a husband and wife, enter into a transaction in which the creditor fails to make a required disclosure, they are entitled to only one award of statutory damages for that violation. This subsection clearly does not limit obligors to one award of statutory damages per transaction. Since it does not even state that obligors are confined to one award for multiple disclosure violations, it is hard to understand how it could be read to limit an obligor to one recovery for two different types of violations: (1) failure to disclose, and (2) failure to honor a valid rescission.

Although subsection (g) clearly limits obligors to one recovery for multiple disclosure violations, nothing in that subsection limits obligors to one recovery per transaction if there is later a failure to acknowledge a valid rescission. Congress is certainly aware of the difference between disclosure violations and rescission violations. In 1982, § 1640(a) was amended to confirm the position of certain courts that obligors are entitled to statutory damages for rescission violations even when their claims for disclosure violations are time-barred. Clearly, if Congress wished to prohibit awards of statutory damages for rescission violations whenever an obligor had previously recovered damages for a disclosure violation, it could have easily said so.

Pursuant to the TILA, an obligor who has previously collected damages for a disclosure violation can later discover a more egregious violation and, more than two years after the first lawsuit, rescind the transaction. Although Congress enacted a one year statute of limitations for disclosure violations, it permitted rescission up to three years from the date of the underlying transaction. See 15 U.S.C. §§ 1640(e) and 1635(f) (1982). Not permitting an additional recovery of statutory damages for a subsequent violation of § 1635(b), however, would severely undermine a creditor's incentive to honor a valid rescission demand. Yet Congress explicitly allowed for rescission suits after disclosure suits and explicitly provided a statutory damages penalty for rescission violations. Stretching the language of subsection (g) to prevent a later recovery for a rescission violation, as defendant proposes, would undercut the penalty Congress clearly decided to impose and I refuse to do so.

V. Equitable Conditioning Rescission

After a creditor has performed its obligations pursuant to a valid rescission, the obligor must tender to the creditor any property the creditor has previously delivered to the obligor. 15 U.S.C. § 1635(b). Public claims that this requires Aquino to return the $5,000.00 she was loaned and requests that I condition rescission upon the return of those funds. Aquino argues that the only property she received in the transaction was the car, and since that was already repossessed by Public, her obligations under § 1635(b) are complete. Both parties can point to courts of appeals opinions in support of their position. Unfortunately, no court of appeals has explicitly acknowledged these varying approaches nor convincingly explained why one approach should be adopted over another.

Aquino's position might be valid in a "credit sale" context where the seller is also the creditor. *See* 15 U.S.C. § 1602(g) (1982). In that situation a seller is simply giving the obligor credit so that he or she can purchase one of the seller's commodities. Allowing the obligor to return the property purchased instead of the monetary equivalent of the credit extended would still return the parties to the status quo.

The transaction between Aquino and Public, however, was quite different. Public did not sell a car to Aquino and it had no incentive to see that Aquino purchased a car from one dealer rather than another, so long as she arranged for credit through Public. There is simply no evidence that Public was so intimately involved with Sheehy that it should be considered the seller's alter ego. In this context I see no reason why an obligor should be permitted to return the property purchased with the proceeds of the credit transaction rather than the monetary equivalent of the credit extended. If an obligor were permitted to return the purchased property, then a creditor would suffer the consequences of an obligor's poor consumer decision.

* * *

Rescission will therefore be conditioned upon plaintiff's return of that portion of the loan proceeds she has not already paid to the defendant in the form of money or property. More specifically, the amount Aquino has already paid Public ($1,768.03), plus the amount for which Aquino's repossessed car was sold by Public ($2,550.00), a total of $4,318.03, shall be deducted from the $5,000.00 in loan proceeds, leaving a balance of $681.97 that Aquino is required to tender to Public. *See* 15 U.S.C. § 1635(b). An appropriate order follows.

Notes on TILA Rescission

1. What is the test for the timeliness of a TILA rescission claim? See Reg. Z § 226.23(a)(3).

2. Will *any* error in the TILA disclosure statement keep the time for rescission open? Id.

3. What should a creditor do when she receives a notice of rescission long after a credit transaction has been consummated? What if she feels that there have been no violations of TILA? Should she do nothing and risk a ruling like *Aquino* if she is wrong? Or should she immediately cancel the security interest and refund the consumer's money, hoping the consumer will be able to tender the loan principal? What if the creditor knows the consumer is filing for bankruptcy, so that giving up the security

interest will virtually assure that she will not be able to collect on the loan? Compare LaGrone v. Johnson, 534 F.2d 1360 (9th Cir.1976) with In re Chancy, 33 B.R. 355 (Bkrtcy.Okl.1983); In re Piercy, 18 B.R. 1004 (Bkrtcy. Ky.1982); In re Wright, 11 B.R. 590 (Bkrtcy.Miss.1981).

Is the solution followed by the *Aquino* court, i.e., allowing the creditor to offset what the consumer owes, and conditioning rescission upon consumer tender, true to the letter or spirit of the Truth in Lending Act? See TILA § 125(b), 15 U.S.C.A. § 1635(b); 12 C.F.R. § 226.23(d)(3) and (4). If the consumer must tender the proceeds of the loan or the reasonable value of the property or services performed before the creditor need eliminate the security interest and return the consumer's money, is the consumer any better off than he was under common law? See Note, "Truth-in-Lending: Judicial Modification of the Right of Rescission," 1974 Duke L.J. 1227.

The vast majority of post–TIL Simplification cases appear to condition rescission on consumer tender almost as a matter of course.

Problem 6

In 1989, Sheffield Loan advanced a loan of $1,000 to Fleur D. Lee, for which she agreed to repay $2125.00 over two years. The loan was secured by a deed of trust on her home, household furniture, and an automobile. Fleur subsequently had some problems making the payments, so she enlisted the assistance of an attorney. Attempts to negotiate more favorable repayment terms proved fruitless. Meanwhile, Fleur's attorney had discovered that Sheffield Loan had failed to adequately disclose a premium for dwelling insurance, and failed to include it in the finance charge.

Fleur then filed suit (one year after the contract was signed) to rescind the loan, and requested a statutory penalty of $1,000 and attorney's fees. Fleur moved for summary judgment. Sheffield argued:

(1) that Fleur was not entitled to rescission because it has been more than three days since the transaction was consummated; and

(2) that if rescission is allowed, Sheffield should be allowed to offset the amount it owes Fleur by the amount of the loan proceeds already paid to her.

(3) that Fleur is not entitled to attorney's fees since she was represented by Legal Services.

How should the trial court rule on the motion?

See TILA § 125, Reg. Z §§ 226.4(b)(8) & (d), and 226.23. See also Harris v. Tower Loan of Mississippi, Inc., 609 F.2d 120 (5th Cir.), cert. denied, 449 U.S. 826, 101 S.Ct. 89, 66 L.Ed.2d 30.

Note on Small Claims Courts

First invented in 1913, "small claims" courts now exist in nearly every jurisdiction, under differing names and in varying relationships to the general court structure of the jurisdiction. Their general purpose is to provide expeditious, inexpensive justice to litigants whose claims are modest in amount and who probably could not justify expending attorney's fees and costs to litigate cases in the regular courts. This laudable purpose is not always realized, however. Small claims courts are open not only to consumer plaintiffs, but also to creditors. Some have criticized the small claims courts for acting as "collection agencies for professional creditors." Nat'l Institute for Consumer Justice, Report, Redress of Consumer Grievances 13 (1973). Yet studies have found that the small claims courts "generally do a good job for the plaintiffs who manage to find their way into them." Id., at 14.

Other problems occur when consumers are plaintiffs in small claims courts. One is the inability of the unadvised plaintiff to determine and use the legal name of the merchant, who may be "doing business as." Another is the difficulty of collecting small claims court judgments, especially against unscrupulous merchants. Most of the protections created for debtors (see Chapters 7 through 9) are available to them, too. Have we made it too difficult for amateur judgment creditors to collect debts?

Small claims courts are characterized by informality and the absence of attorneys. Yet consumers with even relatively small claims may need the advice of counsel.

As illustrated by the preceding cases, consumer protection statutes often provide for statutory damages and attorney's fees to facilitate consumer access to the courts. Should the jurisdictional limits of the small claims courts be waived to allow consumers to recover such extras?

In Wisser v. Kaufman Carpet Co., 188 N.J.Super. 574, 458 A.2d 119 (App.Div.1983), the plaintiff sued in small claims court for a violation of the state Consumer Fraud Act when a carpet company unlawfully refused to install some carpeting without first receiving full payment. The consumer had paid a $1,000 deposit. Plaintiff obtained judgment in the small claims court for $1,000 in damages, which was trebled pursuant to the Consumer Fraud Statute, and was also awarded $500 in attorney fees and $9 in court costs. The jurisdictional limit for small claims court was $1,000 plus "costs." The appellate court refused to award the successful plaintiff any more than $1,000 and $9 for costs. Following is an excerpt from the appellate court opinion in *Wisser*:

> We read these [small claims court] statutes as limiting costs in the small claims division to statutory fees paid to the clerk, witnesses, and court officers * * *. Attorney's fees are not included in small claims division costs. This doubtless reflects the legislative expectation that in most cases parties in the small claims division will appear without counsel. * * *

> We do not mean to inhibit the legislative policy of awarding reasonable attorney's fees under the Consumer Fraud Act. That provision has the salutary purpose of promoting representation and therefore court access for consumer claims involving a minor loss to the individual plaintiff but a major gain to the community through ridding the marketplace of fraudulent and deceitful conduct. Thus, appropriate attorney's fees under the Act may be allowed without regard to the amount involved in the underlying dispute. Where recovery of a substantial counsel fee is in prospect, it is in keeping with

legislative intent to require the action to be brought in a court where ample discovery opportunities are available and all parties are on notice that more is at stake than would be expected in the small claims division.

One final word. A 1978 NYPIRG Study of the City of Buffalo Small Claims Court found that consumers "who follow cases through to the final stage have remarkable success rates. * * * [o]ver 75 percent were awarded all or part of their claim."

SECTION D. ATTORNEY'S FEES

We have seen that consumer protection statutes often include a provision for the award of attorney's fees for the successful consumer plaintiff as a means of opening the court system to consumers with relatively small claims. See, e.g., TILA § 130(a)(3), 15 U.S.C.A. § 1640; Magnuson–Moss Act § 110(d)(2), 15 U.S.C.A. § 2310(d)(2). Most state little FTC Acts and lemon laws also provide for the award of attorney's fees. However, some state laws may provide that fees are available to the "prevailing party," thus placing the unwary consumer in danger of having to pay his adversary's legal fees if he should lose the case. See, e.g., Dillree v. Devoe, 223 Mont. 47, 724 P.2d 171 (1986).

Attorney fee provisions have apparently succeeded in encouraging consumers to go to court with their grievances, judging from the number of reported cases that have been steadily mounting in past few decades. However, there may be some traps for the unwary attorney. Consider the following.

Problem 7

Buck N. Ham bought a compact disk player for $600 on credit from Constant Co., but defaulted in his payments on it because it became inoperable during the warranty period and Constant refused to repair it. Constant dunned him for the late payments, using their standard 30, 60 and 90 day letters. Then Constant brought an action to recover the unpaid balance and stated they might later garnish his wages. This so frightened Buck that he sought counsel from a local attorney, May D. Marion. He brought with him all papers relating to the action and transaction, including a TILA Disclosure Statement. After some study, Marion spotted several material violations of TILA and assured Buck that his troubles were over. They would counterclaim under TILA, get at least $100 for Buck; and Constant would be required to pay Marion's fee. They would also counterclaim for breach of warranty, but since that would require an expensive trial it could be dropped in return for the TILA recoveries. Thus, the procedure would cost Buck nothing. Marion filed the appropriate pleadings and then received a call from Constant's attorney suggesting "a wash"—a settlement in which Constant would dismiss its complaint and Buck would dismiss the TILA counterclaim and release any claim for attorney's fees for Marion.

The settlement offer is a good deal for Buck, but not for Marion. If the litigation proceeds, Buck's recovery is not likely to grow, but Marion's recovery will grow from $0 to a substantial fee.

(A) What should Marion do now in advising Buck?

(B) What should she do next time such a case walks into her office?

Note on "Independent" Claim for Attorney's Fees under TILA

1. In James v. Home Construction Company, 689 F.2d 1357 (11th Cir.1982), the court found that an attorney could have standing to pursue her independent claim for attorney's fees after settlement of a TILA case. In *James*, attorney Diana Hicks represented Roscoe James in a TILA action for rescission and damages. The case was successfully settled, but the issue of fees for Ms. Hicks was left open. After the district court dismissed the case with prejudice pursuant to the settlement, Hicks petitioned the court for award of attorney's fees. The district court held that a TILA plaintiff's attorney did not have standing to seek fees after settlement of the case-in-chief. The Court of Appeals for the Eleventh Circuit reversed.

The Court of Appeals said in part:

Section 1640(a)(3) of the Truth-in-Lending Act creates a legal right to a fee award in a successful action for rescission. The fact that a plaintiff prevails through settlement should not weaken this claim to fees. Contrary to dicta in Smith v. South Side Loan Co., 567 F.2d 306, 307 (5th Cir.1978), suggesting that attorney's fees are the right of the party suing, we find that it is the attorney who is entitled to fee awards in a TILA case, not the client. * * *

* * * The key to the inquiry is the intent of the legislature. One of the congressional goals underlying TILA was the creation of a system of private attorneys general who could effectively enforce the Act without government intervention. The award of attorney's fees, as a practical matter, is a critical and integral part of this plan. In order to effectuate this scheme, attorneys who bring TILA cases should be secure in their expectation of fees from a successful action, and should be able to pursue their right to fees in federal court. If settlement of a TILA case precluded the plaintiff's attorney from seeking a fee award, nothing would prevent indigent clients, who have no financial interest in statutory fee awards, from freely bargaining them away without personal detriment. Such a result would enable creditors who have violated the Act to escape liability for attorney's fees; such a practice would thwart both the statute's private enforcement scheme and its remedial objectives. Congress could not have intended such a result. We therefore find that the Truth-in-Lending Act creates a right of action for attorneys to seek fee awards after settlement of the plaintiff's claim.

2. In Freeman v. B & B Associates, 790 F.2d 145 (D.C.Cir.1986), on the other hand, the attorney did not fare so well. In the *Freeman* case, the

plaintiffs had received a loan from B & B Associates with a grossly understated rate of interest. They sued under the Truth in Lending Act for rescission, penalties and attorney's fees. The plaintiffs accepted an offer of judgment which granted rescission but specifically excluded all liability for attorney's fees. The district court held that the plaintiffs' attorney, David Fox, had an independent cause of action for legal fees under TILA. The District of Columbia Court of Appeals reversed.

The Court of Appeals opinion said, in part:

> While we are sensitive to the concerns underlying the District Court's opinion and the Eleventh Circuit's holding in *James,* we do not think they support the creation of an attorney's independent right of action under TILA for fees. The District Court is correct that a major congressional goal behind TILA was the creation of a system of private enforcement. The court's analysis, however, ignores the fact that Congress specified how this remedial purpose was to be effectuated. The words of the statute show that Congress chose to create its system of private enforcement by giving borrowers access to a source of funds with which to compensate an attorney.

> The words of section 1640 unambiguously vest the right to recover attorney's fees in the client rather than in the attorney. Section 1640 states that "any creditor who fails to comply with any (disclosure) requirement * * * with respect to any person is liable *to such person* in an amount equal to * * * the costs of the action, together with a reasonable attorney's fee as determined by the court." 15 U.S.C. § 1640(a) (emphasis supplied). In other words, under the statute the creditor is liable for attorney's fees to the person to whom the creditor failed to make the required TILA disclosures, i.e., to the borrower. We find nothing in the words of the statute suggesting any right to fees in an attorney which is independent and separate from the right of the borrower-client to collect attorneys' fees.

> Because we find that section 1640 clearly places the right of action for attorneys' fees in the borrower, we will not ignore the words of the statute in pursuit of some disembodied congressional purpose. While the language of TILA "should be construed liberally in light of its broadly remedial purpose," * * * this does not mean that a court may interpret TILA to encompass any policy that increases the total number of TILA suits brought. * * *

> We also regard the District Court's reliance on *James v. Home Construction Company* as misplaced. *James* involved an attorney's standing to pursue his client's claim for attorneys' fees under TILA. *James* is silent on the question of an attorney's right of action where the client has expressly waived any claim to attorneys' fees. * * *

3. Can *Freeman* be reconciled with *James?* Which opinion has the better reasoning? Would either case help May D. Marion in the preceding problem?

Note on Calculating Attorney's Fees

Cases on the calculation of attorneys' fees in consumer protection cases appear with unrelenting frequency in the pages of the appellate reports. Given the "bread and butter" nature of the issue to the practicing bar, this should not be terribly surprising.

The basic issues dealt with by the courts in these cases include:

— Should the attorney fee award be proportionate to the size of the plaintiff's judgment, or should it be based on an hourly fee?

— How should the court handle a case which involves some claims that are subject to a statutory fee award, and some that are not?

— Should there be attorney's fees for appellate work?

— How can the court protect against excessive claims for hours spent on frivolous legal arguments?

— How much of a free hand should the trial court have in determining the amount of attorney's fees?

The answers to these questions will of course often hinge on the precise wording of the relevant statutory provision, but there are issues that appear to be common to all attorney's fees cases. Consider the following as a small sampling of the caselaw.

Problem 8

Same facts as in Problem 7, but this time there is no settlement offer. The case goes to trial and Buck wins a modest judgment ($300 for breach of warranty, and $100 for the TILA violation). Marion, however, had to put in a considerable amount of time researching and trying the case, as well as fending off the various pretrial discovery and other motions filed by Constant. She requests $20,000 in legal fees based on the time expended: defending Buck's rights—200 hours at $100 per hour.

If you were the judge, how would you rule on Marion's request? What criteria would you use? What further information would you require?

Problem 9

Robbin Hood bought a new car from Dale Dodge Dealers. Dale gave Hood a "Limited Warranty" under the Magnuson–Moss Warranty Act, and the car had several defects in breach of that warranty. Dale refused to fix the defects, so Hood consults you. You are aware of the provisions of Magnuson–Moss under which a court "may" allow recovery of a successful plaintiff's attorney's fees from a warrantor. How would you analyze this fact situation to determine whether to accept Hood as a client, and whether to litigate this case if necessary?

Consider the information that you can obtain at the initial interview with Hood, and the imponderables remaining at that point, at which time you must decide whether to accept the case. Do the Magnuson–Moss provisions on plaintiff's attorney's fees assure aggrieved consumers that they will obtain legal representation easily and reliably?   Should they?

HANKS v. PANDOLFO

Superior Court of Connecticut, Appellate Session, 1982.
38 Conn.Sup. 447, 450 A.2d 1167.

COVELLO, JUDGE.

On April 2, 1979, the plaintiffs brought suit claiming damages caused by the defendant's sale of a dented refrigerator. * * * [T]he complaint alleged (1) false, misleading and deceptive representations by the defendant; (2) breach of express and implied warranties; (3) delivery of a defective appliance (a refrigerator with a two foot dent); (4) violation of the Retail Installment Sales Financing Act; (5) two violations of the federal Consumer Product Warranties Act; and (6) unfair trade practices.   The plaintiffs claimed damages and attorney's fees payable to the New Haven Legal Assistance Association, Inc.   The plaintiffs were willing throughout the proceedings to settle the matter for $900 plus $750 attorney's fees.

Examination of the record discloses entry of numerous pleadings. Together with this state of the pleadings, the court had before it counsel's affidavit that she had expended twenty-five and one-quarter hours on the file plus three hours spent in drafting the application and supporting memorandum.   She also submitted a claim with supporting affidavits that the fair value of her services was $100 per hour.   The counsel fees claimed were $2825.   The court awarded $450.

The summary judgment as to liability resolved only the fifth and sixth counts of the amended complaint in favor of the plaintiffs.   These counts dealt exclusively with alleged violations of the federal Consumer Product Warranties Act.   15 U.S.C. §§ 2301 through 2312.   Since the fundamental principle is "that every litigant must bear his own expenses of litigation except as otherwise provided by statute"; Peterson v. Norwalk, 152 Conn. 77, 80, 203 A.2d 294 (1964); this claim for attorney's fees must be dealt with solely within the context of the language contained in that statute.

The federal Consumer Product Warranties Act provides that "(i)f a consumer finally prevails in any action brought under paragraph (1) of this subsection, he may be allowed by the court to recover as part of the judgment a sum equal to the aggregate amount of cost and expenses (*including attorneys' fees based on actual time expended*) determined by the court to have been reasonably incurred by the plaintiff for or in connection with the commencement and prosecution of such action, *unless the court in its discretion shall determine that such an award of attorneys' fees would be inappropriate.*"   (Emphasis added.)

The provision makes four points clear.   First, the use of the permissive language "may" instead of the mandatory language "shall" connotes a clear option of the court to allow or not to allow the recovery of costs whether they be attorney's fees or otherwise.

Second, if the court allows attorney's fees, such fees may be based on actual time expended. Thus, if the court elects to do so, it may totally exclude otherwise relevant considerations and base its fee calculation solely on the time expended, a procedure which presumably would not otherwise be permissible absent the specific language contained in this statute.

Third, whatever method of calculation is used, the costs must be "reasonably incurred."

Finally, the use of the mandatory language "shall" in the last phrase of the provision connotes that a determination must be made that an award of attorney's fees is or is not appropriate. The plain meaning of the language "in its discretion" contained in this phrase, when read together with the other language of the subsection, permits the court to exercise its judgment (1) to award no attorney's fees, or (2) to award attorney's fees based on time only, or (3) to award attorney's fees pursuant to its discretion. Whatever its content, a decision must be made on the issue of counsel fees.

In its articulated memorandum of decision, the trial court accepted as proved the claim that twenty-five and one-quarter hours were expended in pursuing the plaintiffs' claim. The court further found that this amount of time bore a reasonable relationship to the pleadings filed and that the attorney involved was unquestionably well qualified. The court concluded that these factors were outweighed, however, "by the nature of the litigation and the amount involved therein."

The action was initially to recover damages for the sale and delivery of a dented refrigerator. The plaintiffs indicated from the very beginning that the perceived value of the case was $900 plus attorney's fees. Under these circumstances, it is not unreasonable for the court to conclude that these factors outweighed the other relevant considerations bearing on the issue of attorney's fees.

"A court has few duties of a more delicate nature than that of fixing counsel fees. The degree of delicacy increases when the matter becomes one of review on appeal. The principle of law, which is easy to state but difficult at times to apply, is that only in the case of clear abuse of discretion by the trier may we interfere." Hoenig v. Lubetkin, 137 Conn. 516, 525, 79 A.2d 278 (1951). Such is not the case here. There is no error.

DROUIN v. FLEETWOOD ENTERPRISES

Court of Appeal, Third District, 1985.
209 Cal.Rptr. 623, 163 Cal.App.3d 486.

SIMS, ASSOCIATE JUSTICE.

Plaintiff purchased a motorhome manufactured by defendant Fleetwood Enterprises (Fleetwood).

From the date of delivery, plaintiff encountered numerous problems with the motorhome. It was returned for repairs to the dealer, the manufacturing plant in Pennsylvania, and various authorized facilities in several states.

Subsequently, some three months and less than 9000 miles after purchase, while still under express warranties, the motorhome broke down in Arizona. Fleetwood told plaintiff to take the motorhome to Virginia to get it repaired. Fleetwood did not tell her how to get it there.

Plaintiff repaired to the courts to obtain justice. She got some in the trial court and will get some more here.

On July 16, 1980, plaintiff filed her third amended complaint naming as defendants, among others, General Motors Corporation (GM), General Electric Credit Corporation (GECC), and Fleetwood Enterprises, Inc. (Fleetwood).

Plaintiff's first cause of action alleged that defendants GM and Fleetwood breached implied warranties of merchantability and fitness for a particular purpose. Plaintiff's second cause of action alleged defendants willfully breached express warranties to repair defects in material or workmanship. Plaintiff's third cause of action alleged that the acts of defendants previously alleged entitled her to damages, including attorneys fees pursuant to specified provisions of the Magnuson–Moss Warranty—Federal Trade Commission Improvement Act.

* * *

Defendant * * * argues that the amount of attorneys fees awarded by the court is excessive when compared to plaintiff's recovery. Title 15 United States Code section 2310(d)(2), clearly provides that attorneys fees be calculated upon "actual time expended." The Senate Report concerning this language makes its purpose clear: "It should be noted that an attorney's fee is to be based upon actual time expended rather than being tied to any percentage of the recovery. This requirement is designed to make the pursuit of consumer rights involving inexpensive consumer products economically feasible." (Sen. Rep. No. 93–151, 1st Sess. (1973) pp. 23–24.) We believe this rationale applies with equal force to purchases of products which may not be "inexpensive." The trial court did not err in calculating attorneys fees based on actual time expended.

* * *

Problem 10

Fleur D. Lee bought an automobile from Muck Motors. Muck gave Fleur a "Limited Warranty" under the Magnuson–Moss Warranty Act, and the car had several defects, in breach of that warranty. Muck refused to fix the defects, and so Fleur went to the Legal Aid Society for help. At Legal Aid, Dart N. Yan was assigned as her attorney, and Fleur was charged nothing for his services. Dart first contacted Muck, but they still refused to fix the defects, so Dart sued Muck, on Fleur's behalf, for damages both under the UCC and under Magnuson–Moss and won. Fleur was awarded $1,000, the amount established for fixing the car's defects.

Dart then applied for an award of his attorney's fees in the case. He established that he had spent 200 hours of his time on the case, and that attorneys in private practice with his same credentials were paid $100 per hour. Thus, Dart sought a total of $20,000 under 15 U.S.C.A. § 2310(d)(2).

Muck makes three points: (1) Fleur did not have to pay anything to Legal Aid or to Dart. They are supported by donations from the public. Thus, Muck contends that the fee of plaintiff's attorney is $0. Since the court only "may" (not "shall") award fees to a successful consumer, any award to Dart would be "unconscionable." (2) Muck does some quick calculations, based on Dart's salary, and states that 200 hours of his time cost Legal Aid only $2,000. It further says that any award greater than $2,000 would be "unconscionable." (3) Muck also contends that, since only $1000 was in issue, an award of $20,000, or even $2,000, as attorney's fees would be disproportionate to the amount at issue, and therefore "unconscionable."

In determining awards of attorneys' fees under § 2310(d)(2), are any of the above theories persuasive? Is this an appropriate circumstance for use of the unconscionability doctrine?

Are the concepts articulated and used in *Perdue* (Chapter 10, *supra* page 623) applicable to the facts in Problem 10? In Problem 2 of Chapter 10, page 622, we examined the potential use of the unconscionability doctrine in regulating attorney's fees. Are the issues presented by fact situations in that Problem 2 and in this Problem 10 distinguishable?

Query: Should statutory attorney's fees be awarded to attorneys who are representing themselves as consumer plaintiffs? Why or why not? See White v. Arlen Realty & Devel. Corp., 614 F.2d 387 (4th Cir.1980), cert. denied, 447 U.S. 923, 100 S.Ct. 3016, 65 L.Ed.2d 1116; Beslity v. Manhattan Honda, 120 Misc.2d 848, 467 N.Y.S.2d 471 (1983).

Chapter 17

TROOP REINFORCEMENTS: ACTIONS BY PUBLIC AGENCIES

SECTION A. INTRODUCTION

Even those consumer protection laws that afford injured consumers some form of private cause of action usually also assign enforcement responsibility to a public agency which is to police creditor and merchant practices. These agencies include the Federal Trade Commission and others at the federal level, state attorneys general and state consumer protection officers, U3C Administrators (see U3C §§ 6.104–113), and numerous local or municipal offices.

But an enforcement agency without a sufficient range of sanctions to respond flexibly to different types of violations soon becomes an ineffective enforcement agency. Small loan acts, for example, generally gave the supervisory agency only the power to revoke a violator's license to do business (i.e., capital punishment); the result has usually been that, since license revocation is too harsh a device and no other is available, no sanction is imposed.

Consider, from the point of view of the consuming public, the various protective functions a public agency might be expected to perform, and the variety of tools it would need to do that job:

1. A primary agency function should be to discover violations, bring them to a stop and prevent their recurrence, in a wide variety of situations. Some violations may involve misinterpretations of the law; others may be deliberate abuses of consumers. The agency will need investigative authority. It will need both formal and informal procedures to obtain compliance, both internally in the agency and if necessary by access to court. Above all, at times when mass public injury is threatened (for example, through widespread false advertising), the agency must be able to act quickly to protect the public interest. Remedial devices might include informal assurances of discontinuance, and more formal cease and desist orders, or court injunctions.

811

2. In addition to prospective correction of violations, the public agency might be authorized to seek redress of past violations for the affected consumers. This function would require that the agency have the power to enjoin the enforcement of prohibited contract clauses, to require refunds of overcharges, and to obtain rescission or cancellation of prohibited contracts in appropriate cases. Since agency activity requires the expenditure of public funds, the agency might be authorized to recover its own expenses as well as redress for consumers, both to augment the agency's resources and to discourage attempts by violators to fend off agency action by dilatory tactics.

3. A third, and distinct, function of the public agency might be to serve as a strong deterrent to future violations. Lack of a deterrent allows violators to operate without risk. If the violator is later ordered to stop, or even ordered to redress past violations, he has lost nothing but his ill-gotten gains. Where he has little to lose in violating the law, he is less likely to be careful in observing the consumer's rights. In addition, agency inertia or lack of resources may allow violations to continue for an extended time; and no agency can be expected to conduct perfect surveillance or to prosecute every violation committed. Thus a "deterrent" in this context might include civil penalties or punitive damages, and criminal sanctions for egregious violations.

SECTION B. REMEDIES AVAILABLE TO STATE AND LOCAL AGENCIES

State consumer protection agencies (typically the state attorneys general) can usually take advantage of most of the remedies discussed above, although their authority will vary from state to state. The existence of these state public agency remedies is becoming more crucial as the states assume a greater role in consumer protection. Before the 1980's, state agencies were thought of as merely the backup troops for the Federal Trade Commission, which occupied the preeminent position in the battle for consumer protection. However, as deregulatory fever swept the ranks of the federal enforcement agency, the states became more active, particularly in the area of national advertising. State officials voiced their disappointment with Washington, and launched their own attacks on such items as allegedly misleading advertisements for Kraft's "Cheese Whiz," McDonald's "Chicken McNuggets," and Arby's "Lean Meal." The idea of fifty different angles on the law of deceptive advertising has national advertisers yearning for the days when the FTC was more active. At least then there was only one agency to be concerned about. But whether or not state agencies continue to pursue national marketers, or instead concentrate on more localized consumer problems, it is clear that their remedial powers have assumed an increased importance.

Problem 1

Robbin Hood bought a new car on credit from Dale Dodge in Los Angeles, California. The contract of sale contained a "standard warranty" which warranted the car "to be free from defects in material and workmanship for 12 months or 12,000 miles, whichever comes first." The contract also contained the following clause: "Seller's obligation under this warranty is limited to repair or replacement of defective parts without charge to Buyer."

Thirty days after the sale, as Hood was driving on the freeway, a cotter pin in the steering mechanism broke; Hood could not control the car; and it crashed into a bridge abutment. Hood was physically injured and the car was damaged. Dale is willing to stipulate that the cotter pin was defective, and is willing to repair the car; but Dale & Dodge both pointed to the limitation on remedy clause and refused to do more.

You work for the Los Angeles City Attorney's Office. In your opinion, the limitation on remedy clause is "prima facie unconscionable" under UCC § 2–719(3).

(a) Hood accepts the repair offer and signs a release of all claims in exchange for repair of his car. Can you now obtain redress for his personal injuries? Would it be easy to do so? Can you obtain redress for other consumers in Hood's position?

(b) Can you stop Dale and Dodge from continuing to use a contract clause which is "prima facie unconscionable"?

(c) Can you penalize Dale or Dodge for having used such a clause in the past? Is there a need for a penalty here?

The following California statute (enacted in 1977) is a good illustration of consumer protection legislation which concentrates on remedial provisions, rather than substantive provisions. As such, it is the complete antithesis of the U3C, and this type of legislation is probably more widely enacted than the U3C. The substantive provisions are quite broad, akin to the unconscionability doctrine. However, unlike the common law or the UCC use of the unconscionability doctrine, the California statute has teeth—a long shiny row of them, including injunctions, consumer redress, and civil penalties for violations (up to $2,500 for each violation of statute, up to $6,000 for each violation of an injunction). See also the *Toomey* case, infra pages 816–819, to see how the California courts have applied these provisions to cases prosecuted in the 1980s.

CALIFORNIA BUSINESS AND PROFESSIONS CODE

DIVISION 7. GENERAL BUSINESS REGULATIONS

PART 2. PRESERVATION AND REGULATION
OF COMPETITION

CHAPTER 5. ENFORCEMENT

§ 17200. Unfair competition; law governing

As used in this chapter, unfair competition shall mean and include unlawful, unfair or fraudulent business practice and unfair, deceptive, untrue or misleading advertising and any act prohibited by Chapter 1 (commencing with Section 17500) of Part 3 of Division 7 of the Business and Professions Code.

*   *   *

§ 17203. Injunction; orders or judgments

Any person performing or proposing to perform an act of unfair competition within this state may be enjoined in any court of competent jurisdiction. The court may make such orders or judgments, including the appointment of a receiver, as may be necessary to prevent the use or employment by any person of any practice which constitutes unfair competition, as defined in this chapter, or as may be necessary to restore to any person in interest any money or property, real or personal, which may have been acquired by means of such unfair competition.

§ 17204. Actions for injunctions; prosecution by Attorney General, district or city attorneys

Actions for injunction pursuant to this chapter may be prosecuted by the Attorney General or any district attorney or any city attorney of a city having a population in excess of 750,000, and, with the consent of the district attorney, by a city prosecutor in any city or city and county having a full-time city prosecutor in the name of the people of the State of California upon their own complaint or upon the complaint of any board, officer, person, corporation or association or by any person acting for the interests of itself, its members or the general public.

§ 17205. Cumulative remedies

Unless otherwise expressly provided, the remedies or penalties provided by this chapter are cumulative to each other and to the remedies or penalties available under all other laws of this state.

§ 17206. Violations; penalty; actions for recovery; expenses of investigation and prosecution

(a) Any person who violates any provision of this chapter shall be liable for a civil penalty not to exceed two thousand five hundred dollars ($2,500) for each violation, which shall be assessed and recovered in a civil action brought in the name of the people of the State of California by the Attorney General or by any district attorney or any city attorney of a city having a population in excess of 750,000, and, with the consent of the district attorney, by a city prosecutor in any city or city and county having a full-time city prosecutor in any court of competent jurisdiction.

(b) If the action is brought by the Attorney General, one-half of the penalty collected shall be paid to the treasurer of the county in which the judgment was entered, and one-half to the State General Fund. If brought by a district attorney, the penalty collected shall be paid to the treasurer of the county in which the judgment was entered. If brought by a city attorney or city prosecutor, one-half of the penalty collected shall be paid to the treasurer of the city in which the judgment was entered, and one-half to the treasurer of the county in which the judgment was entered.

*   *   *

§ 17207. Violation of injunction prohibiting unfair competition; civil penalty; actions to assess and recover; venue; prosecutors; expenses of investigation and prosecution

(a) Any person who intentionally violates any injunction prohibiting unfair competition issued pursuant to Section 17203 shall be liable for a civil penalty not to exceed six thousand dollars ($6,000) for each violation. Where the conduct constituting a violation is of a continuing nature, each day of such conduct is a separate and distinct violation. In determining the amount of the civil penalty, the court shall consider all relevant circumstances, including, but not limited to, the extent of the harm caused by the conduct constituting a violation, the nature and persistence of such conduct, the length of time over which the conduct occurred, the assets, liabilities, and net worth of the person, whether corporate or individual, and any corrective action taken by the defendant.

(b) The civil penalty prescribed by this section shall be assessed and recovered in a civil action brought in any county in which the violation occurs or where the injunction was issued in the name of the people of the State of California by the Attorney General or by any district attorney, or any city attorney in any court of competent jurisdiction within his jurisdiction without regard to the county from which the original injunction was issued. An action brought pursuant to this section to recover such civil penalties shall take precedence over all civil matters on the calendar of the court except those matters to which equal precedence on the calendar is granted by law.

* * * [The provisions for the allocation of civil penalties and payment of prosecutorial expenses are similar to those in § 17206(b), supra].

Note

For a very readable background on how a similar law was enacted in New York City, and the problems of using it effectively, see P. Schrag, Counsel for the Deceived: Case Studies in Consumer Fraud (1972), especially Chapter 1 ("How Laws Are Passed") and Chapter 5 ("Litigation: The Case of the Kidnapped Lawyers"). See also Note, "D.C. Consumer Protection Procedures Act," 27 Cath.U.L.Rev. 642 (1978).

Problem 2

Enactment of a strong enforcement law such as that above may not automatically translate into effective enforcement in fact. The law may be a paper tiger unless it is *used*.

Try to identify the practical difficulties that would likely remain even after passage of a law like California's. Consider the need for resources in the enforcement agency, the receptivity of the courts, the degree of probable public awareness of the existence of the agency and its powers, the intransigence and possible impecuniousness of merchants and creditors, and so on.

PEOPLE OF THE STATE OF CALIFORNIA v. TOOMEY

California Court of Appeal, First District, 1984.
157 Cal.App.3d 1, 203 Cal.Rptr. 642.

NEWSOM, ASSOCIATE JUSTICE.

Appellant Bill Toomey and his wife are the sole owners of Holiday Funshine, Inc. (hereafter Holiday) established in 1975, through which he sells discount coupons for use at Reno casinos.

* * *

The coupon packages varied slightly, but basically took two forms: those redeemable at individual casinos, which included cash, free token play at a designated slot machine, drink coupons, food credits, and gambling incentive coupons such as "Lucky Bucks," and a "Mini–Bus" package, which provided the buyer with many of the same coupons, to be used at more than one casino during a bus tour. The casino packages were priced at $25 to $30, and were generally represented by solicitations or advertisements to be worth hundreds of dollars.

A complaint was filed on November 4, 1976, by the Attorney General and the District Attorney of Santa Clara County charging Toomey (individually and doing business as Holiday Funshine, Inc.) with unfair business practices (Bus. & Prof.Code, § 17200) and misleading and untrue advertisements (Bus. & Prof.Code, § 17500). A first amended complaint was subsequently filed, adding a cause of action alleging unlawful "bait and switch" business practices.

On February 2, 1978, pursuant to a motion by respondent, the trial court issued a preliminary injunction * * *.

When the preliminary injunction was issued appellant reviewed it with his attorney, but admittedly made no significant changes in his business practices, since he felt his solicitations were not misleading.

The prosecution offered testimony from numerous witnesses who did not receive what they had been led to believe by appellant's advertisements and solicitations. Buyers alleged, for example, that they were not informed of conditions and restrictions placed on the use of the coupons: that "free" token play coupons were generally redeemable only at machines for which, according to the testimony of Robert C. Voss, a senior agent with the Nevada State Gaming Control Board, the rate of return was so low as to make the coupons virtually valueless, and that such coupons could only be redeemed at a rate of 1 each hour for up to 14 consecutive hours, requiring the customers to stay on the premises for absurdly long periods of time.

* * *

Section 17535 authorizes the trial court to enjoin any "person, corporation, (or) firm * * * which violates * * * this chapter," adding that the court may "make such orders * * * as may be necessary to prevent the use or employment * * * of any practices which violate this chapter * * *." (See also § 17203.) Section 17535 vests the trial court with broad authority to fashion a remedy that will prevent unfair trade practices and will deter the defendant and others from engaging in such practices in the future.

Injunctive relief under sections 17203 and 17535 cannot be used, however, to enjoin an event which has already transpired; a showing of threatened future harm or continuing violation is required. Injunctive relief has no application to wrongs which have been completed absent a showing that past violations will probably recur.

Appellant cites the fact that Holiday had ceased sales of its casino coupons prior to the time of trial as establishing the improper imposition of the injunction. But the record shows that Toomey continued to sell other forms of coupons using many of the same deceptive marketing techniques found objectionable by the court when it issued the preliminary injunction. We also find significant the fact that appellant had failed to comply with the terms of the preliminary injunction, continuing his unlawful business practices in contravention of a court order. Thus, the trial court had good reason to feel that appellant's misleading and unfair trade practices would continue. Accordingly, the injunctive relief requested by the People was, in our view, properly granted.

Next, appellant contends that the permanent injunction is too broad in scope, containing proscriptions against otherwise lawful conduct. Relying on the rule that injunctions prohibiting a person from engaging in activities which are constitutionally and statutorily authorized are void as beyond the jurisdiction of the court, appellant cites as overly broad those provisions of the court's order 1) requiring him to establish an impound fund to be used to provide refunds to purchasers; 2) precluding him from selling any product or service to consumers which are to be provided by another party without a valid, binding contract between him and the third party; 3) requiring specified disclosures; 4) prohibiting "an employment relationship or association with any person which (appellant) knows or should know is subject to a court order prohibiting such person from engaging in the activity for which (appellant) may wish to have or associate such person"; 5) barring appellant from using any business name without first notifying the Attorney General's office; 6) mandating the maintenance of records of complaints, refunds and customer correspondence; and 7) requiring appellant to submit to warrantless searches and seizures.

Appellant fails to recognize that the challenged provisions of the permanent injunction are necessary to the objective of preventing future violations. The impound fund and disclosure requirements have an obvious purpose: to deter additional misconduct. The record-keeping, search and business-name notification provisions are important to monitor appellant's business and thereby encourage compliance with the substantive terms of the judgment. The prohibition against employing a person subject to an injunctive order is based upon appellant's prior hiring of Ernie Alfonso—who at the time was subject to a court-ordered restriction against misleading coupon sales—as a sales manager. And the requirement of a valid binding contract with third-party providers of goods or services attempts to solve the problem of casinos failing to honor coupons.

We consider the provisions of the permanent injunction to be properly designed to prevent unfair trade practices and deter appellant and others from future misconduct.

Appellant also argues that the assessment of $150,000 in civil penalties for violations of sections 17200 and 17500—in addition to a $150,000 penalty for violations of the preliminary injunction (§ 17535.5) and restitution (§ 17535)—was excessive as a matter of law. First, appellant complains that the number of violations used as a basis for computing the award was improperly calculated. Second, he submits that the award is not reasonably related to his wealth.

* * *

After calculating the number of solicitations and sales of coupons by Holiday between 1978 and 1981, the trial court determined that appellant committed at least 150,000 violations each of both the preliminary injunction and sections 17200 and 17500. Civil penalties in the amount of $150,000, apparently predicated upon this calculation of violations by the trial court, were imposed.

Appellant complains that the trial court erred by "doubling up" or "piggybacking" the violations; that is, assessing penalties under both sections 17206 and 17536 for a single misleading solicitation. This contention is defeated by sections 17205 and 17534.5, which specifically allow for cumulative remedies, indicating a legislative intent to allow the double fines to which appellant objects.

And we also conclude that the trial court did not err by using the number of sales to calculate the number of corresponding violations. Sections 17206 and 17536 fail to specify what constitutes a single violation, leaving it to the courts to determine appropriate penalties on a case-by-case basis.

* * *

And appellant's claim that the penalties are improper for lack of a showing of reliance by the purchasers is without merit. As an action designed to protect the public rather than benefit private parties, reliance and actual damages need not be established. "(o)nly the violation of statute is necessary to justify an injunctive relief and civil penalties." Thus, use of a "per victim" formula to find 150,000 violations was not error.

Once the trial court arrived at a figure of 150,000 violations, it imposed a penalty of only $1 per violation. When compared with the maximum possible fine of $2,500 per violation, the trial court's assessment was reasonable, if not lenient. * * *

* * *

Appellant also argues that restitution was improperly ordered by the trial court. The flaw in the order requiring restitution to all coupon purchasers, according to appellant, is its inclusion of those who neither testified at trial nor were shown to have relied on the misrepresentations. Appellant would limit restitution only to purchasers who appear at trial and request a refund.

Sections 17203 and 17535 specifically authorize the court to order defendant "to restore to any person in interest any money or property, real or personal, which may have been acquired by means of any (unlawful practice)." Since the Unlawful Business Practices Act seeks to protect the public from continued violations rather than benefit private litigants, reliance and actual damages are not necessary elements to an award under sections 17203 and 17535. Restitution is not intended to benefit the tendees by the return of money, but instead is designed to penalize a defendant for past unlawful conduct and thereby deter future violations. Reliance has no place in this legislative scheme. The evidence shows that misrepresentations and nondisclosures were standard practice in appellant's business. All purchasers were misled, and the public as a whole was deceived. The trial court was fully justified in ordering restitution to all purchasers.

* * *

The judgment is affirmed.

Problem 3

Custom Craft of California produced television commercials which advertised carpeting for $159. While supposedly depicting 270 square feet of carpeting, substantially more carpeting was displayed. The commercials also had a backdrop of many rows of thick and expensive-looking carpets. However, not all of these were the advertised carpeting.

When a person responded to the television advertisement, a salesman visited the potential customer's home. The salesman then ran a short film. Among other things, this film showed two carpets, one supposedly installed by Custom Craft, the other by a department store at about the same time. The Custom Craft carpet "still looks like new," while the department store carpet was "already matted and showing wear—the seams are separating." In fact, the "department store" carpet was an aged carpet chosen by Custom Craft for use in the film. It was simply laid on the floor, not installed. The workers, who were told to make it look worse than it already did, scattered carpet remnants on it; they positioned the carpet to make it seem that the sides were tearing and the corners were lifting from the walls. The "Custom Craft" carpet was said to be installed in the home of a family of five. In fact, it was located in the Custom Craft office.

After the film was shown, the salesmen usually showed customers samples of non-advertised carpets before showing the advertised carpeting. The non-advertised carpet was a better grade of carpeting than the advertised carpet, and came in more colors and styles. Customers were told that the non-advertised carpet came with a ten-year guarantee, that it was a better grade, and that it would last longer than the advertised carpet.

On the other hand, salesmen said of the advertised carpet, "I wouldn't let this junk be installed in my house—it's so cheap," or, "I wouldn't put that in a dog house." In short, a bait and switch operation.

The State Attorney General filed a complaint against Custom Craft under West's Ann.Cal.Bus. & Prof.Code § 17200, see supra page 813. The court found against Custom Craft and has asked the Attorney General to prepare a proposed permanent injunction order and final judgment.

(a) Draft an injunctive order that will conform with the statute's requirements, provide adequate notice to the defendant, stay within the bounds of the first amendment and adequately protect the public.

(b) The trial court indicated that it will refuse to impose civil penalties. Is it required to by the statute?

(c) If the court imposes civil penalties, how should they be calculated?

(d) Would consumer redress be appropriate in this case? Is it authorized by the statute?

Cf. People v. Custom Craft Carpets, Inc., 159 Cal.App.3d 676, 206 Cal. Rptr. 12 (1984).

Note

Courts in other jurisdictions have liberally construed their "little FTC Acts" to provide the state enforcement agency with broad authority to impose consumer redress or restitution or to seek such remedies in court.

Are there any meaningful limits on how far the agencies or the courts can go in ordering consumer redress? Will the award of refunds to consumers who were not deceived result in unwarranted windfalls to consumers? Should consumers therefore have to prove reliance in each case? What about requiring consumers to return the product or at least show a proof of purchase? Is the restitution remedy an appropriate vehicle to achieve the policy goal of deterrence of unfair or deceptive trade practices?

CONSUMER PROTECTION DIVISION OFFICE OF THE ATTORNEY GENERAL v. CONSUMER PUBLISHING COMPANY, INC.

Court of Appeals of Maryland, 1985.
304 Md. 731, 501 A.2d 48.

[Consumer Publishing Company had sold diet pill plans through the mails through the use of false or exaggerated claims. The company was required to make certain disclosures in future advertising, and was also ordered to refund the initial purchase price to certain Maryland residents.]

* * *

The Company argues that the restitution provision of the administrative order must be struck down because there was no evidence that purchasers relied on false impressions created by the Company's advertisements. The Company also argues that the time period covered by the restitution provision is not justified by the evidence in the record. We hold that the Division may enter a general order of restitution without proof of purchaser reliance, as long as the order provides a mechanism for processing individual claims. Nonetheless, we shall vacate the restitution provision of the order because the time period covered is too broad and because the Division's order did not provide a procedure for processing individual consumer claims.

The restitution provision of the Division's order required the Company to restore the initial purchase price, including postage, to all residents of Maryland who purchased the products featured in the advertisements at issue between May 19, 1978, and December 31, 1981.

* * *

The Consumer Protection Act expressly authorizes the Division to order restitution. In § 13–403(b)(1) of the Commercial Law Article, the statute provides:

> "If, at the conclusion of the hearing, the Division determines on the preponderance of the evidence that the alleged violator violated this title, the Division shall state its findings and issue an order requiring the violator to cease and desist from the violation and to take affirmative action, *including the restitution of money or property.*" (Emphasis added.)

In § 13–402(b)(1), the statute is more specific, stating that:

> " * * * any cease and desist order provided for by this subtitle may include a * * * condition for * * * (ii) the restitution by the violator * * * to the consumer of money, property, or any other thing received from the consumer in connection with a violation * * * of this title."

* * *

Traditionally, to be entitled to restitution because of misrepresentation, the plaintiff must prove reliance on a material misrepresentation.

* * *

Over the last thirty years, many states have adopted legislation permitting restitution in cases where the state attorney general or a state agency seeks to prohibit deception, deceptive acts and practices, or misrepresentation in connection with the sale or advertisement of any merchandise. Maryland's Consumer Protection Act is one such statute. These statutes empower courts, and in some instances agencies, to issue orders requiring the restoration of money or other property acquired by any of the practices declared unlawful.

Professors Wade and Kamenshine have suggested that one purpose of such statutes is facilitating consumer redress, and that this purpose is best served by construing the restitution provisions liberally and minimizing the consumer's burden of proof. With regard to reliance, they state:

"In all cases the consumer probably would have to show at least that his purchase was made at the time of the deceptive practice. And if his burden of proof were further increased by requiring him to present evidence of reliance, the result might be less effective implementation of the statute's goals." [20]

* * *

There are few reported cases discussing whether proof of reliance is necessary to support an award of restitution under state consumer protection statutes. Two California cases involve class actions by consumers seeking restitution under California Business and Professions Code § 17535. In Fletcher v. Security Pacific Nat. Bank, 23 Cal. 3d 442, 153 Cal.Rptr. 28, 591 P.2d 51 (1979), the court interpreted California's consumer protection law and concluded that the statute authorizing restitution orders does not require proof of reliance. The court said:

"The general equitable principles underlying section 17535 as well as its express language arm the trial court with cleansing power to order restitution to effect complete justice. Accordingly the statute authorizes a trial court to order restitution in the absence of proof of lack of knowledge in order to deter future violations of the unfair trade practice statute and to foreclose retention by the violator of its ill-gotten gains." 591 P.2d at 55.

" 'To permit the (retention of) even a portion of the illicit profits would impair the full impact of the deterrent force that is essential if adequate enforcement (of the law) is to be achieved. One requirement of such enforcement is a basic policy that those who have engaged in proscribed conduct surrender all profits flowing therefrom.' " 591 P.2d at 57.

* * *

In the instant case the Division relies on the following evidence in support of its general order of restitution: First, the Company itself stipulated that the advertisements in evidence were run in Maryland on certain dates. Second, the pills were available only through mail order. Third, the Company has testified to the amount of its Maryland sales during the relevant period. Fourth, the Company has never contended that Maryland consumers purchased the Company's pills in any other way than from the advertisements in evidence. The hearing officer could reasonably infer from this evidence that most Maryland purchasers of Company products saw the deceptive advertisements. It is also reasonable to infer, as the hearing officer did, that the deceptive

20. Wade & Kamenshine, 37 Geo.Wash. L.Rev. at 1061.

impressions conveyed by the Company's advertising are material and, if believed, would influence a purchaser's decision to buy. While there is no direct evidence that any consumers actually relied on the Company's deceptive or misleading advertisements, we do not believe that such evidence is necessary. In accordance with the authorities previously discussed, we believe that the Division may include a general restitution provision in a cease and desist order without direct proof of consumer reliance.

Although we reject the Company's broad argument that proof of reliance is necessary before a general restitution order may issue, we do recognize that some of those purchasing the Company's products may not have relied on the false impressions created by the advertisements. Some of these consumers may not want refunds. Accordingly, we believe that the Division's order was defective because it did not provide a procedure for processing individual consumer claims. We agree with the cases in other jurisdictions which, under statutes like Maryland's, require that a restitution order provide a procedure for individual determination of consumer restitution claims. The Division may not simply require the mailing of refunds to all Maryland consumers who bought Company products during a certain period. Purchasers should be notified that they may obtain a refund; in order to be entitled to such refund, they should be required to state that they relied on the false impressions created by the advertising. In this way, purchasers who were not deceived will not receive an "automatic" refund. It should not be necessary that each purchaser present additional evidence that he was actually deceived and relied on the misrepresentations in the advertisements. To require proof of reliance, beyond the purchaser's statement, would make recovery difficult and complicated.

* * *

Problem 4

The Attorney General of your state has caught a local car dealer rolling back the mileages of used cars and falsifying disclosure statements, in violation of the Uniform Consumer Sales Practices Act, which has been enacted in your state (see statutory supplement). This Act grants the Attorney General authority to file several types of civil actions: he may seek a declaratory judgment, injunctive relief, seek to recover actual damages for consumers or pursue a class action. UCSPA 9. If the Attorney General sues the car dealer for injunctive relief, but not as a class action (because he could not meet the prerequisites for restitution as a class action), may he obtain an injunction ordering the dealer to pay restitution to individual consumers? If so, must he prove that each individual relied on the false odometer readings in order to receive restitution?

See Celebrezze v. Hughes, 18 Ohio St.3d 71, 479 N.E.2d 886 (1985).

Problem 5

Your Attorney General's Division of Consumer Protection, has received a single complaint that Ronald MacDougall, owner and operator of the MacDog Kennels, refused to refund the deposit of Colonel Tom Sanders. In response, the Attorney General issued an investigative demand which required MacDougall to appear at the office of the Attorney General (some 100 miles from MacDog Kennels) on a set date, and to bring "all written instruments, contracts, and records dealing with business transactions involving consumer deposits for the past year."

MacDougall failed to appear on the specified date, so the Attorney General filed a complaint in the county court seeking an order requiring MacDougall to appear and answer the investigative demand, and enjoining MacDougall from engaging in trade or commerce of any kind within the state pending compliance, and requiring MacDougall to pay all costs of prosecution and investigation of the action. The summons provided that if MacDougall failed to answer the complaint within 30 days, a default judgment could be entered against him. Four months later, a one-page, unsigned, handwritten answer was filed with the court in response to the complaint, in which MacDougall stated that a special order was placed by Sanders for a particular breed of puppy, and that Sanders was told their deposit would not be refunded. Sanders subsequently purchased a puppy elsewhere and demanded a refund from MacDougall, which was refused.

Does MacDougall have a defense against the Attorney General's motion for default judgment? What would you do if you were the judge in this case? Assume the relevant statute is UCSPA section 8 (see statutory supplement). See People v. McWhorter, 113 Ill.2d 374, 101 Ill.Dec. 646, 498 N.E.2d 1154 (1986); In re Attorney General's Investigative Demand, 493 A.2d 972 (Del.Super.1985).

SECTION C. REMEDIES AVAILABLE TO THE FEDERAL TRADE COMMISSION

Traditionally public agencies charged with enforcing consumer protection laws had to rely on administrative cease-and-desist proceedings, which in the case of the Federal Trade Commission proved exceedingly cumbersome and time consuming. In many cases, the offensive practice had long since ceased by the time an order was entered. Unfortunately cease-and-desist orders—either directed by the Commission or by consent—are *prospective* only. They do not undo whatever evil the unlawful practice has already caused. In addition, of course, the cease-and-desist remedy requires a case-by-case adjudication for each alleged violator.

In the 1970s the FTC began asserting the power to order some novel remedies, including corrective advertising and restitution. The Commission also asserted the authority to issue broad Trade Regulation Rules which would have the force of law and bind the entire industry. (We have seen several examples of these "TRRs" in the material on door-to-door sales and holder in due course.) In 1975, Congress significantly expanded the FTC's arsenal of remedies when it passed the Magnuson–Moss Warranty—FTC Improvement Act, which specifically authorized industry-wide rulemaking, civil penalties and consumer redress. In the 1980s, the Commission began attacking consumer fraud through the aggressive use of the courts to obtain preliminary and permanent injunctions, often accompanied by orders freezing the assets of the company and requiring consumer redress. These developments are considered in the following materials.

M. PERTSCHUK, REVOLT AGAINST REGULATION, THE RISE AND PAUSE OF THE CONSUMER MOVEMENT (1982)

Ch. 5 Lessons in Consumer Regulation, 138–46.[*]

* * *

We have learned that we must be accountable for the costs and burdens of regulation. But we will not concede that the economist's useful, but imperfect, tool of cost-benefit analysis dictates policy judgments on what is right and what is just.

* * *

When Detroit warned in the early 1960s that the mandatory installation of seat belts would cost more than consumers were willing to bear, then subsequently priced them around $10 per vehicle, its apparent hypocrisy reinforced our skepticism, steeling our hearts even more against pleas of the hardships of regulation. Our awe for the herculean cost-absorptive powers of U.S. enterprise was simultaneously enhanced. Today, the skepticism remains; the awe has long since dissipated.

* * *

Economists are very good indeed at framing questions that lawyers and consumer advocates have not asked. (Though the economists don't very much like having to deal with the sweaty, humanly imperfect answers to those questions.) They ask, "What do you think you are accomplishing with this rule? Who will benefit, who will pay? What else will happen as a result of this rule; who among competitors will be the winners and who the losers? In curing this marketplace failure, what others may you inadvertently cause, and what healthy market signals will you distort? Is there a less intrusive, less costly way to remedy the problem?"

* * *

To recognize the value of cost-benefit analysis is not to surrender policy judgment to it. Its value lies in informing decision makers and the public of the dollars-and-cents consequences of alternative regulatory decisions. But it does not follow that we must be indentured as policy makers to the bottom line. We must not abandon our capacity to judge.

The numbers themselves are slippery in this kind of calculation. Costs are almost always more readily quantifiable than benefits. But even with the most sensitively calculated cost-benefit equation, a democratic society may give more weight to other shared values than to economic efficiency.

Take product safety, for example. As citizens, and as participants in the democratic political process, we may express our support for regulatory policies that give expression to our reverence for life itself, knowing when we do so that these decisions will not be without cost. We may do this even though, as individual buyers in the actual heat and pressure of purchasing decisions, we may well trade off safety for price. Why should we value our decisions as buyers over our decisions as citizens?

A recent, careful poll by the Opinion Research Corporation mocks the prevailing Washington wisdom that the public no longer supports consumer regulation. Perhaps most intriguing, that poll demonstrates that a substantial majority of the public understands full well that product safety standards add to the cost of consumer products. Even among those so informed, a substantial majority supports continued government regulation of minimum safe performance standards for consumer products. (Of course, casual expressions of desire in shallow polls ought not to be lightly accepted as informed willingness to bear the costs of regulation.)

I retain ample reservations about cost-benefit methodology, but the *questions* it asks are nonetheless appropriate. * * * Let me suggest some of the questions the prudent regulator should ask, and what he or she might do with the answers:

* * *

2. *Will the remedy work?*

In the sixties there were certain goals we pursued because they intuitively seemed self-evidently right. Among them, for example, was the so-called cooling-off rule that we promulgated at the FTC. This gave the consumer in a door-to-door sales transaction the right to change his or her mind and revoke the contract when no longer in the presence of a sometimes coercive or intimidating salesperson in the home. Three years after the effective date of the rule, we were confronted with evidence in the form of surveys that seemed to indicate that consumers rarely exercised the right. Of course, it was possible that the existence of the cooling-off provision had rid the marketplace of coercive selling techniques, but forty years of commission experience with direct selling abuses suggest that so felicitous an explanation was hardly likely. More likely, it appears that the language adopted by the commission was so obtuse and obscure that too few consumers understood their rights.

* * *

4. *Will the benefits flowing from the rule to consumers or to competition substantially exceed the costs?*

In 1969 the Federal Trade Commission, then under the chairmanship of Caspar Weinberger, issued its long-awaited report on automobile quality control and warranty performance. The industry record was dismal, the commission concluded. The country, urged the Weinberger FTC, faced no alternative but to treat the automobile industry as a public utility, following the models of the rail, trucking and aviation industries, regulated in the public interest by the Interstate Commerce Commission and Civil Aeronautics Board. A new automobile regulatory law must be enacted and a new automobile regulatory agency created to set minimum quality performance standards for automobiles, to fulfill such consumer desires as "lemon protection" (the mandatory replacement of the stubbornly defective new car) and to require that loan cars be supplied while cars under warranty were in the shop for repair.

As a Senate Commerce Committee staff member working for consumer advocate Senator Warren Magnuson, I was delighted with the study and felt it demonstrated a genuine commitment to the consumer by Chairman Weinberger. Perhaps, in retrospect, such a regulatory scheme *might* have stimulated a more competitive domestic automobile industry by the year 1981. But I doubt that Caspar Weinberger would today claim his early intellectual offspring, born in that era of high consumerism. A fundamental problem with that report was that nowhere in its pages does one find so much as a discussion of the costs of providing such protection, or of the tradeoffs between such costs and benefits to consumers. Such omissions are not likely to recur when we again see an administration responsive to the needs and concerns of consumers.

* * *

Another example of dubious consumer benefits is the current rule, enforced by the FTC under congressional mandate, that sellers furnish presale warranty information to prospective purchasers in a prescribed format. "Presale availability" of warranty information is sound in principle, but the commission's studies demonstrate that few consumers have taken advantage of the information in the form in which it has been provided, while the requirement has imposed substantial costs on retailers. We have at minimum an obligation to consider a less burdensome, but still effective, means for assuring that those consumers who do desire to see and compare warranty information before purchase will be able to do so. To that end, the commission is considering changes in the presale availability rule.*

Again, however, I would enter a caveat. Even in policing the marketplace for economic injury, as opposed to health or environmental

* [Ed. note: The FTC amended the presale availability rule in 1987. See Chapter 6, supra, at pg. 391.]

injury, a rigid cost-benefit analysis may not be determinative. Values that cannot be reduced to dollars and cents must be considered in policing selling practices. For example, the desire to avoid the intimidation or coercion in their homes by door-to-door salesmen of the elderly, the uneducated poor, or non-English speaking immigrants is a value not easily quantifiable. Even the commission's traditional role in ensuring truth in the marketplace cannot easily be reduced to a cost-benefit formula, since both consumers and sellers have an overriding interest in preserving the integrity—and consumer *perception* of the integrity—of the marketing system. But who could place a dollar figure on "integrity"? It is perhaps for this reason that the advertising community has come to embrace the commission's advertising substantiation requirements, notwithstanding that the Reagan deregulators complain of its burdens.

1. CORRECTIVE ADVERTISING

WARNER–LAMBERT CO. v. FEDERAL TRADE COMM.

United States Court of Appeals, District of Columbia Circuit, 1977.
562 F.2d 749.

J. SKELLY WRIGHT, CIRCUIT JUDGE:

[In 1972, the FTC charged Warner–Lambert, the makers of Listerine mouth wash, with deceptively advertising that Listerine would ameliorate, prevent, and cure colds and sore throats. The company had been making these false claims since Listerine was put on the market in 1879. Following a hearing by an administrative law judge, the Commission ordered Warner–Lambert to cease and desist from making the false claims, and to include the following language in the next ten million dollars of Listerine advertising: "Contrary to prior advertising, Listerine will not help prevent colds or sore throats or lessen their severity."

Warner–Lambert appealed the order. The U.S. Court of Appeals for the District of Columbia held that the Commission had the authority under the FTC Act to shape remedies (such as corrective advertising) that go beyond the simple cease and desist order. The court apparently accepted the Commission's argument that corrective advertising was "absolutely necessary to give effect to the prospective cease and desist order; a hundred years of false cold claims have built up a large reservoir of erroneous consumer belief which would persist, unless corrected, long after petitioner ceased making the claims." The court also concluded that the First Amendment protection of commercial speech presented "no obstacle" to corrective advertising orders necessary to regulate false or misleading advertising. Likewise, the novelty of the remedy was not a problem, since the court concluded that the Commission had long had the power to require affirmative disclosures in advertising that would be misleading without it. The court noted that while the label "corrective advertising" may be new, the concept was actually well established.]

IV. THE REMEDY

Having established that the Commission does have the power to order corrective advertising in appropriate cases, it remains to consider whether use of the remedy against Listerine is warranted and equitable. We have concluded that part 3 of the order should be modified to delete the phrase "Contrary to prior advertising." With that modification, we approve the order.

Our role in reviewing the remedy is limited. The Supreme Court has set forth the standard:

> The Commission is the expert body to determine what remedy is necessary to eliminate the unfair or deceptive trade practices which have been disclosed. It has wide latitude for judgment and the courts will not interfere except where the remedy selected has no reasonable relation to the unlawful practices found to exist.

The Commission has adopted the following standard for the imposition of corrective advertising:

> [I]f a deceptive advertisement has played a substantial role in creating or reinforcing in the public's mind a false and material belief which lives on after the false advertising ceases, there is clear and continuing injury to competition and to the consuming public as consumers continue to make purchasing decisions based on the false belief. Since this injury cannot be averted by merely requiring respondent to cease disseminating the advertisement, we may appropriately order respondent to take affirmative action designed to terminate the otherwise continuing ill effects of the advertisement.

We think this standard is entirely reasonable. It dictates two factual inquiries: (1) did Listerine's advertisements play a substantial role in creating or reinforcing in the public's mind a false belief about the product? and (2) would this belief linger on after the false advertising ceases? It strikes us that if the answer to both questions is not yes, companies everywhere may be wasting their massive advertising budgets. Indeed, it is more than a little peculiar to hear petitioner assert that its commercials really have no effect on consumer belief.

[T]he Commission adduced survey evidence to support both propositions. We find that the "Product Q" survey data and the expert testimony interpreting them constitute substantial evidence in support of the need for corrective advertising in this case.

We turn next to the specific disclosure required: "Contrary to prior advertising, Listerine will not help prevent colds or sore throats or lessen their severity." Petitioner is ordered to include this statement in every future advertisement for Listerine for a defined period. In printed advertisements it must be displayed in type size at least as large as that in which the principal portion of the text of the advertisement appears and it must be separated from the text so that it can be readily noticed. In television commercials the disclosure must be presented simultaneously in both audio and visual portions. During the audio portion of the disclosure in television and radio advertisements, no other sounds, including music, may occur.

These specifications are well calculated to assure that the disclosure will reach the public. It will necessarily attract the notice of readers, viewers, and listeners, and be plainly conveyed. Given these safeguards, we believe the preamble "Contrary to prior advertising" is not necessary. It can serve only two purposes: either to attract attention that a correction follows or to humiliate the advertiser. The Commission claims only the first purpose for it, and this we think is obviated by the other terms of the order. The second purpose, if it were intended, might be called for in an egregious case of deliberate deception, but this is not one. While we do not decide whether petitioner proffered its cold claims in good faith or bad, the record compiled could support a finding of good faith. On these facts, the confessional preamble to the disclosure is not warranted.

Finally, petitioner challenges the duration of the disclosure requirement. By its terms it continues until respondent has expended on Listerine advertising a sum equal to the average annual Listerine advertising budget for the period April 1962 to March 1972. That is approximately ten million dollars. Thus if petitioner continues to advertise normally the corrective advertising will be required for about one year. We cannot say that is an unreasonably long time in which to correct a hundred years of cold claims. But, to petitioner's distress, the requirement will not expire by mere passage of time. If petitioner cuts back its Listerine advertising, or ceases it altogether, it can only postpone the duty to disclose. The Commission concluded that correction was required and that a duration of a fixed period of time might not accomplish that task, since petitioner could evade the order by choosing not to advertise at all. The formula settled upon by the Commission is reasonably related to the violation it found.

Accordingly, the order, as modified, is affirmed.

[The dissenting opinion of Robb, J., is omitted.]

Flat statement: By deleting the phrase "Contrary to prior advertising," the court has gutted this corrective advertising order of whatever effectiveness it might otherwise have had.

Notes

1. As the court noted in *Warner–Lambert,* affirmative disclosure remedies were nothing new to the Commission. In All–State Industries of North Carolina, Inc. v. Federal Trade Comm., 423 F.2d 423 (4th Cir.1970), for example, the Commission ordered a door-to-door aluminum siding seller to disclose that its contracts might be assigned to third-party financers who would be holders in due course. In J.B. Williams v. Federal Trade Comm., 381 F.2d 884 (6th Cir.1967), the Commission's order required the sellers of Geritol (an iron supplement) to "affirmatively disclose the negative fact"

that most tired people are not that way because of an iron deficiency. And in American Home Products Corp. v. Federal Trade Comm., 695 F.2d 681 (3d Cir.1982), the sellers of Anacin and Arthritis Pain Formula were ordered to disclose the aspirin content of those products. See generally Pridgen & Preston, Enhancing the Flow of Information in the Marketplace: From Caveat Emptor to Virginia Pharmacy and Beyond at the Federal Trade Commission, 14 Ga.L.Rev. 635 (1980).

2. How difficult will it be for the Madison Avenue advertising people to bury required "corrective" statements ordered in *Warner–Lambert* amid music, color or other text? One empirical study showed that at the *end* of the Listerine corrective advertising campaign, 57 percent of Listerine users continued to rate cold and sore throat relief as important in their selection of Listerine as a mouthwash. See Wilkie, McNeill & Mazis, Marketing's "Scarlet Letter": The Theory and Practice of Corrective Advertising, 48 J. of Marketing 11, 26 (Spring 1984).

3. The FTC has not actively pursued corrective advertising orders since the *Warner–Lambert* case. In addition to the question of whether corrective advertising actually corrects misimpressions left in the minds of consumers, the Commission may also have been concerned that its discretion to order corrective disclosures is limited by the First Amendment's protection of commercial speech. See Note, Corrective Advertising and the Limits of Virginia Pharmacy, 32 Stan.L.Rev. 121 (1979). See also supra Chapter 1, pages 84–96.

2. RESTITUTION

Notes

As suggested above, prospective cease-and-desist orders—even coupled with corrective advertising if appropriate—do nothing to remedy abuses that have already occurred. The true fly-by-night operator might happily agree to a consent order, having already banked his ill-gotten gains. An effective public enforcement agency therefore needs the power to compel illegal profiteers to give back to their consumer victims the fruits of the unlawful scheme.

As seen in the previous section, state and local laws often specifically authorize public agencies to order, or sue for, this remedy (referred to as restitution or consumer redress). But at the federal level, there was a long period of uncertainty about the Federal Trade Commission's powers in this regard. The matter was partially resolved by legislation and the Commission's success in obtaining restitution as part of injunctive remedies in federal courts.

1. The Commission first sought to obtain restitution for consumers in Heater v. Federal Trade Commission, 503 F.2d 321 (9th Cir.1974). There the Commission attempted to use its general "cease and desist" authority under Section 5 of the FTC Act for this purpose. The Commission claimed it was simply ordering the respondent to cease and desist from continuing the unfair practice of failing to refund consumers' money obtained through unfair practices, and thus the remedy was purely prospective and well

within the cease and desist power. The Ninth Circuit soundly rejected this contention, saying:

> The construction placed by the Commission upon its power to define and prohibit "an unfair act or practice" would, if accepted, operate to invest the Commission with remedial powers which are inconsistent and at variance with the over-all purpose and design of the Act. In particular, it would permit the Commission to order private relief for harm caused by acts which occurred before the Commission had declared a statutory violation, and thus before giving notice that the prior conduct was within the statutory purview.
>
> * * *
>
> [Congress] adopted the general definition standard ["unfair or deceptive acts or practices"] in order to prevent clever circumvention of a more precise definition, thereby insuring the ability of the Commission to define norms of acceptable business behavior. However, to reconcile the Commission's broad power with the need for a specific notice to an individual who must conform his behavior to the terms of the Act, Congress limited the consequences of violation of the Act to a cease and desist order. It withheld from the Commission the power to make a determination which would expose the businessman to liability for acts occurring before the Commission gave the general definition specific meaning in a factual context. In particular, Congress rejected an amendment which provided a private damage suit based on a Commission finding of a violation of the Act. * * *

The Commission later termed the judgment in *Heater* "incorrect," (In the Matter of Holiday Magic, Inc., 84 F.T.C. 748, 1028 (1974)), but never sought certiorari. The *Heater* case was also criticized in the law reviews. See, e.g., Kaplan, The Federal Trade Commission and Equitable Remedies, 25 Am.U.L.Rev. 173 (1975); Note, Restitution for Consumer Fraud Under Section Five of the Federal Trade Commission Act, 10 Va.L.Rev. 69 (1976).

2. The Magnuson–Moss Warranty—Federal Trade Commission Improvements Act of 1975 added a new section 19 to the FTC Act, which specifically authorized the FTC to seek the remedy of consumer redress in the courts. The relevant portion of Section 19 reads:

15 U.S.C. § 57b [FTC Act § 19] Civil actions for violations of rules and cease and desist orders respecting unfair or deceptive acts or practices

(a) Suits by Commission against persons, partnerships, or corporations; jurisdiction; relief for dishonest or fraudulent acts

(1) If any person, partnership, or corporation violates any rule under this subchapter respecting unfair or deceptive acts or practices (other than an interpretive rule, or a rule violation of which the Commission has provided is not an unfair or deceptive act or practice in violation of section 45(a) of this title [FTC Act § 5]), then the Commission may commence a civil action against such person, partnership, or corporation for relief under subsection (b) of this section in a United States district court or in any court of competent jurisdiction of a State.

(2) If any person, partnership, or corporation engages in any unfair or deceptive act or practice (within the meaning of section 45(a)(1) of this title [FTC Act § 5]) with respect to which the Commission has issued a final cease and desist order which is applicable to such person, partnership, or corporation, then the Commission may commence a civil action against such person, partnership, or corporation in a United States district court or in any court of competent jurisdiction of a State. If the Commission satisfies the court that the act or practice to which the cease and desist order relates is one which a reasonable man would have known under the circumstances was dishonest or fraudulent, the court may grant relief under subsection (b) of this section.

(b) Nature of relief available

The court in an action under subsection (a) of this section shall have jurisdiction to grant such relief as the court finds necessary to redress injury to consumers or other persons, partnerships, and corporations resulting from the rule violation or the unfair or deceptive act or practice, as the case may be. Such relief may include, but shall not be limited to, rescission or reformation of contracts, the refund of money or return of property, the payment of damages, and public notification respecting the rule violation or the unfair or deceptive act or practice, as the case may be; except that nothing in this subsection is intended to authorize the imposition of any exemplary or punitive damages.

* * *

3. The FTC has obtained a Section 19 redress order in only a single litigated case to date, a $29 million judgment in FTC v. Glenn Turner, No. 79–474 (M.D.Fla. Sept. 28, 1983). Why do you suppose there have not been more such orders? How would you compare the FTC's burden in a Section 19 redress case with a Section 5 cease-and-desist case?

Note the conditions built into Section 19(a)(2). The Commission cannot demand consumer redress from companies merely because the Commission thinks they acted unlawfully. It is only after the entry of a cease and desist order that the Commission can sue for restitutionary recoveries, and then only with respect to conduct which "a reasonable man would have known under the circumstances was dishonest or fraudulent." However, the Commission often includes refunds, or similar restitution-type payments, in consent orders it negotiates with accused violators.

Problem 6

As an ace FTC consumer protection attorney, you uncover a massive land fraud scheme involving the deceptive sale of undeveloped subdivisions of swampland in Florida and desert in New Mexico. You would like to force the company to pay back the hundreds of thousands of dollars it bilked out of the defrauded buyers. In light of the *Heater* decision, and using Section 19 as quoted above, what steps will you have to go through before you are able to obtain the desired remedy? What happens if some of the consumers settle with the company before you have a chance to get to court with your Section 19 redress case? Will you have to relitigate in court the facts established in a cease and desist proceeding? Will you have to prove that the defendant acted with "dishonest or fraudulent" intent? Can you rely on an earlier cease and desist proceeding for that finding? See AMREP Corp. v. F.T.C., 768 F.2d 1171 (10th Cir.1985), cert. denied, 475 U.S. 1034, 106 S.Ct. 1167, 89 L.Ed.2d 352 (1986); F.T.C. v. AMREP Corp., 705 F.Supp. 119 (S.D.N.Y. 1988).

3. INJUNCTIONS AND RESTITUTION REVISITED

The Commission found a more successful route to the goal of consumer restitution in actions filed under Section 13(b) of the FTC Act. This part of the statute reads as follows:

15 U.S.C. § 53 [FTC Act § 13] False advertisements: Injunctions and restraining orders

(b) Temporary restraining orders; preliminary injunctions

Whenever the Commission has reason to believe—

(1) that any person, partnership, or corporation is violating, or is about to violate, any provision of law enforced by the Federal Trade Commission, and

(2) that the enjoining thereof pending the issuance of a complaint by the Commission and until such complaint is dismissed by the Commission or set aside by the court on review, or until the order of the Commission made thereon has become final, would be in the interest of the public—the Commission by any of its attorneys designated by it for such purpose may bring suit in a district court of the United States to enjoin any such act or practice. Upon a proper showing that, weighing the equities and considering the Commission's likelihood of ultimate success, such action would be in the public interest, and after notice to the defendant, a temporary restraining order or a preliminary injunction may be granted without bond: Provided, however, That if a complaint is not filed within such period (not exceeding 20 days) as may be specified by the court after issuance of the temporary restraining order or preliminary injunction, the order or injunction shall be dissolved by the court and be of no further force and effect: Provided further, That in proper cases the Commission may seek, and after proper proof, the court may issue, a permanent injunction. Any such suit shall be brought in the district in which such person, partnership, or corporation resides or transacts business.

FEDERAL TRADE COMMISSION v. H.N. SINGER, INC.

United States Court of Appeals, Ninth Circuit, 1982.
668 F.2d 1107.

DUNIWAY, CIRCUIT JUDGE:

Defendants appeal from a preliminary injunction and from an order modifying it. We affirm.

I. The Nature of the Case

In its complaint, filed in the district court, the Federal Trade Commission alleged violations of its trade regulation rule "Disclosure Requirements and Prohibitions Concerning Franchising and Business Opportunity Ventures," 16 C.F.R. Part 436 (The Franchise Rule), and sought redress for third parties under Section 19 of the Federal Trade Commission Act, 15 U.S.C. § 57b(a)(1) and (b). It also alleged false promises and false and misleading representations contrary to Section 5(a) of the Act, 15 U.S.C. § 45(a), and sought a permanent injunction under Section 13(b) of the Act, 15 U.S.C. § 53(b) and refunds for third parties as a form of relief ancillary to that equitable relief.

The Commission asked for a preliminary injunction against further violations of the Franchise Rule, freezing the defendants' assets (except for "ordinary business and living expenses") pending a trial on the merits, and requiring an accounting of assets acquired by the defendants as a result of the defendants' activities. The preliminary injunction was sought in accordance with the procedures of F.R.Civ.P. 65(a) and on the authority of both § 13(b) and § 19. The district judge granted a preliminary injunction in terms somewhat different from those requested. Two individual defendants, Quinlan and Weihoff, appeal. * * *

The alleged violations of the law by the defendants arose from the sale of franchises for "Hot Box Products." Franchisees were to distribute frozen pizzas and ovens to retail outlets. They paid substantial amounts for the franchises. The details of the fraud need not concern us. The appellants do not challenge the sufficiency of the evidence to support preliminary injunctive relief against them.

* * *

* * * There are two bases for jurisdiction to issue the preliminary injunction. One is Section 19 of the Act, 15 U.S.C. § 57b(a)(1) and (b) [quoted supra pp. 832–833]:

* * *

It is clear that under this section a district court has jurisdiction to issue a preliminary injunction.

The second legal basis is Section 13(b) of the Act, 15 U.S.C. § 53(b) [quoted supra p. 834]:

* * *

The Commission argues that the second proviso [of Section 13(b)] gives it the power to seek an injunction in the district court in proper cases without also initiating administrative proceedings. The appellants disagree. They read the clause as granting the Commission the power to seek permanent injunctions only under the conditions laid down earlier in the section for the issuance of preliminary injunctions. We agree with the Commission. The proviso in question does not on its face condition the issuance of a permanent injunction upon the initiation of administrative proceedings.

What little legislative history there is supports our conclusion. Section 13(b) was enacted as part of the Trans–Alaska Pipeline Act, P.L. 93–153, but was originally a part of the Senate bill for the Federal Trade Improvement Act of 1973, P.L. 93–637. In the Senate Report on that bill the intent of the final clause of § 13(b) was explained:

> This section would permit the Commission to obtain either a preliminary or permanent injunction through court procedures initiated by its own attorneys against any act or practice which is unfair or deceptive to a consumer, and thus prohibited by section 5 of the Federal Trade Commission Act. The purpose of section 210 is to permit the Commission to bring an immediate halt to unfair or deceptive acts or practices when to do so would be in the public interest. At the present time such practices might continue for several years until agency action is completed. Victimization of American consumers should not be so shielded.

> Section 210 authorizes the granting of a temporary restraining order or a preliminary injunction without bond pending the issuance of a complaint by the Commission under section 5, and until such complaint is dismissed by the Commission or set aside by the court on review, or until the order of the Commission made thereon has become final within the meaning of section 5. The test the Commission would have to meet in order to secure this injunctive relief is similar to the test it must already meet when attempting to secure an injunction against false advertising of food, drugs, devices, or cosmetics.

> Provision is also made in section 210 for the Commission to seek and, after a hearing, for a court to grant a permanent injunction. This will allow the Commission to seek a permanent injunction when a court is reluctant to grant a temporary injunction because it cannot be assured of a (sic) early hearing on the merits. Since a permanent injunction could only be granted after such a hearing, this will assure the court of the ability to set a definite hearing date. Furthermore, the Commission will have the ability, in the routine fraud case, to merely seek a permanent injunction in those situations in which it does not desire to further expand upon the prohibitions of the Federal Trade Commission Act through the issuance of a cease-and-desist order. Commission resources will be better utilized, and cases can be disposed of more efficiently.

S.Rep. 93–151, 30–31. This report sets out a clear and coherent policy underlying the new section and supports the natural reading of the statute.

It is true that the power given to the Commission in the second proviso has rarely been used. We have found only one case where the Commission has sought an injunction in a district court under this section. It was granted. FTC v. Virginia Homes Manufacturing Co., D.Md., 1981, 509 F.Supp. 51. That court described as obfuscatory the argument that the Commission lacked the power because it had never previously attempted to use it. We agree. We hold that § 13(b) gives the Commission the authority to seek, and gives the district court the authority to grant, permanent injunctions in proper cases even though the Commission does not contemplate any administrative proceedings. We hold further that a routine fraud case is a proper case. We further hold that this present case is a routine fraud case and a proper case for the use of this authority.

It is clear that, because the district court has the power to issue a permanent injunction to enjoin acts or practices that violate the law enforced by the Commission, it also has authority to grant whatever preliminary injunctions are justified by the usual equitable standards and are sought in accordance with Rule 65(a).

* * *

The Commission also relies upon § 13(b) [for the authority to request a preliminary injunction freezing defendant's assets to preserve them for a possible order of rescission and restitution]. It argues that, because that section gives the court authority to grant a permanent injunction, it also by implication gives the court authority to afford all necessary ancillary relief, including rescission of contracts and restitution. The power to enjoin is part of what used to be the jurisdiction of equity.

Unless otherwise provided by statute, all the inherent equitable powers of the District Court are available for the proper and complete exercise of that jurisdiction. And since the public interest is involved in a proceeding of this nature, those equitable powers assume an even broader and more flexible character than when only a private controversy is at stake. Power is thereby resident in the District Court, in exercising this jurisdiction, "to do equity and to mould each decree to the necessities of the particular case." Hecht Co. v. Bowles, 321 U.S. 321, 329 (64 S.Ct. 587, 592, 88 L.Ed. 754).

Moreover, the comprehensiveness of this equitable jurisdiction is not to be denied or limited in the absence of a clear and valid legislative command. Unless a statute in so many words, or by a necessary and inescapable inference, restricts the court's jurisdiction in equity, the full scope of that jurisdiction is to be recognized and applied. "The great principles of equity, securing complete justice, should not be yielded to light inferences, or doubtful construction." Brown v. Swann, 10 Pet. 497, 503 (9 L.Ed. 508). As we said in Los Angeles Trust Deed and Mortgage Exchange v. SEC, 9 Cir., 1960, 285 F.2d 162, 182, "Congress must be taken to have acted cognizant of the historic power of equity to provide complete relief in the light of statutory purposes."

Appellants argue that Congress in § 19 explicitly granted the district court power to award rescission and other forms of redress only when a Commission rule had been violated, and thus implicitly restricted the remedy for other violations of the Act to agency processes and to the injunctive relief provided in § 13(b). However, § 19(e) provides: "Remedies provided in this section are in addition to, and not in lieu of, any other remedy or right of action provided by State or Federal law. Nothing in this section shall be construed to affect any authority of the

Commission under any other provision of law." Thus, there is no necessary or inescapable inference, or, indeed, any inference, that Congress intended to restrict the broad equitable jurisdiction apparently granted to the district court by § 13(b). We hold that Congress, when it gave the district court authority to grant a permanent injunction against violations of any provisions of law enforced by the Commission, also gave the district court authority to grant any ancillary relief necessary to accomplish complete justice because it did not limit that traditional equitable power explicitly or by necessary and inescapable inference. * * *

* * *

We hold that the court had the power to make the freeze order. We do not pass upon the validity of all of its terms, because that question is not before us.

* * *

CORNELL, FEDERAL TRADE COMMISSION PERMANENT INJUNCTION ACTIONS AGAINST UNFAIR AND DECEPTIVE PRACTICES: THE PROPER CASE AND THE PROPER PROOF

61 St. John's L.Rev. 503 (1987).*

I. INTRODUCTION

In 1980 the Federal Trade Commission ("Commission") unveiled a new weapon in its consumer protection arsenal: the use of section 13(b) of the Federal Trade Commission Act ("FTC Act" or "the Act") to obtain injunctions against unfair and deceptive practices. In these federal district court actions, the Commission can also secure money judgments to redress consumers' injuries. The Commission pursues these actions without any prior or subsequent administrative proceedings thereby allowing it to move swiftly against targets it could not ordinarily reach through its administrative cease and desist orders, especially those committing "hardcore" fraud. In bringing these actions, the Commission forgoes its traditional roles as expert administrative judge and policymaker. It is the courts, not the Commission, which interpret and apply the FTC Act in these actions. The Commission only prosecutes. Section 13(b) does not clearly delimit the scope of the Commission's new power to seek permanent injunctions. * * *

The source of the Commission's new found injunctive muscle is the second proviso of section 13(b). Congress enacted section 13(b) primarily to authorize the Commission to seek preliminary injunctions during pending administrative cease and desist proceedings. However, Congress added a second proviso, which states "(t)hat in proper cases the Commission may seek, and after proper proof, the court may issue, a permanent injunction."

This simple one line grant authorizes the courts to fashion any equitable remedy reasonably necessary for complete justice in light of the purposes of the FTC Act. In the cases to date, the Commission has used this broad grant of authority to achieve impressive results. In several cases the Commission has swiftly and effectively shut down deceptive schemes through temporary restraining orders, preliminary injunctions, asset freeze orders, and appointments of receivers. The first actions were against companies that sold investments, such as, oil and gas leases and related investments, gemstones, and work-at-home manufacturing operations. The more recent section 13(b) actions have alleged deceptive practices in other areas, including adoption services, home sales, weight reduction plans, and baldness cures. The Commission has secured permanent injunctions against both corporations and individuals and has collected judgments ranging from $65,000 to $6,700,000 to redress consumer injuries. These amounts represent only a small fraction of actual consumer losses. The Commission, like other law enforcement agencies, has found it very difficult to recover money from the defendants running these fraudulent operations. The $6,700,000 judgment in FTC v. International Diamond Corp., for example, was satisfied primarily by the defendant's corporate insurance policies. Meaningful recovery, however, is possible. In FTC v. U.S. Oil & Gas Corp., the receiver collected over $12,000,000 which may be made available for consumer redress. The money already collected represents approximately twenty percent of consumers' losses.

The Commission's section 13(b) actions seeking permanent injunctions fill a void in law enforcement against fraud. The Commission's new jurisdiction extends to any practices in or affecting [commerce], whereas other federal civil agencies which combat fraud have narrow jurisdictional limitations. For instance, the Securities and Exchange Commission (the "SEC") can only regulate securities and related industries and the Commodities Futures Trading Commission (the "CFTC") can only regulate commodities futures contracts and related investments. Most of the Federal Trade Commission's cases to date have been outside both the SEC's and CFTC's jurisdiction.

Through permanent injunctions, the Commission can also reach cases beyond criminal prosecution. Although criminal prosecution carries the threat of much harsher penalties, criminal fraud is very difficult to prove. Criminal prosecutors must prove, beyond a reasonable doubt, the accused's actual knowledge of the falsehood or his reckless indifference to the truth. The Commission has a lower burden of proof, and, as will be developed later, should have to prove less to secure an injunction and a monetary redress judgment. Furthermore, the Commission can secure preliminary injunctions to stop practices during the pendency of its actions.

Section 13(b) actions are a very promising consumer protection enforcement tool. By indirectly authorizing potentially broad remedies, though, section 13(b) leaves open many questions about the scope of the remedy. Section 13(b) states only that the situation must be a "proper case" and that the Commission must make "proper proof," but defines neither term.

Defining "proper cases" requires identifying those situations in which the courts can act effectively as the decisionmaker. Section 5 of the FTC Act declares illegal all unfair and deceptive acts or practices in or affecting commerce. In applying this language, the Commission has argued that courts can effectively act in any case in which a "clear" violation exists. A clear violation, according to the Commission, is any violation of either a trade regulation rule or a statute enforced by the Commission other than the FTC Act, as well as any practice previously declared unfair or deceptive by the Commission in an administrative adjudication.

The clear violation standard, however, does not work well because courts cannot rely on the Commission's adjudicative decisions. In non-rule violation cases, the Commission has always relied on its congressional mantle of administrative expertise to define the meaning of unfair and deceptive practices. Because the Commission's decisions are based on their own expertise, they give courts no guidance beyond the specific practices declared illegal. The section 13(b) cases to date indicate that courts do not rely on Commission precedents, but decide for themselves whether practices are unfair or deceptive. These cases also indicate that courts do not interpret section 5 of the FTC Act consistently with either the Commission or each other.

These inconsistent interpretations of section 5 threaten the Commission's policymaking role. The Commission has used the broad "unfair and deceptive practice" language of section 5 to define and redefine the limits of fair business practices. In doing so, the Commission has often declared certain practices illegal which had previously been considered proper. Extensive judicial interpretations of section 5 may create conflicting lines of authority on the meaning of section 5 unfairness and deception that may inhibit the Commission's ability to maintain the flexible meaning of section 5.

In addition, courts have awarded redress judgments and have issued injunctions enforceable through criminal contempt proceedings to enforce their judgments. The Commission generally can enforce its rulings only through cease and desist orders. These orders cannot impose liability for a past violation of section 5 and are only enforceable through civil penalty proceedings. The stronger judicial remedies may not be necessary or appropriate against some unfairness and deception. Often, it is very difficult to tell whether the complained of practices are harmful, or whether they are actually the fair result of a properly operating market. Congress authorized the Commission to make these close decisions. The generalist courts, in attempting to decide close cases, may actually harm consumers by inhibiting efficient, competitive business practices.

Thus, section 13(b) actions should be formally limited to a particularized set of proper cases that the courts are competent to consider. * * * In order to find a given situation to be a proper case, the Commission should have to establish either a trade regulation rule violation, violation of a statute other than the FTC Act, or a misrepresentation of material fact. This standard is superior to the Commission's clear violation standard because it shifts the court's focus away from the unfair or deceptive language of section 5 to a standard courts are familiar with and competent to handle, thereby eliminating potentially conflicting judicial interpretations of section 5. The proposed standard would provide the same relief actually secured by the Commission in recent cases, but would avoid judicial interpretations of section 5 that are inconsistent with each other and with the Commission's interpretations.

* * *

Notes

1. Does the *Singer* case in effect repeal the restrictive standards of Section 19 for redress actions? Why would the FTC ever seek a redress remedy under Section 19 after the *Singer* decision?

2. Is the FTC treading on dangerous ground by pursuing consumer redress under Section 13(b)? Is it in fact abdicating its policymaking role to generalist courts as suggested in the preceding article? On the other hand, after *Heater* does the FTC have any choice but to go to the courts if it wants to obtain the remedy of consumer redress? Does the standard for a "proper case" under Section 13(b) proposed in the Cornell excerpt protect the FTC's policymaking role while maintaining sufficient flexibility to bring a varity of injunction cases?

3. The FTC has used the Section 13(b) injunction route most aggressively in the area of fraudulent "telemarketing," the deceptive sale of goods or services over the telephone. The FTC has estimated that such fraud costs Americans as much as one billion dollars per year. Statement of the Federal Trade Commission before the Subcommittee on Transportation, Tourism and Hazardous Materials, Committee on Energy and Commerce, U.S. House of Representatives, December 3, 1987, at 2. The Commission also estimated that by 1987 it had secured some 23.5 million dollars in consumer redress mostly through the use of Section 13(b) injunction cases. Id. at 8. Despite this measure of success in helping the victims of telemarketing fraud, some members of Congress have proposed amending the FTC Act to enhance the available remedies. These proposals include:

(1) permitting the FTC to seek consumer redress under Section Five of the FTC Act, and not solely under Sections 19 and 13(b);

(2) extending the mail order rule requiring prompt shipment and/or the three day cooling off rule to telephone sales; and

(3) permitting state enforcement agencies and/or private parties to bring actions under the FTC Act against telemarketers.

How would you evaluate these proposed supplemental remedies? Are they necessary? Helpful?

VISA and MasterCard have testified in favor of allowing a private right of action by financial institutions against telemarketers. These major consumer credit card companies are apparently losing considerable sums of money when consumers cancel charges resulting from telemarketing fraud.

The FTC has already proposed to amend the mail order rule to include telephone sales. FTC, Mail Order Merchandise Rule, Notice of Proposed Rulemaking, 54 Fed.Reg. 49,060 (Nov. 28, 1989).

Problem 7

Farmtech Research Company manufactures a dietary supplement called "Daily Greens." The tablets contain vitamins A, C, and E, the mineral selenium, beta-carotene and dehydrated vegetables. Each tablet provides 3 calories and, taken daily, provides at most the equivalent of 4.2 servings of fresh cabbage per month. The advertisements for Daily Greens tout their value as a food supplement and stress a report of the National Academy of Sciences which found that a regular diet of certain vegetables was associated with a lower incidence of certain cancers. Said the ad: "The National Academy of Sciences thinks a balanced diet may reduce your risk of cancer. Daily Greens were designed to be a part of that balanced diet * * *" In fact, the NAS study carefully qualified its findings on the causal connection between diet and cancer, and sharply distinguished between the consumption of whole food and dietary supplements of particular nutrients.

The FTC has gone to U.S. District Court to enjoin the advertisements and to seek redress for consumers. Can the FTC obtain a permanent injunction without first instituting administrative proceedings against Farmtech? To qualify for injunctive relief under Section 13(a) or (b) of the FTC Act, would the FTC have to meet the same standard of proof as a private litigant seeking an injunction? What standard should the court use? Would the Commission have to show that the ads are false, or could they simply show they are unsubstantiated? Can the Commission obtain redress in an order from the District Court without using the more burdensome procedures of Section 19? Cf. Federal Trade Comm. v. Pharmtech Research, Inc., 576 F.Supp. 294 (D.D.C.1983).

4. CIVIL PENALTIES

The FTC's ability to obtain sizeable civil penalties against offenders can be a very effective deterrent to potential violators. Penalties are meant simply to punish, not to make the victims whole, and thus they can be quite substantial (within the statutory limits of $10,000 maximum per violation). The Commission has long had the authority to go to court to request penalties for violation of a cease and desist order by the party against whom it was issued. The 1975 Magnuson–Moss Warranty—FTC Improvement Act added some important enhancements to the civil penalties remedy. First, Section 5(m)(1)(A) [15 U.S. C.A. § 45(m)(1)(A)] permits the FTC to ask the court to assess penalties

for violations of FTC substantive regulations. Second, Section 5(m)(1)
(B) [15 U.S.C.A. § 45(m)(1)(B)] allows the Commission to go to court to
enforce FTC determinations in final orders issued against *third parties*
if the respondent had "actual knowledge that such act or practice is
unfair or deceptive." Defendants have argued that they are deprived of
due process by being held accountable for violating prior FTC determinations made in a proceeding to which they were not a party. Courts
have rejected this argument, however, because there is a statutory
safeguard providing that issues of fact shall be tried *de novo* if the
defendant was not a party to the original order.

In addition to enforcing the FTC Act itself and its regulations, the
Commission has also been given the authority to enforce other statutes,
such as the Truth in Lending Act. The question has arisen whether
the FTC could use the civil penalty provisions described above for
violations of Regulation Z.

UNITED STATES OF AMERICA v. HOPKINS DODGE, INC.

United States Court of Appeals, Eighth Circuit, 1988.
849 F.2d 311.

DUMBAULD, SENIOR DISTRICT JUDGE.

Appellees (automobile dealers) admittedly engaged in repeated
violations of the "Truth in Lending Act" and regulations thereunder.
Injunctive relief against future violations was awarded by the District
Court's permanent injunction of June 15, 1987 (R. 234–41), 661 F.Supp.
1155. However the Federal Trade Commission (F.T.C.) further sought
civil penalties under 15 U.S.C. 45(m)(1)(B). The District Court granted
appellees' motion for summary judgment with respect to that issue (R.
230) on the ground that the F.T.C. had failed to make specific findings
as required by 15 U.S.C. 45(m)(1)(B). We affirm.

STATUTORY SCHEME

Like the Clayton Act, the Federal Trade Commission Act (which
established the Federal Trade Commission) was enacted to supplement
the provisions of the landmark Sherman Act of July 2, 1890, which
attacked restraints of trade and monopolies in interstate commerce.

The basic thrust of the Federal Trade Commission Act is found in
15 U.S.C. 45. By Section 45(a)(1) "Unfair methods of competition in or
affecting commerce, and unfair or deceptive practices, in or affecting
commerce, are declared unlawful." By section 45(a)(2) the Federal
Trade Commission is empowered and directed "to prevent persons,
partnerships, or corporations * * * from using" such unfair methods
of competition or such unfair or deceptive acts or practices. Section
45(b) provides the procedure by which the F.T.C. shall make "cease and
desist" orders and by which judicial review of such orders by Courts of
Appeals may be had.

Section 45(m)(1)(B) further provides for civil penalties:

> If the Commission determines in a proceeding under subsection (b) of this section that any act or practice is unfair or deceptive, and issues a final cease and desist order with respect to such act or practice, then the Commission may commence a civil action to obtain a civil penalty in a district court of the United States against any person, partnership, or corporation which engages in such act or practice—
>
> (1) after such cease and desist order becomes final *(whether or not such person, partnership, or corporation was subject to such cease and desist order)*, and
>
> (2) *with actual knowledge that such act or practice is unfair or deceptive and is unlawful under subsection (a)(1) of this section.*
>
> In such action, such person, partnership, or corporation shall be liable for a civil penalty of not more than $10,000 for each violation. [Italics supplied by court].

When the Truth in Lending Act became law in 1968, the F.T.C. thus already had functions with respect to practices which were (1) anticompetitive or (2) unfair and deceptive. The scheme of enforcement procedure for provisions of that statute assigned the major enforcement functions to the F.T.C.

15 U.S.C. 1607(c) provides:

> Except to the extent that enforcement of the requirements imposed under this subchapter is specifically committed to some other Government agency under subsection (a) of this section, the Federal Trade Commission shall enforce such requirements. For the purpose of the exercise by the Federal Trade Commission of its functions and powers under the Federal Trade Commission Act, *a violation of any requirement imposed under this subchapter shall be deemed a violation of a requirement imposed under that Act.* All of the functions and powers of the Federal Trade Commission under the Federal Trade Commission Act are available to the Commission to enforce compliance by any person with the requirements imposed under this subchapter, irrespective of whether that person is engaged in commerce or meets any other jurisdictional tests in the Federal Trade Commission Act. [Italics supplied by the court].

A conceivable interpretation of the above-quoted provision might be that it is a self-standing authorization of the use by the F.T.C. of its entire panoply of powers for the purpose of enforcing the Truth in Lending Act, without regard to the procedures prescribed in the Federal Trade Commission Act for exercising the enforcement powers there committed to the F.T.C.

However, the F.T.C. at argument disclaimed reliance upon any such "independent potency" theory, and espoused the more logical view that the italicized language in the above-quoted passage incorporates by reference for enforcement of the Truth in Lending Act the same remedial procedures as are prescribed in 15 U.S.C. 45 for enforcement of the Federal Trade Commission Act.

We must turn then to 15 U.S.C. 45 to determine when and how a civil penalty may be imposed for a violation of the Truth in Lending Act (which by virtue of 15 U.S.C. 1607(c) is to be treated as if it were a violation of the Federal Trade Commission Act).

The first prerequisite required by 15 U.S.C. 45(m)(1)(B) in order to impose a civil penalty upon a non-party to the proceeding in which an administrative determination by the F.T.C. that the particular practice is unfair or deceptive and hence unlawful under Section 45(a)(1) was made is that the F.T.C. must determine "in a proceeding under subsection (b)" of Section 45 "that any act or practice is unfair or deceptive," and that it must then issue "a final cease and desist order with respect to such act or practice."

It was the Commission's failure to make such a determination under subsection (b) of Section 45 of the Act that the practices engaged in by appellees were unfair or deceptive, and its failure to issue a final cease and desist order with respect to such practices that impelled Judge Devitt, correctly, to grant summary judgment in favor of appellees.

APPLICATION TO THE CASE AT BAR

In the light of the foregoing statutory scheme, we proceed to consider what was done by the F.T.C. in the case at bar.

How did the F.T.C. undertake to establish the above-specified first requirement of Section 45(m)(1)(B), namely a final cease and desist order "with respect to such act or practice" made "in a proceeding under subsection (b)" of Section 45?

It furnished appellees copies of four F.T.C. decisions, together with a "synopsis" citing the said decisions in footnotes. Of these four cases, only *Seekonk* (at 82 F.T.C. 1055, R. 156) states as a "conclusion" that respondents "engaged in false, misleading and deceptive advertising, and *utilized unfair and deceptive acts and practices* in the offering for sale, sale and distribution of meat and meat products." [Italics supplied by court] But *Seekonk* is basically a "bait and switch case", a type of abusive practice which apparently, insofar as shown by appellant's brief, was never utilized by appellees. The charges against appellees were essentially for advertising credit terms without conforming to requirements of Regulation Z regarding full disclosure of all terms (annual percentage rate stated as such, number of payments, etc.)

Examination of these four decisions by the F.T.C. in other cases not involving appellees as parties discloses that nowhere in said decisions does the F.T.C. determine that such practice (namely a practice in which appellees admittedly have engaged) is "unfair or deceptive."

This failure to comply with the above-stated first requisite for obtaining a civil penalty against appellees automatically also constitutes failure to meet the requirement of Section 45(m)(1)(B)(2) with respect to appellees' "actual knowledge that such practice is unfair or deceptive and is unlawful under subsection (a)(1)" of Section 45. For though it is established that appellees were furnished copies of those decisions, and hence are chargeable with knowledge of what is contained in those decisions, they were thereby given no knowledge that the practices engaged in by appellees were unfair or deceptive if those decisions did not contain a determination with respect to such practices holding that they were unfair or deceptive and prohibited by the terms of a final cease and desist order. Hence the F.T.C. failed to establish that appellees were liable for a civil penalty.

For the foregoing reasons the judgment of the District Court is Affirmed.

Notes

1. Does it make sense that the FTC can obtain civil penalties for violations of its own cease and desist orders but not for a clear violation of Regulation Z, a detailed regulation that the FTC is specifically charged with enforcing?

2. Is it likely that the car dealers in the *Hopkins* case had actual knowledge of the requirements of Regulation Z? Could the argument be made that it is more fair to charge penalties for a violation of a specific regulation than for a cease and desist order issued against a third party?

Problem 8

Same facts as Problem 1 of this Chapter, supra p. 812–813. Robbin Hood has been hurt by a defect in a Dodge automobile bought from Dale. When Hood seeks compensation for injury, Dale and Dodge point to the limitation on remedy clause limiting recovery to "repair"—and they offer to do that. However, this time you work for the Federal Trade Commission.

(a) Can you obtain redress for Hood's personal injuries? For others who have suffered similar injuries?

(b) Can you stop Dale and Dodge from continuing to use a contract clause which is "prima facie unconscionable"?

(c) Can you penalize Dale or Dodge for having used this clause in the past? Is there a need for a penalty here?

(d) Have your powers been augmented or diminished as you went from working for the state of California to working for the national government? Is there a rational explanation for any differences?

5. TRADE REGULATION RULES

Case-by-case adjudication by a public agency, even with corrective advertising and restitution powers, can be a tremendously inefficient way to police the marketplace. Immense resources may go into the prosecution of a single case, which may then be only a dubious precedent for dealing with other practices which differ somewhat from those enjoined.

For these reasons, the FTC had for years issued industry "guides", suggesting in advance what kinds of practices would incur the Commission's wrath. These guides were not binding, but merely represented the Commission's enforcement policy.

The FTC in about 1970 began promulgating what it called Trade Regulation Rules. These were explicit standards of conduct which the Commission asserted had the force of law—that is, all the FTC would have to prove is that someone violated the letter of the Rule; they would not have to prove deception or unfairness on an ad hoc basis.

One of these Rules required the posting of octane levels on gas pumps. It was quickly challenged, but the Commission's authority was upheld. National Petroleum Refiners Ass'n v. Federal Trade Comm., 482 F.2d 672 (D.C.Cir.1973), certiorari denied, 415 U.S. 951, 94 S.Ct. 1475, 39 L.Ed.2d 567 (1974). The Commission's authority to issue "rules which define with specificity acts or practices which are unfair or deceptive" was enacted into positive law in section 202 of the Magnuson–Moss Warranty—FTC Improvements Act of 1975, amending section 18 of the FTC Act. This specific grant of authority however, was hedged in with extensive administrative procedures for rulemaking, including publishing notice of proposed rulemaking, informal hearings, and cross-examination of witnesses by interested parties.

In the early 1980s the Federal Trade Commission came under political fire for excessive zeal in its regulatory functions. One result was the enactment of the Federal Trade Commission Improvements Act of 1980, which included restrictive provisions on particular proposed rules, and also contained a two-house legislative veto for all FTC consumer protection rules. Congress exercised the veto in 1981 with respect to the FTC's used car rule, but the veto provision was soon struck down in court as a violation of the constitutional requirement of separation of the legislative and executive powers. Consumers Union of U.S., Inc. v. FTC, 691 F.2d 575 (D.C.Cir.1982), summarily aff'd sub nom. U.S. Senate v. FTC, 463 U.S. 1216, 103 S.Ct. 3556, 77 L.Ed.2d 1403 (1983).

The Commission was also facing some difficulties in the courts with respect to its rulemaking procedures, as illustrated by the *Katharine Gibbs School* case, infra p. 848. The result of the combined political and judicial pressure has been a cautious approach to rulemaking at the Commission for most of the 1980s. Many of the rules proposed in the late 1970s have been terminated or the substantive provisions cut back. The few rules that have been promulgated have taken a rigorous "market failure" approach. It is assumed that the free market will automatically produce the greatest consumer welfare, so that consumer protection rules are justified only if the market has failed and the benefits of regulation outweigh the costs. See, e.g., the Credit Practices Rule, 16 C.F.R. Part 444, Statement of Basis and Purpose, 49 Fed.Reg. 7740 (March 1, 1984); and the Ophthalmic Practice Rule, 16 C.F.R. Part

456, Statement of Basis and Purpose, 54 Fed.Reg. 10285 (March 13, 1989).

The trend is a return to case-by-case adjudication. But even this course of action also has its problems. See Ford Motor Co. v. FTC, infra p. 852.

KATHARINE GIBBS SCHOOL, INC. v. FTC
United States Court of Appeals for the Second Circuit, 1979.
612 F.2d 658.

Before VAN GRAAFEILAND and NEWMAN, CIRCUIT JUDGES, and BONSAL, DISTRICT JUDGE.

VAN GRAAFEILAND, CIRCUIT JUDGE.

Twelve petitions have been filed with this Court seeking review of a Trade Regulation Rule issued by the Federal Trade Commission on December 18, 1978, entitled "Proprietary Vocational and Home Study Schools." See 16 C.F.R. § 438. The Rule's broadly stated purpose * * * is "to alleviate currently abusive practices against vocational and home study school students and prospective students." Although the Rule does not define "abusive practices", the Commission's Statement of Basis and Purpose shows that the Commission's concern was with unfair and deceptive advertising, sales, and enrollment practices engaged in by some of the schools.

The more than 7,000 proprietary vocational schools that will be covered by the Rule on its January 1, 1980, effective date are no strangers to regulation. Almost every State has legislation aimed at eliminating some or all of the abuses that trouble the Commission. The United States Veterans Administration and Office of Education have also been active in this area. In 1972, the Commission itself issued a set of guidelines for private vocational and home study schools, and has since instituted proceedings against several schools under section 5 of the Federal Trade Commission Act, 15 U.S.C. § 45.

The Commission decided, however, that all of the foregoing regulatory efforts were inadequate, and, in 1974, it published for comment and public hearing a proposed Trade Regulation Rule. The Commission proceeded originally under the rulemaking power granted it in section 6(g) of the Federal Trade Commission Act, 15 U.S.C. § 46(g), * * *. However, on January 4, 1975, in the midst of the Commission's hearings, Congress passed the Magnuson–Moss Warranty—Federal Trade Commission Improvement Act, Pub.L. No. 93–637, 88 Stat. 2183, Title II of which prescribes with preciseness the Commission's authority to issue rules and general statements of policy and outlines the rulemaking procedures to be followed in connection therewith. Following enactment of this legislation, the Commission changed its hearing procedures to comply with the new statutory requirements. Our primary task on this appeal is to determine whether the Rule finally adopted was within the general powers of the Commission under the Federal Trade Commission Act as refined and limited by the specific provisions of section 57a and, if so, whether the Rule was supported by substantial evidence and was neither arbitrary nor capricious.

Section 5(a) of the Federal Trade Commission Act, 15 U.S.C. § 45(a), declares that "unfair or deceptive acts or practices in commerce" are unlawful, and section 6(g) empowers the Commission to make rules and regulations for the purpose of carrying out this provision. Section 57a(a)(1) redefines this grant of authority by providing that the Commission may prescribe:

> (A) interpretive rules and general statements of policy with respect to unfair or deceptive acts or practices in or affecting commerce (within the meaning of section 45(a)(1) of this title), and

> (B) rules which define with specificity acts or practices which are unfair or deceptive acts or practices in or affecting commerce (within the meaning of section 45(a)(1) of this title). Rules under this subparagraph may include requirements prescribed for the purpose of preventing such acts or practices.

The Magnuson–Moss Act also provides that, after any Commission rule takes effect, a violation thereof shall be an unfair or deceptive act under 15 U.S.C. § 45(a)(1) unless the Commission otherwise provides. It empowers the Commission to commence a civil action for a violation of any rule, in which action the Commission may seek, among other remedies, rescission or reformation of contracts, the refund of money or the return of property, and money damages.

Petitioners contend, and we agree, that in order to comply with section 57a(a)(1)(B) the Commission must define with specificity in the Rule those acts or practices which are unfair or deceptive and may include requirements for preventing them. Petitioners contend further, and again we agree, that the challenged Rule does not comply with these statutory provisions. Instead of defining with specificity those acts or practices which it found to be unfair or deceptive, the Commission contented itself with treating violations of its "requirements prescribed for the purpose of preventing" unfair practices as themselves the unfair practices.[3] We think that Congress expected more than this.

Requirements designed to prevent unfair practices are predicated upon the existence of unfair practices. These unfair practices, which are the statutorily required underpinning for the Commission's "requirements", should have been defined with specificity.

> "Because the prohibitions of section 5 of the Act are quite broad, trade regulation rules are needed to define with specificity conduct that violates the statute and to establish requirements to prevent unlawful conduct." Conf.Rep. No. 93–1408, Joint Explanatory Statement of the

3. The Commission's Rule provides simply that it is an unfair or deceptive act or practice for any school to fail to comply with the requirements of the Rule. 16 C.F.R. § 438.0.

Committee of Conference, reprinted in [1974] U.S.Code Cong. & Ad. News, pp. 7702, 7755, 7763.

The statute requires that the Commission's Statement of Basis and Purpose, which must accompany a Rule, shall include statements as to the prevalence of the acts or practices treated by the Rule and the manner in which such acts or practices are unfair or deceptive. These provisions would be meaningless if the only unfair acts or practices defined in the Rule were possible future violations of its remedial requirements.

We conclude that the Commission erred in failing to comply with the procedural requirements of section 57a(a)(1)(B). We also find several substantive provisions of the Rule to be defective, and the combination of procedural and substantive errors requires that the Rule be set aside. We will remand the Rule to the Commission so that the Commission may comply with section 57a(a)(1)(B) and delete or amend those provisions which we find to be improper.

In the paragraphs that follow, we deal with petitioner's additional claims of error.

I

THE REFUND PROVISIONS

Instead of defining with specificity the advertising, sales, and enrollment practices it deemed unfair and deceptive and setting forth requirements for preventing them, the Commission decided to make it financially unattractive for schools covered by the Rule to accept a student who, for any reason whatever, was unlikely to finish the course in which he or she had enrolled. The Commission did this by directing its attack against the tuition refund policies of the schools.

Although the Commission concededly did not find that existing refund policies were either unfair or deceptive, it directed that they be completely revised so as to make them financially more onerous for the schools. This the Rule accomplishes by requiring schools to make refunds on a strict pro rata basis, the percentage of the refund to be determined by matching the number of classes attended or lessons completed against the total number of classes, hours, or lessons required to complete the course. Refunds on such a pro rata basis do not take into account those costs that are fixed at the time of enrollment, such as salaries for teachers and staff, classroom and boarding facilities, administration overhead, books, and supplies. The Rule does not require a student to return "records, tapes, slides, films, books or any other written course materials" as a condition of obtaining a refund. The cost of other equipment furnished a student must be prorated in the same manner as tuition, unless a separate equipment charge is made in the enrollment contract. Even if a separate charge is made, it will be refunded on a pro rata basis if the equipment is returned, regardless of its then condition or usability. Although the Commission did not fault existing refund policies, it provided, nonetheless, that any failure to comply with its newly prescribed refund regulations would constitute an unfair or deceptive act or practice in connection with the sale or promotion of a course.

These regulations, the Commission says, are designed "to alter the incentive structure for obtaining vocational school enrollments." Elaborating on this subject in its brief, the Commission states that the schools "make little effort to screen candidates to determine if they possess the required verbal, reading or mechanical skills necessary for the courses of study" and that they sign up "unsuitable enrollees". The rationale of the Rule is said to be the "[creation of] structural disincentives to indiscriminate enrollment", which, translated into less dainty language, means "the creation of structural incentives for discriminate enrollment."

The Commission argues that this foray into the field of education is a "reasoned exercise of its legislative judgment" in an area "plainly within its expertise, i.e., unfair selling practices." Commission counsel describes this as an exercise of the Commission's "broad remedial discretion", subject to as little judicial review under the Magnuson–Moss Act as had been exercised prior thereto. We disagree.

When Congress provided that the Commission's rules must define unfair and deceptive acts with specificity, it clearly intended that the Commission's definition would be subject to judicial review. And when Congress, after being informed that the Commission was "strongly opposed" to the substantial evidence standard of review, nonetheless incorporated that standard in the statute, it obviously intended that a Commission rule not receive judicial approval "unless the Commission's action was supported by substantial evidence in the record taken as a whole."

Although courts normally give weight to an agency's interpretation of its own enabling legislation, the judiciary is the final authority on issues of statutory construction. An agency interpretation must be granted deference only when it is consistent with the congressional purpose and when there are no "compelling indications that it is wrong."

Assuming, without deciding, that the Commission has the power to alter the schools' incentive structure for engaging in high pressure or deceptive sales and enrollment practices, its Rule was clearly not so limited in its scope. The Rule penalizes every vocational school for every student dropout, regardless of cause.

This Court is obligated to take a close look at what the Commission has done and to determine whether it has articulated a "rational connection between the facts found and the choice made." We have taken a close look, and we find no rational connection between the Commission's universally applicable refund requirements and the prevention of specifically described unfair and deceptive enrollment practices.

* * *

CONCLUSION

For the reasons above stated, we conclude that the Rule, as presently formulated, is unlawful and must be set aside. The matter is remanded to the Commission for further proceedings not inconsistent with this opinion.

[Omitted portions of the opinion detail the court's findings on other provisions of the Trade Regulation Rule: e.g., mandatory disclosure of job-placement statistics, and preemption of state laws, were struck down; but a required cooling-off period was sustained. Judge Newman filed a sharp dissent, stating his belief that "the Rule is in all respects a lawful response to documented unfair and deceptive practices found by the Commission to exist in the proprietary vocational school field * * *."]

POSTSCRIPT

Some fourteen years after the commencement of rulemaking, the Commission terminated the Vocational Schools rule in 1988. 53 Fed. Reg. 29,482 (Aug. 5, 1988). The reason? The record evidence had grown stale! The Commission also noted that the Department of Education had *proposed* new regulations that *might* cover the same ground.

FORD MOTOR CO. v. F.T.C.

United States Court of Appeals for the Ninth Circuit, 1981, reh. denied 1982.
673 F.2d 1008.

GOODWIN, CIRCUIT JUDGE.

Francis Ford, Inc. petitions this court to review an F.T.C. order finding it in violation of § 5 of the F.T.C. Act, 15 U.S.C. § 45 (unfair trade practices). We have reviewed the petition, and set aside the order.

Francis Ford, Inc. is an Oregon automobile dealership. Its practice in repossessing cars has been to credit the debtor for the wholesale value of the car, charge him for indirect expenses (i.e., overhead and lost profits) as well as direct expenses (i.e., refurbishing) associated with repossession and resale, and sell the repossessed vehicle at retail keeping the "surplus." In doing so, Francis Ford claims it is doing what is commonly done throughout its industry.

The F.T.C. does not approve of the described practice. Nor does it approve of a number of other credit practices now commonly in use in a wide variety of industries. See its investigations of the credit business, and its recent attempted rulemaking. In re Proposed Trade Regulation Rule: Credit Practices, 40 Fed.Reg. 16,347 (1975).

In order to attack Francis Ford's practice, the F.T.C. began in 1976 an adjudicatory action against Ford Motor Co., Ford Credit Co., and Francis Ford, Inc. The commission alleged that the respondents had violated § 5 of the F.T.C. Act by failing to give defaulting customers more than wholesale value for their repossessed cars, and by improperly charging them with indirect expenses such as overhead and lost profits. Parallel proceedings were commenced against Chrysler Corp. and General Motors, their financial subsidiaries, and two dealers. The National Association of Car Dealers sought to intervene to protect the interests of its members but was not allowed to do so. Eventually, all the respondents except Francis Ford settled with the F.T.C.

Shortly after the consent decrees were entered, the administrative law judge held that Francis Ford's credit practices had violated § 5 of the F.T.C. Act, but that the commission had failed to establish that Francis Ford's acts were substantially injurious to its customers. Both Francis Ford and complaint counsel for the F.T.C. appealed to the full commission. The commission deleted the portion of the order favorable to Francis Ford, and affirmed the administrative law judge's decision. The order directed Francis Ford to cease its present credit practices, and to adopt the F.T.C.'s view of proper credit practices under ORS 79.5040 (U.C.C. § 9–504).

The narrow issue presented here is whether the F.T.C. should have proceeded by rulemaking in this case rather than by adjudication. The Supreme Court has said that an administrative agency, such as the F.T.C., "is not precluded from announcing new principles in the adjudicative proceeding and that the choice between rulemaking and adjudication lies in the first instance within the [agency's] discretion." NLRB v. Bell Aerospace Co., 416 U.S. 267, 294, 94 S.Ct. 1757, 1771, 40 L.Ed.2d 134 (1974). But like all grants of discretion, "there may be situations where the [agency's] reliance on adjudication would amount to an abuse of discretion * * *." Bell Aerospace Co., 416 U.S. at 294, 94 S.Ct. at 1771. The problem is one of drawing the line. On that score the Supreme Court has avoided black-letter rules. See id. at 294, 94 S.Ct. at 1772 ("[i]t is doubtful whether any generalized standard could be framed which would have more than marginal utility * * *.") Lower courts have been left, therefore, with the task of dealing with the problem on a case-by-case basis.

The Ninth Circuit recently made such an attempt in Patel v. Immigration & Naturalization Serv., 638 F.2d 1199 (9th Cir.1980). * * * The thrust of the *Patel* holding, therefore, is that agencies can proceed by adjudication to enforce discrete violations of *existing* laws where the effective scope of the rule's impact will be relatively small; but an agency must proceed by rulemaking if it seeks to change the law and establish rules of widespread application.

In the present case, the F.T.C., by its order, has established a rule that would require a secured creditor to credit the debtor with the "best possible" value of the repossessed vehicle, and forbid the creditor from charging the debtor with overhead and lost profits. The administrative decision below so holds. Framed according to *Patel,* the precise issue therefore is whether this adjudication changes existing law, and has widespread application. It does, and the matter should be addressed by rulemaking.

The F.T.C. admits that industry practice has been to do what Francis Ford does—credit the debtor with the wholesale value and charge the debtor for indirect expenses. But the F.T.C. contends that Francis Ford's particular practice violates state law (ORS 79.5040); that the violation will not be reached by the proposed trade rule on credit practices; and that this adjudication will have only local application. The arguments are not persuasive.

By all accounts this adjudication is the first agency action against a dealer for violating ORS 79.5040 by doing what Francis Ford does. Although the U.C.C. counterpart of ORS 79.5040 is enacted in 49 states, nearly word for word, we have been cited to no case which has interpreted the provision to require a secured creditor to credit the debtor for the "best possible price" and not charge him for overhead and lost profits. It may well be that Oregon courts will interpret U.C.C. § 9–504 in the manner advocated by the F.T.C. if the question is put to them. But it is speculation to contend, as does the F.T.C. here, that Francis Ford is in violation of *existing* Oregon law. One of the basic characteristics of law is that potential violators have, or can obtain, notice of it. No notice of the F.T.C.'s view of the law has been pointed out to us.

The F.T.C. could have formulated its position on U.C.C. § 9–504 and its application to the credit practices of car dealerships in its proposed trade rule on credit practices. It did not do so. The pending rulemaking proceeding and this adjudication seek to remedy, more or less, the same credit practices. Although the former is directed against the practices, inter alia, of car dealers in their accounting of deficiencies, and the latter is directed against a car dealer by reason of his practices in failing to account for surpluses, both matters are covered by U.C.C. § 9–504. If the rule for deficiencies is thought by the F.T.C. to be "appropriately addressed by rulemaking," it should also address the problem of accounting for surpluses by a rulemaking proceeding, and not by adjudication.

Ultimately, however, we are persuaded to set aside this order because the rule of the case made below will have general application. It will not apply just to Francis Ford. Credit practices similar to those of Francis Ford are widespread in the car dealership industry; and the U.C.C. section the F.T.C. wishes us to interpret exists in 49 states. The F.T.C. is aware of this. It has already appended a "Synopsis of Determination" to the order, apparently for the purpose of advising other automobile dealerships of the results of this adjudication. To allow the order to stand as presently written would do far more than remedy a discrete violation of a singular Oregon law as the F.T.C. contends; it would create a national interpretation of U.C.C. § 9–504 and in effect enact the precise rule the F.T.C. has proposed, but not yet promulgated.

Under these circumstances, the F.T.C. has exceeded its authority by proceeding to create new law by adjudication rather than by rulemaking.

The order is vacated.

Problem 9

Suppose the FTC decides to investigate telemarketing fraud in the sale of precious gems and metals. Is the FTC now caught in a no-win, procedurally-impossible Catch–22 situation? If it proceeds against consumer abuses on a case-by-case basis, will cease and desist orders be overturned on the basis of the *Ford Motor* decision? If it proceeds with rulemaking, seeking to impose a three day cooling off period for telephone sales, for instance, will its rules be subject to challenge on the authority of *Katherine Gibbs School?* How can the FTC steer between these reefs? Should it simply await further action by Congress (see supra page 847)?

6. NOTE ON PRIVATE RIGHT OF ACTION UNDER THE FTC ACT

1. If a public agency such as the Federal Trade Commission has a useful range of remedial provisions in its legislative authorization, is there any need to provide for "private enforcement" of the FTC Act? There are at least two reasons for allowing individual consumers to enforce such legislation. One is to place the consumer's ability to defend himself in his own hands in cases where the abuse is important to him economically but the agency is spending its resources on more widespread problems. The other is to overcome the possibilities of industry domination of the agency, or agency inertia, red tape or conservatism.

But simply allowing private enforcement of the FTC Act would not be enough. Most individuals would not have the resources to pursue a lawsuit under the FTC Act unless there was also a provision for the award of attorney's fees and costs.

As outlined below, however, the courts have overwhelmingly rejected a private right of action under the FTC Act. But the need for such a legal avenue may well have been superseded by the passage of such statutes as the Magnuson–Moss Warranty Act, Truth in Lending (and other consumer credit statutes), state lemon laws and state little FTC acts, most of which offer a private right of action and attorney's fees for successful consumer plaintiffs. The availability of these legal alternatives led to a halt in the hue and cry for a private right to sue for violation of the FTC Act itself, or its regulations. Nonetheless, the issue is not dead. As noted supra p. 841, the rise in telemarketing fraud has renewed the call for a private right of action under the FTC Act, particularly by financial institutions who are suffering from the effects of cancelled credit card transactions that are sometimes the result of deceptive telephone sales.

2. The leading case on the issue of a private right of action under the FTC Act is Holloway v. Bristol–Myers Corporation, 485 F.2d 986 (D.C.Cir.1973). In an influential opinion dismissing a class action alleging deceptive advertising of the pain reliever *Excedrin,* Circuit Judge Leventhal concluded: "private actions to vindicate rights asserted under the Federal Trade Commission Act may not be maintained."

Judge Leventhal first noted that the FTC Act "nowhere purports to confer upon private individuals, either consumers or business competitors, a right of action to enjoin the practices prohibited by the Act or to obtain damages following the commission of such acts." Thus, to find the desired right of action, the court would have to imply it from the statute or its legislative history. On this point, the court noted:

> Judicial implication of ancillary Federal remedies is a matter to be treated with care, lest a carefully erected legislative scheme—often the result of a delicate balance of Federal and state, public and private interests—be skewed by the courts, albeit inadvertently. This caution is especially apposite in situations where, as here, the substantive prohibitions of the statute are inextricably intertwined with provisions defining the powers and duties of a specialized administrative body charged with its enforcement and where Congress has superimposed a structure of Federal law upon the existing system of common law remedies for fraud and deceit without preempting or superseding the latter.

The court looked to the legislative history of the FTC Act to buttress its conclusion that Congress had not intended the Act to be enforced by individuals. It noted that when the Federal Trade Commission was created by Congress in 1914, it was meant to be "a highly specialized administrative body to which Congress delegated a wide range of visitorial powers in the field of potentially anti-competitive trade practices." The Clayton Act, passed at the same time, contained relatively specific prohibitions of anti-competitive practices, and "was accompanied by a broad range of enforcement devices, including private action." In contrast, "the Federal Trade Commission Act, with its broadly framed proscription, was intended to be the exclusive domain of the specialized agency." Although the Wheeler–Lea Amendments of 1938 "represented a shift in emphasis, from the control of deceptive advertising practices as an incident of antitrust regulation to the avowed purpose of protecting the consumer from fraud," * * * "Congress plainly intended these augmented powers to be exercised within the institutional matrix created by the 1914 Act."

Furthermore, the *Holloway* opinion noted various problems of compatibility of public and private enforcement that would arise should there be a private right of action under the FTC Act. Since the "Act gives the Commission a broad range of flexible enforcement powers, * * * there is need to weigh each action against the Commission's broad range policy goals and to determine its place in the overall enforcement program of the FTC." On the other hand, "private liti-

gants * * * may institute piecemeal lawsuits," and "[t]he consequence would burden not only the defendants selected but also the
judicial system." The court felt that the Commission's statutory role
was to provide "certainty and specificity to the broad proscriptions of
the Act" and that this function would be endangered "if this central
administrative tribunal were replaced by the various Federal courts
invoked by private parties." Judge Leventhal further noted that the
courts lack the expertise to determine whether a particular settlement
would be in the public interest or to shape effective and innovative
remedies in deceptive advertising cases.

The *Holloway* court was not impressed by the allegation that the
Commission had been unable to provide effective enforcement in the
field of false advertising due to insufficient staff and competing demands and thus a private right of action was a necessary supplement,
or that a private action was needed since the FTC apparently could not
award damages to those victimized by false advertising. The court
concluded that these types of complaints were best directed to Congress.

3. Only one case has recognized a private right of action to sue
under the FTC Act, Guernsey v. Rich Plan of the Midwest, 408 F.Supp.
582 (N.D.Ind.1976). In that case, the plaintiffs brought a class action
for injunctive relief and compensatory and punitive damages arising
out of a food/freezer sales plan allegedly in violation of the FTC Act.
The defendant's motion to dismiss was denied.

The *Guernsey* court questioned the ability of the FTC to deal
adequately with consumer fraud. It noted:

> Most defrauded customers have no remedy at all because the Govern-
> ment cannot possibly act in more than a small fraction of all the cases
> of deceit and overreaching against consumers. The Federal Trade
> Commission currently receives about 9,000 complaints a year and is
> only able to investigate one out of eight or nine of these, and, of the
> small fraction investigated, only one in ten results in a cease and desist
> order.

The court distinguished *Holloway* by noting that the defendant
Rich Plan Corporation was already under order by the FTC to cease
and desist from engaging in deceptive acts and practices in the sale of
food/freezer plans. Thus,

> since the Federal Trade Commission has examined the complained of
> practices and found them wanting, one of the hurdles to the private
> enforcement of the Federal Trade Commission Act has been cleared—
> that being that the Federal Trade Commission, with its overview of the
> national economy, is in a better position than a private litigant to
> gauge the injury a deceptive practice will cause [to] the public and to
> balance this against the likely cost of elimination of the practice.

Furthermore, the court found that a private right to sue under
these circumstances would not be at cross-purposes with the FTC Act,
but, on the contrary, would help consumers victimized by violations of
cease and desist orders to receive a just recovery.

4. Is *Guernsey* distinguishable from *Holloway* on the ground that Rich Plan's practices had previously been adjudicated and found to be violations? Does the prior consent decree constitute res judicata in this case?

5. With the notoriously modest budget of the Federal Trade Commission, why is Congress hesitant to provide a private remedy? Wouldn't this be a costless way to improve enforcement?

6. Now that consumers in most states can effectively obtain a private right of action to enforce the FTC Act through their state "little FTC Acts," have the adverse consequences of piecemeal litigation feared by the *Holloway* court come to pass? Is it sufficient that the state courts are usually "guided by" the FTC's interpretation in applying the state laws?

Chapter 18

HEAVY ARTILLERY:
CLASS ACTIONS

Prefatory Note

If individual actions are inefficient and involve too small an amount to interest the consumer's attorney, and if public agencies are not able to keep up with the demand for consumer protection, there remains the heavy artillery weapon of the class action. It is not the purpose of this chapter to examine all aspects of class actions, for that would be a course in and of itself. In Note, Developments in the Law— Class Actions, 89 Harv.L.Rev. 1319 (1976), the authors propose that courts, when deciding whether to certify class actions, look not so much at the technicalities of Rule 23 (Federal Rules of Civil Procedure) but at whether class action availability will promote the remedial policies of the substantive statute. This chapter also will examine the policy problems underlying class action availability for consumer protection issues rather than the technicalities of the various civil procedure rules. Thus, the cases have been chosen because of the quality of their statements on the policies involved. The notes will give the background, as needed, on the applicable technical rules.

Some of the issues to be considered here are:

(1) Should the standard requirements for state or federal class actions be liberalized to further the goals of the underlying consumer protection statute?

(2) What if the named plaintiff has had her claim settled by the defendant? Is she still a good class representative?

(3) In consumer class actions where there is a potential for collecting attorneys' fees under the relevant consumer protection statute, is there a conflict if there is any connection between the plaintiff class and the attorneys representing the class?

(4) Where the settlement of a class action results in the creation of a common fund to cover both the plaintiffs' claims and their attorneys' fees, how will the court balance the interests of the class plaintiffs against the interests of their attorneys, while promoting the statutory

policy of encouraging private enforcement through the provisions for attorneys' fees?

One requirement for a federal class action is the provision of notice to the class plaintiffs. In Eisen v. Carlisle & Jacquelin, 417 U.S. 156, 94 S.Ct. 2140, 40 L.Ed.2d 732 (1974), the U.S. Supreme Court decided that class action plaintiffs must bear the expense of notifying members of the class. Rule 23(c)(2) requires that individual notice be given "to all members who can be identified through reasonable effort" if the class action is brought under Rule 23(b)(3)—which is by far the predominant form of such actions. In Oppenheimer Fund, Inc. v. Sanders, 437 U.S. 340, 98 S.Ct. 2380, 57 L.Ed.2d 253 (1978), the Court required the plaintiffs to bear the cost of identifying the class members in the defendant's records. Also in 1978, the Court resolved a split among the Circuit Courts, holding in Coopers & Lybrand v. Livesay, 437 U.S. 463, 98 S.Ct. 2454, 57 L.Ed.2d 351 (1978), that a denial of class action certification was not appealable under the "death knell" exception to the finality rule.

In state courts, however, there may be a tendency to reduce these notice requirements. Cartt v. Superior Court, 50 Cal.App.3d 960, 124 Cal.Rptr. 376 (1975).

Problem 1

You are employed by Neighborhood Legal Services. Your client, John Little, bought a car from William Scarlet and signed a negotiable promissory note promising to pay $7200 over a four year period. The note did not have the FTC required legend (see supra Chapter Six, pages 413–423). Scarlet negotiated the note to Tuck Trust Company.

One week after the sale and negotiation, the transmission fell out of the car. The car had a new car warranty which was breached by this occurrence, but Scarlet refused to repair or replace the transmission of the car, saying something about owner misuse of the car. Tuck is insisting on payment of installments on the note, regardless of the breach of warranty, alleging that it is a holder in due course of a negotiable instrument. You also have another client, Alan Dale, (on another matter) who has recently bought a car from Scarlet, and signed a negotiable promissory note which did not have the FTC required legend. There has been no breach of warranty on this car yet.

You wish to bring a class action against Scarlet or Tuck for any or all of the violations you have found. Can you successfully do it? For what violation(s)? What remedies can you obtain for the class?—redress for aggrieved consumers?—injunction against future violations?—penalties due to past violations?

Will it matter whether you are in state or federal court? Should it matter? Do you have a choice? The following cases and statutory notes outline the divergence of approach by different courts considering different statutes.

GREGORY C. DIX, et al. v. AMERICAN BANKERS LIFE ASSURANCE COMPANY OF FLORIDA, et al.

Supreme Court of Michigan, 1987.
429 Mich. 410, 415 N.W.2d 206.

LEVIN, JUSTICE.

The named plaintiffs are thirty-nine school employees who purchased tax-shelter annuity policies from defendant American Bankers Life Assurance Company of Florida. The individual defendants, Richard Pawlowski, Danny G. DeWolf, and John D. Martin Sloan, are three of the agents through whom the annuities were secured.

The plaintiffs commenced this action, alleging common-law fraud and deceit, breach of fiduciary duty, and violation of the Michigan Consumer Protection Act.[2] They claimed that the defendants made material misrepresentations and omissions to persuade them to purchase the annuity policies.[3] They requested class certification, asserting that they would represent in this action the claims of over one thousand school employees in Michigan who had purchased annuity policies from American Bankers Life.

* * *

III

The circuit court and the Court of Appeals denied plaintiffs' request for class certification because they found that a class action would not promote the "convenient administration of justice." They held that there were too many practical problems for a manageable class action.

[The circuit court, and the Court of Appeals, 141 Mich.App. 650, 367 N.W.2d 896, in affirming the decision of the circuit court, relied on the Michigan Supreme Court's decision in Freeman v. State–Wide Carpet Distributors, Inc., 365 Mich. 313, 112 N.W.2d 439 (1961)]. *Freeman* is distinguishable from the instant case because it was based solely on a theory of common-law fraud, while the instant case is also

---

2. M.C.L. § 445.901 et seq.; M.C.A. § 19.418(1) et seq.

3. The plaintiffs claimed that American Bankers, through its agents, had made false, deceptive, and misleading representations about the annuity policies and also had omitted important information. The alleged misrepresentations included that the purchasers were establishing a single master annuity account, that the purchasers could freely and without penalty increase or decrease the amount of their annuity-plan deduction, that fees and charges would be paid from the excess interest earned from the purchasers' contributions but not credited to their accounts, that the annuity would never be worth less than the amount contributed, that the break-even point for policies was five

years, that the policy, identified as P–1–7400, was nearly identical to policies sold by Prudential and the Michigan Education Association, and that the purchasers would receive periodic statements detailing the monetary worth of their plans.

In addition to these alleged misrepresentations, the plaintiffs contended that there were serious omissions, including that P–1–7400 was a "front-loaded" plan which extracted a significant percentage of a purchaser's money for fifteen years, that when a payroll deduction was increased the increase would not be attributed to an established account but rather would begin a new account with the same fifteen-year commission charges, and that the break-even point was fifteen years, not five years.

brought under the Consumer Protection Act. We affirm the dismissal of the fraud and deceit and breach of fiduciary duty counts, but reverse the dismissal of the Consumer Protection Act count.

The plaintiffs in *Freeman* were several hundred consumers who had purchased carpet from defendant State–Wide Carpet. They alleged that State–Wide had made fraudulent misrepresentations to induce them to purchase defective carpet. This Court concluded that the request for class certification should be denied, stating that in a fraud action there were too many disparate issues of law and fact for there to be a manageable class action.

The Consumer Protection Act was enacted to provide an enlarged remedy for consumers who are mulcted by deceptive business practices, and it specifically provides for the maintenance of class actions. This remedial provision of the Consumer Protection Act should be construed liberally to broaden the consumers' remedy, especially in situations involving consumer frauds affecting a large number of persons.

We hold that members of a class proceeding under the Consumer Protection Act need not individually prove reliance on the alleged misrepresentations. It is sufficient if the class can establish that a reasonable person would have relied on the representations. Further, a defendant's intent to deceive through a pattern of misrepresentations can be shown on a representative basis under the Consumer Protection Act. So construing the Consumer Protection Act should obviate some of the practical difficulties that Freeman envisioned when an action is brought on a common-law fraud theory.

While, as set forth in *Freeman,* a class action should not be allowed if practical problems would make it unmanageable, the issues of fact and law presented in the Consumer Protection Act count do not differ so much from claim to claim that a class action would not be manageable.

The plaintiffs allege a common scheme of misrepresentation involving a single type of policy. The alleged misrepresentations may differ somewhat from plaintiff to plaintiff, but, if the plaintiffs' allegations are true, they are all substantially similar and are all part of a common scheme, they all stem from the same pattern of misrepresentation, and they all are actionable under the Consumer Protection Act.

The "convenient administration of justice" criterion does not preclude the maintenance of a class action where the individual claims differ slightly with regard to such specifics as the time, place, and exact nature of the injury. No two claims are likely to be exactly similar. Almost all claims will involve disparate issues of law and fact to some degree. The relevant concern here is whether the issues are so disparate as to make a class action unmanageable. We conclude they are not.

* * *

The dismissal of the counts of the complaint alleging fraud and deceit and breach of fiduciary duty is affirmed, the dismissal of the count alleging violation of the Consumer Protection Act is reversed, and the cause is remanded to the circuit court for proceedings consistent with this opinion.

RILEY, C.J., and BRICKLEY, BOYLE, ARCHER and CAVANAGH, JJ., concur.

WALSH v. FORD MOTOR COMPANY

United States Court of Appeals, District of Columbia Circuit, 1986.
807 F.2d 1000.

Before EDWARDS, RUTH B. GINSBURG and STARR, CIRCUIT JUDGES.

Opinion for the Court by EDWARDS, CIRCUIT JUDGE, and RUTH B. GINSBURG, CIRCUIT JUDGE.

Plaintiffs–Appellees, who proposed to represent several million owners of Ford automobiles, initiated the instant suit against Ford Motor Company to pursue breach of warranty claims by means of class actions. The appellees' suit arises under the Magnuson–Moss Warranty–Federal Trade Commission Improvement Act ("Magnuson–Moss" or the "Act"); the essence of appellees' complaint is that certain Ford models suffer from a transmission defect that causes the automobiles to slip out of the "park" position and into "reverse."

In order to obtain class action certification under Rule 23 of the Federal Rules of Civil Procedure, appellees grouped their breach of warranty claimants into three principal categories: one group ("written warranty incidents" class) included all Ford owners who had allegedly experienced a "park-to-reverse" incident within Ford's 12,000 mile/12 month written warranty period; the second group ("implied warranty incidents" class) included every Ford owner who allegedly experienced a park-to-reverse incident; and the third group ("all-owners" class) included all owners of an allegedly defective Ford vehicle, without regard to whether the owner had ever experienced a park-to-reverse incident. Citing a variety of legal objections, Ford opposed class certification; in particular, Ford argued that none of the appellees' proposed claimant groups was a cognizable "class" under Rule 23.

Although the District Court recognized that appellees' proposed class groupings raised some difficult legal issues under Rule 23, the trial judge nevertheless conditionally certified all three classes. The District Court decided to apply Rule 23 only where it is consistent with the terms and intent of Magnuson–Moss; therefore, having found that Magnuson–Moss reflects a congressional intent liberally to allow class actions as a device to facilitate consumers' recovery for breach of warranties, the District Court concluded that appellees' proposed classes should be certified as suggested. The effect of this ruling was to allow appellees to avoid the strict requirements of class certification under Rule 23.

Given the importance of the legal questions at issue, and the enormity of the litigation presently contemplated, the District Court approved appellant's request for interlocutory review under 28 U.S.C. § 1292(b). On November 7, 1985, this court granted interlocutory appeal on the issue of class certification.

Because we find that the District Court's decision to certify appellees' classes was based in significant part on an improper construction of Magnuson–Moss, rather than on a normal application of Rule 23, we vacate and remand for further consideration as to whether any class certification is appropriate under unmodified Rule 23 standards.

* * *

II. DISCUSSION

A. The Interplay Between Rule 23 and Magnuson–Moss

We recognize that certain aspects of a district court's determinations under Rule 23—such as whether common questions of fact or law predominate—are entitled to a measure of deference from an appellate court. However, it is unquestionably the role of an appellate court to ensure that class certification determinations are made pursuant to appropriate legal standards. In the instant case, we find that the District Court's class certification rulings were made under an erroneous legal standard, and must therefore be reversed.

A consistent theme pervading the trial court's opinion is that the remedial purposes of Magnuson–Moss compelled it to bend the requirements of Rule 23 in order to facilitate the maintenance of a class action. Nothing in Magnuson–Moss, however, licenses a district court to manipulate Rule 23 in order to ensure the pursuit of a class action in federal court. Although the Act creates federal jurisdiction over class actions that meet specified jurisdictional requirements, it plainly does not mandate that district courts entertain such actions regardless of whether they are cognizable under Rule 23. Congress passed Magnuson–Moss in part to create additional remedies for breach of warranty, and to allow for the possibility of class actions in federal court. Congress' primary purpose in enacting Magnuson–Moss, however, was to provide minimum disclosure and content standards particularly for written warranties, not to actively promote class actions in federal court.

In short, the District Court was required to analyze the appellees' motion for class certification under traditional Rule 23 standards. We flatly reject the District Court's assessment that Rule 23 may be applied less stringently in Magnuson–Moss cases in order to effectuate the statute's remedial purposes. The Federal Rules of Civil Procedure are to be applied in all civil actions absent a direct expression of congressional intent to the contrary. As will be discussed more fully below, Magnuson–Moss contains no such direct expression. For this reason, and for the reasons that follow, we must remand this case to the District Court to determine what classes, if any, may be certified under Rule 23.

B. Individual Notice

The District Court's most conspicuous departure from Rule 23 standards was its decision to relieve the appellees of their obligation to provide individual notice to all members of the proposed "all-owners" class. Rule 23(c)(2), as interpreted by the Supreme Court in *Eisen* [v. Carlisle & Jacquelin, 417 U.S. 156, 176, 94 S.Ct. 2140, 2150, 40 L.Ed.2d 732 (1974)] requires that individual notice be sent to all class members whose names and addresses may be ascertained through reasonable effort. The appellees did not contend before the District Court that they would be unable to identify the absentee class members through reasonable effort. Rather, they maintained that they would be financially unable to send the requisite notice. *Eisen*, however, explicitly held that individual notice is an absolute requirement of Rule 23(c)(2), not to be "tailored to fit the pocketbooks of particular plaintiffs." Accordingly, unless *Eisen* is somehow inapplicable to class actions brought under Magnuson–Moss, the District Court erred in relieving the proposed representatives of the "all-owners" class of their obligation to provide individual notice to absentee class members.

As noted above, the Supreme Court has held that the Federal Rules of Civil Procedure are to be applied in all civil actions absent a "direct expression" of congressional intent to the contrary. The statutory language of Magnuson–Moss contains no reference to Rule 23(c)(2) or to *Eisen*, much less a "direct expression" that the requirement of individual notice is not to obtain in class actions brought under the Act. When Congress has meant to limit *Eisen* it has known precisely how to do so, as evidenced by its treatment of the notice requirement in the Deepwater Port Act of 1974. In that Act, Congress specified in the statute that when the size of the proposed class exceeded one thousand, Rule 23(c)(2) would be satisfied by notice in the *Federal Register* and in local newspapers. Magnuson–Moss contains no comparable language evincing a congressional intent to modify Rule 23(c)(2).

The District Court, however, found the requisite "direct expression" of congressional intent in the legislative history of Magnuson–Moss. The court relied principally on the following language contained in the Report of the House Interstate and Foreign Commerce Committee:

> The purpose of (the Act's) jurisdictional provisions is to avoid trivial or insignificant actions being brought as class actions in the federal courts. However, if the conditions of this section are met * * * (s)ection 110(d) should be construed reasonably to authorize the maintenance of a class action. * * * (T)his section is remedial in nature and is designed to facilitate relief which would otherwise not be available as a practical matter for individual consumers. In particular, assuming that other requirements for a class action are met, your Committee does not believe that the requirement of individual notice to each potential class member should be invoked to preclude a class action where the identification and notification of the class members is

not possible after reasonable effort by the plaintiff. *In considering whether identification and notification of all members of the class is possible with reasonable effort, the particular circumstances of the plaintiff or plaintiffs should be carefully evaluated by the court, including the question of whether the financial burden of such identification and notification would be likely to deny them relief.* (Emphasis added).

Although the House Committee Report did not mention *Eisen* by name, the trial court read the above language as an indication that Congress meant for *Eisen* not to apply in Magnuson–Moss class actions. As further support for this view, the trial court cited the floor statements of two House members, one of which explicitly mentioned *Eisen*, and both of which embraced the views expressed in the House Report. Finally, the court noted that the Senate–House Conference Committee had adopted the class action provisions contained in the House bill, inferring from this that the Senate concurred in the views expressed in the House Report.

There is a firm presumption that the Federal Rules of Civil Procedure apply in all civil actions; nothing in Magnuson–Moss itself indicates that Congress meant to vitiate or reduce the requirements of Rule 23. The legislative history appellees cite, even if it is properly proposed for our consideration, falls far short of a "direct expression" that Congress intended to truncate the Rule or overrule pro tanto the Supreme Court's decision in *Eisen.*

The appellees would have us rely on that portion of the statute providing that "the representative capacity of the named plaintiffs shall be established in the application of rule 23 of the Federal Rules of Civil Procedure." [15 U.S.C. § 2310(e)]. According to the appellees, the specific mention of Rule 23 in a particular context suggests a congressional intent to dispense with Rule 23 requirements in all other contexts. At a minimum, they argue, the explicit mention of Rule 23 creates an ambiguity concerning *which portions* of Rule 23 Congress meant to apply in Magnuson–Moss class actions.

Although we recognize that some commentators have interpreted the Act in the manner urged upon us by appellees, we firmly reject the suggestion that Magnuson–Moss was intended to preclude application of any Rule 23 requirements. Appellees' argument to the contrary is based on a tortured and, in our judgment, untenable reading of the Act. Before any action—including a class action—alleging breach of warranty under Magnuson–Moss may proceed, the plaintiffs must afford the defendant a reasonable opportunity to cure its alleged breach. Under section 110(e), however, a class action may proceed at an earlier time for the limited purpose of establishing the representative capacity of the named plaintiffs. Section 110(e) further provides that this initial determination of representative capacity is to be made in accordance with Rule 23 standards. The obvious reason for the statutory reference to Rule 23, then, was to clarify that courts are to apply the same standards in making the Magnuson–Moss initial determination of representative capacity as would otherwise be applied in a typical Rule 23 proceeding. We refuse to believe that Congress, in clarifying that Rule 23 would apply to an initial determination of representative capacity, intended, sub silentio, to render the remainder of Rule 23 inapplicable.

To the extent that recourse to legislative history is appropriate, however, we again fail to discern any "direct expression" of congressional intent to eliminate the individual notice requirement as interpreted by the Supreme Court in *Eisen*. The most persuasive piece of legislative history cited by the appellees is the passage in the House Report in which a majority of Committee members opined that the requirement of individual notice should not be permitted to burden the maintenance of class actions under Magnuson–Moss. These views, however, apparently were penned prior to the Supreme Court's decision in *Eisen*, as evidenced by the fact that the majority conspicuously failed to mention *Eisen* by name. It seems most likely that the Committee, far from seeking to displace any Rule 23 requirement, was simply indicating what the legislators thought the Rule meant prior to the Supreme Court's definitive interpretation in *Eisen*.

Of greater significance is the fact that the House Committee's views on individual notice were never considered or adopted by the full Congress. As the District Court observed, the Senate–House conferees adopted the class action provisions contained in the House bill. However, neither the statutory language agreed upon in conference nor the Conference Committee Report made any reference to Rule 23(c)(2) or *Eisen*. At most, then, the House Committee's desire to soften the individual notice requirement was shared only by members of the House, perhaps only by a majority of the House Committee. The matter was never pursued in the Senate, either by means of statutory amendment or in the Conference Committee Report. More important, neither body of Congress focused on the applicability of *Eisen* to class actions brought under Magnuson–Moss, much less expressed a definite intent that *Eisen* not apply.

In short, there is nothing in the language of Magnuson–Moss to suggest that Congress meant to eliminate the individual notice requirement as interpreted by the Supreme Court in *Eisen*. Nor can such an intent be inferred from those pieces of legislative history indicating some congressional discontent with the individual notice requirement. When Congress has intended to limit *Eisen*, it has done so expressly, as in the Deepwater Port Act of 1974. We therefore hold that the District Court erred in relieving the appellees of their obligation to adhere to *Eisen*'s individual notice requirement with respect to any class properly certifiable under Rule 23(b)(3). It is to this latter issue—i.e., whether any class met the standards for certification established by Rule 23(b) (3)—that we now turn. * * *

C. The Predominance Inquiry

As recounted in Part I.B., the District Court conditionally certified three classes, each pursuant to Rule 23(b)(3) of the Federal Rules of

Civil Procedure. Two of the certified classes involved implied warranty claims, one concerned written warranties. For each of the three conditionally certified classes, the District Court announced the requisite Rule 23(b)(3) "find(ing) that the questions of law or fact common to the members of the class predominate over any questions affecting only individual members." That essential finding, we conclude, is flawed and must be vacated so that the District Court can consider the matter anew.

Concerning the applicable law, the District Court correctly stated that under the terms of Magnuson–Moss, state law governs the existence and basic meaning of implied warranties. That court apparently believed, however, that the federal Act alone, uncomplicated by "any State law variations," covered the class members' "claims for breach of written warranty." On the matter of class-wide proof crucial to all three certifications, the District Court determined that differences in the transmission systems at issue were not so material as to impede a threshold finding that common questions of fact predominated.

We hold * * * that, except in the specific instances in which Magnuson–Moss expressly prescribes a regulating rule, the Act calls for the application of state written and implied warranty law, not the creation of additional federal law. The District Court, in this clearer light, should reexamine whether "variations in State law prohibit a finding of predomination for common questions of law." Furthermore, in view of the multiple transmission configurations swept into the certifications, we remand the "class-wide proof" issue for closer inspection by the District Court.

The District Court initially demonstrated full appreciation of the inquiry a court must make to determine whether, as Rule 23(b)(3) requires, "questions of law or fact common to members of the (alleged) class predominate." Thus, the trial judge identified as key to the commonality of law determination in this case "the impact of potentially varying State laws," and as critical to the commonality of fact determination "the availability of class-wide proof." Her analysis veered off course, it appears, because she regarded Magnuson–Moss as an Act intended to facilitate nationwide class actions; she therefore thought it necessary to take a "liberal" or "less strict" approach to Rule 23 certifications. We have already held that Rule 23 applies in Magnuson–Moss cases as it does in federal court cases generally. Had the trial judge felt no Act-prompted pressure to certify, she might not have resisted close analysis of state laws governing the existence, scope, and contours of implied warranties. Furthermore, she might not have assumed that federal law alone governed the alleged written warranty claims. Finally, she might not have proceeded so swiftly to the conclusion that differences in the transmission systems at issue "are either not material or can easily be (handled by establishing) subclasses pursuant to Rule 23(c)(4)."

* * *

[The Court of Appeals then remanded for reconsideration the trial court's conclusion that common legal questions and common factual determinations predominated].

Notes

1. Why would any consumer undertake to underwrite such notice expenses where the recovery will be quite small? Is the practical effect of the *Walsh* and *Eisen* cases to protect class members, to protect warrantors, or to protect judges from working too hard?

2. In addition to meeting the prerequisites of Rule 23, Magnuson–Moss class actions in federal court must also meet stringent statutory prerequisites. The total amount in controversy must be at least $50,000 (with individual claims of at least $25), and there must be at least 100 named plaintiffs. Magnuson–Moss Act § 110(d)(3), 15 U.S.C.A. § 2301(d)(3). Even a class that initially meets this requirement may be decertified if upon discovery or motions for summary judgment or dismissal, it becomes necessary to dismiss the actions of some of the named plaintiffs, and the number drops to below the required 100. *See* Abraham v. Volkswagen of America, Inc., 795 F.2d 238 (2d Cir.1986).

3. Given that Magnuson–Moss incorporates state warranty law by reference, and given that warranty laws vary from state to state (even with most states having adopted the Uniform Commercial Code), how likely is it that a multi-state Magnuson–Moss class action will ever be able to fulfill the requirement of the predominance of a common question of law? Also, will Magnuson–Moss class actions be plagued by the issue of individual factual differences, as are class actions alleging fraud? See Feinstein v. Firestone Tire & Rubber Co., 535 F.Supp. 595 (S.D.N.Y.1982) (no class action allowed because an alleged tire defect did not affect each car in the same way).

4. Why do you suppose the Michigan Supreme Court was more willing to be flexible in allowing the pursuit of a class action claim under the Michigan Consumer Protection Act than the D.C. Court of Appeals was in the Magnuson–Moss context? Do consumers with a Magnuson–Moss breach of warranty claim have access to an alternative forum if they fail to meet the requirements for federal jurisdiction?

Note on TILA Class Actions

The original version of the Truth in Lending Act simply provided for civil liability, but made no special mention of class actions. This resulted in a range of opinion in the courts as to the availability of the class action device in TILA cases. The combination of the $100 minimum penalty damages available to each class member for each violation, plus the availability of attorney's fees meant that a TILA class action could result in a staggering liability for creditors who commit disclosure violations replicated with hundreds of thousands of customers.

In the landmark case of Ratner v. Chemical Bank New York Trust Co., 54 F.R.D. 412 (S.D.N.Y.1972), United States District Judge Frankel denied class certification in a TILA case because the potential $13 million award

(130,000 credit card holders each receiving the $100 minimum penalty) "would be a horrendous, possibly annihilating punishment, unrelated to any damage to the purported class or to any benefit to defendant, for what is at most a technical and debatable violation of the Truth in Lending Act." Other courts followed Judge Frankel's lead, and TILA class actions were becoming scarce.

Congress responded to the situation in 1974 by limiting liability in TILA class actions to the greater of $100,000 (raised to $500,000 in 1976) or 1% of the creditor's net worth. TILA § 130(a)(2)(B), 15 U.S.C.A. § 1640(a)(2)(B). The amendment eliminated the potential for devastating liability, thus encouraging the judicial certification of more TILA class actions. The 1980 TIL Simplification Act added language to the effect that the class action liability ceiling applied not only to a single class action, but also to any "series of class action suits arising out of the same failure to comply by the same creditor." Id.

Problem 2

A trial court determined that a furniture retailer's TILA disclosure statement violated the statute. Since this was a class action against a corporation whose net worth was approximately $150 million, the trial court awarded the then-maximum $100,000 class recovery. The class was composed of 700 credit customers of one of the retailer's 48 stores. On appeal, should this damage award be modified? See Barber v. Kimbrell's, Inc., 577 F.2d 216 (4th Cir.1978).

Should the court consider the fact that it is theoretically possible for customers of the other 47 stores (which used the same forms, and thereby committed the same violation) to bring 47 other class actions for 47 additional awards? Should the court therefore allow an award of only ¹⁄₄₈ of $100,000? Or ¹⁄₄₈ of $1.5 million? Or, should the court delay any award until the one-year TILA statute of limitations has run, and then consider only actual class actions brought? How helpful is the revised section 130 in answering these questions?

Problem 3

(a) Assume a large and wealthy bank supplies non-conforming TILA disclosure statements to dozens of small local retail stores. The bank regularly discounts the consumer paper for which these forms are used. The retail stores are all thinly-capitalized shoestring operations. Their combined "net worth" is about $100,000. The bank on the other hand has a net worth of $5.7 billion. What is the maximum liability of the bank for all the violations in its forms, if the customers from those stores bring a class action? $1,000? $500,000?

(b) What law governs the class action certification if the action is brought in state court?

Note on Class Representation

The ceiling on TILA class action recoveries may mean that each member of the class gets less than twice the finance charge or $100. If the nominal plaintiffs ask that *they* get their full recovery, though other class members will not, are those nominal plaintiffs qualified to represent the class? On the other hand, if by bringing a class action those named plaintifs will only recover a few cents, what incentive is there for them to bring the class action at all? In any type of consumer protection class action, what if the named plaintiffs' claims are fully satisfied pending the litigation? Will they be able adequately to represent the interests of the class? What if the named plaintiff is the class attorney who will be receiving a fee if the case is successful? Does this present a conflict of interest? Consider the following cases.

KAGAN v. GIBRALTAR SAVINGS AND LOAN ASSOCIATION

Supreme Court of California, 1984.
200 Cal.Rptr. 38, 35 Cal.3d 582, 676 P.2d 1060.

REYNOSO, JUSTICE.

May a consumer who notifies a prospective defendant of class grievances under the Consumer Legal Remedies Act and informally obtains individual relief, subsequently bring a class action for damages on behalf of herself and as a representative of the class against the prospective defendant?

Plaintiff Eleanor M. Kagan brought this action individually and as a representative of a class against the Gibraltar Savings and Loan Association (Gibraltar) and various "Doe" defendants. She alleges that Gibraltar engaged in deceptive practices proscribed by the Consumer Legal Remedies Act in falsely advertising that customers would not be charged management fees in connection with Individual Retirement Accounts. Upon a motion by Gibraltar that the action lacked merit, the trial court determined that since the threatened fee had not been deducted from plaintiff's account she "ha(d) not suffered any injury or sustained any damage cognizable under the Consumer Legal Remedies Act." Accordingly, the trial court entered judgment in favor of Gibral- tar.

Plaintiff contends that the Consumer Legal Remedies Act (Civ. Code, § 1750 et seq.) does not permit a prospective defendant to "pick off" prospective class representatives by offering them individual relief not made available to the entire class. As will appear below, we agree.

* * *

[Ms. Kagan opened an Individual Retirement Account with Gibral- tar in April of 1979, in response to Gibraltar's promotional brochure promising "No commissions. No establishment fees. No management fees." Kagan was outraged when Gibraltar informed her by letter in November of 1979] that all IRAs would be charged a $7.50 "trustee fee." On June 2, 1980, Ms. Kagan and her husband (who had also been charged a fee) sent a demand letter to Gibraltar asserting that Gibral- tar's conduct was prohibited by the California Consumer Legal Reme- dies Act (California Civil Code Section 1770), and demanding that the amounts deducted from their accounts be restored and that the false advertising cease. They threatened to sue if relief was not granted within 30 days.]

In a letter dated June 24, 1980, within the prescribed 30–day period, Gibraltar promised to remove and discard from its branch offices the disputed promotional brochures, advised that no trustee fees had been deducted from plaintiff's account, and by check reimbursed plaintiff's husband the $15 in trustee fees which had been charged his account for the years 1979 and 1980.

On July 31, 1980, plaintiff filed the instant class action, on behalf of herself and those other persons who had been induced to establish IRA accounts through Gibraltar's alleged false advertising and misrepresentations. The complaint sought actual damages for the deducted fees, declaratory and injunctive relief preventing future deductions, $5 million in punitive damages and reasonable attorneys' fees and costs.

* * *

Gibraltar contends that since the contested fee was not deducted from plaintiff's account, she no longer "suffers any damage" as required for bringing an individual action under section 1780. Therefore, Gibraltar argues, plaintiff is also precluded from bringing a class action under section 1781, which is expressly limited to "(a)ny consumer entitled to bring an action under Section 1780."

We agree that a consumer who has notified a prospective defendant of an individual grievance and has obtained his or her requested relief cannot subsequently bring either an individual or class action under the Act. However, this is not simply because the consumer no longer "suffers any damage" but because the prospective defendant has remedied the contested practices. Similarly, a prospective defendant receiving notice of a grievance which affects a class of consumers can avert a subsequent class action only by remedying the contested practices as to all affected consumers. The critical inquiry for determining whether a prospective defendant may be subject to an individual or class action is therefore whether the prospective defendant has made all remedies appropriate to the notice which it has received.

The demand letter sent Gibraltar by plaintiff and her husband requested that the "amounts deducted from their accounts for management fees be restored to their accounts, together with interest thereon." It also demanded that Gibraltar "cease its misleading and false advertising practices" and "rectif(y) * * * (its) misconduct in falsely advertising its services, as well as conditioning the conferral of an economic benefit on a contingency which will occur subsequent to the consummation of a transaction." These demands put Gibraltar on notice that its alleged violations of section 1770 affected individuals in addition to plaintiff and her husband, and possibly a broad class of consumers. This notice was formalized by the December 19, 1979, letter from plaintiff's husband to the president of Gibraltar in which he stated: "I believe Gibraltar could be guilty of a major consumer fraud if it attempts to retroactively impose trustee fees." This letter also stated that the intended charge "conflicts with both written and oral representations which were made to myself, my wife and other IRA depositors" and that Gibraltar's oral representation that the fee provision in the agreement would not be operative was presumably "conveyed to anyone else who may have noticed the provision."

As these letters, taken together, put Gibraltar on notice that its alleged violations of section 1770 affected a class of consumers, Gibraltar was under an affirmative obligation to meet the conditions set forth in section 1782, subdivision (c) in order to avert a class action. There is no evidence to indicate that Gibraltar made an effort to meet any of these conditions. Gibraltar did not seek to identify consumers similarly situated to plaintiff, or notify such consumers that it would provide them relief upon their request. Nor did Gibraltar demonstrate that it had provided requested relief to any similarly situated consumers or that it would cease from engaging in the challenged conduct within a reasonable time. Gibraltar made no mention of stopping any of its allegedly false advertising other than withdrawing its promotional brochures. Nor did Gibraltar indicate that it would require its employees to stop making the allegedly misleading oral representations. Additionally, assuming plaintiff's husband is a member of the purported class of IRA depositors fraudulently induced to open IRAs with Gibraltar, Gibraltar's reimbursement to him of the $15 which it acknowledged deducting from his 1979 and 1980 accounts did not include any compensation for the requested interest thereon.

As Gibraltar did not meet the conditions of section 1782, subdivision (c) in response to notification of its alleged class violations of section 1770, a class action for damages pursuant to section 1781, subdivision (a) may lie. * * *

* * *

Gibraltar further asserts that permitting plaintiff to bring a class action is contrary to the well recognized rule that a class representative be a member of the class which she purports to represent * * *, in this case the putative class of persons, induced to establish IRA accounts through Gibraltar's alleged misrepresentations concerning the imposition of fees, whose accounts were actually debited the trustee fee. This argument ignores the clear legislative intent that prospective defendants under the Act not avert a class action by exempting or "picking off" prospective plaintiffs one-by-one through the provision of individual remedies.

Those responsible for drafting the Act specifically sought to preclude such "picking off" of prospective class action plaintiffs:

"The most important point in connection with the settlement of class actions is that settlement with the named plaintiffs will not preclude them from further prosecuting the action on behalf of the remaining members of the class. Note that section 1782(c) precludes the further maintenance of the action only if *all* the described conditions are shown to exist. Those conditions require settlement with all reasonably identifiable members of the class. The term 'maintained' in section 1782(c) was deliberately and carefully chosen just as the term 'commenced' was deliberately avoided. *The intent was to make certain that a person can commence a class action 30 days after he has made a demand on behalf of the class even if the merchant has offered to settle his particular claim in accordance with section 1782(b).* An action so commenced may not be maintained, however, if the conditions for settlement with the class have been met. It is evident that construction of section 1782(c) so as to preclude a person from maintaining any action if his particular claim had been settled would destroy class actions under the statute. That most certainly was not the intent of the legislature." (Emphasis added.)

(Reed, Legislating For The Consumer: An Insider's Analysis Of The Consumers Legal Remedies Act (1971) 2 Pacific L.J. 1, 19.)

* * *

We now hold only that Gibraltar's exemption of plaintiff from the imposition of the trustee fee does not render her unfit per se to represent the class. In determining whether plaintiff's claims are typical of those of the class, and whether plaintiff can fairly and adequately protect the class she seeks to represent, the trial court on remand

"may take into account that the named plaintiff( ) (has) already obtained (her) individual benefits from the action; plaintiffs who have nothing at stake often will not devote sufficient energy to the prosecution of the action; further, the receipt of benefits by the named plaintiffs may sometimes create a conflict of interest between the class and its would-be representatives. * * *

We do note that plaintiff's claims appear to be typical of those of the putative class, and that the tenacity with which plaintiff has thus far pursued this matter is indicative that she has those qualities necessary to fairly and adequately protect the interests of that class. Moreover, plaintiff's demonstrated energy in pursuing this matter would appear to advance the primary purposes for maintaining a class action, by " 'eliminat(ing) the possibility of repetitious litigation and provid(ing) small claimants with a method of obtaining redress for claims which would otherwise be too small to warrant individual litigation.' " (Richmond v. Dart Industries, Inc. (1981) 29 Cal.3d 462, 469, 174 Cal.Rptr. 515, 629 P.2d 23, quoting Eisen v. Carlisle & Jacquelin (2d Cir.1968) 391 F.2d 555, 560.)

* * *

Problem 4

In Illinois, in order to maintain a class action, the court must find:

(1) the class is so numerous that joinder of all members would be impracticable;

(2) there are questions of fact or law common to the class which predominate over any questions affecting only individual members;

(3) the representative party will fairly and adequately protect the interests of the class; and

(4) a class action is an appropriate method for the fair and efficient adjudication of the controversy.

(Ill.Rev.Stat.1977, ch. 110, par. 57.2).

In a class action suit filed in Illinois, Hungry Hanna alleged that the defendant, Harvey's, had advertised and sold "roast beef" sandwiches which in fact were simulated roast beef and not the real thing. Hanna alleged that such advertising violated the Illinois Deceptive Practices Act. The sole remedy under this Act is an injunction that may be granted to a person "likely to be damaged by a deceptive trade practice of another." Ill.Rev.Stat.1977, ch. 121½, par. 313. The proposed class consisted of all Illinois residents who had purchased simulated roast beef sandwiches from Harvey's within the past three years.

Harvey's opposed the class certification on the basis that the class was unmanageable and that Hanna, the only named plaintiff, could not be granted relief under the Deceptive Practices Act because she was not "likely to be damaged" since she clearly is aware that Harvey's uses simulated roast beef. How would you rule if you were the judge in this case and why? Cf. Hayna v. Arby's, Inc., 99 Ill.App.3d 700, 55 Ill.Dec. 1, 425 N.E.2d 1174 (1981); Brooks v. Midas–International Corp., 47 Ill. App.3d 266, 5 Ill.Dec. 492, 361 N.E.2d 815 (1977); Hockley v. Hargitt, 82 Wash.2d 337, 510 P.2d 1123 (1973).

Problem 5

Your friend, Steve Sterling, a hot shot ACLU litigator but with little background in consumer protection, calls you with a problem. It seems he got a solicitation in the mail in which he received some "checks" which he was invited to use, courtesy of his credit card issuer. He accepted the invitation, only to find in his next periodic statement that he was charged a finance charge on the "checks" from the date on which he used them. He looked back at the solicitation as well as the initial and periodic disclosure statements he had received, and concluded that the finance charge was not adequately disclosed. He asks, "Isn't this a violation of some consumer protection law?" You respond, "Well, it sounds like it could be a Truth in Lending violation." Being accustomed to bringing civil rights suits that usually provide attorneys' fees to the victorious plaintiffs, Steve immediately asks whether TIL has such a provision. "Yes," you say, and "you could probably bring a class action on behalf of everyone who responded to the solicitation like you did." "What a great idea," Steve was getting excited now, he could smell revenge on the way. "I'll file a class action, representing myself as the named plaintiff, and we'll really show those creeps. They can't get away with this!" Assuming there has in fact been a TIL violation, is there any problem with the way Steve Sterling wants to handle the case?

Note

In Shroder v. Suburban Coastal Corp., 729 F.2d 1371 (11th Cir.1984), several named plaintiffs, including Gregory Pillon, brought suit against Suburban Coastal for violating TILA and Regulation Z. Plaintiff's attorney was Mr. Gregg Spieler. Plaintiff Pillon was employed in Spieler's office. The court stated that the issue was

> "whether this employment relationship between a named representative and the class attorney is such as to cause a court to properly conclude that this named representative will not fairly and adequately protect the interests of the other class members."

The stated issue was then analyzed as follows:

> The courts have held that basic consideration of fairness requires that a court undertake a stringent and continuing examination of the adequacy of representation by the named class representatives at all stages of the litigation where absent members will be bound by the court's judgment. Susman v. Lincoln American Corp., 561 F.2d 86 (7th Cir.1977), appealed after remand, 587 F.2d 866 (1978). In *Susman,* the court held that the plaintiffs were inadequate to act as class representatives where one plaintiff and one of the plaintiffs' attorneys of record were members of the same law firm. The court, in addition, held that an individual was an inadequate representative of the class where his brother was serving as attorney for the class.

> > Even though plaintiff does not expect to share in any attorney's fees recovered in this cause, there exists the possibility that one so situated will become more interested in maximizing the 'return' to his counsel than in aggressively presenting the proposed class action.

Susman, 561 F.2d at 95. The *Susman* quote stresses that even in cases where the named representative would not benefit financially from the award of attorney's fees, the representative may seek to maximize the return to his attorney. The representative is likely to do this where he has an interest in the representation and goodwill of his law firm which would be enhanced by a large attorney's fee award.

> In this case, Pillon is not an attorney in Spieler's law firm, but continues to be an employee of the law firm. Although Pillon may not share in the award of attorney's fees to Spieler in the event the class is victorious, a clear possibility remains that Pillon is interested in maximizing the return to his employer. Pillon is concerned with his future employment. Consequently, a court could rationally conclude that Pillon would be more concerned with satisfying his employer than with representing the interests of the unnamed class members.

> In *Turoff v. May Co.,* 531 F.2d 1357 (6th Cir.1976), the court held that the named plaintiffs, three of whom were attorneys with the law firm for the class and the fourth of whom was the wife of one of the first three, did not have standing to represent the class.

Because the financial recovery for reasonable attorney's fees would dwarf the individual's recovery as a member of the class herein, the financial interests of the named plaintiffs and of the class are not coextensive. If the interests of a class are to be fairly and adequately protected, if the courts and the public are to be free of manufactured litigation, and if proceedings are to be without cloud, the roles of class representative and of class attorney cannot be played by the same person.

Turoff, 531 F.2d at 1360. Since possible recovery of the class representative is far exceeded by potential attorney's fees, courts fear that a class representative who is closely associated with the class attorney would allow settlement on terms less favorable to the interests of absent class members. *Susman,* 561 F.2d at 91.

In TILA cases, courts may award reasonable attorney's fees to the prevailing class. Since Pillon is not a partner of the firm, it is unlikely that he will receive a percentage of the attorney's fees awarded to Spieler's firm if the class is victorious. In analyzing whether Pillon would be an adequate representative of the class members, we must return to the statement in *Susman* that an individual is an improper representative where there is a possibility that he will be more interested in maximizing the "return" to his attorney than in aggressively presenting the proposed class action. In the present case, this possibility clearly exists. Pillon's employment relationship with the law firm is not minimal. In his deposition, Pillon stressed that even though he does some work for others, his primary employer is Spieler's law firm. His employment gives him a financial stake in the firm which may sway his undivided interests in pursuing the interests of the class. In matters relating to settlement and the settlement amount, Pillon, as a named representative, will play a major role. These decisions will directly affect Spieler and his law firm. There clearly exists the possibility that, in making the above-cited decisions, Pillon will be concerned not so much with other class members as he will be in pleasing his employer.

* * *

And Who Pays the Victorious Consumer's Lawyer?

SKELTON v. GENERAL MOTORS CORPORATION

United States Court of Appeals, Seventh Circuit, 1988.
860 F.2d 250.

CUDAHY, CIRCUIT JUDGE.

This case arises out of a series of class actions brought against General Motors Corporation ("GM") for allegedly substituting less efficient engines and various other automotive parts (including transmissions) into certain lines of GM automobiles. The suits, brought in Illinois, New York and Washington, D.C., culminated when the consolidated class filed a complaint against GM in 1982 (for substituting less efficient transmissions in several lines of GM automobiles), under the Magnuson–Moss Warranty–Federal Trade Commission Improvement

Act, 15 U.S.C. §§ 2301–2312 (the "Magnuson–Moss Act"). The plaintiffs successfully petitioned the court for class certification and then settled with GM in 1985. Pursuant to the settlement, GM agreed to establish a $17 million fund to be distributed among the plaintiffs whose cars were affected by the substitution. As part of the settlement, the plaintiffs agreed that the fund would be the sole source of their attorneys' fees and that the fees would be calculated on an hourly rather than on a percentage-of-the-fund basis.

Class counsel submitted fee petitions based on the hours they expended multiplied by their hourly rate of payment ["lodestar"]. Counsel also requested a 75% enhancement of their fee awards to compensate for the risks undertaken in commencing this litigation. In denying the enhancement, the district court reasoned that the determination of a fee award under common fund principles is not significantly different than under a statutory fee-shifting provision. Thus, the district court held that the fee-shifting provision of the Magnuson–Moss Act is relevant to the award of fees in this case and that, under that provision, counsel are not entitled to an upward multiplier. The court alternatively concluded that, even if the Magnuson–Moss Act does not preclude the award of a multiplier, plaintiffs' counsel in this case are not entitled to a risk multiplier because the litigation never progressed beyond class certification.

I.

The issue presented by this case is whether the principles governing the shifting of attorneys' fees as between a plaintiff and a defendant are equally applicable to the division of a common fund recovery between a plaintiff class and its attorneys. The district court reasoned

> that the standards for determining reasonable attorneys fees in common fund cases and statutory fee cases should not be significantly different. In the court's view, the use of statutory fee guidelines is especially relevant where the litigation is commenced and prosecuted under a federal statute which specifically provides for an award of attorneys' fees.

Skelton v. General Motors Corp., 661 F.Supp. 1368, 1375–76 (N.D.Ill. 1987) (footnote omitted). But there are a number of reasons, based on the development of the respective doctrines and on the logic of the two problems, why these questions must be viewed separately. The factors which separate them are much more significant than those that link them.

Traditionally in the United States, parties to a lawsuit bear their own expenses. Thus, each litigant must pay its own attorney's fees without regard to the outcome of the litigation. This has become known as the "American Rule."

* * *

* * * Congress has created exceptions to the American Rule by inserting fee-shifting provisions in certain statutes. See, e.g., * * * 15 U.S.C. § 1640(a) (Truth in Lending Act); 15 U.S.C. § 2310(d)(2) (Magnuson–Moss Act) * * *. Thus, a plaintiff that prevails in an action brought under a statute with a fee-shifting provision recovers the amount of its attorney's fee from the defendant.

In contrast, when a case results in the creation of a common fund for the benefit of a plaintiff class, a court will exercise its equitable powers to award plaintiffs' attorneys' fees out of the fund. In this type of case, the defendant deposits a specified amount with the court for the benefit of the class in exchange for release of its liability. The attorneys' fee award is then taken as a share of the fund, thereby diminishing the sum ultimately retained by the plaintiff class. Similar to the way a plaintiff's attorney may be compensated by a contingent fee, a plaintiff class pays its attorneys by sharing its recovery with them.

Because there is a difference between statutory fee-shifting cases and common fund cases with respect, inter alia, to who bears the direct burden of compensating plaintiffs' attorneys, different policies may govern the two types of cases. The common fund doctrine (also known as the "equitable fund" doctrine and the "fund-in-court" doctrine) is "based on the equitable notion that those who have benefited from litigation should share its costs." Report of the Third Circuit Task Force, Court Awarded Attorney Fees 14 (Oct. 8, 1985). Statutory fee-shifting provisions, in contrast, reflect the intent of Congress "to encourage private enforcement of the statutory substantive rights, be they economic or noneconomic, through the judicial process." Report of the Third Circuit Task Force, Court Awarded Attorney Fees 15 (Oct. 8, 1985). Defendants who have violated plaintiffs' rights may be required to compensate plaintiffs for the costs incurred in enforcing those rights. Thus, in statutory fee-shifting cases, only parties (usually plaintiffs) may seek reimbursement whereas in common fund cases *attorneys* may seek compensation.

Another difference between the two types of court-awarded fee arrangements concerns the role of the plaintiffs' attorneys. In common fund cases, once the attorneys secure a settlement for the class, they petition the court for compensation from the same fund. Thus, their "role changes from one of a fiduciary for the clients to that of a claimant against the fund created for the clients' benefit." Id. at 20. The court becomes the fiduciary for the fund's beneficiaries and must carefully monitor disbursement to the attorneys by scrutinizing the fee applications. Because statutory fee cases involve the plaintiff (not his attorney) as claimant and continue to be adversary proceedings, these concerns do not arise in the same way.

The district court in this case reasoned, however, that "regardless of any theoretical distinctions between common fund and statutory fee cases, the courts in this circuit employ the same general standards to calculate attorneys fees in both types of cases." Skelton, 661 F.Supp. at

1376. To the extent that, in this circuit, both fee arrangements generally require the court to employ the lodestar approach, this observation is correct. However, when a court must decide whether to compensate attorneys for the risks they incurred in undertaking the litigation, the difference between fee-shifting and common fund arrangements is quite significant.

Panels of this court—as well as commentators and other courts—have expressed the concern that awarding risk multipliers to prevailing plaintiffs in statutory fee cases may inequitably burden defendants. For example, risk multipliers tend to penalize the parties with the strongest defenses. The stronger the defense, the higher the risk involved in bringing the suit and the greater the multiplier necessary to compensate plaintiff's attorney for bringing the action. Thus, defendants with better cases pay higher plaintiff's attorney fees. This consideration does not directly apply in a common fund case. A risk multiplier will not penalize a defendant with a strong defense since the plaintiff class (not the defendant) is responsible for compensating its attorney by sharing its recovery.

Further, assessing risk multipliers against losing defendants in effect requires these defendants to "subsidize" plaintiffs' lawyers for their unsuccessful lawsuits against other defendants. In statutory fee cases, this is "manifestly inconsistent with Congress' intent to award attorney's fees only to prevailing parties." In a common fund case, however, this result cannot directly occur because the specific amount of the fee is charged against the plaintiffs, not the defendant; the defendant's liability is limited to the amount of the common fund, which is available to provide attorneys' fees.

Therefore, the arguments—equitable and statutory—against risk multipliers in statutory fee cases have much less application in common fund cases. This may be the reason that courts awarding fees in common fund cases generally do not express the same reluctance to compensate attorneys for the risk of nonpayment.

* * *

When a case results in a common fund, courts generally follow the "equitable fund doctrine" in determining the attorney fee award. In current practice, the court exercises its equitable powers by first calculating the lodestar, taking into consideration number of hours and how they were spent and the "value of each attorney's services to the class." In re Fine Paper, 751 F.2d at 583. Next, the court may adjust the lodestar to reflect the "contingent nature of the attorney's undertaking." Id. This requires the court to assess the "likelihood of success in obtaining a judgment or settlement," as measured at the time the attorney began work on the case. Id. Thus, where appropriate, equitable fund principles allow for an upward adjustment of the lodestar.

Even in cases initiated under statutes containing fee-shifting provisions, other circuits have applied common fund principles to determine attorneys' fees when resolution of disputes results in the creation of common funds. See, e.g., In re Fine Paper, 751 F.2d 502; City of Detroit v. Grinnell Corp., 495 F.2d 448 (2d Cir.1974). The Second Circuit, in an antitrust class action that resulted in a $10 million settlement explained that it must use common fund principles to determine attorneys' fees because

> the Clayton Act, which provides for the award of attorneys' fees in civil antitrust suits generally, does not authorize award of attorneys' fees to a plaintiff who does not recover a judgment or who settles his claim with the defendant * * *. The only basis for awarding an attorney's fees in such cases is the equitable fund theory doctrine * * *.

Id. at 468–69 (citations omitted). * * *

* * *

Moreover, looking specifically at the Magnuson–Moss Act, the fee-shifting provision, by its terms, does not purport to apply to a fee determination in a case settled in a common fund. The provision provides for the award of attorney's fees as part of the *judgment* if the consumer "finally prevails" in an action brought under the statute. 15 U.S.C. § 2310(d)(2). Nor is there any evidence in the legislative history of Congress' intent to apply the fee-shifting provision to common fund or settlement cases of any kind.

* * *

II.

Having concluded that plaintiffs' counsel are not precluded from seeking a fee enhancer to compensate for contingency we turn to the question whether under the circumstances of this case they are entitled to the risk multiplier they seek. The district court held that a risk multiplier is unnecessary to fully compensate the attorneys because "the action never proceeded very far beyond the initial pleading stages." Skelton, 661 F.Supp. at 1392.

* * *

Here the district court erred in basing its denial of a risk multiplier on the fact that the parties settled at a relatively early stage in the litigation. The point at which plaintiffs settle with defendants (or win a judgment against defendants) is simply not relevant to determining the risks incurred by their counsel in agreeing to represent them. * * * In the present case (as in all similar cases), the early settlement is reflected in the [fact that] lodestar-plaintiffs' counsel worked fewer hours than they would have if the case had gone to trial.

Because we conclude that early settlement is an insufficient basis for denying a risk multiplier, we remand this case to the district court to consider whether class counsel are entitled to compensation for incurring the risk of nonpayment.

* * *

Notes and Questions

1. The so-called "lodestar" formula is a method used in calculating reasonable attorney's fees in many consumer protection matters. The

lodestar is first calculated by multiplying the total number of hours reasonably expended on the case by a reasonable hourly rate of compensation. In determining what is reasonable for the hourly rate, the court may consider the attorney's usual hourly rate, the level of skill required by the particular litigation, judicially imposed time limits, the attorney's reputation and the undesirability of the case. Once the lodestar is set, this sum is sometimes multiplied by a risk factor to compensate the attorney for the risk that she would receive no fee if the case were lost. See Bowers v. Transamerica Title Ins. Co., 100 Wash.2d 581, 675 P.2d 193, 201–204 (1983).

2. Does the approach taken by the *Skelton* court mean that attorneys in Magnuson–Moss and other fee-shifting statutory cases will have an incentive to settle and set up a common fund rather than to take the case to judgment and receive a court-awarded fee that is less likely to include a risk multiplier? Will the court be able adequately to protect the plaintiffs' interests in this respect? On the other hand, will allowing a risk multiplier to be taken in an attorney fee award from a common fund mean that consumers will be more likely to find attorneys to represent them in doubtful or difficult cases? And if attorneys have an incentive to settle, isn't it a good thing to promote settlements, which saves the expense of further litigation?

Problem 6

Howard Helpful is a young attorney with a storefront office and a general practice. When Ima Victim consulted him because she was being pestered by Friendly Finance Co., he discovered an error in Friendly's Truth in Lending disclosure statement. Howard filed a class action under the Truth in Lending Act, which Friendly's attorneys resisted vigorously. After two years, the judge decided that there had been an unintentional, short-duration violation of TILA, and enjoined any further violations. She further decided that, since the violation was in the printed language of the form and no member of the class had read that printing, no member of the class had suffered actual damage and no member would recover monetary damages.

Howard then sought attorney's fees under TILA § 130(a)(3). Since the violation he had discovered was novel, he had worked long and hard on the case. He sought compensation for 500 hours at $30 per hour with a contingency factor multiplier of 1.5, because his theory of the case was entirely original, for a total of $22,500. The judge humphed, said that ordinarily she would permit only 15% of the total recovery as reasonable attorney's fees, but that would be $0, so she would allow Howard "the minimum recovery" of $100.

The case is being appealed on several grounds; one of them is the attorney fee award. On that issue, what are the arguments on appeal, and who should win? Should a rational legal system pay over $20,000 to resolve a dispute in which no one has been hurt?

Chapter 19

DETERRENTS AND NUCLEAR WEAPONS

Prefatory Note

As consumer-merchant or consumer-creditor fighting escalates, there are weapons available which are intended to punish prior conduct. They include: (1) the civil sanction of punitive damages, which may require disgorging ill-gotten gains or may bankrupt the wrongdoer; (2) the criminal sanctions of fines or imprisonment, although the former are usually so light that they may be merely a small cost of doing business, and the latter is rarely accomplished; and (3) the regulatory sanctions of license revocation or suspension, dissolution of the corporation, or an injunction prohibiting a company from doing any further business in the jurisdiction. This approach might best be termed "corporate capital punishment", although it may not affect the corporation's owner nearly so drastically.

Are these "nuclear" weapons effective deterrents? Or are they so rarely used that many violators are willing to take a chance and those who are caught assume they have just been unlucky? What types of cases are most appropriate for the use of nuclear weapons?

SECTION A. PUNITIVE DAMAGES IN INDIVIDUAL ACTIONS

WALKER v. SHELDON

New York Court of Appeals, 1961.
10 N.Y.2d 401, 223 N.Y.S.2d 488, 179 N.E.2d 497.

FULD, JUDGE.

This appeal, here by permission of the Appellate Division on a certified question, calls upon us to decide whether punitive damages may be allowed in a fraud and deceit action.

The complaint alleges that the plaintiff was induced to enter into a contract with the defendant Comet Press and pay it $1,380 by means of a number of false and fraudulent representations made by the individual defendants who are officers of Comet. The representations, as well as the respects in which they are false, are set forth at some length. The complaint also alleges that the misrepresentations were made "in the regular course of [defendants'] business, and as the basis of their business knowing that plaintiff would, as others similarly situated had in the past, act upon said representations". Consequently, the plaintiff seeks, in addition to compensatory damages of $1,380, punitive damages in the amount of $75,000.

The defendants moved to strike certain allegations of the complaint as irrelevant and prejudicial. The court at Special Term denied the motions in their entirety and the Appellate Division, although it modified the resulting orders by directing that some of the recitals be stricken, upheld the allegations which relate to punitive damages.

It was the conclusion of the Appellate Division that, if the plaintiff is able to prove (what in effect she alleges) that the defendants were engaged in carrying on "a virtually larcenous scheme to trap generally the unwary", a jury would be justified in granting punitive damages. We agree with that view.

Punitive or exemplary damages have been allowed in cases where the wrong complained of is morally culpable, or is actuated by evil and reprehensible motives, not only to punish the defendant but to deter him, as well as others who might otherwise be so prompted, from indulging in similar conduct in the future. Moreover, the possibility of an award of such damages may not infrequently induce the victim, otherwise unwilling to proceed because of the attendant trouble and expense, to take action against the wrongdoer. Indeed, such self-interest of the plaintiff has been characterized as "Perhaps the principal advantage" of sanctioning punitive damages because it "leads to the actual prosecution of the claim for punitive damages, where the same motive would often lead him to refrain from the trouble incident to appearing against the wrongdoer in criminal proceedings".

Although they have been refused in the "ordinary" fraud and deceit case, we are persuaded that, on the basis of analogy, reason and principle, there may be a recovery of exemplary damages in fraud and deceit actions where the fraud, aimed at the public generally, is gross and involves high moral culpability. And this court has—in line with what appears to be the weight of authority sanctioned an award of such damages in a fraud and deceit case where the defendant's conduct evinced a high degree of moral turpitude and demonstrated such wanton dishonesty as to imply a criminal indifference to civil obligations. (See Kujek v. Goldman, 150 N.Y. 176, 44 N.E. 773, supra.) In the Kujek case, the plaintiff married Katy Moritz—a domestic employed in the family of the defendant, by whom she had become pregnant—in reliance upon the defendant's fraudulent representation that Katy was "a virtuous and respectable woman". After noting that the plaintiff had sustained actual damages, the court went on to hold that "as the wrong involved not only malice, but moral turpitude also, in accordance with the analogies of the law upon the subject the jury had the right to make the damages exemplary". These exemplary damages, the court declared, were left to the jury "in their sound discretion * * * to amplify the damages [actually caused] by way of punishment and example".

Exemplary damages are more likely to serve their desired purpose of deterring similar conduct in a fraud case, such as that before us, than in any other area of tort. One who acts out of anger or hate, for instance, in committing assault or libel, is not likely to be deterred by the fear of punitive damages. On the other hand, those who deliberately and cooly engage in a far-flung fraudulent scheme, systematically conducted for profit, are very much more likely to pause and consider the consequences if they have to pay more than the actual loss suffered by an individual plaintiff. An occasional award of compensatory damages against such parties would have little deterrent effect. A judgment simply for compensatory damages would require the offender to do no more than return the money which he had taken from the plaintiff. In the calculation of his expected profits, the wrongdoer is likely to allow for a certain amount of money which will have to be returned to those victims who object too vigorously, and he will be perfectly content to bear the additional cost of litigation as the price for continuing his illicit business. It stands to reason that the chances of deterring him are materially increased by subjecting him to the payment of punitive damages.

It may be difficult to formulate an all-inclusive rule or principle as to what is an appropriate case for the recovery of punitive damages, but it is our conclusion that the allegations of the complaint before us, if proved, would justify such an award. The pleading charges that defrauding the general public into entering publishing contracts, such as the one involved in the present case, was the very basis of the defendants' business. What is asserted is not an isolated transaction incident to an otherwise legitimate business, but a gross and wanton fraud upon the public. It follows, therefore, that the courts below were thoroughly justified in refusing to strike the allegations which pertain to punitive damages.

The orders of the Appellate Division should be affirmed, with costs, and the question certified as to each order answered in the affirmative.

VAN VOORHIS, JUDGE (dissenting).

In our view the rules for the allowance of punitive or exemplary damages should not be extended to the facts of this case. The very circumstance that plaintiff asks for compensatory damages of $1,380 and punitive damages in the amount of $75,000 is an excellent illustration of the reasons on account of which the award of punitive damages should be restricted rather than extended to situations where they are not as yet traditionally allowed. In Dain v. Wycoff, 7 N.Y. 191, 193–194 the court used language which is applicable to the present situation: "There can be no reason why twelve men wholly irresponsible should be allowed to go beyond the issue between the parties litigating, and after indemnifying the plaintiff for the injury sustained by him proceed as conservators of the public morals to punish the defendant in a private action for an offence against society. If the jury have the right to impose a fine by way of example, the plaintiff has no possible claim to it, nor ought the court to interfere and set it aside, however excessive it may be. In ordinary cases of misdemeanor, the legislature have restricted the power of the court in the imposition of penalties within certain definite limits. But a jury in civil actions have by this hypothesis an unlimited discretion to determine the crime and upon the measure of redress demanded by the public interest. The right stands upon no principle nor, in reference to actions of this character upon any authority."

* * *

DESMOND, C.J., and DYE and BURKE, JJ., concur with FULD, J.

VAN VOORHIS, J., dissents in an opinion in which FROESSEL and FOSTER, JJ., concur.

Orders affirmed, etc.

HARDY v. TOLER

Supreme Court of North Carolina, 1975.
288 N.C. 303, 218 S.E.2d 342.

MOORE, JUSTICE.

Plaintiff first assigns as error the holding of the Court of Appeals affirming the action of the trial court in allowing defendants' motion for a directed verdict under Rule 50(a) as to the issue of punitive damages.

This action is based upon fraudulent representations made by Toler on behalf of himself and his principal, Pamlico Motor Company, which were relied upon by the plaintiff in purchasing the automobile in question. Defendants represented to the plaintiff that the automobile was a one-owner vehicle which had been driven approximately 23,000 miles, that it had never been wrecked, and that the Chrysler warranty could and would be transferred to plaintiff. Plaintiff offered testimony tending to show that all of these representations were false. The parties stipulated that the car had had two prior owners, had been involved in a wreck, and that the Chrysler warranty would not transfer to plaintiff. Although the plaintiff's evidence and the stipulations of the parties provide ample basis for a recovery based on actionable fraud, this was not sufficient to subject the defendants to punitive damages.

In North Carolina, whether a person may recover punitive damages in an action for fraud depends upon the character of the acts alleged to constitute fraud in each case. Furthermore, it is the general rule that ordinarily punitive damages are not recoverable in an action for fraud.

In *Nunn v. Smith,* 270 N.C. 374, 154 S.E.2d 497 (1967), the Court quoted with approval from *Swinton v. Realty Co.,* 236 N.C. 723, 73 S.E.2d 785 (1953), which held that plaintiffs were not entitled to punitive damages in an action for fraud merely upon a showing of misrepresentations which constituted the cause of action, without more:

" ' * * * " 'Punitive damages' are damages, other than compensatory or nominal damages, awarded against a person to punish him for his outrageous conduct." * * *

*   *   *   *   *   *   *   *   *

" 'We are inclined to the view that the facts in evidence here are not sufficient to warrant the allowance of punitive damages. There was no evidence of insult, indignity, malice, oppression or bad motive other than the same false representations for which they have received the amount demanded.' "

Punitive damages may be awarded only where the wrong is done willfully or under circumstances of rudeness, oppression or in a manner which evidences a reckless and wanton disregard of the plaintiff's rights. The court correctly refused to submit an issue as to punitive damages. This assignment is overruled.

* * *

HUSKINS, JUSTICE (concurring in result).

We have said that punitive damages are damages, other than compensatory or nominal damages, awarded against a person " 'to punish him for his outrageous conduct.' * * * In some cases, in actions to recover damages for fraud, where punitive damages are asked, it is suggested that a line of demarcation be drawn between aggravated fraud and simple fraud, with punitive damages allowable in the one case and refused in the other. In a note in 165 A.L.R. 616, it is said: 'All that can be said is that to constitute aggravated fraud there must be some additional element of asocial behavior which goes beyond the facts necessary to create a case of simple fraud.' " *Swinton v. Realty Co.,* 236 N.C. 723, 73 S.E.2d 785 (1953).

In the case before us defendants represented that the car involved was a one-owner car, had been driven only 23,000 miles, had never been wrecked, and that the warranty could be transferred to plaintiff. Plaintiff purchased the vehicle upon those representations. The truth of the matter was that the car was a second-owner vehicle, had been wrecked, had been driven 80,000 miles when plaintiff bought it, and the warranty could not be transferred. When plaintiff discovered the truth and sought to rescind the contract, Toler denied that the car had been wrecked and said plaintiff must have wrecked it himself. In the face of all that, both defendants *stipulated* at the trial that they knew at the time of the sale that the vehicle had been sold on two previous occasions and had been involved in a wreck prior to the sale to plaintiff. And uncontradicted evidence shows that defendants knew the car had over 80,000 miles on it while telling plaintiff the mileage was only 23,000. In my view such conduct is "outrageous conduct" and contains an additional element of asocial behavior which goes beyond simple fraud and constitutes aggravated fraud. Nothing else appearing, the facts in evidence here are sufficient to warrant the allowance of punitive damages.

I concur in the result reached in this case, however, because G.S. § 75–16 is itself punitive in nature and provides for the recovery of damages in treble the amount fixed by the verdict. Having sought and recovered treble damages, plaintiff's right to punitive damages is thereby excluded. For these reasons I concur in the result reached by the majority.

JUSTICES LAKE and EXUM, join in this concurring opinion.

Notes

1. In Jeffers v. Nysse, 98 Wis.2d 543, 297 N.W.2d 495 (1980), the Wisconsin Supreme Court upheld an award of $3,000 in punitive damages against a housing developer who deliberately misrepresented the heating costs of a home, knowing that the insulation was insufficient. The court (like most in common law fraud cases) stressed that the motive of self-interest was sufficient to support an award of punitive damages, so long as the conduct was deliberate or reckless. There was no need to prove actual malice in the sense of hatred or personal animosity toward the victim. The court in the *Jeffers* case also saw punitive damages as having a deterrent effect:

> "[P]utting the cookies back in the jar" when caught is not enough. If that result were reached, sellers could make any misrepresentation necessary to make a sale. If it was not discovered, or was discovered but not pursued, the seller would make a windfall gain. If the fraud were discovered and successfully proven, the seller would only be liable to make good on his representations. He would suffer no punishment nor would he be deterred from similar conduct in the future.

Id. 297 N.W.2d at 499.

Does the deterrent theory overlook the fact that defendants will incur substantial legal expenses in addition to any actual damages awarded and thus may already be suffering a financial loss in excess of actual damages?

2. Should the materiality of a deliberate and gross misrepresentation dictate whether or not there should be an award of punitive damages? For example, how would a jury or a judge react to a request for punitive damages for the deliberate misrepresentation of the self-defrosting capability of a refrigerator? See Mid–Continent Refrigerator Co. v. Straka, 47 Wis. 2d 739, 178 N.W.2d 28 (1970). Does it make sense under the deterrent theory to factor in the amount of the loss to the victim?

3. Should there be a ceiling on the size of punitive damage awards? If so, what criteria would be relevant in setting such a limit?

4. Should a plaintiff be able to collect punitive damages for fraud in addition to treble damages for violation of the state unfair and deceptive trade practices act? Does it matter how egregious the fraud?

5. Is it appropriate for the court to consider the fact that an award of punitive damages may be "passed on" to future customers in the form of higher prices, or that a company might be put out of business by a large judgment? Or that the liability insurance costs of all companies may be raised? Consider the following from Judge Friendly in Roginsky v. Richardson–Merrell, Inc., 378 F.2d 832 (2d Cir.1967):

> Although multiple punitive awards running into the hundreds may not add up to a denial of due process, nevertheless if we were sitting as the highest court of New York we would wish to consider very seriously whether awarding punitive damages with respect to the negligent—even highly negligent—manufacture and sale of a drug governed by federal food and drug requirements, especially in the light of the strengthening of these by the 1962 amendments, and the present vigorous attitude toward enforcement, would not do more harm than good. A manufacturer distributing a drug to many thousands of users under government regulation scarcely requires this additional measure for manifesting social disapproval and assuring deterrence. Criminal penalties and heavy compensatory damages, recoverable under some circumstances even without proof of negligence, should sufficiently meet these objectives, and the other factors cited as justifying punitive awards are lacking. Many awards of compensatory damages doubtless contain something of a punitive element, and more would do so if a separate award for exemplary damages were eliminated. Even though products liability insurance blunts the deterrent effect of compensatory coverage under such policies * * * to a considerable extent, the total limited, bad experience is usually reflected in future rates, and insurance affords no protection to the damage to reputation among physicians and pharmacists which an instance like the present must inevitably produce. On the other hand, the apparent impracticability of imposing an effective ceiling on punitive awards in hundreds of suits in different courts may result in an aggregate which, when piled on large compensatory damages, could reach catastrophic amounts. If liability policies can protect against this risk as several courts have held, the cost of providing this probably needless deterrence, not only to the few manufacturers from whom punitive damages for highly negligent conduct are sought but to the thousands from whom it never will be, is passed on to the consuming public; if they cannot, as is held by other courts and recommended by most commentators, a sufficiently egregious error as to one product can end the business life of a concern that has wrought much good in the past and might otherwise have continued to do so in the future, with many innocent stockholders suffering extinction of their investments for a single management sin.

> * * * [W]e are convinced that the consequences of imposing punitive damages in a case like the present are so serious that the New York Court of Appeals would subject the proof to particularly careful scrutiny.

6. Judge Friendly in *Roginsky* says he is applying New York law, as he is bound to do under the *Erie* doctrine. *Walker v. Sheldon,* supra Note 1, is the leading New York case, but the *Roginsky* opinion does not mention

it. Does *Roginsky* really attempt to use the policies underlying New York law?

Problem 1

May D. Marion, with offices in North Carolina, runs a "credit repair" scam of the type discussed in Chapter 4, Section A2, at pages 237–240. She advertises in magazines with national circulation. Robbin Hood, a New York resident, who has a very bad credit history, sees her advertisement and responds. Hood paid a fee, and Marion represented that she would repair his negative credit history, but she was not able to do so. In fact, as was pointed out in Chapter 4, Marion's attempts to "dispute" negative items and then negotiate their removal has been uniformly unsuccessful with the credit reporting industry, and she was aware that it had not been successful for previous clients.

Hood wants to sue Marion for this fraud. She is willing to refund Hood's fee to him. You are Hood's attorney. The New York long-arm statute will allow you to sue Marion in New York, but litigation will make sense only if you can recover punitive damages from Marion on the fraud claim. Can you do that? Even though you have jurisdiction in New York, that does not determine which law applies to the transaction—New York or North Carolina law. (See Chapter 15, Section C). If New York law applies, is recovery of punitive damages certain? If North Carolina law applies, how can you argue for recovery of punitive damages?

SECTION B. CRIMINAL SANCTIONS

Many consumer protection statutes contain criminal penalties for violators. See, for example, U3C § 5.301; TILA § 112; FCRA §§ 619, 620. The Motor Vehicle Information and Cost Savings Act prohibits tampering with odometers, and requires accurate disclosure of the mileage or a disclosure that the mileage is unknown upon the transfer of any motor vehicle. Violations are subject to criminal penalties. 15 U.S.C.A. § 1990b–c. Most states have also enacted criminal sanctions for false advertising (so-called "Printers Ink" statutes), or other fraudulent conduct.

BOREN v. STATE

Supreme Court of Arkansas, 1988.
297 Ark. 220, 761 S.W.2d 885.

HAYS, JUSTICE.

In this case, Bill Boren, Jr., appeals a conviction under Ark.Code Ann. § 4–90–204(d) (1987), failure to disclose the alteration of an odometer on a vehicle offered for sale. He has raised two issues on appeal, neither of which has merit.

Bill Boren, Jr. was operating a used car dealership under the name Boren Motor Company. The police received an anonymous tip that there had been some odometer "rollbacks" on cars connected to that dealership. Further investigations were conducted resulting in appellant being charged with four counts of tampering with odometers, Ark. Code Ann. § 4–90–204 (1987) (Ark.Stat.Ann. § 75–2402(4) (1979)).

On May 20, 1987, a jury trial was held in the Circuit Court of Crawford County, Arkansas. When the state rested its case, appellant moved for a directed verdict based on the state's failure to prove knowledge of alteration. The motion was denied and at the close of the appellant's case the motion was renewed and again denied. The jury returned a verdict of guilty on all four counts and imposed a fine of $1,000 on each count and additionally, a term of one year on count two.

I

* * *

Appellant was prosecuted under Ark.Code Ann. § 4–90–204 (1987), which reads in part:

> (d) No person shall sell or offer for sale any motor vehicle with knowledge that the mileage registered on the odometer has been altered so as to reflect a lower mileage than the motor vehicle has actually been driven without disclosing such fact to prospective buyers.

We have not had occasion to interpret our odometer act, Ark.Code Ann. § 4–90–201 (1987) et seq., so we have looked for authority from cases under the federal act, 15 U.S.C.A. § 1981 (1982) et seq., which is very similar to the Arkansas act, and to acts in other states. For the state to prove its case against appellant under § 4–90–204(d) (1987), it was necessary to show that appellant had knowledge that the mileage registered on the odometers had been altered so as to reflect a lower mileage, and that he failed to disclose this fact to prospective buyers.[1]

To prove an alteration of an odometer was done with knowledge and, therefore, intentionally it has generally been held that if it is shown that the alteration took place while the automobile was under the dominion and control of the defendant or his agents the evidence is sufficient.

Evidence of alteration is often circumstantial; usually alteration is shown by contrasting the higher odometer reading prior to the sale to the defendant and the lower reading at the time the defendant sells the vehicle to a customer. Proof of the earlier higher reading has come from testimony of a previous owner, applications for certificates of title on file in the motor vehicle department, testimony of a mechanic or service manager who recorded the mileage on a repair order, or any official records citing the vehicle's odometer reading.

1. While appellant does not raise this point, we note that in order to prove a defendant had knowledge of an odometer rollback, the state need not show any intent to defraud or any evil purpose. In a similar federal statute, the alteration of an odometer is a criminal offense if done "knowingly and willfully." 15 U.S.C. §§ 1984, 1990c. This was interpreted to mean only an intentional violation of a known legal duty, and nothing more was required than to show the intent to do the act. United States v. Studna, 713 F.2d 416 (8th Cir.1983) ("Alterations performed with innocent motives have the same capacity to mislead purchasers as those done with evil motives.")

Here the state presented sufficient evidence to show the automobiles were under the dominion and control of appellant during the time the alteration took place. The state presented evidence regarding the four different cars that were purchased, which essentially related the sales transaction and the odometer reading on each car at the time of purchase. This testimony clearly established, with no dispute from appellant, what the lower reading was at the time of sale to appellant's customers.

The state also presented sufficient evidence to show the cars were under the control of the appellant at the time the vehicles showed a higher reading on the odometer. The four vehicles in question had been purchased from the 166 Auto Auction. Mary Jo Henson, the office manager of the auction presented invoices for each of the four cars. Each invoice identified the car and indicated the mileage registered on the odometer at the time it was auctioned. In each case, there was a difference ranging from 25,000 to 45,000 miles on the readings at the time of auction and the later sale by the appellant. The name of the buyer on each invoice was Boren Motor Company. The state also introduced a privilege license purchased by appellant, showing that Bill Boren, Jr. was authorized to operate under the name Boren Motor Company.

* * *

* * * We find there was sufficient evidence to show appellant's dominion and control over the vehicles during the time that the alteration of the odometers took place.

In addition to knowledge of the alterations, it was necessary for the state to show the vehicles were sold by appellant, without disclosing to the purchasers the alterations and the resultant lower mileage. The purchasers of the cars testified that while appellant had given them a completed disclosure form, there was no other attempt by him to disclose the alteration. In fact, he gave verbal reassurances to two of the customers that the odometers were correct to the best of his knowledge. The disclosure form, however, far from disclosing any alterations, indicated the opposite and there is no way we can find from the form that appellant had disclosed the required information.

Appellant had checked two statements on the disclosure form. The first read: "I hereby certify that the odometer of said vehicle was not altered, set back, or disconnected while in my possession, and I have no knowledge of anyone else doing so." This statement is clearly the antithesis of disclosing that there had been an alteration of the odometer.

The second statement checked by appellant stated: "I certify that to the best of my knowledge, the odometer reading as stated above is not the actual mileage of the vehicle described below and should not be relied upon." Even considering this statement standing on its own, appellant has not given the required disclosure. This statement does not reveal that the reading is actually lower than what has been driven, but only that it is inaccurate. To merely say that the mileage is inaccurate is an ambiguous statement at best and could refer to any number of circumstances. It certainly does not equate to a disclosure that the odometer has been altered so as to reflect a lower mileage than the car has actually been driven. The statement not only misstates the facts as appellant knows them to be, but it deprives the customer of essential information and misleads him or her as to the true circumstances.

* * *

When we also consider the other statement checked on the form—that there had been no alteration of the odometers—the misleading character of the disclosure document becomes overwhelmingly predominant. If appellant were attempting to neutralize or qualify the false statement as to the alterations, by the second statement of inaccuracy, he has failed. When the statement on inaccuracy is read in conjunction with the statement that there has been no alteration, it becomes even clearer that the customer is not only deprived of essential information, but is misled as to the true nature of the facts.

If we were to hold otherwise, a dealer could readily alter the odometers, warrant the opposite on the disclosure statement, and sell cars with impunity by checking a second ambiguous statement on the disclosure form. This cannot have been the intent underlying the required disclosure under state law, or the requirement of the federal disclosures. The purpose of disclosure of odometer information is to "enable the purchaser of a motor vehicle to know how many miles the vehicle has traveled, as a guide to its safety, reliability and value." *Ryan,* supra. If the dealers can manipulate the disclosure forms to suit their purposes, the customers would be better off without the required disclosure.

* * *

Affirmed.

NEWBERN, JUSTICE, dissenting.

The appellant, Bill Boren, Jr., was convicted of four counts of violating Ark.Code Ann. § 4–90–204(d) (1987) which prohibits sale of an automobile with knowledge that the mileage on the odometer shows fewer miles than the automobile has actually been driven without disclosing that fact to the buyer. I agree with Boren's argument that a directed verdict should have been granted in his favor because the state's evidence showed that he disclosed to the buyers of the cars that the mileage shown on the odometers was not accurate and was not to be relied on by the buyers.

The state's witnesses included the purchasers of three cars from Boren Motor Company, owned and operated by Bill Boren, Jr. Chris Fox testified he bought a car from Boren, and Boren told him the odometer mileage was correct to the best of his knowledge. On cross-examination, Fox stated when he bought the car he received from Boren an "Odometer Mileage Statement." It is a statement made on a form which is prescribed by federal regulations, and it contains basic information about the car, including the mileage shown on the odometer at the time of sale. The form has two groups of three alternative statements. Only one in each group of three may be checked by the seller. Fox testified that on the form he received, the box next to the following statement was checked: "I certify that to the best of my knowledge, the odometer reading as stated above is not the actual mileage of the vehicle described below and should not be relied upon." The second "not" was underlined. In the second group, the following statement was checked: "I hereby certify the odometer of said vehicle was not altered, set back or disconnected while in my possession, and I have no knowledge of anyone else doing so." Fox's signature, acknowledging receipt of a copy of the form appears at the bottom. The form is reproduced below.

Section 580.6 Disclosure form.

ODOMETER MILEAGE STATEMENT

(Federal regulations require you to state the odometer mileage upon transfer of ownership. An inaccurate or untruthful statement may make you liable for damages to your transferee, for attorney fees, and for civil or criminal penalties, pursuant to sections 409, 412, and 413 of the Motor Vehicle Information and Cost Savings Act of 1972 (Pub. L. 92-513, as amended by Pub. L. 94-364).

I, _Boren Motor Co._____, state that the odometer of
   (transferor's name - PRINT)

the vehicle described below now reads _25,426_____ miles/kilometers.

Check one box only.

☐ (1) I hereby certify that to the best of my knowledge the odometer reading as stated above reflects the actual mileage of the vehicle described below.

☐ (2) I hereby certify that to the best of my knowledge the odometer reading as stated above reflects the amount of mileage in excess of designed mechanical odometer limit of 99,999 miles/kilometers of the vehicle described below.

☒ (3) I hereby certify that to the best of my knowledge the odometer reading as stated above is NOT the actual mileage of the vehicle described below, and should not be relied upon.

MAKE	MODEL	BODY TYPE
Dodge	Lancer	4 Door
VEHICLE IDENTIFICATION NUMBER 1B3BX48D4FN137345		YEAR 1985

Check one box only.

☒ (1) I hereby certify that the odometer of said vehicle was not altered, set back, or disconnected while in my possession, and I have no knowledge of anyone else doing so.

☐ (2) I hereby certify that the odometer was altered for repair or replacement purposes while in my possession, and that the mileage registered on the repaired or replacement odometer was identical to that before such service.

☐ (3) I hereby certify that the repaired or replacement odometer was incapable of registering the same mileage, that it was reset to zero, and that the mileage on the original odometer or the odometer before repair was _____ miles.

Transferor's Address (seller)   _1418 Fayetteville Rd_____
                                 Street
                                 _Van Buren_____ _AR_   _72956_
                                 (city)   (state) (zip code)

Transferor's Signature (seller) _Bill Boren_____

Date of Statement _3-9-87_____

Transferee's Name and Address (buyer) _Christopher Fox 630 N 4th 13th_
                                        (street)
                                        Van Buren _AR_ _72956_
                                        (city)   (state) (zip code)

Receipt of Copy Acknowledged _Christopher P. Fox_____
                             (transferee's signature - buyer)

                                                                [F9628]

                              *   *   *

The odometer disclosure statement form used by Boren is the one federal law requires dealers to use in states which have not adopted an official form which meets federal requirements. See 49 CFR 580.4, 580.6. We cannot know what the jurors thought, but it may be that they felt Boren had not told the truth when he stated on the form that the odometer on each of the cars was not rolled back while the car was in his possession and that he had no knowledge of anyone else doing so. There was, as the state argues, circumstantial evidence that the rollbacks occurred while the cars were in Boren's possession. That, however, if it is a crime, is not one with which Boren was charged.

The majority opinion is intent on affirming this conviction because "the misleading character of the disclosure document becomes overwhelmingly predominant." It ignores the fact that the form used by Boren is the one he is required to use by federal law. The majority opinion states, "the customer was deprived of essential information and is misled as to the true facts." The point is that Boren was tried and convicted for selling a car with a rolled back odometer without disclosure. He was convicted of violation of a particular criminal law statute and not some vague concept of misrepresentation.

The effect of the majority opinion is not only to ignore the rule that we construe criminal statutes strictly, it ignores the provision in the statute which permits conviction only for sale of a vehicle with a lowered odometer reading "without disclosing such fact to prospective purchasers." Given the failure of the state's evidence to show any sale was made "without disclosure" the judgment of the trial court should be reversed, and the case dismissed.

I respectfully dissent.

PURTLE and DUDLEY, JJ., join this opinion.

Notes

1. Was the crime in the *Boren* case really victimless, since the purchasers should have been put on notice that something was wrong with the odometer reading by Boren's peculiar manner of filling out the disclosure form?

2. Which opinion in *Boren* follows the will of the Arkansas legislature more closely, that of the majority or Judge Newbern's dissent? Did the majority view this as merely a disclosure violation, or something more? Why didn't the Arkansas legislature simply make odometer tampering a crime?

3. The criminal offense of odometer tampering came to the attention of the Supreme Court in Schmuck v. United States, 489 U.S. 705, 109 S.Ct. 1443, 103 L.Ed.2d 734 (1989). Defendant Schmuck purchased used vehicles, rolled back their odometers, and then sold the cars to unwitting dealers at inflated prices, who in turn sold to unwitting consumers. The government charged the defendant under the federal mail fraud act, 18 U.S.C.A. §§ 1341–2. The majority ruled that the mailing element of the statute was met by the mailing of title-application forms by the dealers, and that the defendant was not entitled to a lesser included offense instruction on odometer tampering under the Motor Vehicle Information and Cost Savings Act, 15 U.S.C.A. §§ 1984, 1990c(a).

Justice Scalia, joined by Brennan, Marshall and O'Connor, dissented on the basis that the mail fraud statute does not establish a general federal remedy against fraudulent conduct, with use of the mails as the jurisdictional hook * * *. This federal statute is not violated by a fraudulent scheme in which, at some point, a mailing happens to occur—nor even by one in which a mailing predictably and necessarily occurs. The mailing must be in furtherance of the fraud.

Id., 109 S.Ct. at 1454. Justice Blackmun, writing for the majority, stated that:

Schmuck's scheme would have come to an abrupt halt if the dealers either had lost faith in Schmuck or had not been able to resell the cars obtained from him. These resales and Schmuck's relationships with the retail dealers naturally depended on the successful passage of title among the various parties. Thus, although the registration-form mailings may not have contributed directly to the duping of either the retail dealers or the customers, they were necessary to the passage of title, which in turn was essential to the perpetuation of Schmuck's scheme.

Id., 109 S.Ct. at 1448.

Is the ruling in *Schmuck* likely to lead to an onslaught of consumer cases being prosecuted under the mail fraud statute? Why do you suppose the government took on the apparently difficult task of making this charge stick as a mail fraud case, rather than simply charging Schmuck with a criminal violation of the odometer tampering statute?

Problem 2

The Butcher Block Corporation was engaged in the business of selling bulk beef at retail, which it advertised at unusually low prices in the local newspapers. Customers who responded to the advertisements were shown the sale beef which was fatty, discolored and generally unappetizing. The salesperson would advise the customer that the loss of fat and bone in trimming would make such a purchase unwise. The salesclerk would then show the customer much better looking meat at a higher price, and would allege that there would be minimal loss from trimming such beef. Except in one instance, each customer was persuaded to purchase the more expensive beef. The advertised price for the sale beef was less than the price paid for it by Butcher Block.

The above facts come to your attention as a staff attorney in the state attorney general's office, consumer protection division. (Indeed, your office sent an undercover agent to Butcher Block posing as a customer). Your state has the following criminal statute, which carries a penalty of up to six months in jail and/or a $500 fine:

A person is guilty of false advertising when, with intent to promote the sale or to increase the consumption of property or services, he makes or causes to be made a false or misleading statement in any advertisement * * *

You could also obtain a civil injunction against the following practice under your state's general business law, for a violation of the following section:

No person, firm, partnership, association or corporation, or agent or employee thereof, shall, in any manner, or by any means of advertisement, or other means of communication, offer for sale any merchandise, commodity, or service, as part of a plan or scheme with the intent, design, or purpose not to sell the merchandise, commodity or service so advertised at the price stated therein, or with the intent, design, or purpose not to sell the merchandise, commodity, or service so advertised.

What course of action would you take against Butcher Block Corporation, and why? See People v. Block & Kleaver, Inc., 103 Misc. 2d 758, 427 N.Y.S.2d 133 (Monroe Co. 1980); People v. Glubo, 5 N.Y.2d 461, 186 N.Y.S.2d 26, 158 N.E.2d 699 (1959).

Prefatory Note

The criminal cases discussed thus far all involve a local, presumably closely-held, company in which there is some identity between the person doing the swindling and the owners. The problem is very different for the large, nationwide company whose stock is traded on the New York Stock Exchange, and many of whose shareholders have no effective control of company policy. If one of their officers, employees or agents commits a criminal act, is the company liable? And, are higher levels of management liable?

COMMONWEALTH v. BENEFICIAL FINANCE CO.

Supreme Judicial Court of Massachusetts, 1971.
360 Mass. 188, 275 N.E.2d 33, certiorari denied, 407 U.S. 910, 914, 92 S.Ct. 2433, 2434, 2435, 32 L.Ed.2d 683, 689 (1972).

SPIEGEL, JUSTICE.

[Beneficial Finance Co., Household Finance Co., Liberty Loan Co., and Local Finance Co., along with six of their employees, were convicted of offering or paying bribes or conspiring to do so. Convicted employees included Farrell, a vice president of Beneficial, and Barber & Pratt, public relations men for Household. Two public officials were also convicted: Martin Hanley, who was Deputy Commissioner of Banks and Supervisor of loan agencies, and Morris Garfinkle, who was a member of the Small Loans Regulatory Board (Rate Board).]

[Until 1962, the maximum permitted "small loan" in Massachusetts was $1500. The maximum permitted interest rate for small loan companies was set by the Rate Board, which was composed of five members. In 1962, the state legislature raised the maximum "small loan" amount to $3000, but the maximum permitted interest rate for loans between $1500 and $3000 was to be determined by the Rate Board, after hearings. Hanley and several small loan company employees met and discussed paying money to Hanley "to insure a favorable result from the Rate Board," such payments being called "a program." However, the small loan company employees present at these initial discussions stated that they "had no authority at that time to commit" their corporations to "a program," but that a decision would be made at a later meeting in New York. At the New York meeting, Farrell initiated discussion concerning "a program," which was approved and executed. The court first upheld the convictions of the individual defendants, then turned to an examination of the criminal liability of their corporate employers.]

THE CORPORATE DEFENDANTS.

Having concluded that the evidence was sufficient to establish that the defendants Pratt and Woodcock were part of a conspiracy joined in by Farrell, Glynn and Barber to bribe Hanley and Garfinkle, we turn to the question of whether there was sufficient evidence to support a finding that Beneficial, Household, and Liberty were parties to the conspiracy. * * *

* * * (1) Household was held criminally responsible, in part, for the criminal conduct of Barber and Pratt. Barber and Pratt were employees of Household, but were neither directors nor officers. * * *

1. *Standards of Criminal Responsibility*—The defendants and the Commonwealth have proposed differing standards upon which the criminal responsibility of a corporation should be predicated. The defendants argue that a corporation should not be held criminally liable for the conduct of its servants or agents unless such conduct was performed, authorized, ratified, adopted or tolerated by the corporations' directors, officers or other "high managerial agents" who are sufficiently high in the corporate hierarchy to warrant the assumption that their acts in some substantial sense reflect corporate policy. * * *

[W]e are of opinion that the quantum of proof necessary to sustain the conviction of a corporation for the acts of its agents is sufficiently met if it is shown that the corporation has placed the agent in a position where he has enough authority and responsibility to act for and in behalf of the corporation in handling the *particular* corporate business, operation or project in which he was engaged at the time he committed the criminal act. The judge properly instructed the jury to this effect and correctly stated that this standard does not depend upon the responsibility or authority which the agent has with respect to the entire corporate business, but only to his position with relation to the particular business in which he was serving the corporation. Some of the factors that the jury were entitled to consider in applying the above test, although perhaps not in themselves decisive, are the following: (1) the extent of control and authority exercised by the individual over and within the corporation; (2) the extent and manner to which corporate funds were used in the crime; (3) a repeated pattern of criminal conduct tending to indicate corporate toleration or ratification of the agent's acts. Applying these criteria within the "kinship of the act to authority" test to the present case we next consider the evidence admitted against Household, then Liberty, and lastly, Beneficial.

2. *Household*—Household argues that even applying the "kinship of authority" test to the present case, there is no basis on which the trial court could justify the conclusion that either Pratt or Barber had enough power, duty, responsibility or authority, in handling the matters concerning the Rate Board or involving Hanley in his official capacity, to make the statements and acts of these employees binding upon the corporation.

The judge, without reciting the evidence concerning the relationship between Barber, Pratt and Household, simply ruled that a finding was warranted that the "relationship disclosed by the evidence, whether it be of agency, employment, or office holding, or a combination of them, existed * * * between the individuals Barber and Pratt and the corporation *Household*," and that the "statements, acts and conduct of the individual defendants Pratt and Barber * * * were done and performed by them for and in behalf of *Household*, within the scope of their authority to act for and in behalf of *Household*, and were otherwise in all respects such that they were and constituted the statements, acts and conduct of *Household*."

We agree with the judge that there was sufficient evidence of authority to submit the case to the jury. The evidence shows that Household is a Delaware corporation, engaged in lending money, with its national headquarters and principal place of business in Chicago, Illinois. Household is divided into various geographical divisions as well as into departments and sub-departments. Among the major departments of Household are those described as "Operations," "Advertising," "Auditing" and "Public Relations." The New England area, including Massachusetts, is termed the "Northen Division" within Household's geographical schema. In this area, Household had 91 loan offices. Forty of these were located in Massachusetts.

During the years involved in this case, the "Northern Division" was under the supervision of one Don H. Ellis, a vice-president and "director of supervision" of Household. Ellis testified that although his duties primarily involved "operations," a "Department that serves the public by making loans and collecting the money back," there is communication within the corporate structure between 1 department and another. For example, if the advertising department was conducting activities in the "Northern Division," then Ellis would be so informed.

The director of public relations for Household during the period covered by these indictments was one Harold Haugan. Haugan, like Ellis, was a vice-president of Household, and was so listed on Household's annual report to its stockholders. As director of public relations, it appears that Haugan was equal or superior to Ellis in the corporate hierarchy. The annual report lists the names of these 2 men in such a fashion as to warrant this inference. On the same page of the annual report, just below the listing of the corporate vice-presidents, there is a list of "Other Staff Executives." The defendant Barber is listed among these executives. The annual report also designates Barber as "Divisional Director" of "Public Relations." From the positioning of Barber's name in the annual report, a jury would be warranted in drawing the inference that Barber's status in the corporate hierarchy was comparable to that of Household's controller. In addition, there was evidence that Barber attended a high level executive conference, which was held annually in Fort Lauderdale, Florida.

* * *

Among the duties of Household's public relations men was to "enhance the image of the company." In its general instructions manual, Household counseled its employees to refer problems involving persons in "public life" to the public relations department. Ellis testified that this manual states that "if there is a problem that involves a person in public life, an influential person, you name him, anybody * * * who is antagonistic towards the industry * * * then we refer it to the Public Relations Department."

The Commonwealth argues that the above evidence, specifically concerning Barber's rank in the corporate hierarchy, is sufficient to meet the "high managerial agent" test proffered by Household; that Barber is a "high managerial agent" whose acts, knowledge and admissions constitute the acts, knowledge and admissions of Household. We need not decide whether this evidence, specifically that which may be inferred from the annual report, sufficiently delineates Barber's power and authority within the corporate structure to warrant the conclusion that all requisites of the Model Penal Code standard as construed by the defendants are fulfilled. However, we are of opinion that it could have been found that Barber's authority within the public relations department as "divisional director" clothed him with sufficient authority to deal with Hanley in Hanley's capacity as supervisor of loan agencies. The very nature of public relations activities, together with the specific instructions in Household's manual to refer problems involving persons in "public life" or "influential persons" to the public relations department, warrants the conclusion that Barber and Pratt possessed the authority to deal with the Hanley "program."

The fact that there is evidence that the law department of Household also dealt with the Rate Board proceedings of 1962 does not alter this result. The jury would be warranted in concluding from the testimony of Ellis that there was at least some degree of inter-departmental communication within Household's corporate structure. The fact that Household authorized its law department to deal with the Rate Board hearings did not preempt its public relations department from dealing personally with Hanley. It was within the province of the jury to decide whether Barber, in his position as "divisional director" and Pratt, in his position as Household's sole public relations man in Massachusetts, possessed a sufficient quantum of authority to deal with Hanley. All of the evidence recounted above warranted the submission to the jury of the acts and statements of the other conspirators. This evidence, in toto, more than justifies the conclusion that Household, through its employees Barber and Pratt, acting within the authority conferred on them, conspired to bribe Hanley and Garfinkle. Household's motion for a directed verdict on the conspiracy indictment was, therefore, properly denied.

* * *

Affirmed.

Problem 3

You are an assistant to the U.S. Attorney for Massachusetts. You become aware that the local branch of a nationwide finance company (Friendly Finance Co.) is using disclosure forms which contain several "clear" violations of TILA. In addition, the APRs disclosed always are 1% below the rates you calculate. You write the branch manager a letter pointing out these problems and ask that the forms and calculations be revised. The branch manager responds that the forms are sent to her by Friendly's headquarters in St. Louis, as are the calculation methods.

Your next letter advises the branch manager that you believe that TILA violations are involved, and requests her to contact Friendly's headquarters, bringing your concerns to the attention of corporate officers, and seeks revision of the forms and calculation methods. Friendly's next response is a letter from its General Counsel, stating that she believes that their forms and calculation methods comply with TILA. It further states: "We do not plan to re-examine our forms or calculation methods. We do not believe that any young attorney (especially one who works for the government) knows anything about commerce, and we do not plan to change our present procedures." And they don't.

It is now several months later and the TILA violations continue. If you are *certain* that the forms and calculation methods violate TILA, would you initiate a criminal prosecution of Friendly Finance Co.? If not, why not? If you would, would you seek fines or imprisonment of corporate officers? See TILA § 112.

SECTION C. "CAPITAL PUNISHMENT"—LOSS OF LICENSE AND PUTTING THE VIOLATOR OUT OF BUSINESS

Perhaps the ultimate sanction which can be visited upon someone who persistently engages in fraudulent or unconscionable practices is literally to put them out of business by revoking their license to operate. This remedy is available only to those who are required to be licensed or chartered—such as finance companies, banks, and car dealers.

Reported cases of license revocation are rare, although every licensure system has provisions for such suspension or revocation for cause. Cf., U3C § 2.303. See Miller, "Enforcement of the UCCC: Observations from the Oklahoma and Federal Experience," 51 No. Car.L.Rev. 1229, 1259–60 (1973).

An alternate route to the same end of capital punishment for a business would be for the state attorney general to persuade the court to enjoin it from further operations in the state, under the state little FTC Act. How successful will this strategy be, however, if there is no specific authorization in the statute to put a company out of business for violations?

Finally, some states have laws permitting the attorney general to ask the court to revoke the certificate of incorporation and dissolve a business found to be engaging in persistent fraud. Is this an effective solution, or could the perpetrators simply reincarnate themselves under a different corporate name?

Problem 4

In a state which has enacted the U3C, you are the "Administrator" responsible for enforcement of the Act, and responsible for licensing lenders under section 2.302.

The facts in the *Frostifresh* case, supra page 789, have arisen in your jurisdiction and you are aware that Frostifresh Credit Corporation, the company that finances all of Frostifresh's food/freezer credit plans and which is closely connected with Frostifresh, holds a license issued by your office. You are also aware that about a dozen consumers have successfully sued Frostifresh Credit for fraud and unconscionable practices, and that Frostifresh has previously given your office two separate "assurances of discontinuance" with respect to practices other than its food-freezer sales scheme.

Staff reminds you that the current flap relates to Frostifresh's financing of consumer paper through "puppet" sellers, and not to Frostifresh's direct loan business (for which it needs the license). Staff recommends that you initiate procedures to revoke Frostifresh's license, but they acknowledge that doing so will have certain repercussions:

— The hearing procedure called for in U3C § 2.303, and the probable judicial review of a revocation order, will occupy half the staff of your office for as long as two years;

— It is possible that a court might say that you *can't* revoke a license for conduct arising out of sales financing, but only for conduct incident to the licensed portion of the business—i.e., direct loans.

— Loss of license would probably cause Frostifresh and its puppet sellers to go out of business or bankrupt, in which case consumers who had claims against the company, or who had made downpayments, would be remediless.

— The owners of Frostifresh are thought to have underworld connections, and are known to have substantial political influence, especially with the charirman of the state legislature's appropriations committee.

What course of action would you take?

MARYLAND INDEPENDENT AUTOMOBILE DEALERS ASS'N v. ADMINISTRATOR, MOTOR VEHICLE ADMINISTRATION

Maryland Court of Special Appeals, 1978.
41 Md.App. 7, 394 A.2d 820.

WILNER, JUDGE.

Commercial Law article, § 2–316 describes various ways in which a seller of goods may limit or negate implied warranties that otherwise might be applicable to the sale. Section 2–316.1, however, which immediately follows § 2–316, states that the provisions of § 2–316 "do not apply to sales of consumer goods, as defined by § 9–109." Section 9–109 defines as "consumer goods" those that are "used or bought for use primarily for personal, family or household purposes." No one contests that automobiles, whether new or used, that are bought primarily for personal, family, or household use are "consumer goods" as so defined.

Having excluded sales of consumer goods from the provisions of § 2–316, § 2–316.1 goes on to state in its next succeeding paragraph (hereafter referred to as § 2–316.1(2)):

"Any oral or written language used by a seller of consumer goods and services, which attempts to exclude or modify any implied warranties of merchantability and fitness for a particular purpose or to exclude or modify the consumer's remedies for breach of those warranties, is unenforceable. However, the seller may recover from the manufacturer any damages resulting from breach of the implied warranty of merchantability or fitness for a particular purpose."

The Motor Vehicle Administration (MVA), a unit within the State Department of Transportation, is the agency that licenses, and to a degree, regulates, automobile dealers and salesmen. *See* Transportation article, title 15, subtitles 3 and 4. With more particular reference to this case, § 15–312 provides that a dealer may not willfully fail to comply with the terms of a warranty or guarantee; § 15–315 authorizes MVA to suspend, revoke, or refuse to renew the license of any dealer who fails to comply with any provision of the Maryland Vehicle Law relating to the sale of vehicles, which would include § 15–312; and § 12–104(b), dealing with the general powers of MVA, authorizes it to adopt rules and regulations to carry out those provisions of the Maryland Vehicle Law "that relate to or are administered and enforced by [MVA]".

Presumably in furtherance of this regulatory and rulemaking authority, and with tacit, but nonetheless apparent, reference to Commercial Law article, § 2–316.1, MVA, on May 16, 1976, adopted Regulation 11.02.03.83, which provides:

"A warranty may not contain language which specifically disclaims any implied warranty of merchantability or fitness. Examples of prohibited disclaimers are as follow.

"A. 'This warranty is expressly in lieu of any other warranty, express or implied, including any implied warranty of merchantability or fitness for a particular purpose, and any other obligations or liabilities on the seller's part,' or similar language that could be construed by a consumer to limit his recourse to the terms of express warranties.

"B. 'This vehicle is being sold as is, without any implied or express warranty of merchantability,' or similar language.

"C. 'Sold used with 50–50 warranty. The dealer hereby guarantees this vehicle for _____ days after _____ 19__ with the understanding that necessary repairs made within this period of time will be charged half to the buyer and half to the dealer, of total retail cost of parts and labor used,' or similar language."

The Maryland Independent Automobile Dealers Association, appellant, sued MVA and its administrator initially seeking a declaratory judgment that § 2–316.1 does not apply to the sale of used cars, and that its member dealers therefore have a right to sell used cars on either an express warranty or an "as is" basis. Following the sustaining of a demurrer to this complaint, appellant filed an amended complaint seeking essentially the same relief, but through a challenge to the MVA regulation. The specific relief requested was a judgment declaring that § 2–316.1(2) does not apply to "used motor vehicles", and that the complainants are "thereby not required to comply with the terms thereof", and an injunction restraining MVA and its administrator "from exercising any of the powers respecting the enforcement of the implied warranty provisions of [§ 2–316.1(2)] against the Complainants." This appeal is from the denial of that relief by the Circuit Court for Baltimore County.

Although the parties differ in their statement of the questions presented, it appears that there are but two issues to be decided: (1) does § 2–316.1(2) apply to the sale of used automobiles which otherwise fall within the definition of "consumer goods", and (2) if so, may MVA enforce that section in the manner reflected by its regulation 11.02.03.83?

(1) Statutory Interpretation

There is nothing within § 2–316.1(2) itself that facially would restrict its application to the sale of "new" goods, or, conversely, that would exclude from its provisions the sale of "used" goods. * * *

* * * Paragraph (2) clearly applies to the sale of all "consumer goods", new or used, without regard to whether the seller, in any given case, has a viable action against the manufacturer.

(2) Validity of MVA Regulation

Appellant's contention here is that, even if, under § 2–316.1(2), disclaimers are "unenforceable", there is no warrant for MVA to "enforce" that provision. We find that argument equally lacking in merit. As noted, MVA is specifically authorized to adopt regulations to carry out the provisions of the Vehicle Law that relate to or are administered or enforced by it. One of these, in the subtitle dealing with the licensing of dealers, prohibits dealers from willfully failing to comply with a warranty. Transportation article, § 15–312(7). A disclaimer made in violation of § 2–316.1(2) may well constitute such a failure, thereby subjecting the dealer to disciplinary action by MVA.

If a dealer were charged with a violation of § 15–312(7), MVA would be authorized to investigate the charge and, if it found against the dealer, to suspend or revoke the dealer's license. Transportation article, § 15–315. Obviously, such a procedure involves the "enforcement" of Commercial Law article, § 2–316.1, but in a negative or punitive way. That being plainly authorized (and, indeed, unchallenged by appellant) we fail to see how or why MVA would not also have the authority to adopt an affirmative regulation making clear its intention to enforce that provision, and, at the same time, making clear what types of conduct it will consider to be in contravention of the statute.

ORDER DENYING DECLARATORY RELIEF AFFIRMED; APPELLANTS TO PAY THE COSTS.

Notes

1. The Maryland statute prohibiting the disclaimer of implied warranties was later amended to permit such disclaimers for motor vehicles over six years old with over 60,000 miles. Md.Code Com.Law, § 2–316.1(4) (Supp.1984).

2. What should be the consequences if a person continues to conduct a business without a necessary license—a kind of black market operation? What is the individual consumer's redress?

According to the U3C, § 5.201(1), if a creditor violates the provisions on "authority to make supervised loans" (the licensing requirements), the consumer may recover actual damages plus a penalty of no less than $100 and no more than $1,000. In addition the consumer could recover any finance charge in excess of that permitted to unsupervised lenders. Is this sufficient discouragement to creditors who have lost licenses?

STATE ex rel. LIST v. AAA AUTO LEASING AND RENTAL, INC.
Supreme Court of Nevada, 1977.
93 Nev. 483, 568 P.2d 1230.

OPINION

BATJER, CHIEF JUSTICE.

Appellants commenced an action alleging, inter alia, that respondents engaged in the use of deceptive trade practices prohibited by the Trade Regulation and Practices Act, NRS Ch. 598. The district court dismissed that portion of appellants' complaint which requested respondents be preliminarily and permanently enjoined from engaging in business activities related to the sale, lease or repair of motor vehicles within the state of Nevada. This appeal follows.

* * *

2. Appellants, relying on NRS 598.540(1), contend the district court improperly dismissed that portion of the complaint requesting an injunction. NRS 598.540(1) provides that the commissioner of consumer affairs may apply for an injunction or temporary restraining order prohibiting a person from continuing deceptive trade practices as enumerated in NRS 598.410. The statute further provides: "The court may make orders or judgments necessary to prevent the use by such person of any such deceptive trade practice or to restore to any other person any money or property which may have been acquired by such deceptive trade practices." Appellants argue this language is a clear indication of legislative intent to give the court absolute discretion to take any measure, including completely barring an individual from engaging in a business, necessary to prevent fraud against the public in the form of deceptive trade practices.

Within its police power, the legislature may regulate commercial and business affairs in order to promote the health, safety, morals and general welfare of its citizens and to protect its citizens from injurious activities. Pursuant to this power, the legislature may regulate an otherwise legitimate business which, if conducted improperly, is detrimental to the public, or it may prohibit a business activity which is essentially injurious to the public welfare, provided such legislation is not prohibited by the Constitutions of the United States or Nevada.

Although the Trade Regulation and Practices Act specifically prohibits the use of pyramid promotional schemes, the legislature has nowhere declared business activities related to the sale, lease or repair of motor vehicles to be essentially injurious to the public welfare or injuriously fraudulent. Nor has it declared contracts and agreements relative to such business activities against public policy and voidable.

Courts must construe a statute to give meaning to all of its parts. Upon considering NRS 598.540(1) which permits the commissioner to apply for an injunction prohibiting a person from continuing deceptive trade practices and NRS 598.570 which permits the district attorney to bring an action in the state's name for an injunction against any person who is using, has used or is about to use any deceptive trade practices, we conclude the statutes proscribing the use of deceptive trade practices clearly contemplate only injunctions against the use of such practices and not injunctions which prohibit an individual from engaging in a particular business or occupation.

The district court's order dismissing that portion of the complaint requesting respondents be enjoined from engaging in business activities related to the sale, lease or repair of motor vehicles is affirmed.

THOMPSON, GUNDERSON and MANOUKIAN, JJ., and HOYT, DISTRICT JUDGE, concur.

Problem 5

Therapeutic Hypnosis, Inc. advertised in newspapers, and on the radio and television, that it had a staff of professionally qualified hypnotists who had achieved a high percentage of success in curing people of smoking and overeating. In fact, Therapeutic Hypnosis was the brainchild of one Michael McMillen, who held himself out to be a doctor of psychology, a doctor of theology, a doctor of metaphysical science as well as a college and university graduate, when in fact he had no degree higher than a high school diploma. As the state attorney general, you feel that McMillen and Therapeutic Hypnosis are practicing medicine without a license, defrauding the public, and misusing their state certificate of incorporation. Your state law authorizes you to seek an order enjoining repeated or fraudulent acts in the conduct of any business activity. Can you use the law to effectively put Therapeutic Hypnosis out of business? Would the Nevada court in *AAA Auto Leasing* have come out differently if they had before them the facts raised by McMillen and Therapeutic Hypnosis? Would it have been more efficient for your state to have simply required hypnotists to have a state-granted license to practice? See People v. Therapeutic Hypnosis, Inc., 83 Misc.2d 1068, 374 N.Y.S.2d 576 (Albany Co. 1975).

Index

References are to Pages

ENFORCEMENT AGENCIES
See also, Federal Trade Commission
Civil penalties, 842–846
Functions, 811–812
Injunctions, 834–846
Private right of action, 855–858
Restitution, 831–842
State and local, remedies available,
Injunction, 814, 816–818
Penalties, 814–815, 818
Restitution, 813–814, 819–824

EQUAL CREDIT OPPORTUNITY ACT
See also, Credit Discrimination
CCPA, part of, 6, 107

EXECUTION
See also, Judgment Liens and Execution
Body execution, see Incarceration Critique,
606–609

EXEMPTIONS
Judgment liens, 586
State Laws under CCPA,
States exempted, 762
Truth in Lending Act, 761–762
Wages not garnishable, 570–571

EXTENSIONS AND RENEWALS
See Refinancing

FAIR CREDIT BILLING ACT
See also, Credit and Debit Cards
CCPA, part of, 6, 107

FAIR CREDIT REPORTING ACT
See also, Credit Reporting
Generally, 228 et seq.
CCPA, part of, 6, 107

**FAIR DEBT COLLECTION PRACTICES
ACT**
CCPA, part of, 6, 107

FAIR PACKAGING AND LABELING ACT
Supplementing Federal Food, Drug & Cosmetic Act, 97

"FEDERAL BOX"
See Truth in Lending Act

FEDERAL TRADE COMMISSION
See also, Enforcement Agencies
Advertising, 828–831
Case-by-case adjudication, perils, 848, 852–855
Private right of action, 855–858
Remedies available, 824–858
Restitution, 831–842
Role, 39
Trade regulation rules,
Background, 846–848
Door to door sales, 196–204, 826

FEDERAL TRADE COMMISSION—Cont'd
Holder in due course, 413–414, 423–429,
434–437
Magnuson-Moss Warranty–FTC Improvement Act, 825

FEDERAL TRADE COMMISSION ACT
Generally, 6

FEDERAL RESERVE BOARD
Regulations, 107–108

FINANCE CHARGE
See also, Interest Rates; Time–Price
Doctrine; Truth in Lending Act
Generally, 99–106

FIRST AMENDMENT
See Advertising

FLIPPING
See Refinancing

FOOD PRODUCTS
Federal Food, Drug and Cosmetic Act, 97
Unit pricing, Prices, this index

FORMS
See also, Truth in Lending Act
Credit report, 231–232
Odometer mileage statement, 895

FRAUD
See Misrepresentation

FREEDOM OF SPEECH
Advertising regulation, 84–95, 828–831
Credit reporting, 229–230

GARNISHMENT
Generally, 569–575
Discharge of employee, 575
NCCF Report, 570–571

HOLDER IN DUE COURSE
Credit card issuer liability, 429–434
Disclosure, FTC order on, 413–414
Financer's recourse, 422–423
FTC holder rule,
Effect, 434–437
Purchase money loans, 423–427
Real estate transactions, 427–429
TILA contrasted, 421
Public policy rationale for rejecting protection, 412
Purchase money loans,
Generally, 423–429
FTC holder rule, 423–427
UCC, 425
Uniform Commercial Code,
Generally, 363–369
Close connectedness, 412–413
Uniform Consumer Credit Code, 413

MISREPRESENTATION—Cont'd
Knowledge of falsity, 18–20
Merger doctrine, 24
Mistake, 14
Odometer readings, 23
Opinion versus fact, 13, 16–18
Reliance, 13–14, 18
Silence, known defects, 13, 15–16, 22
Third party, 32–36
Warranties, 18–21, 38–39
Fraudulent concealment, 21–24, 28–31
Fraudulent misrepresentation, 24–28
Negligence, 32–38

MODEL CONSUMER CREDIT ACT
Generally, 5–6

MOTOR VEHICLE INFORMATION AND COST SAVINGS ACT
Criminal sanctions, 890–897

NATIONAL CONSUMER ACT
See also, Model Consumer Credit Act
Generally, 5

NEGOTIABLE INSTRUMENTS
See Holder in Due Course.

PRE-EMPTION
State laws, by federal,
Alternative Mortgage Transaction Parity Act, 675
Credit card billing errors, 760
Credit reporting, 759–760
Depository Institutions Deregulation and Monetary Control Act, 684–685
Fraud, 773
Home mortgage loans, 683–696
Interest Rates, this index
Lemon laws, 753–759
Usury, 669–683
Warranties, 760–761

PRICES
See also, Unconscionability
Credit insurance, 731–732
Credit transactions, see Interest Rates; Truth in Lending Act
Too high, 613–618
Unconscionability, generally, 613–622
Unit pricing, 163–164

PRIVACY
Debt collection, invasion of, 470–472

PRIVITY OF CONTRACT
Warranties, 376, 383–389, 396–398

PUNITIVE DAMAGES
Common law fraud, 888
Deterrence, 888–890
Fraud,
General rule, 886–888
Gross, 883–886

PYRAMID SCHEMES
Generally, 188–192

REAL ESTATE
See also, Uniform Condominium Act
Generally, 406–411
Holder in Due Course, this index
Implied warranty of habitability, 406–409

REBATE ON PREPAYMENT
Actuarial computation of prepayment, 317–323
Rule of 78's computation of prepayment, 317–323
Truth in Lending Act, 318, 322

REDLINING
See Credit Discrimination

REFERRAL SALES
Fraudulent scheme, 185–186
Illegal lottery, as, 186

REFINANCING
See also, Interest Rates; Rebate on Pre-payment
Balloon notes, 332
Flipping, 323–332, 335
Late charges, deferral (extension) charges, 336–337
Long term notes, 332–335
Pyramiding, 338

REGULATION B
See Credit Discrimination

REGULATION Z
See Truth in Lending Act

REGULATORY FLEXIBILITY ACT
Periodic review of rules required, 436

"RENT-TO-OWN" CONTRACTS
CLA, excluded under, 161
State disclosure laws, 162
TILA, excluded under, 159–162
Unconscionability, 619–621

REPOSSESSION
See Security Interests

RETAIL INSTALLMENT SALES ACTS
See also, Time–Price Doctrine
Generally, 5

REVOCATION OF ACCEPTANCE
Generally, 369–377
Reasonable use test, 372

RULE OF 78'S
Actuarial method compared, 317–323
Explained, 317–318

UNFAIR PRACTICES
  See also, Advertising; Federal Trade
    Commission
Distinguished from deceptive, 64–69

UNIFORM COMMERCIAL CODE
Generally, 4–5

**UNIFORM COMMON INTEREST OWNER-
  SHIP ACT**
See Uniform Condominium Act

UNIFORM CONDOMINIUM ACT
Basis for state laws, 409–410

UNIFORM CONSUMER CREDIT CODE
Generally, 5–6

**UNIFORM CONSUMER SALES PRAC-
  TICES ACT**
Deceptive advertising, 184
Origin, enactment, 70

UNIFORM LAND TRANSACTIONS ACT
Warranties, 409

USURY
See Interest Rates

VENUE
Inconvenient, 560–561

WAIVER OF DEFENSES
See Holder in Due Course

WARRANTIES
Assumpsit, part of action of, 38
Disclaimers and remedy limitations,
    Generally, 363–411
  Exclusiveness of remedy, 380–381
  Magnuson–Moss Warranty Act, effects
    of, 390–400
  Non-uniform UCC amendments, 389
  Real estate transactions, 406–411
  Upheld under UCC, 366–367
Implied warranty of merchantability, 378–
    379
Magnuson-Moss Warranty Act, 390–400
  Attorney's fees, 794–798, 803
  Objective test, 391
Presale availability rule, 827
Privity of contract, 396–398
Real estate transactions,
  Implied warranty of habitability, 406–
    409
  Uniform Land Transactions Act, 409
Relation to strict tort liability, 377, 383–
    386
Uniform Commercial Code,
  Generally, 363–364, 369
  Non-uniform amendment, 389

†